Allen's Synonyms and Antonyms

By

F. STURGES ALLEN

Late General Editor of "Webster's New International Dictionary"

REVISED AND ENLARGED EDITION

Edited by T. H. Vail Motter

Assistant Professor of English Literature at Wellesley College

For many years *Allen's Synonyms and Antonyms* has been an invaluable work among books of literary reference for its scope and authority. This new edition, completely revised and brought up to date, contains, in addition to 30 to 40 per cent of new title entries, careful sense discriminations for difficult words based upon a principle devised by Mr. Allen in unpublished material left among his papers. It retains all the admirable features of the original edition, while it has more practical value for the modern student of English. It is especially adapted to the new tendency in English teaching which emphasizes semantic training—or word study.

Distinctive features of *Allen's Synonyms and Antonyms* include: Comprehensiveness of *vocabulary;* fullness of *evidence; cross-referencing* to carefully differentiated subgroups of synonyms; and full *antonym* references.

ALLEN'S

SYNONYMS AND ANTONYMS

424

ALLEN'S

SYNONYMS AND ANTONYMS

by

F. STURGES ALLEN, A.B., LL.B.

Late General Editor of
"Webster's New International Dictionary"

REVISED AND ENLARGED EDITION

EDITED BY

T. H. VAIL MOTTER, Ph.D.

Assistant Professor of English Literature
Wellesley College

HARPER & BROTHERS PUBLISHERS

New York and London

ALLEN'S SYNONYMS AND ANTONYMS

Printed in the United States of America

B-V

PREFACE

IN PREPARING the present edition, the Editor has preserved the basic working plan of the late Mr. Allen's original work. Main entry words constitute the bulk of the text, while the words in smaller type at the foot of the pages are designed to eliminate space-consuming duplication of word-groups under separate entries for each component of a group. A maximum amount of space is therefore devoted to non-recurring items, and unavoidable duplications are minimized.

In compiling the original edition, the first Editor had planned to include as part of his word lists sense discriminations for many terms. Limitations of space, however, abridged his intentions. In this revised edition needed room for the inclusion of sense discriminations and much other new material has been provided by the adoption of wider columns on a larger page, the abbreviation of many stigmatizing terms (such as *rare, archaic, poetic*), the elimination of many cross-reference entries at the foot of the pages in favor of the retention there of only the commonest terms most likely to be sought for, the excision of many foreign words not in common American use, and the deletion of other items through re-editing.

The new material admitted, approximating one-third of the whole, is of two kinds: (1) additional main entry words, synonyms and antonyms, and (2) sense discriminations.

Among the words added to the text are numerous examples of cant, slang and colloquialism, and many common words, perfectly well-known and almost universally used, but which have nevertheless not ordinarily appeared in dictionaries of general use. It is hoped that the usefulness of these inclusions for the reader, the student, the foreign-born student learning English, and writers and speakers generally, will justify their admission.

In place of the little-used foreign words eliminated, the Editor has inserted many British equivalents of American terms, entering them usually under the American word. Look under *radio*, the American term, for *wireless*, the British equivalent; under *fender* for *wing*.

The sense discriminations which comprise more than half the bulk of the new material and which are a distinctive feature of this edition, follow the pattern of Mr. Allen's draft for the letters L-Z left among his papers. In editing and supplementing these notes the present Editor has tried to avoid a purely dictionary function of definition. Sense discriminations, however, are inserted in cases where the user of this book might be baffled by a simple word list, and might be assisted in his selection by the discriminating phrase added in parentheses.

In general these guiding phrases have been added in three kinds of situations: (1) Where, in spite of clear differences in the meanings of words, there is nevertheless confusion in their use. (*Cf. imply-infer; irony-sarcasm; ability-talent.*) (2) Where distinctions clearly exist, but are of so subtle and nice a nature as to escape many users' notice. (*Cf. less-fewer; quantity-amount.*) (3) Where the language's historic habit of adding layer upon layer to the associative senses of many words, leaves even an experienced seeker for the right word often lost amid too many riches. In such cases the parenthetical discriminations will assist where one is struggling with such chameleons as *unspeakable*, or *mistress*.

Suggestions for the use of this book appear in following pages under the title, "How Shall I Say It?" A list of abbreviations used throughout the text appears on page x.

The Editor gratefully offers thanks for advice and help throughout the preparation of the book to his friend and colleague, Professor A. D. Sheffield, literary executor of Mr. Allen; for generous assistance in the preparation of the manuscript to Professor Rudolph Willard, of the University of Texas; and for aid and comfort while the work was passing through the press, to his wife.

T. H. V. M.

Wellesley College,
January 17, 1938.

HOW SHALL I SAY IT?

I

The function of a dictionary of synonyms is at once simple and complex. It is simple because of the things it does not do; complex, paradoxically, because of the apparent simplicity of what it must do: supply immediately the word that is needed for a given context.

Because a dictionary of synonyms must usually serve as a very present help in time of trouble (for what is so troublesome as the idea which will not phrase itself?) it is exempt from the leisurely duties of definition, the satisfaction of philological investigation, or the recording of historical learning. To a work like Weekley's *Etymological Dictionary of Modern English* one turns for the genealogy of *sad*, beginning with its Old English senses of *satisfied, satiated,* and continuing through its mutations, *comfortable, orderly, sober, heavy,* to its modern meaning. In the monumental *New English Dictionary* one may trace the history of *nice* through centuries of semantic change, following that pliant word to the present, when it has come to mean almost everything, and practically nothing. It would seem that the function of a dictionary of synonyms, stripped of such necessities, were indeed simple.

But such is not the case. For although the user of a dictionary of synonyms, temporarily at least indifferent to philology, etymology, semantics, or mere definition, simply desires to find the right word, the task will require the combined ingenuity of the Editor and the industry of the searcher. The Editor's efforts to anticipate the searcher's needs are concluded with the publication of his book; it remains only to suggest to the user how to apply his industry.

For apply it he must. One cannot press a button and produce the desired word. If a synonym were an exact equivalent of another word, interchangeable with it, no need for its existence would arise, and the language might be as comparatively poor in vocabulary as a primitive tongue. But a synonym is merely an approximation of the essential meaning of another word, and always implies its own variant of the first sense. Synonyms are monuments to shades of thought and varieties of experience, and there are few cases indeed when one word will be as good as another. Hence, the richness of our English vocabulary betokens richness and variety of thought and experience.

To help draw up from this well of English the single drop most needed is the function of this book.

II

Finding the right word builds vocabulary. The articulate man who is discriminating in his use of language has possessed himself of a valuable kind of power. How shall he say it?

Let us suppose that a student preparing a theme is at a loss to characterize a certain feminine hat. Having quite literally no words to describe it, he falls back upon the over-worn adjective, *funny.* Let us hope that he realizes the inadequacy of his choice, for the word, in his context, is nearly meaningless, and, since the hat, to the student, is actually anything but funny, positively misleading. Let him turn, then, to the word, *funny,* in this book. If he follows suggestions energetically, he will come upon *odd, fantastic,* and, at last, *grotesque,* and here he is content to stop, for the hat was just that. Since all of these words, met during the hunt, have distinct meanings, none falls into any of the categories which, as explained in the *Preface* above, call for sense discriminations. If, therefore, any of these words is unknown to a consultant, recourse must be had to a defining dictionary to complete the search for the right word. In the end, the victorious hunter will have found his word, pondered the relationships of an interesting series of related synonym-groups, gained respect for the richness of the language, and added to his vocabulary.

A second kind of consultant knows the general word controlling a certain sense-group, but cannot think of the specific equivalent necessary to his context. If the term desired is to denominate a kind of sharpness not altogether admirable, the right words, *wily, cunning, sly,* will appear ultimately to the searcher whether he begins with such general core-sense words as *keen, bright, clever,* or whether he is able to begin as close to his quarry as *shrewd.*

Although a synonym dictionary is not a defining dictionary, its function of helping to supply the needed word assists a third class of searcher who wishes to choose from among a number of words which he regards as generally equivalent, but of whose fine sense distinctions he is ignorant. Is the word desired in a certain context *talent, genius,* or just plain *ability*? In such cases the parenthetical sense discriminations offer guidance.

III

The chief explanatory terms used in this book are here listed:

affected.—This term denotes a use not natural to the user, ranging from ostentation, through excessive fastidiousness, to bad taste. *Delectation* is often an *affected* synonym for *delight, perigrinator* for *pilgrim.*

archaic.—Abbreviated as (*A*). Strictly speaking, ancient words now dead, as *fardel* for *bundle, rutter* for *soldier.* In practice *archaic* words are frequently used for their flavor or tone, and in many instances shade imperceptibly into *rare, poetic* or *learned* uses, described below.

bookish, learned, literary, or poetic.—For convenience these are lumped in the single abbreviation (*B*). The term suggests a specialized use confined to the categories named, and unusual in other contexts. In many instances such words fall also into the class denoted *technical,* described below.

colloquial.—Abbreviated as (*C*). These are words common in ordinary speech, but lacking in the dignity of association necessary for formal or elevated discourse. Examples will appear on nearly every page.

contextual.—Abbreviated as (*contex.*). If often happens that a specific main entry word, such as *outcry,* may properly be represented in a given context by a more general word, such as *noise.* Such a sense is designated as *contextual;* but with the warning to the user that the general word, *noise,* signifies *outcry* only in an appropriate context.

euphemistic.—A word chosen when one does not wish to call a spade a spade, as where *powder room* is used for *toilet, depart* for *die.*

figurative.—Abbreviated as (*fig.*). This term describes the use of a literal word like *rein,* which denotes a specific act, for a general word like *control.*

formal.—These words are distinguished from both *affected* and *technical* uses by the criterion of taste. Formal usage is often required by custom or convention, as *chamber* for *bedroom* in a context of elaborate formality. In certain contexts the same usage would be *affected* or *technical.*

obsolete.—Abbreviated as (*obs.*). This term denotes a word no longer in common use, like *horse-car,* or *cotton* for *succeed.*

obsolescent.—Abbreviated as (*obsolesc.*). Indicates words beginning to fall into disuse, but which cannot be designated as *archaic* or *obsolete.* Of such are *incommodious* for *inconvenient,* and *quiz* for *hoax.*

rare.—Abbreviated as (*R*). When this term is met with in these pages, it signifies "infrequently used in this sense as a synonym for this main entry word."

rhetorical.—This term indicates words which are characteristically used in language artificially or extravagantly elegant, or that specially seeks to convey an extreme or exaggerated effect, as where *marmoreal* is used for *white, wroth* for *angry.*

slang.—Abbreviated as (*S*). When a word as a whole, or in the given sense, has a certain arbitrary use, but is considered as generally below the level of educated speech, it is designated as *slang.*

specific.—Abbreviated as (*spec.*). These are words at the opposite extreme from those designated as *contextual,* for which see above. The searcher who consults the main entry, *ornament, v.t.,* will find all the synonyms there listed as *specific* uses. This indicates that these synonyms have a restricted sense, whose core-sense is the general term, *ornament.* This implies that *to bedeck,* for example, is a synonym for *ornament* only in some specific context where "clothing or covering with decorative objects" is implied. Carried to its extreme, the employment of this device requires the listing, as *specific* synonyms of the word *boat,* many varieties of boats. The Editor has, therefore, included items denoted *specific* wherever they seem to be of wide utility.

technical.—Abbreviated as (*tech.*). This term is added after such words as *pomiform* for *apple-shaped,* which are chiefly of technical, specialized, scientific or professional usage.

IV

Cross references are liberally supplied leading from a word to a synonym under which it also appears, but accompanied by a fresh group of synonyms more closely related in core-sense to the second word. Thus, from *perceive,* which has its own word-group, one is referred to *understand, distinguish, notice,* also synonyms of *perceive,* but each the center of its own word-group. Synonym lists in this book are not duplicated under additional main entries for each word in the list.

The small type words at the foot of the pages are entirely cross references, the words in *italic type* in each case having, under the main vocabulary entry, a list of synonyms including the word referred from. Thus, "**obloquy**: *abuse, discredit*" means: "see in the main vocabulary the words *abuse* and *discredit,* where the word **obloquy** will be found as one of the several synonyms of the group."

V

Dividing numbers are used in many entries where a variety of divergent senses, each with its appropriate synonym-group, has grown up about a single word. Thus, it is convenient to divide the synonyms for *rough* into six numbered word-groups, and a seventh list into which have been assembled eleven additional senses of this versatile word, each a cross-reference to further synonym-groups related to the original sense of *rough*. Where the core-sense of the respective numbered groups is obvious from the words in the group, no additional hints are offered. Frequently, however, defining or discriminating phrases clarify the group senses. Often, too, the antonyms will indicate differences among their respective word-groups.

VI

Abbreviations used in this book follow:

A.	archaic.*
a., adj.	adjective.
abbr.	abbreviation.
adv.	adverb.
Af., Afr.	Africa.
agric.	agriculture.
Am.	America.
Amer.	American.
anat.	anatomy.
antiq.	antiquities.
arch.	architecture.
archæol.	archæology.
astrol.	astrology.
astron.	astronomy.
B.	bookish, literary, learned or poetic.*
Bib.	Biblical.
biol.	biology.
bot.	botany.
Brit.	British.
C.	colloquial.*
Can.	Canada.
cf.	confer (L., compare).
chem.	chemistry.
conj.	conjunction.
contex.	contextual.*
dial.	dialect, dialectal.
dim.	diminutive.
eccl.	ecclesiastical.
econ.	economics.
elec.	electrical.
Eng.	English.
esp.	especially.
etc.	et cetera (L., and so forth).
ethnol.	ethnology.
exc.	except.
exclam.	exclamation.
fem.	feminine.
fig.	figurative, figuratively.*
Fr.	French.
Ger.	German.
her.	heraldry.
hist.	history, historical.
infin.	infinitive.
interj.	interjection.
Ir.	Irish.
loc.	local.
masc.	masculine.
math.	mathematics.
med.	medicine.
metal.	metallurgy.
metaph.	metaphysics.
meteorol.	meteorology.
mil.	military.
min.	mineralogy.
mythol.	mythology.
n.	noun.
New Eng.	New England.
N. Y.	New York.
obs.	obsolete.*
obsolesc.	obsolescent.*
orig.	originally.
p.	participle.
p.a.	participial adjective.
philos.	philosophy.
physiol.	physiology.
pl.	plural.
Port.	Portuguese.
p.p.	participle past.
p.pr.	participle present.
prep.	preposition.
pron.	pronoun.
psychol.	psychology.
R.	rare.*
R.C.Ch.	Roman Catholic Church.
S.	slang.*
Scot.	Scottish, Scotland.
Shak.	Shakespeare.
sing.	singular.
So.	South.
Sp.	Spanish.
spec.	specific.*
superl.	superlative.
tech.	technical.*
theol.	theology.
U. S.	United States.
univ.	university.
v.	verb.
var.	variant (spelling).
v.i.	verb intransitive.
v.t.	verb transitive.
zoöl.	zoölogy.

*Explanation of these terms appears in §III above, pp. viii-ix

ALLEN'S

SYNONYMS AND ANTONYMS

ALLEN'S SYNONYMS

AND

ANTONYMS

abandon, *v. t.* (*leave in the lurch*), quit, desert (*with default of some moral claim*), remit, renounce, forsake (*with the breaking off of some bond or association of sentiment*), drop, discard, surrender; *spec.* evacuate, forswear, maroon, bolt; *see* RELINQUISH, FORGO, ABDICATE.

Antonyms: see KEEP, CONTINUE, ACCOMPANY, APPROPRIATE.

abandoned, *a.* **1.** corrupt, reprobate, unprincipled, depraved, hardened, irreclaimable, incorrigible, irreformable, irredeemable, lost; *spec.* shameless; *see* DISSIPATED.

Antonyms: see CONSCIENTIOUS.

2. forlorn, lorn (*B*), destitute (*R*), castaway, outcast, derelict, deserted, forsaken.

3. *See* UNINHABITED.

abase, *v. t.* **1.** *Often with reflexive pron. as object:* degrade (*lower in moral worth*), debase (*make inferior in quality*), bemean.

2. humble (*lower in dignity*), humiliate, reduce, disgrace, prostrate, lower, mortify (*R*); *spec.* depose, disrank, degrade, demote, discrown (*R*), uncrown, disbench, disbar, unchurch, discepter (*R*), unfrock.

Antonyms: see ADVANCE, ELEVATE, DIGNIFY, RAISE.

abasement, *n. Spec.* degradation, debasing, humiliation, disgrace, *etc.*

abash, *v. t.* disconcert, confound, confuse, discountenance, dash, embarrass, awe; *spec.* shame, overawe; *see* INTIMIDATE.

Antonyms: see CHEER, ENCOURAGE.

abashed, *a.* disconcerted, confounded, confused, ashamed, *etc.*

abate, *v. t. & i.* **1.** *See* ABOLISH.

Antonyms: see BUILD, PRESERVE.

2. reduce, decrease, curtail, diminish, remit, lower, depress, lessen, abridge, slacken, mitigate, relax, slack; *spec.* qualify, intermit, drop, fall (*v. i.*), sink, subside (*from previous agitation*), (*v. i.*), flatten, wane (*v. i.*), allay.

Antonyms: see INCREASE, INTENSIFY.

abbreviate, *v. t.* **1.** *See* SHORTEN.

2. *Referring to words:* shorten, clip, reduce, contract, prune.

abdicate, *v. t.* abandon, relinquish, resign, demit;—*all four contex.*

abdomen, *n.* belly (*inelegant when referring to people*), paunch, pod (*vulgar*), corporation (*C or vulgar*), guts (*pl.; vulgar*); *spec.* epigastrium.

abdominal, *a.* ventral, visceral, hemal (*tech.*), alvine (*R*); *spec.* cœliac, uterine, big-bellied.

abduct, *v. t.* kidnap, rape, ravish (*B often with "away"*), spirit away; *spec.* crimp, shanghai.

abhor, *v. t.* detest, hate, contemn (*B*), despise, abominate, loathe, nauseate (*R*).

Antonyms: see LIKE, LOVE, ADMIRE.

abhorrence, *n.* detestation, despisal, abomination, hatred, antipathy, disgust, loathing, aversion, horror.

Antonyms: see LIKING, LOVE, ADMIRATION, AFFECTION.

ability, *n.* **1.** *Referring to some specific thing to be done:* competency, capacity, power, efficiency, sufficiency.

Antonyms: see INABILITY.

2. *In a general sense:* capability (*often in pl., as in "of great capabilities"*), power, caliber, strength, energy; *spec.* parts (*pl.; A or B*), masterliness.

Antonyms: see INABILITY.

3. *Referring to a concrete quality:* faculty, hang (*C*), gift, art, trick, knack; *spec.* hand; *see* SKILL, ENDOWMENT, TALENT.

Antonyms: see DISABILITY.

abject, *a.* (*sunk to a condition of lost self-respect*), servile, slavish, sneaking, groveling, cringing, hangdog (*C*); *see* OBSEQUIOUS.

Antonyms: see ASSUMING, ASSURED, IMPUDENT, SELF-ASSERTIVE.

abjure, *v. t.* **1.** (*implying a solemn giving up of something one had held before*), recall (*contex.*), forswear, unswear (*R*).

abet: *aid, incite.*
abide: *stay, dwell, tarry, continue, stick, inhere.*
abide, *v. t.: endure, await.*
abiding: *lasting, constant.*

Antonyms: see MAINTAIN, STATE.

2. *See* DISCLAIM.

able, *a.* **1.** qualified (*having the specific gifts and skills that fit one for something*), competent, capable, effective (*chiefly of fitness for service*), sufficient.

Antonyms: see INCAPABLE.

2. clever (*intellectually quick or dexterous*), gifted, talented; *spec.* accomplished, notable (*A or R*).

3. powerful, competent, strong, masterly; *see* SKILFUL, LEARNED.

Antonyms: see WEAK.

abnormal, *a.* (*deviating from type*), exceptional (*unusual in occurrence*), irregular, erratic, anomalous, anomalistic (*R or tech.*), aberrant, eccentric, heteroclite (*R or gram.*), anormal (*R*); *spec.* unnatural; *see* MONSTROUS.

Antonyms: see NORMAL, ORDINARY.

abode, *n.* **1.** residence, habitation (*formal or stilted*), habitance (*A*), dwelling, house, quarters (*pl.; chiefly spec.*), seat (*A or poetic*), home, domicile (*chiefly legal*), tenement (*chiefly spec.*), rest (*R*), hole (*in contempt*), habitat (*chiefly bot. and zoöl.*), fireside (*fig.*), nest (*fig.*), harbor (*B*), cunabula (*B*); *spec.* place, camp (*temporary*), homestead, headquarters, residency, hostel, hospice, barracks (*pl.*); *see* QUARTERS, HOUSE.

2. *See* STAY.

abolish, *v. t.* **1.** (*do away with wholly*), annul, cancel, nullify (*put an end to something previously authorized*), quash, disannul (*emphatic for "annul"*), rescind, remove, abrogate; *spec.* (*chiefly in reference to laws*) antiquate, overrule; *see* REVOKE, INVALIDATE.

Antonyms: see ESTABLISH, CONFIRM, ENACT.

2. (*By force*) overthrow, overturn, subvert, eradicate, remove, extirpate, suppress, exterminate, extinguish, destroy; *see* ABATE, NULLIFY, ANNIHILATE.

Antonyms: see ESTABLISH, CONCLUDE.

abominable, *a.* **1.** odious, detestable, execrable, hateful, damnable, accursed, nefarious, impious (*affronting religious feelings*), hideous, horrible, horrid (*R or B*), nefandous (*R*), unutterable, unspeakable.

Antonyms: see ESTIMABLE, ATTRACTIVE.

2. disgusting, foul, loathsome, loathly (*B*), beastly, vile, revolting, putrid.

Antonyms: see PLEASANT, ATTRACTIVE, BEAUTIFUL.

abominate, *v. t.* abhor, detest, loathe, execrate, hate.

Antonyms: see LOVE, LIKE, ADMIRE.

abortion, *n.* **1.** miscarriage, cast (*referring to beasts only*), slink *or* slinking (*referring to beasts only*).

2. misconception, freak, monstrosity, cometo-naught (*R*).

3. *See* FAILURE.

abound, *v. i.* **1.** exuberate (*R*); *spec.* superabound.

2. overflow, flow, swim, teem; *spec.* luxuriate, revel; *see* SWARM.

abounding, *a.* replete, plenteous (*A*), flowing, full, fertile, fruitful, rife (*R*), flush, teeming, swimming, fat, rich; *see* SWARMING.

Antonyms: see INFREQUENT, DEFICIENT, RARE.

about, *adv. & prep.* **1.** around, round.

2. nearly, approximately, proximately, almost, nigh, well-nigh.

3. round, circuitously; *spec.* alternately, successively.

4. helter-skelter, zigzag.

5. concerning, anent (*Scot.*), touching, of, regarding, on, after, respecting, re (*Latin*).

about, *a.* *As used predicatively after "is," "was," etc.:* **1.** afoot, stirring, going, moving, doing (*C*).

2. near, ready, nigh (*A*).

above, *adv. & prep.* **1.** over, upon, on (*implies contact, where "above," "over" do not*).

2. *adv. See* ALOFT.

3. beyond, exceeding, surpassing, over; *spec.* super- (*a prefix*), hyper- (*a prefix*).

Antonyms: see BELOW.

abrade, *v. t.* rub (*contex.*), wear; *spec.* fret, grind, grate, scour; *see* SCRAPE.

abrasion, *n.* rubbing *or* rub (*contex., implying the wearing off of particles*), attrition, rasping, scouring, wearing *or* wear; *spec.* fret, graze; *see* SCRAPE.

abrasive, *a.* abradent, scrapy; *spec.* fretting, graty (*C*), rough.

abrasive, *n.* abradent, abrader (*R*); *spec.* carborundum, emery, sand, sandpaper, pumice, shagreen, putty, bort, rouge.

Antonyms: see LUBRICANT.

abreast, *a.* (*equally advanced*), beside, alongside; *spec.* aligned, parallel, even.

abridge, *v. t.* **1.** (*To do away with unnecessary space-filling*), abbreviate, compress, brief, reduce, contract (*chiefly spec.*), condense, compact, epitomize (*implying omission of less important parts*); *spec.* razee (*R*), abstract, dock; *see* SUMMARIZE.

Antonyms: see ENLARGE, EXTEND.

2. *See* SHORTEN, DEPRIVE, ABATE.

abridgment, *n.* **1.** *Referring to the act:* condensation, epitomization, compression, reduction, abbreviation, contraction (*implying shortening by the omission of unit parts*), *spec.* elision; *see* SUMMARIZATION.

Antonyms: see ENLARGEMENT, EXTENSION.

2. *Referring to the result: spec.* condensation, epitome (*the contents of a whole, cut down to the main headings*), abstract, summary, sum, compendium, compend (*R*), (*both implying a large content brought within a small compass*), brief, breviary *or* breviale (*A or R*), digest, précis (*tech.; French*), comprisal (*R*), synopsis

aboveboard: *openly.*

abroad: *wide-spread, astray, free, absent, wrong.*

abrogate: *abolish, revoke, invalidate.*

(*an orderly display of essential points to be taken in at one view*), bulletin; *see* SUMMARY.

abrupt, *a.* **1.** steep (*rising at an angle that makes ascent difficult*), precipitous (*cf.* "*precipice*"), sudden (*as of a sharp turn happening unexpectedly*), sharp, angular.

Antonyms: see GRADUAL.

2. offhand, sudden, hasty, unpremeditated, precipitate, tout-de-suite (*French*), out-of-hand, jerky.

Antonyms: see DELIBERATE.

absence, *n.* **1.** awayness (*R*); *spec.* nonattendance, nonappearance, cut (*C*).

Antonyms: see PRESENCE, ATTENDANCE.

2. *See* ABSENT-MINDEDNESS.

3. deficiency, privation (*logic; a loose use*), want; *spec.* destitution.

absent, *a.* **1.** away, abroad (*chiefly spec.*), elsewhere, otherwhere (*R*); *spec.* flown, distant, gone, exiled, banished, oversea, nonattendant.

Antonyms: see PRESENT.

2. deficient, missing, wanting, privative (*logic; a loose use*); *spec.* indigent (*R*), withdrawn, gone.

3. far-away, dreamy, abstracted (*with attention drawn away from things present to some matter of thought*), absorbed (*so concentrated upon a matter as to be oblivious of anything else*), distant, inattentive, vacant, preoccupied, distrait (*R; chiefly as French*), lost, absent-minded, rapt (*R*); *spec.* musing, breathless.

Antonyms: see ATTENTIVE.

absent-mindedness, *n.* abstraction, absorption, *etc. See* ABSENT, **3.**

Antonyms: see ATTENTION.

absolute, *a.* **1.** (*Implying freedom from limitations as to quality or degree*), pure, perfect, consummate, complete, total, entire, round, blank, unqualified, dead, clear, positive, utter, downright, sheer, thorough, thoroughgoing, stark, essential, mere (*R*), regular (*C*), teetotal (*C*), unalloyed, flat (*chiefly C*); *see* THOROUGH.

Antonyms: see PARTIAL, IMPERFECT.

2. (*Unhampered by conditions or controls*), unrestricted, unqualified, unbounded, independent, arbitrary, unreserved, uncontrolled, full, plenary, plenipotentiary (*chiefly spec.*), plenipotent, plenary; *spec.* categorematic; *see* AUTOCRATIC.

Antonyms: see RESTRICTED.

3. unreserved, unequivocal, unqualified, positive, independent, unconditional, unconditioned, peremptory.

Antonyms: see CONDITIONAL.

4. *See* ACTUAL, SELF-EXISTENT.

absolutely, *adv.* purely, utterly, entirely, consummately, flat, flatly, dead, downright, plumb (*S; chiefly U. S.*), doggoned (*C*), damned (*C*), roundly, teetotally (*C*), thoroughly, outright, altogether; *spec.* out.

absolution, *n.* **1.** forgiveness, freeing, justification (*chiefly eccl.*), clearance, shrift (*eccl.*), assoilment (*A*), discharge (*contex.*).

Antonyms: see RETALIATION, PUNISHMENT.

2. *See* ACQUITTAL.

absolve, *v. t. Set free from the consequences of guilt:* forgive, clear, assoil (*A*), wash (*fig.*), shrive (*eccl.*), justify (*chiefly eccl.*), discharge (*contex.*).

Antonyms: see PUNISH.

absorb, *v. t.* **1.** drink (*chiefly used with "in" or "up"*), imbibe, sop, occlude (*tech.*), soak, suck (*chiefly with "up"*), resorb (*R*); *spec.* reabsorb, ingulf *or* engulf, blot, sink.

Antonyms: see EXUDE, REFLECT, EMIT, DIFFUSE.

2. *Referring to mental process:* incorporate, imbibe, drink (*fig.*), take (*contex.*); *spec.* merge.

3. *Referring to things that engage the mind:* occupy, engross, preoccupy, immerse, sink, merge, bury, enwrap (*B*), devour, hold (*contex.*), prepossess.

absorbed, *a.* engaged, preoccupied, occupied, deep, sunk, buried, rapt (*B*), wrapt; *see* ABSENT.

absorbent, *a.* absorptive, bibulous, spongy, spongous (*R*), sorbent (*R*), thirsty (*R or fig.*), sorbefacient (*R*).

absorbing, *a.* engrossing.

absorption, *n.* **1.** imbibition, occlusion (*tech.*); *spec.* resorption (*R*), reabsorption, soaking, *etc.*

Antonyms: see REFLECTION, RADIATION, EMISSION.

2. incorporation, imbibition (*R*); *spec.* merger.

3. engagement, engrossment, preoccupation, prepossession.

abstain, *v. i.* forbear, refrain (*though both* refrain *and* abstain *imply self-imposed restraint,* abstain *often implies an injurious effect to be avoided;* refrain, *a closer curb of the desires and wishes*), withhold, stay, desist, patience (*R*).

Antonyms: see INDULGE.

abstainer, *n.* teetotaler, hydropot (*R*), Rechabite (*fig.*); *spec.* dry, prohibitionist.

abstemious, *a.* (*Whereas the other synonyms tend to refer to food and drink,* austere *implies a reference to character or form.*) ascetic, austere, sober, frugal, abstinent, moderate, temperate; *spec.* temperance (*C*).

Antonyms: see SELF-GRATIFYING, DRINKING, GLUTTONOUS.

abstinence, *n.* abstaining, abstention, withholdment (*R*), nephalism (*R*), self-denial, temperance, refrainment (*R*), forbearance (*R*), teetotalism.

abstract, *a.* **1.** (*Apart from any particular application*), ideal, general, metaphysical, transcendental, imaginary (*R*), theoretical, visionary (*R*); *see* ACADEMIC.

2. *See* ABSTRUSE.

Antonyms: see CONCRETE.

abstract, *n.* abridgment, conspectus, compendium, synopsis, syllabus (*chiefly law and*

abscond: *depart.* | **absent,** *v. t.: withdraw.* | **absolutism:** *autocracy.*

spec.); *spec.* docket, brief, note, headnote; *see* SUMMARY.

Antonyms: see ENLARGEMENT, EXTENSION, WHOLE.

abstract, *v. t.* **1.** withdraw, deduct, disengage, eliminate, remove, subtract, separate (*contex.*); *spec.* embezzle, steal (*figurative or S*).

2. *See* REMOVE, SUMMARIZE, ABRIDGE.

Antonyms: see ADD.

abstraction, *n.* withdrawal, deduction, *etc.*

abstruse, *a.* profound, concealed (*R*), obscure, recondite, abstract, deep, high, dark, acroamatic (*R*), difficult (*contex.*), esoteric (*fig.*), subtle; *spec.* far-fetched.

Antonyms: see EVIDENT, CLEAR.

absurd, *a.* irrational, preposterous, unreasonable, false (*contex.*), fallacious, sophistic (*R*), illogical, incongruous, incoherent, incredible, nonsensical; *spec.* silly, foolish, ludicrous, ridiculous, paradoxical, self-contradictory.

Antonyms: see LOGICAL, REASONABLE, TRUE, CONSISTENT.

abundance, *n.* **1.** more than enough, overflow, plenty, plentitude (*B*), copiousness, profusion, profuseness, plenteousness (*B*), amplitude, affluence, fullness, repletion, freeness, luxuriance, opulence, wealth, richness, prodigality, generosity, foison (*A*), cheap (*A*), routh (*Scot.*); *spec.* flood, exuberance, superabundance, flow, heaviness, lavishness.

Antonyms: see DEFICIENCY, INFREQUENCY, LACK.

abundant, *a.* abounding, copious, generous, luxuriant, plentiful, plenteous (*R or B*), opulent, ample, liberal, profuse, rich, flush (*chiefly spec.*), plenty (*chiefly C*), fat (*R*), free, effuse (*R*), bounteous, bountiful, affluent, numerous (*R*); *spec.* generous, lavish, flowing, exuberant, prodigal, thick, superabundant, profligate, rife, teeming, heavy, unstinted, big.

Antonyms: see DEFICIENT, INFREQUENT, MEAGER, SCANTY.

abundantly, *adv.* aboundingly, copiously, generously, galore (*chiefly C*).

abuse, *n.* **1.** misuse, misusage, ill-use, misemployment (*R or spec.*), abusing, mishandling, outrage, despite (*A*), perversion; *see* ILL-TREATMENT.

2. (*Implying anger and heated words*), reviling, revilement, vilification, vituperation (*implies overwhelming abuse*), malediction (*implies the uttering of curses*), insulting words, invective (*implies intention to discredit*), insultation (*R*), blasphemy (*fig.*), scurrility, libel, opprobrium, obloquy (*implies intent to disgrace*), contumely, rating, ribaldry, tongue-lashing; *spec.* Billingsgate, blackguardism; *see* DEFAMATION, DISPARAGEMENT.

Antonyms: see PRAISE, EULOGY, FLATTERY.

abuse, *v. t.* **1.** misuse, misemploy (*R or spec.*), mishandle, pervert, outrage; *spec.* haze; deceive (*A*), take advantage of (*A*); *see* ILL-TREAT.

Antonyms: see CHERISH.

2. revile, berate (*obs. or R in England*), vilify, vituperate, scurrilize (*R*), blaspheme (*fig.*), slang (*R*), whip (*fig.*), flay, lash, miscall (*R or dial.*), bullyrag (*C*), bawl out (*C*), give hell (*C*), flyte (*A or B*), tongue-lash; *spec.* blackguard (*R*), curse; *see* INSULT, DISPARAGE, DEFAME.

Antonyms: see PRAISE, ENNOBLE, FLATTER.

abusive, *a.* vilificatory, vituperative, insolent, blasphemous (*fig.*), despiteful (*B*), insulting, scurrilous, opprobrious, scandalous, outrageous, foul-mouthed (*contex.*), dyslogistic (*B or learned; used of names, senses, etc.*), contumelious, Thersitical (*fig.*), ribald; *spec.* disparaging, sarcastic, Fescennine (*fig.*); *see* DEFAMATORY.

Antonyms: see PRAISING, LAUDATORY, FLATTERING.

abut, *v. i.* join, butt (*of seams, etc.*); *see* BORDER.

abyss, *n.* deep (*B*), gulf, abysm (*A or poetic*), bottomless pit, hell, swallow (*R*), profound, profundity, chasm, gorge, pit, sink (*chiefly spec.*), void.

Antonyms: see HEIGHT, HEAVEN.

academic, *a.* **1.** collegiate, scholarly, scholastic, clerkly (*A*).

2. conventional, formal, orthodox, cut-and-dried (*C*), budge (*A*).

3. theoretical, speculative; *see* ABSTRACT.

4. belletristic, literary, classical, idealistic, impractical.

accede, *v. i.* **1.** arrive at, enter upon.

2. agree, assent, concur, conform, consent (*implies a greater degree than* assent), acquiesce (*with "in"; implying passive compliance*), concede, yield, subscribe, accord (*with "with"*).

Antonyms: see DISAGREE.

accent, *v. t.* accentuate, stress, emphasize, intensify; *spec.* circumflect (*A*).

Antonyms: see SLUR.

accent, *n.* **1.** stress, emphasis, accentuation, ictus (*tech.*); *spec.* circumflex, prime, secondary, mark, arsis, thesis.

2. *See* EMPHASIS, MODULATION, TONE.

accept, *v. t.* **1.** *See* RECEIVE, HONOR, BELIEVE.

2. recognize, embrace, adopt, take, receive (*referring to laws, etc.*), admit.

Antonyms: see REJECT, DECLINE.

acceptable, *a.* pleasant, welcome, allowable, agreeable, gratifying, grateful (*now only of things*), comfortable, canny (*Scot.*); *spec.* answerable, popular, liked, refreshing; *see* PLEASANT, TIMELY.

Antonyms: see UNACCEPTABLE.

acceptance, *n.* recognition, embracement, reception (*referring to laws, etc.*), taking; *spec.* vogue.

Antonyms: see DECLINATION, REFUSAL, REJECTION.

accepted, *a.* approved; *spec.* popular, conventional, orthodox.

---

access: *attack.*

---

accessible, *a.* approachable, come-at-able (*C*), get-at-able (*C*); *spec.* open, patent (*R*), ready, compassable, convenient, available, obtainable.
Antonyms: see INACCESSIBLE.

accession, *n.* **1.** *See* COMING, ADDITION.
2. agreement, accordance, assent, assentation (*A*), consent, acquiescence, concession, subscription, acceptance (*with "of"*), suffrage (*chiefly spec.*).
Antonyms: see DISAGREEMENT.

accessory, *a.* (*implying something secondary*) **1.** contributing, contributory, auxiliary, supplementary, supplemental, adjective, extra, additional, adjunct, suppletory (*B*), suppletive (*R*), accessary (*the less usual form*); *spec.* incident (*law*), appurtenant.
2. adventitious, appendant, dependent, supervenient, accompanying, bye (*R or spec.*), collateral, accessary (*the less usual form*).
Antonyms: see NECESSARY, ESSENTIAL.
3. abetting, privy, conniving, confederate, participant, assistant, accessary (*the less usual form*).

accessory, *n.* **1.** adjunct, dependent, adjective, belonging, accompaniment, appurtenance, appurtenant, concomitant, incident (*law*), accessary (*the less usual form*); (*C*) appliance, gadget; *spec.* property; *see* ACCIDENT.
2. privy; *spec.* assistant, participant, conniver; *see* ACCOMPLICE.

accident, *n.* **1.** *See* CHANCE, MISFORTUNE, QUALITY, ACCESSORY.
2. accessory, nonessential, external, incident, collateral, unessential.
Antonyms: see ESSENTIAL.

accidental, *a.* **1.** (*happening by chance*), fortuitous, casual, incident; *spec.* stray.
Antonyms: see CONSEQUENTIAL, INTENTIONAL.
2. (*not primary or essential*), nonessential, unessential, accessory, incidental, external, adventitious, collateral, subsidiary, contingent.
Antonyms: see NECESSARY, FUNDAMENTAL, INHERENT, ESSENTIAL.
3. *See* OCCASIONAL.

acclimatize, *v. t.* acclimate, season, naturalize, adapt (*to new conditions*).

accompaniment, *n.* attendance, escort, convoy (*chiefly spec.*), *etc.*

accompany, *v. t.* attend, escort, convoy (*chiefly spec.*), follow; *spec.* cavalier (*R*), esquire (*R*), companion (*R*), chaperon.
Antonyms: see ABANDON.

accompanying, *a.* attendant, accessory, concomitant.

accomplice, *n. spec.* abettor, accessory; *see* ASSOCIATE.

accomplish, *v. t.* complete, fulfill, perform, effect, achieve, do, attain, execute, compass, effectuate, work, manage, contrive, dispatch, consummate, negotiate (*spec. or C*), win, expedite (*R*); *see* FINISH.

accomplished, *a.* **1.** completed, complete, fulfilled, performed, done, consummate, *etc.*
Antonyms: see CRUDE.
2. *Referring to a person, his learning, etc.:* finished, proficient, cultivated, polished (*chiefly spec.*), beseen (*A, as in "well beseen"*); *spec.* learned, versed, read, exquisite.
Antonyms: see BOORISH, RUSTIC.

accomplishment, *n.* **1.** fulfillment, doing, completion, execution, consummation, performance, work, achievement, management, deed, feat (*referring to an act*), negotiation (*spec. or C*); *spec.*, dispatch, triumph.
2. (*usually in pl.*), refinement, embellishment, acquirement, attainment, acquisition; *spec.* graces (*pl.*), proficiency, polish (*used in a generic sense*; as, *"a man without polish"*).

accordingly, *adv.* agreeably, correspondingly, conformably, consistently, so, therefore.

accoucheur, *n.* **accoucheuse** (*fem., French*). obstetrician (*chiefly spec.*), midwife, howdie (*Scot., fem. only*).

account, *n.* **1.** *See* COMPUTATION, CONSIDERATION, IMPORTANCE.
2. reckoning, tally, score (*chiefly spec.*).
3. statement, report, description, narration, relation, recounting, recountal (*R*), rehearsal, recital, recitation, record, history (*chiefly spec.*), story, tale, rede (*A or D*); *spec.* chronicle, travels (*pl.*), summary, detail; *see* ANECDOTE, NARRATIVE.
4. score, tick (*C*), battels (*pl.*; *Univ. of Oxford*), shot (*A*), reckoning.

account, *v. i. spec.* report, return; *see* SETTLE.

accountable, *a.* responsible, answerable, liable, amenable; *spec.* good, solid.
Antonyms: see UNACCOUNTABLE.

accountant, *n.* clerk (*contex.*), bookkeeper; *spec.* actuary (*life insurance*), auditor, cashier, teller, controller, sirkar (*Anglo-Indian*).

accouterments, *n. pl.* equipment, gear (*A*); *spec.* harness, clothing, dress, trappings (*pl.*), gears (*pl.*), machine.

accredited, *a.* credentialed, authorized, sanctioned, acknowledged, accepted, vouched (*with "for"*), attested.

accretion, *n.* **1.** *See* GROWTH, ADDITION, GAIN.
2. concretion, adhesion, coherence.

accrue, *v. i.* (*implies origin in regular growth*), arise, come, grow, inure (*to be operative*), redound (*said of benefits, advantages, etc.*); *spec.* vest, mature, attach, fall (*chiefly with "due"*).

accrued, *a.* due, owing; *spec.* overdue, matured, vested, added (*as regular increase*).

accumulate, *v. t. & i.* heap (*with "up"*), pile (*with "up"*), cumulate, mass, amass (*implies bulk, extent, impressive results*), gather (*esp. with "together"*), agglomerate, aggregate, collect, congest, roll (*with "up"*), acervate (*R*), coacervate (*R*); *spec.* scrape (*with "up"*), garner, store.
Antonyms: see SCATTER.

---

accommodate: *adapt, conform, arrange, furnish, oblige, hold.*
accommodating: *obliging.*
accord, *v. t.: give.*
accord, *v. i.: agree, accede, harmonize.*
accord, *n.: agreement, correspondence, harmony.*
accost: *address, greet.*
account, *v. t.: consider.*

---

accumulation, *n.* amassment, cumulation, agglomeration, conglomeration (*implies absence of design or order*), conglomerate, aggregation, heap, aggregate, collection, gathering, acervation (*R*), coacervation (*R*); *spec.* congeries, huddle, drift, litter; *see* STORE, STOCK.

accuracy, *n.* exactness, precision, propriety, fidelity, justness, truth, *etc.*

accurate, *a.* exact, precise, correct, just, faithful, true, close, critical, strict, nice, particular, proper, exquisite; *see* TRUE.

Antonyms: see INACCURATE, INEXACT.

accursed, *a.* anathematized, cursed (*often in an oath*), execrated, devoted, damned (*chiefly in an oath*), doomed (*A*), blasted (*chiefly a vulgar oath*), hated, abhorred.

Antonyms: see BLESSED.

accusation, *n.* indictment, charge, impeachment, arraignment, denunciation, taxing (*with "with"*), delation (*chiefly by an informer*), impeach (*R*); *spec.* complaint, attack, crimination, recrimination.

Antonyms: see ACQUITTAL.

accuse, *v. t.* charge, indict, impeach, arraign, denounce, task, tax (*with "with"*), attaint (*A*), delate (*chiefly Scot.*); *spec.* article, recriminate, criminate, incriminate, countercharge, report, attack.

Antonyms: see ACQUIT.

accuser, *n. Spec.* plaintiff, prosecutor, complainant, libellant, informer, informant, delator.

accustom, *v. t.* habituate, use (*generally in some phrase as "make or get used to"*), familiarize (*R*), addict, wont, inure, hackney (*used with "in"; chiefly in a bad sense*); *spec.* train, naturalize; *see* TRAIN.

Antonyms: see DISACCUSTOM.

accustomed, *a.* **1.** used (*with "to"*), wont, wonted; *spec.* natural; *see* ADDICTED.

2. *See* CUSTOMARY.

acknowledge, *v. t.* (*generally with implication of public admission*) **1.** allow, grant, admit, agnize (*A*), avouch (*R*), avow, confess (*usually implying an admission of wrong*), recognize, yield, concede, testify (*chiefly Biblical*); *see* ANSWER.

Antonyms: see CONTRADICT, DENY.

2. own (*to acknowledge as referable to one's self*), confess, recognize, admit, avow (*obs. R*); *spec.* father, mother.

3. profess, declare, avow.

4. *Meaning "to receipt for":* receipt.

5. *See* NOTICE.

acknowledgment, *n.* **1.** confession, recognition, admission, allowance, grant, concession.

Antonyms: see DENIAL.

2. profession, declaration, avowal.

acquaintance, *n. spec.* friend, intimate, associate, familiar.

Antonyms: see STRANGER.

acquainted, *a.* **1.** *Referring to things: see* AWARE.

2. *Referring to persons: spec.* familiar (*which see*). *"Acquainted" implies no more than mere personal intercourse and has no general synonym. Cf.* KNOW, *v. t.*

acquired, *a. Spec.* learned, adopted, cultivated, affected.

Antonyms: see INNATE.

acquisition, *n.* **1.** *Referring to the act or action:* gain, acquirement, acquist (*B*); *spec.* purchase, usucaption, conquest; *see* GETTING.

Antonyms: see LOSS.

2. *Referring to the thing:* acquirement (*chiefly spec.*), acquest (*B*); *spec.* spoils (*pl.*), purchase, trade, bargain, buy (*C*); *see* GAIN, ACCOMPLISHMENT.

acquisitive, *a.* grasping, avid, quæstuary (*R*); *spec.* greedy (*here, not so much eager for food, as desirous of gain or possession*).

acquit, *v. t.* **1.** *See* DISCHARGE, PAY, BEHAVE.

2. exculpate, exonerate, clear, discharge, absolve, purge (*R or A, clear of guilt*), assoil (*A*), quit (*A or R*).

Antonyms: see CONVICT, ACCUSE, BLAME.

acquittal, *n.* **1.** *See* ACQUITTANCE.

2. exculpation, acquittance (*R*), clearance, clearing, discharge, purgation (*R*), absolution (*eccl.*); *spec.* compurgation, acquitment (*R*).

Antonyms: see ACCUSATION, CONVICTION.

acquittance, *n.* **1.** *See* DISCHARGE, PAYMENT, ACQUITTAL.

2. *Referring to the document:* release, acquittal (*R, exc. legal*); *spec.* discharge.

acrid, *a.* **1.** pungent, biting, acid, corrosive, virulent, sharp, caustic, rough (*contex.*), mordicant (*R*), acrimonious, vitriolic (*spec. or fig.*).

Antonyms: see BLAND.

2. *See* ACRIMONIOUS.

acridity, *n.* **1.** pungency, roughness (*contex.*), bitingness, acidity, corrosiveness, virulence, causticity.

2. *See* ACRIMONY.

acrimonious, *a.* **1.** *See* ACRID.

2. tart, corrosive, acid, bitter, acrid, sharp, cutting, caustic, pungent, virulent, rancorous, atrabilious (*B*), vitriolic, sour, biting; *see* SARCASTIC.

Antonyms: see SMOOTH, AGREEABLE, GOOD-NATURED.

acrimony, *n.* acerbity, asperity, acidity, heat, acridity, virulence, pungency, rancor, tartness; *spec.* sarcasm, asperity.

acrobat, *n. Spec.* tumbler, vaulter, equilibrist, rope-walker, contortionist, funambulist; *spec.* gymnast.

across, *prep.* on, over, athwart, overthwart (*R*), thwart (*A or B*), cross (*now chiefly dial. or B*).

act, *n.* **1.** *Referring to an act considered as a*

---

ache: *pain.*
achieve: *accomplish, get.*
acid: *sour, rough, acrid, acrimonious.*
acme: *height, top.*
acquaint: *inform.*
acquiesce: *accede.*
acquire: *get, gain, receive, learn.*
acquirement: *acquisition, accomplishment, getting.*
across: *crosswise.*
act: *work, tell.*

---

whole without involving the idea of the time occupied or of its going on: deed, performance, action; *see* ACTION, **1.** DEED.
Antonyms: see NEGLIGENCE.
2. *Referring to the proceeding or course of acting: see* ACTION.
3. action, move, step, turn, deal, movement (*R*), play, proceeding.

act, *v. i.* **1.** perform, work, operate, function, functionate (*R*), go, serve, make; *spec.* do, energize, preside, officiate; *see* WORK, TELL.
2. *Referring to the theater, shows, etc.:* perform, play; *spec.* theatrize (*R*), theatricalize (*R*), mum (*A or B*), mime.
3. move, proceed, deal, stir.
4. *See* BEHAVE, DISSEMBLE.

act, *v. t.* **1.** perform, take (*a part*), represent, impersonate, enact (*R or rhetorical*), play, mince (*R or A, act in a mincing fashion*), assume, support, sustain, render, do (*as a part, an act, etc.*); *spec.* counterfeit, theatricalize (*R*); *see* PERSONATE.
2. *See* PRETEND.

acting, *n.* performance, representation, rendition (*U. S.*); *spec.* histrionism, dramaturgy, mummery, personation.

action, *n.* **1.** act (*R*), doing (*chiefly in pl.*), acting, performance, movement, working, operation; *spec.* effect, motion, play (*of the feelings, passions, etc.*), operation, operance (*R*), touch, process, procedure, business (*theatrical*), function, reaction, response, conation. *If considered as a whole without reference to the element of time these terms are sometimes used as synonyms of "act." See* ACT, **1.**
Antonyms: see INACTIVITY, REST.
2. measure, step, course, procedure, provision, proceeding, démarche (*French*); *spec.* counterstep, precaution; *see* STROKE.
3. *See* BEHAVIOR, TRANSACTION, ACTIVITY, BUSTLE.
4. influence, operation, working, touch; *see* AGENCY.
5. proceeding (*legal*), suit, case, cause, process; *spec.* plea (*hist. or Scot.*), remanet, interpleader, replevin, assumpsit, trespass, libel, counterclaim, prosecution.

active, *a.* **1.** acting, operative, operant (*R*); *spec.* exertive, conative.
Antonyms: see INACTIVE.
2. energetic, vigorous, assiduous, busy, industrious, hustling (*C, U. S.*), vivacious (*chiefly spec.*), animated, bustling (*C, U. S.*), rustling (*C, U. S.*), brisk, humming (*S*), deedful (*R*), pragmatic (*R*), deedy (*dial.*), deliver (*A*); *spec.* strong, sedulous, light, rapid; *see* NIMBLE, LIVELY, RESTLESS.
Antonyms: see SLUGGISH, IDLE, INDOLENT, LAZY.
3. *See* ALERT, AMBITIOUS.

activity, *n.* **1.** energy (*chiefly tech.*), vigor, vivacity (*chiefly spec.*), briskness, actuality (*obs., exc. metaphysics*), hustle (*U. S.; S or C*), operation (*R*), operancy (*R*); *spec.* nimbleness.
Antonyms: see INDOLENCE.
2. *See* ALERTNESS, AMBITION.
3. coil (*A*), bustle, hustle (*U. S.; S or C*), rustle (*U. S.; S or C*), stir, action, turmoil, movement; *see* EXCITEMENT, BUSTLE.
Antonyms: see CALM, PEACE.

actor, *n.* **1.** *Spec.* agent, doer, performer.
Antonyms: see SUBJECT.
2. player, performer, personator, Thespian (*B*), actress (*fem.*), histrion (*R*), impersonator (*chiefly spec.*), dramatis personæ (*Latin; pl.*); *spec.* tragedian, tragédienne (*fem.*), comedian, comedienne (*fem.*), pantomimist, farceur (*French*), caricaturist, burlesquer, star, lead (*S*), diva (*fem.*), ingénue (*fem.*), Pierrot (*masc.*), Pierrette (*fem.*), Columbine, punchinello (*Italian*), buffo (*Italian*), comique (*French*), pantomime (*hist.*), mummer, mime, protagonist, tritagonist. *Cf.* PUPPET.

actual, *a.* real, true, very, factual, positive, concrete, existing, present (*existing at the present time*), existent, veritable, absolute, indeed (*postpositive*), tangible, practical, substantial, substantive, effective (*as opposed to "potential"*); *spec.* sober, right, hypostatic, hypostatical.
Antonyms: see UNREAL, VISIONARY, IMAGINARY, SUPPOSED, FABULOUS, FICTITIOUS, APPARENT.

actuality, *n.* **1.** reality, realism, realness, verity, truth, trueness, substantiality, sooth (*A*), substance, tangibility, effect (*chiefly in "in effect"*), fact.
2. *In a concrete sense:* positive, eternities (*pl.*), reality, truth, verity, *etc.*
Antonyms: see ILLUSION, FICTION, DREAM, DAY-DREAM.

actualize, *v. t.* realize, substantialize, verify (*R*), substantiate, reify (*R*), hypostatize (*tech.*), eventuate (*R*); *see* MATERIALIZE, PERSONIFY.

actually, *adv.* really, truly, veritably, verily, indeed.

actuate, *v. t.* excite, impel, move, activate (*tech.*), start (*often with "off"*); *see* STIMULATE, INCITE.

adapt, *v. t.* prepare (*contex.*), accommodate, fit, conform, suit; *spec.* coördinate, match, square, arrange, adjust, shape, frame, turn, contemper (*A*), attemper, harmonize, naturalize, prepare, assimilate; *see* QUALIFY.

adaptable, *a.* amenable, pliable, pliant, tractable, accommodative, conformable, applicable, adaptive, flexible; *spec.* convenient, versatile, faculative (*biol.*).
Antonyms: see INTRACTABLE, OBSTINATE, UNYIELDING.

adaptation, *n.* preparation (*contex.*), arrangement, accommodation, qualification, design, reworking, *etc.*

add, *v. t.* **1.** join, unite, put (*with "with," "on,"*

activate: *animate.*
acumen: *discernment.*
acute: *pointed, sharp, intense, discerning, sensitive, high.*
adage: *saying.*
adamantine: *hard, unyielding, unfeeling.*

"*to*"), adjoin (*R*), superadd; *spec.* tack, tag (*with* "*on*"), adject (*R*), affix, attach, postfix, interline, interpolate, engraft (*with* "*on*"), annex, append, subjoin; *see* ATTACH.
Antonyms: see ABSTRACT, DEDUCT.
2. compute (*contex.*), sum (*chiefly spec.*), total, foot (*with* "*up*"), cast (*tech.*); *spec.* superadd.
addict, *v. t.* apply, devote, give, habituate (*with* "*to*"); *see* APPLY.
addicted, *a.* (*generally implies a weakness*) accustomed (*contex.*), habituated (*with* "*to*"), given, devoted (*generally implies a good quality*).
addiction, *n.* application, devotion.
addition, *n.* **1.** adjection (*R*), joining, uniting; *spec.* attachment, annexation, subjunction, interlineation, superaddition, *etc.*
2. computation (*contex.*), summation (*chiefly spec.*), totaling, footing (*with* "*up*").
Antonyms: see DEDUCTION.
3. increase; *spec.* raise, enlargement, adjunct, accretion, accession, affix, access, increment, appendage, appendix, annex, annexation, attachment, subscript, codicil, interlineation, interpolation, contribution, supplement, equation, rider, tag, imitation, extension, prolongation, continuation; *see* PREFIX, SUFFIX, POSTSCRIPT.
additional, *a.* extra, further, new, fresh, more, else (*postpositive*), remanent (*R*), supervenient (*R*); *spec.* other, ulterior, supplementary; *see* ACCESSORY, SPARE.
address, *v. t.* **1.** *See* DIRECT, APPLY.
2. accost (*in speech*; *A*), speak, bespeak (*A*); *spec.* apostrophize, petition, salute, memorialize, whisper (*A*), pray, stump (*C*), harangue; *see* GREET.
address, *n.* **1.** speech, talk (*a word suggestive of informality or brevity*), parley, compellation (*A*); *spec.* invocation, valedictory, salutatory, appeal, petition, memorial, prayer, lecture, lecturette (*C or playful*), harangue, eulogy, oration, argument, sermon, salutation, apostrophe; *see* GREETING, SERMON.
2. *See* SKILL, TACT.
adduce, *v. t.* (*the primary notion is "to bring forward"*), instance, cite, bring (*a charge, argument, etc.*); *see* PRESENT.
adequacy, *n.* sufficiency.
adequate, *a.* equal (*with* "*to*"), commensurate (*with* "*to*" *or* "*with*"), commensurable (*with* "*with*"), sufficient (*with* "*to*" *or* "*for*"; *implies fulfilling an end, whereas* adequate *implies meeting a need*), satisfactory (*chiefly spec.*), enough, enow (*A*), ample, competent, due, good, copious; *spec.* proportionate.
Antonyms: see INADEQUATE, DEFICIENT.
adjerent, *n.* follower, satellite (*literary*), dangler; *spec.* hobbler (*obs. or hist.*), retainer, sectary, supporter, upholder; *see* DISCIPLE, PARTIZAN.
adjacency, *n.* **1.** adjoining, contiguity, contiguousness, juxtaposition; *spec.* abutment.
2. *See* NEARNESS.
adjacent, *a.* (*implies nearness, but not necessarily contact; the following synonyms imply contact*), contiguous, conterminous, bordering, adjoining, touching; *spec.* abutting; *see* NEAR.
Antonyms: see APART, DISTANT, SEPARATE.
adjoin, *v. t.* **1.** touch, abut (*chiefly spec.*); *spec.* border, neighbor, side (*A*).
2. *See* ADD.
adjourn, *v. i.* rise, disperse, dissolve.
adjourn, *v. t.* **1.** suspend, continue (*chiefly Scot.*); *spec.* prorogue. *Cf.* DISSOLVE.
2. *See* DEFER.
adjudge, *v. t.* judge (*A*), award, assign, decree, decide, settle, give; condemn, sentence.
adjunct, *a.* added, additional, annexed, connected, auxiliary; *see* ACCESSORY.
adjuration, *n.* conjuration, obtestation, appeal (*contex.*), exorcism (*R*).
adjust, *v. t.* **1.** *See* ARRANGE, ADAPT, HARMONIZE.
2. arrange, dispose, regulate, fix, trim, set, coapt (*R*), rig (*chiefly spec.*); *spec.* register, orient, orientate, size, shape, level, collimate (*R*), square, justify, reconcile, true, modulate (*the voice, tones, light, etc.*), comb, couch (*a lance, etc.*), dress, tune, readjust, harmonize, rectify, systematize, gait, coördinate; *see* TUNE, SIZE, SET, PROPORTION.
Antonym: see DISARRANGE.
adjustment, *n.* arrangement, disposition, trim, *etc.*; *spec.* compromise. *Cf.* ADJUST.
administer, *v. t.* **1.** give, apply, serve, dispense, dispensate (*R*); *spec.* exhibit, distribute.
2. *In law:* settle, dispose (*R*); *spec.* distribute.
3. *Of academic examinations:* supervise, conduct, watch, oversee, proctor, invigilate (*chiefly Brit.*).
4. *See* DELIVER, MANAGE, CONTRIBUTE.
admirable, *a.* good, admirative (*B*), estimable; adorable (*C*); *see* EXCELLENT, FINE, ESTIMABLE, PLEASANT.
Antonym: see CONTEMPTIBLE.
admiration, *n.* **1.** wonder (*A or B*).
2. approval, approbation (*with* "*of*"), esteem (*with* "*for*"), pleasure (*with* "*in*"), reverence (*with* "*for*"), adoration (*with* "*of*").
Antonyms: see ABHORRENCE, CONDEMNATION.
admire, *v. t.* **1.** wonder (*A or B*).
2. approve, approbate, esteem, love (*C*); *spec.* idolize, latrize (*R*), revere, adore, idolatrize.
Antonyms: see CONDEMN, ABHOR, ABOMINATE.
admission, *n.* **1.** admittance, reception, receipt (*R*), adhibition (*R*).
Antonym: see EXPULSION.
2. institution, investiture (*tech.*), initiation,

---

adept, *a.: skilful, tactful.*
adept, *n.: master.*
adhere: *stick.*
adhesive: *sticky.*
adieu: *good-by.*
adjoin: *touch, border.*
adjoining: *adjacent.*
adjudicate, *v. t.: decree.*
adjudicate, *v. i.: judge.*
adjudication: *award, decree, judgment.*
adjunct: *addition, accessory.*
adjure: *bid, ask.*

(*A*) *archaic.* (*B*) *bookish, poetic, literary or learned.* (*C*) *colloquial.* (*Contex.*) *contextual.* (*R*) *rare.* (*S*) *slang.*
See pp. viii–ix.

inauguration, investure (*R*), vesture (*R*); *spec.* collation, incardination.
3. *See* ENTRANCE, ACKNOWLEDGMENT.

admit, *v. t.* **1.** receive, adhibit (*R*), intromit (*R*).
2. install, induct, invest, vest, institute, inaugurate, initiate, enter; *spec.* matriculate, incardinate.
Antonym: see EXPEL.
3. *See* ACKNOWLEDGE.

admixture, *n.* **1.** *See* MIXTURE.
2. mixture, infusion, leaven, tincture, tinge, cast, alloy, spice, sprinkling, seasoning, suspicion, soupçon (*French*), flavor; *see* DASH.

admonitory, *a.* monitory, commonitory (*R*); *see* WARNING, REPROVING.

adopt, *v. t.* **1.** arrogate (*Roman law*), affiliate (*R or fig.*); *spec.* father, mother, naturalize.
2. embrace, espouse, father (*fig.*), take (*a person's side or part*); *spec.* borrow, follow; *see* CHOOSE, COPY.
Antonym: see REJECT.

adoption, *n.* **1.** arrogation (*Roman law*), affiliation (*R or fig.*).
2. embrace (*R*), embracement, espousal.

adult, *n. Spec.* major, Nestor (*fig.*).
Antonyms: see INFANT.

adulterate, *v. t.* falsify (*contex.*), sophisticate, blend, dose (*C or tech.*), debase, doctor (*C*), cook (*C*); *spec.* vitiate (*with "with"*), weaken, simpson (*S*), dash, interpolate, sand, load, fill, dilate, thin, drug, lace, water.
Antonyms: see PURIFY.

adulterated, *a.* impure, sophisticated.

adulterer, *n.* fornicator (*tech.*).

adultery, *n.* fornication (*tech.*), infidelity (*a euphemism*).

advance, *v. i.* **1.** progress, proceed, go, move, make, press, push, march, head (*against force*), incede (*R*); *spec.* inch, creep, drive, gain.
Antonyms: see RECEDE, RETREAT, RETIRE.
2. rise, increase, appreciate (*U. S.*) enhance; *spec.* boom.
Antonyms: see FALL, DEPRECIATE.
3. *See* PROGRESS.

advance, *v. t.* **1.** forward, further, improve, promote, push, shove (*C or S*), speed.
Antonyms: see ABASE, RETIRE.
2. raise, prefer, adduce, suggest, present, venture, propound; *see* PROPOSE, OFFER.
Antonyms: see SUPPRESS, REPRESS.
3. raise, heighten, increase, improve, appreciate (*U. S.*), enhance, boost (*S*); *spec.* boom, bull.
Antonyms: see DEPRECIATE.
4. furnish (*beforehand*), supply; *spec.* imprest (*A*).
5. raise, elevate, exalt, promote, aggrandize (*R*), prefer (*R or A*), *spec.* make, dignify, ennoble.
Antonyms: see ABASE.

advance, *n.* **1.** forwarding, furtherance, promotion, preference; *see* AID.
2. progression, advancement, march, procession (*R*), progress, access (*R*), push, headway, profection (*obs. or astrol.*).
Antonyms: see RECESSION, RETREAT.
3. *Spec.* imprest (*A*).
4. suggestion, preferment, preference, venturing; *see* PROPOSAL, OFFER.
5. rise, appreciation (*U. S.*), raise (*C*), boost (*C or S*), enhancement; *spec.* boom, spurt.
Antonyms: see FALL, DEPRECIATION.

advanced, *a.* **1.** ripe (*as "a ripe age"*).
2. *See* PRECOCIOUS, FORWARD.

advancing, *a.* rising; *spec.* booming.

advantage, *n.* **1.** superiority, precedence, better (*used idiomatically*), odds (*pl. and sing.*), forehand, prize (*R*), leverage (*R*), purchase (*mech. or fig.*); *spec.* spare.
Antonyms: see DISADVANTAGE.
2. *See* GOOD, BENEFIT.

advantageous, *a.* superior, favorable, profitable, gainful, good, clever (*C*), expedient, expediential (*R*), behoveful (*A*), useful, right (*contex.*), wise (*contex.*), advisable; *see* BENEFICIAL.
Antonyms: see DISADVANTAGEOUS, UNWISE, INADVISABLE.

adventurer, *n. spec.* free lance, condottiere (*Italian*), landloper *or* landlouper (*B*).

advertize, *v. t.* **1.** notify, notice, announce, proclaim, publish; *spec.* avow, blaze, blazon (*implies ostentation*), noise, trumpet, warn; PROCLAIM.
Antonyms: see HIDE.
2. *Spec.* circularize, bill, placard, post, poster, cry, quack, push.

advertizement, *n. spec.* notice, bill, placard, poster, ad (*C*), blurb (*C*), ballyhoo.

advice, *n.* **1.** (*in* advice *is implied a knowledge of practical matters, in* counsel *a larger wisdom of a more serious nature*), counsel, rede (*A*), opinion, recommendation, advisement (*A*), admonition, instruction; suggestion (*sing. or pl.*); *spec.* misadvice, miscounsel, dehortation (*R*); *see* EXHORTATION.
2. *See* NOTICE, INFORMATION.

advise, *v. t.* **1.** counsel, rede (*A or B*), recommend, monish (*R*), admonish (*B*), guide (*contex.*); *spec.* disadvise, misadvise, miscounsel, dehort (*R*), exhort.
2. *See* INFORM.

adviser, *n.* **1.** counselor, guide (*contex.*), ad-

---

admonish: *warn, advise, reprove.*
ado: *trouble.*
adolescence: *youth.*
adorable: *estimable, fine.*
adore: *worship, admire, love.*
adorn: *ornament.*
adrift: *afloat.*
adroit: *skillful, ready.*
adult: *grown.*
advent: *arrival, coming.*
adventitious: *accessory, accidental.*
adventure, *v. t.:* *venture.*
adventurous: *venturesome, rash, dangerous, reckless.*
adversary: *enemy, opponent.*
adverse: *opposed, opposing, unfavorable.*
adversity: *misfortune, reverse.*
advertence: *reference.*
advise: *consult.*
advised: *deliberate.*

monisher; *spec.* referendary, comprador (*Oriental*), assessor.

2. *See* INFORMANT.

advocacy, *n.* support; *see* DEFENSE.

advocate, *v. t.* support, favor, plead; *see* DEFEND.

advocate, *n.* **1.** supporter, favorer, pleader; *spec.* intercessor, interpleader, patron (*Roman antiq.*).

Antonyms: see OPPONENT.

2. *See* LAWYER, CHRIST.

aërate, *v. t.* aërify; *spec.* ventilate, inflate.

aëronaut, *n.* aërostat, navigator (*contex.*); *see* AVIATOR.

aëronautics, *n.* aërostatics, aërostation, navigation (*contex.*); *spec.* aërodonetics, ballooning; *see* AVIATION.

æsthetic, *also* esthetic, *a.* tasteful, tasty (æsthetic *being the formal and more exact term,* tasteful *more familiar, and* tasty *C and inelegant*); *see* ELEGANT.

affable, *a.* sociable, conversable, debonair (*B*), talkable (*R*); *spec.* accostable (*R*), approachable, accessible, gracious, courteous, soft-spoken, communicative, free, unreserved.

Antonyms: see ARROGANT, ILL-TEMPERED, SURLY, HAUGHTY, HATEFUL.

affair, *n. Thing done, being done, or to be done:* **1.** business, transaction (*implies dealing with others*), job (*more usually implying an element of seriousness, work, or the like.*)

2. operation (*implying usually something mechanical*).

3. proceeding, undertaking, business (*usually contemptuous*), transaction, job (*applying vaguely to almost anything done or happening which it is not intended to characterize closely as a* duel, fight, battle, intrigue, amour, trick, *etc.*); entertainment, scandal, finances (*pl.*); *see* TRANSACTION, CONCERN, THING.

affect, *v. t.* touch, reach, take (*with "disease," "blow," "fancy," etc., as the subject*), seize (*with "idea" or the like as the subject*), hit (*C*); *spec.* possess, attack, infect, smite, hurt, trouble, move, grip, concern (*implying that one's interests are involved*), interest, pierce, perturb, impress, penetrate, strike, nip (*R*); *see* INFLUENCE, TAINT, THRILL, AGITATE, EXCITE, IMPRESS.

affect, *v. t.* pretend, assume, feign; use, practice, tend (*with "to"*), pose, attitudinize (*B*), act, boast, take (*with "up"*).

affectation, *n.* artificiality, frill (*S*), mannerism (*in* affectation *a conscious effort is implied; a* mannerism, *however, may be unconscious*), emulation (*A*); *spec.* modishness, profession, conventionality, mincingness. *Cf.* AFFECTED.

affected, *a.* **1.** touched, reached, *etc.*; *spec.* infected, tainted, attacked, seized, distempered, concerned, diseased, *etc.* (*implying the influence of, or as of, contagion*).

Antonyms: see UNAFFECTED, INTACT.

2. *See* PRETENDED.

3. artificial, nonnatural (*R*), unnatural, mannered; *spec.* modish, stagy (*C*), conventional, missish, namby-pamby, got-up (*S*), smirking, mincing, minikin (*R*), niminy-piminy (*R*), forced (*implying something assumed or displayed for effect*), mealy; *see* PRETENTIOUS.

Antonyms: see ARTLESS, SINCERE, NATURAL, SIMPLE, UNAFFECTED, FRANK.

affecting, *a.* **1.** moving, impressive (*not implying the special nature of the effect*).

2. moving, touching, pathetic, pitiable, pathetical (*R*), piercing, heart-rending, nerve-racking, tender, feeling, pungent (*implying excitation or expression of the emotions of pity, kindness, etc.*)

affection, *n.* **1.** ailment, trouble, *which see.*

2. emotion, feeling (*without implication as to its nature*).

3. liking (*implying merely desire or inclination toward something*).

4. fondness (*often implying a foolish, or unreasoning or trivial inclination or desire*).

5. love (*usually implying domestic or sexual affection*), passion (*often implying uncontrollable desire, and, specifically, lust*), rage (*C or S; implying, usually, deep or powerful emotion*).

6. regard, bosom (*fig.*), attachment (*contex.*), charity (*Christian religion, A*), storge (*tech.; R*); *spec.* dotage, idolization, latrization (*R*), familism (*R*); *see* LOVE.

Antonyms: see DISLIKE, HATRED, ABHORRENCE, ILL-WILL, INDIFFERENCE.

7. *In a medical sense: spec.* infection, contagion.

affectionate, *a.* fond (*often spec.*), loving, warm, tender, soft (*often spec., and then C or contemptuous*); *spec.* doting, spoony (*A or S*), hot (*S*), amorous; fatherly, motherly, sisterly, brotherly.

Antonyms: see INDIFFERENT, APATHETIC, COLD, DISAGREEABLE, HATEFUL, SHARP, STERN.

affiliate, *v. t.* **1.** *See* JOIN.

2. filiate; adopt; *spec.* father, mother (*with "on"* or *"upon"*).

affirmative, *a.* predicative, declarative, declaratory; assertive; *spec.* insistent, insistive (*R*).

afflict, *v. t. Spec.* strike, beset, smite, ply; *spec.* persecute; *see* TROUBLE, OPRESS.

affliction, *n.* calamity, trouble, pain, misery, sorrow, grief; *spec.* trial, disability, disease, sickness, misfortune, visitation, blow.

afford, *v. t.* **1.** *In the sense of "to have resources or means that are adequate":* carry, manage, bear, go (*C*).

2. *See* FURNISH, YIELD.

afloat, *a.* **1.** floating.

Antonyms: AGROUND.

2. overflowed, submerged, flooded, swamped, swimming; *spec.* anchorless, awash.

---

aerial: *atmospheric, airy, lofty.*
affinity: *relation, liking, attraction.*
affirm: *swear, state.*
affluence: *abundance, wealth.*
affluent, *a.: abundant, rich.*
affront: *insult, offend.*

---

3. launched, started, afoot, astir, going, abroad, circulating.
4. adrift.
aforesaid, *a.* forenamed, forementioned, said, mentioned, beforesaid, named, abovesaid, above-mentioned, afore-mentioned (*R or A*). *"Aforesaid" is now chiefly formal or legal.*
afraid, *a.* **1.** apprehensive, afeard (*A*), fearful (*B*), alarmed, affrighted, terrified, frightsome (*R*), timorous, funky (*S*); *spec.* panic, aghast, scary (*C*), scared (*C*).
Antonyms: see BOLD, RECKLESS.
2. *See* TIMID, APPREHENSIVE.
after, *prep.* **1.** past, beyond, by.
Antonyms: see BEFORE.
2. following.
3. *In the sense of "according to":* to, by.
4. *See* ABOUT, FOR.
aftermath, *n.* aftergrowth, rowen (*chiefly dial. & U. S.*), eddish, rowet (*dial.*); *spec.* fog, aftercrop.
afterpiece, *n.* postlude (*music*).
aftertaste, *n.* tang, taste.
afterwards, *adv.* subsequently, thereupon (*formal*), thereon (*formal*), thereafter (*formal*), so, eft (*obs. or A*), eftsoon *or* eftsoons (*A*), later, then.
Antonyms: see BEFORE, NOW.
again, *adv.* afresh, anew, anon (*chiefly B*) freshly, newly; *spec.* encore.
age, *n.* **1.** oldness, ancientness, ancientry (*B*):—(age *being the general and most common term, and the one commonly used in reference to the life of plants or animals,* ancientness *and* ancientry *implying great* age; antiquity *referring to age in the world's life or history*); anility (*B*), caducity (*R*), senility (*chiefly spec.*), eld (*A and B*), senectitude (*R*); *spec.* date, immemorialness (*R*), maturity, majority.
Antonyms: see CHILDHOOD, INFANCY, YOUTH.
2. period, æon (*often tech.*), eon, lifetime (*fig.*), years (*pl.*), generation; *spec.* Olam (*Hebrew chronology*), kalpa (*Hindu cosmology*), epact, century.
Antonyms: see MOMENT.
age, *v.* antiquate (*implying more or less obsoleteness,* age *being the general term*).
agency, *n.* **1.** action (*contex.*), operation (*contex.*), mediation, intermediation, ministry (*R or spec.*), instrumentality; office; *spec.* hand, working, procurement, procuration.
2. *Spec.* medium, vehicle, contagion; *see* AGENT, MEANS.
3. *Spec.* factorship, commission, proxy, mediumship, factorage, delegacy.
agent, *n.* **1.** actor (*R*), doer, operator (*contex.*), worker, (*contex.*): *implying exertion of power and destiny; spec.* reagent, medium, mediary, means, instrument.
Antonyms: see SUBJECT.
2. *Implying the doing of something for, or in place of, another:* attorney (*chiefly tech. or spec.*), deputy, steward, factor, substitute, representative, emissary, delegate, commissioner, commissary, almoner; servant (*law*), hand (*fig.*); *spec.* agency, instrument, instrumentality, broker, dummy, intermediary, go-between, envoy, lobbyist, minister, proxy, procurator, consignee, syndic, negotiant, co-agent, comprador (*Oriental*); *see* REPRESENTATIVE.
Antonyms: see PRINCIPAL.
3. *See* MEANS.
aggravate, *v. t.* **1.** intensify, heighten, worsen (*B*), exacerbate, increase.
Antonyms: see EXPIATE, MITIGATE, MODERATE, REDRESS.
2. *See* ANNOY, IRRITATE.
aggregate, *n.* amount, total, footing, foot, sum; *spec.* summation.
aggressive, *a.* offensive, attacking, pushful (*C*), enterprising; self-assertive; *spec.* invasive, incursive.
aging, *a.* senescent (*tech.*), oldening (*R*); *spec.* consenescent (*R*).
agitate, *v. t.* **1.** *In a physical sense:* disturb, affect (*contex.*), disquiet, perturb, stir (*often with "up"*), rouse, trouble, excite, convulse (*implies violent shaking or agitation, with a succession of movements*), toss, shake, exercise, discompose, distract, turmoil (*R*), tempest (*R*), commove *or* commote (*R; imply violence*); *spec.* flurry, betoss (*B*), heave.
Antonyms: see CALM, PACIFY.
2. disturb, trouble, disquiet, perturb, convulse, demoralize, solicit (*a Latinism; R*), commove *or* commote (*R; imply violence*), tempest (*R*), turmoil (*R*); *spec.* fret, ruffle, ripple, undulate, curl (*these four imply surface disturbance of a liquid*), flutter, buzz, flurry, heave (*implies spasmodic or intermittent rising and falling*), churn; *see* SHAKE.
Antonyms: see STILL, DEADEN.
3. *See* DISCUSS.
agitated, *a.* **1.** *In a physical sense:* disturbed, shaken, troublous, troubled, unquiet; *spec.* ebullient, boiling, ripply, fretful, ruffled; *see* ROUGH.
Antonyms: see CALM, STAGNANT, QUIET.
2. disturbed, distraught (*emphatic; chiefly B; implying agitation which grows by conflicting emotions or interests*), uneasy, tumultuary (*B*), tumultuous (*emphatic*), shaken, unquiet.
Antonyms: see CALM, PEACEFUL, QUIET.
agitating, *a.* disturbing, disquieting, perturbing, affecting, *etc. Cf.* AGITATE.
Antonyms: see CALMATIVE.
agitation, *n.* **1.** *Referring to the action on the mind:* disturbance, commotion, demoralization, perturbation, excitement, perturbancy (*R*); *spec.* incendiarism, upheaval, demagogism, ebullition.
2. *Referring to the state of mind:* turmoil, tumult, discomposure, unquiet, unquietness;

afoot: *preparing, afloat.*
afresh: *again.*
aft: *astern.*
after, *a.: hind, subsequent.*
agape: *open, wondering.*
aggrandize: *enlarge, elevate.*
aggregate, *v. t.: unite, collect, constitute.*
aggression: *attack.*
aghast: *afraid.*
agile: *nimble.*

spec. heat, trepidation, tremble, twitter (*dial. Eng., or C, U. S.*), twitteration (*R*), ferment, perturbation, perturbancy (*R*), lather (*C*). *The words under sense* **1** *may also be used in this connection.*

Antonyms: see CALM.

3. *Referring to the physical action:* disturbance, commotion, troubling, toss, tossing, jactation (*chiefly med.*), perturbation (*R*); *spec.* upheaval, convulsion, undulation; *see* SHAKING, FLURRY, RUFFLE, UPROAR, FRET, BOILING, EXCITEMENT.

4. *Referring to the physical condition or manifestation: spec.* flurry, ruffle, tumult, curl, fret, ebullience, ebullition, flutter, whitecap, cat's-paw; *see* RIPPLE, SHAKE. *Most of the words under* **3** *may also be used in this sense.*

Antonyms: see CALM.

5. *See* DISCUSSION, DISTURBANCE.

agitator, *n. spec.* demagogue, organizer, agent (demagogue *and its various derivatives imply unscrupulous and unprincipled appeals to passion and prejudice for personal or selfish ends*).

ago, *adv.* back, since, past.

agree, *v. i.* **1.** accord (*with "to" or "with"*), harmonize, consist (*with "with"*), answer (*with "to"*), correspond (*with "with" or "to"*), suit, match, cohere, comport, consort, coincide (*implies exact or identical correspondence without reference to the reason for it*), jump, tally, fit, hitch (*C*), chime, concord (*R*), jibe (*U. S.; C*), gee (*C*), tally, conform (*with "with" or "to"*), comply (*last two imply absence, usually under force or compulsion, of discord, dissension, or variance*).

Antonyms: see DISAGREE, CONFLICT, DIFFER.

2. accord, harmonize, concur, consent (*A*), cotton (*C or Eng.*), assort (*A*).

Antonyms: see OBJECT, QUARREL.

3. covenant, stipulate, meet, engage, close, arrange, bargain (*all implying mutual acceptance of terms offered and asked*); *see* CONTRACT.

4. *See* ACCEDE.

agreeable, *a.* **1.** suitable, accordant, accordable, concordant, conformable, congenial (*implies agreeableness to one's temper, taste, liking*), harmonious, consonant, fit, answerable, congruous, consentaneous (*A*); *see* CONSISTENT, CORRESPONDENT.

Antonyms: see INCONSISTENT, UNSUITABLE, CONTRADICTORY, INHARMONIOUS.

2. pleasant, suave, nice (*a term lacking in dignity*), lovely (*C or emphatic*), gracious, lief (*A*), likable, genial, congenial; *see* AFFABLE, GOOD-HUMORED, COMPLAISANT, SMOOTH.

Antonyms: see DISAGREEABLE, ILL-TEMPERED, ARROGANT, HAUGHTY, HATEFUL, SURLY, ACRIMONIOUS.

3. *See* PLEASANT, ACCEPTABLE.

agreeably, *adv.* **1.** well.

2. *See* ACCORDINGLY.

agreed, *a.* concerted, stipulated, contracted, covenanted, consented, arranged.

agreeing, *a.* **1.** accordant (*obs. or R*), agreeable (*obs. or R*), congruent, consentient *or* consentive (*R; both imply intellectual or mental agreement*), consensual, consentaneous, concentual (*fig.*). *"Agreeing" is not much used as an adjective; the other terms are R or B.*

Antonyms: see DISSENTIENT, DISCORDANT, CONFLICTORY, INHARMONIOUS, DISPUTATIOUS.

2. *Referring to sound:* assonant, consonant.

agreement, *n.* **1.** accord, accordance, concord, consistence, consistency, coincidence, harmony (*implies absence of discord*), chime (*implies a correspondence of proportion or relation*), correspondence, concert (*B, with reference to a plan or course of action*), concinnity (*B; implies adaptation or fitting of parts*), consonance, unison, match, consort (*R*), conformity (*implies correspondence to a pattern*), concentus (*B*), line, keeping, consonancy, congruence, congruity, coherence (*implying a common principle or relationship*), conformation, line (*as, "to be in line with the new movement"*); *see* CONSISTENCY.

Antonyms: see INCONSISTENCY, DISAGREEMENT, CONFLICT, DIFFERENCE.

2. *Referring to the mind:* concert, meeting (*in "meeting of the minds"; legal*), concurrence, consension (*R*), consensus, consentience (*R, implying intellectual or mental agreement*), unanimity, understanding, concentus (*B*), consent (*A*), concent (*fig.*), rapport (*French*).

Antonyms: see OBJECTION, DISAGREEMENT, QUARREL.

3. *Referring to the result of the act:* engagement, transaction, pact, covenant (*chiefly spec.*), convention (*chiefly B, or referring to agreements between nations*), treaty (*a formal agreement between states*), paction (*chiefly spec.*), compact, arrangement, league (*chiefly spec.*), bargain, deal, cheap (*A*); *spec.* interim, concordat (*now between church and state*), cartel *or* (*German*) Kartel (*an agreement to effect a monopoly*), sponsion, affiance, stipulation (*a specific agreement*); *see* PROMISE, CONTRACT.

4. *Of sounds:* assonance, consonance.

5. *See* ACCESSION.

agricultural, *a.* rural, farming, country (*spec.*), prædial (*B or tech.*), georgic (*B*), georgical (*B*), geofonic (*R*).

agriculture, *n.* husbandry, farming, geofonics (*R; usually pedantic*), agronomy (*tech.*).

agriculturist, *n.* husbandman, farmer (*the usual word*), agronomist (*tech.*).

aground, *a.* grounded, aland (*A*); *spec.* ashore, stranded, stuck.

Antonyms: see AFLOAT.

ahead, *adv.* before, on, forward, forth, forthright (*A*).

agog: *eager.*
agonize, *v. i.: suffer, struggle.*
agony: *pain, ecstasy.*
agrarian: *rural.*
ahead: *forward.*

Antonyms: see BACKWARD.

aid, *v. t.* **1.** help, assist, coassist (*R*), comfort (*A, except in law*), favor, bestead (*B*), avail, speed (*B or A*), hand, serve, subserve; *see* SUPPORT:—*without implication as to the nature of, or reason for, the assistance given*).

2. abet:—*implying assistance in doing something wrong.*

3. relieve, succor, befriend:—*implying more or less need of aid.*

4. further, promote, advance, prosper, strengthen, second, foster, nourish, facilitate, bolster (*with "up"*), boost (*C or S*):—*implying action that effects an improvement or advance without reference to its motive.*

5. support, uphold, encourage, back up, sustain, countenance, approve, patronize, subsidize:—*implying action that strengthens a person in maintaining a stand or line of action.*

Antonyms: see HINDER, DEFEAT, BLIGHT, PREVENT, OPPOSE.

aid, *n.* **1.** coöperation (*stilted or spec.*), assistance, help, aidance (*R*), comfort (*obs. or legal*); *spec.* abettal *or* abetment (*in wrongdoing*), sustenance (*R or B*), support, succor, strengthening, service, boot (*A*), suppeditation (*R*), sustainment (*R*), relief; *see* SUPPORT.

Antonyms: see HINDRANCE, DEFEAT, OPPOSITION.

2. furtherance, fosterage, nourishment, advancement, support, favor, sustainment (*R*), promotion, boost (*C or S; U. S.*), maintenance, conducement (*R*); *spec.* patronage.

Antonyms: see OBSTACLE, HINDRANCE, DEFEAT, PREVENTION, OPPOSITION.

3. *See* AIDER.

aider, *n.* **1.** helper, associate, assistant, coadjuter (*R or spec.*), coadjutant (*R*), helpmate *or* (*the original, but now the less usual, form*) helpmeet; *spec.* coworker, coöperator, ally, henchman, tool, stool, decoy, acolyte, second.

2. promoter, furtherer, favorer. *Cf.* AID, *v. t.*

ail, *v. t.* **1.** *Referring to the body:* affect, trouble, distress.

2. *Referring to the mind: see* TROUBLE.

ailing, *a.* invalid, indisposed (*usually slightly unwell*), unwell, ill (*chiefly predicative*), sick (*chiefly U. S. or B*); *spec.* complaining (*C*), diseased (*R, except as a predicate adjective*), sickly, sickish, sicklied (*R*), bad (*contex.*), poorly, peaked, unhealthy, morbid, puling (*C*), pathological (*tech.*), pathologic (*R*), down (*C*), run-down (*C*), unsound, infirm, cacochymic (*obs.*), maladive (*R*), valetudinarian (*B*), valetudinary (*R*), invalidish (*R*); *see* DISEASED.

Antonyms: see WELL, HEALTHY, VIGOROUS, HEARTY.

ailment, *n.* **1.** disorder, ail (*R*), complaint, indisposition, trouble, affection (*all without implication as to its nature*); indisposition (*usually referring to a slight degree of ill-health*).

2. malady, disease, illness, distemper, decline, sickness:—*implying functional disturbances, and in the case of* disease, *often referring to one accompanied by structural changes.*

3. weakness, trouble:—*usually implying a more or less chronic trouble.*

aim, *v. t.* **1.** direct, train, level, point, present; *spec.* fire, shoot, sight.

2. *Referring to a missile:* direct, drive, peg (*C*); *spec.* shoot, throw.

aim, *v. i.* **1.** point, drive (*implying a blow or missile directed with some force*);—*all also used fig.*

2. *See* INTEND.

aim, *n.* **1.** object, mark, target, shot, visie (*Scot.*); *spec.* butt, bull's-eye, white.

2. marksmanship.

3. *See* OBJECT.

aimed, *a.* directed (*contex.*), pointed; *spec.* direct, point-blank, straight.

Antonyms: see AIMLESS.

aimless, *a.* **1.** chance, random, blind, blindfold (*fig.*), undirected; *spec.* harum-scarum.

Antonyms: see AIMED.

2. *See* PURPOSELESS.

air, *n.* **1.** atmosphere, heaven, sky, welkin (*B*), open, aërosphere (*R*); *spec.* miasma, ozone (*often C*).

2. *Spec.* manner, action, bearing, carriage, behavior, show, attitude, mien, look, way, domineer (*C*), bridle, flirt.

3. *Chiefly in pl.:* affectation (*contex.*), frill (*chiefly in pl.; C, U. S.*); *spec.* show, mannerism, style, side, swagger; *see* PRETENSE.

4. *See* WIND, MELODY.

airplane, *n.* aëroplane, plane; crate (*S*), transport, clipper, aircraft, biplane, monoplane, helicopter, *etc.*

airy, *a.* **1.** *See* ATMOSPHERIC (*technical, with reference to the atmosphere, or whole body of air*), GASEOUS, UNSUBSTANTIAL, LIGHT.

2. light, thin, delicate, graceful, tenuous, ethereal, etherial (*the less usual form*), aërial, aëriform (*R*) (*both refer to the nature or substance of air*), celestial (*fig.*).

Antonyms: see CLUMSY, HEAVY.

3. breezy, windy, open, exposed (*to the outer air*).

alar, *a.* *Referring to the wings:* alate, winglike, wing-shaped, winged, alated, pennate (*contex.*).

alarm, *n.* **1.** *See* FEAR.

2. signal, alarum (*A*), warning; *spec.* tocsin, siren, buzzer, bell.

alarming, *a.* frightful, scary (*C*), scaring, terrific (*now R, exc. as an expletive*), dreadful, dread (*rather B or formal*), terrifying, terrible, startling, ghastful (*A*), appalling; *see* HORRIBLE.

Antonyms: see REASSURING.

alarmist, *n.* scaremonger, pessimist, disquietist (*R*); *spec.* terrorist.

alas, *interj.* alack, ohone (*Scot. & Irish*), ah, woe; unfortunately.

Antonyms: see EUHOE.

air, *v. t.: ventilate, express, display.*
aisle: *body, alley.*
akin: *related.*
alacritous: *ready.*
alamode: *stylish.*
alarm, *v. t.: frighten.*

alcoholic, *a.* spiritous, hard, ardent, strong (*contex.*).

alert, *a.* **1.** *See* NIMBLE.

2. *Referring to mental quality:* active, quick, live (*chiefly U. S.*), lively, nimble (*R*), prompt, awake; *see* READY, WATCHFUL.

Antonyms: see SLUGGISH, STUPEFIED.

alertness, *n.* **1.** nimbleness (*cf.* NIMBLE).

2. activity, liveliness, quickness, nimbleness; *spec.* watchfulness.

alienate, *v. t.* **1.** *See* TRANSFER.

2. separate, estrange, wean, disunite, divert, disaffect; *spec.* disacquaint.

alight, *v. i.* **1.** descend, light, perch, settle, rest, drop, pitch, fall, land; *spec.* ground; *see* LODGE.

Antonyms: see RISE.

2. *See* DISMOUNT.

3. *Spec.* detrain.

align, *v. t.* range, line (*with "up"*), straighten; *spec.* collimate (*tech.*).

alike, *a.* **1.** same, like, identical, selfsame (*emphatic*), twin (*of two*); *spec.* consubstantial, duplicate; *see* EQUAL.

Antonyms: see DIFFERENT, DISTINCT.

2. *See* SIMILAR.

alikeness, *n.* **1.** sameness, likeness, identity.

2. *See* SIMILARITY.

all, *a.* whole, any (*in sentences of universal exclusion, as in "there is no hope of any relief," "I cannot give you any encouragement"*), every (*distributive*), each (*implying separation in consideration or treatment*);—*not truly synonyms of "all" nor of each other, but often analogous in use.*

Antonyms: see FEW, MANY.

all, *n.* whole, entirety (*implying unabated quantity or amount*); everything (*implying universal inclusiveness*), everybody;—*specific or partial synonyms only. See* WHOLE.

Antonyms: see PART, NONE.

alley, *n.* walk, passage, opening; *spec.* frescade (*R*), mall, lane, aisle (*an inaccurate use*), byway.

alley, *n.* taw.

all-healing, *a.* panacean (*B*).

allied, *a.* **1.** *See* UNITED, RELATED.

2. *In scientific usage:* kindred, related, congeneric, cognate, akin.

Antonyms: see UNRELATED.

allowance, *n.* **1.** *See* PERMISSION, ACKNOWLEDGMENT.

2. *Spec.* fee, aid, share, subvention, commission, pension (*usually implies retirement*), livery (*historical*), viaticum, pin money, quarterage, pittance; *see* SUBSIDY, FEE, COMMISSION.

3. Ration (*chiefly mil. or formal*), feed (*C*); *spec.* dietary.

4. *In sports:* odds (*pl. & sing.*), law (*tech.*); *spec.* bisque.

alloy, *n.* **1.** *See* MIXTURE, ADMIXTURE.

2. garble (*R*); *spec.* amalgam, spelter (*R*), brass, bronze, latten, temper, pinchbeck, billon.

alloy, *v. t.* **1.** adulterate, mix, temper; *spec.* amalgamate.

Antonyms: see PURIFY.

2. *See* MODERATE, MIX.

alluvium, *n.* deposit (*contex.*), wash (*contex.*); *spec.* geest, drift, gravel, sand, waste, till, delta, warp.

ally, *n.* **1.** associate, confederate.

Antonyms: see ENEMY, OPPONENT.

2. *In scientific classification:* congener.

alms, *n.* dole, charity (*A*), collection (*ecclesiastical*), aid, relief; *spec.* pittance, maundy (*Eng.*).

aloft, *adv.* **1.** above (*contex.*), on high; *spec.* heaven-high, overhead.

2. *See* UP.

alone, *a.* (*postpositive*) solitary, only (*R*), unique, single (*now R*), sole (*A*), isolated, separate, lone (*B or A*), lonely (*emphatic*), lonesome (*R*), solus (*masc.; Latin*), sola (*fem.; Latin*); *spec.* unaccompanied, unattended, forsaken, deserted, abandoned, detached, companionless, desolate:—alone (*now usually follows its noun or is used predicatively*) *implies simply separation from others;* solitary *implies a sense of remoteness from contact with or influence of others;* isolated *implies separation, usually of such a nature as to be considered a hardship;* separate *implies absence of one's fellows;* unaccompanied *implies the absence of companions;* forsaken, deserted, abandoned *implying separation due to being left by or parted from one's companions or associates, especially in violation of duty, or by breaking away from bonds of service, sympathy, or attachment;* lonely *emphasizes the unpleasant emotions aroused by the sense of separation, and in* lonesome *this is now the primary or sole implication.*

alone, *adv.* **1.** solitary, only (*R*), separately, solely, singularly (*R*).

2. *See* ONLY, MERELY.

aloneness, *n.* solitariness, soleness (*A*), singleness (*A or R*), isolatedness, isolation, separatedness, separation, unaccompaniedness, forsakenness, desertedness, desertion, abandonment, loneliness, loneness (*B*), lonesomeness, lonesome (*C*).

alcove: *recess.*
ale: *beer.*
alias, *a.: otherwise.*
alias: *n.: name.*
alien: *foreign.*
alive: *living, lively, swarming, sensitive.*
allay: *appease, abate, mitigate, moderate, calm.*
allege: *state.*
allegiance: *constancy.*
allegorical: *metaphorical.*
all-embracing: *comprehensive.*
alleviate: *mitigate.*
alliance: *union, confederacy, relation, amour.*
allied: *united, related.*
allot: *apportion, appropriate.*
allow: *acknowledge, concede, apportion, permit, grant.*
all-powerful: *omnipotent.*
allude: *refer.*
allure: *attract.*
allurement: *attraction.*
allusion: *reference.*
ally, *v. t.: unite, league.*
almighty: *omnipotent.*
almost: *about.*
almshouse: *poorhouse.*
along, *adv.: lengthwise, forward.*
along, *prep.: by.*
alongside: *abreast.*
aloof: *apart.*

aloof, *a.* apart, distant, off, away.

aloud, *adv.* **1.** out, audibly.

Antonyms: see SILENTLY.

2. *See* LOUDLY.

alphabet, *n.* Christcross-row (*hist. or A*), letters (*pl.*); *spec.* ogham *or* ogam (*Celtic*), glossic, glossotype, palæotype, futhorc *also* futharc (*Runic*).

also, *adv.* besides, moreover, more, likewise, too, further *or* (*less usual*) farther, yet, similarly, withal (*A*), forby (*A*), furthermore *or* (*less usual*) farthermore, therewithal (*A*), eke (*A*), thereto (*A*).

altar, *n.* shrine, sanctuary; *spec.* superaltar, chantry, marae, thymele, Communion table, Lord's table, Holy table, table (*for short*), retable, reredos.

alter, *v. t.* modify, change, vary; *spec.* interpolate, geld, fix (*C*); *see* FALSIFY, CHANGE.

Antonyms: see CONTINUE, MAINTAIN, FIX.

alternate, *v. t.* (*implying a succession of two things by turns*), interchange, vary, rotate; *see* RECIPROCATE.

alternation, *n.* interchange, interchangeableness (*R*), interchangeability (*R*), variation, rotation; *see* RECIPROCATION.

alternative, *n.* (*implies the choice of one of two things*), choice, side, horn (*of a dilemma; rhetoric and logic*), disjunction (*logic*).

although, *conj.* notwithstanding, though, howbeit, albeit, maugre (*A*), despite (*B*).

always, *adv.* **1.** ever (*A or B*), perpetually, eternally, evermore (*A or B*), everlastingly, forever.

Antonyms: see NEVER.

2. *See* CONSTANTLY.

amanuensis, *n.* scrivener, scribe, writer, secretary, (*all three contex.*); *spec.* khoja.

amateur, *n.* (*implies the beginner and nonprofessional*), novice, dabbler, dilettante (*implies elegance and superficiality*), Corinthian (*fig.: one of wealth*).

Antonyms: see PROFESSIONAL, EXPERT.

amateurish, *a.* nonprofessional; *spec.* Corinthian (*fig.*).

Antonyms: see PROFESSIONAL.

amatory, *a.* erotic, amorous, lovesome (*A*); *spec.* gallant (*R*), tender, languorous, languishing, Anacreontic (*R*), Sapphic (*R*), silly (*R or C*), spoony (*A and C*); *spec.* toysome (*A*), erotomaniac, nymphomaniac.

Antonyms: see MAN-HATING, WOMAN-HATING, APATHETIC.

ambiguous, *a.* uncertain, doubtful, indeterminate, equivocal, dilogical (*R*), double, questionable, mistakable; *spec.* left-handed, oracular.

Antonyms: see DEFINITE, UNQUESTIONABLE.

ambition, *n.* **1.** (*implies advancement, usually personal*), *see* DESIRE.

2. energy, activity, push (*C*), emulation (*implies actual attempts whereby ambition is revealed*), aspiration (*generally implies desire of attaining something higher or nobler*).

ambitious, *a.* **1.** *See* DESIROUS.

2. energetic, active, pushing (*C*), pushful (*C*); *spec.* Icarian (*fig.: implying utter failure or ruin*).

Antonyms: see LAZY, UNAMBITIOUS.

3. *Referring to a person, his imagination, etc.: spec.* bold, audacious, aspiring, soaring.

4. *Referring to what shows ambition: spec.* bold, audacious; *see* PRETENTIOUS, SHOWY.

Antonyms: see SIMPLE.

amble, *n.* *Spec.* jog-trot, dog-trot, niggle; *see* PACE.

ambush, *n.* trap (*contex.*), ambuscade, ambushment, blind, bushment (*A*).

ambush, *v. t.* trap (*contex.*), waylay, ambuscade, forelay (*A or dial.*), wait (*A*).

ambush, *v. i.* wait (*A*), lurk (*R*).

amend, *v. t.* **1.** (*implies the correction of a fault, flaw, or error*), improve, reform, mend (*R or dial.*), rectify (*R*); *see* CORRECT, REDRESS.

Antonyms: see SPOIL, IMPAIR.

2. *See* REFORM.

amendable, *a.* improvable, corrigible, reformable; *see* CORRIGIBLE.

amendment, *n.* **1.** improvement, reform, reformation; *spec.* progress; *see* CORRECTION, REDRESS.

2. *See* REFORMATION.

amidst, *prep.* **1.** *Referring to position in or near the middle:* amid (*B or formal*), mid *or* often (*as an aphetic form*) 'mid (*B*), midst *or often* (*as an aphetic form*), 'midst (*A*).

2. *See* AMONG.

ammunition, *n.* supplies (*pl.; contex.*), munition (*often in pl.*); *spec.* missiles (*pl.*), archery, powder, shot (*pl.*), bullets (*pl.*), shell (*pl.*), bomb (*pl.*), torpedo (*pl.*), grenade (*pl.*).

among, *prep.* amongst (*less usual than* **among,** *esp. in the primary local sense*), amidst, in.

amount, *n.* **1.** *See* SUM, AGGREGATE, QUANTITY.

2. deal, lot (*C*); *spec.* quantity.

amount, *v. i.* total, come (*with "to"*).

amour, *n.* **1.** *See* LOVE.

2. love affair, loves (*pl.*), intrigue (*implies illicit and clandestine affair*), gallantry, alliance (*contex.*), passion, amourette (*implying pettiness*); *spec.* intimacy (*euphemistic*); *see* COURTSHIP.

amputate, *v. t.* cut (*with "off"*), sever (*contex.*); *spec.* prune, lop.

amulet, *n.* periapt (*R*), charm, talisman; *spec.* phylactery.

---

already: *before.*
alterable: *changeable.*
altercation: *dispute.*
alternately: *about.*
altitude: *height.*
altogether: *absolutely.*
amalgam: *alloy, mixture.*
amass: *accumulate.*
amaze: *surprise.*
ambrosial: *divine, fragrant.*
ameliorate: *improve, mitigate.*
amenable: *accountable.*
amends: *compensation.*
amenity: *pleasantness.*
amiable: *lovable, kindly.*
amicable: *friendly.*
amiss: *wrong.*
amity: *peace.*
amnesty: *forgetfulness, pardon.*
amorous: *amatory.*
amorphous: *formless.*
ample: *abundant, adequate.*
amplify: *enlarge.*
amplitude: *abundance, size.*

amusing, *a.* diverting, light, funny, odd (*C*), good, delicious (*implying a fine sense of humor highly pleased*), screaming (*C*), howling (*C*); *see* LAUGHABLE.
Antonyms: see DULL, SAD, SERIOUS, SOBER.

analogous, *a.* parallel, correlative, corresponding, similar, cognate, equivalent, correspondent.
Antonyms: see OPPOSITE, CONTRASTING.

analogue, *n.* parallel, correlative, correlate (*R*), parallelism, equivalent.
Antonyms: see OPPOSITE, CONTRAST.

analogy, *n.* parity (*rather B*), correlation, equivalence, parallelism, proportion (*R*), similarity, correspondence.
Antonyms: see CONTRAST, OPPOSITION.

analysis, *n.* **1.** separation, resolution, dissection, division, anatomy (*fig.*), reduction; *spec.* partition, pilpul; *see* DECOMPOSITION, DISINTEGRATION.
2. *In grammar:* parsing, construction; *spec.* scansion.

analytical, *a.* divisive, resolvent, separative.
Antonyms: see COMPOSITIVE.

analyze, *v. t.* **1.** separate, resolve, dissect (*implying purpose of study or criticism and a minute division*), anatomize (*fig.*); *spec.* partition; *see* DECOMPOSE, DISINTEGRATE.
Antonyms: see COMPOSE.
2. *In grammar:* parse, construe; *spec.* scan.

anarchical, *a.* lawless, ungoverned.
Antonyms: see LAW-ABIDING.

anarchistic, *a.* red (*C*), bolshevist (*C*), socialist (*C*), lawless; *spec.* nihilistic, dynamitic, terrorist.

anarchy, *n.* misrule, lawlessness; *spec.* nihilism, dynamitism.
Antonyms: see GOVERNMENT.

anatomize, *v. t.* dissect; *spec.* hominisect, vivisect.

anatomy, *n.* **1.** dissection; *spec.* hominisection, callisection, sentisection, vivisection, phytotomy, topography, zoötomy.
2. *See* SKELETON, ANALYSIS.

ancestor, *n.* predecessor (*contex.*), ancestry (*a collective*), forebear (*orig. Scot.*; *now B*), stock (*a collective*), fore-elder (*R*), forerunner; *spec.* root (*fig.*), patriarch, progenitor, forefather, father (*primarily parent, but loosely equivalent to* forefather), ancestress, grandam (*B; fig.*), progenitress, progenitrix, foremother (*R*).
Antonyms: see DESCENDANT, OFFSPRING.

ancestral, *a.* forefatherly; *spec.* patrimonial, hereditary.

ancestry, *n.* lineage, progeniture, pedigree, progenitorship (*ancestral lineage or descent*).

anchor, 1. *Spec.* kedge, bower, sheet anchor, killick (*chiefly Eng.*), grapnel.
2. *See* HOLD.

anchorage, *n.* riding, berth (*contex.*); *spec.* harborage, roadstead, road.

ancient, *a.* old (*contex.*), early (*contex.*), primitive, high, pristine (*B, and usually in a good sense*); *spec.* prehistoric; *see* ANTIQUATED, OBSOLETE, OLD.
Antonyms: see NEW, MODERN, RECENT.

ancillary, *a.* auxiliary, subordinate.

andiron, *n.* fire-dog.

anecdote, *n.* account (*contex.*), incident (*contex.*), story; *spec.* haggada.

angel, *n.* **1.** spirit (*contex.*), celestial (*contex.*); *spec.* cherub (*often used of a chubby child or a winged child's head*), seraph, virtue, archangel, principality, power, throne, dominion.
2. *See* MINISTER, DEMON, GENIUS.

angelic, *a.* **1.** celestial (*contex.*), seraphic (*often implying zeal and ardor*), cherubic (*often implying childish innocence*).
2. *See* HEAVENLY.

anger, *n.* ill-temper (*contex.*), displeasure (*contex.*), choler (*B*), ire (*B*), wrath, indignation, indignance (*R*), indignancy (*R*), spleen, dudgeon (*A*), madness (*C*), vexation, gall, bile, heat, mad (*S; C, U. S., or dial.*), dander (*C, or dial.*), despite (*A*), corruption (*C or dial.*), irritation (*contex.*); *spec.* fury, frenzy, rage, passion, furiousness, exasperation.
Antonyms: see PLEASURE.

anger, *v. t.* exasperate, madden (*implying uncontrollable rage*), provoke, incense, inflame, excite (*contex.*); *spec.* chafe, enrage, infuriate, huff (*C*), get (*C*).
Antonyms: see PLEASE.

angle, *n.* **1.** corner (*with reference to the space between two meeting lines,* angle *being the exact term*), bend (*primarily spec.*), turn, point; *spec.* cant, nook, elevation, depression, shoulder, elbow (*mechanical, in a pipe, tube, etc., used to join other pieces*), knee, crotch, cusp, bull's-nose.
2. *See* POINT, ASPECT.

angry, *a.* displeased, wrathful, wrathy (*C*), incensed, irate *or* ireful (*B*), wroth (*rhetorical*), dark (*fig.*), hot (*C*), heated, black (*fig.*), mad (*C*), riley (*C, U. S.*), huffy (*C*), exasperated, wood (*A*); *spec.* furious, hot (*C*), sore (*C*), infuriated, infuriate (*B*), passionate, impassionate (*R*), rabid, raging, indignant, fevered, fiery, high, rough.
Antonyms: see PLEASED, APATHETIC, UNIMPASSIONED.

angular, *a.* cornered, sharp, edgy, abrupt, cranky (*esp. dial., Eng.*), angulous (*R*); angular distance (*geography and astronomy*).
Antonyms: see STRAIGHT, CURVED.

animal, *n.* **1.** organism (*contex.*); *spec.* invertebrate, vertebrate, brute (*as distinct from man*), beast (*referring especially to a quadruped, as distinct from birds; or to cattle*), zoön (*tech.*), vermin, creature (*in U. S. esp. of cattle*), critter (*C*), fauna (*a collective*), flesh (*a collective*). "*Animal,*" *except in technical usage, is gen-*

amuse: *divert.*
amusement: *diversion.*
anathema: *curse.*
anchorless: *afloat.*
anent: *about.*
anew: *again.*
anguish: *pain.*
animadversion: *comment, censure.*

erally distinguished from "man" and also is chiefly used of vertebrates.
2. *Spec.* beastliness, brutality, bestiality, brutishness, blood (*fig.*).
animal, *a.* **1.** *Spec.* bestial, brutal, brutish, zoöid (*tech.*), zoic (*tech.*), holozoic (*tech.*).
Antonyms: see SPIRITUAL, HUMAN, VEGETABLE, MINERAL.
2. *See* SENSUAL, UNREASONING.
animate, *v. t.* **1.** energize, inspire (*implying the giving of the breath of life*), quicken (*A*), vivify, vitalize, enliven (*R; implying the giving of life to, in any way*), actuate (*contex.*), inform (*B or spec.*), imbue, activate (*tech.*), spirit (*R*); *spec.* pervade, revive, raise, spiritualize, restore.
Antonyms: see KILL, PARALYZE.
2. *See* ENLIVEN, INCITE, ENCOURAGE.
ankle, *n.* tarsus (*tech.*).
anneal, *v. t.* temper, toughen, harden; *spec.* heat, bake.
annihilate, *v. t.* abolish (*contex.*), destroy, obliterate, dissolve, nullify (*R*), efface (*implying a wiping out or doing away with the appearance of or presence of*), uncreate, blot (*contex.*), unmake (*R*), extinguish, annul, discreate (*R*), nothing (*R*), *see* EXTIRPATE.
Antonyms: see CREATE, PRESERVE.
anniversary, *n.* commemoration, mind day (*obs.*); *spec.* centenary, centennial, triennial quadrennial, quinquennial, sextennial, septennial, octennial, decennial, birthday, birthnight, jubilee (*50th year*), festival, year day (*obs.*).
annotate, *v. t.* gloze, gloss, expound, explain, interpret, commentate (*R*); *spec.* marginalize (*R*), margin, interlineate.
annotation, *n.* **1.** *Referring to the act:* glozing, glossing, commentation (*R*).
2. *Referring to the result:* comment (*explanatory or critical on a passage*), note (*contex.*), footnote, remark (*contex.*), explanation (*contex.*), gloss, scholium (*tech.*), gloze; *spec.* margin (*R*), marginalia (*pl.*), interlineary, postil (*hist.*).
annotator, *n.* commentator, glossist, glossator (*R; especially a medieval one*), glosser, glossographer (*R*), scholiast (*tech.*), editor (*contex.*), scholar (*contex.*).
announce, *v. t.* advertize, intimate, declare (*implying emphatic, legal, or solemn form*), tell, herald, bruit (*B*), notify, signify, signal, annunciate, enunciate (*formal*), enounce (*R*); *spec.* sound, usher, call, denounce (*implying a threat or warning*), presage, advertize, bill, post, cry (*implying oral announcement in public places*), bulletin; *see* PROCLAIM.
Antonyms: see HIDE.
announcement, *n.* intimation, annunciation, notification, declaration (*implying emphatic, solemn or legal form*), notice, advertizement, ad (*C*) enunciation (*formal*); *spec.* indiction, banns (*pl.*), bulletin, obituary, obit (*A*), proclamation, dodger, handbill.
annoy, *v. t.* distress (*contex.*), disturb (*contex.*), vex, touch, plague, torment, harass, irk (*A*), bother, curry (*fig.*), pester, exulcerate (*A*), fret, molest (*A*), displeasure (*R*); *spec.* nag, rag (*C or S*), ruffle, pinprick, earwig, bore; *see* IRRITATE, TROUBLE, TEASE.
Antonyms: see PLEASE, ELATE, PACIFY, CALM.
annoyance, *n.* **1.** distress (*contex.*), disturbance (*contex.*), harassment, exulceration (*R*), molestation (*B*); *see* IRRITATION.
2. *Referring to what annoys:* vexation, plague, thorn, torment, pest, pester, nuisance, gall, bore; *see* IRRITATION, TROUBLE.
Antonyms: see COMFORT.
3. *Referring to the state of mind:* vexation, displeasure, disquiet, ruffle; *see* IRRITATION.
annoying, *a.* displeasing (*contex.*), vexatious, molesting, tantalizing, bothersome, irritating, troublesome, plaguesome (*R*), plaguey (*C*), thorny, painful, worrisome, irksome.
Antonyms: see CALMATIVE, SEDATIVE.
annual, *a.* yearly; *but see* PERENNIAL.
annular, *a.* ring-shaped, round (*contex.*), circular, annulated, annulate, cricoid (*tech.; chiefly spec.*).
anoint, *v. t.* anele (*A*), oint (*A*), inunct (*chiefly spec.; R*), smear (*now only contemptuous*); *spec.* oil, grease, chrism, balsam, salve.
anonymous, *a.* nameless, unnamed, unknown (*a loose contex. use*).
another, *a.* *Spec.* second, other (*A or R*), different.
answer, *v. i.* **1.** *Referring to making defense against a charge, as in law:* defend, plead (*law*); *spec.* reply, rejoin, rebut, surrejoin, surrebut.
2. reply, respond, retort, return (*contex.*), rejoin, replicate (*R*); *spec.* subjoin, recriminate.
3. react, respond; *spec.* counteract.
4. *See* AGREE, SERVE.
answer, *v. t.* **1.** *As in law:* defend.
2. reply, respond, retort, rejoin, say (*contex.*), replicate (*R*), echo.
Antonyms: see QUESTION.
3. acknowledge; *spec.* receipt.
4. solve.
5. *See* SATISFY, SETTLE.
answer, *n.* **1.** *As used in law:* defense, plea; *spec.* rebutter, reply, rejoinder, replication, surrejoinder, surrebutter.
2. reply, response, retort; *spec.* counterblast, countercharge, counterclaim, contraremonstrance, repartee, antiphony, subjoinder, oracle, anthem.
Antonyms: see QUESTION.
3. acknowledgment; *spec.* receipt.
4. solution; *spec.* key, clue.
5. reaction, response.

animated: *living, active.*
animosity: *ill-will.*
annex: *add, attach.*
annexation: *addition, attachment.*
annual: *yearly.*
annul: *abolish, invalidate.*
annunciate: *announce.*
anomalous: *abnormal.*
anon: *soon, again.*
answerable: *accountable, acceptable.*

answering, *a.* responsive, replying, responsory (*A*).

antedate, *v. t.* **1.** precede (*in time*), predate, anticipate (*contex.*).

Antonyms: see POSTDATE.

2. mistime (*contex.*), anachronize (*R*).

antediluvian, *a.* prediluvian, antediluvial, prediluvial, antiquated.

anteprandial, *a.* preprandial;—*both R.*

anteroom, *n.* vestibule; *spec.* hall, lobby, antechamber, receptacle.

anthem, *n.* respond (*R*), responsory; *spec.* offertory, hymn.

anthology, *n.* collection, posy (*R*), florilegium (*R*).

anticipate, *v. t.* **1.** preconceive, foresee (*fig.*), predict, precognosce (*R*), surmise; *spec.* hope, reckon (*used with "that" and a dependent clause*), await, suspect, forefeel (*R*); forebode, intuit (*R or tech.*); *see* EXPECT, FORETASTE.

2. forestall, forerun, devance (*R*), forecome (*R*), prevent (*R*).

anticipation, *n.* **1.** presentiment, foresight, preconception, preassurance (*R*); *spec.* forefeeling (*R*), reckoning, foreboding, hope, prolepsis, intuition; *see* EXPECTATION.

2. forestalment, prevenience (*R*), prevention (*R*); *spec.* prevenance, prematurity.

anticipatory, *a.* **1.** anticipant, anticipative, precognoscent (*R*), presentient (*R*); *spec.* proleptic (*R*); *see* EXPECTANT, HOPEFUL.

2. anticipant, prevenient (*B*), preventing (*R*).

anticlimax, *n.* bathos (*B*), come-down (*C*), let-down (*C*).

antidote, *n.* counteraction (*B*), remedy (*contex.*), alexipharmic (*B*), Theriac (*A; fig.*), mithridate (*A, or hist.*), counterpoison, obvietam (*A or hist.*); *spec.* countercharm, countervenom, bezoar (*A*), emetic.

Antonyms: see POISON.

antiquarian, *n.* antiquary, historian; *spec.* archæologist, archæologer (*R*), archaist (*R*), palæologist.

antiquarianism, *n. Spec.* palæology, archæology, history.

antiquate, *v. t.* age, outdate, unmodernize (*R*).

antiquity, *n.* **1.** age (*contex.*), old (*A or B*), oldness, ancientness.

2. *Referring to the people of antiquity:* eld (*A or poetic*); *spec.* foreworld (*R*).

Antonyms: see MODERNITY, MODERNNESS, NEWNESS, RECENCY.

3. *See* RELIC.

antlers, *n. pl.* horns, head, attire;—*both collectives, and hunting terms.*

anvil, *n.* stithy (*R*); *spec.* teest.

anxiety, *n.* distress (*contex.*), trouble (*contex.*), care, disquiet, concern, concernment, uneasiness, suspense, solicitude, worry; *see* APPREHENSION.

anxious, *a.* distressed (*contex.*), troubled (*contex.*), careful (*B*), uneasy, concerned, solicitous, worried; *see* TIMID, APPREHENSIVE.

Antonyms: see CARELESS, BOLD, CALM, CONFIDENT.

anybody, *n.* any one.

anyhow, *adv.* anyways, anyway, anywise.

anything, *n.* aught (*B*), ought (*the less usual spelling*).

apart, *a.* **1.** separate, aloof, away, aside; *spec.* distant, foreign.

2. *See* UNRELATED.

apart, *adv.* **1.** aloof (*implying more or less considerable distance away*).

2. aside, away (*implying removal from consideration, from the line of action, or from the main body or throng*).

3. separately, individually, independently, isolatedly (*referring to separate consideration, action, or function*).

4. asunder, parted, separated, a-two (*A: referring to two or more objects separate from one another*).

Antonyms: see TOGETHER, ADJACENT, TOUCHING.

apartment, *n.* flat (*chiefly Brit.*). *See* ROOM, SUITE.

apartment house, *n.* tenement, block of flats (*chiefly Brit.*).

apathetic, *a.* dull, phlegmatic, passive, calm (*contex.*), cold, sluggish, cold-blooded, inert (*B*), impassive, unfeeling, unemotional, indifferent, insensible, nerveless, torpid, torpent (*R*); *spec.* languid, languishing, languorous, listless, lethargic, inexcitable, lackadaisical, unconcerned.

Antonyms: see EAGER, EXCITED, ARDENT, ANGRY, IMPETUOUS, COMPASSIONATE, EMOTIONAL, EMPHATIC, ENERGETIC, SUSCEPTIBLE, SPIRITED, AMATORY, AFFECTIONATE, HATEFUL.

apathy, *n.* dullness, sluggishness, inertness (*B*), indifference, unconcern; *spec.* languor, torpor, lethargy, lassitude, calm (*contex.*), *etc.*

apiece, *adv.* individually, each, severally.

apogee, *n.* culmination, height, summit, top.

Antonyms: see NADIR.

apostasy, *n.* **1.** recreancy, tergiversation (*R*), abandonment, perversion, secession, lapse, relapse. *Cf.* BACKSLIDE.

Antonyms: see CONSTANCY.

---

antagonize: *oppose.*
antecedence: *precedence, previousness.*
antecedent: *preceding, previous.*
anterior: *previous, fore.*
antic, *a.: grotesque, frisky, buffoonish.*
antic, *n.: buffoon, caper.*
anticipant: *anticipatory, expectant.*
antipathy: *aversion, abhorrence, incompatibility.*
antipodal: *opposite.*
antipodes: *underworld.*
antiquated: *old, old-fashioned, obsolete, chronic.*
antique: *old, old-fashioned.*
antithesis: *contrast.*
antithetic: *contrasting.*
anyway, anyways: *anyhow.*
apace: *rapidly.*
ape, *n.: simian, imitator.*
ape, *v. t.: imitate.*
aperture: *opening.*
apex: *top, cusp, height.*
aphorism: *saying.*
apiary: *beehive.*
aplomb, *n.: assurance, verticality.*
apocalypse: *revelation, disclosure.*
apologetic: *justificatory, excusatory.*
apology: *justification, excuse, substitute.*
apophthegm: *saying.*
apostrophe: *address.*

---

2. *See* DESERTION.
apostate, *n.* **1.** renegade, recreant, turncoat, pervert *or* (*used from the point of view of the Church left*), vert, transfuge (*R*), tergiversator (*R*); *spec.* backslider.
2. *See* DESERTER.
apostate, *a.* recreant.
apostatize, *v. i.* **1.** renegade, secede, relapse, lapse, fall, vert (*C, Eng.*); *see* BACKSLIDE.
2. *See* DESERT.
appanage, *n.* adjunct, appurtenance, proprium (*tech.*), property (*contex.*), dependency; *spec.* perquisite, prerogative.
apparatus, *n.* **1.** rigging, machine, machinery, mechanism, gear, plant, enginery (*often fig.*), outfit (*C*), appliance, implement, materials, appurtenances (*A*); *spec.* tackle.
2. *See* INSTRUMENT, EQUIPMENT.
apparent, *a.* **1.** *See* EVIDENT.
2. seeming, ostensible, ostensive (*R*), semblable (*R or B*), evident (*R*); *spec.* phenomenal, external, sensible; *see* PROFESSED.
Antonyms: see HIDDEN, ACTUAL.
apparently, *adv.* seemingly, *etc.*, methinks (*A and usually B*). *Cf.* APPARENT, **2.**
apparition, *n.* **1.** (*implies sudden or unexpected appearance*); *see* APPEARANCE.
2. (*implies a supernatural appearance*), specter (*a figure seen in the imagination or by magic*), appearance, phantasm, phantom, image, show, shadow, umbrage (*B*), idol (*B*), eidolon (*B*), phasm (*R*), shape (*now R or contex.*), phantast (*R*), phantasma (*R*); *spec.* double, wraith, fetch, double-ganger, bogy, boodie (*Scot.*), epiphany, Christophany, blue-devils (*C*), illusion; *see* GHOST, SEMBLANCE.
apparitional, *a.* phantom, phantasmic (*R*), phantasmal.
appeal, *v. i.* **1.** (*implies calling on another and higher authority*), turn; *spec.* refer; *cf.* APPEAL, *n.*, **2.**
2. apply, ask, solicit, canvass, ask, pray, sue, entreat (*R*), cry (*fig.*), plead, go (*as to the supreme court*), petition.
appeal, *n.* **1.** *As used in law:* counterplea (*R*); *spec.* recusation, plaidoyer.
2. application, turning, reference, address (*R*), prayer; *spec.* memorial.
3. application, request, asking, call, cry, prayer, entreaty, plea, suit; *spec.* oath, captation.
4. *See* ATTRACTION.
appear, *v. i.* **1.** show (*now C*), emerge, issue, peer (*A*), spring (*chiefly spec.*), offer, develop, come (*as implying purpose*); *spec.* figure, rise, sparkle, coappear, compear (*law*), issue, loom, glimpse (*A*), figure.
Antonyms: see DISAPPEAR, VANISH.
2. *See* SEEM.
appearance, *n.* **1.** appearing, manifestation, show (*C*), rise, apparition (*B: implying something supernatural or remarkable*); *spec.* shadow, reapparition, avatar, glimpse (*faint and transitory*), outcrop, gleam (*of intelligence, etc., implying especially limited, momentary, faint, intermittent or transient* appearance).
Antonyms: see DISAPPEARANCE.
2. species (*tech.*), phase, aspect (*appearance has regard to the outer revelation, while* aspect *reveals more the character and nature*), figure, look, favor (*A*), face, form, shape, surface, shadow, phantasm, ghost (*unsubstantial image or form*), complexion, cast, color, show (*now B, exc. as referring to an illusory or deceiving appearance*), portraiture (*B*), visage (*B*); *spec.* perspective, smoke, facies (*natural hist.*); *see* ASPECT.
3. phenomenon; *spec.* meteor (*esp. tech.*).
4. semblance, guise (*assumed* appearance), seeming; *spec.* likeness.
5. *See* APPARITION.
appease, *v. t.* **1.** *See* SATISFY, PACIFY.
2. slake, quench, assuage, allay, mitigate, calm, lay (*A*); *see* SATISFY.
appeasement, *n.* **1.** *See* SATISFACTION.
2. slaking, assuagement, *etc. Cf.* APPEASE, **2.**
appendage, *n.* **1.** (*implies attachment and subordination*), attachment, pendicle (*chiefly Scot.*), codicil (*fig. or spec.*), rider; *spec.* chatelaine, fob, pendant, tang, crook.
2. *See* PROCESS.
appendix, *n.* (*implies attachment, but greater independence than* appendage) attachment, addition, codicil (*fig. or spec.*), supplement (*implies additions to complete the material*), addendum (*supplying omissions*), excursus, (*spec.*).
appetite, *n.* **1.** belly (*fig.*), hunger, desire, longing, passion (*implies intense longing*), fondness, craving, maw (*fig. or spec.*); *spec.* malacia (*tech.*); *see* THIRST.
Antonyms: see DISGUST, SURFEIT.
2. *See* DESIRE.
appetizer, *n.* **1.** hors d'œuvre (*French*), antipasto (*Italian*), smorgasbord (*Swedish*), tidbit, canape, snack, dish (*contex.*), flavoring (*contex.*).
2. aperitif, cocktail, pick-me-up.
applaud, *v. t.* (*implies loud or emphatic approval*); *spec.* acclaim, clap, cheer, encore, chirrup (*Eng.; S*), claque (*S*); *see* PRAISE.
Antonyms: see CONDEMN, CENSURE.
applaud, *v. i. Spec.* acclaim, clap, cheer, huzza, stomp.
applause, *n.* **1.** *See* PRAISE.
2. *Referring to what is done by way of praise: spec.* plaudit (*chiefly in pl.*), clap, hozanna, huzzas (*pl.*), hand (*C*).
Antonyms: see CONDEMNATION, CENSURE.
apple, *n.* pome (*B*).
apple-shaped, *a.* pomiform (*tech.*).
applicable, *a.* **1.** *See* ADAPTABLE.
2. appliable, suitable, usable, adaptable, pertinent, fit, apposite, devotable; *spec.* appropriate, appropriable.

appall: *frighten, dismay.*
appertain: *belong, relate.*
appetize: *relish.*
appetizing: *palatable.*
appliance: *application, instrument.*
applicant: *asker.*

application, *n.* **1.** apposition, touching, relevancy, pertinency, relation.

2. constancy (*contex.*), assiduity, devotion, appliance, sedulity (*B*), sedulousness, intentness, diligence, industry, attention, apposition (*implies bringing one thing into contact or close proximity with another*); application (*implies a continued and constant effort or attention devoted to the accomplishment of a task or result*); assiduity (*implies zeal or unremittingness in such effort, with less emphasis on the idea of its continuousness, which is chiefly emphasized by* perseverance); activity, industry, diligence, *etc.* (*do not imply continued effort toward a single task*); attention (*often used as nearly synonymous with* application, *emphasizes the closeness of the* application, *rather than the idea of continuousness of effort*).

Antonyms: see CHANGEABLENESS, INDOLENCE.

3. resort, recourse, recurrence.

4. *See* ASKING, APPEAL, APPROPRIATION.

5. *Spec.* poultice, plaster, epithem, stupe, lotion, foment, wash, ointment, cerate, salve, medicament, medication, cream, jelly, dressing, compress.

apply, *v. t.* **1.** put (*with "to," "on," or "upon"*), place, use (*with "to," "on," or "upon"*), lay (*with "to," "on," or "upon"*), bestow (*A*), spread; *spec.* misapply.

2. direct, concentrate, give, devote, address, bend, keep (*implying continued attention or effort devoted to a task*); buckle, put, keep, ply (*R*), turn; *see* ADDICT.

3. *See* APPROPRIATE, RELATE.

apply, *v. i.* **1.** bear (*with "on" or "upon"*), hold, subsist.

2. address (*R*), turn, run, resort, go (*contex.*); *see* APPEAL.

3. attend (*with "to" implies attention*).

4. bear (*with "on," "upon"*), be pertinent, relevant, *or the like:* (*implying a practical connection of one subject with another*).

appoint, *v. t.* (*implies formal or authoritative action*) **1.** ordain, prescribe, fix, order, frame, establish, determine, preappoint (*R*), decree, direct, set, destine, foreordain, dispose; *spec.* redetermine.

2. designate, assign, constitute, set, fix, limit, settle, cast; *spec.* commission, place, name, detail, depute, deputize, delegate, prick, nominate, destine, attach, determine, predetermine, locate; *see* APPORTION, APPROPRIATE.

Antonyms: see FORBID.

3. *See* EQUIP.

appointment, *n.* **1.** ordinance, ordination, ordainment (*R*), establishment, disposition, determination, prescription, decree, direction, settlement, foreordination, predetermination.

2. designation, constitution, settlement, limitation; *spec.* commission, deputation, indiction (*by formal public notice or proclamation*), destination, determination, *etc.; see* APPORTIONMENT, APPROPRIATION.

3. position, post, place, office, job (*C*).

4. engagement, assignation, tryst (*B*), meeting, date (*C*), interview (*spec.*).

5. *See* EQUIP, FURNISH.

apportion, *v. t.* portion (*less usual than "apportion"*), assign, appoint, allow, allocate, allot, measure (*A or fig.*), award (*implies judicial decision*), mete (*R*), give (*contex.*), distribute, deal (*chiefly spec.*); *spec.* award, limit (*U. S. & Canada*), dole, admeasure (*R*), divide, cast (*theatrical*).

apportionment, *n.* assignment, appointment, allowance, allotment, *etc. Cf.* APPORTION.

appreciative, *a.* sensible, sensitive, grateful (*spec.*).

Antonyms: see UNAPPRECIATIVE.

apprehension, *n.* **1.** arrest, capture, seizure.

2. perception, grasp, understanding, intelligence, expectation, opinion.

3. fear (*with "lest" or "that"*), misgiving, mistrust, presentiment, foreboding, anxiety (*with "lest"*), solicitude (*with "lest"*), scruple (*R*).

apprehensive, *a.* fearful (*with "of," "lest," or "that"*), anxious (*with "for fear that"*), solicitous (*with "lest"*), afraid (*with "that"*), jittery (*S*). *"Apprehensive" is used with "of," "lest," or "that."*

Antonyms: see HOPEFUL.

apprehensiveness, *n.* fearfulness, anxiety, solicitude, fear.

approach, *v. i.* **1.** near, advance (*contex.*), approximate, nigh (*R*), advene (*R*), accede (*R*), appropinquate (*R*); *spec.* borrow, verge, draw, board, converge, come.

Antonyms: see DEPART.

2. approximate (*as in quality, form, etc.*), near (*R*); *spec.* resemble.

3. come (*contex.*):—*referring to what draws near in time.*

approach, *v.* **1.** come, draw near *or* nearer, appropinquate (*R*), near, converge (*referring to things moving toward a center*), board (*a ship*)—*with reference to space or time.*

2. *v. i.* come near, approximate:—*in quality, character, or state.*

3. *v. t.* bring near *or* nearer (*locally*), approximate (*A*).

4. accost, address, board (*A*), make up to:—*implying advances toward acquaintanceship, privilege, or the like.*

Antonyms: see AVOID, LEAVE.

approach, *n.* **1.** nearing, appropinquation (*R*), approachment (*R*), approximation, advance (*contex.*); *spec.* convergence, convergency (*R*).

Antonyms: see AVOIDANCE, DIVERGENCE.

---

apposite: *appropriate, relative.*
apposition: *application, relation.*
appraise: *value.*
appreciable: *perceptible.*
appreciate: *value, feel, advance.*
appreciation: *valuation, feeling, advance, understanding.*
appreciative: *sensitive.*
apprehend: *arrest, capture, perceive, understand, expect, fear.*
apprehensible: *understandable, perceptible.*
approachable: *accessible, affable.*

---

2. coming.
3. *In pl.:* advances (*pl.*).
4. access; *spec.* entrance.
approaching, *a.* **1.** nearing, advancing; *spec.* convergent, connivent (*tech.*), coming, ensuing (*implying succession immediately or soon*).
2. *See* COMING (*in time*).
appropriate, *v. t.* **1.** take, spheterize (*R and humorous*); *spec.* misappropriate, condemn, arrogate, convert, embezzle, foreclose, secrete, pocket, usurp; *see* CONVERT, STEAL, CONFISCATE.
Antonyms: see ABANDON, RELINQUISH, FORGO.
2. assign, appoint, allot, apply:—*implying a setting apart to a peculiar use or purpose;* devote (*implying a solemn vow*), dedicate (*implying special formality*), design; *spec.* reserve, misapply, misappropriate.
3. *See* ASCRIBE.
appropriate, *a.* **1.** proper, peculiar, own:—*implying connection as an attribute, quality, or right, and used absolutely or with "to," "for," "unto"* (*A*).
2. becoming, suitable, fit, fitting, meet, condign (*of punishment*), felicitous (*action, remark, etc.*), convenient (*A*), convenable (*obs.*), feat (*A*), competent (*A*), likely, proper, appropriate, apposite, pat (*chiefly spec.*), apt, good, right, sortable (*A*), idoneous (*R*), concinnous (*R*), congruous; *spec.* happy, decent, graceful, applicable; *see* TIMELY:—*implying such connection or relation as adapts or suits one thing to or for another.*
Antonyms: see UNSUITABLE, UNTIMELY.
appropriately, *adv.* becomingly, suitably, *etc.*, apropos. *Cf.* APPROPRIATE, *a.*, **2.**
appropriateness, *n.* becomingness (*R*), suitability, fitness, felicity, *etc.*
appropriation, *n.* taking, application; *spec.* confiscation, arrogation, allotment, secretion, *etc. Cf.* APPROPRIATE, *v. t.*
approval, *n.* approbation, support, sanction, imprimatur (*spec. or fig.*), endorsement, countenance, acceptance, O. K. (*C*); *spec.* favor, fancy, auspices, visé (*French*); *see* ADMIRATION, PRAISE, LIKING.
approve, *v. t.* approbate (*R; chiefly Eng.*), sanction, support, countenance, accept, sustain, pass, endorse, ratify, confirm, second, O. K. (*C*); *spec.* encourage, preconize (*R*), favor, visé; *see* LIKE, PRAISE, ADMIRE.
Antonyms: see CONDEMN, REPROVE, CENSURE.
approximate, *a.* rough, round, close, near;—*referring to approximations, numbers, etc.*
appurtenance, *n.* (*implying something subordinate but necessary*) accessory, belonging, appurtenant, adjunct, appendage; *spec.* paraphernalia (*pl.*), incident (*law*), requisite, property (*theaters*), props (*C; theaters*); *see* ACCESSORY, APPANAGE.
aquiline, *a. Referring to the nose:* hawk-nosed (*R or opprobrious*), beaked, hooked, Roman, prominent (*spec.*).
Antonyms: see PUG-NOSED, SNUB.
arable, *a.* plowable, tillable.
arable, *n.* infield (*Brit.*), earthland (*R*), plowland.
arbitrary, *a.* **1.** *See* ABSOLUTE, CAPRICIOUS, TYRANNICAL, AUTOCRATIC.
2. High-handed, willful, high (*C*).
arbor, *n.* bower; *spec.* pergola, pandal (*Anglo-Indian*).
arboreal, *a.* arboral, arboreous, arborous, dendral (*R*).
arcade, *n.* passage (*contex.*); *spec.* cloister, loggia (*Italian*), gallery.
arch, *n.* cove, fornix (*Latin*); *spec.* ogive, skewback, conch, concha, vault, invert, concameration (*R*), span.
arch, *v. t.* **1.** cove, vault (*chiefly spec.*), embow (*B*), concamerate (*R*); *spec.* hog, hump, hunch.
2. span, overvault (*R*), overarch.
archer, *n.* sagittary (*R*), bowman, bowyer (*R*); *spec.* Sagittarius.
architect, *n.* designer, artist (*contex.*), builder (*contex.*), maker (*R*), constructor (*contex.*), master builder (*tech.*).
architecture, *n.* structure, building, construction.
ardent, *a.* **1.** *See* BURNING, HOT, ALCOHOLIC.
2. eager, impetuous, hot, warm, fiery, burning, fierce, fervent, glowing, feverish, fervid, perfervid (*emphatic for "fervid"; R*), zealous, passionate, enthusiastic, enthusiastical (*A*).
Antonyms: see APATHETIC, INDIFFERENT.
ardor, *n.* eagerness, impetuosity, ardency (*A*), fervor, fever, feverishness, passion, heat, glow, warmth, fire, élan (*French*), fieriness, vehemence, zeal, flame, spirit, soul, verve (*B*), ferventness, fervidity (*R*), perfervor (*R*), enthusiasm.
Antonyms: see APATHY, INDIFFERENCE.
area, *n.* **1.** *Referring to an extent of land:* extent, space, expanse, tract, circuit, compass, field, sphere, range, scope, ground (*contex.*), size, stretch; *spec.* sheet, terrain, terrane; *see* PIECE.
2. extent, expanse, space, room (*now chiefly spec.*).
arena, *n.* **1.** *Spec.* circus, amphitheater, cirque, ring, lists (*pl.*), cockpit, field, Bowl, gridiron, diamond.
2. *See* SPHERE.
argument, *n.* **1.** reason (*contex.*); *spec.* silencer, fallacy, sophism, dilemma; *see* REASON.

approbation: *approval, admiration.*
approximate: *approach.*
approximately: *about.*
appurtenance: *property.*
appurtenant, *a.: accessory.*
appurtenant, *n.: accessory.*
apriori: *deductive.*
apropos: *timely, appropriately.*
apt: *ready, appropriate, disposed.*
aptitude: *talent.*
aqueduct: *channel.*
aqueous: *watery.*
arbiter: *judge, master.*
arbitrate: *decide, judge.*
arbor: *axle.*
arborescent: *branching.*
arc: *curve, band.*
Arcadian: *rural.*
arch, *a.: chief.*
archaic: *old-fashioned.*
archetype: *original, pattern.*
archipelago: *sea.*
arduous: *difficult, laborious.*
argent: *silvery.*
argillaceous: *clayey.*
argosy: *ship.*
argot: *jargon, dialect.*
argue: *discuss, dispute, mean.*

2. *See* DISCUSSION, DISPUTE.
aright, *adv. Spec.* rightly, correctly, justly, properly.
arise, *v. i.* **1.** *See* RISE.
2. originate, spring, issue, rise, proceed, emerge, come, grow, flow, accrue, begin; *see* OCCUR, RESULT.
Antonyms: see DIE.
arising, *n.* **1.** *See* RISE.
2. origination, spring, rise, beginning, birth, *etc. Cf.* ARISE, *v. i.* **2.**
aristocracy, *n.* **1.** *Referring to a form or principle of government:* optimacy (*R*), patriciate (*R*).
Antonyms: see DEMOCRACY.
2. *See* NOBILITY.
3. *As a collective:* quality (*chiefly A or dial.*).
aristocrat, *n.* patrician (*B*), optimate (*B*); *see* NOBLE.
aristocratic, *a.* **1.** *See* NOBLE.
2. patrician (*B*).
Antonyms: see DEMOCRATIC, PLEBEIAN, COMMON.
arm, *n.* **1.** wing (*C or humorous, exc. spec.*); *spec.* brachium, humerus, forearm.
2. branch; *spec.* inlet, estuary, fiord *or* fjord; *see* BRANCH.
3. projection; *spec.* transept, jib, davit, fluke, crane; *see* BOOM.
4. *See* POWER, WEAPON, SLEEVE.
arm, *v. t.* **1.** equip; *spec.* panoply, heel, lead (lĕd), forearm.
2. *See* ARMOR.
armed, *a.* equipped, accoutered, outfitted; *spec.* panoplied, forearmed.
Antonyms: see UNARMED.
armhole, *n.* **1.** *See* ARMPIT.
2. armseye (*tech.*), scye (*R*).
armor, *n. Spec.* panoply, mail, bard.
armor, *v. t.* **1.** *Referring to man or horse:* arm, mail; *spec.* panoply, helm (*A or B*).
2. *Referring to a vessel, aëroplane, etc.:* protect (*contex.*), plate, mail (*R*).
armored, *a.* mailed, mail-clad; *spec.* panoplied, loricate, iron-clad, bullet-proof.
armpit, *n.* armhole, axilla (*tech.*).
arms, *n.* **1.** armament, armor (*A or R*); *see* WEAPON.
2. *In heraldry:* coat of arms *or* (*for short*) coat, bearings (*pl.; often in sing.*), blazon, ensign, blazonment, blazonry.
army, *n.* **1.** host (*A or B*), array (*A*), force, forces (*pl.*), troops (*pl.*), legion *or* (*pl.*) legions (*orig. spec.*), men-of-war (*pl.; now R or hist.*), battalion (*A*); *spec.* fyrd (*hist.*), division, corps, section, squad, company.
2. *See* MULTITUDE, ORGANIZATION.
arrange, *v. t.* **1.** dispose, distribute, allocate (*B*), lay; *spec.* classify, range, rank, trim, organize, systematize, marshal, collocate, form, array, group, defilade, brigade, dress, pitch, echelon, space, size, compose, recompose, order, fix, tidy (*C*), drape, seriate (*R*); *see* ORGANIZE, PACK, ADJUST.
Antonyms: see DISARRANGE, CONFUSE.
2. *In music: spec.* orchestrate, score, instrument.
3. settle, accommodate, determine, reconcile, compose, compound, compromise (*A*); *spec.* adjust, arbitrate, mediate.
4. *See* AGREE, STIPULATE, ADAPT, PLAN.
arrangement, *n.* **1.** disposal, disposure, disposition, allocation (*B*), ordinance (*now only B and implying conformity to some rule or plan of production*); *spec.* systematization, ordination, malarrangement, trim, groupage, organization, defilade, categorization, chronography, collocation, codification; *see* ORGANIZATION, ADJUSTMENT.
Antonyms: see DISORDER.
2. *Referring to the result:* disposal, disposure, disposition, form, shape, *etc.* (*with most of the terms under* **1.,** *above*), lay; *spec.* make-up, orderliness, array, schematism, cosmos (*as opposed to* chaos) (*R*).
3. *In music: spec.* orchestration, instrumentation, score.
4. settlement, accommodation, reconciliation, composite; *spec.* exchange, stipulation.
5. *Referring to the result:* settlement; *spec.* mise (*Eng.; hist.*), bundobust (*Anglo-Indian*); *see* AGREEMENT.
6. *See* ADAPTATION, PLAN, THING.
arranger, *n. Spec.* adjuster, fixer (*C*), disposer, distributer, classifier, marshal, *etc. Cf.* ARRANGE.
arrest, *v. t.* **1.** *See* STOP, RESTRAIN.
2. seize, apprehend, bond (*C*), nick (*C*), nab (*C*), grab (*C*), pinch (*C*), collar (*C*).
arrest, *n.* **1.** *See* STOPPAGE, RESTRAINT, IMPRISONMENT.
2. seizure, apprehension, arrestment (*chiefly Scot.*), arrestation (*a Gallicism*).
arrival, *n.* coming, access (*R*), advent, subvention (*R; chiefly spec.*).
arrive, *v. i.* come, attain (*with "to"*), accede (*R*), subvene (*R; chiefly spec.*), reach (*with "to"*). *"Arrive" takes "at" for its preposition.*
arrogance, *n.* presumption, assumption, pride, overweening, haughtiness, *etc. Cf.* ARROGANT.
arrogant, *a.* (*implies unwarrantable claims to recognition*) presumptuous, overbearing, assuming, assumptive (*R*), magisterial (*B*), fastuous (*R*), high-minded, high, overweening, supercilious, insolent, insulting, contemptuous, snooty (*C*), uppish (*C*), topping; *see* SELF-IMPORTANT, IMPUDENT, HAUGHTY, ROUGH.

---

arid: *dry, uninteresting.*
armament: *arms, equipment.*
armorial: *heraldic.*
armory: *arsenal.*
aroma: *smell.*
aromatic: *odorous.*
around: *about.*
arouse: *wake, rouse, excite.*
arraign: *accuse.*
arrant: *outrageous.*
array, *n.: arrangement, army, body, group, clothing.*
array, *v. t.: arrange, clothe.*

Antonyms: see AGREEABLE, AFFABLE, HUMBLE, SUBMISSIVE, BASHFUL, ABJECT, CONDESCENDING, OBSEQUIOUS.

arrow, *n.* missile (*contex.*), shaft; *spec.* bolt, flight, sumpit, vire (*hist.*), quarrel.

arrow-headed, *a.* sagittate, sagittated (*both tech.*).

arsenal, *n.* armory.

art, *n.* **1.** craft, skill (*A*), knack; *spec.* trade, calling, handicraft (*manual*), cacotechny (*R*), discipline (*in its educational aspect; A*), mystery (*A*).

2. *See* SKILL, INGENIOUSNESS, LEARNING, ABILITY.

3. craft, craftiness, wiliness, deceitfulness, duplicity, artfulness, strategy, cunning, insidiousness (*R*), finesse, design, artifice, ingenuity, policy, slyness, subtlety *or* subtleness (*both now R*), pawkiness (*Scot. or dial.*), foxiness (*R*), foxery (*C*), *see* TRICKINESS;—*mostly with specific implications.*

Antonyms: spec. artlessness, frankness (*see* ARTLESS, FRANK)

artful, *a.* **1.** *See* SKILLFUL, INGENIOUS.

2. crafty, sly, wily, deceitful, cunning, mercurial (*fig.*), cautelous (*A*), subtle (*R*), subtile (*A*), stealthy, politic, insidious (*R*), versute (*R*), foxy (*C*), crooked, fly (*C*), pawky (*Scot. or dial.; chiefly humorous*); *see* TRICKY;—*mostly with specific implications.*

Antonyms: see ARTLESS, FRANK.

article, *n.* **1.** piece; *spec.* contribution, critique, review, essay, feuilleton (*French*), appreciation, notice, paper, skit, study, sketch, apology

2. thing (*contex.*), commodity; *spec.* export, import; *see* GOODS.

3. *See* CLAUSE, ITEM, THING.

artifice, *n.* **1.** (*implies ingenuity*) *See* ART, INGENIOUSNESS.

2. (*implies deception*) device, trick (*a good artifice*), subterfuge, ruse, shuffle, finesse, ingenuity, maneuver, practice, design, contrivance, machination, fetch, trickery, imposture, strategy, stratagem, feint; *spec.* counterplot; *see* TRICK, PRETENSE.

artificer, *n.* craftsman; *spec.* artisan, artist, Dædalus (*fig.*).

artificial, *a.* factitious (*implies a making for some special purpose, as distinct from what arises naturally*), made, false, made-up, manufactured (*spec. or fig.*), painted (*spec. or fig.*); *spec.* labored, unnatural, theatrical, constrained, cultivated; *see* PRETENDED, COUNTERFEIT, CONVENTIONAL.

Antonyms: see NATURAL, GENUINE, UNCONSTRAINED.

artillery, *n.* ordnance, enginery (*A*); *spec.* archery, broadside, battery, onagers, trebuckets (*both A; pl.*); *see* CANNONRY.

artilleryman, *n.* gunner; *see* CANNONEER.

artist, *n.* (*implies skill in the fine arts*): artiste (*French*); *spec.* dilettante, pastellist, painter, sculptor, etcher, engraver, cartoonist, colorist, water-colorist, landscapist, miniaturist, impressionist, cubist, futurist, surrealist, symbolist, dadaist, academician, rapin (*French*), musician, pianist, violinist, organist, *etc.*

artistic, *n.* artful (*A*), dædal (*fig.*); *spec.* painterly (*R*), arty (*C*).

Antonyms: see INARTISTIC.

artless, *a.* **1.** *See* UNCULTURED.

2. (*implies simplicity and directness*): simple, innocent, inartificial, naïve *or* (*less usual*) naïf, natural, guileless, ingenuous, straightforward, plain, unsophisticated; *spec.* rural, rude, homely, homespun, homebred; *see* FRANK.

Antonyms: see ARTFUL, CALCULATING, AFFECTED, PRETENDED, TRICKY, HYPOCRITICAL.

artlessness, *n.* naïveté (*French*), simplicity, unsophistication, ingenuousness, inartificiality (*R*), simpleness, *etc. Cf.* ARTLESS.

as, *adv. & conj.* **1.** like (*vulgar or slovenly*).

2. *See* BECAUSE.

ascend, *v. i.* **1.** *See* RISE, CLIMB, SLOPE.

2. *Referring to going back in time:* mount.

ascend, *v. t.* climb, mount, rise; *spec.* reascend, clamber, top.

Antonyms: see DESCEND.

ascendancy, *n.* control, ascendance, ascendant.

ascent, *n.* **1.** *Spec.* rise (*which see*), climbing (*cf.* CLIMB).

2. slope, rise, gradient (*tech.; Eng.*); *see* HILL.

ascetic, *a.* austere, abstemious, strict; *spec.* puritan, mortified (*R*); *see* ABSTEMIOUS.

Antonyms: see SELF-GRATIFYING, GLUTTONOUS, SENSUOUS, CONVIVIAL.

ascetic, *n. Spec.* fakir, stylite, yogi (*Hindu philos.*); *see* HERMIT.

Antonyms: see BON-VIVANT, GLUTTON, DRINKER.

asceticism, *n.* (*implies rigorous self-discipline*): austerity, abstemiousness; *spec.* yoga *or* yogism.

Antonyms: see SELF-GRATIFICATION.

ascribe, *v. t.* (*implies reference to the source*): **1.** *See* ATTRIBUTE, ACCREDIT.

2. attribute, assign, arrogate (*B*), appropriate.

ascription, *n.* **1.** *See* ATTRIBUTION.

2. attribution, arrogation (*B*), appropriation.

asexual, *a.* neuter (*biol.*), sexless.

ash, *a.* cinerary (*B*), ashen.

ashy, *a.* ashen, cinereous (*B or tech.*), cineraceous (*R*), cineritious (*B or tech.*), favillous (*R*).

aside, *n.* bye; *spec.* byplay, by-end, by-matter; *see* BY-WORK.

ask, *v. t.* **1.** inquire, question, interrogate, speer (*Scot.*):—*implying a calling upon a person in some way for information or for an answer,* question *implying an expressed inquiry, and*

---

arrowy: *rapid.*
arsis: *accent.*
artery: *channel.*
articulate: *joint, pronounce.*
ascendant, *n. horoscope, ascendancy.*
ascertain: *discover, learn.*
ashamed: *abashed.*
ashen: *ash, ashy.*
ashore: *aground.*
aside: *apart.*
asinine: *stupid.*

interrogate *formal or close questioning*; request:—*the more formal term, without implication as to the manner of asking*; beg (*the more usual term referring to alms*), crave (*B or formal*), pray, petition, entreat, beseech, supplicate, implore:—*implying that what is asked is sought as a favor. The terms given last are the stronger ones,* petition *emphasizing the formality of the request,* entreat *and* beseech *the idea of importunity,* supplicate *that of submissiveness, and* implore *the need of the one asking*; dun (*implying repeated and persistent demands, especially for payment of a debt*), importune, move, plead, adjure, conjure, obsecrate (*R*), sue, solicit, earwig (*implies private influence*), knee (*R*), coax.

Antonyms: see FORBID, COMPEL.

2. *With the thing asked for as the object:* request (*implies formality*); *spec.* beg, entreat, implore, supplicate, demand, petition, claim, clamor, canvass, require, seek, exact, solicit, call, invoke, cry, publish (banns).

Antonyms: see REJECT.

3. *See* SUMMON, QUESTION, DEMAND, INVITE.

ask, *v. i.* **1.** *Spec.* beg, beseech, plead, appeal, postulate (*R*), petition, sue, clamor, importune, entreat (*R*).

2. *See* QUESTION.

asker, *n. Spec.* requester, applicant, craver, supplicant, entreater, claimant, suppliant, orator (*law*), *etc. Cf.* ASK, *v. t.*

askew, *a.* crooked, distorted, awry, atwist (*R*), skew, skewed, cock-eyed (*C*); *spec.* loxic.

asking, *a.* **1.** interrogative, interrogational, interrogatory, implorative, postulatory (*R*).

2. *Spec.* requesting, begging, *etc.*, supplicatory, solicitant (*R*), supplicant, suppliant, precative, implorative, postulatory (*R*), precatory (*chiefly legal or tech.*), petitory (*R*), petitionary (*R*). *Cf.* ASK.

asking, *n.* **1.** *Spec.* impetration, imploration (*R*), application, postulation (*R*), prayer, canvass, entreatment (*A*), entreaty, obsecration, beseechment, obtestation (*B*), imploring, instancy (*R*), suit (*B*), suppliance, supplication, rogation, comprecation; *see* APPEAL, ASK.

2. *Referring to what is asked: see* REQUEST.

aspect, *n.* **1.** *See* APPEARANCE, SIDE, FACING.

2. appearance, light, angle (*chiefly C*), complexion, phase, face, view, look.

aspirant, *n.* aspirer, seeker; *spec.* candidate, suitor, competitor, heeler (*C*).

aspirate, *n.* spiritus, breathing, aspiration.

aspirated, *a.* rough (*contex.*), spirated, aspirate (*R*).

assail, *v. t.* **1.** molest; *see* ATTACK.

2. pelt, ply, storm, bestorm (*R*); *spec.* din, hoot, jeer, jibe.

Antonyms: see DEFEND, SHELTER.

assailable, *a.* pregnable.

assassin, *n.* murderer, killer; *spec.* thug, sicarian (*R*).

assassinate, *v. t.* murder (*contex.*), kill, slay, remove; *spec.* morganize (*R; U. S.*), destroy, injure (*of a reputation*).

assay, *n.* trial, test, examination; *spec.* analysis, cupel, cupellation, docimasy.

assembly, *n.* **1.** *See* GATHERING, COMPANY.

2. *Referring to the more formally organized gatherings of persons, spec.:* synod, salon, chapter, plenum, court, moot, convention, convocation, congregation, legislature, congress, senate, house, diet, chamber, camera (*R, or hist.*), cabinet, council, parliament, meeting, chapter, camarilla (*Spanish*), Reichstag (*German*), soviet (*Russian*), comita (*Roman hist.*), muster; *see* CONVENTION, COUNCIL, CONGREGATION.

assess, *v. t.* **1.** charge, levy, impose, apportion.

2. *See* TAX, VALUE.

assessable, *a.* leviable, taxable.

assimilate, *v. t.* **1.** *See* CONFORM, LIKEN.

2. adapt, absorb; *spec.* digest;—*all often used fig. of ideas.*

Antonyms: see EXCRETE.

associate, *n.* **1.** companion, fellow, consociate (*R*), conjunct (*R*):—*implying little or no more than mere accompaniment, usually personal or joint action or effort.*

2. comrade, mate, pal (*C*), brother, buddy (*C*), chum, covey (*S*), crony, gossip, cummer (*Scot.*), billy *or* billie (*Scot.*):—*implying intimate relation in friendship, fortunes, occupation, or the like.*

3. accomplice (*always implying a common evil or unlawful purpose*), confederate (*often so implying*).

4. ally, leaguer:—*implying association under a league or treaty in a matter of some dignity.*

5. partner, copartner (*chiefly legal:—implying association in sharing the results of joint efforts or risk.*)

6. colleague:—*implying equality and association in office or special employment; not used in trade or business.*

7. consort, spouse, mate, comate (*R*):—*referring to husband or wife.*

8. consort:—*referring to a ship convoying another.*

9. attendant:—*implying subordinacy.*

Spec. familiar, intimate, comes (*astron.*), yokefellow, housemate, shipmate, clansman, condisciple (*B*), privy (*R*), compeer, confrere,

askance: *obliquely.*
aslant: *sloping.*
asleep: *sleeping, numb.*
aslope: *sloping.*
asperity: *roughness, acrimony.*
asperse: *sprinkle, disparage.*
asphyxiate: *suffocate.*
aspire: *desire, rise.*
asquint, *adv.: obliquely.*
asquint, *a.: squint-eyed.*
ass: *donkey, blockhead.*
assault: *attack.*
assent, *v. i.: accede.*
assert: *maintain, state, claim.*
assets: *property.*
asseverate: *state.*
assiduous: *diligent, constant, active, persistent.*
assign: *appoint, refer, apportion, appropriate, adjudge, ascribe, attribute, transfer.*
assist: *aid, contribute, serve.*
assize, *n.: edict, court.*

classmate, messmate, convictor (*R*), cohabitant, capitulary, neighbor, association, coadjutor; *see* ALLY, SISTER, COLLEAGUE, ATTENDANT.

associate, *v. t.* **1.** join, unite, link, conjoin, attach (*with "to"*), combine, ally (*chiefly spec.*), mingle; *spec.* pool, syndicate, brigade, regiment, consort, couple, league.

2. *Referring to mental association:* connect, join, unite, link, sort (*R or B*), consort (*R or B*), couple, mingle, correlate.

associate, *v. i.* **1.** unite, combine, join, conjoin, consociate (*R*), mingle; *spec.* missort (*R*), mingle, mix, neighbor, herd, hobnob.

2. companion (*R*), consort (*B or formal*), fellow (*R*), assort (*R*), fellowship, accompany (*R*), train (*S*), consociate (*R*), sort (*dial. or A*), forgather; *spec.* sororize (*R*), fraternize, mingle, mix, neighbor, clique, crony (*R*), herd, haunt (*R, exc. of animals*), missort (*R*), hobnob; *see* CONVERSE.

association, *n.* **1.** *the manner of forming the association:*—joining, connection, conjunction (*R*), linking, combination, alliance, mingling; *see* UNION.

2. *the fact of association:*—company, companionship, fellowship, consociation (*R*), consort (*B*), consortion (*R*); *spec.* comradeship, comradery (*R*), camaraderie (*French*), confraternization (*R*), fraternization, complicity.

3. *the kind of association:*—companionship, company, fellowship, comradeship, accompliceship (*R*), confederacy, alliance, league, colleagueship, partnership, copartnership, attendance, consortship, spousal:—*see* ASSOCIATE; society, club, sodality, circle, academy, institute, profession, Athenæum:—*usually referring, as also* association, *to a body organized, often without incorporation, for some purpose other than trade or commerce;* alliance, league: —*usually referring to states or political bodies*: *or less often to persons engaged in public affairs;* fraternity, brotherhood, sorority, sisterhood, guild, board, order, lodge, monastery, convent, chapter, choir, chantry, congregation, college, communion:—*implying intimate association for mutual help, action, effort, or companionship;* confederacy, confederation:—*referring usually to states or political parties joined by treaty or compact for government or action;* combination, combine, pool, trust, cartel:—*usually referring to organizations, often illegal, in regulation of the conditions of trade, commerce, or traffic;* company (*whether or not incorporated*), firm, corporation, copartnership, partnership, concern:—*referring to business organizations;* band, troop, company, brigade, corps:—*implying primarily military organizations, and hence referring to bodies of men organized temporarily or loosely for joint action;* crew, gang:—*implying organization, usually loose, for a common purpose; often more or less derogatory in sense;* body, organization, consociation:—*general terms;* guild, craft, trade, mystery (*A or hist.*), union:—*with reference to organizations of working men and craftsmen;* connection, clique, clan, carbinarii (*pl.; Italian*), ku-klux, camorra, fratry (*A or hist.*), hong (*Chinese*), hoey (*Chinese*), Burschenschaft (*German*), bond (*Dutch*), somai (*India*); *see* CONVENT, PARTY, COMPANY, PARTNERSHIP, CORPORATION, FIRM, CLUB, UNION, SISTERHOOD.

assume, *v. t.* **1.** take (*as a partner into association*); *spec.* reassume, arrogate.

2. postulate, suppose, fiction (*R*), feign, presume, presuppose, say (*used in the imperative*), hypothesize, hypothetize (*R*), posit, pose (*R*), beg (*chiefly in "to beg the question"*).

Antonyms: see DENY.

3. affect, take (*a character*), invest (*oneself with*), endue (*B*), strike (*an attitude*); *spec.* reassume; *see* ACT.

Antonyms: see DOFF.

4. take (*as in "to take the shape of"*).

5. *See* UNDERTAKE, DON.

6. pretend, feign, sham.

assume, *v. i.* presume, venture.

assumed, *a.* supposed, hypothetical, hypothetic, supposititious, suppositional, suppositive, fictional, fictionary (*R*), feigned, false, unreal, presupposed, presumptive, paper (*C*); *spec.* given.

assuming, *a.* presuming, pretentious, nervy (*C*), presumptuous, immodest (*R*), assumptive, hoity-toity (*usually implying petulance or ill-temper*), superior, forward, lofty; *see* ARROGANT.

Antonyms: see ABJECT, MODEST, UNPRETENTIOUS.

assumption, *n.* **1.** taking; *spec.* reassumption.

2. supposition, supposal (*R*), supposure (*R*), postulation, presupposition, presupposal (*R*), presumption, hypothesis (*tech. or B*).

Antonyms: see DENIAL.

3. *Referring to the thing assumed:* postulate (*logic, etc.*), hypothesis (*tech. or B*), suppose, (*R*), fiction; *spec.* make-believe, datum, data (*as sing. illiterate*), premise, condition, principle. *The terms under sense* **2** *are also used concretely.*

4. affectation, investiture, enduement (*B*), striking, *etc.*

5. presumption, superiority, loftiness, impudence, nerve (*S*), cheek (*S*), brass (*S*), forwardness; *see* ARROGANCE.

assumptive, *a.* **1.** *See* ASSUMING, ARROGANT.

2. suppository, postulative, presuppository.

assurance, *n.* **1.** warrant, certification; *spec.* reassurance.

2. confidence (*contex.*), self-assurance, sufficiency, self-confidence, self-reliance, self-possession, aplomb (*French*), self-trust, self-security, self-sufficiency, plerophory (*R*); *spec.* overconfidence, overboldness, hardihood, overtrust (*R*), bumptiousness, coolness, cocksure-

---

assort, *v. t.: classify, class.*
assortment: *classification, collection, variety.*
assuage: *mitigate, appease, satisfy.*
assuredly: *truly.*

ness, cockiness (*C*), impudence, nerve (*S*), cheek (*S*), brass (*S*), gall (*S*); *see* BOLDNESS, PRESUMPTION, IMPUDENCE.
Antonyms: see TIMIDITY, DOUBT, DISTRUST, BASHFULNESS, EMBARRASSMENT.
3. *See* GUARANTEE, INSURANCE.
assure, *v. t.* **1.** warrant, tell (*contex.*), certify, resolve (*a reflexive*); *spec.* reassure; *see* CONVINCE.
Antonyms: see DISCONCERT, EMBARRASS, INTIMIDATE.
2. *See* INSURE.
assured, *a.* confident, intrepid, bold, fearless, certain:—*implying freedom from disturbing doubts or fears;* self-assured, self-confident, self-reliant, bumptious (*offensively*):—*implying trust in one's own sufficiency;* self-possessed:—*implying only an appearance of self-reliance;* self-assertive; *spec.* cool, overconfident, flush (*R*), Icarian (*fig.*), independent, crank (*dial.*), nervy (*C*), cheeky (*S*), cocky (*C*), presumptuous, immodest; *see* BOLD, IMPUDENT, SELF-ASSERTIVE, DECIDED.
Antonyms: see ABJECT, DOUBTFUL, TIMID, DISTRUSTFUL, BASHFUL, HESITATING.
assuring, *a. Spec.* reassuring, comfortable, encouraging, emboldening, heartening.
Antonyms: see DEPRESSING, HORRIBLE.
astern, *adv.* **1.** aft, abaft (*as in "the gale was abaft"*).
2. *See* BACKWARD.
astir, *a.* stirring, up, afoot, active, moving; *spec.* agog; *see* AFLOAT.
astray, *a.* **1.** lost, wandering, adrift, wrong.
2. abroad, out (*in reckoning*), wide, off (*C*).
astringent, *a.* **1.** constrictive, styptic, shrinking, contracting, constringent (*R*); *spec.* puckery, hæmostatic, rough, binding (*C*).
2. stern, austere, tart, sour.
astrologer, *n.* soothsayer, stargazer (*C*), Chaldean (*fig.*), astrologian (*R*), cock (*fig.; poetic*).
astronomy, *n. Spec.* astrology, astromancy, meteoroscopy, uranology, uranography, astrophysics, astrochemistry, astrophotography.
asylum, *n.* **1.** *See* REFUGE.
2. home (*contex.*), college (*chiefly Eng.*); *spec.* madhouse, sanitarium, bethlehem (*R*), bedlam (*variant of* bethlehem).
at, *prep.* **1.** *Referring to place:* in, to (*U. S. or dial. Eng.*).
2. *Referring to time:* in, to, by.
atheistic, *a.* godless, agnostic, disbelieving, skeptic (*C*), heretic.
athlete, *n. Spec.* boxer, fighter, pancratiast (*R*), acrobat, gymnast, sportsman.
Antonyms: see WEAKLING.
athletic, *a.* **1.** palæstral (*R*); *spec.* agonistic (*B*), gymnastic, acrobatic, sporting.
2. *See* STRONG.
athletics, *n. Spec.* gymnastics, agonistics, acrobatism, sports.
atmospheric, *a.* airy, aërial, elemental (*referring to atmospheric forces*), meteoric (*tech.*).
atomize, *v. t.* comminute, analyze, spray, reduce (*contex.*); *spec.* nebulize, vaporize.
atomizer, *n.* sprayer; *spec.* odorator, nebulizer, vaporizer, gun, nozzle.
atone, *v. i.* pay (*with "for"*), apologize.
atonement, *n.* reconciliation (*restoration of a relationship*), reparation (*restoration of damage or loss*), expiation, redemption.
attach, *v. t.* **1.** seize (*legally*), take, nail (*A or S*), nab (*S*); *spec.* garnishee.
2. join, unite, adjoin (*R*), add:—*implying nothing as to manner, permanence, or security of union;* fasten, fix, barnacle (*fig. and R*):—*implying a degree of permanence or security;* affix, confix (*R*), *spec.* belt:—*usually of a less thing joined to a greater, often unrelated to each other;* annex, append:—*usually implying looseness or lack of intimacy of union;* hitch:—*implying looseness or temporariness;* bind, tie, alligate (*R*):—*implying union by means of something wound or tied about the parts;* connect:—*implies something intermediate;* wed (*fig.*); *spec.* chain, tag, tack, tail, hook, hinge, screw, pin, engraft, solder, subjoin, glue, stick, nail, weld.
Antonyms: see SEPARATE, DETACH.
3. *See* JOIN, ADD, ASSOCIATE, APPOINT, ATTRIBUTE.
attachable, *a. Spec.* fastenable, annexable, connectable, appendable, *etc. Cf.* ATTACH.
attachment, *n.* **1.** joining (*contex.*), union (*contex.*), connection, annexation, affixture (*R*); *spec.* confixation (*R*), subjunction (*R*), appending, binding.
2. *Spec.* fixture, affix, annex, postfix, appendicle (*diminutive*), appendix, accessory, insertion, fixtures (*pl.; chiefly U. S.*), gadget (*C*); *see* APPENDAGE.
3. *See* JOINING, ADDITION, AFFECTION, LOVE.
attack, *v. t.* **1.** assault, assail, engage, encounter, attempt (*A*), aggress (*R; v. i. only*), tackle (*C*), storm (*chiefly spec.*); *spec.* charge, ply, beset (*B*), strike, bait, torpedo, mob, grenade, rush, flank, surprise, fusillade, storm, raid.
Antonyms: see DEFEND, PROTECT, SHELTER.
2. *In a nonphysical sense:* assail, impugn (*B*); *see* DISPUTE, OPPOSE, ACCUSE.
Antonyms: see DEFEND.
3. *See* CENSURE, AFFECT, BEGIN.
attack, *n.* **1.** assault, onslaught, assailment, attempt (*A*), battery (*implying blows*):—*imply the use of force or violence;* aggression, en-

---

astonish: *surprise.*
astound: *surprise.*
astraddle: *bestriding.*
astride: *bestriding.*
astute: *discerning, shrewd, subtle.*
asunder: *apart.*
athwart: *across.*
atmosphere: *air.*
atonic: *weak, unaccented.*
atrabilious: *acrimonious.*
atrocious: *wicked, cruel, outrageous.*
atrocity: *wickedness, cruelty, outrage, monstrosity.*
attach, *v. i.: stick, belong, accrue.*
attain, *v. t.: reach, get, accomplish.*
attain, *v. i.: reach, arrive, come.*
attainment: *accomplishment.*
attaint, *v. t.: contaminate, sully.*

---

counter, encroachment, intrusion, invasion, outbreak, inroad, set, onset, onslaught, offense, oppugnation (*R*); *spec.* charge, stroke, musketade, battery, camisade *or* camisado (*A or mil.*), descent, bombardment, cannonade, raid, sally, surprise, escalade, surprisal, shock, storm.

Antonyms: see PROTECTION, DEFENSE.

2. *In a nonphysical sense:* assault, impugent (*R*), crusade; *see* ACCUSATION.

3. access (*tech. or B*), onset, seizure; *spec.* epidemic; *see* FIT.

4. *See* BEGINNING.

attempt, *v. t.* try, essay, assay (*A*), offer, make, undertake, endeavor (*A*), enterprise (*A*); *spec.* venture.

attempt, *n.* trial, try (*C*), endeavor, venture, experiment, slap (*C or S*), offer (*R*), whack (*S*), shy (*S*), essay (*A or B*), set, assay (*A*), undertaking.

attend, *v. t.* **1.** tend (*now R, A, or U. S., exc. spec.*), serve, mind, nurse, keep; *spec.* guard, stroke, watch, feed, valet, midwife, wash.

Antonyms: see DISREGARD, IGNORE.

2. *In the sense of "to be present at": spec.* frequent, haunt.

3. *See* ACCOMPANY, SERVE, FOLLOW.

attend, *v. i.* **1.** *See* LISTEN, SERVE.

2. wait, hang (*with "upon"*); *spec.* dangle.

3. *In the sense of "to give attention":* tend, look (*with "after"*); *spec.* minister (*usually with "to"*), care (*chiefly with "for"*), serve.

attendance, *n.* **1.** tendance, attention, minding, keeping.

2. waiting (*with "upon"*), hanging (*with "upon"*), tendance (*R*); *spec.* service.

3. *See* ACCOMPANIMENT, SERVICE, RETINUE, COMPANION.

attendant, *a.* **1.** ministerial, attending; *spec.* serving.

2. *See* ACCOMPANYING, SUBSEQUENT.

attendant, *n.* companion, associate; *spec.* shadow, satellite (*chiefly derogatory*), people (*pl.*), barnacle (*fig.*), famulus (*Latin*), chamberlain, escort, acolyte, page, buttons (*C*), peon (*India*), man, boy, orderly, femme de chambre (*French*), courtier, courier, outrider, sergeant, henchman, gillie (*Scot.*), valet, minder, keeper, bodyguard, caddie, cad (*Eng.*); *see* HANDMAID, NURSE, PAGE.

attention, *n.* **1.** consideration, observance, regard, heed, respect, notice, advertence, thought, mind, intentness, concentration, ear (*as in "to give ear," "to have the ear of"*), observancy (*A*); *see* APPLICATION, CARE.

Antonyms: see DISREGARD, INATTENTION, ABSENT-MINDEDNESS.

2. *See* CIVILITY, SERVICE.

attentive, *a.* **1.** considerate, observant, heedful, studious, advertent (*R*), regardful, attent (*A*), awake (*with "to"*), watchful, alert, wide-awake, intent (*with "on"*), intentive (*A*), bent (*R, exc. in "bent on"*), thoughtful, concentrated, mindful; careful, regardant (*R*), regardful; *spec.* searching, resolved, studious (*with "of"*), delicate.

Antonyms: see ABSENT, INATTENTIVE, UNOBSERVANT.

2. *See* POLITE.

attentiveness, *n.* **1.** consideration, regard, heed, intentness, *etc. Cf.* ATTENTIVE.

2. *See* POLITENESS, CIVILITY.

attenuate, *v. t.* **1.** extenuate (*R*), spin (*with "out"*); *spec.* draw, finedraw, rope.

2. *See* THIN, WEAKEN.

attenuated, *a.* thin; *spec.* drawn-out, spun-out, finespun, subtle; *see* SLENDER.

attenuation, *n.* **1.** extenuation (*R*); *spec.* drawing, finedrawing.

2. *Spec.* thinning (*see* THIN, *v.*), thinness (*see* THIN, *a.*), subtlety; *see* SLENDERNESS, WEAKENING, WEAKNESS.

attic, *n.* garret, loft, cockloft (*A; often spec.*), soler (*obs. or R*), sky parlor (*humorous or C*).

attitude, *n.* **1.** *Referring to the body or bodily appearance: see* POSTURE, AIR.

2. *Referring to the mind:* posture, position, set, stand; *spec.* feeling, twist, prejudice, slant (*C*).

attorney, *n.* **1.** *See* AGENT.

2. *In the sense of "attorney at law":* lawyer; *spec.* solicitor, curator, procurator, proctor, barrister, counselor, advocate.

attract, *v. t.* **1.** *See* DRAW, CATCH.

2. draw, magnetize (*fig.*), take, pull; *spec.* drag, allure, inveigle, entice, seduce (*esp. to evil*), solicit, invite, tempt, attempt (*A*), lure, bait, trap, bonnet, decoy (*often fig.*), button (*S*), charm, fascinate.

Antonyms: see REPEL, DISGUST.

attraction, *n.* **1.** *Spec.* affinity, gravitation, gravity, pull; *see* DRAWING.

2. *Referring to the act or action or quality:* draw (*R*), magnetism (*fig.*), pull; *spec.* affinity, allurement, appeal, seduction (*esp. to evil*), charm, enticement, inveiglement, temptation, solicitation, glamour, spell; *see* ATTRACTIVENESS.

3. *Referring to the thing that attracts:* cynosure (*chiefly B*), bait, decoy, magnet, lure, charm. *Most of the terms under* **2** *are similarly used.*

attractive, *a.* **1.** *See* DRAWING.

2. drawing, alluring, seductive (*esp. to evil*), catchy (*C*), seducing (*esp. to evil*), magnetic, allective (*R*); *spec.* enticing, decoying, prepossessing, tempting, taking, catchy, pleasing, psychagogic (*R*), winning, winsome, temptatious (*R*), charming, meretricious (*implies false show*), glamorous (*commercial elegance implying sex-appeal*); *see* PLEASANT.

Antonyms: see REPELLENT, ABOMINABLE, DISGUSTING.

attractiveness, *n.* **1.** *See* ATTRACTION.

2. charm, grace, winsomeness, pleasingness.

attributable, *a.* referable, referrible (*A*), ascribable, imputable, due, chargeable, owing; *spec.* traceable.

attest: *testify, authenticate, evidence.*
Attic, *a.: classic, refined.*
attire, *v. t.: clothe.*
attitudinize: *pose.*

attribute, *v. t.* **1.** refer (*for comparison or classification*), ascribe (*as to source and origin*), assign, impute (*with implications of blame*), lay, attach, accredit, count, give, place, put, charge (*with "to"*), trace (*with "to"*), blame (*with "with"*); *spec.* mother, father, saddle (*with "with"*).
Antonyms: see REFUSE.
2. *See* ASCRIBE.

attribution, *n.* reference, ascription, assignment, *etc. Cf.* ATTRIBUTE, *v.*

auction, *a.* sale (*contex.*); *spec.* subhastation, cant (*chiefly Irish*), survey (*dial. Eng.*).

audible, *a.* sensible (*contex.*), auricular (*R, exc. eccl.*), hearable (*R*).

audience, *n.* **1.** *Referring to the act, fact, or action:* hearing, ear; *spec.* durbar (*East India*), court, conference, appointment.
2. *Referring to those that hear:* auditory (*R*); *spec.* congregation, theater, church, gallery gods (*pl.; C*), gallery, orchestra, pit, house (*C*); *see* HEARER.

auditorium, *n.* auditory (*R*); *spec.* pit, parterre, parquet, cockpit, orchestra, hall, room.

auricular, *a.* aural, heard (*R*), auditory (*referring to the function of the ear*), otic (*R*).

auspicious, *a.* **1.** *See* OMINOUS, PROSPEROUS.
2. favorable, propitious, promising, promiseful, prosperous, successful, white (*B*), lucky, fortunate, bright, hopeful, rosy, flattering, Favonian (*R*), felicitous (*chiefly spec.*); *spec.* brilliant, fair.
Antonyms: see INAUSPICIOUS, ILL-OMENED.

austere, *a.* (*implies loftiness, coldness, or remoteness of manner*) strict (*contex.*), severe, rigid, stern, hard, difficult (*R*), rigorous, Catonian (*R*), astringent (*R*); *spec.* rugged; *see* ASCETIC, ABSTEMIOUS.
Antonyms: see GENTLE, SELF-GRATIFYING.

austerity, *n.* strictness, severity, rigidity, rigor, rigorism, *etc. Cf.* AUSTERE.

authenticate, *v. t.* **1.** *Spec.* canonize.
2. attest, certify, seal (*chiefly spec.*), avouch; *spec.* coattest, consign (*R*), countersign, certificate, test, validate, O. K. (*C*).

author, *n.* **1.** originator, creator, creatress *or* creatrix (*fem.*), breeder (*chiefly spec. or fig.*), doer, maker; *spec.* constructor, deviser, producer, inventor, begetter, father, mother; *see* CREATOR.
Antonyms: see CREATURE.
2. authoress (*fem.; R*), composer; *spec.* writer, scribe, poet, literatist (*R*), quill-driver (*contemptuous*), penner, penman, scribbler, inditer, contributor, co-author, pastoralist, legendary, mythologist (*R*), penny-a-liner, librettist, Goliard (*hist.*), littérateur (*slightly contemptuous*), pamphleteer (*chiefly derogatory*), paragraphist, paragrapher, compiler, essayist, encyclopedist, bluestocking (*A*), penwoman (*R*), pot-boiler (*C*), hack, prosaist, parodist, ecloguist, proser, romancer, columnist, lexicographer, textualist, critic, reviewer, editor, newshawk (*C*).

authoritative, *a.* **1.** potestative (*R*), magisterial (*R*), magistral (*R*); *spec.* official, standard, approved, regular, valid, canonical, orthodox, cathedral.
2. commanding, imperative, dictatorial, imperial (*R or allusive*), jussive (*R*), peremptory, lordly, imperious, imperative; *spec.* masterful; *see* DOMINEERING.
Antonyms: see SUBMISSIVE, OBEDIENT.

authority, *n.* **1.** power, command, dominion, jurisdiction (*chiefly spec.*), rule, sway, right, authorization, warrant (*chiefly spec.*), competency, faculty (*chiefly eccl.*); *spec.* supremacy, headship, sovereignty, canonicity, canonicalness, agency, plenipotence, validity:—*implying the power or right to force obedience.*
2. *See* MAGISTRATE, INFLUENCE.
3. precedent; *spec.* decision, dictum, testimony.

authorization, *n.* permission, license, sanction, warrant, *etc.*:—*implying conferred or delegated power or right.*

authorize, *v. t.* permit, license, sanction, warrant, empower, enable; *spec.* commission, legalize, legitimate, fiat (*R*), dictate.
Antonyms: see FORBID.

authorship, *n.* creation; *see* COMPOSITION; *spec.* pencraft (*R*).

autocracy, *n.* monarchy, despotism, absolutism, tyranny (*chiefly with reference to ancient rulers*), dictatorship; *spec.* czarism, tsarism, kaiserism, Cæsarism.

autocrat, *n.* monarch, despot (*after ancient Greek usage*), tyrant (*chiefly with reference to ancient rulers*), dictator; *spec.* czar *or* tsar (*hist.*), czarina *or* tsarina (*hist.*), Kaiser (*hist.*), emperor, Cæsar (*hist.*).

autocratic, *a.* **1.** arbitrary, despotic (*after ancient Greek usage*), absolute, tyrannous *or* tyrant (*chiefly in reference to ancient rulers*), dictatorial.
Antonyms: see DEMOCRATIC, YIELDING.
2. *See* ARBITRARY.

autograph, *n. Spec.* holograph, sign-manual; *see* SIGNATURE.

autographic, *a.* **1.** autograph, manual (*signature*); *spec.* holographic, holograph.
2. self-recording, ipsographic (*R*).

automatic, *a.* **1.** self-acting, self-regulating, self-moving; *spec.* mechanical, spontaneous, instinctive; *see* AUTOMOBILE, *a.*
2. *See* INVOLUNTARY.

---

attune: *harmonize.*
atwist: *askew.*
auburn: *brown.*
audacious: *bold.*
audibly: *aloud.*
aught: *anything, cipher.*
augment: *increase.*
augur, *v. t.: predict, signify.*
augury: *divination, sign.*
august: *imperial, imposing.*
aura: *emanation, exhalation, sensation.*
aureate: *golden, gilded.*
aureola: *crown, halo.*
auspice: *divination, sign (in pl.), patronage.*
authentic: *reliable, genuine.*
authorized: *accredited.*
automaton: *machine.*

---

automobile, *a.* automatic (*contex.*), self-moving, locomobile, locomotive (*chiefly spec.*), automotive.

automobile, *n.* locomobile (*A*), locomotive (*chiefly spec.*), machine (*C*), motor (*C*), car, auto (*C*), bus (*C*), buzz-wagon (*C*), flivver (*S or C*), Lizzy (*C and A*); *spec.* autocar, motor-car, electric, steamer, runabout, limousine, touring car, roadster, towncar, coupé, coup (*S*), coupelet, sedan, convertible, truck, torpedo, tractor, motorcycle, motocycle, cycle car, jitney (*C or A*), bus, station wagon, taxi (*C*), taxicab.

autumn, *n.* harvest (*A or B*), fall (*chiefly U. S.*).

auxiliary, *n.* secondary, subsidiary, succenturiate (*R*), parergal (*R*); *see* ACCESSORY, ADJUNCT, ANCILLARY.

available, *a. Spec.* ready, handy, convenient, present, free, disposable, usable; *see* ACCESSIBLE.

avalanche, *n.* slide, lauwine (*R*); *spec.* landslide (*chiefly U. S.*), landslip (*chiefly Eng.*), snowslide, snowslip.

avenger, *n. Spec.* revenger, requiter, Ate, Euminides (*pl.*), Erinnyes (*pl.*), Alecto, Megæra, Tisiphone.

average, *a.* mean, passable, mediocre, medial (*chiefly math.*), normal; *spec.* standard; *see* ORDINARY, FAIR.

average, *n.* mean, normal, standard, ordinary, run, rule.

average, *v. i.* run, go; *spec.* equate.

average, *v. t.*, even, divide, equalize.

aversion, *n.* (*suggests voluntary avoidance*), dislike, repugnance, repulsion, antipathy (*suggests an involuntary avoidance*), dyspathy (*R*), *spec.* nausea, horror (*with "of"*), loathing, disgust, Russophobia, negrophobia, anthrophobia, gynæcophobia, Anglophobia, Germanophobia, *etc.*; *see* ABHORRENCE, OPPOSITION.
Antonyms: see LIKING, LOVE, LONGING.

avert, *v. t.* turn (*chiefly with "from" or "away"*), divert, forfend (*A*), prevent, hinder; *spec.* parry, ward (*with "off"*).
Antonyms: see INCUR.

aviary, *n. Spec.* cage, birdhouse, dovecote.

aviation, *n.* aëronautics, flying, flight; *spec.* gliding, soaring, climbing, aëroplaning, hydroplaning, planing (*C*), volplaning.

aviator, *n.* aëronaut, airman, flyer, airwoman, aviatress *or* aviatrix, birdman (*C*), birdwoman (*C*); *spec.* pilot, glider, observer, spotter (*military cant*), bomber, scout, ace, eagle (*C*), Icarus.

avoid, *v. t.* **1.** shun, elude, evade, escape, balk, beware, miss (*contex.*), clear, flee, dodge, blink, run (*contex.*), help (*with a clause introduced by "but"*), blench (*R*), evite (*R*), eschew (*R or A, exc. spec.*), shirk, malinger; *spec.* boycott, double, slip.
Antonyms: see FACE, MEET, APPROACH, INCUR, UNDERTAKE, COURT.
2. *See* INVALIDATE.

avoidance, *n.* elusion, evasion, flight, eschewal, shunning, eschewment (*R*), escape (*R or exc. spec.*), evitation (*R*).

await, *v. t.* tarry, wait, expect (*A*), abide, bide; *spec.* watch.

awake, *a.* **1.** waking; *spec.* open-eyed, alert.
Antonyms: see UNCONSCIOUS.
2. *See* CONSCIOUS, ALERT, ATTENTIVE.

awake, *v. i.* waken, awaken, rouse.

award, *n.* **1.** *See* DECISION.
2. assignment, adjudication, adjudgment (*R*); *see* APPORTIONMENT.

aware, *a.* **1.** cognizant, conscious, sensible, ware (*A*), intelligent (*R*):—*implying knowledge of a fact or condition.*
Antonyms: see UNCONSCIOUS.
2. conversant (*B or formal; with "with"*), informed (*with "of"*), acquainted (*with "with"*); *spec.* familiar (*with "with"*). *"Aware" is used with "of": usually implying knowledge imparted by another.*

awareness, *n. Spec.* cognizance, acquaintance, consciousness, conversance, *etc.*

away, *a. & adv.* **1.** *See* APART, ABSENT.
2. off, hence.

away, *interj.* begone, aroint (*A or B*), hence (*B*), off (*chiefly with "with"*), avaunt (*a word denoting aversion; now B or affected*), go; *spec.* scat, shoo, boo, scram (*S*), beat it (*S*), vamoose (*S*).

awe, *n.* abashment, fear, reverence, veneration, dread, respect.
Antonyms: see CONTEMPT.

awful, *a.* fearful, dread, awesome, dreadful, frightful.

awkward, *a.* (*implies lack of ease and grace*) **1.** ungainly (*with reference to manner of movement*), uncouth (*with reference to manners and speech*), clownish, gauche (*French*), wooden, rustic, grotesque, inept, inapt (*R*), gawky (*C*), maladroit (*B*), ungraceful; *spec.* stiff, bungling, slouchy; *see* CLUMSY.
Antonyms: see GRACEFUL, SKILLFUL.
2. tactless, clumsy, indelicate, uneasy (*R*), boorish.
Antonyms: see SKILLFUL, TACTFUL, DIPLOMATIC.
3. *See* EMBARRASSING, DIFFICULT.

awkwardness, *n.* maladresse (*French*), gaucherie (*French*), rusticity, gawkiness (*C*), ineptitude, ineptness, inaptness (*R*), inaptitude (*R*), ungainliness, uncouthness, clownishness; *see* CLUMSINESS.

axial, *a.* pivotal.

---

autonomous: *self-governing.*
avail, *v.: benefit, aid, serve.*
avaricious: *greedy.*
avaunt: *away.*
ave, *n.: greeting.*
avenge: *vindicate, retribute.*
avenue: *way, road.*
aver: *prove, state.*
averse: *opposed, unwilling.*
avid: *greedy.*
avocation: *business, diversion.*
avouch: *authenticate, state, confirm.*
avow: *state, acknowledge.*
awake, *v. t.: wake, rouse, excite.*
awaken: *wake, rouse, excite.*
award: *apportion, adjudge.*
awash: *floating, afloat.*
awesome: *awful, fearful.*
awry: *askew.*

axiomatic, *a.* self-evident, apodeictic (*B*), necessary; *spec.* gnomic, gnomical, aphoristic.
axis, *n. Spec.* spindle, shaft, arbor; *see* AXLE.
axle, *n.* axis (*R*), shaft; *spec.* axletree, arbor, spindle; *see* PIVOT.
ax-shaped, *a.* dolabriform (*tech.*), securiform (*R*).
azure, *a.* blue (*contex.*), cerulean (*B*), celestic (*B or tech.*), cerule (*B*), cerulescent (*R*), skyey (*C or undignified; R*), sky-colored.

B

babble, *v. i.* **1.** *Referring to inarticulate or meaningless sounds, as of a baby, idiot, etc.:* chatter, clatter, cackle, prate, blather *or* blither (*dial.*), prattle (*implying incoherence, childishness, or sounds of unreasoning things*), patter (*C*), gabble (*C; chiefly derogatory*), chipper (*R*), claver (*Scot.*), deblaterate (*R and humorous or contemptuous*), clack (*chiefly derogatory*), twaddle, gibber (*chiefly spec.*), jargon, jargonize (*R*); *spec.* drivel, rave.
2. *See* CHATTER (*referring to senseless or trivial talk*), MURMUR (*as brooks, leaves, etc.; implying inarticulate or indistinct utterance*), TATTLE.
babble, *v. t.* **1.** chatter, clatter, prattle, prate, blather *or* blither (*dial.*), gabble (*C, chiefly derogatory*):—*implying excess or purposelessness.*
2. *See* TELL, TATTLE.
babble, *n.* **1.** chatter, clatter, prattle, prating, blatter *or* blether *or* blather (*dial.*), bibble-babble, babblement, blateration *or* deblateration (*R and humorous or contemptuous*), blab (*C*), patter, gabble (*C, chiefly derogatory*), jargon, prattlement (*R*), cackle, clack, claver (*Scot.*), clatter, clitter-clatter, prittle-prattle, garrulity, loquacity; *spec.* drivel (*implying childish, senile, or idiotic foolishness*).
2. *See* CHATTER, TATTLE, MURMUR.
baby, *v. t.* humor, indulge.
babyish, *a.* infantine, infantile, childish, simple, dolly *or* dollish (*implying inexpressive prettiness*).
Bacchanal, *n.* **1.** Bacchant (*masc. or fem.*), Bacchante (*fem.*), Bacchanalian, Bacchæ (*pl.; fem.*); *spec.* Thyiad (*fem.*), mænad (*fem.*).
2. *See* REVELER.
bacchic, *a.* **1.** Bacchanalian, Dionysiac, Dionysian, Dionysic.
1. *See* REVELING.
back, *n.* posterior, rear, arrear (*A*), backing, dorsum (*tech.*); *spec.* behind (*C*), breech, butt, cascabel, rearward (*of an army; A*); *see* BUTTOCKS, REVERSE.
Antonyms: see FRONT.
backbone, *n.* **1.** spine, spinal column, rachis (*tech.*), spina (*Latin; tech.*), chine (*tech. or A*), ridgebone (*R*).
2. *See* CONSTANCY, DETERMINATION.
background, *n.* rear, distance; *spec.* scene, ground, groundwork, setting, environment, circumstances, antecedents, education, training, experiences.
Antonyms: see FOREGROUND.
backslide, *v. i.* slide (*contex.; R*), lapse, fall, revert, weaken, tergiversate (*R*); *spec.* refall (*R*); *see* APOSTATIZE, RELAPSE, DESERT.
backward, *adv.* back, arear, hindward, rearward, astern (*naut. or fig.*), abaft (*now only naut.*), baft (*A; now only naut.*).
Antonyms: see FORWARD.
backward, *a.* **1.** rearward, hindward, back, reverse.
Antonyms: see FORWARD, AHEAD.
2. retrogressive, retrograde, regressive, recessive; *see* DEGENERATIVE, REVERSIONARY.
Antonyms: see PROGRESSIVE, PRECOCIOUS.
3. retrospective.
bad, *a.* **1.** *In the very general sense of "not good":* poor, wretched, execrable (*a hyperbolism*), sad (*deplorably bad; chiefly as an intensive with terms of disparagement or censure; often jocular*), miserable, horrid (*C; a weak hyperbole*), awful, (*C*), dreadful (*C*), terrible (*C*), fierce (*C*), rotten (*C*), lousy (*S; intensive*), frightful (*C*), godawful (*S; intensive*), punk (*S*), putrid (*S*).
Antonyms: see GOOD, EXCELLENT, FAIR, FINE.
2. *See* WICKED, HARMFUL, UNPLEASANT, UNSUITABLE, FAULTY, IMPERFECT, INFERIOR, INVALID (*pron.* ĭn-văl′ĭd), AILING, DANGEROUS, SEVERE.
badge, *n.* mark (*contex.*), emblem, token, symbol, sign, ensign (*chiefly spec.*), insignia (*pl.; chiefly spec.*); *spec.* marker, recognizance (*A*), colors (*pl.*), regalia (*pl.*), mon (*Japanese*), crest, favor, laticlave, decoration, cockade, chevron, brassard, weeper, angusticlave, rosette, cordon, ribbon, button, medal, collar, *etc.*
bag, *n.* **1.** container (*cant; contex.*), pouch, case, poke (*dial. or tech., exc. in "pig in a poke"*), receptacle (*contex.*), pocket (*A or spec.*); *spec.* capsule, mail, packet, satchel, sabretache, sachet, sack (*chiefly Brit., when the bag is of paper*), sac, sacklet, reticule, scrip (*A*), purse, ditty-bag, gunny, bunt, cod, knapsack, portmanteau, suitcase, handbag, valise, grip, haversack, dilly-bag (*orig. Australian*).
2. *See* SAC.
bag, *v. t.* pouch, sack, seize, get, kill (*of game*).
bag, *v. i.* pouch, pocket (*R*), belly, bulge (*contex.*), swell (*contex.*).
baggage, *n.* **1.** encumbrances (*pl.*), luggage (*chiefly British*), viaticals (*pl.; R; chiefly mil.*), impedimenta (*pl.; chiefly mil.*), truck (*C*), traps (*pl.; C*), plunder (*S*), things (*pl., C; contex.*), trap (*C*), dunnage (*sailor's S;*) trunks, suitcases, paraphernalia.
2. *See* WANTON, GIRL.

---

axiom: *rule, saying, proposition.*

B

baa: *bleat.*
bachelor: *celibate.*
back, *v. t.: support, mount, drive.*
backbite: *censure, defame.*
backing: *back, support.*
badger: *harass, tease.*
badinage: *pleasantry.*
baffle: *defeat.*
baggy: *bag-shaped, flaccid.*

---

bag-shaped, *a.* baggy, pouchy; *tech.* saccate, utricular, utriculate, utriculose.

bailiff, *n. Spec.* bailie (*Scot.*), pursuivant (*Eng.*), (catchpoll (*B; A*), beagle (*fig.*), bum-bailiff *contemptuous*), constable, granger (*Eng.*), hundreder (*Eng.*).

bake, *v. t.* cook (*contex.; chiefly spec.*); *spec.* burn, roast, fire, kiln, dry, harden.

bake, *n.* cook (*contex.; chiefly spec.*): *spec.* roast.

balance, *n.* **1.** scales (*pl.*), steelyard.

2. poise, evenness, equilibrium, libration (*R*), equipoise, equilibrity (*R*), equiponderance (*B*), equiponderancy (*R*), *spec.* isostasy, stability. *Often used fig. of other than physical forces.*

3. *See* COUNTERPOISE, COMPENSATION, COMPARISON.

4. *Referring to character:* poise, steadiness, composure, equipoise, evenness; *see* SANITY.

5. remainder, surplus, excess (*C in this use*).

balance, *v. t.* **1.** poise, equilibrate (*tech. or B*), equilibrize (*R*); *spec.* equate, trim (*naut.*). *Often used fig. of things or forces other than physical ones.*

Antonyms: see OVERTURN, UPSET.

2. *See* COUNTERPOISE, COMPENSATE, COMPARE, WAVER.

3. *Of accounts:* equate (*R*), square.

balance, *v. i.* poise, equilibrate (*R*), librate (*said of a bird*).

balanced, *a.* **1.** equilibrious, poised; *spec.* stable.

2. *Referring to accounts, total, etc.:* even, square.

bald, *a.* **1.** bare (*contex.*), hairless, peeled (*A or R*), depilous (*R*), pelon (*as a dog; French*); glabrous (*tech.*); *spec.* beardless, whiskerless.

Antonyms: see HAIRY, BEARDED.

2. *See* BARE, MERE, UNADORNED, EVIDENT.

balk, *v. i.* refuse (*R*), jib; *spec.* shy.

balky, *a.* restiff (*A or R*), restive.

ball, *n.* **1.** globe, sphere, orb (*chiefly B and spec.*), round (*chiefly contex.*); *spec.* globule, pellet, pill (*C*), blob, sphericle (*R*), spherule, puck, gutty (*S*), grub, bowl, clew, bullet, croquette, bottom (*A*), cop, marble, jinglet, pigskin (*C*), earthkin, terella, mound, pompon; *see* DROP.

2. dance; *spec.* masquerade, fandango (*now rare, exc. as to foreign countries*), masque, mask, hop (*S*), party, prom (*college S*).

ball, *v. t.* globe (*a reflexive*), orb (*a reflexive*), conglobe, conglobate, englobe, ensphere; *spec.* clew (*all B or R exc. "ball." With "up," C for* confuse, *which see*).

ball, *v. i.* orb (*R*).

ballad, *n.* song, singsong (*chiefly spec.*); *spec.* cantilena (*Italian*), derry (*R*).

band, *n.* **1.** *Chiefly in plural:* bond; *spec.* shackle, chain, fetter, trammel, bilbo, manacle, gyve (*A or B*), handcuff, cuffs (*C, pl.*), binding;—*all implying restraint of personal liberty.*

2. bond, tie, bind, shackle (*B or A*), binder, binding, vinculum (*tech.*); *spec.* bandage, tape, couple, chain, rope, billet, clasp, ligature, ligament, hoop, fillet, girdle, girth, tourniquet, belt, loop, baldric, bandsaw, bandoleer, thong, regula, sliver, reglet, tendon, commissure, breeching, holdback, collar, collet, ferrule, headband, fanon, fascia, parrel *or* parral (*nautical*), becket (*nautical*), cincture, cuff, curb, garter, garland, noseband, cavesson, waistband; *see* STRING, STRAP, RIBBON.

3. stripe, strip, bar, belt, zone, arc, line; *spec.* fascia, vitta, frieze, orle; *see* STREAK.

4. association, organization, company, group, crowd, gang; *spec.* brigade (*of workers*), cohort, union, chorus (*of singers*).

5. *Spec.* brass, woodwind, strings (*pl.*), orchestra.

band, *v. t.* stripe, belt, line; *see* STREAK.

banded, *a.* striped, barred, listed; *spec.* ring-streaked, fasciated, belted.

Antonyms: see UNIFORM.

bandy, *v. t.* **1.** *See* BEAT.

2. toss (*words, names, etc.*), shuttlecock (*R*), exchange (*contex.*).

bank, *n.* **1.** *Spec.* mound, dike, shelf, ridge, wall, slope, hill, ascent, climb, terrace, brae (*Scot.*), embankment, escarpment, terreplein, escarp, glacis; *see* BAR.

2. brim (*A*); *spec.* riverside, levee (*U. S.*), rivage (*B*), shore, beach, ripe (*R*); *see* SHARE.

bank, *v. t.* **1.** *Spec.* embank, dike, terrace, escarp, mound, rampart, wall.

2. *See* CAROM.

bankrupt, *v. i.* break, smash (*S*), bust (*S, U. S.*)

banner, *n.* flag (*contex.*); *spec.* penon, oriflamme, gonfalon, gonfanon.

bantam, *n.* **1.** *See* DWARF.

2. *Referring to a self-important fellow:* cockalorum, whippersnapper, skipjack (*A*), puppy (*C*); *spec.* braggart, jackanapes, upstart.

banter, *v. t. & i.* rally, badinage, joke, roast (*C*), persiflate (*R*), josh (*S*), jig (*dial. or S*), chaff (*C*), quiz, jolly (*C*), kid (*S*), guy (*C*), string (*C*).

baptize, *v. t.* christen, name; *spec.* dip (*C; contex.*), immerse (*contex.*), sprinkle (*C; contex.*), rebaptize.

bar, *n.* **1.** *Spec.* rod, stick, rail, bail, crossbar, batten, boom, tongue, came, concelli (*pl.*),

---

bail, *v. t.: dip.*
bairn: *child.*
bait: *worry, feed, attract.*
balderdash: *nonsense.*
bale, *v. t.: dip.*
bale, *n.: evil, harm, sorrow.*
baleful: *harmful, sorrowful, malevolent.*
balk: *avoid, shirk, defeat.*
balm: *mitigatory.*
balmy: *fragrant, calmative, mitigatory, mild.*
baluster: *post.*
balustrade: *railing.*
ban, *v. t.: curse, forbid.*
banal: *commonplace.*
bandit: *desperado.*
bandy-legged: *bow-legged.*
bane: *harm, pest, evil.*
baneful: *harmful, deadly.*
bang, *v. t.: strike, clap.*
bang, *n.: blow, clap.*
banish: *expel.*
banister: *railing.*
bank, *v. i.: rely.*
bankrupt: *insolvent.*
banquet: *feast.*
banter: *pleasantry.*

crow, fiferail, handspike, slicebar, slice, bull, rave, crosshead, hound, fid; *see* STAKE, ROD.

2. ridge; *spec.* sandbar, overslaugh (*local, U. S.*), spit, swash.

3. *See* BARRIER, BAND, COURT, COUNTER, BARROOM.

4. bank, barrier, ridge;— (*all three contex.*); *spec.* sandbar, shelf, barrage.

5. prevention, hindrance, impediment, check, stop, conclusion (*law*); *spec.* foreclosure, estoppel.

bar, *v. t.* **1.** *See* STOP, PREVENT.

2. prevent, hinder, stop, check, preclude; *spec.* foreclose, exclude, oust, estop.

barbarism, *n. Referring to words or language:* misuse (*contex.*), slip, error, solecism, catachresis (*tech.*); *spec.* malapropism, Gothicism, Gothism (*R*), vandalism (*R*), Gallicism, Latinism, Grecism, *etc.*

Antonyms: see CULTURE.

barbarous, *a.* **1.** *Spec.* Gothic (*A*), vandalic (*R*), heathenish, Hunnish.

2. *See* CRUEL, UNCIVILIZED, HEATHENISH, CACOPHONOUS.

bare, *a.* **1.** naked, nude, exposed, bald; *spec.* stripped, denudate, uncovered, undraped, depilated, unhaired, barked, skinned, peeled, napless, threadbare, worn, blank, gaunt, desolate, callow, breechless, plain, rampick (*A or dial.*), galled; *see* BALD, RAW, NAKED.

Antonyms: see COVERED, CLOTHED, HAIRY, LEAFY.

2. *See* MERE, UNADORNED, UNCOVERED, NARROW, MEAGER, EMPTY.

bare, *v. t.* **1.** denude, denudate, divest; *spec.* unsheathe, bark, skin, shave, discase (*A*), expose, disclose, uncover, strip, unclothe, peel, depilate.

Antonyms: see COVER.

2. *See* EXPOSE, DISCLOSE.

barefoot, *a.* unshod, discalceate (*chiefly said of nuns, friars, etc.*), discalced (*eccl.*).

bareheaded, *a.* hatless, unbonneted (*B*), uncovered.

bargain, *v. i.* **1.** *Spec.* haggle, higgle, stickle, treat, negotiate, dicker (*U. S.*), chop (*A or R*), chaffer, cheap (*A*); *see* BARTER:—*implying an attempt to secure the best terms,* haggle *and* stickle *implying more or less pettiness,* negotiate *commonly referring to large transactions.*

2. *See* CONTRACT.

bark, *n.* rind (*chiefly tech. or B*), covering, skin, peel; *spec.* cortex, liber, cork, tan, dita, cambium, hat, shell.

bark, *v. t.* skin, peel, denude, debark (*R*), strip, decorticate.

bark, *n.* cry (*contex.*), yap (*C*), yelp (*C or spec.*), latration (*B*); *spec.* bay, quest, howl.

bark, *v. i.* speak, cry (*contex.*), latrate (*R*), yap (*C*), yelp (*C or spec.*); *spec.* quest, bay, howl.

barking, *a.* latrant (*B*); *see* BARK.

barracks, *n. pl.* lodgings (*pl.*), quarters (*pl.*); *spec.* bullpen (*S*), dugout (*S*).

barren, *a.* **1.** sterile, fruitless (*R as referring to animals*), unproductive, unfruitful, infertile, dead (*chiefly of soil or land;—referring to absence of life and hence unyielding, as a vein in a mine*), infecund (*R*); *spec.* childless (*contex.*), heartless, naked, neuter, acarpous, infructuose (*R*), desert, unfructuous (*R*), farrow, exhausted, worthless (*both of land*).

Antonyms: see FRUITFUL, LUXURIANT.

2. unproductive, dead, jejune (*B*), otiose (*B*), fruitless; *see* INEFFECTUAL.

Antonyms: see PRODUCTIVE, EFFECTIVE, INGENIOUS.

barricade, *n.* fence, obstruction, barrier, bar; —*all four contex.*

barrier, *n.* obstruction (*contex.*), fence (*chiefly spec.*), bar (*primarily spec.*); *spec.* hedge, chain, boom, rope, bank, entanglement, wall, stockade, fencing (*collective*), gate, barrage, barrage (*French; mil.*), traverse (*R*); *see* BARRICADE.

barroom, *n.* bar, café, tavern, saloon, taproom, speak-easy, cocktail lounge.

barter, *v. t. & i.* bargain, exchange, trade, swap or swop (*C, U. S.; or dial.*), truck, chop (*R or A*).

base, *a.* **1.** *See* LOW, LOWLY, ILLEGITIMATE, INFERIOR (*in quality*), PLEBEIAN.

2. Ignoble, infamous, dishonorable, degraded, vile (*implies baseness by nature*), mean (*implies smallness of spirit*), low, cheap, miscreant (*B*), turpitudinous, illiberal (*R and B*), vulgar (*B*), sordid; *spec.* abject, groveling, menial, villain (*R*), villein (*hist.*), slavish, beggarly, servile, soulless, baseborn; *see* CONTEMPTIBLE.

Antonyms: see NOBLE.

base, *n.* **1.** *See* BOTTOM, SUPPORT, FOUNDATION, BEARING, STEM (*philol.*), RECEPTACLE, BASS.

2. *In the sense of "chief ingredient":* ground, basis, basement (*tech.; chiefly spec.*).

3. *In botany, zoölogy, etc.:* foot, fundus (*tech.*), bottom; *spec.* butt; *see* STALK.

base, *v. t.* **1.** rest (*contex.*), found, ground (*orig. spec.*), put (*contex.*), bottom; *spec.* build.

2. *In a secondary sense:* found, ground, establish, rest, predicate (*U. S.*).

baseness, *n.* ignominy, meanness, infamy, turpitude, *etc. Cf.* BASE, *a.*, **2**.

bashful, *a.* **1.** shy, retiring, diffident, shrinking, timid, strange, shamefaced (*A*), shamefast (*A*), reserved, chary (*R*), boggle (*dial. or C*):—*implying aversion to publicity or lack of self-confidence in intercourse with strangers,* shy *and* shrinking *being rather the strongest terms.*

2. modest, blushful (*R*):—*implying a becom-*

barbarian, *a.: foreign, uncivilized.*
barbarian, *n.: foreigner, savage, boor.*
barbaric: *foreign, uncivilized.*
barbarity: *cruelty.*
bard: *poet, singer.*
bargain: *agreement, contract.*
bark: *vessel, boat.*
barrage: *bar, obstacle.*
barricade: *obstruct.*
barroom: *saloon.*
basal: *foundational, fundamental.*

ing unassumingness in intercourse with others; not necessarily implying diffidence.
3. sheepish:—*implying excessive self-consciousness, either in temperament or because of special circumstances. "Coy" (which see) does not imply anything as to the disposition, but refers merely to the outward acts.*
Antonyms: see ASSURED, BOLD, IMPUDENT, SHAMELESS, ARROGANT, CONCEITED.
bashfulness, *n.* shyness, diffidence, coyness, reserve, timidity, *etc.*
Antonyms: see ASSURANCE, CONCEIT.
basis, *n.* **1.** *See* BASE, BOTTOM, REASON, GROUND.
2. foundation, ground, groundwork, fundamental, principle, premise, corner stone (*fig.*), keystone (*fig.*).
basket, *n.* skep (*local, Eng.*); *spec.* scuttle, seedlip, tap, tapnet, crate, calanthus (*archæol.*), frail, bass, bassinet, canister (*a Latinism or Grecism*), pannier, corbeil, buck, moll, creel, gabion, nacelle, flasket, flat, prickle, pad, corf, canaster, hanaper (*historical*), hamper.
bass, *a.* low, deep, heavy, base (*A*), basso (*Italian*), grave (*R*); *spec.* barytone.
Antonyms: see SHRILL.
bass, *n.* base (*A*); *spec.* thoroughbase, drone, barytone, bourdon.
bastard, *n.* by-blow *or* bye-blow (*A*), love child, whoreson (*law or A*), illegitimate (*formal or legal*), misfortune (*Scot. & dial. Eng.*), come-by-chance (*C*); *spec.* nephew (*euphemistic*), niece (*euphemistic*).
bath, *n.* **1.** immersion, dipping; *spec.* tubbing, pedilavium, shower, douche (*French*), dip (*C*), plunge (*C*); *see* WASH.
2. suffusion, circumfusion, embathing (*B*).
3. wash, lotion; *spec.* dip:—*referring to a liquid applied for some special purpose.*
4. lavatory, laver (*B*); *spec.* tub, demibath, hammam *or* hummum (*Turkish*), sudatory, sudatorium (*Latin*), therm (*A*), thermæ (*pl.; Latin*), sitz bath, vaporarium (*Latin*), caldarium (*Latin*), shower.
5. bain-marie, balneum:—*referring to a vessel or utensil.*
bathe, *v. t.* **1.** immerse, dip, bath (*always literal*), embathe (*B*); *spec.* tub, embrocate, foment, scrub; *see* WASH.
2. suffuse, circumfuse, embathe (*B*).
3. bask, beek (*Scot.*).
battery, *n.* assault, bombardment; accumulator (*Brit. usage for* storage battery).
battleship, *n.* *Spec.* predreadnought, dreadnought, superdreadnought, liner, warship, cruiser, gunboat, destroyer, man-of-war.
bawd, *n.* pimp, procurer, whoremaster (*law*), pander, procuress, panderess (*R*); *spec.* bawdstrot (*obs.*), broker (*obs.*), cadet, maquereau (*French*), mackerel (*A*), madam, hostess; *see* HARLOT.
bawdry, *n.* **1.** pandering, pimping, procuration, panderism; *spec.* proxenetism.
2. *See* OBSCENITY.
be, *v. i.* **1.** exist, consist (*A*), stand, lie, subsist, remain, go (*as in "as things go"*); *spec.* coexist, postexist (*R*), preëxist (*R*), occur, lurk, rank.
2. *See* CONTINUE, OCCUR, CONSTITUTE.
beach, *n.* strand, front (*loc.*), sands (*chiefly Brit.*).
beach wagon, *n.* station wagon.
beadle, *n.* constable, bluecoat *or* bluebottle (*nickname*); *spec.* bedell *or* poker (*Univ. S, Eng.*).
beak, *n.* **1.** *Referring to a bird:* bill, nib, neb.
2. *Referring to an insect:* snout, rostrum (*tech.*), nose; *spec.* proboscis.
3. *Referring to a vessel:* prow, rostrum (*hist.*), beakhead.
4. projection (*contex.*); *spec.* nozzle, nose, horn, umbo (*tech.*).
beam, *n.* **1.** timber, raft (*A or spec.*), balk; *spec.* batten, scantling, truss, tie, trevis (*Scot.*), chevron (*R*), girder, rafter, joist; *see* POLE.
2. *See* WIDTH, QUILL, RAY.
beanlike, *a.* fabaceous (*tech.*).
bean-shaped, *a.* fabiform (*tech.*).
bear, *v. t.* **1.** *See* SUPPORT, KEEP (*in mind*), ENTERTAIN, ENDURE, SUFFER, TRANSPORT, BEHAVE, PRESS, SHOW, CARRY, CAUSE, YIELD.
2. produce, have (*a child, young, etc.*), throw (*spec. only of animals*), drop (*chiefly of animals, esp. sheep*), teem (*A*), cast (*esp. prematurely; chiefly of animals*); *spec.* spawn (*contemptuous*), child (*obs.*), farrow, abort.
bear, *v. i.* **1.** travail (*of women only*), teem (*A*), labor (*of women only; A*), parturiate (*R*); *spec.* litter, yean, ean (*obs.*), cub, pig, pup, farrow, calve, fawn, kitten, foal, whelp, twin, spawn (*contemptuous*).
2. *See* RELATE, APPLY.
bear, *n.* **1.** Bruin (*used as a proper name*); *spec.* grizzly, cub, whelp.
2. *As applied to a person:* rudesby (*A*), crab (*R*), cur (*contemptuous; contex.*), grouch (*C*), sour-puss (*S*).
3. *See* SPECULATOR.
beard, *n.* **1.** *Spec.* whiskers (*pl.*), Charley *or* Charlie (*S*), goatee, imperial, Vandyke, Burnsides (*pl.*), Galloways (*pl.*), beaver (*S*), upholstery (*S*).
2. awn, arista (*tech.*).
bearded, *a.* **1.** hairy (*contex.*), whiskered, barbate (*R*).
Antonyms: see BALD.

basic: *fundamental.*
bastard: *illegitimate, false, irregular, unauthorized.*
batch: *quantity.*
bate, *v. i.: flap.*
bathos: *anticlimax.*
baton: *staff.*
battalion: *division.*
batten: *thrive, fatten.*
batter, *v. t.: beat, bruise, indent.*
batter, *n.: paste.*
battle, *v. i.: fight, contend.*
battle, *n.: fight, contest.*
bauble: *gewgaw, scepter.*
bawl, *v. i.: cry, shout.*
bawl, *v. t.: shout.*
bawl, *n.: cry, shout, outcry.*
bay, *n.: compartment, window.*
bay, *v. i.: bark.*
bayonet, *v. t.: stab.*
bayou: *inlet.*
bays, *pl.: wreath, garland, crown.*
bazaar: *market, fair.*
beach: *ground.*
beacon: *signal, watchtower.*
beam, *v. i.: shine.*
beard: *confront.*

2. *Spec.* awned, barbate, barbed, pogoniate (*tech.*), glochidiate (*tech.*).

beardless, *a.* smooth-faced; *spec.* shaven, unfledged (*fig.*).

bearing, *n.* **1.** *See* ENDURANCE, POSITION, RELATION, TRANSPORTATION, BEHAVIOR, CARRIAGE.

2. base, support, rest; *spec.* journal, plate, step, coak, cock, brass, babbit, tread, trunnion, seating, gudgeon, yoke, saddle, tassel *or* torse, templet, lintel, headstock, tailstock; *see* BUSHING.

3. *In heraldry:* charge, devise; *spec.* well, rest, goutte (*French*), trestle, trivet, traverse, trefoil, tressure, weare, gore, wedge, ferrule, virule, woolpack, flasque, fusil, yard; *see* ARMS.

beast, *n.* **1.** *See* ANIMAL.

2. *As a term of contemptuous opprobrium: spec.* brute, dog, cur, hog, swine, hound, louse (*C*), goat.

beastlike, *a.* theriomorphic (*R*), bestial, beastly (*R*), brutish, brutal (*R*), theroid (*R*), ferine (*R*), feral (*B*).

beastly, *a.* **1.** *See* BEASTLIKE.

2. coarse (*contex.*), abominable (*contex.*), vile; *spec.* swinish, hoggish, piggish, boarish, filthy, gluttonous, greedy; *see* INDECENT.

Antonyms: see REFINED, GENTLEMANLY, LADYLIKE, CHASTE.

beat, *v. t.* **1.** pound, clapperclaw (*A*), contund (*humorous or affected*), belabor (*intensive*), thump (*C*), thwack, whack, pommel *or* pummel, welt (*C or S*), fan (*S*), lam (*S*), whang (*S*); *spec.* mill, bepommel *or* bepummel (*intensive*), drub, tattoo, whale, hammer, bandy, mallet (*A*), malleate (*R*), scutch, flail, flog, lap, beetle, drum, full, batter; *see* RAM, THRASH.

Antonyms: see CHERISH, CARESS.

2. *Referring to making a foam or the like of:* whip, mill, churn (*fig. or spec.*), switch.

3. *Referring to games, contests, etc.:* defeat (*esp. in a game*); *spec.* gammon, whitewash (*C*), skunk (*S*), skin (*C*), wallop (*C*), blank, goose-egg (*S*), distance, lurch.

4. *See* NONPLUS, SURPASS, DEFEAT.

beat, *n.* **1.** *See* BLOW, PULSATION, CIRCUIT, TACK, FLAP, SPONGER.

2. defeat; *spec.* whitewash (*C*), skunk (*S*), blank, *etc.*

3. *In newspaper cant:* scoop.

beatification, *n.* felicitation (*R*), macarization (*R*); *spec.* canonization.

beatified, *a.* blessed.

beatify, *v. t.* heaven (*R*), bless, felicitate (*R*), imparadise (*R*), macarize (*R*); *see* PLEASE, GLADDEN.

Antonyms: see CURSE.

beatitude, *n.* blessing; *spec.* macarism (*R*).

Antonyms: see CURSE.

beautiful, *a.* lovely, lovesome (*A*), beauteous (*B*), handsome, comely (*B*) (*both in lesser degree than* beautiful), bright, lustrous (*fig.*), splendent; *spec.* pretty, dainty, sweet, exquisite (*implies perfection in detail*), graceful, elegant (*vulgar*), charming, glamorous (*commercial elegance implying possession of sex-appeal*).

Antonyms: see UGLY, ABOMINABLE.

beautify, *v. t.* become (*contex.*), adorn, grace, embellish, deck, decorate; *spec.* prettify, improve; *see* ORNAMENT.

Antonyms: see DEFACE.

beauty, *n.* **1.** loveliness, lovelihead (*R*), formosity (*A*), pulchritude (*B*), comeliness, lustre; *spec.* glory, prettiness (*beauty without dignity*), attractiveness, charm, charmer (*now slightly A*).

Antonyms: see UGLINESS, DEFORMITY.

2. belle, fair lady, fair one, beaut (*S*), lulu (*S, A*); *spec.* bellibone (*obs.*).

Antonyms: see HAG.

because, *conj.* since, inasmuch as, as, forwhy (*A*), long *or* along (*A or dial.*), forasmuch as (*A or B*).

becloud, *v. t.* cloud, darken, obscure; *spec.* fog.

become, *v. t.* **1.** befit, suit, beseem, behove (*B*), agree (*with "with"*), accord (*with "with" or "to"*), be meet (*with "for"*):—*implying congruity, appropriateness or the like.*

Antonyms: see MISBECOME.

2. grace, adorn, set (*with "out," "off," "forth"*), beautify:—*implying appropriateness and comeliness with reference to surroundings, place, dress, etc. See* GRACE, BEAUTY.

become, *v. i.* grow, turn, go, fall, drop, wax (*A or B*), come, get;—*mostly idiomates.*

becoming, *a.* **1.** befitting, fitting, fit, suitable, worthy, good, well-becoming, meet, gainly (*R*), graceful (*chiefly spec.*), seemly, beseemly (*R*), decorous; *see* APPROPRIATE, PROPER.

Antonyms: see UNBECOMING, UNSUITABLE, IMPROPER.

2. beautifying, feat (*A or dial.*).

becomingness, *n.* fitness, suitability, comeliness, grace (*chiefly spec.*); *spec.* appropriateness, propriety.

bed, *n.* **1.** couch, lair (*R, exc. of beasts*), doss (*S or cant*), berth (*chiefly spec.*), bunk (*C or spec.*), roost (*S*); *spec.* litter, crib, cot, cradle, trundle, truckle, mattress, pallet, hammock, shakedown, daybed.

2. *See* BEDSTEAD, LAYER, BOTTOM, PIECE.

bed, *v. t.* **1.** lodge, lair (*R, exc. of beasts*), bunk (*C or spec.*); *spec.* cradle, litter, sleep (*C*).

2. *See* REST.

bedcover, *n. Spec.* quilt, bedquilt, blanket, coverlet, coverlid (*R*), counterpane, comforter (*C, U. S.*), bedspread (*U. S.*), spread

bearish: *rough.*
beatific: *blessed.*
beau: *dandy, lover.*
beaver: *visor.*
becalm: *calm, detain.*
beck: *brook.*
beck: *bow, gesture.*
beckon: *gesture.*

(*U. S.*), comfortable (*U. S.*), pall (*A*), rezai (*Anglo-Indian*), palampore, eiderdown.

bedding, *n. Spec.* bedclothes, sheets, blankets, covers, litter, straw, littering, lairage (*R*), brancard.

bedroom, *n.* bedchamber *or* chamber (*formal or pretentious*), bower (*A*), cubicle (*esp. one of a series in a school dormitory*), cubiculum (*jocose*).

bedstead, *n. Spec.* cot, charpoy (*Anglo-Indian*), bed (*C*).

bedtick, *n.* tick, case, cover (*contex.*).

beef, *n. The animal:* bovine, neat (*R*); *spec.* bull, cow, freemartin, ox, steer, heifer, muley *or* mulley, bullock, bossy, roan, taurine (*R*), buffalo, bison, aurochs, carabao, gayal, gaur, zebu, zamouse, yak, musk-ox, urus, anoa, sapiutan, Kerry, Durham, Jersey, *etc.*

beehive, *n.* hive, apiary (*tech.*), alveary (*A, exc. as figuratively used of various old dictionaries*), bike (*Scot. or dial.*); *spec.* dome.

beekeeping, *n.* apiculture.

beer, *n.* lager, ale, bock, stout, porter; *spec.* brew.

beetle, *n.* coleopter (*tech.*), clock (*Eng.*); *spec.* scarab, dung beetle, dorbeetle, June beetle.

befool, *v. t.* **1.** *See* DECEIVE.

2. rig (*S or C*), bejape (*S or C*).

before, *adv.* **1.** *See* FORWARD.

2. earlier, sooner, antecedently, previously, already, beforehand, heretofore, hitherto, beforetime (*A*), erenow (*B or A*).

Antonyms: see AFTERWARDS, NOW.

before, *prep.* **1.** ere (*B or A*).

Antonyms: see AFTER.

2. coram (*Latin: "in the presence of"*).

beg, *v. t.* **1.** *See* ASK.

2. mendicate (*R*); *spec.* quest (*R. C. Ch.*), cadge (*dial. or S*).

Antonyms: see GIVE, REJECT.

beg, *v. i.* **1.** *See* ASK.

2. mendicate (*R*), mump (*cant; obs.*), cadge, cant (*B*), quest (*R. C. Ch.*), panhandle (*S*).

beget, *v. t.* parent (*R*), raise (*R*), gender (*A*), engender (*A or B*), get (*now only of animals*), ingender (*R*), father, procreate (*R*), reproduce.

Antonyms: see KILL.

begetter, *n.* author (*in "author of one's being"*), generator, procreator, father.

begetting, *n.* progeniture, procreation, generation, getting (*A*), get (*chiefly cant*).

beggar, *n.* pauper (*contex.*), mendicant (*B or tech.; esp. of certain ecclesiastics*), mumper (*S*), thigger (*Scot.*), clapperdudgeon (*A*), canter (*A*); *spec.* fakir, jockey (*historical*), bluegown (*Scot.*), gangrel (*A*), vagabond, gaberlunzie (*Scot.*), schnorrer (*Jewish*), dyvour (*Scot.; obsolescent*), dervish, dandy, roundsman, beadsman (*Eng.*), panhandler (*S*).

Antonyms: see RICH PERSON.

begging, *n.* **1.** beggary, mendicity (*R*), mendicancy, mendication (*R*), panhandling (*S*).

2. *See* ASKING.

begging, *a.* **1.** *See* ASKING.

2. mendicant (*B or tech.*), canting (*R*), cadging.

begin, *v. t.* commence, start, gin (*A*), originate, initiate, broach (*chiefly spec.*), inchoate (*B*); *spec.* attack, institute, raise, introduce, reintroduce, recommence, open, inaugurate, auspicate (*the two latter implying formality*), handsel (*Eng.*).

Antonyms: see END, FINISH, COMPLETE.

begin, *v. i.* commence, gin (*A*), proceed, start, arise, originate, enter, open; *spec.* exordize (*R*), recommence, renew.

Antonyms: see END.

beginning, *n.* **1.** commencement, start, outstart, outset, inauguration, opening, institution, inchoation (*B*), inchoacy (*R*), inception, incipience, incipiency, initiation, initiative, ingress (*A*), onset; *spec.* gambit, origination, attack, birth, first, alpha (*B*), fountain, font (*B*). .

Antonyms: see END, FINISH, CATASTROPHE, EVENT.

2. *The place of beginning: spec.* threshold, outset, tee, origin, door, vestibule, gate, springboard, cradle.

3. *See* ARISING.

4. *Spec.* rudiment, forefront, front, embryo, germ, egg, first, outstart, outset, prime, proem (*B*), prelude, incunabula (*pl.; B*), morning (*fig.*), dawn (*fig.*), protasis (*B*).

Antonyms: see COMPLETION, END, OUTCOME.

beginning, *a.* commencing, inauguratory, initiative, initiatory, inceptive, initial, primitive, primary, pristine, prefatory, incipient; *spec.* nascent, rudimentary. *The word "beginning" is unusual as an adjective.*

beguile, *v. t.* **1.** *See* DECEIVE, CHEAT, DIVERT.

2. *In the sense of "to while away":* shorten, pass.

behave, *v. t.* **1.** *As a reflexive verb:* conduct, demean, bear, comport (*B*), deport. carry, quit (*A*), acquit (*A*):—*referring to manner of action.* Behave *as used of persons now commonly implies good or proper conduct. Spec.* misbehave, misconduct, misdemean.

2. *v. i.* act:—*used of persons or things, and without implication of good or bad behavior.*

behavior, *n.* conduct, demeanor, bearing, comportment, deportment, carriage, acquittance, manners (*pl.*), action, semblance (*R*), goings (*pl.; C*), conversation (*A*), havior (*A*), quittance (*A*). *See* AIR.

---

bedeck: *ornament.*
bedew: *wet.*
bedim: *darken.*
bedizen: *ornament.*
bedlam: *asylum.*
befall: *happen, belong, occur.*
befit: *become.*
befog: *cloud, confuse.*
beforehand: *before.*
befoul: *contaminate.*
befuddle: *confuse.*
begem: *ornament.*
beggar, *v. t.: impoverish, belittle.*
beggarly: *poor, base, mean.*
beggary: *begging.*
begrime: *soil.*
begrudge: *envy, grudge.*
beguilement: *deception, cheat, diversion.*
behalf: *side, benefit.*
behave, *v. i.: act.*

---

behead, *v. t.* decapitate, head (*A*), neck (*dial.*), decollate (*B*); *spec.* guillotine, caboche, kill, execute.

behold, *interj.* ecce (*Latin*), lo, la (*dial.*), say (*S*), look (*C*), lookit (*vulgar*).

being, *a.* existing, existent, extant, beent (*metaphysics*), subsistent, subsisting; *spec.* constituted. *"Being" is rare as an adjective.*
Antonyms: see NONEXISTENT.

being, *n.* existence, entity, subsistence, actuality; *spec.* life, essence, quid (*B*), hypaxis (*R, tech.*), existent (*R*), ens, automaton.
Antonyms: see NONEXISTENCE.

belch, *v. i., and t.,* erupt, eject, emit, eructate, burp (*S*).

belfry, *n.* tower (*contex.*), campanile, clocher (*R*), steeple.

belie, *v. t. Spec.* defame, misrepresent, contradict.

belief, *n.* **1.** *Referring to the mental action, condition, habit, etc.:* credit, faith, acceptance, credence, reception (*chiefly Bib.*), thinking (*contex.*), fay (*A*); *spec.* supposition, trust, assurance.
Antonyms: see UNBELIEF, DOUBT, SKEPTICISM.
2. *Referring to what is believed as a matter of faith:* tenet, persuasion, creed, doctrine, dogma; *spec.* supposition, profession, superstition, mumpsimus (*contemptuous or humorous*), tradition, misbelief.
3. *See* CONVICTION, OPINION, CREED.

believable, *a.* credible; *spec.* supposable.
Antonyms: see UNBELIEVABLE.

believe, *v. t.* **1.** trust, credit (*simply as truth or untruth*), swallow (*C, implying credulousness*), hold, accept, receive (*chiefly Bib.*), accredit (*an erroneous use*); *spec.* feel, suppose, fancy, misbelieve, guess.
Antonyms: see DISBELIEVE, DOUBT.
2. *See* CONSIDER.

believe, *v. i.* trust.
Antonyms: see DOUBT.

believer, *n.* truster, accepter, receiver, convert; *spec.* Christian, faithful (*a collective; used with "the"*).
Antonyms: see UNBELIEVER, HERETIC.

believing, *a.* credulous (*now nearly always implying overreadiness to believe*), creditive (*R*), credent (*R*); *spec.* trustful, confiding, fond, easy (*C*), superstitious.
Antonyms: see UNBELIEVING, DOUBTFUL, SKEPTICAL.

believingness, *n.* credulousness (*chiefly spec.*), credulity (*chiefly spec.*), trustfulness; *spec.* fondness, easiness (*C*), superstition.

belittle, *v. t.* **1.** overshadow (*fig.*), minish (*R*), beggar, minimize, underestimate, decry, slight; *spec.* dwarf.
Antonyms: see EXAGGERATE.
2. *See* DISPARAGE.

bell, *n.* **1.** *Spec.* sanctus bell, grelot, gong, doorbell, alarm, ding-dong (*B or C*), jingle, pavillon, tintinnabulum (*B or tech.*), tinkler (*S*), tocsin, chimes (*pl.*), carillon (*a set of bells*).
2. sound (*contex.*), stroke; *spec.* toll, knell, jingle.
3. *See* BUBBLE, TIME, HOUR.

bellow, *n., v. t. & v. i.* **1.** cry (*contex.*), bell (*esp. of deer*), roar, low (*of kine*), blare (*R*).
2. *See* SHOUT.

bellowing, *a.* mugient (*R*), lowing (*of kine*), roaring.

bell-shaped, *a.* campanulate, campanular, campanulous, campaniform;—*all tech. or B.*

belong, *v. i.* pertain, appertain (*formal*), behove (*A*), befall (*A*), attach, concern.

belonging, *a.* pertaining, pertinent, appertaining (*formal*), appertinent (*formal*), accessory or (*less usual*) accessary.

beloved, *n.* dear, idol; *see* LOVE.

below, *adv. & prep.* **1.** *In the sense of "lower than":* beneath, neath *or* 'neath (*B*).
Antonyms: see ABOVE.
2. *In the sense of "directly below": see* UNDER.

belt, *n.* band, strip, zone; *spec.* girdle, girth, bandoleer.

bench, *n.* **1.** seat (*contex.*), settle, settee; *spec.* pew, stool, board.
2. *See* COURT, LODGE.

bend, *v. t.* **1.** strain (*A, exc. of the bow*), draw, stretch (*a bow*).
2. crook, flex (*scientific*), ply (*R*), turn (*chiefly with "over," "out," "in," etc.*); *spec.* spring, strain, crank, deform, circumflex, deflex, buckle, warp, bate, double, geniculate (*R*), hook, knee, elbow, turn; *see* CURVE, STRAIGHTEN.
3. *See* SUBDUE, STRAIN, TURN, APPLY, DIRECT.

bend, *n.* **1.** flexure (*tech.*), flection *or* (*British or spec.*) flexion (*chiefly referring to the act or action; tech.*), turn (*contex.*), crook, bent (*R*); *spec.* warp, buckle, sag, crank, crankle, hook, knee, elbow, scarp, fork, angle, curve.
2. *See* TURN, STOOP, DROOP.

bending, *n.* flection, flexure, crooking; *spec.* circumflexion, genuflexion, reclination.

benedict, *n.* benedick (*alluding to Benedick in Shakespeare's "Much Ado about Nothing"*), neogamist (*R*), newlywed.
Antonyms: see CELIBATE.

---

behest: *bidding.*
behind: *hind, remaining, late, slow.*
behind: *buttocks.*
behold, *v. t.: see.*
beholden: *indebted.*
beholder: *spectator.*
behoof: *benefit.*
behoove, behove, *v. t.: benefit.*
bejewel: *ornament.*
belabor: *beat, ply.*
belated: *delayed.*
belay: *fasten.*
beldam, beldame: *grandmother, hag.*
beleaguer: *surround.*
belike: *probably, perhaps.*
bell, *v. i., flare.*
bell, *v. & n.: bellow.*
belle: *beauty.*
belles-lettres: *literature.*
bellicose: *pugnacious.*
belligerent: *fighting, warlike, combative.*
belly, *v. i.: bag.*
belonging: *accessory, property.*
belted: *banded.*
bemean: *abase.*
bemire: *muddy.*
bemuddle: *confuse.*
beneath: *below, under.*
benediction: *blessing.*

---

benefaction, *n.* **1.** benefit (*R*), beneficence, kindness, favor.
Antonyms: see INJURY.
2. *See* GIFT.

benefactor, *n.* benefiter (*R*); *spec.* patron, Mæcenas (*fig.; B*), Santa Claus (*S*), giver; *see* PROMOTER.
Antonyms: see SPONGER.

benefice, *n. Eccl.:* living; *spec.* parsonage, church, sinecure, vicarage, rectory, mensal, prebend, provostry, commandery, curacy.

beneficent, *a.* **1.** *Referring to persons:* benefic (*R*), beneficial (*A*); *see* KIND, KINDLY.
Antonyms: see EVIL-DOING.
2. *Referring to things: see* BENEFICIAL.

beneficial, *a.* advantageous, helpful, good, beneficient, behooveful *or* behoveful (*A*), gainful (*R*); *spec.* serviceable, bonitarian *or* bonitary, valuable, salutary; *see* CURATIVE, REMEDIAL, HEALTHFUL.
Antonyms: see INJURIOUS, HARMFUL, RUINOUS.

beneficiary, *n. Spec.* usufructuary, probondary, prebend (*R*), chargeant (*R or Scot.*), chargee (*R*), donee, receiver, legatee, grantee, impropriator, impropriatrix, incumbent, pensioner.

benefit, *n.* **1.** avail (*only in "of avail" and "of no, little, etc., avail"*), profit, vail (*obs.*), advantage, behalf (*as in "in behalf of," "on behalf of"*), behoof (*now chiefly legal or B*), good.
2. good, gain, profit, advantage, service, avail, boot (*A, exc. in "to boot"*), benefaction, commodity (*A*), betterment (*R*), behoof (*now chiefly legal or B*); *spec.* bespeak (*actor's cant*), easement.
Antonyms: see INJURY, HARM.

benefit, *v. t.* advantage, profit, help, aid, assist, serve, avail, behoove, behove, good (*obs.*), boot (*A or B*), skill (*A; used only impersonally with "it" as the subject*), improve.
Antonyms: see INJURE.

benefit, *v. i.* help, profit, gain;—*with the impersonal "it."*

benevolent, *a.* **1.** charitable (*referring esp. to almsgiving*), caritative (*R*); *spec.* philanthropic *or* philanthropical, kind, kindly, goodnatured.
Antonyms: see MALEVOLENT.
2. *See* GENEROUS.

bent, *a.* **1.** flexed (*tech.*), crooked, uneven (*contex.*); *spec.* inflexed, reflexed, infractous, geniculate; *see* CURVED.
Antonyms: see STRAIGHT.
2. *See* DETERMINED.

bequeath, *v. t.* **1.** bequeathe (*a variant*), will, give (*contex.*), leave, devise (*usually of real estate*). *"Bequeath" usually refers to personal property.*
2. *See* TRANSFER, GIVE.

bequest, *n.* **1.** willing (*R*), devise, devisal.
2. devise, gift (*contex.*); *spec.* legacy, fideicommissum. *The same distinction holds between "bequest" and "devise" as holds between "bequeath" and "devise."*

bereave, *v. t.* deprive; *spec.* orphan, widow (*chiefly in p. p. or fig.*).

besiege, *v. t.* **1.** invest, encompass, surround, hedge, set (*chiefly with "out"; A*), beset (*R*), siege (*R*), gird (*B*); *spec.* blockade.
2. *See* ASSAIL.

best, *n.* choice, flower, cream, prime, acme, pink, paragon, model, pick; *spec.* élite (*French*).

bestow, *v. t.* **1.** *See* PLACE, DEAL.
2. confer (*as attention, pains*), show (*with "to"*), send (*with "to"*), pay (*a compliment, etc., with the sense of obligation weakened to fitness or the like or lost*), give (*contex.*), spend.
Antonyms: see TAKE.
3. confer; *spec.* lavish, heap, place (*an order, etc.*). *See* GIVE.

bestriding, *a.* astraddle, astride, a-cock-horse (*R or spec.*).

betray, *v. t.* **1.** blow (*S*), give (*with "away"*), squeal (*with "on"; S*), bewray (*A*), sell (*now usually understood as spec.*); *spec.* knife (*S, U.S.*).
2. *See* DISCLOSE, TATTLE, SEDUCE.

betrayal, *n.* **1.** betrayment (*R*), prodition (*R*).
2. *See* DISCLOSURE, SEDUCTION.

betrayer, *n.* Simon (*who betrayed the Troans; fig.*), Judas (*who betrayed Jesus; fig.*); *see* TRAITOR.

betroth, *v. t.* contract (*contex.*), affiance (*formal*), espouse (*B or A*), affy (*A*), engage, bind (*contex.*), promise (*contex.*); *spec.* handfast (*hist.*).

betrothal, *n.* contract (*contex.*), affiance (*formal*), espousal (*B or A*), engagement (*the more usual word*), promise (*contex.*); *spec.* handfast (*hist.*), subarrhation (*hist.*).

betrothed, *a.* engaged, affianced (*formal*).

betrothed, *n.* fiancée (*fem.; French*), fiancé (*masc.; French*), affianced (*R or formal*), intended, engaged (*C*).

better, *a.* **1.** superior, preferable; *spec.* choicer, safer, wiser, *etc.*:—Better *and* superior *are not interchangeable in construction, the idea of comparison being always expressed or implied with* better, *while* superior *may be used absolutely, implying merely excellence.*
Antonyms: see WORSE.
2. *See* IMPROVED.

betterness, *n.* superiority, meliority (*R*), preferableness.

---

beneficence: *benefaction.*
benign: *kind, kindly, gentle, mild.*
benison: *blessing.*
bent: *inclination, trend.*
benumb, *v. t.: numb, dull, stupefy, paralyze.*
berate: *scold.*
berm: *ledge, edge.*
berth: *anchorage, bed, position.*
beseech: *ask.*
beseem, *v. i.: seem.*
beseem, *v. t.: become.*
beset: *stud, surround, harass, attack, invest, besiege, obsess.*
beshrew: *curse.*
beside, *prep.: by.*
beside, *a.: abreast.*
besides: *also.*
besmear: *smear.*
besmut: *blacken.*
besot: *intoxicate, stupefy, stultify.*
bespatter: *spot.*
bespeak: *engage, order, indicate, address.*
besprinkle: *spot.*
bestial: *animal, beastlike, sensual.*
bestir: *rouse, excite.*
bestride: *mount, straddle, ride.*
bet: *wager.*
betide: *happen, befall.*
betimes: *early, immediately.*
betoken: *signify, indicate.*
better, *v. t.: improve, surpass.*

betty, *n.* molly, peggy, moppet, cotquean (*A*), mollycot (*dial. Eng.*), henhussy.

between, *prep.* atween (*A*), betwixt (*A and chiefly B*), atwixt (*A*); *spec.* midway (*R, exc. as adv.*).

Antonyms: see ABOUT, *adv. & prep.*

beverage, *n.* drink, potion (*chiefly med.*), potation (*rhetorical*), drinkable (*C; chiefly in pl.*).

bewildered, *a.* confused, dazed (*cf.* CONFUSE, DAZE), perplexed.

bewitch, *v. t.* **1.** witch, charm, enchant, hypnotize, spellbind, spell, glamour (*R*), trance (*R*), ensorcell (*R*), fascinate; *spec.* voodoo, sirenize (*R*), overlook.

Antonyms: see DISENCHANT.

2. *See* CAPTIVATE.

bewitched, *a.* charmed, enchanted, spellbound, *etc. Cf.* BEWITCH.

bewitchery, *n.* **1.** *In a sense implying a spell cast over one:* witchery, witchcraft, bewitchment, enchantment, captivation (*R*), spell, charm, glamour, fascination (*A or hist.*); *spec.* sorcery.

2. *See* BEWITCHMENT (*referring to the power or faculty*), MAGIC (*referring to the art or practice*), CAPTIVATION.

bewitching, *a.* **1.** witching, enchanting, Circean (*fig.*), charming.

2. *See* CAPTIVATING.

bewitchment, *n.* **1.** *See* BEWITCHERY, CAPTIVATION.

2. *Referring to the power or faculty:* bewitchery (*R*), witchery, witchcraft, spell, enchantment, fascination (*A or hist.*), charm, glamour.

beyond, *prep. Spec.* yond (*A or dial.*), past, exceeding, farther, without, outside, above, after.

biannual, *a.* semiannual, biyearly (*R*).

bid, *v. t.* **1.** *See* OFFER, INVITE.

2. tell, direct, instruct, enjoin, command, order, call (*now chiefly spec.*), charge; *spec.* adjure, conjure, enjoin:—Order *and* command *most imply imperativeness,* order *in particular official commands.* Instruct *implies specific direction,* enjoin *the importance of obeying the command.* Direct *implies some superiority in authority, knowledge, etc.* Bid *is a more general term, often implying little more than a desire or wish; it is now chiefly B,* tell *having replaced it in C use.*

Antonyms: see FORBID.

bidding, *n.* direction, instruction, injunction, enjoinment (*R*), order, dictate, charge, command, commandment (*R of the act*), behest (*B*), mandate, biddance (*R*), prescription, jussion (*R*), imperation (*R*), word (*contex.*), ordinance (*R or spec.*), mandatum, mandment (*law*), voice, hest (*A*); *spec.* imperative, decree, warrant, fiat, commission, countermand, precept, writ.

Antonyms: see FORBIDDANCE.

bier, *n.* feretory (*R*), hearse *or* (*now R*), herse (*A or eccl.*), coffin (*including its stand*); *spec.* catafalque.

big, *a.* **1.** bulky, voluminous, bumper (*crop, etc.; C*), hulking *or* hulky (*C*), whacking (*C*), large (*more formal and dignified than* big, *in general not so emphatic*), decuman (*very large; B*), magnitudinous (*R*), mighty (*rhetorical*), gross, mickle (*A*), tall (*S, U. S.*), great (*implying often importance as well as bulk or magnitude*); *spec.* stout, thick; *see* MASSIVE, LARGE, IMMENSE.

Antonyms: see SMALL, SLENDER.

2. *See* IMPORTANT, PRETENTIOUS, SWOLLEN.

big thing (*of any kind*) bouncer (*C*), whopper (*C*), strapper (*C*), swinger (*C*), whale (*C*).

Antonyms: see PARTICLE.

bill, *n.* **1.** invoice, statement, account, accompts (*A*), reckoning, score, claim, tally, IOU (*C*), charge.

2. note, greenback, goldback (*A*), two-spot (*C*), V (*S*).

3. measure (*legal*), claim, declaration, allegation, indictment, writ, accusation, charge.

bill, *v. t.* charge, enter; *spec.* invoice.

billow, *n.* wave (*contex.*), undulation (*B or tech.; contex.*), swell, surge.

billow, *v. i.* wave (*contex.*), swell, undulate (*contex.*).

billowy, *a.* wavy (*contex.*), undulating (*B or tech.; contex.*), rolling, surging, swelling.

bin, *n.* box (*contex.*); *spec.* pocket, kench (*U. S.*), bunker, hold, crib, hutch, frame.

bind, *v. t.* **1.** hold (*contex.*), truss, confine (*contex.*), fasten; *spec.* tie, vinculate (*R*), wattle, bend, lash (*chiefly naut.*), ligature, ligate, enchain, fillet, ferrule, ferrel, pinion, truss, garter, fetter, enfetter (*R*), frap, fasciate (*R*), braid, band, chain, enchain (*R or B*), bond, cord, rope, wire, reeve, sheaf, thong, withe, hoop, gyve, pin, bandage, lace, enlace (*R*), entangle, interlace (*chiefly fig.*), muzzle, swathe.

Antonyms: see LOOSE.

2. stick jam, jamb (*R*); *spec.* squeeze.

3. *Spec.* braid, tape, *etc.*

4. obligate, hold, oblige (*chiefly law*), engage, restrict (*chiefly law*), astrict (*R*); *spec.* bond, mortgage, pledge, sacrament (*R*), indenture,

bevy: *flock, company.*
bewail: *mourn.*
beware: *avoid.*
bewilder: *confuse, stupefy.*
bezel: *edge.*
bias, *n.: slant, tendency, prejudice, partiality, inclination.*
bias, *v. t.: prejudice, incline*
biased: *partial, prejudiced.*
bibulous: *drinking, absorbent.*
bicker: *quarrel, dispute, murmur.*
bid: *offer, invitation.*
biddable: *obedient.*
bidding, *a.: commanding.*
bide: *await, withstand, endure.*
bifurcate: *forked.*
big-bellied: *corpulent, pregnant.*
bight: *bay, loop.*
bigot: *fanatic.*
bigoted: *narrow.*
bigotry: *fanaticism.*
bigwig: *personage.*
bilateral: *two-sided.*
bilge: *protuberance.*
bilk, *v. t.: defeat, deceive, cheat.*
bilk, *n.: trick.*
bill: *caress.*
billet, *n.: stick.*
billet, *n.: letter, position.*
billet, *v. t.: lodge.*

pin (*with "to"*), indebt (*R*), swear, hypothecate.

Antonyms: see FREE.

5. *See* ATTACH, BORDER, RESTRAIN, FASTEN, CONSTIPATE.

bind, *v. i.* stick, jam, jamb (*R*), hold (*contex.*); *spec.* squeeze.

binding, *a.* **1.** *See* ASTRINGENT.

2. obligatory (*implies necessity*), obligative (*R*), obliging (*R*), imperative (*implies command*), imperious (*R*); *spec.* mandatory (*implies a peremptory command*), incumbent.

Antonyms: see INVALID.

binding, *n.* **1.** holding, confining, confinement, tying, religation (*R*), ligation (*R or B*); *spec.* bandaging, ligature, deligation (*R*).

2. *See* BAND.

3. obligation, committal, obligement (*R*), engagement. "*Binding" is rare.*

4. *See* ATTACHMENT, RESTRAINT.

bird, *n.* fowl (*A, exc. spec. or as a collective*); *spec.* fledgling *or* fledgeling, squeaker, chirper, dicky (*C*), dicky- (*or* dickey-) bird (*C*), cockyolly bird (*nursery or pet name*), cageling, nestling, nestler (*R*), warbler.

birdhouse, *n.* aviary; *spec.* columbarium, columbary, dovecote.

birdlike, *a.* volucrine, avian (*tech.*); *spec.* ornithomorphic (*R*), ornithoid (*R*).

birth, *n.* **1.** nativity (*B or eccl.*), nascency (*R or fig.*), natality (*R*); *spec.* cast, heterogenesis, litter.

Antonyms: see DEATH.

2. *See* OFFSPRING, PRODUCT, DESCENT, ARISING.

birthmark, *n.* nævus (*chiefly spec.; tech.*); *spec.* strawberry, tumor, mole.

biscuit, *n. Spec.* cracker (*U. S.*), hardtack, ship biscuit, cracknel, rusk, pretzel (*U. S.*), saltine, roll, muffin.

bisect, *v. t.* halve, hemisect (*R*), middle (*naut.*).

bishop, *n.* prelate, pontifex (*R*), pontiff (*historical or spec.*), primate, presul (*R*); *spec.* metropolitan, patriarch, pope, exarch, diocesan, archbishop, chorepiscopus (*hist.*), suffragan, co-adjutor, episcopacy (*a collective; with "the"*).

bishopric, *n.* **1.** *See* DIOCESE.

2. bishophood, bishopry, lawn (*fig.*), primacy, prelateship, prelacy, prelature, episcopacy, episcopate; *spec.* exarchate.

bitch, *n.* dog (*contex.*), slut, lady (*cant or euphemistic*); *spec.* brach, brachet.

bite, *v. t.* **1.** fang (*R*); *spec.* nibble, nip, gnaw, gnash, scrunch, champ, chop, savage, snap, tooth (*R*), worry. *Most of these synonyms are also used absolutely or intransitively.*

2. *See* CUT, WOUND, CORRODE, PAIN, HOLD, STING, *etc.*

bite, *n. Spec.* nibble, crunch, scrunch, nip, champ, snap, gnash.

biting, *a.* **1.** mordant (*R*), mordacious (*B*).

2. *See* ACRID, STIMULATING, ACRIMONIOUS, SARCASTIC.

bitter, *a.* **1.** *Spec.* gally, bitterish.

2. *See* ACRIMONIOUS, SEVERE, PAINFUL, SORROWFUL.

bitter, *v. t.* embitter (*emphatic*), sour.

Antonyms: see SWEETEN.

black, *a.* **1.** dark, jet, jetty, pitchy, piceous (*R*), coaly, carbon, coal-black, raven, nigrous, Cimmerian (*fig.; B*), sooty, atramentous (*R*), swart (*chiefly spec.*), inky, sable, ebony, ebon (*B*), atramentaceous (*B*), sombre.

Antonyms: see WHITE.

2. *See* DEPRESSING, MALEVOLENT, WICKED, OUTRAGEOUS, THREATENING.

blackball, *n.* pill (*S*), pip (*C or S*).

blacken, *v. t.* **1.** black, nigrify (*R*), denigrate (*R*), darken; *spec.* soot, ink, besoot (*intensive*), besmutch (*intensive*), besmut (*intensive*), cork, begrime (*intensive*), charcoal, blackwash, ebonize.

Antonyms: see WHITEN.

2. *See* STAIN, SULLY.

blackened, *a.* blacked; *spec.* inked, corked, smutty, *etc.*

bladder, *n. Spec.* vesica, vesicle, cyst, sac, gall, sound (*of a fish*).

bladdery, *a.* bladderform (*R*); vesiculose, vesiculous, cystic, vesicular, vesiculiform (*all tech. or B*).

blade, *n.* **1.** flat; *spec.* spoon, vane, wash, limb, web, languet, spear, brand (*B or A*), snare, colter *or* coulter.

2. *See* CUTTER, FEATHER.

3. spark, bawcock (*A*), dandy, dude, blood, dasher (*A*), galliard (*A*), buck; toff (*C; Brit.*) use *Brit.; spec.* Johnny (*C*), rake, buck, roysterer.

blamable, *a.* culpable (*with "of"*), faultful (*R*), blameworthy, delinquent, faulty, censurable, *spec.* vituperable (*R*); *see* GUILTY, SINFUL, REPREHENSIBLE.

Antonyms: see BLAMELESS, SINLESS, INNOCENT.

blame, *n.* **1.** fault, culpability, blameworthiness, censurableness; *see* GUILT, SINFULNESS, REPREHENSIBILITY.

2. censure, reflection, criticism, dispraise, mispraise (*R*); *see* REPROOF, CENSURE.

blame, *v. t.* (*implies culpability*), censure, criticize, inculpate (*R*), dispraise (*R*), mispraise (*R*); *see* REPROVE, CENSURE.

Antonyms: see ACQUIT, EXCUSE.

blameless, *a.* faultless, unblamable (*R*), innocent, incensurable (*R*), irreproachable, irreprovable (*R*), inculpable (*R*), irreprehensible (*R*), unimpeachable; *see* SINLESS, INNOCENT, GUILTLESS.

Antonyms: see BLAMABLE, SINFUL, GUILTY, REPREHENSIBLE.

---

binder: *band.*
birthplace: *source.*
birthright: *hereditament.*
bit: *morsel, particle.*
bivouac: *camp.*
bizarre: *fantastic, odd, unfamiliar, extravagant.*
blab: *tattle.*
blackguard, *n.: rascal.*
blackguard, *v. t.: abuse.*
black-hearted: *wicked, malevolent.*
blackleg: *cheat.*
blackmail: *extortion.*
blameworthy: *blamable.*

blaming, *n.* censure, criticism, inculpation; *see* REPROOF, CENSURE, ACCUSATION.

bland, *a.* **1.** smooth, inirritant (*R*), velvety, velvet, unctuous.

Antonyms: see ACRID, CORROSIVE, HARSH, PUNGENT.

2. *See* SMOOTH, PLAUSIBLE.

blank, *a.* **1.** *See* ABSOLUTE, EMPTY, BARE, CONFUSED, UNADORNED.

2. thoughtless, vacuous, vacant, inexpressive, unexpressive, dull, expressionless, confused, disconcerted, speechless, confounded.

Antonyms: see EXPRESSIVE, THOUGHTFUL, PLEASED.

blanket, *n.* cover, coverlet, wrap, whittle (*A or dial.*), puff, pouf, comforter, comfortable, comfort, eiderdown, quilt; *spec.* mackinaw, shroud. *See* BEDCOVER.

blaze, *n.* **1.** *See* FLAME, FLASH, OUTBURST.

2. *Referring to a marking on an animal: spec.* mark, spot (*contex.*), star, snip, cloud.

blazon, *v. t.* **1.** *In heraldry*: emblazon.

2. *See* DESCRIBE, DEPICT, SHOW, ADVERTIZE.

blazonry, *n.* **1.** *See* ARMS, SHOW, DEPICTION, DISPLAY.

2. blazoning, emblazonry, blazonment.

bleach, *v. t.* whiten (*contex.*), blanch, decolorize (*chiefly tech.*).

blear, *a.* **1.** *Referring to the person:* blear-eyed, bleared, bleary, dim-eyed, dim-sighted, sand-blind (*A*).

Antonyms: see BRIGHT-EYED.

2. *Referring to the eyes:* bleary, bleared, filmy, cloudy, blurred, dimmed, lackluster, dull, dim, indistinct.

blear, *v. t. & i.* dull, blur, cloud, dim, hoodwink, deceive, blind.

bleat, *v. i. & n.* cry (*contex.*), baa, blat, blate.

bleed, *v. t.* **1.** blood (*A*); *spec.* phlebotomize, venesect, cup, leech, deplete.

2. suffer, feel, ache, smart.

3. extort, overcharge, fleece (*C*), gyp (*S*), drain, soak (*C*).

bleed, *v. i. Spec.* shed, flow, ooze, drop.

bleeding, *n.* bloodletting; *spec.* phlebotomy, venesection.

blend, *v. t.* mix (*contex.*), mingle (*contex.*), combine, prepare, unite, merge, harmonize; *spec.* fuse, amalgamate, interfuse, intergrade, gradate; *see* ADULTERATE.

Antonyms: see SEPARATE.

blending, *a.* confluent (*B*); *see* BLEND.

bless, *v. t.* **1.** *See* CONSECRATE, BEATIFY, CONGRATULATE, PRAISE.

2. *In the sense of "to invoke the divine good will or protection upon"*: sain (*A*).

Antonyms: see CURSE.

blessed, *a.* **1.** blest (*a variant*).

Antonyms: see ACCURSED.

2. *See* GLAD, HALLOWED.

blessing, *n.* **1.** *Implying the invocation or conferral of God's favor and care:* benediction, benison (*A or B*), benedicite (*Latin*), grace (*at table*).

Antonyms: see CURSING.

2. *Referring to that which makes happy or confers well being:* boon, beatitude, benison (*A or B*), bliss. *See* GOOD.

blight, *n.* blast, check, impairment, frustration, corruption, frost, decay, rot, mildew, bunt, ergot, rust, brand, burn, smut, yellows, aphids (*pl.*).

blight, *v.* **1.** *Implying invisible agency, as frost or infection, which interferes with normal growth:* blast, blow, nip; *spec.* mildew, rust, brand, burn, smut, yellow, rot.

2. *Referring to obscure or mysterious malignant influence:* check, blast, strike.

3. decay, infect, thwart, foil, injure, frustrate, impair, destroy, ruin.

Antonyms: see AID, CHERISH, STRENGTHEN.

blighted, *a.* blasted, nipped, stricken; *spec.* rusty, blown, *etc.*

blind, *n.* **1.** shutter, shade, screen, shield, blinker, blinder, cover; *spec.* ambush, shelter.

2. design, ruse, decoy, wile, artifice.

blind, *a.* **1.** sightless, visionless, dark, unseeing, unperceiving, rayless, amaurotic (*technical*), *spec.* eyeless (*often fig.*), moon-eyed, moon-blind, blindfold, blindfolded, stockblind, stark-blind, stoneblind.

2. unperceiving, undiscerning, uncomprehending, unseeing, purblind, dimsighted, blindfold (*fig.*), dark, senseless, insapient (*R*), benighted (*B*); *see* DISREGARDFUL.

Antonyms: see DISCERNING, PROPHETIC.

3. closed (*at the end*), cæcal (*tech.*).

4. *Referring to walls, etc., that have no opening through:* blank.

5. *See* UNINTELLIGIBLE, HIDDEN, ILLEGIBLE, CHANCE.

blind, *v. t.* **1.** blear, darken, purblind, quench (*the eye; B*) *spec.* squint, blink, exoculate (*R*), excecate (*R*), gouge, seel, hoodwink; *see* DAZZLE.

2. darken (*the mind*), benight, hoodwink (*fig.*), deaden, obscure.

blindly, *adv. Spec.* darkly, unseeingly, sightlessly, gropingly, unperceivingly, *etc.*

blindness, *n.* cecity (*R*), amaurosis (*medical*),

---

blanch: *whiten, bleach, pale.*
blandish: *cajole.*
blank, *v. t.: defeat.*
blare: *trumpet, sound.*
blaspheme: *curse, abuse.*
blasphemous: *impious, irreverent, abusive.*
blast, *n.: wind, charge, explosion.*
blast, *v. t.: blow, blight, ruin.*
blasted: *accursed.*
blat, *v. i.: bleat, chatter.*
blat, *v. t.: blurt, tattle.*
blatant: *boisterous, clamorous.*
blaze, *v. i.: flame, shine.*
blaze, *v. t.: advertise.*
blazing: *flaming, flashing.*
blazon: *arms, description, depiction.*
bleak: *exposed, cold, gloomy.*
blear, *n.: blur.*
bleary: *blear.*
blemish, *v. t.: damage, impair, sully.*
blemish, *n.: fault, impairment.*
blench: *shirk.*
blend, *v. i.: unite, harmonize.*
blindfold: *blind.*
blink, *v. i.: wink, flicker, shine.*
blink, *v. t.: avoid, ignore, shirk.*
blink, *n.: wink, moment, flash, flicker.*

---

cataract, anopsia (*medical*); *spec.* sightlessness, darkness, senselessness, benightedness (*B*).
Antonyms: see SIGHT, INSIGHT.
blister, *n.* vesication (*tech.*), vesicle (*tech. or B*); bleb; *spec.* blain (*R*), bullation.
bloat, *v. t.* inflate, swell, puff (*chiefly with "up"*), distend.
Antonyms: see CONTRACT, DEFLATE, SHRINK.
block, *n.* **1.** mass (*contex.*), lump; *spec.* clog (*chiefly Scot.*), clump, scotch, brick, briquette, briquet, square, die, cube, pad, loaf, mold, nub, set, stock (*R*), dado; *see* PIECE.
2. *Referring to buildings:* insula (*Roman antiq.*), island (*R*); *spec.* square.
3. *See* BLOCKING, PATTERN, BLOCKHEAD, QUANTITY, DIVISION, STOP.
4. blockhead, *which see.*
block, *v. t.* **1.** obstruct, jam (*R*), jamb, choke, blockade (*fig. or spec.*), impede, hinder, obstruct, close, bar, check, shut (*with "off"*); *spec.* ram, scotch.
2. *See* STOP, DEFEAT, SHAPE, OUTLINE, PROP.
blockhead, *n.* simpleton, dunce, stupid, fool, ass (*contemptuous*), dolt, dullard, block, stick (*C*), chump (*C or S*), numskull, stock (*R*), dunderhead, blunderbuss, blunderhead, clod, clodpate, clodpoll, cod's-head (*S*), buzzard (*R*), chucklehead (*chiefly dial.*), coof (*Scot.*), pigsconce (*contemptuous; R*), oxhead (*C*), loggerhead, lunkhead (*S, U. S.*), woodenhead (*C*), bonehead (*C*), hardhead (*C*), booby (*C*), doddypoll (*A or R*), cuddy (*chiefly Scot.*), idiot (*S or contemptuous*), dummy (*C*), dumbbell (*C*), nitwit (*C*), driveler (*contemptuous*), idiot (*contemptuous*), imbecile (*contemptuous*), mome (*A*), foozle (*C*), saphead (*S; contemptuous*), sap (*C*), jolthead (*R*), dotterel (*fig.*), wiseacre (*ironical or sarcastic*), wise boy (*C*).
Antonyms: see SCHOLAR, WISEACRE.
blocking, *n.* obstruction, block, jamming, choking, choke, blockade (*fig. or spec.*).
blond, blonde, *a.* fair, light; *spec.* albino, platinum.
Antonyms: see BRUNET.
blood, *n.* **1.** claret (*S*), drops (*pl.; by ellipsis*); *spec.* gore, cruor, grume, ichor (*Greek myth.*).
2. *See* SAP, FAMILY, RELATION, ILL TEMPER, BLADE.
blood, *v. t.* **1.** *See* BLEED.
2. bloody, engore (*R*), bebleed (*A; intensive*).
bloodless, *a.* **1.** anemic *or* anæmic (*chiefly med.*), exsanguine (*R*), exsanguious *or* exsanguinous (*R*), pale, colorless, blanched, pale-faced.
2. *See* PEACEABLE, UNFEELING.
bloodshed, *n.* bloodletting; *spec.* slaughter.
bloodshot, *a.* red (*contex.*); *spec.* inflamed.
bloodthirsty, *a.* cannibal, bloody, bloody-minded, tigerish, sanguinary (*B*), sanguineous (*R*), cruel, inhuman, murderous.
Antonyms: see GENTLE.
bloody, *a.* **1.** red (*contex.*), sanguinary (*unusual in the literal sense*), sanguineous (*R*), hæmatic (*tech.*), sanguine (*B*), ensanguined (*B*); *spec.* crimson (*contex.*), purple (*contex.*), gory, sanguinolent (*chiefly med.*), reeking.
2. *See* HOMICIDAL.
bloom, *n.* **1.** *See* FLOWER (*referring to a single blossom*), FLUSH, EFFLORESCENCE, POWDER, PRIME.
2. *Referring to the state:* flower, blossom, anthesis (*tech.*), efflorescence (*tech.*), florescence (*tech. or B*), blow (*or* blowth *R*).
3. *Flowers collectively:* efflorescence (*tech.*), bloomage (*R*), blossom (*R*), blow.
blotch, *n.* **1.** blot, spot, area (*B; contex.*), patch, smudge, stain; *spec.* stigma.
2. *See* VESICLE.
blouse, *n.* shirt, shirtwaist, waist; *spec.* smock, smock frock, camorra (*Italian*), camise, garibaldi, tunic.
blow, *n.* **1.** stroke, impact, clip (*C*), biff (*C*), buffet (*chiefly spec.*), coup (*French*), smite (*chiefly rhetorical*); *spec.* smite, bang, bat, beat, bounce, ding (*dial.*), thump (*C*), douse (*R*), crack, clout (*dial. or vulgar*), clour (*Scot. or dial. Eng.*), douser (*dial. or S*), punch, plug (*S*), sock (*C*), smash (*C*), dad (*chiefly dial. & Scot.*), push (*chiefly dial.*), lick (*C*), welt (*C or S*), whack (*C*), thwack, slam, crack, wipe (*S*), drub, dump, dash, dab, dazzler (*S*), double-thonger (*C*), cut, clash, clap, bang, floorer (*S*), dunt (*chiefly Scot.*), stinger (*C*), swipe (*C*), counter, sidewinder (*U. S.*), kick, bastinado, punch, left-hander, right-hander, slash, rap, wallop (*S*), plunk (*S*), sockdologer (*S, U. S.*), slug (*C*), whop (*C*), whang (*dial. or C*), tunk (*C or dial.*), bump, stamp, facer (*C*), smack (*C*), thumper (*R*), fisticuffs (*pl.*); *see* CUFF, SLAP.
Antonyms: see CARESS.
2. *See* DISASTER, DISAPPOINTMENT.
blow, *v. i.* **1.** *Spec.* bluster, flaw, whiff, whiffle, fan, breeze (*R*), storm, puff, fuff (*R or Scot.*), blast (*R or A*).
2. *See* EXHALE, BOAST.
3. pant, puff, fuff (*R or Scot.*), gasp.
4. *Spec.* toot, tootle.
blow, *v. t.* **1.** wind (*pron.* wīnd); *spec.* blast, puff, bugle, toot, tootle; *see* TRUMPET.
2. *See* INFLATE, BLIGHT.
3. melt (*of an electrical fuse*), burst, shatter, explode (*of a tire, etc.*).
4. (*C*) *for* spend, *implying recklessness.*
5. (*C*) *for* treat, entertain.
blow, *n.* **1.** blowing, bluster; *spec.* perflation (*R or tech.*), whiff, puff.

---

bliss: *gladness, good.*
blissful: *glad.*
blithe: *glad, cheerful, gay.*
blizzard: *storm, wind.*
bloat, *a.: inflated, swollen.*
bloat, *n.: drunkard.*
blockade, *v. t.: block, besiege.*
blockade, *n.: siege.*
bloodletting: *bleeding, bloodshed.*
bloodsucker: *extortioner.*
bloom: *flower, thrive, flush.*
blossom, *n.: flower, bloom.*
blossom, *v. i.: flower.*
blot, *n.: spot, stain, sully.*
blot, *v. t.: spot, cancel, sully, stain, hide, dry.*
blotch: *spot, stain.*
blow: *flower.*
blowy: *windy.*
blowzy: *red, slovenly.*

2. *See* WIND.
blue, *a.* **1.** azure, cerulean, sky-colored, sky-blue, bluish, aquamarine, ultramarine, indigo, navy, livid (*of the skin*), cold (*of light*).
2. *C:* low, low-spirited, depressed, melancholy, dejected, disheartened, downhearted, depressed, dispirited, sad, despondent, discouraged, gloomy, dismal, bad (*not doing well*), unpromising.
3. strict, severe, scrupulous, precise, illiberal, intolerant, narrow-minded, narrow, puritanical, rigorous, straight-laced.
4. literary, bookish, well-read, high-brow (*C*), scholarly, learned (blue *in this significance is used chiefly of a woman*).
blunder, *v. i.* **1.** err, slip, bungle, boggle (*C*), foozle (*S or often cant and spec.*); *spec.* solecize, muff.
2. stumble, slip, flounder.
blunder, *n.* **1.** (*often implies stupidity or want of knowledge*), error (*contex.*), slip, bungle, boggle (*C*), boner (*C*), mess, fiasco; *spec.* muff, bull, solecism.
2. stumble, slip, flounder; *spec.* Spoonerism, Hibernicism.
blunt, *a.* **1.** dull; *spec.* pointless, round, turned, dullish.
Antonyms: see SHARP, POINTED.
2. (*implies incapacity to feel*), *see* DULL (*implies mental inactivity*), INSENSIBLE.
3. bluff, burly (*A*), abrupt, curt, frank, tactless, downright, forthright (*B*), plump, direct, outspoken, plain-spoken, flat, brusque, uncivil, impolite, rude, rough, round, crisp; *see* ROUGH.
Antonyms: see GENTLE, SMOOTH, SMOOTH-SPOKEN.
blunt, *v. t.* **1.** dull; *spec.* unedge (*R*), turn, round, rebate (*R*).
Antonyms: see SHARPEN.
2. *See* DULL (*mentally*).
blur, *n.* **1.** *See* SMEAR, STAIN, SULLY.
2. *Referring to vision:* blear (*R*), cloud, dimness, indistinctness.
blurt, *v. t.* utter (*contex.*), plump, blat (*C*), bolt (*R*), drop (*C*).
blush, *v. i.* redden, rouge (*R*), ruddy (*R*), flush.
Antonyms: see PALE.
blushing, *a.* rubescent (*B*), erubescent (*R*), flushed, ruddy, rosy.
Antonyms: see PALE.
bluster, *v. i.* **1.** *See* BLOW.
2. bounce (*R*), hector, roister, swagger, defy, threaten, bully, ruffle, gasconade (*B*), vapor (*B*), swell, bravado; *see* RAGE.
Antonyms: see CRINGE, COAX.
bluster, *n.* **1.** *See* BLOW, WIND.
2. bravado, swagger; *spec.* jingo, jingoism, chauvinism (*B*), vaporing *or* vapor (*B*), bluff.
blusterer, *n.* swaggerer, bully, bouncer (*C*), roister *or* (*now more usual*) roisterer, buster (*S*), swasher, swash (*R*), *etc.*
board, *v. t.* **1.** approach (*a ship*).
2. enter (*a train*).
3. entrain (*put aboard a train*).
board, *n.* **1.** *Spec.* deal, plank, panel, slab, clapboard, gangboard.
2. table; *spec.* food, meals, lodging, fare.
3. committee, council, assembly, cabinet, directorate.
4. pasteboard, cardboard.
5. *pl.* theatre, stage.
boarding house, *n.* pension (*French; chiefly referring to a boarding house in continental Europe*).
boast, *v. i.* brag, vaunt, gloat, glory, triumph, (*both with "over"; implying in this use vainglory and exultation*), vapor (*B*), bounce (*R*), blow (*C*), cackle (*S*), bluster, flourish, strut, swagger, exaggerate, crow (*C*), exult, swash, gasconade (*B*), crack (*A*); *spec.* rodomontade (*B*).
boaster, *n.* bragger, brag, braggart, lexiphanes (*R; B*), braggadocio, vaunter, vaporer (*B*), bouncer, cracker, fanfaron (*French*), mother (*contemptuous*), gasconader (*R*), Gascon (*B*), swashbuckler, swaggerer, egoist, hector, kill-cow (*A*), puff (*A*), puckfist (*contemptuous*), Rodomont (*B; fig.*), Thraso (*B; fig.*); *spec.* Scaramouch (*B; fig.*), Tartarin (*B; fig.*).
boastful, *a.* bragging, braggart, vaunting, egotistic, lexiphanic (*R; B*), bouncing (*R*), tongue-valiant (*R*), rodomontade (*R*), Thrasonical (*B; fig.*), Thrasonic (*B; fig.*), mouthy (*C*), flaunty (*R*), self-glorious (*R*), vaunty (*Scot.*), windy (*C*), vainglorious; *see* BOMBASTIC.
Antonyms: see MODEST.
boasting, *n.* boast, brag, bragging, braggery (*R*), braggadocio, braggartism, cockahoop, (*R*), vaunting, vaunt (*B; implies ostentation*), bunk (*C*), bunkum (*C*), *or less often* buncombe, blah (*C or S*), hot air (*C*), humbug, bombast, heroics (*B*), vaporing (*B*), vaporosity (*R*), jactation (*R*), vainglory, side (*S*), dog (*S*), fanfaronade (*R*), rodomontade (*R*), gasconade (*B*), gloriation (*R*), blow (*C*); *see* BOMBAST.
boat, *n.* **1.** vessel (*contex.*), bark (*B*), craft, rowboat; *spec.* sandal, sampan, shallop, shell, outrigger, sailboat, dory, cat, catboat, skimming dish (*C*), skiff, randan, umiak *or* oomiak, sharpy, rocker (*chiefly U. S.*), rum-tum, punt, sculler, torpid (*S, Eng.*), sink (*U. S.*), flat, flatboat, lighter, barge, catamaran, pontoon *or* ponton, tow, dinghy, praam, pinnace, jolly-boat, cockboat, tender, cockleshell, cutter, drover, currach (*Scot. or Irish*), dahabeeyah, canoe, faltboot (*German*), foldboat, speedboat, launch, motorboat, cruiser, auxiliary, gondola, gig, galley, pair-oar, cot (*Irish*), caïque

blubber: *cry.*
bluestocking, *n.: pedant, precisian.*
bluestocking, *a.: precious, pedantic.*
bluff: *cliff.*
bluff, *v. t.: deceive.*
bluff, *n.: pretense.*
blunder, *v. t.: botch, mismanage.*
blur: *smear, sully, blear.*
board, *n.: tack.*
boarish: *swinish, beastly, cruel.*
boat, *v. i.: sail.*

(*French*), coracle, bateau (*chiefly Canada and Louisiana*), scout Bucentaur, sampan (*oriental*), umiak (*Eskimo*), kayak (*Eskimo*), caïque (*Turkish*), dahabeah (*Nile*), yawl, steamer, liner, yacht, houseboat, lifeboat, ferryboat, float; *see* SHIP.

2. sauce boat, gravy boat.

boatman, *n.* boatsman, boater; *spec.* rower, sculler, oar, oarsman, ferryman, barcarole (*Italian*), waterman, wherryman, dandi (*Anglo-Indian*), keelman (*dial. Eng. & Scot.*), lighterman, gondolier, hoveler (*Eng.*).

boat-shaped, *a.* navicular (*B, or tech.*), naviform (*R*), cymbiform (*tech.*), scaphoid (*tech.*).

bodily, *a.* physical (*contex.*), somatic (*tech.*), corporeal (*with reference to the physical nature of the body*), corporal (*now principally with reference to infliction*), carnal (*with reference to bodily appetites*), fleshly, earthly; *spec.* unspiritual, personal.

Antonyms: see ETHEREAL, SPIRITUAL, GHOSTLY.

bodily, *adv.* **1.** corporally, carnally, corporeally.

2. en masse (*French*), wholly, entirely, completely, bodaciously (*dial., Southern U. S.*).

body, *n.* **1.** corpus (*now humorous or grotesque or B*), form, case (*R*), clod (*fig.*), bulk (*disparaging*), carcass (*contemptuous*), hulk (*contemptuous; chiefly spec.*).

Antonyms: see MIND, SOUL, GHOST.

2. carcass (*now contemptuous when used of a human corpse*), form (*contex.*), cadaver (*chiefly spec. and tech.*), lich (*A*), stiff (*S*), corpse (*a human body*), corse (*B*), carrion (*A*), remains (*pl.; euphemistic*); *spec.* kill, mummy, carnage (*a collective with "the"*).

Antonyms: see SOUL, GHOST.

3. trunk, soma (*tech.*), corporation (*humorous or S*), torse *or* torso (*sculpture*); *spec.* waist, bust.

4. *Spec.* (*in the sense of "the main part"*) nave, aisle, cell *or* cella, hull, centrum, enceinte (*French*), buck (*dial., exc., U. S., in "buck board"*), purview, nacelle.

Antonyms: see BORDER, EDGE, BRANCH, RIM, VESTIBULE.

5. mass, form, figure, consistence (*R*); *spec.* bulk, hulk, corpuscle, corpuscule, aggregation, mobile (*R*), atom, atomy, pygmy, mite, particle, piece, fragment, *etc.*

6. corps, force, troop (*chiefly spec.*), array, army (*fig. or spec.*); *spec.* detachment, squad, committee, regiment, battalion, *etc.*

7. *See* BULK, GATHERING, FORCE, PERSON, TRUNK, SUBSTANCE, STRENGTH, QUANTITY, MATERIAL, PRINCIPLE, ASSOCIATION.

bogy, *n.* bogey, demon (*contex.*), specter, spook (*C*), hobgoblin, scarecrow (*fig.*), bugaboo, boggard *or* boggart (*R*), goblin, boggle, bogle, bug (*obs. or dial.*); *spec.* rawhead, bloodybones; *see* BUGBEAR.

boil, *v. t.* seethe (*A or B or a cookery term*), scald, cook (*contex.*), stew; *spec.* wallop (*dial. or tech.*), cree (*dial.*), parboil, decoct (*tech.*), coddle, stew, poach, elixate (*tech.*).

Antonyms: see FREEZE.

boil, *v. i.* **1.** bubble, seethe (*A or B or a cookery term*), ebulliate (*R*), simmer, steam.

Antonyms: see FREEZE.

2. *See* RAGE.

boil, *n.* seethe (*R*); *spec.* wallop (*dial. or tech.*).

boiled, *a.* sodden (*now R*), cooked, stewed.

boiler, *n.* cooker, pot, pan, saucepan, double-boiler, heater, water-heater; *spec.* caldron, copper, kettle, tin.

boiling, *n.* agitation (*contex.*), bubbling, ebullition (*B or tech.*), ebullience (*R*), coction (*B or affected*), gurgitation (*R*), seething, stewing, cooking (*contex.*); *spec.* elixation (*R*), decoction.

boisterous, *a.* (*implies noise and violence*), noisy (*contex.*), riotous, roaring, robustious (*R*), rumbustious (*C*), clamorous, wild (*contex.*), violent, daring, rollicking, unrestrained, uproarious, rampant, rampageous, tumultuous, noisy, turbulent, stormy, furious, vociferous, blatant; *see* ROUGH, CLAMOROUS.

Antonyms: see CALM, MOTIONLESS, SILENT.

bold, *a.* **1.** assured (*B*), stout, stout-hearted, daring, forward, audacious, courageous, fearless, dreadless (*R*), intrepid (*formal*), confident, undaunted, dauntless, hardy, unapprehensive (*R*), nervy (*C or S*), dour (*Scot.*), unfearful (*R*), free, cool, impavid (*R*); *see* BRAVE, RECKLESS, IMPUDENT, INDECENT, VENTURESOME.

Antonyms: see TIMID, AFRAID, FEARFUL, ANXIOUS, COWARDLY, BASHFUL, MODEST.

2. prominent, conspicuous; *see* STEEP, BLUFF, PROJECTING.

boldness, *n.* stoutness, nerve (*C*), crust (*C*), brass (*S*), effrontery, hardihood, audacity, daring, intrepidity, assurance, face, *etc.*

Antonyms: see TIMIDITY, FEAR, ANXIETY, *etc.*

bombast, *n.* boasting, extravagance, rant, stuff (*contex.*), turgescence (*R*), turgidity *or* turgidness (*B*), tumidity (*R*), rodomontade (*B*), mouthing (*contemptuous*), tympany (*R*), loftiness (*contex.*), magniloquy (*R*), sonorousness (*contex.*), magniloquence (*less common than "grandiloquence"*), grandiosity, grandiloquence, grandiloquism (*R*), inflation, heroics (*pl.; sarcastic*), fustian (*contemptuous*), falutin *or* high-faluting (*C*), flatulence (*R*), swellingness (*R*), swollenness (*R*), bombastry, lexiphanticism (*R*), pomposity, gas (*S*), hot air (*S*), Johnsonese (*fig.*), baloney (*S*), huey (*S*); *spec.* spread-eagleism (*U. S.*), euphuism, rant

bob, *n.: plummet, jerk, bow, bunch.*
bob, *v. t.: jerk, dock, refrain.*
bob, *v. i.: bow.*
bobble: *jiggle.*
bode: *forebode, signify.*
boding, *a.: significant.*
bodyguard: *escort, retinue.*
bog: *marsh.*
boggle, *v. i.: shy, object, bungle.*
boggle, *n.: bogy.*
boggy: *marshy.*
bogle: *bogy.*
bogus: *pretended.*
bolster, *n.: cushion, support.*
bolster, *v. t.: cushion.*
bolt, *n.: arrow, lightning, pin, roll.*
bolt, *v. i.: rush, run.*
bolt, *v. t.: swallow, desert.*
bolt, *v. t.: sift.*
bomb: *shell.*
bombard: *cannonade, pelt.*
bombardier: *gunner.*

bombastic, *a.* boastful, sounding, stilted, tumid (*B*), turgid (*B*), grandiloquent, grandiloquous (*R*), turgent (*R*), pompous, plethoric (*B*), flatulent (*R*), puffed, magniloquent (*less usual than "grandiloquent"*), mouthing (*contemptuous*), orotund (*contemptuous; B*), grandiose, grand (*contex.*), lofty, mouthy (*contemptuous*), inflated, windy (*C*), gassy (*C*), fustian (*contemptuous*), magnisonant (*R*), lexiphanic (*R*), hyperbolical, heroic, extravagant, high-flown (*esp. of language*), highfalutin *or* highfaluting (*C*), high-sounding, magnific (*chiefly derisive*), tall (*C*), hot (*S*), toplofty (*C, U. S.*), Herodian (*fig.; R*), Johnsonese *or* Johnsonian (*fig.*), Ossianic (*fig.*), sonorous (*contex.*), swollen, pyrotechnic (*B*), sounding.

Antonyms: see MODEST.

bond, *n.* **1.** union (*contex.*); *spec.* coupler, coupling, couple, link, bonder (*R*), tie, cord, *see* BAND, SHACKLE.

2. nexus (*B or tech.*), tie, link, cord, union, attachment, yoke, connection, similarity, kinship, relationship.

3. *See* CONTRACT, SURETY.

bondage, *n.* serfdom, serfage *or* serfhood; *spec.* helotry *or* helotism (*Greek hist.*), peonage (*Spanish American*); *see* SLAVERY.

Antonyms: see FREEDOM.

bondman, *n.* bondsman (*masc.*), bondmaid (*fem.*), bondwoman (*fem.*), serf; *spec.* villein (*hist.*), carl (*A or hist.*), vassal, thrall, helot (*Greek hist.*), peon (*Spanish American*); *see* SLAVE.

Antonyms: see FREEMAN.

bonnet, *n.* cap, hat, hood; *spec.* tam-o'-shanter, toque, sunbonnet, poke bonnet, poke.

bonus, *n.* gift; *spec.* premium, dividend, extra, honorarium; *see* TIP.

bon vivant. bonne vivante (*French; fem.*), high liver; *spec.* epicure, gourmet, gourmand (*both French: the* gourmand *is more concerned with the quantity of food, the* gourmet *with quality and delicacy*).

Antonyms: see ASCETIC.

bony, *a.* osteoid (*R*), ossean (*R*), osseous (*tech.*); stiff, inflexible, hard.

book, *n.* **1.** volume, tome (*B or tech.*); *spec.* booklet, packet, incunable *or* incunabulum (*a book printed before 1500*), chapbook, folio, quarto, octavo, duodecimo, sixteenmo, twelvemo, *etc.*, legend (*A or eccl.*), miscellany, brochure, livret (*dim.; French*), pamphlet, journal, blotter, ledger, codex, treatise, handbook, compendium, canto, fit (*A*).

2. work, writing, study, publication, production.

3. [*Cap.*] Bible;—*used with "the."*

4. set (*contex.*), packet.

bookworm, *n.* bibliophile, bibliomaniac, scholar, pedant, student (*contex.*), dig, sap, grind, bucker;—*the last four S or C.*

boom, *n.* arm, beam (*contex.*), spar; *spec.* jib, crane; *see* SPAR.

boor, *n.* **1.** *See* RUSTIC.

2. vulgarian (*R*), lout, clown, clodhopper (*contemptuous; C*), lubber, churl, carl (*A or Scot.*), carter (*fig.*), loon, barbarian (*B*), clout (*A*), lobby (*chiefly dial.*), chuff (*A or R*), *spec.* Grobian (*fig.; B*).

Antonyms: see GENTLEMAN.

boorish, *a.* **1.** *See* RUSTIC.

2. vulgar (*implies lack of refinement or taste*), ill-mannered, clownish, loutish, clodhopping (*contemptuous; C*), inurban (*R*), cloddish, uplandish (*R*), outlandish, provincial, churlish, ill-bred, low-bred, barbarian (*R*), coarse, woolen (*R*), illiberal (*R*), carlish (*B*), lubberly, rude, uncultured; *spec.* ungentlemanly; *see* AWKWARD.

Antonyms: see ACCOMPLISHED, REFINED, POLITE.

border, *n.* **1.** bound, bordure (*R*), verge, threshold (*spec. or fig.*), skirt, fringe, hem; *spec.* curb *or* kerb (*British*), brim, brink.

Antonyms: see INTERIOR, BODY.

2. edge, rim; *spec.* hem, edging, forel, selvedge *or* selvage, valance, dado, orphrey, orfray, purfle, mat, margin, trimming, skirting, frill, flounce, furbelow, fringe, welt, binding, rickrack.

3. frontier, coast (*A*), borderland, march (*hist. in pl. and with "the"; or A*), rand (*A, dial., or spec.*); *spec.* outskirt (*R*), outskirts (*pl.*), wayside; *see* BOUNDARY.

Antonyms: see INTERIOR, INLAND.

border, *v. t.* **1.** skirt, verge (*R*), rim, fringe, line (*contex.*), bound, neighbor.

2. edge, rim, margin, marginate (*R*); *spec.* purl, cotise, purfle, bind, dado, hem, frill, flounce, bind, welt, trim.

border, *v. i.* adjoin (*contex.*), neighbor, bound, touch (*contex.*); *see* ABUT.

bore, *v. t.* **1.** pierce (*contex.*), eat (*contex.*); *spec.* gimlet, drill.

2. *See* WEARY.

bore, *n.* wave (*contex.*); eager (*a less usual name*).

borrow, *v. t.* **1.** get (*contex.*), take (*contex.*), hook (*C, contex.*).

---

bonbon: *sweetmeat.*
bond, *a.:* *servile.*
bonfire: *fire.*
bon mot: *witticism.*
bonny: *good-looking, cheerful.*
booby: *blockhead.*
book, *v. t.:* *list.*
bookish: *learned, pedantic.*
boom, *v. i.:* *hum, resound, progress, thrive, advance.*
boom, *v. t.:* *advance.*
boom, *n.:* *hum, resonance, advance.*
boon, *n.:* *good, gift.*
boon, *a.:* *kind, companionable.*
boost, *n.:* *lift, push, advance.*
boost, *v. t.:* *lift, push, raise, advance.*
boot, *v. t.:* *shoe.*
boot, *n.:* *benefit, remedy.*
boot, *v. t.:* *benefit.*
booth: *stall.*
bootless: *useless.*
booty: *plunder, prize.*
booze, *n.:* *carouse, liquor.*
booze, *v. i.:* *drink, carouse.*
borderline: *border.*
bore, *v. t.:* *annoy, tire.*
bore, *n.:* *hole, tube, caliber, annoyance.*
boreal: *northern.*
boredom: *ennui.*
borough: *town.*
borrowed: *imitated.*

Antonyms: see LEND.

2. *See* ADOPT.

bosh, *interj.* fudge, nonsense, baloney (*S*), rot, tommy-rot, poppy-cock (*C*), rats (*C*), Oh yeah (*S*).

bosom, *n.* breast, bust (*esp. of a woman*), heart, affections (*pl.*).

bosom, *a.* gremial (*now only in "gremial veil"*), intimate, close, beloved.

botch, *v. t.* bungle, blunder, muddle, mar, spoil, clamper (*chiefly Scot.*); *spec.* cobble, tinker, butcher (*S*), murder (*S*), bitch (*S*); *see* MISMANAGE, REPAIR.

botchy, *a.* bungling, unskillful.

bottle, *n.* container (*cant*); *spec.* vinaigrette, vial *or* (*more often tech.*), phial, split, siphon, bolthead, demijohn, deadman (*S or C*), matrass, marine (*S*), magnum, Jeroboam (*B and humorous*), carafe *or* caraff, decanter, carboy, cruet, cruse (*A*), costrel, goatskin, tickler (*C*), flagon, flask, flacon, gourd, cornet, canteen, jug (*contex.*).

bottle-shaped, *a.* utriform (*R*).

bottom, *n.* **1.** foot, base, basis (*A*), doup (*Scot.*), root, sole; *spec.* keel, culet, cullet, bilge, heel, sump (*referring to the lowest part of a thing, on which it rests.*)

Antonyms: see TOP, PEAK.

2. bed (*of a body of water*); *spec.* coulee (*U. S.*), channel, basin.

3. intervale, interval, haugh (*Scot. or dial.*); *spec.* swale (*dial.*).

4. *See* DEPTH, SUPPORT, BUTTOCKS, SEAT, ENDURANCE, DREGS.

bottomless, *a.* baseless, fathomless, unfathomable, plumbless (*R*), abysmal (*B*), unending, profound.

boudoir, *n.* cabinet (*R*), bower (*B*).

bought, *a.* boughten (*vulgar, U. S.*), purchased (*pretentious*).

bouncer, *n.* whaler, whacker, whopper, whapper, bumper, buster, smasher, sockdologer (*U. S.*);—*all S or C.*

Antonyms: see DWARF.

bound, *a.* **1.** fastened, confined, tied; *see* BIND.

2. obliged, obligated; *spec.* committed, liege, indentured.

3. *See* CERTAIN.

bound, *v. i.* **1.** *See* JUMP.

2. bounce, rebound, dap (*R*), resile (*R*); *spec.* ricochet, carom, reflect: *of inanimate things, while* jump *suggests volition or purpose.*

bound, *n.* **1.** limit, boundary, confine, border, bourne (*B*), verge: *referring to the line to which a thing extends.*

2. *In the pl.* (*bounds*): territory, area, extent, domain, place, compass, limit, range, reach, pale (*chiefly spec.*), confine (*chiefly in pl.; A or R*), ambit; *spec.* perambulation, division, purlieu; *see* SPHERE, SCOPE: *implying land, space, etc., within certain limits.*

bound, *v. t.* **1.** limit, confine, demarcate (*B; or tech.*), circumscribe, delimit (*chiefly B*), terminate; *see* CONFINE.

2. *See* BORDER.

boundary, *n.* **1.** bounder (*A*), boundure (*A or R*); *spec.* demarcation, monument, landmark, term, Hermes, Herma, herm, cairn, line, marker (*often* markers, *pl.*).

2. limit, bound (*chiefly in pl.*), outline, precinct, confine, verge, buttal (*A or tech.*), butt (*A or R*), bourne (*B*), mete (*chiefly in pl. and legal*), mere (*A*), march (*historical or A*), mark (*historical or A*), rubicon (*fig.*), term (*R*), periphery, circuit, circumference, compass, line (*contex.*), dool (*Scot. & dial. Eng.*), bounder (*A*); *see* BORDER.

boundary, *a.* limitary, terminal (*R*), limital (*R*), bounding, border.

boundless, *a.* **1.** unlimited, infinite, termless, limitless, incomprehensible (*R*), immeasurable, unbounded, illimitable, vast; *spec.* shoreless.

Antonyms: see LIMITED, NARROW.

2. *See* ENDLESS, INEXHAUSTIBLE.

bouquet, *n.* **1.** nosegay, boughpot (*A*); *spec.* posy (*A or C*), buttonhole (*C; Eng.*), boutonnière (*French*), corsage, spray (*funeral*), arrangement (*floral*).

2. *See* SMELL.

bow *n.* **1.** (*pron.* bō), *See* CURVE.

2. fiddlestick (*now familiar or contemptuous*).

bow, *v. i.* **1.** (*pron.* bou) *See* CURVE, STOOP, YIELD.

2. (*pron.* bou) *Spec.* incline, curtsy *or* curtsey, bob, beck (*chiefly Scot.*), nod, duck, scrape, cap, salaam, dip (*C*), kotow, stoop, knee, genuflect, congé (*French*), congee, lout (*A*); greet—*referring to a gesture of courtesy, respect, or deference.*

3. (*pron.* bō) bend, curve.

bow *v. t.* (*pron.* bou), incline, bend; *spec.* prostrate, nod, stoop.

bow *v. t.* **1.** (*pron.* bou), *See* STOOP, OVERCOME, SUBDUE.

2. *Spec.* incline, bend, stoop, lout (*A or dial.; R*);—*referring to a gesture of courtesy, respect, or deference.*

bow, *n.* **1.** (*pron.* bou) *Spec.* obeisance, curtsy, curtsey, bob, reverence, leg (*A or jocular*), beck (*chiefly Scot.*), nod, nid-nod (*C*), scrape, genuflection, salaam, prostration, obedience (*A or dial.*), congé (*French*), congee, duck, inclination, dip.

---

bosh: *nonsense.*
bosom, *v. t.: embrace.*
boss, *n.: employer, controller, overseer.*
boss, *v. t.: direct.*
boss, *n.: stud.*
boss, *v. t.: emboss, stud.*
bossy: *studded.*
bossy: *domineering.*
bother: *trouble, tease.*
bothersome: *troublesome.*
bough: *branch.*
boulder: *rock.*
boulevard: *road, walk.*
bounce, *v. i.: bound.*
bound, *a.: going.*
bounteous: *generous, abundant.*
bountiful: *generous, abundant.*
bounty: *generosity, gift, reward, subsidy.*
bourne: *goal.*
bourse: *exchange.*
bout: *round, course, contest, carouse.*
bovine: *beef.*
bowel: *intestine; in pl.; compassion, interior.*
bower: *bedroom, boudoir, arbor.*
bowery: *shady.*

2. (*pron.* bou), prow, stem, head, prore (*B*), entrance (*tech.*), forepart; *spec.* foreship (*R*), beakhead (*R*), forefoot, forepeak, forehold, foresheets (*pl.*), hawse, luff, forecastle, gripe.

bowl, *n.* **1.** basin, dish, vessel, pan, beaker. *Spec.* mazer (*A or historical*), crater (*Greek antiq.*), tazza, jorum, Jeroboam (*humorous*), bowie (*Scot.*), cogie (*Scot.*), cap (*Scot.*), porringer, brimmer.

2. *See* HOLLOW.

bowl, *v. i.* **1.** *See* ROLL.

2. glide, tool, roll;—*referring to a manner of progress, as of a carriage.*

bow-legged, *a.* bandy-legged.

bowl-shaped, *a.* crateriform (*tech.*).

bowstring, *n.* string, cord, nerve (*B*).

box, *v. i.* fight (*contex.*), spar.

box, *n.* **1.** case, container (*com.*), receptacle; *spec.* canister, chest, trunk, cabinet, casket, cassolette, canteen, coffer, coffin, pyx, cofferdam, caisson, carton, cartouche, buist (*obs. or Scot.*), bin, bunker, caddy, drawer, kist (*Scot. & dial. Eng.*), shrine (*A*), reliquary, monstrance, trunk, case.

2. *Referring to the theater box:* compartment (*contex.*); *spec.* loge (*French*).

3. *See* SEAT, SHELTER.

brace, *n.* bracer (*R*), support (*contex.*), strengthener (*contex.*); *spec.* clasp, buckle, band, clamp, stay, strut, bolt, rope, chain, bracket, truss, girder, tie, rod, rider, rib, crib, prop, shore, buttress, pier, reinforce, reinforcement.

brace, *v. t.* **1.** support, strengthen, stiffen; *spec.* gird, prop, strut, tie, truss, buttress, chain, bracket, rib, stay, reinforce, bone, shore, *etc.*

2. *See* STIMULATE, STRENGTHEN.

bracket, *n.* **1.** brace (*contex.*); *spec.* corbel, console, shoulder, cheek, modillion, gusset, cantilever.

2. *See* SHELF.

3. category, class, classification, group.

4. fixture (*gas or electric*), holder.

braid, *n.* plait, pleat (*A*), brede (*A*), plaiting (*a collective*); *spec.* soutache (*French*), galloon, cue, leghorn (*a collective*), Venetians (*pl.*), lace.

braid, *v. t.* **1.** intertwine (*contex.*), entwine, twine, weave, interweave, twist, intertwist, plat, plait, pleat (*A*), brede (*A*).

2. *See* BIND.

brain, *n.* **1.** headpiece (*fig.*), head, encephalon (*tech.*); *spec.* cerebrum, cerebellum, hindbrain, little brain, gray matter (*C*).

2. *In pl.: see* MIND.

brake, *n.* check (*R*), stop; *spec.* clog, convoy, block, chock, cow, drag, skid.

brake, *v. t.* stop, retard, slow (*with "down"*).

brakeman, *n.* brakesman, guard (*Eng.*). *"Brakeman" is the usual form.*

branch, *n.* **1.** shoot, offshoot, stick (*contex.*), ramus (*tech.*), rame (*R*); *spec.* limb, bough, twig, spray, sprig, spire, start, caulome, bush, phylloclade (*tech.*), offset, sucker, runner, ramulus, ramulet, fork, rootlet; *see* SHOOT.

Antonyms: see TRUNK.

2. division (*contex.*), ramification, divarication (*B*), embranchment (*R*), fork, arm, wing, offshoot, offset, throwoff (*R*); *spec.* stem, loop, spur, bifurcation, billabong (*Australia*), anabranch (*Australia*); *see* ARM.

Antonyms: see BODY.

3. *Referring to a horn:* fork; *spec.* snag, tine, prong, speller, tray, broach, start, bez-antler, pricker.

4. member (*contex.*); *spec.* lodge, tent, court, filiation, chapter, post, corps, language, cell.

branch, *a.* rameous (*R*), ramal (*tech.*).

branch, *v. t. & i.* **1.** divide, fork, furcate, bifurcate, radiate, ramify, divaricate (*B*), offset, outbranch (*B*), digitate (*R*); *spec.* dichotomize, bush.

2. *See* DIVERGE.

branching, *a.* arborescent, ramifying; *spec.* dichotomous, spraying; *see* BRANCHY, DIVERGENT.

branchy, *a.* ramose (*tech.*), ramous (*tech.*), branching; *spec.* ramulose, ramellose, twiggy, sprayey, spriggy.

brand, *n.* **1.** *See* SWORD, BLIGHT.

2. character (*contex.*), stigma (*B*), print, stamp; *spec.* crop, burn (*contex.*).

3. mark, chop (*in China*), *spec.* label, stamp, tally.

4. *Referring to goods:* quality, make, class, grade, chop (*in China*), stamp.

5. (*the primary meaning*) firebrand, flambeau, torch, coal, ember.

6. iron, marker.

brand, *v. t.* **1.** stigmatize (*B*), print, stamp, mark (*contex.*); *spec.* burn (*the original sense of "brand"*), pitch, tiver (*dial. Eng.*).

2. *In commerce:* mark; *spec.* label, tally.

brave, *a.* **1.** bold, audacious, courageous, stalwart, daring, game (*C*), gamy (*C*), dauntless, undaunted, fearless, unafraid, spirited, high-spirited (*B*), lion-hearted (*rhetorical*), valiant, valorous, gallant, doughty (*B*), dour (*Scot.*), stout, stout-hearted, resolute, preux (*French*), galliard (*A*), prow (*A*), yeomanly (*B*); *spec.* manful, intrepid, manly, chivalrous, womanly.

Antonyms: see COWARDLY, UNCHIVALROUS.

2. *See* EXCELLENT, SHOWY.

---

bowl, *v. t.: roll, serve.*
bowlder: *rock.*
box: *slap.*
boxer: *fighter.*
boy: *child, youth, servant.*
boycott, *v. t.: avoid.*
boycott, *n.: conspiracy.*
boyish: *childish.*
bracing: *stimulating.*
brackish: *salt.*
brag, *n.: boaster.*
brag, *v. i.: boast.*
braggadocio: *boasting, boaster.*
braggart, *n.: boaster.*
braggart, *a.: boastful.*
bragger: *boaster.*
bragging, *a.: boastful.*
bragging, *n.: boasting.*
brainwork: *thinking.*
brainy: *intelligent.*
brandish: *swagger.*
brash, *a.: hasty, impetuous, brittle.*
brass, *a.: brazen.*
brassy: *brazen.*
brat: *child.*
bravado, *n.: bluster, defiance.*
bravado, *v. i.: bluster.*
brave, *v. t.: defy, face, challenge, embolden.*
brave, *n.: bully, desperado, warrior.*

---

bravery, *n.* boldness, courage, daring, valor, spirit, *etc.*; *cf.* BRAVE.
Antonyms: see COWARDICE.

bravo, *interj.* excellent! good! fine! swell (*C*).

brawling, *n.* **1.** *See* MURMURING.
2. disputation, quarreling; *cf.* QUARREL.

bray, *n.* & *v. i.* cry (*contex.*), hee-haw (*onomatopoetic; C*).

braze, *v. t.* **1.** brass, brazen.
2. *See* SOLDIER.

brazen, *a.* **1.** brass; *spec.* brassy, brassish.
2. *See* SHAMELESS, HARSH, METALLIC.

brazen, *v. t.* cheek (*S*), face;—*chiefly with "out."*

brazier, *n.* firepan; *spec.* brasero (*Spanish*), hearth, mangal (*R*), scaldino (*Italian*).

breach, *n.* **1.** *See* BREAK, SURF, VIOLATION, WOUND.
2. opening, break, rent, rupture, disruption, ruption (*R or spec.*); *spec.* chasm, fret, split, gap, crack.
3. *Referring to personal relations:* division, rupture, ruption, split, break, schism.

breach, *v. t.* break, rupture, disrupt; *spec.* gap.

bread, *n.* tommy (*S, Eng.*), breadstuff; *spec.* biscuit, eulogia (*hist.*), pone (*Southern U. S.*), manchet (*A*), muffin, roll, rusk, pumpernickel, toast, simnel (*chiefly historical*), showbread, wafer, brewis (*dial.*), bun, crug (*S, Eng.*), host, element (*ecclesiastical*).

break, *v. t.* **1.** *Spec.* disrupt (*R or fig.*), rupture, snap, rive, burst, bust (*S or vulgar*), smash, rend, fragmentize (*R*), stave, chip, bray, brake, craze, fritter, crash (*R*), crumb, comminute, crack, crumple, fracture, fault, tear, cabble, buck, rag, splinter, split, nick, demolish; *see* SHATTER, SCRAPE, BURST.
Antonyms: see JOIN, UNITE, CEMENT, SOLDER.
2. *See* BREACH, DISARRANGE, INTERRUPT, EXCEED, RUIN, DISCHARGE, BANKRUPT, COMMUNICATE, SUBDUE, TAME, VIOLATE, DEGRADE.

break, *v. i.* **1.** part (*contex.*); *spec.* disrupt (*R or fig.*), crash (*R*), burst, bust (*S*), snap, crack, splinter, rend, outburst (*R*); *see* SHATTER, BURST.
2. *Referring to a wave:* comb, wash, crest, topple (*C*).
3. *Referring to a fish:* rise, leap, prime (*R*).
4. *Referring to the voice:* change, mature.
5. *See* FAIL, DAWN, BURST, START, CHANGE.

break, *n.* **1.** breach; *spec.* disruption (*R or fig.*), break-up, rupture, crush, crash, smash, snap, burst, debacle, rent, abrasion, chip; *see* BURST.
2. incontinuity (*R*); *spec.* opening, gap, rent, nick, chasm, hiatus, blank, interval, lacuna (*B*), void, intermission, aperture, rift, fissure, drop, crack; *see* SCRAPE.
3. *Referring to the waves: spec.* wash, combing, breaking.
4. *See* INTERRUPTION, BREACH, START, CHANGE, TRANSITION, RISE.

breakable, *a.* frangible (*B*), fragile; *see* BRITTLE.

breaker, *n.* **1.** *Spec.* crusher, smasher, brayer, cracker, *etc.*
2. wave (*contex.*), comber, white horse, surge (*a collective*).

breaking, *n.* **1.** breakage; *spec.* disruption (*R or fig.*), rupture (*R*), ruption (*R*), fracture (*chiefly spec.*), fraction, infraction (*R*), fragmentation (*R*), crumblement (*R*), irruption (*B*), inbreak (*R*), incrash (*R*), rending, inburst (*R*).

breakwater, *n. Spec.* mole, framework, groyne, jetty, pier (*C, U. S.*).

breast, *n.* **1.** mamma (*of a female; tech.*), mammilla (*of a male; tech.*), bubby (*dial. or vulgar*).
2. *See* BOSOM, COURAGE.
3. brisket.

breastbone, *n.* sternum (*tech.*).

breastplate, *n.* pectoral (*R*), poitrel (*A*), plastron (*hist.*); *spec.* cuirass.

breast-shaped, *a.* mammillary, mammiform; *spec.* mastoid;—*all three tech.*

breath, *n.* **1.** air (*contex.*).
2. respiration, spiration (*R*); *spec.* snore, pant, puff, yawn, wheeze; *see* INHALATION, EXHALATION, SIGH.
3. *See* EXHALATION, WIND, REST, EXERCISE, MOISTURE, TRIFLE.

breathe, *v. i.* **1.** respire, *spec.* pant, puff, pump, snore, wheeze; *see* INHALE, EXHALE, SIGH.
2. *See* STOP.
3. live, exist, be.

breathe, *v. t.* **1.** respire; *see* INHALE, EXHALE.
2. *See* REST, EXHALE, UTTER.

breathing, *n.* **1.** respiration, spiration (*R*); *spec.* eupnœa, dyspnœa, apnœa; *see* INHALATION, EXHALATION.
2. *See* REST, UTTERANCE, ASPIRATE.

breathless, *a.* **1.** blown, pumped (*S*), pooped (*A*), exanimate (*B*), exhausted (*contex.*), all in (*S, U. S.*).
2. *See* LIFELESS.

bred, *a.* reared, raised (*C*); *spec.* educated.

breeches, *n. pl.* **1.** knickerbockers (*U. S.*), knickers (*C*), shorts, breeks (*Scot.*), small clothes, smalls (*C*), hose (*A or hist.; chiefly spec.*); *spec.* buckskins, galligaskins, corduroys; —*all pl.*
2. *See* TROUSERS.

breechless, *a.* trouserless, sansculottic (*hist.*), unbreeched, pantless (*vulgar*).

breed, *v. t.* **1.** *Referring to the female:* grow, create, produce, cherish, form, develop; *spec.* hatch.
2. *Spec.* inbreed, cross, interbreed, intercross, crossbreed, fancy, hybridize.

---

bravo: *desperado.*
brawl: *fight, quarrel, murmur.*
brawn: *flesh, strength.*
brawny: *muscular, strong.*
bray, *v. t.: grind.*
brayer: *pestle.*
breadth: *width;* also, cf. *spacious, roomy, liberal, comprehensive.*
breakage: *breaking.*
breakdown: *collapse.*
breakneck: *dangerous.*
break-up: *decomposition, break.*
breast, *v. t.: oppose.*
breathing, *a.: living.*

3. produce, grow, engender, brew, generate (*R*);—as in "*to breed trouble.*"
Antonyms: see EXTINGUISH.
4. raise (*stock, etc.*).
5. *See* CAUSE, REAR.
breed, *v. i.* **1.** *In the sense of "to bear young":* generate (*R*), reproduce, propagate.
2. *In the sense of "to be born":* originate (*R*).
breed, *n.* stock, brood (*chiefly contemptuous as used of men*); *see* FAMILY, RACE.
breeding, *n.* **1.** stirpiculture (*R*).
2. nurture, education (*R*); *spec.* gentility, gentilesse (*A*); *see* POLITENESS.
breeding place. 1. *Spec.* loonery, hennery, hawkery, gullery, heronry, hatchery, beavery, hoggery, piggery, rookery.
2. *Fig.:* hotbed.
brevity, *n.* **1.** *See* SHORTNESS.
2. *Referring to time:* briefness, shortness, littleness, momentariness, swiftness, transiency, transience.
Antonyms: see LENGTH.
3. *Referring to speech or writing:* briefness, shortness, curtness, terseness, breviloquence (*affected or humorous*), brachylogy (*R*), pauciloquy (*R*); *see* CONCISENESS.
Antonyms: see PROLIXITY.
bribe, *v. t.* corrupt (*contex.*), hire (*contex.*), buy, suborn (*tech.*); *spec.* oil (*S*), anoint (*R; in "to anoint the hand"*), palm (*S*), subsidize, tip, grease (*S*), square (*C*), fix (*C*).
bribe, *n.* gratification (*euphemistic*), perquisite, emolument, bait, tribute; *spec.* sop, graft, grease, baksheesh, tip, boodle (*S*), his (*S; in "he got his"*), hush money (*S*).
bribery, *n.* corruption (*contex.*), subornation (*tech.*), graft, protection; *spec.* subsidizing.
bric-a-brac, *n.* knicknacks (*pl.*); *spec.* scrimshaw, antiques, art goods, curios.
brick, *n.* *Spec.* clinker, clink, grizzle, lump, cutcha (*Anglo-Indian*), quarl, beader, binder, briquette *or* briquet.
bricky, *a.* lateritious (*referring esp. to color; chiefly tech.*).
bride, *n.* wife, Beatrice (*fig.*).
bridegroom, *n.* husband, groom, benedict, Benedick (*fig.*).
bridesman, *n.* best man, groomsman.
bridge, *n.* **1.** span; *spec.* drawbridge, viaduct, bateau, bridge, bascule bridge, overpass, trestle, causeway, communication (*contex.*), Bifrost (*mythol.*) aqueduct.
2. *See* PLATFORM.
3. auction, contract, Culbertson, Sims; *spec.* cards.
4. bridgework (*dental*).
bridge, *v. t. & i.* span, overbridge (*R*), cross, connect, join, unite.
bridle, *n.* **1.** headgear; *spec.* snaffle, branks (*used in punishing a scold; pl.*), check, curb, bit, reins.
2. *See* RESTRAINT.
bridle, *v. i.* bristle.
brief, *a.* **1.** *Implying exclusion of what is diffuse or secondary:* concise, succinct:—*implying a clean-cut directness,* succinct *perhaps more finish in form;* terse *implies polished or elegant conciseness;* condensed *implies reduction from a fuller form,* compendious *implies fullness combined with brevity;* summary *suggests confinement to the main ideas treated;* pithy *and* sententious *imply compactness and force,* pithy *suggesting liveliness and energy, and* sententious *gravity or thoughtfulness;* laconic *implies directness, force, and vigor, often taciturnity, austerity, or brusqueness;* curt *implies excessive brevity, and often brusqueness or rudeness;* epigrammatic *implies pointedness, suggesting wit and ingenuity of expression;* breviloquent (*R*), curtal (*A*); *see* SHORT, CONCISE.
Antonyms: see PROLIX.
2. *Referring to time:* short (*now A, exc. in certain phrases*), transient, little, short-lived, swift, momentary; *see* EPHEMERAL.
Antonyms: see LONG, ENDLESS, ETERNAL, LENGTHY.
brier, *n.* briar (*a variant*), bramble, thorns (*pl.*); *spec.* blackberry, raspberry.
brier, *n.* briar (*a variant*), heath, brierwood.
briery, *a.* briary (*a variant*), brambly, thorny.
bright, *a.* **1.** *Spec.* brilliant, effulgent, refulgent, glaring, lucid, splendid, splendent, resplendent, radiant (*R*), glistening, sparkling, coruscating, flaring, beaming, scintillating, glaring, gay, vivid, splendorous, splendrous, gorgeous, strong (*contex.*), garish, brightsome, light, lightsome, transplendent (*R*), Orient (*B*) *or* Oriental (*esp. of gems, etc.*); *see* LUSTROUS, LUMINOUS, SHINING, FLASHING, GLOWING, DAZZLING, FLAMING.
Antonyms: see DARK, DIM.
2. *Referring to colors: spec.* flaming, flamboyant, fresh, lively, flashy, gay, intense, vivid, deep, clear, luminous, brilliant, vivid; *see* SHOWY. *Most of the terms given under sense* **1** *are also used as synonyms in reference to colors.*
Antonyms: see DULL.
3. *Referring to a career, course of conduct, etc.: spec.* brilliant, dazzling, illustrious, meteoric, purple (*B*), rosy, distinguished, famous.
Antonyms: see OBSCURE.
4. *See* CHEERFUL, CLEAR, INTELLIGENT, AUSPICIOUS, DISCERNING.
brighten, *v. t.* **1.** illuminate, beshine (*R*), illume (*B or fig.*), enlighten (*chiefly B or rhetorical*), embrighten (*R*, light up, irradiate (*B*).

breeze: *wind, disturbance.*
breezy: *windy, lively.*
breve: *summary.*
brew: *concoct, devise.*
brewing: *concoction.*
briar: *brier.*
bridal: *marriage.*
bridle, *v. t.: restrain.*
brief, *n.: letter, writ, abstract, summary.*
brigade, *n.: division, organization.*
brigand: *desperado.*
brighten: *clear, improve.*

2. *Referring to colors:* raise, liven (*C*), lighten.
3. *See* SHINE, ENLIVEN, CHEER.

bright-eyed, *a.* shining-eyed, clear-eyed.
Antonyms: see BLEAR, DIM-EYED.

brightness, *n.* **1.** *Spec.* brilliance, brilliancy, radiance, effulgence, refulgence, refulgency (*R*), lucidity (*R*), splendor, splendidness, resplendence, splendrousness (*R*), splendence (*R*), resplendency (*R*), transplendency (*R*), gaiety, strength (*contex.*), gorgeousness, glister (*chiefly B*), corruscation, sparkle, glint, glitter, scintillation, glare, blaze, flame, iridescence, luminosity, luminousness, Oriency (*esp. of gems*); *see* LUSTER, SHINE, DAZZLE.
Antonyms: see DARKNESS, DIMNESS, OBSCURITY.
2. *Referring to colors: spec.* flamboyance, freshness, flashiness, gayness, gaiety, showiness, intensity, vividness, clarity. *Most of the terms under sense* **1** *are also used of colors.*
Antonyms: see DULLNESS.
3. *Referring to a career, performance, etc.· spec.* brilliance, illustriousness, éclat (*French*) distinction, fame.
Antonyms: see OBSCURITY.
4. *See* INTELLIGENCE, DISCERNMENT.

brindled, *a.* party-colored, banded, brinded, brindle; *spec.* tabby.

bring, *v. t.* **1.** fetch, conduct (*a Latinism*), convoy (*implying protection*), convey (*stressing the means whereby the transport is effected*), deduce (*R*), have (*A*); *spec.* land, retrieve, draw, get, reduce (*R*).
Antonyms: see SEND, REMOVE. Bring *implies transferrence to a place, in contrast to* send, *which implies transport from a place.*
2. *Referring to price, amount, etc.:* fetch, command, realize, come to, produce, yield, get, gain, encash (*R*); *spec.* net.
3. reduce, throw, work; *spec.* reason (*esp. with "into," "out of," etc.*), conjure, pray, laugh, ridicule, lull, *etc.*
4. reflect (*as censure, doubt, etc.*), throw, cast.
5. *See* INDUCE, PRESENT, INTRODUCE, INFLICT.

brisk, *a.* **1.** quick, lively, nimble, swift, alert, spry (*C*), animated, vivacious, sprightly (*of manner of movement or action, implying, liveliness and energy*). *See* ACTIVE, RAPID, STRONG, SHARP.
2. smart, perky, sharp, up-and-coming.

brisket, *n.* breast.

bristle, *n.* hair *or* hairs (*pl.*), brush; *spec.* (*tech.*), seta, setula, setule, vibrissa.

bristle, *v. i.* **1.** *Referring to hair or bristles:* erect (*B or tech.*), stand, stare (*A*).
2. *See* BRIDLE.

bristling, *a.* horrid (*chiefly B*), shaggy, rough, horrent (*chiefly B*), spiny, spiked.

bristly, *a.* setaceous, strigose, strigate, setulose, hispid, setose, scrubby (*R or spec.*), horrent (*chiefly B*), hairy (*contex.*);—*all exc. "bristly," "scrubby," "hairy," and "horrent," chiefly tech.*
Antonyms: see SMOOTH.

brittle, *a.* weak (*contex.*), breakable (*contex.*), fragile (*while* brittle *deals with the nature of the material,* fragile *is more general*), frail (*contex.*), frangible (*B*), brickle (*dial.*), bruckle (*dial.*), brash (*chiefly U. S. and spec.*); *spec.* delicate (*contex.*), short, crisp, shattery (*R*), shivery, cold-short, hot-short; *see* CRUMBLY.
Antonyms: see STRONG, FLEXIBLE, UNBREAKABLE, LIMP.

broad, *a.* **1.** *See* WIDE, SPACIOUS, ROOMY, EVIDENT, COMPREHENSIVE, UNRESTRAINED, GENERAL, LIBERAL.
2. full (*daylight*).
3. pronounced, obvious, marked: *of an accent;* (*brogue, accent, etc.*), Doric (*spec. or fig.; of a dialect, etc.*); risqué, vulgar, obscene:—*of a joke or story.*

broadcast, *n.* transmission, hook-up, message, speech, program:—*of radio.*

broadcast, *v.* disseminate, distribute, scatter, spread, diffuse:—*implying wholesale dissemination;* send, transmit (*of radio transmission*); announce, speak, talk, sing, act, perform, *etc.* —*of radio communication.*

broadside, *adv.* flatways, flatwise, sidewise, sideways.

brogue, *n.* **1.** shoe, brogan.
2. accent, dialect.

broil, *v. t.* **1.** cook (*contex.*), grill, carbonado (*A or B*); *spec.* frizzle, devil, spitchcock.
2. *See* HEAT.

broken, *a.* **1.** *Spec.* disrupt (*R or fig.*), burst, busted (*S or C*), fractured, shattered, gapped, ruptured, torn, rent.
Antonyms: see INTACT, WHOLE.
2. *Referring to one's health:* shaken; *spec.* rundown.
3. *See* INTERMITTENT, ROUGH, VIOLATED.

broker, *n.* **1.** *See* PAWNBROKER, GO-BETWEEN.
2. agent, middleman; *spec.* jobber.

brokerage, *n.* brokage (*A, R, or spec.*), jobbing; *spec.* pawnbrokerage, agency (*contex.*), stock broking.

brooch, *n.* clasp, ouch, fibula (*antiq.*), pin.

brood, *n.* **1.** hatch; *spec.* clutch, covey, cletch *or* clatch (*dial.*), nide (*chiefly Eng.*).
2. *See* OFFSRPING, RACE, BREED.

brook, *n.* stream, streamlet, brooklet, rivulet, rindle (*R or dial.*), rill, beck (*Eng.; or dial.*), burn (*dial. or Scot.*), runnel, runlet, run, streamlet, burnie (*Scot.*), bourn *or* bourne (*chiefly local Eng. or B*), burn (*dial. and Scot.*), branch; (*Southern U. S.*), creek; *spec.* gill (*dial., Eng.*), rillet.

broom, *n.* brush (*contex.*), besom (*now chiefly dial. or B*); *spec.* wisp, pope's-head, brush, whisk, whisker, wing.

brim: *edge.*
brimful: *full.*
brine: *pickle.*
brink: *edge.*
briny: *salt.*
British: *English.*
broach, *n.:* *spit, horn.*
broach, *v. t.:* *transfix, open, begin, spill, introduce, draw, ream.*
broaden: *widen, generalize, liberalize enlarge.*
brood, *v.:* *incubate, consider.*
brook: *endure.*

broom-shaped, *a.* scopiform, fascicular;—*both chiefly tech.*

broth, *n.* broo *or* bree (*Scot.*), liquor; *spec.* brewis (*dial.*), cullis (*now R*), kale; *see* SOUP.

brothel, *n.* bagnio (*B*), bordel (*obs. or A*), bawdyhouse, house of ill repute (*the usual legal term*), cathouse (*S*), whorehouse.

brother, *n.* **1.** *Spec.* cadet (*younger brother*), kid (*S*).
2. *See* ASSOCIATE, FRIAR.

brotherly, *a.* **1.** fraternal.
2. *See* AFFECTIONATE.

brown, *a. Spec.* lurid, foxy, hazel, chelidonian, bay, bayard (*A*), brownish, browny, brunneous (*R*), ferruginous, auburn, adust (*R*), bronze, mahogany, maroon, russet, snuff-colored, smoky, russetish, russety, tan, sorrel, puce, tawny, fallow, tabac, musteline, fawn.

brown, *n. Spec.* bistre, mummy, ecru (*French*).

brown, *v. t.* embrown (*emphatic*); *spec.* tan, russet, scorch, toast.

bruise, *v. t.* **1.** injure (*contex.*), batter, contund (*R*) *or* contuse (*implying injury without breaking the skin*), pound (*R*); *spec.* suggilate (*A or R*).
2. *See* INDENT, CRUSH.

bruise, *n.* **1.** injury (*contex.*), contusion (*tech. or B*), batter (*R*), pound (*R*); *spec.* suggilation (*R or tech.*), ecchymosis, mouse (*S*).
2. *See* INDENTATION.

bruising, *a.* contusive (*B or tech.*).

brunet, *a.* dark, dark-complexioned, brunette (*less usual than "brunet"; chiefly fem.*); *spec.* (*tech.*) melanochroid, melanous, melanistic.
Antonyms: see BLOND.

brunet, *n.* brunette (*femm.*); *spec.* (*tech.*) melanochroi (*pl.*), melanoi (*pl.*).

brush, *n.* **1.** *Spec.* pen, pencil, rigger, sable, pope's-head, fitch, card, air brush.
2. *See* BROOM, TUFT, TAIL.

brush, *v. t.* **1.** *Spec.* whisk; *see* SWEEP.
2. *See* GRAZE.

brushlike, *a.* scopiform (*tech.*), muscariform (*tech.*), brushy (*R*).

brushwood, *n.* **1.** scrub, brush, bush; *spec.* chaparral (*U. S.*), frith (*Eng.*), brake, underbrush, rice (*Eng.*).
2. brush;—*referring to small branches cut up.*

brutalize, *v. t. Chiefly fig. in sense:* animalize (*R*), imbrute (*B*), brutify (*R*), bestialize; *spec.* dehumanize (*R*), dishumanize (*R*), sensualize, harden, debase, demoralize.
Antonyms: see REFINE, SPIRITUALIZE.

bubble, *n.* **1.** globule (*contex.*), bell (*chiefly Scot. or tech.*), blob (*dial. or C*), blobber (*A or dial.*); *spec.* bullule, bead, bleb, bladder, foam.
2. *Referring to the sound:* gurgle.
3. *See* SHOW, FALLACY, TRIFLE.

bubble, *v. i.* **1.** bell (*dial., Scot., or tech.*), effervesce (*B or tech.; often spec.*), intumesce (*tech.; often spec.*), rise (*contex.*), ebullate *or* ebulliate (*R*); *spec.* bead, sparkle, gurgle, yaw, foam; *see* BOIL.
2. gurgle.

bubbling, *a.* effervescent (*B or tech.; often spec.*), effervescive (*B or tech.; often spec.*), ebullient (*now principally with reference to manner or feelings*), bubbly, intumescent (*tech.; often spec.*), fretting (*R implies violent agitation*); *spec.* sparkling, foaming; *see* BOILING.

bubbling, *n.* effervescence *or* (*R*), effervescency (*B or tech.; often spec.*), intumescence (*a stronger term, implying swelling up and bubbling*), ebullience (*R*), ebullition (*B or tech.*), fret (*R*).

bubbly, *a.* bubblish; *spec.* bladdery, blebby, beady.

bucket, *n. Spec.* tub, scoop, kibble, float, piston, pail, blackjack.

buckle, *n.* **1.** clasp, fibula (*antiq.*); *spec.* broach, fastening, fastener.
2. *See* BEND, TWIST.

buckler, *n.* **1.** shield, rondache (*French*), targe; *spec.* rounder.
2. *See* PROTECTOR.

bud, *n.* **1.** sprout, shoot, gemma (*tech.*), burgeon (*B*), tendron (*R*); *spec.* button, gemmule, gemina, knop (*A*), eye, bulbil, bulbet, cabbage, chit.
2. gemma (*biol.*); *spec.* (*zool.*) medusa, medusoid, hydra.

bud, *v. i.* **1.** sprout, shoot, germinate, burgeon (*B*), swell, blossom; *spec.* button.
2. gemmate (*biol.*).
3. disbud; *spec.* chit.

buff, *n.* orange, yellow; *spec.* Isabella, Isabel.

buffer, *n.* bumper, cow-catcher (*U. S.*); *spec.* fender, dolly, cushion.

buffer, *v. t.* cushion.

buffet, *n.* **1.** cupboard, sideboard, low-boy.
2. *See* EATING HOUSE, FOOTSTOOL.

buffoon, *n.* clown (*chiefly spec.*), merry-andrew, fool, jackpudding (*A*), pleasant (*A*), grotesque (*R*), antic, pickle-herring (*R*), merryman (*R*), droll, harlequin, zany (*orig. spec.; R or B*); *spec.* punch, punchinello, Scaramouch, pantaloon, jester, jackpudding, pierrot, Harlequin, mimic, mummer, pantomimist, mime,

---

brotherhood: *association, fraternity, fellowship.*
browbeat: *bully.*
brownie: *fairy.*
browse, *v. t.: graze.*
bruit: *report.*
brummagem: *gaudy.*
brunt: *shock.*
brush, *n.: contest, fight.*
brush, *n.: brushwood, thicket.*
brusque: *blunt, rough.*
brutal: *animal, cruel, rough, coarse, sensual.*
brute, *a.: unreasoning, soulless, insensible, sensual, rough, unconscious.*
brute, *n.: animal, beast, fiend, sensualist.*
brutish: *animal, beastlike, unreasoning, coarse, sensual, cruel, rough.*
buccaneer: *desperado, pirate.*
buck, *n.: deer, dandy.*
buck, *v. i.: jump.*
buck, *v. t.: unhorse.*
bucket, *v. t.: draw, drench, drive.*
bucket, *v. i.: ride.*
budge, *v. i.: move, yield.*
budge, *a.: stiff, pedantic.*
buff: *polish.*
buffet, *v. t.: strike, fight.*
buffet, *v. i.: fight.*

---

mimer, archimime, Goliard (*historical*), gracioso (*Spanish*), comedian.

buffoon, *v. i.* droll, harlequinade (*R*), merry-andrew *or* merry-andrewize (*R*), joke.

buffoonery, *n.* farce, clownery (*chiefly spec.*), foolery, harlequinade, drollery (*B or R*), horseplay, merry-andrewism (*R*), buffoonism, zanyism (*orig. spec.; R*); tomfoolery; *spec.* mimicry, mummery, jokes (*pl.*).

Antonyms: see DIGNITY.

buffoonish, *a.* clownish, buffoon, antic.

Antonyms: see DIGNIFIED.

bugbear, *n.* bug (*A*), bugaboo, scarecrow (*fig. or spec.*), boggard *or* boggart (*R*); *spec.* fetish, mumbo-jumbo; *see* BOGY, *now also C for thing feared or dreaded:* ordeal.

buggy, *a. Spec.* cimicine.

build, *v. t.* **1.** erect, raise, rear, edify (*R*), fabricate (*R or spec.*), construct, fashion, big *or* bigg (*Scot.*); *spec.* mason, substruct, superstruct, reconstruct.

Antonyms: see ABATE, DESTROY.

2. *See* FRAME, BASE, ESTABLISH, CONSTRUCT, COMPOSE.

build, *n.* **1.** *See* STRUCTURE.

2. *Referring to a person:* physique, figure, set, set-up (*C*).

builder, *n.* architect (*chiefly spec.*), erector; *spec.* jerry-builder, carpenter, mason, contractor, promoter.

building, *n.* **1.** *Referring to the operation:* erection, fabric (*now eccl.*), edification (*R in this sense except with reference to spiritual development*), architecture, construction, fabrication (*R or spec.*).

2. *Referring to what is built:* edifice (*usually spec.*), erection (*formal*), fabric, pile (*implying size; often contemptuous*), structure, construction; *spec.* substructure, superstructure, superstruction (*R*), library, hall, rotunda, palace, chamber, camera, store, mansion, coe (*local; mining*), pavilion, cottage, hovel, factory, garage, shelter, court, *etc.; see* HOUSE. *"Building" is commonly used only of an inclosed structure.*

built, *a.* built-up, framed; *spec.* fabricated, pre-fabricated, *knock-down or knocked down.*

bulb, *n.* **1.** bud (*contex.*); *spec.* bulbil, chive, clove, onion, set.

2. *Spec.* tuber, corm, globe (*of an electric light bulb*).

bulb-shaped, *a.* bulbiform, bulbous, bulbed; *spec.* onion-shaped, turnip-shaped.

bulging-eyed, *a.* goggle-eyed, wall-eyed.

bulk, *n.* stall.

bulk, *n.* **1.** *See* SIZE, QUANTITY, BODY.

2. generality, body, mass, heft (*C, U. S.*), most (*with "the"*), staple, gross (*A*); *spec.* majority, many.

Antonyms: see MINORITY.

bulk, *v. i.* **1.** swell, expand, loom; *see* SWELL.

2. *See* WEIGH.

bull, *n.* bovine (*contex.*); *spec.* michy (*S, Australia*), bullock.

bullfighter, *n.* toreador (*Spanish; esp. a mounted bullfighter*); *spec.* banderillero (*Spanish*), picador, matador.

bull's-eye, *n.* aim (*contex.*), center; *spec.* prick (*A*), blank, white, carton (*cant*).

bull-shaped, *a.* tauriform (*tech. or B*).

bully, *n.* **1.** intimidator, bounce (*R, C*), bouncer (*R, except. spec.*), hector, hectorer, brave (*A*), tiger (*S; A*), bulldozer (*C*); *spec.* plug-ugly (*S*), picket.

Antonyms: see FAWNER.

2. *See* BLUSTERER.

bully, *v. t.* intimidate, overbear, bounce (*R, except spec.; C*), hector, huff, browbeat, threaten, domineer, overbear, bulldoze, bullyrag, bluster; *spec.* bluff, outbully, haze (*U. S.*).

Antonyms: see COAX, CAJOLE.

bully, *v. i.* **1.** intimidate, hector, bounce (*C*), huff (*A*), domineer (*contex.*), bulldoze.

Antonyms: see CRINGE, COAX.

2. *See* BLUSTER.

bulwark, *n.* **1.** wall (*contex.*); *spec.* fortification, rampart, parapet, breakwater, barrier.

2. *See* SHELTER.

bumper, *n.* **1.** brimmer; *spec.* cupful, glassful, bowlful:—*implying a drinking vessel filled to the brim.*

2. *See* BUFFER, BOUNCER.

bunch, *n.* **1.** *See* PROTUBERANCE.

2. cluster, bob (*dial. or spec.*); *spec.* bundle, fascicle, fasciculus, hand (*of bananas*), wisp, whisk; *see* TUFT.

3. *See* QUANTITY, GROUP.

bunchy, *a.* **1.** bundled, fasciculate (*tech.*), fasciculated (*tech.*), clustery.

Antonyms: see SCATTERED.

2. *See* PROTUBERANT.

buncombe, *n. Also* bunkum, bunk (*C*), humbug, makebelieve (*contex.*), claptrap (*contemptuous*), talk (*C*), hot air (*C*), blah (*C*), baloney (*S*), hooey (*S*), bull (*S*):—*all implying something said for effect, but possessing no reality, as political promises.*

bundle, *n.* **1.** package, pack, packet, parcel, truss (*R or spec.*), bale (*implies considerable size and weight*); *spec.* roll, fadge *or* fodge (*tech. or dial.*), fardel (*A*), brail, faggot, dossier (*French*), dufter (*Anglo-Indian*), fascine, sheaf, swag (*Australia*), book, peter (*thieves' cant*), bolt, bavin (*A or dial., Eng.*), bottle (*now local Eng.*), hand, bung (*Eng.*), wad (*S*); *see* BUNCH.

bug: *insect.*
bugaboo: *bugbear.*
bugle: *horn.*
build, *v. i.: rely.*
bulge, *v. i.: protuberate, bag.*
bulge, *n.: protuberance.*
bulging: *protuberant.*
bulkhead: *partition, wall.*
bulky: *big.*
bull, *n.: blunder.*
bull, *v. t.: raise.*
bulldoze: *intimidate, bully.*
bullet: *ball, missile.*
bulletin: *statement, publication.*
bullyrag: *bully, tease.*
bulwark: *protect.*
bump, *v. t.: knock.*
bump, *n.: protuberance.*
bumper: *big.*
bumpkin, *n.: rustic.*
bumptious: *self-assertive.*
bumpy: *protuberant, rough.*
bunch, *v. t.: gather.*
bunch, *v. i.: protuberate, gather.*
bunco, *v. t.: cheat.*
bundle, *v. i.: hasten.*

2. *See* GROUP, QUANTITY.
bundle, *v. t.* **1.** pack, packet, truss (*A or spec.*), parcel; *spec.* faggot, hamper (*R*), crate, cask, sack, pug, bag, bale, do up.
2. *See* HASTEN.
bungle, *v. t. & i.* blunder (*R*), boggle (*C*), butcher (*C*), tinker, foozle (*S or often cant and spec.*), bitch (*C*); *spec.* muff; *see* BOTCH.
bunt, *n. Referring to part of a flag or sail:* bag, belly, swell.
buoy, *n.* float (*contex.*); *spec.* spar, marker, dan, dolphin, nun, buoy, nut buoy, can buoy, spar buoy, bell buoy, *etc.*
buoyant, *a.* **1.** floaty (*R*), floating, light.
2. *Referring to the mind:* high-spirited, resilient, volatile (*tending to alternate excess of high and low spirits*), elastic, youthful, confident, sanguine; *see* HOPEFUL.
Antonyms: see HOPELESS, DEPRESSED.
burden, *n.* **1.** burthen (*now chiefly A*), load, weight, incubus (*B; implying something dreaded*), cumber (*B, implies impeding action*), incumbrance *or* encumbrance, incumbency (*R, B*), tax (*esp. excessive*); *spec.* surcharge; *see* LOAD.
2. *In a legal sense:* onus, obligation, charge, weight, incumbency, cumbrance (*R*), encumbrance; *spec.* responsibility, tax.
3. *Referring to what is mentally burdensome:* incubus, weight, load, cumber (*R, B*), cumbrance (*R*).
4. *See* CHARGE, CAPACITY.
burden, *v. t.* **1.** load, load down, weigh down, weight, cumber, encumber (*implies hindering activity*), charge (*now chiefly fig. or naut.*), lade (*A*), tax (*esp. to burden oppressively*), saddle (*orig. spec.*), overload; *see* OVERBURDEN; —*all used also fig.*
Antonyms: see LIGHTEN.
2. *See* OPPRESS, CHARGE.
burdensome, *a.* **1.** heavy, onerous (*formal or B*), oppressive, weighty; cumbersome, taxing —*all used also fig.;* crushing.
Antonyms: see LIGHT.
2. *See* OPPRESSIVE, TROUBLESOME.
bureau, *n.* **1.** *See* OFFICE, DEPARTMENT.
2. chest (*of drawers*), dresser, *spec.* tallboy, highboy, lowboy; *see* SECRETARY.
bureaucracy, *n.* bureaucratism (*R*), officialism, red-tape, red-tapism (*B*), departmentalism, officialdom.
burgher, *n.* citizen, freeman, townsman.
burglar, *n.* housebreaker, cracksman (*S*), yegg (*S*), second story man, Jimmy Valentine; *spec.* robber.
burglarize, *v. t.* burgle (*humorous or C*), rob.
burglary, *n.* housebreaking, effraction (*R*); *spec.* robbery, theft.
burial, *n.* **1.** interment, inhumation, entombment (*orig. spec.*), deposition (*chiefly eccl.*), sepulture (*formal or B*), sepelition (*R*), tumulation (*R*); *spec.* vivisepulture (*R*).
Antonyms: see DISINTERMENT.
2. *See* FUNERAL.
burial, *a.* **1.** mortuary, sepulchral, sepultural (*R*), tombic (*R*).
2. *See* FUNERAL.
burlesque, *a. Spec.* Hudibrastic (*fig.; B*), burlesque-heroic, mock-heroic, heroi-comic (*B*), buffo, macaronic, parodic (*R*); *see* COMIC; RISQUÉ, VULGAR, NUDE; *so popularly understood in the term* "burlesque show."
burlesque, *n.* **1.** *Referring to a literary composition:* parody, travesty, take off (*C*); *spec.* caricature, paratragœdia, mock-heroic, extravaganza, burletta:—burlesque, *properly speaking makes the great comic, and brings it to a lower level; the* heroi-comic *raises the low and comic to an epic level.*
Antonyms: see TRAGEDY.
2. *See* CARICATURE.
burlesque, *v. t.* parody, travesty, take off (*C*); *spec.* caricature, buffoon, buffoonize.
burn, *v. t.* **1.** consume (*by fire*), combust (*A or jocular*), oxidize (*chem. or contex.*); *spec.* carbonize, char, scorch, sear, deflagrate, cremate, cinder (*R*), incinerate, kiln, incense (*R*), coal (*R*), parch, brand, singe, conflagrate (*R*), chark (*R*), coke, broil, flame; *see* ROAST.
2. *To injure by heat: spec.* blister, sear, scald, cauterize.
3. bake.
burn, *v. i.* **1.** consume (*contex.*), oxidize (*chem. or contex. or jocular*), *spec.* flame, flash, glow, deflagrate, flicker, smoke, smother, rage (*contex.*), conflagrate (*R*), flare, fizzle, smolder.
2. *See* DESIRE, SHINE.
burning, *a.* **1.** ardent (*B*), live, living; *spec.* glowing, aflame (*predicative*), flaming, conflagrant (*B*), flamed (*R*), red, raging (*contex.*), ustorious (*R*).
Antonyms: see LIFELESS.
2. *See* ARDENT.
3. consuming, comburent (*R*); spec. caustic.
burning, *n.* consumption (*with "of"; contex.*), combustion, fire; *spec.* flaming, flashing, ustion (*R*), eremacausis (*R*).
burnt, *a. Spec.* charred, incinerated, torrid, parched, *etc.*, samel *or* sammen.
burr, *n.* ring (*contex.*); *spec.* rove, washer.
burrow, *v. i.* dig, work; *spec.* earth, mole, gopher, mine.
burrow, *n.* **1.** cuniculos (*tech.*), excavation (*contex.*); *spec.* mine, earth, wormcast, hole (*C*).
2. *See* LAIR.

---

bung: *stopper, vent.*
bungle, *n.: blunder.*
bungling: *botchy, awkward.*
bunk, *n.: bed.*
bunk, *v. i.: lodge.*
bunker: *bin, hazard.*
bunt, *n.: blight.*
bunt, *v. & n.: push, butt.*
buoy: *float.*
bur: *hull.*
burden, *n.: refrain.*
bureaucrat: *officer.*
burgeon, *v. i.: germinate.*
burgh: *town.*
burial place: *grave, cemetery.*
burn, *n.: brook.*
burn, *v.t.: electrocute.*
burnish: *polish.*
burr: *hull.*

---

burst, *v. t.* break, bust (*C or vulgar*), disrupt (*B, chiefly fig.*), rend, rupture, blow up; *spec.* shatter; *see* EXPLODE.

burst, *v. i.* **1.** break, bust (*C or vulgar*), disrupt (*B, chiefly fig.*), rend, rupture, blow up; *spec.* inburst; *see* EXPLODE.

2. break, outburst, outbreak; *spec.* gush, outblaze (*often fig.*), effervesce, sally, flash, explode, outflame; *see* START.

burst, *n.* **1.** break, rupture, disruption (*B; chiefly fig.*), bust (*C or vulgar*); *spec.* eruption; *see* EXPLOSION.

2. breaking, outburst, outbreak; *spec.* explosion, implosion, outblaze, gush, sally, flash, effervescence, spurt.

3. *See* EFFORT, RUN.

bursting, *a.* disruptive, rending; *spec.* eruptive, erumpent (*R*); *see* EXPLOSIVE.

bury, *v. t.* **1.** inter, inhume, inhumate:—*implying burial in the ground;* sepulcher (*R or spec.*), ensepulcher (*R*), sepulture (*formal or B*); *spec.* entomb, inearth (*chiefly B*), earth (*B*), urn, inurn, tumulate (*R*), tomb (*R*), grave (*A*), mold (*R*); immure, hearse, sod (*C*), plant (*C*).

Antonyms: see DISINTER.

2. *Spec.* cache.

3. *See* COVER, SUBMERGE, IGNORE, FORGET, ABSORB.

bury, *n. Spec.* camp (*dial.*), pie, pit, clamp, cache.

bush, *n.* **1.** shrub, scrog (*chiefly Scot.*), tod (*A or dial.*), cop (*dial.*); *spec.* bushlet.

2. *See* BRUSHWOOD.

bushing, *n.* boaring (*contex.*), coak, bush, bouche, thimble.

bushy, *a.* **1.** bushlike, brushy, dumose (*R*), dumetose (*R*), scroggy (*chiefly Scot.*), bosky, busky, thick (*contex.*), shaggy; *spec.* shrubby, scrubby.

2. *See* ROUGH.

business, *n.* **1.** *See* TASK, WORK, RELATION, OFFICE, TRAFFIC, INDUSTRY, ERRAND, DUTY, CONCERN, AFFAIR.

2. occupation, employment, vocation, avocation (*common in good writers in this sense, but as so used avoided by many as unfortunately destroying the useful distinction between "vocation" and "avocation"*), pursuit, calling, profession (*chiefly spec.*), mystery (*A*), trade (*chiefly spec.*), faculty (*A or hist.*), shop (*chiefly in "to talk shop"; C*), craft (*chiefly spec.*), line (*C*); *spec.* cloth.

Antonyms: see DIVERSION.

business, *a.* commercial, industrial.

buskin, *n.* **1.** shoe (*contex.*), half-boot (*contex.*), cothurnus.

2. *See* TRAGEDY.

bustle, *v. i.* **1.** fluster, flutter, flurry, hustle (*C*), rustle (*C, U. S.*), clutter, stir.

Antonyms: see GLIDE, SIT, IDLE, DAWDLE.

2. *See* RUSTLE.

bustle, *n.* action (*contex.*), fluster, flurry, flutter, stir, ado, to-do, commotion, fuss, tumult, rustle (*C, U. S.*), hustle (*C*).

Antonyms: see LEISURE, DELIBERATION, IDLENESS.

bustling, *a.* rushing, hurried, busy, fussy *or* fussing, tumultuous, humming, rustling (*C, U. S.*), up-and-coming (*C*), live (*C*).

Antonyms: see LEISURELY, IDLE, DELIBERATE.

busybody, *n.* meddler, quidnunc (*B; contemptuous*), pry (*R*), Paul Pry (*fig.*), numquid (*R*), pragmatist (*R*), pragmatic (*R*); *spec.* snoop *or* snooper, butt-in (*C*); *see* GOSSIP.

but, *prep., adv., & conj.* **1.** *See* EXCEPT.

2. however, howbeit (*A*), yet, still, moreover, nevertheless, natheless *or* nathless (*A*), howsomever (*dial. or vulgar*), howsoever (*A*); notwithstanding (*emphatic*).

butcher, *v. t.* **1.** slaughter, kill.

2. *See* MURDER, SPOIL, BUNGLE, MANGLE.

butcherly, *a.* **1.** carnificial (*B or affected*).

2. See CRUEL.

butt, *n.* **1.** *See* STOCK, AIM, OBJECT.

2. laughing-stock, byword, make-game (*R*), target, sport, mockery, mock, laughter (*R*), joke.

3. push, bunt, thrust, buck (*C or dial.*).

butterless, *a.* dry (*toast*), unbuttered.

buttery, *a.* butterish (*R*), butyraceous (*tech.*), butyrous (*R and tech.*).

buttocks, *n.* rump (*esp. of animals*), posteriors (*pl.*), butt (*C, exc. spec.*), behind (*C*), fundament (*chiefly tech.*), nates (*pl.; tech.*), breech, bottom (*C*), seat, tail (*C*), fanny (*polite S*), stern (*C*), doup (*Scot.*), podex (*tech.*), back (*contex.*), arse (*British*), ass (*U. S., vulgar*); *spec.* cushions (*pl.*).

buttony, *a.* knoblike, bossy, buttonlike, umbonal (*tech.*), unbonate (*tech.*), umbonic (*R*).

buttress, *n.* support (*contex.*), brace (*contex.*); *spec.* flying-buttress, counterpart.

buttress, *v. t.* support, prop, brace;—*all three contex.*

buy, *v. t.* purchase (buy *is the simple term, and* purchase *the more pretentious word*), chap (*dial.*), coff (*A, Scot.*), take (*contex.; chiefly spec.*); *spec.* preëmpt, procure, get, ransom, repurchase, redeem, rebuy, discount; *see* BRIBE.

Antonyms: see SELL, HIRE, GRANT.

buy, *n.* purchase, cheap (*A*), bargain (*now spec.*), investment.

buying, *n.* purchase, emption (*chiefly law*); *spec.* preëmption, redemption, coemption.

Antonyms: see SALE.

by, *prep. & adv.* **1.** near, beside, besides (*less usual than "beside"*), to.

2. along, over, through, per (*Latin*); *spec.* past.

---

busky: *bushy.*
busy, *a.: active, occupied, meddlesome.*
busy, *v. t.: occupy.*
butcher, *n.: slaughter.*
butchery: *slaughter, slaughterhouse.*
butlery: *pantry.*
butt: *cask.*
buttery: *pantry.*
buttons: *servant, page, attendant.*
buxom: *plump.*
buzz, *v. i.: hum, ring.*
buzz, *n.: hum, humming.*
buzzard: *hawk.*

3. *See* AT, AFTER.
4. beside (*in comparison*).
5. per (*Latin*), with, of, forby (*A*); *spec.* thereby, therewith, thereof, hereby, herewith.
by-bidder, *n.* straw bidder, Peter Funk (*U. S.*).
bye, *n.* **1.** *See* ASIDE.
2. *In games: spec.* run, goal, hole.
bystander, *n. Spec.* spectator, witness, eyewitness, observer, onlooker.
byway, *n.* sideway (*R*); *spec.* bypath, byroad, sidepath, lane, cut-off, short-cut.
byword, *n.* **1.** *See* SAYING, TALK, NICKNAME.
2. proverb (*word of reproach*).

C

cabinet, *n.* **1.** room, closet; *spec.* boudoir, toilet: *implying a small and retired room.*
2. case, slip (*A*); *spec.* corner cupboard; *see* CHEST.
3. *See* COUNCIL.
cache, *v. t.* bury, hide, store, stow.
cackle, *v. i.* **1.** *Spec.* clack, check, gabble, gaggle, keckle, chuckle, giggle.
2. *See* LAUGH, BABBLE, CHATTER.
cacophonous, *a.* ill-sounding; *spec.* harsh, deafening, raucous. "*Cacophonous*" *is* (*R and B*).
cad, *n.* **1.** *see* ATTENDANT.
2. *In the sense of "a vulgar fellow":* cocktail (*S, R; English*), snob, bounder.
cadet, *n.* son (*contex.*), chevalier (*hist.*); *spec.* duniwassal (*Scot.*), West-pointer (*the official designation of a student at Annapolis is* midshipman).
cæsura, *n. In rhetoric:* break, pause, lengthening; *spec.* comma.
cage, *n.* aviary (*contex.*), enclosure; *spec.* mew.
cajole, *v.* flatter, palaver (*R; chiefly with "ever"*), wheedle, tweedle (*R*), carny *or* carney (*dial. or C, Eng.*), jolly (*C*), kid (*C*), string (*C*), coax, fool, persuade, blarney, cog (*A*), inveigle, blandish:—*all implying persuasion through flattery.*
Antonyms: see BULLY, INTIMIDATE, COMPEL.
cajolery, *n.* flattery, cajolement (*R*), wheedling, blandishment, palaver, jollying (*C*), kidding (*C*), blarney, line (*C; in the expression* "a good line").
Antonyms: see COMPULSION.
cake, *n.* mass (*contex.*); *spec.* brick, block, floe (*of ice*).
cake, *v. i.* bake, harden; *spec.* plaster, crust, encrust.

calamitous, *n.* distressing, troublesome, miserable, unhappy, disastrous, catastrophic, sad, tragic (*C*), dire, ruinous.
calamity, *n.* **1.** trouble, distress, misfortune, misery, unhappiness, affliction.
Antonyms: see HAPPINESS, PLEASURE.
2. *Referring to an instance of what is calamitous:* trouble, misfortune, misery, distress, disaster (*implying unforeseen and adverse forces*), catastrophe (*with implications of finality*), blow, scourge (*implies severe and continued calamity*), curse; *spec.* fatality.
Antonyms: see GOOD.
calculating, *a.* calculative, scheming, politic, designing, wily.
Antonyms: see ARTLESS.
calculous, *a.* gritty, stony.
calculus, *n.* concretion; *spec.* cystolith, dacryolith, gravel, sand, gastrolith, crab's-eye, stone, bezoar.
calendar, *n.* **1.** almanac, rubric (*R*), calends (*pl.; R*); *spec.* clog (*hist.*), fasti (*pl.*), menology, kalendar (*eccl. var.*).
2. list; *spec.* docket, program.
calender, *v. t.* press, iron, smooth;—*all contex.; spec.* water.
calf, *n.* **1.** bovine (*contex.*), offspring (*contex.*); *spec.* maverick (*U. S.*), dogie (*Western U. S.*), slink.
2. *See* CLOWN.
caliber, *n.* **1.** diameter, bore, size (*contex.*).
2. *See* ABILITY, IMPORTANCE, QUALITY.
calibrate, *v. t.* measure, graduate; *spec.* rectify.
call, *v. t.* **1.** *See* NAME, UTTER, SUMMON, CONVENE, PROCLAIM, HAIL, ELICIT, INVOKE, CONSIDER, ENCORE, EVOKE, CONVOKE, ROUSE, VISIT.
2. *In a legal sense:* summon (*as from a lower court*), evoke (*R*), evocate (*R*).
call, *v. i.* cry (*contex.*); *spec.* coo, hoot, shout, yell, toot, neigh, whisper, speak, cooee *or* cooey (*Australia*).
call, *n.* **1.** *Spec.* tally-ho, fanfare, ho, recheat (*A*), coo, coop, cooee *or* cooey (*Australia*), cluck, whistle, roll call, note, yell, shout, whisper, trumpet, taps, reveille, *etc.; see* HAIL, CRY.
2. *Spec.* summons, convocation, appeal, demand, duty, need, invitation, visit.
3. *Spec.* buzzer, bell, horn, annunciator.
callous, *a.* **1.** hard, hardened, indurated, toughened, horny;—*all contex.*
2. *See* INSENSIBLE.
callous, *v. t.* harden, indurate, toughen.

---

bygone: *past.*
bypath: *byway.*
byplay: *aside.*
by-product: *product.*
by-talk: *gossip.*

C

cabal, *v. i.: intrigue.*
cabal, *n.: intrigue, set.*
cabalist: *mystic.*
cable: *rope, conductor, message.*
cablegram: *message.*
caboose: *cookroom, car.*
cadaver: *body.*
cadaverous: *pale.*
cadence: *rhythm, fall, modulation.*
cadent: *rhythmical.*
Cæsar: *autocrat.*
cafe: *eating house, barroom.*
cage, *v. t.: confine.*
cairn: *heap.*
caisson: *box.*
caitiff, *a.: contemptible, mean.*
caitiff, *n.: wretch.*
calash: *hood.*
calculate: *compute, discover, think, expect, intend.*
calculate, *v. i.: rely.*
caliper, *v. t.: measure.*
calipers: *compasses.*
calisthenics: *gymnastics.*
called: *named.*
callow: *featherless, inexperienced, immature.*

---

calm, *a.* **1.** *In a physical sense:* undisturbed, tranquil, reposeful, smooth, serene, imperturbed (*R*), unperturbed (*R*), halcyon (*days, etc.; B or elevated*), still, quiet, placid, peaceful, pacific (*R, exc. in "Pacific Ocean"*), unruffled, motionless, calmy (*A and B*), untroubled:—*all imply absence of motion or agitation;* still *and* quiet *imply absence of sound as well.*

Antonyms: see BOISTEROUS, ROUGH, AGITATED, STORMY, CLAMOROUS.

2. *In a mental sense:* undisturbed, unruffled, quiet, tranquil (*implies natural and inherent calm*), phlegmatic (*implying lack of emotions*), sober, cool, philosophical, composed, reposeful, pacific (*R*), placid (*implying contentment*), impassive (*implying lack of feeling*), unpassionate, equanimous (*R*), marble (*fig.*), marbly (*fig.*), imperturbable (*suggests bravery and determination*), unperturbed, imperturbed, sedate (*suggests decorum*), serene (*more exalted than* tranquil), recollected (*R*), collected, untroubled, douce (*R*), reposeful, canny (*R*); *see* SELF-CONTROLLED, PEACEFUL, UNIMPASSIONED, UNEXCITABLE.

Antonyms: see UNEASY, AGITATED, EXCITED, RAGING, ECSTATIC, IRASCIBLE, ANXIOUS, CONFUSED, *etc.*

calm, *n.* **1.** *In a physical sense:* tranquillity, quiet, quietness, rest, smoothness, repose, serenity, serene (*R*), serenitude (*R*), calmness, stillness, placidity, peace, peacefulness; *spec.* doldrums (*pl.*).

Antonyms: see ACTIVITY, OUTCRY, NOISE, AGITATION, *etc.*

2. *In a mental sense:* composure, repose, equanimity (*formal*), temper (*chiefly in "to lose one's temper," "to keep one's temper," or the like*), tranquillity, quiet, calmness, serenity, serenitude (*R*), serene (*R*), impassiveness, sobriety, sedateness, soberness, placidity, reposedness (*R*), poise, quietude (*R*), quietism (*R*), imperturbation (*R*); *spec.* countenance, indisturbance (*R*); *see* SELF-CONTROL.

Antonyms: see ACTIVITY, AGITATION, COMMOTION, EXCITEMENT, ECSTASY, DISTURBANCE, *etc.*

calm, *v. t.* **1.** *See* STILL.

2. smooth, settle, still, soothe, sedate (*R*), quiet, tranquilize, compose, pacify (*R*), hush, serene (*R*), allay, ease (*mentally*), salve (*the conscience*); *spec.* disfever (*R*), becalm, lull (*by sounds, caresses, etc.*), lullaby; *see* COOL.

Antonyms: see ROUSE, ANNOY, AGITATE, EXCITE, ENLIVEN, DISTURB, IRRITATE.

calmative, *a.* calming, quieting, soothing, tranquilizing, *etc.*, quietive (*R*), sedative; *spec.* dulcet, balmy, lulling. *"Calmative" is less usual and more formal than "calming."*

Antonyms: see ANNOYING, AGITATING, DISTURBING, EXCITING, IRRITATING.

calming, *n.* subsidence.

camp, *n.* encampment, cantonment (*mil.*), leaguer (*R or hist.*), tent, shelter, shack, hut; *spec.* bivouac, roundabout (*R*), douar *or* dowar (*Oriental*), laager (*So. Africa*).

camp, *v. i.* encamp, locate (*contex.*), quarter, lodge (*contex.*); *spec.* bivouac, tent, laager (*So. Africa*), maroon (*So. U. S.*), outspan (*So. Africa*).

Antonyms: see DECAMP.

campaign, *v. i.* fight, serve; *spec.* crusade, electioneer, run.

campus, *n.* yard (*loc., Harvard College, Phillips Exeter Academy*).

can, *n.* **1.** jar, container, tin (*English*); *spec.* cup, glass.

2. *See* TOILET.

3. *See* PRISON.

4. *v. t. See* DISCHARGE.

cancel, *v. t.* **1.** deface (*contex.*), damask (*A or tech., Eng.*); *spec.* obliterate, blot, cross, overscore (*R*), erase, strike out; *see* DELETE.

2. *See* ABOLISH, REVOKE, COUNTERACT.

cancellate, *a.* reticular, reticulate, reticulated, cancellous;—*all tech. B.*

candidacy, *n.* candidateship, candidature.

candidate, *n. Spec.* (*eccl.*), confirmand, aspirant; probationer, licentiate, competent, contestant, nominee.

candidate, *v. i.* sit; *spec.* run.

candle, *n. Spec.* taper (*A*), planet (*cant*), paschal, bougie (*French*), cierge (*French*), dip, pastil.

candlestick, *n.* ceroferary (*R*), candelabrum (*antiq. or eccl.*), chandelier (*chiefly spec.*), candleholders; *spec.* sconce, tricerion, dicerion, paschal, standard, girondole, hearse (*eccl.*).

canine, *a.* doggy (*R; a weak term*), canicular (*R or phrasal*); *spec.* houndy, currish, houndish, doggish.

canine, *n.* **1.** *See* DOG.

2. tooth (*contex.*), cuspid, laniary (*R*).

cannibal, *a.* anthropophagous (*B*), anthropophagic (*R*), anthropophagian (*R; humorously stilted*), hominivorous (*R*); *spec.* ogreish, ogrish, Thyestean, (*fig.*), necrophagous.

cannibal, *n.* man-eater, anthropophagite (*R*), anthropophagist (*R*), anthropophagi (*pl.*); *spec.* ogre, ogress.

cannonade, *v. t.* cannon (*R*); *spec.* bomb, bombard, shell.

cannonading, *n.* cannonry; *spec.* bombarding, drumfire, shelling.

cannoneer, *n.* artilleryman, gunner; *spec.* mitrailleur (*French*).

cannonry, *n.* **1.** *See* CANNONADING.

2. artillery, guns (*pl.*), cannon (*a collective*).

canonize, *v. t.* saint, besaint (*contemptuous*).

canopy, *n.* cover (*contex.*); *spec.* tester, baldachino *or* baldaquin (*eccl.*), tilt, parasol, dome, heaven, hood, majesty (*hist.*), pavilion,

calumniate: *defame.*
calumny: *defamation.*
campaign, *n.: movement.*
campanular: *bell-shaped.*
canal: *channel.*
canard: *report.*
candid: *frank.*
canker, *v. t.: corrupt.*
cankerous: *ulcerous, consuming.*
canny: *shrewd, calm.*
canon: *valley.*
canon: *rule, standard.*
canonical: *orthodox.*

marquee, awning, cope, ciel (*French*), howdah, coverture (*R*).
cant, *n.* **1.** pretense, hypocrisy; *spec. and contemptuous* snivel, whine.
2. *See* JARGON.
cant, *v. i. Spec.* snivel, whine;—*both contemptuous.*
canter, *n.* tittup (*chiefly dial. or humorous*); *see* GAIT.
canter, *v. i.* go (*contex.*), drive (*contex.*), tittup (*chiefly dial. or humorous*).
canvas, *n.* **1.** fabric (*contex.*), cloth (*contex.*); *spec.* scrim, tarpaulin, poldavy, burlap, sacking.
2. *See* PAINTING, SAIL, TENT.
canvass, *v. t.* **1.** *See* EXAMINE, DISCUSS, PEDDLE.
2. solicit, campaign, electioneer.
canvass, *v. i.* solicit.
cap, *n.* **1.** hat (*contex.*), skullcap; *spec.* glengarry, fool's-cap, chaco, coif, busby, caul (*hist.*), coxcomb, biretta (*principally eccl.*) *or* beret *or* berret, biggin (*Scot.*), calotte, calpac (*Turkish*), tam-o'-shanter, tuque, fez, pileus (*antiq.*), tarboosh, kepi, mortarboard, zucchetto (*Italian*), Phrygian cap (*the cap of liberty*).
2. *See* TOP.
capable, *a.* **1.** *See* ABLE.
2. susceptible, admitting.
capacity, *n.* **1.** *See* ABILITY, QUALIFICATION—*with reference to natural ability.*
2. *Referring to capacity to bear or hold:* content, retention (*R*), space, room, burden (*naut.*), size.
caparison, *v. t.* trap, accouter (*contex.*), equip.
caparisoned, *a.* barbed *or* barded (*said of a horse*).
cape, *n. Spec.* pelerine, bertha, vandyke, talma, tippet, capa (*Italian*), fichu (*French*).
caper, *n.* **1.** jump (*contex.*), leap (*contex.*), prance, skip, spring, gambol, capriccio (*Italian*), caracole, gambade *or* gambado, hop, romp, frisk.
2. play, jump, antic, jape, prank, dido (*S or C, U. S.*), conceit, trick, escapade; *see* FROLIC.
caper, *v. i.* **1.** jump (*contex.*), leap (*contex.*), gambol, frisk, prance (*C*), gambado (*B*), prank (*R*), skip, skit (*R*), caracol; *see* FROLIC.
2. *See* PRANCE.
capital, *a.* **1.** metropolitan.
2. *See* FATAL, CHIEF, IMPORTANT, FINE.
3. *Referring to letters:* majuscule, large *or* great (*chiefly spec.*); *spec.* initial.
capital, *n.* **1.** metropolis, seat.
2. *Spec.* stock, principal.
capitol, *n.* statehouse (*loc. U. S.*).
caprice, *n.* **1.** whim, freak (*implying sudden, causeless change or turn of mind*), notion, idea, conceit (*farfetched or affected conception*), fantasy, phantasy, fancy, humor, quip, quirk, vagary, crotchet, fantasticality (*R*), whimsicality (*R*), whimsy, crank, turn, maggot (*now R*), kink, frisk (*R*).
Antonyms: see OPINION, CONVICTION.
2. *See* CAPRICIOUSNESS.
capricious, *a.* whimsical, freakish, freaky, humorsome, fanciful, fantastical, fickle, feminine, inconstant, fitful, crotchety, variable, arbitrary, changeable, erratic, fantastic, fantasted (*R*), whimsy (*R*), whimmy (*C*), vagarious (*R*), wayward, unsteady, notional, puckish (*fig. or spec.*), moony (*C*).
Antonyms: see CONSTANT.
capriciousness, *n.* caprice, fantasticality, fantasy, phantasy, fantasticalness, whimsicality, whimsicalness, humor, notionality.
Antonyms: see CONSTANCY.
captain, *n.* **1.** *See* CHIEF, COMMANDER.
2. *In nautical usage:* master, commander (*often spec.*), skipper (*chiefly spec.*); *spec.* nakhoda (*East Indian*), reis *or* rais (*Arabic*), ressaldar (*India*), rittmaster (*R*), patron (*R*), patroon (*R*), serang (*Anglo-Indian*), coaster.
captious, *a.* **1.** catchy (*C*), tricky, entangling, sophistic, fallacious.
2. *See* CAVILING, FAULTFINDING.
captivate, *v. t.* captive (*A*), enthrall, enslave, fascinate, charm, enchant, bewitch, hold spellbound:—*all implying an overpowering of the mind or will with that which attracts, pleases, or allures.* Enthrall *and* enslave *allude to the helplessness of a slave,* enslave *more consciously than* enthrall; *the other words allude especially to the effect of enchantment;* fascinate *may imply the overpowering effect of terror, horror, or the like;* catch (*C*), *spec.* sirenize (*R*); *see* PLEASE.
Antonyms: see REPEL.
captivated, *a.* infatuated, fascinated, charmed, *etc.*, captive.
captivating, *a.* pleasant (*contex.*), infatuating, enchanting, charming, bewitching, witching, glamorous;—*all implying conquest through pleasing the senses.*
Antonyms: see REPELLENT.
captivation, *n.* **1.** captivity (*R or A*), enthrallment, enslavement, fascination, charm, glamour, enchantment, witchery, bewitchment, bewitching, servitude.
2. *See* SLAVERY.
capture, *v. t.* **1.** seize (*implying power or authority*), take, get (*chiefly C or contex.*), apprehend (*B*), captivate (*A*), captive (*A*), catch;

---

cant, *v. i.: snivel, whine.*
cant, *n.: slope, bevel, inclination.*
cant, *v. t.: incline.*
cant, *v. i.: slope.*
cantankerous: *ill-tempered, perverse.*
cantilever: *bracket.*
cantle: *piece, slice.*
canton, *v. t.: divide.*
canton, *n.: district.*
cantonment, *n.: camp, quarters.*
canvasser: *solicitor.*
cap, *v. t.: cover, overlie, crown, surpass, top.*
capability: *ability.*
capacious: *roomy.*
caparison: *trapping.*
cape: *headland.*
capillary: *filamentous.*
capital, *n.: top.*
capitalist: *financier.*
capitulate: *surrender.*
capitulation: *surrender, summary.*
capsize, *v.: overturn.*
captive, *n.: prisoner.*
captivity: *confinement, captivation.*
captor: *capturer.*

spec. grab (*C*), nab, arrest, collar (*C*), prize, reduce (*a place*), recapture, retake, incaptivate (*R*), jump (*checkers*), castle (*chess*), bag (*hunting*).

Antonyms: see FREE.

2. take (*as a fort*); *spec.* rush, force.

Antonyms: see SURRENDER.

capture, *n.* **1.** seizure, taking, catching, apprehension (*B*); *spec.* arrest, reduction, prize.

Antonyms: see FREEING.

2. *In a concrete sense:* prize, bag, haul.

capturer, *n.* captor, taker, apprehender (*B*), *etc.*

car, *n.* **1.** automobile, motor; *see* VEHICLE.

2. *Referring to railroad cars: spec.* carriage, Pullman, trolley, tram (*Eng.*), tramcar (*Eng.*), smoker (*U. S.*), empty, gondola, box, van (*Eng.*), sleeper, coach, flat, goods wagon (*Eng.*), caboose, cab.

3. *Referring to a balloon: spec.* nacelle, basket, gondola.

4. *In an elevator: spec.* cage.

caravan, *n.* **1.** company (*contex.*), cafila *or* kafila (*Oriental*).

2. *See* VAN.

carbonaceous, *a. Spec.* coaly, charry, plumbaginous.

carbonize, *v. t.* burn (*contex.*); *spec.* char, coke.

card, *n.* **1.** *Spec.* ticket, carte-de-visite (*French*), carte, rose, pass.

2. *Referring to playing cards:* pasteboard (*C or cant*), Devil's picture books (*A or R; pl.*); *spec.* court card, discard, tarot (*French*).

3. wisecracker (*C*), jokes, josher (*C*).

care, *n.* **1.** cark (*A*), concern (*implies anxiety arising from interest or regard*), concernment (*a stronger term than concern*), carefulness, reck (*B*), distress (*implies unhappiness of mind*); *see* TROUBLE, ANXIETY (*implying uneasiness*).

Antonyms: see CARELESSNESS, HAPPINESS.

2. charge, guardianship, ward (*B or formal*), custody, keep, keeping, safekeeping, protection, trust (*R*), guardship (*R*); *spec.* commendam; *see* OVERSIGHT.

3. heed, thought, heedfulness, vigilance, attention, caution, gingerliness, concern, consideration, precaution, guardedness, wariness, regard, reck (*B*), particularity, niceness, notice, pains (*pl.*), painstaking; *see* PRUDENCE.

Antonyms: see CARELESSNESS, NEGLIGENCE, IMPRUDENCE, RECKLESSNESS, RASHNESS.

4. *Referring to that which causes care:* responsibility, anxiety, concern; *see* TROUBLE.

care, *v. i.* **1.** *In the sense of "to concern oneself":* cark (*A*), reck (*B*).

2. heed, notice, consider, think (*contex*); *see* ATTEND.

careful, *a.* **1.** carking (*A*), solicitous, solicitudinous (*R*), concerned; *spec.* meticulous; *see* ANXIOUS, TROUBLED. *"Careful" is now A in this sense.*

2. heedful, attentive, considerate, conscientious, regardful, mindful, respective (*R*), thoughtful, close (*chiefly spec.*), nice, diligent, painstaking, painful, curious (*A*), near (*chiefly spec.*), searching, particular, precise.

Antonyms: see NEGLECTFUL, UNOBSERVANT.

3. cautious, precautious (*R*), cautelous (*A*), prudent, circumspect, gingerly, leery (*S*), vigilant, watchful, wary, chary (*chiefly spec.*), guarded, safe, shy, guardful (*R*), canny (*Scot.; A*), circumspective (*R*); *spec.* noncommittal.

Antonyms: see CARELESS, IMPRUDENT, NEGLIGENT, UNRESTRAINED, RECKLESS, RASH, VENTURESOME.

careless, *a.* **1.** unanxious, unconcerned, untroubled, unapprehensive, free, blithe *or* blithesome (*nearly equal to "happy" in sense; B*), easy (*R*), secure (*B*), cavalier, supine (*chiefly spec.*), inconsiderate (*implying selfishness or indifference*), incurious (*A*), worriless (*R*), poco-curante (*Italian*) insouciant (*French*), nonchalant (*implying indifference*); *see* IMPRUDENT, INDIFFERENT—*implying freedom of care or anxiety.*

Antonyms: see ANXIOUS.

2. heedless, inattentive, inconsiderate, disregardful, harebrained, regardless, thoughtless, unthinking, unmindful, improvident (*chiefly spec.*), imprudent (*implying rashness or thoughtlessness*); neglectful, negligent, uncareful (*R*), mindless, incogitant (*R*), unheedful, unwary, slovenly, unguarded, cursory, casual, unheedy (*R*), incurious (*A*), unobservant, inobservant, incautious, uncareful (*R*), unattentive (*R*); *spec.* offhand, rash, slack; *see* RECKLESS:—*implying neglect or disregard.*

Antonyms: see WATCHFUL, CAREFUL, CONSCIENTIOUS, PRUDENT, VIGILANT.

carelessness, *n.* unconcern, ease, security, nonchalance, *etc. Cf.* CARELESS.

Antonyms: see CARE, CONSIDERATION.

caress, *v. t.* fondle, cherish (*A*), daut (*Scot.*), coddle (*chiefly with a suggestion of excess*), coax (*A*), pet; *spec.* touch, stroke, lap, pat, kiss, bill, hug, dandle, dander (*dial. Eng.*), cuddle, overfondle, pet (*C*), neck (*S*); *see* KISS.

Antonyms: see BEAT, ABUSE, ILL-TREAT.

caress, *n.* fondle (*R*); *spec.* touch, stroke, pat, kiss, hug, dandle.

Antonyms: see BLOW.

caressing, *n.* fondling, dalliance (*B*), cherishment (*R*), cherishing (*R*), petting (*C*), necking (*S*).

caricature, *n.* **1.** *See* BURLESQUE.

2. misrepresentation (*contex.*), misdescription (*chiefly spec.*), burlesque, travesty, parody; *spec.* cartoon:—caricature *deals with line,* parody *follows a known form;* burlesque *treats a serious subject frivolously, the* mock-heroic *treats a low or comic subject seriously.*

caracole: *turn, caper.*
carcass: *body.*
cardboard: *pasteboard.*
cardiac: *stimulating.*
cardinal, *a.: chief.*
cardinal, *n.: prince.*
careen: *incline.*
career, *n.: race, course.*
career, *v. i.: rush.*
careworn: *weary.*
cargo: *load.*
caricature, *v. t.: burlesque.*

carnival, *n.* merrymaking, festival, revelry; *spec.* Mardigras:—*strictly speaking Shrove Tuesday or the period concluded with that day, but now used of any time of organized, deliberate, and excessive merrymaking.*

carnivorous, *a.* flesh-eating, sarcophagous (*R*), zoöphagous (*R*); *spec.* equivorous (*R*), ichthyophagous, omophagous, necrophagous, predaceous, cannibal.

carol, *n.* song, lay; *spec.* noël.

carom, *n.* shot (*contex.*), canon (*chiefly Eng.*), carambole (*R*).

carom, *v. i.* rebound, cannon (*chiefly Eng.*); *spec.* glance.

carom, *v. t. Spec.* bank.

carouse, *n.* carousal, orgy, debauch (*both intensitive*), jamboree (*C, U. S.*), spree (*C*), bat (*S*), bout, buster *or* bust (*C*), binge (*C*), wassail (*A*), fuddle (*C*), rouse (*A*), toot (*C*), bouse, boose or booze (*S, U. S.*), soak (*C*), tear (*C, U. S.*), saturnalia (*pl.: sometimes used as a singular*), bacchanalia (*pl.*).

carouse, *v. i.* rant (*R*), debauch, bum (*vulgar S*), drink (*contex.*), spree (*C*), bouse (*R*), *or* boose *or* (*C*), booze.

carriage, *n.* **1.** *See* TRANSPORTATION, BEHAVIOR, VEHICLE.

2. bearing, mien, air, poise, port, portance (*A*), behavior, conduct, demeanor, presence, front, gest (*A*), personage; *spec.* gait, walk, run, step, tournure (*French*), elevation, lift.

carriage house, remise (*R*), hangar (*French; chiefly spec.*), coach house, garage.

carrion, *n.* flesh (*contex.*); *see* OFFAL.

carry, *v. t.* **1.** *See* TRANSPORT, EXTEND, PROLONG, SUPPORT, BEHAVE, CONDUCT, AFFORD.

2. *Referring to news, messages, information, etc.:* communicate, transmit, bear, take, bring, convey.

3. hold (*as the head, oneself, etc.*), bear (*oneself*); *spec.* port (*mil.*).

4. keep (*as in stock*), hold, have.

carry, *v. i. Referring to a gun, etc.:* reach, shoot.

carry, *n. Spec.* portage.

cartilaginous, *a.* gristly, chondric (*R*).

carve, *v. i.* **1.** *See* CUT, CHISEL, ENGRAVE, SCULPTURE.

2. *Referring to carving at the table:* cut, serve, slice; *spec.* (*all A or R*), mince, lift, flush, display, disfigure, unjoint.

case, *n.* **1.** *Spec.* (*in grammar*) genitive, accusative, nominative, dative, ablative, objective, vocative, locative, subjective, oblique.

2. *See* EXAMPLE, STATE, PATIENT, ACTION, CHARACTER.

case, *n.* **1.** receptacle (*contex.*), holder (*contex.*), container (*contex.; cant*), casing; *spec.* box, chest, cabinet, drawer, bag, valise, sheath, scabbard, cartouche, carton, canister, shell, cellaret, burse, chasse (*French*), shrine pyx, étui (*French*), quiver, holster, housewife, hackle, hutch, coffer, coffin, crate, cartridge, portfolio; *see* CABINET, CASKET.

2. covering, cover; *spec.* sheath, skin, hull, cocoon, shell, carpet, carapace, *etc.*

case, *v. t.* cover (*contex.*), incase, pack; *spec.* bag, sheathe, crate; *see* BOX.

cash, *n.* money, currency, specie, ready-money, *spec.* coin, chink (*S*), brass (*S*), kale (*S*), dough (*S*), mazuma (*S*), jack (*S*), beans (*S*), shekels (*humorous*), spondulicks (*S*), simoleons (*S*), silver, gold, rowdy (*S*), dust (*S*), paper.

cash, *v. t.* encash (*R*); *spec.* realize.

cask, *n.* receptacle (*contex.*), barrel, container (*contex.; cant*), stand (*chiefly A and spec.*) *spec.* cade, caroteel, butt, keg, tierce, hogshead, firkin, castrel, puncheon, pipe, tun, kilderkin.

casket, *n.* receptacle (*contex.*), box (*contex.*), case, pyx *or* pyxis (*R or spec.*); *spec.* reliquary, shrine, coffin:—casket *is a commercial elegance for* coffin, *the more dignified and simple term.*

cast, *v. t.* **1.** *See* THROW, PROJECT, VOMIT, OVERTURN, ABORT, REJECT, REMOVE, SHED, PUT, ADD, APPOINT, PREDICT.

2. run, found; *spec.* recast.

castellan, *n.* governor (*contex.*), keeper (*contex.*), chastelain *or* chatelain, chatelaine (*fem.*).

caster, *n.* **1.** roller (*contex.*), trundle, truckle (*R*), wheel (*contex.*).

2. *See* BOTTLE.

casting, *n.* foundling, cast; *spec.* run, molding.

castrate, *v. t.* geld (*chiefly tech. referring to the male*); *spec.* cut, spay (*the female*), emasculate (*chiefly fig.*), evirate (*referring to the male; R*), steer (*a male calf; R*), unman (*a man*), capon *or* caponize (*a cock*), eunuchize (*R*), twitch (*a beast*).

castrated, *a.* gelt, gelded.

casually, *adv.* happy-go-lucky, haphazard, hitty-missy (*R or dial*).

casualty, *n.* **1.** *See* CHANCE, ACCIDENT.

2. *In pl.;* injured, wounded, hurt, losses (*military*).

cat, *n.* feline (*tech. or B*), Baudrons (*Scottish*), Felix (*both proper names, like "Reynard" for the fox*), puss (*chiefly a call name*), pussy (*chiefly a pet name*), miauler (*fanciful*), grimalkin (*chiefly spec.*), gib (*familiar; chiefly spec.*); *spec.* mouser, rumpy (*C*), tortoiseshell, tomcat (*male*), tommy (*male; C*), tom, tabby, kit, kitten, bobcat, kitty (*a pet name*), kitling (*dial.*), catling, maltese, Angora.

catalogue, *n.* Catalogue *suggests a full list in a*

---

carnage: *slaughter.*
carnal: *bodily, worldly, sensual.*
carol, *v.: sing.*
carousal: *carouse, tournament.*
carp, *v. i.: cavil.*
carping, *a.: faultfinding.*
carton: *pasteboard, box, bull's eye, shot.*
cartoon, *n.: design, caricature.*
cartoon, *v. t.: burlesque.*
cartouche: *box, tablet, scroll.*
carving: *engraving, sculpture.*
cascade: *waterfall.*
casement: *sash, window.*
cashier, *v. t.: discharge.*
casing: *cover, case, covering.*
cast, *n.: exuvium.*
castaway: *abandoned.*
castigate: *punish, reprove.*
castigatory: *punitive.*
casuistry: *prevarication.*
cataclysm: *catastrophe, upheaval.*

---

formal arrangement; list *suggests shortness and informality;* record *suggests something of an official or formal nature;* register *suggests a lesser degree of classification than does* index, which *implies reference to other material;* schedule *suggests a formal list or table; spec.* didascaly, sanctilogy, beadroll (*A or B*).
catalogue, *v. t. Spec.* list, index, record.
catastrophe, *n.* **1.** cataclysm, convulsion; *spec.* debacle, débâcle (*French*), upheaval, paroxysm.
2. ending, dénoûment (*French*).
Antonyms: see BEGINNING.
3. *See* CALAMITY.
catastrophe, *a.* **1.** convulsionary, cataclysmal, cataclysmic, paroxysmal (*R*).
2. *See* CALAMITOUS.
catch, *v. t.* **1.** take, seize, nab (*S or C*); *spec.* nick (*S*), entoil (*A*), land, net, mesh, dredge, lime, gill, ginnle, hook, illaqueate (*R*), grin (*A*), noose, guddle, entangle, enmesh, snap, snare *or* (*emphatic*) ensnare, trawl, trap *or* (*emphatic*) entrap, drag; *see* SEIZE, CAPTURE, TRAP.
Antonyms: see FREE, THROW.
2. attract (*the attention, fancy, etc.*), engage, take, arrest, gain, smite (*rhetorical*), hit (*C*); *see* CAPTIVATE.
3. *Referring to a cold, disease, etc.:* contract, take, get.
4. *Referring to chastisement, reproof, etc.:* receive, get.
5. get (*as a train*), make, nick (*S, Eng.*).
6. trip (*in a fault*), nick (*S, Eng.*), detect (*implies serious effort*).
7. *See* OVERTAKE, DISCOVER, RECEIVE, FASTEN, UNDERSTAND, PERCEIVE, HEAR, PHOTOGRAPH.
catch, *v. i.* **1.** seize, hold; *spec.* hitch.
2. *See* KINDLE, GASP.
catch, *n.* **1.** seize, seizure, hold; *spec.* grasp, grab, snatch, *etc.*
Antonyms: see MISS.
2. *Spec.* trigger, trap, detent, click, dog, latch, barb, buckle, snap, fence, pallet, pawl.
3. *Thing or amount caught: spec.* take, net, fare, trip, trap, draft, haul, shot, field, fly.
4. *See* ROUND.
catching, *a.* inoculable (*R*), contagious, communicable, taking (*chiefly U. S.*), infectious; *spec.* pestilential, pestiferous, noxious.
cathartic, *a.* laxative, physic, purgative, purging, aperient, evacuatory, eccoproctic (*mild; R*), eccritic (*R*), deobstruent (*tech.*), alviducous (*R*), deoppilent (*R or A*), lapactic (*R*).
Antonyms: see CONSTIPATING.
cathartic, *n.* laxative, physic, purgative, purge, aperient, dejector (*R*), eccoproctic (*R*), evacuant, pill (*contex.*).
cathedra, *n.* seat, chair, throne, see (*A*).
cathedral, *n.* duomo (*Italian*); *spec.* secondary.
catholic, *a.* **1.** *See* GENERAL, LIBERAL.
2. (*cap.*) *Short for "Roman Catholic":* Roman, Romanish (*chiefly in derogation*);—Popish, papistical, papish (*used only in derogation*).
Catholicize, *v. t. Romanize.*
cattle, *a.* **1.** *In a general sense: see* STOCK.
2. *Referring to bovines:* beeves (*pl.*), cows (*pl.*), neat (*A; a collective*); *spec.* (*pl.*) red-polls, shorthorns, Lancashires, Jerseys, Holsteins, *etc.*
causable, *a.* inducible, producible.
causal, *a.* **1.** *Spec.* creational.
2. *See* CAUSATIVE.
causative, *a.* inductive, inducive (*R*), productive, causal (*R*), creative (*chiefly spec.*), generative.
cause, *v. t.* produce, effect, effectuate (*R*), gar (*Scot.*), make, have, do (*A*), germinate (*fig. or spec.*), keep (*R; equiv. to "keep up"*), inchoate (*R*), provoke, originate, let (*A or phrasal*), create, generate, occasion, breed, bring, raise, work; *spec.* necessitate, bear, will, induce superinduce; *see* EXCITE, FORM.
Antonyms: see PREVENT.
cause, *n.* **1.** principle (*tech. or B*), origin, producer (*R*), wherefore (*C*), inducement, occasion; *see* MOTIVE, REASON.
Antonyms: see RESULT.
2. *See* ACTION, SIDE.
caustic, *a.* **1.** burning, escharotic (*tech.*), corrosive; *spec.* catheretic.
2. *In mathematics: spec.* catacaustic, diacaustic.
3. *See* ACRID, ACRIMONIOUS.
caustic, *n.* **1.** escharotic (*tech.*), cauter, cautery; *spec.* catheretic, moxa.
2. *Spec.* catacaustic, diacaustic.
cavalry, *n.* soldiery (*contex.*), horse; *spec.* uhlan, rangers; *in the British Army:* Yeomanry, Life Guards, Horse Guards, Dragoon Guards, Dragoons, Hussars, Lancers.
cavalryman, *n.* soldier (*contex.*), knight, horseman, troop, plunger (*mil. R*); *spec.* horse guard, heavy, roughrider, ranger, reiter (*hist.*), dragoon lancer, silladar (*Anglo-Indian*), cuirassier, hussar, matross (*hist., U. S.*), cossack.
cave, *n.* recess, cavern, den (*chiefly spec.*), hole; *spec.* grotto, grot (*B*), lair, nymphæum, Lupercal (*R; A*).
cave-dweller, *n.* caveman, troglodyte (*tech.*).
cave-dwelling, *a.* cavernicolous (*R*), troglodyte (*tech.*), speluncous (*R*).
cavil, *n.* criticism (*contex.*), carping; *spec.* wrangle.
cavil, *v. i.* except (*contex.*), carp, nibble, haggle (*chiefly spec.*), higgle (*chiefly spec.*), stickle; *spec.* quarrel, wrangle.
caviling, *a.* critical (*contex.*), captious, hairsplitting, carping, exceptive (*R*), exceptious (*R*); *spec.* hypercritical.
cavity, *n.* hole, hollow; *spec.* hold (*of a ship*),

cataract: *waterfall, deluge.*
catchy: *attractive, deceptive.*
catechize, *v. t.: teach, question.*
categorical: *dogmatic.*
cater: *provide.*
causeless: *groundless.*
caution, *n.: warning, care.*
caution, *v. t.: warn.*
cautionary: *warning.*
cautious: *careful.*
cavalier, *n.: horseman, knight, gentleman, escort, lover.*
cavalier, *a.: careless, proud.*
cavalierly: *proud.*
cave-in: *collapse.*
cavern: *cave.*

sinus (*tech.*), opening, ventriculus, vacuole, well, diverticulum (*tech.*), pocket, fossa *or* fosse, pit, basin, depression, fossette, druse, lacuna (*tech.*), crypt, cistern, cell, cellar, excavation, atrium, cup; *see* CHAMBER.

Antonyms: see PROJECTION, PROTUBERANCE.

ceiling, *n.* ceil (*R and B*), roof, plafond (*French*); *spec.* cupola.

celebrate, *v. t.* **1.** *See* OBSERVE, PRAISE.

2. proclaim (*implies solemnity and formality*), emblazon, emblaze (*both imply outward manifestation, R*), commemorate (*implies calling to mind*), sing, sound, resound, extol, laud, trumpet, royalize (*R*), renown (*R*); *spec.* historicize, fame (*R*), sonnet (*R*), hymn, concelebrate (*R*), tune, lionize, rime *or* rhyme, berime *or* berhyme (*emphatic; often contemptuous*).

Antonyms: see DEPRECIATE.

celebrate, *v. i.* jubilate, jubilize (*R*), rejoice; *spec.* triumph.

celebration, *n.* **1.** *See* OBSERVANCE (*implies religious or civil ceremonial*), PRAISE, COMMUNION.

2. proclamation, emblazonment, commemoration, laudation, *etc. Cf.* CELEBRATE, *v. t.*

3. *Spec.* festivity, festival, feast, fête (*less solemn or serious than feast*), triumph, ovation, Eucæmia (*Oxford Univ.*), anniversary, biennial, triennial, nativity (*eccl.*), birthday, jubilee, centenary, bicentenary, tercentenary, *etc.*, millennium.

celebrity, *n.* **1.** *See* FAME.

2. notable, name, hero, light, luminary, lion, lioness, star, ace, tycoon (*B, S*), bigwig (*B*), big gun (*S*), big shot (*S*), magnate.

celibacy, *n.* singleness, celibate (*A*), maidenhood, purity, chastity; *spec.* virginity.

celibate, *a.* single, unmarried; *spec.* virgin, chaste.

celibate, *n. Spec.* bachelor, maid *or* maiden (*A or legal, exc. as of women*), spinster, old maid (*fem.; C or contemptuous*), bachelor-girl, virgin, monk, nun, friar, sister, hermit, anchorite, vestal, Diana (*B, fig.*).

Antonyms: see BENEDICT, HUSBAND, WIFE.

cell, *n.* **1.** *Spec.* utricle, vacuole, theca, spore, amœba, corpuscle, plastid, locule, loculus, loculament, locellus, eye, cellule, hæmatid, hæmad, macrocyte.

2. room (*contex.*); *spec.* serdab, vault, reclusory (*R*), concameration (*R*), box (*S*).

3. *See* COMPARTMENT.

celled, *a.* cellate, cellated, cellulate;—*all these tech.*

cell-like, *a.* cytoid (*tech.*).

cellular, *a.* cell-like; *spec.* loculose (*tech.*), loculamentose (*tech.; R*), loculamentous (*tech.; R*), favose (*tech.*), comby (*R*), honey-combed, porous, faveolate (*tech.*).

cement, *n. Spec.* glue, lute, lime, putty, tar, gum, mortar, paste, solder, adhesive. "*Cement*" *is chiefly spec.*

cement, *v. t.* conglutinate (*R*), glue (*primarily spec.*), stick, fasten; *spec.* solder, lime, paste, gum, ferruminate (*A*), mortar, belute (*R*), lute, putty, grout, plaster.

Antonyms: see BREAK.

cemetery, *n.* burial place, graveyard, golgotha (*B*), necropolis (*rhetorical*); *spec.* polyandrium, catacomb, churchyard (*A or hist.*), campo santo (*Italian*).

censer, *n.* thurible, incensory; *spec.* cassolette.

censorius, *a.* critical (*contex.*), culpatory (*R*), condemnatory, reprobative, disapprobatory (*R*), reprehensive, reprehensing (*R*), reprehensory (*R*); *spec.* vitriolic, cynic; *see* FAULT-FINDING.

Antonyms: see APPROVING, PRAISING.

censure, *n.* **1.** blame, condemnation, reproach (*R*), reprehension, reprobation (*R*), objurgation (*R*), reproof, hit (*C*), knock (*S*), criticism, stricture, nip, animadversion (*B*); *spec.* attack, diatribe, backbite, dyslogy (*a nonce word*); *see* BLAME, BLAMING, REPROOF.

Antonyms: see APPLAUSE, APPROVAL, PRAISE, COMPLIMENT.

2. *Referring to direct criticism of a person: see* REPROOF.

censure, *v. t.* **1.** condemn (*implies passing judgment formally or strongly*), reproach, reprehend, reprobate (*intensitive*), reprove (*R*), hit (*C*), knock (*S*), tax (*R*), fault (*R*), slam (*S*), scarify (*fig.*), perstringe (*R*), criticize; *spec.* backbite, attack; *see* BLAME.

Antonyms: see APPLAUD, APPROVE, PRAISE, COMPLIMENT.

2. *Referring to direct censure of a person: see* REPROVE.

census, *n.* lustrum (*Roman A; R*).

cent, *n.* copper (*C*), penny (*a loose usage*).

centenary, *a.* secular; *spec.* centennial, hundredal (*R*).

center, *n.* **1.** *In a physical sense:* middle, midst, centrum, focus, core, navel, omphalos (*R; both fig. or special*), hub (*fig.*), marrow, pith, pole, axis, radiant, metropolis, capital, coom (*Scot.*), bull's-eye.

Antonyms: see CIRCUMFERENCE, EDGE, VERGE, RIM.

2. *In a nonphysical sense:* focus, hub, heart, core, navel, pivot, hinge, kernel, pith, marrow, nucleus, pole, axis.

center, *v. t.* **1.** centralize, concenter (*R or spec.*); *spec.* focus.

2. *See* UNITE.

central, *a.* middle, median, medial, mid; *spec.* focal, nuclear, pivotal, umbilical, metropolitan, chief, leading.

century, *n.* **1.** centennium (*R*), centenary (*R*).

---

cease: *stop.*
ceaseless: *constant, endless.*
cede, *v. t.: relinquish, transfer.*
celebrated: *famous.*
celerity: *rapidity.*
celestial, *a.: heavenly, divine, Chinese.*
censurable: *blamable, reprehensible.*

---

2. *See* HUNDRED.

ceramics, *n.* pottery, earthenware, china, tiles (*pl.*), tiling.

cereal, *n.* **1.** *Referring to the plant:* grain, corn (*chiefly spec., the particular sense varying with the locality*); *spec.* oat, pea, bean, breakfast food (*U. S.*).

2. *See* GRAIN.

cerebrate, *v. i.* mentalize (*R*); *C for* think.

cerebration, *n.* mentalism, mentation; *C for* thought.

ceremony, *n.* **1.** *Referring to the action or procedure:* performance, observance, rite, service (*C*), function (*chiefly spec.*), office, practise; *spec.* sacrament, mummery (*contemptuous*), ordinance (*eccl.*).

2. *Referring to the form: see* FORM.

certain, *a.* **1.** *See* FIXED, DEFINITE, UNAVOIDABLE, UNQUESTIONABLE, CONFIDENT.

2. *In a sense implying unfailing correctness:* sure, assured (*R*), infallible.

Antonyms: see UNCERTAIN, DOUBTFUL, HESITATING.

3. *With "to" and the infinitive:* sure, bound, destined.

certainty, *n.* **1.** certitude (*B*); *spec.* fixity, definiteness (*implies certainty as to detail*), unquestionableness, *etc.*

2. *In a sense implying unfailing correctness:* sureness, assurance (*R*), surety (*implies somewhat greater formality and security than does* sureness), certitude; *spec.* infallibility.

Antonyms: see UNCERTAINTY, DOUBT.

3. *Meaning a thing that is unquestionable or inevitable:* surety, cinch (*S*). *"Sure thing" is chiefly S.*

Antonyms: see CHANCE.

certificate, *n.* declaration, warrant, voucher, testimonial;—*all implying a written certification of the matter in question. Spec.* policy, script, debenture.

chafed, *a.* rubbed, galled, fretted, eaten, foxed (*dial.*), worn; vexed, galled, annoyed, irritated; warmed.

chaffy, *a.* paleaceous, paleate;—*both tech.*

chain, *n.* **1.** catena (*R or tech.*), bonds (*pl.*), fetters; *fig.* bondage; *spec.* painter, fob.

2. *See* ROW, STRING, SERIES, MOUNTAIN.

chair, *n.* **1.** *Spec.* tumbrel, rocker, roundabout (*U. S.*), throne, Cromwell chair, curule chair, faldstool, seat, stool, exedra; *see* CATHEDRA.

2. fellowship, professorship.

chairman, *n.* president, presider; *spec.* toastmaster, moderator, speaker, prolocutor, croupier.

chalky, *a.* cretaceous (*B or tech.*), cretous (*R*), whitish.

challenge, *v. t.* **1.** dare, defy, stump (*C, U. S.*), deraign (*hist. or A*), brave (*R*), charge, denounce.

2. *See* QUESTION.

challenge, *n.* **1.** dare, defy (*C*), defiance, stump (*C, U. S.*).

2. *See* OBJECTION.

chamber, *n.* **1.** *See* ROOM, BEDROOM, COMPARTMENT, ASSEMBLY.

2. *Referring to a room for official business or public assembly:* camera (*R, tech., or spec.*); *spec.* bourse, exchange, curia, hall.

3. cavity, camera (*R or tech.*); *spec.* coffer, cofferdam, kistvaen, casemate, lock, vault, cist, cell, cubicle, closet, appartment; *see* GRAVE.

chambered, *a.* concamerated, camerate; *spec.* septate, locular;—*all tech., exc. chambered.*

chambermaid, *n.* femme de chambre (*French*), biddy (*C*), abigal (*fig.*).

champagne, *n.* simkin (*Anglo-Indian*).

champion, *n.* **1.** protector, defender; *spec.* knight, knight-errant, paladin (*fig.*), warrior.

2. *See* SUPPORTER, VICTOR.

3. prizefighter, champ (*S*).

chance, *n.* **1.** *Referring to a way of happening of events or to a fortuitous state of affairs:* outcome, destiny, lot, fortune (*implies operation of invisible forces*), cast (*A; implies lottery*), hazard (*R; implies a risk taken*), casualty (*A; implies accident*), hap (*R*), peradventure (*B*), venture (*A*); *spec.* toss-up (*C*), gamble.

Antonyms: see CERTAINTY, NECESSITY.

2. *Referring to a particular happening:* occurrence, accident, casualty, contingency, contingence, fortuity, fortune, hap (*R*), peradventure (*B*); *spec.* draw, chance-medley; *see* MISFORTUNE.

Antonyms: see NECESSITY.

3. *Referring to chance generically, a sense often personified:* accident, hazard, haphazard, contingency (*R*), contingence (*R*), hap; *spec.* luck; *see* FORTUNE.

Antonyms: see NECESSITY.

4. *See* OPPORTUNITY, CONTINGENCY.

chance, *a.* accidental, contingent, casual, unplanned, unintentional, chanceable (*A*), chanceful (*A*), stray (*fig.*), blind, blindfold (*fig.*), haphazard, errabund (*R*), harum-scarum (*C*); *see* PURPOSELESS, AIMLESS.

Antonyms: see CONSEQUENTIAL, INTENTIONAL.

chancel, *n.* sanctuary, bema (*eccl.; antiq.*); *spec.* choir.

chandelier, *n.* **1.** candlestick, hearse (*eccl.*), candelabra.

2. pendant (*contex.*), fixture; *spec.* gaselier, electrolier, corona, pendant (*R*), crown, sconce.

---

ceremonial, *a.: formal.*
ceremonial, *n.: form.*
ceremonious: *formal.*
certify: *assure, authenticate.*
certitude: *confidence, certainty.*
cerulean: *azure.*
cessation: *stop, intermission.*
chafe, *v. t.: rub.*
chafe, *v. i.: rub, fret.*
chaff, *n.: pleasantry, refuse.*
chaff, *v. t.: banter.*
chain, *v. t.: bind, fasten.*
chalice: *cup.*
challenge, *v. i.: object.*
challenging: *defiant.*
champaign: *plain, country.*
champion, *v. t.: protect, support.*
championship: *protection, support.*
chance, *v. i.: happen.*

---

change, *n.* **1.** *See* EXCHANGE, REMOVAL, SUBSTITUTION.
2. variation (*implying many and minor changes*), alteration (*implying a change of appearance or form*), alternation (*implying a change between two things*), transition (*with reference to the act of changing from one thing to another*), mutation (*implying a regular process of change*), transmutation (*implying a change in substance, though maintaining the form*), shift (*implying a change in position*); variance, turning, turn (*C*), passing, passage, pass, movement (*chiefly spec.*), revolution, go (*C*), novation (*R*); *spec.* start, bob, break, graduation, risk, vicissitude; *see* TRANSFORMATION (*implying complete alteration*), QUALIFICATION, CONVERSION (*implying change to new purposes*).
Antonyms: see CONSTANCY, CONTINUATION.
3. *Referring to garments:* shift (*now U. S. or dial. Eng.*).

change, *v. t.* **1.** exchange (*often spec.*), commute; *spec.* shift (*one's garments*); *see* EXCHANGE, MOVE, REMOVE.
2. alter, vary, qualify, variate (*R*), modify, transform, mutate (*chiefly spec.*), convert, turn; *spec.* provect, transmute, moderate, diminish, increase, intensify, qualify, transform, shade, convert.
Antonyms: see FIX.

change, *v. i.* alter, vary, variate (*R*), shift (*chiefly spec.*), pass, resolve (*B or spec.*), go (*C or spec.*), mutate (*chiefly spec.*), turn (*chiefly spec.*); *spec.* shape (*as in "things are shaping his way"; C*), glide, sink, jump, break, range, graduate, grade.
Antonyms: see CONTINUE.

changeable, *a.* **1.** movable, variable, mobile, versatile (*R or spec.*), mutable, fluctuating, unfixed, roving; *see* EXCHANGEABLE, MOVABLE: —*implying change in position or form.*
2. alterable, varying, variant, variable, mutable, modifiable, protean, plastic, unstable, kaleidoscopic, inconstant, fickle (*fig.*); *spec.* changeful, vicissitudinous, vicissitudinary (*both B*), chatoyant, shot:—*all implying a capacity for, or a state of, change.*
3. fickle, inconstant, variable, light-headed *or* light, moody, erratic, irregular, irresolute, unsteady, uncertain, unfixed, wavering, restless, indecisive, changing, mutable, shifty (*chiefly spec.*), skittish (*fig.*), volatile (*B*), feathery (*fig., R*), versatile (*B*), mercurial (*B*), unstable, changeful:—*all implying changeability in thought or feeling.*
Antonyms: see CONSTANT, OBSTINATE, FIXED.

changeableness, *n.* **1.** movableness, variableness, *etc.*
2. alterableness, variableness, inconstance.
Antonyms: see APPLICATION.

changeling, *n.* **1.** Proteus (*fig.*); *spec.* waverer, turncoat, renegade.
2. oof.
3. *See* IDIOT, ELF-CHILD.

changing, *a.* **1.** changeful, fluxile (*R*), various (*R or A*), mobile, dynamic *or* dynamical (*tech.*).
2. alterative, modifying, modificatory, Protean (*fig.*).

channel, *n.* **1.** conduit, canal, course, duct, carrier (*contex.*); *spec.* trough (*now U. S.*), gutter, groove, furrow, cloaca, caloriduct (*R*), sewer, main, rabbet, artery, aorta, vein, runway, airway, canyon, cesspipe, pipe, lateral, aqueduct, drain, flute, shoot, cut, intake, leader, canaliculus, coulisse (*French*), cullis, flume, riffle, wadi, conlee, ditch, dike, downcomer, dale, lumen, meatus, launder, main, neck, fishway, katabothron (*R*), lead, run, runnel, runner, sulcation (*R*), donga (*So. Af.*), gullet (*local Eng.*), gully, funnel, gorge, culvert, sluice, raceway *or* race (*chiefly U. S.*).
2. *Referring to the deep part of a waterway:* thread, runway (*R*), ditch (*contemptuous*); *spec.* tideway, gut, sound, strait, swash, raceway *or* race (*chiefly U. S.*), neck, lead, fairway.
3. *Referring to a long depression: spec.* furrow, groove, sulcation (*R*), trough, fluting, dig, scratch, score, gouge, cut, gutter.
Antonyms: see RIDGE.

channel, *v. t. Spec.* gutter, canal (*R*), gully, ravine, chamfer, ditch, canalize, sweal (*A or Scot.*).

channeled, *a. Spec.* guttered, guttery, ditched.

chant, *n. Spec.* hymn, song, melody, canticle, psalm, antiphon, anthem, requiem (*chiefly B*), intonation.

chaos, *n.* **1.** abyss, void, chasm; *spec.* Ginnungagap.
2. *See* CONFUSION.

chapel, *n. Spec.* church, galilee, vestry, cubiculum, crypt, chantry, oratory, Bethesda.

chaperon, *n.* gouvernante (*French*); *spec.* companion, duenna.

chaperon, *v. t.* matronize (*R*).

chapter, *n.* **1.** division (*contex.*), section, passage; *spec.* sura (*in the Koran*), capitular.
2. *See* ASSEMBLY, BRANCH.

char, *v. t.* burn, scorch, carbonize (*tech.*), sear.

char, *n.* burn, scorch, scar; *spec.* charcoal, snuff.

character, *n.* **1.** *See* FIGURE, MARK, NATURE, QUALITY, HANDWRITING, TYPE, STYLE, PERSONALITY, PERSONAGE, REPUTATION.
2. sign, mark, symbol, emblem (*fig. or contex.*), figure (*spec. or contex.*); *spec.* letter, type, hieroglyph, hieroglyphic, polyphone, ideograph, pictograph, descender, hook.
3. personage, eccentric, crank (*C*), nut (*C*), original, erratic (*R*), vagarian (*R*), case (*C or*

---

changeful: *changeable, changing, moving.*
chant, *v. t.: sing, intone.*
chanticleer: *cock.*
chaotic: *formless, confused.*
chap: *person.*
chapfallen: *depressed.*
chaplet: *crown.*
chapped: *cracked.*
chaps: *jaw, chops.*

S, U. S.), oddity (*C*). *"Character" is somewhat C in this sense.*

characteristic, *n.* feature (*implying prominence*), trait (*implying peculiarity or lesser prominence*), attribute, peculiarity, physiognomic (*R*); *spec.* diagnostic (*esp. med.*); *see* QUALITY, DISTINCTION.

charge, *n.* **1.** *See* PRICE, EXPENSE, TAX, ACCUSATION, COMPLAINT, BIDDING, CARE, BURDEN, ATTACK.

2. liability, burden, encumbrance, tax (*orig. spec.*), expense; *spec.* assessment, rate; *see* MORTGAGE.

3. rate tax (*C or S, U. S.*); *spec.* average, demurrage, tariff, terminals (*pl.*), dockage, storage, *etc.*; *see* PRICE.

4. debit (*tech.*), chalk (*spec. or fig.*), score (*spec.*), due, entry.

5. *Referring to firearms, a furnace, etc.:* load; *spec.* round, blast, feed (*fig.*).

charge, *v. t.* **1.** *See* FILL, BID, ASSESS, ACCUSE, ATTACK, PREPARE, LOAD.

2. burden, commission, intrust, tax, encharge (*R*).

3. *Referring to a person:* tax (*C, U. S.*), assess, soak (*S*).

4. *Referring to the amount:* debit (*tech.*), score (*R*); *spec.* peg, size (*Eng. universities*).

5. *Referring to what is charged with a liability:* burden, incumber; *see* MORTGAGE.

charitable, *a.* **1.** *See* BENEVOLENT.

2. eleëmosynary (*B, tech., or euphemistic*).

3. liberal, considerate; *spec.* fair-minded, large-hearted, generous, open-hearted, big-hearted, tolerant, broad-minded (*C*).

charity, *n.* **1.** *See* LOVE, KINDNESS, BENEVOLENCE, ALMS.

2. *Spec.* foundation, bequest, hospital, college (*chiefly Eng.*).

charm, *n.* **1.** *See* BEWITCHERY, BEWITCHMENT, ATTRACTION, ATTRACTIVENESS, CAPTIVATION.

2. *Spec.* talisman, fetish *or* fetich, medicine (*anthropology*), saphie (*North Africa*), obi *or* obeah (*negro*), greegree (*Africa*), amulet.

Antonyms: see HOODOO.

3. incantation, spell, formula; *spec.* words.

charmer, *n.* **1.** *See* MAGICIAN.

2. *Referring to a charming person, esp. a woman, but A in this sense:* witch (*C*), sorceress, enchantress.

chase, *n.* **1.** *In the generic sense:* pursuit, hunting, course, hunt, cynegetics (*R*); *spec.* venery.

2. *See* HUNT, GAME, PURSUIT.

chase, *v. i.* pursue, follow; *spec.* run;—*with "after."*

chaste, *a.* **1.** pure, clean, white (*fig.*), innocent, honest (*R or A*), spotless, modest, undefiled, virtuous.

Antonyms: see UNCHASTE, LEWD, IMMORAL, COARSE, BEASTLY, INDECENT, CORRUPT, LASCIVIOUS, LICENTIOUS.

2. *See* PURE, PROPER.

3. severe, simple, classic.

chastity, *n.* **1.** purity, pureness, innocence, honor, virtue, virtuousness.

2. *See* PURITY.

chattel, *n.* chose (*tech.*), movable, things (*pl.; chiefly spec.*), slave, bondman; *spec.* distress (*sing.*); *see* GOODS.

chatter, *n.* **1.** babble (*R*), jargon, jangle, patter (*C*), gabble (*implying noise, confusion, and little or no meaning*), clatter (*implying noisy talk*), patter (*C*), twaddle *or* twattle (*now dial. or C*), claver (*contemptuous, Scot.*), clack (*contemptuous*), mag (*C*), cackle (*contemptuous or spec.*), gibber, gibberish, jabber, jibber (*R*), prattle, prate (*R*), prating, prittle-prattle (*R*); *spec.* talk.

2. *See* BABBLE, RATTLE.

chatter, *v. i.* **1.** babble, jargon, jargonize (*R*), jabble (*R*), patter (*C*), gabble (*contemptuous*), prattle, jabber, prate, blat *or* blate (*S or contemptuous*); *spec.* talk.

2. *See* RATTLE.

chatter, *v. t.* **1.** patter, prate, rattle (*fig.*).

2. *See* RATTLE.

cheap, *a.* **1.** inexpensive; *spec.* easy (*C*); *see* ECONOMICAL.

Antonyms: see COSTLY.

2. dirt-cheap (*intensive*), reduced, marked-down, half-price, low-priced, popular-priced, moderately-priced, reasonable; attractively-priced:—*the last three imply low cost, but may be merely euphemism for "less expensive."*

3. vulgar, meretricious, catch penny, mediocre, inferior; *spec.* popular; *see* BASE, PALTRY, GAUDY.

cheat, *v. i.* sharp, shark (*R*), swindle.

cheat, *v. t.* **1.** defraud, swindle, beguile, cozen (*now B*), victimize (*contex.*), bilk (*C*), gouge (*C*), fob *or* fub (*R*), daddle (*C*), bob (*A; S*), bucket (*S*), rogue (*R*), shave, rook (*C or S*), gudgeon (*C*), mump (*C; A*), lurch (*A*), ramp (*S*), Jew (*used opprobriously by non-Jews; S*), cozen (*now B*), cony-catch (*A*); *spec.* cog, fleece, thimblerig, bunco, chouse (*C or S*), gyp (*C*), skin (*S*), flim-flam (*S*).

2. *See* DECEIVE.

cheat, *n.* **1.** swindle, beguilement (*esp. the action*), do (*S*), cross (*cant or S*), fraud.

2. defrauder, swindler, sharper, sharker (*R*), cozener (*now B*), gyp (*C*), skinflint, trickster, sharp, Jew (*used opprobriously by some non-Jews; S*), blackleg (*C*), crook (*C*), cony-catcher (*A*), snide (*R*), Greek (*chiefly spec.*) hawk (*fig.*), bilk (*R; C or S*), kite (*R*), shaver

charge, *v. i.: rush.*
chargé: *diplomatic agent.*
chargeable: *attributable.*
charger: *platter, horse.*
charlatan: *quack.*
charm, *v. t.: bewitch, captivate, attract.*
charming: *captivating, pleasant, attractive.*
charnel house: *ossuary.*
chart, *n.: table.*
chart, *v. t.: tabulate.*
charter, *n.: deed, privilege.*
charter, *v. t.: hire.*
chary: *careful, prudent.*
chase, *v. t.: hunt, pursue.*
chasm: *abyss, cleft, break, void.*
chasten: *purify, punish, restrain.*
chastise: *punish.*
chat, *v. i.: converse.*
chat, *n.: conversation.*
chatty: *conversational, communicative.*

(*R*), rascal, lurch (*R*), rogue, rook (*fig.*); *spec.* blackleg (*C*), chouse (*C or S*), scoundrel.
3. *See* DECEIVER, DECEPTION.
cheating, *n.* defrauding, swindlery (*R*), fraud.
check, *v. t.* **1.** *See* STOP, RESTRAIN, REPRESS, SUPPRESS, REJECT, BAR, STUNT, CHOKE, INTERRUPT.
2. mark; *spec.* tick, prick, tally.
3. repulse, squelch, rebuff; *spec.* snub, nip (*C*).
4. countercheck; *spec.* block, scotch, cog, snub, brake, drag, anchor, damp, rein.
5. withhold, forbear, spare, refrain (*R*); *spec.* cease.
check, *n.* **1.** *See* STOP, STOPPAGE, REPRESSION, REVERSE, BAR, RESTRAINT, INTERRUPTION.
2. *Referring to that which checks:* countercheck; *spec.* drag, drogue, block, snub, chock, clog, stop, stopper, damp, damper, blanket (*usually with "wet"*), rein, bridle, inhibition, brake, let (*esp. in "without let or hindrance"*).
3. repulse, rebuff, setback (*U. S.*), backset, thwart (*R*); *spec.* snub.
4. mark; *spec.* tic, prick, tally, dash.
5. *Referring to that by which a thing is controlled, measured, etc.: spec.* standard, control.
6. order, note, draft, cheque (*chiefly Brit.*).
checkered, *a.* checky, chequée *or* chequé (*heraldry*).
check room, *n.* parcel room, left luggage office (*both chiefly Brit.*).
cheek, *n.* **1.** jowl (*R or dial.*); *spec.* gills (*pl.; S*).
2. *See* IMPUDENCE.
cheer, *v. t.* **1.** encourage, inspirit, cherish (*R*), comfort, strengthen, solace, console, hearten:—*implying the giving of courage, hope, or gladness;* comfort, solace, *and* console *implying relief of trouble, grief, distress;* enliven, brighten, encheer (*R*), recreate (*R*), rehearten (*R*), liven (*C*), warm; *spec.* chirrup.
Antonyms: see ABASH, DISCOURAGE, SADDEN, GRIEVE, DEPRESS.
2. *See* APPLAUD.
cheer, *v. i.* shout (*contex.*), jolly (*Eng.*); *spec.* hurrah, hurray, hurra, huzza, yell.
cheer, *n.* **1.** encouragement, comfort, solace, consolation:—*implying the giving of courage, hope, or gladness;* comfort, solace, *and* consolation *usually implying that the recipient of* cheer *is in trouble or distress;* consolement (*R*), enlivenment, recreation (*R*).
2. shout (*contex.*), jolly (*Eng.*); *spec.* tiger, huzza, hurrah, hurray, hurra, hear:—*refer to cries of encouragement, welcome, approbation, etc.*
cheerful, *a.* **1.** light, light-hearted, bright, chipper (*S or C, U. S.*), chirrupy (*C*), lively, merry, jocund (*B*), happy, cheery, genial, debonair (*B*), lightsome, chirpy (*C*), hilarious, jolly, gladsome, heartsome (*chiefly Scot.*), canty (*dial.*), sunny, sunshiny (*C*), buxom (*A*), lusty (*A*), riant (*R*), cheery, genial, blithe, blithesome, bonny (*A or R*), brisk (*chiefly dial.*); *spec.* smiling.
Antonyms: see DEPRESSED, SULLEN, GLOOMY.
2. *See* CHEERING.
cheerfulness, *n.* geniality, hilarity, sunshine, gladsomeness, *etc.*
Antonyms: see DEPRESSION, DISCOURAGEMENT.
cheering, *a.* cheerful, genial, enlivening, inspiriting, strengthening, consolatory, gladsome, lætificant (*R*), heartsome (*chiefly Scot.*), heartening, chirping (*R*), cheery, blithesome, comfortable, cordial (*R*); solaceful (*R*).
Antonyms: see DEPRESSING, GLOOMY.
cheering, *n.* solacement, enlivenment, heartening, *etc.*
cheerless, *a.* dull, gloomy, dreary, dismal, disconsolate, dispiriting, disheartening, unpromising, comfortless, joyless:—*implying absence of that which encourages.* Dull *is the mildest term,* gloomy, dreary, dismal *and* disconsolate *are stronger terms, used of things as well as of persons.* Unpromising *implies merely absence of that which gives hope;* dispiriting *and* disheartening *implies the presence of that which takes away hope or courage;* cheerless, comfortless, joyless *derive their force from the senses of the basic words* cheer, comfort, joy.
cheerlessness, *n.* dullness, dismalness, gloom, *etc.*
cheesy, *a.* caseous (*chiefly tech.*).
chemical, *a. Spec.* alchemical, analytical, synthetical.
chemise, *n.* shift, smock, slip, underthing; *spec.* guimpe.
cherish, *v. t.* **1.** protect, foster, nurture (*the last two imply stimulation of growth*), nurse, coddle, bosom (*R*), indulge, brood; *spec.* enshrine, cosset, pet, entertain, harbor (*mentally*); *see* FOSTER.
Antonyms: see ABUSE, BEAT, BLIGHT, ILL-TREAT.
2. *See* CARESS, LOVE, PRESERVE, ENTERTAIN:—cherish *implies tenderness and affection and frequently indulgence.*
3. treasure, enshrine, prize, revere.
chest, *n.* **1.** case, box, coffer (*chiefly spec.*), hutch (*A or spec.*); *spec.* cist *or* cyst (*antiq.*), clothespress, cabinet, commode, chiffonier, coffin, casket (*euphemistic for* coffin), locker, tallboy, highboy, wangun (*cant*), bureau; *see* TRUNK.
2. thorax (*tech.*); *spec.* breast.
3. treasury, coffer, alms box.
chestnut, *a.* castaneous (*tech.*).
chevron, *n.* **1.** *Spec.* zigzag, dancette.
2. stripe; *see* BADGE.
chew, *v. t. & i.* **1.** masticate (*formal*), chaw

checker: *plaid.*
checkmate: *defeat.*
cheep: *chirp.*
cheery: *cheerful, cheering.*
cherished: *dear.*
cherub: *angel, child.*
cherup: *chirp.*
chevalier: *horseman, knight, lover.*

(*now S or implying vulgarity*), manducate (*R*), grind; *spec.* crunch, crump, munch, mumble, champ, ruminate (*of beasts; of human beings, "to chew mentally"*), gnaw.

2. *See* REND.

chewing, *a.* masticatory, manducatory (*R*);—*both formal or B.*

chicane, *v. i.* pettifog (*in law*).

chicanery, *n.* deceit (*contex.*), trickery, sophistry, chicane (*all implying specious legalism*); *spec.* prevarication, pettifogging, pettifoggery.

chick, *n.* offspring (*contex.*), *fig. for* child; squab (*chiefly spec.*); *see* CHICKEN.

chicken, *n.* **1.** fowl (*contex.*), poult (*R*), biddy (*C*); *spec.* broiler, fryer, peeper, chick, pullet, hen.

2. *C for* girl; flapper.

chicken-breasted, *a.* gibbous (*R or tech.*), pigeon-breasted.

chief, *a.* first, principal, arch (*R*), foremost, capital, cardinal, preëminent:—chief *is used technically of persons in office to imply formal headship*; capital, *of things, to imply that they are first in importance, rank, or class*; cardinal *implies the dependence of other things, referring originally to the hanging of a door on its hinges*; preëminent *implies simply precedence or superiority over all others of the quality or character referred to*; master, high, head, top, supereminent (*R*), main, premier, pivotal, great (*used with "the"*), central, primary, supreme, prime, grand, leading, palmary (*R*), palmarian (*R*), prevailing, main.

Antonyms: see INFERIOR, SECONDARY, SMALL.

chief, *n.* head; *spec.* chieftain, headman, headsman (*R*), cob (*dial.*), cock (*C*), ruler, leader, dux (*chiefly Scot. or spec.*), captain, capitano (*Italian*), cacique (*West Indies*), condottiere (*Italian*), clicker, cid, general (*mil. or eccl.*), foreman, top (*C*), boss (*S*), mogul (*S*), lord (*feudal*), elder, goodman (*Scot. or A*), protopope (*eccl.*), jarl, caboceer (*Africa*) hierarch (*eccl.*), provincial (*eccl.*), ringleader, reis *or* rais (*Arabia*), sheik (*Arabia*), sagamore, sachem, raja *or* rajah, principal, prince, Pope, cardinal, primate, bishop, archbishop, diocesan, metropolitan (*the last seven eccl.*), poligar, prytanis (*fig.*), president, dean (*journalistic cliché*), premier, phylarch, matriarch (*chiefly jocular*), malik (*Hindu*), abuna (*eccl.*), metran (*eccl.*), lumberdar (*India.*), judge (*Bib.*), kehaya (*Turkish*), duce (*Italian*), Führer (*German*); principal, don (*B or cant*), master, head; *see* OVERSEER, SUPERIOR, COMMANDER.

Antonyms: see SUBORDINATE.

chiefly, *adv.* principally, mainly, most, mostly, capitally, cardinally, *etc.*

chieftancy, *n.* chiefship, headship, supremacy, masterdom, primacy.

child, *n.* **1.** *See* OFFSPRING.

2. offspring (*contex.*), kid (*S or C*), kiddie, bairn (*Scot.*), bambino (*Italian*), cub (*jocose or contemptuous*), whelp (*contemptuous*), papoose (*Amer. Ind.*), dandiprat (*obs., juvenile, or A*), dab (*contemptuous*), joey (*Australia; C*), imp (*chiefly spec.*), moppet (*A; a term of endearment*), bud (*a term of endearment*), brat (*contemptuous*), innocent (*as being pure*), cherub (*pl. cherubs; spec. or sarcastic*), lambkin (*a term of endearment*); *spec.* boy, girl, changeling, nestling (*fig.*), elf, tot, elfin (*B; R*), chit (*C*), trot (*C*), urchin, olive-branch (*B and humorous*), young hopeful (*humorous*); *see* SON, DAUGHTER.

Antonyms: see PARENT, FATHER, MOTHER.

childbirth, *n.* parturition (*tech.*), parturience (*tech.; R*), travail (*A*), labor, pains (*pl.*), puerpery (*R*); *spec.* delivery, eutocia, dystocia.

childhood, *n.* infancy (*chiefly legal, exc. spec.*), youth, puerility (*R*); *spec.* minority, pupilage, nonage.

Antonyms: see AGE, MATURITY.

childish, *a.* babyish, boyish, girlish, infantile, infantine, childly, juvenile, youthful *are used of a boy, child, etc., the ordinary terms used whether the term qualified designates something considered as either good or bad. As used of more mature persons, the terms in* -ish *are derogatory, implying the presence of undue or undesirable characteristics.* Childish *is seldom used in speaking of a child, but is used in designating in adults qualities or characteristics considered as pleasing, estimable or desirable in a child*; brattish (*contemptuous*); *see* BABYISH.

Antonyms: see MANLY, WOMANLY, WOMANISH, OLD.

children, *n. pl.* **1.** offspring (*contex.*), kids (*C or S*).

2. childhood (*R*); *spec.* infantry (*jocular*), infancy; *see* YOUTH.

chilly, *a.* cold, cool, chill, icy (*C*).

chime, *v. i. & t.* **1.** ring (*A or spec.*), play (*contex.*).

2. *See* AGREE, HARMONIZE.

chimney, *n.* **1.** fireplace, hearth:—chimney *is A or dialectal in this sense*; *spec.* flue, shoot, stack, smokestack, pipe.

2. *See* CLEFT.

chimney corner, fireside, inglenook (*B*).

chin, *n.* jaw (*S or C*), mentum (*tech.*); *spec.* jowl.

china, *n.* earthenware (*R*), crockery, chinaware, porcelain; *spec.* crackle, belleek, majolica, *etc.*

Chinese, *a.* Celestial (*humorous*), Sinic (*R*), Sinæan *or* Sinaic (*R*); *spec.* Serian *or* Seric.

chip, *n. Spec.* flake, spall, turnings (*pl.*), cuttings (*pl.*), parings (*pl.*), flint; *see* PIECE, SPLINTER.

---

chide: *scold, reprove.*
childlike: *childish.*
chill, *n.: cold, depression.*
chill, *a.: cold, chilly.*
chill, *v. t.: cool, restrain, freeze.*
chilling: *depressing, repellent.*
chime, *n.: bell, melody, harmony, agreement, rhythm.*
chimera: *fancy.*
chimerical: *fanciful, vissionary.*
chink: *cleft, crack.*
chink, *n.: jingle, coin.*
chink, *v. i.: gasp.*

chip, *v.*, cut, nick, break, crack.
chirp, *n. & v. i.* cry (*contex.*), twitter, cheep, cherup, chipper, peep, pipe, pip, yip (*C*), chirk (*dial. or U. S.*), chirrup *or* chirup; *spec.* pule.
chirping, *a.* cheepy.
chisel, *v. t.* cut (*contex.*), carve (*contex.*); *spec.* boast (*masonry*), gouge; *S for* cheat.
chisel-shaped, *a.* scalpriform (*tech.*).
choice, *n.* **1.** *Referring to the act:* preference (*suggests feeling and taste rather than will in choice*), preferment (*R*), selection, election (*suggests deliberation in choice*), option (*emphasizes the power to choose*), discrimination (*implying careful choice*), choose (*R; humorous or C*), optation (*R*), pick, delectus (*R exc. spec.*); *spec.* coöptation, coöption.
Antonyms: see REJECTION.
2. *Referring to the thing chosen:* preference, selection, option, pick, favorite; *spec.* cull (*cant*), delectus; *see* ALTERNATIVE, BEST.
3. *Power of choosing:* option, pick; *spec.* discretion.
choice, *a.* **1.** select, chosen, preferred, picked, recherché (*French*), exquisite, prime.
2. *See* FINE, EXCELLENT.
choke, *v. t. & i.* **1.** suffocate (*contex.*), strangle, strangulate (*chiefly med.*), throttle; *spec.* bowstring, garrotte, grin (*A*), gag.
2. *See* REPRESS, OBSTRUCT, DEADEN, EXTINGUISH.
3. repress (*contex.*), check, swallow, gulp (*used chiefly with "down"*). *"Choke" is used chiefly with "down."*
choose, *v. t.* select, elect (*implying greater consequences than* select), decide (*implying deliberation in choice*), take, opt (*R*), pick, optate (*R*), list (*only as a v. i.; A*); *spec.* coöpt (*A or tech.*), coöptate, cull, draw, prefer, prick, garble; *see* ADOPT.
Antonyms: see REJECT.
choosing, *a.* optative, selective; *spec.* eclectic, elective.
chop, *n.* **1.** *See* JAW.
2. *In pl.* (*chops*): chaps (*pl.; a variant*), choke (*dial.*); *spec.* flews (*pl.*).
chop, *v. t. & i.* cut (*contex.*), hew, hack; *spec.* mince, hackle, lop, haggle.
chop, *n.* **1.** cut (*contex.*), slice (*contex.*), cleave, split, hew, hack; *spec.* lop.
2. bobble, lop, overfall, rip; *spec.* tiderip, ripple.
chopping, *a.* wavy (*contex.*), rough (*contex.*), bobbling, cockling, bobbly, loppy; *spec.* ripply.
chosen, *a.* select, elect (*chiefly spec.; its antonym is* reprobate), picked, predilective (*R*); *spec.* conscript, preferential, predestined; preferred.
chosen, *n. Spec.* elect, élite (*French*).
Christ, *n.* Saver (*R*), Savior *or* Saviour, Jesus, Redeemer, Messiah, Messias, Immanuel, Meditator, Intercessor, Advocate, Judge, Word, Son, Son of Man, Son of God, Lamb, Lamb of God;—*mostly used with "the" or "our."*
christen, *v. t.* **1.** *See* BAPTIZE, NAME.
2. *In the sense of "to use for the first time":* auspicate (*B*), handsel; *spec.* wet (*S*), blood. *"Christen" in this sense is C.*
Christendom, *n.* The Church, Christianity, Zion (*fig.*).
Christian, *n.* Nazarene (*used esp. by Jews and Mohammedans*), saint (*Bib.*), giaour (*used by Turks*), gentile (*used in India*); *spec.* professor (*chiefly Scot. & U. S.*), novice, probationer, Gnostic, Baptist, Methodist, *etc.*
Antonyms: see HEATHEN, HERETIC.
Christmas, *n.* Yuletide (*B or local*), Yule (*B or local*), Christmastide.
chronic, *a.* inveterate, confirmed, seated, settled, rooted, continuing (*contex.*), persistent, unceasing; *spec.* inborn, inbred.
chronological, *a.* datal (*R*), temporal (*contex.*).
church, *n.* **1.** temple, house, house of God, Lord's house, fane (*A or B*), ecclesia (*hist.*), kirk (*Scot. & north of Eng.; chiefly spec.*); *spec.* Ebenezer, cathedral, chapel, Caaba *or* Kaaba, Bethel, meeting-house, basilica, synagogue, tabernacle, duomo (*Italian*), dom (*Ger.*), mosque, kiack, minister, abbey, mensal (*hist.*), martyry, conventicle, samaj (*India*), delubrum.
2. *See* CONGREGATION, CHRISTENDOM.
chute, *n.* shoot, hopper; *spec.* slide.
cigarette, *n.* fag (*C*), gasper (*S, Brit.*), smoke, cig (*C*), coffin-nail (*heavily humorous euphemism*).
cimeter-shaped, *a.* acinaciform (*R*).
cinder, *n. Spec.* coal, breeze; *see* SLAG.
cinder, *v. t. Spec.* scorify.
cindery, *a.* coaly; *spec.* slaggy.
cipher, *n.* **1.** nought, naught (*a less usual form*), 0, nothing, zero, aught (*R and a mistake for "naught"*), ought (*a mistake for "naught"*).
2. cryptogram, cryptology.
3. *See* NUMERAL, MONOGRAM.
cipher, *v. t.* **1.** encipher (*more formal than "cipher"*).
2. *See* COMPUTE.

---

chipper: *chirp.*
chirm: *noise.*
chirography: *handwriting.*
chirrup: *chirp.*
chit: *bud, offspring, child.*
chitchat: *conversation.*
chivalrous: *knightly, generous, polite.*
choler: *anger.*
chopfallen: *depressed.*
choral: *hymn.*
chord, *n.:* *string.*
chore: *task.*
chorus: *refrain.*
chose: *chattel.*
Christianity: *Christendom.*
chronicle, *n.:* *account.*
chronicle, *v. t.:* *record, narrate.*
chronicler: *historian.*
chubby: *plump.*
chuck, *n. & v.:* *cluck.*
chuck, *v. t.:* *throw, stroke.*
chuck, *n.:* *throw, stroke, clutch.*
chuckle: *laugh.*
chum, *n.:* *roommate, intimate.*
chum, *v. i.:* *cohabit.*
chummy: *intimate.*
chump: *blockhead.*
chunk: *piece, lump.*
churchman: *ecclesiastic, minister.*
churlish: *rustic, boorish, surly, rough, ill-tempered, stingy.*
cinch: *girth, hold.*

---

circle, *n.* **1.** disk, radius, round, rondelle (*R or tech. and spec.*), rondure *or* roundure (*R*), rondel (*A*), orb (*rhet. and chiefly spec.*), roundel (*chiefly spec.*); *spec.* carton, discus, roundle (*tech.*), roundlet (*dim.*), circlet (*dim.*). **2.** ring, annulet, annulus (*tech.*), round, roundabout (*R*), gyration (*tech.*), gyre (*chiefly B*), orb (*R or A*), roundel (*chiefly dial.*), O (*fig.*); *spec.* cycle, corona, halo, hoop, meridian, epicycle, ecliptic, cordon, equator, colure, zone, horizon, circlet, roundle, roundlet, spiral; *see* RING.

3. *See* CIRCUIT, SET.

circle, *v. i.* wheel, ring, gyrate; *see* REVOLVE, CIRCUIT.

circuit, *n.* **1.** *See* CIRCUMFERENCE, BOUNDARY, AREA, SPHERE, JURISDICTION.

2. course, round, circling, circle, turn, revolution (*R*), ambit, compass, orbit, tour, circuition (*R*), troll (*A*), circulation (*R*), perambulation (*B and fig.*), circumambience (*nonce use*); *spec.* lap, journey (*contex.*), trip, bout, hookup (*radio*); *see* REVOLUTION.

3. *Referring to the way:* course, round, compass, ambit, circuition (*R*); *spec.* eyre (*A or hist.*), tour, turn, giro (*Italian*), iter (*tech.*), beat, detour, roundabout, lap, ring, cycle; *see* WINDING.

circuit, *v. t.* round, circle, encircle, compass, girdle (*fig.*), surround (*R*), loop, *spec.* circumambulate (*R*), circumnavigate, perambulate, tour.

circuit, *v. i.* course, round, circulate, circle; *spec.* tour, detour; *see* REVOLVE, WIND.

circular, *a.* **1.** round, rounded, globed, globose, globular, orbicular (*elevated or tech.*), orbed (*B*), orby (*R*), spherical, rotund (*R or tech.*), orbiculate (*R*), encircular (*R*), cylindrical; *spec.* discoid, rotate (*R*), disciform, discoidal (*R*), cycloid.

2. round, ringy (*R*), annular, ringlike, orby (*R*), compass (*R or tech.*); *spec.* rotary, gyrant, gyrate, orbital, roundabout.

3. *Of a letter; esp. eccl.:* cyclic, encyclical, pastoral, general.

circularly, *adv.* roundabout, roundwise, round, roundly (*R*).

circulate, *v. i.* **1.** *See* CIRCUIT, REVOLVE.

2. *Referring to money, goods, etc.:* pass, go, run, move.

3. *Referring to rumors, etc.:* run, go; *spec.* evulgate (*R*).

circulate, *v. t.* **1.** *See* DIFFUSE, REPORT.

2. *Referring to money, etc.:* pass.

circulating, *a.* current (*referring to money*), moving (*referring to air*).

circulatory, *a.* circulative, diffusive.

circumference, *n.* periphery (*B or tech.*), circuit, compass, round, perimeter (*geom.*), perimetry (*R*); *spec.* girth, girt, perambulation (*B and fig.*); *see* BOUNDARY.

Antonyms: see CENTER, MIDDLE.

circumlocution, *n.* periphrasis (*B*), periphrase (*R*), roundabout (*R*), indirection, ambage (*R*), circuition (*R*), circumambages (*pl.; R*), circumbendibus (*jocular*), wordiness, verbosity, verbiage.

circumlocutory, *a.* periphrastic, roundabout, indirect, ambagious (*R*), circuitous, wordy, verbose.

circumscribe, *v. t.* **1.** inclose, surround, encompass, encircle, imprison, corral, restrain, limit, confine; *spec.* bound.

2. define, determine, delimit, demarkate, environ; *see* BOUND, RESTRICT, DESCRIBE.

circumstance, *n.* **1.** *See* OCCURRENCE, STATE, FORMALITY, AFFAIR.

2. fact, matter; *see* PARTICULAR.

circumstanced, *a.* conditioned, fixed (*C*), situated.

circumstantial, *a.* minute, detailed, exact, precise, full, detaily (*C; R*); *spec.* fussy; *see* PARTICULAR.

Antonyms: see GENERAL, INDEFINITE.

circus, *n.* hippodrome (*rhetorical; often used as a name for a circus building*), ring, show.

cistern, *n.* reservoir, tank;—*both contex.*

citify, *v. t.* metropolitanize (*R*). *"Citify" is chiefly used in the p. p. "citified."*

citizen, *n.* cit (*contemptuous*); *spec.* burgess, burgher, comburgess, voter, ephebe (*implies, recent attainment of majority*), cosmopolite, communer, freeman, civilian, denizen, resident; *see* TOWNSMAN.

Antonyms: see FOREIGNER.

city, *n.* town, municipality, burg (*C, U. S.*); *spec.* metropolis, metropolitan, capital.

civility, *n.* **1.** *See* POLITENESS.

2. *Referring to the act:* attention, courtesy, devoir (*B, usually pl.:* devoirs), affability; *spec.* bow, salutation, welcome, greeting, attentiveness.

civilization, *n.* civility (*A*); *spec.* reclamation (*the act only*), enlightenment, cultivation, culture (*refers usually to the intellectual and esthetic aspects*), kultur (*Ger.*), polish; *see* REFINEMENT.

civilize, *v. t. Spec.* reclaim, debarbarize, enlighten, cultivate (*chiefly in p. a. "cultivated"*), enrich, develop, soften (*barbarian asperities*); *see* REFINE.

civilized, *a.* civil (*A*); *spec.* enlightened.

Antonyms: see UNCIVILIZED.

---

circle, *v. t.: circuit.*
circlet: *circle, ring, crown.*
circling: *circuit.*
circuitous: *devious, indirect, circumlocutory.*
circuitously: *about.*
circularize: *advertize.*
circumjacent: *surrounding.*
circumfusion: *pouring.*
circumnavigate: *circuit.*
circumscriptive: *restrictive.*
circumspect: *prudent, careful.*
circumstantiate: *evidence, narrate.*
circumvent: *surround, overreach.*
circumvention: *overreaching.*
circumvolution: *rotation, revolution, coil, winding.*
cist: *chamber, tomb.*
citation: *summons, quotation, mention.*
cite: *summons, quote, mention.*
civic: *public.*
civil: *public, polite.*
clabber: *curd.*
clack: *clatter, clap, noise, babble, rattle.*

---

claim, *v. t.* **1.** demand, challenge (*A*), vindicate (*R*); *spec.* counterclaim.
Antonyms: see DISCLAIM.
2. *See* DEMAND, NEED.
3. assert, maintain, state, declare:—claim *is not fully orthodox in this use, except with respect to something which is to be acknowledged as a right.*
claim, *n.* **1.**demand, pretense, pretension; *spec.* plea, counterclaim, condiction (*Roman law*), location (*U. S.*), revendication, plea.
2. demand, lien, bill; *spec.* hold.
Antonyms: see DISCLAIMER.
3. *See* RIGHT.
claimant, *n.* demandant (*now R*); *spec.* pleader, pretender.
clairvoyance, *n.* second sight, clear sight (*R*).
clairvoyant, *a.* clear-sighted (*R*).
clairvoyant, *n.* seer, fortune teller.
clamorous, *n.* noisy (*contex.*), vociferous, clamant (*B*), obstreperous, uproarious, blatant, vociferant, strepitous (*R*), tumultuous; *see* BOISTEROUS.
Antonyms: see CALM, SILENT.
clamp, *n.* clam, cramp, grip, vise (*chiefly spec.*); *spec.* crampiron, horse, dog, yoke, clip, brace, fastener, clasp.
clan, *n.* **1.** *Spec.* tribe, sept, phratry (*Greek antiq. and North Am. Indian*), phyle (*Greek antiq.*), race (*a loose usage*), brotherhood, caste, breed.
2. clique; *see* SET.
clang, *v. i.* clam; *see* RING.
clang, *n.* **1.** clangor, clam; *see* RING, RESONANCE.
2. *See* TIMBRE.
clap, *v. i.* **1.** strike, slap, bang, clack, slam, slat, click.
2. *See* APPLAUD, PUT, IMPOSE, SET.
clap, *n.* **1.** stroke (*contex.*), blow, slap, slam, bang, clack, slat.
2. noise (*contex.*); *spec.* slam, bang, clack, explosion, peal.
3. *See* APPLAUSE.
clapper, *n.* **1.** *Spec.* tongue, clack, bones (*pl.*).
2. *See* TONGUE.
clapping, *a.* clackety, clickety, slapping, slamming, slatting, *etc.*
clasp, *v. t.* **1.** seize, embrace, enclasp (*R or emphatic*), infold *or* enfold, clip; *spec.* twine, clutch, grasp, grip, interlock, entwine, fold, inarm, hug, hook, twine; *see* EMBRACE.
Antonyms: see FREE.
2. fasten; *spec.* buckle, brace, hook, infibulate (*R*).
3. *See* HOLD.
clasp, *n.* **1.** seizure; *spec.* embrace, fold, hug, clutch; *see* EMBRACE.
2. fastening, catch; *spec.* morse, ouch (*A*), fibula, buckle, fermail, hasp.
3. *See* HOLD.
class, *n.* **1.** division (*contex.*), category (*tech. or B*), predicament (*spec. or B*), denomination, department, section, subdivision, sort, species, group, order, rank, range (*R*); *spec.* estate, order, family, genus, species, breed, race (*chiefly B*), tribe (*chiefly C and derogatory*), grade, rate, hierarchy, phylum (*tech.*), quality.
2. *See* KIND, SET, RANK (*in pl.*), NOBILITY, BRAND.
3. *Spec.* form, division, seminar, Philathea, Baraca, classis.
class, *v. t.* classify, place (*contex.*), rank, rate, number, assort (*R*), sort, reckon; posthabit (*R*).
classic, *a.* Attic (*B*).
classical, *a. Spec.* humanistic, canonical *or* canonic, correct:—classical *is used popularly, particularly of music, as an antonym for* popular.
classification, *n.* assortment, grouping, order, arrangement, class, allocation.
classified, *a.* assorted, grouped, indexed, filed, *etc.*
Antonyms: see CONFUSED.
classify, *v. t.* group, categorize (*tech.*), assort, sort (*B*), order, file, index, tabulate; *spec.* grade, distribute, arrange, tribe (*R*), impost (*U. S. customs*), graduate, match, size, pigeonhole, range, brack (*local*), garble (*R, exc. of coins, nuts, etc.*).
Antonyms: see CONFUSE, MIX.
clatter, *n. & v. i.* **1.** *Spec.* clack, clitter, clutter, hurtle; *see* RATTLE, BABBLE.
clause, *n.* **1.** article, particle (*R*); *spec.* paragraph, covenant, proviso, condition, stipulation, reddendo (*Scots law*), reddendum.
2. *See* PART.
claw, *n.* griff (*R*), ungula (*tech.*), talon (*chiefly spec.*), hook (*S*); *spec.* single (*A*), clutch (*chiefly in pl.*), chela, pounce, pincers (*pl.*), tentacle, manus, nipper; *see* NAIL.
claw, *v. t.* scratch, dig (*C or spec.*), hook (*C*), tear, clapperclaw (*A or dial.*).
clay, *n.* argil (*tech.*), cloam (*dial. Eng.*); *spec.* clunch, kaolin, metal, cledge (*local Eng.*), wacke, slip, till, bole, gault (*dial. Eng.*); mud, mire, earth; *also fig. for* human body.
clayey, *a.* argillaceous (*tech.*).
clean, *a.* **1.** unsoiled, pure (*B or fig.*), unsullied (*B*); *spec.* immaculate, unstained, incontaminate (*R*), undefiled (*usually with moral implications*), unsmirched, dirtless, spotless, unspotted, dustless, white, unblemished.

clam: *clamp.*
clamant: *clamorous, urgent.*
clamber: *scramble.*
clammy: *sticky.*
clamor, *n.: outcry, noise.*
clamor, *v. i.: cry, shout, din, ask.*
clamor, *v. t.: shout.*
clamp: *step.*
clangorous: *resonant.*
clank: *ring.*
clannish: *exclusive.*
claptrap: *trickery, nonsense, buncombe.*
clarification: *clearing.*
clarify: *clear.*
clarity: *clearness.*
clash, *v. i.: collide, conflict, disagree, dash.*
clash, *n.: collision, noise, conflict, disagreement.*

Antonyms: see DIRTY, FILTHY, SOILED, FOUL, SMEARY, *etc.*
2. *See* PURE, SKILLFUL, SHAPELY, CLEANLY, CHASTE.
clean, *adv.* **1.** *So as to be clean:* cleanly.
2. *Spec.* absolutely, completely, skillfully.
clean, *v. t.* **1.** cleanse (*more formal and elevated than* clean, *but used frequently as a commercial elegance for* clean), mundify (*R*), clenge (*Scot. & dial.*), purge (*chiefly spec.*); *spec.* purify, wash, lave, launder, deterge, scald, dust, mop, rinse, bream, careen, dress, comb, gill, dredge, pick, grave, scavenge, pure (*cant*), swingle, scour, blow, scrub, elutriate, wipe, willow, clarify, ripple; *see* DRESS, WASH, FAN.
Antonyms: see DIRTY, SOIL, SMEAR, FOUL.
2. *See* CLEAR.
cleaning, *a.* cleansing, mundatory (*R*), purgative; *spec.* purificatory, wash, washing, detersive, depurative, detergent, scouring, purging.
cleaning, *n.* cleansing; *spec.* purge, purgation, scouring.
cleanly, *a.* clean, neat.
clear, *a.* **1.** transparent, limpid (*chiefly spec.*), lucid, pellucid (*intensive*), pellucent (*R*), crystal, crystalline; *spec.* unclouded (*implying freedom from that which obscures or dulls light*), serene; *see* TRANSPARENT.
Antonyms: see TURBID, DREGGY.
2. *Referring to weather:* fair, bright, fine, serene (*R or B*); *spec.* sunny, sunshiny, perfect, unclouded, cloudless.
Antonyms: see FOUL, CLOUDY, RAINY, SNOWY, FOGGY, HAZY.
3. *Referring to tones, implying freedom from dulling or obscuring effects:* liquid, pure; *spec.* mellifluous *or* mellifluent (*rhet.*), crystal, musical, singing, euphonious, fluty, silvery, ringing, sharp.
Antonyms: see HOARSE, DULL.
4. *Referring to weights or amounts:* net, neat (*R*).
5. *Referring to the skin, etc., and implying transparency of the surface; spec.* bright, fresh, healthy, transparent, peachy, fair, blooming.
Antonyms: see SALLOW.
6. *Implying freedom from that which obscures perception, visual or mental:* intelligible (*contex.*), plain, lucid, pellucid (*B*), luminous (*rhet.*), luculent (*R*), perspicuous, sharpcut, sharp, unambiguous, naked (*R*); *spec.* vivid, distinct, definite.
Antonyms: see UNINTELLIGIBLE, OBSCURE, OBTUSE, HIDDEN.
7. *See* DEFINITE, EVIDENT, CONFIDENT, SMOOTH (*in sound*), ABSOLUTE, PURE.
8. Open, free, unobstructed:—*implying freedom from obstruction or obstacles.*
9. Empty, void.
clear, *v. t.* **1.** clarify, fine, refine:—*implying removal of that which clouds, dims, or obscures; spec.* settle, render.
Antonyms: see MUDDY.
2. *See* FREE, DISENTANGLE, ACQUIT, ABSOLVE, AVOID, PURIFY, REMOVE, JUMP.
3. make, net, clean up (*C*), profit, realize, get (*contex.*).
Antonyms: see LOSE.
4. free, rid, sweep, scour.
5. free (*from obstructions, rubbish, weeds, or what not*), sweep (*spec. or fig.*), scour (*spec. or fig.*), clean; *spec.* open, room (*R*), drive, serene (*R*), deobstruct (*R*), deoppilate (*R*), blow, uncloud, evacuate.
Antonyms: see OBSTRUCT.
6. *Spec.* (*referring to land*) deforest, stub, grub, denshire (*Eng.*), burnbeat (*Eng.*), assart (*Eng.*).
7. *See* EVACUATE.
clear, *v. i. Referring to the face, the sky, etc.:* uncloud (*R*), brighten; *spec.* gladden.
Antonyms: see CLOUD.
clearance, *n.* **1.** freeing, riddance, clearing.
2. *See* ACQUITTAL, ABSOLUTION, LICENSE, CLEARING.
clearing, *n.* **1.** clear (*chiefly in "in the clear"*), open (*chiefly in "in the open"*), opening, clearance (*B*); *spec.* assart.
2. *See* ACQUITTAL.
3. clearance; *spec.* clarification, riddance, evacuation, scouring, deforestation, *etc.*
clearness, *n.* **1.** *Spec.* clarity, limpidness, limpidity, *etc.*
2. serene (*R*), serenity (*B or R*); *spec.* cloudlessness.
cleavable, *a.* fissile (*chiefly tech.*); *spec.* scissile, flaggy, laminable, flaky, platy.
cleavage, *n.* **1.** fissility, cleavableness; *spec.* laminableness, lamination, delamination.
2. *See* SPLITTING.
cleave, *v. i.*, cling, adhere, stick, hold fast:—*cleave is now A or B; not to be confused with the following word.*
cleave, *v. t. & i.* divide, split, rend, shear, dissever (*R*); *spec.* plow, delaminate, laminate, fissure, rift, flake, rive, furrow; *see* SPLIT.
cleft, *a.* split; *spec.* riven, reft, rent, multifid (*B*), fissured, cracked, fractured, broken, cut, rimose.
cleft, *n.* split, gap; *spec.* fissure, break, rift, reft (*R*), scissure (*R*), interstice, chasm, opening, crack, crevice, chimney, chink, clof (*Scot.*), rent, flaw, slit, dike (*local, Eng.*), fault; *see* CREVASSE.
clench, *v. t.* **1.** *Now an intensitive of clinch; see* CLINCH, SEIZE, GRASP, STRENGTHEN.
2. grip; *spec.* close (*the fist*), clutch (*the fist*), set (*the teeth*).
clenched, *a.* closed; *spec.* clubbed, set.
clericalism, *n.* sacerdotalism, ministerialism priestcraft.

---

cleanness: *purity.*
cleanse: *clean, purify.*
clear-sighted: *discerning.*
clement: *merciful, mild.*
clergy: *ministry.*
clergyman: *minister.*
clerical: *ministerial.*

clericality, *n.* clericate (*R*), clergy (*A, exc. in "benefit of clergy"*), clergymanship, clerkhood (*A*); *spec.* priesthood, chaplainship, chaplaincy.
clerk, *n.* **1.** clergyman, *see* MINISTER; (*now hist. or A*).
2. Scholar, educated person; (*clerk is A in this sense*).
3. *See* ACCOUNTANT, SECRETARY; recorder, registrar, scribe, scrivener, protonotary, conicopoly (*Anglo-Indian*), typist, stenographer.
4. *See* SALESMAN; counterjumper (*C*).
clever, *a.* **1.** smart (*now chiefly U. S.*), cute (*C*), good, pretty (*A or C*), solert (*A*); *see* ABLE, INTELLIGENT, READY, INGENIOUS, SKILLFUL.
Antonyms: see DULL, STUPID, UNINTELLIGENT, UNSKILLFUL.
2. *See* OBLIGING.
cliché, *n.* bromide, commonplace.
click, *n.* noise, tick, tap; *spec.* clap, snap.
click, *v. i. & t.* sound, tick, tap; *spec.* clap, snap.
clientele, *n.* **1.** dependants (*pl.*), clientry (*a collective*).
2. constituency (*C*), following, clientry (*R*), clientelage (*R*), clientage;—*all collectives.*
3. customers, patrons;—patrons *and* clientele *in this sense are often a commercial elegance.*
cliff, *n.* precipice, crag, steep, bluff, heugh *or* heuch (*Scot.*), linn (*chiefly Scot.*), scaur (*chiefly Scot.*), scar (*R or Eng.*); *spec.* palisade (*usually in pl.*), perpendicular, wall, krantz *or* kranz (*South Africa*).
climate, *n.* clime (*B*); *spec.* weather.
climax, *n.* **1.** *In rhetoric:* graduation (*contex.*).
2. acme (*the highest point itself*), zenith (*refers primarily to the heavens; in its figurative use, a more impressive term than* acme), climax (*implies the ascent which reaches a* climax), culmination (*implies a movement of some extent and duration*), pinnacle, crest.
climb, *v. i.* **1.** ascend, scale, mount; *spec.* clamber, ramp (*of vines, etc.; dial or R*), swarm (*C*), run (*of plants; contex.*), scramble, scrabble.
2. *See* ASCEND; *see also next word.*
climb, *v. t.* ascend, scale, mount; *spec.* clamber, swarm (*C*), shin (*C*), escalade, scramble.
climb, *n.* ascent, mount; *spec.* clamber.
climbing, *a.* scansorial (*tech.*).
clinch, *v. t.* **1.** fasten (*contex.*), secure, clench, turn (*contex.*), clink (*dial. Eng. & Scot.*); *spec.* rivet.
2. *See* SEIZE, GRASP, STRENGTHEN.
3. Conclude, end, confirm, settle.
clip, *v. t.* **1.** cut (*contex.*), snip, shear, retrench (*R*), curtail (*R*); *spec.* prune, dock, pare, beshear (*R*), shear, poll, nip; *see* TRIM.
2. *See* ABBREVIATE.
clip, *n.* **1.** cut (*contex.*), snip, shear; *spec.* nip; *see* TRIM.
2. *See* SHEARS, BLOW, GAIT.
cloak, *n.* **1.** robe (*contex.*), pull (*A*); *spec.* mantle, manteau (*hist.*), mantua (*hist.*), surcoat (*hist.*), cope, pluvial (*hist. or eccl.*), mantlet (*hist.*), domino, mask, burnouse, cardinal, capa (*Spanish*), capote, capuchin, chlamys, cardinal, prince, manto (*Italian or Spanish*), manta (*Spanish*), cowl, Inverness, Joseph (*hist.*), jelab (*Moroccan*), dolman, poncho (*Spanish*), pallium, paletot, palla (*Roman antiq.*), talma, scapular *or* scapulary, roquelaure (*hist.*), sagum, poncho.
2. *See* PRETEXT.
cloak, *v. t.* **1.** clothe (*contex.*), mantle.
2. *See* HIDE.
clog, *n.* **1.** check, weight, drag, trammel; *spec.* log, block.
2. *See* HINDRANCE.
3. dance.
cloggy, *a.* heavy, trammeling.
close, *a.* **1.** *See* CLOSED, NARROW, ACCURATE, PARTICULAR, THICK, COMPACT, APPROXIMATE, CONFINED, HIDDEN, RETICENT, STINGY, NEAR, SHORT, INTIMATE, STOCKY, SEARCHING.
2. oppressive, stale, heavy, stuffy, fusty, stifling; *spec.* musty, sultry, sweltry.
Antonyms: see FRESH.
3. tight, snug, airtight, watertight.
close, *v. t.* **1.** shut, stop, estop (*A*), cork (*spec. or fig.*); *spec.* button, lock, occlude, seal, douse, lute, stopper, plug, dam.
Antonyms: see OPEN, UNFOLD.
2. *See* INCLOSE, SHUT, OBSTRUCT, END, CLENCH.
close, *v. i.* **1.** embrace, clinch, grapple, grip.
2. *See* AGREE.
close, *n.* inclosure, garth (*A*); *spec.* precinct, curtilage, craft.
closed, *a.* close; *spec.* shut; *see* CLENCHED, BLIND.
Antonyms: see OPEN.
closet, *n.* **1.** room (*contex.*), cabinet, cuddy.
2. *Spec.* recess, cupboard, cabinet, buffet, locker, wardrobe, garderobe (*hist.*), cuddy, Ascham.
closure, *n.* **1.** closing, shut (*R*), shutting; *spec.* obstruction, sealing (*with "up"*), blockade, occlusion, infarct (*medical*), embolism.
2. *Referring to debate:* cloture, stoppage (*R*).
clot, *n.* mass, lump, clout, clump; *spec.* gout (*now chiefly in allusion to Shakespeare's use*), gob (*now vulgar*), thrombus, crassamentum, grume, coagulum.
cloth, *n.* **1.** fabric (*contex.*), material (*contex.*)

clew: *ball, guide, corner.*
click: *catch.*
client: *dependent, principal.*
cliffy: *precipitous.*
climacteric, *a.: critical.*
climacteric, *n.: crisis.*
clime: *climate.*
clinch, *v. i.: close.*
clincher: *settler.*
cling: *stick, hold.*
clinging: *sticky.*
clink: *ring.*
clinker: *slag.*
clip, *v. i.: clasp, hold, surround.*
clip, *n.: clamp.*
clipping: *quotation.*
clique: *set.*
cliquish: *exclusive.*
clock: *timepiece, ornament, beetle.*
clockmaker: *horologist.*
clockwork: *machinery.*
clod: *lump, earth, blockhead.*
cloddish: *rustic, stupid.*
clodhopper: *rustic, boor, shoe.*
clog, *v. t.: check, shackle, hamper, obstruct.*
cloister: *convent, arcade.*
clot, *v. t.: coagulate.*

spec. mungo, shoddy, dab (*chiefly dial.*), canvas.
2. dress, raiment; *both* (*A*).
3. *With "the": see* MINISTRY.
4. *In pl. "clothes": see* CLOTHING.

clothe, *v. t.* **1.** dress, apparel (*rather formal or rhet.*), attire (*dignified*), tire (*A*), array (*dignified*), costume, robe (*chiefly spec.*), accouter (*obs. or spec.*), habilitate (*R*), vest (*chiefly fig.*), garb (*chiefly spec.*), beclothe (*R*), invest (*B*), deck, drape, endue (*B*), dizen *or* bedizen (*now usually contemptuous; chiefly spec.*), vesture (*R*), encase *or* incase (*chiefly humorous*), rig (*C or S*), dight (*A or dial.*; *used esp. in romances*), bedight (*A and poetic*), enrobe (*B*), garment (*R*), guise (*A*), tog (*chiefly with "out"; S*); *spec.* jacket, deck, beclout (*R*), breech, cassock, fur, gown, coat, scarf, shroud (*fig.*), uniform, frock, tartan, enclothe, empurple (*R*), crape, coif, swathe, reclothe, reinvest (*R*), caparison; *see* CLOAK.
Antonyms: see STRIP, UNDRESS.
2. *See* INVEST, DISGUISE.

clothed, *a.* clad (*now chiefly B*), enclad (*R*), vested (*heraldry or fig.*), invested, costumed, dight (*A*), robed, habited.
Antonyms: see NAKED, BARE.

clothier, *n.* costumer, outfitter (*chiefly cant*); *spec.* hosier, haberdasher, furnisher, hatter, *etc.*

clothing, *n.* **1.** *Referring to the act:* investment (*chiefly B*), investiture (*B or tech.*).
2. dress, clothes (*pl.*), garments (*pl.*), apparel (*dignified*), habiliment (*chiefly in pl.*, *B*), array (*dignified*), attire (*rather formal; often spec.*), garb (*B*), raiment (*rhet. or B*), costume, robes (*pl.; formal or spec.*), vesture (*B or fig.*), vestments (*pl.; chiefly tech.*), claes (*Scot.*), investiture (*B*), investment (*B*), costumery (*R*), garmenture (*R*), rigging (*C*), wear (*C*), toggery (*S*), togs (*pl.; S*), duds (*pl.; S*), gear (*A or B*), things (*pl.; C*), nulls (*pl.; fig.*); *spec.* robing, gala (*A, exc. with "in"*), finery, rags (*pl.*), tatters (*pl.*), coating, livery, duck, buff (*mil.*), overwear (*R, U. S.*), overclothes (*pl.*), underclothes (*pl.*), slops (*pl.; C*), wardrobe, washing; *see* COSTUME.

cloud, *n.* **1.** meteor (*tech.*), nebula (*R or spec.*), thickness (*R, exc. of the state of fact*); *spec.* cirrus, cumulus, stratus, nimbus, cirrocumulus, rack, colt's-tail, film, messenger, woolpack, mist, fog, fogginess, scud, haze, haziness, mare's-tail, whiff, goat's-hair; *see* FOG.
2. thickening (*contex.*); *spec.* nebula, smoke, fog, vapor, nubecula, puff, scud, mist, fog, film, steam; *see* BLUR, HAZE.
3. *See* MULTITUDE, IMPERFECTION, FAULT, SPOT, STAIN, SCARF.

cloud, *v. t.* **1.** overcloud, overcast, overshadow, becloud (*an intensive*), adumbrate (*R*), obnubilate (*R*), obnebulate (*R*); *spec.* shade, shadow, befog, fog, mist, haze, steam, haziness.
Antonyms: see CLEAR.
2. *Referring to the brow:* darken, shade.
3. *See* DULL, BLEAR, SULLY, WATER.

cloud, *v. i.* **1.** thicken, darken, obscure, fog, befog, envelop, overcast, overshadow.
Antonyms: see CLEAR.
2. *See* SULLY.

cloud-bringing, *a.* nubiferous (*R*).

cloudburst, *n.* rainfall (*contex.*), deluge.

clouded, *a.* **1.** *See* CLOUDY.
2. cloudy; *spec.* moiré (*French*), watered, mottled.
3. *See* DARKENED, HIDDEN.

clouding, *n.* **1.** obnubilation (*R*); *spec.* moiré (*French*), water.
2. *See* OBSCURATION.

cloudy, *a.* **1.** nubilous (*B or tech.*), clouded, nebulous (*chiefly spec.*), thick; *spec.* overcast, foggy, misty, vaporous, fogged, dull, black, filmy, hazy, blurred, overcast, murky, lowering *or* louering, lowery *or* loury, lurid, subnuvolar (*R*); *see* FOGGY.
Antonyms: see CLEAR.
2. *Spec.* muddy, nebulous, smoky, foggy, misty, steamy, indistinct, obscure; *see* HAZY, TURBID.
3. *See* CLOUDED, DARK, HIDDEN, DULL, DEPRESSING, BLEARED.

clown, *n.* **1.** *See* RUSTIC, BOOR, SIMPLETON, BUFFOON.
2. *Meaning a "clumsy fellow": spec.* slouch (*S or C*), swab (*naut. S*), hobnail (*fig.*), lubber (*primarily naut.*), chuckle (*S*), duffer (*S*), muff (*S*), lout (*C*), bumpkin, booby (*C*), nincompoop (*S*), gawky (*C*), gawk (*C*), calf (*C*), hawbuck (*S, Eng.*).
Antonyms: see EXPERT.

club, *n.* **1.** stick (*contex.*), cudgel, truncheon (*A, exc. spec.*), bat, bludgeon, bourdon (*A; spec.* waddy, mace, mere *or* meri, nulla-nulla, leeangle, keerie, baton, batoon (*A*), knobkerrie, lathee (*Anglo-Indian*), knobstick, life-preserver, blackjack, sandbag, night-stick, billy, shillalah, staff, hickory, crab *or* crabstick.
2. *In games: spec.* hockey, hurley, driver, niblick, brassy, cleek, midiron, loftie, mashie, putter, iron, shinny, hurl (*R*).
3. *In cards: spec.* basto, trefoil.
4. association (*contex.*), union, society, guild; *spec.* combination, Rota (*Eng. hist.*), hetæry (*ancient Greek hist.*); *see* SORORITY, FRATERNITY, ASSOCIATION.

club, *v. t.* strike (*contex.*), beat (*contex.*), cudgel, truncheon (*R*), bludgeon; *spec.* bastinado, paddle.

clubfoot, *n.* **1.** *Referring to the foot:* splayfoot, poltfoot (*A*).
2. *Referring to the deformity:* talipes (*tech.*), clubfootedness, splayfoot, poltfoot (*A*); *spec.* varus.

club-shaped, *a.* clavate, claviform;—*both tech.*

clothe, *v. i.: dress.*
clothes: *clothing.*
clout, *n.: rag, blow.*
clout, *v. t.: repair, strike.*
clout, *n.: lump, clot, rustic, boor.*
clownish: *rustic, awkward, boorish.*
cloy: *surfeit.*

cluck, *n. & v.* call (*contex.*), cry (*contex.*); *spec.* chuck.
clump, *n.* **1.** *See* LUMP.
2. group, cluster, bunch, patch; *spec.* thicket, grove, plump (*A*), tuft, *etc.*
clumpy, *a.* **1.** clustery.
2. *See* LUMPY.
clumsiness, *n.*, inaptitude, inexperience, inexpertness, inability, awkwardness, incompetence, unskillfulness.
clumsy, *a.* **1.** *Referring to a person:* awkward, unhandy, ungraceful, heavy, lumberly, lumbering, lumbersome, lumbrous (*R*), graceless (*R*), wooden, left-handed, lubberly (*naut. or fig.*), lubber-like (*naut. or fig.*), booby, boobyish, inelegant; *spec.* elephantine, unskillful, draggy, inapt, lumpish, bungling, incompetent.
Antonyms: see SKILLFUL, GRACEFUL.
2. *Referring to a thing: spec.* unwieldy, bulky, elephantine, cumbrous, heavy, unhandy, bungling, botched, rough, crude, lumberly, lumbering, lumbersome, homemade.
Antonyms: see AIRY.
clustered, *a. Spec.* conglomerate, glomerate (*tech.*).
clutch, *n.* **1.** nest; *spec.* sitting, hatch.
2. *See* BROOD.
clutch, *v. t.* **1.** hold (*contex.*), grip, grasp, engrasp (*R*), clasp, clench, gripe (*R*); *see* EMBRACE, GRAPPLE, SQUEEZE.
2. *See* SEIZE, CLENCH, GRASP.
clutch, *n.* **1.** *Referring to the act:* hold (*contex.*), grip, gripe, grasp, grab, clench, clasp; *see* EMBRACE, GRAPPLE.
Antonyms: see RELEASE.
2. *Referring to the thing that holds:* hold (*contex.*), grip; *spec.* grab, grabber, claw, clasper, grasper, grapple, clamp, crampon, grappler, comealong (*S*), grapnel, lewis, lewisson, gland, fist (*chiefly jocular*), finger, nipper, nip, gripper, gripe, dog, clip, pincers, forceps, chuck, vise, wrench.
Antonyms: see RELEASE.
3. *See* SEIZURE (*in pl.*), GRASP, CONTROL.
coach, *n.* **1.** vehicle (*contex.*), rattler (*S*); *spec.* rattletrap (*S*), stage, tally-ho, drag, four-in-hand, car, carriage (*Eng.*), Pullman.
2. teacher (*contex.*), crammer (*S*), grinder (*S*), coacher (*cant*), tutor. "*Coach*" *is* (*A*).
coach, *v. t.* teach (*contex.*), cram (*cant or S*), tutor. "*Coach*" *is cant.*
coagulate, *v. i. & t.* thicken (*contex.*), clot, run (*dial.; used as a v. i. only*), set, curdle, clod (*A or R*), cruddle (*chiefly dial.*), clabber (*U. S.*); *spec.* solidify, congeal, lopper, caseate; *see* JELLY.
Antonyms: see LIQUEFY.

coagulum, *n.* mass, coagulation, curd (*chiefly spec.*); *see* CLOT.
coal, *n.* **1.** *Referring to the substance: spec.* charcoal, cannel coal, anthracite, cinder, slack, lignite, jet, cobbles (*pl.; Eng.*), duff, dross, culm, coke, carbocoal.
2. *Referring to a lump or piece of coal:* gleed (*A; chiefly spec.*); *spec.* ember (*implies a burning coal*), cinder.
coarse, *a.* **1.** large (*contex.*), crass (*chiefly B*), gross (*B or tech.*), heavy (*chiefly spec.*), thick; rank, rude, crude, clumsy, reedy, gruff (*tech. or Scot.*), homespun, homemade, earthy.
Antonyms: see DELICATE, SMALL, SLENDER.
2. low, vulgar, common, unrefined, crude, gross, unideal (*R*), crass (*B*), inelegant, unpolished, rough, plebeian (*spec. or B*), woolen (*R*), indelicate; *spec.* rude, broad, loose, immodest, ribald, earthy (*R*), rustic, clownish, brutal, brutish, swinish, scurrilous; *see* BOORISH, BEASTLY, LEWD, INDECENT.
Antonyms: see REFINED, SPIRITUAL, INTELLECTUAL, CHASTE.
3. *See* ROUGH.
coarsen, *v. t.* **1.** enlarge (*contex.*), thicken (*contex.*).
2. *See* ROUGHEN, SENSUALIZE.
coat, *n.* **1.** *Spec.* jacket, sack, jemmy (*Eng.; R*), overcoat, greatcoat (*chiefly Eng.*), jacket, ulster, oiler (*U. S.; C*), cut-away, tuxedo (*U. S for* dinner jacket; tux *or* tuck *are the C or S* forms), cassock, secret (*antiq.*), frock, habergeon, buff, tunic.
2. cover, coating; *spec.* set, scumble, wash, glaze, priming, fur, buff; *see* SMEAR, CRUST.
3. pledge (*tech. or B*), pilage (*R*), fell (*R or B*); *spec.* fleece.
4. *See* ARMS, SKIN.
coat, *v. t.* **1.** *See* CLOTHE.
2. cover, overlay, line; *spec.* lute, fur, gum, bark, paint, varnish, enamel, prime, plaster, render, roughcast, crust, wash, silver, glaze, film, plate, paper; *see* CRUST, SMEAR.
coax, *v. t. & i. Spec.* persuade, entice, cajole, urge, honey (*R or A*), wheedle, wangle (*C*), work (*C*), reason (*C*). *There is no general synonym of "coax."*
Antonyms: see BLUSTER, BULLY, COMPEL, INTIMIDATE.
coaxing, *a. Spec.* bland, gentle, winning, persuasive.
coaxing, *n.* suasion (*R*), wangling (*C*), wheedling (*C*), working (*C*), reasoning (*C*).
Antonyms: see COMPULSION.
cobbler, *n.* repairer (*contex.*); *spec.* (*referring to shoes*) clobberer (*dial. Eng.*), sutor (*B*), clouter; (*implying a clumsy worker*) botcher.
cobweblike, *a.* arachnoid (*tech.*), gossamer

cluster: *bunch, clump.*
cluster: *gather.*
clustery: *bunchy, clumpy.*
clutch, *v. i.: grasp, hold.*
clutter, *v. t.: collect, confuse.*
clutter, *v. i.: collect, bustle.*
clutter, *n.: collection, confusion, noise, bustle.*
coachman: *driver.*
coadjutor: *aider.*
coalesce: *unite.*
coalition: *union, combination, confederacy.*
coaly: *carbonaceous, black, dark.*
coast, *n.: shore.*
coast, *v. i.: sail, slide, glide*
coast, *v. t.: sail.*
coastal: *littoral.*
coating: *coat, crust.*
coat of arms: *arms.*
cobble, *n.: stone.*
cobble, *v. t.: pave.*
cobble, *v. t.: repair.*
cobweb: *network, filament.*

(*implies lightness and insubstantiality*); *spec.* cortinate (*tech.*).

cock, *n.* **1.** chanticleer (*B and usually used as a proper name*), rooster (*chiefly U. S. and dial. Eng.*); *spec.* capon, cockalorum (*dim.; C*), cockerel, singer, heeler.

2. spout; *spec.* faucet, tap, valve, plug.

3. *See* WEATHERVANE, CHIEF, HEAP.

cockade, *n.* device; *spec.* black cockade (*Hanover*), white cockade (*Stuart*), rosette, knot.

cocoon, *n.* case (*contex.*), covering (*contex.*); *spec.* pod.

code, *n.* **1.** codex (*R; implies official formulation*); *spec.* system, formulary, law, rule, religion.

2. *See* DIGEST.

codify, *v. t.* systematize, classify, digest, formalize.

coexistent, *a.* contemporaneous, coeval, coetaneous, concomitant; *see* CONTEMPORANEOUS.

coextensive, *a.* equal, coequal; *spec.* coterminous; *see* CONTEMPORANEOUS.

cofferdam, *n.* chamber (*contex.*), box, coffer, caisson.

coffin, *n.* box (*contex.*), casket (*U. S.; a euphemism and elegance in this sense*), hearse (*R*), cist (*archæol.*) kist (*Scot.*); *spec.* sarcophagus, shell.

cogency, *n.* strength, power, force, weight, conviction, *etc.*

cogent, *a.* strong, powerful, potent, good, forcible, forceful, constraining, robustious (*R*), pregnant (*A or B*), weighty, trenchant (*B or rhet.*); *spec.* convincing, urgent, compelling.

Antonyms: see UNCONVINCING.

cogwheel, *n.* cog, wheel, gearwheel, gear; *spec.* lantern, wormwheel.

cohabit, *v. i. Spec.* chum (*C*). "*Cohabit*" *is chiefly spec.*

coheir, *n.* heir, coparcener, parcener.

cohere, *v. i.* **1.** stick, adhere, consist (*A*).

2. *See* AGREE.

coherent, *a.* **1.** sticking, adherent, consistent (*R*).

2. *See* CONSISTENT.

cohesion, *n.* sticking, adherence, adhesion, coherence, cohesiveness, consistence (*R*).

coil, *n.* **1.** *Meaning a "series of rings": spec.* inductorium, helix, tendril, scroll, curl, hank.

2. wind, turn, ring, convolution, round, curl, fold, loop, circumvolution, volute (*chiefly spec.*), volume (*R*), twine, twist, twirl, lap; *spec.* bight, fake, bolster, baluster, worm, corkscrew, roll; *see* SPIRAL.

coil, *v. t. & i.* wind, loop, upcoil (*R*), twist, fold, lap, convolute (*R or B*), convolve, curl, twine, entwine, twirl, clue (*used with "up"; R*); *spec.* roll, spire, spiral (*R*), wreathe, curl, friz, enroll (*R*), belay, fake.

Antonyms: see UNWIND.

coin, *n.* **1.** *Referring to money:* piece, chinker (*S*); *spec.* copper (*C*), dump, doit, cart wheel (*S*), coach wheel (*S, Eng.*), mite, nickel (*C, U. S.*), dime, shilling, quarter, buck (*S*), *etc.*

2. *Referring to coins collectively:* money, currency, specie; *spec.* silver, brass (*dial. or C*), chink (*S*), gold, tin (*S*), copper, change.

coin, *v. t.* **1.** mint, strike, stamp, money (*R*); *spec.* contorniate, counterfeit.

2. *See* INVENT.

coincide, *v. i.* **1.** concur.

2. *See* AGREE.

coincidence, *n.* **1.** concurrence, concomitance, concourse (*A or R*), conjunction, juncture, conjuncture (*R*), conflux, confluence, syndrome (*R or A*).

2. *See* CONTEMPORANEOUSNESS, AGREEMENT.

coincident, *a.* concurrent, concomitant.

coiner, *n.* minter, moneyer (*hist.*); *spec.* counterfeiter.

coin-shaped, *a.* nummular, nummulated, nummiform;—*all tech. or B.*

cold, *a.* **1.** chill; *spec.* cool, coolish, crisp, heatless (*R*), chilly, coldish, frigid, icy, frozen, glacial (*R*), frosty, rimy, chilling, freezing, frore (*now B only*), gelid (*B*), arctic, polar, bleak, nipping, sharp, raw, wintry.

Antonyms: see HOT, WARM, HEATED.

2. *Of a creature or person: spec.* chilly, chill, chilled, shivering, frozen, frostbitten.

3. unfeeling, frigid; *spec.* unemotional, indifferent, phlegmatic, unsympathetic, heartless, unresponsive, indifferent, passionless, unimpassioned, reserved, undemonstrative, stony; *see* APATHETIC, REPELLENT, CRUEL.

Antonyms: see AFFECTIONATE, COMPASSIONATE, KINDLY, FOND.

cold, *n.* **1.** chill, coldness; *spec.* cool, coolth (*R or dial.*), frost, chilliness, gelidity (*R or B*), gelidness (*R*), frozenness (*R*), algidity (*B*), frigidity, iciness, coolness, gelidness (*R*), sharpness.

Antonyms: see HEAT, WARMTH.

2. *Referring to the sensation:* chill, coldness, chilliness.

3. influenza, grippe (*often* grip); *spec.* coryza, gravedo (*R*), rheum, cough, hack, tussis (*medical*), catarrh, rhinitis.

---

cock, *n.: turn, inclination.*
cock, *v. t.: turn, incline.*
cockcrow: *daybreak.*
cocker: *indulge.*
cockerel: *cock.*
cock-eye: *cross-eye.*
cockscomb: *crest, dandy.*
cocksure: *confident.*
cocky: *self-important.*
coddle: *parboil, caress, cherish, indulge.*
codex: *code, manuscript, book.*
codger: *fellow.*
cœnobite: *religious.*
coequal: *equal, coördinate, coextensive.*
coerce: *compel.*
coercive: *compulsory.*
coeval: *contemporaneous.*
coffer: *chest, cofferdam, treasury.*
cogitate, *v. i.: think, consider.*
cogitate, *v. t.: consider, devise.*
cogitative: *thinking.*
cognate: *related, analogous.*
cognizance, *n.: perception, awareness, intelligence, notice, jurisdiction, badge.*
cognizant: *aware, conscious.*
cognomen: *name.*
cohesive: *sticky.*
cohort: *division, band.*
coif: *head-dress.*
coiffure: *head-dress.*
coign: *corner.*
coil, *n.: noise, confusion.*
coke, *n.: coal.*

colic, *n.* bellyache (*now chiefly S*), stomachache, indigestion, gripes (*pl.*), mulligrubs (*pl.; C*), tormina (*tech.*).

collapse, *n.* **1.** *Spec.* cave-in (*C*), breakdown, downfall.

2. *See* FAILURE, FALL, EXHAUSTION.

collar, *n.* **1.** neckband, neckpiece; *spec.* carcanet, bertha, brecham (*Scot.*), collarette, fall, ruff, gorget, tucker, Vandyke, dicky (*New Eng.*), torque *or* torc, fraise, piccadill (*A*).

2. *See* RING.

collarbone, *n.* clavicle (*tech.*), jugulum (*tech. and R*).

collared, *a.* torquate, ringed; *also C for* arrested, seized, taken.

collation, *n.* **1.** *See* COMPARISON, MEAL.

2. *Spec.* harmony, diatessaron.

colleague, *n.* associate (*contex.*), partner, ally, confrère (*French*); *spec.* duumvir, triumvir, centumvir.

collect, *v. t.* **1.** *See* GATHER.

2. gather (*implying merely assemblage*), amass, aggregate, concentrate (*implies assemblage within definite limits*), concenter (*R*); *spec.* scramble (*esp. with "up," "together," etc.*), constellate (*R*), congest, dredge, rake (*esp. with "together," "up," etc.*), muster, bundle, compile, skim, scrape (*esp. with "up" "together," etc.*), round (*with "up"*), collate (*implies formal and orderly bringing together*), recollect; *see* ACCUMULATE.

Antonyms: see SEPARATE, SCATTER, DISTRIBUTE.

3. *See* INFER, COMPOSE.

collect, *v. i.* **1.** meet, assemble, throng, flock; *see* GATHER.

2. gather, mass; *spec.* concentrate, conglomerate, cluster, concenter, congest, clutter, bunch, bundle; *see* LUMP.

collection, *n.* **1.** *See* GATHERING, MEETING.

2. *Referring to the act or action:* gathering; *spec.* massing, recollection, conglomeration, concentration, compilation, concretion, collation, philately, combination; *see* ACCUMULATION.

Antonyms: see SCATTERING, DISTRIBUTION.

3. gathering, aggregation (*implying simply bringing together in a large body*), aggregate, assemblage; *spec.* clump, cluster, parcel, assortment, lot, budget, mass, congeries, colluvies (*B*), heap, pack (*derogatory*), museum, number, conglomerate, conglomeration (*implying haphazard and indiscriminate* collection), conglutination (*R*), combination (*B*), codex (*implying authoritative formulation*), code, chapter, crowd, drove, huddle, jumble, bunch, concentration, body, corpus, round-up (*U. S. & Australia*), sylloge (*R*), cumulation, harvest, file, list, confluency (*R*), chrestomathy, anthology, quest, compilation, clutter, concresence (*R*); *see* ACCUMULATION, SET, CONCRETION.

4. *See* INFERENCE, SELF-CONTROL.

collective, *a.* **1.** aggregate, collected, united, corporate; *spec.* concentrative, congregative.

Antonyms: see INDIVIDUAL, SEPARATE, SCATTERED.

2. *See* COMMON.

collector, *n.* *Referring to a collector of taxes:* tax-gatherer, toll-gatherer (*R or A*), publican (*chiefly Scriptural*), toller (*A or R*), exacter (*A*), tollman (*R*); *spec.* scavenger (*hist.*), gabeller (*hist.*), exciseman, procurator, proctor.

collide, *v. i.* **1.** strike (*usually with "together"*), meet (*contex.*), clash, hurtle, intershock (*R*), interfere, knock, shock, smash, impinge, foul; *spec.* cannon, crash, clash, bump.

2. *See* CONFLICT.

collision, *n.* **1.** striking, impact (*chiefly tech.*), impingement, meeting (*contex.*), clash, hurtle, concussion, shock, smash (*C*); *spec.* smash-up (*C*), accident, crash, jostle, dash.

2. *See* CONFLICT.

colloquial, *a.* conversational; *spec.* informal, popular, unscholarly.

Antonyms: see LITERARY, PEDANTIC, FORMAL.

colonial, *a.* provincial (*A or hist.*).

colonist, *n.* settler, planter (*hist.*), transmigration (*R*); *spec.* emigrant, immigrant, pilgrim.

colonization, *n.* settling, settlement, plantation (*R*).

colonize, *v. t.* **1.** settle, found, people, plant.

2. *Referring to the sending of people to colonize:* transport (*chiefly spec.*), settle; *spec.* exile, banish.

colonnade, *n.* portico (*chiefly spec.*); *spec.* gallery, piazza, arcade, choultry (*Anglo-Indian*), peristyle, amphiprostyle, prostyle, octastyle, enneastyle, decastyle, dodecastyle, arœostyle, proaulion (*archæol.*).

colony, *n.* settlement, plantation (*R*); *implying a special group with common interests:* group, community.

color, *n.* **1.** hue (*chiefly B, except as implying a modification in color*), tincture (*chiefly spec.*), tinct (*A*), *spec.* discoloration, lear, dye, undertone, tone, shade, tinge, glow, flush; *see* TINT.

2. *See* PIGMENT, APPEARANCE, PRETEXT, COMPLEXION, FLUSH, BADGE, FLAG, SALUTE.

3. *Of sound:* quality, timbre, tone.

color, *v. t.* **1.** encolor (*R*), hue (*B*), paint (*spec. or fig.*), dye (*chiefly spec.*), stain (*chiefly spec.*), tone (*chiefly spec.*); *spec.* discolor, tinge, tinct, tint, bloom, complexion (*R*), sip, distemper, wash, crayon, ingrain, illuminate, emblazon.

2. *See* MISREPRESENT.

coloration, *n.* coloring, colorature; *spec.* pigmentation, tonality, chromatism (*tech.*).

color-blindness, *n.* daltonism.

colored, *a.* **1.** hued (*B*), painted (*orig. spec.*), tinted, *etc.*

---

collaborate: *coöperate.*
collapse, *v. i.: fail, fall.*
collate: *collect, compare, examine.*
collateral, *a.: parallel, accessory, secondary, accidental, subordinate, related, coördinate.*
collateral, *n.: pledge, security, accident.*
collected: *calm.*
collectivism: *socialism.*
colleen: *girl.*
collegiate: *academic.*
collocate: *place.*
colloid: *gelatinous.*
colloquy: *conversation.*

---

2. *Spec.* black, red, brown, negro, mulatto.
coloring, *a.* tingent (*R*); *spec.* tinctorial, dyeing, painting, staining.
colorless, *a.* **1.** achromatic (*tech.*), white, hueless (*R*), bleached, blanched, etiolated, faded, tintless (*chiefly spec.*); *spec.* black.
2. *Of people:* hueless, pale, pallid, pale-faced, blanched, bloodless, anemic, faded, leaden, sallow, ghastly, lack luster, pasty, ashen, cadaverous.
3. *Without character or distinction:* dull, faint, muddy, wan, dingy, neutral, indifferent, washed-out, wishy-washy, indistinct, flat (*C*).
colt, *n.* offspring (*contex.*), horse (*contex.*), foal, youngster (*C*), patro (*Sp.*); *spec.* filly (*female*).
column, *n.* pillar, shaft, beam, post; *spec.* atlantes (*pl.*), atlas (*sing.*), cippus, telamon, caryatid; *see* OBELISK, PILLAR.
comb, *n.* **1.** *Spec.* card, ripple, heckle, hackle, hatchel, gill (*cant*).
2. *See* CREST.
3. honeycomb.
combative, *a.* contentious, pugnacious, militant, belligerent; *see* QUARRELSOME.
Antonyms: see PEACEFUL, PACIFIC.
combination, *n.* **1.** *See* UNION, MIXTURE, COOPERATION, CONSPIRACY.
2. *In commerce, politics, etc., referring to the action:* union; *spec.* syndication, pooling, coalition, fusion, merger.
3. aggregate, union; *spec.* (*card games*) tenace, pair, full house, run, flush, *etc.*; *see* COMPOSITE, SERIES, GROUP.
4. association (*which see*), ring, set, union, company, party; *spec.* conjunction, combine (*C, U. S.*), syndicate, cartel *or* (*German*) Kartel, camarilla, Camorra, cabinet, trust, ring (*chiefly U. S.*), gang, cabal, faction, clique, coalition, consolidation, fusion, merger, duumvirate, triumvirate, junto, junta (*R*), cave (*S*).
combinatory, *a.* combinational, coadunative (*R*).
combine, *v. t. & i.* **1.** *See* UNITE, MIX, ASSOCIATE.
2. *In commerce, politics, etc.:* unite; *spec.* syndicate, consolidate, merge, pool, fuse.
combustible, *a. Spec.* burnable, tindery, inflammable.
Antonyms: see INCOMBUSTIBLE.
come, *v. i.* **1.** approach, hither (*R*), attain (*R or A*), advene (*B*); *spec.* immigrate.
Antonyms: see DEPART.
2. *See* ARRIVE, ARISE, APPEAR, RESULT, EMANATE, HAPPEN, FOLLOW, BECOME, DESCEND, DERIVE, ACCRUE, IMMIGRATE, RESULT, REACH, YIELD.
3. fall;—*as a disease, calamity, etc.*
comfort, *n.* **1.** *See* AID, CHEER.
2. comfortableness, ease, self-ease (*R*), luxury; *spec.* peace, satisfyingness (*R*), restfulness, coziness (*implies creature comforts*), content, enjoyment; *see* REST, RELIEF, CONVENIENCE.
Antonyms: see DISCOMFORT, DISTRESS, PAIN.
3. *Of things that give ease:* easement (*R*), luxury; *spec.* solace, consolation (*implies ease in grief*), rest, satisfaction, relief, convenience.
Antonyms: see TROUBLE, ANNOYANCE.
comfort, *v. t.* **1.** *See* CHEER.
2. ease, recomfort (*A*); *spec.* rest, satisfy, quiet; *see* RELIEVE.
Antonyms: see HARASS, DISCOMFORT, DISTRESS, PAIN, WORRY.
comfortable, *a.* **1.** cheering, pleasant, tactful, self-satisfied.
2. easy, easeful, well, luxurious, well-fitted, well-equipped; *spec.* cozy, satisfactory, satisfying, assuring, roomy, snug, convenient, restful.
Antonyms: see UNCOMFORTABLE, DISTRESSING, ANNOYING.
comforter, *n.* **1.** *spec.* cheerer, solacer, aider, helper; *spec.* Holy Ghost. *Cf.* AID, CHEER.
2. *See* BEDCOVER.
comic, *a.* comical; *spec.* burlesque, farcical, ludicrous (*implies absurdity or incongruity*), droll (*implies strangeness or oddity*), *see* FUNNY, LAUGHABLE.
Antonyms: see TRAGIC.
coming, *a.* **1.** *Coming in space:* nearing; *see* APPROACHING.
2. *Coming in time:* ensuing, nearing, approaching, imminent, forthcoming; *see* FUTURE.
coming, *n.* **1.** *See* ARRIVAL.
2. *As to time:* approach, appropinquation (*fig.; A*), advent; *spec.* advance.
3. *As to space:* accession (*now R*); *see* APPROACH.
Antonyms: see DEPARTURE.
command, *n.* **1.** *See* BIDDING, AUTHORITY, CONTROL, DIRECTION, VIEW, FORCE.
2. *Referring to the faculty:* control, authoritativeness.
commander, *n.* controller (*R*), chief, superior, leader, captain (*chiefly spec.*); *spec.* commandant, general, Duce (*Italian*), Führer (*German*), chiliarch, centurion, tagus, heretoga, hetman, drungar, hipparch, killadar, lochage *or* lochagus, sirdar, proconsul, decurion, enomotarch, commendador, shogun, taxiarch, commodore.
commander-in-chief, *n.* generalissimo, generalissima (*R, fem.*); *spec.* tartan.
commanding, *a.* bidding (*R*), magisterial (*B*), imperative, mandative, mandatory, jussive (*R*), peremptory, preceptive.
commemorative, *a.* memorial, recordative (*R*), memorative (*R*), celebrative (*R*).

colossal: *gigantic.*
colossus: *giant.*
coma: *stupor, sleep.*
comatose: *stupefied.*
comb, *v. i.: break.*
combat, *n.: fight, contest, contention.*
combat, *v.: fight, contend.*
combatant, *a.: fighting.*
combatant, *n.: fighter.*
comber: *breaker.*
combustion: *burning.*
come-down: *fall.*
comedy: *drama.*
comely: *good-looking.*
comfit: *sweetmeat.*
comfortless: *disconsolate.*
comical: *laughable.*
commandant: *commander.*
commandment: *bidding.*
commemorate: *celebrate.*

commensal, *n. Spec.* companion (*contex.*), messmate, guest, inquiline (*tech.; R*), trenchmate. *"Commensal" is R.*

comment, *v. i. & t.* remark, observe, commentate (*R*), animadvert (*B; chiefly spec.*), descant (*B*), opine (*stilted or humorous*); *spec.* discourse, touch, gloss (*R*), explain, annotate, interpose, interject.

comment, *n.* remark, observation, reflection, note, animadversion (*R or B; chiefly spec.*), commentary (*chiefly spec.*), descant (*B*), discourse; *spec.* scholiasm, whisper, nothing, interjection, gossip, exegesis, gloss; *see* ANNOTATION, CRITICISM, EXPLANATION.

commercial, *a.* mercantile, mercurial (*B*), mercatorial (*R*); *spec.* shoppy.

commercial traveler, drummer, bagman, traveler (*contex.*), rider (*A*).

comminute, *v. t.* reduce, fritter (*R*), fine (*R*); *spec.* grind, grate, bray, triturate, pulverize, crush, crumb, crumble, harrow, buck (*mining*), mince, hash.

Antonyms: see UNITE.

commission, *n.* **1.** warrant, certificate (*contex.*), patent; *spec.* brevet.

2. *See* AGENCY.

3. authorization (*contex.*); *spec.* errand, mission, message, duty, charge; *see* ORDER.

4. allowance, pay, fee; *spec.* dastoori *or* dustoori (*East India*), rake-off (*S*).

5. *In a bad or evil sense:* doing (*often with "of"*), perpetration (*implies deliberate intent*), commitment (*R*), committal (*A*).

commit, *v. t.* **1.** deliver, consign, intrust *or* entrust, trust, confide, commend, recommend, refer (*R*); *spec.* resign, transfer, assign, recommit, leave.

Antonyms: see WITHDRAW.

2. *See* REFER, DELEGATE, COMPROMISE.

3. consign (*as to memory, writing, etc.*), reduce.

4. send, consign, remit (*R*), remand; *spec.* condemn, relegate; *see* CONDEMN, IMPRISON.

Antonyms: see FREE.

5. *In a bad or evil sense:* do, perpetrate; *spec.* sin (*a sin*), cut (*as in "to cut up pranks"*).

commitment, *n.* **1.** delivery, consignment, consignation, committal, commission (*R*), intrustment, confiding, commendation; *spec.* resignation, transfer.

2. *See* REFERENCE, DELEGATION, BINDING, SENDING, IMPRISONMENT.

3. warrant (*for imprisonment*), mittimus, condemnation, relegation.

4. *Referring to the document:* warrant, mittimus.

5. consignment (*as to memory, writing, etc.*) reduction, committal.

commodity, *n.* thing (*contex.*), article; *spec.* product, ware, drug (*as in "a drug on the market"*).

common, *a.* **1.** general, universal, mutual (*properly only of two*), prevalent, current; *spec.* commutual, reciprocal, joint, collective.

2. popular, exoteric (*B*), vulgar (*A or B*); *see* PUBLIC.

Antonyms: see INDIVIDUAL.

3. usual, ordinary, standard, regular, regulation, conventional, customary, prevailing, vulgar (*A*); *spec.* frequent, familiar; *see* HABITUAL.

Antonyms: see UNUSUAL, EXTRAORDINARY, UNFAMILIAR, ESPECIAL, EXTREME.

4. inferior, ordinary, trivial (*R or A*), vulgar; *spec.* popular, low, base, ill-bred, unrefined, commonplace, illiterate; *see* PLEBEIAN, COARSE.

Antonyms: see ARISTOCRATIC, EXCLUSIVE.

5. *In grammar:* epicene (*a loose and improper use*), neuter, uninflected.

commonplace, *n.* **1.** banality, triviality (*now R*), prosaism, twaddle, prosaicism, prose, cabbage (*fig. or S*); *spec.* platitude (*R or spec.*), fadaise (*French*), truism, blah (*S*), tripe (*S*).

Antonyms: see ODDITY.

2. topic; *spec.* quotation; *see* SAYING.

commonplace, *a.* everyday, common, ordinary, usual, unoriginal, hackneyed, threadbare, stale, tame, trite, trivial (*now R*), banal, plebeian (*B*), Philistine (*B*), prose, prosy, prosaic; *spec.* exoteric, platitudinous, pedestrian, dull, monotonous, tedious, phlegmatic, stolid, humdrum, pointless, sober, jejune, unimaginative.

Antonyms: see ODD, UNUSUAL, ORIGINAL.

commonplace, *v. i.* platitudinize (*R or B*), twaddle.

common-sense, *n.* understanding (*contex.*), mother wit, sense, horse sense (*C*), gumption (*C, U. S.*), savey *or* savy (*S*).

Antonyms: see NONSENSE.

commotion, *n.* **1.** *See* AGITATION.

2. disturbance (*contex.*), stir, breeze (*C*), fuss, ferment, welter, turmoil, hurly-burly, disorder, turbulence, pother, ado, todo, tempest (*fig.*); *see* BUSTLE.

Antonyms: see CALM.

3. *Spec.* sea (*as in "there was a sea on"*), rip, bobble, chop.

communicable, *a.* **1.** impartible, conveyable; *spec.* teachable, transferable; *see* CATCHING.

2. *See* COMMUNICATIVE.

communicant, *n. Eccl.:* communicator, communionist, communer (*esp. U. S.*), partaker, member (*of a church*); *spec.* kneeler.

---

commence: *begin.*
commencement: *beginning.*
commend: *praise, commit.*
commendable: *praiseworthy.*
commendation: *praise, commitment, respect.*
commensurable: *adequate.*
commensurate: *adequate, proportionate.*
commensuration: *proportion.*
commentary: *comment.*
commerce, *n.: traffic, intercourse.*
commerce, *v. i.: traffic.*
comminate: *threaten.*
commingle: *mix.*
commiserate: *compassionate.*
commiseration: *compassion.*
commissary: *agent.*
commissioner: *representative.*
committal: *commitment, reference, delegation, binding, commission.*
committee: *trustee, body.*
commix: *mix.*
commodious: *roomy, convenient.*
commodity: *convenience, thing, goods.*
commonalty: *people.*
commonwealth: *community, state.*
communalism: *socialism.*
commune, *n.: people.*
commune, *v. i.: converse.*

---

communicate, *v. t.* **1.** impart, convey, give, carry, confide; *spec.* deliver, tell, say, write, narrate, express, send, telegraph, cable, signal, wigwag, heliograph, telephone, sing, break, shout, transmit, *etc.*; *see* CARRY.
2. *In reference to disease, emotions, etc.:* impart, convey, give, transmit.
3. *Eccl.:* housel (*hist.*).

communicate, *v. i.* **1.** *Eccl.:* partake, commune (*esp. U. S.*), receive.
2. *Referring to persons:* converse (*now chiefly spec.*), intercommunicate, intercommune (*R*); *spec.* intermessage (*R*), correspond, deal, cable, talk, write, *etc.*; *see* CONVERSE.
3. *Referring to places joined by passageways, etc.:* connect, intercommunicate.

communication, *n.* **1.** impartation, impartment (*R*), conveyance, giving; *spec.* transmittal, transmission, sending, telling, saying, writing, narration.
2. intelligence (*R*); *spec.* message, telegram, cable (*C*), wire (*C*), cablegram, confidence, secret, news, information; *see* LETTER, MESSAGE.
3. *See* INTERCOURSE, PASSAGE.
4. *Referring to the relation of places joined by passageways, etc.:* connection, intercommunication.
5. *Referring to diseases, ideas, etc.:* impartation, giving, conveyance, transmission; *spec.* infection, contagion.

communicative, *a.* communicatory, communicable, transmittive (*R*); *spec.* chatty, talkative.
Antonyms: see RETICENT.

communion, *n.* **1.** *See* COMMUNITY, SYMPATHY, INTERCOURSE, ASSOCIATION.
2. *Eccl.:* liturgy, celebration, concelebration, Eucharist, Sacrament, Lord's Supper, Eulogia (*hist.*), Mass.

community, *n.* **1.** communion, solidarity (*B*), association (*which see*); *spec.* sharing, partnership, society, intercourse.
2. group, body, society, commonwealth; *spec.* body politic (*tech.*), state, neighborhood, district, town, preceptory, phalanstery.

commute, *v. t.* substitute, interchange. *See* EXCHANGE.

commute, *v. i.* (*Of travelling on a commutation ticket*) travel (*chiefly Brit.*).

compact, *a.* **1.** *See* COMPOSED, CONCISE.
2. dense, condensed, compressed, consistent, solid, close, crass (*A*), massive (*chiefly spec. and tech.*), gross (*B and fig.*); *spec.* heavy, saggy, woofy (*R*), packed, snug, tight, thick, close.
Antonyms: see POROUS, SCATTERED.
3. *Referring to things or their arrangement, as rooms, a house, etc.:* close, tight, snug, neat; *spec.* packed.

compactness, *n.* **1.** density, compression (*implies result of force*), body, consistence, consistency, denseness (*R*), solidity, closeness, consolidation, thickness, compactedness, heaviness, conjacency (*R*), snugness, *etc.*
2. neatness.

companion, *n.* associate (*contex.*), fellow (*A, except contemptuous*), shadow (*fig. or spec.*), company; *spec.* match, compeer (*R*), colleague, commensal, escort, chaperon, accomplice, symbiont (*B*), attendant, mate, pal (*C*), chum (*C*), buddy (*C*), side kick (*S*), cobber (*Australian*); *see* SPOUSE, COMRADE.

companionable, *a.* livable, boon (*R or A*); *spec.* clubable; *see* SOCIABLE, CONVIVIAL.

companionship, *n.* association, fellowship, intercourse, company, mateship (*R*), society; *spec.* symbiosis.

companionway, *n.* stairs, steps, stairway, passageway;—*all contex.*

company, *n.* **1.** *See* COMPANIONSHIP, COMPANION, ASSOCIATION, GUEST, FIRM, GANG.
2. assembly, association, party (*C or spec.*), crowd (*C, U. S. and British colonies*), boodle (*contemptuous*), sack (*C*), lot (*contemptuous*), consort (*A*), fellowship (*A or R, exc. spec.*), number (*contex.*), rout (*now chiefly B*); *spec.* bevy, flock, covey, kennel, gang, set, mob, herd, brood, crew, horde, troop, troupe (*theatrical*), platoon, squad, squadron, cohort, gaggle (*derisive*), circle, suite, concourse, vexillum, turma, team, Hanse, watch, table, caravan, faction, taxis, fexillation (*R*), mess, class, cavalcade, claque, command, posse.

comparative, *a.* relative (*contex.*), collative (*tech.*); *spec.* contrastive.

compare, *v. t.* **1.** collate, check (*C*), parallel, balance, parallelize (*R*), counterpoise, paragon (*A or B*), measure, confront, confer (*obs., exc. as imperative, and usually in abbr. "cf."*); *spec.* equal (*R*), equate (*R*); *see* CONTRAST, LIKEN.
2. *In grammar:* inflect.

compare, *v. i.* match; *spec.* vie.

comparison, *n.* **1.** *See* LIKENING.
2. collation, collating, check (*C*), check-up (*S*), confrontation, parallelism, dissimile (*R*), simile, contrast, equating, balance, compare (*with "past" or "beyond"*).
3. parable (*B*), similitude, simile, parabole (*R*), balance, parallelization, analogy (*R*); *spec.* dissimile.

compartment, *n.* division, chamber, section, inclosure, part, partition; *spec.* pane, pigeonhole, cell, closet, cupboard, coupé (*French*), locker, coffer, bay, severy, embayment (*R*), niche, well; *see* PANEL.

compass, *n.* **1.** *See* BOUNDARY, CIRCUMFERENCE, AREA, BOUND, CIRCUIT.
2. sweep (*implying extent of motion*), scope (*implying freedom of observation or range*), *see* REACH.
3. extent, range; *in music:* range, scope, scale, sweep, gamut, register (*of the voice*), diapason.

---

communism: *socialism.*
commutable: *exchangeable.*
commutual: *common.*
compact, *n.: agreement, confederacy.*
compact, *v. t.: consolidate, compose, abridge.*
companionless: *alone.*
compass: *curved.*

4. *Naut.:* needle (*fig.*), pyxis (*R*), box (*fig.; C*); *spec.* dial.

compassion, *n.* **1.** sympathy (*implying feeling with another*), kindness, bowels (*pl.; A or B*), commiseration (*implies expression of emotion for another's troubles*), pity, rue (*A*), ruth (*B or A*), heart, tenderness, piteousness (*A*), pitifulness, mercy (*implies action on behalf of the suffering or condemned*), pathos.

Antonyms: see CRUELTY, MALEVOLENCE, HATE.

2. *See* SYMPATHY.

compassionate, *a.* sympathetic, kind, tender, tender-hearted, merciful, commiserative, ruthful (*A*), piteous (*A*), pitying, pitiful, compassive (*R*).

Antonyms: see UNFEELING, UNCOMPASSIONATE, APATHETIC, MALEVOLENT, HATEFUL, CRUEL, COLD, RELENTLESS.

compassionate, *v. t.* pity, commiserate, bepity (*intensive*), condole.

Antonyms: see CONGRATULATE.

compel, *v. t.* **1.** force, oblige, necessitate, require, coerce, make (*with the infin. without "to"*), coact (*R*), coarct (*R*), drive, enforce (*A or B*), constrain, impel, move, gar (*Scot.*), distress (*R*), compulse (*A*); *spec.* conjure, concuss (*chiefly Scot.*), drum, distrain, hunger (*R*), reduce, press, dragoon, draught, wrest, exact, extract, extort.

Antonyms: see COAX, CAJOLE, ASK.

2. *See* DEMAND.

compellable, *a.* enforceable, coercible, coercive, constrainable, imperative, compulsive.

Antonyms: see UNYIELDING.

compelled, *a.* forced, obliged, constrained, beholden (*A*).

compensate, *v. t.* **1.** offset, counterbalance, balance, equalize, redress (*R*), counterpoise, countervail; *spec.* recoup, redeem, square (*C*).

2. pay (*contex.*), requite, repay, recompense, guerdon (*B*), reward, remunerate (*implies reward*); *spec.* restitute (*R*), indemnify (*implies formal recompense for loss or damage*), recoup; *see* RETRIBUTE.

compensation, *n.* **1.** offset, set-off, balance, counterbalance, countervailing, counterpoise; *spec.* recoupment, redemption.

Antonyms: see LOSS.

2. pay (*contex.*), payment (*contex.; both imply fulfillment of obligation*), recompense, repayment, requital; *spec.* amends, indemnity, indemnification, satisfaction, reward, bribe, reparation, justice, solatium, honorarium, recoupment, restitution, hush money (*S*); *see* RETRIBUTION.

compensatory, *a.* paying (*contex.*), compensative, reparative, amendatory, indemnificatory, *etc.*

compete, *v. i.* contend, strive, vie, rival; *spec.* race.

competition, *n.* contest, contention, rivalship, rivalry, rivalism (*R*), rivality (*R*), concurrence (*now used as French*); *spec.* trial, handicap; *see* RACE, EMULATION.

Antonyms: see COÖPERATION.

competitor, *n.* contestant, rival, antagonist, opponent, aspirant, concurrent (*now chiefly used as French*); *spec.* field (*competitors collectively; fig. or spec.*); *spec.* entrant, claimant; *see* RACER.

compilation, *n.* composition (*contex.*); *spec.* customary *or* custumal, anthology, chrestomathy (*B*), analecta, collectanea, collection, album, notebook.

compile, *v. t.* compose, quilt (*R; fig.*), collect, assemble.

complain, *v. i.* murmur, grunt, grumble, gruntle (*R*), grutch (*A*), lament, repine (*chiefly spec.*), plain (*A*); *spec.* moan, groan, growl, grouse (*C*), bellyache (*S*), scold, mutter, whine, fret.

Antonyms: see REJOICE.

complaining, *n.* faultfinding, complaintive (*R*), murmuring; *spec.* grumbling, growling, grousing (*C*), bellyaching (*S*).

complaining, *a.* **1.** *See* AILING.

2. grumbly (*C*), querimonious (*B*); *spec.* querulous, peevish, whiny, fretting.

complaint, *n.* **1.** *See* AILMENT.

2. murmuring, grumbling, *etc.* murmur, lament, lamentation, plaint (*B*), querimony (*R*), grievance, wail, plain (*A*), repining (*chiefly spec.*); *spec.* growl, grunt, whine.

3. accusation, charge, plaint (*B or law*); *spec.* information, grievance.

complaisant, *a.* complacent (*A*), agreeable (*contex.*), pliant, soft, smooth, yielding, supple, facile (*B*), subservient, buxom (*A*), easy, weak, courtly, yielding; *spec.* gracious, condescending, exorable, submissive; *see* OBLIGING, OBEDIENT.

Antonyms: see PERVERSE, OBSTINATE, DISPUTATIOUS, UNYIELDING, UNACCOMMODATING, DISOBEDIENT, CONTROVERSIAL.

complement, *n.* **1.** *See* COMPLETION, CROWN.

2. total, tale; *spec.* cadre (*French; mil.*).

complete, *a.* **1.** full, entire, perfect, integrate (*R*), integral (*R*), round (*chiefly spec.*); *spec.* intact (*implying unimpairment*), self-contained, dead (*implying cessation of change*), orbed (*R*), orbicular; *see* WHOLE, ABSOLUTE, THOROUGH.

Antonyms: see INCOMPLETE, PARTIAL, INITIAL, CONDITIONAL, IMPERFECT.

2. *See* FINISHED, ACCOMPLISHED.

complete, *v. t.* **1.** consummate, totalize, complement (*R*), round (*used chiefly with "out"*), integrate; *spec.* mature, crown, cap, perfect, perfectionate (*R*).

Antonyms: see BEGIN.

2. conclude, fulfill, mature, realize, perfect, achieve, effect, develop; *see* FINISH, ACCOMPLISH.

compatible: *consistent.*
compatriot: *countryman.*
compeer, *n.:* *equal.*
compendious: *concise.*
compendium: *abridgement.*
competence: *fortune.*
competency: *ability, qualification.*
competent: *adequate, qualified, able.*
complacent: *self-satisfied.*
complement, *v. t.:* *complete.*

completed, *a.* perfected, consummate; *spec.* mature, ripe.

completely, *adv.* **1.** fully, entirely, wholly, totally, utterly, right (*A or dial.*), quite; *spec.* integrally, perfectly, consummately, roundly, cap-à-pie (*French*), out, altogether.

2. *See* ABSOLUTELY, WHOLLY, THOROUGHLY.

completion, *n.* **1.** consummation, perfection, complement (*R*), accomplishment, achievement, fulfillment, integration; *spec.* maturement (*R*).

Antonyms: see BEGINNING.

2. *Referring to the state:* consummation, *etc.* (*as in sense* **1**, above), full, integrity; *spec.* infinity, maturity, ripeness, finish.

3. *Referring to the completing thing:* complement, completory (*R*); *spec.* copestone, coronation (*R or B*), crown, finish, correlate.

Antonyms: see BEGINNING.

4. *See* FINISHING, ACCOMPLISHMENT.

completive, *a.* completory (*R*), perfective, consummative, complementary, conclusive.

complex, *a.* **1.** *See* COMPOSITE.

2. complicated, complicate, intricate, involute (*R*), involved (*all implying multiplicity and manifold interrelation of detail*), perplexed (*implies loss of sense of order*), confused (*implies disorder*); *spec.* entangled, knotty, mazy, inextricable, decomplex, dædal, Dædalian, Gordian, crabbed.

Antonyms: see SIMPLE.

complex, *n.* **1.** *See* COMPOSITE.

2. complexus (*R*), complication, compages (*R*), complexity; *spec.* network, web, tangle, snarl, intanglement, node, maze, labyrinth, knot.

complexion, *n.* **1.** *Of the skin:* hue (*now almost equiv. to "color"*), color, blee (*A*), make-up, temperament (*hist.*), constitution (*med.*).

2. *See* APPEARANCE, ASPECT.

complexioned, *a.* complected (*dial. or C, U. S.*), hued.

complexity, *n.* **1.** complexness (*R*), perplexity, complicatedness, complication, complicacy (*R*), complicity (*R*), intricateness, intricacy, involvedness, involution; *spec.* confusion, inextricability, intricableness, entanglement, maziness.

2. *See* COMPLEX.

compliant, *a.* conformable, compliable (*now R*); *spec.* resigned; *see* COMPLAISANT, OBEDIENT.

Antonyms: see DISOBEDIENT.

complicate, *v. t.* perplex (*implies confusion and uncertainty*), intricate (*R*), involve, complex, compound; *spec.* embarrass, entangle, intertangle (*R*), interlace, decompound.

Antonyms: see SIMPLIFY.

complicity, *n.* association, confederacy, connivance, assistance, conspiracy, privity, guilt.

Antonyms: see INNOCENCE.

compliment, *n.* **1.** praise (*contex.*), honor (*contex.*); *spec.* encomium, eulogy, tribute, panegyric (*all four implying public and formal praise:* panegyric *implies in addition elaborate praise*), flattery (*implies insincerity and excessive praise*), commendation, ovation (*implies enthusiasm and spontaneity*).

Antonyms: see DISPARAGEMENT, CENSURE, REPROOF, CONDEMNATION.

2. *In pl.: see* RESPECT.

compliment, *v. t.* **1.** praise (*contex.*), honor (*contex.*); *spec.* commend, congratulate, eulogize, extol, flatter, favor.

Antonyms: see DISPARAGE, CENSURE, REPROVE, CONDEMN.

2. *See* PRESENT, BESTOW.

comply, *v. t.* conform (*used with "to"*), agree, assent, yield, submit, aquiesce; *see* OBEY.

component, *a.* constituent, constitutive, compositional (*R*), ingredient, integral (*chiefly spec.*), integrant (*chiefly spec.*); *spec.* partial, elemental, essential.

component, *n.* part, constituent, ingredient, principle, element, radicle, material, feature; *spec.* intermixture, member, subdivision.

compose, *v. t.* **1.** make (*contex.*), constitute, form, compound (*implies close and organic union of components*), compact, compile (*implies loose interrelation of the component parts*), build (*chiefly spec.*); *spec.* synthesize, construct, weave, fabricate, mix.

Antonyms: see ANALYZE, DISINTEGRATE.

2. produce, make, do, indite (*B*), frame, build, gignate (*R and jocular*), prepare; *spec.* write, draw, redact, twist, address, compile, recompose, collate, conflate (*R*), sonnetize (*R*), dash (*used with "off"*), improvise, scribble, hexametrize, score, precompose, fable; *see* COMPILE. EXTEMPORIZE.

3. *In printing:* set.

4. *See* ARRANGE.

5. calm (*contex.*), assuage, collect, recover, recollect (*pron.* rek-o-lekt'), recall.

compose, *v. i. Spec.* write, sonnetize, sonnet, sonneteer, pamphletize, elegize, epitaph, epigrammatize, epilogize *or* epiloguize (*R*), prose, poetize.

composed, *a.* **1.** constituted, formed, compact *or* compacted (*A*), compounded, compiled, compaginated (*R*).

2. calm (*contex.*), collected, serene, tranquil, self-possessed, cool, unruffled, unexcited; *see* PEACEFUL.

Antonyms: see EXCITED, UNEASY.

composer, *n.* **1.** maker, doer, poet (*R or A*), constructor, constructer (*R*), framer, former, builder.

2. author (*which see*); *spec.* melodist, melodramatist, symphonist, hymnist, hymnodist, harmonist.

3. *In music:* author.

composite, *a.* compound, complex (*A*), concrete (*B or spec.*), decomposite (*tech.*), com-

---

complication: *complexity.*
complimentary: *laudatory.*
comport, *v. t.: behave.*
comport, *v. i.: agree.*

---

plicate (*A*); *spec.* decompound, colonial, polyzoic, polygenous, conflate *or* conflated (*B*).
Antonyms: see SIMPLE.

composite, *n.* compound, composition, complexus (*tech.*), compo (*S, chiefly Eng.*), complex (*A*), confection (*R or spec.*), combination, compost (*B*); *spec.* breccia, conglomerate, compositum, motley, conserve, pot pourri (*French*), hash (*C*), rehash (*C*).

composition, *n.* **1.** preparation (*contex.*), constitution, make-up, making, formation, confection (*R*), compaction (*R*), synthesis (*B*), framing, compounding, building; *spec.* dispensation; *see* STRUCTURE, MIXTURE.
Antonyms: see ANALYSIS.
2. *Referring to the distinctive character:* constitution, make, make-up, texture, nature.
3. *See* COMPOSITE, COMPROMISE.
4. production, authorship, writing, inditing *or* inditement (*B*); *spec.* invention opus (*often humorous*), work, effort, effusion (*contemptuous*), imagination, conflation; *see* COMPILATION.
5. *In music: spec.* instrumentation, hymnology, hymnody, songcraft.
6. *Referring to literary productions:* production, preparation, piece, opus; *spec.* work, opuscule, screed, book, tome (*contemptuous*), volume, pamphlet, brochure, paper, discourse, disquisition, effusion, dissertation, tract, disputation, essay, thesis, theme, treatise, tractate, study, fiction, poem, novel, sequence, prose, exercise, elucubration (*R*), lucubration (*often humorous*), conflation (*A*), pastoral, scribble, thing (*contemptuous*), number (*often with "little"*; *C*), morceau (*French*), Balaam, extravaganza, niminy-piminy, dithyramb, descant, diatribe, brainstorm, ditty.
7. *Referring to musical productions:* production, opus; *spec.* compilation, drama, oratorio, concertino, concerto, aria, fugue, study, sonata, sonatina, nocturne, intermezzo, madrigal, duet, quartet, sextet, morceau (*French*), melologue (*R*), medley, melopœia, ditty.
8. *In art: spec.* relief, relievo, alto-relievo, basso-relievo, statue, painting, etching, *etc.*
9. typesetting, typography.

compositive, *a.* constitutive, synthetical; *spec.* retextive (*logic; R*).
Antonyms: see ANALYTICAL.

compositor, *n.* composer, typesetter; *spec.* typothetæ (*pl.*), printer.

composure, *n.* calm (*contex.*), serenity, tranquillity, collection, recollection, self-possession; *see* BALANCE, PEACE.

compotation, *n.* drinking (*contex.*), potation, symposium; *spec.* carouse, souse (*S*), bust (*S*), binge (*S*), soak (*S*), booze (*S*), bender (*S*), bat (*S*).

comprehensive, *a.* **1.** *See* INCLUSIVE, UNDERSTANDING.
2. large, wide, widespread, world-wide, extensive, broad, general, wholesale, sweeping, expansive; *spec.* all-embracing, encyclopedic, catholic.
Antonyms: see NARROW.

compromise, *n.* **1.** arrangement (*contex.*), composition, adjustment.
2. *See* ARRANGEMENT, CONCESSION.

compromise, *v. t.* **1.** arrange (*contex.*), compound, commute, adjust, settle.
2. jeopardize, imperil, endanger, risk.
3. prejudice, commit.

comptroller, *n.* controller; *spec.* steward, auditor, overseer.

compulsion, *n.* force, forcing, obligation, necessitation, coercion, coaction (*R*), coarctation (*R*), constraint, impulsion (*R*), pressure, reduction, enforcement; *spec.* necessity, concession (*chiefly Scot.*), distraint.
Antonyms: see COAXING, CAJOLERY.

compulsory, *a.* **1.** compellent (*R*), obligatory, necessitative, coercive, imperative, coercionary (*R*), coactive (*R*), constraining, impelling, moving, imperious; *spec.* violent, inexorable.
2. forced, enforced, obligatory, binding, peremptory, compulsive.
Antonyms: see OPTIONAL.

computable, *a.* calculable, countable, numerable, reckonable, *etc.*

computation, *n.* **1.** calculation, reckoning, account (*now only in a few phrases, as "money of account"*), computus (*hist.*); *spec.* estimation, counting, recount, telling (*A*), numbering, numeration, enumeration, denumeration (*R*), division, multiplication, subtraction, calculus, indigitation (*R*), supputation (*R*), ciphering, rhabdology, daytale *or* daytal *or* datal (*local Eng.*), expansion, capitation, logistics; *see* ADDITION.
2. *Referring to the result arrived at:* result, answer, account, calculation, reckoning; *spec.* score, sum, quotient, multiple, estimate.

computative, *a.* calculative; *spec.* enumerative, numerative.

compute, *v. t. & i.* calculate, reckon; *spec.* count, recount, figure, tell (*A*), numerate, enumerate, cast, number, connumerate (*R*), divide, multiply, subtract, cipher (*C, U. S.*), estimate, tally; *see* ADD.

comrade, *n.* associate, companion, fellow, frater (*Latin*); *spec.* contubernal, classmate, mate, tentmate, schoolmate, messmate, roommate, crony (*intimate*), buddy (*C*), partner, pardner (*C*), pal (*C*), brother (*fraternity*);

compost: *fertilizer.*
compote: *preserve.*
compound, *n.: inclosure.*
compound, *a.: composite.*
compound, *n.: composite, derivative.*
compound, *v. t.: compose, complicate, arrange, pay.*
comprehend: *understand, include, imply.*
comprehensible: *understandable.*
comprehension: *understanding, intelligence, inclusion.*
compress, *v. t.: squeeze, condense, crowd, consolidate, constrict, abridge.*
comprise: *include.*
compunction: *regret.*
compunctious: *regretful.*
concatenate: *connect.*
concatenation: *connection, series.*
concave: *hollow, hole.*
conceal: *hide.*
concealed: *hidden, secret.*
concealment: *hiding, secrecy.*

kick, *or* side kick (*S*), bunkie (*S*), boy friend (*C*), girl friend (*C*), coachfellow, playmate, playfellow, chum (*C*); *see* INTIMATE.

concede, *v. t.* **1.** *See* ACKNOWLEDGE, GRANT, RELINQUISH.
2. allow, grant, yield.

conceit, *n.* **1.** conception, idea.
2. judgment, opinion.
3. conceitedness, self-esteem, self-complacency, self-conceit, self-exaltation, inflation, self-pleasing (*R*), self-glorification, self-sufficiency, sufficiency, self-satisfaction, self-admiration, megalomania (*implying notions of grandeur*), egoism (*implying excessive self love*), egotism (*implying more self conceit than* egoism); vanity (*implying especially emptiness and futility*), pride (*generally a far stronger term than conceit*), overweening, overweeningness, outrecuidance (*French; R*), assurance, puppyism (*implying silliness and emptiness*).
Antonyms: see BASHFULNESS, MODESTY, HUMBLENESS.
4. *See* IMAGINATION.
5. notion, caprice (*emphasizing suddenness and willfulness*), quip (*implying wit and oddity*), quirk (*implying suddenness and oddity*), fancy (*implies playfulness and imagination*), device (*A*), crochet, maggot (*emphasizes the fantastic*), crank, trick; *see* CAPRICE.

conceited, *a.* self-complacent, self-satisfied, self-assured, proud (*intensitive in this sense*), self-pleased, self-conceited, egotistical, egotistic, vain, overweening, priggish, self-opinionated, self-opinioned, self-sufficient, inflated, blown (*B*), conceity (*C, chiefly Scot.*).
Antonyms: see BASHFUL, MODEST.

conceive, *v. t.* **1.** form (*in the womb*).
2. form (*in the mind*), frame, ideate (*R*), brain (*R*), beget, engender, create, imagine.
3. *See* IMAGINE, DEVISE, THINK, UNDERSTAND.

concentrate, *v. t.* **1.** concenter (*R*), converge, strengthen, gather, collect; *spec.* reconcentrate; *see* DISTILL, INTENSIFY, CONDENSE, UNITE, FOCUS.
Antonyms: see SEPARATE, SCATTER, DISPERSE, DIFFUSE.
2. *Referring to the mind, attention, ideas, etc.:* focus (*fig.*), center, fix, consolidate (*fig.*) recollect; *spec.* rally, localize; *see* APPLY.

concentrated, *a. Spec.* condensed, intent (*of a person*), fixed, intensified, *etc.*
Antonyms: see DIFFUSE.

conception, *n.* **1.** conceiving; *spec.* superfetation *or* superfœtation.
2. *Spec.* embryo, fetus *or* fœtus.
3. *See* IMAGINATION, THINKING, UNDERSTANDING, IDEA, PLAN.

conceptual, *a.* conceptive, concipient (*A*).

concert, *n.* **1.** *See* COÖPERATION, CONSPIRACY, AGREEMENT.
2. entertainment, consort (*A or hist.*); *spec.* aubade (*French*), madrigal, serenade, recital, program, musical, matinee.

concession, *n.* **1.** *See* ACCESSION, ACKNOWLEDGMENT, RELINQUISHMENT, GRANT.
2. cession, allowance, granting, grant, yielding, conferral, conferment; *spec.* compromise.

conciliate, *v. t.* **1.** win (*favor, a person, etc.*), square (*a person; C*); *spec.* curry (*favor*).
2. reconcile (*as theories, differences*).
3. *See* PACIFY.

concise, *a.* brief (*contex.; implies limited length*), terse (*implies point and effectiveness*), condensed (*implies reduction in extent*), short (*contex.*), pithy (*implies concentration and matter*), compact (*implies economy in space*), sententious (*implies energy and brevity*); compressed, succinct, summary; *spec.* laconic, holophrastic, curt, epigrammatic, compendious.
Antonyms: see PROLIX, WORDY, VERBOSE, DISCURSIVE.

conciseness, *a.* brevity, shortness (*contex.*), concision (*R*), syntomy (*R*), shortness (*contex.*), terseness, commatism (*B*), succinctness, compactness; *spec.* laconism, *etc.*

conclude, *v. t.* **1.** *See* END, INFER, DECIDE.
2. effect, make, drive, close; *spec.* compound, clinch, sign (*C*).
Antonyms: see ABOLISH, PREVENT.

conclusion, *n.* **1.** *See* END, EVENT, INFERENCE, DECISION.
2. effecting, making, closing, effectuation.

concoct, *v. t.* cook (*frequently with "up"*), devise (*contex.*), prepare, invent, hatch, brew, contrive; *see* PLAN.

concoction, *n.* **1.** devising, preparation (*contex.*), planning, invention, brewing.
2. device, preparation, invention; *spec.* lie, mixture, dose, scheme, plot, brew.

concomitant, *a.* accompanying, concurrent; *spec.* simultaneous, coincident, coexistent, accessory; *see* CONTEMPORANEOUS.

concourse, *n.* **1.** *As to persons or animals:* confluence, conflux, concurrence, congress (*R*); *see* GATHERING.
2. *See* CONFLUENCE, JUNCTION.

concrete, *a.* **1.** *See* COMPOSITE, ACTUAL, PARTICULAR, SOLID.
Antonyms: see ABSTRACT.
2. *In reference to numbers:* material (*theol. and philos.*), denominate (*R*).

concrete, *n.* **1.** composite, compound, concretion.
2. cement; *spec.* conglomerate, beton, tabby, ferroconcrete, asphalt.

---

conceitedness: *conceit.*
conceivable: *thinkable, imaginable.*
concent: *harmony.*
concentric: *parallel.*
concept: *idea.*
concern, *n.: affair, thing, interest, importance, care, relation, firm.*
concern, *v. t.: affect.*
concerned: *affected, careful, anxious.*
concerning: *about.*
concert, *v. t.: plan.*
concert, *v. i.: conspire, coöperate.*
conclude: *end, finish, eventuate.*
conclusive: *final, decisive, convincing.*
concord, *n.: agreement, peace, harmony.*
concord, *v. i.: agree.*
concordant: *agreeable, harmonious.*
concordat: *agreement.*
concrete: *solidify.*

---

concretion, *n.* **1.** *See* SOLIDIFICATION, ACCRETION.
2. *The thing formed:* collection (*contex.*), concrement (*R*), concrescence (*R*), concrete; *spec.* calculus, knot, congelation, accretion, crystallization, geode, dacryolite, dacryolith.
concubinage, *n.* cohabitation, living ("together" *or* "in sin"); *spec.* hetærism *or* hetairism.
condemn, *v. t.* **1.** disapprove (*contex.*), discommend (*R*), reprobate (*implies strong condemnation as unworthy*), disallow (*A*), disfavor, reprehend, discountenance, denounce (*implies formal public and vigorous condemnation*), deprecate; *spec.* anathematize, damn (*intensitive*), execrate (*implies violent condemnation*), hoot, hiss; *see* CENSURE (*implying adverse criticism*).
Antonyms: see CONDEMN, APPLAUD, APPROVE, PRAISE, COMPLIMENT.
2. sentence, doom, judge (*A*), adjudge; *spec.* damn (*A*), lag (*cant*).
3. consign, commit (*contex.*), devote, doom.
4. *See* CONVICT, CONFISCATE, APPROPRIATE.
condemnable, *a.* **1.** disapprovable, disallowable, damnable (*intensitive*); *see* BLAMABLE, REPREHENSIBLE.
2. convictable, adjudgeable.
3. consignable, committable, devotable.
condemnation, *n.* **1.** disapprobation, discommendation (*R*), reprehension, disapproval, blame, frown, reprobation, depreciation, damnation (*intensitive*); *see* CENSURE.
Antonyms: see JUSTIFICATION, APPLAUSE, APPROVAL, PRAISE, ADMIRATION, COMPLIMENT.
2. conviction, convictment (*R*), sentence, doom, judgment (*R*).
3. consignment, commitment (*contex.*), committal, doom (*R*).
condemnatory, *a.* **1.** disapprobatory, denunciatory, damnatory, reprobative, reprehensive, deprecatory, minatory, threatening; *see* CENSORIOUS.
Antonyms: see APPROVING, LAUDATORY, PRAISING.
2. convictive.
3. consignatory, devotive, doomful.
condensation, *n.* **1.** thickening, concentration, coercion (*tech., and chiefly spec.*); *spec.* liquefaction (*of a gas*), distillation, collection, steam, moisture, inspissation, solidification.
2. abridgment, abbreviation, curtailment, reduction, shortening, epitomy, compression, concentration.
Antonyms: see DEVELOPMENT, ENLARGEMENT.
condense, *v. t. & i.* **1.** thicken, concentrate, densify (*R*), coarct (*R*); *Spec.* inspissate, liquefy; *see* DISTILL, SOLIDIFY.
Antonyms: see DILUTE, EVAPORATE, VAPOR.
2. abridge (*contex.*), abbreviate, reduce, curtail, shorten, compress, concentrate; *spec.* epitomize.
Antonyms: see DEVELOP, ENLARGE.
condescend, *v. i.* stoop, deign, descend, vouchsafe.
condescending, *a.* gracious (*of very exalted persons*).
Antonyms: see ARROGANT.
condescension, *n.* **1.** *Referring to an action or to an act:* stoop.
2. condescendence, graciousness, grace, humility; *spec.* complaisance.
condition, *n.* **1.** provision, proviso, prerequisite, postulate, precondition; *spec.* assumption, contingency, terms (*pl.*), defeasance, stipulation, demand, clause, agreement.
2. *See* QUALIFICATION, STATE, RANK, LIMITATION.
conditional, *a.* subject, conditioned, limited, restricted, provisional, provisory, provisionary, prerequisite; *spec.* contingent, dependent, subject.
Antonyms: see ABSOLUTE, COMPLETE.
conduct, *v. t.* **1.** *See* GUIDE, ESCORT, MANAGE, HOLD, BEHAVE, TRANSPORT, TRANSMIT.
2. *In the sense of "to carry on as an enterprise":* run, operate, carry (*often with "along," "on," etc.*); *spec.* push, drive, wage.
conductor, *n.* **1.** *See* LEADER, GUIDE, ESCORT, MANAGER.
2. guard (*on a train; Eng.*); *spec.* tripper.
3. transmitter, conveyor; *spec.* cable, line, lead, bus, buster.
cone-shaped, *a.* conical, conic, coniform (*R*), pyramidal.
confection, *v. t.* prepare, form, mix, create.
confederacy, *n.* **1.** association, league, alliance, compact (*the agreement only*), union, coalition, confederation, federation; *spec.* pentapolis.
2. conspiracy.
confederate, *a.* leagued, allied, confederated, federated, federal, associated.
confer, *v. i.* **1.** *See* CONVERSE, CONSULT.
2. talk, parley, palaver, powwow (*fig. or spec.*).
conference, *n.* **1.** *See* CONVERSATION, CONSULTATION.
2. talk, parley, palaver, powwow (*fig. or spec.*).
confess, *v. t.* **1.** *See* ACKNOWLEDGE.
2. disclose (*contex.*), tell, reveal, unbosom, disbosom (*R*); *spec.* unburden, spill (*S*), blow (*S*).
Antonyms: see HIDE, DENY.

---

concupiscent: *desirous, lascivious.*
concur: *coincide, agree, coöperate.*
concurrence: *coincidence, concourse, confluence, agreement, coöperation, correspondence, junction.*
concurrent: *coincident, confluent, concomitant, coöperative, joint, correspondent.*
condign: *appropriate.*
condiment: *flavoring.*
condition, *v. t.: stipulate, limit.*
conditioned: *circumstanced.*
condole: *sympathize.*
condolence: *sympathy.*
condone: *excuse.*
conduce: *tend, contribute.*
conducive: *contributory.*
conduct, *n.: management, direction, procedure, behavior, pursuit, doing.*
conduit: *channel.*
confab: *conversation.*
confabulate: *converse.*
confabulation: *conversation.*
confect: *preserve.*
confection: *preparation, composition, sweetmeat, preservation.*
confectionery: *factory, sweetmeat.*
confederate: *ally, conspirator.*
confederation: *confederacy.*
confer: *bestow.*

---

3. shrive, shrift (*R*).
confession, *n.* **1.** *See* ACKNOWLEDGMENT.
2. shrift (*chiefly spec.*).
3. *Referring to a body of believers in one faith:* communion, church.
confessional, *n.* stall, box (*C*).
confidant, *n.* confidante (*fem.*), confidente (*French; fem.*), confident (*French; masc.*), gossip (*A*), intimate, privado (*obs.*).
confidence, *n.* **1.** *See* ASSURANCE.
2. assurance, certitude, self-confidence, positiveness, clearness, cocksureness, boldness, surety (*R*); *spec.* insistency, certainty, credit.
3. communication, privacy, secret.
confident, *a.* **1.** *See* ASSURED, BOLD.
2. assured, sure, hopeful, optimistic, certain, positive, clear, cocksure, secure (*B*); expectant; *spec.* insistent.
Antonyms: see ANXIOUS, TIMID.
confidential, *a.* **1.** private, secret, fiducial, fiduciary, trust.
2. *See* INTIMATE, TRUSTED.
confinable, *a.* restrainable, imprisonable.
confine, *v. t.* **1.** imprison, prison (*B*), mew (*B*), incarcerate (*B*), carcerate (*B*), restrain, immure; *spec.* mure (*orig. spec.*), pew (*fig. or spec.*), circumscribe (*R*), kennel (*fig. or spec.*), embound (*R*), restrict, pen (*fig. or spec.*), restringe (*R*), close, inclose (*obs., exc. spec.*), jail, pinch, shop (*cant*), bail, cauldron (*R*), box, house, closet, chamber (*A*), cabin (*R*), crib (*A*), pound, impound, cub (*chiefly dial.*), pin, embar (*R*), impark (*R*), shackle, dam, dungeon, jug (*S*), lock (*used chiefly with "up," "into," etc.*), endungeon (*R*), bastille *or* bastile, cloister, coop, penfold, gate (*Eng. univ.*), yard, impale (*R*), enchain, incave, encage, embank, intern, constrain, enjail (*R*), labyrinth, cage; *see* DETAIN.
Antonyms: see FREE.
2. fasten (*contex.*), hold, secure, detain, restrain; *spec.* tie, jess, braid, brail, bind, button, chain, constrict, enchain, rope, *etc.*; *see* BIND.
Antonyms: see LOOSE.
3. bound, limit, restrict, circumscribe, astrict (*R*), restringe (*R*), pinch (*R*), narrow, cram; see RESTRICT. *Many of the words given under sense* **1** *may be used figuratively in this sense.*
confined, *a.* **1.** incarcerate (*A*), restrained, pent, imprisoned, mewed, *etc.*; *see* BOUND.
Antonyms: see FREE.
2. restricted, limited, narrow, close, cramp; *see* NARROW.
Antonyms: see UNLIMITED, UNINCLOSED, WIDE.
3. bedrid, bedridden, helpless.
confinement, *n.* **1.** imprisonment, incarceration (*B*), carceration (*R*), immurement (*orig. spec.*), prisonment (*R*), restraint, constraint, durance (*chiefly B and in the phrase "in durance vile"*), ward (*A*), *spec.* duress, claustration, captivity, chains, inclosure, limbo, prison, detainment (*R*), custody.
Antonyms: see FREEDOM.
2. fastening (*contex.*), holding (*contex.*), securing (*contex.*), detention; *spec.* chains, restraint.
3. limitation, limiting, restriction, circumscription, narrowness (*as of opportunity*), limit, crampedness, crampness (*R*); *see* RESTRICTION.
4. childbed.
confining, *a.* limitative, limiting, restrictive, circumscriptive, binding, limitary.
confirm, *v. t.* **1.** establish, fix, strengthen; *spec.* bishop; *see* STRENGTHEN.
Antonyms: see ABOLISH, WEAKEN.
2. ratify (*implies authoritative action*), sanction (*implies approval*), validate (*implies putting into effect*), roborate (*R*), corroborate, avouch, vouch (*R or tech.*), approbate *or* approve (*chiefly Scots law*); *spec.* homologate (*chiefly Scots law*), countersign, indorse, seal, reconfirm (*R*).
Antonyms: see INVALIDATE, DISPUTE.
3. establish, verify, corroborate, accredit, support, substantiate, sustain, clinch (*C*), uphold; *see* PROVE.
Antonyms: see DISPROVE, DISCREDIT, CONFUTE.
confirmable, *a.* verifiable; *see* PROVABLE.
confirmation, *n.* seal, support, sanction, verification, corroboration.
confirmatory, *a.* **1.** ratificatory, sanctionative, corroborant (*R*); roborative (*R*), corroborative (*A*); *spec.* signatory, obsignatory (*R*).
2. corroboratory, corroborative, corroborant, supportive.
confiscate, *v. t.* take (*contex.*); seize, appropriate, forfeit (*R or hist.*); *spec.* condemn, sequestrate, sequester.
conflagrant, *a. See* BURNING.
conflict, *n.* **1.** *See* CONTENTION, FIGHT.
2. confliction (*R*), encounter, rencounter (*R*), collision, clash; *see* INTERFERENCE, DISAGREEMENT.
Antonyms: see AGREEMENT.
conflict, *v. i.* **1.** *See* FIGHT.
2. clash, encounter, rencounter (*R*), collide; *spec.* interfere; *see* DISAGREE.
Antonyms: see AGREE, CONFORM.
conflictory, *a.* conflicting, conflictive (*R*), collisive (*R*), clashing; *spec.* discordant, interfering, disagreeing, antagonistic.
Antonyms: see AGREEING.
confluence, *n.* **1.** *Meaning "a flowing together"*: junction, joining, union, conflux, meeting, concourse, concurrence.
Antonyms: see DIVERGENCE.
2. *See* CONCOURSE.
confluent, *a.* joining, meeting, uniting, commingling, concurrent, tributary.
Antonyms: see DIVERGENT.

---

confide, *v. t.: commit, tell.*
confide, *v. i.: trust.*
confiding, *n.: commitment.*
confiding, *a.: trustful, believing.*
configuration: *form, construction.*
confine, *n.: boundary.*
conflagration: *fire.*
conflux: *confluence, concourse.*

conform, *v. t.* adjust (*suggests arrangement of minor differences and discordances*), accommodate (*emphasizes obliging effort towards conformity*), shape, assimilate (*emphasizes formal likeness*), liken (*R*); *spec.* serve; *see* ADAPT, HARMONIZE.

conform, *v. i.* **1.** agree (*contex.*) *used with "with"*), harmonize, shape; *spec.* assimilate (*used with "to"*).

Antonyms: see CONFLICT.

2. *See* COMPLY, CORRESPOND.

conformable, *a. Spec.* agreeable, adaptable, consistent, correspondent, compliant.

confront, *v. t.* **1.** (*implies hostility or distrust*); *see* FACE, OPPOSE, COMPARE.

2. contrapose (*R*), counterpose (*R*).

confuse, *v. t.* **1.** *See* ABASH.

2. perplex (*contex.*), confound, distract, disconcert, flurry, addle, flutter, fluster, flustrate, bewilder, flabbergast (*C*), wilder (*R*), muddle, bemuddle (*intensive*), fuddle, befuddle (*intensive*), mist (*fig.*), bemist (*intensive*), mess (*C*), clutter (*dial.*), muss (*C, U. S.*), fuss (*C, U. S.*), dizzy, mix (*C*), bumbaze (*R*), maze (*R*), entangle, bemaze (*R*), bemuse (*R*), blank (*A or R*), dazzle, muddify (*R*), muddy (*fig.*), gravel, bedevil (*R*), befog, fog (*R*), demoralize (*C or spec.*); *spec.* rattle, dumfound, dumfounder; *see* STUPEFY, DISCONCERT, DISCOMFIT.

3. disorder (*contex.*), mix, jumble, ravel (*R*), embroil, embrangle (*R*), entangle, mingle, muddle, commingle; *spec.* blend, confound, mess, derange; *see* DISARRANGE.

Antonyms: see ARRANGE, CLASSIFY, DISTINGUISH, ELUCIDATE.

confused, *a.* **1.** abashed, embarrassed; *see* ABASH.

2. flabbergasted (*C*), confounded (*B, intensive*), bemazed (*intensive*), puzzleheaded, faggy, misty, flustery (*R*), flustered, turbid, mixed (*C*), distracted, distract (*A*), muddy (*fig.*), addled (*B*), muddleheaded; *spec.* blank, dim, capernoitit (*Scot.*), thunderstruck, thunderstricken, astonished, overwhelmed, *see* STUPEFIED.

Antonyms: see CALM, METHODICAL, SELF-CONTROLLED.

3. mixed, jumbled, jumbly, topsy-turvy, upside-down, higgledy-piggledy (*contemptuous*), promiscuous, messy (*C*), macaronic (*B*); *spec.* chaotic, troublous, indiscriminate, mussy (*U. S.*).

Antonyms: see ORDERLY, CLASSIFIED.

confusedly, *adv.* helter-skelter (*implies hurry and confusion*), higgledy-piggledy (*implies disorder*), jumbly, hurry-scurry (*implies haste and disorder*).

confusing, *a.* perplexing, distracting, flustering, *etc.*

confusion, *n.* **1.** *See* ABASHMENT, DISCOMFITURE, STUPEFACTION.

2. *Referring to the state of mind:* perplexity (*implies inner confusion*), distraction (*suggests disturbance from without*), disconcertedness (*implies sudden confusion*), flurry (*implies intense and temporary agitation*), blankness, flutter (*humorous, implying ineffectual agitation*), flutteration, muss (*U. S.*), fluster, flustration, dither (*C*), bewilderment, wilderment (*R*), puzzle (*implies complication*), muddle, fuddle (*chiefly spec.*), disconcertion (*R*), disconcertment (*R*), fluster, flusterment (*R*), dazzle (*R, suggests overwhelming splendor*), dazzlement (*R*), puzzlement (*R*), mist, muddiness (*fig.*), muddlement (*R*); *spec.* dumfounderment, entanglement, dumfoundedness, demoralization; *see* STUPEFACTION, DISARRANGEMENT.

Antonyms: see CALM, SELF-CONTROL.

3. *Referring to the physical condition:* disorder (*contex.*), ravelment (*R*), jumble (*implying disorder and absence of meaning*), chaos (*implies absence of organic law*), muss (*U. S.*), higgledy-piggledy (*contemptuous*), jumblement (*R*) babel (*implies confusion of sound*), coil (*A*), imbroilment, imbroglio (*chiefly spec.*), hugger, mugger (*C, suggests secrecy and haste*), moil (*suggests ineffectual labor and drudgery*), muddle, fuddle, clutter (*dial. or C*); *spec.* tangle, tanglement, entanglement, promiscuity; *see* DISARRANGEMENT.

Antonyms: see ARRANGEMENT, METHOD, SYSTEM, ORDER.

confute, *v. t.* (*implying conclusive victory in argument*), confound (*A*), convince (*A*), convict (*A*), refute (*suggests more equal argument than does* confute), redargue (*Scot.*), overthrow, overturn, overcome, refute; *spec.* disprove, silence, overwhelm, overthrow.

Antonyms: see CONFIRM, PROVE.

congeal, *v. t. & i.* solidify (*contex.*), fix, set, stiffen, harden, thicken, freeze (*chiefly spec.*); *spec.* pectize (*R*), gelatinize, jelly, jell (*C*), coagulate, ice (*R*); *see* CRYSTALLIZE.

Antonyms: see SOFTEN, LIQUEFY.

congealed, *a.* solidified, set, frozen (*chiefly spec.*), *etc.*; *spec.* pectous.

congenital, *a.* connate (*chiefly spec.*), connascent (*R*), innate (*chiefly spec.*), inborn, connatural, inherited.

congratulate, *v. t.* felicitate, gratulate (*A*), macarize (*R*), hug (*oneself*), plume (*oneself*), pride (*oneself*), flatter (*oneself*); *see* COMPLIMENT.

Antonyms: see COMPASSIONATE.

congratulatory, *a.* gratulatory (*R*), congratulant (*R*), congratulating (*R*), complimenting, complimentary.

congregate, *a.* met (*contex.*), assembled.

conform, *a.: consistent, correspondent.*
confrère: *colleague.*
congener: *ally.*
congenial: *agreeable.*
congeries: *collection, accumulation.*
congest: *accumulate, collect, congest.*
conglomerate, *n.: mass, accumulation, collection.*
conglomerate, *v.: collect.*
conglomeration: *accumulation, collection.*

congregate, *v. i.* assemble, gather, convene (*implies formality and importance*), collect; *spec.* throng, muster, flock, swarm, cluster, crowd, herd (*fig. of men*), shoal; *see* MEET, CROWD.
Antonyms: see SEPARATE, SCATTER.

congregation, *n.* **1.** assemblage, assembly, gathering, collection, body; *see* MEETING.
2. church, synagogue, chapter; *spec.* parish (*U. S.*), body, order, propaganda (*R. C. Ch.*).

conical, conic, *a.* cone-shaped, coniform (*R*), cone-like.

conjectural, *a.* suppositional, supposititious (*B*), hypothetical (*B*), theoretical (*chiefly tech.*); *see* SUPPOSED.
Antonyms: see UNQUESTIONABLE.

conjecture, *n.*, guess, guesswork, *surmize*, supposition, hypothesis, assumption, presumption, fancy, imagination, suspicion, *etc.*

conjecture, *v. i.*, suppose, hypothecate, surmize, guess, infer, think, assume, presume, imagine, fancy, suspect.

conjure, *v. i.* **1.** juggle (*R*), charm (*R*), incant (*A or R*), chant.
2. *See* JUGGLE.

connect, *v. t. Spec.* concatenate, link, interlink, interconnect, associate, ally, relate, hyphen, hyphenate, hyphenize; *see* JOIN, UNITE, ATTACH, ASSOCIATE, RELATE.
Antonyms: see DETACH, DISCONNECT.

connect, *v. i. Spec.* lock, interlock, interdigitate (*R*), interosculate, meet, join, touch; *see* COMMUNICATE.

connection, *n.* **1.** *Spec.* attachment, junction, union, concatenation, interosculation, linking; *see* ASSOCIATION, RELATION, INTERCOURSE, COMMUNICATION.
Antonyms: see DETACHMENT.
2. *See* RELATION, BOND, DENOMINATION.

connivance, *n.* winking; *cf.* collusion, cooperation, consent.

connive, *v. i.* wink; *nearly related are:* collude, coöperate, consent.

connivent, *a. Nearly related are:* collusive, cooperative; *see* ACCESSORY.

connoisseur, *n.* expert, virtuoso (*masc.; Italian*), virtuosa (*fem.; Italian*); *spec.* critic, judge, collector, epicure, lapidary.

conquer, *v. i.* prevail, overcome, overthrow, win; *spec.* triumph.

conquerable, *a.* vincible (*R*), vanquishable, overcomable (*R*); *spec.* vulnerable.
Antonyms: see UNCONQUERABLE.

conquering, *a.* victorious, victor (*R or B*).

conqueror, *n.* defeater, conqueress (*fem.*), victor, victress (*fem.*), victrix (*fem.; Latin*), winner, subjugator, subduer, discomfiter, master, hero; *spec.* humbler, reducer, prostrator.

conquest, *n.* **1.** (*implying importance, skill and energy*); *see* ACQUISITION, OVERCOMING.
2. victory, win (*C*), winning, mastery; *spec.* triumph; *see* DEFEAT.

conscientious, *a.* upright, religious, faithful, strict, scrupulous, exact, particular; *spec.* careful, painstaking, meticulous (*suggests excessive conscientiousness in details*), honorable, honest, incorruptible, just.
Antonyms: see ABANDONED, DECEITFUL, DISHONEST, CARELESS, UNPRINCIPLED.

conscious, *a.* **1.** sensible (*implies physical sensitivity*), cognizant (*implies recognition and judgment*), percipient (*tech. or B*), awake (*fig.*), sentient; *see* AWARE (*stresses recognition of that which is without*).
Antonyms: see UNCONSCIOUS.
2. self-conscious; *spec.* guilty.
Antonyms: see INNOCENT.
3. *See* INTENTIONAL.

consciousness, *n.* sensibility, sense, mind, sentience (*R or B*), perception, sensation, *etc.*

conscribe, *v. t.* enlist (*contex.*), enroll, draft, impress, press.

conscription, *n.* enlistment (*contex.*), drafting, impressment, press.

consecrate, *v. t.* **1.** *To pronounce words of consecration over:* bless, seal (*R*), sacrament (*R*); *spec.* dedicate, taboo, sanctify, devote.
Antonyms: see CURSE.
2. *To make consecrate (in fact):* hallow, sanctify, sacrament (*R; fig.*), bless.
Antonyms: see DESECRATE.

consecration, *n.* **1.** blessing (*A*), sacring; *spec.* sanctification, dedication, devotion.
2. hallowing, sanctification, devotion.

consecrative, *a.* hallowing, consecratory, sanctifying.

consequence, *n.* **1.** *See* RESULT, INFERENCE, IMPORTANCE, SELF-IMPORTANCE.
2. succession (*contex.*), sequence, consecution, sequent.

consequential, *a.* **1.** necessary, derivable, consequent, sequential; *see* INFERABLE.
Antonyms: see ACCIDENTAL, CHANCE.
2. *In reference to results:* indirect, secondary; *spec.* eventual (*R*).

congress: *meeting, intercourse.*
congruence: *agreement, consistency.*
congruent: *agreeing, consistent.*
congruity: *agreement, consistency.*
congruous: *agreeing, consistent.*
conjoin: *join, unite.*
conjugal: *matrimonial.*
conjugate, *a.: joined, united, married, related.*
conjugate, *v. t.: inflect.*
conjugate, *v. i.: unite.*
conjunct: *joined, united.*
conjunctive, *a.: joining, uniting, joint.*
conjure, *v. t.: ask, invoke, bring, effect.*
conjurer: *magician, juggler.*
connate: *congenital, related, united.*
connected: *joined, united, adjunct, constant, related.*
connotation: *meaning.*
connote: *mean.*
connubial: *matrimonial.*
conquer, *v. t.: defeat, overcome.*
consanguineous: *related.*
consanguinity: *relation.*
conscript: *drafted.*
consecrated: *holy.*
consecutive: *successive.*
consensual: *agreeing.*
consensus: *agreement.*
consentaneous: *agreeing, consistent, unanimous.*
consentience: *agreement.*
consentient: *agreeing, unanimous.*
consequent: *resulting, inferable, consequential.*
consequentialness: *self-importance.*
consequently: *therefore.*
conservation: *preservation.*

3. important (consequential *A in this sense*); *see* SELF-IMPORTANT.

conservative, *a.* **1.** preservative. *Cf.* PRESERVE.

2. unprogressive (*a derogatory term*); *spec.* misoneistic (*R*), Tory (*Eng.*), blue (*Eng. politics*), stand-pat (*C*), reactionary.

conservative, *n. In politics:* mossback (*S; chiefly U. S.*), hunker (*local, U. S.*), Tory (*Eng.*), stand-patter, republican (*U. S.*).

consider, *v. t.* **1.** deliberate (*implies time and careful thought*), cogitate (*implies reflection and meditation*), ponder, ponderate (*R*), brood (*implies continuous and concentrated thought*), contemplate, meditate, ruminate, chew (*C or fig.*), study, speculate (*A or R*), turn, revolve, roll (*R*), forethink (*R*), perpend (*A*), treat; *spec.* weigh, muse, design (*R*), digest, envisage (*B*), precontrive (*R*), premeditate (*R*), preconsider (*R*); *see* RECONSIDER, ENTERTAIN.

2. regard, heed, mark, notice, mind, scan; *spec.* entertain, review, consult, esteem.

Antonyms: see DISREGARD, IGNORE.

3. think, opine (*emphasizes personal view or thought*), opinionate (*R*), regard, believe, view trow (*A or B*), judge, hold, deem, count, account, reckon, take, call, esteem, make; *spec.* rate, estimate, value, repute, gauge, misesteem; *see* INFER.

4. respect, regard.

Antonyms: see INSULT, IGNORE.

consider, *v. i.* **1.** think, reflect, deliberate, meditate, brood, mull (*C, U. S.*), study, ponder, pore, cogitate (*B*), muse (*chiefly spec.*), ruminate, speculate.

2. *See* CARE.

considerable, *a.* large, sizable (*chiefly spec.*), substantial, substantive, impressive, good, round, important, goodish, goodly, gey (*Scot.*), tolerable, pretty, fair, respectable; *spec.* material, noteworthy, comfortable, decent (*chiefly C*), handsome, tidy (*C*).

Antonyms: see SMALL.

consideration, *n.* **1.** thinking, thought, forethought, deliberation (*suggests mature and often corporate thought and study*), cogitation (*B*), pondering (*suggests the earnest deliberation of an individual*), ponderation (*R*), think (*dial. or C*), speculation (*R; implies venturesome meditation*), contemplation (*implies long and calm thought*), meditation, study, ponderment (*R*), reflection, rumination; *spec.* premeditation (*implies careful thought in advance of action*), preconsideration (*R*), precogitation (*R*), predeliberation (*R*), muse, musing, counsel, view, introversion, envisagement (*B; see* RECONSIDERATION.

Antonyms: see THOUGHTLESSNESS.

2. care (*implies watchful and cautious thought*), regard (*emphasizes the fixing of attention*), heed (*emphasizes the paying of attention*), notice, mindfulness, respect (*R*); *spec.* afterthought, review, retrospect, retrospection.

Antonyms: see CARELESSNESS, DISREGARD, IMPUDENCE.

3. importance, respect, esteem, note.

4. account, opinion, judgment, esteem, estimation, reckoning, regard, weight, view; *spec.* misestimation, misestimate.

5. *See* REASON, COMPENSATION, ATTENTIVENESS, ATTENTION.

6. fee, gratuity, pay, money, charge, recompense, compensation, stipend.

consign, *v. t.* **1.** *See* DELIVER, COMMIT.

2. send, remit, remand, resign; *spec.* condemn, assign, devote; *see* ABANDON.

3. address, bill, send.

consignation, *n.* **1.** *See* DELIVERY, COMMITMENT.

2. sending, consignment, remission (*R*), remand, resignation; *spec.* condemnation, devotion, abandonment.

consigner, *n.* sender, consignor, deliverer; *spec.* vendor, shipper, freighter, bailor, principal.

consignment, *n.* **1.** *See* DELIVERY, COMMITMENT, CONSIGNATION.

2. goods (*contex.*), shipment, order, lot, allotment.

consist, *v. i.* **1.** subsist, lie.

2. *See* INHERE, AGREE.

consistency, *n.* **1.** agreement (*contex.*), congruence, congruency, congruity, coherency, coherence, conformability, conformity, correspondence, compatibility, harmony, accordancy, consonance, consonancy; *spec.* self-consistency, consequence (*logic*), reconcilability.

2. density, firmness, thickness, texture (*spec.*), nature (*spec.*).

consistent, *a.* **1.** *See* COMPACT, FIRM.

2. agreeable (*contex.*), accordant, coherent, consentaneous (*R*), congruous, congruent, conformable, conform (*A*), correspondent, compatible, consonant, harmonious; *spec.* self-consistent, consequent (*logic*), symmetrical, reconcilable, cosmic (*fig.*), concordial (*R*).

Antonyms: see INCONSISTENT, ABSURD.

consolidate, *v. t.* **1.** compact, firm, compress, settle, knit, solidify, strengthen; *see* CONCENTRATE.

2. *See* JOIN, UNITE, COMBINE, UNIFY.

consonant, *b.* articulation; *spec.* letter, sound, explosive, explodent, sonant, surd, whisper, breath, subvocal, subtonic, continuant, stop, check, mute, liquid, semi-liquid, cerebral, fricative, trill, sibilant, glottal, lingual, labial, bilabial, dental, labiodental, interdental, nasal, guttural, palatal, velar, alveolar.

---

conservator: *custodian, guardian.*
conserve, *v. t.: preserve.*
conserve, *n.: sweetmeat.*
considerate: *careful, obliging, charitable, attentive, kindly.*
considerative: *thoughtful.*
considered: *deliberate.*
consistence: *firmness, compactness.*
consistory: *court.*
consolation: *cheer.*
consolatory: *cheering.*
console, *v. t.: cheer.*
console, *n.: bracket.*
consonant: *agreeable, agreeing, consistent, harmonious.*
consort, *n. spouse, mate, ship.*
consort, *v. i.: associate, agree.*
conspectus: *outline.*

---

conspicuous, *a.* (*implies attracting attention*) notable (*implies distinction*), prominent (*implies standing out above the rest*), eminent *implies a greater degree of distinction than* prominent), salient (*suggests the obvious and striking*), famous (*implies considerable publicity*), great (*contex.*), outstanding, signal (*implies the outstanding*), striking, noticeable, marked, staring; *spec.* notorious, glaring (*esp. of what is bad*), flagrant, outrageous (*all four implying a bad eminence*), gaudy, rampageous, obvious, brilliant, celebrated, distinguished, remarkable.
Antonyms: see OBSCURE, UNNOTICEABLE.

conspiracy, *n.* confederacy, concert, combination, plot (*contex.*), plan (*contex.*), coöperation (*contex.*), complot (*B*), conspiration (*R*), covin (*A; law*), synomosy (*literally, a sworn conspiracy; R*), practice (*A*), machination (*B; implies cleverness and crafty wiles; contex.*); *spec.* intrigue (*contex.*), boycott, collusion, cabal.
Antonyms: see DISAGREEMENT, CONTENTION.

conspirator, *n.* conspiratress (*fem.*), confederate, plotter, complotter (*R*); *spec.* colluder, Cataline (*fig.*), caballer, coconspirator (*R*), intriguer, intrigant (*masc.; French*), intrigante (*fem.; French*).

conspiratory, *a.* collusive, covinous (*chiefly legal*).

conspire, *v. i.* combine (*contex.*), confederate (*R*), concert (*emphasizes working together*), plot (*contex.*), complot (*B*), machinate (*B; contex.*), consult (*A*), practice (*A*), collogue (*dial.*); *spec.* cabal, intrigue, collude, plan, (*contex.*), trinket (*A or R*), coöperate (*contex.*).
Antonyms: see DISAGREE, CONTEND.

constancy, *n.* steadfastness, stability, fidelity, loyalty; *spec.* faith, faithfulness, endurance, truth, devotion, honor, perpetuity, continuousness, trustiness, continuity, uniformity, persistence, permanence, eternity, *etc. Cf.* CONSTANT.
Antonyms: see CHANGE, APOSTACY, VACILLATION.

constant, *a.* **1.** steadfast, fast, firm, unwavering, continued, stanch, unalterable, unswerving, abiding, enduring, fixed, settled, tenacious, diligent, assiduous, sedulous, unshaken, unmoved, steady, staid (*R*), stable, rocky (*R*); *spec.* persevering, persistent, pertinacious, Sisyphean (*fig.*); *see* DETERMINED.
Antonyms: see CHANGEABLE, CAPRICIOUS.
2. true, loyal, leal (*B or Scot.*), faithful, feal (*A*), tried, devoted, trusty, trustworthy; *see* RELIABLE.
Antonyms: see TREACHEROUS, INCONSTANT, TREASONABLE, UNFAITHFUL, UNRELIABLE.
3. *In a sense implying absence of change or variation:* invariable, invariant (*R, exc. math.*), unchanging, fixed, uniform, steady, stable, invaried (*R*), unvaried, unwavering, undeviating, regular, persistent.
Antonyms: see CHANGEABLE, VACILLATING, CAPRICIOUS, UNSTABLE.
4. *In a sense implying continuation in time:* continual, continued, persistent, sustained, enduring; *spec.* permanent, abiding, perpetual, eternal, endless, unremitting, everlasting, regular, momentary (*R*); momently (*R*), hourly.
Antonyms: see TRANSIENT.
5. *In a sense implying unbroken continuance:* continuous, continual, unbroken, regular, even, uniform, uninterrupted, steady, sustained, unremitting, unremitted, unintermitted, incessant, incessable (*R*), ceaseless, unceasing, connected, perennial, pauseless, running, endless.
Antonyms: see INTERMITTENT.

constantly, *adv.* stead-fastly, firmly, unchangingly, uniformly, continually, perpetually, always, regularly, evenly, *etc. Cf.* CONSTANT, *a.*

constipate, *v. t.* bind (*C*), tie (*with "up"*), confine (*R*), astrict (*R*), astringe (*R*).
Antonyms: see PHYSIC.

constipated, *a.* bound (*C*), costive (*tech.*), tied up.
Antonyms: see LOOSE.

constipating, *a.* binding (*C*), costive (*tech.*).
Antonyms: see CATHARTIC.

constituency, *n.* principal; *spec.* electorate, voters (*pl.*), district.

constituent, *a.* **1.** *See* COMPONENT.
2. *Spec.* elective, appointive, electoral.

constituent, *n.* **1.** *See* COMPONENT.
2. principal; *spec.* elector, voter.

constitute, *v. i.* form, be, make (*often with "up"*), spell; *spec.* aggregate (*C*), total; *with a cognate object, as in "fifty-two cards constitute a pack."*

constitution, *n.* **1.** *See* APPOINTMENT, ESTABLISHMENT, STRUCTURE, TEXTURE, COMPOSITION.
2. nature (*contex.*), make-up, organization, make; *spec.* temperament, complexion (*A*), physique; *see* DISPOSITION.
3. decree (*contex.*), law, edict; *spec.* fundamental law, organic law.

constitutional, *a.* **1.** natural, organic, hectic (*obs.*); *spec.* temperamental, diathetic.
2. *See* ESSENTIAL.
3. *In law:* organic, politic (*R*); *see* LAWFUL.

constraint, *n.* **1.** *See* COMPULSION, CONSTRICTION.
2. *Referring to a compelling force:* pressure, press, force, stress, duress (*chiefly spec.*), distress, pinch, cramp (*R*).
3. restraint, repression, reserve; *see* EMBARRASSMENT, STIFFNESS, SELF-CONTROL.
Antonyms: see EASE, FAMILIARITY.

constrict, *v. t.* squeeze (*contex.*), compress (*contex.*), bind, contract, cramp, astrict (*R*), astringe (*R*), constringe, constrain (*B*); *spec.* strangulate, choke, tighten; *see* CONFINE, NARROW.

---

consternation: *fear.*
constitute, *v. t.: appoint, establish, create, compose, make.*
constituted: *being.*
constitutive: *component, creative.*
constrain: *compel, confine, restrict.*
constrained: *stiff, forced.*
constraining: *compulsory.*

Antonyms: see FREE, ENLARGE, DISTEND, INFLATE.

constriction, *n.* **1.** compression, tightness, squeezing, contraction, constraint (*B*), narrowing, astriction (*R*), contingency (*R*).

Antonyms: see INFLATION.

2. contraction, stricture, closure; *spec.* intake, neck, choke; *spec.* narrowing.

construct, *v. t.* **1.** *In reference to physical things:* make, build, form, frame (*emphasizes building and structure*), confect (*R, suggests lightness and delicacy*), configurate (*R, emphasizes form and pattern*), configure, compose, join, fabricate (*often suggests deception or falseness*); *spec.* erect, draw, forge, contour.

Antonyms: see DESTROY, ABATE, DEMOLISH.

2. *In reference to ideas, plans, etc.:* create (*contex.*), conceive, design, build, fabricate, contrive, weave, frame.

Antonyms: see DESTROY, ABOLISH.

construction, *n.* **1.** *The act:* making, building, formation, erection, fabrication, composition; *spec.* malconstruction, manufacture.

2. *The thing:* form, building, structure, fabrication, figure (*chiefly spec.*), contrivance, conformation (*chiefly spec.*), configuration (*chiefly spec.*), frame; *spec.* formation, drawing, erection.

3. *As to immaterial things or qualities:* composition, contexture, structure, conformation, configuration; *spec.* frame-up.

4. *See* EXPLANATION, MEANING.

constructive, *a.* tectonic (*B*), constitutive; (*C for* helpful).

consult, *v. i.* talk (*contex.*), advise, confer, counsel, commune (*A or R*), powwow (*chiefly U. S.*), colloque (*C*), confabulate (*R*).

consult, *v. t.* **1.** advise with, confer with;—*no single-word synonyms.*

2. *See* CONSIDER.

consultant, *n.* conferrer, counselor, adviser, consulter.

consultation, *n.* talk (*contex.*), conference, counsel, advice (*A*), colloquy, parley (*chiefly spec.*), pourparler (*French*), powwow (*spec. or chiefly U. S.*), palaver (*chiefly spec.*); *spec.* indaba, interview.

consultative, *a.* advisory, consultory (*R*).

consume, *v. t.* **1.** destroy, eat, canker (*fig.*); *see* WASTE, BURN, DECOMPOSE, CORRODE.

Antonyms: see RENEW.

2. *Meaning "to use up":* devour, swallow (*fig.; chiefly with "up"*); *spec.* absorb, take, eat, drink, use, wear, kill, outwear (*R*), dissolve; *see* EXPEND, ERODE.

Antonyms: see RENEW, PRODUCE.

consumer, *n.* **1.** destroyer.

2. user (*contex.*), devourer, cormorant (*fig.*), eater, barathrum (*fig.*).

Antonyms: see PRODUCER.

consuming, *a.* destroying, cankerous (*fig.*); *spec.* depascent (*R*), erodent.

consumption, *n.* **1.** destruction; *see* BURNING, DECAY, CORROSION.

2. *Meaning "a using up":* use (*contex.*), devourment; *spec.* absorption, dissolution, eating, drinking; *see* EXPENDITURE, WEAR.

3. tuberculosis, t. b. (*C*), phthisis, wasting.

consumptive, *n.* lunger (*S or C*), hectic (*R or tech.*), pulmonic (*R*), t. b. (*C*).

contact, *n.* **1.** touch (*contex.*), touching, tangency (*tech.*), contingence (*R*), taction (*R*).

2. *In elec.: meaning "a touching piece": spec.* contactor, brush, terminal.

contact, *v. t., In commercial usage:* meet, communicate with, reach, get in touch with.

container, *n.* holder; *spec.* wrapper, package, bottle, box, bag, case, cask, empty, barrel, cash, *etc.; see* RECEPTACLE.

contaminate, *v. t.* **1.** corrupt (*implies moral contamination*), infect (*generally implies bacterial contamination*), taint, attaint (*R*), pollute (*implies extensive contamination*), soil, inquinate (*R*), defile (*intensitive; moral contamination*), sully (*emphasizes blot on reputation*), foul, befoul (*intensive*), file (*dial. or A*), vitiate, poison, empoison (*intensive; B*), envenom (*intensive; B*); *spec.* debauch, degrade, deprave, stain, dirty.

Antonyms: see PURIFY, ELEVATE.

2. *See* FOUL, VITIATE.

contaminated, *a.* corrupt, corrupted, polluted, pollute (*R*), maculate *or* maculated (*R*), cankered (*B*), *etc.*

contamination, *n.* **1.** *The act:* corruption, attaint (*R*), tainture (*R*), infection, maculation (*R*), defilement, tainting, stain, soil (*R*), filing (*dial. or A*), sullying, pollution, inquination (*R*), vitiation, fouling; *spec.* debauchment, degradation, depravation, stain.

2. *That which corrupts:* corruption, taint, stain, infection, pollution, poison, foulness, impurity; *spec.* depravity, filth, obscurity, filthiness, immorality, abomination.

3. *Spec.* fouling, vitiation, infection.

contaminative, *a.* corruptive, tainting, infectious, poisonous, depraving, defiling, polluting, infective, *etc.*

Antonyms: see ELEVATING.

contemn, *v. t.* **1.** *Referring to the mental attitude: see* DESPISE, ABHOR.

2. scorn, flout; *see* RIDICULE. *This sense refers to the act, which may not agree with the inward or mental attitude.*

Antonyms: see HONOR.

---

constringe: *constrict.*
construe, *v. t.: explain, translate, understand, interpret.*
construe, *n.: translation.*
consuetude: *custom, habit.*
consul: *magistrate, diplomatic agent.*
consummate, *a.: absolute, perfect, accomplished, completed, burning.*
consummate, *v. t.: complete, perfect, accomplish.*
consummation: *completion, perfection, end, accomplishment, death, height.*
contagious: *catching, infectious.*
contain: *include, hold, restrain (oneself).*

---

contemporaneous, *a.* coexistent (*contex.*), contemporary, monochronous (*R*); *spec.* coetaneous (*R and B*), coeval, concomitant, coinstantaneous, coincident, simultaneous, coterminous, synchronous, collateral, synchronical (*R*), synchronal; *see* COEXISTENT.

contemporaneousness, *n.* coexistence (*contex.*), contemporariness, *etc.*

contempt, *n.* **1.** disdain (*implies haughty contempt*), scorn (*implies anger as well as contempt*), despisal (*emphasizes looking down on object of contempt*), contumely (*R, implies insolence in contempt*), dislike, disesteem (*R*), misprison (*B*), misprise (*R*), misprisal (*R*); *spec.* pity (*fig.*), superciliousness (*emphasizes a sense of superiority*), despite (*B; implies abuse and defiance*).

Antonyms: see RESPECT, AWE, POLITENESS.

2. *See* DISCREDIT.

contemptible, *a.* despicable, mean, unvenerable (*R*), base, vile, low, abject, pitiful, pitiable, sorry, wretched, ignominious, caitiff (*R*), scald (*A*), scurvy, dirty (*vulgar or very contemptuous*), lousy (*C*); *see* PALTRY.

Antonyms: see ADMIRABLE, ESTIMABLE, PRAISEWORTHY.

contemptuous, *a.* disdainful, ludibrious (*R*), scornful, contumelious (*B*), despiteful (*A*), pitying (*fig.*), supercilious, insolent, sneering, cynic, cavalier (*B, implies haughtiness and indifference*), cavalierly (*R*).

Antonyms: see RESPECTFUL, POLITE.

contend, *v. i.* **1.** contest (*R*), engage, fight (*fig.*), battle (*fig. or spec.*), struggle, strive, conflict (*R*), *spec.* fight, buffet, tussle, combat, vie, rival, cope, wrestle (*cant*), war, spar, scramble, scrap (*C*), jostle (*fig.*), tilt; *see* FIGHT, QUARREL, DISPUTE.

Antonyms: see AGREE, CONSPIRE, COÖPERATE.

2. compete, contest (*R*), rival (*A*), strive, vie, struggle, rivalize (*R*).

contention, *n.* **1.** *Referring to the action:* contest, fight (*fig. or spec.*), colluctation (*R*), conflict, variance, debate, controversy (*implies a verbal contention of considerable duration*), polemics (*an intenser word than* controversy), logomachy (*B*); *spec.* combat, strife, struggle, wrestle, wrangling, feud, scrap (*C*), wrestling, scramble; see FIGHT, DISPUTE, QUARREL, LITIGATION.

Antonyms: see AGREEMENT, CONSPIRACY, COOPERATION.

2. *See* COMPETITION, CONTEST.

contentious, *a.* strifeful (*R*), gladiatorial (*fig.*), litigious (*R, exc. spec.*); *spec.* stormy; *see* QUARRELSOME, DISPUTATIOUS, COMBATIVE.

contents, *n. pl.* content (*A*), lining (*fig.*); *spec.* furniture (*R*), filling, stuffing, cargo, load, matter, subject-matter, topic, theme.

contest, *n.* **1.** contention, struggle, engagement, encounter, strife, combat (*fig. or spec.*), fight (*fig. or spec.*), battle (*fig. or spec.*), concurrence (*a Gallicism*), rencounter (*B*); *spec.* bout, scrap (*C*), tussle (*C*), tilt (*often fig.*), set-to (*S*), brush, skirmish, scrimmage (*C*), scrummage (*R, C*), bully, debate, duel, pool, grapple, match, game, pentathlon, decathlon, draw, rubber, passage, rough-and-tumble (*C*), scuffle, tournament, handicap, wrestle; *see* FIGHT.

Antonyms: see COOPERATION.

2. *See* CONTENTION, COMPETITION.

contestant, *n.* contender; *spec.* rival, entry, competitor, tilter, juster; *see* FIGHTER, DISPUTANT.

contingency, *n.* **1.** possibility, chance, prospect, situation, likelihood, case.

2. *See* CONDITION.

contingent, *a.* **1.** possible.

2. *See* CONDITIONAL.

continuance, *n.* **1.** continuation, duration, abidance (*R*), currency, course, lasting, persistence, endurance, perduration (*R*), last (*R*), run, stay, during (*R*); *spec.* pendency, standing.

Antonyms: see STOP, STOPPAGE.

2. persistence, persistency, perseverance, continuation (*R*), duration, maintenance.

3. *See* CONTINUATION, PROLONGATION, EXTENSION, STAY.

continuation, *n.* **1.** continuance, maintenance, sustenance, support; *spec.* pursuance, perpetuation; *see* RENEWAL, EXTENSION, PROLONGATION.

Antonyms: see CHANGE, STOPPAGE.

2. *Spec.* supplement, sequel.

3. *See* CONTINUANCE.

continue, *v. i.* **1.** *See* EXTEND.

2. be (*contex.*), last, endure, persist, remain, subsist, abide, stand, run, rest, perdure (*R*), dure (*A*), stay; *spec.* hold, drag (*esp. with* "*on,*" "*along,*" *etc.*), hang (*C; with* "*on*"), linger (*esp. with* "*on*"), stick (*C*), dwell, keep, live, perennate (*R*).

Antonyms: see CHANGE, STOP.

3. persevere, persist, proceed, pursue, insist (*A*), carry on (*chiefly Eng.*), go (*esp. with* "*on,*" "*along*"), keep (*chiefly spec.*); *spec.* flow, plug (*C or S*).

Antonyms: see STOP, HESITATE, DESIST, VACILLATE.

continue, *v. t.* **1.** *See* EXTEND, PROLONG, KEEP, MAINTAIN, SUSTAIN.

2. *Spec.* perpetuate, spin, perennate (*R*); *see* RENEW.

contemplate, *v. t.: consider, intend, respect, see.*
contemplation: *consideration, intention, sight.*
contemplative: *thoughtful, meditative.*
contemporary: *contemporaneous.*
contender: *contestant, fighter, disputant.*
content, *n.: contents, meaning, capacity, substance.*
content, *a.: satisfied, happy.*
content, *n.: satisfaction, happiness.*
content, *v. t.: satisfy, gladden, pacify.*
contentment: *satisfaction, happiness.*
contest, *v. i.: contend.*
context: *text.*
contexture: *texture.*
contiguity: *adjacency, expansion.*
contiguous: *adjacent.*
continence: *self-control.*
continent, *a.: self-controlled.*
continent, *n.: receptacle, mainland.*
continual: *constant.*

Antonyms: see ALTER.

3. pursue, carry, run, resume.

Antonyms: see ABANDON, INTERMIT, STOP.

continued, *a.* **1.** sustained, protracted, uninterrupted, unbroken, continuous, prolonged, resumed, gradual, successive; *spec.* sostenuto (*Italian*).

2. *See* CONSTANT.

continuing, *a.* enduring (*implying length of continuance*), durable (*with reference to substance and construction*), during (*R*), lasting, persevering, persistent; *spec.* chronic, perennial (*implying continuous growth*), steady, permanent (*implying fixed position and durability*).

continuity, *n.* **1.** *See* CONSTANCY.

2. *Spec.* continuum, contiguity, unbrokenness, sequence.

continuous, *a.* **1.** *See* CONSTANT.

2. unbroken.

contort, *v. t.* twist, wrench (*implies violence and suddenness*) writhe (*implying continued pain*), wreathe; *see* DISTORT.

contraband, *a.* forbidden, banned, outlawed.

Antonyms: see INNOCENT.

contract, *v. i.* **1.** agree (*contex.*), bargain (*less dignified than* contract), covenant (*spec. or B; implies solemnity and formality*), stipulate (*with reference to special details*), engage, dicker (*C*).

2. shrink, shrivel (*spec. or fig.*), dwindle, collapse; *spec.* pucker, pinch; *see* NARROW.

Antonyms: see SWELL, DILATE.

3. *See* DIMINISH.

contract, *v. t.* **1.** stipulate, bargain, promise, covenant (*spec. or B*); *spec.* undertake, indenture; *see* BETROTH.

2. *See* INCUR, EFFECT, MAKE, CATCH, FORM.

3. reduce, diminish, shorten; *spec.* syncopate, shrink, pucker, pinch; *see* CONSTRICT, NARROW, DIMINISH, ABBREVIATE, ABRIDGE.

Antonyms: see STRETCH, BLOAT, ENLARGE, DISTEND, INFLATE.

contract, *n.* agreement (*contex.*), promise (*contex.*), bargain, pact (*chiefly spec.*), cheap (*A*), covenant (*usually involves the government*), stipulation (*chiefly spec.*), convention (*chiefly international law*), obligement (*civil law*); *spec.* undertaking, condition, suretyship, charter (*implies governmental recognition*), lease, bond, barter, exchange, coup *or* cowp (*Scot.*), option, debenture, indenture, cowle (*Anglo-Indian*), trade (*U. S.*); *see* BETROTHAL.

contracted, *a.* shrunken, diminished; *spec.* shriveled, withered, puckered, pinched, constricted, collapsed, corky, clung, cramp.

contraction, *n.* **1.** agreement, stipulation (*chiefly spec.*), bargaining, covenanting; *spec.* undertaking.

2. shrink, shrinking, shrinkage, shriveling (*spec. or fig.*), withering, reduction, diminution, abbreviation, abridgment; *spec.* pucker, cramp, pinching, syncope, syncopation, systole, narrowing, collapsed; *see* CONSTRICTION.

Antonyms: see DILATION.

3. *See* SHRINK, ABRIDGEMENT.

contractor, *n.* undertaker (*chiefly spec.*), bargainer *or* bargainor, covenanter *or* covenantor (*spec. or B*), stipulation (*chiefly spec.*); *spec.* sweater, padrone (*Italian*), impresario (*Italian*), lumper.

contradict, *v. t.* **1.** gainsay (*B*), contravene (*R*), deny, belie, counter, controvert, dispute, negative, traverse (*chiefly law*), denegate (*R*), disallow (*R*); *spec.* counterargue (*R*), contrapose (*logic*), disprove.

Antonyms: see ACKNOWLEDGE.

2. *See* OPPOSE.

contradiction, *n.* **1.** gainsay (*R*), countering, gainsaying (*B*), denial, controversion, dispute, negation, traverse (*law*), denegation (*R*), disallowance (*R*); *spec.* contraposition, antinomy.

2. *See* OPPOSITION, INCONSISTENCY.

contradictory, *a.* contradictive, negatory, contrary.

Antonyms: see AGREEABLE.

contrast, *v. t.* compare (*with emphasis on the differences*), oppose, antithesize (*R*), differentiate, set against.

contrast, *n.* comparison (*contex.*), difference, opposition, antithesis; *spec.* foil; *see* OPPOSITE.

Antonyms: see ANALOGUE, ANALOGY.

contrasting, *a.* different, contrastive, antithetic, contrasty (*C*), contrastful.

Antonyms: see ANALOGOUS.

contravene, *v. t.* oppose, thwart, counter, defy, deny; *see* VIOLATE, DEFEAT.

contribute, *v. t.* **1.** give (*contex.*), donate (*impressive*); supply, furnish; *spec.* subscribe, raise, shell out (*C or S*), put in, chip in (*C*).

2. help, aid, assist, subserve (*R*), administer (*B*), minister (*B*), conduce, go (*an idiomatic use*).

contribute, *v. i.* tend, conduce, serve, redound, go; *spec.* minister.

contributing, *a. Spec.* contributory, accessory, secondary, assisting.

contribution, *n.* **1.** gift (*contex.*), donation (*formal*); *spec.* subscription, *see* SUBSIDY.

2. conducement (*R*), help, subservience (*R*), administration (*B or R*), ministration (*B*).

Antonyms: see HINDRANCE, PREVENTION.

3. help, aid, assistance; *spec.* instrumentality.

Antonyms: see HINDRANCE.

4. tax, tribute, levy, impost, dues (*pl.*), scot, gavel (*obs. or hist.*); *spec.* quarterage.

5. *See* ARTICLE.

contributor, *n.* **1.** giver (*contex.*), donor (*impressive*); *spec.* subscriber, backer (*C*), angel (*theatrical parlance*).

continuous: *continued, constant.*
continuum: *continuity.*
contortionist: *gymnast.*
contour: *outline.*
contrarious: *perverse, opposing.*
contrary, *a.: opposite, opposing, contradictory, perverse, inconsistent, unfavorable.*
contrary, *n.: reverse.*
contrast, *v. t.: compare.*
contretemps: *misfortune.*

2. author (*contex.*); *spec.* correspondent, editor, writer.
3. conducer, helper, aider, ministrant (*B*).
contributory, *a.* contributing, helpful, conducive, contributary (*R*), contributive, subservient, serviceable, instrumental, dispositive (*B*), ministrant (*B*); *see* ACCESSORY.
Antonyms: see HINDERING, PREVENTIVE.
contrivance, *n.* thing (*contex.*), device, contraption (*C*), fangle (*R*), fanglement (*R*), fake (*S*), fakement (*S*); jiggumbob (*C; humorous*); *spec.* invention, construction, machine, gimcrack (*C*), gadget (*C*), article (*humorous*), number (*humorous*), whatnot (*C*), jiggumascrew (*S*), do-funny (*C*), whigmaleerie (*Scot.*). *See* DEVISING, INVENTION, ARTIFICE, PLAN, FORMATION, CONSTRUCTION, INGENIOUSNESS.
contrive, *v. t.* **1.** *See* DEVISE, CONSTRUCT, INVENT, PLAN.
2. effect, manage, do (*contex.*), wangle (*C*), finesse (*C*), make (*contex.*); *see* ACCOMPLISH.
contrive, *v. i.* plan, plot, shift; *spec.* conspire.
control, *v. t.* command (*implies authority*), dominate (*implies power and will*), sway (*implies effective influence*), govern (*implies administrative ability*), rule, regulate, order, rein (*fig.*), predominate (*R*); *spec.* ride, direct, carry, hold, grip, gripe, obsess, caucus (*Eng.*), officer, prevail, master, preponderate, boss (*S*), buffalo (*S*); *see* RESTRAIN (*with reference to unruly forces*), RULE, DIRECT, MANAGE.
control, *v. i.* prevail, reign.
control, *n.* **1.** controlment (*R*), command, mastery, mastership, domination, power, dominion, paramountcy (*B*, *or spec.*), regulation, regiment (*R*), disposition, disposal, reign (*fig.*), governance (*A*), government (*chiefly spec.*), reins (*pl.; fig.*), sovereignty, prepotence *or* prepotency (*R*), predomination (*R*), curb, restraint, predominance (*R*), prevalence (*R*), prepollence *or* prepollency (*R*), preponderance, preponderancy, preponderation (*R*); *spec.* empire, clutches (*pl.; fig.*), hand, jussion (*R*), grip, gripe; *see* RULE, ASCENDANCY, RESTRAINT, DIRECTION, MANAGEMENT, COMMAND, (*the faculty*), SELF-CONTROL.
Antonyms: see UNCONTROL.
2. *See* DOMAIN.
controller, *n.* **1.** control (*R*), dominator, rector (*R*), swayer, governor, ruler, manager, regulator; *spec.* commander, arbitrator, master, master, mistress, disposer, director, boss (*chiefly spec.; S*), regent (*R*); *see* RULER.
2. *See* ACCOUNTANT, COMPTROLLER.
controlling, *a.* commanding, governing, predominant, uppermost, sovereign, master, prepollent (*R*), prepotent (*B*), paramount, dominant, dominative, ascendant, preëminent, preponderant, regnant (*spec. or fig.*), regent (*R*), gubernative (*R or B*), regulative, governmental; *spec.* hegemonic (*R*), prevalent; *see* RULING.
controversial, *a.* **1.** disputatious, contentious, eristic (*B*), polemic *or* polemical (*B or tech.*); *see* FORENSIC.
2. *See* QUESTIONABLE, COMPLAISANT.
controversialist, *n.* disputant, disputer, contestant, antagonist (*contex.*), polemic (*B or tech.*), arguer, eristic (*B, R*), polemist (*R*), polemicist (*R*).
convalesce, *v. i.* recover (*contex.*), recuperate (*contex.*).
convene, *v. i.* gather, assemble, collect, congregate (*R*), muster (*chiefly spec.*); *spec.* reconvene; *see* MEET.
Antonyms: see SEPARATE, SCATTER, STRAY.
convene, *v. t.* gather, assemble, collect, muster (*chiefly spec.*); *spec.* reconvene; *see* CONVOKE.
Antonyms: see SEPARATE, SCATTER, DISSOLVE.
convenience, *n.* **1.** *Spec.* adaptability, fitness, accessibility, handiness, availability, suitableness, serviceableness; *see* INSTRUMENT.
2. advantage, commodity (*A*), opportunity, accommodation; *spec.* easement, ease, commodiousness (*A*), comfort.
Antonyms: see INCONVENIENCE.
convenient, *a.* **1.** *See* ADAPTABLE, ACCESSIBLE, AVAILABLE, SERVICEABLE.
2. advantageous, commodious (*A*), comfortable, easy.
Antonyms: see INCONVENIENT.
convent, *n.* association (*contex.*), cloister (*chiefly B or tech.*), monastery (*usually implies a house of monks, while* convent *implies a house of nuns*), cenoby (*R*); *spec.* abbey, priory, nunnery, fratry (*A or hist.*), house, cell (*tech.*), math (*Hindu*), friary, friars (*pl.*), commandery.
convention, *n.* **1.** assembly, gathering, body, house (*spec.*), pow-wow, congregation, congress (*chiefly spec.*); *see* MEETING, ASSEMBLY.
Antonyms: see SCATTERING.
2. *See* CONVOCATION, GATHERING, AGREEMENT, CONTRACT, CUSTOM, CONVENTIONALITY, RULE.
3. custom, usage, practice, formality, conventionalism, conventionality (*chiefly spec.*), convenance (*French*); *see* FORMALITY;—*used with "a" or in the pl.*
conventional, *a.* customary, agreed, stipulated, accepted, cut-and-dried (*C*), artificial, right, orthodox (*chiefly spec.*), correct, proper, positive, approved, sanctioned, expected, usual, conservative; *spec.* stiff, contractual, academic, canonical, prim, old-fashioned; *see* FORMAL.
Antonyms: see UNCONVENTIONAL, HOMELIKE.
conventionality, *n.* **1.** conventionalism, convention, rightness, correctness, propriety, orthodoxy (*chiefly spec.*), positiveness; *spec.* stiffness; *see* FORMALITY.

---

contrite: *regretful.*
contrition: *regret.*
controversy, *n.: dispute, quarrel.*
controvert: *dispute, contradict.*
controvertible: *questionable.*
contumacious: *disobedient, obstinate.*
contumacy: *disobedience, obstinacy.*
contumelious: *abusive, impudent, contemptuous.*
contumely: *abuse, impudence, contempt.*
contuse: *bruise.*
contusion: *bruise.*
conundrum: *riddle, question.*
convalesce: *recover.*
convection: *transfer.*
convenience: *oblige.*
conventicle: *meeting, church.*
conventual: *ecclesiastic, monk, nun.*

---

2. *See* CONVENTION, CUSTOM.
converge, *v. t. & i.* center (*contex.*), concentrate merge, meet, join, unite, focus.
Antonyms: see SCATTER.
conversation, *n.* discourse (*B*), confabulation (*C*), confab (*C*), talk, converse (*B*), speech, colloquy (*esp. spec.*), tell (*dial.*), collocution (*R*); interlocution (*R*); *spec.* palaver, chat, chatter, chit-chat, gossip, gossiping, gossipry, indignation (*R*), parley, conference, interlocutory, coze (*R*), word (*with "a"*), episode, tête-à-tête (*French*), causerie (*French*); *see* DIALOGUE.
conversational, *a.* confabulatory (*C, B*), confabular (*R*), colloquial (*chiefly spec.*), interlocutory (*R*); *spec.* chatty, dialogic, cosy (*Eng.*), easy, breezy, informal, familiar.
conversationalist, *n.* conversationist (*less common than "conversationalist"*), talker, converser, confabulator (*R*); *spec.* dialogist.
converse, *v. i.* **1.** deal (*A, exc. spec.*), commerce (*obs.*), commune (*A or spec.*), common (*obs.*), intercourse (*R*), traffic; *spec.* associate. *"Converse" is now chiefly spec. but is broader than "commune."*
2. speak, discourse (*B; whereas* converse *implies interchange of thoughts,* discourse *may imply a continued presentation by a single person; or dial.*), confabulate (*B or stilted*), talk (*less formal than* speak), confab (*C*), collogue (*C or humorous*), colloque (*R*); *spec.* chat, gossip, confer (*implies purpose*), coze (*B, R*), dialogue, dialogize (*R*), parley.
converser, *n.* **1.** confabulator (*R*); *spec.* interlocutor, dialogist, interlocutress (*fem.*), interlocutrix (*fem.*), conferee.
2. *See* CONVERSATIONALIST.
conversion, *n.* **1.** change (*contex.*), reformation, transmutation, metamorphosis, reduction, resolution; *see* TRANSFORMATION.
2. regeneration, rebirth, salvation; *spec.* proselytization, proselyting, Protestantization.
3. appropriation (*contex.*); *spec.* embezzlement; *see* THEFT.
4. *See* EXCHANGE.
convert, *v. t.* **1.** change, turn, regenerate, save, reform; *spec.* disciple (*R or A*), proselyte, proselytize, Protestantize.
2. change, alter, resolve, reduce, transmute, exchange, turn; *see* TRANSFORM.
Antonyms: see FIX.
3. appropriate (*contex.*); *see* STEAL, EMBEZZLE.
convert, *n.* neophyte (*chiefly spec.*), convertite (*A; often spec.*), disciple; *spec.* vert (*C*), pervert (*contemptuous*), apostate, catechumen, marrano (*hist.*), proselyte, proselytess (*fem.; R*).
convertible, *a.* conversible (*R*), exchangeable, transformable, transmutable; *spec.* interchangeable, liquid, equivalent.
Antonyms: see FIXED.
convex, *a.* curved, bowed, bent, arched, protuberant, swelling, bulging; *spec.* prominent, embowed (*B*), gibbous *or* gibbose, hog-backed.
Antonyms: see HOLLOW.
convict, *a.* condemned;—*not a good synonym.*
convict, *v. t.* **1.** condemn (*not a good synonym*), convince (*A*).
Antonyms: see ABSOLVE, ACQUIT.
2. convince (*of sin, etc.; R*).
convict, *n.* criminal (*contex.*), jailbird (*S*), prisoner; *spec.* felon, expiree, emancipist (*Australia*), bushranger, Derwenter (*Australia*), lagger (*cant*), termer (*cant*), trusty (*cant*), lifer (*cant*).
conviction, *n.* **1.** condemnation;—*not a good synonym.*
Antonyms: see ACQUITTAL.
2. *Referring to the act of convincing:* convincement, convictment (*R*), satisfaction (*R*).
3. *Referring to the state or belief:* belief (*contex.*), convincement (*R*), convictment (*R*), satisfaction (*R*), persuasion; *spec.* possession, obsession, penitence (*conviction of sin*).
Antonyms: see CHANGEABLENESS, CAPRICE, CAPRICIOUSNESS, UNCERTAINTY.
convince, *v. t.* assure (*contex.*), satisfy, persuade; *spec.* possess, obsess.
convincing, *a.* satisfactory, satisfying, conclusive, persuasive (*now A or R*), moving, impelling; *see* COGENT.
Antonyms: see UNCONVINCING.
convivial, *a.* sociable (*implies companionability, while* convivial *emphasizes joviality*), companionable (*contex.*), festive, gay, jolly, jovial, good (*contex.*).
Antonyms: see APATHETIC, ASCETIC.
convocation, *n.* **1.** gathering, assembling, convention, call (*contex.*), calling (*used esp. with "together"*), summons.
2. *See* ASSEMBLY.
convoke, *v. t.* convene, assemble, summon, call (*esp. with "together"*), convocate (*A*); *spec.* resummon, reconvene.
Antonyms: see DISSOLVE.
convolution, *n.* twist, volume *or* volute (*B or tech.*), whorl; *see* COIL, CURL.
cook, *v. t.* **1.** prepare (*contex.*), do (*chiefly in the p. p.*); *spec.* overdo, boil, fry, bake, roast, braise, barbecue, buccan, griddle, grill, pan, jug, coddle, devil, frizzle, steam, *etc.*; *see* ROAST, BROIL, STEW, PARBOIL, FRY.
2. *See* DEVISE, FALSIFY, FAKE, RUIN.
cook, *n.* **1.** cooky (*C*), doctor (*chiefly naut.; S or cant*), chef, *spec.* magirologist (*R*), magirist (*R*), dietitian.

---

conversable: *sociable.*
conversant: *aware.*
converse, *n.: intercourse, conversation.*
converse, *a. & n.: opposite.*
convey: *transport, transfer, transmit, communicate, carry.*
conveyance: *transportation, transfer, transmission, communication, vehicle.*
convocate: *convoke.*
convolute: *curled.*
convoy, *v. t.: accompany.*
convoy, *n.: accompaniment, escort.*
convulse: *agitate, shake.*
convulsion, *n.: agitation, spasm, fit, catastrophe.*
convulsive: *spasmodic.*
coo, *v. i.: cry, woo.*
coo, *n.: cry.*

---

2. *Spec.* boil, fry, fricassee, broil, *etc.*
cookery, *n.* cuisine (*tech. or B*), kitchen, cooking; *spec.* magirology (*R*), magiric (*R*), gastrology.
cooking, *n.* preparation (*contex.*), coction (*B or affected*).
cookroom, *n.* *Spec.* (*naut.*) cab, galley, caboose, kitchenette; *see* KITCHEN.
cookshop, *n.* trattoria (*Italian*), grill, restaurant, diner.
cool, *v. t.* **1.** chill, colden (*R*), refrigerate (*chiefly spec.*), frigorify (*R*), congeal, harden, set, infrigidate (*R*); *spec.* ice, freeze, quench, defervesce.
Antonyms: see HEAT, WARM.
2. calm, quiet, appease; *spec.* chill, freeze, quench, ice (*fig.*); *spec.* disfever (*R*). "*Cool*" *is chiefly used with* "*off*" *or* "*down.*"
3. *See* DEPRESS.
cool, *v. i.* refrigerate, colden (*R*), chill; *spec.* shiver, freeze, defervesce (*R*).
cooling, *a.* **1.** refrigerative, refrigerating, refrigeratory, refrigerant, frigorific (*chiefly tech.*), *spec.* freezing, defervescent (*R*).
Antonyms: see HEATING.
2. Chilling, refreshing, calming, appeasing.
coöperate, *v. i.* combine, concur, concert, cowork (*R*), coact (*R*); *spec.* collaborate, colleague (*R*), conspire, concur; *see* CONNIVE.
Antonyms: see CONTEND.
coöperation, *n.* combination, concurrence (*implies independent action toward a common end*), (*contex.*), concert (*emphasizes common direction*), concourse (*R*), coworking (*R*), coaction (*R*), synergy (*R*); *spec.* collaboration, conspiracy (*implies wrong or illegal action*), collusion (*implies secrecy and wrong*); *see* CONNIVANCE (*implies approval without participation*), AID.
Antonyms: see COMPETITION, CONTENTION, CONTEST.
coöperative, *a.* coöperant (*R*), coactive (*R*), concurrent, collaborative; *spec.* coefficient, synadelphic (*R*), conspiratory; *see* HELPFUL, CONNIVENT.
coördinate, *a.* equal, coequal, collateral (*R or spec.*), harmonized.
coördinative, *a.* *Spec.* equalizing, paratactic, organizing, harmonizing, systematizing.
copper, *a.* cupreous (*R*), cuprous (*chiefly tech.*), coppery, copperish, copper-colored; *spec.* cupric.
coppice, *a.* underwood, copse, hay (*dial. Eng.*), shrubby.
copulate, *v. i.* unite (*sexually*), couple (*chiefly spec.*).
copy, *n.* **1.** reproduction, representation, likeness, facsimile, counterfeit (*R*), replica; *spec.* transcript, counterscript, duplicate, carbon-copy, counterpart, tracing, transfer, offprint, rewriting, electrotype, ectype, replica, reflex, photostat, rotograph, photograph.
Antonyms: see ORIGINAL.
2. *See* IMITATION, PATTERN.
3. matter; *spec.* flimsy (*S*), manuscript, typoscript *or* typescript.
copy, *v. t.* **1.** reproduce; *spec.* transcribe, take, duplicate, electrotype, rewrite, transfer, trace, pounce, offprint, etch, photostat, photograph, engross, rewrite; *see* MANIFOLD.
Antonyms: see ORIGINATE.
2. adopt, borrow, follow; *spec.* echo (*fig.*), repeat; *see* IMITATE, RESEMBLE.
copyist, *n.* **1.** reproducer (*R*); scribe; *spec.* transcriber, writer, scrivener, duplicator, typist, typewriter (*now being replaced by* "*typist*").
2. *See* IMITATOR.
cord, *n.* *Spec.* braid, funicle, cordon, gimp *or* guimp, twist; *see* STRING, ROPE, BAND, BOND, RIB, BOWSTRING.
cordage, *n.* cording; *spec.* roping, ropework, tackle, service, sennit, sinnet.
cordial, *a.* **1.** *See* STIMULATING.
2. sincere, hearty, heartfelt, heartwhole, heartful (*R*), warm, ardent, vigorous, earnest.
Antonyms: see DISTANT.
3. *See* FRIENDLY.
cordiality, *n.* good will, sincerity, heartiness, heartfulness (*R*), empressment (*French*), warmth, ardency (*R*), ardor, vigor, depth, earnestness.
Antonyms: see DISTANCE.
cordlike, *a.* restiform (*tech. or B*).
core, *n.* **1.** carpel (*tech.*).
2. nucleus, center, heart, interior, inside; *spec.* drawback, mandrel, mandril.
3. gist; *see* PITH, SUBSTANCE.
corky, *a.* suberic, subereous (*R*), suberose;—*all three tech. or B.*
corner, *n.* **1.** *Spec.* angle, predicament.
2. angle, coign (*chiefly in* "*coign of vantage*"), coin (*A*), quoin (*chiefly spec.*), cantle (*chiefly spec.*), nook (*chiefly spec.*); *spec.* horn, crook, dog's-ear, shot, clew.
3. monopoly, advantage, control.
corner stone, coin *or* (*usually*) quoin (*both obsolescent*), headstone (*A*).
cornerwise, *adv.* diagonally, cater (*dial.*); *spec.* bendwise.
coronet, *n.* **1.** crown; *spec.* tiara.
2. *See* WREATH.
3. cushion (*of a horse's foot*).

cool, *a.: cold, chilly, calm, deliberate, composed, indifferent, unemotional, bold, impudent, unexaggerated, self-controlled.*
coolish: *cold.*
coolness: *cold, assurance, self-control, boldness, deliberation.*
coop: *pen.*
coördinate: *equalize, adapt, organize.*
copartner: *associate, partner.*
cope, *v. i.: contend.*
cope, *n.: vault.*
copious: *adequate, abundant, diffuse, prolix.*
coquet, *n.: flirt.*
coquetry: *flirtation.*
coquette: *flirt.*
coquettish: *flirtatious.*
cord, *v. t.: string.*
cordial, *n.: stimulant, liqueur.*
cordon: *line, guard.*
cork, *n.: bark, float, stopper.*
cork, *v. t.: stopple, blacken.*
corn, *n.: grain.*
corn, *v. t.: granulate, feed.*
corner, *v. t.: perplex, monopolize.*
cornered: *angular.*
corollary: *inference, result.*
corona: *circle, crown, chandelier.*
coronal: *crown.*
coronary: *crown.*
coronet, *v. t.: crown.*

corporal, *n.* pall (*A*), mortcloth (*Scot.*).
corporation, *n.* **1.** association, company, incorporation, society, firm (*C*), organization; *spec.* city, borough.
2. *Referring to the abdomen:* potbelly (*vulgar*); *see* ABDOMEN.
corpselike, *a.* cadaverous (*B or tech.*), deathlike; *spec.* ghastly.
corpulent, *a.* fat, big-bellied (*now chiefly vulgar*), bellied (*vulgar*).
correct, *a.* **1.** right (*has ethical implications lacking in* correct), rightful (*R*), regular (*implies conformity*), true, perfect, strict; *spec.* faultless, straight (*fig.*), pure, grammatical; *see* LOGICAL, ACCURATE, PROPER, TRUE, EXACT, CONVENTIONAL.
Antonyms: see INCORRECT, ILLOGICAL, INACCURATE, IMPROPER, UNTRUE, INEXACT, UNCONVENTIONAL, UNTIMELY.
2. *Referring to artistic style, taste, etc.:* pure, Attic; *spec.* classical, academical, academic, faultless, neat.
correct, *v. t.* **1.** rectify, right, repair, remedy, righten (*R*), amend, mend, emend (*implies editorial correction*); *spec.* emendate, castigate (*a text*), reform; *see* REDRESS.
Antonyms: see FALSIFY.
2. *See* PUNISH, REPROVE, COUNTERACT.
correction, *n.* rectification, repair, remedy, amend, emendation (*textual*), reparation, *etc.*
corrective, *a.* **1.** correctory (*R*), correctional, amendatory (*R*), rectificatory, remedial; *spec.* emendatory, reformative.
2. *See* PUNITIVE.
3. counteractive, neutralizing.
correctness, *n.* **1.** rightness, right, truth, strictness, trueness, perfection, rectitude; *spec.* accuracy, propriety, logicality, exactness, fidelity, conventionality, faultlessness, grammaticalness.
2. *As to artistic taste, style, etc.:* taste, purity, pureness, purism (*R, exc. as concrete*); *spec.* faultlessness, sumpsimus (*B*).
correlate, *n.* correlative; *spec.* reciprocal, complement, counterpart, correspondent.
correspond, *v. i.* **1.** agree, concur (*used with "with"*), conform (*used esp. with "to"*), answer (*used with "to"*), suit (*used with "with"*), square (*used with "to"*), quadrate (*R*), tally (*used with "with"*), respond (*R*), match (*used with "with"*); *spec.* harmonize, homologize (*chiefly tech.*), correlate; *see* RECIPROCATE.
Antonyms: see DISAGREE.
2. communicate (*contex.*), write.
correspondence, *n.* **1.** agreement, conformity (*emphasizes the bringing into harmony with something external*), conformableness, accord (*emphasizes the state of agreement*), respondence (*R*), respondency (*R*), tally, concurrence, coincidence (*often emphasizes accidental identity; spec.* correlation, proportion, equivalence, parallelism, homology (*chiefly tech.*), uniformity, adaptation (*suggests a deliberate* correspondence); *see* CONSISTENCY, RECIPROCITY.
2. communication (*contex.*), intercourse (*contex.*), communion (*R*), rapport (*French*).
3. *Collectively:* letters (*pl.*), writing, writings (*pl.*), letter-writing.
correspondent, *a.* agreeable, responsive (*R*), conformable, conform (*obs.*), concurrent, corresponsive (*R*), corresponding, answering; *spec.* uniform, proportional, ratable, correlative, complemental, relative, equivalent, homologous (*chiefly tech.*); *see* CONSISTENT, RECIPROCAL, ANALOGOUS.
Antonyms: see INCONGRUOUS, ABSURD, INCONSISTENT.
correspondent, *n.* **1.** *Spec.* correlate, homologue (*chiefly tech.*).
2. communicator (*contex.; R*), writer.
3. *See* CONTRIBUTOR.
corrigible, *a.* **1.** correctable (*R*), amendable, rectifiable; *spec.* emendable.
2. submissive, amenable, tractable.
corrode, *v. t.* consume, gnaw, bite, canker (*R*), cancer (*R*), rust; *spec.* dissolve, waste, wear. (*fig.*), eat (*esp. with "away"*); *spec.* etch:—*all implying slow or gradual action.*
corrosion, *n.* consumption, gnawing; *spec.* etching, rust.
corrosive, *a.* **1.** corroding, consuming, gnawing, eating, mordant; *spec.* caustic, cankerous, burning.
Antonyms: see BLAND.
2. *See* ACRID, ACRIMONIOUS.
corrugate, *v. t.* furrow, wrinkle; *spec.* pucker.
Antonyms: SMOOTH.
corrugated, *a.* wrinkled, furrowed.
corrupt, *a.* **1.** *See* DECOMPOSED, ADULTERATED.
2. corrupted, wicked (*intensitive, emphasizing the breaking of religious and moral law*), demoralized (*emphasizes the breakdown of the morality*), immoral (*emphasizes the absence of moral restraint*), amoral (*emphasizes the absence of moral law*), impure, dissolute (impure *and* dissolute *suggest sexual immorality,* dissolute *in the stronger sense*), depraved, vicious, rotten (*C or strongly denunciative*), putrid (*a very strong term*), lousy (*S, intensive; emphasizes social rather than moral qualities*), rantipole (*R*), Neronian (*fig.*); *see* GRACELESS, DEBAUCHED, CONTAMINATED, ABANDONED, LICENTIOUS, DISSIPATED, DISHONEST, SINFUL.

---

corporal: *bodily.*
corporate: *united, material.*
corporeal: *bodily, material.*
corps: *body.*
corpse: *body.*
corpus: *body.*
corpuscle: *particle, cell.*
corpuscule: *particle.*
correctional: *corrective.*
correlate, *v. t.: relate.*
correlate, *v. i.: correspond, reciprocate.*
correlation: *relation, analogy, reciprocation.*
correlative: *related, reciprocal, analogous.*
corresponding: *correspondent, analogous, reciprocal.*
corridor: *gallery, hall.*
corroborate: *confirm.*
corrupt, *v. i.: decompose.*

Antonyms: see UNCORRUPTED, INNOCENT, PURE, SINLESS, CHASTE.

corrupt, *v. t.* demoralize (*emphasizes confusion of morals*), vitiate (*emphasizes weakening of the morals*), debase, degrade, deprave (*all three emphasize the lowering of morals in order of intensity*), defile (*emphasizes moral pollution; an intensitive*), canker, debauch; *see* BRIBE, CONTAMINATE, PERVERT.

Antonyms: see PURIFY, REFORM.

corruption, *n.* **1.** *The act:* demoralization, vitiation, depravation, debauchery, degradation.

2. *The state or quality:* wickedness, contamination, perversion, defilement, pollution, poison (*fig.*), immorality, impurity, corruptness, rust (*fig.*), demoralization, vice, vitiation, depravity, depravation (*R*), depravedness (*R*), depravement (*R*), viciousness, filth, vitiosity, rottenness, putridity (*R*), putrefaction, debauchery, degradation; *see* CONTAMINATION, DISHONESTY, DISSIPATION, BRIBERY.

Antonyms: see PURITY.

corruptive, *a.* demoralizing, depravatory, vitiatory (*R*), perversive, debauching, degrading, *etc.*; *spec.* contaminative.

Antonyms: see PURIFICATORY, REFORMATIVE.

corset, *n* bodice (*obs.*), stays (*pl.*), foundation, support, girdle.

cortical, *a.* corticate, corticose;—*all tech.*

corybant, *n.* devotee (*contex.*), priest (*contex.*), orgiast.

cosmetic, *n. Spec.* powder, paint, color, henna, paste, rouge, lipstick, enamel, cream, make-up (*a collective*), whitewash, wash, lotion, tonic, skinfood.

cosmic, *a.* **1.** universal; *spec.* pancosmic (*R*), extraterrestrial (*R*).

2. *See* VAST, GRAND.

cost, *n.* **1.** charge, price.

2. *See* EXPENSE, EXPENDITURE, LOSS.

cost, *v. t.* require;—*only approximate; there are no close synonyms.*

costly, *a.* **1.** expensive, high-priced, high, chargeful (*obs.*), dear, precious (*very costly*); *spec.* valuable, Orient, Oriental, noble, golden (*fig.*), extravagant, exorbitant, overcostly, overdear, dispendious (*R*).

Antonyms: see CHEAP.

2. Pyrrhic (*fig.; esp. in "Pyrrhic victory"*).

3. *Spec.* rich, sumptuous, gorgeous.

costume, *n.* attire, dress, clothes (*pl.*), clothing, apparel, garb, get-up, outfit (*C*), guise, rig (*C*), rigout (*C*); *spec.* livery, uniform.

costumer, *n.* clothier, outfitter (*chiefly cant*), tailor; *spec.* haberdasher.

cot, *n.* **1.** *See* COTTAGE, SHED.

2. cover, sheath, stall; *spec.* fingerstall, thumbstall.

cottage, *n.* house, room (*B or A*); *spec.* bower, chalet, casino (*Italian; in English, it implies a large and public place of recreation*), lodge, cot (*B*), bungalow.

cottager, *n.* cotter, cottar, cottier (*all three English; in America,* cottager *implies living in a summer cottage*).

couch, *n.* **1.** cot; *see* BED, LITTER.

2. *Spec.* lounge, dormeuse, settee, divan, pulvina (*French*), chaise-longue (*French*), pouf (*French*), vis-à-vis (*French*), davenport, day-bed, *see* SOFA.

couch, *v. t.* **1.** lower (*as a spear; contex.*) *spec.* level.

2. *See* LOWER, REST, EMBROIDER, EXPRESS.

cough, *v. i. & t. Spec.* expectorate (*tech. or B*), hem, hack.

cough, *n.* tussis (*med.*); *spec.* hem, hack, expectoration (*B or tech.*).

cough, *a. Tech.:* bechic, tussal, tussicular, tussive. *"Cough" is the noun used attributively.*

council, *n.* assembly (*contex.*); *spec.* congregation, chapter (*monastic*), chamber, senate, junta (*Spanish and Italian*), divan (*Oriental*), cabinet, duma, ministry, directory (*hist.*), directorate, committee, board, corporation, syndicate, diet, convocation, synod, college (*of cardinals, etc.*), consistory, vestry, husting (*hist.*), decurion (*Roman or Italian hist.*), rada, soviet.

councilor, *n. Spec.* senator, minister, decurion (*Roman and Italian hist.*), elder, Nestor (*fig.*), director, vestryman, fellow, *etc.*

count, *n.* nobleman; *spec.* earl (*Eng.*), landgrave, graf (*Ger.*), palatine, palgrave (*hist.*).

count, *v. t.* **1.** compute (*contex.*), enumerate, tell (*chiefly spec.*), score (*fig. or spec.*), notch (*spec. or fig.*), check.

2. *See* NAME, INCLUDE, MAKE, ATTRIBUTE, CONSIDER.

count, *v. i.* **1.** compute, number; *spec.* muster.

2. *See* RELY, TELL, MATTER.

counter, *n.* **1.** computer, checker.

2. *Spec.* chip, dib, fish, dump, lot.

counter, *n.* table (*R or contex.*), board (*R*); *spec.* bar.

counteract, *v. t.* destroy (*contex.*), cross, oppose; *spec.* undo, nullify, defeat, cancel, neutralize, correct, frustrate, off-set, hinder, impede; *see* COUNTERPOISE.

corrupted: *corrupt, contaminated.*
corruptness: *corruption.*
corsage: *waist.*
corsair: *pirate.*
cortège: *retinue.*
coruscate: *flash.*
corvine: *crowlike.*
corybantic: *orgiastic.*
coryphee: *dancer.*
cosmogony: *creation.*
cosmopolitan: *world-wide.*
cosset: *cherish, foster, indulge.*
costate: *ribbed.*
costive: *constipated.*
costless: *free.*
costume, *v. t.: clothe.*
cosy: *sheltering, comfortable, sheltered;—a variant of cozy.*
cot: *bed.*
cote: *shed.*
coterie: *set.*
cothurnus: *buskin.*
cotter: *key.*
cotter, cottar: *cottager, peasant.*
couch, *v. i.: lie, lurk.*
counsel, *n.: consultation, consideration, advice, lawyer.*
counsel, *v. i.: consult.*
counsel, *v. t.: advise.*
counselor: *adviser, lawyer.*
countable: *computable.*
countenance, *n.: face, approval.*
countenance, *v. t.: approve.*
counter, *a.: opposing, opposed.*
counter, *n.: stern.*
counter, *v. t.: oppose, contradict.*
counter, *n.: parry.*

counter-balance, *v. t.* counterpoise (*implies opposing an equal weight*), balance, equate, compensate (*implies opposing equivalent forces or factors*).

countercharge, *v. i. & t.* answer, recriminate, reply.

counterclaim, *n.* set-off; *spec.* recoupment.

counterfeit, *a.* false, spurious, sham, bogus, fake, flash (*cant*); *spec.* forged, make-believe; *see* PRETENDED, ARTIFICIAL.

counterfeit, *v. t.* **1.** imitate, forge; *spec.* personate, copy, fake; *see* PRETEND, ACT.

2. *See* RESEMBLE.

counterfeit, *n.* impostor (*A*), imitation, forgery (*chiefly spec.*), sham, fake, fraud, gyp (*C*); *spec.* duffer (*S*), doublet, Brummagem, pinchbeck, dummy, swindle, imposture.

counterfeiter, *n.* imitator (*contex.*); *spec.* forger, coiner, pretender, dissembler, impostor.

countermine, *v. t. & i.* counterwork.

counterpart, *n.* **1.** copy, duplicate, double.

2. likeness, similitude; *spec.* picture, image, like, match, parallel, pendant, twin.

3. *Spec.* opposite, obverse, correlate, twin, tally, reciprocal, complement, supplement, parallel; *see* REVERSE.

counterpoise, *n.* **1.** balance, counterbalance, counterweight, equipoise; *spec.* makeweight, offset.

2. *See* COMPENSATION.

counterpoise, *v. t.* **1.** counteract (*suggests opposing equal force rather than equal weight*), balance, counterbalance, equiponderate (*B and fig.*), equilibrate (*chiefly fig.*), equilibrize (*R*), equipoise (*R*), counteract (*chiefly in reference to immaterial things*); *spec.* offset.

2. *See* COMPENSATE.

countersign, *v. t.* sign (*contex.*); *spec.* validate, indorse, attest.

countersign, *n.* signal, sign; *spec.* password, shibboleth (*hist. or fig.*), watchword.

counting, *n.* computation (*contex.*), account.

countless, *a.* innumerable, innumerous (*R*), myriad (*chiefly B*), infinite (*A or R*), numberless, uncountable, uncounted, unnumbered; *cf.* INCALCULABLE.

countrify, *v. t.* ruralize, rusticate.

country, *n.* **1.** land, region, district.

2. *See* STATE, PEOPLE.

3. *Spec.* countryside, champaign (*B*), field (*A*), plain, waste, wild, heath, fields (*pl.*), forest, meadows (*pl.*), valley, mountain, uplands (*pl.*), lowlands (*pl.*), *etc.*

country house, garden house (*Eng.*); *spec.* countryseat, seat, villa, farmhouse.

countryman, *n.* **1.** compatriot (*B*), landsman (*R*).

2. *See* RUSTIC, PEASANT.

county, *n.* shire (*not an exact synonym, though the district is usually conterminous; Brit.*), parish (*Louisiana*); *spec.* landgraviate (*Ger.*), palatinate.

coup-de-grâce, *n.* (*French*), death-blow, finishing-stroke, finisher (*C*), quietus (*contex.*).

couple, *v. t.* **1.** join, unite, bind, tie, link, yoke (*chiefly spec. or fig.*), pair, bracket, shackle (*fig. or spec.*); *spec.* double; *see* LEASH.

Antonyms: see UNCOUPLE.

2. *See* JOIN, UNITE, ASSOCIATE.

coupling, *n.* tie, link, couple, shackle (*chiefly fig. or spec.*), union, connection, joint, splice, weld, welding; *spec.* turnbuckle.

courage, *n.* boldness (*emphasizes the absence of timidity*), audacity, intrepidity, daring, hardihood, bravery (*like* courage, *implies more spiritual qualities than* boldness), valor (*emphasizes personal bravery*), prowess (*implies skill in action*), fortitude (*emphasizes endurance*), spirit, breast (*B*), pluck, pluckiness, sand (*S*), grit (*C*), guts (*S, or intensitive*), gizzard (*C*), backbone, heart (*B*), mettle, nerve, spunk (*C, implies quickness of spirit*), stout-heartedness, high-heartedness (*B*), stoutness (*B*), courageousness (*like* courage, *implies moral and spiritual courage*), dash, chivalry, gallantry (*suggests magnificent and courtly bravery*), derring-do (*B and A*), dauntlessness (*an elevated term*), heroism (*implies noble self-sacrifice*), resolution, firmness, manhood, manliness, virtue (*spec. and B*); *spec.* pot-valiance, Dutch courage.

Antonyms: see COWARDICE.

courageous, *a.* bold, intrepid, dauntless, daring, audacious, brave, valorous, valiant, nervy (*S*), game (*C*), high-hearted (*B*), fortitudinous (*R*), unfearful, undismayed, unafraid, fearless, heart-whole (*R*), stout, stanch *or* staunch, stalwart, mettlesome, plucky, spunky (*C*), hardy (*B*), lion-hearted (*fig.*), gingerous *or* gingery (*R*); *spec.* heroic, resolute, chivalrous, firm; *see* BRAVE.

Antonyms: see COWARDLY.

courier, *n.* runner, messenger, express, post rider *or* post (*chiefly hist. and spec.*), poster (*R*); *spec.* postman (*hist.*), estafette (*French*), kavass (*Turkey*).

course, *n.* **1.** motion (*contex.*), currency (*R*), passage, career (*B*); *see* PROGRESS.

2. way, track, route, line, tack (*fig. or spec.*), path, road, ground; *spec.* thread, lane, orbit, meander, circuit, circle, ambit, random (*R*), traverse, march, stadium, diaulos, walk, trajectory, traject (*R*), itinerary, racecourse, speedway, parkway.

3. progress, happening, sequence, current-movement, run, tenor; *spec.* drift, trend, conduct, process, lapse; *see* ROUTINE.

4. *See* ACTION, SERIES, CONTINUANCE, CHANNEL, CHASE.

---

countermand, *v. t.: revoke.*
counterpane: *bedcover.*
countervail: *compensate.*
counterwork: *countermine.*
countrified: *rustic.*
country, *a.: rustic, rural.*
coup: *master-stroke.*
couple, *n.: leash, pair, two.*
couple, *v. i.: unite.*
couple, *v. t.: associate.*
course, *v. t.: pursue, drive.*

---

5. *Referring to action, work, etc.:* round, bout, turn, run, spell; *spec.* heat, pull.
6. curriculum (*chiefly spec.*), cursus (*tech.*), college (*R or local*), program.
7. set (*of dishes at table*), service (*A*); *spec.* dessert, hors d'œuvres (*French*); antipasto (*Italian*).

court, *n.* **1.** inclosure, garth (*A*); *spec.* curtilage (*chiefly legal and tech.*), peristyle, courtyard, quadrangle, parvis, patio, piazza, campus (*R*).
2. tribunal, bench (*chiefly tech.*), judicatory (*chiefly Scot.*), bar (*fig.*), curia (*chiefly spec.*), judicature (*R*), jurisdiction (*fig.*); *spec.* dicastery, shiremote *or* shiremoot (*hist.*), husting (*Eng.*), exchequer (*Eng.*), hallmote (*hist.*), rota, divan (*Turkish*), court-martial, leet, Marshalsea (*Eng.*), sanhedrin, College, mallum (*hist.*), consistory, brotherhood (*Eng.*), chapter, lodge, Inquisition, conservancy, presbytery.
3. attention, addresses (*pl.*); *spec.* homage.
4. castle, hall, palace; *see* HOUSE, RETINUE, ASSEMBLY.

court, *a.* curial, aulic (*R or spec.*) *"Court" is the noun used attributively.*

court, *v. t.* **1.** cultivate, haunt.
2. woo, spark (*C*), squire, sue, gallant (*R*), gallantize (*R*).
3. invite, solicit, allure; *see* SEEK.
Antonyms: see AVOID.

court, *v. i.* woo, spark (*C*), philander (*chiefly spec.*), spoon (*S, A*), bill (*chiefly in "bill and coo"*), sue, call.

courtesy, *n.* **1.** courtliness (*implying stateliness of manner*), courteousness, gentilesse (*hist.*), gentility, civility (*emphasizing polite conduct*), politeness, breeding (*implying gentle breeding*), manners (*implying good manners*), urbanity; *spec.* chivalry.
2. favor, permission, kindness, goodness, allowance, consideration, compliance.
3. salutation, welcome, greeting, regards (*pl.*), respect *or* respects, remembrances, greeting, duty, devoirs (*pl., French*), love (*A*).
4. curtesy, courtesy, bow, obeisance, salute; *spec.* kiss, embrace.

courtly, *a.* **1.** aulic (*R*).
2. *See* POLITE, DIGNIFIED, REFINED.

courtship, *n.* courtliness (*A*); amour, wooing, courting, love-making, suit, love (*chiefly in "make love"*), service (*R or A*).

cousin, *n.* relative (*contex.*), coz (*for "cousin"; chiefly used in fond or familiar address*), cousiness (*fem.; R*); *spec.* catercousin, cousin (*German*); *spec. for* lover.

cover, *v. t.* **1.** encover (*R*), overcover (*R*); *spec.* overwhelm, drown (*fig.*), protect, invest, clothe, cloak, overspread, veil, envelop, sheathe, roof, deck, skim, jacket, shadow, bury, mantle, leather, keckle, hoodwink (*fig.; R*), case, encase, cap, overbuild, overlay, pave, bury, cope, crumb, cushion, copper, coif, clapboard (*U. S.*), canopy, carpet, drape, tent, lay, mulch, shoe, jacket, overcanopy (*R*), shingle, lag, infilm (*R*), flake, face, front, loricate (*R*), net, muffle, dome, house, mat, fledge, gravel, crape, drift, cowl, helmet, curtain, armor, lead, lath; *see* TOP, OVERSPREAD.
Antonyms: see BARE, UNCOVER, STRIP.
2. *See* HIDE, DISGUISE, INCUBATE, SHELTER, INCLUDE.
3. *Tech. or cant:* serve, line; *spec.* top, tup, horse.

cover, *n.* **1.** covering; covert (*R or B*); *fig. or spec.* coverlet (*fig.*), coverlid (*fig.*), drape, casing, case, coat, vesture, curtain, cot, lid, cap, helmet, headpiece, ferrule, ferrel, jacket, face, facing, blanket, tablecloth, board, blind, boot, tick, bedtick, tilt, awning, canopy, tent, pavilion (*B*), shoe, down (*R*), dome, capping, skin, screen, envelope, house *or* housing, frontal, lorication (*R*), robe, vesture, tarpaulin, roofing, volva, baldachin, baldaquin, tester, husk, screen, muffle, mulch, panoply, pall, mantle, cloak, film, leathering, overcast, coating, overlay, veil, sheathing, mantling, blanket, shed, shelter, *etc. The word "covering" is generic or less individual than "cover" and often applies to an inseparable layer or envelope to which cover would seldom apply.*
2. *Referring to a book:* binding, case, lid (*chiefly U. S. and dial. Eng.*).
3. blind, cloak; *see* PRETEXT, DISGUISE.

covered, *a.* covert (*now R*); *spec.* cased, blanketed, cuculate, hooded, crusted, crustate, crustaceous, obtected, *etc.*
Antonyms: see BARE.

covering, *n.* cover, coverture (*B*); *fig. or spec.* casing, casement (*R*), weather-boarding, clapboarding, coating, sheathing, shingles (*pl.*), tiles (*pl.*), roofing, tegument, headgear, envelope, crust, panoply, *etc.*; *see* COT, SKIN. *Many words under "cover" are used also in a generic sense (in which they do not take the article "a" or "an") as specific synonyms of "covering."*

cow, *n.* bovine (*contex.*), kine (*pl., A*); *spec.* heifer, humlie *or* humblie (*Scot.*), dairy (*a collective; chiefly Eng.*), critter.

coward, *n.* recreant (*implies one who has renounced through fear*), caitiff (*B*), nithing *or* niddering (*A or hist.*), wheyface (*C or contemptuous*), Scaramouch (*fig.*), milksop (*C or contemptuous*), hare (*fig.*), chicken (*fig.*); *spec.* dastard, craven, poltroon, cur (*contemptuous*), quitter (*S*), slacker (*C*), deserter, shirker.

cowardice, *n.* recreancy (*R*), faint-heartedness, fear, timidity (*implying baseness and*

---

courteous: *polite.*
courtesan: *harlot.*
cove, *n.: recess, inlet, retreat.*
cove, *v. t.: arch.*
covenant, *n.: agreement, contract.*
covenant, *v. i.: contract.*
covert, *a.: covered, secret, sheltered, hidden, secluded.*
covert, *n.: thicket, shelter, protection, feather.*
covertness: *secrecy.*
coverture: *covering, hiding, protection.*
covet: *desire.*
covetous: *desirous, greedy.*
covetousness: *desire, greed.*
covey: *brood, flock, company.*
covin: *deception.*
covinous: *deceitful.*
cow, *v. t.: intimidate.*
cow, *v. i.: shrink.*

---

fear), funk (*C*); *spec.* dastardliness, dastardice, (*obs.*), poltroonery.
Antonyms: see BOLDNESS, BRAVERY, COURAGE.
cowardly, *a.* recreant (*R*), faint-hearted, fearful, timid, base, niddering (*A*); *spec.* dastardly, pusillanimous, craven, dastard, poltroonish (*R*), white-livered, unmanly, unwomanly, yellow (*S*). *Cf.* TIMID.
cowherd, *n.* herder, neatherd (*A*, herdsman, herd; *spec.* oxherd, cowboy.
cowhouse, *n.* byre (*Eng. or B*), cowshed, shippon *or* shippen (*Scot. & dial. Eng.*), barn (*contex.*).
coy, *a.* bashful (*contex.*), shy, demure, coquettish, reserved, chary; *see* DISTANT.
crabbed, *a.* **1.** *See* ILL-TEMPERED, IRASCIBLE,
2. irregular, cramped, cramp, illegible.
Antonyms: see SMOOTH.
crab-shaped, *a.* cancriform (*tech.*).
crack, *v. i.* **1.** snap; *spec.* pistol (*R*), pop, bang, explode; *see* CRACKLE.
2. break (*contex.*), fracture (*contex.*), burst (*contex.*); *spec.* chap, flaw, split, chink, craze, fissure.
crack, *n.* **1.** break (*contex.*), fracture (*contex.*); *spec.* crevice, crackle, craze, chink, flaw, star, cleft, spring, brack, split, chop, fissure, slit, cranny, rift, rent, chap.
2. *See* BLOW, SHOT, MOMENT, EXPERT.
3, snap; *spec.* pop, explosion; *see* CRACKLE.
cracked, *a.* broken, fractured; *spec.* crazed, crazy, crackled, crannied, starred, chapped, split, chappy.
cracker, *n.* **1.** snapper; *spec.* popper, firecracker.
2. *See* BOASTER, BISCUIT.
3. poor white, tacky (*Southern U. S.*).
crackle, *v. i.* break (*contex.*), snap (*of fire*), crack (*contex.*), crepitate (*B or tech.*), decrepitate (*B or tech.*).
crackle, *n.* break (*contex.*), crack (*contex.*), crepitation (*B or tech.*), crackling, decrepitation (*B or tech.*), snapping.
crackling, *a.* crepitant (*tech. or B*).
crackling, *n.* **1.** *See* CRACKLE.
2. *Chiefly in pl.:* greaves *or* graves (*pl.; Eng.*), scraps (*pl.*).
cradle, *n.* **1.** bed (*contex.*), cunabula (*pl.; R*), support, frame; *spec.* scythe.
2. *See* SOURCE.

crane, *n.* **1.** derrick, lift; *spec.* jenny, davit.
2. *See* BOOM.
3. heron.
cranelike, *n.* gruiform (*tech.*).
cranium, *n.* **1.** head; *see* SKULL.
2. brainpan, pericranium (*affected or humorous*).
crank, *n.* **1.** *See* HANDLE, CONCEIT, CAPRICE.
2. erratic (*R*), vagarian (*C or R*); *spec.* monomaniac, freak, vegetarian. *"Crank" is more or less* (*C*).
crape, *n.* crêpe (*French*); *spec.* mourning (*which see*), weeds (*S*).
crash, *v. i.* **1.** break, shatter, smash, shiver.
2. *See* COLLIDE.
crash, *n.* **1.** *See* NOISE, FAILURE.
2. collision, shock, smash, smash-up, accident (*generally automobile*).
crayon, *n.* pencil, pastel, chalk.
creak, *v. i. spec.* squeak, grind, scroop, grate, rasp, screak, crank (*R*), screech, stridulate.
creak, *n. spec.* squeak, grind, grinding, scroop, stridor, creaking, rasp, grating, grate (*R*), scream, screak, screech.
creaking, *a.* creaky; *spec.* squeaking, strident, stridulous, scrooping, grinding, grating, discordant, screaky, squeaky, raspy, rasping.
cream, *n.* **1.** head (*as risen on milk; Brit.*), crème (*French*), scum (*R*); *spec.* froth.
2. *Spec.* emulsion, crème (*French*), cosmetic, cordial.
3. *See* BEST.
creamy, *a.* creamlike; *spec.* luscious, soft.
create, *v. t.* **1.** make, form, fashion, originate, constitute, produce, raise, rear; *spec.* concreate (*R*), co-create (*R*), erect, procreate; *see* DESIGN, INVENT, IMAGINE, CAUSE, RECREATE.
Antonyms' see ANNIHILATE, NULLIFY, UNMAKE, ABOLISH, EXTINGUISH.
2. *See* ESTABLISH, CONSTRUCT.
creation, *n.* **1.** formation, production, origination, making, constitution, doing (*R*), facture (*R*); *spec.* erection, cosmogony, procreation, concreation; *see* INVENTION, DESIGN, IMAGINATION, CAUSATION.
2. *Referring to the thing created:* creature (*now B*), formation, facture (*R*), production, origination; *spec.* cosmos, universe, world; *see* INVENTION, DESIGN, IMAGINATION.
Antonyms: see CREATOR.

---

cowboy: *cowherd.*
cower: *stoop, cringe.*
cowhide: *leather, whip.*
cowl: *hood, tub.*
coxcomb: *cap, dandy, jackanapes.*
coxswain: *steersman.*
cozen: *deceive, cheat.*
cozy: *sheltering, comforting, sheltered.*
craft: *art, skill, trade, vessel.*
craftiness: *art.*
craftsman: *artificer.*
crafty: *artful.*
crag: *cliff.*
craggy: *precipitous.*
cram, *v. t.: crowd, stuff, press, surfeit, teach, study.*
cram, *v. i.: gormandize.*
cramp, *n.: clamp, restrain, spasm.*
cramp, *a.: narrow, crabbed.*
cramp, *v. t.: constrict, restrain, fasten.*
cramped: *stiff, crabbed.*
crane, *v. t.: stretch.*
crank, *v. t.: bend, turn.*
crank, *a.: rickety, unstable, spirited.*
crankle: *bend.*
cranky: *irascible, odd, rickety, winding, zigzag.*
crannied: *cracked.*
cranny: *crack.*
crape, *v. t.: pucker.*
crapulence: *excess.*
crapulent: *dissipated.*
crapulous: *dissipated.*
crass: *coarse, crude, dense, stupid.*
crate, *n.: basket, case.*
crater: *bowl, mouth.*
craunch: *crunch.*
cravat: *neckcloth.*
crave: *ask, desire, need.*
craven, *a.: cowardly.*
craven, *n.: coward, quitter.*
craving: *desire.*
craw: *crop, stomach.*
crawl, *v. i.: creep, cringe, insert.*
crawling: *creeping.*
crawly: *creepy.*
craze, *v. t.: derange.*
craze, *n.: derangement, fad, crack.*
crazy: *cracked, rickety, deranged, frantic, unwise.*
crease, *n.: wrinkle, pucker.*

(*A*) *archaic.* (*B*) *bookish, poetic, literary or learned.* (*C*) *colloquial.* (*Contex.*) *contextual.* (*R*) *rare.* (*S*) *slang.*
See pp. viii–ix.

3. *See* ESTABLISHMENT.
4. gown, dress, hat.
creative, *a.* **1.** creant (*R*), formative, originative, productive, constituent, constitutive, poetic (*R*); *spec.* plastic, procreative, generative, demiurgic; *see* CAUSATIVE, IMAGINATIVE, INVENTIVE.
Antonyms: see ANNIHILATIVE, NULLIFACATORY.
2. *See* CONSTITUTIVE.
creator, *n.* God, author (*contex.*), maker, fashioner, poet (*R*), originator, producer; *spec.* Demiurge (*philos.*), Brahma, inventor, designer, imaginer.
Antonyms: see CREATURE, CREATION.
creature, *n.* **1.** creation, being, thing (*contex.*); *spec.* breather (*B*), animal, creation (*collective*), mortal; *see* PERSON.
Antonyms: see CREATOR, AUTHOR.
2. minion; *spec.* dependent, tool.
credential, *n. Spec.* testimonial, introduction, passport, pass, card, certificate, exequatur. *"Credential" is used chiefly in the pl.*
credible, *a.* believable, likely, swallowable (*R*, *C*), trustworthy; *spec.* probable, conceivable.
Antonyms: see INCREDIBLE.
credit, *n.* **1.** *Spec.* credibility; *see* BELIEF, REPUTATION, HONOR.
2. trust, tick (*C*), score (*A or dial.*); *spec.* chalk, talley.
Antonyms: see CASH.
3. *Spec.* payment, set-off.
credit, *v. t.* **1.** *See* BELIEVE, HONOR.
2. accredit.
3. trust.
creditable, *a.* honorable, accredited; *see* REPUTABLE.
creed, *n.* belief, symbol (*theol.*); *spec.* tenet, doctrine, persuasion, credo (*chiefly tech.*), views (*pl.*), dogma (*implying a definite belief*).
creep, *v. i.* **1.** crawl, dawdle, park (*C*, *intensitive*); *spec.* formicate (*R or med.*), worm, swarm, grovel.
2. *Referring to plants:* run, trail, advance (*contex.*).
3. *Meaning "to go stealthily":* steal.
4. *Referring to the sensation:* crawl; *spec.* formicate (*R*), swarm.
creeper, *n.* **1.** crawler; *spec.* reptile.
2. *Spec.* runner, flagellum (*tech.*).
3. crampon, crampet.
creeping, *a.* **1.** crawling, reptant (*R*), repent (*R*), reptile (*chiefly spec.*); *spec.* formicant (*med.*), serpent (*R*).
2. *Referring to a plant:* running.
creepy, *a.* crawly; *C for* scary.
crenate, *a.* scalloped, notched, indented; *spec.* knurled.
crescent, *n.* **1.** meniscus (*math.*), lunule (*tech.*), lune (*chiefly tech.*), half-moon (*a loose usage*), semilune (*a loose usage*), demilune (*chiefly spec.*), lunette, lunula, lunulet.
2. Islam (*fig.*).
crescent-shaped, *a.* convexo-concave (*contex.; tech.*), crescent, crescentic, crescentiform (*formal*); semilunar (*formal*), semilunary (*a loose usage*), bow-shaped, bowed, meniscal (*R or tech.*), sigmoid (*tech.*), horned, lunulate, moony (*R*), lunular, lunar, lunary, lunate.
crest, *n.* **1.** crown; *spec.* tuft, comb, copplecrown (*obs. or dial.*), topknot, top, tip, horn, plumicorn (*R*), cockscomb.
2. *See* DECORATION, PLUME, HELMET, RIDGE.
3. *The top of a wave: spec.* comb, curl.
crested, *a. Spec.* muffed, tufted, copplecrowned (*A or dial.*).
crevasse, *n.* cleft (*contex.*); *spec.* schrund (*Ger.*), chimney.
crib, *n.* **1.** *See* MANGER, BEDSTEAD, FRAME.
2. *Spec.* translation, key, cab, horse, pony, trot;—*all but "translation" and "key" S.*
crier, *n.* caller, announcer; *spec.* croaker, crower, bellman, muezzin, herald, proclaimer.
crime, *n.* offense (*contex.*), felony, misdemeanor, outrage, arson, robbery, murder, rape, incest, burglary, theft, manslaughter, mayhem, perjury, treason, embezzlement; *see* WRONG, TRANSGRESSION, SIN.
criminal, *a.* **1.** unlawful, illegal, illicit, criminous (*R*); *spec.* felonious, burglarious, murderous, treasonous.
Antonyms: see LAWFUL.
2. guilty (*contex.*), criminous (*chiefly spec.*), crimeful (*R*).
Antonyms: see INNOCENT.
3. wicked (*contex.*), wrong, sinful (*implies moral rather than legal guilt*), crimeful (*R*), villainous.
criminal, *n.* offender (*contex.*), malefactor (*B*), culprit, sinner; *spec.* felon, burglar, murderer, thief, robber, perjurer, incendiary, traitor, embezzler, defaulter, convict, jail bird (*C*), gallow-bird.
crimson, *n.* red (*contex.*), cramoisy (*A*); *spec.* magenta.
cringe, *v. i.* cower (*implies crouching and shrinking from fear*), stoop (*implies humility and submission*), wince (*implies shrinking and drawing back from fear*); crouch (*fig. or spec.; implies servility*), spaniel (*fig.; R*), crinkle (*obs. or dial.*), fawn (*implies servile seeking for favor*), truckle (*implies obsequiousness*); *spec.* crawl, grovel, sneak; *see* SHRINK.
Antonyms: see BLUSTER, BULLY, SWAGGER.
cringe, *n.* crouch, stoop; *see* SHRINK.
Antonyms: see SWAGGER.

---

credence: *belief.*
credent: *believing.*
credulity: *believingness.*
credulous: *believing.*
cremate: *burn.*
crepitant: *crackling.*
crepitate: *crackle.*
crepuscle: *twilight*
crepuscular: *twilight.*
crescent, *a.*: *waxing, crescent-shaped.*
crest, *v. t.*: *crown, top.*
crest, *v. i.*: *break.*
crestfallen: *depressed.*
cretaceous: *chalky.*
crevice: *cleft.*
crew: *force, company, gang.*
crib: *steal, plagiarize.*
crick: *spasm.*
cricket: *stool.*
criminate: *accuse, involve.*
crimp, *v. t.*: *gash, impress, wrinkle.*
crimp, *n.*: *flute, wrinkle.*
crimpy: *wrinkly, curly.*

---

cringing, *a.* abject, servile, spaniel (*fig.*), fawning; *see* OBSEQUIOUS, CRINGE.
cripple, *n.* lameter *or* lamiter (*Scot.*); *spec.* paralytic, halt.
cripple, *v. t.* disable (*contex.*), lame; *spec.* paralyze, maim, injure, hurt, disable, incapacitate.
crippled, *a.* lame, lamish (*R*); *spec.* paralyzed, maimed, injured, hurt, disabled, incapacitated.
crisis, *n.* **1.** turn, turning-point, hinge (*fig.*), climacteric (*B*). rub (*fig.*), pinch (*fig.*).
2. *See* JUNCTURE.
crisscross, *v. t.* cross, gridiron.
critic, *n.* judge; *spec.* connoisseur, diatribist (*R*), reviewer, verbalist, verbarian (*R*), censurer, censor, zoilist (*fig.*), expert, specialist.
critical, *a.* **1.** critic (*R*); *spec.* dissective, exacting, hypercritical, supercritical; *see* caviling.
2. *Spec.* judicious, accurate.
3. decisive; *spec.* climacteric, climacterical, exigent, dangerous, *etc.*
criticism, *n.* **1.** judgment (*contex.*), critique; *spec.* dissection, analysis, comment, epicrisis (*tech.*), appreciation, review, reviewal (*R*), animadversion, hypercriticism, nip, zoilism (*fig.*), diatribe; *see* CENSURE, CAVIL, REPROOF.
2. critique; *spec.* dialectic, dialectics.
criticize, *v. t.* judge, do (*contex.*); *spec.* dissect, review, flay, hypercriticize, pan (*C*), slam (*S*); *see* CENSURE, BLAME, REPROVE.
croak, *v. i. & t.* **1.** cry (*contex.*), quark (*R*).
2. forbode (*contex.*), grumble, *"Croak" is not a synonym of "complain"; "croak" refers to the future; "complain" to the past or to what is fixed upon.*
3. *S for* die.
croaking, *n.* **1.** crying (*contex.*), coaxation (*R*).
2. foreboding (*contex.*), grumbling.
crock, *n. Spec.* dish, jar, pot, pitcher, pig (*Scot.*), plate, *etc.*
crocket, *n.* ornament, crotchet.
crocodilian, *n.* reptile (*contex.*); *spec.* gavial, alligator, crocodile, cayman.
Crœsus, *n.* Dives (*fig.*); *spec.* nabob, magnate (*implies financial power as well as wealth*), plutocrat (*C*), millionaire, billionaire, stinking-rich (*S; intensitive*);—*applied to a very rich man* (*what constitutes great riches varying with the time and place*). *"Crœsus" is fig.*
crook, *n.* **1.** *See* CURVE, BEND, SINUOSITY.
2. hook, pothook, cammock (*Scot.; chiefly spec.*); *spec.* staff; *see* CROSIER.
3. evildoer (*contex.*); *spec.* malefactor, cheat, swindler, rogue, rascal, scoundrel.
crooked, *a.* **1.** cranky (*R*), crank (*Scot.*); *see* BENT, CURVED, ANGULAR, SINUOUS, WINDING, ASKEW, ZIGZAG, TWISTED.
Antonyms: see STRAIGHT.
2. *See* DISHONEST, INDIRECT, DEVIOUS, DECEITFUL, TRICKY, ARTFUL, INTRIGUING.
crop, *n.* **1.** craw, ingluvies (*tech.*); *spec.* gebbie (*Scot.*), gorge.
2. *See* HANDLE, WHIP, HARVEST.
cropper, *n.* fall (*contex.*), plumper.
crosier, *n.* crozier, crook, pastoral, staff.
cross, *n.* **1.** gibbet, crucifix (*implies the presence of the corpus on the cross*), crux (*tech.*); *spec.* christcross *or* crisscross (*A*), crosslet, rood (*A or spec.*), tau, gamma.
2. mark (*contex.*), signature (*contex.*), christcross (*R*), crisscross.
3. *See* TRIAL, TROUBLE, CROSSING, CROSSWAY, CROSSBREEDING, HYBRID.
cross, *v. t. & i.* **1.** *Meaning "to make the sign of the cross on or over":* sign (*A*), sain (*A*), bless (*A or B*).
2. intersect, decussate (*B or tech.*), intercross (*R*), cut (*fig.; contex.*), transit (*R*); *spec.* crisscross, gridiron.
3. traverse, thwart (*R*), cut (*chiefly spec. and used with "over"*); *spec.* bestride, overstride, overstep, stride.
Antonyms: see ADJOIN, PARALLEL.
4. traverse, overpass (*R*), pass, transverse (*R*), transpass (*R*), thwart (*A*), overthwart (*R*); *spec.* swim, overswim (*R*), raft, overstep, repass, recross, leap, jump, *etc.*
5. interbreed, mix, crossbreed, intercross (*R*), hybridize; *spec.* cross-fertilize. *"Interbreed" and "cross" or "crossbreed" are often distinguished.*
6. *See* CANCEL, OPPOSE.
cross, *a.* **1.** transverse, thwart (*A or R*), traverse (*R*), overthwart (*R*).
2. *See* OPPOSING, ILL-TEMPERED, RECIPROCAL.
crossbreeding, *n.* cross, crossing, interbreeding, hybridization, hybridizing; *see* CROSS-FERTILIZATION.
crossed, *a.* **1.** crutched (*eccl.*).
2. *See* HYBRID.
cross-eye, *n.* strabismus (*tech.*), cock-eye.
cross-fertilization, *n.* crossbreeding, allogamy (*tech.*).
crossing, *n.* **1.** cross, overpassing, traversing, traverse (*A*).
2. intersection, decussation (*B or tech.*); *spec.* lease (*weaving*).
3. *See* OPPOSITION, CROSSWAY.
4. *Spec.* miscegenation; *see* CROSSBREEDING.
crossroad, *n.* crossway, cross (*R*), concourse (*a collective; B*), intersection.
cross-shaped, *a.* decussate (*chiefly bot.*), cru-

crinkle, *v. i.: wrinkle, ripple.*
crinkle, *v. t.: wrinkle, curl.*
crinkle, *n.: twist, wrinkle, ripple.*
crinkly: *ripply, wrinkly.*
crisp, *a.: curly, brittle, blunt, sharp, definite, lively, cold, stiff.*
crisp, *v. t.: curl, ripple, harden, wave.*
crisscross, *n.: cross.*
crisscross, *v. t.: cross.*
crisscross, *adv.: crosswise.*
crisscross, *a.: cross.*
criterion: *standard.*
critique: *criticism.*
crock, *n.: soot, smut.*
crockery: *earthenware.*
crone: *woman.*
crony: *comrade.*
crook, *v. t. & i.: bend, curve, zigzag.*
crop, *v. t.: top.*
crossbar: *whippletree.*
crossbred: *hybrid.*
crossbreed: *cross.*
cross-examination: *question.*
cross-fertilize: *cross.*
cross-grained: *perverse.*
crosshatch: *engrave.*
crossness: *ill-temper.*
cross-question: *question.*
crossruff: *seesaw.*

cial (*chiefly anat.*), cruciform, cruciate, cruciferous (*bot.*).
crosstie, *n.* tie, sleeper (*chiefly British*).
crossway, *n.* cross; *spec.* crossing, crosswalk; *see* CROSSROAD.
crosswires, *n. pl.* reticule, reticle;—*both tech.*
crosswise, *adv.* across, traverse (*R*), thwartwise (*R or A*), athwart, transversely, transverse (*R*); *spec.* crisscross, thwartship, askew, awry, sidewise, sideways.
Antonyms: see LENGTHWISE.
crouch, *v. i.* bend (*contex.*), squat, drop; *spec.* cower, stoop; *see* CRINGE.
crouch, *n.* bend (*contex.*), squat, droop; *see* CRINGE, STOOP.
crow, *n.* **1.** raven, crake (*dial. Eng.*); *spec.* blackneb (*Scot.*), scaldcrow (*local*), chough (*Cornish*), jay (*Cornish*), hoodie *or* hoody (*Scot.*), corbie (*Scot.*), grayback, gorcrow, daw, jackdaw.
2. cry (*contex.*), song (*contex.; B or tech.*), cock-a-doodle-doo (*C*).
crow, *v. i.* **1.** cry (*contex.*), sing (*contex.; B or tech.*), chanticleer (*R*).
2. *See* EXULT.
crow, *a.* corvine (*B or tech.*).
crowbar, *n.* gravelock (*obs. or dial. Eng.*), crow, lever; *spec.* pry, pinch, pinchbar, jemmy, betty.
crowd, *n.* **1.** gathering, concourse (*B*), horde, press, drove (*disparaging*), mass, mob (*chiefly disparaging*), host, herd (*disparaging*), swarm, ruck (*disparaging*), rout, rabble, pack, cram, jam, crush, huddle, throng.
2. *See* MULTITUDE, POPULACE, PRESSURE.
crowd, *v. t.* **1.** *See* HASTEN, PUSH.
2. *Referring to persons brought uncomfortably close together:* gather, huddle, overcrowd, crush, press, scrouge (*C*), cram, wedge, shoulder (*chiefly spec.*), serry (*R*), hustle, pack, jam.
3. *Referring to things put together very or too closely: spec.* pack, jam, swarm, huddle, cram, overcrowd, tuck, ram, compress; wedge.
4. *Referring to the place in which things or persons are brought or placed too close together: spec.* pack, jam, cram, wedge, overcrowd, overcharge, throng, gorge, congest.
crowd, *v. i.* **1.** *See* HASTEN.
2. gather, collect, congregate, huddle; *spec.* throng, mob, press, crush, herd, serry (*R*), swarm, cram, wedge, huddle, nestle, jug, shoal; *see* SNUGGLE.
Antonyms: see SCATTER, STRAGGLE.
crowded, *a.* **1.** full, packed, jammed, *etc.*
2. thick, serried (*B*), thronged, *etc.*
Antonyms: see THIN.
crowding, *n.* **1.** press, throng, jam; *spec.* huddlement.
2. *See* PRESSURE.
crowlike, *a.* corvine, corvoid (*chiefly spec.*); —*both tech.*
crown, *n.* **1.** chaplet, coronal, corona (*Latin*), ring (*contex.*), crownal (*A*), circlet, diadem (*now chiefly B*); *spec.* crownlet, coronet, aureola, aureole, bays (*pl. used with "the"*), festoon, laurel, wreath, garland, fillet.
2. head-dress, head-piece; *spec.* pschent (*Egyptian*).
3. top, crest; *spec.* copplecrown, topknot, cockscomb.
4. top, climax, complement.
5. top (*contex.*), sinciput, poll, vertex.
6. *See* SOVEREIGNTY, SOVEREIGN, HEIGHT, PERFECTION, REWARD, CREST.
crown, *a.* coronary. *"Crown" is the noun used attributively.*
crown, *v. t.* **1.** coronate (*R*), diadem (*R, exc. in p. p. diademed*); *spec.* coronet, laurel; *see* WREATHE.
2. top, surmount; *spec.* culminate (*R*), cap, head, pinnacle (*R*), crest.
3. enthrone.
crowned, *a.* incoronate (*R*), diademed; *spec.* garlanded, wreathed, laureled, laureate.
crowning, *n.* coronation (*the formal word for the ceremony*).
crownlike, *a. Spec.* garlandish, garlandy.
crucifixion, *n.* **1.** *Spec.* Calvary.
2. *See* REPRESSION.
crucify, *v. t.* **1.** execute (*contex.*), hang (*A*).
2. *See* REPRESS.
crude, *a.* **1.** raw, unfinished, unprepared; *spec.* rough, unwrought, unmanufactured, half-baked, unbaked, green, undiluted, unfulled, unburnt, unrefined, undressed, unmalted, undigested, untamed, rawish, uncut, *etc.*
2. raw, unfinished, crass, imperfect; *spec.* plain, rude, tasteless, rough, gross, artless, incondite (*R*), harsh, inartistic, half-baked, immature, ineloquent, sketchy, rough, bold, bare, unfair, brutal, highhanded, *etc.*; *see* CLUMSY.
Antonyms: see ACCOMPLISHED, NICE, SUBTLE, REFINED, SKILLFUL, ELEGANT.
3. *See* UNRIPE, ROUGH, COARSE.
cruel, *a.* **1.** cold-blooded, cold, unfeeling, hard-hearted, hard, harsh, unkind (*a euphemism*), heartless, fell (*B; implies extreme or deadly cruelty*), felon (*B*), severe; *spec.* devilish, atrocious, savage, barbarous, Draconian, swinish, boarish, brutal, butcherly, brute, inhuman, brutish, sanguinary, tigerish, wolfish, fiendish, iron, merciless, ruthless, pitiless, ferocious (*implying active or violent cruelty*), truculent (*implies bullying*), incompassionate, sadistic (*implies pleasure in cruelty*).
Antonyms: see GENTLE, COMPASSIONATE, KINDLY, KIND, MERCIFUL.
2. *Figuratively: spec.* severe, sharp, hard, unfavorable, *etc.*
cruelty, *n.* cold-bloodedness, coldness, harshness, unkindness (*euphemistic*), fellness (*B*); *spec.* deviltry, devilry, atrocity, truculence, barbarity, savagery, savageness, sadism, *etc.*

crotch: *fork, angle.*
crotched: *forked.*
crotchet: *hook, note, caprice, fad.*
crotchety: *capricious, fanciful.*
croup: *rump.*
crucial: *decisive.*
crucifix: *cross.*
cruciform: *cross-shaped.*
cruet: *bottle.*

Antonyms: see COMPASSION, GENTLENESS, MERCY.
cruise, *v. i.* range; *see* VOYAGE, SAIL.
cruise, *v. t.* navigate, range, sail, manœuvre.
cruiser, *n.* man-of-war, powerboat; *spec.* corvette, battle cruiser.
crumbly, *a.* breakable (*contex.*), friable, crump (*Scot. & dial. Eng.*), soft (*contex.*), crummable (*R*); *spec.* rotten, short, brittle, pulverizable (*contex.*), slack, moldery (*R*), brashy.
Antonyms: see STRONG.
crunch, *v. t. Implies sound as well as crushing or grinding:* chew (*contex.*), cranch *or* craunch (*obs.*), grind, crush, press, scrunch.
crupper, *n.* **1.** *Referring to part of a harness or saddle:* loop (*contex.*), dock.
2. *See* RUMP.
crush, *v. t.* **1.** bruise (*R*), press (*contex.*), pash (*A*); *spec.* mash, smash, squash, grind, jam, cranch *or* craunch (*obs.*), crunch, scrunch.
2. *See* PRESS, OVERCOME, OPPRESS, CROWD, DESTROY.
crush, *n.* **1.** pressure (*contex.*), pash (*A*); *spec.* mash, grind, crunch, squash.
2. *See* PRESSURE.
crust, *n.* **1.** coat (*contex.*), coating (*chiefly spec.*), cake, skin (*contex.*), incrustation, crustation (*R*), rind (*chiefly spec.*), encrustment; *spec.* shell, hull, efflorescence, druse, pie crust, case, scurf (*R*), sinter, scale.
2. *See* SCAB.
crust, *v. i.* cake; *spec.* effloresce, overcrust.
crust, *v. t.* incrust *or* encrust, cake, incrustate (*R*); *spec.* bark, enamel.
cry, *v. i.* **1.** *Referring to persons: spec.* shout, exclaim, clamor, call, blare, bray (*spec. or humorous*), chuckle, cluck, coo, croak, crool, croon, croup, crow, chirp, chirrup, holla, hollo, holloa, hoop, hoot, howl, lulliloo, peep, pule, screak, screech, shrill, squall, squeak, squawk (*humorous*), squeal, whimper, yang (*R*), whoop, yell, yoop (*R*); *see* SHOUT, SCREAM, BELLOW, ROAR.
Antonyms: see LAUGH, SMILE.
2. *Referring to animals: spec.* call, note, baa, bay, bell, howl, sing, blare, blat, bleat, boo, bow-wow, bray, cackle, cauk (*dial.*), caterwaul, caw, cawk, cheep, chirm, chirp, chirr, clutter, cluck, clock (*R*), coo, crake, croak, cronk (*dial.*), cuckoo, drum, gabble, gaggle, hee-haw (*C*), honk (*U. S. & Can.*), hoot, juck, juke, jug, keckle, low, mew, miaow, mewl, miaul, moo, neigh, open, peep, pew, potrack (*R*), purr, quack, scape, screak, scream, screech, shriek, shrill, squeak, squawk, trumpet, twitter, weet, whimper, yelp, yowl; *see* BARK, BELLOW, CHIRP, CROW, ROAR.
3. lament, weep, keen (*Irish*); *spec.* squall, wail, moan, whimper, sob, bellow, bawl, snivel, blubber.
Antonyms: see REJOICE, LAUGH.
4. *See* APPEAL, MOURN.
cry, *v. t.* **1.** utter (*contex.*); *spec.* shout, exclaim, proclaim, advertise.
2. *See* HAWK.
cry, *n.* **1.** *Referring to persons:* utterance (*contex.*); *spec.* shout, exclamation, scream, clamor, call, blare, boo, boohoo, bray (*A or humorous*), cackle, chirm, chirk, chirrup, chuckle, check, coo, croak, crool, croup, crow, gabble, hollo, holloa, hoot, hosanna, howl, lulliloo, lure, peep, quaver, roar, screak, screech, shriek, shrilling, snivel, sob, squall, squawk, squeal, wail, whimper, whoop, yang (*R*), yoop (*C*), yell; *see* BELLOW, SHOUT, SCREAM.
2. *Referring to animals: spec.* note, call, baa, bark, bay, bell, blare, blat, bleat, boation (*R*), boo, boom, bow-wow, bray, buller (*Scot.*), bumble (*cant, dial.*), cackle, caterwaul, caw, cawk, cheep, chirm, chirp, chirr, clock (*R*), chuckle, cluck, coo, crake, croak, cronk (*dial.*), gabble, gaggle, gobble, gobblement (*R*), growl, hee-haw (*C*), honk (*U. S. & Can.*), hoot, howl, juck *or* juke, jug, keckle, low, mew, mewl, miaow, maul, moo, neigh, pheal (*R*), purr, quack, scape, screak, scream, screech, shriek, shrill, song, squall, squawk, squeak, squial, trumpet, twitter, wail, weet, weke, whimper, whoop, yelp, yowl; *see* CHIRP, BELLOW, ROAR, CROW.
3. *See* APPEAL, WATCHWORD.
4. weep (*R*), lamentation, keening (*Irish*); *spec.* boohoo, wail, whimper, squall, sob, bawl.
Antonyms: see LAUGH.
crystal, *a.* **1.** crystalline (*esp. as opposed to "amorphous"*), crystalloid (*tech. and esp. as opposed to "colloid"*), crystalliform (*tech.*); *spec.* drusiform, glacial.
2. *See* CLEAR.
crystal, *v. i.* crystallize.
crystal-gaze, *v. i.* scry. *"Crystal-gaze" is R, exc. in the form "crystal-gazing."*
crystal-gazer, *n.* seer (*contex.*), scryer.
crystallize, *v. i.* solidify (*contex.*), congeal (*contex.*), crystal (*R and B*); *spec.* candy, shoot.
cub, *n.* offspring (*contex.*), puppy, whelp.
cube, *n.* **1.** solid (*contex.*), die (*chiefly architectural*), hexahedron (*geom.*).
2. *In mathematics:* power.
cuckold, *n.* cornute (*A*), cornuto (*A*); *spec.* wittol.
cuckold, *v. t.* horn (*obs.*), cornute (*A*).
cuckolded, *a.* horned, cornuted (*A*), forked (*obs. or A*).
cudgel, *n. & v.* club, stick; *spec.* bastinado, crab, bludgeon, baton, batoon (*A*).

---

cruise: *sail, voyage.*
crumb, *v. t.: comminute.*
crumble: *disintegrate.*
crump: *chew.*
crumple: *wrinkle.*
crunching: *pressure.*
crusade, *n.: war, movement.*
crusade, *v. i.: war, campaign.*
cruse: *bottle, jug, jar.*
crushing: *pressure.*
crutch: *staff, fork.*
crypt: *vault.*
cryptic: *hidden.*
cuddle, *v. t.: embrace.*
cuddle, *v. i.: snuggle.*
cuddy: *donkey, closet.*

---

cue, *n.* **1.** queue, pigtail *or* (*for short*) tail (*C or humorous*); *spec.* braid, plait, roll, *etc.*
2. *See* FILE.
3. *Spec.* stick.
cuff, *n.*, hem, sleeve, edge, band.
cuff, *n.* blow (*contex.*), buffet, slap, fisticuff.
cuff, *v. t.* strike (*contex.*), slap, box, buffet, handicuff (*C*), fisticuff.
cul-de-sac, *n.* (*French*), pocket, impasse (*French*), no-thoroughfare, dead end.
culminate, *v. i.* top (*C*), end, conclude, finish.
cult, *n.* **1.** cultus; *spec.* worship.
2. *See* DEVOTION, RITE, HOMAGE.
cultivate, *v. t.* **1.** farm, till (*now chiefly spec.*), work, culture (*R*), labor (*R*); *spec.* garden, hoe, rake, weed.
2. *Referring to working on plants:* grow, husband (*R*); *spec.* hoe, earth, weed.
3. *See* CIVILIZE, REFINE, PURSUE, COURT, FOSTER.
cultivation, *n.* **1.** farming, tillage (*now chiefly spec.*), husbandry, culture, tilth (*R or B*).
2. *Referring to work on plants:* growth, culture; *spec.* care, attention.
3. *See* CIVILIZATION, REFINEMENT, PURSUIT, FOSTERAGE.
culture, *n.* **1.** *See* CULTIVATION.
2. *Spec.* education, development, enlightenment, civilization, humanism, humanity (*A*), literature (*A*); *see* REFINEMENT.
Antonyms: see BARBARISM.
cuneiform, *n.* writing (*contex.*), print (*contex.*); *spec.* sphenogram.
cunning, *a.* **1.** *See* SKILLFUL, ARTFUL, PRETTY.
2. interesting (*contex.*), cute (*C*).
cup, *n.* **1.** *Spec.* chalice (*B, elevated, or eccl.*), mazer (*obs. or hist.*), goblet, noggin, mug, pannikin, porringer, jorum (*C*), stein (*German; but not used in Germany*), cannikin, cyathus, tazza (*Italian*), cyclix, calix, can, bumper, bowl (*B*), chark (*Russian*), beaker, rhyton, standard, taster, bucket, gourd, goddard (*obs. or dial.*).
2. *See* SHARE.
cupbearer, *n.* Ganymede (*hist. or fig.*), Hebe (*hist. or fig.*).
cupboard, *n.* closet; *spec.* buffet, locker, press.
cupid, *n.* love, Eros (*Greek*). "*Cupid*" *is the Latin god.*
cup-shaped, *a.* calciform (*R*), poculiform (*tech.*), cupped, cuppy (*R*); *spec.* cupular, cupulate, cotyliform, cotyloid, calathiform, cyathiform.
curable, *a.* healable, remediable, mendable (*obs. or dial.*), recoverable, medicable.
Antonyms: see INCURABLE.
curate, *n.* minister (*contex.*), rector, vicar, assistant (*contex.*), priest (*contex.*).
curative, *a.* beneficial, restorative, curatory, healing, remedial, medical (*R*), consolidant (*R*), salutary, sanative (*R*), sanatative, sanatory; *spec.* medicable (*R*), medicinal, incarnative (*R*), recuperative, recuperatory, vulnerary.
curb, *n.* **1.** *See* CONTROL, RESTRAINT, MARKET.
2. inclosure; *spec.* collar, puteal.
curd, *n.* coagulum; *spec.* clabber, bonnyclabber, junket.
curdle, *v. t. & i.* coagulate; *spec.* separate.
cure, *n.* **1.** *See* MINISTRY, REMEDY, RECOVERY.
2. preservation (*R or affected*); *spec.* ensilage, corning, smoking, jerking, *etc.*
cure, *v. t.* **1.** heal, remedy (*R*), recover, sanitate (*R*), sanitize (*R*), restore, mend (*A*), leech (*A*); *spec.* cicatrize, incarn (*R*).
Antonyms: see DISEASE.
2. preserve; *spec.* ripen, ensilate, ensile *or* ensilage, kipper, season, jerk, dry, smoke, pickle, salt, put (*with "up," "down"*).
curiosity, *n.* **1.** curiousness, inquiringness, inquisitiveness (*implies persistent and often meddlesome curiosity*); *spec.* pryingness, prying, questioning, interrogation.
Antonyms: see INDIFFERENCE.
2. article (*contex.*), curio, bric-à-brac (*a collective*), rarity, oddity, knick-knack, souvenir (*spec.*).
curious, *a.* **1.** *See* NICE, ODD, ELABORATE.
2. inquiring, inquisitive (*chiefly used in a bad sense*); *spec.* seeking, inquisitorial, inquisitional, zetetic, interrogative, prying, meddling, nosey, snoopy, meddlesome, investigating, questioning, scrutinizing, mousing, percontatorial (*R*), supercurious, overcurious.
Antonyms: see INDIFFERENT.
curl, *n.* **1.** roll (*contex.*), convolution (*tech. or B*), volute (*tech. or B*); *see* TWIST, COIL, SPIRAL.
2. *Referring to the hair:* buckle (*A*), ringlet, feak (*R*); *spec.* cannon, curlicue, frizz, frounce, frizzle, kink, lovelock, kinkle, favorite, spit (*for* spit curl), roll, permanent, wave, toupee (*implies an arrangement of false hair*).
3. *Referring to the state:* buckle; *spec.* crispation (*R*), crispature (*R*), wave.
4. *See* CREST.
curl, *v. i.* roll (*contex.*); *see* WAVE, RIPPLE.
curl, *v. t.* **1.** roll (*contex.*); *see* TWIST, COIL, SPIRAL.
2. *Referring to the hair: spec.* kink, frizz, frounce, frizzle, crinkle, crimp, crisp.

---

cue: *suggestion, part, humor.*
cuisine: *kitchen, cookery.*
cull, *v. t.: choose.*
culm: *stalk.*
culmination: *top, height.*
culprit: *transgressor.*
cultivated: *artificial, refined.*
cultured: *refined.*
cultus: *cult.*
culvert: *drain.*
cumber, *v. t.: hamper, burden.*
cumber, *n.: burden.*
cumbersome: *hindering, burdensome, unwieldy.*
cumbrous: *unwieldy, clumsy.*
cumulate: *accumulate.*
cumulus: *heap, cloud.*
cuneiform: *wedge-shaped.*
cunning, *n.: skill, art.*
cupidity: *greed.*
cupidous: *greedy.*
cupped: *cup-shaped.*
cuppy: *cup-shaped, pitted.*
cupreous: *copper, copper-colored.*
cur: *dog, coward, wretch.*
curacy: *ministry.*
curator: *custodian.*
curb, *v. t.: restrain, subdue.*
curd: *coagulum.*
curdle: *coagulate.*
curé, *n.: minister.*
curfew: *ringing.*
curio: *curiosity.*
curiousness: *curiosity.*

curled, *a.* rolled (*contex.*), convolute (*B or tech.*), volute (*B or tech.*), waved; *spec.* coiled, cyclical, involute; *see* CURLY.

curly, *a.* wavy; *spec.* curled, kinky, frizzly, frizzy, crimpy, kinkled, spiry (*R*), fuzzy, crisp, wreathy.

curly-haired, *a. Referring to a dog: spec.* feathery.

current, *a.* **1.** *See* PREVALENT, PASSING, PRESENT.

2. *Referring to money, etc.:* circulative (*R*), circulating, used.

3. accepted, received, abroad, afloat, standard, fashionable; *spec.* general, rife.

4. *Referring to expense, etc.:* occurrent (*R*), incidental.

current, *n.* **1.** *See* COURSE.

2. stream; *spec.* tide, race, rip, draught, underset, undertow, roost (*local; British*).

curry, *v. t.* **1.** comb (*contex.*), currycomb, groom.

2. *Figuratively: spec.* tickle, scrape, beat, blight, plague; *see* THRASH.

curse, *v. t.* **1.** maledict (*R*), blaspheme (*implies cursing God*), devote (*R and B*), execrate (*B*), anathematize (*B and properly, formal*), bless (*euphemistic or ironical*), damn, bawl (*with "out"; C; of a person*), ban (*A*), blank (*euphemistic*), cuss (*vulgar or C, and euphemistic; U. S.*), shrew *or* beshrew (*A*), pest (*A*); *spec.* hoodoo.

Antonyms: see BLESS, BEATIFY, CONSECRATE.

2. *See* ABUSE, BLASPHEME, ANNOY, TROUBLE.

curse, *v. i.* blaspheme, profane (*R*), pest (*R*), anathematize (*B and, properly, formal*), execrate (*B*), fulminate (*fig. or tech.*), swear.

curse, *n.* **1.** malediction (*implies calling down evil upon a person*), execration (*B*), oath (*implies a profane invocation of the deity*), imprecation, anathema (*properly, formal*), ban (*implies formal exclusion; less solemn than* anathema), blessing (*euphemistic or ironical*), malison (*A*), profanity; *spec.* maranatha (*literally, "The Lord is at hand"; because of its occurrence in I Corinthians 16.23 it is occasionally misunderstood as an intensitive synonym for* anathema), excommunication, hoodoo, damn, damme (*obs. or A; orig. a vulgar ejaculation*).

Antonyms: see BLESSING, BEATITUDE.

2. *Spec.* trouble, calamity, plague, bane, pest.

cursed, *a.* **1.** damnable, execrable (*now weakened in force*), infernal (*C and euphemistic*), confounded (*now euphemistic*); *see* ACCURSED.

2. *See* HATEFUL.

cursing, *n.* malediction, execration. damnation, profanity.

Antonyms: see BLESSING, PRAYER.

cursing, *a.* execratory, execrative, damning.

cursory, *a.* passing, transient, running, desultory (*implies absence of aim and continuity*), unmethodical; *spec.* hasty, hurried; *see* CARELESS, SUPERFICIAL, DISCURSIVE (*implies extensive wandering*).

curt, *a.* **1.** *See* SHORT, BRIEF.

2. brief (*contex.*), short, snappish, snappy; *spec.* tart, brusque.

Antonyms: see GRACIOUS.

curtain, *n.* screen, ridel *or* riddel (*A or eccl.*), veil (*chiefly fig.*); *spec.* drop, purdah (*East India*), portière (*French*), arras, lambrequin (*U. S.*), drapery, drapes (*pl.; cant*), valance, shade.

curtain, *v. t.* screen (*contex.*), veil (*chiefly fig.*); *spec.* shade.

curtsy, curtsey, *n.* civility (*contex.*), bow; *see* LEG.

curvature, *n.* **1.** *Referring to the action or act:* bend, curve, bending, curving, curvation; *spec.* camber (*chiefly tech.*), rounding, procurvation, incurvation, recurvation, recurvature, convexity, convexness (*R*), concavity, winding, concaveness (*R*), flexion, retroflexion, sheer.

2. *See* CURVE.

curve, *n.* **1.** *Referring to the state or the form produced:* bend, curvature, incurvature, inflection (*B*), compass (*tech.*), bent (*R*); *spec.* bow, crook, round (*A*), roundabout, arc, flex, arch, bight, sinus, decurvation, recurvation, retroflex, recurvature, sweep, epicycloid, conchoid, catenary, curl, sheer, ellipse, evolute, cycloid, extrados (*architecture*), logistic, polhode, ogee, epitrochoid, herpolhode, gadroon, twist, incurvation, wind, circle, wave, convexity, convex (*R*), concavity, concave (*R*), geanticlinal, geosynclinal, oxbow, coil, sinuosity, turn, spiral.

2. *See* CURVATURE.

3. *Referring to a curved thing: spec.* bend, curl, bow, cambrel (*obs. or dial.*), crook, crescent, lune, half-moon, arc, arch, hook.

curve, *v. t. & i.* bend, turn, inflect, round, crook; *spec.* bow, embow, twist, arch, arc, decurve, camber, incurve, incurvate, recurve, recurvate, reflect, wind, hook, spire, coil.

Antonyms: see STRAIGHTEN.

curved, *a.* bent (*primarily spec.*), bowed, bow-shaped, curvate (*R*), crooked, curvilinear; *spec.* roundish, rounded, spherical, arched, arc-like, inbent, reflex, incurved, campylotropous, embowed (*B*), retorted (*R*), concave, convex, bulging, sweepy, arcuate, crumpled, camerated, compass, circinate, circinal, crescent, falcate, falcated, rotundate, elliptic, circular, oval, tortile (*R*), recurved, recurvate; *see* SINUOUS, WINDING.

Antonyms: see ANGULAR, STRAIGHT.

curvet, *n.* jump (*contex.*), leap (*contex.*), courbette (*French*), vault.

cushion, *n.* **1.** pillow; *spec.* pad, woolsack,

---

curlicue: *curl.*
curmudgeon: *niggard.*
curriculum: *course.*
currish: *canine, irascible, mean.*
currycomb: *curry.*
cursive: *running.*
curtail: *shorten, abate, diminish, clip, deprive.*
curtate: *short, shortened.*
curtilage: *court.*
curtsy, curtsey, *v. i.: bow.*

---

bolster, panel, mat, wad, compress, buckram, pillion, bass, hassock, quilt.
2. *See* BUFFER.
cushion, *v. t.* **1.** *Spec.* pad, protect, bolster, cover, seat, wad, quilt.
2. rest, pillow.
cushioned, *a. Spec.* padded, gamboised, quilted.
cushion-shaped, *a.* pulvinate (*tech.*).
cusk, *n.* torsk.
cusp, *n.* point (*contex.*), apex, peak, cuspis (*tech.*); *spec.* horn.
custodian, *n.* guardian, guardianess (*fem.; R*), keeper, custodier (*Scots law*), custos (*Latin*); *spec.* conservator, curator, curatrix (*fem.*), warden, concierge (*French*), janitor, janitress, tutor, sacrist, sacristan.
custom, *n.* **1.** practice (*emphasizes habit of action*), use (*now R*), praxis (*R, emphasizes practice as distinct from theory*), usage (*suggests corporate habit and custom*), consuetude, wont (*now chiefly B*), fashion (*chiefly spec.*), dustoor (*East India*); *spec.* rite (*implies ritual habit*), localism, way, manner, procedure, prescription, institution (*implies formal recognition of custom*); *see* CONVENTION, HABIT (*suggests rather the tendency to repeat,* custom *the fact of repeating*).
2. *See* CONVENTIONALITY, TAX.
3. patronage, support, trade.
customary, *a.* accustomed, wonted, usual, consuetudinary (*R*), ordinary (*contex.*), regular, normal; *spec.* everyday, natural, traditional, traditionary, nomic, prescriptive; *see* CONVENTIONAL, HABITUAL.
Antonyms: see UNACCUSTOMED, UNCONVENTIONAL, OBSOLETE, OCCASIONAL, ODD.
customer, *n.* **1.** buyer, purchaser, patron.
2. *See* FELLOW.
cut, *v. t. & i.* **1.** incise (*B, except in p. a. "incised"*), incide (*R*), separate (*contex.*); *spec.* carve, cleave, truncate, lance, scarify, bite, dissect, shear, poll, shave, skive, scissor, snip, saw, bite, scythe, slice, slit, slash, knife, mince, chop, barb, poll, chisel, sculpture, chip, mow, reap, gouge, hack, hash, nick, hew, facet, saber *or* sabre, score, scotch, flitch, gash, crimp, crease, hog, shred, lop, dock, carbonado, roach, clip, crop, trim, castrate, whittle, pare, *etc.*
2. *See* SEPARATE, PENETRATE, CROSS, SHORTEN, SWITCH, DIMINISH, REDUCE, DEPART (*v. i.*).
3. *Referring to the sensibilities:* hurt, bite, sting, pain, wound.
4. ignore, snub; *see* SLIGHT.
5. harvest, gather, reap.
cut, *n.* **1.** *Referring to an act:* cutting (*R*), incision (*B or tech.*), incisure (*R*), *spec.* gash, nick, discission (*R*), bite, crop, scotch, shave, shear, clip, snip, carve, slit.
2. *Referring to the place or form made by cutting: spec.* cutting, gash, slash, nick, incision (*B or tech.*), scotch, notch, channel, furrow, passage, groove, jad, facet.
3. *Referring to a piece or part cut off or out: spec.* cutting, clipping, shaving, peel, scrap, mowing, crop, harvest, fall, snip, paring, slice.
4. *Referring to a piece of meat or food cut off: spec.* joint, sparerib, flitch, clod, collop, chop, slice, steak, crop, round, shoulder, neck, brisket, rump, *etc.*
5. *See* ENGRAVING, STYLE, SWITCH, PASSAGE, SARCASM, TAUNT, SLIGHT, ABSENCE.
cut, *a. Spec.* gashy, shorn, tonsured, slashed, carved, carven (*B*), hacked, cleft, *etc.*
cuttable, *a.* sectile (*B or tech.*), secable (*R*); *spec.* cleavable.
cutter, *n. Spec.* cleaver, diamond, écraseur (*French*), colter *or* coulter, cropper, carver, clipper, chopper, microtome, mower, hewer, hook, blade, shear, sickle, scythe, knife, *etc.*
cutting, *a.* **1.** sharp, incisive (*B*), incisory (*R*), sectorial (*B*); *spec.* edgy.
2. *Referring to language, etc.:* sharp, biting, stinging, wounding, snide (*C*); *see* ACRIMONIOUS, SARCASTIC.
cutting, *n.* **1.** *Referring to the action:* cut (*R*), incision (*B*), section (*chiefly tech.*), scission (*R*); *spec.* tonsure, excision, concision, shaving, clipping, *etc.*
2. *See* CUT.
cycle, *n.* **1.** *See* CIRCLE, ROUND.
2. period, eon; *spec.* saros, age.
3. wheel (*C*), machine (*C*), bike (*S*); *spec.* bicycle, tricycle, quadricycle, tandem, pneumatic, quartet, quintet, quintuplet, hydrocycle, motorcycle, scooter.
cyclic, *a.* **1.** circular;—*chiefly of poems, periods of time, etc.*
2. *See* RECURRENT.
cylinder, *n. Spec.* rundle, cannon, drum, cage, barrel, fly, roll; *see* ROLLER.
cylindrical, *a.* cylindraceous (*R*), cylindric (*R*), cylindriform (*R*), round (*contex.; spec.*), cyclindroid.
cynic, *n.* **1.** *See* PHILOSOPHER.
2. misanthrope, pessimist (*contex.*), sour-puss (*S*).
cynical, *a.* **1.** *See* SURLY.
2. *Spec.* Diogenic.
3. misanthropic; *spec.* sneering, satirical, censorious.

D

dab, *v. t.* **1.** *Implies lightness and swiftness:* strike (*contex.*), tap, touch; *spec.* peck, slap, pat, blow.

---

curvilinear: *curved.*
cuspid: *canine.*
cuspidate, cuspidated: *pointed, ornamented.*
cuspidor: *spittoon.*
custody: *care, imprisonment.*
cut-and-dried: *prearranged, conventional.*
cutaneous: *skin.*
cute: *cunning, shrewd, clever.*
cuticle: *skin.*
cutlass: *sword.*
cutty: *short.*
cycloid: *circular.*
cyclopean: *gigantic, massive.*
cyclorama: *show.*
cynosure: *attraction.*
cyst: *chest, sac.*
cystic: *vesicular.*
czar: *monarch.*

2. *See* SPOT.

dab, *n.* **1.** stroke (*contex.*), tap; *spec.* peck, slap, pat, blow.

2. *See* LUMP, SPOT, LITTLE.

dabble, *v. t.* wet (*contex.*), spatter.

dabble, *v. i.* **1.** puddle, muddle, potter, mess; *spec.* splash, paddle, patter, plouter (*chiefly Scot.*).

2. potter, trifle, smatter; *see* POTTER.

dabbler, *n.* **1.** mudlark (*C*).

2. dabster, potterer, smatterer, trifler, amateur; *spec.* sciolist (*B*). *Cf.* BUNGLE.

Antonyms: see EXPERT.

daffodil, *n.*, asphodel (*A or hist.*), narcissus, jonquil, daffa-down-dilly (*A and B; also* daffodilly).

daffy, *a.*, daft, crazy, silly, imbecile, balmy (*C*), nutty (*C*), *etc.*

dagger, *n.* **1.** weapon (*contex.*), point (*R*), tickler (*S*), skene (*A or hist.*), parazonium (*Greek antiq.*), prog (*R*); *spec.* poniard (*B*), bodkin (*A*), ataghan, creese, crease, kris, kuttar, misericord, dirk, stiletto, stylet, poignado *or* poinado (*A*), left-hander, khanjar, dudgeon (*A*).

2. *In printing:* obelisk; *spec.* diesis (*double dagger*).

daily, *a.* diurnal, quotidian (*R*).

Antonyms: see NOCTURNAL.

dainty, *a.* **1.** *See* PALATABLE, PARTICULAR, FASTIDIOUS (*suggests hypercritical taste*), NICE.

2. beautiful, pretty, elegant (*implying taste and richness*), delicate (*implying fineness of texture and work*), neat (*implying trimness*), trim, tricksy (*R*), exquisite (*implying delicacy and excellence: a superlative*), choice, precious (*C*).

Antonyms: see UGLY, CLUMSY, COARSE.

3. nice; *spec.* squeamish, fastidious, exquisite.

dais, *n.* tribune (*contex.*), platform (*contex.*); *spec.* estrade (*R*), half-pace, footpace.

dam, *n.* obstruction (*contex.*), barrier (*contex.*), weir; *spec.* barrage.

dam, *v. t.* obstruct (*contex.*), bay; *spec.* pond (*Eng.*), impound.

dance, *n.* **1.** measure (*B*), saltation (*esp. characterized by leaping steps; R*); *spec.* valse, courante, courant, country-dance, waltz, strathspey (*Scot.*), sun dance, tango, turkey-trot, bunny-hug, onestep, twostep, Boston, fox-trot, rhumba, continental, Charleston, barn-dance, square dance, Virginia reel, Morris dance, german, saraband, schottische, shuffle, roundelay, round, tarantella, rigadoon, Romaika, roly-poly, ridotto (*Italian*), juba (*U. S.*), tambourin, pas, passepied, grandfather, morris, minuet, hay, pavan (*hist.*), dance of death, gavotte, hobble, hoe-down (*U. S.*), break-down, hornpipe, gallaird (*hist.*), gallopade, galop, bolero, contre-dance, country dance, cotillion *or* cotillon, corroboree, brawl, cachucha, canary, cancan, caper, carmagnole, polka, reel, kantikoy, quadrille, fling, jig, lavolta (*hist.*), farandole (*French*), fandango (*Spanish*), chemise (*cant*), strip-tease, *etc.*

2. party (*contex.*), assembly (*contex.*); *spec.* ball, hop (*S or C*), promenade, prom (*collegiate*), nautch (*India*).

dance, *v. i. & t.* **1.** foot (*chiefly with "it"; R*); *spec.* step, trip (*it*), tread (*contex.*), waltz, tripudiate (*R*), rigadon, minuet, jig, pirouette, polonaise, poussette, polk, reel, quadrille, leap, fox-trot, onestep.

2. play, bob, jiggle, jig, jigger, bobble; *spec.* caper, jump, dandle.

dancer, *n.* Terpsichore (*fig.*), danseuse (*fem.; French*), ballerina (*French*); *spec.* flinger, kicker, coryphee, matachin, hoofer (*S*), artist (*contex.*, as *"strip-tease artist"*).

dancing, *n.* footing (*contex.*), orchestics (*the art; R*), Terpsichore (*as an art; fig.*).

dancing, *a.* **1.** saltatorial, saltatory;—*both B.*

2. *See* JIGGLY.

dancing girl. *Spec.* bayadere (*India*), geisha (*Japanese*).

dandy, *n.* **1.** fop, coxcomb *or* (*less usual*) cockscomb, exquisite, fopling, popinjay, beau, jackanapes (*A*), man milliner (*contemptuous; A*), jack-a-dandy (*A*), prick-me-dainty (*A*), buck (*A*), bawcock (*obs.*), toff (*S, Eng.*), skipjack (*A*), dudine (*female dude; C and R*), swell (*A*), dude (*one excessively dandified*); *spec.* fashionables (*pl.*), smoothie (*C*).

Antonyms: see SLOVEN, RAGAMUFFIN.

2. *See* FINE ONE.

dandy, *a.* foppish, smart (*A or obs.*), exquisite, dudish (*implying excess*), coxcombical, jackanapish (*R*), buckish (*A*), dandified, lardy-dardy (*S; also* la-di-da *implying excessive elegance and obstentation*).

Antonyms: see SHABBY, SLOVENLY.

dandyism, *n.* foppery, foppishness, exquisitism (*implying pose*), exquisiteness (*implying pose*), macaronism (*R*), dudism (*implying ostentatious elegance*), coxcombery, jackanapery (*R*), jack-a-dandyism (*A*), peacockery (*implying pride and ostentation*).

danger, *n.* hazard (*implies chance danger*), risk (*suggests active and probable danger*), peril (*suggests great and imminent danger*), jeopardy (*suggests exposure to certain danger*), peril,

D

dabster: *dabbler, expert.*
dado: *border.*
daft: *foolish, deranged, daffy.*
daggle: *draggle, soil, wet.*
dainty: *delicacy, sweetmeat.*
dale: *valley.*
dalliance: *trifling, idling, caressing.*
dally: *trifle, idle, toy.*
damage, *n.: detriment, loss, harm, injury, impairment.*
damage, *v. t.: harm, injure, impair.*
damaged: *spoiled.*
damaging: *harmful, injurious.*
damn: *condemn, curse, ruin.*
damnable: *condemnable, abominable, cursed.*
damnation: *ruin, condemnation.*
damnatory: *ruinous, condemnatory.*
damp, *n.: moisture.*
damp, *a.: moist.*
damp, *v. t.: moisten, restrain, deaden.*
dampen: *moisten, restrain.*
dampening: *depressing.*
damsel: *girl.*
dandle: *jiggle, caress.*
dangerless: *safe.*

jeopardy; *spec.* venture, rock (*something dangerous; fig.*).

Antonyms: see SAFETY.

dangerous, *a.* bad (*contex.*), risky, hazardous, perilous, jeopardous (*R or obs.*), chancy (*C*), dangersome (*R*), unsafe, precarious (*suggests lack of security or continuance*), riskful (*R*), parlous (*a form of* perilous); *spec.* critical, ticklish (*C*), nice, kittle (*Scot. or B*), delicate, serious, ugly, nasty, adventurous, breakneck, thorny.

Antonyms: see SAFE.

dangle, *v. t.* hang, pendulate (*R*); *spec.* swing, jiggle.

dapple, *a.* spotted, variegated; *spec.* dapple-gray.

dapple, *v. t.* spot, variegate.

dare, *v. t.* **1.** *See* CHALLENGE, FACE, DEFY.

2. undertake, venture;—*not close synonyms.*

dare-devil, *n.* devil (*C*), madcap.

dark, *a.* **1.** *Spec.* obscure (*implies overshadowing*), tenebrous (*B*), gloomy, rayless, dingy, dim, dimmish, murk (*A or B*), murky, blind, caliginous (*B*), obfuscous (*R*), Cimmerian (*alluding to the Cimmerians, fabled to live in perpetual darkness*), dun, dunny, dunnish, cloudy (*often fig.*), umbrageous (*B*), fuliginous, sooty, grimy, somber, atramentous (*B*), swarthy, swart, tawny, drumly (*chiefly Scot. or B*), gloomy, muddy, murksome (*R*), nightly, crepuscular (*often fig.*), nonluminescent (*formal*), nonluminous (*formal*), dead, crepusculine (*R*), dirty, torchless, shadowy, unsunned (*R*), sunless, rayless, cloudy, darkful, darkish, darksome (*vaguer and weaker than "dark"; chiefly B*), deadly, grimed, umbery (*R*), fuscous (*chiefly nat. hist.*), dusky (*implies low light*), opaque, fuscescent (*R*), black, coaly, carbonaceous (*R*), dull, ebony, pitchy, inky, inkish (*R*), lightless, nigrescent (*R*), funereal, unillumined; *see* DIM, SHADY, BLACK, DULL.

Antonyms: see BRIGHT, MOONLIGHT, LUMINESCENT, SHINING, FAIR.

2. *Referring to the understanding: see* MYSTERIOUS, ABSTRUSE.

3. *Referring to the complexion:* swarthy (*implies black*), tawny (*implies yellow or brown*), dusky, swart (*stronger than tawny*); *spec.* grimy, ebony.

Antonyms: see FAIR, PALE.

4. *See* GLOOMY, DEPRESSING, WICKED, IGNORANT, HIDDEN, SECRET, RETICENT, THREATENING.

dark, *n.* darkness, blackness; *spec.* obscurity (*implying low visibility*), tenebrousness (*B*), tenebrosity (*B*), dinginess (*implying smoke or grime*), duskiness, dimness, murkiness, murk (*chiefly B*), caliginosity (*B*), dun, umbrageousness (*B*), ebony, swarthiness, swartness, tawniness, gloom, shadow, pitchiness, inkiness.

Antonyms: see LIGHT, MOONLIGHT.

darken, *v. t.* **1.** dark (*A or B*), denigrate (*R*); *spec.* darkle, dim, black, blacken, shade, muddy, eclipse, dun, dull, disluster (*R*), ebonize, dusken (*R*), cloud, fog, disilluminate, encloud (*intensive; R*), gloom, obumbrate (*B*), obtenebrate (*R*), overshadow, shade, murk (*R*), obfuscate (*R*), obnubilate (*R*), overgloom (*R*), overshade (*R*), overcloud, overcast, obfuscate, blur, becloud (*intensive*), bedim (*intensive*), bedarken (*intensive*), bescreen (*intensive*), begloom (*intensive*), sable (*chiefly B*), umber (*R*), somber.

Antonyms: see LIGHT, BRIGHTEN.

2. *Spec.* dim (*the eyes or sight, or the sight of*), blur, purblind, blear, blind, obscure, obfuscate (*R*), mist.

3. *Referring to the understanding: spec.* dull, benight, obscure, mystify, cloud, becloud.

Antonyms: see ENLIGHTEN.

4. *See* DEPRESS, SULLY.

darken, *v. i.* **1.** dark (*A or B*); *spec.* darkle (*B*), cloud, dusk (*B*), dim, dull, dusken (*R*), gloom, umber (*fig.*).

2. *In the sense of "to grow angry looking":* darkle, cloud.

darkened, *a. Spec.* obscured, obfuscate, clouded, cloudy, ustulate (*R*), infuscate (*R*).

darkening, *n.* obscuration (*contex.*); *spec.* blackening, clouding, *etc.*

darkness, *n.* **1.** dark; *spec.* obscurity, dimness, dinginess, dusk, duskness, duskiness, tawniness, gloom, gloominess, swartness, swarthiness, griminess, caliginousness (*B*), murkiness, somberness, dullness, shadow, shadowiness, shadiness, duskishness, caliginosity (*A*), tenebrosity (*B*), smokiness, umbrageousness (*B*), fuliginosity (*B*), sootiness, muddiness, dimmit (*dial. Eng.*), lightlessness, murk (*chiefly Scot.*), night, opacity, eclipse, dunness (*R*), shades (*pl.*), *etc.; see* SHADING.

Antonyms: see BRIGHTNESS.

2. *Spec.* obscurity, mystery, abyss, abstruseness, gloom, depression, wickedness, ignorance, blindness, secrecy.

darling, *a.* beloved, favorite, pet (*which see*), sweetheart, sweetie (*S*), friend (*S*).

Antonyms: see DISLIKED.

dart, *n.* **1.** spear (*chiefly spec.*), weapon (*contex.*), lance, javelin (*spec.*), gavelock (*obs. or hist.*), banderilla, jerid *or* jereed, whisk.

2. *Referring to the motion: spec.* jump, bolt (*implies suddenness*), flit, shoot (*generally implies speed*), leap, spring, whisk (*implies speed and lightness*), pounce, flirt.

dart, *v. t.* **1.** throw, hurl (*implies speed and power*), cast, dartle; *spec.* shoot, flirt, launch, jaculate (*R*).

2. direct (*a look, etc.*).

dart, *v. i.* shoot, scoot (*C*); *spec.* leap, jump, pounce, spring, rush, dash, dartle, rocket, bolt,

---

dangle, *v. i.: hang, attend.*
dangling: *hanging.*
dank: *moist.*
dapper: *dandy, small, smart.*
dapple: *spotted, variegated.*
dare: *challenge, defiance.*
dare-devil, *a.: reckless.*
daring: *bold, brave, defiant.*
darling, *n.: dear, pet.*
darn: *repair.*

hurtle (*implies sudden and violent motion*), flit, flirt (*implies sudden jerky motion*), whip, whisk, scoot, rush, whir.

dash, *v. t.* **1.** propel (*implies direction*), strike, beat (*implies repetition*), knock, pash (*now chiefly dial. Eng.*), slam (*suggests a loud and sudden impact*); *spec.* smash (*C*), swash, ding, slap, crash; *see* SPLASH, KNOCK.

2. *See* SHATTER, THROW, RUIN, DEPRESS, ABASH, FLAVOR, COMPOSE.

dash, *v. i. Implying motion with sudden speed:* run, sprint, speed, fly (*contex.*), hurry, rush, dart; *spec.* clash, smash, lash; *see* SPLASH, RUSH.

Antonyms: see LAG.

dash, *n.* **1.** *See* PROPULSION, SHOCK, LINE, BLOW, RUSH, ENERGY, SHOW.

2. admixture (*contex.*), little (*contex.*); *spec.* touch, intimation (*C*), tinge, spice, sensation (*C or S*), lace (*of spirits*), flavor, relish; *see* TRACE.

date, *n.* **1.** time; *spec.* epoch (*implies the beginning of a new order*), day, age, era (*refers generally to a specific order of things*), aeon *or* eon (*implies a very long period of time*), moment (*a very short period of time*), misdate.

2. *See* DURATION, APPOINTMENT.

3. (*C*) *for* engagement, appointment.

date, *v. t.* time, place (*chronologically*), *spec.* misdate.

dateless, *a.* undated; *also,* eternal.

datum, *n. Spec.* element, premiss, condition, material (*a collective*).

daughter, *n.* child (*contex.*), girl (*contex.*); *spec.* cadette, daughterkin, daughterling, daughter-in-law, stepdaughter, infanta, dauphiness.

Antonyms: see PARENT, FATHER, MOTHER.

dauntless, *a. Implying strength of spirit as well as fearlessness:* brave (*contex.*), bold, unaffeared (*A*), unaffrighted, unappalled, courageous.

dawdle, *v. i.* **1.** trifle, potter, idle, diddle, loaf (*C*).

Antonyms: see BUSTLE.

2. *See* DELAY.

dawn, *n.* daybreak, break of day.

dawn, *v. i.* **1.** daw (*Scot.*), morrow (*R*), break (*chiefly with "day" as the subject*).

2. *See* ARISE.

dawning, *n.* daybreak.

day, *n.* **1.** daytime; *spec.* sunshine, light.

Antonyms: see NIGHT.

2. *A day of a certain kind: spec.* lay-day (*commercial*), dripper (*C*), roaster (*C*), scorcher (*C*), doomsday, holiday, Sabbath, Sunday.

3. *See* DATE.

daybreak, *n.* dawn, dawning, break (*chiefly in "break of day"*), dawing (*Scot.*), daylight, morn (*B*), cockcrow (*fig.*), greking (*obs. or Scot.*), daypeep (*B*), dayspring (*B*), aurora (*fig.*).

Antonyms: see NIGHT.

daydream, *n.* dream (*contex.*), reverie, conceit, fancy, castle in the air, air castle, château en Espagne (*French*), pipe dream (*C*), illusion.

Antonyms: see ACTUALITY.

daylight, *n.* light (*contex.*); *spec.* sunshine, sunlight, daybreak.

daze, *v. t. Implies suffering from an excess of reaction:* confuse (*implies temporary loss of power of speech and action*), confound (*A, intensive*), stupefy, bewilder, stun; *spec.* dazzle, blind.

daze, *n.* confusion, stupor, bewilderment; *spec.* dazzle, dazzlement, stand.

dazzle, *v. t. Implies overpowering light:* confuse, daze, blind, bedazzle (*intensive*), overpower (*contex.*); *spec.* stupefy, bewilder.

dazzle, *n.* **1.** dazzlement, daze, confusion;—*referring to the state.*

2. brilliancy, brightness;—*referring to the effect of light or display.*

3. *See* SHOW.

dazzling, *a.* bright (*contex.*), blinding, overpowering (*contex.*);—*referring to light or display.*

dead, *a.* **1.** *See* LIFELESS, ABSOLUTE, UNQUESTIONABLE, DIRECT.

2. *Referring to a person that has died:* deceased (*euphemistic or pretentious*), perished (*by privation*), defunct (*R*), late (*a euphemism, conventional in certain connections*), exanimate (*R*), ci-devant (*French*), croaked (*C*).

Antonyms: see LIVING.

3. mat, dull, flat.

Antonyms: see LUSTROUS, POLISHED.

4. *Referring to living matter that has died: spec.* mortified, gangrenous, sphacelate, necrosed.

5. *Referring to things that have ceased to function, act, etc.:* defunct; *spec.* obsolete, extinct, extinguished, sleeping, inert, lifeless, still, stagnant, lusterless, out (*referring to fire*), flat, useless.

dead, *n.* **1.** decedent (*U. S.; chiefly law*), deceased (*euphemistic; usually with "the"*), defunct (*formal; usually with "the"*), croaker (*S*). *"Dead" is chiefly used collectively with "the."*

2. *See* SILENCE.

deaden, *v. t.* **1.** *Spec.* dull, benumb, numb, stupefy, anesthetize, paralyze.

2. *Referring to sounds or sounding things:* muffle, damp, bemuffle (*intensive*), dumb (*R*), mute, soft-pedal; *spec.* pug.

3. *Referring to velocity, activity, etc.;* check, brake; *spec.* smother (*a fire*), damp (*a fire*), stagnate, repress, choke.

Antonyms: see AGITATE.

deadhouse, *n.* mortuary; *spec.* morgue.

deadlock, *n.* standstill, impasse (*French*), halt, stand.

---

dashing: *lively, showy, energetic.*
dastard: *coward, cowardly.*
daub, *v. t.: smear.*
daub, *n.: smear, plaster.*
daunt: *intimidate, dismay.*
davit: *crane.*
dawn: *daybreak.*
daylight: *sunlight.*
daystar: *morning star, sun.*
daze, *v. t.: stupefy.*
daze, *n.: stupor.*

---

deadly, *a.* **1.** mortal, fatal, deathly (*R*), fell (*B*).
2. implacable, lethal (*B or journalistic*), fatal, killing (*referring to gait, pace, habits, etc.*), mortiferous (*R*), mortific (*R*), deathful (*R*), mortifying (*R*), funest (*R*), lethiferous (*R*); *spec.* murderous, baneful, poisonous, pestilent, pestilential, pestiferous, noxious, *etc.*
3. *See* DEATHLIKE.

deaf, *a.* earless (*fig.*), surd (*A*), unhearing.

deafen, *v. t.* **1.** deave (*obs. or Scot. and dial.*), stun (*with noise*).
2. *See* DROWN.

deal, *n.* **1.** *See* SHARE, AMOUNT, QUANTITY.
2. lot, heap;—*all three* (*C*).
3. bargain, arrangement, treatment, order, apportionment, justice (*in "a square deal"*).

deal, *v. t.* **1.** *See* APPORTION.
2. *Referring to a blow, etc.:* give, bestow, deliver, fetch, lay (*used with "on"*), plant, place, administer, strike.

deal, *v. i.* traffic, converse, practice (*R*); *spec.* contend (*used with "with"*).

dealer, *n.* monger (*chiefly in combination*), merchant (*Scot. or U. S. in sense of retailer*), trader, chapman (*A*); *spec.* copeman (*A*), coper (*A*), cadger, hawker, badger, huckster, tallyman, stallman, jobber, middleman, agent, drover (*cattle dealer*).

dealing, *n.* **1.** intercourse.
2. traffic; *spec.* negotiation, conduct.
3. giving, bestowal, delivery, placing, planting; —*referring to a blow, etc.*

dear, *a.* **1.** loved, beloved; *spec.* cherished, precious, favorite, prized, bosom.
2. *See* HEARTFELT, COSTLY.

dear, *n.* darling, deary (*amatory, conjugal, or familiar*), beloved, mavourneen (*Irish*), lovey (*in affectionate address*), honey (*chiefly Irish, dial. Eng., or negro U. S.*), pigsney (*A*); *spec.* pet, favorite, moppet (*contemptuous as used of a man*), sweetie (*familiar and vulgar*).

death, *n.* **1.** decease (*legal, slightly euphemistic, or rhet.*), demise (*pretentious, except of exalted personages*), quietus (*R or B*), dying, departure (*euphemistic*), expiration (*R*), expiry (*B*), finish (*vulgar or C*), finis (*figurative; R*), exit (*B or affected*), parting (*euphemistic*), ending (*now C*), end, dissolution (*C*), mortality, consummation (*fig., B*), passing (*euphemistic*), pass (*R*), defunction (*R*); *spec.* predecease, euthanasia *or* euthanasy.
Antonyms: see BIRTH.
2. *Referring to the dying of tissues, etc.: spec.* mortification, gangrene, necrosis.
3. *Referring to the cause of death: spec.* quietus, coup de grâce (*French*), finish (*vulgar or C*).
4. *Referring to the state:* dormition (*fig.*), sleep (*fig.*), darkness (*fig.*), grave (*fig.*), tomb (*fig.*).
Antonyms: see LIFE.
5. *See* EXTINCTION, DESTRUCTION.

death bell, passing bell, knell.

deathlike, *a.* deathly, deadly, deathy, deathful (*R*), mortal.

debit, *n.* entry (*contex.*), charge, score.

debit, *v. t.* enter (*contex.*), charge, score.

débris, *n.* **1.** ruins (*pl.*); *see* RUBBISH.
2. *In geol.: spec.* detritus, eluvium.

debt, *n. Spec.* due (*chiefly in pl.*), arrear, liability, obligation (*chiefly in pl.*).

début, *n.* appearance, coming-out. *"Début" is French.*

débutant, *n. masc.,* **débutante,** *n. fem.* come-outer (*S*), deb (*C*); *spec.* subdeb (*C*), bud (*U. S. journalistic cant*), rose (*S; U. S.*).

decade, *n.* decennary, ten.

decamp, *v. i.* depart, go, run, abscond.

decay, *v. i.* **1.** *See* DECLINE, DECOMPOSE.
2. *Referring to things falling into ruin; spec.* dilapidate, disintegrate, crumble, ruin, ruinate, perish.
Antonyms: see RENEW.
3. *Referring to fruits, etc.:* rot, molder; *spec.* rust, blight, blet.

decay, *n.* **1.** *See* DECLINE, DECOMPOSITION.
2. *Referring to becoming or being ruined: spec.* dilapidation, disintegration, crumbling, waste, ruin, ruination, disrepair, decayedness, decrepitude, irrepair (*R*), unrepair.
Antonyms: see RENEWAL.
3 *Referring to fruits, etc.:* rot, mold, spoil; *spec.* blight, rust, spur, blet.

decayed, *a.* **1.** dilapidated; *spec.* decrepit, disjasked (*Scot.*), forworn (*A*), tumbledown, ruinous, ruined, antique (*jocose*).
2. *See* DECOMPOSED.
3. *Referring to fruit, vegetables, etc.:* unsound, rotten, moldy, spoiled; *spec.* druxy, doted *or* doated, spurred, ergotized, bletted, doddered, *etc.*

deceitful, *a.* deceptive (*which does not imply intent to deceive, nor necessarily any evil purpose, while the others do*), cunning (*implying subtlety and baseness*), covinous (*A*), two-faced, indirect, underhand, underhanded, deceivable (*A*), insincere, circumventive, false; *spec.* crooked, double-tongued, double-hearted, dodgy (*C*), evasive, hypocritical, fraudulent, fraudful (*R*), guileful, juggling, Jesuitical (*opprobriously used by non-Catholics*), histrionic (*B or R*), theatrical (*implying ostentation and unreality*), dissembling, intriguing, insidious, tricky, trickish, tricksy, snaky, treacherous.

dealing: *intercourse, traffic.*
dean: *senior.*
dearth: *deficiency.*
deathless: *immortal.*
deathly: *deathlike.*
debacle: *rush, catastrophe, upheaval.*
debar: *exclude, refuse, prevent.*
debark: *disembark.*
debark: *decorticate.*
debase: *abase, degrade, adulterate, corrupt.*
debase: *decline.*
debate, *v.: dispute, discuss.*
debate, *n.: dispute, discussion.*
debauch, *v. t.: corrupt.*
debauch, *v. i.: dissipate, carouse.*
debauch, *n.: carouse.*
debauched: *dissipated.*
debauchery: *corruption, dissipation.*
debenture: *certificate, security.*
debilitate: *weaken, enervate.*
debit: *charge.*
debouch: *issue.*
decadence: *decline.*
decadent: *declining.*
decapitate: *behead.*
decease, *n.: death.*
decease, *v. i.: die.*
decedent: *dead.*
deceit: *deception.*

Antonyms: see CONSCIENTIOUS, FRANK.

deceitfulness, *n.* cunning, covin (*A*); *spec.* guile, fraud, *etc.*

deceivable, *a. Spec.* delusible, gullible, illusionable (*R*), credulous.

deceive, *v. t.* mislead; *spec.* delude, fool, befool (*intensive*), bejape (*obs.*), begunk (*Scot.*), bamboozle, gyp (*C*), begyp (*jocose*), beguile, gull, flatter, hoax, humbug, hoodwink, bubble (*R*), circumvent, outwit, trick, bucket (*S*), cozen, best, cajole, bilk, do (*S*), cheat, mock, chisel (*S*), chouse (*S*), jilt, overreach, defraud, doodle (*S*), hallucinate, illude (*implying false hopes*), cog, blear, bluff, misinform, mock, tantalize, jilt (*one's expectations*), hocus-pocus (*A or R*), juggle, dupe, fob, flimflam (*cant*), flam (*cant*), kid (*S*), diddle (*C or S*), skin (*C*).

Antonyms: see UNDECEIVE.

deceiver, *n.* misleader; *spec.* deluder, bamboozler, beguiler, hoaxer, humbug, humbugger, hoodwinker, circumventor *or* circumventer, outwitter, tricker, cozener, cheater, cheat, swindler, swindle, defrauder, double-dealer, pretender, Sinon (*fig., implying treachery*) Judas (*fig.*), trickster, charlatan, faker, impostor, impostress, sharper, cogger (*obs. or A*), hallucinator, hypocrite, illuder (*R*), juggler, dodger (*often S*), faitour (*A*), duper, rogue, knave, duffer, diddler (*C or S*).

deception, *n.* **1.** *Referring to the action, fact, habit, practice, etc.:* deceit; *spec.* cheat, misleading, delusion, fooling, bamboozle (*generic*), bamboozlement, bambosh (*S, A*), beguilement, hoax, humbugging, humbug, humbuggery, humbugism, hoodwinking, circumvention, outwitting, outwittal (*R*), tricking, trickiness, trickishness, trickery, trick, hocus-pocus, flimflam (*cant*), flummery (*empty talk, etc.*), illusion, fancy, cozenage (*A*), flam (*cant or C*), gullery (*A*), gulling, duplicity, guile, finesse, stratagem, pretense, sham, covin (*A*), hallucination, disguise, disguisement, defraudation (*R*), defraudment (*R*), hypocrisy, hypocrisis (*R*), do (*S or C*), indirectness, insidiousness, hanky-panky (*S*), chicanery, pettifogging, quibbling, sophistry, subterfuge, dodgery (*R*), dupery, subreption (*R*), guile, double-dealing, mockery, gyppery.

2. *Referring to the thing that deceives: spec.* artifice, cheat, fraud, humbug, mockery, flam (*cant*), trick, decoy, snare, ambush, sham, sell, cantel (*A*), dodge, hoax, gag (*S*), imposture, cog, bosh (*S*), juggle, ruse, wile, stratagem. *Many of the words in sense* **1** *are synonyms also in this sense.*

deceptive, *a.* misleading, deceitful (*which see*); *spec.* delusive (*implying deceptive impression of reality*), delusory, catchy (*S*), tricksy, hallucinative (*implying unreality*), hallucinatory, fairy (*as if done by a fairy*), illusory, fallacious, false, subjective, disingenuous.

decide, *v. i.* **1.** determine (*implies an authoritative investigation*), settle (*implies previous doubt and uncertainty*), fix, conclude (*implies preceding deliberation*), resolve (*implies formal expression*), decree (*implies authoritative decision*); *spec.* misdecide.

2. adjudge (*tech.*), adjudicate, dijudicate (*R*), decern (*Scot.*); *spec.* arbitrate, umpire, pass (*upon a question*).

decide, *v. t.* **1.** determine (*implies results of careful study*), settle (*implies ending previous uncertainty*), resolve, conclude (*implies preceding deliberation*); *spec.* predetermine, decern (*Scots law*); adjudge (*R*), adjudicate (*tech.*), judge; arbitrate, award, decree, deraign (*law, hist., or obs.*), dijudicate (*R*), rule, hold.

2. *To bring a person to a decision:* determine, resolve (*R*).

decided, *a.* positive, strong, pronounced; *spec.* marked; *see* ASSURED.

Antonyms: see DOUBTFUL, HESITATING.

decipher, *v. t.* **1.** translate, interpret, decode; *spec.* read.

2. *Referring to mental character:* read, trace, make out.

decision, *n.* **1.** *Referring to the act of the mind:* determination, settlement, conclusion; *spec.* resolution, discretion, judgment, finding. *See* SPIRIT.

2. *Referring to the delivery of a decision or to the thing decided upon:* adjudgment, adjudication, judgment, decerniture (*Scots law*); *spec.* arbitration, award, decree, decreement, pronouncement, sentence, edict, definition, decreet (*Scots law; C*), halacha *or* halakah, decretal; *see* VERDICT.

decisive, *a.* **1.** determinative, resolutive *or* resolutory (*in law spec.*), conclusive, adjudicative, decretive, decretory.

Antonyms: see INDECISIVE.

2. determinative, definitive (*implies finality or completeness*), conclusive (*implies satisfying doubts*), final, peremptory (*implies compulsion*), determinant; *spec.* critical, crucial, fateful.

deck, *n.* **1.** *Spec.* orlop, texas (*Western U. S.*), hurricane deck, splinter deck, poop deck, main deck, quarterdeck.

2. pack (*of cards*).

declaim, *v. i.* speak, recite, harangue (*chiefly spec.*), rant (*chiefly spec.*), spout (*contemptuous*), mouth (*contemptuous*); *spec.* perorate (*B*).

declamatory, *a. Spec.* rhetorical, bombastic, elocutionary, loud, grandiloquent, oratorical.

declaratory, *n.* declarative, predicative, affirmative, expository.

declare, *v. t.* **1.** *Spec.* proclaim, acclaim, find (*law*), denounce (*as being bad*).

2. *See* STATE, DISCLOSE, ACKNOWLEDGE.

declination, *n.* **1.** *See* DEVIATION, DESCENT.

2. refusal, declension, nonacceptance, rejec-

---

decent: *appropriate, modest, proper, shapely, considerable, fair.*

decern: *decide.*

deck, *v. t.: ornament, cover, clothe.*

---

tion, veto (*implies authoritative refusal*); *spec.* declinature (*Scots law*), repudiation, repulse, detrectation (*R*).
Antonyms: see ACCEPTANCE.

declinatory, *a. In an active sense:* deteriorative, degeneratory, degenerative, degradational, depreciatory, depreciative.

decline, *v. i.* **1.** *See* DEVIATE, DESCEND.
2. deteriorate (*implies falling away in quality*), decay, impair, worsen (*R*), fail; *spec.* ebb, fall (*often with "away"*), set, weaken, wane, derogate, degenerate (*implies falling away in character or nature*), degrade (*implies falling away in station*), debase, depreciate (*implies falling away in value*), fade (*implies loss of color or outline*), flag (*implies loss of energy*), retrograde (*implies falling back to previous lower position*), wither, recede, retrogress (*R*), rot, lapse, dwindle, diminish; *see* LANGUISH.
Antonyms: see IMPROVE, PROGRESS.
3. *See* REFUSE.

decline, *v. t.* **1.** bend, bow, depress.
2. refuse, reject; *spec.* repudiate (*implies denial of responsibility for a thing*), repel, repulse, renegue (*R*).
Antonyms: see ACCEPT, RECEIVE.
3. *See* INFLECT.

decline, *n.* **1.** *See* DESCENT.
2. deterioration, decay, impair (*R*), impairment, declination (*obs.*), decadence (*implies moral decline*), decadency, degeneration, degradation, debasement, depreciation, derogation, failure, ebb, depravation (*implies corruption and immorality*), languishment, retrograde, retrogression, retrogradation, wane, diminution, *etc.*
Antonyms: see PROGRESS, RECOVERY.
3. *See* DISEASE, AILMENT.

declining, *a. In an active sense:* decadent, deteriorating, degenerating.

declivitous, *a.* sloping, steep. "*Declivitous*" *is used esp. in reference to downward slope.*

declivous, *a.* sloping. "*Declivous*" *usually means* descending.

decomposable, *a.* perishable, resoluble, corruptible (*A or B*), resolvable; *spec.* putrescible, putrefiable (*R*).

decompose, *v. t. & i.* **1.** decompound (*R*), dissolve, resolve, disintegrate (*chiefly spec.*), analyze (*esp. spec.*); *spec.* electrolyze, thermolyze, hydrolyze.
Antonyms: see SYNTHESIZE.
2. *Referring to natural decomposition, destroying physical integrity and soundness:* consume, decay, rot (*often spec.*), spoil, mold, corrupt (*A or R*), faint; *spec.* (*of loathsome and stinking rottenness*) putresce, putrefy.

decomposed, *a.* **1.** decompounded, dissolved, disintegrated, *etc.*
2. decayed, corrupt (*A or R*), rotten, moldy, spoiled; *spec.* putrid, putrescent, carious (*chiefly tech.*), green; *see* TAINTED.
Antonyms: see SWEET.

decomposing, *a.* **1.** decompounding (*R*), disintegrative, disintegratory, analytic; *spec.* thermolytic, electrolytic, proteolytic, hydrolytic.
2. decaying, rotting, spoiling, molding, corruptive (*A or R*); *spec.* putrefactive, putrefacient.

decomposition, *n.* **1.** decompounding, dissolution (*implies destruction of the organizing forces*), resolution (*implies reduction to component elements*), disintegration (*chiefly spec.*), analysis (*esp. for study*), break-up; *spec.* thermolysis, hydrolysis, electrolysis, proteolysis, electrolyzation.
Antonyms: see SYNTHESIS.
2. *Referring to natural decomposition:* decay, corruption (*R or A*), spoiling (*R*), rot; *spec.* dry rot, putrefaction, putridity, putrescence, caries, cariosity.

decoration, *n.* **1.** *See* ORNAMENTATION, ORNAMENT.
2. *Spec.* medal, badge, crest, cockade, feather, crown, epaulette, *etc.*

decorticate, *v. t.* excorticate (*R*); *spec.* debark, disbark, skin, peel, busk, pill (*A*), rind, rend (*a tree*).

decorum, *n.* propriety; *spec.* modesty, behavior (*implying good behavior*).
Antonyms: see MISBEHAVIOR.

decoy, *n.* **1.** trap.
2. enticement, lure; *spec.* stool, flare.

decoy, *v. t.* attract, entice, lure.

decree, *v. t.* decide, command, order, ordain, appoint, rule (*chiefly spec.*); *spec.* adjudge, adjudicate, enact, decern (*now chiefly Scot. and tech.*): *all implying authority.*

decree, *n.* decision, command, edict (*implies generally the order of a king or emperor*), fiat, order, ordinance (*now chiefly spec.*), ordination, enactment, law (*chiefly spec.*), dispensation (*theol.*), ordainment (*R*), enaction (*R*), rule (*chiefly spec.*); *spec.* firman, sanction (*hist.*), decretal, novel, rescript, constitution, assize, pragmatic, psephism, recess (*hist.*), hatti, interdict, irade.

decreeing, *a.* decisional, enactive, decretial (*R*), decretive (*R*), decretory.

decretive, *a.* **1.** decisive, decreeing, ordinative.
2. *See* DECREEING.

dedicate, *v. t.* **1.** appropriate (*contex.*), give (*contex.*), devote (*implies exclusive use*), consecrate (*implies liturgical dedication*), vow, hallow (*A*), bless (*eccl.*), sanctify (*A, implies making sacred or holy*); *spec.* promise, surrender.
2. *Spec.* inscribe (*as a book*); *see* CONSECRATE, INSCRIBE.

dedication, *n. Spec.* appropriation, devotion, consecration, blessing (*liturgical*), *etc.*

dedicatory, *a.* dedicative, consecrative, consecratory, votary, votive.

deduct, *v. t.* abstract, remove, defalcate (*R*),

decorate: *ornament, honor.*
decorative: *ornamental.*
decorous: *becoming, proper.*
decorum, *v. t.: propriety.*
decrepit: *weak, weakened.*
decrepitate: *roast.*
decrepitate: *crackle.*
decrepitude: *weakness.*
decrescence: *diminution.*
decretal: *decree.*
decussate: *cross.*
deduce: *infer, derive.*

subtract (*esp. of numbers*); *spec.* rebate, recoup (*law*).
Antonyms: see ADD.

deduction, *n.* **1.** *See* INFERENCE.
2. abstraction, removal, subtraction (*esp. of numbers*); *spec.* recoupment (*law*).
Antonyms: see ADDITION.
3. *Referring to the thing deducted:* defalcation (*R*); *spec.* discount, drawback, draft, tare, reprise, rebatement, rebate, off-reckoning, off-take.

deductive, *a.* inferential, a priori (*Latin; tech.*).

deed, *n.* **1.** action (*with reference to the doing itself*), act (*with reference to what is done*), exploit (*implies an unusual deed*), feat (*implies skill or strength*), gest (*A or B, implies courtesy or nonchalance*), do (*C*), jest (*A or B, implies amusement*), fact (*obs., A or idiomatic*), effort; *spec.* accomplishment, derring-do (*pseudo A*), prowess (*chiefly in pl.; B*).
2. instrument (*contex.*), document (*contex.*); *spec.* release, quitclaim, land-boc (*obs.*), charter, indenture, infeudation, remise.
3. *See* ACTION.

deed, *v. t.* convey (*contex.*); *spec.* quitclaim, release, remise.

deep, *a.* **1.** profound (*very deep*); *spec.* depthless, bottomless, abysmal (*intensitive*).
Antonyms: see SHALLOW, SURFACE.
2. *See* ABSTRUSE, DISCERNING, SUBTLE.
3. *Referring to evils in which one may be involved:* serious, grave, profound, extreme, great.
4. *Referring to emotions deeply felt:* deep-felt, deep-seated, profound, intimate, heartfelt, cordial (*chiefly spec.*); *spec.* heavy, sound, dead, hearty, thorough, inveterate, ingrained.
Antonyms: see SUPERFICIAL.
5. *Referring to sleep:* profound, heavy, fast.
Antonyms: see LIGHT.
6. *Referring to colors:* strong, intense, rich.
7. *See* LOW, BASS, ABSORBED.
8. involved; sunk;—*referring to a person involved in vice, disgrace, etc.*

deep, *n.* **1.** abyss, profound (*B*), gulf (*B*); *spec.* ocean.
Antonyms: see SHALLOW.
2. *See* DEPTH.
3. *Spec.* mystery, incomprehensible (*used with "the"*), riddle.

deepen, *v. i.* *There are no synonyms.*
Antonyms: see SHOAL.

deepen, *v. t.* strengthen, intensify, increase.

deeply, *adv.* *Spec.* profoundly, abstrusely, soundly, mortally, intimately.

deepset, *a.* sunken.

deer, *n.* **1.** doe (*female*), buck (*male*), fawn (*young*); *spec.* stag, hart, havier, hind (*female*), spire, spay (*male*), hearst (*a hunting term*), roe, roebuck (*masc.*), fallow, deer, elk, reindeer, caribou, russ, moose, maral, wapiti, venada.
2. *Referring to deer flesh:* venison.

deer, *a.* cervine.

deface, *v. t.* mar (*implies considerable injury*), disfigure (*suggests more permanent injury than deface*), disfeature (*R*), defeature (*R*), dedecorate (*R*), disvisage (*R*), disfashion (*R*); *spec.* deform (*suggests structural injury*), distort (*implies twisting out of shape*), mutilate (*implies intentional injury*), maim (*implies physical disability*), (*fig.*), mangle (*implies considerable, clumsy and painful injury*), garble (*implies rendering misleading*), bemangle (*intensive*), skew, twist, wrench, blur, blotch, haggle, hack, uglify, cancel, foul (*make ugly*), dog's-ear, scar, soil, tarnish, *etc.*
Antonyms: see BEAUTIFY, ORNAMENT.

defacement, *v. i.* disfigurement, deformation, deformity, *etc.*

defamation, *n.* traduction, vilification, aspersion, calumny; *spec.* slander, libel.

defamatory, *a.* traductory, calumniatory, abusive; *spec.* libellous, scandalous.

defame, *v. t.* traduce (*implies exposing to scorn and ridicule*), vilify (*implies defamation of character*), slur (*implies indirect defamation*), asperse (*implies sprinkling with injurious charges*), belie, calumniate (*implies charging falsely and maliciously*), vilipend (*B; spec.*), slander, scandal (*A*), scandalize (*R*), backbite, libel.
Antonyms: see PRAISE, ENNOBLE.

default, *n.* **1.** *See* FAULT.
2. omission, failure; *spec.* neglect.

defeat, *v. t.* **1.** frustrate (*implies rendering ineffectual*), checkmate, balk (*implies putting obstacles in the way*), block (*implies closing the way*), spoil, foil, baffle (*implies puzzling or bewildering*), thwart, cross, circumvent (*implies outwitting by stratagem*), outwit, contravene, blank, stump (*C*), stale (*implies making ineffectual because of too great familiarity*), dish (*C*), disappoint; *spec.* nullify, euchre (*C*), neutralize, double, puzzle, halt, *etc.*
Antonyms: see AID.
2. overcome, overpower, overthrow, overwhelm, conquer, discomfit, have, beat, thrash (*C*), wallop (*C*), skin (*C*), trounce, lick (*C*), whip (*C*), drub (*C*), master, vanquish, cast (*tech., law, or obs.*), fail, repulse, checkmate, confound (*A*), euchre (*spec. or fig.*), lurch (*spec. in games, or fig.*), throw, floor (*in argument, etc.; C*), overmatch (*R*), bilk (*cribbage or fig.*); *spec.* counterwork, countermine, counterplot, rout, derout (*emphatic*), outargue, outplay, outvote, sack (*S*), trim (*C*), take.
Antonyms: see AID.

defeat, *n.* **1.** frustration, checkmate, balk, fail, bafflement, thwarting, circumvention, outwittal (*by strategy*), contravention.
Antonyms: see AID.
2. overthrow, conquest, discomfiture, best, thrashing (*C*), drubbing (*C*), whipping (*C*),

---

defalcate: *embezzle.*
default, *n.: deficiency, failure, fault.*
default, *v. i.: fail.*
defaulter: *insolvent.*

---

walloping (*C*), beating, licking (*C*), mastery, vanquishment, overcoming, cast (*law or obs.*), checkmate, confusion (*R*); *spec.* rout, derout (*emphatic*), lurch, reverse.

Antonyms: see VICTORY, SUCCESS.

defecate, *v. i.* cack (*obs. or dial. Eng.*), evacuate, foul (*R*), dung (*now of animals only*), stool, go (*contex.*).

defective, *a.* **1.** *See* DEFICIENT.

2. *Spec.* deranged, feeble-minded, imbecile, idiot, daffy, balmy (*C*), nutty (*S*), potty (*S*).

defend, *v. t.* **1.** *See* PROTECT.

2. maintain (*in the status quo*), uphold, vindicate (*as being true or correct*), sustain, support, champion (*the truth, a cause, etc.*), espouse (*a cause*); *spec.* justify, plead, advocate.

Antonyms: see ASSAIL, ATTACK.

3. oppose (*a claim, lawsuit, etc.*).

defense, *n.* **1.** *See* PROTECTION.

2. maintenance, upholding, vindication (*as true or correct*), support, espousal (*of the truth, a cause, etc.*); *spec.* justification (*of action*), advocacy, apologia (*B*).

Antonyms: see ATTACK.

3. *Spec.* justification, excuse (*of conduct, action*), apology (*implies explanation*), plea, vindication, denial, answer.

defensible, *a.* **1.** fencible (*of a fort, etc.*), tenable, armed, armored, protected.

2. maintainable, supportable, vindicable (*as right or true*), tenable; *spec.* excusable, justifiable.

Antonyms: see INDEFENSIBLE.

defer, *v. t.* delay, postpone, procrastinate (*property, putting off 'til tomorrow*), put off, adjourn (*properly, spec.*), suspend, wait; *spec.* table, stay, perendinate (*R*), respite (*R*), reserve, shelve.

deference, *n.* respect (*implying honor and recognition*), reverence (*implies a very deep respect, as for a deity*); *spec.* submissiveness (*without the implication of courtesy which marks* deference), obeisance (*implies deferential attitude of body*), regardfulness, complaisance.

deferential, *a. Spec.* submissive, obeisant, regardful; *see* COMPLAISANT.

deferment, *n.* deferral (*R*), delay, postponement, retardation, procrastination, adjournment *or* (*R*), adjournal (*properly, spec.*), prorogation, suspension, suspense (*in law spec.*), wait, pause, frist (*A*); *spec.* respite, reprieve, mora, cunctation (*B and R*), breathing, moratory, moratorium, truce.

defiance, *n.* **1.** defial, dare (*C*), daring, daringness (*the quality*), challenge, bravado, bravery (*A or R*), defy (*C*), disregard, despite (*B*); *spec.* diffidation (*chiefly feudalism*), opposition, resistance, rebellion, disobedience, challenge.

2. *Referring to the quality: spec.* contempt, stubbornness, despite (*B*), recalcitrance, rebelliousness, disobedience, contumaciousness.

defiant, *a.* daring (*now chiefly C*), disregardful, challenging; *spec.* contumacious, resistant, disobedient, mutinous, despiteful, recalcitrant, rebellious, insolent, stubborn, refractory.

Antonyms: see SUBMISSIVE, RESIGNED, OBEDIENT.

deficiency, *n.* **1.** defect (*chiefly spec.*), want, lack, deficit, defalcation, shortage, wantage (*R*), deficience (*R*), absence, default (*A or spec.*);—*referring to that which is either not present or not available.*

Antonyms: see EXCESS, EXTRA.

2. insufficiency, inadequacy, failure, dearth, scarcity, famine, want, lack, penury, poverty, shortness, default (*A or R*), meagerness;—*referring to the fact of being deficient.*

Antonyms: see ABUNDANCE, EXCESS.

3. *See* IMPERFECTION.

deficient, *a.* poor, defective (*implies deficiency in certain details*), insufficient, inadequate (*emphasizes failure to meet specific requirements*), incomplete, imperfect (*emphasizes lack of completion*), short (*implies missing what is expected*), scarce (*implies a shortage*), scant (*implies just missing the full measure*), wanting (*used with "in"*), lacking.

Antonyms: see ABUNDANT, ABOUNDING, EXCESSIVE, SPARE.

define, *v. t.* **1.** delimit, determine, bound, demarcate, limit, delimitate (*R*), bound, circumscribe, demark (*R*);—*referring to land or used fig.*

2. *Referring to words, ideas, etc.:* determine, formalize, precise (*R*); *spec.* individuate, individualize.

3. *See* DESCRIBE.

definite, *a.* determinate, distinct, certain, positive, limited, fixed; *spec.* clear-cut, sharp-cut, clear, plain, downright, sharp, crisp (*tones, etc.*), explicit, express, formal, vivid, specific, unequivocal, flat, particular, precise, exact.

Antonyms: see AMBIGUOUS, INDEFINITE, INDISTINCT.

definition, *n.* **1.** delimitation, demarcation:—*both meaning "to mark off the boundaries."*

2. *Referring to words, ideas, etc.:* determination, meaning, explanation, formalization; *spec.* individuation.

3. *See* DESCRIPTION.

deflate, *v. t.* exhaust (*contex.*), empty (*contex; R*); *spec.* flatten.

Antonyms: see INFLATE, BLOAT.

deflower, *v. t.* **1.** disflower (*strip of flowers*).

2. violate, devirginate (*R*), rape (*contex.*), ravage, despoil.

deform, *v. t.* **1.** misshape, spoil, disform (*R*), disfigure; *spec.* spring, distort, strain (*tech.*), bemonster (*R*), mar. *"Deform" as used in physics does not imply anything more than change of shape or structure.*

2. *See* DEFACE.

---

defecate: *clear, purify, excrete.*
defect: *deficiency, imperfection, fault.*
defile, *v. & n.: march.*
defile, *n.: pass, ravine, march.*
defile, *v. t.: dirty, foul, contaminate, corrupt, sully, violate, desecrate.*
defilement: *dirtying, fouling, contamination, corruption, soiling, sullying, violation.*
definitive: *decisive.*
deflagrate: *burn, explode.*
deflect: *turn.*

deformed, *a.* deform (*A*), misfashioned, malformed, misshapen, inform (*A*).
Antonyms: see SHAPELY, WELL-SHAPED.

deformity, *n.* **1.** informity (*R*), misshapenness, malformation, monstrosity (*great deformity*), misshape (*R*), misfigure (*R*), disfigurement; *spec.* crookedness, varus, misproportion.
Antonyms: see BEAUTY.
2. *See* DEFACEMENT.

defraud, *v. t.* cheat (*implies cunning*), bilk (*implying a hoax*), hoax (*implies a practical joke*), hornswoggle, rook (*C*), gudgeon (*R*), swindle (*implies violation of trust*); *spec.* bunco, dupe (*implies taking advantage of credulity*), chouse (*C*), bamboozle (*C*), gyp (*C, implies petty fraud*).

defray, *v. t.* pay, liquidate, settle, meet, satisfy, answer, bear, discharge, disburse (*R*).

defrayal, *n.* payment, liquidation, bearing, discharge, settlement, *etc.*

defy, *v. t.* dare, challenge, oppose; *spec.* beard, confront, disregard, brave, face, disobey, mock, outdare, scorn.
Antonyms: see OBEY.

degeneracy, *n. Implying usually moral degeneracy:* deterioration, debasement, degeneration, degenerateness, degradation, retrogradation; *spec.* depravity.

degenerate, *a.* degraded, debased, lowered, sunk, fallen, retrograded; *spec.* decadent.
Antonyms: see EXALTED.

degenerate, *v. i.* decline, deteriorate, sink, fall, degrade, retrograde.

degenerate, *n.* retrograde; *spec.* rotter.

degeneration, *n.* decline, deterioration, retrogradation, retrogression, debasement, fall, decay (*moral*); *spec.* caducity (*R*), caseation, involution, decadence, perversion.
Antonyms: see REGENERATION.

degenerative, *a.* retrogressive, declinatory (*R*), backward, lower.

degradation, *n.* **1.** dishonor, abasement, humiliation, debasement, disgrace, shame;—*referring to the condition.*
2. abasement, debasement, dishonoring, disgrace, fall, humbling, humiliation, deposition; *spec.* disbarment, disranking;—*referring to the act.*
Antonyms: see ELEVATION.
3. degeneracy, degeneration.
4. debasement, lowering, prostitution (*fig.*); *spec.* perversion, misuse, corruption, contamination, vitiation.
Antonyms: see ELEVATION.

degrade, *v. t.* **1.** dishonor, reduce, debase, disgrade, abase, lower, sink, disrate, break, disrank, disgrace, shame, humiliate, depose; *spec.* unchurch, disennoble, disbar, disbench, disestablish, disorb, unmiter, dethrone, disenthrone, unpriest, uncowl, unfrock, uncrown, outcast, unking.
Antonyms: see ELEVATE, DIGNIFY, ENNOBLE, ORDAIN.
2. abase, debase, lower, prostitute (*fig.*); *spec.* pervert, misuse, alloy, adulterate, vitiate, contaminate.
Antonyms: see ELEVATE.

degraded, *a.* abased, debased, abject, depraved, low, fallen) *spec.* vile, perverted, corrupt, prostituted.
Antonyms: see ELEVATED, EXALTED.

degree, *n.* **1.** *See* ROW, SHELF, GRADUATION, MEASURE, EXTENT, AMOUNT.
2. step, stage, grade, rank, order, point (*which one or something has reached or arrived at*); *spec.* remove (*in the line of descent*), interval, space (*music*); line (*music*), tone.
3. intensity, pitch, plane, point, measure, intension (*B*), grade, gradation, height, potence (*R*); *spec.* shade.

dehisce, *v. i.* gape, open.

dehorn, *v. t.* poll; *spec.* hummel *or* humble (*Scot.*).

dehort, *v. t.* dissuade (*obs.*), disadvise; *spec.* discourage.

deify, *v. t.* **1.** apotheosize, consecrate (*Roman antiq.*), divinify (*R*), exalt, god (*R*), shrine (*R*), immortalize; *spec.* co-deify, idolize, canonize (*to raise formally to the rank of saint*).
2. worship.

deity, *n.* **1.** god (*esp. male*), spirit, goddess (*fem.*), godlet (*dim.*), godhead (*emphasizes the divine essence*), godkin (*dim.*), godling (*dim.*), divinity, numen (*esp. local or minor; R*), power, Providence (*emphasizes God's foresight and consequent provision*), omnipotent, creator, Maker, Ruler, Father, King, Messiah, Trinity; *spec.* heaven (*a collective*), all-father, manu, monad, monas (*R*), faun, patron, patroness, oversoul, kami, demiurge, lar, fury, Trimurti, Triton, Woden, Pan, panice, Dagon, Moloch, Mammon, Fortuna, Apollo, Mars, Vulcan, Neptune, Mercury, Venus, Juno, Minerva, Hercules, Ares, Hephæstus, Poseidon, Hermes, Aphrodite, Hera, Athena; *see* DEMON, DEMIGOD.
Antonyms: see HUMAN.
2. *Referring to the state or quality: see* DIVINITY.

delay, *v. i.* linger (*implies delay in departing*), loiter (*implies slow purposeless movement*), tarry, stay, dawdle (*implies idleness and ineffectuality*); *spec.* idle, hang (*C*), poke (*C*), park (*C, intensitive*), dilly-dally, dally, lag, drag, stop, dwell, filibuster.
Antonyms: see HASTEN, HURRY.

delay, *n.* **1.** *See* DEFERMENT, RETARDATION.
2. lingering, loitering, tarrying, tarry (*R*), stay, linger (*R*), moration (*R*), tarriance (*B and R*), lagging; *spec.* stop, demurrage, respite, reprieve, truce.
Antonyms: see SPEED.

delayed, *a.* belated, lated (*B*), late, slow (*as of*

---

deforest: *disafforest.*
deft: *skillful.*
defunct: *dead.*
degrade: *decline, degenerate.*
deign: *condescend.*
deject: *depress.*

---

a train, etc.), held (*usually with "up" or "back"*).

delectable, *a.*, delightful, pleasing, pleasant, enjoyable, charming, delectable *is B or A*.

delegate, *n.* agent (*contex.*), representative, deputy, commissioner, secondary (*R*), alternate, substitute, proxy.

delegate, *v. t.* **1.** transfer (*contex.*), commit, intrust.

2. depute, commission, appoint, deputize (*U. S.*).

delegation, *n.* **1.** *Referring to the thing delegated:* commitment, intrustment, committal, assignment.

2. *Referring to the person to whom delegation is made:* deputation, commissioning, appointment, deputization (*U. S.*).

3. representative. "*Delegation*" *is chiefly used as a collective.*

delete, *v. t.* cancel, erase, cut (*frequently with "out"*), remove, dele, elide, retrench (*from a book*); *spec.* obliterate, expunge, efface.

deliberate, *a.* **1.** intentional, prepense (*B or legal; usually postpositive*), premeditated, advised, considered, set, resolved, studied, planned; *spec.* aforethought, mature, cool, careful, thoughtful, collected.

Antonyms: see IMPETUOUS, ABRUPT, IMPULSIVE, THOUGHTLESS.

2. unhasty (*R*), leisured, measured, slow; *spec.* leisurely.

Antonyms: see BUSTLING, HASTY.

deliberation, *n.* **1.** *See* CONSIDERATION.

2. slowness, coolness, deliberateness, caution, thought.

Antonyms: see IMPETUOSITY, BUSTLE, HASTE.

delicacy, *n.* **1.** luxury, dainty, tidbit, titbit, regale (*R*).

2. frailty, fragility, tenderness, softness, slightness.

3. *Spec.* nicety, fineness, tenderness,weakness, dangerousness, accuracy, sensitiveness, discrimination, distinction, refinement, subtlety, exactness, fastidiousness, consideration, difficulty, virtuosity (*technical skill and delicacy*).

delicate, *a.* **1.** *See* PALATABLE, WEAK, BRITTLE, SLIGHT, ETHEREAL, SENSITIVE, SLENDER.

2. *Spec.* nice, fine, tender, frail, weak, dangerous, accurate, sensitive, refined, subtle, exact, exquisite, fastidious, considerate, minikin (*now contemptuous*), difficult, discriminating.

Antonyms: see GROSS, COARSE, ROUGH, HARDY.

delight, *v. i.* *Spec.* luxuriate, feast, riot, roll, revel.

delight, *v. t.*, rejoice, charm, please, enchant, gratify.

delight, *n.*, pleasure, joy, enjoyment, gratification, charm, enchantment, happiness, delectation (*affected*).

delineate, *v. t.* **1.** trace, draw, line, mark, figure, describe, depict, inscribe (*chiefly spec.*), pencil (*often spec.*), touch (*lines*); *spec.* sketch, outline, plan, foreshorten, map, blazon (*particularly, armorial bearings*), emblaze, lineate (*R*), trick, retrace.

2. *See* OUTLINE, SKETCH, DEPICT, DESCRIBE.

delineation, *n.* **1.** tracing, drawing, lining, marking, figuring, inscription (*chiefly spec.*), penciling (*often spec.*), touching; *spec.* trace, sketching, planning, fore-shortening, blazoning.

2. *Referring to the figure so made:* tracing, drawing, inscription (*chiefly spec.*), figure; *spec.* sketch, plan, map, blazonry, diagram, elevation, perspective.

3. *See* OUTLINE, SKETCH, DEPICTION, DESCRIPTION.

delinquency, *n.* *Spec.* fault, misdeed, offense, transgression:—*implying minor offenses.*

delinquent, *n.* offender, culprit, malefactor, transgressor.

delirious, *a.* **1.** deranged, raving, light-headed, wandering; *spec.* frenzied, nutty (*S*).

2. excited, frenzied, mad.

delirium, *n.* **1.** derangement, raving, deliration (*R*), wandering, light-headedness; *spec.* frenzy; *see* DELIRIUM TREMENS.

2. excitement, frenzy.

delirium tremens, jimjams (*S*), blue devils (*fig.; C*), blues (*pl.: C*), d.t.'s (*C*), horrors (*pl.; used with "the"*).

deliver, *v. t.* **1.** free, liberate (*implies release from bondage or bonds*); *spec.* rescue (*implies deliverance from peril*), ransom, redeem, release (*implying delivery from pain, bondage, or obligation*), emancipate (*implying deliverance from bondage, physical or otherwise*), manumit (*implies freedom from slavery*); *see* SAVE.

Antonyms: see ENSLAVE, IMPRISON.

2. transfer, give, pass (*esp. with "over"*), render; *spec.* consign, commit, surrender, hand, intrust, relinquish, resign, extradite, impart.

3. free, disburden, rid; *spec.* accouch.

4. *See* EMIT, DEAL (*a blow, etc.*), EJECT, PROJECT, DISCHARGE, SERVE, THROW, UTTER, IMPART, COMMUNICATE.

deliverance, *n.* **1.** freeing, delivery (*R*); *spec.* rescue, ransom, release.

2. *See* UTTERANCE, JUDGMENT, VERDICT.

deliverer, *n.* **1.** freer (*R*), liberator; *spec.* rescuer, ransomer, releaser, redeemer, savior.

2. transferer, deliverer (*tech.*), transferor, giver, renderer; *spec.* conveyancer (*legal*), committer, surrenderer, *etc.*

3. freer (*R*), ridder; *spec.* exterminator (*of vermin*).

delivery, *n.* **1.** freeing, deliverance, redemption, salvation (*from bondage of sin or peril*), release (*from captivity, imprisonment or obligation*), liberation (*from bonds or bondage*), manumission (*of slaves*).

2. transfer, transference (*emphasizing the action*), transferal (*R*), passing (*esp. with "over"*), rendering, rendition, tradition (*tech.*), giving;

---

dele: *delete.*
delectation: *pleasure, delight.*
deliberate: *consider.*
delinquent: *blamable.*
deliquesce: *melt, diminish.*

spec. consignation, consignment, assignment, commitment, intrusting, impartment, impartation, handing, resignation, extradition, surrender.

3. *See* CHILDBIRTH, DEALING (*of a blow*), EMISSION, EJECTION, PROJECTION, DISCHARGE, THROWING, UTTERANCE.

dell, *n.* valley (*contex.*), vale (*contex.*), dingle.

Delphic, *a.* Delphian, Pythian, Pythic, oracular.

delusion, *n.* **1.** derangement, deception. *An "illusion" or "hallucination" is a "delusion" only if the mind is deceived into a false belief.*

2. misbelief.

demagogue, *n.* leader (*contex.*), orator (*contex.; now often synonymous with demagogue*), politician (*contex.*).

demand, *v. t.* **1.** ask (*contex.*), require, requisition (*formal*); *spec.* exact.

Antonyms: see GIVE, OFFER, TENDER.

2. *See* CLAIM (*as due, etc.*), NEED.

demand, *n.* **1.** requisition, requirement, require (*R*), ultimatum; *spec.* draft, exaction, strike, run.

Antonyms: see GIFT, OFFER, TENDER.

2. call, request; *spec.* market, sale, run, exigency.

3. *See* CLAIM, INQUIRY.

demandable, *a.* requirable, exigible.

demerit, *n.* merit (*R; contex.*), indesert (*R*), undesert, fault, blame, desert (*chiefly in pl.*), ill desert.

demerit, *v. t.* underserve (*R*).

demigod, *n.* semideity (*R*), semigod (*R*); *spec.* hero (*Greek antiq.*), heroine (*fem.*), Prometheus, Epimetheus, Hercules, Perseus, *etc.*

demobilize, *v. t.* disorganize (*R*), scatter, disperse, disband.

democracy, *n.* **1.** *Spec.* democratism, Jacobinism, Jeffersonianism.

Antonyms: see DICTATORSHIP, ABSOLUTISM, ARISTOCRACY, MONARCHISM.

2. *See* GOVERNMENT, STATE.

democrat, *n. Spec.* Jeffersonian (*U. S.*), hardshell (*U. S.*), Bourbon (*U. S.*), Jacobin, ultrademocrat, new dealer (*U. S.*).

democratic, *a. Spec.* Jeffersonian, Jacobinic, Jacobinical, ultrademocratic, liberal, republican.

Antonyms: see TOTALITARIAN, COMMUNISTIC, FASCIST, MONARCHICAL, ARISTOCRATIC, AUTOCRATIC.

democratize, *v. t. Spec.* Jacobinize, popularize.

demolish, *v. t.* **1.** destroy (*contex.*); *spec.* abate (*law*), raze, rase (*R*), overthrow, level, pulverize, unbuild (*R*), ruin.

Antonyms: see CONSTRUCT.

2. *See* RUIN, SPOIL.

demon, *n.* **1.** *In the general sense, of Greek mythology, of a supernatural being between god and man:* deity (*contex.*), spirit (*contex.*), numen (*R*), daimon (*tech. or B*), intelligence (*B*); *spec.* angel, ghost, genius, lar, sylph, manito, devil, specter, fiend, diablotin (*French*), imp, dev, genie, jinn (*prop. pl.*), jinnee (*sing.*), hag (*A*), harpy, demogorgon, Triton, satyr, manes (*pl.*), lares (*pl.*), penates (*pl.*), empusa, incubus (*masc.*), succubus (*fem.*), lemur, barghest, ghoul, Lamia, ogre, ogress, deuce, puck (*also* pook, pooka *or* phooka), vampire, scarecrow, bug, bogy, bogey, colt-pixie, fairy, fay (*B*), Erlking, familiar, kelpie *or* kelpy (*Scot.*), jotun, hobgoblin, sprite *or* (*A variant*) spright, kobold, Brownie, bogle, gnome, goblin, troll, nixie, nix, poker (*U. S.; C*), pixy *or* pixie, redcap, Poltergeist (*German*), Robin Goodfellow. *In ordinary English usage "demon" is an evil spirit.*

2. *See* DEVIL.

demonic, *a. Spec.* Mephistophelean, Mephistophelian, Mephistophelic, ghoulish, gnomish, elvish, elfin, infernal, elfish, devilish.

demonize, *v. t.* diabolify, diabolize, devilize;—*all three R or B.*

demonology, *n.* diabology, diabolology, devilism, devilry, deviltry, diablerie (*French*); *spec.* Satanology.

demonstrative, *a.* **1.** proving, probative.

2. expressive; *spec.* cordial, emotional, unreserved; *see* EFFUSIVE, COOL.

Antonyms: see IMPASSIVE, UNEMOTIONAL.

demonstrativeness, *n.* expressiveness; *spec.* cordiality, empressment (*French*), ardor, unreservedness, emotion (*contex.*), emotionality, emotionalism.

demoralize, *v. t.* **1.** corrupt, infect, undermine (*morally*), deprave.

2. disconcert, embarrass, agitate, discomfit, disorganize, confuse, unnerve, buffalo (*S*).

denaturalize, *v. t.* denature.

dendriform, *a.* dendroid, arborescent, arboriform, dendritic;—*all tech. or B;* treey, treelike.

deniable, *a.* contradictable, traversable.

denial, *n.* **1.** *See* REFUSAL, CONTRADICTION, TRIAL.

2. negation, disaffirmation, negative, disaffirmance; *spec.* forswearing, repudiation, rejection, sublation (*logic*), disallowance, disclaimer (*chiefly law*), disclamation (*R*).

Antonyms: see ACKNOWLEDGMENT, ASSUMPTION.

denomination, *n.* **1.** *See* NAMING, NAME.

2. class (*which see*), kind; *spec.* (*in religion*) body, connection (*chiefly spec.*), persuasion, sect, communion, church, faith.

denominational, *a.* sectarian, sectarial.

---

deluge: *flood.*
demarcate: *define, distinguish, divide, separate.*
demarcation: *definition, boundary distinction, division.*
demean: *degrade, abase, behave.*
demeanor: *behavior.*
demented: *deranged.*
demesne: *estate.*
demise: *transfer, death.*
demise: *transfer, die.*
demit: *dismiss, abdicate, relinquish.*
demonstrate: *prove, show.*
demount: *descend.*
demur, *v.: object.*
demur, *n.: objection.*
demure: *sober, proper, modest.*
denominate: *name.*

---

denote, *v. t.* **1.** *See* SIGNIFY, INDICATE, EXPRESS, MEAN.
2. mark, stamp, stigmatize (*esp. as evil*), brand (*esp. as evil*), betoken.
denounce, *v. t.* **1.** proclaim, portend, indicate: —*is A in this sense.*
2. *See* ACCUSE.
3. condemn, fulminate (*violently*), vituperate (*abusively*), slam (*S*).
Antonyms: see APPROVE.
denouncer, *n.* fulminator, inveigher, vituperator.
dense, *a.* **1.** *See* COMPACT (*referring to constituent particles or parts*), THICK (*referring to visibly separate parts or objects*), STUPID.
2. *Referring to ignorance, etc.:* intense, crass (*B*), gross, profound, dumb; *spec.* impenetrable, utter, absolute.
density, *n.* **1.** *See* COMPACTNESS (*referring to the constituent particles or parts*), THICKNESS (*referring to visibly separate parts or objects*), STUPIDITY.
2. *Referring to ignorance, etc.:* intensity, crassness (*B*), profoundness, dumbness, dumheit (*jocular*); *spec.* impenetrability, absoluteness.
dentate, *a.* toothed, serrate; *spec.* jagged, denticulate, notched. "*Dentate*" *is tech.*
denude, *v. t.* bare; *spec.* abrade, erode; *see* BARK, STRIP.
denunciation, *n.* condemnation (*contex.*), fulmination (*violent*), vituperation (*abusive*), diatribe (*bitter and violent*); *spec.* flyting, invective, philippic, slam.
deny, *v. t.* **1.** *See* REFUSE, CONTRADICT, ABJURE, DISCLAIM.
2. negate, disaffirm, negative; *spec.* forswear (*on oath*), sublate (*a term of logic*), disallow, disclaim.
Antonyms: see ACKNOWLEDGE, ASSUME, CONFESS.
deodorizer, *n.* deodorant; *spec.* pastil, pastille, fumigator, incense.
depart, *v. i.* **1.** go (*often with "away"*), leave, remove (*formal or affected*), move (*C*), withdraw, part (*A*), recede (*R*); *spec.* flee, congee (*A*), fly, flit, beat it (*S*), scoot.
2. *Referring to sudden or secret departure:* abscond, decamp, skip (*S*), flit (*C*), slide, cut (*S or C*), mosey (*S, U. S.*), mizzle (*S*), vamose (*S*), evaporate (*C*), fold up (*C*); *spec.* elope.
Antonyms: see STAY, APPROACH, COME.
3. *See* DIE.
4. differ, deviate, vary.
departing, *a.* going, leaving, parting.
Antonyms: see COMING.
department, *n.* **1.** division, subdivision, section, part, province, branch, sphere;—*referring to a subject or to a complex whole.*
2. district, county, shire;—*referring to a territorial part.*
3. office, bureau.
departure, *n.* **1.** going, leave, leaving, removal (*formal or affected*), withdrawal (*formal*), parting, decession (*R*); *spec.* flight, exit, exition (*R*), flit (*R*), hegira (*spec. or fig.*), congé (*French; a formal departure*), furlough.
Antonyms: see COMING.
2. absconding, decampment.
3. *See* DEATH, DEVIATION, VARIATION, DIGRESSION, DIFFERENCE.
depend, *v. i.* **1.** *See* HANG, RELY.
2. hinge, turn, hang, rest;—*referring to the depending of an undecided matter upon something else.*
dependable, *a.* reliable, trustworthy, steady.
dependence, *n.* **1.** hanging, suspension.
2. hinging, turning, hanging, resting.
3. *See* RELIANCE, SUPPORT.
dependency, *n.* **1.** dependence;—*esp. in sense of state or fact of depending.*
2. dependent; *spec.* subject, colony, province.
Antonyms: cf. SOVEREIGNTY.
dependent, *a.* **1.** hanging, suspended.
2. *See* CONDITIONAL, RELATIVE, SUBORDINATE, ACCESSORY.
dependent, *n.* **1.** *See* DEPENDENCY.
2. *Spec.* client, creature.
depict, *v. t.* **1.** delineate (*esp. in lines*), do (*contex.; chiefly C*), portray, render (*esp. in reference to technique*), reproduce, figure, depicture (*R*), picture, represent; *spec.* draw, table (*R*), line (*chiefly in "line in," "line out," "line off," etc.*), linearize (*R*), lineate (*R*), paint, blazon, sketch, emblaze, emblazon, crayon, pencil, symbolize, chalk, limn (*B*).
2. *See* DESCRIBE.
depiction, *n.* **1.** delineation (*esp. in lines*), portrayal, rendition, reproduction, representation, depicture (*R*), portraiture, blazonry, blazon.
2. *See* DESCRIPTION.
depilate, *v. t.* unhair, grain (*skins*); *spec.* clean.
deplete, *v. t.* **1.** empty; *spec.* drain, evacuate, reduce, exhaust.
Antonyms: see FILL.
2. *See* EXHAUST.
depopulate, *v. t.* unpeople, depeople (*A*); *spec.* disman (*R*), desolate.
Antonyms: see PEOPLE.
deport, *v. t.* **1.** behave (*oneself*).
2. remove, banish.
depose, *v. t.* **1.** degrade, remove, impeach, oust; *spec.* dethrone, disenthrone, disthrone (*R*), discrown, unthrone (*R*), disestablish (*a church*), unfrock (*a clergyman*), break (*an officer*).
Antonyms: see ENTHRONE.
2. *See* TESTIFY.
deposit, *v. t.* **1.** *In the sense of "to put for safe keeping, to commit to another":* lodge, put, place, depose (*A*); *spec.* intrust, bail, store, leave, bank (*C*).

---

denotation: *meaning.*
dénouement: *explanation, catastrophe.*
dent, *n.:* *indentation.*
dent, *v. t.:* *indent.*
dent, *n.:* *notch, tooth.*
dependable: *reliable.*
deplorable: *lamentable.*
deplore: *mourn.*
deploy: *extend.*
deport: *behave, remove, banish.*

2. *In the sense of "to lay or put down, to place at rest":* place, lodge, put, lay, depose (*A*); *spec.* dump (*chiefly U. S.*), plant, ground, repose, plank (*with "down" or "out"; S*), land, couch, store, precipitate.

Antonyms: see DISLODGE.

3. precipitate (*as from a solution*).

deposit, *n.* deposition, layer; *spec.* precipitate, precipitation, settling (*chiefly in pl.*), silt, sublimate, diluvium (*geol.*), loess, tartar, sinter, sediment, grounds (*pl.*), *see* PRECIPITATION.

depositary, *n.* **1.** *Spec.* bailee, trustee, bank, banker.

2. *See* DEPOSITORY.

depositing, *n.* placing, putting, lodging, lodgment; *spec.* consignation, intrusting, bailment.

deposition, *n.* **1.** degradation; *spec.* dethronement, discrownment, impeachment.

2. testimony (*contex.*); *spec.* affidavit.

3. placing, putting, lodgment, reposition (*R*); *spec.* discharge, precipitation, settling.

4. *See* DEPOSIT.

depository, *n.* **1.** bailee.

2. depositary, storehouse; *spec.* warehouse, storage.

depraved, *a.* immoral, vicious, evil, wicked; *spec.* corrupt, contaminated, abandoned, degraded, low, perverted, degenerate.

Antonyms: see ELEVATED.

depravity, *n.* wickedness, immorality, vice, evil; *spec.* corruption, contamination, degradation, perversion, lowness, degeneracy.

Antonyms: see ELEVATION.

depreciate, *v. t.* **1.** depress (*in value, price, etc.*), lower, undervalue, mark down, decry, deprecate (*spec.*).

Antonyms: see ADVANCE.

2. *See* DISCREDIT, DISPARAGE.

depreciate, *v. i.* decline, fall, drop; *spec.* slump (*S or cant*), tumble.

Antonyms: see ADVANCE.

depreciation, *n.* decline, fall, drop, decrease; *spec.* slump (*S or cant*), tumble.

Antonyms: see ADVANCE.

depredator, *n.* plunderer; *spec.* thief, robber, pirate, brigand, marauder.

depress, *v. t.* **1.** *See* LOWER (*as to position in space*), DEPRECIATE.

2. dull (*in activity, as trade*), deaden.

3. dispirit, deject, prostrate, discourage, oppress, dishearten, sadden, contrist (*A*), enfeeble, dash, damp, dampen, dismalize (*R*), vaporize (*R*), vapor (*R*), oppress, bow, cool (*chiefly with "off" or "down"*), quail, sink, desolate, frigidize (*R*), hip (*C, R*), disanimate (*R*), downweigh (*R*), darken;—*mostly specific.*

Antonyms: see ELATE, CHEER, GLADDEN, ENLIVEN.

depressed, *a.* **1.** lowered (*in space*).

2. dulled (*as trade*), deadened.

3. dispirited, dejected, downcast, discouraged, disheartened, despondent, despairing, desperate (*A*), prostrate, crestfallen, saturnine (*B*), disconsolate, cheerless, sad, gloomy, melancholy, oppressed, rueful, lugubrious (*B*), doleful, dolorous (*now B*), dismal, sorrowful, downhearted, dull, chopfallen, chapfallen, dolent (*A*), mopish, low, vapored (*R*), damp (*A*), somber, melancholic, melancholious (*R*), heartsick, sick, drooping, darksome (*R*), glum, heavy, heavy-hearted, half-hearted, droopy (*R*), hypped, hyppish, *or* hippish (*C*), forlorn, hopeless, woeful, low-spirited, hypochondriac, dumpish, dumpy (*C*), desolate, wretched, lonely, lonesome, dyspeptic (*fig.*);—*mostly specific.*

Antonyms: see CHEERFUL, ELATED, GLAD, BUOYANT.

depressing, *a.* dispiriting, dejecting (*R*), discouraging, disheartening, cheerless, sad, saddening, gloomy, melancholy, atrabilious (*B*), doleful, rueful, lugubrious, woeful *or* woful, dreary (*A*), somber, dismal, dampening, damping, dark, grievous, oppressive, disconsolate, dolorous, melancholy, black, cloudy, Cimmerian (*fig.*), chilling, frigid (*R*), heavy, gray, leaden, dusky, dark, dull, dolorific (*R*), painful. *Most of these synonyms are more or less specific.*

Antonyms: see CHEERING, ASSURING.

depression, *n.* **1.** lowering (*in space*).

2. *See* CAVITY, HOLLOW.

3. dispiritedness, dejection, dejectedness, discouragement, despondency, damp, hopelessness, desperation (*A*), cheerlessness, sadness, gloom, gloominess, melancholy, melancholia, atrabiliousness (*B*), dole (*A*), dolefulness, dolor (*B*), sorrow, grief, distress, dreariness (*A*), dismalness, woe, woefulness, blue devils (*pl.; C*), blues (*pl.*), dispiritment (*R*), disheartenment, desolation, disconsolation, dullness, despair, brokenness, despairingness (*R*), downheartedness, lowness, dumps (*pl.; now C and usually humorous*), dumpishness, hypochondria, hypos (*pl.; C*), hyp (*C*), hyps (*pl.; C*), mopishness, ruefulness, doldrums (*pl.*), dismality, hip (*C*), neariment (*A*), drearihood *or* drearihead (*A*), chill, heaviness, mulligrubs (*C*), megrims (*pl.*), spleen, qualm, black dog (*C*), chill, darkness, lugubriosity *or* lugubriousness (*B*). *Most of these synonyms are more or less specific.*

Antonyms: see CHEER, ELATION.

4. crash (*financial*).

deprivation, *n.* deprival (*R*), privation (*R*), dispossession, loss; *spec.* divestiture, divestment, bereavement, robbery, deforcement (*A; esp. of lands*), stripping, denudation, abridgment, curtailment, docking, dockage, despoilment, despoliation, spoliation, plunder, pillage, rifling.

Antonyms: see RESTORATION.

deprive, *v. t.* dispossess; *spec.* divest, bereave, rob, deforce (*A; esp. of land*), strip, debar, shear, denude, drain, abridge, curtail, dock, despoil, spoil, plunder, reave (*now chiefly in p. p. "reft"*), pillage, rifle, relieve (*euphemistic*

(*A*) *archaic.* (*B*) *bookish, poetic, literary or learned.* (*C*) *colloquial.* (*Contex.*) *contextual.* (*R*) *rare.* (*S*) *slang.* *See pp. viii–ix.*

and C or S), oust (*law*), shorten (*R*), mulct, lose, destitute.
Antonyms: see INVEST, PRESENT.

depth, *n.* **1.** deepness, bathos (*R*), profundity, profoundness, abyss, drop;—*referring to depth in space.*
Antonyms: see SHALLOWNESS, HEIGHT.
2. *Referring to that which is deep in space:* deep.
Antonyms: see HEIGHT.
3. *Spec.* abstruseness; *see* DISCERNMENT, SUBTLETY.
4. deep (*of winter, etc.*), dead (*of night, winter, etc.*).
5. *In reference to emotions or experiences:* profoundness, profundity, intimacy, intensity, heaviness, soundness (*of sleep*), cordiality, heartiness, thoroughness, inveteracy, inveterateness; *spec.* nadir (*fig.*).
Antonyms: see HEIGHT.
6. *Referring to colors:* strength, intensity, richness, brilliance.
7. lowness, heaviness; *spec.* bassness;—*referring to sound.*

deputy, *n.* **1.** agent (*contex.*), delegate, representative, secondary (*R*), second, locumtenens (*Latin*), substitute, vice (*R*); *spec.* vicegerent, vicar, viceroy, kaimakam, lieutenant, undersheriff, tipstaff (*Eng.*).
2. *In France* deputy *is equivalent to* legislator, member (*of the House of Deputies*).

derange, *v. t.* **1.** *See* DISARRANGE, DISTURB, CONFUSE, DISORGANIZE.
2. *Referring to functions, mental processes, etc.:* upset, disorder, distemper (*R, exc. in p. p. "distempered"*), unbalance, unsettle, disturb, perturb, discompose, confuse, ruffle.
3. *Referring to the mind:* craze, shatter, unsettle, perturbate (*R*), unhinge, insanify (*R*), distract (*now R*), dement, dementate (*R*), crack (*chiefly C*), bemad (*R*), madden (*now esp. with anger*), frenzy (*now usually with some passion or suffering*), mad (*R*), loco (*C, U. S.*).

deranged, *a.* insane, crazy, demented, dement (*R*), unsound (*chiefly said of the mind*), daft, nonsane (*R or nonce*), distempered (*B*), lunatic, unbalanced, unsettled, mad (*implying frenzy or violent delusion*), brainsick, disordered; *spec.* maniac, maniacal, morbid, raving, distraught (*B*), distracted, distract (*A*), moonstruck, witless (*now R*), idiotic, flighty, foolish, imbecile, cretinous, frantic (*now R*), feeble-minded, weak-minded, doting *or* dotard, doughbaked (*dial. or C*), possessed, locoed (*C, U. S.*), dotty (*C or S*), dotish *or* doatish, fatuous (*now R*), mattoid, cuckoo (*C*), potty (*C*), nutty (*C*), nuts (*S*), screwy (*S*), daffy, daft, balmy, off (*contex.*), loony (*C*); *see* DELIRIOUS.
Antonyms: see SANE, RATIONAL.

deranged person. *Spec.* lunatic, imbecile, idiot, fool, changeling (*A*), dotard, madman, madwoman (*R*), madling (*R*), maniac, monomaniac.

derangement, *n.* **1.** *Spec.* disarrangement, disturbance, confusion, disorganization, disorder.
2. *Referring to functions, mental processes, etc.:* upsetting, disordering (*the act*), disorder (*the resulting condition*), distemper (*R; exc. med.*), unbalancing, disturbance, perturbation (*R*).
3. *Referring to the mind:* alienation (*tech.*), craziness, insanity, katatonia (*a form of insanity; tech.*), insaneness, aberration, craze (*as, "in a craze"*), mania, madness, dementia, dementedness, distemperature (*R*); *spec.* rage (*B*), bug (*C*), distraction, delirium, deliration (*now B*), demonomania, idiocy, idiotism, cretinism, imbecility, fatuity, frenzy, furiosity (*chiefly Scots law*), delusion, kleptomania, lycanthropy, lypomania *or* lypothymia, paranoia, paraphrosyne *or* paraphrenitis, paraphrenia (*R*), perturbancy (*R*), perturbation (*R*), unbalance (*R*), vesania (*R*), crack.
Antonyms: see SANITY.

derelict, *n. An abandoned thing, as a vessel, tract of land, etc.: spec.* wreck, outcast, dereliction.

derivation, *n.* **1.** *See* INFERENCE, DERIVATIVE.
2. getting, obtaining, drawing, taking, extraction (*as of comfort from some fact or circumstance*).
3. origination, origin, source, root; *spec.* etymology.

derivative, *n.* derivate, derivation; *spec.* compound, paronym (*R*).

derive, *v. t.* **1.** *See* INFER, TRACE.
2. get, obtain, draw, take, extract (*chiefly spec. or fig.*), deduce.

derive, *v. i.* arise, come, originate, spring; *spec.* descend.

descend, *v. i.* **1.** fall, drop, sink, subside (*chiefly B*), settle; *spec.* gravitate, plunge, precipitate, tumble, stumble, stoop, swoop, pounce, souse, alight, demount, dismount, decline, droop, slump, dip, set (*as the sun*), trip.
Antonyms: see RISE.
2. slope, dip, drop, pitch, decline (*R*), lurch, topple, glide.
3. *See* CONDESCEND, DERIVE, *v. i.*
4. *Of duties, rights, etc.:* devolve, pass, come, go, fall, succeed (*R*).
5. *Of family descent:* spring, issue (*now only law*), come, arise.
6. *To make an incursion:* assault, attack, invade, fall, pounce, swoop.

descendant, *n.* descendent, offspring, progeny, child, bairn (*Scot.*), issue (*chiefly legal*), posterity (*chiefly collective pl.*), scion (*R*), imp (*B*), offset (*R*), offshoot (*R*), posteriors (*pl.*), son, daughter, *etc.*; *spec.* epigone (*R*), spawn (*contemptuous*), chip (*C*), brat (*scornful or humorous*), kid (*C*), kiddy (*S*), heir.
Antonyms: see ANCESTOR.

descendental, *a.* empirical, positive, naturalistic, realist;—*opposed to "transcendental."*

deride: *ridicule.*
derision: *ridicule.*
derival: *inference.*
derogate: *decline, detract.*
derogatory: *discreditable, disparaging.*

descending, *a.* descendant *or* descendent (*both R*), down (*tech. or C*), cadent (*R*), declivous, falling, settling, sloping, *etc.*; *spec.* catadromous, downright, wheeling (*B*).

Antonyms: see RISING.

descent, *n.* **1.** descension (*R*), fall, drop, sinking, subsidence, cadence (*R*), settlement (*chiefly spec.*), down (*chiefly in "ups and downs"*), downfall, downcome, comedown (*C*), droop (*B*); *spec.* gravitation, plunge, precipitation (*B*), tumble, slump, lapse, stoop, swoop, souse, alighting, dismount, declension, declination, dip, downrush, pounce.

Antonyms: see RISE.

2. slope, declivity, decline, declination, slide, glissade, glide, dip, pitch, drop.

3. devolution, passing, succession (*R*), devolvement; *spec.* evolution.

4. ancestry, lineage, pedigree, progeniture, progenitorship (*R*), origin, original (*R*), extraction, engendrure (*A*); *spec.* paternity, parentage, birth, filiation.

describable, *a.* portrayable, paintable, depictable, drawable, definable, figurable, representable, characterizable;—*with specific implications.*

Antonyms: see INDESCRIBABLE.

describe, *v. t.* **1.** *To tell in words:* picture, depict, portray, paint, depaint (*emphatic*), limn (*B*), delineate, draw, figure, represent, tell (*with "about"*), narrate, relate, record, report; *spec.* outline, define, characterize, qualify. sketch, adumbrate (*R*), blazon, image, empicture (*R*), epithet, epitomize, gazetteer, detail, miniature, misdescribe, portraiture (*R*), phrase.

2. *See* DELINEATE.

description, *n.* **1.** *Describing in words:* picturing, depiction, depicture (*R*), portrayal, portrayment (*R*), portrait, portraiture, painting, limning (*B*), delineation, representation, report, narrative, relation; *spec.* drawing, sketching, sketch, outlining, outline, definition, figuring, imaging, characterization, adumbration (*R*), blazonry *or* blazonment, blazon, cacotype, collation, signalment (*R*), periegesis (*R*), presentment, prospectus, hypotyposis (*R*), image (*R*), likeness, iconography.

2. *See* KIND.

descriptive, *a.* depictive, delineative, delineatory, definitive, figurative, representative; *spec.* adumbrative, graphic, lifelike, graphical (*R*), vivid, lively.

desecrate, *v. t.* contaminate, profane, defile, unhallow (*R*), pollute, violate; *spec.* deconsecrate, secularize.

Antonyms: see CONSECRATE.

desecration, *n.* contamination, defilement, profanation, sacrilege (*R*), violation, pollution.

desert, *a.* **1.** abandoned, unfrequented, desolate, empty, uninhabited.

2. *See* WASTE, WILD, BARREN.

desert, *n.* solitude, wilderness, wild, waste; *spec.* Sahara (*fig.*), karoo.

desert, *v. t.* fail; *spec.* disappoint, jilt, bolt; *see* ABANDON.

desert, *v. i.* leave, quit; *spec.* apostatize, renegade, skirt (*of a dog deserting from the hunting-pack*), backslide.

deserter, *n.* runaway, runagate (*B or A*), fugitive, transfuge (*R*), transfugitive (*R*), rat *or* ratter (*S*); *spec.* recreant, Damas (*fig.*), renegade, turncoat, apostate, traitor, truant, backslider.

desertion, *n.* apostasy, recreancy, backsliding.

deserve, *v. t.* merit; *spec.* earn, demerit.

deserved, *a.* condign (*A, exc. of punishment*), just, rightful, merited, due, meet.

deserving, *a.* worthy, meritorious, good (*contex.*).

design, *v. t.* **1.** *See* INTEND, PLAN, DEVISE.

2. devise, create, plan, project; *spec.* outline, delineate, invent, sketch, cartoon, model, weave.

design, *v. i.* **1.** devise, create, invent, plan;—*referring to artistic work.*

2. *See* INTEND.

design, *n.* **1.** *See* PLAN, INTENTION, ADAPTATION, ARTIFICE, ART.

2. device, contrivance, creation; *spec.* figure, model, cartoon, diaper, print, imprint, weave, pattern, blazonry, bearing, blazon, colophon, trade mark, stamp.

designated, *a. Spec.* specified, mentioned, named, given, stipulated, indicated, called for.

desirable, *a.* pleasing, optable (*R*), fair; *spec.* covetable, preferable.

desire, *v. i.* wish (*less intense than desire*), want (*implies need*), long, yearn (*chiefly elevated or B; implies tenderness and restlessness*), crave (*connotes urgent appetite*), aspire (*implies ambition*), lust (*implies inordinate physical desire*), pleasure (*R*), burn, gasp, pant, raven (*implies rapacity*), list (*B*), thirst, itch, reck (*R*), rage (*intensive*), hanker (*chiefly C*); *cf.* DESIRE, *n.*

desire, *v. t.* wish, want, desiderate, greed (*R*), hope, crave, covet, ambition (*R*).

desire, *n.* **1.** conation (*tech.*), wish, want, appetite (*spec. or fig.*); *spec.* longing, yearning, appetency, craving, crave (*R*), avidity (*implies eagerness*), covetousness (*implies intense longing for what is another's*), covetise (*A*), avarice (*implies greed*), cupidity (*A*), concupiscence (*for the flesh*), (*chiefly spec.*), lust (*connotes disapprobation of the thing desired*), aspiration, ambition, eagerness, burning, panting, greed, greediness, rapacity (*implying violence*), rapaciousness, ravenousness, desidera-

descrial: *discovery.*
descry: *discover, perceive, see.*
desert: *due, demerit.*
deserted: *abandoned, unfrequented, alone.*
deshabille: *undress.*
desiccate: *dry.*
designate: *indicate, appoint, mention.*
designation: *indication, appointment, name.*
designing: *scheming.*

tion, desiderium (*B*), optation (*R*), itching, itch (*usually contemptuous*), yen (*S; U. S.*), fever, calenture (*B*), device (*obs. or R, exc. in "left to one's own devices"*), letch (*R*), hunger, hungriness, hanker, gluttony (*fig.*), breathing (*used with "after"*), list (*A or B*); lickerishness *or* liquorishness (*B*), lechery, orexis, voraciousness.

Antonyms: see AVERSION.

2. desideratum; *spec.* hope, passion, godsend.

desirous, *a.* wishful; *spec.* wistful, avid, avidious (*R*), covetous, avaricious, cupidous (*R*), concupiscent, concupiscible, lustful, aspiring, ambitious, eager, greedy, grasping, rapacious, thirsty, thirstful, lickerish *or* liquorish, hungry, edacious (*B*), voracious, gluttonous, desiderative (*often tech.*).

desist, *v. t.* stop, cease, stay, quit (*C*); *spec.* pause, forbear.

Antonyms: see CONTINUE.

desk, *n. Spec.* table, faldstool, escritoire, lectern, stand, secretary, ambo (*eccl.*).

desolate, *a.* **1.** *See* ALONE, LONELY, UNFREQUENTED, UNINHABITED, DEPRESSED, GLOOMY.

2. waste; *spec.* ruinous, tumbled-down *or* tumble-down, ravaged, desert, barren, wild, bleak, inhospitable.

desolate, *v. t.* **1.** *See* DEPOPULATE, DEPRESS, DEVASTATE.

2. waste, ravage, destitute (*R*), devastate, havoc (*R*); *spec.* ruin, sack, pillage, burn.

desolation, *n.* **1.** *Spec.* loneliness, unfrequentedness, uninhabitedness, desertedness, depression, cheerlessness.

2. wasteness (*R*), waste; *spec.* devastation, ruin, ruinousness, desertion, barrenness, ravage, wildness, bleakness, dreariness.

desperado, *n.* desperate (*obs.*); *spec.* blackguard, brave, bravo, hero (*R and B; contex.*), apache (*French*), freebooter, ruffian, brigand, bandit, highwayman, buccaneer, filibuster, pirate, marauder, robber, plunderer, raider, despoiler, looter, assassin, mohock, plug-ugly (*S or cant; U. S.*), rowdy, highbinder, warrior (*Amer. Indian*), bully, rapparee (*hist.*), berserk, berserker, moonlighter, mosstrooper, thug, yeg, gangster.

despisal, *n.* contempt, abhorrence, scorn, disdain, aversion, detestation.

despise, *v. t.* abhor (*implies intense hatred*), disesteem, contemn (*B; the verb of* contempt), scorn (*connotes lively and intense contempt*), disdain (*connotes highminded aversion*), despite (*A; like* despise, *implies looking down on what is contemptible*), misprize (*R*); *spec.* spurn, scout, ridicule, ignore.

Antonyms: see HONOR, ESTEEM.

despond, *v. i.* despair (*implying utter loss of hope*).

Antonyms: see HOPE.

destination, *n.* **1.** appointment, ordainment, predetermination, ordination (*chiefly spec.*), foreordainment.

2. *See* PURPOSE.

3. goal, bourne (*chiefly B*), terminus (*chiefly tech.*); *spec.* haven, harbor, port, station.

destine, *v. t.* **1.** appoint, predestine, predestinate, ordain (*implying divine or authoritative appointment*), fate, predetermine, foreordain, order, shape, weird (*R*); *spec.* foredoom, doom.

2. *See* ADDRESS.

destiny, *n.* **1.** lot (*connotes chance*), doom (*connotes an unhappy destiny*), fate (*connotes an impersonal and blind necessity*), ordinance (*R*), kismet (*B*), star (*R*), constellation, planet, fortune, wierd (*suggests a mysterious and unquestionable fate*).

2. *See* FATE.

destitute, *a.* **1.** *See* DEVOID.

2. poor (*contex.*), penniless, moneyless, ruined (*contex.*), broke (*C*), down and out.

destroy, *v. t.* **1.** *See* DEMOLISH, KILL, ANNIHILATE, EXTINGUISH, ABOLISH, COUNTERACT, DEVASTATE.

2. annihilate (*intensive; connotes complete destruction*), demolish (*concerns a structure or organization*), ruin, ruinate, unform (*R*), perish (*A*), subvert, fordo (*A*); *spec.* blot (*used with "out"*), break, shatter, shipwreck, devastate, dismantle (*implies stripping of what is movable*), consume (*implies fire or a corrosive*), raze (*implies complete tearing down*), rend (*implies tearing violently apart*), spoil, efface, crush (*used with "out"*), erode, dissolve, desolate, abate, kill, explode, sap (*fig., implies the work of concealed forces*), shatter (*connotes a complete and sudden destruction, as of a breakable*), murder (*of human beings*), dissolve (*implies complete disappearance from sight*), eradicate, root (*with "up" or "out"*), wreck (*connotes destruction through accident or unintelligent guidance, or violence)—referring to material, or fig. to immaterial, things.*

Antonyms: see BUILD, ESTABLISH, CONSTRUCT, PROTECT.

3. root (*with "up" or "out"*), fordo.

destroyer, *n.* destructor (*R*), ruin, demolisher, razer, wrecker (*usually connotes a professional* destroyer), *etc.*; *spec.* biblioclast, iconoclast, vandal, *etc.*

destructible, *a.* destroyable, perishable, eradicable.

Antonyms: see INDESTRUCTIBLE.

destruction, *n. Spec.* demolition, ruin, ruination, death, killing, spoliation, wreck, devastation, annihilation, shipwreck, vandalism, dissolution, holocaust, erosion, *etc. Cf.* DESTROY.

destructive, *a.* demolitionary, ruinous, subversionary, annihilative, exterminative, extinctive, extirpatory, eradicatory, consump-

---

despair, *n.: depression, hopelessness.*
despair, *v. i.: despond.*
despairing: *depressed, hopeless.*
despatch: *var. of* DISPATCH.
desperate: *depressed, hopeless, extreme, frantic, heroic, reckless, great.*
desperation: *depression, hopelessness, recklessness.*
despondency: *depression.*
despondent: *depressed.*
despot: *autocrat, tyrant.*
despotic: *autocratic, tyrannical.*
desquamate: *scale.*
destitute: *devoid, poor.*
destitution: *absence, poverty.*

---

tive; *spec.* pestiferous, internecine, interdestructive, fatal, pernicious.
Antonyms: see CREATIVE.

detach, *v. t.* **1.** separate, disconnect (*chiefly spec.*), unfix, loose, unloose, free, disunite, disjoin, dissever; *spec.* disengage, draft, disjoint, disanchor.
Antonyms: see ATTACH, CONNECT, JOIN.
2. *See* DETAIL.

detachment, *n.* **1.** detaching, freeing, separation, disconnection (*chiefly spec.*), unfixing, loosening, disuniting, disjoining, disjunction, disseverance; *spec.* disengagement.
Antonyms: see CONNECTION, JOINING.
2. *Spec.* aloneness, separation.
3. *See* DETAIL.

detail, *n.* **1.** item, particular, minutia (*chiefly in pl.* "*minutiæ*"), circumstance, feature.
2. *Spec.* circumstantiality, account.
3. *In mil. use:* body, party, squad, detachment; *spec.* picket, patrol, party.

detail, *v. t.* **1.** describe, report, mention, explicate (*R*), itemize (*special*).
2. *In mil. use:* appoint, detach, tell off.

detailed, *a.* full, circumstantial, particular, minute, itemized (*chiefly spec.*).

detain, *v. t.* **1.** *See* WITHHOLD.
2. hold, stay, keep, delay, retard, retain; *spec.* confine, check, buttonhole, buttonhold, becalm, embay (*B*).
Antonyms: see HASTEN.

detective, *n. Spec.* spotter (*S*), mouser (*S*), Pinkerton, dick (*S*).

detention, *n.* **1.** withholding.
2. holding, stay, keeping, delay, detainment (*R*), detainer, retention; *spec.* confinement, check, demurrage.

deteriorate, *v. i.* decline, worsen, pejorate (*R*), disimprove (*R*), impair; *spec.* degenerate, rust, oxidize, corrode, shrink, shrivel, dry up, fade, mold, molder, wear, spoil, go bad, rot, decay.
Antonyms: see IMPROVE.

determinate, *a.* **1.** *See* DEFINITE.
2. definitive, conclusive.

determination, *n.* resolution, resoluteness, resolve, constancy, backbone, sturdiness, grit (*C*), firmness, stamina, pluck (*C*).

determined, *a.* resolute, resolved, bent (*with* "*on*"), stalwart, possessed (*C or spec.; with* "*to*"), set, bound.

detract, *v. i.* subtract, derogate;—*esp. so as to impair or injure, as reputation, happiness, etc.*

detriment, *n.* loss, disadvantage, prejudice, harm, damage, ruins (*pl.; A*), cost, injury; *spec.* mischief, hurt.

detruncate, *v. t. To cut off:* crop, lop.

deuce, *n.* **1.** *See* TWO.
2. tie;—*lawn tennis.*
3. devil.

devastate, *v. t.* desolate, destroy, ravage, waste, harry, havoc (*R*), scour; *spec.* plunder, sack, strip, pillage, rob, ruin.

devastation, *n.* desolation, destruction, ravaging, ravage, waste, havoc, ruin, vastation (*R*); *spec.* plunder, sack, stripping, pillage, ruination, depredation.

develop, *v. t.* **1.** *See* DISCLOSE, UNFOLD.
2. unfold, evolve, expand, disenvelope (*R*); *spec.* ripen, unravel, elaborate, explicate (*R or logic*), breed, mature, force, gestate;—*referring to the completion, perfection, or the like, of something by bringing out its possibilities.*
Antonyms: see CONDENSE.
3. deduce, educe, unfold;—*referring to the bringing out of something latent.*
4. produce, form, grow, breed, engender.
5. promote, exploit, market, expand, improve, build, boom.

develop, *v. i.* **1.** evolve, unfold, expand, grow, enlarge; *spec.* boom, flower, segment, progress, ripen, mature; *see* RIPEN.
2. *See* FORM, GROW, APPEAR.

development, *n.* **1.** disclosure, unfolding, revelation.
2. unfolding, unfoldment (*R*), evolvement, evolution (*often spec.*), expansion; *spec.* unraveling, elaboration, explication (*R or logic*), maturing, maturation, maturement (*R*), forcing, gestation, culture, upgrowth, uprise (*C*), boom, histogenesis, descent, progress.
Antonyms: see CONDENSATION.
3. deduction, educement, eduction, unfolding.
4. *See* PRODUCT, FORMATION, GROWTH.
5. promotion, exploitation, expansion, improvement, building, boom, sale.

deviate, *v. i.* turn, depart, incline, decline, vary, sheer (*chiefly spec.*), swerve, yaw (*nautical*), jibe (*also* gybe; *both nautical*), tack, divert (*A*), digress (*R in the literal sense*), exorbitate (*A*), excurse (*R*), veer (*chiefly naut.*), slue, slew, wander (*chiefly fig. or spec.*), stray (*chiefly spec.*), deflect (*R*), diverge, stagger;—*used literally and fig.*

deviation, *n.* turn, turning, departure, variation, wandering, strayiug, veer (*chiefly spec.*), tack, jibe, yaw, deflection, declination, divergence, sheer (*chiefly spec.*), swerve, stagger, sweep, inclination, diversion, digression (*R in the literal sense*), exorbitation (*R*); *spec.* disorientation, excursion, drift.

device, *n.* **1.** *In an immaterial sense:* contrivance, arrangement, design, plan, stratagem, scheme, invention, project, expedient, concoction, conceit, brew (*fig.*).
2. *Referring to a material thing:* contrivance

---

desuetude: *disuse.*
detect: *discover, perceive.*
detection: *discovery, perception.*
deter: *restrain, prevent.*
deterge: *clean, remove.*
determination: *definition, discovery, direction, constancy, decision, end.*
determinative: *decisive, ending.*
determine, *v. t.: define, decide, discover, end, direct.*
determine, *v. i.: decide, end.*
deterrence: *restraint.*
deterrent: *restraint, preventive.*
detest: *abhor.*
detestable: *abominable, hateful.*
dethrone: *depose.*
detonate: *explode.*
detour, detour: *circuit.*

(*connotes an ingenious invention*), arrangement, design, invention, contraption (*C*), gadget (*connotes a simple but ingenius mechanism*), thingumabob (*C*), appliance (*connotes meeting a particular end*), fangle (*obs.*), fanglement (*R*); *spec.* crochet, curwhibble (*R*), tool, instrument, shift.

3. emblem, emblazonment, blazon, bearings, *spec.* cockade, pageant (*hist.*), cipher (*of letters*), monogram, legend, motto.

4. *See* IDEA, CONTRIVANCE, TRICK, EXPEDIENT.

devil, *n.* **1.** [*cap.*, "*the Devil*"] Demon (*contex.*), Satan, Deuce (*in expletive use*), Dragon, Old Serpent, Satanas (*A*), Beelzebub, Old Harry (*euphemism*), Lucifer (*R or B*), Deil (*Scot.*), Auld Hornie (*Scot.; C*), Old Nick (*euphemism*), Davy Jones (*sailors' S*), Tempter, Archfiend, Archenemy, Prince of Darkness, Foul Fiend, Enemy, Adversary, Apollyon, Mephistopheles, Mephisto, Lubberfiend, Evil One. *Also popularly:* Old Nick, Old Limmie, Old Clootie, Old Teaser, Old One, *etc.*

Antonyms: see GOD.

2. *See* DEMON, WRETCH.

devilish, *a.* **1.** [*cap.*] Satanic, Satanical, Luciferian (*R*).

2. demonic, demoniac, diabolical, fiendish, satanic, satanical, serpentine (*R*), snaky, infernal, hellish, inhuman.

Antonyms: see HEAVENLY, HUMAN.

devilry, *n.* mischief (*contex.*), devilment, deviltry, diablery, diablerie (*French*).

devious, *a.* **1.** *Departing from the direct course:* roundabout, circuitous, indirect, rambling, crooked.

Antonyms: see STRAIGHT.

2. *Following an irregular course:* deviating, deviatory, wandering, rambling, straying.

devise, *v. t.* **1.** *To think up:* contrive (*implies skill and ingenuity*), invent (*implies making something new*), conceive, concoct, plan, design, imagine (*obs.*), brew (*fig.*), shape, cook (*usually with "up"*), cogitate (*formal or B*), excogitate (*R*), cast (*obs.*), plot, scheme, project, formulate, fudge (*often with "up"*), fabricate, manufacture, frame, elaborate; *spec.* machinate, hatch, spin, forge (*evil*), forecast (*obs.*).

2. *See* BEQUEATH.

devising, *n.* devisement (*R*), contrivance, contrival (*R*), premeditation, devisal (*R*), imagination (*obs.*), concoction, projection, framing, machination.

devoid, *a.* destitute, void, forlorn (*B*); *spec.* bare, free, empty;—*all used with "of."*

devotee, *n.* devotionalist, devotionist (*R*), votary, fanatic, fan (*C, general*), enthusiast, zealot; *spec.* oblate, corybant, bacchanal, bacchant, bacchante (*fem.*);—*used of religious devotees and fig.*

devotion, *n.* **1.** *See* CONSECRATION, DEDICATION, APPROPRIATION, APPLICATION, ADDICTION, CONSTANCY.

2. zeal, cult, prayerfulness, exercitation, piety, devoutness.

3. worship; *spec.* meditations (*pl.*), vigils (*pl.*). *The word "devotion" is often used in the plural, collectively.*

devour, *v. t.* **1.** eat, swallow, raven, wolf (*S*), gorge, glut, gulp (*esp. with "down"*), scoff (*S*).

2. *See* CONSUME.

devourer, *n.* eater, consumer, cormorant (*fig.*), locust (*fig.*); *spec.* epicure, gormandizer.

devourment, *n.* **1.** eating, ligurition (*R*).

2. *See* CONSUMPTION.

devout, *a.* **1.** pious (*connotes fulfillment of religious obligations*), religious, holy (*emphasizes spiritual character*), prayerful, heavenly-minded.

Antonyms: see IRRELIGIOUS.

2. *See* SINCERE.

devoutness, *n.* piety, devotion.

dew, *n.* moisture, precipitation;—*both contex.*

dew, *v. t.* wet (*contex.*), moisten (*contex.*), bedew (*intensive*).

dewy, *a.* moist (*contex.*), roral (*R*), roscid (*R*).

diagonal, *a.* cornerwise, bias.

diagonally, *adv.* cornerwise, bias.

diagram, *n.* delineation, plan, chart, scheme (*R*), plat (*chiefly spec.*), outline; *spec.* plot, sketch, section, graph (*tech.*), blueprint, tracing, picture (*contex.*).

diagram, *v. t.* delineate, plan, outline, plot, sketch, chart, trace, plat (*U. S.*); *spec.* graph (*C*).

dialect, *n.* language (*contex.*), lingo (*contemptuous*); *spec.* patter, patois (*French*), argot, cant, jargon, idiom, vernacular, intonation, brogue.

dialogue, *n.* conversation (*contex.*), talk (*contex.*); *spec.* snip-snap, flyte, collogue.

diameter, *n.* width (*contex.*); *spec.* thickness, bore, caliker, module.

diametric, *a.* utter (*used before "opposite"*), absolute, exact, precise, *etc.*

diarrhea, *n.* laxity, looseness, lask (*obs. or vet.*), skit (*dial.*), flux, discharge; *spec.* cholera, cholerine, dysentery, lientery, scour, purge.

dictate, *v. t.* **1.** *See* SPEAK.

2. bid, prescribe, order, direct, enjoin, command; *spec.* impose.

dictation, *n.* **1.** *See* SPEAKING.

2. bidding, injunction, order, prescription, *etc.*

dictator, *n.* ruler, leader, autocrat, Duce (*Italian*), Führer (*German*).

dictatorial, *a.* commanding, autocratic, authoritative, injunctive, magisterial (*B*), domineering, directory (*R or B*), dogmatic, peremptory, overbearing, highhanded.

Antonyms: see OBEDIENT.

diction, *n.* expression, style (*contex.*), wording, phraseology; *spec.* form, idiom, usage (*contex.*).

dictionary, *n.* wordbook, lexicon (*chiefly spec.*), vocabulary; *spec.* thesaurus, encyclopedia,

devolve, *v. i.: pass, descend.*
devolve, *v. t.: transfer.*
devote: *consecrate, dedicate, appropriate, apply, addict, condemn.*
devoted: *accursed, addicted, constant.*
diadem: *crown.*

manual, gradus (*short for "Gradus ad Parnassum"*), glossary, gloss (*R*), gazetteer.

dictum, *n.* saying, dictate, say-so (*dial. or U. S.*), say (*B or obs.*).

die, *v. i.* **1.** expire, perish, decease (*B or ostentatious elegance*), demise (*elevated or B*), depart (*euphemistic*), croak (*S*), drop (*chiefly C*), end (*now R*), pass (*A, or euphemistic*), succumb (*rhet.*); *spec.* fall, drown, hang, suffocate, suicide, push daisies (*soldiers' S*), go west (*S*), kick (*"in" or "the bucket"; S*), cash (*with "in"; S*).

Antonyms: see LIVE, GROW, GENERATE, GERMINATE, REVIVE.

2. *See* GANGRENE, STOP, VANISH, FADE, DISAPPEAR.

die, *n.* **1.** dice (*R*), bones (*pl.; C*), devil's bones (*pl.; C or in obloquy*), ivories (*pl.; S*); *spec.* demy, dispatcher (*S*), dispatch (*S*), fulham, doctor (*old S*), goads (*pl.; cant*).

2. stamp; *spec.* punch, swage, matrix, hub.

3. *See* FATE.

diet, *n.* **1.** *See* FOOD.

2. regimen.

differ, *v. i.* **1.** disagree (*used with "with"*), vary (*used with "from"*), diverge (*used with "from"*), deviate (*used with "from"*), depart (*used with "from"*), discept (*R*), disaccord (*used with "with"*), discrepate (*R*).

Antonyms: see AGREE.

2. dissent, disagree, disaccord.

Antonyms: see AGREE.

3. *See* DISPUTE, QUARREL.

difference, *n.* **1.** disagreement, variance, variation, dissemblance (*A*), divergence (*connotes considerable variation from the norm*), deviation (*emphasizes the parting from the norm*), departure, heterogeneity, odds (*emphasizes disagreement*), disaccord, distinction (*emphasizes difference as noticeable*), distinctness, discongruity, dissimilarity, distinction, dissimilitude (*R*), separateness, inconformity, nonconformity (*suggests obedience to a principle*), unlikeness, contrast, interval, diversity, disparity, dispart, inconsistence, inconsistency, contradiction, contradictoriness, repugnance (*connotes dislike*), antagonism (*implies hostility*), inimicality (*R*), hostility, hostileness, adverseness, irreconcilability, irreconcilableness, incongruity, incongruousness, incompatibility, incompatibleness (*implies temperamental differences*), discordance, discordancy, dissonance, dissonancy, inharmoniousness, contrariety, contrariness, discrepation (*R*), converseness, opposition, oppositeness, antithesis, antitheticalness, disparity, differentia, nuance (*French*). *Most of these words are more or less specific in their implications.*

Antonyms: see AGREEMENT, RESEMBLANCE, SAMENESS.

2. dissension, disaccord, disagreement; *spec.* controversy (*implies extended argument*), dispute, altercation, discord, quarrel, bicker, contention, strife, brabble, feud (*connotes a family quarrel of long standing*), fray (*implies a noisy brawl*), jar (*emphasizes shock and discord*), jangle (*implies a noisy and continued discord*), wrangle, embroilment, variance.

Antonyms: see AGREEMENT.

different, *a.* **1.** disagreeing, variant, divergent, deviative, distinct, dissimilar, unlike, diverse, divers (*A; both emphasize plurality rather than difference*), contrastive, contrasting (*emphasizing differences in detail*), contrastful (*R*), inconsistent, contradictory, repugnant (*emphasizing dislike or loathing*), antagonistic, antagonistical, inimical, hostile, adverse (*all five emphasizing hostility*), irreconcilable, heterogeneous, incongruous, incompatible, discordant, dissonant, inharmonious, contrary, converse, inconformable, disparate, contradistinct, discrepant, discriminate (*A*), otherguess (*C*), otherwise (*used only predicatively*); —*referring to things which differ from each other in some quality or attribute. Most of these words have specific implications. "Different" is the most general term.*

Antonyms: see ALIKE, SAME.

2. distinct, separate, other (*than*), nonidentical, unidentical; *spec.* various;—*not implying any difference in kind or character, but merely non-identity.*

Antonyms: see SAME.

differentiate, *v. t.* difference, specialize, discriminate (*emphasizing careful discernment*), sever; *spec.* disequalize, desynonymize, despecificate.

difficult, *a.* **1.** difficile (*A*), hard, troublesome, uneath (*A*), nice, tough (*C*), uneasy (*R*), stiff; *spec.* arduous (*connotes need of continuous effort*), Herculean, skillful (*R*), ticklish, uphill, crabbed, cramp, nice, awkward, wicked (*C*), mean (*C*), hot (*S*), knotty, spiny, thorny, laborious, painful, delicate (*demanding skill and judgment*), obscure (*implies factors only partially understood*), abstruse (*implying remoteness from ordinary life*), mysterious (*connoting conditions not understood*), exacting, stiff, labored.

Antonyms: see EASY.

2. *See* EMBARRASSING, AUSTERE, UNMANAGEABLE.

difficulty, *n.* **1.** hardness; *spec.* arduousness, laboriousness, niceness, delicacy, obscurity, abstruseness, crabbedness.

Antonyms: see EASE.

2. *Spec.* crux, exigency, knot, nodus, perplexity, trouble, obstacle (*implies a hindrance encountered in the way*), obstruction (*connotes something put in the way*), impediment (*connotes something hindering advance*), predicament, dilemma (*implies a choice of two diverse or contrasting conditions*).

3. *See* OBJECTION.

---

diet: *food, regimen.* | **diet:** *assembly, session.* |

---

4. embarrassment (*implies a hindrance to action*), quandary (*implies confused or puzzled state of mind*); *spec.* complication, disagreement, imbroglio.

diffuse, *a.* **1.** wide-spread, scattered, perfuse (*R*), dispersed (*implies being driven widely apart*), dissipated (*implies ineffectual squandering*), disseminated (*implies being widely sown*), dispelled, distributed, disgregate (*R*); *spec.* interdiffuse, effuse, diffusive.

Antonyms: see CONCENTRATED.

2. *See* PROLIX.

diffuse, *v. t.* spread, scatter, strew, disperse, dissipate, disseminate, dispel, distribute, disgregate (*R*); *spec.* suffuse, interdiffuse, effuse, circulate, broadcast (*fig.*).

Antonyms: see CONCENTRATE.

diffuse, *v. t. & i.* spread, scatter, strew, disperse, dissipate, disseminate, dispel, distribute, dispense, dispensate (*R*); *spec.* circulate, radiate, disject, dispread (*A*), dot, dissolve, shed, evaporate, propagate, disgregate (*R*).

Antonyms: see CONCENTRATE.

diffusion, *n.* spreading, spread, strewing, dispersion, dissipation, dissemination, broadcasting, dispelling, distribution, dispensation, dispensing; *spec.* circulation, osmose, osmosis, effluve (*R*), dissolution, cosmopolitanism, propagation, diffluence (*R*), diaspora (*Jewish hist.*), centrifugence.

diffusive, *a.* spreading, scattering, strewing, dispersive, dissipative, disseminative, dispelling, distributive, distributory, dispensative, dispensatory; *spec.* circulatory, circulative, effluent, centrifugal, diffugient (*R*), catalytic, osmotic.

dig, *v. t.* **1.** delve (*A or B, exc. fig.*), grave (*R and A*), excavate; *spec.* costean, grub, dike, ditch, mine, tunnel, scoop, burrow, hollow, spade, root, rootle, spud, rout (*chiefly dial.*), hoe, shovel, mattock, channel, quarry.

2. *To dig up:* exhume (*formal*), dishumate (*B and chiefly fig.*), dishume (*R*), disinhume (*R*), unbury (*R*), unearth, delve (*A or B*), grub; *spec.* disentomb, disinter (*formal*), mine, quarry, expose (*contex.*), reveal (*contex.*).

dig, *v. i.* **1.** grub.

2. work (*contex.*), drudge; *spec.* study.

digest, *n.* abridgment (*contex.*), synopsis (*implies a general view of a subject in brief*), syllabus (*implies an ordered outline*), outline, compendium (*implies the whole presented in small compass*), abstract (*connotes a brief presentation of the important points*), epitome (*implies the substance presented under ordered heads*); *spec.* code, pandect (*connotes a complete* digest).

digestible, *a.* light.

digestion, *n.* decoction; *spec.* bradypepsia (*now R*), eupepsy (*R*), indigestion.

digestive, *a.* peptic (*R*); *spec.* bradypeptic (*R*), eupeptic (*R*).

digging, *a. Referring to animals:* fossorial, fodient (*R*), burrowing, effodient (*R*).

digging, *n.* **1.** dig, delving *or* delve (*A or B*), excavation.

2. excavation (*often with reference to archæological exploration*), exhumation (*formal*), unearthing; *spec.* unburial (*R*), disinterment.

digit, *n. Spec.* finger, thumb, toe, dewclaw.

dignified, *a.* stately, grave (*with reference to countenance*), noble (*implies loftiness of station*), courtly (*denotes manner*), majestic, august (*implies venerability and station*), imposing, portly (*with reference to size; of a human being*), grand, lofty, buskined (*fig.; B*).

Antonyms: see UNDIGNIFIED, BUFFOONISH.

dignify, *v. t.* honor (*contex.*), elevate, promote, lift, exalt; *spec.* dub (*denotes conferring of knighthood*), glorify, idealize, transform (*contex.*), canonize (*denotes formal recognition as a saint*), crown, ennoble.

Antonyms: see ABASE, DEGRADE.

dignifying, *a.* honorific (*formal or B; contex.*), exalting, dignificatory, elevatory (*R*); *spec.* glorifying, doxological (*R*), ennobling.

dignitary, *n.* dignity, official; *spec.* canon, bishop, prelate, governor, *etc.;—implying high rank in office.*

dignity, *n.* **1.** worth, majesty, nobleness, highness, nobility; *spec.* greatness, glory, grandeur, excellence.

Antonyms: see INSIGNIFICANCE.

2. stateliness, augustness, gravity, decorum; *spec.* portliness.

Antonyms: see BUFFOONERY.

3. rank, elevation, station, place, standing, degree, eminence, honor; *spec.* preferment, prelacy, papacy, governorship, *etc.*

4. *See* DIGNITARY.

digress, *v. i.* **1.** *See* DEVIATE.

2. *Referring to discourse, thought, etc.:* deviate, wander, ramble, amble, excurse (*R*), divagate (*R*), evagate (*R*).

digression, *n.* **1.** *See* DEVIATION.

2. *Referring to discourse*: deviation, departure, divagation, excursion, excursus (*formal and intentional digression on a particular aspect of the main subject*), discursion, ecbasis (*R*), evagation (*R*); *spec.* ecbole (*R*), episode.

dike, *n.* **1.** *See* CHANNEL, DITCH.

2. bank, barrier, wall; *spec.* estacade, levee.

Antonyms: see TRENCH.

dilapidated, *a.* decayed, decadent, ruined, rundown, tumble-down.

dilapidation, *n.* decay, unrepair, ruin, disintegrity (*R*).

Antonyms: see INTEGRITY, REPAIR.

dilapidative, *a.* disintegrative, disintegratory, ruinous.

dilatable, *a.* swellable (*R*), extensible, distensible.

dilatation, *n.* expansion, swelling, swell, enlargement, dilation; *spec.* distention, ectasia, aneurism, diastole, varix.

Antonyms: see CONTRACTION.

dilate, *v. i. & t.* **1.** enlarge, expand (*implies*

---

digressive: *discursive.* | **dike,** *v. t.: ditch, drain, bank.* | **dilatory:** *slow.*

---

opening out or widening naturally), amplify (*connotes marked increase*), swell; *spec.* distend (*implies pressure within*), dome, intumesce.
Antonyms: see CONTRACT.
2. enlarge (*in discourse*).
diligent, *a.* **1.** *See* INDUSTRIOUS (*with emphasis on attention to work*), CONSTANT.
2. assiduous (*implies constant attention*), sedulous (*implies careful attention*), studious (*connotes earnestness*),—*referring to actions.*
diluent, *a.* diluting, thinning; *spec.* solvent.
dilute, *a.* diluted, wishy-washy (*C*), drowned (*C; of liquor*).
dilute, *v. t.* thin, weaken, attenuate, reduce; *spec.* adulterate, water (*usually with "down"*).
Antonyms: see CONDENSE, THICKEN.
dim, *a.* **1.** dark (*connotes no light*), dusky, (*connotes partial darkness*), faint (*denotes weak impression*), dull (*connotes little brilliance or luster*), obscure (*suggests heavily overclouded light*), vague (*implies that not sharply defined*); *spec.* misty, pale, hazy, foggy, dreamy.
Antonyms: see BRIGHT.
2. *See* DULL (*mentally*).
dimension, *n.* measure, extent, proportion (*chiefly in pl.*), girt or girth, size.
diminish, *v. t. & i.* lessen, belittle (*implies contempt*), decrease, minify (*R*), minish (*R*), rebate (*R*), reduce, abate (*A*), retrench; *spec.* melt, minimize, narrow, contract, shrink, shrivel, dwindle, lower, taper, shorten, cut, abbreviate, abridge, curtail, attenuate, dwarf, deliquesce, reef, decline, remit (*R*), ease.
Antonyms: see INCREASE, ENLARGE, MAXIMIZE.
diminishing, *a.* diminutive (*A and R, in this sense*), decrescent (*B*), reductive; *spec.* contractive, deliquescent, lessening, decreasing, *etc.*, decrescendo.
diminution, *n.* diminishment, lessening, decreasing, decrement (*B and R*), retrenchment, decrescence (*B*), reduction, abatement; *spec.* shrinkage, shortening, loss, abbreviation, abridgment, curtailment, attenuation, deliquescence, taper, relaxation, remission, defalcation (*A*), rebatement (*R*), drawback, decline, decrescendo, *etc.*
Antonyms: see INCREASE, ENLARGEMENT.
dimness, *n.* dark, darkness, obscurity, *etc. Cf.* DIM, *a.*
Antonyms: see BRIGHTNESS.
din, *n.* noise, bruit (*A*), racket, rumor (*A*); *spec.* clamor, turmoil, hubbub, tumult, uproar, clang, clash, crash, clatter, hullabaloo (*C*), pandemonium (*fig.*), chaos (*contex.*), rumble.
Antonyms: see SILENCE.
din, *v. t.* ring; *spec.* clamor, clang, clash, clatter.
dining, *n.* aristology (*art of dining*), deipnosophism (*R*), eating.
dining room. *Spec.* ordinary (*Eng.*), triclinium (*Roman antiq.*).
dinner, *a.* prandial (*affected or jocose*).
dinner, *n. Spec.* dinnerette.
diocese, *n.* bishopric, bishopry, episcopate, see, province, district (*both contex.*); *spec.* exarchate, eparchy, metropolis, patriarchate.
dip, *v. t.* **1.** immerse, plunge (*suddenly*), dive (*R*), immerge (*R*), douse (*into water*), implunge (*R*); *spec.* bathe, souse, duck, ingulf *or* engulf (*R*), pickle, baptize, soak (*intensive*).
2. *See* WET.
3. *To remove by dipping:* lade, bale, bail, scoop, ladle; *spec.* bucket.
4. bob (*as a flag*), lower.
dip, *v. i.* **1.** immerse, plunge, dive; *spec.* bathe, duck.
Antonyms: see EMERGE.
2. *See* DESCEND.
3. go (*into a subject, book, etc.*).
dip, *n.* **1.** plunge, immersion, dive, immergence; *spec.* douse, bath, intinction, baptism.
Antonyms: See EMERGENCE.
2. *See* DESCENT.
3. bob (*as of a flag*).
diplomacy, *n.* **1.** diplomatics (*R*); *spec.* kingcraft, intrigue.
2. *See* TACT.
diplomatic, *a. Spec.* temporizing, artful, politic; *see* TACTFUL, SCHEMING.
Antonyms: see AWKWARD.
diplomatic agent, diplomatist, diplomat; *spec.* proxenus, chargé (*French*), ambassador, envoy, legate, internuncio, internuncius, consul, plenipotentiary, minister, nuncio, resident.
direct, *a.* **1.** *See* STRAIGHT, IMMEDIATE.
2. straightforward, dunstable (*A or B*), downright, upright, flat, plump; *spec.* pointed, frank, honest, sincere, express, unequivocal, dead.
Antonyms: see AMBIGUOUS, INDIRECT, WANDERING.
3. *Referring to descent:* lineal.
direct, *v. t.* **1.** address (*a letter, remarks, etc.*), destine (*contex.*).
2. aim, point, head, address, turn, bend, determine; *spec.* guide, con (*naut.*), incline, dispose, orient, orientate, level, shape, present, motion, intend (*a Latinism*), dart, guide, lead, steer, run, push, *etc.*
3. *See* BID, MANAGE, CONTROL, REFER (*one to a person, to a place in a book, etc.*).
directable, *a.* amiable, turnable, determinable; *spec.* guidable, leadable, steerable, dirigible, tractable.
direction, *n.* **1.** addressing, address, superscription.
2. aim, aiming, pointing, addressing, turning, turn, determination; *spec.* bent, orientation,

dilemma: *predicament.*
dilettante: *amateur.*
diligence: *application.*
diluvium: *deposit, drift.*
dim-eyed: *blear.*
ding: *dash.*
dingle: *valley.*
dingle, *v. & n.: ring.*
dint: *indent.*
dire: *threatening.*

leading, guidance, steering, compass, piloting, bearing, inclination, intention (*R*).
3. *See* BIDDING, CONTROL, REFERENCE (*as in "reference to a person, book," etc.*).
4. conduct, control, disposal, disposition, surveillance, supervision, oversight; *spec.* command.
5. way, road (*chiefly spec.*), path, course, run, bearing, line, point; *spec.* quarter, side, sense, lead, east, west, north, south, *etc.*, trend.

directly, *adv.* **1.** *Spec.* straight, exactly, lineally, immediately, soon.
2. straightforwardly, downrightly, *etc.*, plump, plumply, flatly, *etc.*

dirge, *n.* monody (*Greek literature*), coronach (*Scot. & Irish*), threnody, requiem (*B, except eccl.*), elegy; *spec.* myriologue (*R*), office (*for the dead*).

dirigible, *a.* directable, navigable.

dirt, *n.* **1.** *Spec.* filth (*intensive, denoting something disgusting*), grime (*implies dirt rubbed or worn in*), clart (*dial.*), mire (*connotes moisture and density*), muck (*connotes manure in moist or decayed state*), fouling, mud, sludge (*implies a deposit of sediment*), dust, impurity, *etc.*
2. *See* EARTH.
3. *Spec.* meanness, sordidness, obscenity, nastiness.
4. (*S*) *for* money.

dirt eating, geophagy.

dirtied, *a.* defiled, polluted, pollute, fouled.

dirtiness, *n. Spec.* filthiness, filth, foulness, *etc.*
Antonyms: see PURITY.

dirty, *a.* **1.** *Spec.* grimy, filthy, foul, clart *or* clarty (*dial.*), unclean, uncleanly, impure (*R*), miry, muddy, mucky, nasty, vile, soily, cindery, grubby; *see* FILTHY, FOUL.
Antonyms: see CLEAN, SPOTLESS.
2. *See* DISCREDITABLE, MEAN, INDECENT, STORMY.

dirty, *v. t.* defile, foul, soil, sully (*chiefly fig.*), filthify (*R*); *spec.* grime, pollute, dust, muddy, mire, colly (*A, or dial.*), begrime, slobber (*chiefly dial.*), tar, bedraggle, smirch, tarnish, spot.
Antonyms: see CLEAN, PURIFY.

dirtying, *n.* defilement, fouling, soiling, *etc.*

dis-. *The prefix "dis-" has usually a stronger force than the prefixes "un-" and "in-"; as in "unrelated," "disrelated"; "unsatisfied," "dissatisfied"; "inability," "disability," etc.*

disability, *n.* **1.** *Referring to the condition:* inability (*while* disability *connotes loss of ability,* inability *emphasizes absence of power or capacity*), incapacity, disablement; *spec.* disqualification (*connotes failure to attain to a standard*), incompetence (*emphasizes lack of skill or knowledge*), superannuation (*implies excessive age*), unfitness.
Antonyms: see ABILITY.
2. *Referring to a defect:* incapacity, cripplehood (*R*), crippleness (*R*), crippledom (*R*), lameness (*chiefly spec.*); *spec.* palsy, paralysis, impotence, handicap, superannuation.
Antonyms: see ABILITY.

disable, *v. t.* **1.** incapacitate, discapacitate (*R*), disenable; *spec.* disqualify, unfit, invalidate, weaken.
Antonyms: see ENABLE.
2. incapacitate, impair, cripple, becripple (*intensive*), lame (*chiefly spec.*), maim, exhaust, prostrate; *spec.* palsy, paralyze, strangle, choke, throttle, dishabilitate (*Scots law*), disempower (*R*), gravel, silence, demoralize, unnerve, founder, dry-founder, hamstring, cramp, disarm, hock, hough.

disabled, *a.* incapacitated, crippled, lamed, lame, halt (*B or dignified*), halting, *etc.; spec.* palsied, superannuate, hoofbound, foundered, groggy (*C*), hors de combat (*French*), game.

disadvantage, *n.* **1.** inconvenience, discommodity, disinterest (*R*); *spec.* hindrance, detriment, handicap, drawback, check, disservice, penalty.
Antonyms: see ADVANTAGE, GOOD.
2. *See* LOSS.

disadvantageous, *a.* inconvenient, awkward, discommodious; *spec.* unfavorable, detrimental, harmful, injurious, hurtful.
Antonyms: see ADVANTAGEOUS.

disafforest, *v. t.* deforest (*law or forestry*), disforest, diswood (*R*), deafforest (*R*).

disagree, *v. i.* differ (*contex.*), dissent, clash, conflict; *spec.* quarrel, dispute, vary, diverge.
Antonyms: see AGREE, CONSPIRE, CORRESPOND.

disagreeable, *a.* unpleasant, distasteful, *spec.* nasty (*C in U. S.*), repulsive, nauseous (*intensive*), cantankerous, grouchy (*C*), uncongenial, hateful, offensive.
Antonyms: see AGREEABLE, AFFECTIONATE.

disagreeing, *a.* **1.** different, conflictory, conflicting, incongruent, incongruous, inaccordant, discordant, jarring, clashing, contradictory, contrary, repugnant, divided (*as persons*), factious, inconsonant, discrepant.
2. *See* DISSENTIENT.
The word "disagreeing" is seldom used adjectively.

disagreement, *n.* **1.** difference (*connotes merely the fact of unlikeness*), discord (*connotes conflict*); clashing, clash, disunion, disunity.
Antonyms: see SECESSION.
2. conflict, division, incongruence, incongruousness (*emphasizes lack of harmony and consistency*), inaccordance, inaccordancy (*R*), contrariety, discord, discordance, discordancy, opposition, variance, division, clash, difficulty; *see* DISSENSION.
Antonyms: see AGREEMENT, CONSPIRACY.
3. *See* DIFFERENCE, DISPUTE, QUARREL.

disappear, *v. i.* **1.** vanish, evanish (*emphatic; B*), die (*used with "away," "out," or "down"*),

---

disadvise: *discourage.*
disaffect: *alienate, displease.*
disaffirm: *deny.*
disaffirmance: *denial.*
disagreeable: *unpleasant.*
disallow: *deny, reject, refuse.*
disannul: *invalidate.*

evanesce, sink, go; *spec.* melt, dry, evaporate, dive, dissolve (*often with "into"*), fly (*with "away"*), skip (*C*), fade (*C*, *except spec.*), beat it (*S*), scoot (*S*).
Antonyms: see APPEAR.
2. *See* DECAY, END.
disappearance, *n.* **1.** vanishment (*R*), vanishing, evanescence, evanishment (*R*), dissolution, evanition (*R*), fade-out (*S*).
Antonyms: see APPEARANCE.
2. *See* OBSOLESCENCE.
disappearing, *a.* vanishing, evanescent, *etc.*; *see* OBSOLESCENT.
disarm, *v. t.* unarm, disweapon (*R*); *spec.* diswhip (*R*), dismail (*A*), dishelm, unsting (*R*); dismantle (*of a ship or fortress*).
Antonyms: see ARM.
disarrange, *v. t.* **1.** disorder, disturb, derange, mix up, mix, disarray (*chiefly mil.*), dislocate; discompose (*obs.*); *spec.* confuse, tangle, entangle, embroil, topsy-turvy (*R*), topsy-turvyfy (*R; humorous*), muss (*U. S.; often used with "up"*), mess (*C*), upset, jumble, ruffle, dishevel, rumple, tousle, rummage (*often used with "over"*), break, unsettle, misplace, mislay, misfile, tumble.
Antonyms: see ARRANGE, ADJUST, TIDY.
2. *See* DISCONCERT.
disarrange, *a.* topsy-turvy, hugger-mugger, discomposed, *etc.*
disbelief, *n.* discredit, unbelief (*implies only non-belief*); *spec.* incredulity (*implies inability or unwillingness to believe*), infidelity (*implies lack of belief*), scepticism (*implies a critical attitude in the absence of sure knowledge*), rationalism (*implies disbelief in the supernatural*), agnosticism (*connotes suspension of judgment through absence of knowledge*).
disbelieve, *v. t.* discredit, miscredit (*R*); *spec.* doubt, reject.
discerning, *a.* bright, discriminating, discriminative (*both implying ability to make careful distinction*), discriminant (*R*), nice (*implies fineness of judgment*), subtle (*implies refined analysis*), acute (*emphasizes sharpness of perception and understanding*), clear-sighted, clear-headed, long-headed (*implies foresight*), sharp, percipient (*R*), long-sighted, perspicacious (*implies clearness and understanding*), deep, sagacious, keen, astute, piercing, judicious (*often spec.*), eagle-eyed, Argus-eyed (*fig.*); *spec.* discreet, searching.
Antonyms: see BLIND.
discernment, *n.* **1.** *See* DISTINCTION, DISCOVERY, PERCEPTION.
2. discrimination, sagacity (*implies penetration and judgment*), acumen (*implies experience and understanding*), shrewdness (*implies sharpness of mind and practical intelligence*), sharpness, brightness, depth, penetration, perspicacity, perspicaciousness (*R*), insight (*implies understanding*), clear-headedness, astuteness (*implies cleverness and skill*), keenness, long-headedness, sharpness, judiciousness (*often spec.*); *spec.* discretion, tact, judgment.
Antonyms: see STUPIDITY.
discharge, *v. t.* **1.** *See* UNLOAD.
2. shoot, fire; *spec.* volley, empty, play, turn, direct;—*in reference to a bow, gun, hose, etc.*
Antonyms: see LOAD.
3. project, expel, shoot, fire, throw; *spec.* direct, deliver, play, explode,—*in reference to missiles.*
4. dismiss, cashier, discard, remove, fire (*S*), drop (*U. S. colleges and schools*), send down (*Oxford and Cambridge*), sack (*S*), can (*C*), bounce (*S, U. S.*), dispost (*R*), kick (*used with "out"; C*), depose (*chiefly spec.*); *spec.* disemploy (*R*), retire, demit (*A*), degrade, displace, expel, break (*C*), drop, promote (*in some other business or organization*), pension, liquidate (*absolutistic euphemism*).
Antonyms: see HIRE, APPOINT.
5. *See* FREE (*as from obligation, confinement, etc.*), ACQUIT, PERFORM, PAY, SATISFY, DEFRAY, EMIT, EXPEL, EXCRETE.
6. diselectrify (*R*).
discharge, *v. i.* **1.** *See* UNLOAD.
2. *Referring to a stream:* disembogue, empty, fall, flow.
3. *Referring to a sore, etc.:* run, flow; *spec.* gleet, maturate.
discharge, *n.* **1.** unloading.
2. shooting, firing, fire; *spec.* play, aim, direction,—*in reference to a bow, gun, etc.*
3. projection, expulsion, firing, shooting; *spec.* play, delivery, round, burst, salvo, salute, fusillade, volley;—*in reference to missiles.*
4. dismissal, remove (*R*), cashierment (*R*), discardment (*R*), bounce (*R, U. S.*), sack (*S*), removal, deposition (*chiefly spec.*); *spec.* disemployment (*R*), demission (*A*), degradation, displacement, expulsion, liquidation (*euphemistic*), congé (*French*), destitution (*A*).
5. *See* ACQUITTAL, ACQUITTANCE, PERFORMANCE, PAYMENT, SATISFACTION, ANNULMENT, DEFRAYAL, EMISSION, EXPULSION, EXCRETION, FREEING (*as from obligation, confinement, etc.*).
6. outflow, run-off, disemboguement, emptying;—*referring to flowing waters, etc.*
7. *Referring to a sore, etc.:* flow, flux, issue; *spec.* profluvium, defluxion, rheum, lochia, ichor, gleet.
disciform, *a.* circular, discoidal, discoid, rotate.

---

disappoint: *desert, defeat.*
disapprove: *condemn, reject.*
disarray: *disarrange, undress.*
disaster: *misfortune.*
disastrous: *unfortunate.*
disavow: *disclaim.*
disband: *scatter.*
disbandment: *dispersal.*
disbar: *degrade.*
disbark: *decorticate.*
disbelief: *unbelief.*
disbeliever: *infidel.*
disbench: *abase, degrade.*
disburden: *free, unload.*
disburse: *expend.*
discard: *reject, abandon, disuse.*
discern: *distinguish, discover, perceive, see.*

---

disciple, *n.* adherent (*implies close following*), follower, co-follower, believer, convert, sectary (*R*), sectator (*R*), progeny (*collective pl.; fig.*), pupil (*implies youth in age, faith, or learning*), scholar (*emphasizes interest and application*), student (*implies study of a particular body of instruction*); *spec.* chela (*Hinduism*), evangelist, apostle, missionary.

disciplinarian, *n.* martinet.

disciplinary, *a. Spec.* penitentiary.

discipline, *n.* **1.** *See* TRAINING, ART, ORDER, PUNISHMENT.

2. control (*not a good synonym*), government.

discipline, *v. t.* **1.** tutor.

2. *See* TRAIN, PUNISH, WHIP.

disclaim, *v. t.* deny, renounce (*implies former adherence or acceptance*), repudiate (*implies refusal to accept as right or just*), disown (*implies rejection as one's own*), disavow (*implies refusal to accept responsibility for a thing*), disacknowledge (*R*); *spec.* abjure (*implies renunciation of claim or allegiance*).

Antonyms: see CLAIM, AVOW.

disclaimer, *n.* denial, abjuration, renunciation, repudiation, disowning, disavowal, disclamation (*R*), disownment, disacknowledgment (*R*).

Antonyms: see CLAIM.

disclose, *v. t.* **1.** *See* UNCOVER.

2. show, reveal (*as not known*), divulge (*as of a secret*), exhibit, expose (*as hidden*), uncover (*as covered*), discover, bare, unveil, display, parade, flaunt (*implies a challenge*), manifest, evince (*by some sign or token*), betray, bewray (*A*), publish, tell, blab, whisper, declare, meld (*cards*), spill, demonstrate, uncloak, unburden, unbundle (*R*), speak, confess, unshroud, unfold, uncurtain, develop, uncase, divulgate (*B*), unearth, open, discloud, blow (*now S*), evulgate (*R*), communicate;—*all having more or less specific senses.*

Antonyms: see HIDE.

disclosing, *a.* exhibitory, manifestive, expositive, revelative, revelatory, evincive.

disclosure, *n.* **1.** *Spec.* uncovering.

2. show, showing, revelation, reveal (*R*), revealment, uncovering, discovery (*A*), unveiling, baring, unfolding, development, exhibition, exposure, exposal, exposé (*French*), display, parade, flaunt, flaunting, manifestation, monstration, evincement, divulgement, divulgation (*B*), divulgence, betrayal, bewrayal (*A*), apocalypse (*R or B*), publication, publicity, telling, blabbing, whispering, whisper, declaration, *etc.;—all more or less specific in meaning.*

Antonyms: see HIDING.

discomfit, *v. t.* **1.** *See* DEFEAT.

2. embarrass (*implies hindrance of action*), disconcert (*implies disturbance of mind*), confound, confuse, abash, demoralize; *spec.* squelch (*C or S*).

discomfiture, *n.* **1.** *See* DEFEAT.

2. embarrassment, confusion, abashment, demoralization, disconcertion, disconcertedness.

discomfort, *v. t.* distress; *spec.* annoy, disturb, embarrass, pain, grieve.

Antonyms: see COMFORT.

discomfort, *n.* uneasiness, distress; *spec.* malaise (*French*), disease (*A*); *see* ANNOYANCE, EMBARRASSMENT, PAIN, GRIEF.

Antonyms: see COMFORT, WELL-BEING.

disconcert, *v. t.* **1.** *Referring to plans, etc.:* disarrange, upset, disturb, ruin (*C, intensive*), spoil.

2. *Referring to persons:* disturb, upset, bewilder, demoralize, unbalance, faze (*C*), buffalo (*S*); *see* ABASH, CONFUSE, EMBARRASS, DISCOMFIT.

Antonyms: see ASSURE.

disconcertedness, *n.* disarrangement, upset (*C*), demoralization, disconcertion; *spec.* abashment, confusion, embarrassment, discomfiture.

Antonyms: see ASSURANCE.

disconnect, *v. t.* detach, separate, disunite, disjoin, disjoint, dissociate, uncombine (*R*); *spec.* sever, uncouple, unscrew, disengage, dislink, free.

Antonyms: see CONNECT, JOIN.

disconsolate, *a.* **1.** sorrowful, melancholy, woeful, gloomy, spiritless, glum, forlorn; *spec.* inconsolable, comfortless, desolate; *see* HOPELESS, SAD.

2. *See* DEPRESSING.

discontent, *n.* **1.** discontentedness, discontentment, miscontent (*R*), miscontentment (*R*), malcontentment (*R*), malcontent (*R*), dissatisfaction, dissatisfiedness, heartburn (*fig.*); *see* LONGING.

Antonyms: see SATISFACTION.

2. discontentee (*A*), malcontent (*the usual word in this sense*).

discontented, *a.* discontent, uncontented, discontentful (*A*), miscontent (*A*), malcontent dissatisfied, glum; *spec.* weary, sour (*S*), soured (*S*).

Antonyms: see SATISFIED.

discontinuous, *a.* incontinuous (*R*), broken, discrete, disjunct (*R*), disconnected, interrupted; *see* INTERMITTENT, RECURRENT, INCONSEQUENT.

Antonyms: see CONTINUOUS.

discontinuousness, *n.* discontinuity, brokenness, discreteness, discretion (*R*), disjunction (*R*), disconnectedness, *etc.*

discord, *n.* **1.** *See* DISAGREEMENT, DISPUTE, QUARREL, DISSENSION, UPROAR.

2. *Referring to sound:* discordance, discordancy, dissonance, disharmony, jar (*R*), cacophony (*chiefly music or pedantic*), jangle; *spec.* wolf.

Antonyms: see HARMONY.

discordance, *n.* **1.** *See* DISAGREEMENT, DIFFERENCE, DISCORD.

2. harshness, cacophony (*chiefly music or B*), dissonance, discordancy.

Antonyms: see HARMONY, MELODY.

discordant, *a.* **1.** *See* DISAGREEING, DIFFERENT, DISPUTATIOUS, QUARRELSOME, CLASHING.

discolor, *v. t.: color, stain.*
discommode: *inconvenience.*
discompose: *agitate.*
discontent, *v. t.: displease.*
discontent, *a.: discontented.*

2. harsh, dissonant, inharmonious, inconsonant, unsweet (*R*), sour (*C or S*), disharmonic (*R*), cacophonous (*chiefly music or B*), untunable (*R*), unmelodic, tuneless, rough, jarring, jangling, jangly (*R*), rude, clashing, ragged.
Antonyms: see AGREEING, HARMONIOUS, MELODIOUS.

discourage, *v. t.* **1.** depress, dishearten, dismay, (*implies confusion and loss of spirit*), daunt (*implies intimidation and dismay*); *spec.* unman (*a man*).
Antonyms: see CHEER, ENCOURAGE, EMBOLDEN.
2. *See* RESTRAIN.
3. discountenance, disfavor, disapprove; *spec.* disadvise, dissuade (*R*), dehort (*R*), veto, pan (*C*);—*in reference to a proposed action.*
Antonyms: see FAVOR.

discouragement, *n.* **1.** depression, disheartening, disheartenment, dismay.
Antonyms: see CHEER.
2. *Referring to that which discourages:* damper, deterrent, wet blanket (*C*).
3. discountenance, disfavor; *spec.* disadvisement, dissuasion (*R*), dishortation (*R*).

discouraging, *a.* **1.** *See* DEPRESSING.
2. discountenancing, disfavoring, disapproving; *spec.* dissuasive (*R*), dehortative (*R*), dehortatory (*R*).

discourse, *n.* **1.** *See* CONVERSATION, TALK.
2. composition, exercitation (*R*), dissertation, disquisition, preachment, peroration (*R or B*), descant (*B*), rhesis (*R*), lucubration (*often derogatory*); *spec.* thesis, excursus, speech, oration, treatise, homily, eulogy, colloquy, exhortation, address, soliloquy, recital, sermon.

discourse, *v. i.* dissertate (*formal*), dissert (*R*), lucubrate (*often derogatory*), expatiate; *spec.* speak, write, treat, yarn (*C*), sermonize; *see* DISCUSS.

discover, *v. t.* **1.** ascertain, spot (*S*), identify, invent (*R*), detect, discern, recognize, find, get, elicit, contrive, devise; *spec.* distinguish, calculate, descry, espy, spy, sight, hear, feel, sense, learn, strike, determine, unearth, disinter, exhume, smell, catch.
2. *See* UNCOVER.

discoverable, *a.* ascertainable, determinable, detectable, discernible, distinguishable, calculatable, reperible (*R*), findable, sensible, *etc.*

discovery, *n.* **1.** ascertainment (*emphasizes attaining certainty*), device, design, invention (*implies finding out what was unknown previously*), contrivance (*implies a clever device or mechanism*), detection (*implies discovery of what was concealed*), disclosure, discernment (*implies sharp and careful observation*); *spec.* distinction, distinguishment, determination, finding, calculation (*implies working with known factors*), descrial, espial, spying, sighting, hearing, feeling, sensing, learning, strike, striking, hitting, unearthing, mare's nest (*humorous*), find (*C*), exposure, exposé.
2. *Spec.* uncovering.

discredit, *n.* **1.** disrepute, disparagement, disrespect, disesteem, misesteem, dishonor, disgrace, ill-favor, ill-repute, shame, scandal, humiliation, ignominy, disfavor, infamy, contumely, contempt, attaint, obloquy, opprobrium, reproach, odium. *Most of these synonyms have specific implications.*
Antonyms: see HONOR.
2. *Referring to that which brings disesteem, etc.:* disgrace, dishonor, blot, smirch, stain, reproach, *etc.*
Antonyms: see HONOR.
3. *See* DISBELIEF.

discredit, *v. t.* **1.** disparage (*connotes slight or depreciative comment*), decry (*implies public condemnation*), dishonor, disgrace, shame, scandalize, stigmatize, attaint, stain, defame (*A*), impeach (*implies legal or formal charges against one in official position*), derogate (*R or A*), depreciate (*implies undervaluation*), compromise, infamize (*R*), blot, infame (*A*), dispraise (*R*), disfame (*R*), endamage (*R*), degrade, smirch. *Most of these synonyms have specific implications.*
Antonyms: see CONFIRM, HONOR, FLATTER.
2. *See* DISBELIEVE.

discreditable, *a.* disreputable, disrespectable, dishonorable, unworthy, derogatory, derogative, disgraceful, degrading, shameful, inglorious, scandalous, ignoble, dishonest (*A*), ignominious, blameworthy, infamous, contumelious, opprobrious, foul, reproachful, odious, unworshipful (*R*), indign (*R*), dirty, shady, crooked. *Most of these synonyms have specific implications.*
Antonyms: see HONORABLE.

discursive, *a.* **1.** *See* WANDERING.
2. digressive, rambling, wandering, desultory, touch-and-go (*C*), cursory, unconnected, vague, loose, excursive (*R*), long-winded.
Antonyms: see CONCISE.

discuss, *v. t. & i.* debate (*to discuss formally*), discourse (*v. i.; implying discussion at length*), talk (*C; often implies informality*), canvass (*implies reviewing in detail*), treat (*implies specific detail*), conjabble (*C*); *spec.* reason, dialogize (*with another*), argue (*implies dispute*), sift, ventilate (*so as to make public*), criticize (*implies sharp evaluation*), critique, review,

---

discount, *v. t.: buy.*
discount, *n.: deduction, interest.*
discountenance: *abash, condemn, discourage.*
discourse, *v. t.: narrate, discuss, speak.*
discourteous: *impolite.*
discourtesy: *impoliteness.*
discreet: *judicious, prudent.*
discrepant: *disagreeing, different.*
discrete: *discontinuous, separate, distinct.*
discretion: *decision, choice, will, prudence.*
discriminate: *differentiate, distinguish.*
discriminating: *discerning, delicate, nice.*
discrimination: *distinction, discernment, delicacy, nicety.*
discriminative: *nice, distinctive, discerning.*

---

dispute (*implies persistent questioning*), agitate, moot.

discussion, *n.* debate (*formal discussion*), canvass, treatment, parlance (*A*), parle (*A*), parley (*A*), démelé (*French*); *spec.* agitation, argument, ventilation, pilpul, dialogism, excursus, disputation, review.

disease, *n.* **1.** ailment (*does not imply acute malady*), malady (*a general term*), disorder, sickness, distemperature (*R*), ill (*B*), complaint, distemper, misaffection (*R*), evil (*A exc. in phrases*); *spec.* pest, infection, contagion, dyscrasia, intemperies (*R*), idiopathy, pestilence, plague, cacoëthes, deuteropathy, decline, epizoötic, epizoöty, enzoötic.
Antonyms: see REMEDY.
2. *See* UNHEALTH.

disease, *v. t.* disorder, indispose (*chiefly in p. p., "indisposed"*), distemper, affect; *spec.* infect.
Antonyms: see CURE, DISINFECT.

diseased, *a.* ailing (*contex.*), ill, sick, distempered, sickly, unsound, unwell, dyscrasic (*R*), affected; *spec.* sickish.

disembark, *v. t. & i.* land, debark.

disembarrass, *v. t.* relieve, debarrass (*R*).
Antonyms: see EMBARRASS.

disembodied, *a.* incorporeal, unbodied (*R*), disincarnate (*R*), ecstatic (*R*).
Antonyms: see MATERIAL.

disembowel, *v. t.* eviscerate, embowel (*R*), disbowel (*R*), bowel (*R*), gut, viscerate (*R*), deviscerate (*R*), exenterate (*R; exc. fig.*); *spec.* paunch, gib, draw, gill (*R*), gralloch, dress (*of game, fish, or fowl*).

disenchant, *v. t.* disencharm (*R*), disillusion, unwitch (*R*), disentrance, release, free, restore.
Antonyms: see BEWITCH.

disentangle, *v. t.* disengage, untangle, ravel, unravel, disentrammel (*R*), untwine, elaqueate (*R*), clear, disinvolve (*R*); *spec.* comb, tease.
Antonyms: see ENTANGLE.

disfavor, *n.* **1.** *Spec.* dislike, condemnation, discredit, slight, disparagement, displeasure, discouragement.
2. *See* UNKINDNESS.

disguise, *v. t.* hide, conceal, cover, cloak, clothe, mask, veil, dissemble (*usually implying evil intent*), dissimulate (*usually implying evil intent*), veneer (*fig.*), color, shroud, muffle;—*implying a hiding or obscuring by a false or counterfeit appearance, the words mostly having specific implications suggested by their literal senses.*

disguise, *n.* concealment, cover, cloak, mask (*spec. or fig.*), veil, dissemblance, dissimulation, veneer, color, shroud, muffler, masque, masquerade (*spec. or fig.*), camouflage,—*mostly having specific implications.*

disguised, *a.* feigned, cloaked, masked, veiled, hidden, concealed, incognita (*fem.*), incognito (*masc.*), camouflaged.

disgust, *n.* **1.** distaste (*contex.*), repletion, surfeit, nausea, loathing.
Antonyms: see PLEASURE.
2. dislike (*contex.*), aversion (*connotes an active dislike of some standing*), abhorrence (*connotes horror and detestation*), repugnance (*implies a hostile attitude*), abomination (*connotes intense loathing and disgust*), loathing, displeasure (*R*).
Antonyms: see APPETITE.

disgust, *v. t.* **1.** displease (*contex.*), sicken, nauseate, revolt (*a contex. sense*), turn (*contex.*)
Antonyms: see PLEASE, ENTICE.
2. *See* REPEL.

disgusting, *a.* **1.** displeasing (*contex.*), distasteful (*contex.*), nauseating, nauseous, loathly (*B*), loathful (*now R*), loathsome, sickening, foul, revolting, repulsive.
Antonyms: see PLEASANT.
2. abominable, revolting, foul, repulsive, shocking, hateful, repugnant, abhorrent, odious, lousy (*S*), putrid (*C*).
Antonyms: see ATTRACTIVE.

dish, *n.* vessel (*contex.*); *spec.* crock, plate, platter, bowl, cup, saucer, tureen, pitcher, tray, doubler (*large; A or dial.*), plat (*French*), epergne, bonbonnière (*French*), skillet, saucepan, spider, casserole, pan, gravy boat, tumbler, goblet, caraffe, *etc.*

dishevel, *v. t.* disorder, touse, tumble, tousle, ruffle, muss.

disheveled, *a.* disordered, tously, tousled, unkempt, tumbled, mussy, mussed (*often with "up"*).
Antonyms: see DISHEVEL.

dishonest, *a.* untrustworthy (*contex.*), crooked, faithless, false, dishonorable; *spec.* corrupt, sinister, knavish, fraudulent, deceitful, disingenuous, slippery, perfidious, treacherous, shyster (*usually of a lawyer*).
Antonyms: see HONEST, CONSCIENTIOUS, VIRTUOUS.

dishonesty, *n.* untrustworthiness (*contex.*), crookedness, faithlessness, falsity, improbity (*R*), falsehood; *spec.* knavery, knavishness, fraud, fraudulence, perfidiousness, perfidy, treachery, corruption.
Antonyms: see HONESTY, VIRTUE.

disinclination, *n.* indisposition, indisposedness; *spec.* unwillingness, reluctance, reluctancy, grudgingness, aversion (*connotes habitual unwillingness*), dislike, distaste, disaffection, repugnance (*intensive*).
Antonyms: see INCLINATION.

disinfect, *v. t.* sanitize, sanitate, cleanse (*implies thoroughness*), sterilize; *spec.* fumigate, listerize, asepticize, steam, cauterize.
Antonyms: see DISEASE, POISON.

disingenuous, *a.* artful, deceitful.

disdain, *n.: contempt.*
disdain, *v. t.: despise.*
disenthrall: *free.*
disenthrone: *depose.*
disfavor, *v. t.: dislike, condemn, discourage.*
disfigure: *deface, deform.*
disfurnish: *strip, dismantle.*
disgorge: *vomit, eject, relinquish.*
disgrace: *discredit, abase, degrade.*
disgraceful: *discreditable.*
disgruntle: *displease.*
dish, *v. t.: serve, ruin, hollow.*
dishabille: *undress.*
disincline: *indispose.*
disinclined: *opposed, unwilling.*

disinherit, *v. t.* disown, exheredate (*R*), cut off.

disinheritance, *n.* disowning, exheredation (*R*), disherison (*tech. or B*), disinherison (*R*), disownment.

disintegrate, *v. t. & i.* decompose, resolve (*R*), break (*with "up" or "down"*), separate (*contex.*); *spec.* dissolve, analyze, crumble, crumb, decay, weather, disgregate, diffuse, fall (*with "to pieces"*).
Antonyms: see COMPOSE.

disintegration, *n.* decomposition, resolution (*R*), analysis, *etc.*

disinter, *v. t.* dig (*contex.*), dishume, unbury, exhume, unearth, disinhume; *spec.* disentomb, uncharnel (*R*).
Antonyms: see BURY.

disinterment, *n.* digging (*contex.*), exhumation; *spec.* disentombment.
Antonyms: see BURIAL.

disjoint, *v. t.* **1.** joint; *spec.* break.
2. *See* DISUNITE, DISCONNECT, DISLOCATE.

disk, *n.* circle; *spec.* saucer, button, squail, paten, roundel, roundlet, sabot, flan, discus, quoit (*class antiq.*), umbrella (*zoöl.*).

disk-shaped, *a.* placentoid (*tech.; R*).

dislike, *n.* **1.** *Spec.* disfavor, antipathy (*connotes involuntary dislike*); aversion (*connotes habitual dislike*), distaste, disrelish, disgust, repugnance, repulsion, displeasure, objection, disinclination, dyspathy, misliking, detestation, abhorrence, abomination, unfriendliness, ill-will, disaffection, dislove (*nonce word*), hostility, enmity, dispeace (*R*), animosity, hate, hatred, malevolence, malice, spite (*A or dial.*). *The words from "dislike" to "abomination" refer especially to an emotion or feeling prompting avoidance and aroused by contact with or experience of, the object in question; the words from "unfriendliness" to "malevolence" refer especially to the emotion, feeling, or attitude aroused by some more intimate relation involving self-interest.* Dislike *is the broadest term, applying to any degree of emotion.*
Antonyms: see AFFECTION, ENJOYMENT, LIKING.
2. *See* UNWILLINGNESS, OPPOSITION.

dislike, *v. t. Spec.* distaste, disrelish, disfavor, loathe, detest, abhor, abominate, hate, mislike (*R*), resent. *See* DISLIKE, *n., above.*
Antonyms: see LIKE, ENJOY.

disliked, *a. Spec.* detested, hated, loathed, abhorred, despised, contemned, *etc.*
Antonyms: see BELOVED.

dislocate, *v. t.* **1.** displace, disjoint; *spec.* (*referring to bones*) luxate, slip, put (*with "out"*), disarticulate, exarticulate (*R*), splay.
2. *See* DISARRANGE, DISORGANIZE.

dislocated, *a.* shotten.

dislodge, *v. t.* **1.** displace, dispel, unlodge (*R*); *spec.* unrest (*R*), dismount, unnest.
Antonyms: see DEPOSIT, FIX.
2. remove, expel, oust; *spec.* uncamp (*R*), eject, evict, dispossess.

dismantle, *v. t.* **1.** *See* STRIP.
2. unfurnish, strip, disfurnish; *spec.* unrig, dismast, disarm.
Antonyms: see EQUIP.
3. destroy (*contex.*); *spec.* raze, disembattle, wreck.

dismay, *v. t.* **1.** discourage (*contex.*), appall (*connotes overcoming the spirit through sudden and great fear*), daunt (*connotes deprivation of activity*).
Antonyms: see ASSURE.
2. *See* FRIGHTEN.

dismay, *n.* discouragement, consternation (*implies complete confusion,* terror.

dismember, *v. t.* **1.** disjoint, dislimb (*R*), limb (*R*), piecemeal (*R*), rend, maim; *spec.* joint.
2. *See* MUTILATE.

dismiss, *v. t.* **1.** *To send away: spec.* dissolve, disperse.
Antonyms: see RECALL.
2. *See* DISCHARGE.
3. *To put away, as out of consideration: spec.* scout, banish.

dismount, *v. i.* alight, descend.

dismount, *v. t.* **1.** *See* DISPLACE, DISLODGE.
2. *Spec.* unhorse, dishorse.

disobedience, *n.* nonobedience (*connotes mere failure to obey*), disobeyal (*R*), mutiny (*implies concerted insubordination*), noncompliance *or* noncompliancy (*emphasizes fact of failure to comply*), nonobservance, disregard (*implies conscious neglect*); *spec.* insubordination (*implies unruly defiance of authority*), recalcitrance (*implies stubbornness*), contumacy (*emphasizes stubbornness and perverseness*), recusancy, recusance (*implies objection on principle to an established regulation*), undutifulness, rebellion, insurrection (*against constituted authority*), indiscipline, defiance, unruliness, waywardness, frowardness (*A*), perverseness (*implies willful and obstinate* disobedience).
Antonyms: see OBEDIENCE.

disobedient, *n.* nonobedient, mutinous (*chiefly spec.*), noncompliant, disregardful; *spec.* insubordinate, contumacious, recalcitrant, recusant, undutiful, rebellious, unsubmissive (*R*), perverse, rebel, froward (*A*), unruly, wayward, defiant.
Antonyms: see OBEDIENT, COMPLAISANT, COMPLIANT.

disobey, *v. t.* **1.** *Spec.* ignore, defy, resist, rebel (*with "against"*),—*in reference to persons.*
2. transgress, disregard, ignore, shirk, rebel (*with "against"*),—*in reference to commands.*
Antonyms: see OBEY.

disorder, *n.* **1.** disarrangement, misarrangement, deray (*A*), misorder (*R*), disarray, chaos, *spec.* confusion, hodgepodge, topsy-turvy, ir-

---

disjoin: *disunite, disconnect.*
disjoint: *disunite, disconnect, dislocate.*
dislodgment: *displacement, removal, expulsion.*
disloyal: *unfaithful.*
dismal: *depressing, depressed, cheerless.*

regularity, litter, jumble, medley, muddle, mess, deordination (*R*), entanglement, tangle, dishevelment, muss (*U. S.*), untidiness.

Antonyms: see ARRANGEMENT.

2. *See* DISTURBANCE, DERANGEMENT, DISORGANIZATION, DISEASE, AILMENT.

disorderly, *a.* **1.** *Spec.* irregular; immethodical, desultory (*implies lack of orderly connection*), messy (*C*), untidy, orderless, unsystematic, hugger-mugger, chaotic, confused, anomalous (*implies failure to fit into an order or classification*).

Antonyms: see ORDERLY.

2. irregular, lawless; *spec.* riotous, rough, anarchic, turbulent, troublous, tumultuous, rowdy, rowdyish, boisterous, topsy-turvy, rough-and-tumble, mobbish, mutinous, unquiet.

Antonyms: see LAW-ABIDING.

disorganization, *n.* disarrangement, disruption, disorder, derangement, confusion, jumble, muddle; *spec.* demoralization, embarrassment, dislocation.

Antonyms: see ORGANIZATION.

disorganize, *v. t.* disarrange, disorder, derange, upset, disrupt; *spec.* demoralize, dislocate, demobilize, jumble, muddle.

Antonyms: see ORGANIZE.

disparage, *v. t.* **1.** *See* DISCREDIT.

2. depreciate, asperse, decry, defame, deprecate, traduce, belie (*A or R*), calumniate, scandalize (*R*), blackmouth (*R*), denigrate (*B*), blacken, detract (*R*), mince (*R*), diminish (*A*), lessen (*A*), disconsider (*R*), disprize (*A*), derogate (*A*), dehonestate (*R*); *spec.* bedaub, belittle, minimize, vilify, underpraise, backbite, slur, slander, libel.

Antonyms: see COMPLIMENT, PRAISE, ENNOBLE.

disparagement, *n.* **1.** *See* DISCREDIT.

2. depreciation, decrial, defamation, aspersion, reflection, traduction, scandalization, calumny, calumniation (*implies malice and false report*), denigration (*B*), blackening, detraction, diminution (*R*), disconsideration (*R*), derogation; *spec.* dehonestation (*R*), dispraise, blasphemy, vilification, slurring, backbiting, slander, libel.

Antonyms: see COMPLIMENT, PRAISE.

disparaging, *a.* depreciatory, depreciative, calumnious, calumniatory, detractive, condemnatory, slighting, derogatory, light, vilificatory, pejorative (*R or spec.*); *spec.* slanderous, libelous.

Antonyms: see LAUDATORY.

dispel, *v. t.* **1.** *See* SCATTER, DISLODGE.

2. dissipate, banish, resolve, dissolve, scatter, expel, remove, disperse, calm, quiet;—*in reference to doubts, fears, etc.*

disperse, *v. i.* scatter; *spec.* diffuse, dissolve, disband.

Antonyms: see CONVENE, GATHER.

displace, *v. t.* **1.** move (*contex.*), remove, translocate (*R*), unplace (*R*); *spec.* remove, disjoint, spring, start, shift, slip, dislodge, unseat, disseat (*chiefly fig.*), misplace, transpose, disroot, displant, dismount, dislocate, disturb, fault, unship, disorb (*R*), disnest, disniche.

Antonyms: see FIX, REPLACE.

2. *See* REPLACE, DISCHARGE.

displacement, *n.* **1.** moving, removal, translocation (*R*), unplacement (*R*); *spec.* disjointure (*R*), start, shift, transposition, transfer, slip, dislodgment, unseating, dislocation, disturbance, leap, fault, unshipment, dismounting, heterotopy (*tech.*), parallax.

Antonyms: see FIXATION, REPLACEMENT.

2. *See* REPLACEMENT, DISCHARGE.

3. conduct, administration, direction.

4. transfer; *spec.* bestowal, gift, sale.

displease, *v. t.* disgruntle (*C*), disturb, dissatisfy, disaffect, discontent, mislike; *spec.* disgust, offend, vex, anger, annoy.

Antonyms: see PLEASE.

displeasure, *n.* dissatisfaction, disaffection, discontention; *spec.* annoyance, indignation, anger, vexation, offense, distaste, disgust.

Antonyms: see PLEASURE.

disport, *v. i.* play, sport, merrymake (*chiefly in p. pr.*), shrove (*R*), carol, gambol; *spec.* rant, frolic, revel, wanton.

dispose, *v. t.* **1.** *See* ARRANGE, ADJUST, INCLINE.

2. appoint, direct, determine, settle.

disposed, *a.* inclined, prone, minded, propense (*R*), affectioned (*A*), inclining, ready, tending; *spec.* apt, addicted. Disposed, apt, inclined, *and* tending *are also used of physical objects, whereas the rest are confined to mental attitudes.*

Antonyms: see UNWILLING, OPPOSED, AVERSE.

disposition, *n.* **1.** *See* ARRANGEMENT, ADJUSTMENT, CLASSIFICATION, APPOINTMENT, CONDUCT, DIRECTION, STATE (*of affairs, etc.*).

2. constitution (*refers to fundamental physical organization*), temperament, temper (*refers particularly to mental characteristics*), humor, spirit (*with reference to character of mind*), nature, birth, mood, turn, vein, frame (*refers to physical build*), stomach (*fig.*), conditions (*A, pl.*), cue, grain.

3. inclination, inclining (*refers to natural taste*), tendency (*refers to habit*), disposedness (*R*), affection (*R*), proneness, propensity, aptitude (*with emphasis on natural fitness*), inclining, bent; *spec.* fancy, notion.

---

disorder, *v. t.: disarrange, confuse, derange, disorganize, disease.*
disown: *disclaim, disinherit.*
disparate: *unequal, different.*
disparity: *inequality, difference, disproportion.*
dispassionate: *impartial, unimpassioned.*
dispatch, *v. t.: send, kill, expedite, accomplish.*
dispatch, *v. i.: hasten.*
dispatch, *n.: sending, killing, expedition, haste, message.*
dispensable: *unnecessary.*
dispensate: *distribute, administer.*
dispensation: *distribution, diffusion.*
dispense: *distribute, administer, excuse.*
disperse, *v. t.: scatter, diffuse, distribute, dispel.*
dispirit: *depress.*
display, *v. t.: unfold, show, disclose.*
display, *n.: unfolding, show, disclosure.*

4. *Spec.* transfer, bestowal, gift, sale, endowment, donation.

dispossess, *v. t.* remove, forjudge (*A or law*), expropriate (*chiefly spec.*); *spec.* disseize; *see* EJECT, DISLODGE.

disproof, *n.* refutation, confutation, confutement (*R*), disprovement (*R*), rebutter, rebuttal, rebutment (*R*); redargution (*chiefly Scot. or law*).

Antonyms: see PROOF.

disproportion, *n.* misproportion, disparity, irregularity, incommensurability, incommensurableness, incommensurateness; *spec.* asymmetry, clumsiness.

Antonyms: see PROPORTION.

disproportionate, *a.* unproportionate, disparate, incommensurable, incommensurate, excessive, off-center.

Antonyms: see PROPORTIONATE.

disprove, *v. t.* refute, confute, rebut, negative, redargue (*chiefly Scot. or law*), convict (*A*).

Antonyms: see PROVE, CONFIRM, VERIFY.

disputable, *a.* controvertible, questionable, debatable, discussible, disputant; *spec.* litigable, impugnable, contestable.

Antonyms: see UNQUESTIONABLE.

disputant, *n.* disputer, contestant (*contex.*), contender (*contex.*), controversialist, controverter, controvertist; *spec.* debater, jangler, wrangler, dialogist, dialectic, pilpulist, polemic.

disputatious, *a.* **1.** *Spec.* controversial, captious, disputative, contradictious, polemic.

2. contentious, discordant, disputative, bickering, wrangling, strifeful, jarring, quarrelsome, litigious, dissentious.

Antonyms: see AGREEING, COMPLAISANT.

dispute, *v. t.* contradict, controvert, differ, disagree; *spec.* argue, attack, debate, impugn, discept (*R*), challenge, question, litigate, deraign (*hist.; law*).

Antonyms: see CONFIRM.

dispute, *v. i.* **1.** controversialize (*R*), differ, disagree; *spec.* debate, argue, arguify (*C*).

2. contend, differ, disagree, altercate; *spec.* quarrel, bicker, brabble (*A*), brawl, jangle, wrangle, jar, flite *or* flyte (*A*), strive, spat (*C*), squabble, tiff.

dispute, *n.* **1.** controversy, contradiction, disceptation (*R*); *spec.* debate, argument.

2. contention, contest, difference, argument, disagreement, discord; *spec.* quarrel, jangle, dissension, jar, strife, snarl (*C*), wrangle, squabble, bicker, brawl, brabble (*A*), spat (*C*), tiff, bickerment (*R*), impugnation (*R*), impugnment (*R*), polemic.

3. *Spec.* issue.

disqualification, *n.* disablement, disability; *spec.* superannuation, minority, sex, insanity, *etc.*

Antonyms: see QUALIFICATION.

disqualify, *v. t.* disable; *spec.* superannuate, unfit.

Antonyms: see QUALIFY.

disregard, *v. t.* ignore (*implies intention*), neglect (*implies failure to heed*), overlook (*R or spec.*), pretermit (*R*); *spec.* dissemble, disobey, slight (*implies some contempt*), defy.

Antonyms: see OBSERVE, ATTEND, CONSIDER, MENTION, EMPHASIZE.

disregard, *n.* ignoration (*R*), inattention, neglect, dissembling, preterition (*R*), pertermission (*R*); *spec.* oblivion, disobedience, slight, defiance, heedlessness, unheeding.

Antonyms: see OBSERVANCE, ATTENTION, EMPHASIS, CONSIDERATION.

disregardful, *a.* neglectful, inattentive, disregardant; *spec.* deaf, blind, careless, heedless, oblivious, disobedient, slighting, defiant.

Antonyms: see ATTENTIVE.

disrepair, *n.* decay, impairment, unrepair, ruin, neglect, irrepair (*R*).

Antonyms: see REPAIR.

disrespect, *n.* **1.** *See* DISCREDIT, INCIVILITY.

2. disesteem, misesteem; *spec.* irreverence, contempt, disdain (*connotes scorn*), *etc.;—referring to the attitude of mind.*

Antonyms: see ESTEEM.

disrespect, *v. t.* disesteem; *spec.* despise, spite, loathe, abhor, abominate.

Antonyms: see ESTEEM.

disrespectful, *a.* irrespectful (*R*); *spec.* irreverent, contemptuous, impolite, slighting, boorish, rude, insolent, scornful.

Antonyms: see RESPECTFUL.

dissect, *v. t.* **1.** *To cut up: spec.* anatomize, vivisect, transect (*R*).

2. *See* ANALYZE, CRITICIZE.

dissemble, *v. i.* pretend, feign, possum (*C, R*), dissimulate, act (*chiefly spec. or fig.*).

dissembler, *n.* deceiver, pretender, feigner, dissimulator, actor, disguiser (*R*); *spec.* hypocrite, counterfeiter, Judas, puritan (*obs.*).

dissembling, *a.* deceitful, dissimulating; *spec.* hypocritical, canting, ironical.

Antonyms: see FRANK.

dissembling, *n.* **1.** deceit, dissimulation, dissemblance, pretense, disguising; *spec.* hypocrisy, irony, cant.

2. *See* DISREGARD.

dissension, *n.* disagreement, discord, division, contention, strife, friction; *spec.* faction, party, partizanship.

Antonyms: see PEACE.

dissent, *v. i.* differ, disagree.

dissent, *n.* difference, disagreement; *spec.* nonconformity, recusancy.

dissenter, *n.* differer (*contex.*), dissentient, dissident, come-outer (*C, U. S.*); *spec.* recusant, nonconformist, puritan, Brownist (*hist.*), Raskolnik, sectary, sectarian, heretic, infidel.

---

disqualified: *unqualified.*
disrank: *degrade.*
disrobe: *undress.*
disrupt, *v. t.: break, burst, breach, disorganize.*
disseminate: *scatter, diffuse.*
dissent: *disagree.*

---

dissentient, *a.* disagreeing (*contex.*), dissenting, dissentious, inacquiescent; *spec.* recusant, factious, dissident, nonjuring.
Antonyms: see AGREEING.
dissentious, *a.* inacquiescent (*R*), recusant (*chiefly eccl.*); *spec.* inflammatory, incendiary, strifeful.
dissipate, *v. i.* **1.** *See* SCATTER, DIFFUSE.
2. debauch, riot (*R*); *spec.* Corinthianize, rake.
dissipated, *a.* **1.** *See* SCATTERED, DIFFUSE.
2. corrupt (*contex.*), debauched, dissolute, rakehell (*A*), fast, abandoned; *spec.* Corinthian, wild, raking, rakish, unsteady, licentious, crapulent, crapulous, lecherous, profligate.
dissipater, *n.* **1.** *Spec.* scatterer, diffuser, waster.
2. dissipator (*a variant spelling*), debauchee; *spec.* rake, ranter (*R*), lecher (*A*), palliard (*A*), rioter (*R or A*), profligate, rakehell (*A*), rakeshame (*A*), rip (*C or dial.*), roué (*French*), rounder (*C*), Corinthian.
dissipation, *n.* **1.** *Spec.* scattering, diffusion.
2. corruption (*contex.*), debauchery, debauch, debauchment, dissoluteness, fastness; *spec.* prodigalism, raking, rakery (*R*), riot (*R*), riotousness, crapulence, crapulency.
3. *Referring to an act or occasion:* debauch; *spec.* spree (*C*), bout, bum (*S*), orgy, drunk (*S*), toot (*S*), binge (*S*), souse (*C*), bender (*C*).
dissolve, *v. t.* **1.** *See* DECOMPOSE, DISINTEGRATE.
2. *Referring to happiness, troubles, doubts, etc.:* destroy, annihilate (*R*), consume, diffuse, end (*contex.*); *spec.* abrogate, annul, explain.
3. *Referring to a legislature, parliament, etc.:* dismiss, end (*R*); *spec.* prorogue.
Antonyms: see CONVENE, CONVOKE.
4. *To cause to become a solution: spec.* cut, lixiviate, leach.
dissolve, *v. i.* **1.** decompose, disintegrate, resolve (*R*), melt.
2. *See* DISAPPEAR, SCATTER.
dissuade, *v. t.* **1.** turn, divert.
Antonyms: see INDUCE.
2. *See* DEHORT.
dissuasion, *n.* turning, diversion, discouragement.
distance, *n.* **1.** remoteness, separation, farness; —*referring to state, fact, or degree.*
Antonyms: see NEARNESS.
2. space (*with reference to the distance intervening between two points of reference*), remove (*R as referring to space*), interval, way (*used with "long," "short," etc.*), interspace, length (*spec. or idiomatic*); *spec.* difference, westing, easting, elongation, longitude, drift, pitch, drop; —*referring to interval in space, time, degree, etc.*
3. *Referring to a distant place: spec.* offing; *see* BACKGROUND.
4. aloofness, offishness, stiffness, repellency; *spec.* reserve, reservation, coldness, frigidity, superiority, condescension, unresponsiveness.
Antonyms: see CORDIALITY.
distant, *a.* **1.** remote, separate, apart (*postpositive*), far-away, far-off, inaccessible, unapproachable, away (*postpositive*); *spec.* different, ulterior, yonder.
Antonyms: see NEAR, ADJACENT, IMMEDIATE.
2. offish, aloof (*predicative*), repellent, uncommunicative, strange; *spec.* bashful, reserved, reticent, cold, cool, freezing, frigid, unneighborly, superior, condescending, unresponsive, high-hat (*C*), snooty (*S*).
Antonyms: see CORDIAL.
distend, *v. t.* dilate, expand, extend, swell; *spec.* plump, bloat, enlarge, fill, inflate.
Antonyms: see CONSTRICT, CONTRACT.
distill, distil, *v. t. & i.* **1.** *See* DROP, EXTRACT.
2. evaporate, concentrate, condense; *spec.* cohobate (*old chem.*), rectify.
distillate, *n. See* EXTRACT.
distillation, *n.* **1.** evaporation, distillment (*R*); *spec.* cohobation, descent.
2. *See* DISTILLATE, EXTRACT.
distinct, *a.* **1.** different (*contex.*), remote, several, discrete (*emphasizes discontinuity*), explicit (*implies clearness and absence of ambiguity*), discriminate (*marked by distinguishing differences*), disjunct (*emphasizes separation*).
Antonyms: see SAME, ALIKE.
2. *See* DEFINITE, CLEAR (*in meaning*), EVIDENT, SEPARATE.
distinction, *n.* **1.** separation, demarcation, differentiation, discretion, discernment, discrimination, distinguishment (*R*), contradistinction.
2. difference, remoteness, discreteness, severance, discrimination.
3. *Spec.* separateness, distinctiveness.
4. repute, renown, eminence (*emphasizes elevated station*), rank, note (*chiefly used with "of"*), mark (*chiefly used with "of"*), éclat (*French*), kudos (*Greek*), superiority, eximiousness (*R*), notability; *spec.* fame (*R*), signality, greatness.
distinctive, *a.* distinguishing, differentiative, discriminative; *spec.* diagnostic, diacritic *or* diacritical, individual, characteristic.
distinguish, *v. t.* **1.** *To mark as different:* differentiate, separate, difference, demarcate, mark (*often used with "off"*), differ (*R*); *spec.* accentuate.
Antonyms: see CONFUSE.
2. *To perceive or treat as distinct:* separate, demarcate, differentiate, difference, discriminate, discern, tell, secern (*R*), single, differ (*R*), decern (*R*), sever, severalize (*R*); *spec.* classify, discover, contradistinguish.
Antonyms: see CONFUSE.
3. signalize, signal (*R*), mark, singularize.
distinguished, *a.* superior, eminent, conspicu-

---

disserve: *injure.*
dissident: *dissentient.*
dissimilar: *different.*
dissimulate: *disguise, dissemble.*
dissimulation: *disguise, dissemblance.*
dissipate: *scatter, dispel, diffuse, waste.*
dissociate: *separate.*

---

ous, noted, marked, eximious (*R*); *spec.* shining, famous, extraordinary, laureate.
Antonyms: see OBSCURE.

distort, *v. t.* **1.** deform; *spec.* screw, wring, wrench, torment (*R*), twist, contort, writhe, wrest, warp, deface, knot, gnarl.
2. *See* PERVERT;—*referring to meaning.*

distorted, *a.* deformed, Gordian (*fig.*), knotted, gnarled, contorted, *etc.*

distortion, *n.* **1.** deformation; *spec.* twist, contortion, screw, warp, defacement, contortuosity (*nonce word*), knot, buckle.
2. *See* PERVERSION;—*referring to meaning.*

distress, *n.* discomfort (*contex.*), dolor (*B*), unease (*A*), misease (*A*), anguish, agony; *spec.* trouble, calamity, torment, press, affliction, pain, tribulation, care, hurt, misery, gnawing, trial, hardship, harassment, confusion, privation, need, want, pressure, grief, sorrow, exigency, anxiety, *etc.*; hell (*S or very strong*).
Antonyms: see COMFORT, ENJOYMENT, RELIEF.

distress, *v. t.* discomfort, trouble; *spec.* press, harrow, straiten, harry, worry, bother, rack, harass, gripe (*R*), lacerate, tear, hurt, torment, pain, grieve, sadden, pinch, jar (*now usually considered S or inelegant*).
Antonyms: see COMFORT, RELIEVE.

distressing, *a.* distressful, uneasy; *spec.* tormentful (*R*), dolorific (*B*), carking (*A and B*), heavy, calamitous, grievous, bitter, harrowing, severe, sorry, gnawing, pinching, miserable, troublesome, sad, painful, griping, heartrending.
Antonyms: see COMFORTING, COMFORTABLE.

distribute, *v. t.* **1.** dispense (*implies a central supply or source*), dispensate (*R*), divide (*implies apportioning a whole*), part (*A*), dispart (*R*), disperse (*implies scattering what has been assembled*); *spec.* prorate (*chiefly U. S.*), spread (*emphasizes extension*), partition (*emphasizes planned division*), scatter (*suggests strewing widely*), parcel (*implies small divisions*), morsel (*R*), deal (*principally of cards; implies giving out in regular portions*), dole (*implies rationing in small portions*), allocate (*implies assignment*), allot (*implies setting apart for a particular reason*), mete (*emphasizes measuring forth*), share, apportion, send, diffuse, circulate; *see* SPREAD.
Antonyms: see COLLECT.
2. *See* CLASSIFY, ADMINISTER (*as justice*).

distribution, *n.* **1.** dispensation, division, partition; *spec.* dispersion, prorating (*chiefly U. S.*), scattering, parceling, parcelment, deal, dole, apportionment, sharing, allotment, allocation, diffusion; *spec.* spreading.
Antonyms: see COLLECTION.
2. *Spec.* classification, administration (*as of justice*), spreading.

district, *n.* place, region, quarter (*chiefly spec.*); *spec.* division, subdivision, section, riding, regency, wardenry, ward, neighborhood, province, presidency, precinct, prefecture, department, county, shire, township, town, canton (*R, exc. of Switzerland*), lathe (*Kent, Eng.*).

distrust, *v. t.* doubt (*connotes lack of certainty*), mistrust (*implies suspicion*), misdoubt, suspect (*connotes mistrust*), fear (*implies anxiety*), misgive (*implies misapprehension*); *spec.* jealouse (*obs., Scot., or dial.*).

distrust, *n.* doubt, mistrust, suspicion, misdoubt, misgiving; *spec.* jealousy, heartburn.
Antonyms: see TRUST, ASSURANCE, RELIANCE.

distrustful, *a.* doubtful, mistrustful, diffident (*A*), strange, dubious, suspicious; *spec.* shy, jealous, uneasy, fearful.
Antonyms: see ASSURED, RELIANT, UNSUSPICIOUS.

disturb, *v. t.* **1.** *Referring to the mind:* stir, trouble, agitate; *spec.* annoy, distract, fuss (*C*), muss (*C; with "up"*), distress, vex, worry, disconcert, discompose, muddle, disquiet, bother (*C*), shake, upset.
Antonyms: see CALM, PACIFY.
2. *Referring to things: see* AGITATE.
3. *Spec.* move, disarrange, derange, disorder, confuse, unsettle, shake, molest, interrupt, remove, convulse.

disturbance, *n.* **1.** *Referring to the mind:* agitation, inquietude (*R*); *spec.* turmoil, annoyance, vexation, distress, distraction, worry, disconcertion, discomposure, distemperature, muss, mess, perturbation.
Antonyms: see CALM.
2. *Referring to things: see* AGITATION.
3. *Spec.* moving, removal, disarrangement, derangement, disorder, confusion, unsettlement, molestation, interference, convulsion.
4. *Referring to disturbance among people:* disorder, disquiet, distemperature (*R*), breeze (*C*), inquietation (*R*), inquietude (*R*), curfuffle (*Scot.*); *spec.* commotion, tumult, coil (*A*), sedition, insurrection, kick-up (*C*), row (*C*), to-do (*C*), dust (*S or C*), shindy (*S*), scene, pother (*C or A*), fracas, uproar, muss (*C, U. S.*), convulsion, bother, fuss (*C*), botheration (*C*), bobery (*S*), bluster, conflict, fight, hoity-toity (*R*), rumpus (*C*), stew (*C*), grithbreach (*hist.*), row-de-dow (*R*), outbreak, ruption (*R*), rout, riot, ruffle (*R*), dispute, ruction (*C*), bustle, clutter, stir, anarchy, brawl, hubbub, combustion (*now B and R*), scrimmage, turn-up (*C, R*).

disturbing, *a.* disquieting, disturbant (*R*); *spec.* agitative, troublous, uncomfortable, perturbative (*R*), perturbatory (*R*), *etc.*
Antonyms: see CALMATIVE.

disunion, *n.* **1.** division, separation, severance, disjoining, disseverance, dissociation, disjointure, disjunction; *spec.* disconnection, detachment, dissension.
Antonyms: see UNION.

---

distasteful: *disgusting, unpalatable, offensive.* | **distract:** *divert, derange, disturb, confuse, frenzy.* | **distracted:** *deranged, confused.*

(*A*) *archaic.* (*B*) *bookish, poetic, literary or learned.* (*C*) *colloquial.* (*Contex.*) *contextual.* (*R*) *rare.* (*S*) *slang.*
See pp. viii–ix.

2. separation; *spec.* schism, secession, withdrawal *or* withdrawing.
3. *See* DISAGREEMENT.
disunite, *v. t. & i.* **1.** separate, secede, withdraw, leave, disjoint; *spec.* dissever, rend, dissociate, disconnect, detach, disjoint.
Antonyms: see UNITE.
2. alienate, estrange, divide.
disuse, *v. t.* abandon, obsolete (*R*), discard, shelve (*fig.*); *spec.* discontinue, neglect, disaccustom (*A*), abandon.
Antonyms: see USE, EXERCISE.
disuse, *n.* **1.** abandonment, nonuse, nonemployment, disusage, discarding; *spec.* discontinuance, neglect, nonobservance.
Antonyms: see USE.
2. desuetude (*B*), disusage, nonuse, inusitation (*R*); *spec.* neglect, nonobservance.
ditch, *v. t.* trench, channel, dike (*now R*); *spec.* moat, drain, vallate (*R*).
ditch, *n.* fosse (*tech. or B*), trench; *spec.* canal, graff (*hist.*), grip (*dial. or hunting*), drain, coupure, moat.
dive, *v. i.* **1.** plunge, descend, submerge; *spec.* sound.
2. *See* DISAPPEAR.
dive, *n.* **1.** plunge; *spec.* header (*C*).
2. *See* RESORT.
diverge, *v. i. Spec.* radiate (*implying a central point of separation*), branch, ramify, divaricate, fork, deviate (*implies a given course*), differ.
divergent, *a. Spec.* radiant, radial, radiative (*R*), branching, forking, furcate, divaricating, deviating.
Antonyms: see PARALLEL, CONFLUENT.
diversified, *a.* **1.** diverse, manifold, multifold, varied, mixed, multivarious (*R*), variate (*R*), multifarious, heterogeneous, diversiform, variform (*formal or B*), various.
Antonyms: see UNIFORM.
2. *See* VARIEGATED.
diversify, *v. t.* **1.** variate, vary, varify (*R*).
2. *See* VARIEGATE.
diversion, *n.* **1.** turning; *spec.* deviation, derivation, dissuasion.
2. amusement, pastime, dispart (*A*), entertainment, beguilement, play, recreation, derivation (*A or tech.*), sport, relaxation; *spec.* trifling, fun, solacement *or* solace.
Antonyms: see BUSINESS, WORK.
3. *Referring to that which amuses; used with the article "a" and having a plural:* amusement, merriment, merry-making, recreation, play, game, entertainment, sport, pastime, relaxation, divertissement (*French*), solacement *or* solace, derivation (*A*), distraction (*R*); *spec.* entremets (*French*), avocation (*R*).
diversity, *n.* **1.** *See* DIFFERENCE.
2. variety, diversification, manifoldness, multifariousness, multiformity, variation; *spec.* heterogeneity, heteromorphism (*chiefly tech.*), multiformity.
Antonyms: see UNIFORMITY.

divert, *v. t.* **1.** turn, disorientate (*fig. or spec.*), deviate, deflect, switch.
2. turn (*from a purpose, etc.*), draw; *spec.* dissuade.
3. distract (*contex.*), amuse, delight, derive (*A*), solace, entertain, recreate, beguile, disport; *spec.* tickle, regale.
Antonyms: see WORK, TIRE, WEARY.
diverting, *a.* amusing, entertaining, recreative, divertive, *etc.*
divide, *v. t.* **1.** sever (*implies complete separation, often with violence*), disunite (*emphasizes dissolution of unity*), separate, carve (*implies skill and energy*), cleave (*connotes speed and force*), cut (*spec. or fig.*); *spec.* scind (*R*), section, sectionize (*R*), part, parcel (*connotes division into small parts*), bisect, dispart, dissever, subdivide, dismember, junk (*R*), split, rend (*implies violence*), tear, segment, halve, quarter, third, disconnect, disjoint, class.
Antonyms: see JOIN, UNITE.
2. *To mark or partition off (a continuous thing) into parts, or to consider as so marked off or partitioned:* separate, demarcate (*R*), partition (*spec. or fig.*); *spec.* graduate, lot, compart, subdivide, parcel, district, canton, chapter.
3. *See* DISTRIBUTE, APPORTION, DISUNITE, SHARE, COMPUTE, MEASURE.
divide, *v. i.* **1.** separate, part, sever (*implies separation for ever; B*) cleave (*spec. or fig.*), cut (*spec. or fig.*); *spec.* bisect, dispart, subdivide, dismember, split, halve, quarter.
Antonyms: see UNITE.
2. *See* BRANCH, SHARE.
divide, *n.* watershed, water parting, shed; *spec.* coteau (*Canada and U. S.*).
divided, *a.* parted; *spec.* biparted (*R*), bipartite, digitate, lobulate, lobulated, lobulose, lobate, multipartite, disulcate, *etc.*
Antonyms: see UNITED.
divination, *n.* **1.** prediction, divining, soothsaying, auspice (*chiefly spec.*), hariolation (*R*), riddling (*R*), augury; *spec.*, stargazing, astrology, spatulamancy, rhabdomancy, theomancy, haruspicy *or* haruspication, ornithomancy, mantology (*R*), mantic (*R*), hieromancy, hieroscopy, gyromancy, hydromancy, graptomancy, geomancy, bibliomancy, lithomancy, hariolation (*R*), spodomancy, halomancy, dowsing; *all refer to special kinds of omen reading.*
2. *See* GUESS.
divine, *v. i.* **1.** predict, vaticinate, soothsay, hariolate (*R*), prophesy; *spec.* dowse.
2. *See* GUESS.
divine, *a.* **1.** superhuman, godlike, deific, deiform, godly, spiritual, heavenly, celestial, ambrosial (*spec. or fig.*).
Antonyms: see EARTHLY, HUMAN.
2. *See* RELIGIOUS.
3. fine, superior, excellent, ambrosial (*fig.*).
4. *Feminine* (*C*) *for* admirable, attractive, charming, beautiful, *etc.*

distraction: *diversion, derangement, disturbance, confusion, frenzy.* | **diurnal:** *daily.* | **divaricate:** *branch.*

diviner, *n.* **1.** predictor, Chaldean (*fig.*), augur, soothsayer; *spec.* geomancer, dowser, astrologer, stargazer, fortune-teller, gypsy.
2. *See* GUESSER.

divinity, *n.* **1.** deity, godhead, godhood, godship, deityship (*R*).
2. godlikeness, deiformity (*R*).
3. *See* DEITY, THEOLOGY.

divisible, *a.* separable, partible, severable, dividual (*R*), dividuous (*R*), *etc.; spec.* commensurable.
Antonyms: see INSEPARABLE.

division, *n.* **1.** *Act of dividing or state or fact of being divided:* severance, parting, separation, cutting (*spec. or fig.*), disparting; *spec.* disuniting, section (*connotes cutting*), splitting, split, scissure (*connotes splitting*), partitionment, parcelment, disseverance (*R*), subdivision, rending, partition, partage (*R*), schism, segmentation, lobation, fracture, breaking, deduplication, dismemberment, dearticulation, disconnection, diæresis, digitation, bisection, bipartition, trisection.
Antonyms: see JOINING, UNION.
2. *A part formed by (physical) division:* part; *spec.* subdivision, section, parcel, fragment, cut, lobe, lobule, cloot (*Scot. and dial. Eng.*), *etc.*
3. *A marking off or treating as marked off:* separation, demarcation; *spec.* partitionment, graduation, parcelment, districting.
4. *A part marked off or taken as being separated:* part, section; *spec.* subdivision, segment, member, movement, column, passus, canto, fit (*A*), verse, decade, chapter, book, compartment, cell, court, category, kind, sort, branch, department, canton, ordinary, lot, parcel, faction, party, sect, district, block, *etc.*
5. *Mil. and naval: spec.* battery, company, brigade, battalion, organization, army, classis, cohort, decury, maniple, tercio, tertia, class, squadron, fleet, command, troop, squad.
6. *Of territory: spec.* province, territory, state, government, presidency, consulate, dominion, county, shire, department, ward, township, town, district, circar (*India*), canton, cantonment, commune, commot, residency, mahal (*India*), eparchy, eyalet (*Turkish*), vilayet (*Turkish*).
7. *See* CLASSIFICATION, CLASS, COMPUTATION, DISTRIBUTION, DISUNION, DISAGREEMENT, SHARING, SHARE, BRANCH.
8. *Thing that divides:* partition; *spec.* line, wall, fence, *etc.*

divorce, *n.* divorcement; *spec.* repudiation, separation, diffarreation, dissolution.
Antonyms: see MARRIAGE.

divorce, *v. t.* unmarry (*R*); sunder, part, separate; *spec.* repudiate.
Antonyms: see MARRY.

dizziness, *n.* giddiness, vertigo (*tech.*), swim.

dizzy, *a.* **1.** giddy, giddyish (*R*), vertiginous, vertiginate (*R*), light-headed.
2. dizzying, giddy.
3. (*C*) *for* foolish, crazy, mad, daring (*implying rashness*).

dizzy, *v. i.* swim.

do, *v. t.* **1.** *Every kind of action may be reviewed as a particular form of doing, and the senses which the verb "do" may represent are as numerous as the forms of activity represented by the words which the verb may govern. It is impossible, therefore, to give a complete list of the various verbs which may be replaced by "do." The most important ones, however, are here listed. Spec.* inflict, administer, render, perform, achieve, commit, practice, cook, celebrate, cause, compose, transact, conduct, conjure, contrive, deceive, settle, conclude, depict, give, misdo, misexecute, make, manage, prepare, pickle, proceed, render, show, give, serve, solve, use, exert, produce, translate, review, dig, act, ruin, swindle, visit, finish, slur, slight, spoil, *etc. See the above words in the vocabulary (upper or lower).*
2. (*C*) *for* cheat, trick, swindle.

do, *v. i.* **1.** *See* ACT, FARE.
2. answer, suffice, suit, serve.

dock, *v. t.* **1.** cut, clip, curtail (*R*), bobtail (*a horse*), truncate.
2. *See* DEPRIVE, SHORTEN, ABRIDGE.

docked, *a.* curtail (*R*), curtailed (*R*), bobtail; *spec.* cock-tailed.

doctor, *n.* doc (*C*), physician, medical (*C*), medic (*C*), M.D. (*C*), doser (*contemptuous*), leech (*A*), healer (*often spec.*), curer; *spec.* specialist, homœopath, homœopathist, allopath, allopathist, osteopath, hydropath, hydropathist, chiropractor, surgeon, dentist, orthodontist, chiropodist, alienist, oculist, optometrist, aurist, veterinarian, vet (*C*), doctress (*now R*), doctrine (*feminine; C; jocose*).

doctor, *v. t.* **1.** treat, leech (*A*); *spec.* quack.
2. *See* ADULTERATE, FALSIFY, FAKE.

doctor, *v. i.* leech (*A*), practice.

doctrine, *n.* tenet, dogma, dogmatism (*chiefly derogatory*); *spec.* creed, formula, theory, opinion, teaching.

document, *n. Spec.* writing, handwriting (*A*), instrument, monument (*R or spec.*), muniment (*law*), diploma (*hist. or spec.*), record, charter, charta, parchment, paper, patent, manuscript, photostat, autograph, holograph, Round Robin, brevet, certificate, passport, commission, power, pleading, *etc.*

document, *v. t.* evidence, prove.

dodge, *v. i.* **1.** jink (*chiefly Scot.*); *spec.* duck, flinch, jump, jerk.
2. evade, escape (*used of* dodging *detection*), shuffle, palter, shift; *spec.* hedge, trim, prevaricate, quibble.

dodge, *n.* **1.** *Spec.* duck, jump, jerk, twitch.

divulge: *disclose, tattle.* | **do,** *n.: act, deed.* | **docile:** *teachable, manageable.*

2. evasion, deceit, artifice, trick, scheme.
3. device, expedient, scheme, plan.

doer, *n.* facient (*R*); *spec.* performer, actor, author, committer, perpetrator, maker, *etc. Cf.* DO.

doff, *v. t. To lay or put off:* cast, douse (*C*); *see* REMOVE. Doff *is literary and has a flavor of archaism.*
Antonyms: see DON.

dog, *n.* **1.** canine (*chiefly tech.*), cur (*contemptuous or derogatory*), whelp (*chiefly contemptuous*); *spec.* pup, puppy, toy, tike, terrier, trundletail, turnspit, spaniel, springer, setter, dachshund (*Ger.*), Dachl (*Ger.*), skirter shock, rache *or* ratch (*A*), reporter (*U. S.*), pug, pye-dog *or* pie-dog (*Anglo-Indian*), pariah dog, pointer, poodle, mastiff, lurcher, hound (*spec. exc. A or B*), harrier, hunter, gazehound, griffon, guara, finder, deerhound, staghound, dingo, dhole (*India*), courser, collie, colly, bulldog, beagle, Saint Bernard, basset, brindle, buckhound, bandog, tiedog (*obs. or R*), bitch, brach, brachet, slut, lady (*euphemistic*);—*all those from* bitch *on being feminine.* Dog *is often used specifically of a male dog.*
2. *See* FELLOW, CLAMP.

dog days, canicular days (*B*), canicule (*R*).

dogma, *n.* doctrine, tenet.

dogmatic, *a.* **1.** *See* DIDACTIC, DOCTRINAL.
2. positive, categorical, pragmatic, pragmatical, magisterial (*B*), thelical (*R*); *spec.* opinionated, peremptory, dictatorial.
Antonyms: see DOUBTFUL, HESITATING.

doing, *a. In the sense of "going on":* up, on;—*in predicative use.*

doing, *n.* **1.** feasance (*tech.*), facture (*B*), transaction; *spec.* conduct; *see* CREATION, MAKING.
2. *See* ACTION, COMMISSION, ACCOMPLISHMENT, PERFORMANCE.

doings, *n. pl.* gear (*sing.; A or dial.*), ongoings (*pl.*); *see* ACTION.

doll, *n.* **1.** plaything (*contex.*), toy (*contex.*), dolly, mammet (*A*); *spec.* puppet (*A*), baby, betty (*girl doll*), benedict (*boy doll*).
2. *Of a young woman:* cutie (*C*), lala paluza (*S*), peach (*S*), *etc.*

dollar, *n.* sinker (*S, U. S.*), simoleon (*S*), plunk (*S, U. S.*), wheel (*S*), cartwheel (*S; connotes silver dollar*), berry (*S*), bone (*S*), bean (*S*); *spec.* rixdollar (*hist.*), duro (*Spanish*), peso (*Mexican*), cob (*obs.*).

domain, *n.* **1.** *See* ESTATE, LORDSHIP, BOUND, CONTROL, SPHERE.
2. realm, reign (*R*), dominion, bourn *or* bourne (*R or B*), territory, possession; *spec.* kingdom, province, empire, empery (*B*), obedience, sultanate, khanate, daimiate, lordship, signory, dukedom, county, palatinate.

dome, *n.* vault; *spec.* cupola, tholus, canopy, beehive.

domestic, *a.* **1.** home, homely (*R*), household, domal (*R*), familiar, family; *spec.* menial (*servant; now contemptuous*).
2. domesticated;—*fond of domestic life.*
3. internal, interior, intestine, inland, native, home; *spec.* home-bred.
Antonyms: see FOREIGN.
4. *See* TAME.

domestic, *n.* servant, familiar (*R*); *spec.* maid, girl (*C*), cook, chambermaid, man, valet, boy (*colonial British*), butler, scullion (*A*).

domesticate, *v. t.* domesticize; *spec.* civilize, naturalize; *see* TAME.

domineer, *v. i.* tyrannize, lord.
Antonyms: see FAWN.

domineering, *a.* tyrannical, masterful, tyrannic (*R*); *spec.* authoritative, bossy (*C*), bullying, high-handed.
Antonyms: see OBSEQUIOUS, SERVILE.

domineering, *n.* tyranny, bossing (*C*).

don, *v. t.* assume (*spec. or affected*), wear.
Antonyms: see DOFF.

done, *a. Spec.* performed, executed, finished, *etc. Cf.* DO, *v. t.*

donkey, *n.* **1.** ass, jack (*male*), jackass (*male*), onager (*wild*), jenny (*female*), burro (*Southwestern U. S.*), cudidy (*chiefly Scot.*), dicky *or* dickey (*properly he-ass; S or C*), moke (*S*), neddy. *"Ass" is the common word when used of the wild forms.*
2. *See* BLOCKHEAD.

door, *n.* **1.** barrier; *spec.* trap, trapdoor, hatch, heck (*chiefly Scot.*).
2. *See* DOORWAY, PASSAGE.

doorkeeper, *n.* porter, portress (*fem.*), janitor, janitress (*fem.*), janitrix (*fem.*), doorward (*A*), ostiary (*chiefly eccl.*), tiler (*Freemasonry*), usher (*A or spec.*), concierge (*in France, etc.*).

doorpost, *n.* durn (*now dial.*).

doorway, *n.* passage (*contex.*), door, portal (*a dignified term*); *spec.* postern, entrance, exit, hatchway, durns (*pl.; now dial.*).

dose, *n.* portion; *spec.* potion, powder, pill.

dot, *n.* spot (*contex.*), speck; *spec.* point, tittle (*B*), peck, speckle, prick, pinprick.

dot, *v. t.* **1.** spot (*contex.*), speck; *spec.* point, speckle, punctuate, sprinkle, stipple, island.
2. *See* DIFFUSE, SCATTER.

dotted, *a.* spotted; *spec.* punctate, punctated, consperse (*R*), sprinkled, irrorate, speckled, bipunctate.

dotting, *n.* spotting; *spec.* punctuation, punctulation.

dot-shaped, *a.* punctiform.

double, *a.* **1.** twofold, duplicate, duple (*R or math.*), duplex (*tech. or R*), dual; *spec.* dualis-

doggerel, *n.: verse.*
doggerel, *a.: trivial.*
doldrums: *dullness, depression.*
dole, *n.: share, distribution, gift, alms.*
dole, *v. t.: distribute, apportion, give.*
dole, *n.: depression, sorrow, grief.*
doleful: *depressed, lamentable, sorrowful, depressing, gloomy.*
dolor: *depression, sorrow, distress.*
dome, *v. t.: vault, cover.*
domicile, *n.: abode.*
domicile, *v. i.: dwell.*
domicile, *v. t.: establish, settle.*
dominion: *control, government, empire, domain, authority, rule.*
donate: *give.*
donation: *gift.*
doom, *n.: judgment, destiny, condemnation.*
doom, *v. t.: condemn, destine.*
dormant: *sleeping, inactive.*
dose, *v. t.: drug, adulterate.*
doting: *fond.*
double, *n.: counterpart, fold, turn, evasion, trick.*

tic, geminous (*R*), geminate, paired, binary, binate, binal (*R*), biform, biformed, bifront.
2. *See* AMBIGUOUS, INSINCERE, FOLDED.
double, *v. t.* **1.** multiply, redouble, duplicate, geminate (*R*); *spec.* repeat, facsimile, increase.
2. *See* FOLD, DEFEAT, AVOID, COUPLE.
doubled, *a.* duplicated, reduplicate, conduplicate (*R or tech.*).
double-entendre, *n.* (*French*), equivocation; *spec.* pun, dittology.
doubling, *n.* duplicature (*chiefly math.*), gemination (*R*), duplication, conduplication (*B*), duplation (*R*).
doubly, *adv.* twice, twofold, extra; *also A for* deceitfully.
doubt, *n.* **1.** uncertainty, question, dubiety (*B*), dubiousness, doubtfulness, incertitude, undecidedness; *spec.* misdoubt, skepticism (*implies suspended judgment*), incredulity (*implies unbelief*), suspicion (*implies distrust and questioning*), disbelief (*emphasizes rejection*), distrust (*implies lack of confidence*), perplexity (*implies confusion of mind*), hesitation (*implies wavering uncertainty*), irresolution, wavering, indecision, suspense;—*referring to the state of mind.*
Antonyms: see ASSURANCE, TRUST, BELIEF, CERTAINTY.
2. *See* UNCERTAINTY;—*referring to facts, events, etc.*
doubt, *v. i.* question, dubitate (*B or affected*); *spec.* misdoubt, hesitate, mistrust, disbelieve.
Antonyms: see BELIEVE, TRUST.
doubt, *v. t.* question, query (*B*), dubitate (*R or affected*), misdoubt; *spec.* suspect, distrust, disbelieve.
Antonyms: see BELIEVE, TRUST.
doubtful, *a.* **1.** undecided, questioning, doubting, undetermined, irresolute, uncertain, dubious, dubitant (*R*); *spec.* skeptical, hesitant, perplexed, distrustful, wavering, incredulous; *see* BELIEVING;—*referring to the state of mind.*
Antonyms: see ASSURED, DECIDED, DOGMATIC, TRUSTFUL, CERTAIN.
2. *See* UNCERTAIN;—*referring to facts, events, etc.*
dovecot, dovecote, *n.* birdhouse (*contex.*), columbarium, dovehouse, columbary.
dovetail, *v. t.* **1.** mortise (*contex.*), tail, cog, cock.
2. *See* JOIN.
dower, *n.* **1.** portion (*of a widow*), thirds (*a loose usage*), dowry, dot (*French*), share (*contex.*).
2. *See* DOWRY, ENDOWMENT.
dower, *v. t.* dot (*R*), tocher (*Scot.*), portion, endow;—*referring to bestowment on bride.*
down, *adv.* downward, downwards, groundward, earthward, netherwards (*R*), downwardly; *spec.* downstairs, below (*on shipboard*), hellward, floorward.
Antonyms: see UPWARD, HEAVENWARD.
down, *a.* downward, descending; *spec.* sloping, downmost.
down, *n.* **1.** *See* PLUMAGE.
2. pubescence, lanugo (*tech.*), hair, wool, fluff.
downcast, *a.* **1.** *See* DEPRESSED.
2. lowered (*eyes, glance*), dejected (*eyes; R*).
Antonyms: see UPTURNED.
downs, *n. pl.* upland, wold (*Eng.*), fell (*Eng.*), moor.
downy, *a.* **1.** feathery (*contex.*), pubescent, fluffy, lanuginous (*tech.*), hairy; lanuginose (*tech.*); *spec.* silky, sericeous (*tech.*), thrummy (*R*), cottony, pappose (*R, also* pappus), flossy.
2. *See* SOFT.
dowry, *n.* **1.** *Referring to that of a bride:* dower, dote (*R*), dot (*French*), tocher (*Scot.*), share (*contex.*).
2. *See* DOWER (*of a widow*), ENDOWMENT.
dowser, *n.* diviner (*contex.*), hydroscopist rhabdomancer (*R*), rhabdomantist.
drab, *a. & n.* dun, brownish, yellow, yellowish gray, dull, monotonous.
drabble, *v. i. & t.* draggle.
draconian, *a.* draconic, dracontine (*R*), severe, rigorous, harsh, cruel.
draconic, *a.* dragonlike, dracontine, dracontian, dragon.
draff, *n.* dregs; *spec.* swill.
draft, *n.* **1.** *See* DRAWING, LOAD, DRINKING, DRINK, INHALATION, CURRENT, OUTLINE, DEDUCTION.
2. demand; *spec.* order, check *or* (*chiefly British*) cheque, bill (*of exchange*).
3. depth (*enough to float a vessel*).
4. *Mil.:* conscription.
5. *In form,* drafts, *construed as sing.:* checkers (*U. S.*).
draft, *v. t.* **1.** *See* OUTLINE.
2. *Mil.: spec.* impress, press, conscribe (*R*), conscript, commander (*South Africa*).
drafted, *a. Spec.* conscript, impressed, pressed.
draggle, *v. t. & i.* **1.** drabble, trail, betrail (*intensive*), bedraggle (*intensive*).
2. *See* STRAGGLE.
dragnet, *n.* dredge, drag, trammel.
dragon, *n.* monster (*contex.*), drake (*R*); *spec.* serpent, saurian, dragonet.
drain, *v. t.* **1.** empty (*contex.*); *spec.* emulge (*R*), tap, milk (*fig.*), dike, trench, sluice, sewer, ditch.
Antonyms: see FILL.
2. *See* EXHAUST, DEPRIVE, DRINK.
3. drip, percolate.
drain, *n.* **1.** *See* DRAINAGE.
2. channel (*contex.*); *spec.* plumbing, ditch, culvert, leader, fox, sewer, cesspool.

doughty: *brave, strong, formidable.*
douse: *lower, doff, extinguish.*
douse: *dip, drench.*
downcast: *throw.*
downcome: *descent, fall.*
downright: *vertical, absolute, evident, frank, definite.*
downward: *down.*
drabble: *draggle.*
drag, *v. t.: draw, attract, dredge, search, drawl, introduce.*
drag, *v. i.: draw, delay, continue, drawl.*
drag, *n.: coach, brake.*

drainage, *n.* **1.** drain, draining; *spec.* sewerage, run-off.
2. *Spec.* sewage, seepage;—*referring to matter drained off.*
dram, *n.* drink (*contex.*); *spec.* thimbleful, pony, sip.
drama, *n.* **1.** composition, play, piece, scenario, script, typescript; *spec.* comedy, comedietta, tragedy, farce, burlesque, travesty, sketch, interlude, monodrama, monologue, melodrama, melotragedy, pastoral, masque, operetta, opera, opera-bouffe, review, burlesque, vaudeville, pantomime, tragicomedy, trilogy, proverb, mystery, miracle play *or* (*R*) miracle, cinema, movies, talkies.
2. dramaturgy (*B*), dramatics, theatricals.
3. the stage, the theater, the movies, the talkies.
dramatic, *a.* theatrical, theatric (*R*), dramaturgic (*B*), Thespian (*B*), scenic, scenical; *spec.* melodramatic, melodramatical, tragic, farcical, Atellan, comic, burlesque. *For discriminations see* THEATRICAL.
dramatist, *n.* playwright, dramaturge; dramaturgist; *spec.* tragedian, writer, scenarist.
dramatize, *v. t.* *Spec.* melodramatize, operatize (*R*), burlesque, farcify (*R*).
drape, *v. t.* **1.** cover (*contex.*); *spec.* hang, tapestry, pall.
2. *See* ARRANGE, HANG.
drape, *n.* **1.** *See* COVER, DRAPERY.
2. adjustment, hang, cast. Drape *is C or cant.*
drapery, *n.* furniture, hangings (*pl.*), drapes (*C or cant*); *spec.* tapestry, curtains.
draw, *v. t. & i.* **1.** drag (*implies resistance*), haul (*connotes transportation*), pull (*implies force*), tug (*implies strain and effort*), hale (*implies compulsion*); *spec.* tow (*implies pulling after a rope or chain*), lug (*implies difficulty and awkwardness*), attract (*emphasizes emotional or intellectual, rather than physical, drawing power*), trail (*connotes helplessness or reluctance*), snake (*C or S, U. S.*), train (*R*), entrain (*R*), tear, rush, trawl, bunt, bouse *or* bowse, brail, draggle, hook, unsheathe, tighten, poker, strict (*A*).
Antonyms: see PUSH, THRUST, DRIVE.
2. *See* ATTRACT, INHALE, UTTER, EXTRACT, ROUSE, CHOOSE, ELICIT, DERIVE, INFER, REMOVE, DIVERT, BRING, EMPTY, SEARCH, STRETCH, ATTENTUATE, EXTEND, DISEMBOWEL, INDUCE, GET, EXTORT, DELINEATE, DEPICT, DESCRIBE, CONSTRUCT.
3. *Of water, liquor, etc.:* skink (*to draw liquor: A*); *spec.* tap, broach, bucket, rack, siphon, exhaust (*air from a vessel*).
4. unshot (*a gun, etc.; R*).
5. trace (*a line*), run; *spec.* protract, retrace.
6. write, compose, formulate, draft.
drawing, *n.* dragging, draft, traction, pulling, *etc.*
drawingknife, drawknife; *spec.* drawshave, shave, jigger.
drawing-room, *n.* withdrawingroom (*A*), salon (*French*), saloon (*U. S.*).
drawl, *v. t. & i.* drag;—*referring to speech.*
dream, *n.* **1.** vision; *spec.* nightmare, daymare (*R*).
Antonyms: see ACTUALITY.
2. *See* DAYDREAM.
dream, *a.* somnial (*R*), somniative (*R*).
dreamland, *n.* *Spec.* cloudland, fairyland, reverie.
dreamlike, *a.* unreal; *spec.* illusive, dreamy, speculative, imagined.
dredge, *v. t.* drag.
dreggy, *a.* impure, feculent, dreggish; *spec.* turbid, foul, polluted.
Antonyms: see CLEAR.
dregs, *n. pl.* refuse (*contex.*); *spec.* sediment, lees (*pl.*), grounds (*pl.*), fæces (*pl.*), fæcula *or* fecula, outcasts (*pl.*), offal, scum, offscourings (*pl.*), sordes (*tech.*), sordor (*R*), foots (*pl.*), bottoms (*pl.*), tilts (*pl.*), taplash (*obs. or dial.*).
drench, *n.* **1.** dose, potion;—*referring to physic given to an animal.*
2. wetting (*contex.*); *spec.* souse, douche, soaking.
drench, *v. t.* **1.** dose (*contex.*), physic;—*referring to an animal.*
2. wet (*implies a thorough wetting*); *spec.* douche (*chiefly tech.*), douse, souse, soak, bucket.
Antonyms: see DRY.
dress, *v. t.* **1.** arrange (*contex.*); *spec.* line (*used with "up"*), preen.
2. prepare (*contex.*); *spec.* clean, roughdress, scapple *or* scabble, finish, taw, pick, drove, baste, machine, burl, scutch, hackle, shamoy, hatchel, barber, side, curry, bard, liquor, comb, manicure, jig, draft, *etc.*
3. equip, furnish; *spec.* dub, deck, ornament.
4. *See* CLOTHE, REPROVE, SCOLD.
dress, *v. i.* **1.** align (*mil.*), straighten.
2. prepare (*contex.*); *spec.* vest (*chiefly eccl.*), clothe, busk (*A or Scot.*).
Antonyms: see UNDRESS, STRIP.
dress, *n.* **1.** *See* CLOTHING, COSTUME.
2. *Of a woman's or girl's outer clothing:* gown (*formal*); *spec.* frock (*chiefly Brit.*), suit, habit, jam (*A*).
3. *Of the mode in which one is dressed, or the dress and equipment as a whole:* attire, tire (*A, R*), toilet, array (*B or formal*), trim, garb (*chiefly B*), gear (*chiefly A*), get-up (*C*), rig, costume, vesture (*B*), regalia, make-up, bedizenment, dizenment (*R*), bravery, trappings, disguise *or* disguisement, cloth, motley, dishabille.
dress, *a.* habilimental (*R*), habilimentary (*R*), habilatory (*R*), vestiary (*R*).
dressing gown, kimono, bathrobe, gown.

---

drawing, *a.: attractive.*
dread: *fear, awe.*
dreadful: *fearful, alarming.*
dreary: *cheerless, gloomy, depressing, lonely, sad, monotonous, uninteresting, dull.*
dredge: *sprinkle.*

dressing room, tiring-room, wardrobe, anteroom, *etc.*

dressmaker, *n.* modiste (*French*), seamstress.

dressy, *a.* **1.** fond of dress;—*no single-word synonym.*

2. showy, ornamental, elaborate.

dried, *a.* desiccated (*tech. or cant*), baked, baken (*A*), anhydrous, dehydrated, anhydride (*tech.*), evaporated, kiln-dried.

drift, *n.* **1.** *See* PROPULSION, COURSE, MEANING, TENDENCY.

2. movement (*contex.*), driftage.

3. deviation (*distance away due to drift*), driftway; *spec.* leeway.

4. *In geology:* deposit, diluvium; *spec.* till, detritus.

5. *In mining, etc.:* excavation, passage, drive; *spec.* gallery, tunnel, level.

drink, *v. t.* **1.** consume (*contex.*), imbibe (*spec. or jocose*), discuss (*humorous*), demolish (*S*), quaff (*chiefly B*); *spec.* dispatch, bibble, swizzle (*C*), sip, sipple, lap, drain, swill (*vulgar or denoting vulgar excess*), swig (*C or S*), guzzle, suck (*vulgar or spec.*), surround (*C*), tope (*C*), crush (*B, R*), tipple, buzz (*S or cant*), crack.

2. *To cause to drink:* drench (*R*), lush (*S*).

3. salute, toast, wassail (*A or B*). *"Drink to" is the usual term,* drink *alone being R or C in this sense.*

4. *See* ABSORB, HEAR, SEE.

drink, *v. i.* imbibe, quaff (*B*); *spec.* sip, sipple, lap, guzzle (*C or S*), bib (*A*), bibulate (*jocose*), bibble, soak (*C*), refresh, hobnob, swill (*vulgar or implying vulgar excess*), swizzle (*C*), pull (*used with* at, on, *etc.; C*), tea, fuddle, boose *or* booze (*S*), bouse (*R*), tipple, carouse, lush (*S*), nobble (*R*), nip, sot, liquor (*S*), grog, dram, pot (*A*).

drink, *n.* **1.** *Liquid to be drunk:—distinguished from meat (solid food). There are no synonyms in this sense.*

2. *See* BEVERAGE, LIQUOR.

3. *The act:* drinking, draft, quaff (*B or humorous*); *spec.* pull (*C*), suck (*C*), sip, swig (*C*), lap.

4. *A portion to drink:* draft *or* draught, potation (*B or humorous*), potion (*chiefly med. or spec.*); *spec.* dram, finger, pony, eye-opener, nip, toothful (*C*), suck (*C*), split, pot (*A*), grace, cup, libation (*humorous*), peg (*Anglo-Indian; S*), nightcap, sip, tickler (*C*), tiff (*obs. or chiefly dial.*), caulker (*S*), drop, bumper, rouse (*A*), toddy, chaser, brimmer (*C*), bracer (*C*), snifter (*C*), snoot-full (*S*).

drinkable, *a.* potable, potatory (*R*).

drinker, *n.* imbiber (*formal or affected*), quaffer (*B*); *spec.* drunkard, soaker (*C*), soak (*C*), lapper, tippler, bibber, sipper, bouser, boozer, toper, guzzler, tosspot (*A*), hobnobber, compotator, whetter, rum-hound (*C*), sponge (*C*).

drinking, *a.* potatory (*R*); *spec.* ebrious (*R and affected*), bibulous, groggy.

Antonyms: see ABSTEMIOUS.

drinking, *n.* consumption, draft, potation (*B*), sorbition (*R*), imbibition (*R or affected*), bibation (*R*), bibition (*R*), bibulation (*R*), libation (*C, B*); *spec.* tippling, compotation, drink, pot (*fig.*), cups (*pl.; fig.*), cupping, rummer.

drip, *v. t. & i.* **1.** drop, weep (*fig.*); *spec.* leak, dribble, trickle.

2. *To be wet:* drop.

drip, *n.* **1.** dripping, drop; *spec.* dribble, trickle.

2. *In architecture:* larmier, corona; *spec.* label, dripstone.

3. drippings (*pl.*), droppings (*pl.*);—*that which drips.*

drive, *v. t.* **1.** move (*contex.*), propel (*implies motion forward*), impel (*emphasizes the imparting of motion*), force, push, thrust, ram (*implies violent impact*); *spec.* throw, actuate, turn, revolve, drift, puff, tide, run, hammer, dint, ding (*A or dial.*), press, strike, blow, expel, shoot, beat, roll, slide, *etc.;—in this sense implying that the resulting motion of the driven body is, as a whole, the direct result of applied force.*

Antonyms: see DRAW.

2. *Of any force, impulse, or actuating cause, producing action by stimulating or bringing into activity some other force: spec.* compel, impel, incite (*connotes stimulation to move*), chase, run, herd, huddle (*implies confusion*), hustle, smoke, ferret (*used with "out"*), shame, rush, pelt, dog, hound, hunt, kick, hurry, hoot, hunger (*R*), beat, constrain, urge, frighten, worry, dispel, dissipate, reverberate (*R*), repercuse, retund (*R*), culbut, *etc.*

Antonyms: see RESTRAIN.

3. direct, tool (*chiefly spec.; cant*); *spec.* spank, call (*Scot.*), trot, back, hoy, gallop, canter, amble, bucket (*C or cant*), walk, run, *etc. In this sense the word* drive *suggests a greater or less degree of participation in the management of direction; the word* ride *emphasizes the idea of being carried in a vehicle or on an animal, and does not necessarily imply any participation in the management or direction. So one* drives *one's own car, or* drives *in another's as his guest: but a passenger generally* rides *in a public conveyance, though he may take the driver's place, and then he would* drive. Ride *alone is used of traveling on the back of an animal.*

4. *See* TRANSPORT, STRIKE, PROSECUTE, URGE, CONCLUDE.

5. excavate (*horizontally*), hole, drift;—*distinguished from "sink."*

drive, *v. i.* **1.** advance; *spec.* rush, dash, float, drift, rack, scud.

2. vehiculate (*R*), tool (*chiefly spec.; cant*);

---

dribble: *drip, slobber.*
drill, *v. t.: sow.*
drill, *n.: exercise, training.*
drill, *v. t.: piece, exercise, train.*

---

spec. rattle, bowl (*used with "along"*), coach, spank (*C*), charioteer, bucket.
3. *See* STRIKE, URGE.
drive, *n.* **1.** driving; *spec.* drift, battue.
2. journey (*contex.*), excursion (*contex.*), ride, joy-ride (*S*).
3. excavation, drift.
4. *See* DRIVEWAY, URGENCY, ENERGY.
driver, *n.* **1.** propeller, impeller; *spec.* carrier, sail.
2. engineer, engine-driver, captain, pilot, reinsman (*R, U. S.; spec.*), Jehu (*humorous*), charioteer, wagoner, waggoner, curricleer (*R or nonce*), coachman, cabman, cabby (*C*), hackman, mahout, carnac (*French*), driveress (*nonce word*), vetturino (*It.*), jarvey (*S*), *Eng.*, dragsman, tripper, teamster, muleteer, drover, cameleer, motorist, motorcyclist, motorman, chauffeur, chauffeuse (*fem.*), truck driver, truckman, bus driver, busman.
driveway, *n.* drive; *spec.* sweep.
drizzle, *n.* rain (*contex.*), spray (*contex.*), drow (*Scot.*).
droop, *v. i.* **1.** hang, incline; *spec.* bend, dangle, loll, lop, nod, nutate (*R*), sink, flag, weep, sag, slouch, drop, fall, fade, wither, wilt.
2. *See* DESCEND, LANGUISH.
droop, *v. t.* hang (*as the head*), incline; *spec.* dangle, bend, loll, nod, sink, slouch, drop.
Antonyms: see ERECT.
droop, *n.* hang (*R*), inclination; *spec.* slouch, sag, pendency, bend.
drooping, *a.* **1.** hanging; *spec.* nutant (*R*), nodding, cernuous (*chiefly bot.*), weeping, pendent, sagging.
2. *Spec.* declining, languishing, descending, depressed.
Antonyms: see ERECT.
drop, *n.* **1.** ball (*contex.*), globule, gutta (*tech.*), tear (*chiefly spec.*), pearl (*chiefly spec.*); *spec.* blob, gout (*A*), bead, droplet, dewdrop, raindrop.
2. *See* PARTICLE, PENDANT, DESCENT, FALL, BREAK (*in a surface*), DISTANCE, CURTAIN.
drop, *v. i.* **1.** *Spec.* drip, pearl, bead, distill, bleed (*fig.*), plump.
2. *See* DESCEND, FALL, CROUCH, SINK, DEPRECIATE.
drop, *v. t.* **1.** *Spec.* drip, distill, shed.
2. *To let, or cause to, fall: spec.* fell, plump, dump (*chiefly U. S.*), lower, droop.
3. *See* FELL, MAIL, UTTER, OMIT, DROOP, LOWER, ABANDON, STOP.
4. *C for* hint, reveal, suggest.
drop-shaped, *a.* guttate (*tech.*), guttiform (*tech.*), pearly, beady.
dropsical, *a.* hydropic, hydroptic (*R*); *spec.* œdematous.
dropsy, *n.* hydrops (*tech. or obs.*), hydropsy (*now R*); *spec.* hydrothorax, hydrarthrosis, œdema.
dross, *n.* **1.** refuse (*contex.*), recrement (*tech.*), slag (*usually dross in a fused glassy combination of basic drossy substances*), scoria (*usually cindery or porous dross, as cellular lava*); *spec.* scum, cinder, clink, sullage.
2. *See* REFUSE.
drossy, *a.* slaggy, scoriaceous; *spec.* scummy, cindery.
drove, *n.* **1.** herd; *spec.* string.
2. *See* CROWD, COLLECTION.
drown, *v. t.* **1.** *See* SUFFOCATE.
2. overwhelm, overpower; *spec.* (*of sound*) deafen, deaden, outcry, outroar.
drudge, *v. i.* work (*contex.*), fag (*often spec. in Eng. school cant*), grind, slave, plod, dig, plow, grub, hack, scrub.
drudge, *n.* worker (*contex.*); *spec.* grub, hack, grubstreeter (*B*), packhorse (*fig.*), devil *or* deviller (*C*), scrub, plodder, slave, fag (*in an Eng. school*), grind, penny-a-liner.
drudgery, *n.* work (*contex.*); *spec.* fag (*R*), grind, hackwork (*chiefly depreciatory*), journeywork, slavery.
drug, *n.* **1.** medicine, physic (*chiefly spec.*), medicinal, dope (*chiefly spec.*, preparation, remedy*: S*); *spec.* elixir.
2. *See* COMMODITY.
drug, *v. t.* medicate, dose, physic (*chiefly spec.*), dope (*chiefly spec.; S*); *spec.* stupefy.
druggist, *n.* apothecary (*obs. in England, and less common than* druggist *in U. S.*), pharmaceutist *or* pharmacist (*tech.*), pharmacopolist (*R*), chemist (*Brit., or ostentatious elegance, U. S.*).
drugstore, *n.* druggery (*R*), pharmacy, chemist's shop (*Brit., or ostentatious elegance, U. S.*).
drum, *n.* **1.** tabor (*R or spec.*), tambour (*chiefly spec.*); *spec.* tambourine, tomtom, kettledrum, gumby, tabret, *etc.*
2. cylinder; *spec.* die, tympanum (*R*), tambour, vase.
3. *See* GATHERING.
4. beat, drub, thrum.
drum, *v. t.* **1.** *See* GATHER, EXPEL, COMPEL.
2. drub, thrum.
drumbeat, *n.* rub-a-dub, tan-tan (*nonce*), dub, tuck (*chiefly Scot.*); *spec.* tattoo, roll, taps (*pl.*).
drunkard, *n.* drinker, inebriate, lushington (*S*); *spec.* bloat (*C*), sot, toper, boozer (*C*), dipsomaniac, sot, bum (*S, U. S*).
drunken, *a.* intoxicated, tight (*C*), inebrious, bousy *or* boozy; *spec.* sottish, soaked (*C*), corny (*S*), pied, pie-eyed (*C*), stewed (*C*), boiled (*C*), sodden (*C*), fuddled, primed, screwed (*C; British*), groggy, spifflicated (*C*).
Antonyms: see SOBER.
dry, *a.* **1.** waterless, unwet (*R*), unmoistened,

drivel, *v. t.: slobber, utter.*
drivel, *v. i.: slobber, babble.*
drivel, *n.: slobber, nonsense.*
drizzle: *rain.*
drizzly: *rainy.*
droll, *n.: buffoon, wit.*
droll, *a.: laughable.*
droll, *v. i.: jest.*
drone, *n.: idler, sluggard.*
drone, *v. i.: idle.*
drone, *n.: hum.*
drone, *v.: hum, monotone.*
drowse: *sleep.*
drowsy: *sleepy, sluggish.*

arid (*chiefly spec.*), siccaneous (*R*), moistless (*R*), droughty *or* drouthy (*R, exc. spec.*), dryish, anhydrous; *spec.* dried, desiccated, corky, dry-shod, dryfooted, husky, parched, juiceless, drinkless, sapless, exsuccous (*R; also fig.*), thirsty.
Antonyms: see WET, MOIST, SOAKED.
2. *See* SOUR (*wine*), PROHIBITION.

dry, *v. t.* exsiccate (*tech.; R*), desiccate (*tech.*), parch, dehydrate (*tech.*), evaporate (*R*); *spec.* buccan, drain, blot, passulate (*R*), sear, kiln, kiln-dry, stove, sammy.
Antonyms: see WET, MOISTEN, DRENCH, SOAK, WATER.

dry, *v. i.* desiccate, dehydrate, exsiccate (*R*); *spec.* sear (*R*).
Antonyms: see SOAK.

dryer, *n.* desiccative, desiccant, siccative, exsiccator (*R*), dehydrator (*tech.*), exsiccant (*R*).

drying, *a.* siccative, exsiccant (*R*), exsiccative (*R*), desiccant (*tech.*), desiccative; *spec.* torrefactive (*R*).

dryness, *n.* dryth (*obs. or dial. Eng.*), aridity (*chiefly spec.*), aridness, drought *or* drouth (*R, exc. spec.*).
Antonyms: see MOISTURE.

d-shaped, *a. Spec.* deltoid (*like Greek* Δ).

dub, *v. t.* **1.** *See* KNIGHT, HONOR, NAME.
2. *Spec.* dress, trim, grease.

duck, *n.* dilly (*C or dial.*), quack (*humorous*); *spec.* duckling, flapper, drake, pintail, sprigtail, calloo, callow, dundiver, garrot, gadwall, Harlequin, hardhead (*U. S.*), golden-eye, granny, waterwitch, merganser, mallard, teal, old-wife, old-squaw, shoveler, scaup, eider, eider duck, dungbird.

duck, *v. i. & t.* **1.** *See* DIP.
2. lower (*contex.*), bob (*jerkily*), bend, dodge, bow.

duct, *n.* channel (*contex.*), canal, ditch; *spec.* pipe, conduit, tube, chimney, funnel, flue.

ductile, *a.* **1.** malleable, tensile; *spec.* extensible, tractile (*R*), tough.
Antonyms: see REFRACTORY, UNYIELDING, RIGID.
2. *See* PLASTIC, MANAGEABLE, PLIANT.

due, *a.* **1.** owed, owing, mature, dueful (*A*), rightful; *spec.* payable; *see* ACCRUED.
2. *See* DESERVED, PROPER, ADEQUATE, ATTRIBUTABLE.

due, *n.* **1.** droit (*law*), right; *spec.* charge, fee, toll, tribute, levy, duty, tax; *see* DEBT.
2. desert, merit (*chiefly in pl.*).

duel, *n.* fight (*contex.*), rencounter (*B*), monomachy (*R*); *spec.* holmgang (*R*).

duet, *n.* composition (*contex.*), duo (*Italian*), duetto (*R*).

dull, *a.* **1.** *See* STUPID, CHEERLESS, DEPRESSING, BLUNT, DARK.
2. *Referring to capacity of feeling:* dim (*implies lack of brightness or distinctness*), insensitive, unfeeling, inapprehensive, gross (*connotes lack of sensitivity*), Bœotian (*fig.*), fat, saturnine (*B*), obtuse, muzzy (*C*), stolid, blunt, sluggish, inert; *spec.* numb, languid, besotted, cloudy.
Antonyms: see SENSITIVE.
3. *Referring to mental capacity or condition as to interest:* spiritless, heavy, dumpish (*implies melancholy and low spirits*), unanimated, listless (*implies lack of inclination*), torpid (*implies low vital energy*), dead, inanimated, lifeless, indifferent, crass (*connotes thick-wittedness*); *spec.* apathetic (*implying lack of feeling*), phlegmatic, inapprehensive (*R*), sleepy, numb, depressed, dark, lumpish, Bœotian (*fig.*).
Antonyms: see SHARP, SHREWD, PRECOCIOUS, WITTY.
4. *Referring to sensations, as pain:* obtuse (*R*), heavy.
5. *Referring to what affects the mind or attention:* vapid (*implies loss of liveliness*), uninteresting, tedious, insipid, tame, dry, jejune (*B*); *spec.* tiresome, insulse (*R*), drear (*chiefly B*), drearisome (*R*), dreary, humdrum, monotonous, routine, commonplace, prosaic, prosy, ponderous, irksome, frigid, flat.
Antonyms: see AMUSING, CLEVER, WITTY.
6. *Referring to colors:* sober, obscure, sad, plain, colorless, somber, grave, sordid, drab, dun; *spec.* dirty, muddy, gray, dead, lifeless.
Antonyms: see VIVID, BRIGHT, GLOWING.
7. *Referring to a surface:* lusterless, lackluster, opaque, matt, dead, rayless (*R*), flat.
Antonyms: see BRIGHT, IRIDESCENT.
8. *Referring to sounds:* flat, dead, deadened, muffled, softened, indistinct, shut (*R*).
Antonyms: see CLEAR, SHRILL.
9. *Referring to a market:* flat, inactive, quiet, slack; *spec.* UNRESPONSIVE.

dull, *v. t.* **1.** *See* STUPEFY, DEPRESS, DARKEN, BLUNT.
2. *Referring to mental activity:* deaden, obtund (*chiefly med.*), hebetate (*R*), numb, benumb bedull (*intensive*), blunt, jade (*by wearying*), retund (*R*), dullify (*C*), damp or dampen (*as the appetite, desire, ardor, etc.*), blur, besot (*with dissipation*), torpify (*R*); *spec.* cloud.
Antonyms: see STIMULATE.
3. *Referring to a surface:* unpolish (*R*), scrape, roughen, deaden; *spec.* tarnish.
4. *Referring to colors:* deaden, somber (*R*), sober, reduce, tone down.

dullness, *n.* **1.** *Spec.* cheerlessness, darkness, bluntness, stupidity, depression, flatness, deadness.
2. insensitiveness, unfeelingness; *spec.* torpor, sluggishness, meropia, numbness, languidness.
3. spiritlessness, dumpishness, lifelessness, heaviness, doldrums (*pl.; fig.*), ennui, boredom; *spec.* apathy, lethargy, sleepiness, *etc.*
4. uninterestingness, tediousness, tedium, jejuneness, insipidity, frigidity, monotony, *etc.*

---

drub: *beat.* | **dry,** *n.: prohibitionist.* | **dual:** *double.*

5. *Referring to colors:* sobriety, obscurity, plainness, flatness, *etc.*

Antonyms: see BRIGHTNESS.

6. *Referring to a surface* (lusterlessness, mattness, opacity, *etc.*

duly, *adv.* rightly, right, fitly, appropriately, deservedly, properly.

dumb, *a.* **1.** voiceless, mute, inarticulate, speechless, tongue-tied, tongueless.

2. *See* SILENT, NOISELESS.

3. (*C*) *for* stupid, unintelligent, dull, dull-witted.

dumb, *v. t.* gag (*fig. or in transferred senses*), disvoice (*R*).

dump, *n.* **1.** *See* COUNTER.

2. dumpling (*person of rounded outline*).

dump, *n. Spec.* tip, tipple (*local, U. S.*).

dung-eating, *a.* coprophagous.

dungeon, *n.* **1.** donjon, keep.

2. *Spec.* oubliette (*French*); *see* VAULT, PRISON.

dupe, *n.* victim (*contex.*), dotterel (*fig.*), pigeon (*cant*), gull, cully, fool (*A*), stale (*A*), sucker (*C*), lick (*C*), greenhorn, farmer (*C*).

dupe, *v. t.* deceive, fool, victimize (*C*), pigeon (*cant*), gull; *spec.* cheat.

duplicate, *n.* double; *spec.* copy, replica, facsimile, carbon.

duration, *n. Spec.* continuance, date, term, tenor, longitude (*R*), time, durance (*A*).

during, *a.* pending, within, in, through, over (*a period of time*).

dust, *n.* dirt (*contex.*), powder, pother (*R*); *spec.* smother, coom *or* coomb (*Scot. or local Eng.*), breeze, cully, slack, culm, ashes, pouce, pounce, smoke.

duty, *n.* **1.** obligation, ought (*R*), devoir (*A*).

2. obligation, part, charge, business (*spec. or fig.*); *spec.* office, function, task, burden, trust, commission.

Antonyms: see PRIVILEGE.

3. *See* TAX.

dwarf, *n.* diminutive, pygmy *or* pigmy (*often spec.*), droich (*Scot.*), hop-o'-my-thumb (*B*); *spec.* bantam, midge, midget, runt (*contemptuous, exc. of animals*), Lilliputian (*spec. or fig.*), fingerling (*R*), dandiprat (*A*), micromorph (*tech. and R*), manikin, Negrito, Negrillo.

Antonyms: see GIANT.

dwarf, *a.* dwarfish *or* pygmy, pigmy, dwarfly (*R*), undershapen (*R*), undersized, runtish (*contemptuous, exc. of animals*), undergrown, runty (*U. S.*); *spec.* scrubby.

Antonyms: see GIGANTIC.

dwarf, *v. t.* **1.** stunt, bedwarf (*intensive*).

2. *See* DIMINISH, BELITTLE.

dwell, *v. i.* **1.** *See* DELAY, CONTINUE.

2. abide (*implies continuance*), reside (*formal*), domicile (*chiefly legal*), live, harbor (*A*), wont (*R*), inhabit (*R*), stay (*C*), tenant (*R, implying temporary sojourn*), sojourn, lodge (*connotes temporary quarters*), home, keep (*R*); *spec.* house, cabin, kennel, den, tabernacle, tent, room, sojourn, tarry.

3. harp (*in "to harp on"*).

dweller, *n.* inhabitant, abider, liver (*chiefly U. S.*), habitant (*R*), residentiary, resident (*chiefly formal or tech.*); *spec.* denizen. *"Inhabitant" and "resident" are the two common terms.*

dwelling, *n.* abode (*chiefly B*), tenement (*chiefly tech.*), inhabitation, lodging, lodge (*chiefly spec.*); *spec.* house, cottage, establishment, tent, tepee, shanty, shack, dugout, manse, mansion, castle, hutch (*contemptuous*), hut, gunyah (*Australia*), hermitage, igloo (*Eskimo*), familistery, bourock (*Scot.*), cot, barrack, bothy, chalet, cell, den, bungalow, court, doghole, embassy, cabin, bower, drosty, booth (*A*), tabernacle, appartment, maisonette, penthouse.

dye, *n.* **1.** *See* COLOR.

2. pigment (*contex.*); *spec.* grain, dyestuff.

dye, *v. t.* color (*contex.*), strain, grain (*spec. or B*), imbue (*B*); *spec.* tinge, shade, double-dye, ingrain.

dying, *a.* moribund (*B*), fey (*A*), mortal; *spec.* commorient.

dyspeptic, *a.* **1.** indigestive.

2. *See* IRASCIBLE.

E

eager, *a.* **1.** *See* SPIRITED, STRENUOUS.

2. anxious, desirous, keen, fervent, fervid (*these two suggest warmth, ardency; often religious zeal*), forward, hotheaded, hot (*C*), zealous, ardent, agog (*predicative*); *spec.* vehement, earnest.

Antonyms: see APATHETIC.

eagle, *n.* erne (*now chiefly spec.*); *spec.* ringtail, sore-eagle, griffin, harpy, eaglet.

ear, *n.* head (*of various composite fruits, as cereals*); *spec.* spike.

ear, *n.* **1.** *Referring to the external ear:* lug (*chiefly Scot.*), shell (*chiefly B*), concha (*tech.*), conch (*R*); *spec.* prick-ear, crop-ear.

2. projection (*contex.*), lug; *spec.* loop, canon, cannon.

3. *See* HEARING, ATTENTION, AUDIENCE.

earache, *n.* otalgia (*tech.*).

eardrum, *n.* drum (*contex.*), tympanum (*tech.*).

eared, *a.* spiked (*like corn*).

earlier, *a.* old (*contex.*), former, previous, elder.

Antonyms: see LATER.

early, *adv.* betimes, soon; *spec.* timely.

early, *a.* rathe (*B*); *spec.* timely, auroral, matutinal *or* matinal, rareripe, ratheripe *or* rathripe (*B*), precocious.

Antonyms: see LATE.

---

dummy, *a.: pretend.*
dummy, *n.: mute, blockhead, agent, counterfeit, model.*
dumpish: *depressed, dull, stupid.*
dun, *a.: drab.*
dun, *v. t.: ask.*
duplicate: *v. t.: double, copy, repeat.*
durance: *duration, imprisonment, confinement.*
duress: *imprisonment, constraint.*
dusky: *dim.*
dust, *v. t.: dirty, powder, clean.*
dwindle: *decline, diminish.*

E

eagle-eyed: *sharp-sighted, discerning.*
earlier: *before.*
earliest, *a.: first, original.*

earmark, *v. t. Spec.* crop, dog's-ear, dog-ear.
earnest, *n.* **1.** payment (*contex.*), installment (*contex.*), handsel; *spec.* God's penny (*now dial.*), earnest-money.
2. *Referring to an indication of what is to come:* pledge, promise, handsel, foretaste.
earnest, *a.* **1.** intent (*concentrated*), serious, intense (*implying tension*); *spec.* eager, impassioned, animated, cordial.
Antonyms: see INSINCERE, TRIFLING, PLAYFUL.
2. *See* IMPORTANT.
earnestness, *n.* earnest (*only in "in earnest," "in real earnest," etc.*), impressment (*R*), seriousness, intentness.
Antonyms: see PLAY.
earnings, *n. pl.* **1.** pay (*sing.; contex.*), gettings (*pl.; A*), wages (*pl. or sing.; chiefly spec.*), salary (*sing.; chiefly spec.*), gravy (*S; easy or superfluous* earnings).
2. *See* PROFITS.
earth, *n.* **1.** planet (*contex.*), ball (*fig.*), globe, terrene (*R*), terra (*tech.*), Tellus (*fig.; B*), world (*more often used generically for the whole of humanity or affairs, whereas* earth *relates to the terrestrial globe*); *spec.* counterearth, Midgard (*mythol.*).
2. world (*as the home of man and other creatures*), mold *or* mould (*B or obs.*).
3. *Referring to the solid substance of the earth:* ground, clod (*B*), glebe (*B or rhetorical*), land, mold *or* mould (*B or obs.*); *spec.* rock, sand, mud, muck, dirt (*C; often derogatory or contemptuous*), clay, loam, hard pan (*chiefly U. S.*), dust, *etc.*
4. *Referring to that part of the ground in which plants grow:* soil, mold *or* mould (*B or spec.*); *spec.* loam, humus, dirt (*C*), muck.
5. *Referring to worldly things or state:* world (*used with "the"*).
6. *See* MANKIND, BURROW.
earth-born, *a.* **1.** terrigenous (*R*).
2. *See* HUMAN, WORLDLY.
earthen, *a.* earth; *spec.* stone, dirt, clay, mud, *etc.;—the nouns used attributively.*
earthenware, *n.* crockery; *spec.* cloam, cloom (*obs. or dial. Eng.*), china, delf *or* delft, pottery, stoneware, crouchware, porcelain, Wedgwood ware, pebble *or* pebbleware, majolica, terra-cotta, Belleek, *etc.*
earthly, *a.* **1.** terrestrial, earthy (*R*).
2. unspiritual, nonspiritual; *spec.* material, mundane, worldly, sensual, bodily, temporal.
Antonyms: see DIVINE, SPIRITUAL, ETHEREAL.
3. conceivable, possible.
earthquake, *n.* quake, shock, seism (*R*); *spec.* microseism.
earthworm, *n.* angleworm, dew-worm; *spec.* lobworm.
earthy, *a.* **1.** earthlike, cloddy (*depreciatory*), terrene (*R*), glebous (*R*); *spec.* muddy, clayey, dusty, elemental (*fig.*), wholesome (*fig.*), simple (*fig.*).
2. terrestrial.
3. *See* MATERIAL, GROSS, COARSE.
earwax, *n.* cerumen (*tech.*).
ease, *n.* **1.** comfort (*positive well-being, as compared to the sense of absence of strain implied by* ease).
2. easiness; *spec.* carelessness, freedom, relief, facility, leisure, liberty, convenience, rest, repose, content, unconstraint, unconcern, quiet, naturalness (*of manner*).
Antonyms: see CONSTRAINT, DIFFICULTY.
ease, *v. t.* **1.** *See* COMFORT, MITIGATE, RELIEVE, DIMINISH.
2. facilitate, smooth, favor.
easily, *adv.* easy (*C or vulgar*); *spec.* conveniently, carelessly, smoothly, glib, readily, gently, *etc.*
east, *n.* **1.** dawn (*B*), dayspring (*B*), orient (*B or A*), rise (*fig.*).
Antonyms: see WEST.
2. east country, eastland (*now B*); *spec.* Orient.
eastern, *a.* eastwardly, eastward, east (*more C and usual than "eastern"*), eoan (*R*), auroral *or* aurorean (*B*), orient *or* oriental (*R, exc. as capitalized and spec., of the Levant*), easterly.
Antonyms: see WESTERN.
easterner, *n.* oriental (*R, exc. as capitalized and spec.*), easterling (*A, exc. hist.*).
easy, *a.* **1.** comfortable.
2. *Spec.* free, unembarrassed, unconstrained, smooth, effortless, tractable, tranquil, quiet, careless, smooth, ready, facile, natural, graceful, mild, manageable, airy, soft, gentle, moderate, indolent, unconcerned, easy-going, restful, compliant, complaisant, credulous, loose, wealthy.
Antonyms: see SEVERE.
3. facile, light; *spec.* convenient.
Antonyms: see DIFFICULT.
easy-going, *a.* easy, jog-trot, happy-go-lucky; *spec.* careless.
eat, *v. t.* **1.** consume (*contex.*), devour, discuss (*humorous*), demolish (*S*), mandicate (*R*); *spec.* engorge (*R*), touch, gormandize, gluttonize, dispatch (*C*), table (*R*), gorge, wolf (*S*).
2. *See* CONSUME, CORRODE, ERODE, WEAR.
eat, *v. i.* feed (*now chiefly of animals*), victual (*R*); *spec.* gorge, pick *or* peck (*fig., C, or S, exc. of birds*), raven, gormandize, mess, lunch, board, common (*chiefly in school and college use*), dine, dinner (*R*), sup, supper (*R or C*), collation (*obs.*), breakfast, grub (*S*).
eatable, *a.* edible, esculent (*tech. or B*), ciborious (*R*).
Antonyms: see UNEATABLE.
eatable, *n.* edible, esculent (*B or tech.*), comestible (*learned and usually humorous or affected*), gustable (*R*).
eater, *n.* consumer, devourer; *spec.* epicure,

---

earmark, *v. t.: mark.* | **earn:** *gain.* | **earnest-money:** *earnest.*

---

gorger, glutton, diner, luncher, gourmet (*French*), gormandizer, gormand, gourmand (*French*).
eating, *a.* **1.** eadacious (*chiefly humorous*).
2. *Spec.* corrosive, erosive, gnawing.
eating, *n.* **1.** consumption, devourment, manducation (*R*), eat (*obs., S, or cant*), repast (*R*).
2. gastrology.
3. *Spec.* consumption, corrosion, erosion, fretting, *etc.*
eating house, restaurant; *spec.* cafe, chophouse, coffeehouse, tea room, cafeteria, quick-and-dirty (*C, U. S.*), diner (*U. S.*), roadhouse, lunchroom, hash-house (*C, U. S.*).
eaves, *n. pl.* overhang.
ebony, *n.* **1.** *Referring to the wood:* ebon (*now B*).
2. *See* DARK.
eccentric, *a.* **1.** *Spec.* decentered.
2. *Spec.* elliptic, parabolic, hyperbolic.
3. peculiar, queer, odd, oddish, strange, bizarre, singular, erratic, unpredictable, wild, cranky, outré (*French*), quaint, outlandish; *spec.* fantastic, abnormal, whimsical.
eccentric, *n.* crocheteer (*R*), hobbyist, monomaniac, crank (*C*), curiosity, quiz (*R*), original; *spec.* guy.
eccentricity, *n.* peculiarity, queerness, oddity, oddness, strangeness, idiosyncrasy, singularity, erraticness, crankiness, quaintness, outlandishness; *spec.* fantasticalness, abnormality, whimsicality.
ecclesiastic, ecclesiastical, *a.* church (*the attributive use of the noun*), churchly; *spec.* religious.
ecclesiastic, *n.* *Spec.* churchman, conventual, prior; *see* MONK, NUN, MINISTER.
echo, *n.* **1.** reverberation (*learned or tech.*), reply, return, repercussion (*R*), reflection (*R or tech.*); *spec.* re-echo.
2. *See* REPETITION, IMITATION.
echo, *v. t.* **1.** reverberate, return; *spec.* re-echo.
2. *See* REPEAT, COPY.
echo, *v. i.* reverberate, resound, reply, ring, redound (*R*); *spec.* re-echo.
economical, *a.* economizing, saving, careful, sparing, thrifty, provident, parsimonious (*R*), frugal; *spec.* cheap.
Antonyms: see EXTRAVAGANT, WASTEFUL.
economics, *n.* political economy, chrematistics (*often spec.*), plutonomy (*R*), plutology (*R*).
economist, *n.* political economist, chrematist (*chiefly spec.; R*); *spec.* physiocrat.
economize, *v. t.* save, husband, stint, scant, spare, scrimp (*C*), skimp (*C*).
Antonyms: see WASTE.
economize, *v. i.* save, stint, scant, spare, retrench, scrimp (*C*), skimp (*C*).
economy, *n.* economizing, economization (*R*), saving, thrift, thriftiness, savingness, providence, parsimony (*R*), sparing, husbandry, husbanding, skimping (*C*), scanting (*C*); *spec.* retrenchment.
Antonyms: see WASTE, EXTRAVAGANCE.
ecstasy, *n.* rapture (*of bliss only*), transport (*with implication of being carried out of one's self*), rapt (*R*), raptus (*R*), paroxysm, intoxication, enthusiasm, ravishment (*R*); *spec.* trance, frenzy, agony, madness, nympholepsy.
Antonyms: see APATHY, CALM.
ecstatic, *a.* transported, rapt, enrapt, enraptured, rapturous, rhapsodical, raptured; *spec.* enthusiastic (*R*).
Antonyms: see APATHETIC, CALM.
eddy, *n.* countercurrent (*contex.; R*), swirl; *spec.* whirlpool.
eddy, *v. i.* swirl, gurge (*R*).
edge, *n.* **1.** *Referring to a projecting part where two surfaces meet at an angle: spec.* featheredge, face, beard, bit, burr, hip, groin, arris, bezel, waney, gunwhale *or* gunnel, crest, hem, verge.
2. *Referring to the place where a surface terminates:* verge, margin, limit (*chiefly in pl.*), bound, brim (*chiefly spec.*), side, coast (*A*), bordure (*chiefly her.*), lip, rim, brink, border; *spec.* skirt (*chiefly in pl.*), hem, outskirt (*chiefly in pl.*), limb, exergue, list, selvage *or* selvedge, footing, fringe, listing, edging, leech, deckle edge, berm, curb, bezel, bank.
Antonyms: see BODY, CENTER.
3. intensity; *spec.* sharpness, zest, keenness, bitterness, sting.
edge, *v. t.* **1.** *See* SHARPEN.
2. border, rim, margin, skirt, marginate (*R*); *spec.* fringe, befringe (*R*), purl, belace.
edged, *a.* **1.** *See* SHARP.
2. marginate (*tech.*), listed, margined, bordered, *etc.*
edging, *n.* edge (*contex.*); *spec.* skirt (*R*), welt, welting, frill.
edict, *n.* **1.** decree (*contex.*); *spec.* bull, capitulary, constitution.
2. *See* DECISION.
edit, *v. t.* **1.** redact (*tech. or B*); *spec.* revise, arrange, digest.
2. conduct (*for publication, as a periodical*).
editing, *n.* redaction; *spec.* revision, recension, emendation.
edition, *n.* redaction; *spec.* (*referring to the number printed at one printing*) issue, impression, impress, printing.
editor, *n.* **1.** redactor (*tech. or B*), redacteur (*French*), reviser; *spec.* scholar.
2. conductor (*as of a periodical*).
editorial, *n.* leader (*chiefly British*); *spec.* leaderette (*chiefly British*).
educated, *a.* lettered, literate (*learned*), cultured, schooled, trained.
Antonyms: see UNEDUCATED.
education, *n.* **1.** breeding (*bringing up*).
2. *See* TEACHING, TRAINING.
3. training, culture.

---

ebb, *n.: outgo, decline.*
ebb, *v. i.: outflow, decline.*
ebullition: *boiling, bubbling, agitation.*
éclat: *distinction.*
eclectic: *choosing.*
eclipse, *n. obscuration, darkness.*
eclipse, *v. t.: obscure, darken, outshine.*
edible: *eatable.*
edifice: *building.*
edify: *improve.*
educate: *train, teach.*
educational: *instructive.*
eduction: *drawing.*
eerie: *fearful, weird.*

effface, *v. t.* remove (*contex.*), obliterate, erase (*properly spec.*), expunge, excise (*properly spec.*), delete *or* dele (*tech.*), outblot (*B*), strike (*esp. with "out," etc.*); *spec.* dislimn (*R*), rase (*R*), snuff, sponge.
Antonyms: see INTERPOLATE.

effect, *n.* **1.** consequence, fruit (*fig.*); *spec.* superconsequence, impress, outcome.
2. *Referring to mental effect on a person:* impression, impressure (*R*), ensemble (*French*), impress.
3. *See* MEANING, ACTION, ACTUALITY.
4. *In pl.:* goods.

effect, *v. t.* bring (*with "about"*), cause, produce, effectuate, have; *spec.* operate, work, force, accomplish, drive, contrive, negotiate, compass, conclude, make, contract, execute, perform, conjure.

effective, *a.* **1.** causative, active, operative, dynamic, dynamical.
2. *As implying power or potency in producing results:* efficacious, effectual, efficient, good (*of persons*), perficient (*R*), proficient, prevalent (*R*), deedful (*R*).
Antonyms: see BARREN, INEFFECTUAL, UNPRODUCTIVE.
3. *In reference to affecting a person's opinion, feeling, or the like:* impressive, forceful, efficacious, telling, fetching (*C*), pointed; *spec.* cogent, stinging, cutting, striking, convincing.

effectiveness, *n.* causativeness, effectuality, efficaciousness, efficiency, point, forcefulness, cogency, virtue, duty.

effeminacy, *n.* womanishness, invirility (*R*), woman (*R, exc. as equiv. to womanliness*), femininity, feminity (*R*); *spec.* tenderness, weakness, delicacy.

effeminate, *a.* womanish, ladylike (*properly spec.*), soft, silken (*fig.; used of men*), unmanly (*used of men*), tender, weak, delicate, effete (*often loosely used in this sense*).
Antonyms: see MANLINESS.

effeminate, *n.* milksop, mollycoddle, tenderling (*R*); *spec.* betty, molly, pansy (*S*), daisy (*S*), violet (*S*), fairy (*S*), sissy.

effeminate, *v. t.* soften, emolliate (*R*), emasculate (*a man*).
Antonyms: see TOUGHEN.

effete, *a.* exhausted.

effloresce, *v. i.* *Referring to a formation on minerals, salt solutions, etc.:* bloom; *spec.* crust.

efflorescence, *n.* bloom, florescence, pulverulence, powder; *spec.* crust.

effort, *n.* **1.** exertion (*positive and strenuous exercise of strength, will, etc., whereas* effort *usually implies a single action rather than continued activity*), endeavor, strife, stretch, strain, stress, push (*fig.; C*), spurt *or* spirt, trouble (*implying inconvenience*), pains (*implying solicitude or special care*), attempt, try; *spec.* breath, burst, struggle.
2. *See* DEED.

effusion, *n.* **1.** *See* OUTFLOW, UTTERANCE, EXPRESSION, COMPOSITION.
2. demonstration (*of feeling*), gush, slopping over (*contemptuous; C*).

effusive, *a.* **1.** *See* LUXURIANT.
2. demonstrative (*which see*), gushing, exuberant.
Antonyms: see IMPASSIVE, UNEMOTIONAL.

egg-shaped, *a.* oviform, oval, ovate, ovoid, ovodial (*R*), ovicular (*R*), ellipsoidal (*a loose usage*); *spec.* obovate.

egoism, *n.* **1.** individualism, self-feeling; *spec.* suicism (*R*), selfishness, self-seeking, self-opinionatedness, weism (*R*), solipsism (*philos.*); *see* SELFISHNESS.
2. *See* EGOTISM.

egoistic, *a.* **1.** individualistic, self-regarding, self-centered; *see* SELFISH.
2. *See* EGOTISTIC.

egotism, *n.* conceit, egoism (*less offensively self-centered than* egotism), suicism (*R*).

egotistic, *a.* egotistical, conceited (*contex.*), egoistic, self-obtruding.

eight, *n.* *Referring to a group of eight things:* octave (*chiefly spec.*), ogdoad (*B*), octonary (*chiefly spec.*), octad, octet *or* octette (*R*).

eight-angled, *a.* octangular (*tech.*).

eightfold, *a.* octuple (*B or tech.*).

eighth, *n.* octave (*mus.*); *spec.* suboctave (*R*).

eight-sided, *a.* octahedral (*tech.*), octahedric (*tech.*), eight-square (*chiefly naut.*).

ejaculate, *v. t.* **1.** *See* EJECT.
2. *To utter:* blurt, bolt; *spec.* exclaim.

eject, *v. t.* **1.** emit, expel, ejaculate (*chiefly physiol.*), cast (*used with "out"; R*); *spec.* fire, belch, spew, eructate, eruct, erupt, eliminate (*obs. or humorous*), spit, spout, squirt, deliver, void, evacuate, disgorge, regorge; *see* VOMIT.
Antonyms: see INJECT.
2. *To drive from a place or position:* remove, oust, expel, dispossess, bounce (*S*); *spec.* disseize, evict, unnest, unkennel, unhouse.

ejection, *n.* **1.** emission, expulsion, ejaculation (*chiefly spec.*); *spec.* delivery, firing, belching, belch, spewing, eructation, eruption, spouting, squirt, squirting, delivery, voidance, outthrow (*R*), disgorgement.
Antonyms: see INJECTION.
2. ouster, expulsion, dispossession, disseizing, eviction, removal.
3. ejecta (*pl.*), ejectamenta (*pl.*); *spec.* spew, vomit.

elaborate, *a.* labored, operose (*R*); *spec.* studied, perfected, complicated, detailed, curious, dressy.
Antonyms: see SIMPLE, ELEMENTARY.

elaborate, *v. t.* work out, develop, labor, devise.

elaborateness, *n.* elaboration, detail, nicety, complication, *etc.*

---

effectual: *effective.*
effectuate: *accomplish.*
effervescent: *bubbling, lively.*
effigy: *figure.*
effrontery: *impudence.*
effuse, *a.: diffuse, spreading.*
egg, *v. t.: incite, urge.*
egregious: *outrageous.*

---

elaboration, *n.* **1.** development, painstaking, perfection, devising.
2. *See* ELABORATENESS.
elastic, *a.* **1.** resilient (*chiefly tech.*), springy; *spec.* expansive.
Antonyms: see PLASTIC, INELASTIC.
2. *See* BUOYANT (*in mind*).
elate, *v. t.* excite, enliven, exhilarate, exalt, elevate (*now R*), flush, animate; *spec.* please, gladden, puff, inflate.
Antonyms: see DEPRESS, ANNOY.
elated, *a.* elate (*A or B*), exalted (*closest to the sense, in* elated, *of being uplifted*), exultant (*stressing enthusiastic expression of* elation), swollen, flushed, exhilarated, animated; *spec.* joyful, glad, inflated, puffed-up.
Antonyms: see DEPRESSED.
elation, *n.* excitement, enlivenment, exaltation, flush, elevation (*now R*), animation; *spec.* joy, pride.
Antonyms: see DEPRESSION.
elbow, *n.* ancon (*tech.*), joint (*contex.*).
elbow, *v. t.* push, nudge (*gently*); *spec.* jostle.
elbowlike, *a.* anconal, anconoid;—*both tech.*
elect, *v. t.* choose; *spec.* return, predestinate, tap (*loc., Yale Univ.*).
elect, *a.* chosen; *spec.* predestinated.
elect, *n. Spec.* predestinate.
election, *n.* choice; *spec.* by-election, predestination.
elective, *a.* **1.** choosing; *spec.* constituent.
2. optional, optative, selective, electoral (*chiefly spec.*).
elector, *n.* chooser; *spec.* constituent, voter.
electorate, *n.* constituency.
electric, *a.* **1.** *Spec.* voltaic, faradaic, thermoelectric, piezoelectric, *etc.*
2. *See* THRILLING, EXCITING, STIMULATING.
electrified, *a.* live (*rail, etc.*).
electrify, *v. t.* **1.** electrize; *spec.* galvanize, faradize.
2. *See* THRILL, EXCITE, STIMULATE, STARTLE.
electrocute, *v. t.* shock; execute, burn (*S, U. S.*).
elegance, *n. Spec.* grace, refinement, courtliness, daintiness, featness (*A*), nicety, finish, cultism, Gongorism, purism, finery.
elegant, *a. "Elegant" implies good taste and more or less ornateness, grace, discrimination, or the like, such as is associated with cultivation. Hence, with this implication: spec.* æsthetic (*B*), graceful, refined, courtly, Chesterfieldian, Ciceronian, dainty, shapely, trim, feat (*A*), nice, genteel, silken *or* silky, chaste, cultured, neat, polished, finished.
Antonyms: see CRUDE.
elegist, *n.* threnodist, monodist.
element, *n.* **1.** *See* COMPONENT, PART.
2. *Formerly: spec.* earth, air, fire, water.
3. *For chem., see the dictionaries.*
4. *Spec.* datum, condition, moment *or* momentum (*tech. or B*), factor, principle, germ, rudiment, fundamental, principium (*R*), primary.
5. *In the Christian religion: spec.* host, bread, wine, eulogia (*hist.*), Eucharist.
elementary, *a.* **1.** component (*R*). *See* SIMPLE, UNCOMPOUNDED.
2. initial, rudimentary, inchoate (*just begun*), incipient (*just beginning, but implying growth to come*), primary (*first, in time*), fundamental (*necessary as prerequisite to what follows*), basal *or* basic, primordial.
Antonyms: see ELABORATE.
elephant, *n. Spec.* foal, tusker, mammoth, mastodon.
elevate, *v. t.* **1.** *See* RAISE (*physically*), ELATE.
2. *To raise in rank, etc.:* raise, advance, exalt, aggrandize; *spec.* dignify, promote, ennoble.
Antonyms: see ABASE, DEGRADE.
3. *To raise the mental or moral character of:* raise, lift, exalt; *spec.* refine.
Antonyms: see CONTAMINATE, DEGRADE.
elevated, *a.* **1.** *See* HIGH, UPTURNED.
2. *Referring to mental or moral character:* high, lofty, grand, sublime, soaring, empyreal (*fig.*), grandiose, high-flown, buskined (*B*), noble, magnificent.
Antonyms: see VILE, DEGRADED, DEPRAVED.
elevating, *a.* ennobling, inspiring, exalting.
Antonyms: see CONTAMINATIVE.
elevation, *n.* **1.** *See* RAISING, DELINEATION.
2. raising, advancement, exaltation, aggrandization; *spec.* dignification, promotion, ennoblement.
Antonyms: see DEGRADATION.
3. raising (*morally or intellectually*), lifting, exaltation; *spec.* refinement.
Antonyms: see DEGRADATION.
4. *Referring to state or position or elevated rank, as in character: spec.* height, dignity, eminence, eminency.
Antonyms: see DEGRADATION, DEPRAVITY.
5. *Referring to an elevated object or place:* height, eminence (*chiefly B*); *spec.* hill, swell (*of land*), mountain.
Antonyms: see HOLLOW.
elevator, *n.* lift, hoist (*chiefly spec.*); *spec.* whim, dumbwaiter; storehouse (*for grain*).
eleventh, *a.* undecennary (*tech. or learned*).
elf, *n.* demon (*contex.*), sprite, fairy, imp (*chiefly spec.*), elfin, pygmy, puck, pixy; *spec.* urchin.
elfish, *a.* demonic (*contex.*), impish (*chiefly spec.*), fairy, elfin, elvish; *spec.* mischievous, weird.
elicit, *v. t.* draw (*used with "forth" or "out"*), extract (extract *implies force in drawing out*), extort (*implies the bringing out of a reluctant witness, etc.*), call (*used with "out"*), evoke,

eld: *age, antiquity.*
elder, *a.: earlier, old, superior.*
elder, *n.: senior.*
elderly: *old.*
eldest: *oldest.*
elect: *chosen.*
electioneer: *campaign.*
elegiac: *mournful.*
elegy: *dirge.*
elide: *delete.*
eligible: *qualified.*
eliminate, *v. t.: expel, excrete, omit, ignore, suppress, abstract.*

fetch (*C or R*), educe, expiscate (*humorous or Scot.*); *spec.* wrest *or* wring, extort, pump.
elite, *n.* chosen (*pl.*), flower (*collective sing.*); *see* CHOSEN, BEST.
elocution, *n.* utterance; *spec.* delivery, oratory, eloquence.
elocutionist, *n. Spec.* reader, speaker.
eloquence, *n.* facundity (*R*); *spec.* oratory.
eloquent, *a.* facund (*R*); *spec.* Ciceronian, oratorical.
else, *a.* other, different, besides *or* beside (*predicatively used*), more.
Antonyms: see ALIKE.
else, *adv.* differently, otherwise.
elucidate, *v. t.* clarify, illucidate (*R*), illuminate, illustrate; *spec.* explain, interpret, demonstrate.
Antonyms: see CONFUSE.
elucidative, *a.* illustrative, demonstrative, clarifying, illucidative, illuminative, illuminatory; *spec.* explanatory, interpretative.
Antonyms: see CONFUSING.
elusive, *a.* elusory, evasive, lubricous (*B*), slippery (*fig.*), subtle, shifty, baffling, shy; *spec.* deceptive, equivocatory, illusory.
emaciate, *v. t.* thin, waste, extenuate (*R*), disflesh (*R*).
emaciation, *n.* leanness, tabescence (*R*).
emanate, *v. t.* emit, effuse; *spec.* exhale, evaporate, radiate.
emanate, *v. i.* flow, proceed, issue, come; *spec.* exhale, evaporate, radiate.
emanation, *n.* **1.** emission, effluence, effluvium (*thing emanated*), efflux; *spec.* aura, exhalation, mephitis (*noxious*).
2. *Referring to impalpable things:* evaporation, radiation.
emasculate, *v. t.* **1.** *See* CASTRATE.
2. weaken, unman; *spec.* effeminate, effeminize.
embalm, *v. t.* preserve (*both fig. and literal*), cherish (*fig. only*); scent, perfume.
embankment, *n.* **1.** embanking.
2. mound (*R*); *spec.* dike, levee, mole, bulwark, bund (*Anglo-Indian*), promenade.
embarrass, *v. t.* **1.** discomfort, demoralize, disconcert, discomfit; *spec.* nonplus, involve, bother, abash, encumber, trouble, harass, annoy, shame, mortify, hamper, confuse, confound (*completely* confuse).
Antonyms: see DISEMBARRASS.
2. *See* COMPLICATE.
embarrassing, *a.* demoralizing, awkward, difficult, disconcerting, bothersome, *etc.*
Antonyms: see ASSURE.
embarrassment, *n.* discomfort, disconcertion, disconcertedness (*loss of presence of mind*), discomfiture; *spec.* cumber, confusion, shame, difficulty, mortification, constraint, abashment (*total loss of self-possession, often from sense of inferiority*), involvement, pressure, trouble, vexation, perplexity, *etc.*
Antonyms: see ASSURANCE.
embassy, *n.* **1.** commission, embassade (*A*), embassage (*A*).
2. legation, embassage (*A*), embassade (*A*).
3. residence (*contex.*), legation.
embattle, *v. t.* crenel (*R*), crenellate (*R*).
embed, *v. t.* bed, impaste (*R*), enlay (*chiefly spec.*).
embellish, *v. t.* enrich; *spec.* vary, emblazon, emblaze.
embezzle, *v. t.* misappropriate, misapply, convert, peculate (*chiefly spec.*). *"Embezzling" is accomplished by fraud or breach of trust in relation to property already legally in one's possession; "stealing" by wrongfully getting possession of property with intention to appropriate it.*
embezzle, *v. i.* misappropriate, defalcate, peculate (*chiefly spec.*).
embitter, *v. t.* **1.** *Referring to the taste: see* BITTER.
2. *Referring to the mind:* envenom, empoison (*B*), rankle (*R*), sour, exacerbate (*make more bitter; B*).
Antonyms: see SOFTEN.
3. *Referring to persons:* exasperate, poison, envenom; *spec.* exacerbate (*B*).
Antonyms: see SOFTEN.
embodiment, *n.* bodiment, insubstantiation (*R*), image, incorporation; *spec.* incarnation, personification, personation (*R*), impanation, avatar (*theosophy*), epiphany, representation.
embody, *v. t.* incorporate, corporate (*R*), body, insubstantiate (*R*); *spec.* incarnate, impersonate, enflesh (*R*), encarnalize (*R*), personify, represent, comprise, impanate, pillar.
Antonyms: see SPIRITUALIZE.
embolden, *v. t.* hearten, encourage, embrave (*R*), nerve, inspirit; *spec.* reassure.
Antonyms: see DISCOURAGE.
emboss, *v. t.* **1.** *Referring to a surface:* ornament (*contex.*), boss; *spec.* knot, pounce (*hist.*).
Antonyms: see INDENT.
2. *Referring to projecting parts:* raise, boss; *spec.* knot.
embrace, *v. t.* **1.** clasp (*contex.*), clutch (*contex.*), clip (*A or dial.*), fathom (*R*), halse (*Scot.*), hold (*contex.*), bosom (*fig.*), fold, infold *or* enfold (*intensive*), entwine (*intensive*), grapple, embosom (*intensive*), hug; *spec.* cuddle, lock, enlock (*intensive; R*), nurse.
2. *See* INCLUDE, ADOPT, ACCEPT, RECEIVE.
embrace, *n.* **1.** clasp (*contex.*), clip (*A*), embracement (*R*), hold (*contex.*), fold, hug.
2. *See* EMBRACE, ADOPTION, ACCEPTANCE, RECEPTION, ESPOUSAL.
embrasure, *n.* **1.** *Spec.* splay.

---

elope: *depart.*
elude: *evade, avoid.*
elusion: *evasion, avoidance.*
emaciated: *thin.*
emancipate: *free.*
embalm: *preserve.*
embark, *v. t.: ship, invest.*
embark, *v. i.: engage.*
emblazon: *delineate, depict, embellish, celebrate.*
emblem: *symbol, badge.*
emblematic, emblematical, *a.: symbolic.*

---

2. opening (*contex.*), vent (*R*); *spec.* porthole (*mil.*).
embroider, *v. t.* ornament (*contex.*), work; *spec.* branch, lace, tambour, couch.
embroidered, *a.* ornamented (*contex.*), worked; *spec.* orphreyed *or* orfrayed.
embroidery, *n.* ornamentation (*contex.*), needlework, work; *spec.* orphrey *or* orfray, sampler, spatterwork, needlework, insertion, orris, phulkari (*East Indian*).
embroil, *v. t.* involve, perplex, trouble, disorder.
embryo, *n.* **1.** *Spec.* fetus *or* fœtus, conception (*fig.*), corcle *or* corcule (*bot.*), mole *or* mola.
2. *See* BEGINNING.
emerge, *v. i.* **1.** issue; *spec.* peep, outcrop (*also fig.*), appear.
Antonyms: see SINK, DIP.
2. *See* ARISE.
emergence, *n.* **1.** issuance, emergency; *spec.* outcrop, peeping, appearance, emersion (*chiefly astron.*).
Antonyms: see DIP.
2. *See* ARISING.
emetic, *a.* vomitory, vomitive (*R*), eccritic (*R*).
emetic, *n.* puke (*not now in polite usage*), vomitory (*tech. or R*), vomitive (*R*), vomit (*R*), eccritic (*R*); *spec.* castor oil, rhubarb, *etc.*
emigrant, *n.* migrant; *spec.* colonist, redemptioner (*U. S.*).
Antonyms: see IMMIGRANT.
emigrate, *v. i.* depart (*contex.*), migrate.
Antonyms: see IMMIGRATE.
emigration, *n.* departure (*contex.*), migration; *spec.* exodus.
emission, *n.* **1.** emitting, discharge; *spec.* projection, radiation, exudation, emanation, expression, exhalation, delivery.
Antonyms: see ABSORPTION.
2. *See* ISSUANCE.
emit, *v. t.* **1.** discharge, deliver, emanate (*R or spec.*); *spec.* shoot, spirt, dart, dartle, squirt (*undignified*), jet, evolve, radiate, breathe, exhale, effuse, bleed (*fig.*), express, shed, gush, vent, puff, throw, hurl, foam, outpour.
Antonyms: see SWALLOW, ABSORB.
2. *See* ISSUE, UTTER.
emotional, *a.* **1.** emotive.
2. sentimental (*to excess or affectedly*), pathematic (*R*), feeling, pathetic (*R*), effective; *spec.* maudlin, mawkish, demonstrative, sickly (*C*), sicklied, intense, languorous, languishing, unctious (*R*), unctuous, mushy.
Antonyms: see APATHETIC.
emotionalize, *v. i.* sentimentalize; *spec.* gush, languish.
emperor, *n.* monarch (*contex.*), czar, cæsar, kaiser; *spec.* kaiserling (*chiefly dim.*), imperator (*hist.*), Mikado.
emphasis, *n.* **1.** *See* ACCENT, FORCE.
2. significance, weight, accentuation, accent, stress.
Antonyms: see DISREGARD.
emphasize, *v. t.* accentuate, stress, mark, punctuate; *spec.* underline, underscore, enforce.
Antonyms: see DISREGARD.
emphatic, *a.* forcible, forceful, impressive, decided, strong, significant; *spec.* intensive, expressive, positive, important, earnest, energetic, unequivocal, distinct.
Antonyms: see APATHETIC.
empire, *n.* **1.** domain (*contex.*), dominion (*contex.*), imperium (*formal or hist.*).
2. *See* DOMAIN.
employee, *n.* employé, agent (*R or tech.*), help (*a collective*); *spec.* man, hand (*these two often with "hired" prefixed*), servant, clerk. "*Employee" is chiefly U. S.*
Antonyms: see EMPLOYER.
employer, *n.* governor (*S*), boss (*cant or S*), master (*chiefly legal*).
Antonyms: see EMPLOYEE.
emptiness, *n.* **1.** hollowness, voidness, vacuity (*B*), inanition (*chiefly spec.*), vacuousness (*R*), inanity (*R*), vacancy, vacantness; *spec.* exhaustion, depletion, *etc.*
Antonyms: see FULLNESS.
2. *See* HOLLOWNESS (*of a sound*), HUNGER.
3. *Referring to an empty space:* inane (*B*), void (*the usual word*), vacuity (*B or tech.*), hollow; *spec.* vacuum (*tech.*).
4. unsubstantiality, vanity, hollowness, uselessness; *spec.* frivolity, vanity, unsatisfying, unsatisfactoriness, meaninglessness, triviality, unfeelingness, fruitlessness, senselessness, insincerity, inanity, stupidity, *etc.*
empty, *a.* **1.** hollow, vacant (*as opposed to* occupied, *whereas* empty *is the opposite of* full, *and implies measurement of quantity number or quality*), vacuous (*R*), inane (*R*); *spec.* blank (*free from marks or writing*), clear, unloaded, unfilled, emptied, exhausted, depleted, destitute (*implies dearth, drought, calamity, penury, etc.*), free.
Antonyms: see FULL.
2. *See* HOLLOW (*of a sound*), HUNGRY, DEVOID.
3. unsubstantial, vain, useless; *spec.* void, foolish, trivial, unsatisfying, meaningless, frivolous, unfeeling, fruitless, senseless, insincere, inane, stupid, *etc.*
Antonyms: see SIGNIFICANT, PITHY.
empty, *v. t.* **1.** void (*B or tech.*), deplenish (*R*), deplete; *spec.* buzz (*Eng.*), disglut (*R*), drink, clear, draw, exhaust, gut (*fig.*), evacuate, bottom (*R*), drain.
Antonyms: see FILL, STUFF.
2. *See* DISCHARGE.
emulate, *v. t.* rival.

emendate: *correct.*
eminent: *elevate, distinguished, conspicuous.*
emotionless: *unfeeling.*
emphasizing: *intensive.*
empiric: *quack.*
employment: *use, occupation, business, service.*
emporium: *market, warehouse, shop.*
empower: *enable, authorize.*
empressment: *cordiality, demonstrativeness.*

emulation, *n.* rivalry, vying, competition (*for some specific object*), strife.
emulous, *a. Meaning:* desirous of equaling or excelling; strifeful;—*no exact synonyms.*
enable, *v. t.* empower.
Antonyms: see DISABLE.
enact, *v. t.* **1.** decree, make, pass.
Antonyms: ABOLISH, REVOKE.
2. *See* ACT.
enamel, *n.* ornamentation (*contex.*), glaze; *spec.* cloisonné (*French*).
enamor or **enamour,** *v. t.* captivate, smite (*chiefly in p. p., "smitten"*). *"Enamor" takes "of"; "captivate" usually "with."*
enchase, *v. t.* **1.** *See* SET, VARIEGATE.
2. ornament (*contex.*); *spec.* chase, engrave, inlay, emboss.
encircle, *v. t.* **1.** surround, embrace, encompass, environ; *spec.* span, twine, ring, enring (*intensive*), rim, infold *or* enfold, orb (*elevated*), loop, inorb (*R*), inarch, necklace.
2. *See* CIRCUIT.
encore, *v. t.* recall, call (*chiefly in "call before the curtain"*).
encourage, *v. t.* **1.** animate, strengthen, hearten, enhearten (*intensive*), heart (*A*), fortify, chirrup (*chiefly spec.*), inspirit; *spec.* reanimate, cheer, abet, embolden, incite, urge, stimulate, assure, reassure, comfort.
Antonyms: see ABASH, DISCOURAGE, OPPRESS, FRIGHTEN.
2. *See* APPROVE, AID.
encroach, *v. i.* advance, accroach (*R*), trench (*esp. of immaterial things*), infringe; *spec.* usurp (*R*), invade, trespass, intrude.
encroachment, *n.* advancement, infringement, infraction, trenching, inroad, invasion; *spec.* trespass, intrusion, purpresture.
encumber, *v. t.* **1.** *Implying a hindering by something that burdens:* cumber, embarrass; *spec.* burden, overburden, hamper, obstruct, hinder, clog, drag, load, obstruct, hinder, perplex.
2. lumber, burden;—*to weigh down with what is useless.*
Antonyms: see UNLOAD.
3. *With financial implication:* burden, charge; *spec.* mortgage.
encumbrance, *n.* **1.** cumber (*R*), cumbrance, cumberment (*R*), embarrassment, clog; *spec.* burden, hindrance, obstruction, hamper, baggage.
2. burden, charge; *spec.* mortgage, debt.
encyclopedia, encyclopædia, *n.* cyclopedia *or* cyclopædia (*the less usual term*), thesaurus (*now R*).
encysted, *a.* bagged, capsuled, saccate (*R*).
end, *n.* **1.** limit, extremity;—*in reference to space, and now only in "ends of the earth."*
2. *Referring to the terminating part of anything:* tip, extremity (*the very end*), termination (*B*), terminal (*chiefly tech. or spec.*), extreme (*B or formal*), terminus (*B or formal*), desinence (*chiefly spec.; R*); *spec.* fag-end, butt *or* butt-end, stub, remnant, tail, thrum, chump, crop (*tech.*), tag, ravel, fall, foot, horn, head.
Antonyms: see BEGINNING.
3. *Referring to the end or termination of a course, series, etc.:* conclusion, termination, determination (*formal*), close, closure (*R, exc. spec.*), stoppage; *spec.* finish, finis (*Latin*), end-all, period (*A*), consummation, destruction, annihilation, dissolution, finale (*Italian; music*), final (*music*), ending.
Antonyms: see BEGINNING.
4. *Referring to a terminating event, act, etc.:* dénoûment (*French*), catastrophe, wind-up (*C*), finish-up (*R*), finish, finale (*Italian*), ending.
Antonyms: see BEGINNING.
5. *Spec.* (*in reference to discourse*) exodium, catastrophe, finale (*Italian*), ending, peroration, epilogue, appendix.
Antonyms: see BEGINNING.
6. *In reference to lapse of time:* period (*A*), ending, lapse, expiration, expiry, termination.
Antonyms: see BEGINNING.
7. *Referring to the last part of life:* evening, close, extremity (*A*).
Antonyms: see INFANCY.
8. *See* DEATH, RESULT, OBJECT, INTENTION.
end, *v. t.* **1.** terminate (*a more formal word than "end"*), conclude (*formal*); *spec.* finish, stop, close, cease, discontinue, dissolve, abolish, destroy, annihilate.
2. *To form an end to:* terminate, determine (*formal*); *spec.* head, tail, fetch up.
Antonyms: see BEGIN.
3. *See* KILL.
end, *v. i.* **1.** terminate (*more formal than "end"*), conclude (*formal*); *spec.* finish, cease, stop, expire, lapse, discontinue, dissolve, determine (*formal*).
Antonyms: see BEGIN.
2. *To cease to exist: spec.* go, die, vanish, disappear, fall.
Antonyms: see BEGIN.
3. *To finish a discourse:* close, conclude; *spec.* perorate.
Antonyms: see BEGIN.
4. *See* DIE, EVENTUATE.
endanger, *v. t.* imperil, jeopard (*R*), adventure (*R*), jeopardize, peril (*R*), risk, hazard, jeopardy (*R*); *spec.* compromise.
endeavor, *v. i.* try (*the common word*), seek, attempt, offer, struggle, strive, essay (*B or A*), labor; *spec.* study.
endeavor, *n.* trial, try, attempt, effort, struggle, striving, essay (*A or B*), exertion, offer.
ending, *n.* **1.** *See* END, DEATH.

enable: *empower.*
encamp: *camp.*
encase: *incase.*
enceinte: *pregnant.*
enchain: *bind, confine.*
enchant: *bewitch, captivate, please.*
encomiast: *praiser.*
encomiastic: *laudatory.*
encomium: *eulogy.*
encompass: *surround, encircle.*
encore: *again.*
end: *final.*

2. *In reference to words:* suffix, postfix, termination, terminant (*R*).
ending, *a.* terminating, terminative (*R*), concluding, conclusive (*obsolesc.*), conclusory, determinating, determinative, *etc.; spec.* finishing, *etc.*
endless, *a.* **1.** *Referring to either time or space:* never-ending (*chiefly of time*), interminable, termless (*chiefly of time*), boundless, indefinite, indeterminable, dateless, interminate, illimitable, unlimited, immeasurable, infinite (*oftener of space than time*), unending (*chiefly of time*).
Antonyms: see SHORT, BRIEF, TERMINABLE.
2. *Referring to time only:* eternal, everlasting, ceaseless, perpetual; *spec.* undying.
Antonyms: see BRIEF.
3. *See* IMMORTAL, CONSTANT, PURPOSELESS.
endless, *adv. Spec.* interminably, boundlessly, indefinitely, infinitely, evermore, constantly.
endow, *v. t.* **1.** *See* DOWER (*a bride*).
2. enrich, dow, estate (*R*); *spec.* benefice, portion, reinvest.
3. enrich (*used with "with"*), furnish, gift (*chiefly in p. p., as an adjective*).
endowment, *n.* **1.** *Act of endowing:* dotation (*B*).
2. *Referring to property given by way of endowing:* fund, property, foundation (*U. S.*); *spec.* studentship, fellowship, scholarship, professorship, chair (*fig.*), living, *etc.*
3. gift, power, dower, dowry; *spec.* ability; *see* TALENT.
endue, *v. t.* indue, clothe, invest; *spec.* reinvest, grace;—*in reference to permanent gifts or powers of mind or body.*
endurable, *a.* bearable, tolerable, supportable, abidable, sustainable, sufferable; *spec.* withstandable, weatherable, livable, stomachable.
Antonyms: see UNBEARABLE.
endurance, *n.* **1.** *See* CONTINUANCE, CONSTANCY, PATIENCE.
2. *The act of enduring or lasting:* bearing, abiding, support, sustenance (*B or tech.*), tolerance (*chiefly tech.*), standing, withstanding, durance (*A*), sufferance.
3. *Staying power:* backbone, bottom, guts (*S*), sand (*C*); *spec.* fortitude, constancy, energy.
4. *The act of enduring or suffering to be:* tolerance, toleration, abidance, stomaching, enduringness (*R*); *spec.* permission, forbearance, vitality.
endurant, *a.* tolerant, patient (*of evil*).
endure, *v. i.* **1.** *See* CONTINUE.
2. abide, bear, suffer; *spec.* wear, last.
endure, *v. t.* **1.** *Referring to the capacity or power to suffer unharmed or unimpaired:* bear, abide (*B*), support, sustain, suffer, tolerate, coendure (*spec.*), stand, withstand, bide (*A*), undergo, stay; *spec.* weather.
2. *Referring to the will to put up with:* tolerate, abide, stand, brook, digest (*A*); *spec.* stomach, swallow, pocket, permit, receive.
endways, endwise, *adv.* **1.** *See* UPRIGHT, LENGTHWISE.
2. distad (*tech.*);—*towards the end.*
enema, *n.* injection (*contex.*), clyster.
enemy, *n.* opponent, adversary, antagonist (*"opponent," "adversary," and "antagonist" not implying the ill-will or malevolence implied by "enemy"*), unfriend (*R*), Philistine (*fig.*), foe (*A or rhetorical, exc. in mil. use; often a collective in mil. use*), foeman (*A or B*), hostile (*chiefly U. S. and of an American Indian*); *spec.* archenemy, Devil.
Antonyms: see FRIEND, ALLY.
energetic, *a.* active, vigorous, mettlesome, mighty; *spec.* hearty, hard, strenuous, trenchant, forceful, forcible, strong, powerful, dashing, emphatic, enterprising, live, robust; *spec. see* ENTERPRISING.
Antonyms: see APATHETIC.
energize, *v. t.* potentialize (*R*), activate (*tech.; chiefly chem. and biol.*), dynamize (*chiefly med.*); *spec.* animate.
Antonyms: see WEAKEN, ENERVATE.
energy, *n.* **1.** action;—*not a good synonym.*
2. activity, go (*C*), vigor, mettle, spirit, force, might, intensity, dash, life, animation. *Most of these words have specific implications or associations suggested by their general senses.*
Antonyms: see WEAKNESS, WEARINESS.
3. power, force, potency, strength; *spec.* impetus, impulse, momentum, vis viva (*tech. Latin*), magnetism, electricity.
Antonyms: see INERTIA.
4. *Only in reference to persons, ideas, etc.:* spirit, vigor, backbone (*C*), life, animation, pith, verve, drive, vim (*C*), fizz (*C*), go (*C*), go-ahead (*C*); *spec. see* ENTERPRISE.
Antonyms: see WEAKNESS.
enervate, *v. t.* weaken, devitalize, unnerve, paralyze, soften; *spec.* debilitate, emasculate.
Antonyms: see STRENGTHEN, ENERGIZE.
enfeoff, *v. t.* infeft (*Scots law*); *spec.* subfeu (*R*).
enfeoffment, *n.* infeudation, infeftment (*Scots law*); *spec.* subinfeudation.
enforce, *v. t.* **1.** *See* COMPEL, EMPHASIZE, STRENGTHEN.
2. *In reference to laws, duty, etc.:* execute, sanction.
3. enfranchise (*R*); *spec.* naturalize, endenizen (*B*).
engage, *v. t.* **1.** *See* PLEDGE.
2. bind, obligate; *spec.* betroth.
3. *Spec.* bespeak, hire, enlist, book, retain, brief, fee.
4. *To win over:* gain.
5. *To seize and hold, fasten upon:* occupy, interest; *spec.* bite, arrest, catch, attract.
Antonyms: see SLIDE.
6. attack, encounter; *spec.* reëncounter (*R*).
engage, *v. i.* **1.** *See* CONTEND, FIGHT, PROMISE, ENTER, AGREE, CONTRACT.
2. embark (*used with "in"*); *spec.* enlist.
3. interlock, interact; *spec.* gear, pitch, mesh.
engine, *n.* **1.** *See* INSTRUMENT, MEANS.
2. *Of machines for converting a force into mechanical power* (*this now being the usual sense*

enervate: *weaken.*
enfeeble: *weaken.*
enfold: *envelop, clasp, fold.*
engender: *develop.*

of "engine"): spec. steam engine, electrical engine, *etc.*, turbine, jinny, corliss, motor, diesel.

3. *Of military engines: spec.* matafund, arbalest, ballista, mangonel, lombard, springal.

engineer, *n.* machinist (*contex.*); *spec.* driver, hydraulician, mechanician, pioneer.

English, *a. Spec.* Anglican (*mostly referring to the Church of England*), British (*referring to what is or belongs to Great Britain; now esp. used in referring to political or imperial affairs*).

Englishman, *n.* Englander, Englisher (*chiefly Scot.*), John Bull (*a nickname*), gringo (*Spanish Amer.; contemptuous*); *spec.* Harry, Tommy (*S*), milord.

engrave, *v. t.* **1.** grave (*A or B*), cut, carve, sculpture, chisel, incise; *spec.* intaglio (*R*), etch, enchase, hatch, crosshatch, mezzotint; *—in reference to forming figures on a surface.*

2. *See* PRINT.

engraved, *a.* graven, sculptured, incised, cut; *spec.* intagliated.

engraver, *n.* graver (*R, exc. of a tool*); *spec.* die cutter, lapicide, etcher, burin (*a tool*).

engraving, *a.* carving, glyptic (*chiefly spec.*), sculptural.

engraving, *n.* **1.** graving, carving, sculpture (*R*), chiseling; *spec.* intaglio, glyptography, fretwork, chalcography, cerography, gypsography, stylography, petroglyph, heliogravure, photogravure, heliography;*—in reference to the art or process.*

2. graving, carving, sculpture (*R*), glyptic (*chiefly spec.*); *spec.* intaglio, fretwork, chalcograph, cut (*esp. a woodcut*), plate (*one on metal*), triptych, diptych, lithoglyph, taille-douce (*French*), mezzotint, cerograph, heliograph, photogravure, heliogravure;*—referring to the figure produced.*

enjoy, *v. t.* **1.** like, relish, joy (*A*).

Antonyms: see DISLIKE.

2. experience, have (*some experience*).

enjoyment, *n.* **1.** relish, gusto, gust, zest, fruition (*B or dignified*).

Antonyms: see DISLIKE, DISTRESS.

2. pleasure, gratification, luxury.

enlarge, *v. t.* **1.** increase, extend, widen, aggrandize (*learned*), greaten (*A*), amplify, largen (*R*), magnify (*R*); *spec.* augment, broaden, ream, dilate, distend, drift, explain, thicken, drill, bore (*chiefly with "out"*).

Antonyms: see DIMINISH, ABRIDGE, CONDENSE, CONSTRICT, CONTRACT.

2. *See* MAGNIFY.

enlarge, *v. i.* **1.** increase, expand, widen; *spec.* augment, broaden, dilate, distend, swell.

2. *See* EXPATIATE.

enlargement, *n.* **1.** increase, extension, widening; *spec.* broadening, aggrandizement (*learned*), amplification, augmentation, distension, dilatation, expansion.

Antonyms: see ABRIDGEMENT, ABSTRACT, CONDENSATION, DIMINUTION.

2. *Only of a thing formed by an enlargement: spec.* bulb, knot, ganglion.

enlarging, *a. Spec.* expatiatory, crescent, expansive.

enlighten, *v. t.* **1.** *See* BRIGHTEN.

2. lighten (*A*), illume (*R or B*), illuminate (*formal*), illumine (*R*); *spec.* educate, civilize instruct, inform.

Antonyms: see DARKEN, NONPLUS, PERPLEX.

enlightenment, *n.* illumination, light, lightening; *spec.* culture, civilization, education, learning.

Antonyms: see IGNORANCE.

enlist, *v. t.* list, enroll, levy, recruit (*all mil.*).

enliven, *v. t.* **1.** *See* ANIMATE, CHEER.

2. animate, exhilarate, rouse, invigorate, actuate (*learned*), spirit, inspirit, inspire, quicken, quick (*A*), fire, brisk (*chiefly with "up"*); *spec.* spice, brighten, elate, reanimate.

Antonyms: see CALM, DEPRESS.

enmity, *n.* dislike (*contex.*), ill-will, animosity; *spec.* pique; *see* MALEVOLENCE, HATRED.

Antonyms: see LOVE.

ennoble, *v. t.* dignify, exalt, raise; *spec.* greaten (*R*), elevate, glorify, nobilitate (*R*), baronize.

Antonyms: see DEGRADE, DEPRECIATE, ABUSE, DEFAME.

ennui, *n.* tedium, boredom; *see* WEARINESS.

Antonyms: see VIVACITY, GAYETY.

enormous, *a.* large (*contex.*), titanic, tremendous, huge, immense, colossal, gigantic, elephantine, vast, prodigious (*B or contemptuous*).

Antonyms: see SMALL.

enrich, *v. t.* **1.** richen (*R*); *spec.* millionize, endow.

Antonyms: see IMPOVERISH, PLUNDER.

2. *See* EMBELLISH, FERTILIZE.

enriching, *a.* locupletive (*R*).

enshrine, *v. t.* **1.** inshrine (*a variant*), contain (*contex.*); *spec.* entemple (*R*), tabernacle, enchase (*R*).

2. *See* PRESERVE, CHERISH.

ensign, *n.* **1.** flag (*contex.*); *spec.* gonfanon, gonfalon, hatchment, eagle, pennon.

2. *See* BADGE.

enslave, *v. t.* **1.** enthrall (*chiefly fig.*), slave (*R*), thrall (*A*), yoke (*figurative*), beslave (*emphatic*), vassal (*R*); *spec.* helotize.

Antonyms: see FREE, DELIVER.

2. *See* CAPTIVATE.

---

engineer, *v. t.: manage.*
engorge: *surfeit, satiate, obstruct.*
engross: *copy, absorb, monopolize.*
engulf: *swallow, absorb.*
enhance, *v. i.: advance, increase.*
enhance, *v. t.: intensify, exaggerate, advance.*
enhearten: *encourage.*
enigma: *question, riddle, mystery.*
enigmatic: *mysterious.*
enjoin: *bid, dictate, forbid.*
enjoyable: *pleasant.*
enormous: *immense.*
enough: *adequate.*
enquire: *question.*
enrage: *anger.*
enrapt, enraptured: *ecstatic.*
enrapture: *transport, please.*
enravish: *transport.*
enroll: *list, enlist.*
ensconce: *shelter, conceal, establish.*
ensemble: *whole, effect.*

---

enslaved, *a.* bond.
enslavement, *n.* **1.** enthrallment; *spec.* vassalage, serfage, serfdom.
Antonyms: see FREEING.
2. *See* CAPTIVATION.
entail, *n.* tail, tailye *or* tailzie (*Scot.*).
entangle, *v. t.* **1.** *In a physical sense:* tangle, ravel, perplex (*R*), involve, embrangle (*B*); *spec.* mesh, enlace, inmesh, entrap, mat.
Antonyms: see DISENTANGLE, UNRAVEL.
2. *See* CONFUSE.
entangled, *a.* complex, foul (*chiefly naut.*), afoul (*predicative*).
entanglement, *n.* **1.** tangle, maze, embranglement (*B*), ravelment (*R*), involvement, intertanglement (*R*), perplexity, cobweb (*implying fineness*); *spec.* node, knot.
2. *See* CONFUSION.
enter, *v. i.* **1.** *To go or come in: spec.* pierce, penetrate.
Antonyms: see ISSUE.
2. *To go into or commence upon a subject-matter, book, undertaking, etc.:* dip, dive, take up, begin, commence.
3. *To become busied, occupied, etc.:* engage; *spec.* start, go (*used with "into"*).
enter, *v. t.* **1.** *In a physical sense: spec.* penetrate, pierce, trespass, invade, board (*a ship or, U. S., a railroad train*), force.
2. *To cause to go into, undertake, etc.:* insert, enroll, place (*as* to enter *a candidate*).
3. *See* BEGIN, JOIN, LIST, RECORD.
entering, *a.* entrant, incoming, ingoing.
enterprise, *n.* **1.** project, emprise (*A*); *spec.* scheme, adventure, attempt.
2. energy, push (*C*), go-ahead (*C*).
Antonyms: see LAZINESS.
enterprising, *a.* energetic, go-ahead (*C*), pushing (*C*), pushful (*C*).
Antonyms: see LAZY.
entertain, *v. t.* **1.** receive, hospitize (*R*); *spec.* harbor, guest (*R*), shelter.
2. *Referring to opinions, etc.:* hold, cherish, bear, have; *spec.* nurse.
Antonyms: see REJECT.
3. *See* DIVERT, FEEL.
4. treat (*C*), regale (*B*); *spec.* fête, breakfast, dine, dinner, tea, wine, supper (*R*).
entertainer, *n. Spec.* hospitator (*R*), harborer (*A*), host, hostess.
Antonyms: see SPONGER.
entertainment, *n.* **1.** reception; *spec.* hospitation (*R*), harboring.
2. *See* DIVERSION.
3. treat (*C*), regalement; *spec.* fête, Friday, gaudy (*Eng.*), refection, lunch, tea, dinner, spread (*C*), banquet, supper, breakfast, beanfeast (*Eng.*).
enthrone, *v. t.* regalize (*spec. or fig.*), throne, seat (*contex.*).
Antonyms: see DEPOSE.
enthuse, *v. i.* (*C, chiefly U. S.*), rave (*C*), kindle; *spec.* poetize, warm, fanaticize.
enthusiast, *n.* fanatic (*although an* enthusiast *is often carried beyond reason, a* fanatic *is most extreme, esp. in religion*), bigot (*one filled not only with* enthusiasm, *esp. in the realm of religion, but obstinately inaccessible to other views*), zealot (*a* fanatical *partisan*); booster (*C, U. S.*), fan (*S, U. S.*).
entice, *v. t.* attract, tempt, train (*R*), allure, lure; *spec.* wile, decoy, inveigle.
Antonyms: see REPEL, DISGUST, FRIGHTEN.
enticement, *n.* attraction, allurement, temptation, lure; *spec.* decoy.
enticing, *a.* attractive, inviting, alluring, tempting, soliciting; *spec.* decoying. *"Entice" implies success in allurement; "enticing" does not.*
Antonyms: see REPELLENT.
entirety, *n.* entireness, wholeness, integrality, integrity.
entitle, *v. t.* **1.** intitule (*chiefly tech.*), betitle (*derogatory*).
2. *See* QUALIFY, NAME.
entrails, *n. pl.* **1.** viscera (*R*), insides (*C or dial.*), guts (*vulgar, or C as fig.*), intestines, puddings (*chiefly dial. and Scot.*). *The singular form, "entrail," is R.*
2. *See* VISCERA.
entrain, *v. t.* board.
entrance, *n.* **1.** *Referring to the action:* entry, ingress (*B*), ingression (*R*), progress, beginning (*the* entering *upon or going into a place or undertaking*); entrée (*French*), incoming, ingoing, income (*R*); *spec.* illapse (*R*), trespass, début (*in society; French*).
Antonyms: see ISSUE.
2. *Referring to the privilege or right:* admission, access, entrée (*French*).
3. *Referring to the place or means of entering:* entry, staircase (*these two often used of a section or division of a college residence hall or dormitory served by one* entrance), aperture, ingress; *spec.* door, mouth, inlet, doorway, adit, vestibule, hall, hallway, lobby, portal, propylon, propylæum, porte-cochère (*French*), postern, gorge (*fortification*), gate, foregate, stile.
Antonyms: see EXIT.
entry, *n.* **1.** *See* ENTRANCE.
2. listing; *spec.* enrollment (*the setting down, generally with some solemnity, of a record or a competitive name*), registry, registration, post, posting, credit.
3. entrant (entry *is often vulgarly and always incorrectly used as a synonym for* entrant).

ensnare: *snare, catch.*
ensue: *follow.*
ensuing: *coming.*
entail: *settle, impose, necessitate.*
enthrall: *enslave, captivate.*
enthusiasm: *ecstasy, frenzy, ardor, fanaticism.*
enthusiastic: *ardent, enthusiastic.*
entire: *complete, absolute, whole, intact.*
entity: *being, thing.*
entranced: *transported.*
entreat: *ask.*
entreaty: *asking, appeal.*
entrée: *entrance.*
entrepôt: *depository.*
entrust: *commit.*
enumerate: *compute, mention.*
enunciate: *announce, pronounce.*

envelope, *n.* covering, inclosure (*B or elevated*); *spec.* incasement, casement (*R*), casing (*close*), mantle, involucre, pack, capsule, film, skin, integument, facing, mantling, shroud, vesture (*R*), perianth, mist, veil, konseal, wrap, spathe.

envelop, *v. t.* cover, wrap (*chiefly spec.*); *spec.* invest, overroll, pack, jacket, enshroud, infold *or* enfold, web, shroud, mantle, involve, encompass.

envious, *a.* jealous, grudging.

envy, *v. t.* grudge, begrudge.

envy, *n.* grudgingness, grudging, jealousy, jealousness.

ephemeral, *a.* short-lived; *spec.* fugitive, occasional, mushroom, fungous.

Antonyms: see ETERNAL, LASTING, LONG-LIVED.

epic, *a.* epopœan (*R*); *spec.* Homeric.

epic, *n.* epopee (*R*), epopœia (*A*), epos; *spec.* Homeric, Iliad, rhapsody, Dunciad.

epicure, *n.* epicurean, palatist (*R*), opsophagist (*R*), deipnosophist (*learned*), aristologist (*learned*), bon vivant (*masc.; French*), bonne vivante (*fem.; French*), gourmet (*French*), gourmand.

episcopacy, *n.* **1.** pontificality (*R*), prelacy (*hostile term*), prelatism (*hostile term*).

2. *See* BISHOPRIC.

episcopal, *a.* pontifical *or* pontific (*chiefly hist. or spec.*), prelatical *or* prelatic (*chiefly a hostile term*).

episcopalian, *n.* prelatist (*a hostile term*).

epizoötic, *n.* *Spec.* murrain. *"Epizoötic" is used of animal diseases only, and corresponds to "epidemic" as applied to man.*

equable, *a.* even (*while* equable *implies an inherent quality,* even *is confined to fact*), even-tempered, uniform (*unchanging*), steady (*regularity, esp. of movement*).

equal, *a.* **1.** alike (*postpositive*), like; *spec.* coordinate, level, coequal (*R*), commensurate, coextensive, parallel, corresponding, equipollent (*B*), equivalent, equiponderant (*R*), quits (*used with "with"*), even, isopsephic (*R; tech.*), isonomic (*R*), coeval, coetaneous, coeternal, identical, tantamount, equipotential, isotropic, isotopic.

Antonyms: see UNEQUAL.

2. *See* ADEQUATE, IMPARTIAL.

equal, *n.* fellow, match, peer, compeer (*B*); *spec.* coördinate, parallel, countervail, equivalent.

equal, *v. t.* **1.** *See* EQUALIZE.

2. match, even (*R*), fellow (*used with "with"; B*); *spec.* peer, tie, commeasure, countervail (*A*), rival, parallel, number.

equality, *n.* parity, equalization, equation (*tech. or spec.*), egality (*obs. or French*), par (*chiefly in "on a par"*), level; *spec.* match, equivalence, peerdom (*R*), equipollence, equipoise, tie, coevality (*R*), coequality, owelty (*law*), identity, isopolity, isonomy, equilibrium, isotopy, parallelism.

Antonyms: see INEQUALITY.

equalization, *n.* **1.** equaling, equation.

2. *See* EQUALITY.

equalize, *v. t.* equal, equate (*chiefly math.*), even; *spec.* par (*R*), coördinate.

equally, *adv.* alike, evenly, indifferently (*chiefly spec.*).

equal-sided, *a.* *Spec.* isosceles.

equanimity, *n.* **1.** evenness (*of temper*).

2. *See* CALMNESS.

equestrian, *a.* mounted.

equine, *a.* caballine (*R; B*), hippic (*R*), solidungulate (*tech.*).

equine, *n.* horse, solidungulate (*tech.*), soliped (*tech.*).

equip, *v. t.* furnish, outfit, provide; *spec.* harness (*A*), accouter, appoint, dress, accommodate, arm, gird, spar, rig.

Antonyms: see DISMANTLE.

equipage, *n.* turnout (*C*).

equipment, *n.* **1.** *Referring to the action:* furnishing, accoutering, accouterment, equipage, provision, appointment.

2. *Referring to things:* furniture, furnishings, tackle (*chiefly spec.*), gear (*chiefly spec.*), harness (*esp. mil.*); *spec.* apparatus, plant, accouterment (*often in pl.*), dress, fitting (*chiefly in pl.*), appointment, outfit, rigging, rig, armament (*chiefly mil.*).

erect, *a,* upright, unrecumbent (*R*), straight, vertical, perpendicular.

Antonyms: see DROOPING, STOOPING.

erect, *v. t.* **1.** raise, rear; *spec.* pitch, prick, ruffle, perfect, pedestal.

Antonyms: see DROOP.

2. *See* BUILD, CONSTRUCT, CREATE, ESTABLISH.

erect, *v. i.* rise; *see* BRISTLE.

erection, *n.* **1.** raising, rearing, *etc.*

2. *See* BUILDING, CONSTRUCTION, CREATION, ESTABLISHMENT.

erode, *v. t.* destroy (*contex.*), eat, wear, consume, fret (*away*); *spec.* rub (*used with "off"*), denude, wash (*often used with "away"*).

erosion, *n.* destruction (*contex.*), eating, consumption (*R*); *spec.* denudation, fret (*R*), eola-

envenom: *poison, embitter, contaminate.*
environ: *encircle, surround.*
environment: *surroundings.*
environs: *surroundings, neighborhood.*
envisage: *visualize.*
envoy: *diplomatic agent, postscript.*
epicurean: *luxurious, palatable, sensual.*
epigram: *saying, poem.*
epigrammatic: *concise.*
episode: *digression, occurrence.*
epitaph: *inscription.*
epithet: *name.*
epitome: *abridgment.*
epoch: *date, period.*
equanimity: *calm, peace.*
equilibrate: *balance, counterpoise.*
equilibrium: *balance, equality.*
equipoise: *balance, equality.*
equitable: *just.*
equity: *justice.*
equivalent, *a.: equal, analogous, correspondent, convertible, reciprocal.*
equivalent, *n.: equal, analogue.*
equivocal: *ambiguous, uncertain, questionable.*
equivocation: *ambiguity, prevarication.*
era: *date, period.*
eradicable: *destructible.*
eradicate: *abolish.*
erase: *efface.*
erosive: *eating.*
erotic: *amatory.*

tion (*geol.*), washout, watergall (*only of the place eroded*).

err, *v. i.* mistake, nod, slip (*often used with "up"*), trip; *spec.* fall, wander, stray, stumble, blunder, hallucinate, misbelieve, sin, bull (*with "it" as object*).

errand, *n.* business (*contex.*), commission, message, mission, trip.

erroneous, *a.* false, untrue, mistaken (*used only of persons*), erring (*used only of persons*), errant (*R*); *spec.* fallacious, devious, misguided (*used only of persons*).

Antonyms: see TRUE.

error, *n. Spec.* erroneousness, obliquity, mistake, solecism, absurdity, blunder, wrong, parepochism (*R*), parachronism, corrigendum, fault, erratum, errancy, trip, stumble, slip, fallacy, flaw, misbelief, metachronism, misprint, untruth, misstep.

Antonyms: see TRUTH.

erupt, *v. t.* eject, belch; *spec.* (*of volcanoes*) vesuviate (*R*).

Antonyms: see SWALLOW.

eruption, *n.* **1.** *See* EJECTION, OUTBREAK.

2. *Spec.* efflorescence, rash, erythema, brash, blain, exanthema, tetter, vesicle, blotch, malanders *or* mallenders, eczema, hives, heat.

escape, *v. i.* **1.** scape (*A*), evade (*now R*); *spec.* fly, slip, run, decamp, double.

2. *See* ISSUE, LEAK.

escape, *n.* **1.** scape (*A*), escapement (*R*), scapement (*R*); *spec.* avoidance, bolt, evasion (*from confinement; R*).

2. *See* ISSUE, OUTLET, OUTFLOW, LEAK, LEAKAGE.

escort, *n.* **1.** *See* ACCOMPANIMENT.

2. attendant, companion, conductor; *spec.* cavalier, burkundaz (*Anglo-Indian*), psychopomp, safe-conduct, convoy, envoy, gallant, squire, esquire, bodyguard, date (*C, U. S.*).

escort, *v. t.* accompany (*contex.*); *spec.* gallant, squire, conduct; *spec.* marshal, convoy, guard, walk, support, hand.

escutcheon, *n.* achievement, scutcheon; *spec.* shield, hatchment, inescutcheon.

especial, *a.* special, particular; *see* SPECIAL, UNCOMMON.

Antonyms: see COMMON.

esplanade, *n.* maidan (*Anglo-Indian*); *spec.* marina (*Italian and Spanish*), bund (*in the far East*), drive, promenade, mall.

esquire, *n.* **1.** armiger, squire.

2. *See* GENTLEMAN, OWNER, SQUIRE, ESCORT.

essence, *n.* **1.** *See* BEING, SUBSTANCE, EXTRACT.

2. quiddity (*B*), isness (*R*), hypostasis (*tech.*), principle, hyparxis (*tech; R*), form, inwardness.

3. *With various special implications suggested by the original senses:* sense, gist, core, kernel, marrow, pith, elixir, quintessence, flower, soul, spirit, life, heart, substance.

essential, *a. Spec.* substantial, indispensable, constituting, constitutional, intrinsic, inward, fundamental, elementary, needful, vital; *see* NECESSARY.

essential, *n.* substantial, secret, life (*in sense of first principle*), vitals (*pl.*).

Antonyms: see ACCESSORY, ACCIDENT.

establish, *v. t.* **1.** confirm, fix, settle, stabilify (*R*), stabilitate (*R*), stablish (*A*), stable (*R*), secure, set, firm; *spec.* sustain, instate, domicile *or* domiciliate (*chiefly legal*), home, install, intrench (*with suggestion of firm or permanent* establishment), pitch, root, rear, land (*S or C*), ensconce, ground, foot (*R*), make.

Antonyms: see WEAKEN, ABOLISH.

2. found, institute, constitute, create, erect (*chiefly spec.*), make (*as an order, rule, etc.*), raise, plant; *spec.* ordain (*A*), organize, build, appoint, ground.

Antonyms: see ABOLISH.

3. *See* CONFIRM.

establishment, *n.* **1.** confirmation, fix, settlement, fixation, stablishment (*R*), securement, firming.

2. creation, constitution, plantation (*R*), institution, erection, foundation, stabiliment (*R*); *spec.* instatement (*R*), organization, installment, installation, upbuilding, ordainment.

3. creation, institution, concern; *spec.* organization, works (*pl.*), dwelling, church, school, college, plant.

estate, *n.* **1.** *See* STATE, RANK, PROPERTY.

2. *Spec.* demesne, lordship, reversion, domain, feu, feud, curtesy, mesnalty, jointure, lay fee, leasehold, dower, plantation, hacienda (*Spanish*), term, freehold.

esteem, *v. t.* **1.** *See* CONSIDER.

2. respect (*usually of persons*), prize, regard (*usually of persons*), favor, value, admire, appreciate; *spec.* revere, reverence, venerate, worship.

Antonyms: see DESPISE, DISRESPECT.

esteem, *n.* **1.** *See* CONSIDERATION.

2. respect, regard, favor, admiration, estimation; *spec.* reverence, worship.

3. standing, rank, value, worth.

Antonyms: see CONTEMPT, DISRESPECT, ILL WILL.

estimable, *a.* admirable, precious, valuable, creditable; *spec.* adorable, worshipful, respectable.

Antonyms: see ABOMINABLE, CONTEMPTIBLE.

estrange, *v. t.* **1.** *See* TRANSFER.

2. alienate, disunite.

Antonyms: see WIN.

---

errantry: *knighthood.*
erratic: *wandering, abnormal, eccentric, odd, capricious.*
erstwhile: *formerly.*
eructate: *eject, vomit.*
erudite: *learned.*
erudition: *learning.*
escapade: *caper.*
escape, *v. t.: avoid.*
escheat: *revert.*
eschew: *avoid.*
esculent: *eatable.*
espial: *discovery.*
espousal: *bethrothal, adoption, defense.*
espouse: *betroth, adopt, defend.*
espy: *discover.*
esquire: *escort.*
essay: *attempt.*
estimate, *v. t.: consider, value, compute.*
estimation: *consideration, valuation, computation.*
estrange: *alienate.*

---

estuary, *n.* arm (*contex.*), frith, firth, lough (*Anglo-Irish*).
etching, *n.* **1.** *See* CORROSION.
2. engraving (*contex.*); *spec.* zinco (*Eng.*), acquaint.
eternal, *a.* **1.** perpetual, timeless, endless, sempiternous (*R*), sempiternal, everlasting, immortal, eviternal (*chiefly spec.; R*), eterne, (*A or B*); *spec.* coeternal.
Antonyms: see EPHEMERAL, BRIEF, TEMPORARY.
2. *See* CONSTANT, ENDLESS.
eternalize, *v. t.* perpetuate, immortalize, eternize; *spec.* monument, monumentalize.
eternally, *adv.* perpetually, evermore (*A*), forever, everlastingly, ever (*B or A*).
eternity, *n.* **1.** perpetuity, eternalness, everlastingness, timelessness, endlessness, sempiternity; *spec.* coeternity.
Antonyms: see MOMENT.
2. *See* CONSTANCY, ENDLESSNESS.
ethereal, *a.* **1.** *See* AIRY, HEAVENLY.
2. delicate (*contex.*); *spec.* light, tenuous, fragile, flimsy, fairy.
Antonyms: see EARTHLY, BODILY.
ethics, *n. sing. & pl.* morals (*pl.*), morality; *spec.* hedonics, eudemonism.
etymology, *n.* derivation, pedigree (*fig.*).
eucharist, *n.* **1.** Communion, Mass, Housel (*hist.*), Oblation; *spec.* liturgy, viaticum.
2. Mass, element.
euhoe, *interj.* (*Latin*), evoe (*Latin; less correct than "euhoe"*); *spec.* eureka, hurrah, bravo.
Antonyms: see ALAS.
eulogist, *n.* praiser (*which see*), encomiast, panegyrist; *spec.* laureate.
eulogize, *v. t.* approve (*contex.*), praise, compliment, panegyrize.
eulogy, *n.* eulogium, eulogism (*R*), approval, praise, panegyric, encomium; *spec.* monody (*R*).
Antonyms: see ABUSE.
euphemistic, *a.* soft (*contex.*), euphemous (*R*); *spec.* extenuatory.
evacuate, *v. t.* **1.** empty, clear; *spec.* (*referring to the bowels*) purge, scour, empty.
Antonyms: see FILL, OCCUPY.
2. *See* LEAVE.
3. eject (*contex.*); *spec.* (*esp. referring to excrement*), discharge, defecate, void.
evacuate, *v. i.* defecate.
evacuation, *n.* **1.** clearing, discharge; *spec.* (*referring to the bowels*), passage, motion, purgation, catharsis.
2. *See* LEAVING (*cf.* LEAVE).
evade, *v. t.* avoid, elude; *spec.* dodge, bilk, bluff, funk (*S*), pass the buck (*S, U. S.*).
evaporate, *v. i. & t.* emanate, vaporize, volatilize; *spec.* distill.
Antonyms: see CONDENSE, SOLIDIFY.
evasion, *n.* **1.** avoidance, elusion; *spec.* shuffling, double, doubling, quibbling, dodge, bluffing, funking (*S*).
2. deceit, subterfuge, shuffle, put-off (*C*), shift; *spec.* dodge, prevarication (*direct untruthfulness*), tergiversation (*twisting, avoiding or turning one's back to truth*), equivocation (*ambiguity; saying one thing and meaning another*).
evasive, *a.* deceitful (*contex.*), slippery; *spec.* dodgy (*C*), tergiversant (*R*), prevaricative, shifty.
even, *a.* **1.** *Referring to adjoining surfaces:* level, equal (*A*), smooth, flat, regular; *spec.* flush.
Antonyms: see UNEVEN, IRREGULAR.
2. *Referring to the temper, motion, action, etc.:* uniform, regular, equal, level, smooth; *spec.* equable, easy (*C*); *see* EVEN-TEMPERED.
3. *See* EQUAL, ABREAST, IMPARTIAL.
even, *v. t.* level, smooth; *spec.* scabble *or* scapple, grade, float.
even, *adv.* just (*often used with "now"*), yet.
evening, *n.* eve (*B or rhetorical*), even (*B, dial., or C*).
Antonyms: see MORNING.
evening, *a.* vesperal (*R*), vespertine (*B*), vespertinal (*R*).
evening star. Vesper, Hesper (*B*), Hesperus (*B*).
Antonyms: see MORNING STAR.
event, *n.* **1.** *See* OCCURRENCE.
2. result, conclusion, issue, end, sequel, outcome, hap (*esp. A*); *spec.* turn-up (*C*), futurity.
Antonyms: see BEGINNING.
even-tempered, *a.* even (*chiefly B*), equable, equanimous, equal.
Antonyms: see IRRITABLE.
eventful, *a.* **1.** chanceful (*R*), full (*contex.*).
Antonyms: see UNEVENTFUL.
2. *See* IMPORTANT.
eventuate, *v. i.* end, conclude, issue; *spec.* result.
eversion, *n.* extroversion (*tech.*), exstrophy (*tech.; R*).
every, *a.* each (*implies one by one, whereas* every *implies the existence of all*).
everyday, *a.* customary (*contex.*), accustomed (*contex.*), workaday; *spec.* commonplace, homely.
everywhere, *adv.* throughout, passim (*Latin*).
Antonyms: see NOWHERE.
evidence, *n.* attestation, token, stamp, testimony (*properly spec.*), witness (*spec. or fig.*); *spec.* demonstration, record, muniments (*pl.*) voucher, deposition, proof, trace.
evidence, *v. t.* attest, support, tell; *spec.* circumstantiate, certificate, show, prove, confess (*B*), document, vouch, testify.

---

etiquette: *manners.*
eulogism: *eulogy.*
euphonious: *smooth, melodious.*
evade: *escape.*
evanescence: *disappearance, transience.*
evaporative: *volatile.*
eventual: *final.*
eventuality: *occurrence.*
ever: *always, once, eternally.*
everlasting: *endless, eternal, constant.*
evermore: *constantly, endlessly.*
everything: *all.*
evict: *eject.*
eviction: *ejection.*

evidency, *n.* apparency, evidence (*R*), indubitableness, obviousness, palpableness, seemingness, plainness.

evident, *a.* **1.** apparent, plain, obvious, broad, unmistakable, palpable (*spec. or fig.*), patent, open, naked, conspicuous (*R*), manifest, distinct, clear, bald, unhidden (*R*), downright, overt.
Antonyms: see ABSTRUSE.
2. *See* VISIBLE, APPARENT.

evil, *n.* **1.** *See* WICKEDNESS.
2. *With "a" or "an"*: harm, ill, curse, blast, bale (*now chiefly B*), cancer (*fig.*), canker (*fig.*), bane, disease, malefice (*A*).
Antonyms: see GOOD.

evildoer, *n.* malfeasant (*B or tech.*), malefactor (*esp. criminally*), malefactress (*fem.*).

evildoing, *a.* malfeasant (*B or tech.*), malefactory, maleficent.
Antonyms: see BENEFICENT.

evocate, *v. t.* evoke; elicit; *spec.* exorcize (*R*), invoke.

evoke, *v. t.* evocate, call; *see* ELICIT.

evolution, *n.* **1.** development (*contex.*); *spec.* phylogeny, ontogeny, ontogenesis, physiogeny, phylogenesis.
2. *See* MOVEMENT, FIGURE (*dancing*).

ewe, *n.* sheep (*contex.*); *spec.* crocodile (*dial.*), crock (*chiefly Scot.*).

exacerbate, *v. t.* irritate, exasperate (*both weaker senses than* exacerbate).

exact, *a.* **1.** *See* STRING, ACCURATE, DEFINITE.
2. precise, diametric (*opposite*), absolute, direct; *spec.* express (*chiefly with allusion to Heb. i. 3, as in, "the express image"*).
3. delicate, accurate, precise, nice, fine; *spec.* sensitive, true.

exact, *v. t.* **1.** *See* ASK, EXTORT.
2. take (*vengeance, etc.*), have.

exacting, *a.* **1.** *See* CRITICAL, DIFFICULT.
2. extortionary, extortive, exactive.

exaction, *n.* **1.** *See* DEMAND.
2. extortion, squeeze (*C*), requisition; *spec.* mulct, contribution (exaction *may mean not only the act of* exacting, *but also that which is* exacted).

exactly, *adv.* just, even (*chiefly A or Biblical*), precisely, full, fully, quite, plumb *or* plum; *spec.* flat, faithfully, literally.

exactness, *n.* **1.** *See* STRICTNESS, ACCURACY, DEFINITENESS.
2. delicacy, exactitude, nicety, precision, punctiliousness (*in forms and conventions*), accuracy; *spec.* sensitiveness, trueness.

exaggerate, *v. t.* magnify, enhance, stretch (*C*); *spec.* overspeak (*R*), overpicture (*R*), overdraw, overtell (*R*), overdo, overstate, overcolor, overcharge, romance, hyperbolize (*rhetoric*).
Antonyms: see BELITTLE.

exaggerated, *a.* hyperbolical (*rhetoric*), outré (*French*), tall (*C, U. S.*), overdone, excessive.

exaggeration, *n.* excess, enhancement; *spec.* hyperbole (*rhetoric*), overstatement.

exalted, *a. Spec.* elevated, elated, high, lofty, highflown (*chiefly disparaging*), magnificent, magnific, sublime, magnifical, proud, lordly; *spec.* buskined.
Antonyms: see LOW, DEGRADED, DEGENERATE.

examination, *n.* inspection, scrutiny, investigation, search, research (*esp. spec.*), exploration, scrutation (*R*), scan (*R*), perusal (*A*), survey, examen (*R or tech.*); *spec.* review, test, mid-term, mid-semester, final, exam (*C*), quiz, disquisition (*R*), probation (*U. S. or obs.*), collation, overhaul (*R*), consideration (*A*), reconnaissance *or* reconnoissance, perscrutation (*R*), assay, post-mortem, prying, inquiry, interrogation, inquisition; *spec.* catechism, collections (*pl.; Eng. schools*), school (*Oxf. University*), tripos, responsions (*pl.*), exercise, little go (*Eng.*), great go *or* greats (*Eng.*).

examine, *v. t. & i.* **1.** investigate, inspect, scrutinize, peruse (*A*), dissect, examinate (*B*), consider (*A*), overlook, search, scan, introspect (*primarily spec.; R*), overhaul, survey; *spec.* collate, rummage, explore, reconnoitre, ransack, probe (*as a wound*), canvass, review, bottom, feel, bolt, sift, sniff, try, test, candle, anatomize.
2. question, interrogate, cross-examine (*implying repeated and close questioning*), quiz (*U. S.*), catechize; *spec.* pry (*v. i. only*), sound (*in order to get the views of, etc.*), probe.

example, *n.* **1.** *One that serves to illustrate:* sample, specimen, piece, instance (*of a case in point, rather than a material portion or sample*), case, representative (*typical*), illustration, exemplar, essay, exemplification (*formal*); *spec.* demonstrate, monument.
2. *One that serves as a model or pattern:* pattern, sample, type, standard, model, foregoer (*A*); *spec.* sampler, lead (*pron. led*).
3. *See* WARNING.

example, *v. t.* represent, illustrate, exemplify; *spec.* sample.

excavate, *v. t.* **1.** *See* HOLLOW.
2. form (*contex.*); *spec.* dig, burrow, delve (*A*), hole, drive, drift, groove.

excavation, *n.* cavity (*contex.*), hole (*contex.*); *spec.* burrow, cutting, delve (*B*), pit, den, digging, beard, mine, shaft, stope, quarry, drift, drive, countermine.

exceed, *v. t.* **1.** transcend, overstep, pass, overgo (*R*), overpass (*R*); *spec.* stretch.
2. surpass, transcend, excel, overpeer (*R*), outpeer (*R*), cap, ding (*A or dial.*); *spec.* outdo, pass (*R*), outgo, outreach (*R or naut.*), break, out-Herod, outstrip, outplay.

exceed, *v. i. Spec.* surpass, excel, overabound.

excellence, *n.* worth, virtue, perfection, excel-

---

evil, *a.: wicked, harmful, injurious, malevolent.*
evil-looking: *ugly.*
evince: *disclose, show.*
eviscerate: *disembowel.*
evolve: *develop, emit.*
exalt: *praise, elevate, advance, elate.*
exasperate: *anger, irritate.*
exceeding: *above.*
excel, *v. t.: exceed, surpass.*
excel, *v. i.: exceed.*

---

lency, fineness, goodness (*R*), grace, superiority; *spec.* preëminence, greatness, purity.
Antonyms: see FAULT.

excellent, *a.* admirable, worthy, splendid (*C*), tiptop (*C*), superexcellent, brave, choice, first-rate, transcendent, exquisite, prime, sterling, superordinary, unexceptionable, divine (*fig.*), heavenly (*fig.*), crack (*S or C*), grand (*C*), great (*chiefly U. S. and C*), swell (*C*), admirable, golden, jolly (*C, chiefly Brit.*), rum (*cant*), surpassing, extreme.
Antonyms: see FAULTY, BAD, IMPERFECT, FAIR.

except, *v. t.* exclude, omit; *spec.* reserve, forprize (*R*).
Antonyms: see INCLUDE.

except, *prep.* unless, saving, save, but, excepting, batting (*obs. or B*).

exception, *n.* **1.** exclusion, omission; *spec.* reservation, limitation, reserve, forprize (*R*), salvo.
2. *See* OBJECTION.

excess, *n.* **1.** excessiveness, immoderation, immoderacy (*R*), immoderateness, superabundance, exuberance, exuberancy, superfluity, inordinacy (*R*), inordinateness, extremism (*R*), extremeness, transcendence, transcendency; *spec.* Caligulism (*fig.*), extravagance, extravagancy, extremity, extreme, exorbitance, exorbitancy, fulsomeness, unrestraint, nimiety, redundance, exundance (*R*), overabundance, overmuchness (*R*), superfluence (*R*), violence, unreasonableness.
Antonyms: see CONSTRAINT.
2. *Referring to the thing that is in excess, or to the degree of excess:* superabundance, redundancy, plethora, overmuch (*R*), superfluity, superflux (*R*), surfeit, surplus, surplusage, overplus; *spec.* oversupply, overflow, flood, overstock, glut, over, extra, plurality, epact (*astron.*), overweight, majority.
Antonyms: see DEFICIENCY.
3. *Referring to excess in indulgence:* immoderation, intemperance (*chiefly spec.*); *spec.* crapulence (*B*).

excessive, *a.* immoderate, inordinate, extravagant; *spec.* extreme, exorbitant, nimious (*chiefly Scots law*), exuberant, superabundant, exundant (*R*), overgreat, overlarge, redundant, overmuch, fulsome, deadly (*C*), undue, transcendent, unreasonable, outrageous, supernumerary, woundy (*C; A*), overdone, overflowing, superfluous, surplus, spare, dithyrambic (*B*), devilish, fiendish, cruel, *etc.*
Antonyms: see DEFICIENT.

excessively, *adv.* superabundantly, extravagantly, *etc.*, overly (*Scot. and C., U. S.*), ultra- (*in compounds, as in "ultra-conservative"*), consumedly (*B and affected*), over, too, too-too (*humorous*).

exchange, *n.* **1.** change (*contex.*); *spec.* interchange, conversion, commutation, reciprocation, transposal, transposition, substitution, barter, cambism, shuffle.
2. premium, agio, batta (*Anglo-Indian*).
3. *Referring to the business place: spec.* change (*the form "'change," as in "on 'change," is due to an erroneous supposition*), bourse, market, rialto (*R*), bazaar, fair.

exchange, *v. t.* change (*contex.*); *spec.* interchange, reciprocate, commute, substitute, transpose, transhift (*R*), counterchange, barter, bandy.

exchangeable, *a.* changeable (*contex.*), commutable, interchangeable.

excise, *v. t. To cut off:* remove (*contex.*), excide (*R*), exscind (*chiefly B or fig.*), exsect (*R*); *spec.* resect, efface.

excision, *n.* cutting, exscision (*chiefly B or fig.*), exsection (*R*); *spec.* resection, effacement.

excitable, *a.* nervous, irritable, hot-brained, hot-headed, inflammable, inflammatory (*R*).
Antonyms: see UNEXCITABLE.

excitation, *n.* **1.** *The act or action:* causing, arousing, rousing, provocation (*esp. spec.*), excitement (*R*); *spec.* electrification (*often fig.*), incendiarism.
2. *See* EXCITEMENT.

excitative, *a.* excitive, excitory, inflammatory (*usually spec.*); *spec.* incendiary (*fig.*), irritative (*chiefly biol.*).

excite, *v. t.* actuate (*B*), move, cause, call (*used with "up," "into activity," etc.*), raise, rouse, arouse, waken, awake, awaken, stimulate, incite, inflame, summon (*used with "into activity," etc.*), inspire, quicken, inebriate (*fig.*), stir, bestir, kittle (*Scot.*), disturb, kindle, impassion, enchafe (*A*), fire, electrify (*often fig.*), ferment (*fig.*), whet, irritate (*chiefly biol.*), impel, prompt, provoke, anger, agitate, heat, elate, enfrenzy (*R*);—*mostly idiomatic or specific.*
Antonyms: see CALM.

excited, *a.* nervous, ebullient (*R*), heated; *spec.* incensed, intoxicated, frenzied, fevered, feverish, restless, hot, tense, delirious, frantic, wild.
Antonyms: see APATHETIC, CALM, SELF-CONTROLLED, UNIMPASSIONED.

excitement, *n. The state or feeling:* excitation, disturbance, tension, activity, bustle (*C*), ferment, fermentation (*fig.*), heydey (*B*), incensement (*R*); *spec.* intoxication, inebriation (*R*), heat, ebullience (*B*), ebullition (*B*), inflammation, overwork, irritation (*chiefly biol.*), stir, breeze, flurry, flutter, ruffle, agitation, elation, erethism, delirium, hustle, franticness, electrification (*often fig.*).
Antonyms: see APATHY, CALM, SELF-CONTROL.

exciting, *a.* disturbing, electric (*fig.*), stirring, incentive, provocative, excitant (*R*), *etc.*
Antonyms: see CALMATIVE, SEDATIVE.

exclaim, *v. t. & i.* shout, cry, ejaculate, vociferate, reclaim (*R*), conclamate (*R*); *spec.*

---

except: *object.*
exceptional: *abnormal, unusual, special.*
excerpt, *v. t.: extract, quote.*
excerpt, *n.: extract, quotation.*

---

wail, howl (*chiefly contemptuous*), ululate (*R*), exululate (*R*), hoot (*often fig. in contempt*), hoop, hollo, hollow, holla, shrill, outshrill (*B*), whew.

exclamation, *n.* **1.** shout, cry, interjection, vociferation; *spec.* howl (*chiefly in contempt*), ululation, ecphonesis (*rhetorical; R*), bounce.

2. *A word exclaimed: spec.* interjection. *There are numberless exclamations; a few common ones are:* highty-tighty, hoity-toity (*somewhat contemptuous or disapproving*), hilloa, hillo, bounce, boo, bo, boh, cripes, ha, heck, hollo, hollow, holloa, halloo, hoicks, huzza, hurrah, hurray, hurra, hurroo, hush, hushaby, hello, gosh, chut, bully, doggone, bravo, marry (*A*), he, ho, hic, hey, hey-ho, hi, heyday, whoop-la, why, zounds (*A*), yoicks, haw, huh, hoo, evviva (*Italian*), evoe (*B*), hosanna, pooh, alas, gramercy, hist, whist, eureka, ugh, twang, tush, tut, whew, wow.

exclamatory, *a.* interjectional, interjectionary (*R*), interjectory.

exclude, *v. t.* **1.** debar, bar; *spec.* prohibit, lock (*often used with "out"*), out, prevent, blackball, ostracize.

Antonyms: see INCLUDE, IMPLY.

2. *See* EXPEL.

exclusion, *n.* **1.** debarring, debarrance (*R*), debarration (*R*), barring, debarment; *spec.* prohibition, preclusion, prevention, lock-out, ostracism, disfellowship (*R*).

2. *See* EXPULSION.

exclusive, *a.* **1.** excluding, sole, exclusory; *spec.* prohibitive, preclusive, inaccessible, preventive.

Antonyms: see INCLUSIVE.

2. *Spec.* clannish, cliquish.

3. refined, special, particular (*a vulgar sense perpetrated in modern advertizing*).

Antonyms: see COMMON.

excommunicate, *v. t.* expel, curse, unchurch.

excrement, *n.* dirt (*obs.*), ordure (*B*), dung (*now cant or inelegant*), feces *or* fæces (*chiefly tech.*), dejection (*R*), dejecture (*R*), rejectamenta (*pl.; R*), egesta (*pl.; tech.*), soil (*esp. in "night soil"*), egestion (*R*); *spec.* buttons (*pl.*), fumet, stool, frass, cast, crottels (*pl.*), fiants (*pl.*) *"Excrement" is learned or tech.*

excrescence, *n.* outgrowth; *spec.* appendage, burr, knot, wolf, gall, horn, fungus, nail, condyloma, wart, caruncle, lump, sitfast.

excrescent, *a.* outgrowing; *spec.* superfluous.

excrete, *v. t.* expel, discharge, pass, egest (*R*); *spec.* evacuate, eliminate, defecate.

Antonyms: see ASSIMILATE.

excretion, *n.* expulsion, discharge, egestion (*R*); *spec.* elimination, evacuation, dejection, diuresis, perspiration, metasyncrisis (*med.*), saliva, bile, *etc.*

Antonyms: see SECRETION.

excretitious, *a.* expulsory, excrementitious, excrementitionary; *spec.* evacuant, dejectory, depurative, emunctory.

excursion, *n.* **1.** *The act or action:* expedition; *spec.* sally, trip.

2. journey, trip; *spec.* outing, ride, voyage, sail, pilgrimage, tramp, ramble, jaunt, tour, walk.

3. *See* DEVIATION, DIGRESSION.

excursionist, *n. Spec.* tripper (*C*), tourist, voyager, rambler, walker, driver, rider.

excusable, *a.* allowable, dispensable (*A*), defensible, pardonable, venial.

Antonyms: see UNPARDONABLE, INEXCUSABLE, FLAGRANT.

excusatory, *a.* dispensative, dispensatory, excusative, apologetic.

excuse, *n.* **1.** defense, excusal (*R*), pardon, remission, remittal (*R*); *spec.* apology, condonation, extenuation, justification, indulgence, forgiveness, dispensation, essoin (*law*), amnesty.

2. *The thing offered by way of excuse:* plea, defense; *spec.* justification, reason, ground, apology, color.

Antonyms: see PUNISHMENT.

excuse, *v. t.* **1.** pardon, remit, overlook; *spec.* condone, forgive, extenuate, essoin, dispense, justify, furlough.

Antonyms: see PUNISH.

2. *See* FREE.

execute, *v. t.* **1.** *To carry out, as a plan, purpose, command:* perform, do, effectuate, effect; *spec.* enforce, fulfill, wreak (*vengeance*); *see* ACCOMPLISH, FILL.

2. *To go through actions, operations, movements, etc., constituting:* do (*as a dance, a somersault*), perform; *spec.* perpetrate (*as a joke; C*), play (*as a trick*), turn (*a handspring*); *see* FINISH.

3. make (*a deed, conveyance, will*).

4. *See* MAKE.

5. kill (*contex.*); *spec.* garrote, impale, behead, draw, decimate, crucify, guillotine, hang, gibbet, shoot, strangle, drown, electrocute (*a word often condemned as barbarous but which appears to have established itself*).

execution, *n.* **1.** doing, effecting, effectuating, performance; *spec.* enforcement, filling; *see* ACCOMPLISHMENT.

2. doing, performance; *spec.* perpetration (*C*), playing.

3. *The manner of executing: spec.* pianism (*cant*), mechanism, technique, touch, brush.

4. killing (*contex.*); *seec.* auto-da-fé (*Portuguese*), decimation, guillotinade, euthanasia, crucifixion, hanging, strangling, electrocution (*see "electrocute," under* EXECUTE.)

executioner, *n.* killer (*contex.*), deathsman (*R or B*); *spec.* headsman, hangman, carnifix, lictor (*Roman antiq.*), Jack Ketch (*hist.*), tormentor (*a Latinism*), slaughterman (*R*).

executor, *n.* doer, accomplisher, performer, executive (*chiefly spec.*).

excogitate: *devise.*
excoriate: *skin.*
excoriated: *raw.*
excruciate: *torture.*
exculpate: *acquit.*
excursive: *discursive.*
excursus: *discussion, digression.*
execrable: *abominable, bad.*
execrate: *curse.*
execrated: *accursed.*
execration: *cursing.*
executed: *done.*

exegesis, *n.* exposition.
exercise, *n.* **1.** *The act or action:* exertion (*esp. with conscious effort or force*), exercitation (*B*), use, practice (*often spec.*), working, operation; *spec.* play, plying, wielding, breather, breath.
2. *The course of exercise:* training, practice, drill, drilling, discipline; *spec.* goosestep, school; *see* TRAINING.
3. *The act of showing or of putting into practice:* use, practice, having, exhibition; *spec.* operation, enforcement.
4. *See* AGITATION.
5. trial, test; *spec.* composition, examination, quodlibet (*Latin; hist.*), theme (*obs.*), study, étude (*French*).
exercise, *v. t.* **1.** exert, practice, use, operate, work; *spec.* play, wield, ply, breathe, walk, run, trot, course, prosecute.
Antonyms: see DISUSE.
2. train, drill, school, discipline, practice; *spec.* enter (*cant*), teach, tutor; *see* TRAIN.
3. use, have, do, practice, show, exhibit, prosecute.
4. *See* AGITATE.
exhalation, *n.* **1.** aura (*B or tech.*), efflation (*R*), emission, breath (*R*), exhalement (*R*), emanation, halitus (*R*); *spec.* reek, blast, transpiration, fume, miasma, steam, smoke, evaporation. *Some of these words are used only concretely, of the thing exhaled.*
2. breath (*contex.*), expiration; *spec.* exsufflation, puff.
Antonyms: see INHALATION.
exhale, *v. t.* **1.** breathe, emanate, emit; *spec.* transpire, respire, reek, outbreathe, fume, furnace, vapor, gasp, steam, smoke, evaporate, blow.
2. breathe (*contex.*), expire, vent (*R*); puff; blow, spout.
exhale, *v. i.* breathe (*contex.*), expire; *spec.* exsufflate, spout, blow, puff.
Antonyms: see INHALE.
exhaust, *v. t.* **1.** *See* DRAIN, EMPTY, DRAW, DISCUSS.
2. weaken, deplete, overcome, spend, overspend (*R*), overtire, pump, extenerate (*R; fig.*), prostrate, outwear, wear out, outweary (*R*); *spec.* impoverish, overcrop, breathe.
Antonyms: see STRENGTHEN, REFRESH, REST, RESTORE.
exhaust, *n.* exhaustion, education (*obs.*).
exhausted, *a.* forspent (*A*), fordone (*A*), effete (*B*), dead, forworn (*A*), outspent (*R*), outworn; *spec.* breathless, forfoughten (*obs. or Scot.*).
Antonyms: see STRONG, FRESH.
exhaustion, *n.* **1.** *Spec.* draining, emptying, emptiness.
2. weakening, prostration, exhaustedness, depletion; *spec.* inanition, exinanition (*R*), collapse, impoverishment.
exhaustive, *a.* **1.** emptying.
2. *Referring to a discussion:* complete, full, thorough.
exhort, *v. t.* advise, urge.
exhortation, *n.* advice, urging, protreptic (*R*), hortation (*B*), prone (*R; eccl.*), paraenesis (*R*), hortative (*R*).
exhortative, *a.* exhortatory, cohortative (*esp. gram.*), hortative, hortatory, urgent.
exigency, *n.* demand, need, necessity, distress, difficulty, extremity, urgency, strait, juncture, pressure, pinch; *spec.* crisis.
exigent, *a.* demanding, exacting, urgent, necessary, distressful, pressing; *spec.* critical.
exiguous, *a.* scanty, small, slender.
exile, *n.* **1.** outcast.
2. *See* EXPULSION.
exit, *n.* **1.** departure; *spec.* death.
2. *A way out:* outlet, egress, escape; *spec.* doorway, gate, window, skylight, *etc.*
Antonyms: see ENTRANCE.
exorbitant, *a.* excessive, Sibylline (*fig.*); *spec.* greedy.
Antonyms: see MODERATE.
exorcise, *v. t.* lay, down (*C*); *spec.* exsufflate.
exorcism, *n.* laying, downing (*C*); *spec.* exsufflate (*R*).
exordium, *n.* beginning, proem (*B*), introduction; *spec.* preface.
exoteric, *a.* **1.** *Referring to disciples:* unintiated, outer.
2. *Referring to opinions:* public.
3. *Referring to an author, etc.:* commonplace.
expand, *v. t. & i.* **1.** *See* OPEN, DEVELOP.
2. spread, widen, bulk, outspread; *spec.* stretch, outspread; *spec.* outstretch, mushroom, unfurl, display, dilate, distend, open.
Antonyms: see SHRINK, PRESS.
3. develop.
expanse, *n.* expansion (*less usual than "expanse"*), area, stretch, spread; *spec.* contiguity, continuity, sheet, field, sea (*fig.*), outspread, (*R*).
expansion, *n.* **1.** spread, widening; *spec.* stretch, dilation, diastole.
2. *See* EXPANSE, DEVELOPMENT.
expansive, *a.* wide; *spec.* comprehensive, elastic, dilatable, extensible.
Antonyms: see CONFINED.
expatiate, *v. i.* enlarge, descant, dilate, expand.
expect, *v. t.* contemplate, anticipate, think, trust, await, hope, look, calculate (*used with an*

exemplify: *example, typify.*
exempt: *free.*
exemption: *freeing, freedom.*
exert: *exercise.*
exertive: *active.*
exfoliate: *scale, shed.*
exhibit, *n.:* *show.*
exhibition: *show.*
exhibitory: *disclosing.*
exhilarate: *elate, enliven.*
exhort, *v. t.:* *advise, urge.*
exhort, *v. i.:* *preach.*
exile, *v. t.:* *expel.*
exist: *be.*
existence: *being.*
existent: *being.*
exodus: *emigration.*
exonerate: *acquit.*
exorable: *complaisant.*
exorbitance, exorbitancy: *excess.*

infinitive clause or with "that"; chiefly local, U. S.), apprehend.
expectancy, *n.* **1.** anticipation, hopefulness, apprehension.
2. prospect, abeyance (*law*).
expectant, *a.* anticipator, anticipant, hopeful.
expectation, *n.* anticipation, contemplation, thought, trust, hope.
expectorate, *v. i.* **1.** raise; *spec.* cough.
2. *See* SPIT.
expediency, *n.* advantage, advisability, policy; *spec.* opportunism.
expedient, *a.* wise (*contex.*), politic; *spec.* timeserving, opportunist; *see* WISE, ADVANTAGEOUS.
expedient, *n.* device, shift; *spec.* kink, trick, stopgap, dodge (*C*), ruffle, resort, resource, makeshift, subterfuge.
expedite, *v. t.* **1.** dispatch, hasten, hurry, quicken; *spec.* facilitate.
Antonyms: see HINDER.
2. *See* ACCOMPLISH.
expedition, *n.* **1.** haste, dispatch, hastening, hurrying.
2. journey, campaign, quest (*medieval romance*); *spec.* crusade, commando (*South Africa*).
expel, *v. t.* **1.** eject, extrude; *spec.* shoot, oust, discharge, evaporate, excrete, dislodge, dispel, egest, eliminate, belch.
Antonyms: see ADMIT, INJECT.
2. *In reference to putting a person out of some place:* remove, exclude; *spec.* evict, estampede (*R*), exsibilate (*R*), deforce (*R*), fire (*S, U. S.*), bounce (*S or cant, U. S.*), disseize, bolt, oust.
Antonyms: see ADMIT.
3. *Explusion from a group:* exclude, fire (*S, U. S*).; *spec.* outcast (*R*), excommunicate, disparish, unchurch, drum (*used with "out"; esp. mil.*), disfellowship (*U. S.*), disown (*in the Society of Friends*). *See* DISCHARGE.
4. banish, exile, exclude, drive (*used with "out"*); *spec.* deport, expatriate, epatriate (*R*), depatriate (*R or obs.*), transport, relegate, ostracize, denationalize, exostracize (*R*), ride (*chiefly with "from"*). *See* DISCHARGE.
expend, *v. t.* consume (*contex.*), outlay, disburse spend, use, employ.
expenditure, *n.* consumption (*contex.*), outlay, outgo, disbursement, expense (*A*); *spec.* profusion, cost.
Antonyms: see INCOME.
expense, *n.* **1.** expenditure, outlay; *spec.* cost, charge.
2. *See* CHARGE.
experience, *n.* knowledge, acquaintance, encounter; *spec.* sufferance, enjoyment, trial, taste, adventure, time.
Antonyms: see INEXPERIENCE.
experience, *v. t.* have, know, see, meet, encounter, undergo; *spec.* suffer, enjoy, share, try, realize, taste, lead, receive, prove (*A*).
experienced, *a. Spec.* old, practiced, wise, salted (*S or C*), veteran, expert.
Antonyms: see INEXPERIENCED.
experimental, *a.* trial.
expert, *a.* adroit; *spec.* proficient, scientific.
expert, *n.* crack (*C or S*), adept, dabster (*C*), dab (*C; chiefly spec.*), proficient, master, sharp (*S*), sharper (*S*), shark (*S*), whiz (*S*); *spec.* specialist, technician, technicist (*R*), technologist, virtuoso (*masc.*), maestro, virtuosa (*fem.*), connoisseur.
Antonyms: see CLOWN, DABBLER; *also cf.* BUNGLE.
expiate, *v. t. To atone for:* redeem, assoil (*A*), purge (*chiefly law*); *spec.* mend, ransom.
Antonyms: see AGGRAVATE.
expiation, *n.* atonement, redemption, piation (*R*); *spec.* cross (*of Christ*), satisfaction, satispassion (*theol.*), ransom.
expiatory, *a.* piacular (*R*), redemptive; *spec.* lustrative, lustral.
expired, *a.* run (*as time; often with "out"*), over (*C*).
explain, *v. t.* expound, solve, elucidate, resolve, explicate (*R*), unfold, dissolve (*R*); *spec.* demonstrate, construe, clear, interpret, enucleate (*B*), innuendo (*law*), untie (*fig.*), undo (*R*), unriddle, unravel, untangle, glossate, gloss, define, describe, develop, detail.
Antonyms: see OBSCURE.
explainable, *a.* accountable, interpretable, explicable.
explainer, *n.* expounder; *spec.* hierophant, exponent.
explanation, *n.* **1.** account (*matter-of-fact*), interpretation (*with the explainer's point of view*), elucidation (*throwing light*), exposition (*orderly and analytical*), explication (*often critical or exegetical*), construction; *spec.* definition, description.
2. *Referring to what explains:* explication, key; *spec.* comment, commentary, exegesis, secret, innuendo, catastrophe.
explanatory, *a.* interpretative, elucidative, elucidatory, explanative (*R*), expository, expositive, expositional, exegetical.
explicit, *a.* **1.** *See* DEFINITE.
2. express; *spec.* written, outspoken, positive, plain.
Antonyms: see IMPLIED.
explode, *v. t.* **1.** *See* DESTROY.
2. burst, detonate; *spec.* fire, pop, spring, deflagrate, crack.
exploit, *v. t.* utilize (*contex.*); *spec.* milk (*C*), work (*C*).
exploration, *n.* search, prospecting, prospect, probe; *spec.* inquisition.
explore, *v. t.* search, plumb (*fig.*), fathom, outsearch (*R*); *spec.* prospect.
explosion, *n.* **1.** *Spec.* destruction.
2. bursting, burst; *spec.* fulmination, detona-

expensive: *costly.*
expert, *a.*: *skillful.*
expiration: *exhalation, end, death.*
expire: *exhale, die, end.*
expletive: *oath.*
explicable: *explainable.*
exploded: *obsolete.*
exploit: *deed.*

tion, fulguration, blast, clap, crack, shot, report, pop.
3. *See* OUTBREAK.
explosive, *n. Spec.* lyddite, cordite, fulminant (*R*), dynamogen, rackarock, fulminate, dynamite, roburite, gelignite, guncotton, herculite, gunpowder, trinitotoluol, TNT (*abbr.*).
expose, *v. t.* **1.** disclose, unearth (*fig.*), flay (*fig.*), decorticate; *spec.* unmask, bare.
Antonyms: see HIDE, SECLUDE.
2. subject (*used with "to"*); *spec.* venture, risk, post, weather, pitch, gibbet (*fig.*), bare, abandon.
Antonyms: see PROTECT, SHELTER.
exposed, *a.* **1.** bleak, raw, airy, bare, open, shelterless, windy.
Antonyms: see SHELTERED, UNEXPOSED.
2. *With "to":* liable, subject.
3. *See* BARE.
expostulate, *v. t.* remonstrate.
exposure, *n.* **1.** disclosure; *spec.* show-up (*C*), unmasking.
2. *Usually with "to":* subjection; *spec.* abandonment.
Antonyms: see PROTECTION, SHELTER.
3. liability, subjection (*used with "to"*), liableness (*R*).
express, *n.* **1.** *See* DISPATCH.
2. agency (*contex.*), dispatch.
express, *v. t.* **1.** squeeze (*esp. with "out"*).
2. *See* EXTORT, SEND, HASTEN.
3. represent, symbolize, present, show, denote, testify (*A*), betoken; *spec.* delineate.
4. *Referring to the conveying of an idea by words, actions, etc.: spec.* state, emit, manifest, tell, declare, frame, present, have (*used with "it"*), enunciate, language (*R*), broach, breathe, dictate (*obs. or A*), expound, deliver, impress (*with "upon"*), couch, dash, vent, air, word, utter, voice, clothe, cough, hoot, communicate, blush, nod, signify, smile, sound, speak, hymn, figure, write, wave, pantomime (*R*), look, glance, glare, gesticulate.
Antonyms: see IMPLY.
5. *See* SEND.
expression, *n.* **1.** squeezing (*used esp. with "out"*).
2. representation, symbolization, presentation, presentment, show, denotation; *spec.* delineation, token.
3. *Spec.* statement, utterance, emission, wording, breath, communication, vent, signification, *etc.*
4. diction; *spec.* eloquence, idiom, brevity, *etc.*
5. *Referring to the thing expressed: spec.* effusion, phraseology, locution, phrase, term, word, look; *see* SAYING.
expressionless, *a.* unmeaning, null (*R*), wooden (*fig.*), vacant, blank; *spec.* soulless, fishy (*fig.*), dull.
Antonyms: see EXPRESSIVE.
expressive, *a.* demonstrative, eloquent, significant, significatory, significative, meaning (*R*); *spec.* forceful, wise, emphatic, epigrammatic.
Antonyms: see MEANING, BLANK, EXPRESSIONLESS.
expulsion, *n.* **1.** ejection, ejectment (*chiefly law*); *spec.* explosion, defenestration, elimination, dislodgment, discharge.
Antonyms: see ADMISSION, INJECTION.
2. banishment, exile, exilement, deportation, relegation (*chiefly Roman law*), transportation (*chiefly spec.*), expatriation, ostracism, petalism (*ancient hist.*), rustication.
Antonyms: see ADMISSION.
3. ejectment, exclusion, eviction, ousting.
4. excommunication (*eccl.*), exclusion, excision (*R*).
5. excretion, discharge, catharsis (*tech.*); *spec.* diuresis, evacuation.
expulsive, *a. Spec.* expulsory (*R*), ejective, eliminant, eliminative (*physiol. and chem.*), explosive, ecbolic (*med.; R*), excommunicative, excommunicatory.
expunge, *v. t.* (*the first five, with* expunge, *apply normally to records, parliamentary or court remarks, etc.*), remove, efface, blot out, cancel, erase; destroy, annihilate.
expurgate, *v. t.* emasculate, expurge (*R*), castrate; *spec.* bowdlerize.
extemporaneous, *a.* **1.** extemporized, unpremeditated, spontaneous, extempore, improvised, improvisatory, improvisatorical (*R*), offhand, impromptu.
2. *See* OCCASIONAL.
extempore, *adv.* impromptu, extemporaneously, offhand.
extemporize, *v.* compose (*contex.*), improvise.
extemporizer, *n.* improvisator, improviser, improvisatore.
extend, *v. t.* **1.** *Spec.* continue, lengthen, elongate, widen, drag, enlarge, pass (*chiefly with "to"*), run, stretch, produce (*chiefly with "to"*), draw, distend, protend (*R*), prolong, protract, cöextend, string, deploy (*mil.*), diffuse, carry, wiredraw.
Antonyms: see ABRIDGE.
2. *Spec.* reach, protrude, thrust, outstretch (*chiefly B*), shoot, portend (*R*), porrect (*R*).
3. *See* ENLARGE.
extend, *v. i.* reach, go, come, continue, range, run, proceed; *spec.* (*physically*) ride, project, protrude, ramify, cross, outlie (*R*), lie, outreach (*B*), outspan (*R*), grow, stream, stretch.
Antonyms: see SHORTEN, WITHDRAW.
extensible, *a.* produceable, productile (*R*), extendible, extensile, protractile; *spec.* ductile, malleable, plastic, pliable, dilatable.
extension, *n.* **1.** *Spec.* continuation, continu-

export: *ship.*
exposition: *explanation, exegesis, show, statement.*
expositive: *disclosing, explanatory.*
expound: *state, express, explain.*
exquisite, *a.: accurate, fastidious, choice, accomplished, intense, excellent.*
exquisite, *n.: dandy.*
extant: *being.*

ance, lengthening, widening, enlargement, stretching, production, protraction, prolongation, distention, coextension, deployment, diffusion, deploy.

Antonyms: see ABRIDGEMENT, RETIREMENT, ABSTRACT.

2. *Spec.* protrusion, projection, porrection (*R*), protension (*R*), ramification, wing, annex.

3. *See* COMPREHENSION.

extensive, *a. Spec.* wide, widespread, far-reaching, far-flung, dissipated, divergent, nationwide, statewide.

Antonym: see INTENSIVE.

extent, *n.* **1.** *See* VALUATION.

2. extension, measure; *spec.* reach, continuance, amplitude, size, expanse, dimension, measurement, proportions, degree, compass, stretch, content (*tech.*), gauge, length (*also fig.*), field, latitude, range, scope, breadth, width, height, distance, area.

extenuative, *a.* excusatory, palliatory; *spec.* euphemistic.

extenuative, *n.* palliative; *spec.* euphemism.

exterior, *a.* **1.** outer, external, outward, outside, extern (*R*); *spec.* outmost, outermost, superficial, outlying, foreign, extrinsic.

Antonyms: see INTERIOR.

2. *See* FOREIGN.

exterior, *n.* outside; *see* SURFACE.

exterminate, *v. t.* annihilate, abolish, uproot, extirpate (*a forcible uprooting*), eradicate (*a less violent uprooting*).

externalize, *v. t.* objectify, objectize (*R*), entify (*R*); *see* VISUALIZE.

externally, *a.* outwardly, outside, outward.

extinction, *n.* destruction (*contex.*); *spec.* annihilation, death, suffocation.

extinguish, *v. t.* destroy (*contex.*); *spec.* annihilate, quench, choke (*often with "out" or "off"*), quell, subdue, douse (*S or cant*), dout (*now dial.*), remove, suppress, slake (*R*), stifle, smother, suffocate; *see* SNUFF.

Antonyms: see KINDLE, CREATE, BREED, FOSTER, PRESERVE.

extinguished, *a.* destroyed (*contex.*); *spec.* dead, out.

extirpate, *v. t.* destroy, abolish, deracinate (*R*), weed (*chiefly used with "out"*), uproot; *spec.* annihilate; *see* EXTERMINATE.

Antonyms: see PLANT.

extort, *v. t.* elicit, extract, exact, draw, wring, wrest, pinch, screw, shave (*C or S*), force, squeeze. *For discriminations see* ELICIT.

extortion, *n.* elicitation, oppression, rapacity, overcharge, exaction; *spec.* tribute, expression, blackmail, garnish (*hist.*).

extortionate, *a.* unreasonable (*contex.*), exacting, vampire (*fig.*), vampiric (*fig.*), bloodsucking (*fig.*).

Antonyms: see MODERATE.

extortioner, *n.* exacter, extortionist, wringer, wrester, caterpillar (*fig.*), blood-sucker, (*fig.*) vulture (*fig.*), flayer (*fig.*), fleecer, griper (*R*), vampire (*fig.*), harpy (*fig.*).

extra, *a.* additional, accessory, spare.

extra, *n. Spec.* accessory, et ceteras (*pl.; Latin*), sundries (*pl.*), additions (*pl.*), paraphernalia (*pl.*), odd.

Antonyms: see DEFICIENCY.

extract, *v. t.* **1.** derive, elicit, draw, remove; *spec.* distil, squeeze, extort.

Antonyms: see INJECT.

2. *See* REMOVE, WITHDRAW.

extract, *n.* **1.** *Spec.* essence, decoction, magistery (*R*), distillate, distillation.

2. *See* QUOTATION.

extraction, *n.* **1.** elicitation, derivation; *spec.* distillation, squeezing, *etc.*

2. *See* DESCENT.

extraordinary, *a.* unusual, singular, uncommon, remarkable, exemplary (*A*), portentous (*humorous*), phenomenal, prodigious (*humorous, exc. spec*); *spec.* transcendent, parlous (*C or humorous*), inconceivable, distinguished, amazing, monstrous, marvelous, abnormal, enormous.

Antonyms: see COMMON.

extravagance, *n.* **1.** excess, profusion, profuseness, prodigality, lavishness, exuberance; *spec.* superabundance, enormity, monstrosity, wildness, furor, *etc.*

Antonyms: see ECONOMY.

2. hyperbolism (*rhet.*); *spec.* bombast, fantasticality, fantasticalness, grotesqueness, grotesquerie, *etc.*

extravagant, *a.* **1.** profuse, profusive (*R*), prodigal, lavish; *spec.* wasteful, profligate (*though both* prodigal *and* profligate *imply reckless thoughtlessness for the morrow,* profligate *carries also the overtone of debasement*), rampant, wild, rank, spendthrift.

Antonyms: see ECONOMICAL, STINGY.

2. *Spec.* bombastic, fantastic, fantastical, wild, furious, eccentric, bizarre, grotesque, odd, baroque, rococo.

Antonyms: see MATTER-OF-FACT, MODERATE.

extravasation, *n.* stigma.

extreme, *a.* **1.** remotest, utmost, farthest, uttermost (*A or formal*), last, ultra (*chiefly tech.*), limitary.

Antonyms: see NEAREST.

2. *See* FINAL.

3. greatest, utmost, uttermost (*A or formal*), supreme, outside (*C*); *spec.* precious (*C*), horrible (*C*).

4. excessive, deep (*chiefly spec.*); *spec.* bad, drastic, intense, desperate (*C*), egregious, impossible, outrageous, immoderate, deadly (*C*), eternal (*now vulgar*), heroic, high, radical, unspeakable (*C*), monstrous (*C*), *etc.*

extreme, *n.* **1.** *See* END.

2. utmost, limit, extremity; *spec.* excess, pink, height.

extremely, *adv.* very, so (*chiefly C*).

---

extenuate: *mitigate.*
external: *exterior, accidental, foreign.*
extol: *praise, celebrate.*
extradite: *deliver.*
extraneous: *foreign.*

exudation, *n.* emission, discharge, sweat (*chiefly spec.*), ooze (*only of what exudes*), percolation.
exude, *v. i. & t.* emit, transude, discharge, sweat (*chiefly spec.*), ooze; *spec.* weep, percolate, infiltrate, filter, strain, lixiviate.
Antonyms: see ABSORB.
exult, *v. i.* rejoice, vaunt, insult (*A*), crow (*C*), jubilate, maffick (*C*); *spec.* gloat, triumph, glory.
Antonyms: see MOURN.
exultant, *a.* rejoicing, jubilant.
exultation, *n.* gladness, rejoicing, insultation (*A*); *spec.* gloat, gloating, triumph, jubilation.
Antonyms: see MOURNING.
exuvium, *n.* (*tech. or B*); skin, cast, slough.
eye, *n.* **1.** oculus (*tech. or spec.*), orb (*B or rhetorical*), optic (*chiefly in pl., and C*), glim (*S*), peeper (*S*), lamps (*pl.; S; formerly B*), piercer (*S*), goggler (*S*), orbit (*an erroneous use*); *spec.* eyelet, oculus, cock-eye, wall-eye, stemma, facet.
2. *See* VISION, LOOK.
3. eyehole; *spec.* collar, eyelet, peephole.
eye, *v. t. Spec.* watch, ogle.
eyeball, *n.* apple (*of the eye*).
eyebrow, *n.* brow, supercilium (*tech.*).
eyeglass, *n. Spec.* monocle, pince-nez (*French*), nippers (*pl.; S*), lorgnette, lorgnon (*French*), spectacles (*pl.*), glasses (*pl.*).
eyelashes, *n. pl.* cilia (*tech.*), eyewinkers.
eyelass, *a.* exoculated (*B*), blind.
eyelid, *n.* lid, palpebra (*anat.*); *spec.* haw.
eyesore, *n.* dissight *or* desight (*R*).
eyewash, *n.* collyrium, eyewater.

F

fable, *n.* **1.** apologue.
2. *See* UNTRUTH, STORY.
fable, *v. t.* feign, invent;—*referring to what is told in words.*
fabric, *n.* **1.** building.
2. cloth, texture (*A*), contexture, stuff (*chiefly spec.*), tissue (*chiefly spec.*), web (*chiefly spec.*), woof (*R*), material, medley; *spec.* textile (*chiefly tech.*), network, homespun, diagonal, webbing, *etc.*
3. *See* TEXTURE.
fabricate, *v. t.* **1.** *See* CONSTRUCT.
2. *Referring to a made-up tale, story, etc.*: devise, compose; *spec.* spin, coin, forge.
fabulous, *a.* fictitious; *spec.* romantic, legendary, feigned; unbelievable, incredible; huge (*often of an incredibly large fortune, etc.*).
Antonyms: see ACTUAL.
face, *n.* **1.** countenance (*B*), features (*pl.*), visage (*generally stresses outward appearance*), favor (*A*), front (*S or fig.*), physiognomy (*chiefly implying the inner qualities shown by the* face), mazard (*A and jocular*), phiz (*C and jocular*), mug (*S*), brow (*R or obs.*); *spec.* grimace.
2. *See* BOLDNESS, APPEARANCE, COVER, EDGE, ASPECT, PRESENCE, SURFACE, FACET.
3. front, forefront (*chiefly spec.*); *spec.* escarpment, breast, disk, pedion, obverse, head.
face, *v. t.* **1.** *To have the face towards:* front, confront, envisage (*R*); *spec.* respect, frontier.
2. oppose, front, breast, confront, buck (*S, U. S.*), brave, cope (*R*); *spec.* outbrazen, nose, beard, buffet, defy, dare.
Antonyms: see AVOID.
3. *To show to the face of* (*a person*): confront;—*often with "with."*
4. cover; *spec.* veneer, revet, line, campshed (*local, Eng.*).
5. *See* BRAZEN.
face, *v. i.* front, head (*chiefly spec.*), give (*a Gallicism*); *spec.* look (*often fig.*).
facet, *n.* face (*contex.*); *spec.* templet, lozenge, table (*in gems*), cut, culet.
facetious, *a.* humorous.
face-to-face, *a. Spec.* tête-à-tête (*French*), vis-à-vis (*French*), respectant (*her.*).
facing, *n.* **1.** cover (*contex.*); *spec.* lining, envelope, shoe, veneer, skin.
2. frontage, outlook; *spec.* exposure.
3. confrontation, confrontment (*R*).
faction, *n.* **1.** combination, division, side; *spec.* clique, sect; *see* PARTY.
2. *See* DISSENSION.
factory, *n.* workshop, shop, mill, manufactory (*formal*), officina (*Spanish*), works (*chiefly Brit.*), mint (*often spec.*); *spec.* hattery, pottery, bloomery, bakery, confectionery, brickyard, *etc.*
faculty, *n.* **1.** *See* ABILITY, ART, TALENT.
2. *Of the mind's faculties:* power, sense, wits (*pl.; chiefly spec.*); *spec.* instinct, intellectuals (*pl.; A*), reason.
3. department, school (*hist.*); *spec.* seminarists (*pl.*).
fad, *n.* custom, craze, rage, hobby, mania, monomania, frenzy, delirament (*R*), whim-wham (*A or R*), furor; *spec.* fashion, pursuit, tulipomania, vinomania, crotchet, dipsomania, *etc.*
fade, *v. i.* **1.** *See* DECLINE, WITHER.
2. vanish (*often used with "away"*), faint; *spec.* die (*used with "out"*), dim, pale, dissolve, disperse.
Antonyms: see INTENSIFY.

---

extricate: *free.*
extrinsic: *foreign, accidental, external.*
extrude: *expel.*
exuberance: *abundance, excess.*
exuberant: *abundant, excessive, prolix.*

F

fable: *narrative.*
facetiousness: *pleasantry.*
facile: *easy, complaisant, ready, fluent, skillful.*
facilitate: *aid, ease.*
facsimile: *copy, duplicate.*
fact: *occurrence, actuality, truth.*
factious: *disagreeing, dissentient.*
factitious: *artificial, false.*
factor: *agent, element.*
factorage: *agency.*
factual: *actual.*
facture: *creation, making, doing.*
faculative: *optional.*
fag: *drudge, tire.*
fagot: *bundle.*

---

fail, *v. i.* **1.** lack, collapse, miss, miscarry, abort, fizzle (*chiefly U. S.*); *spec.* flunk, bust (*both school S, U. S.*), pluck (*school S, Brit.*), (*these three both v. i. and v. t.*); err, default.
Antonyms: see SUCCEED.
2. break, bankrupt, default, defalcate (*R*), smash (*S*), swamp (*C*).
Antonyms: see SUCCEED.
3. *See* DECLINE, SINK, SICKEN.

failure, *n.* **1.** fail (*obs., exc. in "without fail"*).
2. *See* DECLINE.
3. deficiency, default, omission, nonact (*R*), nonexecution; *spec.* abortion, collapse, fizzle (*C*), miscarriage, flunk (*U. S.; school S*), lapse, muff, fiasco, breakdown, slip, negligence, frost (*S*), dereliction, delinquency, nonsuccess.
Antonyms: see SUCCESS.
4. bankruptcy (*in U. S. spec.*), insolvency (*in U. S. spec.*), break, default, defalcation (*R*); *spec.* smash (*C*), crash.
5. might-have-been (*C*).

faint, *a.* **1.** *See* TIMID.
2. weak, languid, listless, dolcho farniente (*Italian*), sickly, gone (*C*).
Antonyms: see POWERFUL.
3. *See* INDISTINCT, DIM.
4. *Referring to sounds:* soft, small, gentle, thin.

faint, *n.* swoon, deliquium (*A*); *spec.* lipothymia.

faint, *v. i.* **1.** decline, fade.
2. swoon, go (*contex.*), swelter (*R*).
Antonyms: see REVIVE.

faintness, *n. Spec.* swoon, lassitude.

fair, *a.* **1.** good-looking, dexter (*R*); *spec.* beautiful, shapely, clean, clear, legible, distinct (*these three, of writing*), glossy, smooth, sweet, favorable, cloudless (*these two, with* clear, *used of the weather*).
2. *See* DESIRABLE, IMPARTIAL, FAVORABLE, AUSPICIOUS, JUST, UNOBSTRUCTED, CLEAR.
3. medium, passable, fairish (*R*), so-so (*C*), moderate, indifferent, tolerable, respectable, reasonable, decent, ordinary; *spec.* average.
Antonyms: see EXCELLENT, BAD.
4. blond, blonde, clear, white (*C, U. S.*); *spec.* lily, lilied.
Antonyms: see DARK.

fair, *n. Spec.* bazaar, exchange, kermis, show.

fairly, *adv.* fair, well, middling (*usually qualifying an adjective, as "good"*).

fairy, *n.* demon (*often spec.*), spirit (*contex.*), fay, sprite *or* (*A*) spright; *spec.* Titania, browny, elf, nix, fairyhood (*a collective*).

fairyland, *n.* faërie *or* faëry (*A*), fairydom; *spec.* dreamland.

fake, *v. t.* falsify (*contex.*), sophisticate, counterfeit (*contex.*); *spec.* deacon (*cant or C*), doctor (*C*), duff (*S or C*), nobble (*S*), fudge, cook (*S*), edit (*euphemistic*), pack.

fake, *n.* contrivance, fakement; *spec.* adulteration, fraud, cheat.

fakir, *n.* ascetic (*contex.*), dervish.

falcon, *n.* hawk (*contex.*); *spec.* tercelgentle (*male*), merlin, lanner (*esp. fem.*), lanneret (*masc.*), tartaret (*obs.*), sakeret (*masc.; A*), saker (*esp. fem.*), shahin *or* shaheen, sorefalcon.

fall, *v. i.* **1.** descend (*formal*), drop, sink, lapse (*B and R*); *spec.* drop, calve (*dial. or tech.*), cave (*used with "in"*), pitch, drip, slump (*dial.*), plop, rain, plump, squab, cataract, topple, drizzle, droop, tumble, slant, distill, lodge, collapse, shed.
Antonyms: see RISE, STAND.
2. *See* DESCEND (*come to a lower level*), END, ACCRUE, BECOME, APOSTATIZE, DECLINE, DIE, DEPRECIATE, LOWER (*referring to the countenance*), SURRENDER, ABATE, SUBSIDE, OUTGO, PASS, OCCUR.
3. *Referring to prices, etc.:* decline, drop, sink; *spec.* slump (*cant or C*), tumble.
Antonyms: see ADVANCE.

fall, *n.* **1.** descent, downfall, downcome, comedown (*C*), labefaction (*R*), drop (*often spec.*); *spec.* shower, downrush, downpour, deluge (*hyperbolical*), cropper (*C; chiefly in "to come a cropper"*), discharge, cave-in (*chiefly C*), dripple, flap (*C*), flop, plop, tumble, spill (*C*), plump (*C*), squash, dogfall, eavesdrip, eavesdrop, crowner, collapse.
Antonyms: see RISE.
2. *See* DESCENT, RUIN, SURRENDER, TACKLE, WATERFALL.
3. *Referring to prices, etc.:* decline, drop; *spec.* slump (*C or cant*), tumble.
Antonyms: see ADVANCE.

fallacy, *n.* **1.** error, deception; *spec.* sophism, absurdity, sorites, bubble, idol, idolum *or* idolism, paralogism.
Antonyms: see TRUTH.
2. deceptiveness (*cf.* DECEPTIVE).

fallible, *a.* errable (*R*), deceivable (*R*).
Antonyms: see INFALLIBLE.

falling, *a.* descending, cadent (*A*); *spec.* precipitant, deciduous, incident, dripping, *etc.*
Antonyms: see RISING.

falling, *n.* descent; *spec.* dripping, distillation, drip-drop, incidence, ptosis (*R*), prolapsus.

fallow, *a.* uncultivated, unplowed, untilled, unused (*fig.*), lea, ley *or* lay (*Eng.*); *spec.* yellow.
Antonyms: CULTIVATED (*see* CULTIVATE).

false, *a.* **1.** *See* UNTRUTHFUL, UNFAITHFUL, UNTRUE, ERRONEOUS, DECEPTIVE, ABSURD, DISHONEST.
2. pseudo (imitative, counterfeit; *chiefly B*), spurious (*like* pseudo, *not the genuine article, but implying intent to deceive*), bastard (*chiefly in contempt*), counterfeit, supposititious, hollow, bogus, fictitious, fictive (*R*); *spec.* pretended, forged, made-up, impostrous (*R*), artificial, factitious.
Antonyms: see TRUE, NATIVE.

---

fail, *v. t.: desert.*
failing: *fault.*
faint-hearted: *cowardly, timid.*
faith: *belief, constancy, trust.*
faithful: *constant, accurate, trustworthy, conscientious.*
faithless: *unfaithful, untruthful, dishonest, treacherous.*
fall, *v. t.: drop.*
fallacious: *absurd, erroneous, deceptive.*

---

falsify, *v. t.* alter, sophisticate; *spec.* fake, cook (*S*), interpolate (*by adding*), doctor; *see* ADULTERATE, FAKE.

falsity, *n.* **1.** falsehood; *spec.* absurdity, deceptiveness, *etc.*; *see* DISHONESTY.
2. spuriousness, supposititiousness, hollowness, fictitiousness, fictiveness (*R*); *spec.* pretension, artificiality.

falter, *v. i.* **1.** stumble stagger, dodder, hobble, totter, hesitate, waver.
2. *Referring to speech:* hesitate, halt; *spec.* stammer, stutter, stumble, quaver, waver, lisp, hem.
3. *See* HESITATE.

falter, *n.* **1.** stumble, stagger, dodder, totter, hesitation, waver.
2. balbuties (*tech.*), halt, hesitation (*contex.*); *spec.* stammer, stutter, stumble, quaver, waver, lisp.
3. *See* HESITATION.

fame, *n.* **1.** *See* REPUTATION.
2. honor (*contex.*), repute *or* reputation (*contex.*), renown, illustriousness, luster, illustration (*R*), distinction, kudos (*pedantic or humorous; Greek*), celebrity, lionism, lionhood, *or* lionship (*fig.*), note, consideration; *spec.* glory, eminence, greatness, conspicuousness, tongue (*fig.*).
Antonyms: see OBSCURITY.

fame, *v. t.* **1.** *See* REPORT.
2. eternize (*R*), immortalize. *The verb "fame" is rare.*

familiar, *a.* **1.** *See* DOMESTIC, AWARE.
2. intimate, homely (*A*), common (*contex.*); *spec.* hobnobby (*R*), hailfellow (*R*), free, overfamiliar, unconstrained.
Antonyms: see UNFAMILIAR, FORMAL.
3. *See* COMMON.

familiarity, *n.* **1.** intimacy, homeliness (*A*); *spec.* freedom, conversation (*B*).
2. *See* KNOWLEDGE, ACQUAINTANCE.

family, *n.* **1.** household, brood (*contemptuous*), cletch *or* clutch (*contemptuous*), people (*used with "my," "his," etc.*), stock, house; *spec.* mine, his, theirs, *etc.* (*all these uses being chiefly C*).
2. lineage (*formal*), house, race, kin, strain, blood (*fig.*), breed (*chiefly contemptuous*); *spec.* dynasty.
3. *See* KINDRED, KIND, CLASS.

family, *a. Spec.* patronymic; *see* DOMESTIC.

famish, *v. t. & i.* starve, pinch, clam (*dial.*).
Antonyms: see NOURISH, FEAST, FEED.

famishment, *n.* starvation, pinch.
Antonyms: see NUTRITION.

famous, *a.* distinguished, celebrated, renowned, noted, notable, notorious (*implying some derogation or disapproval; whereas* notable *means worthy of note, and* noted, *the simple fact of being known*), great (*contex.*), illustrious, bright, brilliant, lustrous, famed, Roscian (*fig.*); *spec.* fabled, historied, storied, heroic, glorious, historical, immortal (*forever*).
Antonyms: see OBSCURE.

fan, *n.* **1.** *Spec.* punkah *or* punka (*East Indies*), flabellum, fanner (*chiefly tech.*), winnower, blower, colmar (*hist.*), van, thermantidote (*R or local*).
2. *See* ENTHUSIAST.

fan, *v. t.* **1.** clean (*contex.*), blow, winnow (*chiefly spec.*).
2. *See* STIMULATE, INCREASE.

fanatic, *n.* enthusiast, bigot, zealot, visionary; *spec.* sectarian. *For discriminations see* ENTHUSIAST.

fanaticism, *n.* enthusiasm, bigotry, zealotry.

fanciful, *a.* **1.** capricious, fantasied, conceited (*dial. or A*), maggoty (*now contemptuous*), chimerical, fantastic, fantasque (*R*), curious, crotchety.
Antonyms: see UNIMAGINATIVE, MATTER-OF-FACT.
2. *See* ODD.

fancy, *n.* **1.** *See* IMAGINATION (*the faculty*).
2. *The thing imagined:* imagination, fantasy, phantasy, notion, idea, thought; *spec.* antic, phantasm, hallucination, delusion, megrim, reverie, vapor, specter, vision, belief, chimera *or* chimæra, day-dream.
3. *See* CONCEIT, CAPRICE, APPROVAL, LIKING, TASTE.

fan-shaped, *a.* flabellate (*tech.*), flabelliform (*tech.*).

fantastic, *a.* **1.** *See* IMAGINARY, CAPRICIOUS.
2. fanciful, romantic; *spec.* grotesque, bizarre; *see* ODD.
Antonyms: see PLAIN.

fantasy, *n.* **1.** *See* IMAGINATION, FANCY, CAPRICE.
2. fantasia (*music.*).

far, *adv.* widely, wide, remotely, distantly, long, *etc.*
Antonyms: see NEAR.

fare, *v. i.* **1.** *See* GO, OCCUR, LIVE.
2. do, come on (*C*). *"Fare" is more formal than "do."*

fare, *n.* **1.** *See* FORTUNE.
2. food, table, board (*becoming A*).

farewell, *n.* goodby, adieu, leave taking, leave (*short for "leave taking"*), parting, valediction (*properly the words said*), valedictory (*the words*).
Antonyms: see GREETING.

farm, *n.* grange; *spec.* plantation, barton (*Eng.*), estansia (*Sp.*), location (*Australia*), fazenda (*Sp.*), farmstead, hacienda (*Sp. Amer.*), ranch (*western U. S. & Canada*), stud, dairy, mains (*Scot.*).

far-sighted, *a.* **1.** hypermetropic (*tech.*), longsighted, hyperopic (*tech.*); *spec.* presbyopic.

---

familiar: *associate, domestic, demon, friend.*
fancy, *v. t.: imagine, believe, like.*
fane: *church, temple.*
fanfare: *call.*
fantastic: *oddity.*
farcical: *comic.*
farm, *v. t.: cultivate, lease.*
farmer: *agriculturist.*
farming: *agriculture.*

Antonyms: see NEAR-SIGHTED.

2. provident; *see* SAGACIOUS.

farther, *a.* further (*chiefly in secondary or fig. senses*); *spec.* beyond, past.

farthest, *a.* furthest (*chiefly in secondary or fig. senses*), uttermost, final, extreme, endmost, last.

Antonyms: see NEAREST.

fascinate, *v. t.* **1.** bewitch, charm, spellbind (*chiefly cant*); *spec.* dare (*only in "to dare larks"*).

Antonyms: see REPEL.

2. *See* CAPTIVE.

fashion, *n.* custom; society; mode (*formal, implying elegance*), vogue (*suggesting changing or passing* fashion), style (*the approved* fashion, *implying distinction*), craze, fad, rage (*these three suggesting the violent fluctuations of temporary favor*).

fast, *a.* **1.** *See* FIRM, CONSTANT, UNFADING, RAPID, DISSIPATED, DEEP.

2. ahead (*referring to time*).

fasten, *v. t.* **1.** fix, secure (*formal*), confine; *spec.* catch, tie, lock, gird, infix, marl, bolt, chain, belay, pin, lace, strap, cobble, cleat, bond, clasp, infibulate (*R*), button, batten, tether, paste, cement, stick, peg, screw, seal, seize, spike, surcingle, skewer, toggle, wedge, tack, lash, latch, rivet, rope, mortise, knot, key, fish, dowel, forelock, hasp, hoop, collar, crank, cotter, cramp, cable, clinker, buckle, stanchion, halter, gum, bind, dog.

Antonyms: see LOOSE, UNFASTEN.

2. *See* ATTACH, HOLD, KEEP, IMPOSE.

fastening, *n.* confinement; *spec.* clinch, clip, breeching, lace, lacing, tie, tether, clasp, tacking, latch, lashing, lock, fast, headfast, holdfast.

fastidious, *a.* particular, nice, dainty, delicate, exquisite, fine, precise; *spec.* finical, finicking, chary, picksome (*Eng.*), priggish, pernickety (*contemptuous*), overnice, starch, niminy-piminy, squeamish, cockney (*Eng.*), missish, proper (*a euphemism*); *see* PRECIOUS.

Antonyms: see NEGLIGENT, GROSS.

fat, *a.* **1.** greasy, pinguedinous (*R*), fatty, unctious *or* unguinous (*chiefly spec.*), sebaceous (*physiol.; often spec.*), pinguid (*R*); *spec.* lardy, oily, tallowy.

2. corpulent, gross, stocky (*contex.*), polysarcous (*R; tech.*), fleshy, ventricose (*R*), obese (*a formal or book word*); *spec.* puffy, paunchy (*inelegant*), pot-bellied (*vulgar*), pursy, portly, pudgy, fubby, squab, plump, plumpy.

Antonyms: see THIN, LANKY.

3. *See* DULL, PRODUCTIVE, PROFITABLE.

fat, *n. Spec.* grease, sebum (*tech.*), blubber, tallow, seam (*obs. or R*), spermacetti, suet, oil, yolk, lumber (*esp. in horses*).

fate, *n.* **1.** necessity, destiny.

2. dispensation, cup (*fig.; chiefly Scriptural*), experience, portion (*one's share; usually spec.*), doom (*spec. or fig.*).

3. fortune.

4. weird (*A*), Mœræ (*Greek; pl.*), Parcæ (*Latin; pl.*); *spec.* Clotho, Lathesis, Atropos, Norn.

fateful, *a.* fatal, inevitable, necessary, predestined, predestinate (*A*), doomful, karmic (*spec. or fig.; R*); *spec.* tragic.

father, *n.* **1.** parent (*contex.*), sire (*chiefly B, exc. of beasts, esp. horses*), getter (*obs., exc. of horses*), genitor (*R*), fatherling (*nonce word*), governor (*S*), dad (*childish or familiar and undignified*), daddy (*pet form of "dad"*), papa (*now chiefly childish or affected*), pater (*Latin or S*), dada (*child's word*), pa, pop (*both C*); *spec.* (*in a loose use of "father"*) stepfather, father-in-law, foster-father, pater-familias. *These words except "parent," "sire," "getter," "genitor" and, occasionally, "father" are used only of the human parent.*

Antonyms: see CHILD, MOTHER.

2. *See* ANCESTOR, GOD, PRIEST, CONFESSOR.

father, *v. t.* **1.** beget, sire.

2. *see* ADOPT, ACKNOWLEDGE.

3. attribute, impose; *see* AFFILIATE.

fatherhood, *n.* paternity, progenitorship (*R*).

fatherless, *a.* orphan (*contex.*), unfathered, sireless, dadless (*nonce*).

fatherly, *a.* parental (*contex.*), paternal, fatherlike, gubernatorial (*S*).

fathomless, *a.* **1.** immeasurable, measureless, deep, abyssal, abysmal.

Antonyms: see SHALLOW.

2. *See* UNINTELLIGIBLE.

fatness, *n.* fleshiness, obesity, obeseness, corpulence, corpulency, polysarcia (*tech.*), grossness (*R*), pinguitude (*R*), pinguidity (*R*), plumpness; *spec.* embonpoint (*French*).

fatten, *v. i. & t.* fat (*esp. used with "up"*), pinquefy (*R*); *spec.* saginate (*R*), brawn (*dial.*), batten, plump.

Antonyms: see WASTE.

faucet, *n.* cock, tap; *spec.* spigot, spile, stopcock.

fault, *n.* **1.** *Spec.* failing, default, error, obliquity, blemish, peccadillo, blunder, defalcation, lapse, delinquency, vice, cloud (*fig.*), spot, flaw, shortcoming, defect, imperfection, demerit, infirmity, weakness, foible (*a harmless* weakness), offense.

Antonyms: see EXCELLENCE, WORTH.

2. *See* BLAME, NEGLIGENCE, CLEFT.

faultfinding, *a.* censorious, captious, cynical *or* cynic (*now chiefly spec.*), critical, carping, nagging.

faultless, *a.* **1.** *See* CORRECT, BLAMELESS.

2. perfect, irreproachable, immaculate, spotless.

faulty, *a.* vicious, bad; *spec.* ill, blameworthy, transgressive, blamable, imperfect.

---

farthest: *extreme.*
fashion, *v. t.: make, create.*
fashionable: *stylish.*
fatal: *deadly, fateful.*
fatherhood: *paternity.*
fathom: *sound, understand, explore.*
fatigue, *n.: weariness.*
fatigue, *v. t.: tire.*
fatiguing: *tiresome.*
fatuous: *foolish, stupid, deranged.*

Antonyms: see GOOD, EXCELLENT.

favor, *n.* **1.** *Spec.* esteem, benignity, popularity; *see* APPROVAL.

2. *See* AID, APPEARANCE, GIFT, BADGE, LETTER.

3. *Spec.* benefaction, grace, boon, benefit, kindness, dispensation, indulgence.

favor, *v. t.* **1.** *See* APPROVE, OBLIGE.

2. countenance, patronize; *spec. see* AID.

Antonyms: see DISCOURAGE.

3. *See* SAVE, SUPPORT, INDULGE, RESEMBLE, EASE.

favorable, *a.* **1.** *See* AUSPICIOUS.

2. advantageous; *spec.* fair, helpful, good, golden, salutory.

Antonyms: see UNFAVORABLE.

3. well-inclined, well-minded, benign, friendly, favoring, gracious, propitious.

Antonyms: see OPPOSED.

favorite, *n.* **1.** dear, minion (*now contemptuous*); *see* DARLING, PET.

2. *See* CHOICE.

favoritism, *n.* partiality; *spec.* nepotism.

fawn, *v. i.* cringe, cower (*whereas* fawn *implies unworthy flattery and abasement,* cringe *and* cower *add the suggestion of cowardice*), crawl, toady, truckle.

Antonyms: see DOMINEER.

fawner, *n.* cringer, toady, sycophant, truckler, toadeater, bootlicker (*C or S*); *spec.* flunky.

Antonyms: see BULLY.

fawning, *a.* cringing, abject, servile, sycophantic, toadying, truckling, toadyish; *see* OBSEQUIOUS.

Antonyms: see DOMINEERING.

fawning, *n.* cringing, sycophantism, toadyism.

fear, *n.* alarm (*sudden agitation*), dread (*with implication of anxiety long drawn out*), phobia (*tech. or R and humorous for a habitual* fear *of a specific nature*); *spec.* consternation (*with implication of inhibition of judgment or action*), panic (*overwhelming* fear), funk (*S*), misdoubt, misgiving, affright (*R*), terror (*intense* fear), trepidation (*lighter and more controllable by the mind than* fear), scare, fright, fray (*A*), horror, eeriness, awe, apprehension, pantophobia, mysophobia, agoraphobia, hydrophobia, claustrophobia, superstition, reverence.

Antonyms: see BOLDNESS, HOPE.

fear, *v. t.* apprehend, dread, redoubt (*obs. or R*); *spec.* misdoubt, revere.

fear, *v. i. Spec.* misgive.

feared, *a.* dread, redoubted (*rhetorical*).

fearful, *a.* **1.** *See* AFRAID.

2. dreadful, fearsome (*R*), terrible, ghastful (*A*), ghastly (*obs.*), redoubtable (*rhetorical*); *spec.* dire, awful, grim, grisly, awesome, gruesome *or* grewsome, frightful, horrible, appalling, horrendous (*R*), eerie *or* eery, apprehensive (*R*), tremendous (*now R*).

Antonyms: see BOLD.

3. *See* TIMID, GREAT.

feast, *n.* **1.** *See* FESTIVAL, MEAL.

2. *Spec.* banquet, regale (*R*), junket (*often spec.; U. S.*), gaudy (*Eng.*), fête (*French*), tuck-out (*S*), barbecue, brideale *or* bridale, Gregory (*Anglo-Irish*), wine, potlatch, give-ale (*hist.*), infare (*local Eng.*), hockey *or* hookey (*dial. Eng.*), symposium.

feast, *a.* epulary (*R*).

feast, *v. i.* feed (*inelegant; contex.*), epicurize (*R*); *spec.* fête (*R*), cosher (*Ireland*), luxuriate.

Antonyms: see FAMISH.

feast, *v. t.* feed (*contex.*); *spec.* banquet, regale, fête, wine.

Antonyms: see FAMISH.

feastday, *n.* fiesta (*Italian*), saint's day; *spec.* red-letter day.

feasting, *n.* epulation (*R*); *spec.* banqueting, regalement (*R*).

feat, *n.* **1.** *See* ACCOMPLISHMENT, DEED.

2. stunt (*C*); *spec.* split (*gymnastics*), giant swing, cartwheel.

feather, *n.* **1.** plume (*B or rhetorical, exc. spec.*), pen (*obs.*); *spec.* plumule, covert, scapular, down (*a collective*), eiderdown (*a collective*), beam, quill, filoplume, interscapular, remex, primary, principal, pinion, streamer, flag.

2. *See* PLUMAGE, TUFT.

3. *In mechanics: spec.* spline, rib, flange, key, web, fin, tongue, vane.

4. *Referring to part of an oar:* blade, flat, broad.

feather, *v. i. Spec.* fledge.

feather, *v. t.* **1.** implume (*R or rhetorical*), plume (*R or rhetorical, exc. spec.*); *spec.* (*of an arrow*) flight, fledge, wing, fletch.

2. *To remove the feathers from:* deplume, deplumate; *spec.* pinion.

feathered, *a.* plumed (*chiefly spec.*), plumous (*R*); *spec.* winged, penniferous (*R*), pennigerous (*R*), plumate; *see* FEATHERY.

feather-footed, *a. Referring to a dog:* rough-footed, rough-legged.

featherless, *a.* impennate (*chiefly spec.*); *spec.* unfledged, callow.

featherlike, *a.* penniform, pennate (*R*), pinnate, plumiform;—*all four B or tech.*

feathery, *a.* **1.** feathered, plumose (*chiefly spec.*), plumy (*chiefly spec.*); *spec.* plumate, fledgy (*R*), downy.

2. *Referring to a dog:* curly-haired.

feature, *n.* **1.** lineament, point.

2. *See* FACE, CHARACTERISTIC.

febrifuge, *a.* antifebrile, antipyretic.

fecal, fæcal, *a.* dungy (*chiefly spec.*), stercoraceous (*B or tech.*), excrementitious (*B or tech.*).

---

favorite, *a.: darling, pet.*
favoritism: *partiality.*
fawn, *n.: deer.*
fawn, *v. t.: bear.*
fawn, *a.: brown.*
fay: *fairy.*
faze: *disconcert, intimidate, worry.*
feasible: *possible.*
feat: *elegant, skillful.*
febrile: *feverish.*

---

fee, *n.* **1.** benefice, fief, feud, feudatory.
2. *See* ESTATE, PAY, TIP.
3. payment (*contex.*), allowance (*contex.*); *spec.* portage, entrance, tuition, toll, towage, ferriage, honorarium, costs (*pl.*), premium, procuration, retainer.
feed, *v. t.* **1.** aliment (*R*); *spec.* gorge, nurture, meal (*R*), grub (*S*), mess, fodder, forage, suckle, diet, breakfast, dine, dinner (*R*), lunch (*C*), supper (*C*), graze, hay (*R*), soil, corn (*R*), bait, water, pap.
Antonyms: see FAMISH.
2. *Spec.* fuel (*a stove or fire*), fire (*an engine*), supply, gratify, nourish.
feed, *v. i.* **1.** *Referring to the action as taking place:* eat.
2. *Referring to an action as contemplated or habitual:* eat, fare, live (*contex.*); *spec.* subsist, board, meal, diet, gorge, dine, breakfast, lunch, *etc.* "*Feed*" *in this sense is R or S.*
Antonyms: see FAMISH.
feeding, *n.* feed, cibation (*obs. or R*), eat (*S*).
feel, *v. t.* **1.** *See* PERCEIVE.
2. examine, test, touch; *spec.* handle, fumble, palpate, sound, probe, explore, thumb, finger.
3. experience, entertain, make, taste, find, bear; *spec.* believe, discover.
feel, *v. i.* **1.** *See* PERCEIVE, SEEM.
2. *Spec.* grope, fumble.
feeler, *n.* tactor (*tech.*); *spec.* palp, palpus, whisker, vibrissa, tentacle, antlia, barbel, pedipalp.
feeling, *n.* **1.** sentience; *spec.* touch.
2. experience; *spec.* sensation, perception, consciousness, affection.
3. *The faculty or capacity:* sensibility, emotionality, soul, feelingness, blood (*fig.; human feelings*); *spec.* heart strings (*pl.*), demonstrativeness, unction, sympathy, antipathy, cænesthesis.
Antonyms: see INSENSIBILITY.
4. emotion, sentiment, affection; *spec.* fire (*fig.*), hate, hatred, hope, despair, sympathy, pathos, love, gladness, anger, pang, pain, sorrow, joy, *etc.*
Antonyms: see INSENSIBILITY.
5. *See* ATTITUDE.
feint, *n.* pretense; *spec.* artifice, stratagem, expedient, trick.
felicity, *n.* **1.** *See* GLADNESS, APPROPRIATENESS, GOOD, FORTUNE, READINESS.
2. *Referring to a speech, action, etc.:* inspiration, hit, stroke, bull's-eye (*C*).
feline, *a.* cattish, catty (*C*), feliform (*R*).
fell, *v. t.* drop (*especially with a blow or shot*), down, floor, ground; *spec.* prostrate, throw, grass (*chiefly S*), sandbag, cut (*with "down"*), hew (*with "down"*), saw (*with "down"*), *etc.*
Antonyms: see RAISE.
fellow, *n.* **1.** *See* ASSOCIATE, EQUAL, PERSON.
2. dog (*playful, humorous, or contemptuous*), customer (*C; usually with "queer," "ugly," etc.*), cove (*S and vulgar in U. S.*), Jack (*contemptuous*), Gill (*S*), cull *or* cully (*S and contemptuous*), gaffer (*rural Eng.*), joker (*S*), Johnny *or* Johnnie (*contemptuous or familiar*), cuss (*in reproach, contempt, or humorously; S and C, U. S.*), cuffin (*thieves' cant*), codger (*disrespectful and chiefly vulgar*), devil (*C or S*), wight (*now chiefly jocose*), varlet (*a low fellow; A*), coistrel (*in contempt; A*), knave (*a low fellow; A*), chal (*Gipsy*), wallah (*Anglo-Indian*), shaver (*C*), chap (*C*), guy (*C*).
3. don (*Eng. universities*), dean (*in Oxford and Cambridge; British*).
fellowship, *n. Spec.* brotherhood, comradeship, membership; *spec.* stipend, grant, scholarship.
female, *n.* she (*R, exc. as attributive*), petticoat (*C or humorous*); *spec.* woman (*the generic term*), lady (*implying refinement and position, and not to be used for the generic term*), girl, cow, hen, bitch, queen, worker.
Antonyms: see MALE.
female, *a.* she (*chiefly in combination*), feminine (*the usual, generic adjective for what pertains to woman, as opposed to* masculine), womanly (*implying inner qualities of womanhood*), womanish (*somewhat derogatory*), ladylike (*now rather an old-fashioned designation of favorable behaviour in a woman, and when used of a man, denoting emphasis on affectation or over-delicacy*), effeminate (*unmanliness*); *spec.* pistillate.
Antonyms: see MALE, MANLY.
feme-sole, *n. Spec.* widow, spinster;—*referring to a woman at the time unmarried.*
femininity, *n.* femineity (*R*), feminality (*R*), femality (*R and humorous*), muliebriety (*R*), feminacy (*R*), feminineness, feminility (*R*), feminity (*R*), womanliness (*the word in ordinary use and chiefly spec.; "femininity" being the more formal word and also usually spec.*), womanishness (*usually derogatory*).
Antonyms: see MANLINESS.
fence, *n.* **1.** *See* PROTECTION.
2. *In fencing:* guard; *spec.* parry.
3. inclosure, hay (*A*); *spec.* barricade, stockade, paling, palisade, hoarding, counter, pale (*A*), barrier, palisado (*R*), hedge, ha-ha, weir.
4. *As to stolen goods:* receiver, lock (*cant*).
fence, *v. i.* guard (*against*); *spec.* parry, evade.
fence, *v. t.* inclosure; *spec.* wire, pale (*R*), palisade, palisado (*R*), hedge (*often with "in" or "about"*), impale (*chiefly B*), picket.
fender, *n.* duffer; *spec.* pudding, pad, hurter, scotchman; shield, wing (*chiefly Brit.*).

feces: *excrement.*
feckless: *spiritless, weak.*
fecund: *fruitful.*
federal: *confederate, united.*
federate: *unite.*
feeble: *weak, indistinct.*
feeble-minded: *irresolute, defective.*
feel, *n.:* *touch.*
feeling, *a.:* *sentient, affecting, emotional.*
feign: *imagine, pretend, assume.*
felicitate: *congratulate.*
felicitous: *glad, appropriate.*
felicity: *gladness, appropriateness.*
feline, *n.:* *cat.*
fell, *a.:* *fierce, cruel, harmful, painful, deadly, destructive.*
fell, *n.:* *skin, down.*
felon, *a.:* *wicked, cruel.*
felon, *n.:* *convict.*
felony: *crime.*
feminine: *female, womanish.*
fend: *repel, protect.*

ferment, *n.* **1.** zyme (*tech. or R*); *spec.* enzyme, diatase, pepsin, yeast, leaven (*now chiefly Bib.*), barm.
2. *See* FERMENTATION, EXCITEMENT, AGITATION, UPROAR, FRET.
ferment, *v. i.* **1.** work.
2. *Spec.* fret, simmer.
fermentation, *n.* **1.** ferment, working; *spec.* zymosis (*R*).
2. *See* EXCITEMENT.
fern, *n. Spec.* brake, osmund, bracken, hart's-tongue, maidenhair.
fern-shaped, *a.* filiciform (*tech.*), filicoid (*tech.*), fernlike.
ferny, *a.* bracky, brackeny.
ferocity, *n.* **1.** *See* VIOLENCE, ARDOR, IMPETUOSITY.
2. unkindness, ferociousness, truculence (ferocity *for show and to impress*), savageness, savagery, dourness (*Scot.*), grimness (*B*); *spec.* vandalism, sternness, angriness, malignancy, pitilessness, murderousness, brutality.
Antonyms: see KINDNESS, GENTLENESS.
ferrule, *n.* band (*contex.*), ring, shoe, collet, virole (*R*); *spec.* thimble, cap.
ferrule, *v. t.* bind, shoe, cap, ring.
ferry, *n.* bac (*French*); *spec.* ghaut *or* ghat (*Anglo-Indian*), pont (*So. African*).
ferry, *v. t.* transport (*contex.*); *spec.* row, sail, steam, pull.
ferryman, *n.* waterman (*contex.*); *spec.* Charon.
fertilize, *v. t.* **1.** *See* FRUCTIFY.
2. enrich, fat (*R or B*), fatten; *spec.* manure, compost, bone, warp (*Eng.*), guano, salt, phosphate, nitrify.
fertilizer, *n.* dressing; *spec.* compost, marl, manure, dung, phosphate, bone-dust, lime, guano.
ferule, *n.* palmer (*obs. or R*); *spec.* rod, ruler.
fester, *n.* sore (*contex.*), ulcer, pustule.
fester, *v. i.* ulcerate, rankle (*B*), suppurate (*tech.*).
festival, *n.* **1.** carnival (*properly spec.*), feast (*chiefly spec.*), fiesta (*Italian*); *spec.* fête (*French; on a large scale*), fête champêtre (*French*), holiday (*now usually called a "holy day"*), pardon (*Roman Catholic Church or obs.*), gaudy day (*Eng.*), gala day, jubilee, festivity, harvest home, kirn (*Scot.*), hoolee *or* hooli (*East Indian*), dusserah (*Hindu*), hypapante, encænia, panegyris *or* panegyry.
2. *See* FESTIVITY.
festive, *a.* **1.** convivial, festal, festivous (*R*), feastful (*A*); *spec.* jolly, uproarious, carnival.
Antonyms: see MOURNFUL.
2. *As being fond of merriment; see* GAY.

festivity, *n.* **1.** festiveness, conviviality, merrymaking.
2. festival, merrymaking; *spec.* celebration, rejoicing, revel, high jinks (*boisterous* festivity).
fetid, *a.* malodorous, foul, olid (*R*), rank, nidorous (*R*), stinking, graveolent (*B; rhetorical, affected, or euphemistic*); *spec.* gamy, rancid.
Antonyms: see FRAGRANT.
fetish, *n.* fetich (*a variant*), charm; *spec.* juju, medicine.
feudatory, *n.* vassal, beneficiary; *spec.* prince, palatine.
fever, *n.* **1.** heat, fire (*fig.*), pyrexia (*R*); *spec.* feveret, febricula, ague, typhus, typhoid, dengue, hectic, remittent, calenture, intermittent, quintan, tertian, quotidian, quartan.
2. *Referring to a feverish state:* febricity (*R*), feverishness, febrility (*R*), fieriness.
3. *See* DESIRE, ARDOR.
fevered, *a.* excited; *spec.* angry.
feverish, *a.* **1.** febrile, feverous (*R*), fevered, pyretic (*R*), pyrectic (*R*), pyrexial (*R*), pyrexic (*R*), pyrexical (*R*), febricitant (*R*), febricose (*R*); *spec.* febriculose (*R*), inflamed, fiery.
2. *See* EXCITED, ARDENT.
few, *a.* sparse, small (*with "number"*).
Antonyms: see ALL, MANY, NUMBERLESS.
few, *n.* handful;—*a collective.*
fewness, *n.* paucity (*B or formal*), scarcity, sparsity, sparseness.
fiber, *n.* **1.** filament; *spec.* staple, fibrile *or* fibrilla, strand, bast, sunn, oakum, istle, henequen, hemp, jute, cotton, piña, rafia, ramie, pita, manila, coir.
2. *See* TEXTURE.
fiberlike, *a.* fibrous, fibriform (*R*), fibrine (*R*), fibry; *spec.* fibrilliform.
fiction, *n.* **1.** *See* IMAGINATION (*the action*).
2. *The thing imagined:* imagination, invention, forgery, figment (*an unreliable, fragmentary or implausible* fiction), fantasy, concoction, fabrication (*implies intent to deceive*), story, fable, novel, allegory, epic, assumption.
Antonyms: see ACTUALITY.
fictitious, *a. Spec.* mythical, dummy, invented, imaginary, assumed, fabled, fabulous, artificial; *spec.* paper.
Antonyms: see ACTUAL.
fiddle, *v. i.* **1.** play; *spec.* bow. *Curiously, though* fiddle *as a verb has no equivalent except the general term "play," the verb* fiddle *as well as the noun, is now rather contemptuous or familiar.*
2. *See* POTTER, FIDGET.

ferocious: *fierce.*
ferret: *drive.*
fertile: *fruitful.*
fervent: *hot, ardent.*
fervid: *hot, ardent.*
fervor: *heat, ardor.*
festal: *festive, holiday.*
festoon, *n.: wreath.*
festoon, *v. t.: wreathe.*
fetch, *v. t.: bring, captivate, draw, heave, deal, elicit.*
fetching: *effective.*
fête, *n.: entertainment, festival.*
fête, *v. t.: entertain, feast.*
fetter, *v. t.: shackle, hamper.*
fettle, *n.: condition.*
feud: *quarrel.*
fevered: *feverish, excited.*
fewer: *less.*
fiancé, fiancée: *betrothed.*
fiasco: *failure.*
fiddle, *n.: violin.*
fidelity: *constancy, truthfulness, accuracy.*

fidget, *v. i.* fidge; *spec.* fiddle, twiddle.

field, *n.* **1.** *Spec.* clearing, glebe (*B or eccl.*), paddock (*chiefly dial. Eng.; in Australia not spec.*), croft (*Brit.*), meadow, patch.
2. *See* COMPETITOR, EXTENT, EXPANSE, SPHERE.
3. battlefield; *spec.* plain (*chiefly B*), Armageddon (*fig.*).

fiend, *n.* **1.** *See* DEMON, MONSTER.
2. demon (*of cruelty*), shaitan (*C*), brute, hellhound, cat (*esp. of a woman*), wolf, tiger; *see* MONSTER.

fierce, *a.* **1.** *See* VIOLENT, ARDENT, IMPETUOUS.
2. unkind (*contex.*), ferocious; *spec.* glaring, dragonish, truculent, catawampous (*S, chiefly U. S.*), fell (*chiefly B*), savage, Vandalic (*hist.*), breme (*obs. or B*), dour (*Scot.*), grim, cruel, stern, angry, malignant, pitiless, merciless, murderous, inhuman, tigerish, wolfish.
Antonyms: see KIND, GENTLE.

fiery, *a.* **1.** hot, igneous (*B or tech.*), red (*fig.*), empyreal *or* empyrean (*fig.*); *spec.* flaming, lurid.
2. *See* ARDENT, IMPETUOUS, FEVERISH, IRRITABLE, ANGRY.

fight, *n.* **1.** contention (*contex.*), contest (*contex.*), encounter, rencounter (*R*), conflict (*formal*), combat (*primarily spec.*), affair (*contex.*); *spec.* cuff (*R*), bicker (*now chiefly Scot.*), bustle (*A*), brawl, battle, affray, fray, mêlée (*French*), mellay (*A*), ruffle, engagement, action, quarrel, sciamachy, digladiation (*R*), duomachy (*R*), pell-mell (*R*), duel, brush, theomachy, tourney, just *or* joust, tilt, spar, scrap (*C*), scrimmage, naumachia, skirmish.
2. *See* CONTENTION, CONTEST.
3. pugnacity, pluck, game (*R*).

fight, *v. i.* **1.** contend, conflict (*R*), combat, contend, battle, warfare (*R*); *spec.* ruffle (*A*), camp (*obs. or dial.*), war, battle, scuffle, box, spar, strike, tilt, just *or* joust, bicker, brawl, duel, militate, crab, claw, scratch, buffet, skirmish, strive, fistify (*nonce word*).
2. *See* CONTEND.

fight, *v. t.* **1.** encounter, combat (*now chiefly fig.*), engage; *spec.* buffet (*chiefly fig.*), war (*R*), worry.
2. *Cause to fight:* pit, match.
3. *See* OPPOSE.

fighter, *n.* combatant, contestant, champion (*A, R, or spec.*), contender (*contex.*), combater (*R*); *spec.* battler, warrior, militant (*R*), duelist dueler (*R*), slasher, tilter, juster, jouster, guerilla, gladiator, skirmisher, pugilist, boxer, sparrer, cuffer, pancratiast.
Antonyms: see PACIFIST.

fighting, *a.* *Spec.* combatant, militant, belligerent, pugilistic, skirmishing, boxing, *etc.*

fighting, *n.* contention (*contex.*); *spec.* combating, warring, duel (*with "the"*), fisticuffs (*pl.*).

figlike, *a.* ficoid (*tech.*), caricous (*R*), ficiform (*tech.*).

figural, *a.* *Spec.* graphic, diagrammatic.

figurative, *n.* **1.** descriptive; *spec.* symbolic.
2. *Rhet.:* metaphorical, figured (*R or spec.*); *spec.* allegorical, fabular.
3. *See* FLORID (*of speech*), ORNATE (*in art*).

figure, *n.* **1.** character (*contex.*), number, digit; *spec.* cipher, one, two, *etc.*
2. *See* FORM, PERSON, SYMBOL.
3. *Referring to the thing having a particular form:* shape; *spec.* image, effigy, design, diagram, sculpture, cylinder, square, ball, triangle, ellipse, ovoid, oval, parabola, diamond, parallelogram, rhombus, ghost, sector (*geom.*), carving, casting, molding, *etc.*
4. *In dancing:* evolution; *spec.* entrechat (*French*), quadrille.
5. *In rhetoric:* image, trope, ecbasis (*R*); *spec.* metaphor, similitude, simile, metonymy, irony, litotes, diasyrm, aporia, diaporesis, hendiadys, *etc.*

filament, *n.* fibor (*contex.*); *spec.* thread, film, strand, cirrus, barbel, gossamer, hair, threadlet, cobweb, harl, wire.

filamentous, *a.* filamentary; *spec.* threadlike, fibrous, stringy, filar, thready, hair-like, filiform (*tech.*), capillary, fibrillose, filose, cirrous (*tech.*).

file, *v. t.* *Spec.* record, lodge, pigeonhole, thread, string.

filibuster, *n.* obstructionist.

filigree, *n.* wirework.

filing, *n.* abrasion (*contex.*); *spec.* limation (*fig.*; *R*).

filings, *n. pl.* limail (*tech.*).

fill, *v. t.* **1.** *Spec.* inject (*chiefly used with "with"*), stuff, cram, pack, line, congest, crowd, crown, overflow, fulfil (*A*), infill (*R*), brimful, brim, bumper, replenish, chink (*C, U. S.*), saturate, suffuse, plug, stop (*chiefly Brit. for the dental operation*), charge.
Antonyms: see DEPLETE, DRAIN, EMPTY, EVACUATE.
2. *See* DISTEND, PERVADE.
3. trim (*a sail*).
4. *Referring to orders, commissions, etc.:* execute, discharge, do, perform.

fillet, *n.* **1.** band (*contex.*); *spec.* (*for the hair*) bandeau, vitta (*B*), snood, sphenodome, infula (*Roman antiq.*).
2. *In architecture: spec.* orlo, tænia, platband, stria.

filling, *n.* *Spec.* packing, replenishment, repletion, fill, charge, stuffing.

film, *n.* skin (*contex.*); *spec.* membrane, nebula, scale, veil, pellicle, scum, lamina, gauze, cloud.

filmy, *a.* *Spec.* clouded, flimsy, cloudy, finespun, gauzy, pellicular.

---

fidgety: *uneasy.*
fiducial: *trustful, confidential.*
fiduciary: *confidential.*
fiendish: *devilish, cruel.*
fieriness: *ardor, heat, fever, irascibility.*
fig: *trifle.*
figment: *fiction.*
figure, *v. t.: depict, delineate, describe, ornament, compute, symbolize.*
figure, *v. i.: appear, compute.*
figured: *ornamented.*
figurehead: *dummy.*
filch: *steal.*
file, *n.: list, line.*
file, *n. & v.: march.*
filibuster, *v. i.: delay.*
filly: *colt.*

For explanation of terms used, see pp. viii–ix; for abbreviations, see p. x.

filter, *v. t. & i.* **1.** strain, filtrate, percolate (*usually spec.*).
2. *See* EXUDE.
filth, *n.* **1.** dirt, sordes (*tech.*), sordor (*R*), vileness, foulness, obscenity (*B*), filthiness, ordure (*A*), nastiness.
2. *See* DIRTINESS, CORRUPTION.
filthy, *a.* **1.** dirty, foul, nasty, sordid (*B*), obscene (*B*), vile; *spec.* impure, mucky, dungy, hoggish.
2. *See* INDECENT.
fin, *n.* **1.** flipper, pinna (*zoöl.*); *spec.* sail.
2. *See* FEATHER (*in mechanics*).
final, *a.* end (*the noun used attributively*), last, terminal, latest, ultimate, extreme; *spec.* eventual, conclusive, decisive, unappealable.
finality, *n.* terminality, ultimateness, extremity; *spec.* decisiveness, eventuality, conclusiveness.
finances, *n. pl.* circumstances (*contex.*), affairs (*contex.*).
financial, *a.* fiscal (*chiefly U. S. & spec.*); *spec.* bursal.
financier, *n. Spec.* investor, lender, cambist, capitalist.
fine, *n.* punishment (*contex.*), penalty, mulct, amercement, assessment, forfeit (*often spec.*); *spec.* geld, wite, bloodwite, wergild.
fine, *v. t.* penalize (*contex.*), amerce, mulct, sconce (*Oxford University*); *spec.* log.
fine, *a.* **1.** refined, clear, pure. *See* PURE.
2. admirable, brave (*B*), choice, superior, handsome; *spec.* glorious, grand (*also as S*), imposing, delicate, nice, subtle, swell (*S*), nifty (*S*), divine, heavenly, superfine (*an intensive*), fancy, splendiferous (*C*), bully (*S*), dandy (*C*), nobby (*C, cant*), finical, surpassing, magnificent, superb, transcendent, spanking (*C*), rum (*cant*), crack (*S or C*), recherché (*French*). *As S or C intensives:* adorable, tearing, ripping, splendid, rattling, stunning, elegant, great, boss, smashing, tearing, bouncing.
Antonyms: see BAD, INFERIOR.
3. *See* SMALL, SLENDER, SENSITIVE, NICE, FASTIDIOUS, EXACT, CLEAR.
fine, *interj.* bravo! *Many of the words under "fine" and "excellent" are more or less used as interjections in corresponding senses.*
fineness, *a.* excellent, delicacy, superiority, subtlety, subtility (*now R*), *etc. Cf.* FINE.
fine one, crack (*C*), rattler (*S*), screamer (*S*), clipper (*S*), bouncer (*C*), dandy (*C*).
finery, *n.* ornament; *spec.* frippery, gaudery (*R*), gewgawry (*R*), gimcrackery.
finger, *n.* **1.** digit (*chiefly tech.*), mudhooks (*pl.; S*); *spec.* minimus, index, pointer, fingerlet.
2. technique;—*in music.*
3. *See* POINTER.
finial, *n. In architecture:* ornament (*contex.*), terminal; *spec.* crop.
finish, *v. t.* **1.** *See* END, DRESS, KILL.
2. accomplish, crown, complete, consummate, fulfill, do, execute, round (*esp. with "out"*).
Antonyms: see BEGIN.
finish, *v. i.* **1.** conclude, end;—*in the sense of "to have done."*
2. *See* END, DIE.
finish, *n.* **1.** *See* END, DEATH, PERFECTION, ELEGANCE.
2. surface (*contex.*); *spec.* dress.
finished, *a.* **1.** done, accomplished, over (*in predicative use; C*), complete, rounded, round.
Antonyms: see INCOMPLETE, UNFINISHED.
2. perfect; *spec.* fine, elegant.
Antonyms: see UNFINISHED.
finishing, *n. Spec.* end, conclusion, termination, completion, *etc.*
finite, *a.* definable, limited, terminable.
Antonyms: see INFINITE.
finiteness, *n.* limitedness, limitation, finitude, finity (*R*).
fin-shaped, *a.* pinniform (*tech.*), finny.
fire, *n.* **1.** *Spec.* flame, coal, blaze, conflagration, beacon, bale (*A*), bale-fire, ingle, bonfire, smudge, needfire, spark, smother.
2. *See* BURNING, FEVER, ARDOR.
fire, *v. t.* **1.** *See* IGNITE, HEAT, EJECT, EXPEL, EXCITE, ENLIVEN.
2. discharge, explode; *spec.* play.
firearm, *n.* piece, gun (*C, exc. as spec.*), popgun (*contemptuous*); *spec.* pistol, revolver, rifle, mitrailleuse (*French*), Martini, musket, jezail, bulldog, escopette (*U. S.*), fusil (*obs. or hist.*), fusee (*obs. or hist.*), galloper, harquebus, gingall, jingall, culverin, hackbut, hagbut, chassepot (*French*), carbine, carabine, cannon, gun, petronel, saket, falconet.
fireman, *n. Spec.* stoker.
fireplace, *n.* hearth, fireside, grate (*fig.*); *spec.* range, hob, cupola, cockle, tisar.
firework, *n.* **1.** pyrotechnic;—*both usually pl.*
2. *Spec.* squib, girandola, rocket, pinwheel, petard, bomb, serpent, saucisson (*French*), jack-in-the-box, maroon, flowerpot, fizgig, wheel, jet, gerbe.
firm, *a.* **1.** *See* FIXED, CONSTANT, COURAGEOUS.
2. stable (*unlikely to change or be moved*), solid, coherent, consistent, consistency, steady, stout, stanch, strong, stiff, tight, secure, fast; *spec.* hard, braced, tied, inflexible, nailed, bolted, *etc.*
Antonyms: see SHAKY, TOTTERING, WEAK, UNSTEADY, RICKETY, LOOSE.
firm, *v. t.* **1.** steady, stabilize, stabilify (*R*), solidate (*R*); *spec.* consolidate, brace, jack (*U. S.*), nail, bolt, screw, *etc.*
Antonyms: see WEAKEN.
2. *See* ESTABLISH.

filtrate: *filter.*
fine, *v. t.: purify.*
finedraw: *sew, attenuate.*
fine-grained: *smooth.*
fine-spun: *attenuated, slender, subtle, filmy.*
finesse: *art, artifice.*
finger, *v. t.: handle, steal.*
finger, *v. i.: play, toy.*
finical: *fastidious.*
finis: *end, death.*
finish: *v. i.: end.*

firm, *n.* association, concern, house; *spec.* partnership, corporation, company.
firmness, *n.* **1.** *Spec.* fixedness, courage.
2. constancy, unyieldingness, backbone (*C*).
3. stability, solidity, steadiness, stoutness, stanchness, strength, stiffness, tightness, consistency, security, fastness, solidness; *spec.* coherence.
Antonyms: see INSTABILITY.
first, *a.* **1.** *Referring to time or order:* earliest, premier (*R*), erst (*obs.*); *spec.* primary, primal, prime, pristine, eldest, aboriginal, maiden, original.
Antonyms: see LAST, FINAL.
2. foremost, front, head.
3. *See* CHIEF.
first, *adv.* firstly (*avoided by some*), imprimis (*Latin*), erst (*A and B*); *spec.* formerly.
first-class, *a.* excellent, prime, scrumptious (*U. S.; C*), palmary (*R*), palmarian (*R*).
Antonyms: see INFERIOR.
fish, *n.* fin (*fig.*); *spec.* fishlet, fishing, fry (*collective pl.*).
fish, *a.* piscine (*B or tech.*), ichthyic (*R*).
fish, *v. i.* **1.** *Spec.* angle, bob, dap, dib, dibble, torch, flyfish, troll, gig, guddle (*Scot.*), grig, drive, shrimp, spoon, whiff, spin.
2. *See* SEEK.
fisher, *n.* fisherman, piscator (*B, often pedantic*), piscatorian (*R*), piscatorialist (*R*); *spec.* angler, peterman (*local Eng.*), wormer (*C*), jacker, dibber, drifter, trawler, trapper.
fishery, *a.* **1.** piscary (*tech.*).
2. *See* FISHING.
fishhook, *n.* angle (*B or R*); *spec.* sockdolger (*S, U. S.*), limerick, carlisle, sproat, kirby, *etc.*
fishing, *n.* piscatory (*B*), piscatorial (*B*), halieutic (*R*).
fishing, *n.* fishery, piscation (*R*), halieutics (*the art; R*).
fishlike, *a.* fishy, ichthyomorphic (*B or tech.*), ichthyoid (*B or tech.*), pisciform (*B or tech.*).
fishline, *n.* line (*contex.*); *spec.* drail, boulter, bultow, greatline, gimp, spiller, whiffing.
fishpond, *n.* piscina (*R*).
fishway, *n.* zigzag.
fist, *n.* **1.** hand (*contex.*), nieve *or* nief (*A*), duke (*S*), daddle (*dial.*).
2. *See* CLUTCH, HANDWRITING.
fit, *n.* **1.** sit, set (*by many condemned as not in good usage*); *spec.* hang, drape.
2. *See* PREPARATION.
fit, *v. t.* **1.** *See* BECOME, PREPARE, QUALIFY.
2. adapt; *spec.* adjust, justify, dovetail, fay (*U. S. or shipbuilding*), joint, concinnate (*R*).
fit, *v. i.* **1.** sit, set (*by many condemned as not in good usage*); *spec.* hang.
2. *See* SUIT.
fit, *n.* **1.** *Referring to a disorder:* access (*tech. or literary*), attack, qualm, lunes (*pl.; A*), paroxysm; *spec.* touch, outbreak.
2. *Referring to a nervous upset: spec.* pet, heat, tantrums (*pl.*), freaks (*pl.*), fury, fume, passion, huff, gale (*U. S.*), spell, convulsion, spasm, turn.
five, *n. Of five things grouped; with "a" or "an": spec.* quinary (*R*), quintuple (*R*), quintuplet, quintet, quintette, pentad, quincunx, cinnque.
five-angled, *a.* pentangular, pentagonal;—*both B or tech.*
fivefold, *v. t.* quintuple, quintuplicate (*R*).
fix, *v. t.* **1.** fasten, immobilize (*R*), plant, firm; *spec.* lock, root, bind, stay, cement, ship, nail, screw, congeal, freeze, clinch (*"clench" is now R in this sense*), tie, bind, *etc.*
Antonyms: see DISLODGE, DISPLACE.
2. *See* ESTABLISH, PLACE, ADJUST.
3. decide, seal, nettle; *spec.* appoint, define, harden.
Antonyms: see CHANGE, CONVERT, ALTER.
4. *Spec.* (*in figurative or transferred uses*) set, corroborate, enchain, rivet, nail, confirm, implant, fossilize, grave *or* engrave, impress, imprint, number, concentrate, absorb, settle, harden.
fix, *v. i.* set (*which see*); *spec.* harden.
fixation, *n. Spec.* congelation, implantation, fixture (*R*), immobilization, establishment.
Antonyms: see DISPLACEMENT.
fixed, *a.* **1.** firm, set, secure, fast, immovable (*R*), immobile; *spec.* certain (*as in "a day certain"*), sessile, irremovable, stationary, inerratic, *etc. Cf.* FIX, *v. t.*
Antonyms: see CHANGEABLE, PORTABLE, PROTRUSILE.
2. constant; *spec.* intransformable, ineradicable, concentrated, unchangeable, settled, unchanging, definite, certain, unshakable, upset, steadfast.
Antonyms: see CHANGEABLE, CONVERTIBLE.
fixture, *n.* attachment, fittings (*pl.*), equipment.
flaccid, *a.* limp, baggy, soft (*contex.*).
flag, *n.* layer (*contex.*), flagstone, flagging (*collective sing.*), slab.
flag, *n.* **1.** bunting (*collective sing.*); *spec.* streamer, pennon, pendant, pennant, colors (*pl.*), bluepeter, banderole, bandrol, burgee, brattach (*Gaelic*), raven, jack, union, fanion, guidon, Dannebrog, tricolor (*French*).
2. *See* TAIL.
flag, *v. t.* signal.
flagon, *n.* stoup, gun (*S, Eng.*).
flagrancy, *n.* grossness, outrageousness; *spec.* notoriety.
flagrant, *a.* **1.** *See* FLAMING.

---

fiscal: *financial.*
fissure, *n.: crack, cleft.*
fit, *a.: appropriate, becoming, qualified, prepared.*
fitful: *intermittent.*
fitting, *a.: appropriate, becoming.*
fitting, *n.: equipment.*
fizz, *n.: hiss, energy.*
fizzle, *v. i.: hiss, burn, fail.*
fizzle, *n.: hiss, failure.*
flabbergast: *confuse.*
flagellate, *a.: whip-shaped.*
flagellate, *v. t.: whip.*
flaggy: *cleavable.*
flagitious: *wicked.*
flail, *v. t.: beat.*
flake, *n.: rack.*
flake, *n.: hurdle, scale, lamina, flame.*
flake, *v. i.: scale.*
flaky: *cleavable, laminate.*

---

2. gross, glaring, grievous (*A*), monstrous, atrocious, heinous, outrageous; *spec.* violent, shameful, notorious, wicked, nefarious, flagitious, scandalous.
Antonyms: see EXCUSABLE, UNIMPORTANT.
flame, *n.* **1.** blaze, light, flare, low (*chiefly Scot.*); *spec.* flake, flamelet.
2. *See* ARDOR, SWEETHEART.
flame, *v. i.* **1.** burn (*contex.*), blaze.
2. *See* BURN (*with zeal*), SHINE.
flaming, *a.* **1.** blazing; *spec.* flaring.
2. bright (*contex.*), flaring, lambent, blazing.
flange, *n.* flanch (*R*), rib, rim; *spec.* feather, collet.
flank, *v. t.* **1.** border; *spec.* wing.
2. *See* ATTACK.
flap, *n.* **1.** *Spec.* lap, lappet, leaf, lug, lapel, fly, tab, tuck, apron.
2. beat (*contex.*), stroke (*contex.*), flaff (*chiefly Scot.*); *spec.* flutter, slat, flop.
flap, *v. t. & i.* beat (*contex.*), strike (*contex.*), flaff (*chiefly Scot.*); *spec.* flutter, slat, flop, bate, winnow.
flapper, *n.* *Spec.* flytrap, chowry (*India*), whisk, swingle.
flare, *v. t.* **1.** *See* DISPLAY.
2. spread; *spec.* bell.
flaring, *a.* **1.** *See* FLAMING.
2. spreading; *spec.* funnel-shaped, infundibuliform, bell-mouthed.
flash, *v. i.* blaze (*contex.*), burst (*as "out," "into flame," etc.*), fulgurate (*B; R, exc. fig.*); *spec.* gleam, blink, fulminate, flicker, bicker, glimpse (*A*), glimmer, shimmer, glisten, glance, scintillate, sparkle, corruscate, glint, twinkle.
flash, *n.* blaze (*contex.*); *spec.* flicker (*a fitful flash*), flaught (*chiefly Scot.*), burst, fulguration (*B; R, exc. fig.*), gleam (*a light shining out of relative darkness*), blink, fulmination, bicker, glimpse, glimmer, shimmer, glisten, glance, spark, scintillation, corruscation, sparkle, glint, flip (*R*), twinkle.
flashing, *n.* bright (*contex.*), blazing (*contex.*), fulguration (*R or fig.*), glistening, glittering, *etc.*
flashy, *a.* showy, brilliant, Bowery (*fig.*), loud.
flask-shaped, *a.* lageniform (*tech. or R*).
flat, *a.* **1.** plane (*more tech.*), plain (*an unusual spelling*), level; *spec.* flattish, complanate, homaloid.
Antonyms: see UNEVEN, HILLY.
2. *See* HORIZONTAL, UNIFORM, MONOTONOUS, DULL, BLUNT, DIRECT.
flat, *adv.* **1.** *See* ABSOLUTELY, EXACTLY.
2. flatly (*R*), flatling (*B*); *spec.* horizontally, lengthwise, flatways, flatwise, broadside, *etc.*
flat-footed, *a.* *In zoöl.:* plantigrade (*tech.*).
flatten, *v. t.* flat (*R or spec.*); *spec.* smooth, level, lower, fell, depress, abate (*of wind*), squash, squelch, strike.
flattened, *a.* *Spec.* deplanate (*tech.*), compressed, flatted, oblate.
flatter, *v. t.* **1.** *Spec.* adulate (*B*), compliment, gloze (*R*), butter (*fig.*), beflatter (*intensive*), blarney, beslobber (*intensive*), blandish, smooth, soft-soap (*C; fig.*), slaver (*fig.*), oil (*fig.*); *see* CAJOLE.
Antonyms: see INSULT, ABUSE, DISCREDIT.
2. *Reflectively:* congratulate.
flatterer, *n.* adulator (*B*), pickthank (*A*), flattercap (*R or dial.*), Damocles (*fig.*).
flattering, *a.* **1.** adulating (*B*), buttery (*C; fig.*), silken (*fig.*), silky (*fig.*), sweet, candied (*fig.*), fair, pickthank (*A*).
Antonyms: see ABUSIVE.
2. *See* PROMISING, AUSPICIOUS.
flattery, *n.* *Spec.* adulation (*B*), lipsalve (*fig.*), gloze, blandiloquence (*R*), flamm (*cant*), daub (*dial.*), flummery (*fig.*), slaver (*fig.*), taffy (*S, U. S.*), sugar plum (*fig.; an instance of flattery*), sugar (*fig.*), soap (*S; fig.*), soft soap (*S; fig.*), honey (*fig.*), soft sawder (*fig.; S U. S.*), blarney; *see* CAJOLERY.
Antonyms: see INSULT, ABUSE.
flat-topped, *a.* tabular (*formal or B*).
flatulent, *a.* windy, gassy, ventose (*B*).
flavor, *n.* **1.** *See* SMELL, TASTE.
2. admixture (*contex.*); *spec.* dash, lacing, lace, seasoning.
flavor, *v. t.* taste (*R*); *spec.* spice, bespice (*intensive*), curry, lace, pepper, salt, saffron (*R*), lemon, ginger, onion, season, dash.
flavoring, *n.* *Spec.* seasoning, relish, condiment, zest, spice, salt, pepper, *etc.*
flaw, *n.* **1.** crack; *spec.* brack, feather, wind shake, honeycomb.
2. *See* FAULT.
flea, *a.* pulicine (*B*).
fleay, *a.* pulicous, pulicose;—*both tech. or B.*
flee, *v. i.* depart (*contex.*); *spec.* run, slope (*S*), skedaddle (*C; orig. U. S.*), fly (*now the more common term; "flee" being rhetorical or A*).
Antonyms: see STAY.
flee, *v. t.* avoid (*contex.*), run (*R*), fly.
fleece, *n.* **1.** toison (*R or B*).
2. *See* WOOL.
fleece, *v. t.* cheat, pluck (*C or fig.*), shave (*C*), plunder, sweat (*S or cant*); *spec.* bleed (*C; fig.*), skin (*C; fig.*), strip, flay (*fig.*).
fleet, *n.* *Spec.* division (*contex.*), armada, caravan, convoy, flotilla, marine, navy (*B or rhet., exc. spec.*).
flesh, *n.* **1.** muscle, beef (*spec. or C*); *spec.* brawn, carrion, game.
Antonyms: see SKIN.

---

flamboyant: *wavy, bright.*
flank, *n.: side.*
flashy: *showy.*
flaunt: *disclose, wave.*
flaw, *v. t.: crack.*
flaw, *n. : wind.*
flay, *v. t.: skin, criticize.*
fleabitten: *spotted.*
fleck, *v. t.: spot, streak, speckle, freckle, dot.*
fledge: *feather.*
fleecy: *fluffy.*
fleeing: *fugitive.*
fleer: *smile, jeer.*
fleet, *v. i.: glide, hasten, speed, vanish.*
fleet, *a.: rapid, transitory.*
fleeting: *transitory.*

---

2. *Referring to fruit:* pulp, meat; *spec.* sarcocarp.
3. *See* MEAT, KINDRED.
flesh, *a.* creatic (*tech.; R*); *spec.* fleshy, fleshly.
flesh-eating, *a.* carnivorous.
flesh-eating, *n. Spec.* hippophagy, hippophagism;—*both formal or tech.*
fleshlike, *a. Spec.* sarcoid (*tech.*).
fleshy, *a.* **1.** *See* FAT, BODILY.
2. sarcous (*tech.*), carnose (*R*), carnous (*R*), carneous (*R*), meaty (*R or spec.*).
3. *Referring to roots:* carnose (*R*), pulpous (*R*), pulpy.
flexibility, *n.* flexility (*R*), pliability, pliantness, pliancy; *spec.* suppleness, litheness, limberness, withiness, willowiness, lissomeness.
flexible, *a.* **1.** flexile (*chiefly tech.*), bendable, pliable, pliant; *spec.* supple, lithe, limber, withy, willowy, lissom (*B*), buxom (*A and B*), limp.
Antonyms: see STIFF, BRITTLE, RIGID.
2. *See* ADAPTABLE.
flicker, *v. i.* **1.** *See* FLUTTER, MOVE.
2. flame (*contex.*), flutter, waver, glimmer (*less suggestive of dying out than the other words*), blink.
flicker, *n.* **1.** *See* FLUTTER, MOTION.
2. flame (*contex.*), flutter, waver, wavering, glimmer, blink.
flickering, *a.* flaming (*contex.*), intermittent (*contex.*), fluttering, wavery (*R*), wavy, glimmering.
flight, *n.* departure (*contex.*), fleeing; *spec.* stampede (*headlong and disorderly flight*), rout (*implying defeat and pursuit or being completely supplanted*), scurry, helter-skelter, scamper, debacle, hegira *or* hejira, regifuge (*R*).
flight, *n.* **1.** flying, volation (*R*), fly, volition (*R*), wing, volatility (*the power of flight; R*); *spec.* soaring, soar, mounting, flit, flutter, hover, glide.
2. *See* FLOCK, ARROW.
3. *Referring to utterance of wit, venting of tears, etc.: spec.* sally, burst, strain, stretch.
4. *Referring to motion of missiles, falling leaves, etc.: spec.* rain, shower, storm, flutter.
5. *Referring to steps:* pair, gradatory (*R*); *spec.* ghaut *or* ghat (*Anglo-Indian*).
flighty, *a.* **1.** volatile, barmy (*R or B*), giggish (*R*), shuttle-witted (*A; fig.*), bird-witted (*fig.*).
2. *See* DERANGED.
flimsy, *a.* unsubstantial, slight, thin (*contex.*), frail; *spec.* filmy, sleazy, sleezy, paper, papery, gossamer, gossamery, jerry-built.
Antonyms: see FIRM, STRONG.
flipper, *n.* limb (*contex.*), pinna (*tech.*), flapper (*R*); *spec.* wing.
flirt, *v. i.* **1.** *See* MOVE, DART.
2. *Spec.* coquet, gallant, philander (*used of the male; with "with"*), dally, play, wanton.
flirt, *n.* **1.** *See* THROW, JERK, MOVEMENT, DART.
2. *Spec.* coquet (*male or female*), coquette (*female*), wanton; *spec.* philanderer (*male*).
flirtation, *n. Spec.* coquetry, flirting, dalliance (*these three imply relatively innocent behavior*); wantonness, philandering (*these imply disregard for accepted moral standards*).
flirtatious, *a.* flirtish (*R*), flirty (*R*); *spec.* coquettish, coquet.
flit, *v. i.* **1.** hasten, dart.
2. *See* DEPART.
3. fly, flutter, flicker, twinkle, skit.
float, *v. i.* **1.** buoy (*R, exc. spec.*); *spec.* live, swim, ride, waft, drift (*contex.*), drive, tide.
2. *Referring to objects poised in the air, in water, etc.:* buoy, hang; *spec.* swim, trail, stream, watch (*of a buoy*), fluff, waft, fly.
Antonyms: see SINK.
3. *See* GLIDE.
float, *v. t.* **1.** support (*contex.*), buoy; *spec.* swim, launch, flash, flush, waft.
Antonyms: see SINK.
2. *See* OVERFLOW.
float, *n.* **1.** floatage, floater; *spec.* raft, catamaran, swimmer, camel, buoy, outrigger.
2. *In fishing:* dobber (*local, U. S.*); *spec.* cork, quill, darby.
3. *Of a wagon with its display, in a procession:* pageant (*A or hist.*).
floating, *a.* **1.** afloat, natant (*tech. or R*), superfluitant (*R*), supernatant (*R*), swimming.
2. *See* WANDERING.
3. unfunded; *spec.* variable;—*referring to a debt, etc.*
flocculent, *a.* gossypine (*R*), cottony (*chiefly spec.*), flocky (*R*), floccose, woolly (*primarily spec.*).
flock, *n.* **1.** *See* COMPANY, MULTITUDE, GROUP.
2. *Referring to a group of gregarious animals:* plump (*A, or dial. Eng.*); *spec.* troop, herd, pack, drove, swarm, shoal *or* school, bevy, covey, team, wing, flight, fling (*Brit.*), game, kit (*cant*), gaggle, loft. *All the terms are secondarily applied to human beings, with implications of respect, fear, contempt, etc., implied by the literal senses, as "bevy" to maidens and ladies, "herd" to a rabble of persons, etc.*
flock, *v. i.* congregate; *spec.* school, herd, swarm, shoal.
flock, *n.* clump (*contex.*); *spec.* lock, flake, tuft, dag, floccule, flocculus.
flock, *v. i.* gather (*contex.*); *spec.* tuft.
floe, *n. Spec.* field, sheet, pan, cake, flake.
flogging, *a.* plagose (*humorous*).
flood, *n.* **1.** *Spec.* deluge, Niagara (*fig.*), wave, rage, flush, inundation, confluence, cataclysm, tide, debacle, torrent, freshet *or* (*less usual*), fresh, overflow, waterfall, cloudburst, countertide, spate (*chiefly Scot.*), downpour, water (*contex.*), bore, eager.
2. *See* FLOW, ABUNDANCE, EXCESS.

flex, *v. t.: bend.*
flick, *v. t.: whip, snap.*
flick, *v. i.: flutter.*
flick, *n.: stroke, snap.*
flimflam, *n.: deception.*
flinch: *shrink.*
fling, *v. i.: flounce.*
flip: *throw, snap.*
flippant: *frivolous.*
flirt, *v. t.: throw, dart.*
floaty: *buoyant.*
flog, *v. t.: beat, lash.*
flood, *v. t.: overflow.*

flood, *a.* diluvial *or* diluvian (*chiefly spec.*); *spec.* cataclysmic *or* cataclysmal (*tech. or B*).
floodgate, *n. Spec.* stanch, weir, penstock.
floor, *n.* **1.** bottom (*contex.*), flooring; *spec.* pavement, parquet, stage, deck, contignation (*R or obs.*).
2. *See* STORY.
floor, *v. t.* **1.** cover (*contex.*), lay; *spec.* deck, plank, pave.
2. *See* FELL.
floorcloth, *n.* covering (*contex.*); *spec.* carpet, linoleum, oilcloth, rug, *etc.*
florid, *a.* **1.** flowery, ornate, embellished; *spec.* rococo, figurative, figured, luxuriant.
Antonyms: see PROSAIC.
2. *See* RED, RED-FACED.
flotation, *n.* floatage; *spec.* supernatation.
flounce, *v. i. & n.* **1.** *Spec.* flounder, fling, throw, whop, flop, struggle, tumble, toss, plunge, blunder, slosh, twitch, plouter (*chiefly Scot.*).
2. *See* RUSH, JERK.
flounce, *n. & v. t.* furbelow.
flour, *n.* powder (*contex.*), meal (*now chiefly spec.*); *spec.* sujee *or* suji (*East India*), tapioca, farina, cones (*cant*).
flourish, *v. t.* swing (*contex.*), upsway (*R*); *spec.* brandish, wave, whisk, sweep, flaunt, shake.
flourish, *n.* **1.** *See* SHOW.
2. swing (*contex.*); *spec.* shake, brandish, brandishment, wave, whisk, sweep, flaunt.
3. *Referring to writing, etc.:* stroke, quirk; *spec.* paraph.
4. *In music:* floriation (*R*); *spec.* cadenza, fanfare *or* fanfarade, tantara, tarantara, blast, tantivy.
flow, *v. i.* **1.** run; *spec.* stream, spew, spring, gutter, dribble, pour, purl, gurgle, drain, draw, flush, trickle, gush, rush, ripple, flood, tide, regorge (*R*), reflow (*R*), outflow, effuse, extravasate, well (*used with "out" or "up"*), in flow (*R*), inflood, interflow, bleed, discharge, roll, glide, geyser.
2. *See* PASS, GO, GLIDE, ISSUE, EMANATE, ARISE, WAVE, RISE.
3. abound, run;—*as with gold, milk and honey, etc.*
flow, *n.* **1.** run (*R or spec.*); *spec.* tide, stream, dribble, pour, drain, trickle, gush, geyser, rush, flowage, determination, current, flash flood, fluxion (*R, exc. med.*), flux (*R, exc. med. or fig.*), flush, dribbling, streaming, bore, wave, guggle, discharge, tide, ripple, defluence (*R*), defluxion, catarrh.
2. *Spec.* passage, glide, issue, emanation, blow, abundance, rise.
flower, *n.* **1.** blossom, bloom, blowth (*R*), blow (*R*); *spec.* floweret, floscule, flowerage (*collective*), floret, inflorescence (*collective; tech.*), drop.
2. *In pl.:* bloom (*a collective*).
3. *Referring to the state: see* BLOOM.
4. *See* BEST, ESSENCE, ELITE.
flower, *v. i.* **1.** blossom, bloom, blow, effloresce (*R*); *spec.* emblossom, tassel (*chiefly U. S.*).
2. *See* DEVELOP.
flowery, *a.* **1.** bloomy, blossomy, flowerful (*R*), *florulent* (*chiefly in decorative art*); *spec.* floscular (*R*), flosculous (*R*), florigerous (*R*).
2. *See* FLORID.
flowing, *a.* **1.** running, current (*now R*), fluent (*R and fig., exc. spec.*); *spec.* quick (*R*), dribbling, gushing, fluxional, living (*Biblical usage*), decursive (*R*), confluent, decurrent (*R*), defluent (*R*), refluent, interfluent (*R*), influent, profluent (*R*), excurrent (*chiefly tech.*), scaturient (*R*), circumfluent *or* circumfluous.
Antonyms: see STAGNANT, MOTIONLESS, STILL.
2. *See* ABUNDANT.
flue, *n.* duct (*contex.*); *spec.* chimney, tunnel.
fluent, *a.* **1.** *See* FLOWING.
2. *Referring to speech, expression, etc.:* ready, facile, flowing, easy, voluble; *spec.* glib.
Antonyms: see DUMB.
fluff, *n.* down, fuzz, floss; *spec.* flue, lint.
fluffy, *a.* downy, fuzzy; *spec.* fleecy, cottony, linty, woolly.
fluid, *a.* **1.** running, fluent (*R*), fluxible (*A*); *spec.* gaseous, liquid.
Antonyms: see SOLID.
2. *See* UNSTABLE.
fluid, *n. Spec.* liquid, gas, aura, humor (*A*).
fluidify, *v. t. Spec.* gasify, liquefy.
flurry, *n.* **1.** excitement, agitation, bustle, fluster, confusion.
2. *See* RAIN, SNOW, WIND.
flurry, *v. t.* excite, agitate, confuse.
flush, *v. i.* **1.** *See* FLOW.
2. redden (*contex.*), mantle (*of the cheek*); *spec.* blush, fluster.
flush, *v. t.* **1.** flood; *spec.* wash.
2. redden (*contex.*), inflame.
3. *See* ELATE.
flush, *n.* **1.** *See* FLOW, FLOOD, THRILL, ELATION, HEIGHT.
2. redness (*contex.*), color (*contex.*), rubicundity (*R; rhetorical or stilted*), glow; *spec.* blush, bloom, hectic (*R*).
Antonyms: see PALLOR.
flush, *v. t.* start (*used esp. with "up"*), rise; *spec.* retrieve.
flushed, *a.* **1.** red (*contex.*), flush, rubicund (*R; rhetorical or stilted*), ruddy, glowing; *spec.* hectic, blushing, blushful (*R*), blowsed *or* blowsy, blooming.

---

flooded: *afloat.*
flossy: *silky, downy.*
flourishing: *prosperous, luxuriant.*
flown: *gone.*
fluctuate: *vary, waver, swing.*
fluke: *arm, lobe.*
flume: *channel.*
flummery: *nonsense, porridge, flattery.*
flunk, *v. i.: fail.*
flunkey: *manservant, footman.*
fluorescent: *luminescent.*
flurry, *v. t.: bustle.*
flush, *v. i.: rise.*
flush, *a.: abounding, abundant, flushed, even.*

Antonyms: see PALE.
2. *See* ELATED.
flute, *n.* **1.** pipe (*chiefly spec. or C*), flauto (*Italian*); *spec.* diaulos (*Greek antiq.*), fife, tibia, flautine (*Italian*), poogye (*Hindu nose flute*), piccolo.
2. channel (*contex.*), groove; *spec.* goffer, gauffer, crimp.
flute, *v. i.* play (*contex.*), pipe (*contex.*); *spec.* tibicinate (*R*), fife.
flutist, *n.* player (*contex.*), fluter (*R*), piper (*contex.*), fluatist; *spec.* fifer, tibicen.
flutter, *n.* **1.** *See* FLAP.
2. agitation, twitter (*C or dial.*), flutteration (*C or S*), twitteration (*S*); *spec.* play, tremble, confusion.
flutter, *v. i.* play, wave.
fly, *v. i.* **1.** *Spec.* circle, wing, flit, clip (*A*), flitter, sail, flutter, soar, kite, glide, flicker, hover, swoop, dive, float, rode, outfly (*B*), plummet (*to dash to earth*), rocket (*to mount suddenly and vigorously*), sweep, flush, hang, wheel (*to fly lazily in great circles*).
2. flee, shun, escape.
3. *See* MOVE, GLIDE, FLOAT, DEPART, SPREAD, VANISH, DISAPPEAR.
fly, *v. t.* **1.** *In hunting with a hawk:* chase.
2. *See* FLEE.
fly, *n.* **1.** *Spec.* tsetse, bot, bott, dun, grannom, dunfly, dipter (*tech.*), drake, gnat, midge, bluebottle, ichneumon, breeze.
2. *Referring to artificial flies:* bait, *spec.* hackle, harl, palmer, butcher, governor, grackle, grannom, Dobson (*U. S.*), dun, dunfly, dropper, heckle, goldfinch, hornet.
flyer, *n.* **1.** volator (*R*); *spec.* bird, bat, squirrel, sauropter, saurian.
2. *See* AVIATOR.
flying, *n.* **1.** volation (*R*), volitation (*R*), flight.
2. *See* AVIATION.
flying, *a.* volant (*R*), volitant (*R*); *spec.* circumvolant.
foam, *n.* froth (*less dignified than "foam"*); *spec.* scum, cream, mantle, head, spume, lather, suds (*C; pl.*).
foam, *v. i.* froth; *spec.* scum, cream, mantle, spume, head.
foam, *v. t.* befoam (*an intensive*), froth; *spec.* scum, mantle, spume (*R*).
foamy, *a.* frothy; *spec.* creamy, spumous, spumy, spumescent, lathery.
focus, *v. t.* center, concenter, converge, concentrate, focalize;—*all but "focalize," contex.*
Antonyms: see SCATTER.
fodder, *n.* feed, provend (*A*); *spec.* provender, chaff, browse, wintering, ensilage, silage, ramoon (*East India*), hay, oats, beans, *etc.*
fog, *n.* **1.** cloud (*contex.*), mist (*contex.*), brume (*R*), nebula (*R*); *spec.* haze, smother.
2. *See* HAZE.
foggy, *a.* **1.** cloudy (*contex.*), thick, misty (*contex.*), hazy, brumous (*B*), nebulous (*R*).
Antonyms: see CLEAR.
2. *See* HAZY, DIM, CONFUSED.
fogy, *n.* fogram, fogrum, fossil, foozle;—*all (C) or (S), and used esp. with "old."*
foil, *n.* **1.** *See* SHEET.
2. foliation; *spec.* trefoil, quatrefoil, cinquefoil, sexfoil.
3. *In art, etc.:* contrast, set-off; *spec.* blank.
foist, *v. t.* **1.** *See* INTRODUCE.
2. palm.
fold, *n.* **1.** folding, double, doubling, turn, plication (*tech.*), plicature (*tech.*); *spec.* lap, coil, induplication (*R*), foldure (*R*), ply, plait *or* pleat, tuck, wimple (*A or Scot.*), plica, ruga folio, anticline, isocline, syncline, wrap, bosom, nook (*Scot.*), wrinkle.
2. *See* CLASP, EMBRACE.
fold, *v. t.* **1.** double, turn, plicate (*tech.*); *spec.* lap, coil, plait *or* pleat, tuck, ruckle (*R*), interfold, wrap, infold.
Antonyms: see UNFOLD.
2. *See* CLASP, EMBRACE.
folded, *a.* plicate (*tech.*); *spec.* lapped, induplicate, double, *etc.*
follow, *v. t.* **1.** accompany (*contex.*), attend (*contex.*); *spec.* heel, dodge, tag (*C*), dog, hound, hunt, bedog (*intensive*), trail.
Antonyms: see LEAD, PRECEDE, PREFACE.
2. trace, run; *spec.* retrace.
3. *See* PURSUE, SUCCEED, ADOPT, OBSERVE, COPY.
follow, *v. i.* **1.** *Spec.* heel, tag, attend, hunt.
2. come (*contex.*), attend, succeed, ensue, emanate (*R*); *spec.* result.
follower, *n.* **1.** sectary *or* sectator (*R*); *spec.* successor, pursuer, heeler.
Antonyms: see FORERUNNER, PREDECESSOR.
2. *See* ADHERENT.
following, *a.* sequent (*chiefly spec.*), subsequent (*chiefly spec.*), sequacious (*R*), sequential (*R*) succeeding, successive, attendant, ensuing, consecutive.
Antonyms: see PRECEDING, PREFATORY.
following, *n.* **1.** followers (*pl.*); *spec.* clientele, clientelage, clientage, clientry, retinue.
2. *Of the act: spec.* succession, consecution, pursuing.
Antonyms: see PRECEDENCE.
foment, *v. t.* **1.** bathe; *spec.* embrocate.
2. *See* FOSTER, INCITE.
fond, *a.* **1.** *See* FOOLISH, PET.

fluster, *n.: confusion.*
fluster, *v. i.: flurry, bustle.*
fluster, *v. t.: flush, confuse.*
flustery: *confused.*
flustrate: *confuse.*
fluted: *channeled.*
flutter, *v. t.: agitate, confuse.*
fly, *n.: flight, length, loft.*
flyte, *v. i. & n.: dispute.*
flyte: *v. t.: abuse.*
foal, *v. t.: bear.*
fob, *n.: pocket, chain.*
fob, *v. t.: deceive.*
foe: *enemy.*
fœtus: *embryo.*
fog: *aftermath.*
fog, *v. t.: cloud, perplex.*
foil: *defeat.*
foison: *abundance, strength, means.*
foliage: *leafage.*
foliation: *foil, leafage, leafing.*
folio: *word, leaf.*
folk: *kindred, people, nation.*
folly: *foolishness.*
fondle: *caress.*
fondling: *pet.*

2. affectionate; *spec.* (*as implying excess or bad judgment*; overfond, doting.
Antonyms: see COLD.
3. partial (*used with "to"; C*); *spec.* greedy (*used with "of"*).
fondness, *n.* **1.** affection.
2. desire (*contex.*), appetite, partiality (*used with "to" or "for"*), taste, relish.
font, *n. Of type:* fount, letter (*tech.*).
font, *n.* **1.** *Eccl.:* laver, delubrum (*R*).
2. *See* FOUNTAIN, SPRING.
food, *n.* nourishment, nutriment, nutrition, nurture (*B*), aliment (*chiefly tech.*), nouriture (*R*), foodstuff (*chiefly spec. and commercial*), ingesta (*pl.; tech.*), meat (*A, exc. in "meat and drink"*), victuals (*pl.; now chiefly tech. or somewhat inelegant*), viands (*pl.*), tackle (*S*), scran (*S*), scraps (*pl.*), creature (*B or dial.*), provisions (*pl.*), provant (*R*), provand (*R*), proviance (*B or R*), provend (*A*), provender (*now humorous or referring to food for animals*), pabulum (*referring to food for animals or plants, exc. as humorous*), prog (*S*), peck (*S*), grub (*S, dial., or cant*), cram (*dial. Eng.*), belly timber (*A or dial.*), bellycheer (*A*), tuck (*S*), crug (*S, Eng.*), tack (*chiefly in "hardtack"*); *spec.* ration, board, fare, cates *or* acates (*pl.; A*), bit (*chiefly dial.*), livery (*hist.*), diet, dish, dietary, slops (*pl.; S or cant*), bait, delicatessen (*pl.*), mash, manna, flummery, scrapple (*U. S.*), browse, bite, bread, flesh, greens, *etc. Cf.* FEED.
food, *a.* cibarious (*R*), cibarian (*R*).
fool, *n.* simpleton, dolt, dupe, butt, lunatic, idiot, imbecile, moron, dope (*S*), cheese (*S*), fish (*S*), sap (*S*), nut (*C*), *etc.*
fooling, *n.* **1.** foolery, tomfoolery; *spec.* nonsense, buffoonery.
2. *See* DECEPTION.
foolish, *a.* **1.** *See* UNWISE.
2. senseless, silly, empty-headed, fatuous, fond (*A*), inane, goosish (*R, C*), goosy (*R, C*), desipient (*R*), brainless, weak, mad (*wildly* foolish), simple, light-minded, empty, daft, harebrained; *spec.* lunatic, soft, buffoonish, crazy, idiotic, imbecile, vain, inept, cracked; phoney (*U. S., S denoting* foolish *in sense of being incomplete, not genuine or wholly sound. In this category belong also* screwy, nutty, nuts, dopey, dippy, flooey, haywire).
Antonyms: see WISE.
3. deranged (*contex.*), sawney (*C*); *see* IMBECILE.
foolishness, *n.* **1.** *See* UNWISDOM.
2. foolery (*chiefly concrete*), folly, fondness (*A*), desipience (*R*), silliness, jackassery (*contemptuous*), fatuity, fatuousness (*chiefly the quality*); *spec.* lunacy, inanity, vanity, dotage, idiocy (*C*), infatuation, ineptness, madness, levity, lunacy.
Antonyms: see WISDOM.

foot, *n.* **1.** extremity (*affected or humorous*), pedal (*humorous or affected*), dewbeater (*S; chiefly in pl.*), paw (*esp. spec.*); *spec.* pad, heel (*fig., or the hind foot*), hoof, harefoot, splayfoot, clubfoot.
2. *See* BOTTOM, BASE, END, INFANTRY, AGGREGATE.
3. *In prosody:* unit; *spec.* dactyle, tribrach, trochee, iambus, diabrach, pyrrhic, dochmiac, dichoree, diiamb, *etc.*
foot, *a.* pedal (*affected or humorous, exc. as spec.*).
foot, *v. i. Spec.* walk, hoof (*S*);—*used with "it".*
football, *n.* **1.** pigskin (*C*), leather (*C*).
2. *Of the game: spec.* rugger (*S*), rugby, soccer (*S*), association.
footlights, *n. pl.* floats (*cant*).
footman, *n.* servant (*contex.*), Jeames (*humorous*).
footpath, *n.* footway; *spec.* sidewalk, berm.
footprint, *n.* step *or* footstep, vestige (*B*); *spec.* prick, track, trace, pug (*Anglo-Indian*), seal, pad, ichnite, ichnolite, ornithichnite.
foot-shaped, *a.* pediform (*tech.*).
footsoldier, infantryman, footman (*R*), peon (*India*), grabby (*S and opprobrious*), infantry (*a collective*); *spec.* peltast.
footstep, *n.* **1.** footfall, tread (*chiefly spec.*); *spec.* clamp, tramp, pad.
2. *See* FOOTPRINT, STEP.
footstool, *n. Spec.* ottoman, buffet, hassock.
for, *prep.* after.
forbearance, *n.* abstention, desistance; *see* ENDURANCE, PATIENCE, TOLERATION.
forbearing, *a. Spec.* patient, sparing, mild; *see* TOLERANT.
forbid, *v. t.* **1.** prohibit, enjoin; *spec.* interdict, ban, taboo, proscribe, debar, inhibit, disallow, veto, embargo.
Antonyms: see BID, ASK, APPOINT, PERMIT.
2. *See* PREVENT.
forbiddance, *n.* prohibition (*formal*), forbiddal; *spec.* veto, interdiction, ban, inhibition, debarment, proscription, taboo, disallowance, embargo.
Antonyms: see BIDDING, APPOINTMENT, PERMISSION.
forbidden, *a.* prohibited (*formal*); *spec.* interdicted, taboo, prescribed, contraband, unlawful.
forbidding, *a.* **1.** prohibitory (*formal*); *spec.* interdictory, interdictive (*R*), inhibitory *or* inhibitive.
2. *See* REPELLENT.
force, *n.* **1.** energy, power; *spec.* principle, dyname, vehemence, strain, head, might, birr (*chiefly Scot.*), cram, dint (*in "by dint of"*), vim (*C*), vis (*Latin*), rapture (*R*), wrench,

foodstuff: *food.*
fool, *n.: simpleton, buffoon, imbecile.*
fool, *v. t.: deceive.*
foolhardy: *venturesome.*
foot, *v. t.: add.*
fop: *dandy.*
forage, *n.: food.*
forage, *v. t.: search, feed.*
forage, *v. i.: plunder, search.*
foray, *v. t. & i.: plunder.*
forbear, *v. t.: check.*
forbear, *v. i.: abstain.*

twist, stress, tension, compression, shear, brunt; *see* ENERGY.
2. *Of language, ideas, etc.:* energy; *spec.* emphasis, pith, nervousness, sway, efficacy, cogency, snap (*C*), pithiness.
3. *See* VIOLENCE, COMPULSION, CONSTRAINT.
4. body, corps, array (*rhetorical*); *spec.* crew, posse, posse comitatus (*Latin*), army, command, tercio, impi (*Kaffir*), detachment, patrol, regiment, squadron, battalion, fleet, convoy, *etc.*

force, *v. t.* **1.** effect (*R*); *spec.* squeeze, press, elbow, pinch, drive, burst, bear, inch, rush, hustle, repel, inject.
2. *See* VIOLATE, COMPEL, ENTER, EXTORT, DEVELOP.

forced, *a.* artificial, unspontaneous (*R*); *spec.* harsh, strained, constrained, compulsory.

forceful, *a.* **1.** energetic, mighty; *spec.* active, dynamic, vigorous, virile, *etc.*
2. *See* EFFICACIOUS, EXPRESSIVE, COGENT, EMPHATIC, VIOLENT.

forcible, *a.* **1.** energetic; *spec.* vehement, heady; *see* ENERGETIC.
Antonyms: see WEAK.
2. *See* VIOLENT.
3. efficacious, effective, forceful; *spec.* (*of language, ideas, etc.*) sinewy, nervous, pithy, robustious (*R*), important; *see* COGENT, EMPHATIC.

ford, *n.* crossing (*contex.*), shallow (*contex.*), fordage, wade (*C*); *spec.* ghaut *or* ghat.

ford, *v. t.* cross (*contex.*), wade.

fore, *a.* anterior, forward; *spec.* first, front, foregoing.
Antonyms: see HIND.

forebode, *v. t.* **1.** anticipate (*contex.*); *spec.* threaten, croak, misbode, presage, surmise, mistrust. "*Forebode,*" "*foreboding,*" *etc., are often used as implying expected evil.*
2. *See* PREDICT, SIGNIFY.

foreboding, *a.* anticipative (*contex.*), forebodeful, presageful, presentient (*R*); *spec.* croaking, croaky, *etc. Cf.* FOREBODE.

foreboding, *n.* anticipation (*contex.*), presage, presentiment (*dignified*), boding, premonition, presension (*R*), bode (*A*), bodement (*R*); *spec.* preapprehension (*R*), croaking, *etc. Cf.* FOREBODE.

foreground, *n.* front, fore (*R*); *spec.* forefront.
Antonyms: see BACKGROUND.

forehead, *n.* metopon (*tech.*), brow, front (*B or rhetorical*).

forehead, *a.* metopic (*tech.*), frontal.

foreign, *a.* **1.** exterior, outside, external, peregrine (*R*), strange (*A, exc. spec.*), outlandish (*chiefly spec.*), outland (*A*), alien (*chiefly spec.*); *spec.* exotic, extraneous, extrinsic, barbaric, barbarian, oversea, tramontane (*R*), unnative (*R*), metic.
Antonyms: see NATIVE, DOMESTIC, INLAND.
2. *See* UNNATURAL, APART, IRRELEVANT, UNRELATED.

foreigner, *n.* alien (*chiefly spec.*), stranger (*chiefly Bib.*), outsider (*contex.*), outlander (*A or B*), extern (*R*); *spec.* exotic (*R*), ultramontane, barbarian, tramontane (*R*).
Antonyms: see NATIVE, CITIZEN.

foreignism, *n.* alienism (*chiefly spec.*); *spec.* exoticism, Gallicism, Briticism, Irishism, *etc.*

foreknow, *v. t.* foresee, precognize (*R*).

foreknowledge, *n.* prognostication (*B*), prescience (*chiefly spec.*), presension (*R*), presensation (*R*), precognition (*B*), prenotion (*R*); *spec.* preacquaintance (*R*).
Antonyms: see IGNORANCE.

forensic, *a.* controversial, argumentative, rhetorical.

forerun, *v. t.* precede, precourse (*R*), precurse (*R*); *spec.* anticipate, foreshadow, introduce, prelude.

forerunner, *n.* **1.** predecessor, precursor; *spec.* apparitor (*tech. or hist.*), pioneer, prelude (*only fig.*), harbinger (*chiefly B*), outrunner, prodromus (*R*), herald.
Antonyms: see FOLLOWER.
2. *See* ANCESTOR.

forerunning, *a.* precursory, precurrent (*R*), prodromal (*R*).

foresee, *v. t.* anticipate, previse (*R*), forelook (*R*), preview (*R*), prevision (*R*); *spec.* prognosticate, forecast.

foreseeing, *a.* prescient (*chiefly spec.*), precognizant (*R*), previsive (*R*).

foreshadow, *v. t.* signify, indicate, shadow, prefigure, foreshow, adumbrate (*B*); *spec.* presage.

foreshadow, *n.* antitype.

foresight, *n.* anticipation, prescience (*chiefly spec.*), preview (*R*), prevision (*R*), onsight (*R*), prospection (*R*), forelook, prospect (*B*); *spec.* providence, forecast.

forest, *n.* woodland, wildwood (*B or R*).
Antonyms: see PRAIRIE.

forester, *n.* woodman; *spec.* woodward, landreeve.

forestry, *n.* woodcraft, silviculture; *spec.* dendrology.

foretaste, *n.* earnest, pregustation (*R*), antepast (*B*), handsel (*chiefly Eng.*); *spec.* prelibation (*chiefly fig.*).

foretaste, *v. t.* pregust (*R*), anticipate.

forethought, *n.* forecase (*R*); *spec.* providence, anticipation, premeditation.
Antonyms: see AFTERTHOUGHT.

---

forcing: *compulsion.*
fore, *n.: front.*
forebear, *n.: ancestor.*
forecast, *n.: foresight, prediction.*
forecast, *v. t.: foresee, predict, devise.*
foreclose, *v. t.: appropriate, bar.*
forefather: *ancestor.*
forego: *precede.*
foregone: *previous.*
foreground: *front.*
forehand: *advantage.*
foremost, *a.: first, chief.*
foreordain: *appoint, destine.*
forepart: *front.*
forestall: *anticipate, prevent.*
foretaste: *anticipate.*
foretell: *predict.*
forever: *eternally, always.* **Also cf.** *constant.*
foreword: *preface.*

---

forfeit, *n.* fine (*contex.*), forfeiture; *spec.* deodand.
forfeit, *v. t.* lose; *spec.* escheat.
Antonyms: see GAIN.
forfeitable, *a. In law: spec.* lapsable, escheatable, caducary.
forge, *n.* furnace, smithy (*now chiefly literary*), smithery (*R*), stithy (*R*); *spec.* bloomery, hearth.
forge, *v. t.* **1.** smith (*R*), stithy (*R*); *spec.* tilt, extund (*R*).
2. *See* DEVISE, CONSTRUCT, FABRICATE, INVENT, COUNERFEIT.
forger, *n.* **1.** worker (*contex.*), smith; *spec.* blacksmith, whitesmith, goldsmith (*A*), silversmith, (*A*), tilter, Cyclops, Vulcan, Hephæstus, Hephaistos.
2. *See* COUNTERFEITER.
forgery, *n.* **1.** smithing (*R*), smithery (*R*).
2. *See* FICTION, COUNTERFEIT
forget, *v. t.* **1.** disremember (*chiefly dial.*) bury (*fig. or C*), oblivionize (*R*), unknow (*R*); *spec.* unlearn.
Antonyms: see REMEMBER, RECALL.
2. *See* OMIT.
forgetful, *a.* **1.** forgetting (*R, exc. spec.*), leaky (*contemptuous or undignified*), short (*referring to the memory*), oblivious, unmindful.
Antonyms: see RETENTIVE.
2. *See* NEGLECTFUL.
forgetfulness, *n.* forgetting, oblivion, Lethe (*fig.*), forgetness (*R*), obliviousness, obliviscence (*R*), forget (*R*); *spec.* amnesty, limbo, absent-mindedness.
forgiveness, *n.* remission (*R*), pardon (*spec. or fig.*); *spec.* absolution, amnesty.
forgiving, *a.* excusing, remissive (*R*), placable.
Antonyms: see UNFORGIVING.
forgo, *v. t.* abandon, forbear (*by the exercise of self-restraint*); *spec.* remit.
Antonyms: see KEEP.
forgoing, *n.* abandonment, forbearance; *spec.* remittal, remission.
forgotten, *a.* unremembered, gone, disremembered (*chiefly dial.*), lost.
Antonyms: see RETRIBUTION.
fork, *n.* **1.** divarication (*B*), crotch (*a homely word, now chiefly U. S. and dial. Eng.; chiefly tech. or spec.*), crutch (*R*); *spec.* tormentor.
2. *See* BRANCH.
fork, *v. i.* branch (*contex.*), furcate (*B or tech.*), divaricate (*B or tech.*); *spec.* bifurcate, trifurcate.
forked, *a.* forky (*R or spec.*), crotched (*see* FORK), furcate (*B*), divaricate (*B*); *spec.* bifid, biforked, bifurcate, trifurcate, lituate.
forking, *a.* branching; *spec.* dichotomous.
forking, *n.* branching, furcation (*B*), divarication (*B or tech.*); *spec.* dichotomy, trichotomy, bifurcation.

form, *n.* **1.** shape (*more concrete and a less elevated term than "form"*), figure, mold (*orig. spec.*); *spec.* model, impression, cast, conformation, fashion (*a word that is becoming A in this sense*), figuration, configuration, outline, build, format, get-up (*C*), set-up (*C*), cut, contour, confection, crystal, *etc.*
2. ceremony, rite (*chiefly spec.*), ceremonial, observance, formality; *spec.* conventionality, office, mystery (*chiefly in pl.*), ordinance, performance (*often contemptuous*), liturgy, sacrament, sacramental, use, augury, baptism, etiquette, cult, hierurgy, punctilio.
3. *See* BODY, PATTERN, KIND, ESSENCE, DICTION, SEAT, STATE, ARRANGEMENT, ORDER, CLASS, TYPE.
form, *v. t.* make, produce, efform (*R*), shape, fashion, (*dignified*), inform, constitute; *spec.* coin (*often depreciatory*), develop, organize, conceive, create, fabricate, found, emboss, describe, block, model, mold, mingle, mix, arrange, construct, reconstruct, generate, compose, build, turn, cause, contract.
form, *v. i. Spec.* develop, make, come, grow.
formal, *a.* **1.** ceremonial, ritual, ceremonious; *spec.* official, conventional, functional, perfunctory, perfunctionary (*R*), set, model, outward, solemn, academic, liturgical, Pharisaic *or* Pharisaical, external, sacramental.
Antonyms: see INFORMAL.
2. *See* DEFINITE.
3. *Referring to manners, actions, language, etc.:* rigid, ceremonious, stiff, unbending, precise; *spec.* prim, starch, punctilious, buckram (*fig.*), stilted, rigid, affected, bombastic, *etc.*
Antonyms: see UNCEREMONIOUS, COLLOQUIAL, HOMELIKE, INTIMATE, FAMILIAR.
formality, *n.* **1.** convention, conventionality, formulism, custom, circumstance, red tape (*chiefly spec.*), wiggery (*fig.; R*), punctuality (*A*), punctualness (*A*), red-tapism (*chiefly spec.*); *spec.* punctilio, perfunctoriness.
2. *See* FORM.
formalize, *v. t.* **1.** *See* DEFINE.
2. *Spec.* conventionalize, ceremonialize.
formation, *n.* formature (*R*); *spec.* invention, coinage, malformation, production, contrivance, development, composition, creation, growth, coagulation (*fig.*), conformation, generation, genesis, construction, potence, echelon, terrane.
formative, *a.* fashioning, informative (*R*); *spec.* creative, morphotic, plastic, shaping, modeling, cosmoplastic.
former, *a.* earlier, prior, previous, cidevant (*French*), sometime (*indefinite*), whilom (*A or B*), past, bygone, heretofore (*R*), quondam (*indefinite; B*); *spec.* preceding, late.
Antonyms: see SUBSEQUENT.

---

forgather: *gather, meet, associate.*
forge, *v. t.: invent, devise.*
forge, *v. i.: overreach.*
forgive: *excuse, absolve.*
forgiveness: *excuse, absolution.*
forlorn: *abandoned, depressed, hopeless, lamentable, devoid.*
formalist: *precision.*

---

formerly, *a.* heretofore, quondam (*R*), erst (*A or B*), erstwhile (*A*), once (*C*).

formidable, *a.* fearful, redoubtable (*often humorously ironical*); *spec.* doughty (*A or rhetorical*), difficult, dangerous, impassable, *etc.*

formless, *a.* inform, chaotic, shapeless, amorphous (*tech. or learned*).

formula, *n.* **1.** form, formulary, rule; *spec.* (*eccl.*) credo, belief, confession.
2. recipe (*used chiefly in medicine or cookery*), receipt (*used chiefly in cookery*), prescription (*med.*).

formulate, *v. t.* state, formularize, formulize, frame, devise; *spec.* schematize, draw, institute.

formulation, *n.* statement, devising, formularization, formulization.

fortification, *n.* defense, stronghold, fastness, bulwark (*B*), fort (*chiefly spec.*); *spec.* fieldwork, citadel, fortlet, hold (*A*), capitol, fortalice, fortress, rampart, rampire (*A*), redoubt, breastwork, redan, earthwork, tower, martello-tower, bastile, sconce, keep, donjon, curtain, surtout, lodgment, lunette, tenaille, gabionade, traverse, tambour, contravallation, flanker, castle, star, circumvallation, tetragon, rath (*Irish hist.*), mount *or* mound (*hist.*), presidio (*Spanish*), burg (*German*), Kremlin (*Russian*), zareba (*in the Sudan*), gurry (*Anglo-Indian*), pillbox (*S*), post.

fortify, *v. t.* **1.** strengthen; *spec.* brace (*oneself or one's spirits*), encourage, brandy.
2. fence (*B or A*), fort (*R*), fortress; *spec.* rampart, rampire (*A*), fraise, stockade, wall, mound, battle (*obs. or B*), embattle, mure, entrench, counterscrap, countermure.

fortunate, *a.* **1.** *See* AUSPICIOUS.
2. prosperous, chancy (*Scot.*), happy, lucky, blessed; *spec.* successful, timely, providential.
Antonyms: see UNSUCCESSFUL, UNFORTUNATE, UNLUCKY.

fortunately, *adv.* happily, well, *etc.*

fortune, *n.* **1.** accident, chance, luck, hap (*A*); *spec.* goodhap (*A*); *see* MISFORTUNE.
2. luck, cast (*obs. or dial.*), lines (*pl.; after Ps. xvi, 6*), fare; *spec.* prosperity, success, felicity, misfortune.
Antonyms: see MISFORTUNE.
3. *See* FATE, WEALTH.
4. competence, sufficiency, pile (*C*); *spec.* independence, plum (*obs. S, Eng.*).

forward, *a.* **1.** onward, advancing, progressive, progressing.
Antonyms: see BACKWARD.
2. *See* FORE, READY, BOLD.

forward, *adv.* onward *or* onwards (*esp. in space*); on, along, forth, forthward (*A*); *spec.* before, ahead, frontward, frontwards, forthright (*A*), advanced, advancing.
Antonyms: see BACKWARD.

foster, *v. t.* aid (*contex.*), promote, cherish, nurture (*R, exc. spec.*), nurse (*fig. or spec.*); *spec.* foment, cosset, nuzzle (*fig.*; *R*), mother (*fig.*), cultivate, patronize, cradle, nourish, harbor, encourage.
Antonyms: see EXTINGUISH.

fosterage, *n.* aid (*contex.*), promotion, nurture, nourish, nourishment; *spec.* fomentation, cultivation, patronage, encouragement.

foul, *a.* **1.** dirty (*contex.*), impure, filthy, immund (*R*), sordid (*with filth or offensive dirt*), tetrous (*R*), obscene (*A or R*); *spec.* rank, festering, squalid, loathful (*R*), noisome, feculent, loathsome, loathly (*B*), loathy (*R*), dreggy, polluted, disgusting, fetid, muddy.
Antonyms: see CLEAN.
2. *See* DIRTY, ABOMINABLE, ENTANGLED, UNFAIR, DISCREDITABLE.
3. *Of weather: spec.* unfavorable (*contex.*), black, dirty, nasty, rough, wet.
Antonyms: see CLEAR.

foul, *v. t.* **1.** dirty, defile, contaminate; *spec.* bemire, pollute, sully.
Antonyms: see CLEAN.
2. *See* CONTAMINATE.

fouling, *n.* dirtying, defilement, *etc.*

foulness, *n.* **1.** dirtiness, impurity, filth; *spec.* feculence, squalor, squalidity (*R*), squalidness, loathsomeness, loathfulness, pollution, bilge, putridity, *etc.*
2. *See* CONTAMINATION.

foundation, *n.* **1.** base, basis, support, groundwork, bottom, substruction (*R*), substructure (*R*), tablement (*R*); *spec.* ground, rest, bed, bedding, groundsel, stereobate, socle, pierreperdu (*French*), sill, grillage, riprap (*U. S.*), fond (*French*).
2. *See* ENDOWMENT, BASIS, REASON.
3. *Spec.* college, fellowship, monastery, church, *etc.*

foundational, *a.* fundamental, basic, basal.

founder, *n.* establisher, author, projector, father, patriarch, organizer, foundress (*fem.*), builder; *spec.* œcist (*R*), heresiarch.

four, *n.* tetrad. *Referring to a group:* quartet, quartette, quartetto (*Italian; chiefly in music*), tetrad, quaternion, quarternity (*R*); *spec.* quatre (*R*); tiddy, quatuor (*music; R*).

four-angled, *a.* quadrangular (*B*).

fourfold, *a.* quadruple, quaduplicate;—*both* (*B*).

four-footed, *a.* quadruped, quadrupedal (*R*), four-foot (*B or obs.*).

four-handed, *a.* quadrumanous, quadrumane, quadrumanal;—*all three tech. or B.*

fourpence, *n.* groat, flag (*C or cant, Eng.*).

forsake: *abandon.*
forsooth: *truly.*
forswear: *abjure, abandon, deny.*
forswearing: *denial;* cf. *abjure.*
forth: *ahead, out.*
forthcoming: *coming.*
forthwith: *immediately.*
fortitude: *courage.*
fortnightly: *biweekly.*
fortress: *fortification.*
fortuitous: *accidental.*
fortuity: *chance.*
forward, *a.: fore, precocious, assuming, impudent.*
forward, *v. t.: advance, send.*
fossil: *remains, fogy.*
fossilize: *petrify.*
fouled: *dirtied.*
found, *v. t.: cast.*
found, *v. t.: base, establish, colonize.*
found, *v. i.: rely.*

four-sided, *a.* quadrilateral, tetrahedral;—*both tech. or B.*

fourth, *n.* quarter, quartern (*obs. or R*).

fourway, *a.* quadrivial (*of roads; B or R*).

fowl, *n.* **1.** *See* BIRD.

2. gallinacean (*tech.*), chicken (*primarily spec.*), poultry (*a collective*); *spec.* hen, biddy (*now chiefly C or humorous*), cook, capon, chick, pullet, broiler, roaster.

fox, *n.* Charley *or* Charlie (*used as a prop. name*), reynard (*quasi proper name*), lowrie (*quasi proper name; Scot.*); *spec.* vixen, whelp, cub.

fox hunter, pink (*cant*).

foxy, *a.* **1.** alopecoid (*tech.*), vulpine (*B or tech.*), vulpecular (*R*).

2. *See* ARTFUL.

fragment, *n.* **1.** part (*contex.*), division (*contex.*), fraction (*R*); *spec.* crumb, flinders (*pl.*), fritters (*pl.; R*), smithers (*pl.; C*), smithereens (*pl.; C*), orts (*pl.*), frustum (*R*), calf, sliver, shiver, splinter, morsel, chip, shard, shred, brickbat, potsherd, crock, sippet.

2. *See* PART.

fragrant, *a.* sweet; *spec.* aromatic, spicy (*a stronger term than aromatic*), balmy, ambrosial *or* ambrosian, perfumy (*R*).

Antonyms: see FETID, ILL-SMELLING, RANK.

frame, *n.* **1.** *See* STRUCTURE.

2. framework; *spec.* case, curb, yoke, griff, gate (*R*), tenter, sash, easel, rack, cadge *or* cage, casement, chase, brake, coffin, hurst, crib.

3. *See* DISPOSITION.

frame, *v. t.* **1.** *See* ADAPT, INCLINE.

2. construct, enframe (*R*), form; *spec.* set, build, erect.

3. devise, form; *see* INVENT, COMPOSE, PRONOUNCE.

4. *See* EXPRESS.

frank, *a.* free, ingenuous, plain, plain-spoken, outspoken, free-spoken, direct, point-blank, unequivocal, outright, Dunstable (*fig.; B*), candid, downright, unreserved, open-hearted, naïve, sincere, liberal, open, undisguised, guileless, artless, genuine, unartful, free-hearted.

Antonyms: see HYPOCRITICAL, AFFECTED, ARTFUL, DECEITFUL, SECRET, DISSEMBLING, INTRIGUING, LYING, SNEAKING.

frank, *v. t.* send, transport;—*both contex.*

frankfurter, *n. Spec.* sausage, wiener (*C, U. S.*), hot dog (*C, U. S.*), dog (*C, U. S.*).

frankincense, *n.* incense (*contex.*), olibanum; *spec.* thus (*not a real frankincense*).

frantic, *a.* excited (*contex.*), frenzied, frenetic, desperate, transported, crazy (*spec.* or *C*), distraught (*B*), distract *or* (*more usually*) distracted; *spec.* passionate, ecstasied *or* ecstatic, mad, horn-mad, infuriate, delirious, madding (*B*), mœnadic, must, daft, giddy, furibund (*B*), raging, furious, maniac, deranged, zealous, rabid (*B*).

franticness, *n.* excitement, desperateness, desperation, distractedness, frenzy, furor, fury, mania, *etc.*

fraternity, *n.* brotherhood; *spec.* friary, society (*contex.*), club (*contex.*), synomasy (*R*).

fray, *v. t.* rub, wear, frazzle (*U. S. and dial. Eng.*); *spec.* fret, shred, tatter, ravel. "*Fray*" *is often used with "out."*

freak, *n.* **1.** *See* CAPRICE.

2. lusus naturæ (*Latin*), abnormality, monstrosity (*chiefly spec.*); *spec.* sport, mutation, comicality, Judy (*fig.*), abortion.

freaky, *a.* **1.** *See* CAPRICIOUS.

2. abnormal, sportive, monstrous (*chiefly spec.*); *spec.* abortive.

freckle, *n.* spot (*contex.*), blemish (*a contex. sense*), fleck, lentigo (*tech.*), ferntícle (*obs. or dial.*).

freckle, *v. t.* spot (*contex.*), discolor (*contex.*), fleck.

free, *a.* **1.** independent, frank; *spec.* emancipated (*R*), emancipate (*R*), manumitted, liberated, unenslaved, libertine (*obs. or hist.*), frank (*obs.*), ransomed, sui juris (*Roman law*), free-born.

2. self-governing, autonomous (*B or tech.*), independent.

3. *Referring to physical freedom:* loose, unconfined, unrestricted, bondless, untrammeled, unrestrained, quit, uncontrolled, inadherent, unimpeded, unattached, uncombined, solute, clear (*as a rope*), unentangled.

Antonyms: see CONFINED.

4. costless, expenseless, gratuitous, gratis (*a less dignified term than "gratuitous"*), chargeless.

5. exempt; *spec.* immune, privileged.

6. *See* AFFABLE, GENEROUS, CARELESS, AVAILABLE, DEVOID, EMPTY, LIBERAL, LOOSE, BOLD, FAMILIAR, VOLUNTARY, SPONTANEOUS, FRANK.

free, *v. t.* **1.** liberate, release, deliver, rescue, loose (*chiefly spec.*); *spec.* redeem, ransom, manumit, emancipate, disenslave (*R*), disenthrall (*B*), enfranchise (*tech. or B*), forisfamiliate (*Roman law*), unvassal (*R*), enlarge (*R or law*), discharge, parole (*fig.*), slip, disentwine, disimprison, disincarcerate (*R*), disimmure (*R*), disbody (*R*), disembody (*R*), relax (*Scots law*), unbind, clear, extricate, unleash, uncloister (*R*), unchain, unpen, unfetter, uncage, disembed, disyoke, eliminate, evolve, disembarrass, disencumber.

Antonyms: see PLEDGE, PAWN, FASTEN, CATCH,

foyer: *lobby.*
fracas: *disturbance.*
fractional: *partial.*
fracture, *n.*: *breaking, crack.*
fracture, *v. t.*: *break, crack.*
fragile: *brittle, weak.*
fragmentary: *dividual.*
fragrance: *smell.*
fragrant: *odorous.*
frail: *brittle, weak, slight, delicate.*
franchise: *privilege.*
frangible: *breakable.*
fraternal: *brotherly.*
fraternize: *associate.*
fraudulent: *deceitful, dishonest.*
fray: *fight.*

GRASP, CLASP, CONFINE, CONSTRICT, IMPRISON, IMPOUND, SHACKLE, TRAP.
2. *Referring to freeing from what holds fast:* disengage, liberate, clear; *spec.* disentangle.
3. *Referring to freeing from evil, oppression, etc.:* deliver, relieve (*R, exc. spec.*), rid (*emphatic*); *spec.* disburden, unburden, debarrass (*R*), disencumber, dispossess, emancipate, discharge, clear, disengage, disembroil.
Antonyms: see BIND, COMMIT, ENSLAVE.
4. exempt; *spec.* privilege, excuse, immunize, frank (*R*).

freebooter, *n.* desperado (*contex.*); *spec.* pirate, berserk, berserker, viking, buccaneer.

free-born, *a.* ingenuous (*chiefly Roman hist.*).

freedman, *n.* libertine (*Roman hist.*); *spec.* deditician (*Roman hist.*).
Antonyms: see BONDSMAN.

freedom, *n.* **1.** independence (*free from subjection*), liberty (*with implication of previous restraint now absent*); *spec.* emancipation, manumission, release, delivery, ransom, rescue.
Antonyms: see BONDAGE, SLAVERY.
2. unrestraint, play, disengagement, enlargement, discharge, disimprisonment, disembodiment, *etc.*
Antonyms: see CONFINEMENT.
3. self-government, independence, autonomy (*B or tech.*).
4. license (freedom *granted and subject to recall or regulation; sometimes the abuse of* freedom), swing (*often C*), lattitude, breadth; *spec.* ease, discretion.
5. exemption, impunity; *spec.* immunity, privilege.
6. *See* EASE, FAMILIARITY, READINESS, BOLDNESS.

freeholder, *n.* franklin (*obs. or hist.*), charterer (*hist.*); *spec.* yeoman.

freeing, *n.* **1.** liberation, emancipation, manumission, deliverance, enfranchisement, release, ransom, disenthrallment, *etc.*
Antonyms: see ENSLAVEMENT.
2. *Spec.* discharge, disembarrassment, exemption, clearing, quittance, disencumberment, disengagement, delivery, releasement (*R*), riddance, loosing, dispensation, relief, deliverance, enlargement, elimination, disembodiment, disincarceration, disimprisonment, disengage, immunization, redemption, *etc.*
3. exemption; *spec.* privileging.

freely, *adv. Spec.* gratis. *Cf.* FREE, *a.*

freeman, *n. Spec.* noble, ceorl (*Eng. hist.*), burgess, burgher, liveryman, citizen.

free-thinker, *n.* libertine (*disparaging*), antinomian (*B*); *spec.* skeptic, unbeliever.

freeze, *v. t.* **1.** congeal (*contex.*), chill (*contex.*), befreeze (*intensive*).
Antonyms: see BOIL.
2. *See* STICK.

freeze, *v. i.* **1.** cool; *spec.* regelate.
Antonyms: see BOIL.
2. *See* STICK.

freeze, *n.* congelation, cooling; *spec.* frost.

freight, *n.* goods (*chiefly Brit.*); *see* LOAD.

freightage, *n. Spec.* cartage, wagonage, ferriage, *etc.*

freighter, *n. Spec.* loader, forwarder, shipper, vessel.

French, *a.* Gaulish (*B or humorous*), Gallic, Gallican (*B or hist.*); *spec.* Romance, creole, Frenchy, Frenchified.

Frenchify, *v. i. & t.* Gallicize.

Frenchman, *n.* Parleyvoo (*humorous*), Frog (*S*); *spec.* creole.

frenzy, *n.* excitement (*contex.*), passion, transport, ecstasy (*chiefly spec.*); *spec.* rapture, fury, delirament (*R*), heat, rage, furiosity (*R*), furor, orgasm, furiousness, burn (*fig.*), chafe (*A*), rave (*R*), œstrus *or* œstrum, must, distraction, delirium, derangement, enthusiasm, fanaticism, fad; *see also* TRANSPORT.

frenzy, *v. t.* excite, transport, ecstasy (*chiefly spec.*), rap (*chiefly spec.*); *spec.* ravish, rapture, distract, enrapture, impassion, furify (*R*), madden, enrage.

frequency, *n.* **1.** oftenness (*R*), oftness (*A*), thickness (*in space or time*), quotiety (*R*), howmanyness (*R*); *spec.* repetition, habitualness.
Antonyms: see INFREQUENCY.
2. commonness (*cf.* COMMON).

frequent, *a.* **1.** often (*A or R*), thick (*in space or time*); *spec.* many, daily, hourly, rapid, minutely, momentary.
Antonyms: see INFREQUENT.
2. *See* COMMON.

frequent, *v. t.* haunt (*often spec.*); *spec.* infest, affect, visit, use (*R*), attend, ghost (*R*), overrun.

frequentation, *n.* haunting, infestation, visitation, use (*R, exc. spec.*), attendance.

frequenter, *n.* haunter, resorter, habitué (*French*), *etc.*

fresh, *a.* **1.** new, recent; *spec.* green, warm, unfaded.
Antonyms: see ANCIENT.
2. *Referring to meat, vegetables, etc.:* caller (*Scot.*); *spec.* green, uncured, unsmoked, undried, crisp.
Antonyms: see WITHERED.
3. *Referring to water, food, etc.:* unsalted, sweet.
4. *Of the air, etc.: spec.* pure, sweet, refreshing.
Antonyms: see CLOSE.
5. *Spec.* unexhausted, energetic, blooming, clear, strong, vivid, brilliant, additional, green, dewy, unobliterated, brisk.
6. impertinent, disrespectful, presumptuous, *etc.* (*all S uses of* fresh).
Antonyms: see EXHAUSTED, TIRED, WEARIED.

freshen, *v. t.* refresh, revive, liven; *spec.* renew, brighten, quicken, brisk *or* brisken.

freshman, *n.* novice; *spec.* plebe (*U. S.; C*) puny (*Eng.*), bejan (*Scot., but obs. at Edinburgh*).

free-handed: *generous.*
free-hearted: *frank.*
free lance: *adventurer.*
frenetic: *frantic.*
frenzied: *frantic.*
freshet: *flood.*
freshly: *again.*

freshness, *n.* **1.** newness, recency; *spec.* greenness.
2. *Spec.* brilliance, bloom, dewiness, verdure, vigor, flush, glow, energy, strength, *etc.*
Antonyms: see WEARINESS.
fret, *v. t.* **1.** erode, gall, chafe; *see* FRAY.
2. *See* AGITATE, ANNOY, IRRITATE.
fret, *v. i.* **1.** erode, chafe; *spec.* fray.
2. chafe, fume, stew (*C*); *spec.* worry, repine, ferment, boil (*C or S*).
3. *Referring to water, etc.:* roughen, ripple, babble.
fret, *n.* **1.** erosion, chafe; *spec.* breach.
2. agitation, chafe, stew (*C*), fume; *spec.* ferment, fermentation, worry.
friar, *n.* **1.** ecclesiastic (*contex.*), frate (*Italian*), shaveling (*opprobrious*), brother; *spec.* mendicant, breviger (*hist.*), carmelite, Franciscan (*Gray Friar*), Dominican (*Black Friar*), Augustinian, Minimite (*R*), Minim, Minor, tertiary, discalceate, limiter (*hist.*), cordelier (*Franciscan*), calender (*Mohammedan; a loose use*).
2. *See* MONK.
friary, *n.* association (*contex.*), friars (*pl.*), convent.
friend, *n.* **1.** intimate (*contex.*), Damon (*fig.*), familiar, acquaintance (*less intimate than* friend).
Antonyms: see ENEMY.
2. approver (*cf.* APPROVE).
friendliness, *n.* amicability, amity, cordiality; *spec.* brotherliness, neighborliness, kindliness, kindness, *etc.*
Antonyms: see OPPOSITION.
friendly, *a.* **1.** amicable, cordial; *spec.* brotherly, kindly, neighborly, lovesome (*A*), friendlike.
Antonyms: see UNFRIENDLY.
2. *See* FAVORABLE.
frighten, *v. t.* fright (*R or B*), fear (*A*), affray (*R*), affright (*chiefly B*), alarm (*suggesting the causing not only of* fright, *but of apprehension*), scare (*a more C synonym for* fright), fray (*A*), funk (*S*); *spec.* appall, shoo, terrify, terrorize, dismay, gally (*dial. or whaling*), horrify, freeze, cow (*to reduce to terrified or spiritless surrender*), daunt (*to break down the courage of*), startle, consternate, intimidate (*implies threatening, show of force, etc. for the purpose of subduing the spirit*), stampede, drive.
Antonyms: see ENCOURAGE, ENTICE.
frill, *n.* **1.** edging; *spec.* jabot, purl, ruching, ruche (*French*).
2. *See* AFFECTATION.
fringe, *n.* border, edge, fimbriation (*tech.*), fimbrilla (*dim.; tech.*); *spec.* phylactery (*erroneous*), bullion, macramé, bang, fimbria.
fringe, *v. t.* border, edge, fimbriate (*tech.*).
fringed, *a.* bordered, edged, fimbriate (*tech.*), fringy, jubate (*tech.; R*); *spec.* ciliate *or* ciliated, cirrated.
frisky, *a.* lively (*contex.*), antic; *see* FROLICSOME.
frivolity, *n.* frivolousness, lightness, emptiness, foolishness, fribble, levity, flippancy, trifling, flimsiness, silliness, volatility, flightiness, giddiness, frippery, trumpery.
frivolous, *a.* light, empty, foolish, light-minded, light-headed, fribble, contemptuous, trifling, frippery (*contemptuous*), giddy, flimsy, silly, volatile, flighty, frivol (*C or S*), fribblish (*R*), butterfly (*fig.*), unideaed (*R*), jiggish (*R*), trumpery; *spec.* overlight, flippant, hoity-toity.
frock, *n. Spec.* gown, dress, overall, coat, jersey.
frog, *n.* **1.** amphibian (*contex.; tech.*), paddock (*Scot.*); *spec.* frogling, tadpole.
2. *Referring to part of a horse's foot:* cushion, frush.
froglike, *a.* batrachoid, raniform;—*both tech.*
frolic, *n.* play, caper, sport, lark, skylark (*C*), prank, trick (*C*); *spec.* romp, rollick, escapade, racket (*S*), spree (*C*), hoity-toity (*R*), gambol, curvet, frisk, merrymaking, cantrip (*chiefly Scot.*).
frolic, *v. i.* play, prank (*R*), sport; *spec.* rollick, caper, romp, lark, skylark (*C*), freak, frisk, gambol, curvet, wanton, spree (*C*).
frolicsome, *a.* playful, frolic, sportful, sportive, prankful (*R*), prankish (*R*); *spec.* frisky, frisk, larkish (*C*), larky (*C*), larking (*C*), rompish, romping, rompy, wild, skittish, hoity-toity, capersome.
from, *prep.* fro (*Scot. and dial.*); *spec.* with, off, of.
Antonyms: see TOWARD.
front, *n.* **1.** *Spec.* forehead, face, look.
2. fore (*chiefly tech. or a quasi noun*), forepart, forefront (*emphatic*), foreside (*obs. or tech.*); *spec.* van, head, beginning, foreground, proscenium (*tech., exc. B as fig. or transferred*), heading, breast, frontage, belly; *see* FOREGROUND.
Antonyms: see BACK.
3. *Referring to a building:* face, façade, frontal, frontispiece (*R*).
Antonyms: see BACK.
4. *Referring to an army, etc.:* van; *spec.* vanguard.
5. *See* CARRIAGE.
front, *v. t.* **1.** *See* FACE, OPPOSE, MEET, COVER.
2. lead (*go in front*), head (*by having the front place*), face.
frontier, *n.* border, coast (*A*).
frontlet, *n.* band, frontal; *spec.* chamfrain, forestall.
frost, *n.* **1.** *See* FREEZE.
2. *Referring to white frost:* hoarfrost, rime (*B or tech.*), cranreuch (*Scot.*), hoar (*R*).
frosted, *a.* hoary.

---

fret: *ornament, variegate.*
fretful: *irascible, agitated, gusty.*
friction: *rubbing, dissension.*
fright: *fear.*
frightened: *afraid.*
frightful: *alarming.*
frigid: *cold, dull, distant.*
frippery: *finery, show.*
frisk: *caper, frolic, search.*
fritter, *v. t.: break, waste, trifle.*
frivol, *v. i.: trifle.*
frontage: *front.*
frontal: *frontlet, front.*

---

frown, *v. i.* scowl, lower *or* lour, gloom, glout (*R*), glower, cloud (*contex.*).
Antonyms: see SMILE.
frown, *n.* scowl, lower *or* lour, gloom (*chiefly Scot.*), flout (*R*), glower, cloud (*contex.*).
frowning, *a.* scowling, lowering *or* louring, lowry *or* loury, glooming, glowering, clouded (*contex.*), cloudy (*contex.*), threatening.
fructification, *n.* fecundation, fertilization, impregnation; *spec.* masculation, orthogamy, heterogamy, autogamy, self-fertilization.
fructify, *v. t.* fecundate, fertilize (*chiefly spec.*), impregnate (*cause to become pregnant; chiefly spec.*); *spec.* fruit.
fructifying, *a.* fructificative (*R*), fecundatory (*R or tech.*), fertilizing, fructiferous (*R*).
frugal, *a.* **1.** sparing, chary; *spec.* abstemious, economical.
2. *See* SCANTY.
fruit, *n.* **1.** *Spec.* fruitlet, fruitling (*R*), fruitage (*a collective*), follicle, drupel, drupelet, key, samara, legume, mericarp, cremocarp.
2. produce (*a collective sing.*), vegetable (*with no definite distinction from "fruit" in popular use*).
3. *See* PRODUCT, EFFECT, OUTCOME, GOOD, PROFIT.
fruit, *v. i.* fructify; *spec.* bear.
fruit-bearing, *a.* frugiferous (*R*), fructuous (*chiefly spec.*).
fruit-eating, *a.* frugivorous, fructivorous;—*both tech.*
fruitful, *a.* **1.** productive, fertile, fecund (*A or R*), prolific, feracious (*R*), fructuous (*chiefly spec.*); *spec.* teeming, polyphorous (*R*), teemful, promising, potent, pregnant, uberous (*R*); plenteous (*chiefly B*), good, broody *or* breedy (*dial. or C*), exuberant, eugenesic (*R*), fat *or* fatty, rich, gleby (*R*), proliferous;—*many of these terms are used, figuratively or by transfer, of the mind, imagination, etc.*
Antonyms: see BARREN, UNPRODUCTIVE.
2. *See* PRODUCTIVE.
fruit grower, horticulturist (*contex.*): *spec.* orchardist, orchardman.
fruit growing, horticulture (*contex.*); *spec.* pomiculture (*R*), pomology.
fruiting, *n.* fruitage.
fry, *v. t.* cook (*contex.*); *spec.* sauté, frizzle, fricassee.
fry, *n. Spec.* fricandeau, frizzle, fricassee.
fuel, *n.* firing (*Eng. or A*); *spec.* kindling, breeze.
fugitive, *a.* **1.** fleeing; *spec.* runaway, hideaway (*R*).
2. *See* TRANSITORY, EPHEMERAL.

fugitive, *n.* fleer (*R*); *spec.* runaway, vagabond, wanderer, refugee, runagate (*contemptuous*).
fulcrum, *n.* support.
Antonyms: see LEVER.
full, *v. t.* thicken (*contex.*); *spec.* mill.
full, *a.* **1.** replete (*a stronger and more formal term than "full"*), plenitudinary (*R*), plenitudinous (*R*); *spec.* brimful, flush, swollen, chock-full *or* choke-full (*somewhat C*), crammed, crowded, packed, stuffed, overflowing, puffy.
Antonyms: see EMPTY.
2. satisfied, sated *or* satiated; *spec.* gorged (*implying gross gormandizing*), crammed (*C*), stuffed.
3. loose, flowing; *spec.* baggy, foldy (*R*), pouched, pouchy.
4. *Referring to the voice:* rounded, orotund (*B*), rotund (*formal or tech.*).
5. *See* ABSOLUTE, ABOUNDING, COMPLETE, EXHAUSTIVE, DETAILED, CIRCUMSTANTIAL, PLUMP, STRONG.
full, *n.* completion, utmost.
full-blooded, *a.* **1.** plethoric, sanguine, sanguineous, hæmatose (*R*);—*all formal or B.*
2. *Referring to breed, etc.:* pure, true.
Antonyms: see HYBRID.
fuller, *n.* hammer (*contex.*), hardy (*blacksmithing*).
fullness, *n.* **1.** repletion, repleteness (*less usual*), impletion (*R*), plenitude (*B*), plenum (*R*); *spec.* circumstantiality, puffiness, satiety.
Antonyms: see EMPTINESS, VACANCY.
2. *Spec.* completeness, absoluteness, plumpness, rotundity, abundance, *etc.*
fulvous, *a.* yellow, fulvic (*R*); *spec.* tawny, tan.
fumigate, *v. t.* **1.** reek, suffumigate (*R*), fume; *spec.* smoke, match, disinfect.
2. *See* PERFUME.
fun, *n.* **1.** *Spec.* humor, wit, drollery, waggishness, waggery (*R*).
2. *See* DIVERSION, PLAY.
function, *n.* **1.** activity, duty, office, province, service.
2. *See* ACTION, CEREMONY.
3. *In math.:* *spec.* sine, cosine, secant, cosecant, logarithm, intermediate, faculty, *etc.*
function, *v. i.* act (*contex.*), functionate (*R*), serve.
fund, *n.* accumulation, stock, supply; *spec.* box, reserve, pool, bank, capital, endowment.
fundamental, *a.* basic, basal, underlying, ground, bottom, basilar (*R*); *spec.* cardinal; *see* ELEMENTARY, ESSENTIAL.
Antonyms: see ACCIDENTAL.
funereal, *a.* **1.** burial (*contex.*), funeral, feral

frosty: *cold, gray.*
froth, *n.: foam, nonsense.*
froward: *perverse.*
frowzy: *slovenly, red, red-faced, moldy.*
frozen: *congealed, cold.*
fruition: *enjoyment.*
fruitless: *barren, ineffectual.*
frustrate: *defeat.*
fuddle, *v. t.: confuse.*
fuddle, *v. i.: drink.*
fudge, *v. t.: fake.*
fudge, *n.: nonsense.*
fulcrum, *n.: support.*
fulfill: *accomplished, satisfy, obey, perform.*
fulfillment: *accomplishment, satisfaction, obedience, performance.*
fulgent: *luminous.*
fuliginous: *dark, smoky.*
fulminate, *v. i.: explode, flash, curse.*
fulminate, *v. t.: explode, denounce.*
fulsome: *excessive.*
fulsomeness: *excess.*
fumble: *feel, mismanage.*
fume, *v. i.: smoke, exhale, fret.*
fume, *v. t.: smoke, exhale, fumigate.*
fume, *n.: smoke, exhalation, smell, fret, fit.*
fumy: *smoky, vaporous.*
functionary: *officer.*
fundament: *buttocks.*
fundamental, *n.: basis, element.*
fundus: *base.*

(*R*), exequial (*R*), epicedial (*R*), funebrial (*R*), sepulchral; *spec.* funerary, elegiac.
2. *See* DARK, GLOOMY, SORROWFUL.
fungus, *n. Spec.* mushroom, toadstool, bunt, fuzzball, bullfist, puffball, mold, rust, smut, agaric, mildew, tuckahoe, champignon, truffle, morel, *etc.*
funnel, *n.* channel, tunnel (*R*); *spec.* infundibulum.
funnel-shaped, *a.* choanoid (*tech.*), infundibuliform (*tech.*).
funny, *a. Spec.* humorous, facetious, grotesque; *see* COMIC, LAUGHABLE, ODD.
fur, *n.* skin (*contex.*), coat (*contex.*); *spec.* flix (*R*), flick (*dial.*), calaber, ermine, ermines, erminites, erminois, budge, miniver, pean, pashm, sable, kolinsky, woom (*cant*), vair, beaver, seal, *etc.*
furl, *v. t. Naut.:* stow, hand.
furled, *a.* in (*used predicatively*).
furnace, *n. Spec.* cupola, forge, calcar, kiln, chauffer, reverberatory, revolver, retort, roaster.
furnish, *v. t.* **1.** provide, supply, dight (*A or dial.*); *spec.* equip, accommodate, endow, store.
2. supply, produce, give, yield, find, provide, afford (*B*); *spec.* advance, lend, sell, rent, *etc.*
furnished, *a.* equipped, found, beseen (*A*), *etc.*
furnishing, *n.* **1.** *Referring to the action:* provision, supplial, suppliance (*R*), furnishment (*R*); *spec.* purveyance, equipment, accommodation, endowment.
2. *Often in pl.:* equipment.
3. provision, supply, yield; *spec.* product, find, advance, loan, *etc.*
furniture, *n.* furnishing (*often in pl.*), equipment; *spec.* drapery, coverlet, hangings, bedding.
furrow, *n.* depression (*contex.*); *spec.* trench, channel, track, seam, groove, rut, cut, wrinkle, line, drill, scratch.
furrow, *v. t. Spec.* channel, seam, plow, wrinkle, intrench (*R*), trench, ditch, rut, corrugate, cleave, cut.
furrowy, *a. Spec.* guttery, rutty, wrinkly.
further, *adv.* besides, beside, else; *see* ALSO.
fury, *n.* **1.** *See* FRENZY, ANGER, FIT, VIOLENCE.
2. Diræ (*Latin; pl.*), Erinnyes (*Greek; pl.*), Eumenides (*Greek, euphemistic; pl.*); *spec.* Tisiphone, Megæra, Alecto.
3. *See* TERMAGANT.
furze, *n.* gorze, whin.
fusible, *a.* meltable (*R*), fluxible (*A*), fusile (*R*).
Antonyms: see REFRACTORY.
fuss, *n.* disturbance, ado (*chiefly B*), to-do (*C*), pucker (*C*), fidge (*C*); *spec.* commotion, tumult, stir, pother, boggle, fizz (*C*), bustle, fluster, fiddle-faddle, fidfad (*R*), fret, worry.
fuss, *v. i.* pucker (*C; R*), fike (*Scot.*), fidge (*C*); *spec.* potter, boggle, fizz (*C*), bustle, fret, worry.
future, *a.* coming, forward (*commercial*); *spec.* prospective.
Antonyms: see PAST.
future, *n.* futurity (*dignified*), futurition (*philos.*), by-and-by (*chiefly B in suggestion*), to-come (*R*), yet (*used with "the"; R*), to-be (*R*); *spec.* tomorrow (*often fig.*), ulterior, hereafter.
Antonyms: see PAST, PRESENT.

G

gadfly, *n.* fly (*contex.*), breeze, gadbee (*dial. or B*), clog (*Scot. & dial. Eng.*).
gaff, *v. t. Spec.* spear, hook, gambeer.
gain, *n.* **1.** *See* ACQUISITION, BENEFIT, PROFIT.
2. addition (*contex.*), accretion (*contex.*); *spec.* advantage, graft, plunder, booty, clean-up (*U. S.*), winning, emolument, gettings (*pl.; A*), superlucration (*R*), gravy (*C, U. S.*).
Antonyms: see LOSS.
gain, *v. t.* **1.** get, acquire, reap (*fig.*), obtain; *spec.* procure, earn, gather, superlucrate (*R*), net, clear, profit.
Antonyms: see FORFEIT.
2. *See* INCUR, WIN, REACH.
gait, *n.* **1.** step; *spec.* slouch, swing, clip (*C*), amble, hobble, canter, dog trot, gallop, jog, jog trot, rack, pace, singlefoot (*U. S.*), lope, trot, run, walk, shamble, saunter, stalk, stride, hobble, swing, roll, volley, piaffer.
2. *See* CARRIAGE.
gaiter, *n.* legging (*contex.*), continations (*pl.; S*); *spec.* squatterdash, spats (*pl.*), gambado.
gallant, *n. Spec.* blade, escort, gigolo, cicisbeo (*a* gallant *of a married woman*).
gallery, *n.* **1.** *Spec.* corridor, loft, balcony, veranda, portico, cantarina, traverse, triforium, loggia, drift.

---

funk, *n.: fear.*
funk, *v. t.: evade.*
funk, *v. i.: shrink.*
furbish: *polish, renovate, renew.*
furcate, *a.: forked.*
furious: *angry, violent, frantic, extravagant.*
furor: *frenzy, fad.*
further, *a.: farther, additional.*
further, *v. t.: aid, advance.*
furtherance: *aid.*
furthermore: *besides.*
furtive: *thievish, secret, sneaking, stealthy.*
fuse, *v. t.: liquefy, smelt, unite.*
fusillade: *discharge.*
fusion: *liquefaction, union.*
fuss, *v. t.: disturb, confuse.*
fustian, *n.: bombast.*
fusty: *moldy, close, old-fashioned.*
futile: *ineffectual, trivial.*
futurity: *future, event.*
fuzz: *fluff.*

G

gab: *talk.*
gabble: *babble, chatter, cackle.*
gad: *wander.*
gag, *v. t.: choke.*
gag, *v. i.: retch.*
gag, *n.: deception, interpolation.*
gage: *pledge, surety.*
gain, *v. i.: benefit, graft, advance.*
gainful: *advantageous, profitable, beneficial.*
gainsay: *contradict.*
gait, *v. t.: adjust.*
galaxy: *assembly.*
gale: *wind, fit.*
gall, *n.: annoyance, impudence.*
gall, *v. t.: fret, vex.*
gallant, *a.: showy, brave, polite.*
gallant, *v. t.: court, escort.*
gallant, *v. i.: flirt.*
gallantness: *bravery, amour.*
gallantry: *bravery, show, politeness.*
galled: *vexed.*

---

2. *Referring to part of an audience: spec.* gods (*pl.; cant or S*).
gallop, *v. t. & i. Spec.* canter, run.
gallop, *n.* gait (*contex.*); *spec.* tantivy, canter.
gallows, *n.* bough (*A*), tree (*A*), gibbet (*obs.*).
gallows, *a.* patibulary (*R*).
gallowsbird, *n.* (*C*), criminal (*contex.*), hempstring, hempseed (*nonce; Shakespeare*).
gamble, *v. i.* **1.** play (*contex.*), game, gaff (*Eng. S or colonial*); *spec.* dice, throw, punt, plunge.
2. *See* WAGER.
gamble, *v. t.* risk (*contex.*), wager.
gamble, *n.* chance; *spec.* wager, risk, plunge, pyramid.
gambler, *n.* **1.** player (*contex.*), sport (*cant*); *spec.* gamester, gamestress (*fem.*), dicer, hazarder, plunger, punter.
2. wagerer (*cf.* WAGER).
game, *n.* quarry.
game, *n.* **1.** *See* SPORT.
2. diversion (*contex.*); *spec.* contest.
3. *See* RIDICULE, PLAN.
4. *Referring to a single contest: spec.* pancratium, Olympic, Marathon.
5. hunt, chase; *spec.* victim, butt.
Antonyms: see HUNTER.
gamekeeper, *n.* ranger (*A*); *spec.* venerer (*R*).
gang, *n.* **1.** company, crew.
2. *See* SET, ASSOCIATION.
gangrene, *n.* death (*contex.*), necrobiosis (*tech.*), mortification, necrosis (*tech.*).
gangrene, *v. i.* die, mortify, necrose (*tech.*).
gangrenous, *a.* dead, mortified, necrose (*tech.*), cankerous (*R*).
gap, *n.* **1.** *See* BREACH.
2. opening (*contex.*), break, vacancy, gape (*R*), space; *spec.* lacuna, jump, hiatus, chasm, pass, ravine, rictus, yawn, intermission, pause.
gape, *v. i.* open (*contex.*), hiate (*R*), gaup *or* gawp (*dial.*), inhiate (*R*); *spec.* yawn, dehisce.
gaping, *a.* agape, hiant (*chiefly hist.*); *spec.* yawning, ringent, patulous, patulent (*R*), dehiscent, loculicidal.
garden, *n. Spec.* potagerie (*French*), herbary, nursery, Lyceum.
gardener, *n.* mallee (*Anglo-Indian*); *spec.* horticulturist, florist.
gardening, *a.* hortulan (*R*), hortensial (*R*), hortensian (*R*); *spec.* topiary.
gardening, *n.* horticulture; *spec.* floriculture, olericulture, viniculture.
gargle, *v. t.* rinse (*contex.*), wash, gargarize (*R*).
gargle, *n.* wash (*contex.*), gargarism (*med.; R*), collutory (*tech.*).
garment, *n.* **1.** confection (*a Gallicism*), rag (*derogatory*), cloth (*obs.*), vestment (*rhetorical or spec.*), wearable (*C*); *spec.* shroud (*B or A*), covering, habit, abolla, slops (*pl.*), frock, fur, gown, *etc.*
2. *In pl.: see* CLOTHING.
garret, *n.* attic, soler (*obs. or R*).
garrison, *n.* post (*U. S.*).
garter, *n.* sock suspender (*chiefly Brit.*).
gas, *n.* **1.** fluid (*contex.*); *spec.* choke, damp, flatus, mafette, argon, oxygen, hydrogen, nitrogen, chlorine, *etc.*
2. *See* BOMBAST.
3. gasoline (*U. S.*), petrol (*Brit.*), fuel.
gaseous, *a.* fluid (*contex.*), gassy, gasiform, airy (*now R or spec.*); *spec.* aeriform.
gash, *v. t. & n.* cut (*contex.*), crimp (*chiefly spec.*), scratch, score, slash, scotch.
gasoline, *n.* petrol (*Brit.*), gas (*cant or C*).
gasp, *v. i.* breathe (*contex.*), catch; *spec.* chink, pant, labor, choke (*contex.*).
gastronomic, *a.* esurient (*an incorrect use; properly "pertaining to love of eating or appetite"*).
gate, *n.* **1.** opening (*contex.*), passageway (*contex.*), portal (*elevated term*), gateway (*often used fig. for sense of unfolding opportunity*), port (*now chiefly Scot.*), pylon (*archæol.*), arch, toran, porte-cochère (*French*), floodgate, sluice, turnpike, wicket, lich-gate.
2. door (*contex.*), shuttle, portcullis, wicket, lattice, hatch.
gatekeeper, *n.* porter (*the more formal term*).
gather, *v. t.* **1.** assemble (*whereas* gather *commonly implies nothing more than the fact of bringing together,* assemble *and* collect *imply choice and selection, and* group *implies in addition, arrangement*), collect, group; *spec.* lump, mass, huddle, herd, rake (*with "up"*), crowd, congregate, rally, aggregate, flocculate (*R*), forgather, ingather, cluster, drum, whip, cull, glean, bring in, harvest, shock, clump, stack, bunch, convene, mobilize.
Antonyms: see SCATTER, SEPARATE, DISPERSE.
2. *In sewing, etc.: spec.* shirr, pucker, full.
3. *See* ACCUMULATE, WIN, INFER, GAIN.
gather, *v. i.* **1.** assemble, collect, group, congregate, forgather, aggregate; *spec.* bunch, convene, huddle.
Antonyms: see DISPERSE, SCATTER, STRAY.
2. *See* INCREASE, SUPPURATE.
gather, *n.* gathering; *spec.* shirr, pucker.
gathering, *n.* **1.** *The act or action:* assembly, assemblage, collection, forgathering, grouping; *spec.* congregation, convention, aggregation, mobilization, clustering, *etc.*
2. *Those gathered, considered collectively:* assemblage, body, collection, group; *spec.* crowd,

---

gally: *bitter.*
galore: *abundantly.*
game, *a.: disabled.*
game, *v. i.: gamble.*
game, *a.: brave, constant.*
gamesome: *frolicsome, merry.*
gamester: *gambler.*
gamut: *scale, compass.*
gamy: *brave, constant, ill-smelling.*
gang: *set, association.*
gaol: *prison;—var. of jail.*
gap: *breach.*
garb, *n.: costume, clothing.*
garb, *v. t.: clothe.*
garble: *deface, pervert.*
garish: *showy, bright.*
garland: *wreath.*
garment: *clothe.*
garner, *n.: granary.*
garner, *v. t.: accumulate, store.*
garnish, *n.: ornament.*
garnishment: *ornamentation.*
garret: *attic.*
garrison, *v. t.: man.*
garrote: *strangle.*
garrulous: *talkative.*
gascon, *a.: boasting.*
gascon, *n.: boaster.*
gauche, *a.: awkward.*
gaud: *gewgaw.*

---

throng, bunch, drum, convention, congregation, aggregation, rally, herd, flock, cluster; *see* ASSEMBLY, CONVENTION.
3. *See* ACCUMULATION.
gaudy, *a.* showy; *spec.* tawdry, tinsel, garish, flashy, gimcrack, brummagem, cheap.
Antonyms: see SIMPLE, MODEST.
gauge, *v. t.* **1.** measure, estimate.
2. adjust.
gauge, *n.* **1.** *See* MEASURE, EXTENT.
2. *Spec.* templet, fence, manometer.
gawk, *n.* simpleton (*contex.*), clown, gawky, booby, jay (*C or S*); *spec.* calf (*C*), sight (*C*).
gay, *a.* **1.** lively, vivacious, airy, blithe, gaysome (*R*), merry, jolly, jovial (*more B than "jolly"*), mirthful, galliard (*A*); *spec.* wild, riotous, festive, light-hearted, mad, hilarious, gleeful, gaudy, jaunty, sportive, sprightly, convivial, frolicsome, gamesome, merrymaking, frivolous, jubilant, showy.
Antonyms: see SAD, SULLEN.
2. *See* BRIGHT.
gayety, *n.* **1.** liveliness, vivacity, vivaciousness, airiness, joyance, merriness, merriment, mirth, mirthfulness, galliardise (*A*); *spec.* hilarity, hilariousness, jauntiness, sportiveness, merrymaking, frivolity, jubilance.
Antonyms: see ENNUI.
2. *See* BRIGHTNESS.
gaze, *v. i.* look (*contex.*); *spec.* muse (*B*), pore, stare, ogle, gape, glower, gloat, glare, leer.
gelatinous, *a.* colloid (*tech.*), tremellose (*tech.*); *spec.* gelatiniform.
gelding, *n.* neuter (*R*); *spec.* ridgeling, ridgel.
gem, *n.* jewel, stone; *spec.* solitaire, scarab, hyacinth, diamond, ruby, sardine, sapphire, tiger's-eye, moonstone, bloodstone, opal, amethyst, topaz, turquoise, pearl, emerald, garnet, carbuncle, *etc.*
gemlike, *a.* gemmy, gemmeous (*R*).
genealogy, *n.* history (*contex.*), generation (*R*); *spec.* pedigree, tree.
general, *a.* **1.** universal (*with* catholic, *implies no exception to the generally widespread and inclusive quality*), catholic (*chiefly eccl.*); *spec.* cosmic (*literally like* universal, *pertaining to the cosmos or* universe; *more commonly both are used fig.*), œcumenical, heavenwide, nationwide, statewide; generic (*contex.*).
Antonyms: see PARTICULAR, MINUTE, NARROW, INDIVIDUAL, LOCAL, SPECIFIC.
2. *In a less inclusive sense:* widespread, common (*shared by many together*), wide, broad (*less emphatic than "wide"*); *spec.* generic, main, impersonal, popular, current, indefinite, bird's-eye, usual, customary.
Antonyms: see CIRCUMSTANTIAL, PARTICULAR.
generalize, *v. t.* broaden, universalize, spread.
generate, *v. t.* **1.** beget (*chiefly spec.*), breed (*chiefly spec.*), create (*contex.*), reproduce (*biol.*), produce (*young*), procreate, conceive (*in the womb*), engender, propagate; *spec.* spawn (*contemptuous*), bear, pullulate, inbreed.
Antonyms: see KILL.
2. *See* CAUSE.
generate, *v. i.* breed, reproduce, grow, produce, conceive, propagate (*chiefly tech.*); *spec.* hatch, segment, increase, proliferate, teem, multiply, inbreed.
Antonyms: see DIE.
generation, *n.* **1.** begetting, breeding, production, genesis (*R*), reproduction, procreation, propagation (*chiefly tech.*); *spec.* increase, proliferation, isogamy, theogony, ontogeny, histogenesis, heterogenesis.
2. *Referring to those living during a certain period:* age, descent.
generative, *a.* **1.** reproductive, progenitive, creative, genial (*R*), genital (*chiefly spec.*); *spec.* proligerous (*R*), proliferous, conceptive, germinative, gametal.
2. *See* PRODUCTIVE, CAUSATIVE.
generosity, *n.* **1.** greatness, large-heartedness, magnanimity (*formal*), nobility, magnanimousness; *spec.* loftiness, courage.
Antonyms: meanness (*see* MEAN); *see* SELFISHNESS.
2. generousness, free-heartedness, liberality, handsomeness (*R*), bounty, frankness (*obs.*), freedom (*R*); *spec.* benevolence, royalty, munificence, prodigality, lavishness.
Antonyms: stinginess (*see* STINGY).
3. *See* ABUNDANCE.
generous, *a.* **1.** great (*contex.*), magnanimous (*formal*), ingenuous, large-hearted, great-hearted, big-hearted (*more C*), noble; *spec.* lofty, courageous, chivalrous, beneficent.
Antonyms: see MEAN.
2. *Referring to the opposite of "stingy":* free-hearted, open-hearted, open-handed, open (*C*), free, liberal, free-handed, frank (*obs.*), handsome, large (*A*), bounteous, bountiful; *spec.* munificent, lavish, prodigal, benevolent, stintless.
Antonyms: see STINGY, GREEDY, PALTRY, SELFISH.
3. *See* ABUNDANT.
genius, *n.* **1.** demon (*contex.*), spirit (*contex.*); *spec.* python (*New Testament*), jinni, jinn (*pl.; improperly used as sing.*).
2. angel (*chiefly with "good" or "bad"*), spirit (*chiefly with "a good" or "a bad"*).
3. *See* CAPACITY, SPIRIT, TALENT.
gentile, *n.* **1.** *See* HEATHEN.
2. non-Jew, uncircumscision (*with "the"*).
gentle, *a.* **1.** well-born, generous (*A*), good.
2. *See* TAME.
3. mild (*a weaker word than "gentle"*), light, soft, moderate; *spec.* benign, silken, soothing, kind, lenient, low, complaisant, amiable, *etc.*

gauge, *v. t.: measure, adjust.*
gaunt: *thin, repellent.*
gauzy: *filmy.*
gawky: *awkward.*
gear, *n.: dress, clothing, equipment, apparatus, cogwheel, goods.*
gelid: *cold.*
generic: *general.*
genie: *demon.*
genre: *style.*
genteel: *polite, noble, elegant, stylish.*
gentile, *a.: heathen, racial.*

Antonyms: see ROUGH, SEVERE, SHARP, STERN, VIOLENT, HARSH, FIERCE, CRUEL, AUSTERE, BLOODTHIRSTY, BLUNT, OUTRAGEOUS.
4. *Referring to a slope, climb, etc.:* moderate, gradual, slight, easy.
Antonyms: see PRECIPITOUS.

gentleman, *n.* **1.** gent (*vulgar*), aristocrat, caballero (*Spanish*), duniwassal (*chiefly spec.; Scot.*); *spec.* esquire (*Eng.*), hidalgo (*Spanish*), cavalier.
Antonyms: see BOOR.
2. *See* MAN.

gentleness, *n.* **1.** mildness, lightness, softness, moderateness, moderation; *spec.* easiness, benignity, faintness, soothingness, kindness, lenience, complaisance, amenity, milkiness (*R*).
Antonyms: see VIOLENCE, SHARPNESS, CRUELTY, FEROCITY, SEVERITY.
2. *Referring to a slope, climb, etc.:* moderateness, gradualness, slightness, easiness.

genuine, *a.* **1.** true, right, real, veritable, proper (*R*), indeed (*predicative*); *spec.* Simon Pure, honest, 100% (*C, U. S.*), true-blue; *see* AUTHENTIC.
Antonyms: see ARTIFICIAL.
2. *See* SINCERE, FRANK.

germ, *n.* **1.** germen (*now only fig.*), embryo, seed (*now chiefly spec.*), seminium (*R*), seminary (*R*).
2. *See* ELEMENT.
3. microörganism, seed (*spec. or fig.*); *spec.* microbe, bacterium.

germicide, *a. Spec.* antiseptic, bactericide.

germinate, *v. i.* grow (*contex.*), germ (*now fig.*), burgeon, germin (*A*), germinate (*R*), generate; *spec.* sprout, shoot, pullulate (*R*), blade, bud, vegetate, catch, set.
Antonyms: see DIE.

germinate, *v. t.* cause (*contex.*), germ (*R*); *spec.* sprout.

gestural, *a.* gesticulative, gesticular, gesticulatory, pantomimic (*chiefly spec.*), pantomimical (*R*).

gesture, *n.* **1.** motion (*contex.*), gest (*A*); *spec.* gesticulation, beck, sign, fig, wave, puff, signal.
2. *In a generic sense:* gesticulation, chironomy (*R*), dumb, show, pantomime (*chiefly spec.*).

gesture, *v. i.* motion, gesticulate, pantomime (*R*), sign; *spec.* wave, ramp, beckon, signal.

gesturing, *a.* gesticulant (*R*).

get, *v. t.* **1.** obtain, procure, raise, gain, secure, have, acquire; *spec.* achieve, take, win, glean, borrow, sponge, wangle (*C, for get by devious means*), impetrate, find, draw, elicit, wheedle, coax, derive, learn, attain, forage, mine, snatch, hire, catch, capture, *etc.*
Antonyms: see MISS.
2. *See* NONPLUS, INDUCE, TAKE (*oneself*), BEGET.

gettable, *a.* obtainable, come-at-able (*C*), havable (*R*).
Antonyms: see INACCESSIBLE.

getting, *n.* obtainment, obtainal (*R*), obtention (*R*), procurement, securement (*R*), procuration; *spec.* impetration, acquirement, elicitation, derivation, *etc.; see* ACQUISITION.

gewgaw, *n.* trifle, trinket, toy (*obs., exc. spec.*); *spec.* kickshaw, knickknack, gimcrack, fizgig, gaud (*B*), bauble, falderal *or* folderol, fallal, flapdoodle (*contemptuous; C*), flamfew (*R*).

ghastly, *a.* **1.** *See* FEARFUL.
2. pale, deathly, corpselike, ghast (*A or B*); *spec.* cadaverous, lurid.

ghost, *n.* **1.** *See* SOUL, DEMON, APPEARANCE.
2. apparition, larva (*obs. or hist.*), larve (*hist.*), spirit, specter, phantom, phantasm (*B or rhetorical*), phantasme (*R*), revenant (*rather B or cant*), shadow (*R*), shade (*chiefly spec.*), sprite *or* (*A*) spright (*R*), spook (*C*).
Antonyms. see BODY.

ghostly, *a.* **1.** *See* SPIRITUAL.
2. ghostlike, spectral, spookish (*C*), phantasmal, phantom, shadowy, ghosty (*jocular*), spooky (*C*).
Antonyms: see BODILY.

giant, *n. Spec.* giantess, colossus, jumbo (*C*), Goliath (*fig.*), polyheme (*R*).
Antonyms: see DWARF.

gibbet, *n.* gallows, patible (*R*); *spec.* cross, rood (*A*).

gift, *n.* **1.** *See* GIVING.
2. present, liberality (*R*), donation (*chiefly spec.*); *spec.* bonus, premium, prize, dole, contribution, mite, favor, testimonial, gratification, offering, boon, oblation, gratuity, bounty, propine (*A or Scot.*), largess, fairing, benevolence, donary (*R*), grant, tip, benefaction, cumshaw (*Chinese ports*), baksheesh, concession, honorarium, merced (*Spanish*), dash *or* dashee (*African coast*), pittance, alms, charity, pilon (*southwestern U. S.*), pilonce (*Texas*), pilonvillo (*Texas*), lagniappe (*New Orleans*), donative, legacy, bequest, devise, benefit, enam (*India*), batta (*Anglo-Indian*), bribe, handsel, favor, mortuary, khilat *or* khelat (*East India*), feu, ormolu, congiary (*Roman hist.*), nuzzer (*Anglo-Indian*).
Antonyms: see DEMAND.
3. *See* ENDOWMENT, ABILITY, TALENT.

gig, *n.* chaise; *spec.* whisky, tilbury.

gigantic, *a.* **1.** immense, colossal, elephantine, Titanic (*spec. or fig.*), Herculean (*spec. or fig.*), Cyclopean (*spec. or fig.*), Brobdingnagian *or* (*incorrectly*) Brobdignagian (*spec. or fig. and ironical*), monstrous (*spec.*) *or* (*C*) monster.
Antonyms: see DWARF.

---

gestate: *develop.*
gestation: *pregnancy.*
gesticulate: *gesture.*
get, *v. i.: become.*
get, *n.: offspring, begetting.*
get-up: *form.*
geyser: *spring.*
ghoul: *demon.*
gibber: *chatter.*
gibbous: *convex, humpbacked, protuberant.*
gibe: *jeer.*
giddy: *dizzy, frivolous.*
gifted: *able.*
giggle: *laugh.*

2. *See* ENORMOUS.

gild, *v. t.* adorn, deaurate (*R*), engild (*B; often fig.*); *spec.* begild, overgild.

gilded, *a.* aureate (*B*), inaurate (*R*).

gin, *n.* liquor (*contex.*), ribbon (*S; cant*), satin (*S*), eyewater (*S*), deadly (*S*), juniper (*S*), jacky *or* jackey (*S*); *spec.* schiedam, Hollands, schnapps.

gird, *v. t.* **1.** encircle (*contex.*); *spec.* girt, bind, belt, surcingle.

2. *See* INVEST, PREPARE, BRACE, SURROUND, BESIEGE.

girdle, *n.* band (*contex.*), girth, cingle (*B; chiefly spec.*); *spec.* brail, cincture (*B*), belt, cingulum (*tech.*), truss, sash, cummerbund (*Anglo-Indian*), scarf, cestus (*Roman antiq.*), zone (*B or Greek antiq.*), zoster (*Greek antiq.*).

girdle, *v. t.* bind (*contex.*), encircle (*contex.*), girth, engird (*B*), engirdle (*B*), circuit (*contex.*).

2. *Referring to a tree:* ring, ringbark.

girdled, *a.* precinct (*R*); *spec.* succinct.

girl, *n.* **1.** child (*contex.*), maid (*A or playful*), lass (*chiefly dial.*), lassie (*chiefly Scot.*), maiden (*elevated*), damsel, damoiselle (*French*), colleen (*Anglo-Irish*), wench (*A or derogatory*), girly (*C*), tot (*obs. or R*); *spec.* girleen (*Anglo-Irish*), giglet, dell (*A, cant*), flapper (*S*), lassock (*Scot.*), missy, minx, hussy, baggage, cummer (*Scot.*), gill (*R, exc. in "Jack and Gill"*), whelp (*contemptuous*), cub, skirt (*S, U. S.*), Jane (*S, U. S.*).

2. *See* DOMESTIC.

girlhood, *n.* lassiehood (*chiefly Scot.*), maidenhood, girlishness (*R*), maidhood (*R*).

girlish, *a.* childish, maidenish, girly (*C*), maidenly (*commendatory*), S. S. and G. (*cant for* "sweet, simple and girlish," *usually contemptuous*).

girth, *n.* **1.** band (*contex.*), girdle, bellyband (*sometimes spec.*); *spec.* roller, cinch, surcingle.

2. *See* CIRCUMFERENCE, GIRDLE.

gist, *n.* **1.** reason, ground, basis;—*referring to a legal action.*

2. *See* ESSENCE.

givable, *a.* dative (*law*), grantable, conferable, bestowable, *etc.*

give, *v. t.* **1.** present, confer, bequeath (*A or spec.*), grant; *spec.* donate (*chiefly U. S.*), contribute, dole, lend, heap (*with "upon"*), distribute, begrudge, club, offer, produce, emit, utter, entail, devise, entrust, *etc.*

Antonyms: see BEG, DEMAND.

2. *In various secondary senses: see* AFFORD, COMMUNICATE, REQUITE (*give in return*), ADMINISTER, ADDICT, APPLY, ATTRIBUTE, DELIVER, DEAL, SHOW, GRANT, ADJUDGE.

give-and-take, *n.* giff-gaff (*Scot. and dial. Eng.*).

giver, *n.* presenter, donor (*tech., spec. or formal*), donator (*R*), conferrer, granter; *spec.* contributor.

giving, *n.* **1.** gift (*chiefly of a single act*), presentation, conferment, present (*R*), conferral, largition (*R*), bestowal, bestowment, grant (*chiefly spec. or formal*), donation (*chiefly spec.*); *spec.* disposal, disposition, dation, conveyance, dealing, colportage, collation.

2. *See* COMMUNICATION, DELIVERY, PRODUCTION, *etc.*

glad, *a.* happy, content, joyful; *spec.* blithe, festal, blessed, blithesome, beatific, blissful; *see* ECSTATIC.

gladden, *v. t.* please (*contex.*), happify (*now R*), happy (*obs.*), content, contented, rejoice; *spec.* gratify, beatify, blithen, exhilarate, transport; *see* CHEER.

Antonyms: see SADDEN, GRIEVE, DEPRESS.

glade, *n.* opening, laund (*A*), lawn (*A*).

gladiator, *a.* *Spec.* retiarius, swordsman, andabate, secutor.

gladness, *n.* pleasure (*contex.*), felicity, happiness, content, rejoicement (*R*), rejoicing; *spec.* joy, joyance (*B*), bliss, blitheness, transport, *etc.; see* ECSTASY.

glance, *v. i.* **1.** strike (*contex.*), slant, glint (*chiefly Eng.*); *spec.* skip, ricochet, glide, skim.

2. *See* FLASH.

3. look (*contex.*); *spec.* flash, run, glimpse, blink, peep, peek.

glance, *n.* **1.** stroke (*contex.*), glint (*chiefly Eng.*); *spec.* glide, skip, skim, ricochet, graze.

2. *See* FLASH, INTIMATION.

3. look (*contex.*); *spec.* flash, blink, glimpse, cast, blush (*only in "at first blush"*), ray, beam, coup-d'œil (*French*), peep, ogle, peek.

gland, *n.* kernel (*R or dial*); *spec.* glandule, prostate, sweetbread, thymus, pancreas, liver, parotid, *etc.*

glass, *n.* **1.** *Spec.* glazing (*collective*), obsidian, crystal, Pele's hair, chark (*Russian*), hæmatinon, smalt, *etc.*

2. *Referring to a thing made of glass: spec.* bumper, tumbler, goblet, lens, mirror, slide, goggles (*pl.*), blinkers (*pl.; C*), telescope, microscope, eyeglass, spectacles (*pl.*), binocle, binocular, hourglass, chromatic, *etc.*

glasshouse, *n.* *Spec.* hothouse, greenhouse, coolhouse, conservatory, stove.

glassy, *a.* vitreous (*more tech. than "glassy"*), vitric (*chiefly as opposed to "ceramic"*), hyaline (*chiefly tech. and spec.*), hyaloid (*R, exc. anat.*); *spec.* hyalescent, subvitreous.

glaze, *n.* **1.** coat (*contex.*), coating (*contex.*); *spec.* glost, varnish, enamel. *"Glaze" is often*

gingerly: *careful.*
girt, *v.: gird.*
girt, *n.: circumference, dimension.*
given: *addicted, assumed.*
glabrous: *smooth.*
glacé: *smooth, iced.*
glacial: *crystal.*
glacis: *bank, slope.*
glair, *n.: white, shine.*
glair, *a : smooth.*
glamour: *magic, attraction, bewitchery bewitchment, captivation.*
glare, *v. i.: shine, gaze.*
glare, *n.: brightness, show.*
glaring, *a.: fierce, bright, showy, conspicuous.*
glaze, *v. t.: polish.*

used in the U. S. spec. of thin ice or the surface of ice.
2. *See* LUSTER.
glide, *v. i. Spec.* lapse (*chiefly fig.*), glissade, fleet, illapse (*R*), slide, slip, sail, fly, float, flow, coast, skate, swim, skim.
Antonyms: see BUSTLE, JERK.
gliding, *a. Spec.* lapsing, slipping, sliding, perterlabent, flowing, *etc.*
globular, *a.* globose, globate; *spec.* pilular, pilulous.
globule, *n.* sphere, spherule, globelet (*R*); *spec.* drop, bulb, bead, pill, pellet, button, bullet.
gloom, *n.* **1.** gloominess, shade, shadow, obscurity; *see* DARK, DARKNESS.
2. *See* CHEERLESSNESS.
gloomy, *a.* **1.** dreary, drear (*chiefly B*), cheerless, doleful; *spec.* bleak, funereal, desolate, morbid.
Antonyms: see CHEERFUL, CHEERING, GLAD.
2. *See* CHEERLESS, DARK, DEPRESSED, DEPRESSING.
glory, *n.* **1.** *See* FAME, DIGNITY, HONOR, BEAUTY, BRILLIANCE, PROSPERITY.
2. *Spec.* gloriole (*R*), aureole, halo, nimbus, vesica.
gloss, *n.* **1.** *See* LUSTER.
2. *Spec.* (*in figurative or transferred senses*) veneer, whitewash (*C*), color, varnish, veil, smooth.
glove, *n. Spec.* gauntlet, muffler *or* muffle, mousquetaire, mitt, mitten.
glow, *v. i.* **1.** radiate (*contex.*), incandesce (*tech.*); *spec.* burn.
2. *Referring to colors: spec.* blaze, fire, bloom, blush, flush.
3. *Referring to bodily feeling: spec.* burn, swelter, sizzle (*C*), toast, roast (*C*), cook (*C*), bake (*C*), boil (*C*).
4. *Referring to the emotions: spec.* burn, fire, inflame (*R*), consume.
glow, *n.* **1.** luminosity, incandescence (*tech.*); *spec.* burning.
2. *Referring to colors:* warmth, flush; *spec.* blaze, brilliance, bloom, redness, flush.
3. *See* ARDOR.
4. *Referring to bodily feeling:* warmth; *spec.* heat, swelter, toast (*C*), roast (*C*), sizzle (*C*).
glowing, *a.* **1.** bright (*contex.*), luminous, candent (*tech. or B*), excandescent (*R*), incandescent; *spec.* burning.
2. *Referring to colors:* bright (*contex.*), warm; *spec.* blazing, rutilant (*R*), blushing, blooming, red.

Antonyms: see DULL.
3. *See* ARDENT.
gloze, *v. t.* **1.** *See* ANNOTATE.
2. *In figurative or transferred senses: spec.* gloss, veneer, varnish, veil, color, smooth, whitewash (*C*).
glue, *n.* mucilage, paste.
glutton, *n.* sensualist (*contex.*), gormandizer (*more emphatic than "glutton"*), gourmand (*obs.*), hog (*scornfully contemptuous*), gorger (*R*), pig (*contemptuous; often playful*), surfeiter, gorger, cormorant (*fig.*), bellygod (*A*), gastrophile (*R*), crammer (*C*), stuffer (*C*), gastrophilist (*R*), gastrophilite (*R*), ravener (*B*), guttler (*R*), helluo (*B*), poke-pudding (*Scot.; humorous*).
Antonyms: see ASCETIC.
gluttonous, *a.* **1.** gourmand, greedy, ravenous (*intensive*), piggish (*contemptuous; often playful*), hoggish (*scornfully contemptuous*), gormandizing.
Antonyms: see ABSTEMIOUS, ASCETIC.
2. *See* DESIROUS.
gluttony, *n.* **1.** gormandizing (*of the act*), gulosity (*R*), bellycheer (*A*), hoggishness (*contemptuous*); piggishness (*contemptuous*); *spec.* gastrophilism (*R*).
2. *See* DESIRE.
gnawing, *a.* **1.** rodent (*R, exc. tech.*).
2. *See* CORROSIVE, DISTRESSING.
go, *v. i.* **1.** move (*contex.*), gang (*chiefly B; Scot.*); *spec.* repair, proceed, pass (*chiefly used with "on," "along," "down," "through," etc.*), draw (*with "on," "along," "through," "back," etc.*), rampage, hie (*A or B*), stalk, take (*used with "to"*), labor, jaunt, run, rip (*C*), forcereach (*chiefly naut.*), range, carry, round, idle, jog, egress (*R*), extravagate (*R*), lollop (*C*), mill, bolt, pat, fare (*A or B*), determine, gallivant, step, happen, hap (*R or A*), strike, march, bundle (*chiefly used with "off"*), clump, force, advance, retreat, resort, depart, flow, speed, return, revert, exceed, transgress, dip, boat, ride, falter, glide, crawl, ferry, ply, travel, glance, walk (*see* GAIT, *n.*), amble, canter, pace, gallop, lope, rack, trot, hasten, hop, leap, sail, steam, float, fly, swarm (*in a multitude*), tiptoe, tumble, *etc.*
2. *In figurative or transferred senses: see* DEPART, ENTER, AVERAGE, CIRCULATE, BE, BECOME, APPEAL, EXTEND, CONTRIBUTE, END, ACT, DESCEND, PASS, DISAPPEAR, RESORT.

gleam, *n.: light, flash, appearance.*
gleam, *v. i.: shine, flash.*
glean: *harvest, get.*
glebe: *earth, field.*
gleeful: *pleased, gay.*
glen: *valley.*
glib: *fluent, smooth.*
glimmer: *flash, flicker.*
glimpse, *n.: flash, appearance, view, glance, sight.*
glimpse, *v. i.: flash, glance.*
glimpse, *v. t.: see.*
glint, *n.: flash, luster, glance.*
glint, *v. i.: flash, glance.*
glisten, *n.: flash.*
glisten, *v. i.: flash, shine.*
glitter: *flash.*
glittering: *lustrous, shining, flashing.*
gloat: *exult, rejoice, gaze.*
globe: *ball, earth.*
gloom, *v. i. frown, darken.*
glorious: *famous, fine.*
glory: *exult.*
gloss, *n.: annotation.*
gloss, *v. t.: annotate.*
gloss, *v. t.: polish, gloze.*
glossary: *dictionary.*
glossy: *lustrous, smooth.*
gloze, *n.: annotation.*
glum: *sullen, depressed.*
glut: *surfeit, satiate, oversupply, obstruct.*
glutinous: *sticky.*
gnarl: *protuberance.*
gnarled: *distorted.*
gnash: *bite.*
gnaw: *bite.*
gnome: *demon.*
gnomen: *pointer.*
go, *v. t.: afford, wager.*
go, *n.: energy, turn, success, fad.*
goad, *v. t.: prick, incite, urge.*

goal, *n.* **1.** *Spec.* mark, bye, post, port, home, bourne (*chiefly B*), bourn, hail (*Scot.*), meta (*Roman antiq.*).
2. *See* OBJECT, DESTINATION.
goat, *n. Spec.* buck, billy-goat (*C*), nanny (*C*), nanny-goat (*C*), kid, goatling, angora, jaal-goat, ibex, pasan, pasang, markhor; *spec.* butt, victim (*C, U. S., probably from* "scape-goat.")
goatlike, *a.* caprine (*tech. or B*), goatish, goatly (*nonce word*), hircine (*chiefly spec.*), hircinous (*R*), goaty (*chiefly spec.*); *spec.* capriform.
go-between, *n.* agent (*contex.*); *spec.* broker, Mercury (*fig.*), dealer, middleman, pander.
Antonyms: see PRINCIPAL.
goblin, *n.* demon (*contex.*), sprite *or* (*A*) spright (*contex.*), bogy, bogle, boggle, bogey; *spec.* kobold, nix, brownie, trull.
god, *n.* **1.** *See* DEITY.
2. [*cap.*] *Referring to the Christian god:* Deity (*with "the"*), King-of-Kings (*with "the"*).
Antonyms: see DEVIL.
godparent, *n.* sponsor, gossip (*obs.*); *spec.* godfather, godmother.
goer, *n. Spec.* proceeder, farer, traveler, speeder (*C*), exodist (*R*), walker, runner, *etc.*
goggle-eyed, *a.* bulging-eyed.
goglet, *n.* guglet, serai (*India*), surahee (*India*), chatty (*India*), olla (*Spanish America*), monkey pot.
going, *a.* **1.** *Spec.* traveling, proceeding, bound, outward-bound.
2. *See* AFLOAT.
going, *n.* **1.** *See* DEPARTURE.
2. *Spec.* proceeding, traveling, travel, troop, tour, exit, troll, progress, march, walk, run, *etc.*
3. *Referring to the condition of the ground, etc., for going: spec.* wheeling (*C*), racing, walking, running, rowing, skating, *etc.*
gold, *n.* **1.** aurum (*tech.; chem.*); *spec.* dust, gilding, gilt, or (*her.*).
2. *See* WEALTH.
golden, *a.* **1.** aureate (*B*), Pactolian (*fig.*); *spec.* auriferous, prime (*number; A*).
2. yellow, inaurate (*R; chiefly zoöl.*).
3. *See* EXCELLENT.
goldness, *n.* aureity (*B*).
gone, *a.* **1.** departed; *spec.* flown.
2. *See* ABSENT, WORNOUT, FAINT, FORGOTTEN.
good, *a.* buckra (*southern U. S.; negro dialect*); *spec.* goodly, goodish, satisfactory, excellent, favorable, admirable, adequate, beneficial, advantageous, agreeable, appropriate, considerable, competent, healthy, sound, real, honorable, responsible, righteous, becoming, kind, honest, frank, convivial, religious, well-behaved, *etc. "Good" is used as a synonym of almost any adjective denoting a quality that is approved.*
Antonyms: see BAD, FAULTY.
good, *interj.* bravo.
good, *n.* **1.** *Spec.* boon, godsend; *spec.* kalon (*Greek*), fruit, benefit, advantage, blessing, benison (*A or B*), bliss, beatitude, felicity.
Antonyms: see EVIL, DISADVANTAGE, CALAMITY, PEST.
2. *In pl.: see* GOODS.
goodby, *interj.* adieu (*A, affected, or used in pleasantry*), farewell (*now A or rhetorical; chiefly spec.*), vale (*R; Latin*), bye-bye (*C*), so-long (*S*).
Antonyms: see GREETING.
good-for-nothing, *n.* ne'er-do-well, scalawag.
good-looking, *a. Spec.* comely, fair (*chiefly B or rhetorical*), beautiful, handsome pretty (handsome *may be used of either a man or a woman;* pretty, *of a woman, implies more fragility and delicacy than does* handsome; *used of a man it is derogatory*), prettyish, minion (*R*), dainty, goodly, seemly (*R or A*), sightly, personable (*chiefly B*), bonny (*Scot., exc. as used in Eng. for local or lyrical effect*), well-favored (*A*), specious (*A*), likely (*R*), proper (*A*), shapely, canny (*dial.; not Scot.*), fine, graceful, elegant, delicate, *etc.*
Antonyms: see HOMELY.
good nature, kindness (*contex.*); *spec.* amiability, cleverness (*U. S., C*), good humor, good temper, grace, complaisance, accommodatingness.
Antonyms: see ILL-TEMPER.
good-natured, *a.* kind (*contex.*); *spec.* clever, amiable, good-humored, good-tempered, complaisant, accommodating, agreeable.
Antonyms: see ILL-TEMPERED, ACRIMONIOUS, SULLEN.
goodness, *n. Spec.* satisfactoriness, excellence, favorableness, admirableness, adequacy, beneficence, advantageousness, agreeableness, appropriateness, soundness, reality, honorableness, responsibility, righteousness, *etc.*
goods, *n. pl.* chattels, commodity (*a single article*), gear (*a collective*), effects, freight (goods *is chiefly Brit. in this sense*), things, movables (*law*); *spec.* traps (*C*), contraband, invoice, consignment;—*the last three collectives.*
goose, *n.* **1.** honker (*U. S. & Can.; C or S*); *spec.* gander, cagmag, goslet (*U. S.*), gosling, wavey, solan, graylag, gannet, barnacle, whitehead, brant.
2. *See* SIMPLETON.
gore, *v. t.* pierce (*contex.*); *spec.* tusk, horn, stab, hook.

go-ahead, *a.: enterprising.*
go-ahead, *n.: energy.*
gobbett: *piece.*
gobble: *v. t.: swallow.*
gobble, *n. & v. i.: cry.*
goddess: *deity.*
godhead: *divinity.*
godless: *atheistic, irreligious.*
godlike: *divine.*
godly: *divine, religious, righteous.*
goggle, *v. i.: turn.*
good, *interj.: bravo.*
goodby, *n.: farewell.*
goodfellowship: *camaraderie.*
good-humored: *good-natured.*
goodish: *good, considerable.*
goodly: *considerable.*
good will: *cordiality.*
goody, *a.: righteous.*
goody, *n.: sweetmeat.*
gore: *blood, triangle.*
gorge, *n.: throat, stomach, ravine.*
gorge, *v. t.: surfeit, devour, crowd.*
gorge, *v. i.: gormandize.*
gorged: *full.*
gorgeous: *bright, showy.*

Gorgon, *n. Spec.* Stheno, Euryale, Medusa.
gormandize, *v. i.* stuff, cram, gorge.
gospel, *n.* news (*contex.*), evangel, evangely (*A*); *spec.* Protevangel, Protevangelium.
gospel, *a.* evangelic, evangelical; *spec.* synoptic.
gossip, *n.* **1.** *See* GODPARENT.
2. busybody, gossiper, tattler, talebearer, tittle-tattler, quidnunc (*B*); *spec.* granny (*contemptuous*).
3. conversation, tittle-tattle, small talk, talk, by-talk, gup (*Anglo-Indian*), gossipry (*R or A*), gossipred (*R*), gossiping, tales (*pl.*); *spec.* chit-chat, claver, report *or* (*R*) reportage, scandal, slander (*these two carry more serious implications than* gossip), dirt (*cant*).
gossip, *v. i.* converse, talk, tattle, tittle-tattle, chatter, prattle, clatter; *spec.* comment, dish the dirt (*cant, U. S.*).
gourd, *n.* cucurbit (*tech.*), calabash (*chiefly spec.*); *spec.* pumpkin, squash, cusha, crookneck, Hubbard, luffa, melon.
gouty, *a.* arthritic (*tech.*), podagral (*properly spec.*).
governess, *n.* teacher (*contex.*), tutoress, gouvernante (*French*); *spec.* duenna.
government, *n.* **1.** control (*contex.*), gubernation (*R*), regency (*R, exc. spec.*), dominion, ordinance (*A*), rulership (*R*); *spec.* discipline, self-government, autonomy.
Antonyms: see ANARCHY.
2. *Referring to some particular mode or system of organization and governing: spec.* archology (*the science; R*), politics, polity (*B or tech.*), regimen, economy, duarchy *or* (*a bad spelling*) dyarchy, diarchy, triarchy, tetrarchy, pentarchy, heptarchy, hecatontarchy, timocracy, dynasty, gerontocracy, gynæcocracy, gynarchy, gynocracy (*R*), kingship, regency, protectorate, democracy, hierocracy, hierarchy, hagiocracy, theonomy, hetærocracy, stratocracy (*R*), logocracy, mesocracy, hamarchy, communalism, dulocracy, imperialism, Cæsarism, kingdom, foolocracy (*R*), episcopacy, congregationalism, methodism.
3. *Referring to the governing body:* signory (*chiefly spec.*); *spec.* administration, duumvirate, triumvirate.
4. *See* STATE.
5. *In grammar:* regimen (*tech.*), rection (*R*).
governmental, *a.* **1.** controlling.
2. political; *spec.* dynastic.
governor, *n.* **1.** *See* CONTROLLER.
2. ruler; *spec.* regent, vicegerent, prefect (*Roman hist.*), president (*chiefly hist.*), proveditor (*Venetian*), reis *or* rais, satrap, bey, dey, emir, killadar, kehaya, monarch, mudir, politarch, sirdar, proconsul, podesta (*Italian*), resident, eparch, beglerbeg, burgrave, harmost, toparch, castellan.
3. father (*cant*).
governorship, *n. Spec.* regency, vicegerency, prefecture, *etc.*
gown, *n.* garment (*contex.*); *spec.* dress, robe, smock, frock, cassock, gaberdine, frock, slip, sack (*obs.*), peignoir, negligee, négligé (*French*), mantua, caftan, nightgown, nightdress.
grace, *n.* **1.** *See* FAVOR, MERCY, VIRTUE, ATTRACTIVENESS.
2. *Spec.* embellishment, elegance, easiness, honor.
3. *Referring to saying grace at table: spec.* petition, blessing, thanks.
grace, *v. t.* become, beautify, endow, adorn.
graceful, *a.* **1.** easy, elegant; *spec.* (*of physical actions*) gainly (*R*), sylphlike, sylphine, sylphish, lightsome (*R*). *The use of* slender *as implying gracefulness is erroneous; it is not connected with the word* grace.
Antonyms: see AWKWARD, CLUMSY.
2. *See* APPROPRIATE, HAPPY.
gracile, *a.* slender.
gracious, *a.* **1.** *See* ACCEPTABLE.
2. kindly (*contex.*); *spec.* affable, good-natured, complaisant, condescending.
Antonyms: see CURT, SURLY.
3. *Referring to God, Christ, or the Virgin Mary:* mild (*A or B*), benignant, benign.
gradual, *a.* **1.** gradational, gradatory (*R*).
Antonyms: see ABRUPT, SUDDEN.
2. *See* SLOW, GENTLE.
graduate, *n.* alumnus (*masc.*), alumna (*fem.*); *spec.* postgraduate.
graduate, *v. t.* **1.** laureate (*hist.*).
2. *See* PASS, CLASSIFY, CALIBRATE.
graft, *n.* **1.** *In horticulture:* scion (*tech.*), slip, graff (*A*).
2. *See* GAIN.
graft, *v. t.* **1.** engraft, ingraft, inoculate, graff (*A*), imp (*A*); *spec.* inarch, bud.
2. get (*contex.*).
grail, *n.* platter, sangrail.
grain, *n.* **1.** fruit (*contex.*), coryopsis (*bot.; tech.*), verry (*chiefly spec.*), seed (*a popular usage; the* seed *botanically being the part inside of the husk or hull*); *spec.* kernel.
2. *As a collective sing.:* corn (*Brit.*), cereal (*tech.*); *spec.* grist, sharps (*pl.*), hards (*pl.*), middlings (*pl.*), cracklins (*pl.*), groats (*pl.*).
3. *As the name of a kind of fruit or the plant bearing it:* cereal (*the more tech. term*), corn (*Brit.*); *spec.* wheat, corn (*U. S.*), maize (*B, tech., or Brit.*), rye, oats (*pl.*), spelt, millet, dhurra, tsamba, cuscus, lentil, ragi, raggee. Grain *and* cereal *in the ordinary narrow use refer only to grasses or their fruits; in an extended sense they include others besides grasses, as* peas, beans, buckwheat.

gory: *bloody.*
gorze: *furze.*
got-up, *a.: affected.*
gourmand: *epicure.*
gourmet: *epicure.*
gown, *v. t.: clothe.*
grab, *v. t.: seize, capture.*
grab, *n.: seizure, clutch.*
grace, *v. t.: beautify, honor.*
gradate: *blend, shade.*
gradation: *series, degree, rank.*
grade, *n.: degree, class, slope, brand, rank, intensity.*
grade, *v. t.: graduate, even.*
grade, *v. i.: change, shade.*
gradient: *slope.*

4. particle (*contex.*), kernel (*chiefly spec.*), kern (*R*).
5. *See* MEASURE, TEXTURE, DISPOSITION.
6. *Referring to a dye: spec.* kermes, cochineal.
7. *Referring to a small hard particle: spec.* granule, granulation, sand, granula (*R*), pellet.
grain, *v. t.* **1.** *See* GRANULATE, DYE, PAINT.
2. roughen (*contex.*), granulate; *spec.* pebble.
grammarian, *n.* grammatist (*chiefly disparaging*), grammaticaster (*contemptuous*); *spec.* chorizontes (*pl.; Greek antiq.*).
granary, *n.* storehouse (*contex.*), garner, grange (*A*).
grand, *a.* chief, fine; *spec.* grandiose, noble, eminent, majestic, cosmic, magnificent, magnific, elevated, dignified, impressive, courtly, Miltonic, stately, Michelangelesque, grandisonant (*R*), splendid, splendent, large, bombastic, imperial, palatial, superb.
Antonyms: see SMALL, MEAN, INSIGNIFICANT.
grandchild, *n.* oy *or* oe (*Scot.*); *spec.* granddaughter, grandson.
grandeur, *n. Spec.* dignity, impressiveness, glory, magnificence, splendor, majesty, nobility, grandiosity, greatness, pomp.
grandfather, *n.* grandparent, belsire (*A*), goodsire (*Scot. or obs.*), grandsire (*A or dial., exc. of animals*), granddad *or* grandad (*childish or in familiar affection*), grandpa *or* grandpapa (*familiar*).
grandmother, *n.* grandparent, beldam *or* beldame (*A or B*), grannam (*obs. or dial.*), grandmamma (*C*), granny (*familiar, endearing, or contemptuous*), grandam *or* grandame (*A*).
grandness, *n.* fineness; *spec.* eminence, elevation, dignity, impressiveness, courtliness, grandeur.
grant, *v. t.* **1.** *Referring to a request, desire, etc.:* give (*contex.*); *spec.* allow, indulge, gratify, satisfy, fulfill, concede, hear, humor.
2. *See* CONCEDE, GIVE, TRANSFER, ACKNOWLEDGE.
grant, *n.* **1.** *Spec.* indulgence, gratification, fulfillment, satisfaction, concession.
2. *See* CONCESSION, GIFT, GIVING, TRANSFER, ACKNOWLEDGMENT.
grantee, *n.* recipient (*contex.*); *spec.* licensee, lessee, releasee, beneficiary, devisee, legatee, concessionnaire (*French*).
grantor, *n.* giver (*contex.*); *spec.* ceder (*R*), lessor, releasor, devisor, legator.
granular, *a.* grainy, graniform; *spec.* granose (*R*), granulose, saccharoid, saccharine.
Antonyms: see MASSIVE.
granulate, *v. t.* **1.** comminute (*B or tech.*), corn (*chiefly tech.*), grain; *spec.* pearl, grate.
2. *See* GRAIN.
granulated, *a. Spec.* grumous (*bot.*).
grape, *n.* fruit (*contex.*), berry; *spec.* cutthroat (*local, U. S.*), raisin (*bot.*), concord, delaware, niagara, *etc.*
grapelike, *a.* botryoid (*tech.*), grapy.
graphic, *a.* **1.** delineative (*a bookish word*); *spec.* drawing, pointing, descriptive, pictorial, etching, picturesque, figural, diagrammatic.
2. *See* DESCRIPTIVE.
graphite, *n.* plumbago (*tech.*), lead (*popular*).
grapple, *v. t. & i. & n.* close (*chiefly v. i.*), clutch; *spec.* tackle (*U. S.*), clinch *or* clench (*U. S.*), lock, embrace.
Antonyms: see FREE.
grasp, *v. i.* reach (*contex.*); *spec.* clutch;—*all used chiefly with "at" or "after."*
grass, *n. Spec.* cereal, bent, eddish, hay, couch, fiorin, fog, drawk, drauk, timothy, redtop, *etc.*
grassland, *n.* green (*R, exc. spec.*), sward (*more B than "grassland"*); *spec.* grass-spot, lawn, greensward, pasture, meadow, mead (*chiefly B or dial.*).
grassy, *a.* grasslike, herby; *spec.* gramineous, graminaceous, gramineal, graminiform, sward.
grassy, *a.* grasslike, herby; *spec.* gramineous, graminaceous, gramineal, graminiform, swardy, benty, couchy, foggy.
grate, *v. t.* **1.** *See* ABRADE.
2. emit (*contex.*), utter (*contex.*); *spec.* grind (*used with "out"*), rasp.
grate, *v. i.* **1.** *See* RUB.
2. *Referring to the noise and usually fig.: spec.* jar, grind, creak, scroop, rasp, screak, scrunch, squeak, crank (*R*), stridulate, groan.
grate, *n.* frame (*contex.*); *spec.* grating, screen, basket.
grating, *a.* **1.** rubbing (*cf.* RUB, *v. i.*).
2. scrapy; *spec.* grinding, rusty, screaky, creaky, scrooping, squeaky, raspy.
grating, *n.* **1.** rubbing (*cf.* RUB, *v. i.*).
2. *Spec.* grind, scroop, screak, creak, squeak, scratch, rasp, stridulation.
grating, *n.* **1.** frame (*contex.*), grate (*now unusual*), grid (*chiefly spec.*); *spec.* grille *or* grill, crotch (*local Eng.*), hurdle, portcullis, heck (*chiefly Scot.*), grizzly.
2. *In optics:* gitter.
grave, *n.* burial place, hearse (*A*), cell (*chiefly B*), chamber (*contex.*), tomb (*often spec.*), sepulcher (*more pretentious than* grave), sepulture (*A*); *spec.* charnel-house, Davy Jones's locker (*naut. cant*), mausoleum, mastaba (*Egyptology*). Grave *as strictly used applies only to an excavated cavity in the ground.*
gravel, *n.* **1.** stone (*contex.; a collective*), stones (*contex.; pl.*), chesil (*Eng.*), grit (*now R*), grail (*A or B*); *spec.* shingle (*chiefly Eng.*), beach (*Eng.*), alluvium, ballast.

---

grandee: *magnate.*
grandiloquence: *bombast.*
granny: *gossip, grandmother.*
graph: *diagram.*
grasp, *v. t.: take, hold, understand.*
grasping: *greedy.*
grateful: *thankful, acceptable.*
gratify: *please, gladden, grant.*
gratifying: *acceptable, pleasant.*
gratis, *adv.: freely.*
gratis, *a.: free.*
gratuitous: *free, groundless.*
gratuity: *gift.*
grave, *a.: important, serious, dignified, low* (in sound), *dull* (in color).
gravel, *v. t.: stone, disable, dull plus.*

---

2. *See* CALCULUS.
gravestone, *n.* stone, monument, tombstone; *spec.* ledger, headstone, footstone, shaft, cross, *etc.*
gray, *a.* **1.** grey (*var. spelling, by some used with different implications from "gray"; "gray" is chiefly U. S., "grey" chiefly British*); *spec.* grayish, grizzly *or* grisly, grizzled, hoar, hoary, griseous (*B*), blae (*obs. or Scot. and dial. Eng.*), ashen, ash-colored, pearly, leaden, lead-colored, cloudy, clouded, misty, foggy, perse (*A*), pearled, leady, frosty, canescent, gray-haired, drab.
2. *See* DEPRESSING, DULL.
gray, *v. t. Spec.* cloud, pearl, grizzle.
gray-haired, *a.* gray, hoar (*B*), hoar-headed (*B*); *spec.* silver-haired, grizzly, grizzled.
graze, *v. t. & i.* **1.** rub (*contex.*); *spec.* shave, brush, raze (*R*), scrape, scratch, glance.
2. *See* ABRADE.
graze, *n.* **1.** rub (*contex.*); *spec.* shave, brush, scrape, scratch, glance.
2. *See* ABRASION.
graze, *v. i.* **1.** feed (*contex.*); *spec.* pasture, browse, depasture (*tech.*).
2. *See* TEND.
grazing, *n.* **1.** *Referring to the act: spec.* pasture (*R*), pasturage, depasturation (*tech.*), depasture (*tech.*).
2. *Referring to what is fed on:* pasture, pasturage, range (*U. S.*).
grease, *a.* fat; *spec.* lard, axung, tallow, butter, slush, suet, oil, drippings (*pl.*), dubbing.
grease, *v. t.* **1.** lubricate (*B, exc. spec.*); *spec.* butter, oil, dub, lard, anoint, garnish.
2. *See* BRIBE.
greasy, *a.* **1.** fat, unctuous; *spec.* oily, lardy, yolky (*of wool*).
2. *See* SMOOTH, SLIPPERY.
great, *a.* **1.** *See* BIG.
2. *See* PREGNANT, LONG, CHIEF, FINE, DEEP, GENEROUS, OUTRAGEOUS, EXCELLENT, IMPORTANT, FAMOUS.
3. *Referring to degree, intensity, etc.: spec.* passing (*A*), pronounced, decided, mighty (*rhetorical or chiefly C*), vast, fearful (*C*), dense, desperate (*C*), deuced (*S or C*), plaguey (*S*), devilish (*S*), thundering (*S or C*), mortal (*C*), magnificent (*obs., exc. as a title or S*), terrible (*C*), terrific (*C*), dreadful (*C*), divine (*C*), rousing.
Antonyms: see SMALL, UNIMPORTANT, MINUTE.
greater, *a.* more, major (*not used with "than"*); *spec.* better.
greatest, *a.* **1.** most, best (*in "best part"*), maximum, maximal.
2. *See* EXTREME.
greatly, *a.* well, vastly (*C*), highly, hugely, immanely (*R*).
greatness, *n.* **1.** *See* SIZE.
2. *Spec.* dignity, distinction, fame, muchness, grandeur, generosity, importance, *etc.*
greed, *n.* desire, greediness, cupidity, avidity; *spec.* omnivorousness, avarice, covetousness, graspingness, rapacity, rapaciousness, insatiableness, pleonexia (*R*), hunger (*often fig.*), thirst (*often fig.*), exorbitancy, gluttony.
greedy, *a.* desirous, cupidous (*R*), covetous; *spec.* avid, avaricious, omnivorous, insatiable, pleonectic (*R*), ravenous, rapacious, grasping, gripple (*A*), hungry, thirsty, exorbitant, gluttonous, piggish (*C*), hoggish (*vulgar or intensive*).
Antonyms: see GENEROUS.
Greek, *a.* Grecian (*chiefly spec.*), Hellenic (*chiefly spec.*), Hellenian (*R*), Helladian (*R*), Helladic (*R*); *spec.* Greekish, Dorian, Doric, Ionian, Ionic, Spartan, Bœotian, Thracian, Romaic, Italic.
Greek, *n.* Grecian (*R*), Hellene, Hellenic (*the language*), Greekling (*contemptuous*).
green, *a.* **1.** Verdant (*chiefly spec.*); *spec.* glaucous, porraceous (*R*), citrine *or* citrinous, cæsious, chlorine *or* chlorochrous, olivaceous, olive, smaragdine.
2. *See* FRESH, IMMATURE, INEXPERIENCED, IGNORANT.
green, *n.* **1.** vert (*her.*); *spec.* viridian, verditer, reseda, celadon, mignonette, pistachio, bice, corbeau (*French*).
2. *See* VERDURE.
greenish, *a.* green, glaucous, virescent (*B*), viridescent (*R*).
greet, *v. t.* **1.** address (*contex.*), receive; *spec.* accost, salute, hail, welcome.
2. *See* RECEIVE.
greeting, *n.* **1.** address (*contex.*), reception; *spec.* accost, salutation, salute, hail, ave, welcome, colors (*pl.*); *see* RESPECT, *n.*
Antonyms: see FAREWELL, GOODBY.
2. *See* RECEPTION.
greyhound, *n.* grew *or* grewhound (*Scot.*); *spec.* sapling, tumbler.
griddlecake, *n.* slapjack (*U. S.*); *spec.* scone, crumpet.
gridiron, *n.* grill, brander (*Scot.*), brandiron (*dial.*), brandreth (*obs.*).
grief, *n.* discomfort (*contex.*), dole (*A*).
grieve, *v. t.* discomfort (*contex.*), distress (*contex.*), pain (*chiefly spec.*), hurt (*chiefly spec.*), sadden, sorrow (*R*); *spec.* agonize, torture, torment, aggrieve, trouble, oppress, afflict.
Antonyms: see PLEASE, GLADDEN.
grimace, *n.* face, mow (*now R*), mop (*now R*); *spec.* mouth, mug (*theatrical S*).

---

graven: *engraved.*
gravid: *pregnant.*
gravitate: *descend, tend.*
gravitation: *descent, tendency.*
gravity: *seriousness, sobriety, dignity, importance, attraction.*
gravy: *dressing, juice.*
greaten: *enlarge.*
Grecian: *Greek.*
greenery: *verdure.*
greenhorn: *novice.*
gregarious: *social.*
grief: *sorrow.*
grievance: *complaint.*
grieve: *sorrow.*
grieved: *sorrowful.*
grievous: *depressing, sad, intense, flagrant, sorrowful, troublesome.*
grill: *broil.*
grill, grille: *grating.*
grim: *fierce, stern, fearful.*

grimace, *v. i.* mow (*now R*), mop (*now R*); *spec.* mouth (*R*), mug (*theatrical S*).

grind, *v. t.* **1.** comminute (*contex.; B*), crush; *spec.* whet, triturate, masticate, crunch, bray, mull (*dial. Eng.*), pestle (*R*), roll, mill.

2. *See* ABRADE, SHARPEN, GRATE, OPPRESS.

grind, *v. i.* **1.** comminute (*contex.; B*), crush; *spec.* triturate, roll, mill, lap.

2. *See* TURN, GRATE, DRUDGE, STUDY.

grit, *n.* dirt (*contex.*); *spec.* sand, gravel, powder.

grits, *n. pl.* grain (*contex.; a collective*), groats (*pl.*); *spec.* oatmeal (*a collective; sing.*), hominy (*a collective; sing.*).

gritty, *a.* dirty (*contex.*), calculous (*R*); *spec.* muddy, sandy, stony, gravelly.

groan, *v. i.* **1.** moan.

2. *See* SUFFER, COMPLAIN, GRATE.

groan, *n.* moan.

groin, *n.* angle (*contex.*), edge, rib.

groom, *n.* **1.** hostler *or* ostler (*orig. spec.*), coistrel (*A*); *spec.* palfrenier (*A*), nagsman (*cant*), tiger (*in livery*), equerry.

2. *See* BRIDEGROOM.

groom, *v. t.* **1.** tend (*contex.*), fettle (*dial.*); *spec.* brush, rub, comb, curry, currycomb.

2. *See* TIDY.

groove, *n.* **1.** channel (*contex.*); *spec.* furrow, rut, flute, cannelure, channelure, canaliculation, sulcus, gutter, chamfer (*obs. or R*), chase, rebate, rabbet, rifle, croze, mortise, vallecula, cut, score, gain, glyph.

2. *See* ROUTINE.

groove, *v. t.* channel (*contex.*); *spec.* furrow, gouge, chase, croze, rebate, throat, quirk, rifle, dado, ditch (*R*), excavate, mill, score.

grooved, *a.* channeled (*contex.*); *spec.* sulcate, guttered, fossulate, canaliculate, contorniate, valleculate.

groove-shaped, *a.* sulciform (*tech.*).

grope, *v. i.* feel, search, grabble (*chiefly spec.*), puzzle (*only fig.*).

gropingly, *a.* blindly.

gross, *a.* crass (*chiefly spec.*); *spec.* big, bulky, coarse, coarse-grained, thick-skinned, dense, fat, flagrant, dull, heavy, stupid, brutal, brutish, callous, unrefined, insensitive, whole, vulgar, obscene, sensual, earthy.

Antonyms: see NICE, DELICATE, REFINED, FASTIDIOUS.

grossness, *n.* crassness; *spec.* size, bulkiness, coarseness, fatness, flagrancy, dullness, stupidity, brutality, vulgarity, obscenity, sensuality.

ground, *n.* **1.** *See* EARTH, LAND, BASE, BASIS, FOUNDATION, REASON, EXCUSE, GIST (*in pl.*), DREG (*in pl.*), DEPOSIT, VIEWPOINT.

2. *As in "on that ground," etc.:* basis, reason; *spec.* antecedent.

ground, *v. t.* **1.** *See* BASE, ESTABLISH, FELL, TEACH.

2. *In a nautical sense:* strand (*orig. spec.; more dignified than "ground"*); *spec.* beach, sand, shore (*R*).

groundless, *a.* causeless (*as having no valid cause*), uncalled-for, baseless, unfounded, ungrounded, reasonless, unsolid (*R*), gratuitous (*chiefly spec.*); *spec.* misgrounded, idle, unprovoked, unasked, unsought, unsolicited, unjustifiable, wanton (*willful as well as unjustifiable*).

Antonyms: see REASONABLE.

group, *n. Spec.* assembly, assemblage, combination, block, bunch, family, nest, knot, body, cluster, flock, flight, plexus, division, clump, round, roundlet, bundle, claque, flush, shock, shook, stack, sheaf, gens, clan, sept, tribe, race, party, clique, system, species, genus, variety, horde, order, class, phylum, kingdom, force, army, array, corps, battalion, regiment, company, squadron, battery, fleet, command, glomerule, school, class, crew (*organized body of workers, as the* crew *of a train, ship, etc.*), outfit (*C*), organization.

group, *a.* gentile (*as the gentile name*), gentilitial (*R*), gentilitious (*R*); *spec.* family.

group, *v. t. & i.* assemble; *spec.* arrange, classify, cluster, clump, tuft.

grove, *n.* wood (*contex.*), tope (*Anglo-Indian*), tuft (*B or R*); *spec.* pinery, pinetum.

grow, *v. i.* **1.** live, wax (*A or B*), form; *spec.* luxuriate, fungus, fungate, spindle, shoot, vegetate, develop.

Antonyms: see DIE.

2. *See* ARISE, DEVELOP, BECOME, THRIVE, ACCRUE, GERMINATE, INCREASE, EXTEND, GENERATE.

grow, *v. t.* produce, raise *or* breed (*referring to plants or, U. S., animals*), rear (*chiefly spec.*); *spec.* cultivate.

growl, *v. i.* **1.** gnarl (*R*), gnar (*B*), girn (*Scot.*); *spec.* grumble, snarl.

2. *See* COMPLAIN.

growl, *n.* **1.** gnarl (*R*), gnar (*B*), girn (*Scot.*); *spec.* grumble, snarl.

2. *See* COMPLAINT.

grown, *a.* adult, mature (*chiefly spec.*), full-grown; *spec.* ripe.

Antonyms: see IMMATURE.

growth, *n.* **1.** development, thrift (*healthy*); *spec.* germination, increase. *Cf.* GROW.

---

grime, *n.: dirt.*
grimy: *dirty.*
grin: *snarl, smile.*
grip, *n.: hold, clutch, control, handle, handbag, handclasp.*
grip, *v. t.: seize, clutch, impress, control.*
grip, *v. i.: hold, close.*
gripe, *v. t.: seize, hold, pain, control, affect.*
gripe, *n.: hold, control* (in pl.), *pain, colic.*
grisly: *gray, fearful.*
grist: *grain.*
gristly: *cartilaginous.*
grizzle, *v. t. & i.: whiten.*
grizzly, *a.: gray.*
groggy: *intoxicated, weak.*
gropingly: *blindly.*
gross: *bulk.*
grotesque: *funny.*
grotto: *cave.*
grounded: *aground.*
groundward: *down.*
groundwork: *foundation, basis, background.*
grovel: *creep, cringe.*
groveling: *abject.*

---

2. production, rearing (*chiefly spec.*); *spec.* cultivation, culture, *etc. Cf.* GROW.
3. *Something that has grown:* formation, product; *spec.* sprout, spire, shoot, flush, accretion, excrescence, vegetation, sucker, fleece (*in fig. sense of feathery part of grasses, etc.*), stand (*relative number on a given area*). *Cf.* GROW.
4. *See* INCREASE.
5. adulthood.

grudge, *v. t.* **1.** give, begrudge, grutch (*R or A*).
2. *See* ENVY.

grudge, *n.* ill will. *"Grudge" is now rarely used of the general feeling of "ill will," but rather of a particular instance, with synonyms as follows:* grutch (*R*), down (*C*); *spec.* spite.

guarantee, *v. t.* undertake, insure *or* ensure, assure, guaranty (*R*), warrant; *spec.* secure, vouch.

guarantee, *v. i.* undertake, vouch; *spec.* agree, contract.

guarantee, *n.* **1.** guarantor; *spec.* surety, voucher, warrantor, insurer, bailor, bail, contractor.
2. guaranty (*referring to the act or thing*).

guaranty, *n.* **1.** *Of the act:* guarantee, undertaking, warranty; *spec.* security, insurance, assurance, vouch (*A*), voucher.
2. *Of the thing:* guarantee, warrant; *spec.* security, voucher, agreement, contract.

guard, *v. t.* **1.** protect, keep (*now chiefly spec.*), ward (*A*); *spec.* watch, overwatch, safeguard, escort, attend, tile (*Freemasonry*), patrol, picket.
2. watch, check.

guard, *v. i.* watch, ward (*A*); *spec.* beware, patrol, sentry (*R*).

guard, *n.* **1.** *Of the act or fact:* protection, watch, ward (*A*), keep (*chiefly spec.*); *spec.* custody, escort.
2. *Referring to persons:* protector, watch, keeper (*chiefly spec.*), safeguarder, guardian (*more formal than "guard"*), warden (*B or A, exc. spec.*), warder (*B or A, exc. spec.*); *spec.* picket (*of one or more*), death-watch, escort, patrol (*chiefly collective sing.*), watchman, safeguarder, safeguard, sentinel, sentry (*the usual military term*), vanguard (*collective sing.*), wardsman (*R*), cordon (*collective pl.*), rearguard (*collective pl.*).
3. *Referring to things: spec.* protection, protector, shooter, pad, ward, tsuba (*Japanese*), button, fob, catch, hood, cowcatcher, pilot (*U. S.*).
4. *See* CONDUCTOR.

guarded, *a. Spec.* protected, close, cautious, careful.

guardian, *n.* **1.** protector, guard; *spec.* custodian.
2. *In law: spec.* curator, conservator, tutor.

guardianship, *n.* **1.** care, protection; *spec.* custody.
2. *In law: spec.* curatorship, tutorship, tutelage, tutorage, tutory (*R*), ward, wardship, matronage.

guess, *v. t. & i.* **1.** conjecture, surmise, suspect (*chiefly spec.*), think (*contex.*), jalouse (*Scot.*), suspicion (*C for "suspect"*); *spec.* mistrust, divine, predict, theorize, imagine, foresee.
Antonyms: see KNOW.
2. *See* BELIEVE.

guess, *n.* conjecture, surmise, shot (*C*), surmisal (*R*); *spec.* mistrust, suspicion, cast, divination, prediction, theory, imagination, foresight.

guesser, *n.* conjecturer, surmiser; *spec.* Œdipus (*fig.*), mistruster, diviner, *etc.*

guest, *n.* visitor; *spec.* convival (*at a feast; obs.*), umbra (*Roman hist.*), shadow (*a Latinism*), diner, company (*a collective*), parasite.

guidance, *n.* **1.** direction, conduction, conduct, pilotage (*chiefly spec.*); *spec.* steering, leading, lead, marshaling, manuduction (*R*), steerage (*naut. or R*), escort.
2. *See* MANAGEMENT.

guide, *v. t.* **1.** direct (*while* guide *implies personal direction, supervision or suggestion,* direct *is generally impersonal, as by signs, written instruction etc.*) conduct, pilot (*chiefly spec.*), show; *spec.* manuduct (*R*), cicerone, lead, run, marshal, steer (*naut. or fig.*), escort, motion, misdirect, misguide, rein.
2. *See* MANAGE, ADVISE.

guide, *n.* **1.** director, conductor, Mercury (*fig.*), pilot (*chiefly spec.*); *spec.* marshaler, leader, cicerone, sightsman (*R*), steersman, steerer.
2. *Referring to things: spec.* landmark, lodestar, cynosure (*B*), key, clew, clue, thread, directory, index, fence, screed, trail, trace, guidebook, bridle.
3. *See* MANAGER, ADVISER.

guidebook, *n. Spec.* Baedeker, itinerary, roadbook, ruttier (*A*).

guidepost, *n.* waypost; *spec.* fingerpost.

guiltless, *a.* innocent, blameless; *see* INNOCENT.
Antonyms: see BLAMABLE.

guilty, *a.* blamable, nocent (*R*); *spec.* criminal, self-accusing, conscious.
Antonyms: see BLAMELESS, INNOCENT.

guitar, *n. Spec.* vina, sancho, samisen (*Japanese*), sitar (*Anglo-Indian*).

gullet, *n.* **1.** œsophagus (*tech.*).
2. *See* NECK, THROAT.

---

grub, *v. i.: dig, drudge, eat.*
grub, *v. t.: dig, clear, uproot.*
grub, *n.: larva, food.*
grubby: *dirty.*
grubstake: *support.*
grudging, *n.: envy.*
gruel, *n.: porridge.*
gruesome, *a.: fearful.*
gruff, *a.: rough, surly.*
grum, *a.: ill-tempered, sullen.*
grumble, *v. i.: complain, mutter, growl, rumble.*
grumpy, *a.: ill-tempered, dissatisfied.*
grunt, *v. i.: complain.*
guardhouse: *shelter, prison.*
guerdon: *reward.*
guerilla: *fighter.*
guffaw: *laugh.*
guild: *association.*
guile: *deceitfulness, deception.*
guileful: *deceitful.*
guileless: *simple.*
guilt: *blame.*
guise: *costume, appearance, pretense.*
gulf: *inlet, abyss.*
gull, *v. t.: deceive, dupe.*
gull, *n.: dupe.*

---

gully, *n.* valley (*contex.*); *spec.* arroyo (*local, U. S.*).
gummy, *a.* gumlike, gummous (*R*), gummose (*R*); *spec.* mucilaginous.
gun, *n.* **1.** cannon; *spec.* pompom, big Bertha (*C*).
2. firearm, weapon, shooter (*C*), pelter (*humorous*); *spec.* musket, rifle, pistol, revolver, matchlock, Gatling. *The following are U. S. gangster terms:* gat, rod, iron, roscoe, oscar, blow, heater, dewey.
gunboat, *n. Spec.* tinclad (*C*).
gunner, *n.* **1.** shooter (*contex.*); *spec.* musketeer, carbineer.
2. artilleryman, artillerist, cannoneer, gun (*C or cant*); *spec.* bombardier, culverineer.
3. hunter.
gurgle, *v. i. & n.* **1.** gurgle; *see* FLOW, BUBBLE.
2. *See* LAUGH.
gusty, *a.* unsteady, fretful, puffy.
gutter, *n.* channel (*contex.*); *spec.* cannel *or* kennel (*British*).
guttural, *a.* **1.** throat (*the noun used attributively*).
2. *Of sounds:* throat, thick, throaty.
guzzle, *v. t.* consume, drink, bum (*S, U. S.*), ingurgitate (*R*).
gybe, *v. i. & n.* shift.
gymnasium, *n.* calisthenium (*R*), gymkhana (*Anglo-Indian or transferred*), palæstra *or* palestra (*chiefly Greek antiq.*).
gymnast, *n.* athlete (*contex.*); *spec.* contortionist, equilibrist, ropewalker, turner.
gymnastic, *a.* athletic (*contex.*), gymnic (*R*); *spec.* calisthenic.
gymnastics, *n.* athletics (*contex.*); *spec.* calisthenics.
gypsy, *a.* Egyptian, Romanian (*R*), Bohemian, Romany (*cant*); *spec.* Tzigany.
gypsy, *n.* **1.** Egyptian, Bohemian, caird (*Scot.*), rom (*male; cant*), Romany, faw (*dial. Eng.*); *spec.* Tzigany.
2. *Referring to the language:* Roman.

H

habit, *n.* **1.** *See* DRESS, GARMENT.
2. custom, use (*chiefly B for "custom"*), wont (*chiefly B for "custom"*), usage, habitude (*R*), consuetude (*R*), practice, rule; *spec.* cacoëthes, knack, trick.
habitual, *a.* common (*contex.*), accustomed, customary, usual, wonted, consuetudinary (*R*); *spec.* hackneyed, settled, confirmed, inveterate, great.
Antonyms: see OCCASIONAL.
hack, *n.* **1.** *See* HORSE.
2. author (*contex.*), drudge, penny-a-liner, hodman (*B*); *spec.* jobber.
hag, *n.* beldam *or* beldame (*B or R*), witch, harridan, vixen, termagant, shrew.
Antonyms: see BEAUTY.
hail, *v. t.* **1.** *See* GREET.
2. call; *spec.* hollo.
hail, *v. i.* call; *spec.* ave, hollo, hello.
hail, *n.* call; *spec.* hollo, hello, ave.
hair, *n.* filament (*contex.*); *spec.* bristle, hairlet, eyelash, kemp, whisker, villus.
hair, *n. Referring to the natural covering or coat of hair: spec.* frizzle, fur, wool, down, thatch (*fig.; humorous*), carrots (*red; humorous or derisive*), crine (*R*), beard, mustache, pile, grizzle, mane, pubescence, wool, pubes.
hair, *a.* pilar (*R*), crinal (*R*).
hair-dresser, *n.* coiffeur (*French*); *spec.* barber.
haired, *a. Spec.* (*her.*) maned, crined.
hairiness, *n.* hirsuteness, hirsuties (*tech.*), hispidity, crinosity (*R*), pilosity (*R*).
hairlike, *a.* hairy (*R*), filamentous; *spec.* capilliform, capillaceous (*R*), threadlike, villous.
hairy, *a. Spec.* hairish, hispid (*chiefly tech.*), bristly, hirsute (*B*), shaggy, crinite, kempy, comose *or* comous, pilose *or* (*R*) pilous, peline (*R*), pileous (*R*), rough, tomentose, woolly, capillate, capillose, villous, furry, pubescent.
Antonyms: see BALD, BARE.
halberd, halbert, *n.* bill; *spec.* spontoon, brown bill, lochaber, battle-ax.
half, *n.* moiety (*legal or formal*); *spec.* hemisphere, mediety.
halfbreed, *n. Spec.* mestizo (*masc.*), mestiza (*fem.*), mulatto, mule, half-cast, creole (*contex.*).
half-fledged, *a.* pin-feathered.
halfpenny, *n.* bawbee (*Scot.*), make (*S*), mail (*obs. or hist.*).
hall, *n.* **1.** *See* ABODE.
2. building (*contex.*); *spec.* dormitory, auditorium, dining-hall (*esp. in Brit. colleges*), casino, college, burse (*Eng.*), pantheon, prytaneum (*Greek antiq.*).
3. room (*contex.*), hallway; *spec.* anteroom,

---

gully: *valley, channel.*
gulp: *swallow, choke.*
gumption: *common sense.*
gush, *v. i.: flow, emotionalize.*
gush, *n.: flow, effusiveness.*
gushing: *flowing, effusive.*
gust: *taste, enjoyment.*
gust: *wind.*
gusto: *enjoyment*
gut, *n.: intestine, abdomen, channel.*
gut, *v. t.: disembowel, plunder.*
gutter, *v. t.: channel.*
gutter, *v. i.: flow.*
guttery: *channeled.*
guy, *n.: eccentric.*
guy, *v. t.: ridicule.*
guy: *support.*
gyrate, *a.: circular.*
gyrate, *v. i.: revolve.*
gyve: *shackle.*

H

habiliment: *clothing.*
habitable: *inhabitable.*
habitat: *abode.*
habitation: *occupation, abode, residence.*
habituate: *accustom.*
habitude: *habit.*
habitué: *frequenter.*
hack: *chop, cough.*
haggard: *thin.*
haggle, *v. t.: chop.*
haggle, *v. i.: cavil, bargain.*
hailstone: *pellet.*
hairless: *bald.*
hairsplitting, *a.: caviling.*
hairsplitting, *n.: refinement.*
halcyon: *calm.*
hale, *a.: healthy.*
hale, *v. t.: draw.*
half-baked: *crude.*
half-hearted: *depressed, insincere, timid.*
hallow: *consecrate, observe.*

---

lobby, divan, atrium (*Roman antiq.*), impluvium (*Roman antiq.*), durbar (*East India*), sala (*Spanish*).
4. passage (*contex.*); *spec.* corridor, gallery.
hallowed, *a.* holy, consecrated, blessed.
Antonyms: see UNHOLY.
hallucination, *n.* deception, fancy; *spec.* paræsthesia *or* paresthesia, zoöscopy, phosphene, photism, afterimage, photogene.
halo, *n.* **1.** circle, burr (*chiefly spec.*), aura, brough (*Scot.; chiefly spec.*); *spec.* corona.
2. *See* GLORY.
halter, *n.* **1.** *Spec.* hackamore (*U. S.*).
2. *For hanging criminals:* rope, rope's end, tether (*R*).
halve, *v. t.* divide, dimidiate (*R*); *spec.* bisect.
ham, *n.* **1.** *In quadrupeds:* hock.
2. thigh; *spec.* gammon.
hammer, *n. Spec.* beetle, maul *or* mall, mallet, tapper, rammer, commander, bush-hammer, fuller, woolstock, sledge, skelper, helve, martel, mash, striker, plexor, flatte, bucker, gavel, cock.
hammer, *v. t.* strike (*contex.*), beat (*contex.*); *spec.* drive, tilt, ram, draw.
hammer-shaped, *a.* malleiform (*R*).
hamper, *v. t.* hinder, embarrass, trammel (*primarily spec.; a stronger word than "hamper"*), entrammel (*intensive*), fetter, cumber *or* encumber (*primarily spec.*); *spec.* clog, shackle.
hamper, *n.* hindrance, embarrassment, encumbrance, encumberment (*R*), trammel.
hamstring, *v. t.* hough, hock; *spec.* spade.
hand, *n.* **1.** extremity (*contex.*), manus (*tech.*), paw (*in contempt or jocular*), pud (*a child's word*), dabble (*dial.*), mauley (*S*), famble (*S*); *spec.* fist, forefoot.
2. *See* AGENCY, OWNERSHIP, CONTROL, ABILITY, HANDWRITING, SIGNATURE, WORKER, EMPLOYEE, SIDE, POINTER.
3. *In cards: spec.* dummy, flush, straight, full house, carte blanche, crib, *etc.*
handbag, *n.* bag, grip (*C*), gripsack (*C, U. S.*); *spec.* portmanteau (*chiefly Brit.*), Gladstone bag *or* (*for short*) gladstone, satchel, valise, weekend case, overnight case, briefcase, attaché case, *etc.*, carpetbag, suitcase, luggage (*collective, for the pl.*), carryall (*Eng.*), scrip.
handbook, *n.* manual, vade mecum (*Latin*), enchiridion (*B*); *spec.* guidebook.
handbreadth, *n.* palm.
handbred, *a. Spec.* cade.
handclasp, *n.* grip, clutch, grasp.
handful, *n.* **1.** gripe (*local, Eng.*), fistful; *spec.* wisp.
2. *See* FEW.
handicap, *n.* **1.** *See* CONTEST.
2. penalty (*cant*).
handicap, *v. t.* penalize (*cant*); *spec.* weight.
handkerchief, *n.* wiper (*R*), wipe (*S*), sudarium *or* sundary (*primarily spec.; a bookish word*), fogle (*S*), rag (*cant or S*); *spec.* Barcelona (*obs.*), bandanna, Madras, foulard, romal (*Mexico and southwestern U. S.*), vernicle.
handle, *n.* grip, stale (*dial. or tech.*); *spec.* spindle, handstaff, crop, snead (*chiefly Scot. & dial.*), grasp, brake, helm, haft, loom, helve, lug, hilt, snath *or* snathe, bow, bail, tiller, stalk, ear, palm, crutch, withe, shaft, sally, tote, tale (*R*), rounce, pull, crank.
handle, *v. t.* **1.** touch (*contex.*), paw (*chiefly spec. or contemptuous*), hand (*R*), manipulate; *spec.* feel, fumble, finger, thumb, fist, palm, gentle, manhandle, smooth.
2. haft, hilt, helve.
3. *See* MANAGE, TREAT.
handled, *a.* anaste (*R*).
handling, *n.* touching (*contex.*); *spec.* manipulation, thumbing, fingering, contrectation (*R*).
hand-propelled, *a.* manumotive (*R*).
hand-shaped, *a.* maniform (*R*); *spec.* palmate.
handwriting, *n.* chirography, paw (*C or jocular*), scription (*R*), scripture (*R*), fist (*jocular or cant*), script, hand, calligraphy (*primarily spec.*); *spec.* character, cacography, graphology, penmanship, courthand.
hand-written, *a.* manuscript.
hang, *v. t.* **1.** suspend, depend (*R*); *spec.* dangle, drape, droop, swing, sky (*cant*).
2. execute (*contex.*), patibulate (*humorous; nonce*); *spec.* gibbet, truss (*R*), supercollate (*R and ludicrous*), noose, halter.
hang, *v. i.* **1.** depend, suspend (*R*); *spec.* dangle, lop, dingle-dangle (*intensive*), stream, flow, trail, droop.
2. die (*contex.*), swing (*C*).
3. *Spec.* impend, hover, lean.
4. *See* FLY, STICK, ATTEND, DELAY, STAY.
hang, *n.* **1.** *Spec.* dangle (*R*), drape, droop.
2. *See* ABILITY, FIT.
hanger-on, *n.* dependent, parasite, bur *or* burr (*fig.*); *spec.* client.
Antonyms: see SUPPORTER.
hanging, *a.* **1.** dependent; *spec.* pendulous, pendulant (*R*), decumbent, flaggy, pendent *or* pendant, pensile, penduline (*R*), drooping, dangling.
2. supporting, suspensory, suspensorial.
hanging, *n.* **1.** dependence, danglement (*R*).
2. execution (*contex.*); *spec.* gibbet.
3. *See* DRAPERY.
hangman, *n.* Jack Ketch (*a popular name*), ketch (*C*).
happen, *v. i.* **1.** *See* OCCUR, CHANCE.
2. *With an indirect object:* chance (*now R*),

hallowed: *holy.*
hallucinate: *delude.*
hallucinative: *deceptive.*
halt, *v. i. & n.: stop.*
halt, *a.: disabled.*
halt, *v. i.: limp.*
hamlet: *village.*
hampering: *hindrance.*
hand, *v. t.: deliver.*
handclap: *applause, moment.*
handcuff: *manacle.*
handicraft: *art, trade.*
handiness: *convenience, skill.*
handsel: *earnest, foretaste.*
hank: *coil.*
hanker: *desire.*
hap, *n.: chance, accident, event.*
haphazard, *n.: chance.*
haphazard, *adv. casually.*
happiness: *gladness.*
happy: *glad.*
happy-go-lucky, *a.: easy-going.*
happy-go-lucky, *adv.: casually.*
hara-kiri: *suicide.*

bechance (*R*), betide (*only in 3d person, and mostly in "woe betide"*), befall (*A*).

3. come, fall; *spec.* strike, stumble;—*with "on" or "upon."*

harangue, *n.* address (*contex.*), declamation, speech (speech *is the ordinary term,* address *is more formal,* declamation *more oratorical, and* harangue *more with implication of bombast or demagoguery*); *spec.* rigmarole, spiel (*C, humorous*), gab (*C, humorous*), jaw (*C, depreciatory and humorous*); *see* TIRADE.

harass, *v. t.* distress (*contex.*), badger; *spec.* dragoon, heckle, curse, beset, worry, annoy, gall, harry, haggle, embarrass, afflict, depress.

Antonyms: see COMFORT, PROTECT.

harassed, *a.* distressed (*contex.*); *spec.* hag-ridden.

harbor, *n.* **1.** *See* REFUGE.

2. port, haven (*a word now becoming B*); *spec.* mole, cothon, seaport, portlet, bunder (*Anglo-Indian*).

hard, *a.* **1.** firm, solid (*as opposed to what is* fluid, gaseous, *or* liquid), rigid (*as opposed to* pliable, soft), sclerous (*tech.*), indurated, dure (*B*), dour (*Scot.*), untender (*R*); *spec.* adamantine (*chiefly B or tech.*), resistant (*R*), stony, marble, iron, steely, icy, flinty, brazen, brassy (*often fig.*), dintless, rocky, *etc.; see* RIGID.

Antonyms: see SOFT.

2. *See* (*in almost numberless secondary or figurative uses*), ENERGETIC, DIFFICULT, ALCOHOLIC, AUSTERE, CRUEL, UNFEELING, STINGY, SEVERE, VIOLENT, STUBBORN, HARSH, STRONG, TIGHT, FIRM, *etc.*

harden, *v. t. & i.* **1.** firm (*chiefly tech. or B*), solidify; *spec.* steel, immarble (*R*), stone (*R*), enharden (*R*), indurate, crust, braze, callous, chill, crisp, congeal, freeze, case-harden, vulcanize.

Antonyms: see SOFTEN.

2. toughen, inure, indurate, callous (*R*).

3. *Referring to the feelings, morals, etc.;* obdurate (*R*), obdure (*R*), indurate, callous (*fig.*); *spec.* sensualize, brutalize, Molochize (*nonce word*), savagize (*R*), braze *or* brazen (*R*), stiffen, confirm.

Antonyms: see SOFTEN.

hardiness, *n.* **1.** *See* BOLDNESS.

2. strength, endurance, robustness, sturdiness, stoutness, vigor, toughness.

hardly, *a.* **1.** *See* BOLD, COURAGEOUS.

2. strong, enduring, robust, robustious, sturdy, stout, tough, rugged.

Antonyms: see DELICATE, WEAKLY.

hardness, *n.* **1.** firmness, solidity, induration; *spec.* adamant, *etc.*, sclerosis, scirrhosity.

2. *Spec.* austerity, cruelty, *etc.* (*cf.* AUSTERE, CRUEL, *etc.*).

hardy, *adv.* **1.** *Spec.* severely, harshly (*cf.* SEVERE, HARSH.)

2. scarcely, barely, merely, just.

hare, *n.* Bawd (*a dialect proper name, like "Reynard" for the fox*), cutty (*Scot.*), puss *or* pussy (*as a quasi proper name*), wat (*now chiefly dial.*); *spec.* leveret, leparine, lagimorphic.

harem, *n.* seraglio, serail (*R*); *spec.* zenana.

harlot, *n.* harlotry (*chiefly B*), prostitute (harlot *and* harlotry *are general terms not necessarily implying indiscriminate promiscuity*), paramour (*originally quite lacking the opprobrium attaching to* harlot; *now a euphemism for* harlot), courtesan (*rather euphemistic*), trull (*A, contemptuous*), meretrix (*R*), whore, drab (*B*), scarlet woman, harridan (*a worn-out* strumpet), limmer (*Scot.*), strumpet; *spec.* hetæra *or* hetaira (*Greek antiq.*), street walker, night walker, sultana, minion (*R*), doxy (*cant or S*), tart (*S, with implication of comparative youth and impudence*), concubine, moll (*S, U. S.; more properly a synonym for* mistress), bag (*S*), broad (*S*), *etc. See* BAWD.

harlot, *a.* **1.** meretricious (*chiefly spec.*).

2. *See* LEWD.

harlotry, *n.* prostitution (*esp. for hire*), strumpetry; *spec.* hetærism, hetairism.

harm, *n.* **1.** evil, hurt, ill, injury, damage, lesion (*B, exc. spec. in med.*), mischief, execution (*chiefly in "to do execution"*), scathe (*A; chiefly as a generic sing.*), grame (*A*); *spec.* bale (*B*), desecration, abuse, bane, waste, breaking, beating, misfortune, ruin, *etc.*

2. *Referring to the violation of legal rights: see* INJURY.

3. *See* DETRIMENT.

harm, *v. t.* **1.** hurt, injure, damage, scathe (*A*); *spec.* abuse, desecrate, break, beat, waste, *etc.*

Antonyms: see BENEFIT.

2. *Referring to legal harm: see* INJURE.

harmful, *a.* **1.** evil, ill (*now chiefly rhetorical, exc. as occurring in proverbs or in certain phrases*), bad (*a mild word*), hurtful, injurious, noisome (*chiefly spec.*), maleficent (*chiefly B*), malefic (*chiefly spec.*), mischievous; *spec.* damaging, baleful, inimical, dire, direful, fell, baneful (*B or rhetorical*), pestiferous, malignant, sinister, sinistrous (*R*), noxious, nocent (*R*), deleterious, destructive, disadvantageous, unfortunate, pernicious, *etc.*

Antonyms: see BENEFICIAL, HARMLESS.

2. *See* INJURIOUS (*referring to harm to legal rights*).

harmless, *a.* hurtless, innocent, innocuous, innoxious (*R*), safe, inoffensive, unharmful (*R*), unhurtful (*R*); *spec.* woundless (*R*).

Antonyms: see HARMFUL.

harmonious, *a.* **1.** *See* AGREEABLE, CONSISTENT, SMOOTH, ORDERLY.

2. harmonial (*R*), harmonic (*more technical than "harmonious"*), symphonic *or* symphonious, consonant, spheral (*B*), melodous, smooth (*contex.*), concinnous (*R*), tunable (*R*), tune-

harangue, *v. i.: declaim.*
harbinger, *n.: forerunner, predecessor.*
harbinger: *v. t.: signify.*
hardened: *insensible, abandoned.*
hard-hearted: *unkind, cruel.*
hardihood: *boldness.*
harebrained: *changeable, careless, rash.*
hark, harken, *v. i.: listen.*
hark, harken, *v. t.: hear.*
harlequin: *buffoon.*

ful, musical, concordant, undiscording (*R*); *spec.* sympathetic.
Antonyms: see INHARMONIOUS, DISCORDANT.
harmonize, *v. i.* **1.** *See* AGREE, SYMPATHIZE.
2. tune, chime, blend, chord.
harmonize, *v. t.* **1.** attune, melodize, concent (*R*).
2. unite, reconcile, conform.
3. *See* ADJUST, ADAPT.
harmony, *n.* **1.** *See* AGREEMENT, CONSISTENCY, UNITY, SMOOTHNESS, ORDER.
2. smoothness (*contex.*); *spec.* melody, concert (*now R*), tune (*as in "in tune"*), chord, cadence, concord, monochord (*R*), concent (*A*), consonance, chime, descant (*hist.*), concentus (*B*), symphony (*B*), unison, diapason, diaphony, organum, faburden (*hist.*).
Antonyms: see DISCORD, DISCORDANCE.
3. *Referring to a literary work showing consistency of parallel passages: spec.* diatessaron.
harness, *v. t.* hitch (*U. S.*); *spec.* saddle, inyoke, yoke, span, inspan (*South Africa*), trap.
Antonyms: see UNHARNESS.
harp, *n. Spec.* clairschach (*Celtic*), kanoon.
harpoon, *v. t.* strike, peg (*cant*).
harpy, *n.* **1.** demon (*contex.*).
2. *See* EXTORTIONER.
harsh, *a.* **1.** *Spec.* rough, acid, acrimonious, dure (*B*), bearish, brutal, cruel, rude, churlish, hard, unfeeling, unkind, ungenial, sharp, crude, coarse, brute, brutish, intender (*R*), sour, severe, blunt, round, astringent, acrid, rugged.
Antonyms: see GENTLE, BLAND, UNCTUOUS.
2. *Referring to sounds:* cacophonous (*R or B*), unmelodious; *spec.* metallic, brazen, hard, hoarse, strident, iron, scabrous (*R*), raucous, unsweet (*R*), ragged, discordant, grating.
Antonyms: see SMOOTH, SWEET.
harshness, *n. Spec.* hardness, cruelty, crudity, crudeness, unkindness, ungentleness, acidity, astringency, dissonance, raucity (*R*), *etc.*
harvest, *n.* **1.** yield, product, harvestry, crop, gather (*R*); *spec.* vintage, rabi (*Anglo-Indian*).
2. *See* PRODUCT.
harvest, *v. t.* crop (*R*), reap (*primarily spec.*); *spec.* glean, hay, vindemiate (*R*), crop.
Antonyms: see SOW.
harvester, *n.* harvestman, reaper; *spec.* gleaner.
harvest home. maiden (*Scot.*), kirn (*Scot.*).
harvest queen. *Spec.* harvest doll, kirn baby (*Scot.*), maiden (*Scot.*).
has-been, *n.* quondam (*obs.*), back number (*C*), old hat (*S*).
haste, *n.* quickness, hurry, precipitation *or* precipitancy, precipitance (*R*), speed, festination (*R*), rush (*headlong haste; often in a slang way, any haste*), press, expedition, dispatch, expeditiousness; *spec.* posthaste (*R as a noun*), rashness, bustle, hustle, impetuosity, hastiness.
Antonyms: see DELIBERATION.
hasten, *v. t.* quicken, hurry, dispatch, speed, urge, press, hurry-scurry, precipitate, express, festinate (*R*); *spec.* rush, spur, crowd, bundle, hustle.
Antonyms: see DETAIN, RETARD.
hasten, *v. i.* quicken, go, hurry, press, hie (*A or B*), dispatch, expedite, forward, haste (*B*); *spec.* scorch, fleet, hustle (*C*), spurt, rustle (*C*), fly, clip (*C*), race, spur, wing, crowd (*A or R*), scurry, run, peg (*C*), powder (*C*), drive, post, hurry-scurry.
Antonyms: see DELAY.
hastily, *adv.* quickly, hurriedly, expeditiously; *spec.* hotfoot, post (*A*), posthaste, rashly, recklessly, helter-skelter, hurry-scurry, *etc.*
hasty, *a.* quick, hasteful (*R*), hurried, precipitate; *spec.* precipitant (*R*), expeditious, rash, brash, running, hot-headed, rapid, passing, cursory, abrupt, helter skelter, pell mell.
Antonyms: see DELIBERATE.
hat, *n. spec.* cap, derby (*U. S.*), bowler (*Eng.*), billycock (*Eng.*), gibus, sombrero, sundown (*U. S.*), sugar loaf, turban, castor, squam (*U. S.*), wideawake, tiara, lid (*S*), tile (*S*), petasus, kausia, leghorn, dicer (*S*), slough (*S*), shovel, mushroom (*S*), felt, garibaldi, miter, turban, mitra, busby (*Brit.*), shako, capeline, copintank (*obs.*), caubeen (*Irish*), kiss-me-quick, jerry, Christie (*Canada*).
hate, *n. This word, as distinguished from* hatred, *denotes especially the actual feeling or emotion; while* hatred *denotes especially merely the attitude of mind. See* HATRED.
Antonyms: see COMPASSION.
hate, *v. t.* dislike (*chiefly implies only mild disapproval, but contex. may be synonymous with* hate), abhor (*implying profound repugnance*), detest (*implying deep* dislike *or antipathy*), execrate (*involves invoking dire punishment or uttering imprecations or curses*), abominate (*carries suggestion of dislike of something ill-omened or shameful*); *spec.* loathe (*implying absolute disgust*).
hateful, *a.* **1.** disagreeable (*contex.*); *spec.* spiteful, rancorous; *see* MALEVOLENT.
2. disagreeable (*contex.*), offensive, cursed, abominable, detestable, odious; *spec.* spiteful, annoying, invidious.
Antonyms: see KINDLY, KIND, APATHETIC, AFFABLE, AFFECTIONATE, AGREEABLE, COMPASSIONATE.
hatred, *n.* dislike, hate, abhorrence, heartburn, detestation, execration; *spec.* malevolence, malignity, enmity, abomination, odium. *See* HATE.
Antonyms: see AFFECTION, COMPASSION, LOVE.

---

harness, *n.: equipment.*
harp, *v. i.: dwell.*
harrow: *plunder, distress.*
harry: *plunder, distress.*
hash, *v. t.: comminute.*
hasp, *n.: clasp.*
hassock: *tuft, footstool.*
hastiness: *haste.*
hatch, *v. t.: engrave, inlay.*
hatch, *v. t.: incubate, devise.*
hatch, *v. i.: generate.*
hatch, *n.: offspring.*
hatch, *n.: door, gate.*
hatchment: *escutcheon.*
hatchway: *doorway.*

---

haughtiness, *n.* arrogance, hauteur (*French, but nearly Anglicized*).

haughty, *a.* proud (*contex.*), arrogant, lordly, supercilious, overproud, hoity-toity (*familiar or deprecating*).

Antonyms: see AFFABLE, AGREEABLE, HUMBLE, SERVILE.

have, *v. t.* **1.** possess, hold; *spec.* own.

Antonyms: see LACK.

2. *See* GET, EXPERIENCE, ENJOY, EXERCISE, ENTERTAIN, REMEMBER, BEAR, KEEP, DEFEAT, STATE, LEARN, CAUSE, EFFECT.

hawk, *n.* Jack (*male; chiefly spec.*); *spec.* eyas, brancher, buzzard, kite, windhover, falcon, harrier, gerfalcon, haggard, hobby, sore, lanner, intermewer, staniel, lanneret, kestrel, henharrier, henhawk, goshawk, tercel *or* tiercel, tercelet *or* tiercelet, saker, sakeret.

hawk, *v. t.* sell, peddle, cry.

hawker, *n.* seller, dealer, peddler; *spec.* colporteur.

hawking, *n.* falconry (*chiefly spec.*).

hazard, *n.* *Spec.* chance, adventure, danger, stake, bunker (*golf*).

haze, *n.* **1.** *Spec.* cloud, gauze (*R*), fog, mist, smoke, fume, miasma, pall, smother.

2. *See* OBSCURITY, DIMNESS.

hazy, *a.* **1.** dim (*contex.*), thick, misty, cloudy, smoky, foggy, fumy; *spec.* miasmatic.

Antonyms: see CLEAR.

2. *See* DIM, INDISTINCT.

head, *n.* **1.** headpiece (*A or C*), nob (*S*), noddle (*C or jocular*), mazard (*A and jocular*), garret (*S*), poll (*obs., exc. C, dial.,* or *in "poll tax," etc.*), pate, pash (*obs.*), sconce (*A and jocular*), knob (*S*), dome (*S*), costard (*contemptuous or humorous*), coxcomb (*humorous; chiefly spec.*), brain (*fig.*), top (*C*), pow (*Scot. and dial.*); *spec.* occiput (*tech.*), sinciput (*tech.*), calvarium (*tech.*), jowl, gorgoneion, skull, face.

Antonyms: see TAIL.

2. *Referring to the hair of the head:* crop (*S*); *spec.* mop, bush, shock.

3. *See* UNDERSTANDING, PERSON, INDIVIDUAL, FRONT, ANTLERS, BOW, SOURCE, HEADING, FORCE, FOAM, PROTUBERANCE, TOP.

4. chief; *spec.* leader, dean, conductor, paterfamilias, provost, master, præpositus, hegumen (*eccl.*), mother (*eccl.*), superior (*eccl.*), cream, face.

5. *Referring to an inflorescence: spec.* capitulum (*tech.*), spike, glomerule, cabbage.

headache, *n.* cephalalgia (*tech.*).

headband, *n.* band, vitta (*B*); *spec.* fillet.

headdress, *n.* headgear, coiffure (*French*), headtire (*A*); *spec.* barb, chignon, cob, coif, bridle, tower, butterfly, stephane, commode, headcloths (*pl.*), capuchon, polos, tutulus, hennin (*hist.*).

headed, *a.* *Referring to plants: spec.* capitate, capitellate, kerned.

heading, *n.* **1.** *See* FRONT.

2. *Referring to part or all of a book, manuscript, etc.: spec.* title, head, caption (*chiefly U. S.*), headline, lemma (*B*), capitulary (*R*), rubric.

headland, *n.* head (*mostly in place names*), foreland; *spec.* promontory, cape, cliff, bluff, escarpment, ness (*mostly in place names*), reach (*obs. or U. S.*), peak (*local*), horn (*R*), nook (*R*), tongue, spit, hook, reef, maze (*R*).

headless, *a.* acephalous (*tech.*).

headlong, *a.* headfirst; *spec.* pell-mell, hurry-scurry.

headpiece, *n.* hat; *spec.* casque (*now B or hist.*), crest, helmet, headstall.

headship, *n.* primacy (*dignified*), supremacy; *spec.* chieftaincy, captaincy, chiefdom.

heal, *v. i.* *Spec.* incarn (*R*).

health, *n.* soundness, haleness (*R*), eucrasy (*R*), healthfulness (*R*), tone (*chiefly spec.*), euphoria (*R*), sanity (*A, exc. spec.*), heal (*Scot.*); *spec.* vigor, hardiness.

Antonyms: see UNHEALTH.

healthful, *a.* **1.** *Referring to things:* beneficial, healthsome (*R*), wholesome, salutary, salutiferous (*R*), salubrious (*chiefly spec.*), healthy (*a use avoided by some*); *spec.* laudable.

Antonyms: see UNHEALTHFUL, PATHOLOGIC, POISONOUS.

2. *Referring to persons: see* HEALTHY.

health resort. sanitarium, sanatorium.

healthy, *a.* **1.** *Referring to persons:* sound (*now used chiefly in the predicate*), hale (*chiefly spec.*), sane (*R, exc. spec.*), healthful, hygeian (*R*); *spec.* well, lusty, hearty.

Antonyms: see AILING, UNHEALTHY.

2. *See* HEALTHFUL (*referring to things*), GOOD.

heap, *v. t.* **1.** pile, coacervate (*R*); *spec.* stack, cop (*dial. Eng.*), clamp (*tech.*), dress (*Scot.*), hill, huddle, mound.

2. *See* GIVE, BESTOW.

3. *Referring to that on which things are heaped: spec.* overfill, pile, cumber.

heap, *n.* **1.** accumulation (*contex.*), cumulus (*R*), coacervation (*R*); *spec.* huddle, pile, entassement (*R*), imbroglio (*R*), hill, mound, tumulus, mountain, ruck, stack, cop (*Eng.*), barrow, cairn, cache, bing, mow, haymow, rick, hayrick, cock, haycock, haystack, dump, kitchen-midden (*archæology*), clam.

2. *See* DEAL.

heaped, *a.* tumulary (*R*), cumulate (*contex.*), massed (*contex.*).

hear, *v. t.* **1.** perceive (*contex.*), listen, hark (*at-*

---

haul: *draw.*
haunch, *n.: hip, quarter, coxa.*
haunt, *n.: resort.*
haunt, *v. t.: frequent, obsess, attend.*
haunting: *recurrent.*
haven: *harbor, refuge.*
having: *possession.*
havoc: *devastation.*
hay, *n.: fodder.*
hay, *v. i.: harvest.*
hazard, *n.: chance, venture, danger, stake.*
hazard, *v. t.: endanger, venture.*
haze, *v. t.: abuse.*
head, *a.: chief.*
head, *v. t.: behead, lead, oppose, top, direct.*
headsman: *chief, executioner.*
headstrong: *obstinate.*
headway: *advance, motion.*
heady: *obstinate, intoxicating.*
heal: *cure.*
healing: *curative.*

---

tentively; B), list (*A*), drink (*used with "in"*), catch, hearken (*B*); *spec.* forehear (*R*), mishear, overhear, receive.
2. *See* DISCOVER, GRANT, TRY.
hear, *v. i.* perceive; *spec.* listen, hark (*chiefly as an imperative or interj., or B*), hearken.
heard, *a.* auricular (*B*).
hearer, *n.* auditor, audient (*R*), listener; *spec.* pittite.
hearing, *n.* **1.** *Referring to the faculty or sense:* audition (*tech.*), ear (*often spec.; in sing. only*).
2. *Referring to the opportunity or privilege of being heard:* audience, audition.
3. *See* TRIAL.
4. sound, earshot, ear, range (*contex.*).
hearse, *n.* **1.** *See* GRAVE.
2. *Spec.* catafalque.
hearse, *v. t.* enhearse *or* inhearse (*R*); *spec.* bury, shroud.
heart, *n. Spec.* mind, soul, reins (*pl.; a Biblical use*), spirit, feeling, courage, temperament, center, essence, breast, meaning.
heart, *a.* pectoral (*tech. or B*).
heartburn, *n.* **1.** cardialgia (*tech.*).
2. *See* HATRED, DISTRUST.
heartful, *a.* deep, cordial (*now R or B*); *spec.* dear.
hearth, *n.* **1.** fireplace, hearthstead (*R*); *spec.* hearthstone.
2. *See* FIREPLACE, FORGE.
heartily, *adv.* cordially, sincerely, inly.
heart-shaped, *a.* hearted, cordiform, cordate, cardioid;—*mostly tech. or B.*
heartwood, *n.* duramen (*tech.*).
hearty, *a.* **1.** cordial (*chiefly spec.*), sincere; *spec.* deep.
2. strong, vigorous, robust; *see* HEALTHY.
Antonyms: see AILING.
hearty, *n.* comrade, good fellow; sailor (*contex.*), roisterer (*in this sense in Brit. university S, as antonym of* aesthete).
heat, *n.* **1.** caloric (*A or B*), caloricity (*A or B*), fire (*spec. or fig.*), fieriness (*spec. or fig.*); *spec.* hotness; fierceness, warmth, warmness, torridity, ferventness, fervidity *or* fervidness *or* (*more commonly*) fervor (*B*), calorie, glow, pressure (*as in the S phrase "turn on the heat"*).
Antonyms: see COLD.
2. *See* EXCITEMENT, ARDOR, FIT, ACRIDITY, GLOW, FEVER, FRENZY, AGITATION, ROUND, HEIGHT.
heat, *v. t.* **1.** calorify (*R*), calify (*R or obs.*), fire (*spec. or fig.*), enchafe (*A and B*), hot (*C or illiterate*); *spec.* bake, warm, inflame, burn, broil, scorch, calcine, decrepitate, incandesce, stove, superheat, mull.
Antonyms: see COOL.
2. *See* EXCITE, INFLAME.
heat, *v. i.* calorify (*R*), warm (*chiefly spec.*); *spec.* incandesce.
heated, *a.* **1.** *Spec.* warm, fiery, broiling, sizzling, burning, *etc.*; *see* HOT.
Antonyms: see COLD.
2. *See* EXCITED, ANGRY.
heater, *n. Spec.* calefactory, pome, stove, etna.
heathen, *a.* ethnic (*B*); *spec.* gentile, pagan, infidel, unchristian, paganish, heathenish, barbarous.
heathen, *n. Spec.* gentile, pagan, infidel, paynim, gentoo.
Antonyms: see CHRISTIAN.
heathendom, *n.* heathenism, ethnicism (*B*), heathenry, infidelity (*R*), heathenesse (*A*); *spec.* pagandom, paganity (*R*), gentilism.
heather, *n.* ling (*northern Eng.*); *spec.* brier, briar, white heath.
heathery, *a.* heathy, lingy.
heating, *a.* calescent, calorific, pyrogenic (*R*), calefacient, calefactive *or* calefactory (*R*), calorifacient, incalescence;—*all, exc. "heating," B or tech.*
Antonyms: see COOLING.
heating, *n.* calefaction (*rhetorical or tech.*); *spec.* incalescence (*R*), warm (*C*), warming.
heaven, *n.* **1.** *In a physical sense:* sky (*in pl. with "the," spec.; in sing., chiefly with "the," spec.*), firmament (*now B or rhetorical*), cope (*B*), welkin (*A or dial.*), sphere (*B*); *spec.* canopy, empyrean, hyaline (*B*), crystalline.
2. *Referring to the abode of the blessed: spec.* Paradise (*chiefly B*), Zion (*Biblical*), Canaan (*chiefly devotional*); *spec.* Asgard (*Scandinavian religion*), Elysium (*Greek religion*).
Antonyms: see HELL.
3. *See* DEITY, HAPPINESS.
heavenliness, *n.* heavenhood (*R*), celestiality (*R*), celestitude (*humorous*).
heavenly, *a.* **1.** celestial, uranic (*R*); *spec.* ethereal, empyreal *or* empyrean.
Antonyms: see TERRESTRIAL.
2. divine (*contex.*), celestial, supernal (*B*), heavenlike; *spec.* ethereal (*B*), elysiac (*Greek religion*), Paradisiacal, Paradisiac, Paradisaic, Paradisaical, Paradisial, Paradisian, Paradisic (*R*), Paradisical (*R*), Olympian (*Greek religion*), Olympic (*R*), angelic.
Antonyms: see INFERNAL, DEVILISH, WORLDLY.
heavenward, *a.* **1.** up, upwards, aloft, skyward.
Antonyms: see DOWNWARD.
2. Zionward (*R*).
heaviness, *n.* **1.** weight, heft (*dial. or C*); *spec.* ponderousness, ponderosity.
2. *See* DEPRESSION, DEPTH, DULLNESS, *etc. Cf.* HEAVY, *a.*, **2.**
heavy, *a.* **1.** weighty, hefty (*dial. Eng. and C or dial. U. S.*), sad (*dial., exc. in comb. or in spec. uses, as* sadiron), leaden (*fig. and intensive*); *spec.* ponderous.
Antonyms: see LIGHT, AIRY.

hearken, *v. t.: hear.*
hearken, *v. i.: hear, listen.*
hearsay: *report.*
hearten: *cheer, encourage, embolden.*
heartless: *unfeeling, cruel, cold.*
heartrending: *distressing.*
heart-sick: *depressed.*
heartwhole: *cordial.*
heath: *moor, heather.*
heave, *v. t.: lift, raise, utter, throw, agitate.*
heave, *v. i.: rise, swell, retch.*
heave, *n.: lift, rise, wave.*

2. *See* BURDENSOME, BASS, OPPRESSIVE, DULL, DEPRESSED, SOBER, LOW, IMPORTANT, STUPID, SLEEPY, COARSE, CLOSE, STIFF, ABUNDANT, DISTRESSING, VIOLENT, DEPRESSING, CLOGGY, LOUD, MASSIVE, STEEP, STRONG.

Hebrew, *a.* Semitic, Jewish, Judaic, Hebraic, Israeltish, Israelitic.

Hebrew, *n.* Semite, Jew, Israelite, Israel (*collective pl.*), kike, yid, sheeney (*all three vulgar S; U. S.*).

hedge, *n.* **1.** hedgerow, hay (*A*); *spec.* bullfinch (*Eng.*), frith, quickset.

2. *See* BARRIER.

hedge, *v. i.* evade, dodge, trim; *spec.* temporize, straddle (*C*), pass the buck (*S*).

height, *n.* **1.** elevation, eminence (*B or A*), highness (*R*), celsitude (*R; chiefly fig.*); *spec.* altitude, head.

Antonyms: see ABYSS, DEPTH.

2. *Referring to distance from the top to bottom:* celsitude (*humorously affected or grandiose*), tallness, loftiness; *spec.* altitude, stature.

Antonyms: see DEPTH.

3. *Of a high place:* elevation.

4. *Referring to the greatest extent or degree of something, as heat, feeling, etc.:* top, apex, noon (*fig.*), culmination, climax, vertex, pinnacle, pitch (*R*), crown, meridian, summit, acme, apogee, zenith; *spec.* heyday, heat, stress, flush, ne plus ultra (*Latin*), sublimity (*R*), sum, perfection, consummation, top (*C, with "the"*).

Antonyms: see DEPTH.

heighten, *n.* **1.** elevate (*by raising*).

2. *See* STRENGTHEN, INTENSIFY, AGGRAVATE.

heir, *n.* inheritor, heritor (*R*), heiress (*fem.*), inheritress *or* inheritrix (*fem.*), heritress *or* heritrix *or* heretrix (*fem.*); *spec.* representative, heir apparent, master (*Scot.*), coheir, coheiress, coparcener, parcener.

heirship, *n.* inheritance, heritance (*R*); *spec.* coparcenary, coparcenery, coparceny, parcenary.

hell, *n.* **1.** *Referring to the place of the departed souls: spec.* Sheol (*Hebrew*), Hades (*Greek*), shades (*Latin*), underworld, grave (*with "the"; fig.*), inferno (*usually taken in sense* **2**, *below*), Elysium (*Greek*).

2. *As the place where the damned are tormented: spec.* abyss, inferno (*now chiefly in allusion to Dante's "Inferno"*), Tartarus (*Greek*), Gehenna (*Hebrew*), pit (*with "the"; often called "the bottomless pit"*), Hades (*an erroneous use, chiefly by way of a euphemistic oath*), Pandemonium (*Greek*), Tophet (*fig.*), malebolge.

Antonyms: see HEAVEN.

3. *See* DISTRESS.

helm, *n.* tiller;—*primarily the steering gear as a whole.*

helmet, *n.* headpiece, helm (*A or B*), casque (*now only hist., B, or French*); *spec.* crest, skullcap, sallet, salade, burgonet, basinet, morion, heaume.

helmeted, *a.* **1.** galeated (*R*).

2. *zoöl.; spec.* galeated.

helmet-shaped, *a.* galeated; *spec.* cassideous, cassidiform;—*all three B or tech.*

helpful, *a.* aiding (*contex.*); *spec.* assistant, contributory, aidful (*R*), furthersome (*chiefly Scot.*), beneficial, comfortable, favorable, auxiliary, serviceable; *see* COÖPERATIVE.

Antonyms: see HINDERING, RUINOUS.

helpless, *a.* silly (*A*), unhelpful (*R*), impotent; *spec.* defenseless, naked, abandoned, blank, prostrate, resourceless, shiftless.

Antonyms: see INGENIOUS.

hem, *v. t.* **1.** sew (*contex.*), hemstitch; *spec.* table (*naut.*).

2. *See* SURROUND.

hemisphere, *n.* semiglobe (*R*), semisphere (*R*).

hemp, *n. Spec.* bhang (*India*), hashish *or* hasheesh, hards.

hempen, *n.* hemp (*the noun used attributively*), hempy.

hen, *n.* bird (*contex.*), fowl (*contex.*), biddy (*C*); *spec.* sitter, pullet, poulard.

hence, *adv.* **1.** away (*contex.*), hereout (*R*), herefrom (*R*).

Antonyms: see HERE.

2. *See* THEREFORE.

heraldic, *a.* armorial.

heraldry, *n. Spec.* blazonry.

herbaceous, *a.* herbous (*R*).

herbage, *n.* vegetation (*contex.*), herb (*R or B*), verdure.

herbarium, *n.* hortus siccus (*Latin*), herbary.

herbivorous, *a.* poëphagous (*R*); *spec.* granivorous, graminivorous.

herby, *a.* herbose; *spec.* grassy.

herd, *n.* **1.** *Spec.* drove, troop, rout (*R*), pack, game (*obs. or R*); *see* FLOCK.

2. *See* CROWD.

herd, *v. i.* **1.** associate (*contex.*); *spec.* pig, crowd.

2. drove (*referring to the action of a drover*).

herder, *n.* herdsman (*the usual term for a male herder*), herd (*chiefly in composition*); *spec.* ranchero (*U. S.*), gooseherd, shepherd, shepherdess, pasturer (*R*), pastor (*R*), pastoress (*R*), pastoral (*R*), herdess (*R*), herdboy, cowboy (*U. S. and colonial Eng.*), goatherd, cow-

---

hecatomb: *slaughter.*
heckle: *harass, question.*
hectic: *flushed.*
hectic, *n.: consumptive.*
hector: *bully.*
heed, *v. t.: notice, consider.*
heed, *v. i.: notice, care.*
heed, *n.: notice, attention, consideration, care.*
heedful, *a.: attentive, careful.*
heedless, *a.: disregardful, careless.*
heel, *v. t.: arm.*
heel, *v. i.: follow.*
heft, *n.: weight, bulk.*
heft, *v. t.: lift.*
hellish: *infernal, devilish.*
hello: *hollo.*
helmsman: *steersman.*
helter-skelter, *adv.: about, confusedly, hastily.*
hem, *v. i.: cough, falter.*
hem, *n.: edge, border.*
herald, *n.: crier, predecessor.*
herald, *v. t.: announce, forerun.*
herb: *plant.*
herd, *v. t.: drive, tend, gather.*

---

herd, hayward, neatherd, vaquero (*Western U. S.*).
here, *adv.* **1.** hither (*B or affected*), hitherward *or* hitherwards (*A*).
Antonyms: see HENCE.
2. *See* NOW.
hereafter, *adv.* henceforth, henceforward.
Antonyms: see NOW.
hereditament, *n.* **1.** heritage (*chiefly spec.*), patrimony, heritance, birthright, inheritance; *spec.* heirloom.
2. *See* INHERITANCE.
hereditary, *a.* **1.** inheritable, heritable, transmissible, descendant *or* descendent, descensive (*R*); *spec.* transmissible, patrimonial.
2. *Referring to disease, traits, etc.:* heritable, transmissible.
heredity, *n.* transmission; *spec.* telegony.
heresy, *n.* unbelief, heterodoxy, dissenting, recusancy, schism (heresy *implies an unorthodox opinion, often religious, tending to promote* schism *or separation;* schism *sometimes implies the dissenting view, but more often the resultant separation*); *spec.* Lollardism, Lollardry, Lollardy.
Antonyms: see ORTHODOXY.
heretic, *n.* unbeliever, heterodox (*R*), recusant, dissenter; *spec.* Lollard, infidel.
Antonyms: see BELIEVER.
heretical, *a.* unbelieving, heterodox, dissenting (*chiefly spec.*), recusant.
Antonyms: see ORTHODOX.
heritage, *n.* inheritance (*implying simply what has been inherited or passed down, whereas* heritage *is a more B or elevated term for the same*), patrimony (*an inheritance from one's father*), hereditament (*spec.*).
hermaphrodite, *a.* bisexual; *spec.* gynandrous, androgynic, androgynous.
hermit, *n.* recluse, solitaire (*R*), solitary, anchoret, anchorite, anchoress (*fem.*), hermitess (*fem.*); *spec.* eremite, Guillemen (*hist.*), ascetic, Hieronymite, marabout.
hernia, *a.* rupture (*less tech. than hernia*), ramex (*obs.*); *spec.* epiplocele, exomphalos, bubonocele.
hero, *n.* **1.** *See* DEMIGOD.
2. heroine (*fem.*), protagonist (*B*); *spec.* lion, paladin.
hesitate, *v. i.* **1.** stop, pause, scruple (*chiefly spec.*); *spec.* halt, stand, falter, waver, stickle, stick, doubt, crane (*C, Eng.*), trifle, boggle, demur, shrink, shilly-shally.
Antonyms: see CONTINUE.
2. *See* FALTER.
hesitating, *a.* undecided (*contex.*), doubtful (*contex.*), indecisive, hesitant, hesitative, hesitatory (*R*); *spec.* suspensive (*R*), faltering, scrupling, faltering, *etc.*
Antonyms: see ASSURED, DOGMATIC, CERTAIN, DECIDED, READY.
hesitation, *n.* **1.** doubting, doubt, uncertainty, indecision;—*the four being contex. senses; spec.* stop, stick, stickle, boggle, scruple, stand, shrink, falter.
2. *See* FALTER.
heterogeneous, *a.* diverse, unhomogeneous (*R*), diversified, miscellaneous, mixed; *spec.* omnigenous, hybrid *or* (*R*) hybridous, indiscriminate.
Antonyms: see HOMOGENEOUS.
hexahedral, *a. Spec.* cubic, cubical, cubiform, cuboid, cuboidal.
hiatus, *n.* gap (*contex.*); *spec.* lacuna (*tech.*), blank.
hiccup, *n.* hick (*R*); *spec.* (*as the name of the ailment*) hiccups (*often construed as a sing.*), singultus (*tech.*).
hidden, *a.* **1.** *Referring to physical things:* hid (*chiefly predicative*), concealed, covered, covert (*obs.*), secreted, secret (*chiefly A or B, exc. spec.*), dern (*A or Scot.*); *spec.* close, cloaked, masked, screened, ensconced, planted (*cant*), enshrouded, obscure, obscured, occult (*R*), latitant (*R*), recondite (*R*), undiscovered, clouded, cloudy, suppressed, veiled, blotted, shadowed, shrouded, overlaid, stored, obumbrate (*tech.*), dark, blind, disguised, lurking, snug, latent (*R; for discrimination see* INACTIVE).
Antonyms: see APPARENT.
2. *Referring to things seen (perceived) by the mind:* hid (*chiefly predicative*), inward, concealed; *spec.* covered, screened, shrouded, obscured, disguised, mysterious, mystic *or* mystical, oracular, occult, esoteric, covert, latent, secret, clandestine, cryptic, surreptitious, underhand *or* underhanded, sly, blind, illegible, unintelligible, insidious, lurking, private, fraudulent, unknown, unacknowledged, unavowed, *etc.*
Antonyms: see APPARENT, CLEAR, UNCONCEALED.
hide, *v. t.* **1.** *Referring to physical objects:* conceal, cover; *spec.* mask, cloak, bemask (*R*), stow, screen, bescreen, secrete, ensconce, plant, shroud *or* enshroud (*B*), den (*chiefly reflexive*), obscure, occult (*R*), disguise, protect, bury, cloud, becloud, earth, suppress, veil, embosom, bushel (*R*), blot, burrow, shadow, eclipse, overlay, store.
Antonyms: see DISCLOSE, EXPOSE, INDICATE, SHOW.
2. *Referring to things seen by the mind: spec.* bury, hoard, gloze, eclipse, sweeten, repress, smother, omit, cavern, den, earth (*B, rhetorical, or cant*). *See also definition,* **1,** *above.*
Antonyms: see INDICATE, ADVERTIZE, ANNOUNCE, PROCLAIM, CONFESS, DISCLOSE, EXPOSE.
hiding, *n.* concealment, cover, celation (*R; chiefly spec.*); *spec.* disguise, occultation (*R*

heroic, *a.: brave, extreme.*
heroic, *n.: poem, bombast.*
hesitant: *hesitating.*
heterodoxy, *a.: heresy.*
heterogeneity: *diversity, difference.*
hew: *chop, fell.*
heyday: *height, prime.*
hibernate: *winter.*
hide, *n.: skin.*
hidebound: *narrow.*
hideous: *ugly, horrible, abominable.*
hieratic: *priestly.*

or chiefly astron.), eclipse, coverture, latitation (*R*).
Antonyms: see DISCLOSURE, INDICATION, SHOW.

high, *a.* **1.** elevated, lofty (*often rhetorical or B*), eminent (*B or A*); *spec.* towering, mountained (*B*), aërial, soaring; over-ripe (high, *so used chiefly of meats and game, is S*); drunk (*S*).
Antonyms: see LOW.
2. *Referring to distance from top to bottom:* lofty (*often rhetorical or B*), tall.
Antonyms: see LOW.
3. *Referring to a price:* fancy, dear, stiff (*S*); *spec.* costly.
4. *Referring to sounds:* high-pitched, high-toned, acute (*chiefly music and phonetics*); *spec.* shrill, sharp, piercing, cracked, creaking, intense, forceful, rank.
Antonyms: see LOW.
5. *See* ARBITRARY, ARROGANT, EXTREME, STRONG, EXALTED, ANGRY, NORTHERN, SOUTHERN, LATE, ANCIENT, LOUD, IMPORTANT, ABSTRUSE, PLEASED.

higher, *a.* upper, superior, supernal (*B*).
Antonyms: see LOWER.

highest, *a.* **1.** *Referring to place:* uppermost, supreme (*R*), top, summit.
Antonyms: see LOWEST.
2. *Referring to degree, rank, etc.:* supreme, superlative, utmost, crowning, consummating.
Antonyms: see LOWEST.

highest, *n. Spec.* meridian, maximum, zenith.

highlander, *n. Spec.* hillsman, mountaineer, tartan.

high priest, pontiff (*B or rhetorical*); *spec.* pope (*Roman Catholic*), protopapas *or* protopope (*Greek Church*).

hill, *n.* **1.** elevation, ascent, rise, rising; *spec.* monadnock (*chiefly U. S.*), knoll, hillock, mound, knob (*chiefly U. S.*), know (*Scot.*), highland, dune, down, hummock, holt, monticule, mount (*B or A*), mountain, butte (*western U. S.*), drum (*local or geol.*), swell, ridge, kop (*South Africa*), kopje (*South Africa*), drumlin, steep, hilltop, hillside, Alpine, Himalayan.
Antonyms: see HOLLOW, VALLEY, PLAIN.
2. *See* HEAP.

hilly, *a.* rising (*contex.*); *spec.* knolly, hillish, hillocky, mountainous, mountainy (*R or C*), rolling.
Antonyms: see PLAIN.

hind, *a.* hinder (*in reference to two*), posterior, rear, rearward (*R*), postjacent (*R*), posterial (*R*); *spec.* posticous, hindmost, after, behind.
Antonyms: see FORE.

hinder, *v. t.* **1.** delay, retard, impede (*properly spec.*); *spec.* embarrass, restrain, obstruct, clog, encumber *or* cumber, discourage, belate, hamper, bar, check, counteract.
Antonyms: see EXPEDITE.
2. *See* PREVENT.

hindering, *a.* **1.** delaying, impedimental, impeditive (*R*); *spec.* obstructive, cumbering, cumbersome, *etc.*
Antonyms: see HELPFUL, CONTRIBUTORY.
2. *See* PREVENTIVE.

hindermost, *a.* last, back, hindmost.

hindrance, *n.* hinderance (*R*), hindering, let (*A*), remora (*R*), delay, delayal (*R*), retardation, impediment (*properly spec.*); *spec.* embarrassment, obstruction, obstructive, cumbrance, encumberment, encumbrance, incumbrance, discouragement, cramp, debarrent (*R*), clog, drawback, hamper, hampering, counteraction, check, difficulty, contrariety, bar, balk, disadvantage, impedance (*elec.*), shoe, brake, *etc.*
Antonyms: see AID, CONTRIBUTION.

Hindu, *n.* Indian, gentile (*R*) *or* gentoo; *spec.* Mahratta (*man*), Mahratti, Hindustani.

hinge, *n.* **1.** joint (*contex.*); *spec.* butt, strap.
2. *See* CENTER, CRISIS.

hip, *n.* **1.** *Referring to one side only:* thigh. Thigh *and* hip *are not proper synonyms, but are often used as synonyms.*
2. *Referring to both sides taken together:* haunch (*chiefly spec.*), coxa (*tech.; R*); *spec.* rump.

hip, *a.* ischiadic, ischial, sciatic, ischiatic;—*all tech.*, sciatic *being the more usual term.*

hipped, *a.* hipshot.

hire, *v. t.* get, engage, employ, buy (*fig.*); *spec.* fee, bribe, ship, job, hack, charter, lease. Hire *emphasizes the idea of the payment to be made.*
Antonyms: see BUY, DISCHARGE, LET.

hire, *n.* reward, pay; *spec.* salary, wages, wage, compensation, emolument, honorarium, rent, stipend (*A, exc. Scot.*), bribe, freight.

hired, *a.* mercenary (*now spec.*), paid; *spec.* hackney.

hireling, *n.* mercenary (*now spec.*); *spec.* myrmidon.

hiss, *v. i. Spec.* fizz, fizzle, siffle, hizz (*R*), sibilate, siss (*dial. and C, U. S.*), sizzle, sizz (*chiefly U. S.*), goose (*theat. cant*), spit.

hiss, *n. Spec.* fizz, fizzle, siss (*dial. Eng. and C, U. S.*), sizzle, sibilation, siffle (*R*), spit.

hissing, *a.* sibilant, sibilous (*R*).

historian, *n.* historiaster (*in contempt*); *spec.* memorialist, biographer, logographer (*Greek antiq.*), chronicler, historiographer.

historic, historical, *a. Spec.* authentic. Historic *is chiefly used of what constitutes history*; historical, *of what relates to history.*

historicize, *v. t.* record (*contex.*), historize (*R*), historify (*R*); *spec.* celebrate. Historicize *is R.*

---

high-flown: *bombastic.*
high-handed: *arbitrary, willful, domineering.*
highland: *plateau, hill, mountain.*
high-minded: *arrogant, spiritual, refined.*
high-sounding: *pretentious, bombastic.*
high-spirited: *spirited.*
high-strung: *spirited.*
hilt: *handle.*
hindermost: *last.*
hinge, *v. i.: turn, depend.*
hint, *n.: intimation, tip, trace.*
hint, *v. t.: intimate.*
hippish, *a.: depressed.*
hirsute: *hairy.*

---

history, *n.* **1.** *See* NARRATIVE.
2. account (*contex.*), record, story; *spec.* memorials, memoirs, historiette, anecdote, commentary, chronicle, biography, autobiography, career, genealogy, prehistory.
3. historiology.

histrionic, *a.* theatrical (*these two words, properly implying merely what relates to the theatre as distinguished from the drama, are often used with the suggestion of that aspect of the theatre which is false, make-believe, artificial, affected or insincere*). *See* THEATRICAL, DECEITFUL.

histrionics, *n. pl.* theatricals, acting, dramatics; *spec.* tantrums (*contex.*).

hoard, *v. t.* hide (*contex.*), accumulate (*contex.*), store, save; *spec.* miser (*R*), treasure (*chiefly with "up"*).

hoard, *n.* accumulation (*contex.*), store, savings (*chiefly spec.*); *spec.* treasure (*often fig.*).

hoard, *n.* fence; *spec.* billboard.

hoarse, *a.* **1.** throaty, thick, husky; *spec.* roupy, croaking.
Antonyms: see CLEAR.
2. *See* HARSH.

hoax, *n.* deception (*contex.*), quiz (*obsolesc.*), hum (*S or C*), humbug (*R; now chiefly spec.*), cod (*S*), gammon (*S or C*), string (*S*), sell (*C*), trick, take-in; *spec.* canard, gag, jolly, josh (*S*), rig.

hoax, *v. t.* deceive (*which see*), trick (*which see*), sell (*C*), gammon (*C*), hum (*S or C*), string (*S*); *spec.* rig, josh (*S*), jolly, gag (*cant or S*), kid (*S*).

hockey, *n.* bandy *or* bandy ball (*R*), shinny; *spec.* hurley, polo.

hod, *n. Spec.* boss (*a plasterer's term*).

hoe, *n.* sarcle (*a Latinism*); *spec.* scuffler, scuffle, hacker.

hoe, *v. t.* cultivate (*contex.*); *spec.* weed, scuffle.

hoist, *n.* **1.** *See* RAISE;—*referring to the act.*
2. elevator (*which see*); *spec.* crane, gin, shears, derrick, teagle, sling, whip.

hold, *v. t.* **1.** have, keep, retain; *spec.* grasp, clasp, grip, pin, gripe, clip (*R or A*), pinion, clutch, embrace, fasten, fix, lock, cramp, catch, seize, bite, stay.
2. *Referring to a meeting:* conduct.
3. contain, receive; *spec.* carry, accommodate, stow.
4. *See* HAVE, KEEP, CONTROL, OBSERVE, OCCUPY, MANAGE, ABSORB, DETAIN, RESTRAIN, ENTERTAIN, CONSIDER, BIND, CARRY, CHECK, DECIDE.

hold, *v. i. Spec.* cling, cleave, stick (*as to one's post*), adhere (*as to one's opinions*), fasten.

hold, *n.* **1.** keeping, retention; *spec.* grasping, gripe, grip, clasp, anchor (*fig.*), bite, clutch, purchase, embrace, handhold, holdfast, control, possession, seizure.
2. *Referring to the thing that holds: spec.* lock, mortise, clutches (*pl.*), grip, cinch.
3. *See* CLAIM.
4. *Referring to a thing that one may hold to:* holdfast; *spec.* nail, lodgment, foothold, horn, rooting.

holder, *n.* **1.** holding; *spec.* handle, chuck, portcrayon, holdfast, container, case, zarf.
2. *See* POSSESSOR, OWNER.

holdfast, *n.* hold, holder; *spec.* tentacle, sucker, disk.

holding, *n.* property (*contex.*), tenement, tenantry, tenancy; *spec.* feu.

hole, *n. Spec.* aperture, void, cavity, perforation, hollow, fenestra (*anat.*), crater, slot, cell, cranny, chamber, interstice, eye, pore, porosity, depression, eyelet, mesh, bore, bye, concave, cave, pit, den, chasm, abyss, recess, gulf, leak, vug, box, mortise, sinus (*anat.*), limber (*naut.*), denehole (*archæology*), well, finger, burrow.
Antonyms: see PROJECTION.

holey, *a.* holy (*R or dial., variant*); *spec.* gulfy, cuppy, crannied, chinky, porous, chambered, *etc.*

holiday, *n.* **1.** *See* FESTIVAL.
2. *Spec.* playday, playtime, vacation.

holiday, *a.* festal, ferial (*R*).

holiness, *a.* **1.** sanctity (*B; implies a special state of sacredness acquired by merit*), sanctitude (*R*), sanctanimity (*R*), sinlessness, perfection, saintliness, sanctimony, hallowedness, consecration, righteousness (*implies consistent rectitude and obedience to divine law, with no suggestion of freedom from sin or special spiritual purity*), sanctification. *Cf.* HOLY.
2. hallowedness (*cf.* HALLOWED).

hollo, *v. i.* hollow (*R or obs.*), holla (*R or obs.*), hello (*by many considered undignified; a form which arose about 1880*), hallo, halloo (*esp. used as a hunting term or of shouting to call attention*), halloa (*R*); *spec.* soho.

hollow, *a.* **1.** *Spec.* cavernous, cavernulous, cavitary (*R*), cellular, porous, concave, cuppy, holey, empty, dimply.
Antonyms: see CONVEX, PROTUBERANT, PROJECTING.
2. *Referring to a sound:* reverberated, empty, sepulchral, deep, muffled.
Antonyms: see SOLID.
3. *See* INSINCERE, EMPTY, UNFEELING.

hollow, *n.* depression (*contex.*), hole, concave, hollowness (*R*), incavation (*R*); *spec.* dish, sinus, bosom, cove, cup, pocket, dimple, sag, dip, cupule, delve (*B*), basin, pan, bowl, sink (*U. S.*), scoop, excavation, punty *or* ponty, punt, kick, arch, trough, vola, valley, conch, conceptacle, countersink, indentation, scrobicule, pit.

---

hitherto: *before.*
hive: *swarm.*
hoary: *gray, old, frosty.*
hobble, *v. i.: falter.*
hobble, *v. t.: shackle.*
hobble, *n.: gait.*
hobby: *horse, fad.*
hobgoblin: *bogy.*
hobnob: *drink, associate.*
hocus-pocus: *deception.*
hodgepodge: *stew, mixture.*
hog: *swine, beast, glutton.*
hold, *v. i.: apply.*

Antonyms: see PROJECTION, HILL, ELEVATION, PROTUBERANCE.

hollow, *v. t.* excavate, concave; *spec.* dish, gull (*tech. or dial.*), recess, slot, pit, chamber, scoop, tunnel, cup, cave (*R*), cavern (*R*), *etc.*; *see* INDENT.

Antonyms: see EMBOSS.

hollow-backed, *a. Referring to a horse:* sway-backed.

hollowed, *a.* incavate (*R*), depressed; *spec.* cupped, chambered, *etc.*

Antonyms: see PROTUBERANT.

hollowness, *n.* **1.** *Of the state:* cavity, concavity, depression, emptiness; *spec.* cellulosity, porosity, sunkenness, cuppiness, *etc.*

2. *See* EMPTINESS, INSINCERITY, FALSITY.

holly, *n.* hollin *or* hollen (*A or dial.*), Christmas (*fig.*); *spec.* yapon, toyon.

holy, *a.* **1.** sinless; *spec.* saintly, sainted, hallowed (*set apart for* holy *purposes*), blessed *or* blest, sanctified (*rendered stainless, without sin, R*), consecrated (*set apart for religious purposes*), sacred (*a less intense synonym for* holy, *which implies inner merit, whereas* sacred *suggests set apart for religious or ecclesiastical uses*).

Antonyms: see SINFUL.

2. *See* HALLOWED, DEVOUT.

holy spirit, Paraclete, Comforter (*alluding to John xiv: 16*), Third Person (*theol.*), Dove (*fig.*).

homage, *n. Spec.* court, devotion, cult (*formal or B*).

home, *a.* **1.** *Spec.* family, domestic, homeward, homing.

2. *See* INTIMATE.

home-bred, *a.* plain, rude; *see* UNCULTIVATED.

homeless, *a. Spec.* outcast, harborless (*A or B*), houseless.

homelike, *a.* homish (*less dignified than homelike*), homely (*A*), homy *or* homey (*C*); *spec.* intimate, simple, plain, unpretending.

Antonyms: see CONVENTIONAL, STIFF, FORMAL.

homely, *a.* **1.** *See* DOMESTIC, SIMPLE, UNPRETENTIOUS, UNCULTIVATED.

2. plain, ill-favored; *spec.* unpretty, unpersonable (*R*), unlovely, featureless (*R*), uncomely (*R*), coarse, ugly, homespun.

Antonyms: see GOOD-LOOKING.

homemade, *a. Spec.* homespun.

homicidal, *a.* murderous; *spec.* bloody, patricidal, matricidal, *etc.*

homicide, *n.* **1.** murder (*obs. or hist., exc. spec.*), manslaughter (*chiefly spec.*); *spec.* matricide, parricide, patricide, regicide, sororicide, fratricide, suicide.

2. manqueller (*A*), manslaughterer (*chiefly spec.*), murderer (*obs. or hist., exc. spec.*); *spec.* parricide, patricide, matricide, sororicide, fratricide, suicide, regicide.

homogeneous, *a.* alike (*contex.; post-positive*), uniform, like; *spec.* same, similar, congruous, consubstantial (*B or tech.*), unigenous (*R*).

Antonyms: see HETEROGENEOUS.

honest, *a.* good, moral; *spec.* just, righteous, square, sound, direct, frank, upright, conscientious, sincere, genuine, pure, virtuous, uncorrupted, incorruptible.

Antonyms: see DISHONEST.

honesty, *n.* goodness, probity, morality; *spec.* justness, justice, righteousness, uprightness, virtue, purity, *etc.*

Antonyms: see DISHONESTY.

honey, *n.* **1.** nectar (*B or fig.*).

2. *See* SWEETNESS, LOVABLENESS, DEAR.

honey, *a.* melleous (*R*), mellaginous (*R*), mellic (*R*).

honey-bearing, *a.* melliferous (*R*).

honor, *n.* **1.** *See* DIGNITY, FAME, CONSTANCY, UPRIGHTNESS, VIRTUE, CHASTITY, JUSTICE, POSITION.

2. *Referring to what does one credit:* credit, ornament; *spec.* distinction, crown, glory.

Antonyms: see DISCREDIT.

3. *Referring to what is bestowed in order to honor: spec.* ornament, title, distinction, dignity, decoration, compliment, worship, reverence.

honor, *v. t.* **1.** dignify (*contex.*); *spec.* adore, worship, idolize, idolatrize, grace, hallow, credit, decorate, compliment.

Antonyms: see VIOLATE, CONTEMN, DESPISE, DISCREDIT.

2. *Referring to a note, bill, etc.:* accept, pay.

honorable, *a.* **1.** good (*contex.*), worthy; *spec.* worshipful, admirable, famous, esteemed, respected, noble, elevated, reputable.

Antonyms: see DISCREDITABLE.

2. *See* CONSCIENTIOUS, JUST, UPRIGHT, VIRTUOUS, SINCERE, CREDITABLE, RESPECTABLE.

honoring, *n.* dignification (*contex.*); *spec.* worship, idolization, hallowing, crediting, decoration, compliment.

hood, *n.* **1.** *The garment for the head and neck: spec.* capuche, capuchin, calash (*hist.*), coif, cowl, trotcozy (*Scot.*).

2. *Any of various contrivances: spec.* canopy, chimneypot, calash, blower.

3. *Of an automobile:* bonnet (*chiefly Brit.*).

hooded, *a.* cucullate (*tech.*).

hoodoo, *n.* **1.** curse.

2. *Of what brings bad luck: spec.* genius (*used with* bad), jinx (*S*), Jonah (*fig.; C*).

Antonyms: see CHARM.

hoof, *n.* ungula (*tech.*); *spec.* cloot (*Scot. and dial. Eng.*), dewclaw, coffin.

hook, *n.* **1.** *Spec.* uncus (*tech.*), hamus (*tech.*),

---

holocaust: *sacrifice, destruction, slaughter.*
holograph: *autograph.*
home: *abode, goal, house.*
homespun: *homemade, coarse, homely, artless.*
honorarium: *fee.*
hoodlum: *rowdy.*
hoodoo, *v. t.: curse.*
hoodwink: *blind, deceive.*
hoofed: *ungulate.*

---

uncinus (*tech.*), gaff, cleek (*Scot.*), buttonhook, fishhook, slingdog, dog, agraffe, crotchet, tug, strike, clasp, clamp.
2. *See* HEADLAND.

hook, *v. t. Spec.* strike (*to hook a fish*).

hook-beaked, *a.* uncirostrate, hamirostrate;—*both tech.*

hooked, *a.* **1.** *See* HOOK-SHAPED.
2. *Provided with a hook or hooks:* hamose *or* hamous (*both R*), hamate *or* (*R*) hamated (*tech.*), hamular (*tech.*), hamulate *or* hamulose (*both R*).

hook-shaped, *a.* hooked, hooklike, uncinate (*B or tech.*), unciform (*B or tech.*), uncinal (*B or tech.*), ancistroid (*tech.*); *spec.* unguiform.

hoopskirt, *n.* skirt (*contex.*), hoop (*C*); *spec.* crinoline, farthingale.

hope, *n.* feeling (*contex.*), desire (*contex.*), expectation, anticipation; *spec.* trust, belief.
Antonyms: see FEAR; *also cf.* HOPELESS.

hope, *v. t. & i.* desire (*contex.*), expect, anticipate; *spec.* trust.
Antonyms: see DESPOND.

hopeful, *a.* expectant, anticipative, anticipatory; *spec.* sanguine, rosy, roseate, fond, sanguineous (*R*), optimistic, melioristic.
Antonyms: see APPREHENSIVE, HOPELESS.

hopeless, *a.* **1.** depressed (*contex.*), unhopeful (*R*); *spec.* abject, despondent, disconsolate, despairing, despairful, desperate, forlorn.
Antonyms: see BUOYANT, HOPEFUL.
2. *Referring to things: spec.* abandoned, desperate, irredeemable, irretrievable, incurable.

hopelessness, *n. Spec.* despondence, despair, desperation, *etc.*

horizon, *n.* circle (*contex.*), sky line, verge (*R*).

horizontal, *a.* flat, even (*R, exc. spec.*), level.
Antonyms: see VERTICAL.

horizontal, *n.* flat, level.

horn, *n.* **1.** *Spec.* antler, spike, branch, dag, broach, cornicle.
2. *Referring to wind instruments: spec.* saxhorn, althorn, saxophone, saxtuba, bugle, conch, cornet, cornet-a-pistons (*French*), krummhorn, *etc.*
3. *Spec.* cornucopia, crest, end, alternative, corner, beak.
4. keratin.

horned, *a.* **1.** cornigerous (*tech.*), cornuate *or* cornuted (*B*); *spec.* crescent-shaped.
2. *See* CUCKOLDED.

hornless, *a. Referring to cattle or sheep, etc.: spec.* muley, hummel *or* humble (*Scot.*), dodded (*dial. Eng.*), polled, pollard.

horn-shaped, *a.* corniform (*B*).

horny, *a.* corneous (*tech.*); *spec.* hornish, cornified, keratose (*tech.*).

horologist, *n. Spec.* clockmaker, horologer, watchmaker.

horoscope, *n.* ascendant, nativity, geniture (*R*).

horoscopist, *n.* genethliac (*R*).

horrible, *a.* **1.** alarming (*which see*), horrifying, horrific (*B*), horrid (*properly suggesting inner revulsion; but actually used C for a mild expression of dislike*), shocking, hideous (*R, exc. spec.*), horrendous (*R or B; properly with suggestion of causing the hair to stand on end*); *spec.* Gorgonian (*fig.*), horrisonous.
Antonyms: see ASSURING.
2. *In weakened sense: see* WICKED, OUTRAGEOUS, MONSTROUS, ABOMINABLE.

horse, *n.* **1.** steed (*B or rhetorical*); *spec.* pad, prancer (*cant or, as used of any horse, S*), caple *or* capul (*formerly chiefly B; now dial. Eng.*), dobbin, courser (*rhetorical*), charger, bidet (*B*), hobby (*A or historical*), cocktail *or* curtal, Bucephalus (*fig.; B or rhetorical*), weed (*S or cant*), scrow, neighor (*R*), crock, prad (*S*), geegee (*C*), pony, barb, daisy-cutter (*cant*), cob, stepper (*C or S*), clipper, jade (*contemptuous*), hack, rip (*S or C*), skate (*S*), plug (*C or S*), pinto (*Western U. S.*), mustang (*U. S.*), nag, mount, remount, rouncy (*A*), runt, jennet *or* genet, roadster, naggy, stallion, mare, colt, foal, filly, gelding, pot (*cant*), plater (*cant*), palfrey, Pegasus, punch, kyang, Percheron, hunter, thoroughbred, gigster (*R*), hackney, clicker, saddler (*C., U. S.*), Hambletonian, Waler (*Anglo-Indian*), Galloway, drayhorse, Houyhnhnm, galloper, dweller, balker, filler, rosinante, roarer, whistler, thriller, wheeler, leader, rogue, Turk, Arab, tarpan, tit (*obs. or R*), trotter, pacer, ambler, runner, rider, roan, chestnut, sorrel, gray, bay, black, ginger, grizzle, stalking-horse, dun, cayuse, ass, mule, hinny, zebra. *The term "horse" is specifically used of an adult gelded male as distinguished from a "stallion," "mare," or "colt."*
2. *As a collective pl.:* cavalry.
3. *Spec.* clamp, jack, hobbyhorse, clotheshorse, sawhorse.

horse, *v. t.* mount; *spec.* remount.

horseman, *n.* rider, pricker (*A*); *spec.* cavalryman, chevalier (*hist. or A*), knight (*hist.*), hussar, gaucho, yeoman (*Eng.*), demilance, jockey.

horsemanship, *n.* manage *or* manége (*French*); *spec.* equitation.

horses, *n. pl.* horseflesh (*a collective*).

hospital, *n.* infirmary (*chiefly spec.*); *spec.* fermary (*obs. or hist.*), cockpit, lazaretto *or* lazaret, pesthouse, valetudinarium, sanitarium *or* sanatorium.

---

hoop, *n.: ring.*
hoop, *v. t.: bind.*
hoot, *n.: cry.*
hoot, *v. i.: cry, jeer.*
hoot, *v. t.: assail, drive, express.*
hop: *leap, dance.*
hopper: *chute.*
horal: *hourly.*
horde: *group, crowd.*
horrent: *bristly, bristling.*
horrid: *bristling, repellent, abominable, offensive, bad.*
horrific: *horrible, shocking.*
horrify: *frighten, shock.*
horror: *tremble, fear, abhorrence, aversion:* (in pl.) *delirium tremens.*
hortative, *a.: exhortatory, advisory.*
hospitable, *a.: cordial.*

hospitality, *n.* xenodochy (*R*), cordiality (*contex.*).

hot, *a.* **1.** heated (*contex.*), ardent (*B*), torrid, fervid (*B*), fervent (*B*); *spec.* parching, roasting, incandescent *or* candent, fiery, flaming, boiling, swelty.

Antonyms: see COLD.

2. *See* EAGER, ANGRY, ARDENT, EXCITED, ACRID, VIOLENT, PUNGENT.

hothead, *n.* madbrain, hotspur.

hound, *n.* **1.** dog (*contex.*); *spec.* beagle, dachshund, talbot, limer (*A*), leash hound, bloodhound, kibble, great Dane.

2. *See* WRETCH.

hour, *n.* **1.** bell (*naut.*), ghurry (*Anglo-Indian*).

2. time (*contex.*); *spec.* prime (*eccl.*), matin (*eccl.*), laud (*eccl.*), complin (*eccl.*), vespers (*pl.; eccl.*).

hourly, *a.* **1.** horal (*R*), horary (*R*).

2. *See* CONSTANT, FREQUENT.

house, *n.* **1.** building (*contex.*), dwelling (*contex.*); *spec.* court, cottage, cot (*chiefly B*), hovel, bungalow, shack, château, hutch, shanty, hut, dome (*B or rhetorical*), barn (*fig.*), barrack, barracoon, kennel, shed (*B*), rabbitry, cabin, ranch (*U. S.*), rancho (*Spanish*), box, lodge, gatehouse, humpy (*Australia*), crib (*thieves' S*), cruive (*Scot.*), croo (*Scot. and Irish*), sty.

2. *See* ABODE, TEMPLE, LAIR, THEATRE, CHURCH, FIRM, ASSEMBLY, FAMILY.

3. Home *is loosely used as a synonym for* house; *but* home *implies the dwelling of a family group as well as the spiritual connotations of the group.*

house, *a.* domal (*R*).

house, *v. t.* shelter (*contex.*); *spec.* booth (*R*), cote, barrack, roof (*R*), hive, hut, temple, palace (*R*), impalace (*R*), kennel, hovel (*R*).

housekeeper, *n. Spec.* matron, housewife.

housekeeping, *n.* ménage (*French*) *or* menage (*chiefly spec.*), householdry (*R*); *spec.* housewifery, notability (*obs.*).

housewife, *n.* wife (*A*); *spec.* cotquean (*of a laborer; obs.*).

how, *n. Spec.* whereby, why, what.

howl, *n.* **1.** cry (*contex.*); *spec.* bawl, ululation (*B*), yowl.

2. *See* EXCLAMATION.

hoyden, *n.* girl (*contex.*), romp, tomboy (*C*).

hub, *n.* **1.** nave, block.

2. *See* CENTER.

hue, *n.* cast (*obs.*), form (*A*), appearance (*A*); tone (*more technical than "hue"*), blee (*A*); complexion; *spec.* color, tint.

hull, *n.* **1.** pericarp (*tech.*); *spec.* husk, glume, chaff (*a collective*), bran (*a collective*), shell, pod, rind, bur *or* burr, skin, shuck, bark, shale (*A or R*), flight, palea, lodicule, bract, scale, calyx, legume, silique, peel, capsule, glumelle (*R*), stone, putamen.

2. *See* BODY.

hull, *v. t.* strip (*contex.*); *spec.* pod, shell, husk, shuck, decorticate, peel.

hum, *n. Spec.* croon, bum (*chiefly dial.*), bumble, burr, murmur, thrum, bombination (*R*), boom, buzz, whiz, drone, bombus (*med.*).

hum, *v. i.* **1.** *Spec.* croon, bum (*chiefly dial.*), burr, thrum, bombinate (*R*), bombilate (*R*), boom, buzz, whiz, drone, murmur.

2. *See* SING.

human, *a. Spec.* hominal (*nat. hist.*), hominine (*R*), humanistic, earth-born (*contex.*), mortal, humane.

Antonyms: see SUPERHUMAN, INHUMAN, DIVINE, DEVILISH.

human, *n.* earthling (*R; contex.*), clod (*depreciative*); *spec.* Christian, man, woman, child, boy, girl.

Antonyms: see DEITY, ANIMAL.

humble, *a.* **1.** lowly (*now somewhat A or rhetorical*), low (*R, exc. spec.*); *spec.* low-born, poor, undistinguished, meek, inglorious, unambitious, unescutcheoned (*R*), obscure.

Antonyms: see PROUD, HAUGHTY, PRETENTIOUS, ARROGANT, CONCEITED.

2. *See* LOWLY.

humility, *n.* abasement, humbleness; *spec.* submissiveness.

Antonyms: see PRIDE.

humor, *n.* **1.** *Referring to the four bodily fluids of the old physiology: spec.* blood, phlegm, choler, melancholy.

2. mood, cue; *see* DISPOSITION.

3. *Referring to other bodily fluids: spec.* eyewater (*R*), crystalline, pus, serum.

4. *See* CAPRICE, FUN.

humorist, *n. Spec.* joker, jester, wag, wit.

---

host: *army, multitude.*
host: *sacrifice, element, entertainer.*
hostage: *pledge.*
hostelry: *inn.*
hostile, *a.: unfriendly, opposed.*
hostile, *n.: enemy.*
hostility: *unfriendliness, opposition;* (in pl.) *war.*
hot bed: *breeding place.*
hotchpotch: *mixture.*
hotel: *inn.*
hotfoot: *hastily.*
hot-headed: *eager, reckless, impetuous, hasty.*
hound, *v. t.: hunt, drive, incite.*
house, *v. i.: dwell.*
housebreaking: *burglary.*
household, *n.: family.*
household, *a.: domestic.*
housemaid: *maidservant.*
housing: *shelter.*
hovel: *shed, house.*
hover, *v. i.: fly.*
hover, *n.: flight.*
however: *but.*
hubbub: *disturbance, din.*
huckster: *peddler.*
huddle, *v. i.: crowd, gather, shrink.*
huddle, *v. t.: crowd, gather, heap, drive.*
huff, *v. t.: anger, offend.*
huff, *n.: pet, quarrel.*
huffy, *a.: angry.*
hug, *v. t.: embrace, caress.*
hug, *v. i.: snuggle.*
hug, *n.: embrace, caress.*
huge, *a.: enormous.*
hulk: *vessel, body.*
hulking: *big.*
humble, *v. t.: abase.*
humbug, *v. t.: deceive, hoax.*
humbug, *n.: deception, hoax, deceiver.*
humdrum, *a.: dull.*
humid: *moist.*
humidity: *moisture.*
humiliate: *abase.*
humiliation: *abasement.*
hummock: *hill, protuberance.*
humor, *v. t.: grant.*
humorous: *funny.*
humorsome: *capricious.*

---

humpback, *n.* hunchback.
humpbacked, *a.* humpback, cyphotic (*tech.*), bow-backed (*R*), hunched, gibbous (*chiefly spec.*).
humped, *a.* hunchy, gibbous (*chiefly tech.*); *spec.* humpbacked.
hundred, *n.* century, centred (*hist.*), centrev *or* centref (*Welsh; hist.*).
hunger, *n.* **1.** desire (*contex.*), appetite, hungriness, emptiness (*fig.*); *spec.* voracity, polyphagia (*med.*), esurience (*humorously pedantic*), famine, bulimia (*med.*), greed.
Antonyms: see SURFEIT.
hunger, *v. i. Spec.* famish, starve.
Antonyms: see SURFEIT.
hungry, *a.* **1.** hungered (*A*), ahungered *or* anhungered (*R, A*); *spec.* famished, starved, edacious (*now chiefly humorous*), lickerish, lickerous (*obs.*), voracious, esurient (*now humorously pedantic*), polyphagous (*med.*), greedy, ravenous, empty, insatiate, avid, sharp-set (*R*), peckish (*C*), dinnerless, supperless, *etc.*
Antonyms: see SURFEITED.
2. *See* DESIROUS, GREEDY.
hunt, *v. t.* **1.** chase; *spec.* still-hunt, stalk, run, trail, track, trap, hound.
2. *See* DRIVE, FOLLOW, SEEK, SEARCH, PURSUE.
hunt, *v. i.* **1.** *Spec.* shoot, poach, stalk, forage, hawk, jack, trap, snare, kangaroo, wolf, grouse, ferret.
2. *See* SEARCH, SEEK.
hunt, *n.* **1.** *Spec.* chase, drag, stalk, still-hunt.
2. *See* GAME, SEARCH
hunter, *n.* huntsman (*male; a more formal word than* hunter), huntress (*female*), huntswoman (*female; R*), nimrod (*fig.*), Endymion (*fig.*), jager *or* jaeger (*German or Swiss*); *spec.* stalker, shikari (*Anglo-Indian*), gunner, forager, trapper, poacher, boarhunter, pigsticker, jacker, deerstalker, ferreter, falconer.
Antonyms: see GAME.
hunting, *a.* venatorial (*R*), venatic *or* venatical (*R*), venary (*R*); *spec.* cynegetic (*R*).
hunting, *n.* venery, venation (*B*); *spec.* chase, pigsticking, rabbiting, hawking, falconry, *etc.*
hurry, *v. t. & i.* **1.** *See* HASTEN.
2. *In a sense implying the feeling of urgency, but not necessarily resultant speed:* drive, whip (*fig.*).
Antonyms: see DELAY, LAG.
hurtful, *a.* unwholesome, noxious, noisome (*formerly equivalent to* noxious, *bringing harm, but now implying a bad smell*), pernicious (*working destruction or injury, chiefly not of a material sort*), baneful (*causing or bringing death or great harm*), harmful.
husband, *n.* spouse (*formal*), goodman (*Scot. or A*), man (*Scot. or dial.*), lord (*B, jocular, or ironical*), hubby (*familiar and C*); *spec.* benedict, bridegroom.
Antonyms: see WIFE, CELIBATE.
hussy, *n.* woman (*contex.*), girl (*contex.*), jade (*sometimes playful*), limmer (*Scot.*), minx (*often playful*), baggage, slut (*like all these synonyms, derogatory, but* slut *is rarely playful, and always implies disgusting slovenliness*).
hut, *n.* **1.** house (*contex.*); *spec.* wicki-up, yurt, mia-mia (*Australian*), hutment.
2. *See* DWELLING.
hybrid, *n.* crossbreed (*chiefly spec.*), mongrel (*chiefly spec.; a disparaging term*), cross; *spec.* outcross, lurcher, bigener (*bot.; R*), mameluco (*South America*), mulatto, quadroon, octaroon, half-breed, half-blood, half-caste (*East India*), mule, mestee *or* mustee (*West Indies*), mestizo (*Spanish America and Philippine Islands*), quintoon, terceroon, mustafina, mustafino (*Spanish American*), creole.
hybrid, *a.* crossed, cross (*R*), mixed-breed, crossbred (*chiefly spec.*); *spec.* mongrel, graded, half-blood, half-blooded, half-breed.
Antonyms: see FULL-BLOODED.
hygiene, *n.* soteriology (*R*), hygiastics (*R*), hygienics (*R*), hygiology (*R*).
hymn, *n.* hymnic (*R*); *spec.* psalm, canticle, pæan, choral, sanctus, triumph, troparion, hymeneal, sequence, prose, hallel, recessional, processional, magnificat, laud, Exultet, Gloria, prosodion, dithyramb *or* dithyrambic, mantra, Orphic.
hymnist, *n.* composer (*contex.*), hymnodist; *spec.* laudist.
hypnotic, *a.* magnetic (*contex.; obs.*), ectenic (*R*), mesmeric (*obs.*).
hypnotism, *n. In allusion to former practitioners or obs. theories:* magnetism, Braidism, Mesmerism.
hypocrisy, *n.* deceit (*contex.*); *spec.* dissembling, Tartufferie (*fig.*), Tartuffism (*fig.*), cant, Phariseeism (*fig.*), Pharisaism (*fig.*), snivel, sanctimony.
Antonyms: see ARTLESSNESS; *also cf.* FRANK.
hypocrite, *n.* deceiver (*contex.*); *spec.* dissembler, Tartuffe (*fig.*), pretender, Pecksniff (*fig.*), Pharisee (*fig.*), four-flusher (*cant*), bluffer (*C*).
hypocritical, *a.* deceitful (*contex.*), double-faced; *spec.* dissembling, Tartuffian (*fig.*),

hump, *n.: protuberance.*
hump, *v. t.: arch.*
hunch, *n.: protuberance.*
hunch, *v. t.: arch.*
hunk: *piece, chunk.*
hunker: *conservative.*
hunks: *niggard.*
hurl: *project, throw, dart, utter.*
hurt, *v. t.: harm, injure, grieve, pain, offend.*
hurt, *n.: harm, injury, pain.*
hurtful: *harmful, injurious, painful.*
hurtle, *v. i.: collide, clash, clatter, rush.*
hurtle, *v. t.: project, throw.*
husband, *v. t.: economize.*
husbandman: *agriculturist.*
husbandry: *economy, agriculture, management.*
hush, *v. t.: silence, calm.*
hush, *n.: silence.*
husk: *hull.*
husky: *hoarse, strong.*
husting: *council.*
hustle, *v. t.: crowd, push, hasten, drive, jostle, put.*
hustle, *v. i.: hasten, work, bustle.*
hustle, *n.: haste, activity, bustle.*
hustling: *active.*
hutch: *house, chest.*
hymn, *v. t.: celebrate, praise.*
hypochondria: *depression.*
hypothecate: *pledge.*
hypothecation: *pledging.*
hypothesis: *condition.*

Tartuffish (*fig.*), Pharisaic (*fig.*), Pharisaical (*fig.*), sanctimonious.
Antonyms: see ARTLESS, FRANK.
hysteria, *n.* convulsion (*contex.*), hysterics (*pl.; C*); *spec.* tarantism, conniptions (*pl.; vulgar, U. S.*), vapors (*pl.*), lata, miryachit, jitters (*pl. with "the" S, U. S.*), heebejeebies (*pl. with "the"; S, U. S.*).
hysterical, *a.* convulsive (*contex.*), hysteric (*R*).

I

I, *pron.* ego (*metaphysics*).
ice, *n.* crystal (*now R*); *spec.* floe, glacier, frazil (*Can. and U. S.*), icicle.
iceberg, *n.* berg; *spec.* calf.
ice-covered, *a.* glaciate.
iced, *a. Spec.* frosted, glacé (*French*), frappé (*French*).
idea, *n.* thought, conceit (*A*), concept, conception, intention (*chiefly logic*), notion (*chiefly spec.*), intellection (*chiefly tech.*), impression; *spec.* wrinkle, phantom, design, fancy, memory, feeling, motif (*French*), recept, theory, plan.
idealize, *v. t. Spec.* exalt, abstract, spiritualize, disrealize (*R*), sublime *or* sublimate, refine, heighten, perfect.
identical, *a.* alike (identical *implies absolute congruence, similarity or alikeness; all its synonyms tend to be looser in application*) same, tantamount (*equality in nonmaterial things or matters*), equal, equivalent (*implying that similar things roughly approximate one another, whereas* equal *suggests greater accuracy and more exact correspondence*).
idle, *a.* indolent; *spec.* loafing, dawdling, playing.
Antonyms: see BUSTLING.
idle, *v. i. Spec.* laze, lazy (*R*), loaf, dawdle, lounge, loll, slack (*C*), dally, drone, trifle, moon, truant, play.
Antonyms: see BUSTLE, WORK.
idleness, *n.* indolence; *spec.* loafing, dawdling; *see* INACTIVITY.
Antonyms: see BUSTLE.
idler, *n. Spec.* loafer, droner, lounger, dawdler, do-nothing, do-little, drone, buckeen (*Irish*), nonworker (*nonce word*).
Antonyms: see WORKER.
idling, *n. Spec.* lazing, loafing, dalliance, *etc.*
idol, *n.* **1.** image, simulacrum (*B*), god (*contex.*); *spec.* teraphim (*pl.*), joss (*Chinese*), Mumbo Jumbo, pagod, Dagon, *etc.*
2. *See* BELOVED.
idolatry, *n.* worship (*contex.*), fornication (*a Biblical term*).
idyl, *n.* eclogue, pastoral.
if, *conj.* gin *or* gif (*Scot.*), provided; *spec.* though.
ignis fatuus, will-o'-the-wisp, jack-o'-lantern (*now R*), jack-o'-the-wisp (*obs.*), fata morgana (*Lat.*).
ignitable, *a. Spec.* inflammable.
ignite, *v. t. Spec.* fire, kindle, light, inflame (*B or R*), strike.
ignoramus, *n.* ignorant (*R*), illiterate, simple.
Antonyms: see SCHOLAR, LITERATE.
ignorance, *n.* **1.** unscience (*R or obs.*), darkness (*fig.*), inscience (*R*), nescience (*B*), ignorantness (*R*); *spec.* ineducation, illiteracy, illiterateness, illiterature (*R*), benightment, rusticity, dark, darkness, imprescience, blindness (*fig.*).
Antonyms: see LEARNING, ENLIGHTENMENT, KNOWLEDGE.
2. unawareness.
Antonyms: see FOREKNOWLEDGE.
ignorant, *a.* **1.** nescient (*B*), unknowing (*R*), inscient (*R*); *spec.* unlearned, inerudite, illiterate, uninformed, untaught, benighted, borrel *or* borel (*A*), dark, lay, grammarless, unstudied, unread, unexpert (*R*), green; *see* UNEDUCATED.
Antonyms: see LEARNED, WELL-INFORMED.
2. *See* UNAWARE.
ignore, *v. t.* disregard; *spec.* pass, overlook, bury, elude, sink, blink, overjump, skip, disimagine (*R*), cut (*C*), overslaugh (*U. S.; R*), disobey, suppress, eliminate, forget.
Antonyms: see ATTEND, NOTICE, CONSIDER, MENTION.
ill-composed, *a.* incondite (*B*).
ill-considered, *a.* unbaked (*fig.*), indigested *or* ill-digested (*fig.*); *spec.* wild.
illegible, *a.* undecipherable, unreadable; *spec.* blind, hidden.
Antonyms: see LEGIBLE.
illegitimate, *a.* **1.** unlawful; *spec.* unauthorized, irregular, spurious, inconsequent.
Antonyms: see LAWFUL.
2. bastard, natural; *spec.* baseborn, base (*A*),

I

icy: *cold, distant, indifferent, unemotional.*
ideal, *a.: abstract, theoretical.*
ideal, *n.: type.*
idealism: *romanticism.*
idealistic: *romantic.*
ideate: *conceive.*
identical, *a.: alike, same.*
identify: *recognize.*
identity: *likeness, sameness, individuality.*
idiocy: *imbecility, foolishness.*
idiom: *language, dialect, form, expression, diction.*
idiosyncrasy: *peculiarity.*
idiot: *imbecile, simpleton, blockhead.*
idiotic: *imbecile, irrational, foolish.*
idle: *groundless, ineffectual, purposeless, inactive, unemployed, unused, indolent.*
idleness: *unemployment.*
idling: *inactivity, indolence.*
idolater: *worshiper.*
idolize: *worship, honor, admire, love.*
idyllic: *poetic.*
igneous: *fiery.*
ignoble: *lowly, base.*
ignominious: *discreditable, contemptible.*
ignominy: *discredit.*
ill, *a.: wicked, unjust, unkind, faulty, harmful, ailing, diseased.*
ill, *n.: harm, ailing.*
ill-bred: *impolite.*
illegal: *unlawful.*
illegitimate, *n.: bastard.*
ill-favored: *homely, offensive.*
illiberal: *ungentlemanly, narrow, stingy.*
illimitable: *endless, infinite.*
illiterate: *ignorant.*
ill-judged: *unwise.*
illness: *sickness, ailment.*

---

hedgeborn (*A*), misbegotten.
Antonyms: see LEGITIMATE.

illogical, *a.* inconsequent, invalid; *spec.* absurd, unreasonable, incoherent.
Antonyms: see LOGICAL.

ill-omened, *a.* sinister, sinistrous, left-handed; *spec.* inauspicious.
Antonyms: see AUSPICIOUS.

ill-shaped, *a. Spec.* distorted, misshapen, lopsided, ugly, ill-proportioned.

ill-smelling, *a.* malodorous (*B*), offensive, nosey (*C*), rank, cacodorous (*a R hybrid; humorous or contemptuous*), inodorous (*R*), graveolent (*B; rhetorical, affected, or euphemistic*); *spec.* foul, stinking, gamy, rancid, noisome, fetid, goatish, buckish, rotten, *etc.*
Antonyms: see FRAGRANT.

ill temper, temper; *spec.* ill-nature, ill-humor, crossness, blood (*chiefly with "bad" or in "to get" or "have one's blood up"*), cankeredness (*R*), bile (*fig.; now chiefly C*), spleen (*fig.*), black dog (*fig.*), grouchiness, groutiness (*U. S.; C*), moroseness, doggedness; *see* ANGER.

ill-tempered, *a. Spec.* ill-natured, ill-humored, crabbed, unlovely, cross, shrewd (*obs.*), ugly (*U. S.*), sour, surly, grum, grumpy *or* grumpish, unamiable, morose, malignant, unkindly, sullen, sulky, bearish, cynical *or* cynic, churlish, cantankerous (*C*), dogged (*R*), snarly, currish *or* (*R*) doggish, snappish, shrewish, vinegarish *or* vinegary, vinaigrous (*R*), spleeny, splenetic, spleenish, vixenish, bilious, crusty, nasty, cranky, frumpy (*a trivial or C term*), frumpish (*R*), cankered, dorty (*Scot.*), grouchy *or* grouty (*U. S.; C*), angry, irritable.
Antonyms: see AFFABLE, AGREEABLE.

ill-treat, *v. t.* abuse, injure, ill-use, mistreat (*chiefly spec.*), maltreat (*chiefly spec.*), misuse; *spec.* bedevil, spite, mishandle, mohock (*R or hist.*), violate, outrage, rape.
Antonyms: see CARESS, CHERISH, PROTECT.

illuminate, *v. t.* **1.** *See* LIGHT, BRIGHTEN, ENLIGHTEN, INSPIRE, ELUCIDATE.
2. ornament (*contex.*), illumine; *spec.* miniate, rubricate, emblaze.

illusion, *n.* **1.** *Referring to the act: see* DECEPTION.
2. *Referring to the thing:* deception (*contex.*), unreality (*emphasizing the unreal quality*); *spec.* apparition, dream.
Antonyms: see ACTUALITY.

illustrate, *v. t.* **1.** *See* EXAMPLE.
2. picture; *spec.* Grangerize.

illustration, *n.* **1.** *Referring to the action: see* ELUCIDATION.
2. *Referring to the thing:* picture, figure; *spec.* diagram, plate, chart, drawing, crayon, iconography, frontispiece, cut, cartoon, caricature, lampoon.

ill will, dislike (*contex.*); *spec.* enmity, hostility, malice, dole (*Scot.*), grudge (*R*), spleen, spite, cankeredness (*R*), rancor *or* rancour (*R or B*), malevolence, malignity, malignancy, venom, malignance (*R*), animosity.
Antonyms: see AFFECTION, LOVE, ESTEEM.

image, *n.* **1.** representation (*contex.*), imago (*B*), figure, copy, simulacre *or* simulacrum (*B; primarily spec.*), shape (*contex.*), effigy (*chiefly spec.*); *spec.* parhelion, doll, dolly, picture, icon, shadow, statue, painting, drawing, guy, idol, reflection, embodiment (*an abstraction, when used in sense of* image), counterpart, magot.
2. *See* APPARITION.

imagery, *n. Spec.* images (*pl.*), imaginations (*pl.*), figures (*pl.*), engraving, statuary, paintings (*pl.*), *etc.*

imaginable, *a.* conceivable; *spec.* feignable, believable, supposable; *see* THINKABLE.

imaginary, *a.* unreal (*contex.*), fancied (*chiefly spec*); *spec.* fancy, invented, ideal, fictitious, shadowy, figmental (*B*), notional, visionary, fantastic, fantasied *or* phantasied, conceivable, abstract, poetic.
Antonyms: see ACTUAL.

imagination, *n.* **1.** *Referring to the faculty or action:* conception (*contex.*), fancy (*chiefly spec.*), fiction, creation; *spec.* fantasy, conceit, description.
2. *In reference to the thing imagined: see* FANCY.

imaginative, *a.* creative (*contex.*), fanciful, fictive, visionary (*R*); *spec.* dreamy.
Antonyms: see UNIMAGINATIVE, IMITATIVE, PRACTICAL.

imagine, *v. t.* devise (*contex.*), conceive (*contex.*), fancy (*chiefly spec.*), think (*contex.*), create (*contex.*); *spec.* suppose, feign, fantasy (*A*), picture, frame, figure, prefigure, dream, chimerize (*R*), believe, guess, assume, pretend, *etc.*

imbecile, *a.* **1.** deranged (*contex.*), foolish, innocent (*obs. or dial.*), silly (*A or spec.*), daft (*chiefly predicative; now R*); *spec.* senile, anile (*R*), driveling, idiotic, half-witted.
Antonyms: see INTELLIGENT.
2. *See* FOOLISH.

imbecile, *n. Spec.* defective, driveler, idiot, mooncalf (*chiefly dial. or B*), nidget (*A*), fool, half-wit (*R*), cretin.

imitate, *v. t.* copy, reproduce; *spec.* ape, borrow, mimic, counterfeit, mock, emulate, echo, follow, forge, duplicate, pattern (*R*), zany (*R*).
Antonyms: see INVENT.

imitated, *a. Spec.* second-hand, borrowed, counterfeit, mock, mimic, imitation (*the noun used attributively*), forged, pretended, feigned, false (*contex.*).
Antonyms: see NEW, ORIGINAL.

imitation, *n.* **1.** *Spec.* mimicking, mimicry, apery, mock (*R*), forgery, parrotism *or* parrotry (*fig.*), *etc.*
Antonyms: see INVENTION.
2. *In reference to the result of the action: spec.* copy, counterfeit, forgery, mockery, echo, duplicate, counterpart, pretence, reproduction, *etc.*

---

illusory: *deceptive.*
illustrious: *famous.*
imbibe: *absorb, drink.*
imbrue: *stain.*
imbue: *impregnate, animate.*

Antonyms: see INVENTION.

imitative, *a. Spec.* mimic, mimetic, counterfeit, Brummagem (*Eng.*), apish, copying, sequacious (*B*), echoic, reflective.

Antonyms: see INVENTIVE, IMAGINATIVE.

imitator, *n.* copyist, copier; *spec.* ape, parrot, mimic, echo, counterfeiter.

immaterial, *a.* **1.** incorporeal (*chiefly spec.*), unsubstantial *or* (*R*) insubstantial, inessential (*B*), metaphysical (*tech.*), matterless (*R*); *spec.* bodiless *or* (*R*) imbodied, incorporate (*R*), inconcrete, aerie, insensible, unfleshly (*R*), mental, spiritual, spectral.

Antonyms: see MATERIAL.

2. *See* UNIMPORTANT.

immateriality, *n.* incorporeality, immaterialness (*R*), bodilessness, unsubstantiality *or* (*R*) insubstantiality, inessentiality (*R*), metaphysicalness; *spec.* aeriness, mentality, spirituality.

immature, *a.* undeveloped; *spec.* tender, unripe, unfledged, impuberal (*R*), green, callow, beardless, young.

Antonyms: see GROWN.

immaturity, *n.* undevelopedness; *spec.* impuberty, greenness, unripeness, *etc.*

immediate, *a.* **1.** *Spec.* primary, next, direct, proximate.

Antonyms: see INTERMEDIATE, DISTANT.

2. *Spec.* (*referring to such nearness in time as is without any intervening action or the like*) instant, instantaneous, prompt. "*Immediate*" *and* "*prompt*" *are loosely used where there is only relative proximity.*

Antonyms: see DISTANT.

immediately, *adv.* **1.** directly, direct (*C*), next, proximately, betimes.

2. instantly, presto (*primarily a juggler's or magician's term; hence chiefly exclamatory or rhetorical*), instanter (*Latin or emphatic*), forthwith, straightway (*A or rhetorical*), straight (*A*), straightly (*A or obs.*), forthright (*A*), therewith (*A or formal*), eftsoon *or* oftsoons (*A*); *spec.* now.

immense, *a.* large (*contex.*), enormous, prodigious (*B or contemptuous*), great, tremendous, huge, vast (*chiefly spec.*), vasty (*R; now chiefly a B affectation*); *spec.* elephantine, gigantic, colossal, huge, titanic, infinite (*hyperbolical*), stupendous, mountainous, monstrous.

Antonyms: see MINUTE, SMALL.

immensity, *n.* **1.** largeness (*contex.*), greatness, immenseness (*R*), enormousness, tremendousness, hugeness, enormity (*R*), prodigiousness, vastity (*R*), vastness; *spec.* giganticness, colossalness, titanicness, infinity, monstrousness.

2. *Naming a thing of great size:* mountain, enormity, monstrosity; *spec.* vastity, vast, gulf, abyss.

immersion, *n.* mersion (*chiefly spec.; R*); *spec.* dip, bath, swim, baptism, absorption.

immigrant, *n.* incomer, comeling (*A*); *spec.* visitor, greener (*S*), colonist.

Antonyms: see EMIGRANT.

immigrate, *v. i.* come (*contex.*).

Antonyms: see EMIGRATE.

imminent, *a.* impendent (*R*), impending (*implying, literally, something hanging overhead and likely either to descend, or to threaten indefinitely; whereas* imminent *suggests something, often an evil, about to happen immediately*), instant (*R*).

immoral, *a.* wicked (*contex.*), evil, wrong, wrongful, vicious, loose (*somewhat euphemistic*), gay (*euphemistic*), rotten (*intensive and usually vulgar*); *spec.* licentious, abandoned, dishonest, indecent, treacherous, *etc.*

Antonyms: see RIGHTEOUS, UPRIGHT.

immorality, *n.* wickedness, impurity, vice, viciousness, perversity, *etc.*

immortal, *a.* **1.** deathless (*a homelier word than* immortal), undying, never-dying, imperishable; *spec.* endless.

Antonyms: see MORTAL.

2. *See* FAMOUS.

immortalize, *v. t.* fame; *spec.* deify.

immovable, *a.* **1.** moveless (*R*), fixed, immobile, immotile (*R*), stationary.

Antonyms: see CHANGEABLE, MOVABLE.

2. *See* MOTIONLESS, UNYIELDING.

impact, *n.* stroke, blow, impingement (*tech. or B*); *spec.* percussion, appulse, brunt, bump, touch, slam. *Many of the words mentioned under* "*stroke*" *are used in the closely allied sense of* "*impact.*"

impair, *v. t.* deteriorate, damage, harm, injure; *spec.* mar, spoil, flaw, vitiate, touch, ruin, blemish, shatter (*fig.*), reduce, dilapidate, deface, crush, break, wear, *etc.*

Antonyms: see AMEND, IMPROVE.

impair, *v. i.* deteriorate, decline; *spec.* vitiate, shatter, ruin, break, wear, *etc.; see* SPOIL.

Antonyms: see IMPROVE.

impairment, *n.* deterioration, damage, harm, injury; *spec.* mar, blemish, shattering, break, wear, *etc.*

impartial, *a.* just, fair, equal (*B*), even (*A*); *spec.* disinterested, dispassionate, unpassionate, unbiased, unprejudiced, indifferent (*R, exc. tech.*), unwarped.

Antonyms: see PARTIAL, PREJUDICED, UNFAIR.

impartiality, *n.* justice, impartialness (*R*), fairness, equality (*B*), evenness (*R; A*); *spec.*

immaculate: *clean, faultless.*
immanent: *inherent.*
immature: *undeveloped.*
immerse: *dip, bathe, baptize.*
immigrate: *migrate.*
immitigable: *implacable.*
immobile: *immovable, motionless, fixed, impassive.*
immoderate: *excessive.*
immoderation: *excess.*
immodest: *improper, indecent.*
immolate: *sacrifice, kill.*
immune: *free, unpunished, unhurt.*
immure: *confine.*
immutable: *unchangeable.*
imp, *n.: child, demon, elf.*
imp, *v. t.: graft.*
impale: *transfix, torture, punish.*
impalpable: *intangible.*
imparity: *inequality.*
impart: *communicate.*

dispassion, dispassionateness, impassionateness, indifference, indifferency (*R*).
Antonyms: see PARTIALITY.
impassable, *a.* impermeable (*chiefly spec.*); *spec.* impervious, imperviable (*R*), passless (*R*), waterproof, airtight, watertight, tight, intranscalent (*R*), innavigable (*R*), unnavigable, impenetrable.
Antonyms: see PASSABLE.
impassive, *a.* **1.** *See* INSENSIBLE.
2. inexpressive, immobile, immovable; *spec.* stoical, impassible, undemonstrative, unimpressionable, unimpressible, stolid, apathetic, calm.
Antonyms: see DEMONSTRATIVE, EFFUSIVE, VEHEMENT.
impassioned, *a.* passionate; impassionate (*R*); *spec.* frenzied, angry, frantic, furious.
impel, *v. t.* **1.** move (*contex.*), impulse (*R*); *spec.* drive, send, kick, throw, push, *etc.*
Antonyms: see RESTRAIN.
2. *Referring to the mind or inclinations:* excite, move, permove (*R*), constrain; *spec.* compel, actuate, urge, drive.
Antonyms: see RESTRAIN, STOP.
impelling, *a.* **1.** impulsive, propulsive, driving.
2. moving, exciting, constraining; *see* INCENTIVE; *cf.* IMPEL.
impenetrable, *a.* **1.** dense (*contex.*), proof, impermeable, impervious, imperviable (*R*).
Antonyms: see PERVIOUS.
2. unintelligible.
impenitent, *a.* nonrepentant, irrepentant (*R*), unrepentant, obdurate, uncontrite (*R*); *spec.* unconverted.
Antonyms: see REGRETFUL.
imperceptible, *a.* unsensible (*R*), indistinguishable, insensible, imperceivable (*R*), inappreciable, unperceivable (*R*), inapprehensible, indiscernible; *spec.* undiscoverable, inaudible, invisible, infinitesimal.
Antonyms: see PERCEPTIBLE.
imperfect, *a.* deficient, unperfect (*R*), faulty, bad, poor; *spec.* incomplete, crude, rude, rudimentary, dough-baked (*dial. or C*), half-baked (*C*), lame, defective, flawy (*R*), catalectic, foxy (*cant*), unsound, illogical, decayed, inelegant, *etc.*
Antonyms: see ABSOLUTE, COMPLETE, EXCELLENT.
imperfection, *n.* fault, defect, default (*R*), imperfectness; *spec.* speck, incompleteness, defectiveness, deficiency, faultiness, incompleteness, incompletion (*R*), illogicality, inelegance, unsoundness, brack (*chiefly dial.*), taint, shot, cloud.
Antonyms: see PERFECTION.
imperial, *a.* **1.** imperatorial (*R*); *spec.* august.
2. *See* SOVEREIGN.
imperiousness, *n.* domineeringness.
imperishable, *a.* endless; *see* IMMORTAL.
Antonyms: see TRANSIENT.
impetuosity, *n.* impetuousness, ardency, vehemence, fury, fire, violence, ferocity, fierceness, headiness, headlongness, hot-headedness, brashness (*chiefly spec.*), rush, bull-headedness (*C*), haste; *spec.* frenzy, passion.
Antonyms: see DELIBERATION.
impetuous, *a.* ardent, fiery, vehement, violent, fierce, headlong, hot-headed, brash (*chiefly spec.*), bull-headed (*C*); *spec.* swift, breakneck, rushing, passionate, hasty, mad-brained, madheaded, frantic, furious, ferocious.
Antonyms: see DELIBERATE, APATHETIC.
impious, *a.* **1.** *See* IRRELIGIOUS.
2. irreverent (*contex.*), profane; *spec.* blasphemous.
impish, *a.* demoniac; *spec.* puckish, puck-like.
implacable, *a.* *Spec.* impropitiable, immitigable, deadly; *see* UNFORGIVING, MORTAL.
Antonyms: see MERCIFUL.
implant, *v. t.* **1.** fix; *spec.* insert.
2. *See* INTRODUCE.
implication, *n.* **1.** interlacing, complication.
2. meaning (*contex.*), involvement *or* (*R*) involution, comprisal (*R*), comprehension; *spec.* connotation, inference, assumption; *see* IMPLY.
3. *Referring to what is implied: see* INFERENCE.
implicative, *a.* implicating.
implied, *a.* implicit, involved, comprised; *spec.* tacit, connoted, inferred, assumed.
Antonyms: see EXPLICIT.
imply, *v. t.* mean, import, involve, implicate (*less common than* imply), comprise, comprehend; *spec.* connote, suppose, presuppose, infer (*drawing out the meaning from a statement or situation, whereas* imply *denotes putting the meaning into it*), assume.
Antonyms: see EXPRESS, EXCLUDE.
impolite, *a.* ill-bred (*properly spec.*), rude, discourteous, unmannerly, disrespectful, respectless (*R*); *spec.* ungentlemanly, ungentle, ungracious.
Antonyms: see POLITE.
impoliteness, *n.* ill-breeding (*properly spec.*), rudeness, unmannerliness, discourtesy; *spec.* ungentleness, scurviness, shabbiness, disre-

impartible: *indivisible.*
impartment: *communication.*
impasse: *cul-de-sac.*
impassible: *insensible, impassive.*
impassionate: *angry, impassioned, earnest.*
impatient: *irritable, intolerant, uneasy.*
impeach: *accuse, discredit.*
impeccable: *sinless.*
impecunious: *poor.*
impede: *hinder.*
impediment: *hindrance, obstacle.*
impedimenta: *baggage.*
impend: *hang.*
impending: *imminent.*
imperative: *commanding, urgent.*
imperil: *endanger.*
imperious: *domineering.*
imperishable: *immortal.*
impermeable: *impassable.*
impersonal: *general.*
impersonate: *embody, typify, act.*
impersonator: *actor.*
impertinent: *irrelevant, impudent.*
imperturbable: *calm.*
impetus: *energy, momentum.*
impiety: *irreligion.*
impinge: *collide, strike.*
impingement: *collision, impact.*
implant: *fix, insert, introduce.*
implement: *instrument.*
implicate: *imply, involve.*
implicit: *implied, trustful.*
implore: *ask.*
impolitic: *unwise.*
imponderable: *weightless, imponderous.*

spect, disrespectfulness, ungentlemanliness, inurbanity, inurbaneness (*R*).

imponderable, *a.* **1.** weightless.
2. *See* UNSUBSTANTIAL.

importance, *n.* account, concern *or* (*less common*) concernment, import, interest, weight, significance, moment (*now chiefly with* great, small, little, *or the like*), consequence, matter; *spec.* caliber (*fig.*), ponderance (*R*), ponderosity (*chiefly B and spec.*), estimation, materialness, magnitude, notability, regard, esteem, figure, greatness, largeness, stress, value, self-importance, seriousness.
Antonyms: see INSIGNIFICANCE; *also cf.* IMPORTANT.

important, *a.* notable, interesting, significant, weighty, considerable, momentous (*a stronger term than the noun "moment"*); *spec.* eventful, material, esteemed, consequential, substantial, big (*C or humorous*), live, earnest, heavy, high, large, great, grave, ponderous, valuable, serious, self-important, critical.
Antonyms: see UNIMPORTANT, TRIVIAL, INSIGNIFICANT.

importunity, *n.* importunacy (*R*), importunateness, asking (*contex.*), urgency.

impose, *v. t.* **1.** *See* SUPERPOSE.
2. put, father (*spec. or fig.*), place (*contex.*), fasten, fix; *spec.* entail, dictate, force, clap, saddle, charge, tax, quota (*R*), levy, inflict, enforce.

imposing, *a. Spec.* dignified, grand, magnificent, grandiose, superb, courtly, august, imperial, royal, regal, lofty, stately, palatial, haughty, majestic, monumental, exalted, sublime.
Antonyms: see INSIGNIFICANT.

impossible, *a. Spec.* infeasible *or* unfeasible, insuperable, impracticable, ineffectible (*R*), hopeless.
Antonyms: see POSSIBLE, PROBABLE.

impostor, *n.* deceiver (*contex.*); *spec.* counterfeiter, humbug, bunyip (*Australia*), deceptress (*fem.*), mountebank, charlatan, quack, bluff, shyster (*cant*), parvenu (*French*), sharp (*C*), shark (*S*), confidence man, crook (*C*), deadbeat (*C*), sponger (*C*), piker (*C*), fourflusher, bluffer.

impound, *v. t.* confine (*contex.*), pound, pinfold.
Antonyms: see FREE.

impoverish, *v. t.* **1.** *Spec.* pauperize, beggar, ruin, ruinate, depauperate (*R and B; chiefly fig.*).
Antonyms: see ENRICH.
2. *See* EXHAUST, INSOLVENT.

impracticable, *a.* **1.** impossible (*contex.*), infeasible, ineffectible.
2. *See* INTRACTABLE, USELESS.

impregnable, *a.* unconquerable.

impregnate, *v. t.* **1.** *See* FRUCTIFY.
2. *Spec.* fill, saturate, permeate, imbue, imbrue, pervade (*less emphatic than "permeate"*), soak, interpenetrate, medicate, embalm, dye, tinge, *etc.*

impress, *v. t.* levy, enlist, press, crimp; *spec.* draft, requisition, confiscate.

impressible, *a.* impressionable, sensitive; *spec.* movable, tender, waxy (*often derogatory*), waxen (*R*), soft, plastic.
Antonyms: see INSENSIBLE.

impressive, *a. Spec.* effective, speaking, powerful, telling, striking, splendid, frappant (*French*), effecting; *spec.* emphatic, solemn.
Antonyms: see INEFFECTUAL, UNCONVINCING, INSIGNIFICANT.

imprison, *v. t.* confine, quod (*S*), secure (*R*), stock (*obs. or spec.*), jail, commit, incarcerate, lock up, hold (*contex.*).
Antonyms: see FREE, DELIVER.

imprisonment, *n.* confinement, incarceration, durance; *spec.* custody, arrest, duress.

improbable, *n.* unlikely (*implying even less likelihood than* improbable); *spec.* implausible.
Antonyms: see PROBABLE.

improper, *a.* wrong; *spec.* indecorous, inappropriate, unseemly (*a stronger term than "improper"*), unbecoming, undue, fie-fie (*jocular*), incorrect, unfit *or* unfitting, unsuitable, wrong, illegitimate, irregular, immodest, imprudent, discourteous, *etc.*; *see* INDECENT.
Antonyms: see PROPER, APPROPRIATE, TIMELY, BECOMING.

impropriety, *n.* unpropriety (*R*); *spec.* indecorum, indecorousness, unsuitability, unsuitableness, *etc.*, indecency, immodesty, imprudence, solecism.

improvable, *a.* betterable (*R or C*), amendable; *spec.* cultivable.

improve, *v. t.* better (*a homelier and stronger term than* improve), amend *or* mend; *spec.* edify, ameliorate *or* (*less common*) meliorate, cultivate, brighten, refine, soften, increase raise, *etc.*
Antonyms: see SPOIL, IMPAIR.

improve, *v. i.* better; *spec.* ameliorate, meliorate, brighten, mend, refine, soften, increase, *etc.*
Antonyms: see DECLINE, DETERIORATE, IMPAIR.

imprudent, *a.* **1.** careless (*which see*), incautious; *spec.* thriftless, improvident.
2. *See* UNWISE.

---

import, *v. t.*: *introduce, imply.*
import, *v. i.*: *matter.*
import, *n.*: *meaning, importance, article.*
importunate: *persistent, urgent.*
importune: *ask, urge, ply.*
impotent: *weak, helpless, powerless.*
impractical: *visionary.*
imprecate: *invoke.*
imprecation: *curse.*
impresario: *manager.*
impress, *v. t.*: *print, mark, fix, affect.*
impression, *n.*: *printing, mark, edition, idea, effect.*
impressionable: *impressible.*
impressment: *earnestness.*
imprest: *advance.*
imprimatur: *approval.*
imprint, *v. t.*: *mark, fix, print.*
imprint, *n.*: *print, mark.*
impromptu, *adv.*: *extempore.*
impromptu, *a.*: *extemporaneous.*
improvident: *careless.*
improvisatory: *extemporary.*
improvise: *extemporize, invent.*

impudence, *n.* impudency (*R*), impudentness (*R*), impertinence, procacity (*R*), cheek (*S*), cheekiness (*S*), boldness, bold-facedness, forwardness; *spec.* brazenness, brazen-facedness, presumption, insolence, contumely, brashness, bumptiousness, pertness, sauciness, malapertness (*A*), petulance (*R*), hardiness, hardihood, nerve (*S*), nerviness (*S*), effrontery, gall (*S*), lip (*vulgar S*), front (*R or vulgar*), face (*S, U. S.*), sauce (*C*), jaw (*vulgar, S*), insolency (*R*), protervity (*R*), abuse, contempt, arrogance, defiance, shamelessness, intrusiveness, *etc.*

Antonyms: see CONSIDERATION, POLITENESS.

impudent, *a.* impertinent, cheeky (*S*); *spec.* pert, saucy, bold *or* bold-faced, brazen *or* brazen-faced, insolent, arrogant, brash, bumptious, malapert (*A*), forward, cool, hardy, nervy (*C*), lippy (*vulgar S*), brassy (*S*), hubristic (*R*), protervous (*R*), contumelious, abusive, contemptuous, defiant, unblushing, blushless (*R*), intrusive, unbashful (*R*), shameless, assured, rude.

Antonyms: see POLITE, RESPECTFUL, OBSEQUIOUS, ABJECT, BASHFUL.

impulse, *n.* **1.** *In reference to the act:* impulsion; *spec.* drive, push, throw, kick, send, nisus. *Cf.* IMPEL, *v.*

Antonyms: see STOPPAGE.

2. *In reference to the force or energy:* influence, shock; *spec.* throw, push, *etc.*

3. *In reference to action upon the mind:* influence; *spec.* ate (*B*), incitement.

4. *In reference to the action of the mind:* inclination.

5. *See* MOMENTUM.

impulsive, *a.* **1.** *See* IMPELLING.

2. hasty; *spec.* heedless, careless, mad-brained, mad-cap, wild.

Antonyms: see DELIBERATE.

in, *adv.* within; *spec.* inwards.

Antonyms: see OUT.

inability, *n.* disability; *spec.* disqualification.

Antonyms: see ABILITY.

inaccessible, *a.* unaccessible (*R*), uncomeatable (*C*); *spec.* unapproachable *or* (*R*) inapproachable.

Antonyms: see ACCESSIBLE, GETTABLE.

inaccurate, *a.* incorrect, inexact; *spec.* erroneous.

Antonyms: see ACCURATE.

inactive, *a.* idle (*chiefly spec.*), quiet; *spec.* donothing (*C*), fainéant (*French; reproachful; B*), quiescent, dormant, slumbering (*a homelier equivalent of "dormant"*), sluggish, inert, passive, drowsy, effortless, restive (*R*), peaceful, sleepy, restful, inanimate, lifeless, deedless (*B or R*), dull, stagnant, motionless. Latent *is not a synonym of* inactive; latent *implies only the fact of* being hidden, *and not* inactivity.

Antonyms: see ACTIVE, LIVELY.

inactivity, *n.* inaction, inactiveness; *spec.* donothingness (*C*), do-nothingism (*C*), fainéance (*French; reproachful; B*), quiescence, dormancy, slumber, sleep, sleepiness, sluggishness, inertness, passiveness, drowsiness, peacefulness, repose, indolence, idling, deedlessness, dolce far niente (*Italian*), inexertion (*R*), inertion (*R*), stagnation, rest, hibernation (*fig.*), peace, dullness, lifelessness, spiritlessness, motionlessness, sloth, slothfulness, inanition, torpor, exhaustion.

Antonyms: see ACTION; *also cf.* ALERT.

inadvisable, *a.* inexpedient, unprofitable; *see* UNADVISABLE.

Antonyms: see ADVANTAGEOUS.

inalienable, *a.* indeprivable, imprescriptible, untransferable, indefeasible, unforfeitable.

inartistic, *a.* inartificial (*R*), artless (*more emphatic than* inartistic); *spec.* crude.

Antonyms: see ARTISTIC.

inattention, *n.* inadvertence, inobservance, inobservancy (*R*), unmindfulness, unobservance (*R*); *spec.* oscitance (*R*), oscitation (*R*), oscitancy (*R*), nonadvertence *or* nonadvertency (*R*), slip, inapplication, carelessness, absent-mindedness, disregard.

Antonyms: see ATTENTION.

inattentive, *a.* inadvertent, unmindful, unobservant, unobserving, unheedy (*R*); *spec.* oscitant (*R*), incurious (*B*), careless, absent, disregardful.

Antonyms: see ATTENTIVE.

inaudible, *a.* unhearable; *spec.* silent, quiet (*contex.*).

inauspicious, *a.* unauspicious (*R*), unfavorable (*a weak word*); *spec.* ill-starred, ominous, unpropitious, unlucky.

Antonyms: see AUSPICIOUS.

incalculable, *a.* inestimable, infinite, unknown, sumless, untold, incomputable, unreckonable; *cf.* COUNTLESS.

incapable, *a.* *Spec.* unable, incompetent, disqualified.

Antonyms: see ABLE.

incendiary, *n.* conflagrator (*R*), firer (*R*); *spec.* arsonist (*R*).

---

impugn: *attack.*
impugnity: *freedom.*
impure: *dirty, foul, adulterated, licentious, immoral, corrupt, dreggy.*
imputable: *attributable.*
impute: *attribute.*
inability: *disability.*
inaction: *inactivity.*
inadequate: *deficient.*
inadvertent: *inattentive.*
inane: *empty, foolish.*
inanimate: *lifeless, dull.*
inanition: *emptiness, exhaustion.*
inanity: *emptiness, foolishness.*
inappreciative: *insensible.*
inapprehensive: *dull.*
inapproachable: *inaccessible.*
inappropriate: *unsuitable.*
inapt: *unsuitable, awkward.*
inarticulate: *dumb, jointless.*
inartificial: *inartistic, artless, simple.*
inaugurate: *admit, begin.*
inborn: *innate, instinctive.*
inbred: *innate, chronic.*
inbreed: *generate, breed.*
incandescence: *glow.*
incandescent: *hot.*
incantation: *conjuration.*
incapacitate: *disable.*
incapacity: *disability.*
incarcerate: *confine.*
incarnate, *v. t.: embody.*
incase: *inclose, clothe.*
incautious: *imprudent.*
incendiary, *a.: dissentious.*

---

incense, *n.* **1.** censery (*R*); *spec.* frankincense.
2. *See* FRAGRANCE.

incentive, *a.* incitive, provocative; *see* IMPELLING.

incentive, *n.* propellate (*R*), incitement (*less usual than* incentive); *spec.* mainspring, provocative, instigation, provocation, goad, spur, stimulus, reason.

incise, *v. t.* incide (*R*), cut (*contex.*); *spec.* engrave, scarify.

incision, *n.* cut (*contex.*), insection (*R*); *spec.* scarification.

incite, *v. t.* **1.** actuate, instigate, move; *spec.* provoke, goad, hound, drive, impel, prod, push, sick (*C or undignified*), egg (*with "on"*), halloo, stimulate, animate, force, excite, reason, urge, spur, encourage, abet, coax, cheer, solicit, suggest, *etc.*
2. create (*contex.*), cause (*contex.*), raise, call (*chiefly with "into being" or "up"*); *spec.* foment (*fig.*), ferment (*fig.*).
Antonyms: see RESTRAIN, PREVENT.

incitement, *n.* **1.** *In reference to action:* actuation, motion (*R*); *spec.* call, fomentation (*fig.*), instigation, provocation, goading, impulsion, egging, spurring, instance, stimulation, animation, excitement, reasoning, encouragement, solicitation, abetment, coaxing, cheering, suggestion, *etc.*
Antonyms: see RESTRAINT, PREVENTION.
2. *In reference to what incites: see* INCENTIVE.
3. creation (*contex.*), causing (*contex.*), fermentation; *spec.* fomentation, raising, calling.

incivility, *n.* disrespect, rudeness; *spec.* slight, impudence.

inclination, *n.* **1.** disposition; *spec.* predilection, tendency, leaning, mind, set, penchant (*French*), bias, appetency, itch (*usually contemptuous*), cacoëthes (*B for "itch"*), twist, turn, propensity, proclivity, predisposition, proneness, bent, hankering, propenseness (*R*), propension (*R*), dislike, liking, taste, fear, *etc.*
Antonyms: see DISINCLINATION.
2. deviation (*contex.*), pitch (*chiefly tech., and usually spec.*); *spec.* tilt, tip, cant, obliquity, droop, slant, rake, ramp, leaning, incline (*R*), batter, declivity (*down*), acclivity (*up*), slope, cock, recumbency, hade, heel, list.
3. *See* BOW.

incline, *v. t.* **1.** *See* BOW.
2. deviate (*R; contex.*), pitch (*chiefly spec.*); *spec.* recline, droop, bow, slant, skew, rake, lean, cock, slope, tilt, tip, lurch, careen, heel.
3. dispose, lean (*R*), bend, bias, predispose, oversway (*R*), inflect (*R*), move, frame.
Antonyms: see DISINCLINE.

incline, *v. i.* **1.** *See* BOW.
2. deviate (*contex.*), slant, pitch (*chiefly spec.*); *spec.* droop, stoop, bow, rake, slope, hang, careen, lurch, list, hade, slouch.
3. lean, tend.

incline, *n.* **1.** slope, inclination; *spec.* acclivity (*upward*), declivity (*downward*), grade, escalator.
2. *See* INCLINATION.

inclined, *a.* **1.** *See* DISPOSED.
2. sloping, oblique, inclining, slant, slanting, slantwise; *spec.* drooping, canted, skew, recumbent, leaning, declivitous, *etc. Cf.* INCLINATION.
Antonyms: see VERTICAL, HORIZONTAL, PARALLEL.

inclining, *a.* **1.** *See* INCLINED.
2. dispositive (*B*).

inclose, *v. t.* enclose (*a variant*), encompass, circumclude (*R*), include (*now R, exc. in the p. p. or in a nonmaterial sense*), close; *spec.* embosom (*R*), bosom, circumscribe, circummure, core, embed, pen, coop, lock (*fig.*), seal, enlock (*R*), embay (*often fig.*), sphere (*R*), encircle, incase *or* case, corral (*chiefly U. S.; often fig.*), envelop, surround, hedge, incapsulate, bower, cavern, englobe (*R*), enshrine *or* shrine, encyst, box, incave *or* incavern (*R*), inwall, dike, emball (*R*), embox (*R*), impark, encapsule, encoffin (*R*), incoffin (*R*), wall, park, palisade, pale (*R*), rail, paddock, kraal, embower, coffin, rope, cabinet, capsule, caldron (*R*), casket, castle, cupboard, chamber, coffer. *The word "inclose" suggests prevention of either egress or ingress.*

inclosure, *n.* **1.** encompassment, circumclusion (*R*); *spec.* embosomment (*R*), circumscription, embedment, encirclement (*R*), inspherement (*R*), envelopment, surrounding, incapsulation, *etc.*
2. *Referring to that by which a thing is inclosed: spec.* wall, list (*B*), envelope, case, box, curb, girdle (*often fig.*), cincture (*often fig.*).
3. *Referring to the inclosed place: spec.* close (*chiefly A*), pen, fold, sty, coop, stall, shed, hatch, crib, chest, bin, brake, envelope, crew (*dial.*), crawl (*colonial Eng.*), corral, stockade, fold, park, hay (*A*), intake, lock, pound, sept (*R*), pale (*R*), yard, enceinte (*French*), college (*local Eng.*), garth (*Eng.; chiefly in "cloister garth"*), dock, cofferdam, paddock, kheda *or* kedda, cote, court, compound (*Anglo-Indian*), precinct.

include, *v. t.* comprehend (*chiefly spec.*); *spec.* comprise, intercept, contain, embody, involve, incorporate, number, cover, count, subsume, embrace.
Antonyms: see OMIT, EXCEPT, EXCLUDE.

---

incense, *v. t.: burn, anger.*
incentive: *impelling.*
inception: *beginning.*
incertitude: *doubt.*
incessant: *constant.*
inch, *v. i.: advance.*
…ch, *v. t.: force.*
inchoate, *a.: initial.*
inchoate, *v. t.: begin.*
incidence, *n.: falling.*
incident, *a.: falling, accessory, accidental.*
incident, *n.: occurrence, accessory.*
incidental: *accidental, current.*
incinerate: *burn.*
incipient: *initial, elementary, beginning.*
incised: *engraved.*
incisive: *cutting, sharp.*
inclement: *severe.*
inclining: *disposition.*

---

inclusion, *n.* comprehension, comprisal, incorporation.
inclusive, *a.* **1.** inclusory, comprehensive.
Antonyms: see EXCLUSIVE.
2. *With an implication of great scope or inclusion: spec.* unexclusive (*R*), sweeping, all-embracing, compendious, wide, liberal, comprehensive.
Antonyms: see NARROW.
incombustible, *a.* fireproof (*a homelier word, of more specific associations*).
Antonyms: see COMBUSTIBLE.
income, *n.* **1.** entrance (*R*), incoming (*chiefly in pl.*).
Antonyms: see OUTGO.
2. *Spec.* gain, return, earnings (*pl.*), revenue, receipts (*pl.*), perquisite.
Antonyms: see EXPENDITURE.
incoming, *a.* entrant (*R*), inward (*emphasizing the idea of direction*).
incoming, *n.* entrance; *spec.* inrushing, inflow.
Antonyms: see OUTFLOW.
incompatibility, *n. Spec.* antipathy, inconsistence.
incompatible, *a. Spec.* antipathetic, uncongenial, inconsistent, unsympathetic.
incomplete, *a.* deficient, partial; *spec.* inexhaustive, unaccomplished, unfinished.
Antonyms: see COMPLETE, FINISHED, THOROUGH.
incongruous, *a.* incongruent, disagreeing; *spec.* grotesque, unconstituted, absurd.
Antonyms: see CORRESPONDENT.
inconsequent, *a.* **1.** illogical, inconsequential (*less common than* inconsequent); *spec.* disconnected, discontinuous, loose, desultory, inconsecutive, fragmentary, snippy *or* snippety (*contemptuous; C*), inconclusiveness.
Antonyms: see LOGICAL.
2. *Spec.* bitty (*C*), scrappy, discontinuous, fragmentary.
3. *See* UNIMPORTANT, INCONSISTENT.
inconsistency, *n. Spec.* illogicality, inconsonance, repugnance, inconsequence, incoherence, *etc.; see* CONTRADICTION.
Antonyms: see AGREEMENT.
inconsistent, *a.* **1.** illogical (*contex.*), different (*contex.*), incompatible (*chiefly tech.*), incompassible (*tech.*), discrepant, variant (*contex.*), inconsonant (*a mild term*); *spec.* intolerant, inconsequent, incoherent, contradictory *or* (*less usual*) contradictious *or* (*R*) contrariant, self-contradictory, incombinable, nonsequential, incongruous, irreconcilable, contrary, repugnant, antagonistic, solecistic (*B*), changeable.
Antonyms: see CONSISTENT, AGREEABLE, CORRESPONDENT, LOGICAL.
2. *In reference to æsthetic ideas:* inconsonant, dissonant, discordant, inaccordant.
Antonyms: see CONSISTENT.
inconvenience, *n.* **1.** incommodiousness (*becoming obs., exc. spec.*), incommodity (*now R, exc. spec.*); *spec.* disadvantageousness, untimeliness, troublesomeness, annoyingness, difficulty, *etc.*
Antonyms: see CONVENIENCE.
2. *Referring to what gives inconvenience: spec.* disadvantage, trouble, annoyance, difficulty.
Antonyms: see CONVENIENCE.
inconvenience, *v. t.* incommode (*now chiefly spec.*), discommode (*R*); *spec.* disaccommodate.
inconvenient, *a.* incommodious (*obsolesc. exc. spec.*), discommodious (*obs. or R*), disconvenient (*obs. or R*), awkward (*fig., exc. spec.*); *spec.* disadvantageous, untimely, troublesome, annoying, difficult, *etc.*
Antonyms: see CONVENIENT.
inconvertible, *a.* inexchangeable.
incorrect, *a. Spec.* inaccurate, wrong, unsound, untrue, false, faulty, improper, unbecoming, erroneous, illogical, *etc.*
Antonyms: see CORRECT.
incorrectness, *n.* inaccuracy, untruth, faultiness, *etc.*
incorrigible, *a.* abandoned; *spec.* recidivous.
increase, *v. t.* grow (*fig. or chiefly spec.*), augment) *spec.* enhance, multiply, lengthen, eke (*A*), greaten (*A*), exaggerate, inflate, fan (*chiefly fig.*), reinforce, redouble, raise, swell, thicken, heighten, magnify, intensify, extend, enlarge, inflate, strengthen, generate, develop, double, triple, *etc.*
Antonyms: see ABATE, DIMINISH, RELAX.
increase, *v. i.* grow, wax (*R or A, exc. spec.*); *spec.* appreciate (*chiefly of property*), enhance, multiply, lengthen, rise, gather, accrue, mount, swell, thicken, heighten, intensify, extend, enlarge, *etc.*
Antonyms: see DIMINISH, RELAX.
increase, *n.* increasement (*R*), increment (*chiefly spec.*), growth, addition, augmentation; *spec.* enhancement, multiplication, gain, crescendo, lengthening, exaggeration, rise, spurt, inflection, reinforcement, redoubling, swell, swelling, accession, accretion, enlargement, addition, accumulation, heightening, intensification, thickening, inflation, generation, *etc.*
Antonyms: see DIMINUTION.
increasing, *a.* growing, lengthening, crescent (*B equivalent of "growing"*), crescive (*R*), increscent (*chiefly spec.*), incretionary (*R*); *spec.* multiplying, *etc.*
Antonyms: see DIMINISHING.

incognito: *disguised.*
incoherent: *illogical, inconsistent.*
incommode: *inconvenience.*
incomparable: *unequaled.*
incompassionate: *cruel.*
incompatible: *different.*
incompetence: *disability.*
incompetent: *incapable.*
incomprehensible: *unintelligible.*
inconceivable: *unthinkable.*
inconclusive: *indecisive.*
inconformable: *different.*
inconsequential: *inconsequent, unimportant.*
inconsiderable: *unimportant, small.*
inconsiderate: *careless, indifferent, thoughtless.*
inconsolable: *disconsolate.*
inconsonant: *inconsistent.*
inconspicuous: *unnoticeable.*
inconstant: *changeable.*
incontestable: *undeniable.*
incontinent: *unrestrained, licentious.*
incontrovertible: *undeniable.*
incorporate: *embody.*
incorporeal: *immaterial.*
incorrigible: *abandoned.*

incredible, *a.* unbelievable; *spec.* absurd, nonsensical.
Antonyms: see CREDIBLE.
incubate, *v. t.* sit, brood, cover; *spec.* hatch.
incumbent, *a.* **1.** *Spec.* superincumbent, superjacent (*R*), overlying, brooding.
Antonyms: see UNDERLYING.
2. *See* BINDING.
incur, *v. t.* get; *spec.* run, contract, gain, acquire.
Antonyms: see AVOID, AVERT.
incurable, *a.* remediless, irremediable (*R, exc. fig.*), immedicable (*R*), unmedicinable (*R*); *spec.* hopeless.
Antonyms: see CURABLE.
indebted, *a.* obligated, beholden (*now A or B*).
indecent, *a.* **1.** *See* IMPROPER.
2. improper (*contex.*), obscene, lewd, blue (*euphemistic or C*), immodest, coarse (*contex.*), unclean (*fig.*); *spec.* bold, filthy, nasty, dirty (*a vulgar or very strong word*), shameless, immoral, smutty. *Various words given under* filthy *are often used as synonyms of* indecent.
Antonyms: see CHASTE, MODEST.
indecision, *n.* doubt, hesitation, irresoluteness *or* irresolution; *spec.* shilly-shally, vacillation.
indecisive, *a.* inconclusive.
Antonyms: see DECISIVE.
indefensible, *a.* defenseless, insupportable;—*spec.* inexcusable, excuseless, untenable.
Antonyms: see DEFENSIBLE.
indefinite, *a.* indefinitive (*R*); *spec.* unlimited, obscure, nameless, indefinable, indecisive, uncertain, undefined, vague, general, uncircumstantial, impersonal, inexplicit, indescribable, indesignate, endless, nondescript.
Antonyms: see DEFINITE, CIRCUMSTANTIAL.
indent, *v. t. Spec.* notch, serrate, tooth, incise, jag (*R*), recess, engrail, pink, scallop, scollop.
indent, *v. t.* hollow (*contex.*), dent *or* (*now less common*) dint, print; *spec.* pick, dinge, batter, punctuate, bruise, peck, pit, dimple.
Antonyms: see EMBOSS.
indentation, *n.* depression (*contex.*), hollow (*contex.*), indenting (*R*), indenture (*R*), indention (*R, exc. spec.*), print, dent *or* (*now less common*) dint; *spec.* peck, pick, pit, kick (*cant*), dimple, recess, notch, jag, tooth, serration, incisure, cut, bruise, embrasure, scallop, scollop, crenel *or* crenelle, inlet. *"Indentation" is a more formal term than "dent."*
indented, *a. Spec.* notched, jagged, cut, erose, crenate.

indenture, *n.* **1.** *See* INDENTATION.
2. agreement, indent (*R*); *spec.* deed, certificate, chirograph.
indescribable, *a.* unnamable, unmentionable, nameless.
Antonyms: see DESCRIBABLE.
indestructible, *a. Spec.* indiscerptible (*R*), inextinguishable, imperishable, endless.
Antonyms: see DESTRUCTIBLE.
indicate, *v. t. Spec.* imply, infer, show, evince, denote, depict, designate, specify, particularize, tell, mark, signify, betoken *or* (*R*) token, signalize, bespeak, index (*R*), suggest, register, hint, label, describe, name, demonstrate, contra-indicate, foreshadow, sign, evidence, disclose, presign (*R*), symptomatize, *etc.*
Antonyms: see HIDE, OBSCURE.
indication, *n. Spec.* implication, inference, show, sign, index, indicium (*chiefly in pl.*), designation, specification, suggestion, evincement, denotation, denotement (*R*), particularization, telling, mark, signification, betoken, token, registry, hint, label, description, mention, evidence, disclosure, symptom, *etc.*
Antonyms: see HIDING, OBSCURATION.
indicative, *a.* indicatory, indicial (*R*); *spec.* designative, evincive, significatory, significant, significative, indicant, indexical (*R*), suggestive, symptomatic, demonstrative, *etc.*
indictment, *n.* accusation (*contex.*), dittay (*Scot.*).
indifference, *n.* **1.** indifferency (*R*); *spec.* coldness, frigidity, dryness, coolness, lukewarmness, nonchalance, easefulness (*R*), ease, easiness, stoicism, distance, listlessness, insouciance (*French*), Laodiceanism (*fig.*), Spartanism (*fig.*), adiaphorism, apathy, carelessness, dullness, insensibility, frivolity, incuriosity, incuriousness, equality.
Antonyms: see AFFECTION, INTEREST, ARDOR, CURIOSITY.
2. *Spec.* mediocrity, ordinariness, unimportance.
indifferent, *a.* **1.** *Spec.* cold, cool, calm, frigid, dry, light, lukewarm, nonchalant, insouciant (*French*), easeful (*R*) *or* easy, adiaphorist *or* adiaphoristic *or* adiaphrous (*tech. or B*), Laodicean (*fig.*), tossy (*R*), unconcerned, easy-going (*C*), inconsiderate, stoical, listless, distant, unmoved, Spartan (*fig.*), incurious, uninquiring, uncurious (*R*), apathetic, perfunctory, dull, insensible, careless.
Antonyms: see AFFECTIONATE, ARDENT, CURIOUS.

incredible: *unbelievable, absurd.*
incredulity: *unbelief, doubt.*
increment: *increase, addition.*
incriminate: *accuse, involve.*
incubus: *demon, nightmare.*
inculcate: *teach, inspire.*
inculpate: *involve.*
incunabula: *beginning.*
incurious: *indifferent, careless.*
incursion: *invasion.*
incursive: *aggressive, invasive.*
indecorous: *improper.*
indecorum: *impropriety.*
indeed, *adv.: actually.*
indefatigable: *untiring.*
indefeasible: *inalienable.*
indelible: *ineffaceable.*
indelicate: *coarse, indecent, awkward.*
indemnify: *compensate.*
indenture: *bind.*
independence: *freedom, assurance, fortune.*
independent: *free, assured, absolute.*
indeterminable: *endless.*
indeterminate: *uncertain.*
indict: *accuse.*
indigence: *poverty.*
indigenous: *native, inborn.*
indigested: *ill-considered.*
indignant: *angry.*
indignation: *anger.*
indignity: *insult.*

2. *See* MODERATE, FAIR, UNIMPORTANT.

indirect, *a.* devious; *spec.* circuitous, tortuous, oblique, sidelong, squint, secondary, mediate, circumlocutory, roundabout, deceitful, consequential.

Antonyms: see DIRECT.

indirection, *n.* deviousness, deviation; *spec.* circuity, circuitousness, obliquity, obliqueness, secondariness, mediacy, circumlocution, deceitful, roundabout.

indiscriminate, *a.* confused, miscellaneous, heterogeneous (*all three suggesting lack of plan, selection or consistency*); promiscuous (*implying, in addition to the sense of lack of plan or selection, the suggestion of sharing or common use often contrary to good taste or accepted custom*).

indistinct, *a.* obscure; *spec.* nebulous, thick, misty, feeble, hazy, uncertain, dreamy, dull, blurred, faint, inarticulate, indistinguishable, indefinite, confused, broken, *etc.*

Antonyms: see DEFINITE.

individual, *a. Spec.* definite, several (*used with a pl.; technical or B*), special, separate, particular, single, concrete, proper, inseparable, same, respective.

Antonyms: see COMMON, COLLECTIVE, GENERAL, MUTUAL.

individual, *n.* unit, one, singular (*R*); *spec.* head (*often collective pl.*), particular, person, incident.

individuality, *n.* selfness (*R*), singularity, definiteness (*contex.*); *spec.* identity, eccentricity (*contex.*), idiosyncrasy (*contex.*); *see* PERSONALITY.

individualize, *v. t.* singularize, peculiarize.

individually, *adv.* separately, definitely, severally, apart (*a predicative*); *spec.* apiece, distributively.

indivisible, *a.* inseparable, impartible.

indolence, *n.* idleness, otiosity (*B*), ease; *see* INACTIVITY.

Antonyms: see ACTIVITY, APPLICATION, WORK.

indolent, *a.* idle, otiose (*B*); *spec.* easy, easeful (*R*), easy-going (*C*), fat (*C or S*).

Antonyms: see ACTIVE, OCCUPIED.

indoor, *a.* intramural (*B*).

Antonyms: see OUTDOOR, OPEN-AIR.

indorse, *v. t.* **1.** endorse (*a variant*); *spec.* visé (*French*), docket, countersign.

2. *See* APPROVE.

induce, *v. t.* **1.** *Spec.* lead, cause, occasion, win, draw, bring, get, have, drive, motive, motivate (*R*), persuade, procure.

Antonyms: see DISSUADE.

2. *See* CAUSE, INFER.

inducement, *n.* **1.** *Referring to the act: spec.* causation (*R*), occasioning, persuasion, motivation (*R*), drawing, procurement, *etc.*

2. *Referring to the thing: spec.* cause, persuasive, consideration.

3. *See* CAUSE.

indulge, *v. t.* **1.** *Spec.* coddle, favor, humor, cosset, license, foster, cocker, pet, tolerate, pamper, spoil, excuse, gratify.

Antonyms: see PERSECUTE.

2. *See* GRANT.

indulge, *v. i. Spec.* revel, wallow.

Antonyms: see ABSTAIN.

indulgence, *n.* **1.** *Spec.* favor, humoring, licensing, indulgency, easiness, lenience *or* leniency, lenity, toleration, tolerance, pampering, gratification, self-gratification, self-indulgence, gentleness, fostering, excuse.

Antonyms: see SEVERITY; *cf.* PERSECUTE.

2. *See* GRANT.

indulgent, *a.* favoring, humoring, easy, lenient; *see* PAMPERING, SELF-GRATIFYING.

industrious, *a.* **1.** diligent, operose (*R*), worksome (*R*), laborious, hard-working; *spec.* sedulous.

Antonyms: see LAZY, INACTIVE.

2. *See* ACTIVE.

industry, *n.* **1.** *See* APPLICATION.

2. diligence, operosity (*R*), laboriousness, industriousness.

Antonyms: cf. LAZY.

3. *Spec.* trade, business, manufacture, art, painting, farming, gardening, *etc.*

ineffaceable, *a.* indestructible (*contex.*), indelible, inexpungible, inerasable.

ineffectual, *a. Spec.* ineffective, inefficient, inefficacious, useless, futile, unproductive, barren, empty, vain, blank, fruitless, infructuous (*B for "fruitless"*), infructuose (*R*), resultless (*R*), idle, inoperative, vain, dead, void, unavailing, lame, inofficious (*R*), ill, virtueless, Danaidean (*fig.*), Sisyphean (*fig.*), unsuccessful, dintless.

Antonyms: see EFFECTIVE, IMPRESSIVE.

inelastic, *a.* nonelastic; *spec.* plastic.

Antonyms: see ELASTIC.

ineloquent, *a.* plain-spoken, plain; *spec.* rude, crude.

inequality, *n.* inequalness (*R*), inconstancy, variableness, inequity (*with implication of unfairness, injustice*), imparity (*R*), odd (*R*),

indirectly, *adv.: circuitously, secondarily, sideways, sideway.*
indiscreet: *unwise.*
indiscrete: *united.*
indiscretion: *unwisdom.*
indispensable: *essential.*
indispose: *disease, weaken, disincline.*
indisposed: *ailing, unfriendly.*
indisposition: *ailment, disinclination.*
indisputable: *undeniable.*
indissoluble: *insoluble, inseparable.*
indite: *compose.*
individualism: *personality, egoism.*
individualize: *define.*
individuate: *define.*
indivisible: *inseparable.*
indomitable: *unyielding, unconquerable.*
indubitable: *unquestionable.*
induct: *admit, introduce, usher.*
indurate, *v. t.: harden, strengthen.*
industrial: *business.*
indwell, *v. t.: inhabit.*
indwell, *v. i.: inhere.*
indwelling: *inherent.*
inebriate, *a.: intoxicated.*
inebriate, *n.: drunkard.*
inebriate, *v. t.: intoxicate, excite.*
inebriety: *intoxication.*
inedible: *uneatable.*
ineffable: *inexpressible.*
ineffective: *ineffectual.*
inefficacious: *ineffectual.*
inefficient: *ineffectual.*
inelegant: *coarse, clumsy, unrefined.*
ineligible: *unqualified.*
inept: *unsuitable, awkward.*
inequitable: *unjust, unequal.*
ineradicable: *fixed.*

diversity, disparity; *spec.* inadequation (*A*), inadequacy.
Antonyms: see EQUALITY.

inert, *a.* **1.** dead (*spec. or fig.*).
2. *See* INACTIVE, DULL, SLUGGISH, LAZY, APATHETIC, INCORROSIVE.

inertness, *n.* **1.** deadness (*R*).
2. inertia (*the more common word*); *spec.* inactivity, dullness, sluggishness, laziness, apathy, incorrosiveness.

inexact, *a.* loose, rough, crude (*derogatory*), careless.
Antonyms: see ACCURATE.

inexcusable, *a.* unallowable, indefensible, unpardonable.
Antonyms: see EXCUSABLE.

inexhaustible, *a.* intarissable (*R*), exhaustless, boundless, inexhaustive; *spec.* bottomless, wasteless.
Antonyms: see LIMITED.

inexperience, *n.* noviceship (*chiefly spec.*), noviciateship (*R*), strangeness, novitiate (*chiefly spec.*), greenness (*C or undignified*), freshness; *spec.* callowness, rawness, unsophistication, untrainedness, youth; *cf.* NOVICE.
Antonyms: see EXPERIENCE.

inexperienced, *a.* unexperienced, green (*C or undignified*), fresh, new, griffinish (*Anglo-Indian*), untried, strange; *spec.* callow, raw, unversed, unsophisticated, undisciplined, unacquainted, young.
Antonyms: see EXPERIENCED.

inexpressible, *a.* unexpressible (*R*), inexpressive (*A*), unexpressive (*A*), ineffable (*more intensive, or of loftier sentiment, than* inexpressible); *spec.* unutterable, inutterable (*R*), utterless (*R*), incommunicable, unspeakable.

inextinguishable, *a.* unquenchable (*a stronger word than* inextinguishable), quenchless.

infallible, *a.* **1.** inerrable (*R*), unerring, oracular (*fig.*); *spec.* undeceivable.
Antonyms: see FALLIBLE.
2. *See* CERTAIN.

infancy, *n.* **1.** childhood (*contex.*), babyhood, babyism (*R*), infanthood (*R*); *spec.* cradlehood (*R*).
Antonyms: see AGE, END.
2. *See* MINORITY.

infant, *n.* **1.** child (*contex.*), babe (*now chiefly affected or rhetorical*), baby (*now chiefly spec.*); *spec.* weanling, foundling.
Antonyms: see ADULT.
2. *See* MINOR.

infantry, *n.* footsoldiers (*pl.; a nontechnical term*), foot (*a collective*), infantrymen (*pl.*).

infantryman, *n.* soldier (*contex.*), footsoldier, doughboy (*S, U. S.*), grabby (*depreciatory; S, Eng.*); *spec.* Thomas Atkins *or* (*usual*) Tommy Atkins *or* Tommy (*C, British*), Sammy (*C, U. S.*), Froggy (*S*).

infatuate, *v. t.* affatuate (*R*), captivate; *spec.* besot (*contemptuous*).

infatuated, *a.* captivated, mad, infatuate (*R*); *spec.* mad, besotted (*contemptuous*).

infatuation, *n.* foolishness (*contex.*), captivation; *spec.* besotment *or* besottedness (*contemptuous*), madness.

infection, *n.* **1.** affection, infestation (*R*).
2. medium; *spec.* contagion, virus, germ, blight, bacillus, bacterium, pest, pestilence.
3. *See* DISEASE, CONTAMINATION.

infer, *v. t.* **1.** conclude, draw; *spec.* deduce, induce, syllogize, derive, reason, gather, construe, generalize, particularize, glean, collect, guess, presume.
2. *See* INDICATE, IMPLY, MEANING.

inferable, *a. Spec.* deducible, consequent, consequential, generalizable, derivable, straight.

inference, *n.* conclusion, collection (*R*); *spec.* deduction, induction, derivation, illation (*tech. or B*), consequence, corollary, sequela, generality, generalization, generalism, implication (*this is a synonym of* inference *only in so far as an* implication *dropped, say, by a speaker, becomes the* inference *drawn by his hearer*), particularism, misconclusion, guess, presumption, derival.

inferential, *a. Spec.* deductive, inductive, illative, speculative.

inferior, *a.* **1.** *See* LOWER.
2. deterior (*R*); *spec.* bad, poor, mean, little (*now R*), base, petty, paltry, shabby, indifferent (*euphemistic*), tolerable (*often euphemistic*), dicky *or* dickey (*S or C*), subordinate, humble, junior.
Antonyms: see CHIEF, FINE, SUPERIOR, FIRST-CLASS.

inferior, *n.* puny (*Eng.*); *spec.* subordinate, junior.
Antonyms: see SUPERIOR.

inferiority, *n.* **1.** *Referring to position in place:* subjacency (*R*).
2. *Referring to rank, quality, etc.: spec.* subordinacy, juniority.
3. *Referring to quality, etc.:* poorness, meanness, baseness, littleness, indifference (*euphemistic*), tolerableness, shabbiness.

infernal, *a.* **1.** infern (*B and R*), underworld; *spec.* chthonian.
2. *Spec.* hellish (*now R*), Hadean (*R*), Tartarean, Tartarian (*R*), Stygian, Plutonian.
Antonyms: see HEAVENLY.

---

inertia: *inertness.*
inestimable: *incalculable, invaluable.*
inevitable: *unavoidable.*
inexcusable: *unjustifiable.*
inexorable: *unyielding.*
inexpedient: *unadvisable.*
inexpensive: *cheap.*
inexplicable: *unexplainable.*
inexpressive: *inexpressible, blank.*
inexpugnable: *unconquerable.*
inexpungible: *ineffaceable.*
infamous: *discreditable, base.*
infantile: *childish, babyish.*
infect: *disease.*
infectious: *catching, contaminative.*
infelicitous: *unhappy.*
inferno: *hell.*
infest: *frequent.*
infestation: *frequentation.*
infidel, *a.: heretic, heathen.*
infidel, *n.: heathen, unbeliever.*
infidelity: *heathenism, disbelief, treachery, adultery.*
infiltrate: *exude, pervade.*

---

3. *See* DEVILISH.
infinite, *a.* **1.** *See* ENDLESS, IMMENSE.
2. unlimited, immeasurable, interminate, unmeasured (*contex.*), measureless, illimitable, limitless, boundless; *spec.* coinfinite, inexhaustible, infinitesimal.
Antonyms: see FINITE, LIMITED, MEASURABLE.
infinity, *n.* **1.** *Spec.* endlessness, immensity.
2. *Spec.* infinite, infiniteness, infinitude, unlimitedness, immeasurableness, interminateness, unmeasuredness, measurelessness, illimitableness, boundlessness, limitlessness, inexhaustibleness, inexhaustibility, infinitesimalness.
inflate, *v. t.* **1.** distend (*contex.*), expand (*contex.*), puff (*orig. spec.*), swell; *spec.* intermesce, bloat, blow, sufflate (*R*), aërate.
Antonyms: see CONSTRICT, CONTRACT.
2. *See* ELATE, INCREASE.
inflated, *a.* **1.** *Spec.* puffy, swollen, bloat, bloated, overblown, turgid (*B*), bladdery.
2. *See* BOMBASTIC, CONCEITED, ELATED.
inflation, *n.* **1.** distension (*contex.*); *spec.* sufflation (*R*), puffiness, aëration, bloat, bloatedness, turgidity, tympanites *or* tympanism, vesiculation, insufflation.
2. *See* BOMBAST, CONCEIT, SWELLING (*with anger*), INCREASE.
inflect, *v. t. & i.* **1.** *See* CURVE.
2. *In grammar: spec.* decline, conjugate, compare.
3. modulate (*as the voice*).
inflict, *v. t.* administer (*humorous*), do (*used with "to"*), give (*a somewhat informal word*); *spec.* lay, impose, bring, land.
infliction, *n.* administration (*humorous*); *spec.* laying-on, imposition.
inflow, *n.* influx (*more often fig. than "inflow"*), influxion (*R*); *spec.* indraft, inrush, inrun (*R*), inpour, inset, flow, flood, instream, instreaming.
Antonyms: see OUTFLOW.
influence, *n.* **1.** power, potency (*B equiv. of "power"*); *spec.* effect, bias, credit, pull (*U. S.; S, chiefly political*), propulsion, impulse, control, magnetism, magic, authority, spell.
2. *Referring to a person:* power, potency (*B*), potentate (*obs.*); *spec.* authority, prestige.
influence, *v. t.* affect, actuate, sway; *spec.* control, persuade, bias, bribe, conjure.
influential, *a.* strong; *spec.* effective, effectual (*R*), substantial, powerful, weighty (*chiefly B or rhetorical*), momentous (*R*), controlling, potent (*chiefly rhetorical*).
influenza, *n.* grippe, la grippe, grip, flu (*C*).
inform, *v. t.* **1.** *See* FORM, ANIMATE.
2. acquaint, apprise, possess (*A*); *spec.* notify, teach, appraise (*becoming R or tech.*), tell, enlighten, instruct, tip (*S*), certify, advise, advertize (*chiefly B or tech.*), notice (*chiefly tech.*), flag, warn.
informal, *a.* *Spec.* unofficial, inofficial, unconventional.
Antonyms: see FORMAL, OFFICIAL.
informant, *n.* *Spec.* tipster (*C*), tipper (*C*), notifier, adviser, teacher, advertizer, teller, appriser, relator, preacher (*S or R*), squealer (*S*), intelligencer (*R*), newsmonger, accuser, warner.
information, *n.* *Spec.* notice, enlightenment, intelligence, instruction, teaching, tip (*C or cant*), advertizement, advice, word, complaint, message, warning.
informed, *a.* posted (*C*); *see* AWARE.
infrequency, *n.* *Spec.* rarity, sparseness.
Antonyms: see ABUNDANCE, FREQUENCY.
infrequent, *a.* unfrequent (*R*), uncommon (*a stronger word than "infrequent"*); *spec.* sparse, scarce, rare, thin, occasional, sporadic.
Antonyms: see FREQUENT, ABOUNDING.
infrequently, *adv.* seldom, uncommonly; *spec.* rarely, sparsely.
Antonyms: see OFTEN.
ingenious, *a.* inventive, deviceful (*R*); *spec.* subtle, artful, clever, fertile, dædal (*B*), dædalian (*B*), tricky.
Antonyms: see HELPLESS, BARREN.
ingeniousness, *n.* ingeniosity (*R*), inventiveness, ingenuity; *spec.* art, artifice, artfulness, cleverness, trickiness, contrivance.
ingot, *n.* lingot (*A*); *spec.* pig, sow, bloom.
ingrate, *n.* viper (*fig.*), snake; *spec.* traitor.
ingratiate, *v. t.* insinuate;—*an approximate synonym only.*
ingratiating, *a.* insinuating, smooth, silken, silky.
Antonyms: see REPELLENT.
ingratitude, *n.* ungratefulness, unthankfulness.
Antonyms: see THANKFULNESS.
inhabit, *v. t.* occupy, indwell (*R*); *spec.* people.
inhabitable, *a.* habitable (*now chiefly used with "not"*); *spec.* lodgeable.
Antonyms: see UNINHABITABLE.
inhalation, *n.* breath (*contex.*), draft, inspiration; *spec.* sniff, snuff, snuffle.
Antonyms: see EXHALATION.
inhale, *v. t. & i.* breathe (*contex.*), draw, inspire, inbreathe; *spec.* sniff, snuff, snuffle.
Antonyms: see EXHALE.
inharmonious, *a.* different (*contex.*), inhar-

---

infinitude: *infinity.*
infirm: *weak, unstable, ailing.*
infirmary: *hospital.*
infirmity: *ailment, fault.*
inflame: *kindle, heat, excite, anger, flush.*
inflamed: *feverish, bloodshot.*
inflammable, *a.: combustible, excitable.*
inflammatory: *kindling, excitative, irritating, dissentious.*
inflexible: *rigid, unyielding, firm.*
influx: *inflow.*
infold: *envelope, clasp.*
inform, *a.: formless, deformed.*
inform, *v. i.: tell.*
informative, *a.: instructive.*
infraction: *violation, encroachment.*
infringement: *violation, encroachment.*
infuriated: *angry.*
infuse: *introduce, inspire.*
ingenuity: *ingeniousness.*
ingenuous: *generous, artless, frank.*
inglorious: *humble, discreditable.*
ingrained: *deep.*
ingrate: *ungrateful.*
ingredient: *component.*
inhabitant: *dweller.*

monic; *spec.* disharmonious, discordant, tuneless.
Antonyms: see HARMONIOUS, AGREEABLE.
inhere, *v. i.* exist (*contex.*), abide (*contex.*), inexist (*R*), coinhere, belong (*used with "to"*), consist, subsist, lie, reside, indwell (*R or B*).
inherence, *n.* **1.** inherency, inexistence, inhesion; *spec.* indwelling, immanence, intrinsicalness, residence (*R*).
2. inbeing, immanence.
inherent, *a.* subsistent, proper (*with "to"*); *spec.* indwelling, intrinsic (*belonging as a part or quality of a thing, as opposed to the external or accidental association implied in its opposite,* extrinsic), immanent, inalienable, inseparable, essential (*necessary to a thing's being what it is, whereas* inherent *refers to a quality or attribute absolutely and permanently a part of a thing*).
Antonyms: see ACCIDENTAL.
inherit, *v. t.* take, heir (*R*).
inheritable, *a.* capable (*of inheriting*);—*said of the person.*
inhuman, *a.* **1.** unkind; *see* CRUEL, FIERCE, DEVILISH.
2. *Of what is merely not human:* nonhuman; *spec.* supernatural, superhuman.
Antonyms: see HUMAN.
initial, *a.* **1.** first, commencing, initiatory, initiary (*R*), inchoate; *spec.* introductory, rudimentary, opening, incipient, liminal (*R*), original; *see* BEGINNING.
Antonyms: see COMPLETE, LAST.
2. *See* ELEMENTARY.
inject, *v. t.* **1.** introduce (*contex.*), intromit; *spec.* transfuse, syringe, insufflate, indart, interject.
Antonyms: see EJECT, EXPEL, EXTRACT.
2. *See* FILL.
injection, *n.* **1.** *Referring to the act:* introduction, intromission, immission (*R*).
Antonyms: see EJECTION, EXPULSION.
2. *Of the thing: spec.* enema, clyster.
injunctive, *a.* bidding, dictatorial, commanding.
injure, *v. t.* **1.** hurt (*a less formal word than* injure), harm, wrong, prejudice (*tech.*); *spec.* outrage, mischief (*A*), touch, disserve, misserve, aggrieve (*R or tech.*), damage, detriment (*R*), impair, disavail (*R*), endamage (*B or R*).
Antonyms: see BENEFIT.
2. *See* HARM (*in reference to other than legal rights*), ILL-TREAT, DAMAGE.
injurious, *a.* **1.** evil, hurtful, harmful, wrongful, prejudicial, damaging, prejudicious (*R*), detrimental, mischievous; *spec.* contrarious, tortious.
Antonyms: see BENEFICIAL.
2. *See* HARMFUL.
injury, *n.* **1.** harm, wrong, hurt, prejudice, damnification (*tech.*), impairment, impair (*A*), damage, mischief; *spec.* detriment, disservice.
2. *See* HARM, DAMAGE.
3. *Concretely, as used with the article "a" or "an":* hurt (*chiefly spec.*), harm (*R*), damage (*R*), mischief (*R*), iniquity, injustice, wrong; *spec.* disservice, outrage, tear, impairment, detriment.
Antonyms: see BENEFIT.
injustice, *n.* injury, unjustness, iniquity, wrong, inequity.
Antonyms: see JUSTICE.
ink, *n.* atrament (*R*); *spec.* sepia.
inkstand, *n.* standish (*R*).
inkwell, *n.* reservoir; *spec.* inkhorn, inkstand.
inland, *a.* **1.** interior; *spec.* midland, mediterranean (*R*), up-country, upland.
Antonyms: see FOREIGN.
2. *See* DOMESTIC.
inland, *n.* interior; *spec.* midland, upcountry, upland, hinterland, in-country (*Scot.*).
Antonyms: see BORDER.
inlay, *v. t.* *To adorn by inlaying: spec.* hatch, niello, tessellate.
inlet, *n.* **1.** *See* ENTRANCE.
2. recess, arm; *spec.* cover, creek, fleet (*local, Eng.*), inrun, bay, bight, nook, gulf, frith, firth, fiord, bayou (*southern U. S.*).
Antonyms: see OUTLET.
inmate, *n.* dweller; *spec.* intern, guest, inhabitant.
inn, *n.* house, hotel (*chiefly spec.; in the U. S.* hotel *is the ordinary term for any* inn), hostel (*often A, but in Europe a residence for students*), hostelry (*A or B*), tavern (*spec., exc. local U. S.*), public house (*legal*), pub (*vulgar and C; British*); *spec.* ordinary (*Eng. or local U S.*), locanda (*Italian*), posada (*Spain*), asteria (*Italy or Italian; R*), resthouse (*in the East*), sala (*India*), choulty (*Anglo-Indian*), caravanserai (*in the Orient*), fonduk (*North Africa*), fonda (*Spanish*), serai (*in the Orient*), khan (*in the Orient*).
innate, *a.* inborn (*the Anglo-Saxon term*), native (*implying close relation to geographical origin*), inbred, indigenous (*naturally belonging*), natural (*and therefore easy*), congenital (*pertaining to biological origin*), original; *spec.* intrinsic *or* intrinsical; *see* INSTINCTIVE.
Antonyms: see ACQUIRED.
innkeeper, *n.* landlord (*contex.*), innholder (*R*), taverner (*R*), victualer (*now chiefly local*), Boniface (*fig.*), host, hostess (*fem.*), hostler (*A*); *spec.* khanjee, padrone.
innocence, *n.* *Spec.* sinlessness, purity, blame-

inheritance: *heritage.*
inhibit: *restrain, prevent, forbid.*
inhibition: *restraint, forbiddance, prevention.*
inhospitable: *cool, desolate.*
inimical: *unfriendly, opposed.*
inimitable: *unequaled.*
iniquitous: *unjust, wicked.*
iniquity: *injustice, wickedness, sin.*
initiate, *n.*: *novice.*
initiate, *v. t.*: *begin.*
initiative, *a. & n.*: *beginning.*
injudicious: *unwise.*
injunction: *bidding.*
injunctive: *bidding, dictatorial.*
inner: *interior.*
inning: *turn.*

lessness, chastity, guiltlessness, simplicity, harmlessness.
Antonyms: see COMPLICITY.
innocent, *a. Spec.* sinless, pure, blameless, artless, chaste, guiltless, simple, harmless.
Antonyms: see WICKED, BLAMABLE, SINFUL, CONSCIOUS, CORRUPT, CRIMINAL, GUILTY.
innocent, *n. Spec.* child, dove, lamb, simpleton;—*as being innocent by nature.*
Antonyms: see SINNER, TRANSGRESSOR.
innovate, *v. i.* neologize (*in language or religion*), novelize (*R*).
innovation, *n.* novation (*R*), neologization (*R*), neology *or* neologism (*chiefly spec.*), novelty.
innutritious, *a.* unnutritious, innutrient (*R*), innutritive (*R*), jejune (*B*), lean (*A or R*), heartless (*fig.; R or dial.*), inalimental (*R*).
Antonyms: see NOURISHING.
inoculate, *v. t.* infect; *spec.* invaccinate, vaccinate.
inoculation, *n.* infection; *spec.* invaccination (*R*), vaccination, clavelization, variolation, ovination (*R*).
inodorous, *a.* odorless (*the homelier, but more emphatic, word*); *spec.* scentless.
Antonyms: see ODOROUS.
inoffensive, *a.* offenceless (*R*), unoffending; *see* HARMLESS, UNOBJECTIONABLE.
Antonyms: see OFFENSIVE.
inorganic, *a.* unorganized; *spec.* disorganic, mineral.
Antonyms: see ORGANIC.
inpouring, *n.* infusion (*R, exc. fig.*).
inscribe, *v. t.* **1.** *Referring to what is recorded by inscribing: spec.* emblaze, superscribe, subscribe, indorse, letter, tablet, write.
2. *Referring to what is marked upon: spec.* mark, superscribe, subscribe, letter, engrave, line, address.
3. *See* DEDICATE.
inscription, *n. Spec.* carving, delineation, superscription, subscription, indorsement, epigram (*R*), epigraph, epitaph, petroglyph, exergue, lapidary, epigraphy (*a collective*), colophon, writing, engraving, address, dedication.
insect, *n.* arthropod (*tech.*); *spec.* hexapod (*tech.*), bug (*chiefly dial. or popular, U. S., exc. in reference to the bedbug*), buzzard (*dial.*), hammer, larva, ephemerid, ephemera, butterfly, laborer, worker, nit, coleopter, mosquito, fly, *etc.*
insectile, *a.* entomic (*R*), insectan (*R*), insectiform (*formal or tech.*).
insensibility, *n.* insensateness (*R*), insensibleness, insentience (*R*), unfeelingness, senselessness (*chiefly spec.*); *spec.* torpidity, anæsthesia (*tech.*), insensitiveness, impassiveness, induration, brass (*fig.*), marble (*fig.*), stone (*fig.*), steel (*fig.*), apathy, dullness, indifference, bluntness, deafness, deadness, lifelessness, numbness, callousness, sluggishness, unconsciousness.
Antonyms: see FEELING; *also cf.* SENSITIVE.
insensible, *a.* **1.** *In reference to physical sensation:* unfeeling, insentient, senseless; *spec.* torpid, inirritable, anæsthetic (*tech.*), insensitive, dull, obtuse, insensate, impassible, impassive, indifferent, dullish, lifeless, benumbed, callous, thick-skinned, unconscious, insusceptible, sluggish.
Antonyms: see SENSITIVE, SENTIENT.
2. *In reference to the perception of, or experiencing of, ideas, emotions, etc.:* unfeeling, insentient (*R*), apathetic, callous, senseless (*R*); *spec.* torpid, blunt, insensitive, insusceptible, impassible, impassive, indifferent, deaf (*fig.*), hardened, thick-skinned (*fig.*), pachydermatous (*humorous or affected*), inirritable, insensate, unaffected, inappreciative, unmoved, dead, lifeless, benumbed, callous, sluggish, unconscious.
Antonyms: see IMPRESSIBLE, SENSITIVE, SUSCEPTIBLE, SENTIMENT.
inseparable, *a.* undividable, indivisible, undepartable (*R*), inseverable; *spec.* indissoluble, indiscerptible (*B*), indissociable (*R*), inseparate (*R*), individual (*R*).
Antonyms: see DIVISIBLE.
insert, *v. t.* introduce (*more formal or B than* insert); *spec.* infix, interpose, inwork, work, interpolate, intercalate, inset, enter (*chiefly tech.*), insinuate, intromit (*R*), inmit (*R*), interline, implant, parenthesize, sink, inlay, subtrude (*R*), intrude, inweave, interpage.
Antonyms: see WITHDRAW, REMOVE.
inserted, *a. Spec.* parenthetical, intercalary, intermediate, intervening, intercalated, interbedded, interstratified, embolismic, epagomenic (*R*), incut.
insertion, *n.* **1.** *Referring to the act: spec.* infixion, introduction, implantation, epenthetic (*phonetic*), immission (*R*), intromission, intercalation, interpolation, insinuation, embolism.
Antonyms: see WITHDRAWAL, REMOVAL.
2. *Referring to what is inserted: spec.* panel, insert, inlay, inset.
insight, *n.* discernment, perception, penetration, perceptiveness (*R*), perceptivity (*R*), perspicuity (*an improper use*); *spec.* clairvoyance, intuition.
Antonyms: cf. BLIND.
insignificance, *n.* **1.** meaninglessness (*cf.*

innocuous: *harmless.*
innuendo: *intimation.*
innumerable: *countless.*
inoffensive: *offenceless, harmless, unobjectionable.*
inoperative: *ineffectual.*
inopportune: *untimely.*
inordinate: *excessive.*
inquest: *question, jury.*
inquietude: *uneasiness, disturbance.*
inquire: *question.*
inquiring: *curious.*
inquiry: *question, examination.*
inquisition: *question, examination.*
inquisitive: *curious.*
insane: *deranged, unwise.*
insatiable: *greedy.*
insatiableness: *greed.*
inscrutable: *unintelligible.*
insecure: *unsafe, uncertain.*
insensate: *insensible, unwise.*
insensitive: *insensible.*
insentient: *insensible.*
inside, *n.: interior, nature,* (in pl.) *viscera.*
inside, *a.: interior.*
inside, *adv.: within.*
insidious: *deceitful.*
insignia, *n. pl.: badge.*

MEANINGLESS).

2. smallness, nothingness; *spec.* sniffetiness (*R*), triviality, poorness, unimportance.

Antonyms: see DIGNITY, IMPORTANCE.

insignificant, *a.* **1.** *See* MEANINGLESS.

2. small, simple (*depreciatory*), nothing (*in predicative use*); *spec.* sniffety (*R*), trivial, poor, unimportant.

Antonyms: see IMPOSING, GRAND, IMPORTANT, IMPRESSIVE.

insincere, *a.* deceitful, empty, hollow; *spec.* half-hearted, pretended, double, farcical, unfaithful, hypocritical, disingenuous, *etc.*

Antonyms: see EARNEST, SINCERE.

insincerity, *n.* deceitfulness, emptiness, hollowness; *spec.* half-heartedness, doubleness, farcicality, unfaithfulness, hypocrisy, disingenuousness, pretence, *etc.*

Antonyms: see SINCERITY; *also cf.* EARNEST.

insoluble, *a.* irresoluble (*R*), insolvable; *spec.* (*in a secondary sense*) indissoluble, unexplainable, irreducible.

Antonyms: see SOLUBLE.

insolvent, *a.* **1.** *Inability to meet debts:* bankrupt, failed (*R*); *spec.* defaulting.

2. *Very low in resources* (*a loose use of* insolvent)*:* impoverished, broken, broke (*S*), stony (*C*), hard up, on one's uppers.

insolvent, *n.* bankrupt, defaulter, lame duck (*stock-exchange; S*).

inspiration, *n.* **1.** *See* INHALATION.

2. *In reference to mental enthusiasm, emotion, etc.: spec.* inflatus, embreathment (*R*), entheos (*obs. or R*), inbreathing, enthusiasm (*R; as infused by the deity*), theolepsy (*R*), fire, prophecy, frenzy.

3. *See* SUGGESTION.

inspire, *v. t.* **1.** *See* INHALE, EXCITE, SUGGEST.

2. *Spec.* inbreathe, embreathe (*R*), conceit, illumine, animate, cheer (*contex.*), arouse (*contex.*), inculcate, infuse (*with "into"*), instill.

instability, *n.* **1.** unstableness (*tech.*); *spec.* tenderness, crankiness, unsteadiness, waveringness, wavering, changeableness, weakness.

Antonyms: see FIRMNESS.

2. *In reference to the mind, opinion, etc.: see* CHANGEABLENESS.

installment, *n.* **1.** *See* ESTABLISHMENT.

2. payment (*contex.*); *spec.* portion, handsel (*Eng.*), earnest, kist (*East Indian*).

instep, *n.* arch (*a loose usage,* instep *properly being the upper part only*).

instill, *v. t.* **1.** introduce, drop, drip, distill (*R*).

2. *See* INFUSE.

instinct: *a. Spec.* imbued, animated, moved, actuated; *see* animated.

instinctive, *a.* inborn, innate; *spec.* intuitive.

institution, *n.* **1.** *See* ESTABLISHMENT, ADMISSION, BEGINNING, LAW, CUSTOM.

2. organization; *spec.* academy, college, hospital, school, church, prison, museum, theater, store, factory, *etc.*

instructive, *a.* teaching, didactic (*B*), informative, docent (*R*); *spec.* preceptive, educational, pedagogic, pedagogical, propaedeutic, prophetic (*R*), tutory (*R*).

instrument, *n.* **1.** *See* AGENT.

2. device (*contex.*), appliance, implement (*chiefly spec.*), engine (*now B, exc. spec.*); *spec.* utensil, tool, apparatus, weapon, convenience.

3. *Referring to what affects the mind: spec.* organon *or* organum (*B and tech.*), organ.

4. document (*contex.*), paper; *spec.* deed, bond, deed poll, specialty, note, mortgage, bill, check *or* cheque, power, grant, settlement, writ, *etc.*

insult, *v. t.* abuse (*contex.*); *spec.* outrage, affront, sauce, cheek (*S*).

Antonyms: see CONSIDER.

insult, *n.* abuse (*contex.*), insultation (*R*); *spec.* outrage, affront, sauce, cheek (*S*), indignity, insolence.

Antonyms: see FLATTERY.

insuperable, *a.* insurmountable, invincible, unconquerable.

insurable, *a.* assurable (*chiefly British*), coverable (*cant*).

insurance, *n.* **1.** assurance. *In the United States* insurance *is now the term in general popular and technical use for all kinds of contracts. In Great Britain* insurance *is the general term in popular use, but in technical usage* assurance *is used in the names and literature of the majority of the life insurance companies, and* insurance *is similarly used for fire, marine, and accident insurance.*

2. *See* GUARANTY.

insure, *v. t.* **1.** assure, cover (*cant or C*); *Spec.* underwrite.

2. *See* GUARANTEE.

insurer, *n.* **1.** *In reference to the one assuming*

---

insinuate: *insert, introduce, intimate, ingratiate.*
insinuating: *penetrating, ingratiating.*
insipid: *tasteless, dull.*
insist: *state.*
insistent: *affirmative, confident.*
insolence: *impudence.*
insolent: *impudent.*
insomnia: *sleeplessness.*
insouciant: *careless, unconcerned.*
inspect: *examine.*
inspiring: *elevating, stimulating, cheering.*
inspirit: *enliven, encourage, cheer, rouse.*
instance, *n.: urgency, incitement, example, occasion.*
instance, *v. t.: adduce.*
instancy: *urgency.*
instant, *a.: urgent, immediate.*
instant, *n.: moment.*
instantaneous: *immediate.*
instate: *establish, place, admit.*
instigate: *incite.*
instill: *introduce, inspire.*
instinct, *n.: faculty.*
instinctive: *innate.*
institute, *v. t.: establish, admit, begin.*
institute, *n.: school.*
instruct: *teach, inform, bid.*
instrument, *v. t.: arrange.*
instrumentality: *agency, agent, contribution.*
insubordinate: *disobedient.*
insubstantial: *immaterial.*
insubstantiate: *embody.*
insufferable: *unbearable.*
insufficient: *deficient.*
insular: *island, isolated, narrow*
insulate: *isolate.*
insupportable: *unbearable, indefensible.*

---

the obligation: assurer, underwriter.
2. *In reference to the one securing protection:* insurant, insured, assured, insuree (*R*), assurer.
insurgence, insurgency, *n.* disturbance (*contex.*), outbreak, uprising *or* rising, insurrection, revolt, rebellion; *spec.* revolution, mutiny, sedition.
insurgent, *a.* insurrectional, insurrectionary; *spec.* seditious, rebellious, rebel, revolting, mutinous, revolutionary.
insurrect, *v. i.* rebel, rise, revolt.
intact, *a.* unaffected (*contex.*), entire, whole, integral, uninjured, unblemished, unimpaired, unsullied, complete, sound.
Antonyms: see AFFECTED, BROKEN, TORN.
intangible, *a.* impalpable (*often spec.*), untouchable (*R*), intactile (*R*); *spec.* aërial, airy, spiritous, phantom.
Antonyms: see TANGIBLE.
intellectual, *a.* **1.** thoughtful (*contex.*); *spec.* imaginative, spiritual; *see* INTELLIGENT.
Antonyms: see COARSE.
2. *See* MENTAL.
intellectual, *n. Referring to a person:* intellectuality (*R*), intelligence (*R*), mind, talent.
intelligence, *n.* **1.** *As referring to a faculty of the mind:* intellect, mentality, understanding (*often spec.*), brain *or* (*pl.*) brains (*C*), nous (*spec., exc. in educated C use*); *spec.* reason, cognition, cognizance, apperception, apprehension, comprehension, sense, intelligency (*R*), memory, imagination, thought, consideration, insight.
2. *As referring to a fact or quality admitting of degrees or comparison: spec.* brightness, sagacity, quickness, readiness, shrewdness, cleverness, smartness, keenness, subtlety, subtility (*R*), sharpness, knowingness, wit.
Antonyms: see STUPIDITY.
3. news (*B*); *see* INFORMATION.
intelligent, *a.* **1.** *As having the faculty of intelligence:* intellectual, understanding, sensible, cognitive (*B or tech.*).
2. *As having an unusual degree of intelligence: spec.* bright, apprehensive (*R*), sagacious, shrewd, clever, smart (*in one sense now chiefly U. S.*), keen, subtle, sharp, knowing, instructed, knowledgeable, brainy (*C*), well-informed, adept, learned, scient (*R*), downy (*S*), wide-awake, gnostic (*humorous*), cunning (*A*), wise, canny (*in a good sense; A Scot.*), leery (*S*), cute (*C*), quick-witted, intuent (*R*), fly (*S*).
Antonyms: see UNINTELLIGENT, IMBECILE, STUPID.
intelligibility, *n.* easiness (*contex.; C*); *spec.* plainness (*C*), evidentness, palpability, palpableness, perspicuousness, perspicuity, lucidness, lucidity.
intelligible, *a.* easy (*contex.; C*); *spec.* plain, clear, obvious, manifest (*rather B or formal*), evident, open, palpable, perspicuous, lucid.
Antonyms: see UNINTELLIGIBLE.
intend, *v. i.* propose, mean (*chiefly with an infinitive clause as its object; now chiefly spec.*), calculate (*C, U. S.*), purpose (*R*); *spec.* design, contemplate, aim, destine (*chiefly in the passive*), will, direct.
intense, *a.* **1.** strong, violent, tense, sharp, potent, extreme, keen, high; *spec.* acute, exquisite, grievous, poignant, deep, dense, sore, marked, passionate, vivid.
Antonyms: see WEAK.
2. *See* EARNEST.
intensify, *v. t. & i.* heighten, intensate (*R*), strengthen, enhance (*chiefly spec.*); *spec.* concentrate, sharpen, raise, whet, deepen, thicken, embody, aggravate, strengthen.
Antonyms: see ABATE, FADE, WEAKEN, RELAX.
intensity, *n.* **1.** strength, power, intension (*B*), tension *or* (*less common*) tensity; *spec.* degree, pitch, accent, point, grade, potency, potence (*R*), keenness, violence, sharpness, extremity, soreness, height, vividness, vividity (*R*), passionateness, passion, edge, depth, energy, density.
Antonyms: see WEAKNESS.
2. earnestness (*cf.* EARNEST).
intensive, *a.* intensitive (*R*), intensative (*R*), intensifying; *spec.* emphasizing, concentrated.
Antonyms: see EXTENSIVE.
intention, *n. Referring to the will or action of the mind:* meaning (*A or obs.*), intent (*now chiefly legal*), mind (*as in "I have a mind to go"*), purpose, end, aim; *spec.* design, contemplation, calculation (*C, U. S.*), distinction, will, thought, counsel, view, forepurpose (*R*), direction.
intentional, *a.* purposed, purposive, conscious, conscientious, designed, intended; *spec.* spontaneous, willing, willful, voluntary, contemplated, deliberate, advised, free, *etc.*
Antonyms: see UNINTENTIONAL, CHANCE, ACCIDENTAL.
intentionality, *n.* willingness, voluntariness, purposeness (*R*), willfulness, *etc.*
interact, *v. i. Spec.* interplay, engage, mesh, reciprocate.
interceptive, *a.* stopping, checking, inclusive.
intercourse, *n.* communication, dealings (*pl.; familiar*), conversation (*R, exc. spec.*), commerce (*now chiefly B and A*), consuetude (*a Latinism*); coitus, congress (*R*), intimacy (*euphemism*); *spec.* connection, consortion (*R*), intercommunion (*R*), communion (*elevated*

insurmountable: *insuperable, unscalable.*
insurrection: *insurgence.*
insusceptible.: *insensible.*
integer: *number, whole.*
integral: *component, intact.*
integrate: *complete.*
intellect: *intelligence, thinker, mind.*
intellection: *understanding, idea.*
intemperance: *excess.*
intend, *v. t.: mean.*
intended, *a.: intentional.*
intended, *n.: betrothed.*
intent, *a.: attentive, earnest.*
intent, *n.: intention, meaning, object.*
inter: *bury.*
intercede: *interpose.*
intercept: *stop, include.*
interchange: *exchange, alternate.*
interdict, *v. t.: forbid.*
interdict, *n.: decree.*

and chiefly B), fellowship, community, converse, intelligence (*R*), practice (*A*), truck (*C*), neighborship, correspondence.
Antonyms: see NONINTERCOURSE.
interest, *n.* **1.** *See* RIGHT, BUSINESS, ADVANTAGE, PARTY.
2. *As in "a matter of interest":* feeling, concern, concernment (*B*).
Antonyms: see INDIFFERENCE.
3. premium, usury (*obs. or A, exc. spec.*), use (*A*), usance (*A*), discount.
Antonyms: see PRINCIPAL.
interest, *v. t.* **1.** *See* AFFECT.
2. engage; *spec.* grip, absorb, excite, occupy, hold, amuse, frighten, please, horrify, *etc.*
interesting, *a. Spec.* exciting, cunning (*U. S.*), funny, pleasing, *etc.*
Antonyms: see UNINTERESTING.
interfere, *v. i.* **1.** *Chiefly in reference to horses:* hitch, strike; *spec.* overreach, forge, grab, click.
2. *See* COLLIDE, CONFLICT, INTERPOSE.
interior, *a.* **1.** internal, inner, intern (*B or A*), inward, intraneous (*R*), inside; *spec.* inmost, innermost, within (*always predicative*), intimate (*B or tech.*), intracanal, intralobular, intramolecular, intramundane, intramural, intraocular, intrapetalar, intrapetiolar, intraseptal, intrauterine, intravascular, intravenous, intraventricular.
Antonyms: see EXTERIOR, SURFACE.
2. *See* MENTAL, SPIRITUAL, DOMESTIC, *etc.*
interior, *n.* **1.** inside; *spec.* bowels (*pl.; fig*)., womb (*fig.*), heart (*fig.*), recess, belly (*fig.*), center.
Antonyms: see SURFACE, EXTERIOR, BORDER.
2. *See* INLAND, SPIRIT.
interiorly, *adv.* internally, inwardly, within, inly.
interlace, *v. t.* **1.** unite, bind, entangle;—*all three contex.*
2. *See* DIVERSIFY.
3. complicate (*contex.*); *spec.* knit, weave, lace, pleach, twist, interknit, implicate (*R*), impleach (*R*), intervolve, interweave, interlard, interwreathe, plait, plash, twine, intertwine, intertwist, trellis (*R*), raddle (*R*).
interlaced, *a.* interwoven, knit, implicate (*R*); *spec.* matted, matty (*R*).
interlay, *v. t. Spec.* interlaminate, interbed, interlap, interleave.
interleave, *v. t. In reference to a book:* interfoliate (*R*).
interlude, *n.* interact, entr'acte (*French*); *spec.* exode *or* exodium, ritornelle, ritornello (*Italian*), intermezzo (*Italian*); *see* INTERVAL.
intermarriage, *n.* alliance, marriage.
intermediacy, *n.* intermediateness, intervention.
intermediary, *n. Spec.* intermediate, agent, middleman, medium, mean, intermedium, go-between (*often depreciatory*), intervener, interagent.
intermediate, *a.* mediate (*R*), medial (*chiefly spec.*); *spec.* intermediary, median (*chiefly in scientific use*), middle, interjacent, medium, mean, mesne, intervening, intervenient, transitional, interlobate, interlobular, interlocular, intermaxillary, intermolecular, intermundane, intermuscular, internarial, internasal, interneural, interoceanic, interopercular, internodal, interosseal, interosseous, interplanetary, interpolar (*R*), interpleural, interradial, interramal, interrenal, interparietal, interscapular, intersidereal (*R*), interstellar, interseptal, interstrial, interspatial, interstitial, interspinal, interspinous, intertrochlear, intervalvular, intervascular, intervenient, interventricular, intervertebral, intervisceral.
Antonyms: see IMMEDIATE.
intermission, *n.* **1.** cessation, interruption (*contex.*), intermittence (*less common than "intermission"*), skip; *spec.* lull, pause, rest, suspension, intermittency (*R*).
2. *See* INTERVAL, GAP.
intermit, *v. t.* abate, suspend, respite (*R*), interrupt.
Antonyms: see CONTINUE.
intermittency, *n.* **1.** *Spec.* fitfulness, periodicity.
2. *See* INTERMISSION.
intermittent, *a.* discontinuous, remittent, broken, intermissive (*R*); *spec.* spasmodic, fitful, capricious, gusty, squally, periodical, periodic, flickering.
Antonyms: see CONSTANT.
interpellate, *v. t.* question (*in parliamentary usage, a formal inquiry of an officer, committee, etc.*).
interpolate, *v. t.* **1.** *Spec.* falsify, adulterate.
2. add (*contex.*), insert, interpose, introduce; *spec.* interline, interlineate, interjaculate.
Antonyms: see EFFACE.
interpolation, *n.* addition (*contex.*), insertion, gag (*S or cant*); *spec.* interlineation, *etc.*
interpose, *v. t.* insert, introduce, interpone (*obs. or Scots law*), interlocate (*R*); *spec.* interject, sandwich; *see* INTERPOLATE.
interpose, *v. i. Spec.* intermediate, mediate, intercede (to interpose *on behalf of some one or some cause*), intervene (*suggesting coming between opposing forces with a plan of solution*), interfere, (*to place one's self in the way troublesomely*), tamper, meddle, intermeddle, intromit (*chiefly Scot.*), interrupt.
interposition, *n.* **1.** insertion, introduction; *spec.* interjection, interpolation, intercalation, interlocation, gag.
2. *Spec.* intermediation, mediation, interven-

---

interim, *n.: interval.*
interject: *inject, interpose, comment.*
interline: *add, insert.*
interlocutor: *conserver.*
interloper: *intruder.*
intermeddle: *interpose.*
intermediary: *mediatory, intermediate.*
interment: *burial.*
interminable: *endless.*
intern, *n.: inmate.*
internecine: *destructive.*
interpellate: *question.*
interplay, *v. i.: interact.*

---

tion, interference, meddling, intermeddling, interposal (*R*), intromission (*chiefly Scot.*).

interrupt, *v. t. Spec.* intercept, obstruct, stop, pretermit, break, intersect, cut, check, quit, interlude, *etc.*

interruption, *n. Spec.* break, interception, obstruction, stoppage, stop (*R, exc. in certain phases*), pretermission, intersection, cut, break, check, quitting, cut-off (*chiefly C, exc. tech.*), cæsura, *etc.*

intersect, *v. t.* cross (*contex.*), cut (*spec., exc. fig.*), countersect (*R*); *spec.* intervein, interrupt.

Antonyms: see PARALLEL.

intersecting, *a.* crossing (*contex.*), secant (*chiefly tech.*), across (*used predicatively*), intersectional, intersecant, cutting (*spec., exc. fig.*), *etc.*

Antonyms: see PARALLEL.

intersection, *n.* **1.** crossing (*contex.*), intercrossing; *spec.* decussation, chiasma.

2. *Spec.* road, crossway (*often in pl.*), crossing, cross (*R*), carfax (*obs. or local Eng.*), crosspath, crossroad (*often in pl.*).

interspace, *n.* interval, skip (*R*); *spec.* interlude (*fig.*), gap, intervolute, interstice.

intersperse, *v. t.* intermingle; *spec.* lard, interlard, shed (*R; chiefly in p. p.*), sprinkle *or* (*less usual*) intersprinkle, intersow (*R*), scatter, diversify.

interval, *n.* **1.** *Referring to time:* distance (*only in "distance of time"*), skip, space; *spec.* spell, pause, recess, interregnum (*often fig.*), meantime, elapse (*R*), intermedium (*R*), interlude, interim, parenthesis (*R*), interruption, difference, interlunation.

2. *In reference to a difference of sounds in pitch:* skip; *spec.* discord, step, dissonance, complement, tone, diastem, diesis, diaschisma, ditone, heptachord, tritone, semitone, second, third, fifth, quint, *etc.*

3. *See* INTERSPACE, BOTTOM.

intestinal, *a.* visceral (*contex.*), enteric (*R or tech.*); *spec.* duodenal, rectal.

intestine, *n.* viscera (*contex.*), bowel (*homelier or more familiar; R in sing.*), gut (*now vulgar, exc. in tech. use*); *spec.* ileum, jejunum, colon, cæcum, rectum, duodenum, chitterlings (*pl.*).

intimacy, *n.* **1.** closeness, nearness; *spec.* familiarity, depth.

2. *See* AMOUR, INTERCOURSE.

intimate, *a.* close (*referring to likeness of interest, etc.*), near (*a weaker term than* close), strict (*R*); *spec.* bosom, particular, homelike, home, familiar, special, deep, confidential, chummy (*C*).

Antonyms: see FORMAL.

intimate, *n.* associate (*contex.*); *spec.* friend, chum (*C or S*), familiar; *see* COMRADE.

intimate, *v. t.* **1.** *See* ANNOUNCE.

2. *As implying indirection in statement:* indicate (*contex.*), hint, suggest; *spec.* insinuate, sneer, innuendo (*R*), slur (*R*).

intimation, *n.* **1.** *See* ANNOUNCEMENT, DASH.

2. indication (*contex.*), implication, hint, suggestion; *spec.* insinuation, innuendo, sneer, slur, item (*obs. or local U. S.*), inkling, glance, tip (*C*), lead (*C*).

intimidate, *v. t.* frighten, daunt, quail (*chiefly B*); *spec.* subdue, terrorize, rally, bullyrag, browbeat, faze, overbear, bulldoze, cow, overawe, craven (*chiefly B*), abash, bully.

Antonyms: see ASSURE, CAJOLE, COAX.

into, *prep.* intil (*Scot.*); *spec.* within.

intoed, *a.* pigeon-toed.

intolerance, *n.* impatience (*used with "of"*), intoleration (*R*); *spec.* incompatibility, incompatibleness.

intolerant, *a.* impatient (*used with "of"*), incompatible, narrow-minded.

Antonyms: see TOLERANT, PATIENCE.

intone, *v. t.* intonate; *spec.* chant, recite, accentuate, monotone, sing.

intoxicant, *n. Spec.* delirifacient, bhang (*India*), delirant, toxicant.

intoxicate, *v. t.* inebriate; *spec.* besot, tipsify (*C and R*), disguise (*A*), fuddle (*C*), befuddle (*an intensive*), fox (*R*), mellow, stew (*S*), corn (*S*), maudlinize (*R*), tipple, poison, excite, stupefy.

Antonyms: see SOBER.

intoxicated, *a.* **1.** inebriate *or* inebriated *or* inebrious (*often euphemistic*), drunk (*the ordinary, blunt word*), ebriate *or* ebriose (*R and humorous*), bowzy *or* boozy (*S*), disguised (*A*), drunken (*more dignified and less emphatic than* drunk; *chiefly used as an attributive*); *spec.* tipsy (*less emphatic than* drunk), foxed (*R*), merry, whiskyfied (*humorous*), muddy (*contex.*), vinolent (*R*), jolly (*euphemistic*), maudlin, tight (*S*), high (*S or C*), mellow (*euphemistic*), groggy (*S or C*), glorious, screwed *or* screwy (*S*), corned *or* corny (*S or C*), cut (*S*), stewed (*S*); *see* DRUNK.

Antonyms: see SOBER.

2. exhilarated (*often fig.*); *see* EXCITED.

intoxicated person, drunk (*C or cant*), inebriate.

intoxicating, *a.* intoxicative (*R*), inebriative, intoxicant, inebriating, hard (*U. S.; C; contrasted with "soft"*), heady (*C*), methystic (*R*); *spec.* delirifacient, delirant.

intoxication, *n.* **1.** inebriation, inebriety (*chiefly spec.*), drunkenness, ebriosity (*R*), disguise (*A*), ebriety (*R or euphemistic*); *spec.* stupefaction, sottishness, grogginess (*C or S*), besottedness, tipsiness (*C*), temulency (*R*), temulence (*R*), opiism, kef *or* keif *or* kief, dipsomania (*spec.*).

2. *See* EXCITEMENT, ECSTASY.

intractable, *a.* **1.** unmanageable, tough (*C*), untractable (*R*), ungovernable, uncontrol-

interpretation: *explanation, meaning, translation.*
interregnum: *interval.*
interrogate, interrogation, interrogatory: *question.*
intervene: *occur, interpose.*
interview, *n.: conference.*
interview, *v. t.: question.*
intestine, *a.: domestic.*
intolerable: *unbearable.*

lable; *spec.* refractory (*chiefly spec.*), stubborn, obstinate, restive, mulish, cross-grained (*C*), contrarious, indocile, perverse, unruly, indisciplinable, irreconcilable, self-willed, impracticable.
Antonyms: see ADAPTABLE, MANAGEABLE.
2. *See* REFRACTORY.
intrench, *v. t. Spec.* circumvallate, dike.
intrigue, *v. i.* plan (*contex.*), deceive (*contex.*), scheme, maneuver *or* manœuvre, plot, machinate, wirepull (*chiefly in p. pr.*); *spec.* conspire, cabal.
intrigue, *n.* **1.** plan (*contex.*), deception (*contex.*), scheme, plot, maneuver *or* manœuvre, machination, intriguery; *spec.* cabal, wirepulling, Machiavellianism, conspiracy.
2. *See* AMOUR.
intriguer, *n.* intriguist, schemer, plotter, maneuverer, machinator; *spec.* wirepuller, Machiavellian, Machiavel (*fig.*).
intriguing, *a.* deceitful (*contex.*), planning (*contex.*), crooked, tortuous; *spec.* Machiavellian, wirepulling, *etc. also used C for* attractive, interesting, fascinating.
Antonyms: see FRANK.
introduce, *v. t.* **1.** *See* INSERT.
2. *Referring to causing a thing, subject matter, etc., to come into a sphere of action, thought, consideration, etc.: spec.* bring, immit (*R*), intertrude (*R*), intromit (*R*), insinuate, inject, infuse, start, interfuse (*R*), instill, inoculate, implant, initiate, usher, import (*chiefly commercial*), herald, ingest, infiltrate, induct, present, inwork, table, broach, inweave, initiate, read, immigrate, prelude, begin, precede, foist, drag (*in*).
Antonyms: see WITHDRAW.
introduction, *n.* **1.** *See* INSERTION.
2. *Spec.* initiation, injection, insinuation, intrusion, induction (*R*), opening, import (*chiefly commercial*), beginning, *etc.*
Antonyms: see WITHDRAWAL.
3. *Referring to the thing that introduces: spec.* prodome *or* prodromus (*R*), exordium, preface, protasis, proem, primordium (*R*), prelusion (*R*), preliminary, prelude, preludium (*R*), credential, isagogue (*R*), prolusion (*R*), prologue, prolocution (*R*), preamble.
introductory, *a. Spec.* initial, introductive, inductory (*R*), precursory, proemial, prodromal (*R*), initiary (*R*), intromissive (*R*), ingestive, exordial, preliminary, isagogic (*R*), prelusive (*R*), manuductory (*R*), preludial (*R*), prolusory (*R*), propædeutic.
introspection, *n.* self-examination, self-reflection, introversion, inlook (*R*).
introspective, *n.* self-examining, subjective, introverted.
introvert, *v. t.* turn (*often with "inside out"*); *spec.* invaginate, intussuscept.
intrude, *v. t.* **1.** *See* INSERT.
2. *Spec.* obtrude, interpose.
Antonyms: see WITHDRAW.
intrude, *v. i. Spec.* obtrude, impose, interlope, intervene, encroach, interfere, trespass (*often fig.*).
Antonyms: see WITHDRAW.
intruder, *n. Spec.* obtruder, imposer, interloper, stranger, *etc.*
intrusion, *n.* **1.** *See* INTRODUCTION.
2. *Spec.* obtrusion, interposition, intervention, irruption, imposition, encroachment, invasion, trespass (*often fig.*), intravasation.
intrusive, *a.* **1.** *Spec.* obtrusive, intervenient, irruptive (*R*), institutive (*R*), invasive, epenthetic.
invalid, (*pron.* ĭn-văl′ ĭd), *a.* **1.** void, null, nugatory, bad, unsound.
Antonyms: see VALID, BINDING.
2. *See* ILLOGICAL.
invalid (*pron.* ĭn′vȧ-lĭd), *n.* valetudinarian (*chiefly spec.*), patient (*spec.*).
invalidate, *v. t.* abolish, nullify, annul, disannul, unmake, void (*R*), avoid (*R or tech.*), undo (*R*), vitiate, vacate (*chiefly spec.*), invalid (*R*), infirm (*R*); *spec.* cancel, abrogate, quash, reverse, repeal.
Antonyms: see CONFIRM.
invalidity, *n.* nullity, voidness, nugatoriness (*R*).
invaluable, *a.* unvaluable (*R*), priceless, inestimable, impayable (*French*).
Antonyms: see WORTHLESS.
invasion, *n. Spec.* intrusion, visitation, incursion, inroad (*often used fig.*), irruption (*R*), creagh *or* creach (*Irish and Scot.*), raid, foray, infall (*R*), encroachment.
Antonyms: see RETREAT.
invasive, *a.* aggressive, intrusive, incursive.
inveigh, *v. i.* declaim; *spec.* rail, thunder.
invent, *v. t.* originate, devise, contrive, conceive, create; *spec.* spin, frame, fabricate, forge, design, coin (*often depreciatory*), mint, improvise, feign (*R*), concoct.
Antonyms: see IMITATE.
invented, *a.* fictitious, contrived, forged, *etc.*
invention, *n.* **1.** origination, devising, fiction, conception, creation; *spec.* design (*R, exc. of the thing invented*), improvisation, fabrication, mintage, coinage, device (*R, exc. of the power of devising*), contrivance, creation, concoction, ingenuity (*referring only to inventive quality or character*).
Antonyms: see IMITATION.

---

intransigent: *irreconcilable, radical.*
intrench, *v. t.: circumvallate, dike, establish.*
intrench, *v. i.: encroach.*
intrepid: *bold.*
intricacy: *complexity.*
intricate: *complicated.*
intrinsic: *inherent.*
intromit: *introduct, insert.*
introversion: *introspection.*
introvert: *reverse.*
intrust, *v. t.: trust.*
intuition: *knowledge, insight.*
intuitive: *perceptive.*
inure: *accrue, accustom, toughen.*
invade: *enter, violate, attack.*
invaginate: *reverse.*
invalid: *ailing.*
invariable: *constant.*
invective: *denunciation.*
inveigle: *cajole.*

---

2. *See* DISCOVERY.

inventive, *a.* concoctive, creative, ingenious.
Antonyms: see IMITATIVE.

invest, *v. t.* **1.** *See* CLOTHE, ADMIT, ENVELOP.
2. *Referring to insignia of office or the functions or privileges of office: spec.* vest, seize, gird.
Antonyms: see DEPRIVE.
3. endue *or* indue (*now R or alluding to Biblical use*), clothe, endow.
Antonyms: see DEPRIVE.
4. surround (*contex.*); *spec.* besiege (*the formal military term*), beset, beleaguer (*now R*), blockade.
5. *In reference to funds:* place (*contex.*), put (*contex.*); *spec.* sink, embark, fund, venture, risk.

investigate, *v. t.* examine; *spec.* study, scrutinize, sift, search, overhaul, scrutate (*R*), research (*R*), perscrutate (*R*), indagate (*R*), inquisition (*R*), question.

investigation, *n.* examination; *spec.* study, scrutiny, search, overhauling, scrutation (*R*), research (*R*), perscrutation (*R*), inquisition (*R or tech.*), indagation (*R*), inquiry, dialectic, pilpul.

investigation, *n.* **1.** *See* CLOTHING.
2. investment (*a less usual term*), investure (*R*), vestment (*R*).
3. admission, installation; *spec.* ordination, vestment, investure (*R*).
4. enduement *or* induement; *spec.* endowment.

inviolability, *n.* inviolableness, inviolacy (*R*), *spec.* hallowedness (*R or A*), holiness, sanctity, sacredness, sacrosanctity, sacrosanctness (*R*).

inviolable, *a. Spec.* hallowed (*now A, Biblical, or rhetorical*), holy, sacramental, sacred, sacrosanct (*a formal word for* sacred).

inviolate, *a.* intemerate (*B*), invitiate (*R*), unblemished, inviolated, undefiled.

invisible, *a.* unseeable (*a less usual term*), viewless (*R*); *spec.* undiscernable, unapparent, hidden.
Antonyms: see VISIBLE.

invitation, *n.* invitement (*R*), bid (*C or S*), call (*spec. or fig.*), calling; *spec.* biddance *or* bidding (*spec. or fig.*), solicitation, challenge, *etc.*

invite, *v. t.* **1.** ask, call (*spec., exc. fig.*), bid (*spec., exc. fig.; often S*); *spec.* solicit, challenge, court.
2. *See* ATTRACT, ENTICE, ALLOW.

invocation, *n.* summoning, conjuration, attestation (*A*); *spec.* oath.

invoke, *v. t.* **1.** *See* ASK.
2. summon, invocate (*R*); *spec.* attest (*A*), conjure, wish.

involuntary, *a. Spec.* automatic, spontaneous, mechanical, will-less (*R*).
Antonyms: see VOLUNTARY.

involute, *a.* **1.** *See* COMPLEX.
2. inrolled (*R*); *spec.* spiral.

involution, *n.* **1.** *See* COMPLEXITY.
2. involvement; *spec.* inclusion, implication, complexity, complication, engagement, embarrassment, degeneration, multiplication, envelopment, entanglement.

involve, *v. t.* **1.** *See* INCLUDE, IMPLY, COMPLICATE, ENVELOP, ENTANGLE.
2. implicate (*referring more to the imputed blame or fault than to the personal consequence*); *spec.* inculpate, incriminate, criminate, commit, entangle *or* (*R*) tangle, mire.

invulnerable, *a.* unassailable, woundless (*R*).
Antonyms: see VULNERABLE.

irascibility, *n.* irritability, biliousness (*fig. or C*), fieriness, *etc. Cf.* IRASCIBLE.

irascible, *a.* hot-blooded (*suggesting a native fullness of feeling or passion as the cause*), quick, ireful (*R or rhetorical*), iracund (*R*), irritable, dyspeptic, impatient, choleric (*becoming B*), bilious (*fig. or C*); *spec.* passionate, petulant, passionful (*R*), testy, tetchy *or* (*now more usual*) touchy, cranky, waspish, brainish (*A*), impatient, snappish, currish, snarly (*C*), fiery, fretful, fretty (*a weaker term than* fretful), hasty, crabbed, splenetic *or* splenitive (*R*) *or* spleeny *or* spleenish (*all four fig.*), restless, nettlesome, peevish, nettly (*R*), peppery (*C*), pettish (*C*).
Antonyms: see CALM, PEACEFUL, PATIENT.

iridesce, *v. i. Spec.* opalesce, opalize (*R*).

iridescence, *n. Spec.* opalescence, iris, irisation (*R*), nacreousness, rainbow, prismaticness, sunbow, versicolor (*R*).

iridescent, *a. Spec.* opalescent, opalesque (*R*), opaline, nacreous, nacrous, prismatic.
Antonyms: see DULL.

Irishman, *n.* Hibernian, Teague (*a nickname*), Mick (*a jocular or contemptuous nickname*), Paddywhack (*C; a contemptuous or jocular nickname*), Paddy (*a contemptuous or jocular nickname; C*), Greek *or* Grecian (*S*), Bogtrotter (*a contemptuous nickname*), harp (*S*), Irishry (*a collective pl.*); *spec.* Fenian, Sinn-Feiner.

irksome, *a.* wearisome, tiresome (*these two, with* irksome, *imply what causes fatigue or distaste*), tedious, humdrum (*imply monotony and consequent distaste*), fatiguing, vexatious, annoying, boring (*contex.*), irritating.

iron, *a.* ferrous (*tech.*); *spec.* ironish (*R*), irony, chalybeate, ferruginous, ferrous, ferric, ironclad.

irony, *n.* sarcasm (*a bitter jest or taunt in which what is implied is expressed by opposites, and which is intended to hurt, often taking its victim unawares or at a disadvantage; it is the cruel intent or bitterness that distinguishes* sarcasm *from* irony, *which is the witty statement of truth, observation, etc., by opposites.* Irony *may be gentle or cutting, but is not unfair*), satire (*a holding up*

inventory: *list.*
inverse, *n.: opposite, reverse.*
inveterate: *chronic, habitual, deep.*
invidious: *hateful.*
invigorate: *strengthen, refresh.*
invincible: *unconquerable.*
invocation: *address.*
invoice, *n.: list, goods.*
involved: *complex.*
inward: *interior, incoming, mental, spiritual, hidden, essential.*
irate: *angry.*
ironical: *dissembling, sarcastic.*

to ridicule, not necessarily using irony); *see* RIDICULE.

irrational, *n.* unreasoning, unthinking, unreasonable (*chiefly spec.*); *spec.* brainless, brute, brutish, reasonless, insane, absurd, unwise, foolish, idiotic, fantastic, *etc.*

Antonyms: see RATIONAL, REASONABLE.

irreconcilable, *n.* different, inconsistent; *spec.* intransigent.

irregular, *a.* **1.** exorbitant (*now R, A, or spec.*); *spec.* illegitimate, inordinate, heteromorphous, disorderly, improper, abnormal, informal, uneven, changeable, unsettled, baroque, eccentric, ragged, unequal, heteroclite (*R*), erratic, unmeasured (*R*), uncanonical, unsystematic, bastard, crabbed, unparliamentary, snatchy, foul, licentious, tortuous, unequal.

Antonyms: see REGULAR, PERIODIC.

2. *Referring to surface: spec.* unequal, uneven, humpy, hummocky, hillocky, rough, hilly, mountainous, knotty, bunchy.

Antonyms: see EVEN.

irrelevant, *a.* unrelated, extraneous, foreign, impertinent (*chiefly legal*), illogical, inconsequent, unessential *or* inessential.

Antonyms: see RELATIVE.

irreligious, *a. Spec.* impious, ungodly, godless, irreverent, ribald, indevout *or* undevout, profane, blasphemous, wicked.

Antonyms: see RELIGIOUS, DEVOUT.

irremissible, *a.* **1.** *See* UNFORGIVABLE.

2. obligatory, irrenunciable.

irreparable, *a. Spec.* irremediable, irretrievable, hopeless, remediless, irrecoverable, irreplaceable, unchangeable.

irrepressible, *a. Spec.* insuppressible, unsmotherable (*R*), unquenchable, incoercible.

irresistible, *a.* resistless (*a terser, more emphatic word than* irresistible), overpowering, overwhelming, killing (*C or S hyperbole*), stunning (*C or S hyperbole*), knockdown (*C or S*), knockout (*S*).

irresolute, *a.* indecisive, spineless, unconfirmed (*R*); *spec.* unsteadfast, changeable, inconstant, undecided, unstable, feebleminded, hesitating, fickle.

irresponsible, *a.* unaccountable.

irrevocable, *a. Spec.* irreversible, irrepealable.

irritable, *a.* touchy; *spec.* peevish; *see* IRASCIBLE, EXCITABLE.

irritate, *v. t.* **1.** excite (*contex.*), touch (*contex.*), rile (*C and now chiefly U. S.*), aggravate (*C*); *spec.* nag, rasp (*by harshly offending the sensibilities*), roughen (*C*), spite, ruffle, roil (*equiv. of* rile; *U. S. and dial.*), jar (*C*), grate, nettle, inflame, prod, fret, exacerbate, annoy, anger, worry, *etc.*

Antonyms: see CALM, PACIFY.

2. *Med. and physiol.: spec.* inflame, exacerbate, rub, counterirritate.

irritated, *a. Spec.* warm, nettled, exacerbated, *etc.*

irritating, *a. Spec.* irritative, exciting, nettling, grating, excitatory, irritant, provocative, inflammatory, annoying, angering, worrying, provoking, *etc.*

Antonyms: see CALMATIVE.

irritation, *n.* **1.** excitement (*contex.*), irritancy (*R*); *spec.* anger, ill temper, annoyance, worry, *etc.*

2. *Referring to what irritates: spec.* provocation, aggravation (*C*), gall (*fig.*), annoyance, vexation, itch, burn, acridity, *etc.*

island, *n.* isle (*now usually poetic, exc. spec.*); *spec.* holm, holme, islet, ait, eyot, islot *or* ilot (*R*), inch (*Scot.*), key *or* cay, calf, knoll.

Antonyms: see MAINLAND.

island, *a.* insular (*formal*), insulary (*R*).

island, *v. t.* insulate (*formal*), enisle (*R*), isle (*R*).

islander, *n.* insular (*formal*), insulary (*R*), islandman (*R or local*), isleman (*R or spec.*).

isolate, *v. t.* separate, insulate (*R, exc. spec.*); *spec.* segregate, quarantine.

isolated, *a.* insulated, insular; *spec.* segregate (*R*), alone (*a postpositive*), solitary, incommunicable.

issuable, *a.* utterable (*now R or spec.*).

issue, *n.* **1.** *Referring to the act of coming out:* issuance (*U. S.*); *spec.* exit, escape, process (*R*), flow, outburst, outspring (*R*), egress, sally, sortie, procession, emergence, emanation, debouchment, exudation, emigration, outflow, discharge, effervescence, *etc.*

Antonyms: see ENTRANCE.

2. *Referring to the act of sending out:* emission (*chiefly spec.*); *spec.* utterance, envoy (*A*), mise (*chiefly Eng.*), delivery, discharge.

3. *Of what issues or is issued: spec.* discharge, stream, emission, flux, outpour, catarrh, edition, offspring, produce, *etc.*

4. *See* OUTCOME, EVENT, DISPUTE, RESULT, EFFECT, *etc.*

issue, *v. i.* **1.** depart (*contex.*), egress; *spec.* exit, emanate, debouch, flow (*often fig.*), gush (*by flowing violently*), furnace, burst (*used with "out," "forth," etc.*), escape, stream, proceed, sally, sortie, appear, emerge, come (*chiefly with "out," "forth," etc.*), rise, spout, spurt, spirt, run (*fig.*), well (*chiefly with "up," "forth," etc.*), effervesce, exude, arise, descend, spring, outspring (*B*).

Antonyms: see ENTER.

2. *See* EVENTUATE, RESULT, ACCRUE.

issue, *v. t.* **1.** deliver (*contex.*); emit; *spec.* expedite, discharge.

2. *Spec.* publish, give, utter, outgive (*B*).

isthmus, *n.* neck, tarbet (*local, Scot.*).

itch, *n.* **1.** psora (*tech.; R*); *spec.* scabies,

irradiate: *light, brighten.*
irreclaimable: *abandoned.*
irredeemable: *abandoned, hopeless.*
irrefragable: *undeniable.*
irremediable: *incurable, irreparable.*
irremovable: *fixed, permanent.*
irreproachable: *faultless, blameless.*
irretrievable: *irreparable.*
irreverent: *disrespectful, impious.*
irrigate: *water, wash.*
itch, *v. i.: desire.*

pruritus, prurigo, prurience, mange.
2. *See* DESIRE, INCLINATION.
itchy, *a.* scabious (*tech.*), psoric (*tech.*); *spec.* mangy, prurient.
item, *n.* detail, particular; *spec.* entry, article, local, term, paragraph.
itinerant, *a.* traveling, wandering, nomadic, itinerary, peripatetic *or* peripatetical (*often humorous*).
itinerary, *n. Spec.* route, circuit, guidebook.
ivory, *a.* eburnean *or* euburnian (*R*), eburnine (*R*); *spec.* ivorylike, eburneoid (*R*).
ivy, *a.* hederaceous (*R*), hederal (*R*), hederic (*chem.*).

J

jack, *n. Referring to cards:* knave, varlet (*obs.*); *spec.* bower, pam (*obs.*).
jackanapes, *n. Spec.* pert (*obs.*), puppy (*C*), coxcomb, saucebox (*C*).
jacket, *n.* coat (*contex.*).
janitor, *n.* concierge (*French; chiefly spec. in Eng.*); *spec.* doorkeeper, custodian.
jar, *n.* crock (*contex., obs. or B*); *spec.* dolium, can (*loose for* glass jar), hydria, cruse, guggler.
jar, *v. i.* **1.** *See* GRATE.
2. shake (*contex.*); *spec.* jolt, jounce.
jargon, *n.* **1.** *See* CHATTER.
2. cant, canting, slang; *spec.* gibberish, argot, babel, dialect, chinook, shop.
jaw, *n.* **1.** jawbone, mandible (*tech. and chiefly spec.*), maxilla (*tech. and chiefly spec.*), jowl (*now R, exc. spec.*), choller (*dial. Eng. and Scot.*), chap *or* chop (*now obs. or R, exc. of brutes or as contemptuous*).
2. *In pl.: spec.* mouth, throat, entrance.
jeer, *v. i. & t.* ridicule (*contex.*), scoff, jape, jibe, gibe, flout, gird (*A*), frump (*A*), fleer, gleek (*obs.*); *spec.* mock, taunt, jest, hoot.
jeer, *n.* scoff, flout, gibe, jibe, jape, fleer, gird (*A*), frump (*A*), gleek (*obs.*), hit (*C*), outfling (*R*); *spec.* mock, taunt, shy (*S*), quip, sarcasm, sneer, jest, bob (*C*).
jeerer, *n.* ridiculer (*contex.*), scoffer; *spec.* taunter, sneerer, ribald (*R*), *etc.*
jeering, *a.* ridiculing, scoffing, frumpish (*R*); *spec.* ribaldrous, *etc.*
jelly, *v. t.* congeal (*contex.*), coagulate (*contex.*), gelatinize (*B or tech.*), gelatinate (*R*), jell (*U. S.; C*).
jelly, *n.* gelatin (*B or tech.*); *spec.* jujube, blancmange, blancmanger, aspic.
jerk, *v. i. & t.* **1.** move (*contex.*), pull (*contex.*); *spec.* twitch, jet, jigget (*C*), flip, yank (*C*), bob, flirt, fling, flounce, hitch, tweak, flick, perk, jig, jog, dodge, jiggle, pluck.

Antonyms: see GLIDE.
2. *See* THROW.
jerk, *n.* motion (*contex.*), pull (*contex.*); *spec.* twitch, toss, hitch, jet, flick, flirt, yank (*C*), bob, fig, jog, joggle, flip, fling, throw, dodge, spasm, jiggle, jigget (*C*).
jerky, *a.* abrupt; *spec.* twitchy, jiggety (*C*), jiggish, hitchy, tossing, yanking (*C*), spasmodic, *etc.*
jest, *n.* **1.** *See* JEER.
2. *The specific jest:* joke (*an undignified word*); *spec.* chestnut (*S*), Joe Miller (*S or humorous*), jokelet (*humorous*), gag, farcicality (*R*), jolly (*C*), pleasantry, jape (*chiefly a literary archaism*), drollery, witticism, crack (*S*), wisecrack (*S*), jibe (*implying pointed attack*).
3. *Generic; having the quality of a jest:* play (*contex.*), sport (*as in "done in sport"*); *spec.* japery, joking, waggery, joke (*rather undignified*), waggishness, prank, humor, jocosity, jocularity, repartee (*French*), comeback (*C*).
Antonyms: see EARNESTNESS.
jest, *v. i.* droll (*B*), bound (*A*); *spec.* joke, jape (*R, exc. as a literary archaism*), jolly, quiz, banter.
jester, *n.* farceur (*French*); *spec.* joker, japer, jokesman (*nonce word*), jokesmith (*humorous*) jokist (*R*), quiz, quizzer, jokester (*contemptuous*), buffoon, wag, droll (*R, exc. hist.*), wit, joculator (*hist.*), minstrel (*hist.*), jongleur (*hist.*), Goliard (*hist.*).
jesting, *a.* merrymaking (*contex.*), sportive, jocose; *spec.* joking, jocular, japish, droll, joky (*C*), jokesome (*R*), jollying (*C*), waggish, ribald, quizzical, farcical, witty.
jewel, *n.* gem (*spec.*); *see* TREASURE.
jewel, *v. t.* bejewel (*an intensive*), engem (*R*), enjewel (*R*).
Jewry, *n.* Jewdom (*R*), Hebrewdom (*R*); *spec.* ghetto, Israel (*a collective*), Sephardim, Ashkenazim.
jiggle, *v. t. & i. Spec.* play, jibbet (*C*), dance, jigger (*C*), bob, jig, noddle, bobble, popple, jog, joggle, chop, dangle, dandle, trot (*C*).
jiggle, *n.* dance, bob, bobble, popple, jig, noddle, jog, joggle, dangle, jigget (*C*).
jiggly, *a.* jiggety (*C*), dancing, jiggish (*C*), bobby, popply, joggly, choppy.
Antonyms: see FIRM.
jilt, *v. t. To cast off a lover:* deceive (*contex.*).
jilt, *n.* light-o'-love (*A*).
jingle, *v. i., t., & n. Spec.* tinkle, clink, chink, clank, jangle, clang.
jingling, *a.* clanky, jingly, clinky, jangling, jangly (*R*).

---

itching: *desire.*
itemize: *particularize.*
iterate: *repeat.*

J

jab: *thrust, stab.*
jabber: *chatter.*
jack, *v. t.: raise.*
jackass: *donkey, blockhead.*
jacket, *v. t.: clothe, cover, envelop.*
jade, *n.: horse, hussy.*
jade, *v. t.: tire, dull.*
jag: *projection, indentation.*
jail, *v. t.: confine, imprison.*
jam, *n.: crowd, crush.*
jam, *v. t.: block.*
jam, *v. i.: stick.*
jangle, *v.: chatter, dispute, jingle.*
jangle, *n.: dispute, discord, jingle.*
jangly: *discordant, jingling.*
jape, *v. i.: jest, jeer.*
jape, *n.: jest, trick, caper.*
jar: *shock, distress.*
jaunt: *excursion.*
jealousy: *vigilance, distrust, envy.*
jeopardize: *endanger.*
jet, *v. t.: jerk, emit, spout.*
jibe, *v. i.: agree.*
jibe, *v. i. & n.: jeer.*
jig, *v.: dance, jerk.*
jilt: *desert.*

jingoism, *n.* bluster (*contex.*), jingo, Chauvinism; *spec.* imperialism, nationalism, patriotism.

job, *n.* **1.** work (*contex.*); *spec.* chore (*U. S.*), char (*Eng.*).

2. *See* BUSINESS, AFFAIR.

join, *v. t. & i.* unite; *spec.* connect, meet (*v. i.*), conjugate (*R*), concorporate (*eccl. or B*), concrete, coarticulate (*R*), conjoin (*a stronger and more literary term than "join"*), marry (*fig.*), wed (*fig.*), combine, affiliate, consolidate, compact, compaginate (*R*), compound, assemble, Siamese (*fig.*), consolidate, joint, couple, coadunate (*R*), coapt (*R*), coagment (*R*), yoke, fay, enter, associate, attach, add, interlace, hinge, lock, gear, solder, link, leash, rabbet, piece, tenon, band, splice, dovetail, miter, dowel, seam, scarf, joggle, enlink (*R*), catenate, construct, rejoin.

Antonyms: see SEPARATE, BREAK, DETACH, DISCONNECT.

joined, *a.* united; *spec.* combined, connected, coadunate (*R*), conferruminate, consolidate, conjugate, conjunct (*chiefly B*), conjoined, concorporate (*eccl. or B*), joint.

Antonyms: see SEPARATE.

joining, *n.* union, juncture (*more formal than* joining); *spec.* connection, jointure (*R*), join (*R or C*), junction, juncture, assemblage, joinder (*R*), combination, conjunction, conjuncture (*now R, exc. of circumstances or events*), consolidation, conjugation, concourse, combine (*U. S.; C*), contexture, coaptation (*R*), contignation (*R*), catenation, composition, compaction, coadunation, attachment, annexation, addition, conspiracy, *etc.*

Antonyms: see DIVISION; *also cf.:* SEPARATE.

joining, *a.* unitive (*R*), uniting; *spec.* connective, combinative, contextive (*R*), concretive, copulative, conjunctive, associating, interosculating, interosculant (*R*), *etc.*

joint, *n.* **1.** union; *spec.* junction, connection, connexus (*R*), link, seam, miter, knee, knot, node, joggle, fillet, mortise, variator, hinge, splice, communication, scarf, dovetail, elbow, weld, butt, lap, *etc.*

2. *Referring to part of an animal:* articulation; *spec.* saddle, elbow, knee, atlas, hip, shoulder, ankle, hock (*in a quadruped*), knuckle, chine.

3. *See* RESORT.

joint, *v. t.* **1.** articulate (*chiefly spec.*).

2. *See* DISJOINT.

joint, *a.* joined, united, conjoint; *spec.* conjunctive, concurrent, solidary (*chiefly tech.*), correal, articulated, hinged, *etc.*

Antonyms: see SEPARATE.

jointless, *a.* inarticulate.

jostle, *v. t.* push (*contex.*), hustle (*chiefly spec.*); *spec.* shove, elbow, shoulder.

jostle, *n.* push, hustle; *spec.* shove, elbowing, jostlement (*R*).

journal, *n.* **1.** record (*contex.*), diary (*chiefly spec.*); *spec.* daybook, gazette.

2. *See* PERIODICAL, BEARING.

journalist, *n.* author (*contex.*), pressman (*R or cant*), gazetteer (*hist.*); *spec.* reporter, publicist (*a loose use*).

journey, *n.* progress (*R, exc. spec.*); *spec.* excursion, expedition, junket (*often implying a nosey or busybody sort of* journey, *like a Congressional`* junket), errand (*in its widest sense dignified and chiefly B*), jaunt, peregrination (*R or stilted*), voyage (*now R, exc. of a long* journey *by water*), pilgrimage, meander, passage, Odyssey (*fig.*), cruise, tour, trip, run, trek (*South Africa or C*), hike (*C*), wayfaring (*A*), travel, walk, ride, drive, wander, row, sail.

journey, *v. i.* go (*contex.*), travel (*chiefly spec.*), peregrinate (*R*), progress (*A, exc. spec.*); *spec.* jaunt, voyage, pilgrimage (*esp. with "it"*), meander, pass, tour, hike (*C*), wander, ride, row, sail, drive.

journeyer, *n. Spec.* traveler, excursionist, expeditionary (*R*), messenger, jaunter, peregrinator (*R*), voyager, pilgrim, wanderer, cruiser, tourist, tripper, trekker, hiker (*C*), wayfarer (*A*), walker, rider, driver, rower, sailer.

judge, *n.* **1.** magistrate (*contex.; a formal word*), decider (*contex.*), judicature (*a collective pl.*), judicator (*R*), judger (*R*), judgeress (*fem.; R*), judiciary (*chiefly hist. and spec.*), justiciar (*R, exc. hist. and spec.*), justicer (*A*), Rhadamanthus (*fig.*), hakim (*Oriental*), doomsman (*A or B*), doomster (*A or B*), doomer (*A*), moderator (*B or spec.*), justice (*chiefly spec.*), deemster (*obs. or A, exc. spec.*); *spec.* cadi (*Oriental*), cadilesker (*Turkish*), surrogate, probate, bencher (*A*), heliast, dicast, sentencer (*not a technical term*), arbitrator, arbiter, referendary, umpire, brehon (*Irish hist.*), podesta (*Spanish*), quorum (*collective pl.*), squire, kazi (*Oriental*), Inquisitor, ordinary, recorder, puisne, censurer, Christ (*as judging at Doomsday*).

2. *See* CRITIC.

judge, *v. t. & i.* **1.** decide (*contex.*), adjudicate (*formal*), doom (*A, exc. spec.*); *spec.* pronounce, decree, acquit, arbitrate, try, umpire, condemn, sentence, find.

---

jingoism: *bluster.*
job: *thrust, stab.*
jockey, *n.: horseman.*
jockey, *v. t.: cheat, manage, maneuver.*
jocosity: *jest.*
jocund: *cheerful.*
jog, *v. t.: jerk, push, remind.*
jog, *v. i.: go, jiggle.*
jog, *n.: jerk, push, jiggle, reminder.*
joist: *beam.*
joke, *n.: jest, butt.*
joke, *v. i.: jest.*
joke, *v. t.: banter.*
jolly: *gay, excellent.*
jolly, *n.: jest.*
jolly, *v. t.: banter, cajole.*
jolt: *shock.*
josh: *banter, hoax.*
jounce: *shock.*
journeyman: *worker.*
joust: *fight.*
jovial: *gay, convivial.*
jowl: *head.*
joy, *n.: pleasure, happiness.*
joyance: *pleasure, happiness.*
joyful, *a.: pleased, happy.*
joyless, *a.: unhappy, cheerless.*
joyous: *pleased, happy.*
jubilant: *pleased, gay, exultant.*
jubilee: *anniversary, festival, merry-making.*

---

2. decide, consider; *spec.* apprehend, measure, think, guess.

judgment, *n.* **1.** decision, adjudication, judicatory (*R*), judicature (*R*), doom (*A, exc. spec.*), judication (*R*), deliverance (*chiefly spec.*); *spec.* arbitration, condemnation, decree, forjudger, acquittal.

2. decision, consideration, estimation; *spec.* inference, condemnation, censure.

3. decision, thought (*contex.*); *spec.* opinion, conceit, proposition, estimate, sentiment, inference, guess, criticism.

4. sense, discretion; *spec.* counsel (*A or obs.*), judiciousness, wit (*now R, exc. in pl. and in certain phrases*), eye, fancy, circumspection, sensibility, rationality, taste.

judicial, *a.* **1.** legal (*contex.*), judiciary, judicatory, judicatorial (*R*); *spec.* judicative, juridical.

Antonyms: see LAY.

2. sensible, judicious; *spec.* discriminating, discreet, judgmatical *or* judgmatic (*C*), critical, understanding, cautious, *etc.*

judicious, *a.* judgmatic, sensible, prudent, wise.

Antonyms: see UNWISE.

jug, *n.* vessel (*contex.*); *spec.* pitcher, ewer, graybeard, cruse, toby, prochoös, jack, tankard, blackjack.

juggle, *v. i.* conjure, trick.

jugglery, *n.* conjury, magic (*seemingly so*); *spec.* legerdemain.

juice, *n.* humor (*A*); *spec.* blood, sap, verjuice, broo (*Scot.*), gravy.

juicy, *a.* succulent (*B or tech.*); *spec.* bloody, sappy.

jump, *v. i.* **1.** spring, leap (*a livelier word than* jump), bound; *spec.* vault, skip, hop, dance, lunge, buck, pounce.

2. *See* DART, START, CHANGE.

jump, *v. t.* **1.** *Cause to jump:* spring, leap; *spec.* vault, skip, hop.

2. *Referring to jumping over a thing:* spring, leap, vault (*often spec.*), clear (*contex.*), negotiate (*cant*), overvault (*R*), overspring (*R*), overleap (*R*), take.

jump, *n.* **1.** spring, leap; *spec.* vault, skip, hop, saltation (*R*), saltus (*R*), dance, lunge, pounce.

2. *See* DART, START, TRANSITION.

3. *Referring to the space across which an electric spark passes:* gap.

junction, *n.* **1.** *See* JOINING.

2. *Referring to a place where things come together, but do not become united in the way ordinarily suggested by* joint: juncture, conjunction; *spec.* commissure, seam, chiasm, osculature, concurrence.

juncture, *n.* **1.** *See* JOINING, JUNCTION.

2. *Referring to circumstances: spec.* emergency, conjunction, contingency, pass, predicament, concurrence, combination, union, crisis.

junior, *n. Spec.* youngster (*mil.; C*), boots (*S*), fag (*Eng. schools*).

Antonyms: see SENIOR.

jurisdiction, *n.* **1.** court; *spec.* justiciary (*Scot.*), soke, inspectorate, cognizance, liberty, courtship, leet, circuit, danger.

2. *See* AUTHORITY.

3. *Referring to a person's sphere of control or influence:* sphere, range, compass, reach, circuit, ambit (*R or B equivalent of* circuit), province, round, orbit.

jurisdictional, *a.* jurisdictive (*R*); *spec.* justiciable, cognizable.

jurist, *n.* jurisprudent (*often spec.*), legist (*B*); *spec.* Justinianist, Civilian, Romanist, publicist, jurisconsult.

juror, *n.* juryman (*a less technical term*); *spec.* recognitor.

jury, *n.* panel, country (*tech.*), inquest (*usually spec.*).

just, *a.* **1.** true (*contex.*), right, white (*S, U. S.*), square (*S*); *spec.* well-founded, equitable, prætorian (*R*), honorable, honest, legitimate, fair.

Antonyms: see UNJUST.

2. *See* RIGHTEOUS, UPRIGHT, DESERVED, CONSCIENTIOUS, IMPARTIAL, LAWFUL, REASONABLE, ACCURATE.

just, *adv. Spec.* exactly, even; *see* HARDLY.

justice, *n.* **1.** justness (*the quality*), equitableness, right, truth (*contex.*); *spec.* honesty, honor, equity, legitimacy, legitimateness, Astræa (*a personification*), Nemesis (*a personification*).

Antonyms: see INJUSTICE.

2. *Spec.* righteousness, uprightness, conscientiousness, impartiality, truth, lawfulness, reasonableness, right, accuracy, sincerity, desert, count.

3. *See* JUDGE.

justification, *n.* **1.** defense, righting, warrant; *spec.* legitimation, legitimization, vindication, reason, approval, apology.

Antonyms: see CONDEMNATION.

2. *See* EXCUSE.

justify, *v. t.* **1.** defend, warrant; *spec.* legitimate, support, legitimatize (*R*), legitimize, vindicate, approve, deraign (*law, hist., or obs.*).

Antonyms: see CONDEMN.

2. *See* EXCUSE, ADJUST, FIT.

K

keel, *n. Spec.* rocker (*chiefly U. S.*), kedge.

keep, *v. t.* **1.** hold; *spec.* withhold, possess, re-

judicious: *judicial, prudent, wise.*
juggle: *conjure, deceive.*
jumble: *confuse.*
junction: *joint, joining, meeting.*
jungle: *thicket.*
junker: *noble.*
junket: *feast, journey.*
junta: *council, clique.*
juridical: *judicial, legal.*
jurisprudence: *law.*
jurisprudent: *lawyer, jurist.*
just, *v. & n.: fight, tournament.*
justifiable: *defensible.*
justness: *justice, accuracy.*
jut, *v. i.: project.*
juvenile, *n.: child.*

K

keen: *sharp, sharp-sighted, intense, intelligent, painful, eager, shrill, pungent, discerning.*
keep, *v. i.: dwell, continue.*

serve, preserve, retain, bear (*in mind*), save, have.

Antonyms: see ABANDON, RELINQUISH, FORGO.

2. *See* OBSERVE, MAINTAIN, PRESERVE, GUARD, ATTEND, SUPPORT, DETAIN, CAUSE, CONTINUE, APPLY.

keeper, *n. Spec.* guardian, custodian, preserver, conservator (*chiefly tech. of officials or persons legally appointed to conserve something*), warden, warder, holder, retainer, constable, bearward, parker, attendant, armature, castellan.

keeping, *n. Spec.* custody, care, guard, agreement, maintenance, observation, retainer (*R, exc. law*), retention, support, harmony, preservation, *etc.*

kennel, *n.* **1.** *See* HOUSE.

2. pack (*of dogs*).

kerchief, *n.* kercher (*obs. or dial.*), curch (*Scot.*), headkerchief (*R*); *spec.* neckpiece, handkerchief.

kerosene, *n.* potogen (*R*), paraffin oil (*Eng. or tech.*), paraffin (*Eng.*).

kettledrum, *n.* drum (*contex.*), kettle (*C*), timbal (*chiefly A or hist.*); *spec.* naker (*hist.*), atabal.

key, *n.* **1.** clavis (*B*); *spec.* wrest.

2. lock (*mach.*); *spec.* cotter, spline, stop, feather, pin, *etc.*

3. *Referring to an explanation, translation, etc.: spec.* translation, crib, horse (*school S*), pony (*S*), trot (*school S*).

4. *In music:* tonality (*tech. and R*); *spec.* natural, sharp, flat, mode.

5. *Of a musical instrument: spec.* manual (*R*), digital (*tech.*), pedal, stop.

keyboard, *n. Spec.* manual, pedalier.

kick, *v. t.* strike (*contex.*), spurn (*chiefly B*), foot (*R or obs. now; often implying scorn*), calcitrate (*R; B*); *spec.* football, toe, hack, punt (*football*), drive.

kick, *v. i.* **1.** strike (*contex.*), calcitrate (*R*); *spec.* spurn (*R, exc. B*).

2. *See* RECOIL, OBJECT.

kick, *n.* **1.** strike (*contex.*), calcitration (*R*), spurn (*obs.*); *spec.* punt, hack.

2. *See* RECOIL, OBJECTION.

3. stimulus, thrill (*S senses of* kick).

kid, *n.* offspring (*contex.*); *spec.* yeanling *or* eanling.

kidney, *n.* reins (*pl.; A*).

kill, *v. t.* **1.** destroy, finish (*now chiefly C, exc. spec.*), dispatch, quell (*R or A*), quench (*R or A*), disanimate (*R*), end (*not a dignified word*), fordo (*A*), corpse (*vulgar, Eng.*), dead (*dial. or illiterate*); *spec.* slay (*now chiefly B or rhetorical*), slaughter, massacre, outkill (*R*), smite (*A*), deaden (*R*), butcher, decimate, drown, assassinate, purge (*a euphemism employed for political* assassinations), burn, martyr, stone, lapidate (*B equiv. of* stone), lynch, tomahawk, immolate, jugulate (*R*), decapitate, garrote, guillotine, crucify, hang, gibbet, brain, deacon, burke, winterkill (*U. S.*), pot, snipe, murder, noose (*R*), lance, spear, pike, pith, neck (*tech. or dial.*), homicide.

Antonyms: see ANIMATE, BEGET, GENERATE, REVIVE.

2. *See* DESTROY, DEFEAT, VETO, CONSUME.

killed, *a. Spec.* lost, slain, inanimate.

killer, *n.* slayer (*usually A or spec.*), manqueller (*A*), manslayer; *spec.* Drawcansir (*fig.*), cutthroat, slaughterer, smiter, decapitator, hangman, guillotiner, garroter, matador, murderer, assassin, gangster, trigger-man, knacker, giganticide (*R*), deicide, insecticide, lyncher, macropicide (*R*), massacrer, potter, sniper, bactericide, fungicide, *etc.*

killing, *n.* **1.** destruction, dispatch, quell (*R*), bloodshed (*in a generic or collective sense*), death (*in a generic or collective sense*); *spec.* massacre, homicide, murder, slaughter, slaying, butchery, cervicide (*R*), martyring, martyrization, mactation (*R*), decapitation, custom, assassination, hanging, drowning, *etc.*

2. *See* DESTRUCTION.

kill-joy, *n.* wet-blanket, spoil-sport (*all C*).

kind, *n.* **1.** *See* NATURE.

2. division (*contex.*), species (*B or tech.*), sort (*a vaguer term than "kind"*), genus (*chiefly tech.*); *spec.* class, type, genre (*French*), cast (*a vague word*), manner (*now only in "what manner of"*), denomination, description, race, brood, swarm, crew, crowd, stamp, brand, form, make, family, breed, shade, stripe (*usually derogatory*), strain, style, persuasion (*jocular*), tap (*C*), color, class, gender (*gram.*), sex, make, *etc.*

kind, *a.* good-natured, humane, mild (*A or R*), benign (*B*), boon (*A*); *spec.* soft, beneficent, benevolent, tender, cosmophil (*nonce word*), good, gracious, kindly, sweet, friendly, brotherly, kind-hearted, compassionate, accommodating, amiable.

Antonyms: see UNFEELING, UNKIND, FIERCE, CRUEL, HATEFUL.

kindle, *v. t.* **1.** ignite (*more B than* kindle), fire (*C or tech.*), enkindle (*an intensive; A*), light; *spec.* flash, inflame, emblaze (*R*), conflagrate (*R*), ignify (*R*).

Antonyms: see EXTINGUISH.

2. *See* EXCITE.

kindle, *v. i.* ignite, catch, light, *etc.*

kindleable, *a.* ignitable.

kindling, *a.* ignescent (*R*), inflammatory (*R or B*); *spec.* conflagrative.

kindling, *n.* **1.** *Spec.* fuel, tinder, touchwood, lightwood.

2. ignition, lighting; *spec.* inflammation.

kindly, *a.* well-disposed, hearty, genial, benignant, beneficent, benign (*chiefly B*), be-

---

keepsake: *reminder.*
keg: *cask.*
ken, *n.: knowing, knowledge.*
ken, *v. t.: know, understand.*
kid, *v. t.: deceive, hoax, banter.*
kidnap: *abduct.*
kiln, *n.: furnace, oven.*
kiln, *v. t.: burn, bake, dry.*
kin: *kindred, relationship.*

---

nevolent, debonair (*A*), gracious (*B or R*); *spec.* sweet, friendly, considerate, neighborly, open-hearted, sympathetic, brotherly, gall-less, loving, thoughtful, humane, amiable.
Antonyms: see MALEVOLENT, COLD, STERN, CRUEL, HATEFUL, SHARP.

kindness, *n.* **1.** tenderness, mildness (*A or R*); *spec.* humanity, benignity, benevolence, grace, goodness, beneficence, favor, gentleness, charity, blood.
Antonyms: see UNKINDNESS, FEROCITY, SHARPNESS.
2. *See* BENEFACTION.

kindred, *n. pl.* family, kin (*now a less usual term than* kindred), kinspeople (*U. S.*), kinsfolk (*C or dial.*), sib (*A*), kinship (*R*), flesh (*fig.*), folks (*C*), relations (*pl.; C*), relatives (*pl.*), mine (*C*), folk, cousinry, cousinhood, cousinage (*obs.*).

kindred, *a.* **1.** *Referring to persons:* related.
2. *Referring to things:* congenial (*R*), connate (*R*), connected, connatural (*R*), congeneric *or* congenerate, cognate, congenerous (*R*); *spec.* conjugate, sympathetic.
Antonyms: see UNRELATED.

kingly, *a.* royal, regalian (*R*), regal, basilic (*R*), kinglike, princelike (*now R*), princely (*A or spec.*); *spec.* palatine.
Antonyms: see PLEBEIAN.

kiss, *v. t.* **1.** caress (*contex.*), salute (*A*), lip (*a word suggestive of coarseness or used of the lower animals*), osculate (*R*), exosculate (*R*); *spec.* bill, peck (*humorous*), bekiss (*intensive*), smack, buss (*an A equiv. of* smack).
2. *See* TOUCH.

kiss, *n.* **1.** caress (*contex.*), salute (*A*), osculation (*R*); *spec.* smack, peck (*humorous*), buss (*A equiv. of* smack).
2. *See* TOUCH.

kissing, *a.* oscular (*B*), osculatory (*B*).

kitchen, *n.* **1.** *Spec.* galley, scullery.
2. cuisine (*tech. or pretentious*), cookroom (*C*).

kite, *n.* hawk, milvine (*tech.*); *spec.* elanet, glide (*chiefly Scot. & dial. Eng.*), swallowtail, gledge.

knead, *v. t.* work; *spec.* malaxate (*R*), petrie, massage.

kneel, *v. i.* bow, knee (*R*); *spec.* kowtow *or* kotow.

kneepan, *n.* patella (*tech.*), kneecap, rotula (*R*), whirlbone (*R*); *spec.* stiflebone.

knife, *n.* **1.** *Spec.* whittle (*A or dial.*), chive (*thieves' cant*), whinger (*A or R*), toothpick (*S, U. S.*), bowie knife, bistoury, slice, razor, scalpel, serpette, trivet, parang, lancet, lance, fleam, jackknife, gully (*Scot. & dial. Eng.*), cuttoe (*obs. or R*), machete, bolo.
2. blade (*contex.*); *spec.* plow *or* plough, shears (*pl.*), shave.

knife-shaped, *a.* cultrate, cultriform;—*both tech.*

knight, *n.* younger (*obs. or A*); *spec.* champion, chevalier, cavalier, knight-errant, errant, paladin (*fig.*), bachelor, maltese, companion, horseman, Ritter (*German*), knighthood (*a collective*).

knight, *v. t.* dub.

knighthood, *n.* knights (*pl.*), chivalry, knightlihood (*R*); *spec.* errantry.

knightly, *a.* knightlike, cavalierly (*R*), chivalric *or* chivalrous.

knob, *n.* **1.** protuberance (*contex.*), boss; *spec.* stud, knop, knurl, nub (*chiefly dial.*), lump, button, nubble, knot, knub, knobble, bob, bur, bud, croche (*tech.*), cascabel, pommel, whelk.
2. *See* HILL.

knobby, *a.* bossy; *spec.* nubby, lumpy, knobbly, knotty, whelky.

knock, *v. t. & i.* **1.** strike (*contex.*); *spec.* rap, rat-tat, rattle.
2. *See* CENSURE.

knock, *n.* **1.** stroke (*contex.*); *spec.* rap, rat-a-tat, rat-tat.
2. *See* CENSURE.

knot, *n.* **1.** *See* KNOB, DISTORTION.
2. interlacement (*contex.*); *spec.* sheepshank, becket, rosette, bow, picot, clovehitch, granny, hitch, Turk's-head, wallknot, kettlestitch, cat's-paw, bend, bowline, burl.
3. *See* DIFFICULTY, COCKADE, GROUP.

knot, *v. t.* **1.** interlace (*contex.*); *spec.* kink.
2. *See* WEAVE, GNARL.

knotted, *a.* **1.** Gordian (*fig.; B*); *spec.* convoluted, nowed.
2. *See* DISTORTED.

knotty, *a.* **1.** *Spec.* gnarled, knurly, nodose, nodous (*R*), nodulose, geniculate, snaggy.
2. *See* COMPLEX.

know, *v. t.* cognize (*tech.*), can (*A*), wit (*A*), savey *or* savvy (*S*), ken (*Scot.*); *spec.* have, intuit (*tech. or B*), intue (*R*), recognize, receive (*R*), understand, infer, experience.
Antonyms: see GUESS.

knowable, *a.* cognizable (*tech.*), cognoscible (*tech.*); *spec.* perceptible.
Antonyms: see UNKNOWABLE.

knowing, *a.* **1.** *Referring to the capacity of knowing, understanding, or perceiving: see* INTELLIGENT.
2. *Referring to having knowledge previously acquired:* cognizant (*tech. or B*), fly (*S*), aware; *spec.* conscious, sensible, informed, percipient. Knowing *in this sense is rather R.*
Antonyms: see UNAWARE.

knowing, *n.* cognition (*tech. or B*), ken (*obs. or R*); *spec.* perception, apperception, inference, sensibility, consciousness.

knowingness, *n.* **1.** *See* INTELLIGENCE.
2. awareness, flyness (*S*); *spec.* sciolism (*B or R*), cunningness.

---

king: *monarch.*
kingdom: *domain, group.*
kink, *v. t.: twist, curl, loop, knot.*
kinsfolk: *kindred.*
kinship: *relation, kindred.*
kinsman: *relative.*
kit: *set.*
knack: *ability.*
knave: *rascal, jack.*
knavery: *dishonesty, rascality.*
knell, *v. t.: summon.*
knell, *v. i.: ring.*
knickerbockers: *breeches.*
knickknack: *gewgaw.*
knife, *v. t.: stab, betray.*
knit: *weave, interlace, consolidate, wrinkle.*
knoll: *hill.*

knowledge, *n.* cognition (*tech. or B*), cognizance (*tech. or B*), cognoscence (*R*), ken, wit (*A*), *spec.* pansophy (*R*), panthology (*R*), mastery, command, kenning (*Scot. and dial. Eng.*), gnosis, consciousness, recognition, intuition, identification, perception, guptavidya (*theosophy*), information, news, instruction, prescience, know how (*C*), cunning, experience, skill, science, acquaintance, familiarity (*used with "with"*), privity.

known, *a. Spec.* understood, assumed, given.
Antonyms: see UNSUSPECTED.

knuckle, *n.* **1.** joint (*contex.*); *spec.* (*in quadrupeds*) hock.
2. *Pl.; in reference to the weapon: spec.* knuckleduster (*sing.*), cestus (*sing.*).

L

label, *n.* **1.** mark (*contex.*), ticket (*chiefly spec.*); *spec.* tag (*chiefly U. S.*), slip, docket, tally.
2. *In architecture:* drip.

labor, *v. i.* **1.** *See* ENDEAVOR, WORK, ELABORATE, GO.
2. *Referring to a woman in childbirth:* travail (*A*).

laboratory, *n.* work place (*contex.*).

labored, *a.* **1.** *See* ELABORATE.
2. *Spec.* artificial, forced, heavy, ponderous.
Antonyms: see SPONTANEOUS.

laborious, *a.* **1.** arduous (*B*), toilsome, toilful (*R*), hard (*of a slow, difficult task*), laborsome (*R*); *spec.* heavy, tedious, sweaty, difficult, slavish. *See* WORK.
2. *See* INDUSTRIOUS.

labyrinth, *n.* maze (*of that which is mentally confusing, as contrasted with the idea of structural intricacy suggested by* labyrinth).

labyrinthine, *a.* labyrinthian, labyrinthic, Dædalian (*fig.*).

lace, *n.* **1.** fastening (*contex.*); *spec.* string, cord, band, latchet (*dial. or Bib.*), thong, braid, strap.
2. fabric (*contex.*), netting; *spec.* bobbinet, Valenciennes, Duchesse, pillow lace, passement (*hist.*), net, guipure, tatting, edging, allover, insertion, Mechlin, point.
3. admixture (*contex.*), flavor, dash.

lace, *v. t.* **1.** fasten, enlace (*B*).
2. *See* INTERLACE.
3. adulterate, flavor.

lacerate, *v. t. Spec.* tear, distress, wound.

lachrymatory, *n.* tear bottle.

lacing, *n. Spec.* enlacement (*R*), flavor.

lack, *v. i.* **1.** *See* FAIL.
2. want (*suggesting need or desire;* lack, *more the simple fact of deficiency*).

lack, *v. t.* want; *spec.* need.
Antonyms: see HAVE.

lackey, *n.* **1.** servant; *spec.* footboy, footman, valet, flunky (*rather derogatory*).
2. *See* FAWNER.

lad, *n.* youth, boy, jockey (*chiefly Scot.*), laddie (*chiefly Scot.; esp. by way of affection*).

ladder-shaped, *a.* scalar, scalariform (*both B*).

ladies' man, gallant (*R, exc. spec.*).

ladle, *n.* dipper (*chiefly U. S.; usually spec.*); *spec.* bail, bale, scoop (*chiefly cant*), simpulum, shank, cyathus (*classical antiq.*).

lady, *n.* **1.** *See* MISTRESS, LADYLOVE.
2. *As used with "Our":* Virgin Mary.
3. gentlewoman (*A*); *spec.* ladykin, mem sahib (*India*), begum (*India*), countess, baroness, duchess, czarina, czarevna, *etc.*
4. dog, bitch.
5. wife.

ladybird, *n.* cow-lady (*dial. Eng.*), ladycow (*dial. Eng.*), ladybug (*chiefly U. S.*).

lady in waiting, duenna (*Spanish; spec.*).

lady-killer, *n.* masher (*S*).

ladylove, *n.* lover (*only of one who loves in return*), Dido (*fig.; usually of one who is deserted*), paramour (*A; now usually in an evil sense*), mistress (*implying domination over the male; often with an evil suggestion*), sweetheart (*sentimental suggestion*).

ladyship, *n.* ladyhood (*used only of the quality;* ladyship *being often used in designation or address*).

lady's maid, tirewoman (*A*).

lag, *v. i.* delay (*contex.*).
Antonyms: see HURRY, RUSH, DASH.

lagging, *n.* delay (*contex.*); *spec.* retardation, hysteresis (*elec.*).

lagoon, *n.* pond, bayou, lake, *etc.* (lagoon *always suggests shallowness*).

lair, *n.* bed (*contex.*); *spec.* den, form (*of a hare or R deer*), nest, couch, house, earth, burrow, lodge, kennel.

laity, *n.* people (*contex.*), laymen (*pl.*), temporalty (*eccl.*).
Antonyms: see PROFESSION, MINISTRY.

lake, *n.* lough (*Anglo-Irish*), loch (*Scot.*), mere (*chiefly B*); *spec.* pond (*smaller than* lake), tank (*India*), lakelet, salina, tarn.

lake, *a.* lacustrine (*chiefly spec.*), lacustral (*R*), lacustrian (*R*).

lamb, *n.* offspring (*contex.*); *spec.* sheep, yeanling, eanling, yearling, lambling (*R*), lambkin (*R*), cade, cosset.

lambrequin, *n. Spec.* cornice, curtain, mantling (*her.*).

lamentable, *a.* regrettable, sorrowful, deplorable (*moving profound regret*), sad, ruthful (*A*), rueful, pitiful, pitiable (*both suggesting sorrow tinged with contempt at another's misfortune*), piteous (*moving compassion*), miserable, mourn-

---

knowledgeable: *intelligent*

L

laborer: *worker.*
lacerate: *rend, distress, wound.*
laconic: *brief.*
ladle, *v.: dip.*
ladylike: *womanly, refined, effeminate.*
lame, *a.: disabled, crippled, ineffectual.*
lame, *v. t.: disable, cripple.*
lamed: *disabled.*
lament, *v. i.: mourn, complain, sorrow.*
lament, *v. t.: regret, mourn.*
lament, *n.: lamentation.*

---

ful, melancholy, doleful, woeful, pathetic; *spec.* commiserable (*B*), forlorn.
Antonyms: see LAUGHABLE.

lamentation, *n.* **1.** lament, moan (*R*), plaint (*B*), mourning, wail, greet (*Scot.*); *spec.* jeremiad (*fig.*), bawl, wailing, weeping, dirge.
Antonyms: see REJOICING, MERRYMAKING, REVELRY.
2. *Referring to the experience or feeling, apart from expression: see* SORROW.

lamina, *n.* lamination (*used chiefly in pl.*); *spec.* scale, leaf, foliation (*B or tech.*), stratification (*B*), sheet, fold, thickness, lift, flake, layer, stratum (*B*), blade, plate, lamella, film. *"Lamina" and "lamination" are both* (*B*).

laminate, *a.* laminaceous, foliaceous, laminar, lamellar, laminated, stratified, straticulate (*R*), laminal, foliated, laminose, laminous, flaky, leafy, bedded;—*all more or less* (*B*), *exc. the last three words.*

lamp, *n.* lucerne (*R*); *spec.* sconce, lantern (*French hist.*), cresset, crusie, crusy (*Scot.*), Davy, lampion.

lance, *n.* **1.** *Spec.* demilance, dart, lancegay (*hist.*), sarissa (*antiq.*).
2. *See* LANCER.

land, *n.* **1.** *Referring to the solid surface:* earth.
Antonyms: see SEA.
2. *Referring to some particular region of the earth:* country; *spec.* frontage, district, grounds, lunge (*for horse training*), links (*pl. or collective sing.*), parade (*mil.*), wold *or* weald, Cockaigne, Thule, El Dorado (*fig.*), Beulah (*fig.*), desert, plains (*pl.*), mainland, continent, island, campus, yard, odal, premises (*pl.; law*), yoke, hundred, farm, country, motherland, reservation, *etc.*

landlady, *n.* **1.** *See* LANDOWNER.
2. *Spec.* hostess.

landlocked, *a.* inclosed, mediterranean (*B*).

landlord, *n.* **1.** *See* LANDOWNER.
2. *Spec.* host, innkeeper.

landmark, *n.* boundary; *spec.* hoarstone, merestone, mere (*A*), meith (*Scot.*), guide.

landowner, *n.* landholder, territorialist (*R*); *spec.* landlord, landlady, patroon (*U. S.*), agrarian.

landscape, *n.* picture (*contex.*), paysage (*French*); *spec.* treescape.

landsman, *n. Spec.* landlubber, horse marine (*both sailors' S; contemptuous*).
Antonyms: see SAILOR.

language, *n.* **1.** speech, tongue (*B, of some nation or people*); *spec.* idiom (*as proper to a people or country*), slang, parlance (*chiefly used with "common"*), lingua (*Latin; used chiefly in "lingua franca"*), accent, pasilaly (*A*), pasigraphy (*a loose use*), oration (*considered grammatically*), vernacular (*mother tongue, as vs. literary level of speech*), vulgar (*R*), cryptology, dialect, patois (*of the humbler classes*).
2. *See* VOCABULARY, DICTION.

languid, *a.* weak (*contex.*), listless, lukewarm; see APATHETIC, FAINT.

languish, *v. i.* sicken (*contex.*), decline (*contex.*), sink, droop, pine, dwine (*A or Scot.*).

lanky, *a.* **1.** lean (*contex.*), lank, slabsided (*S, U. S.*), flatsided (*C*), rangy (*primarily spec.*).
Antonyms: see FAT, SQUAT, STOCKY.
2. *See* STRAIGHT.

lantern, *n.* **1.** lanthorn (*A*), light; *spec.* jack-o'-lantern (*U. S. and dial. Eng.*), bull's-eye.
2. *Spec.* cupola, tholus (*tech.*).

lapdog, *n.* dog (*contex.*), messan (*Scot.*).

large, *a.* **1.** *See* COMPREHENSIVE.
2. big; *spec.* largish, heroic (*often humorous*), goodly (*implying generous, comforting, etc., size*), hugeous (*R*), liberal, generous, long (*C*), exorbitant (*A*), Babylonian (*fig.*), bulky, voluminous, immense, considerable (*not enough to be very important*), coarse, grand, elephantine, colossal, broad.
Antonyms: see SMALL, MINUTE.

largen, *v. i. & t.* enlarge; *spec.* broaden.

larva, *n. Spec.* caterpillar, grub, hopper, worm, flyblow, cankerworm, looper, scolex, slugworm, slug, cysticercus, eruca (*R*), caddis.

larval, *a.* **1.** personate (*zoöl.*), masked.
2. larvalike, larviform; *spec.* eruciform (*R*).

lascivious, *a.* sensual (*contex.*), lustful; *spec.* licentious, lecherous, lickerish *or* liquorish, fleshly, venereous (*B*), petulant (*R*), lubricous (*R*), lubricious (*R*), concupiscent, goatish, prurient, wanton (*used esp. of women*), lewd, libidinous, salacious (*B*), Cyprian (*fig.*).
Antonyms: see PURE, CHASTE.

lash, *n.* **1.** (*a stroke with a pliant implement*), stroke (*contex.*), whip; *spec.* swinge, scourge, flogging.
2. whip; *spec.* scourge (*a lash that cuts flesh*), rope's-end, thong, cat-o'-nine-tails, scorpion.
3. stroke;—*referring to satire, sarcasm, etc.*
4. *Spec.* eyelash, flabellum (*zoöl.*).

lash, *v. t.* **1.** strike (*contex.*), whip; *spec.* scourge, swinge, flog.
2. *See* ABUSE.

lash, *v. i.* **1.** strike (*contex.*), whip; *spec.* scourge, swinge, flog.
2. *See* RUSH, DASH, FLASH, INVEIGH.

lashing, *n.* fastening; *spec.* (*naut.*) gammon, gripes (*pl.*).

last, *a. Spec.* hindmost, hindermost, extreme, final, lowest, utmost, farthest, latest (*nearest of a past series to the present, where* last *implies completing the series*), preceding.
Antonyms: see FIRST, INITIAL.

lasting, *a.* continuing, abiding, durable (*implying successful resistance to wear or disintegration*), endurable (*R*); *spec.* perdurable,

---

land, *v. t.: disembark, catch, deposit.*
land, *v. i.: disembark, alight.*
landslide: *avalanche.*
languorous: *apathetic, faint, emotional.*
lap, *v.: drink, play, touch.*
lapel: *flap.*
lapse, *n.: failure, apostasy, course, passing, end, fall.*
lapse, *v. i.: fall, apostatize, end, pass.*
lard: *fat.*
large: *comprehensive, big.*
large-hearted: *generous.*
lark: *frolic.*
lassitude: *apathy, faintness.*
last, *v. i.: continue, endure.*

wearing, perdurant (*R*), stable (*implying resistance of forces tending to upset*), diuturnal (*R*), endless, immortal, perennial, permanent, fixed.

Antonyms: see EPHEMERAL, TEMPORARY, PASSING.

late, *a.* **1.** *Spec.* latish (*R*), behind (*in respect to time or things*), backward (*esp. in respect to growth*), latesome (*obs. or dial.*), tardy, tardive (*R*), impunctual (*R*), slow, high, overdue, behindhand (*always predicative*), latest, last.

Antonyms: see EARLY.

2. *See* DEAD, RECENT.

later, *a.* latter, posterior, inferior (*R*); *spec.* puisne (*law*).

Antonyms: see EARLIER.

lateral, *a.* side (*the noun used attributively; less formal or tech. than* lateral).

lattice, *n.* latticework; *spec.* grate, grating, transenna, trellis, cancelli (*pl.*), espalier.

laudatory, *a.* praiseful; *spec.* encomiastic, commendatory, fine, complimentary, panegyrical *or* panegyric, eulogistic.

Antonyms: see ABUSIVE, CONDEMNATORY, DISPARAGING.

laugh, *v. i. Spec.* giggle, teehee, sneer, grin, hee-haw, guffaw, snicker, snigger, sniggle, ha-ha, snort, fleer, cackle, haw-haw, titter, chuckle, chortle (*C*), cachinnate (*B*), convulse.

Antonyms: see CRY, SOB, WAIL, WEEP.

laugh, *n. Spec.* giggle (*implying foolish levity*), teehee, sneer, grin, gurgle, horselaugh (*coarse, loud*), hee-haw, haw-haw, guffaw (*vulgar, boorish*), laughter, snicker (*implying a partly suppressed manner, with audible catches of breath*), ha-ha, snort, fleer, cackle (*contemptuous*), tittle, snigger, sniggle, chuckle (*implying an amused satisfaction*), chortle (*C*), cachinnation (*pedantic, or humorous*), convulsion.

Antonyms: see CRY, SOB, SIGH.

laughable, *a.* funny (*provoking amusement*); *spec.* facetious, facete (*A*), quizzical, droll (*implying oddity*), drollish, witty, ludicrous, ridiculous (*stirring derision*), risible (*R*), amusing, grotesque, jocular; waggish, farcical, burlesque; *see* COMIC.

Antonyms: see LAMENTABLE.

laughing, *a. Spec.* risible, merry, sparkling, rippling (*contex.*), giggly.

Antonyms: see WEEPING.

laughter, *n.* laughing (*emphasizing the idea of action*); *spec.* titteration (*R*), gigglement, risibility, convulsion, cachinnation (*B; often derogatory*).

Antonyms: see WEEPING, LAMENTATION; *also cf.* CRY.

lava, *n. Spec.* coulee, slag, pumice, bomb.

lavatory, *n.* washroom, cloakroom. *See* BATH, TOILET.

lavish, *v. t.* bestow (*contex.*); *spec.* squander, waste, deluge, pour, shower, rain.

Antonyms: see STINT.

law, *n.* **1.** *Referring to civil laws:* rule (*R*); *spec.* act, statute, enactment, doom (*hist.*), canon (*now chiefly hist. or eccl.*), ordonnance (*in Continental Europe*), ordinance (*esp. one passed by minor body or official*), decree, institution, constitution (*esp. Roman law or eccl.*), edict, plebiscite (*one passed by the people in general, or spec. Roman hist.*), capitular *or* capitulary, rescript, decision, byrlaw (*dial. or hist.*).

2. jurisprudence (*science of law*).

3. *See* LITIGATION, PROFESSION, ALLOWANCE.

law-abiding, *a.* lawful; *spec.* orderly, ruly.

Antonyms: see ROWDYISH, LAWLESS, ANARCHICAL, DISORDERLY.

lawful, *a.* legitimate (*valid by law, or sanctioned by authoritative standards*), legal (*more formal than "lawful"*); *spec.* juristic *or* juristical, licit (*R*), quiritary *or* quiritarian (*Roman law*), just, right, rightful, unprohibited, warrantable, valid, jural (*R; equiv. of "juristic"*), civil, forensic (*in relation to the courts*), constitutional.

Antonyms: see UNLAWFUL, CRIMINAL.

lawless, *a.* unruly, ruleless (*R*), unregulated, disorderly (*contex.*); *spec.* riotous; *see* ANARCHICAL.

Antonyms: see LAW-ABIDING.

lawyer, *n.* man-of-law (*A*); *spec.* advocate, attorney, solicitor (*chiefly Eng.*), barrister (*chiefly Eng.*), proctor, counselor *or* counsel, pettifogger, shyster (*cant or contemptuous*), sergeant, gownsman (*Eng.*), judge, rabbi (*Jewish*), bencher (*Eng.*), canonist, silk (*Eng.; C or S*), conveyancer, Civilian, Romanist, procurator, procurer (*R*), leader (*at the bar*), brehon, cognitor (*Roman law*), cadi (*Mohammedan*), writer (*Scot.*).

lax, *a.* **1.** *Referring to the bowels: see* LOOSE.

2. slack (*suggesting want of vigor*), relaxed, loose, liberal (*euphemistic*); *see* NEGLIGENT, IMMORAL.

Antonyms: see STRICT.

lay, *a.* popular (*without the technicalities of professionals*), laic (*R*), nonprofessional, unprofessional; *spec.* temporal, secular, civilian.

Antonyms: see PROFESSIONAL, MINISTERIAL, PRIESTLY, JUDICIAL.

lay, *v. t. Spec.* deposit, put, calm, allay, bring, attribute, exorcise (*of spirits, etc.*), apply, bet, cover, inflict.

layer, *n. Spec.* couch (*esp. of varnish, malt, etc.*) bed, coping, course (*of masonry, etc.*), lift, belt, footing, seam, sill, ply, overlay, floor, cordon, lap.

layman, *n.* laic (*R or tech.*), nonprofessional *spec.* secular.

Antonyms: see PRIEST.

latest: *late.*
lather: *foam.*
latitude: *extent, freedom, region.*
latter: *later, subsequent.*
laudable: *praiseworthy, healthful.*
launched: *afloat.*
laureate: *crowned, distinguished.*
lavish, *a.: abundant, extravagant, unstinted.*
lawn: *grassland.*

laziness, *n.* idleness, indolence, sloth (*B*).

lazy, *a.* inert (*indisposed to exert oneself*), idle, indolent, slothful (*sluggishly indolent*); *spec.* sluggard, slack, shiftless (*lacking resourcefulness or ability to find expedients*), drony, dronish *or* droning, osculant (*R*), sleepy.
Antonyms: see ACTIVE, AMBITIOUS, ENTERPRISING, INDUSTRIOUS.

lead (lĕd), *n.* Saturn (*tech.*); *spec.* pipe, channel, plummet.

lead (lēd), *v. t.* **1.** *See* GUIDE, DIRECT, INDUCE, EXPERIENCE.
2. precede, front (*R*); *spec.* head, deduct *or* deduce, precent (*R*), captain.
Antonyms: see FOLLOW.

leaden, *n.* **1.** lead, Saturnine (*A or her.*), plumbous (*R*); *spec.* leady.
2. lead-colored, plumbous (*chiefly R*); *spec.* livid, gray, leady.
3. *See* HEAVY, DEPRESSING.

leader, *n.* **1.** *See* GUIDE, CHIEF, DRAIN.
2. *Referring to one who precedes or conducts to some place or in a course:* conductor; *spec.* guide, header, lead, heretoga (*Old Eng. hist.*), bellwether, choragus (*esp. in the Classic drama*), forehorse, demagogue (*hist.*), coryphæus (*primarily Classic antiq.*), cantor *or* precentor, cob (*dial. Eng.*), mahdi (*Mohammedan*), stretcher, whip (*angling*).

leadership, *n.* chieftaincy, headship, head, lead; *spec.* captaincy, captainship, commandership, hegemony (*political science*).

leaf, *n.* **1.** *Spec.* blade, phyllome (*tech.*), leaflet, foliole (*tech.*), bract (*tech.*), bracteole (*tech.*), bractlet (*tech.*), frond (*popular usage*), cotyledon (*tech.*), flag, pad (*U. S.*), needle, petal (*tech.*), sepal (*tech.*).
2. *Spec.* lamina, folio, lamella, flap, fold, interleaf, inset, valve, valvelet.

leafage, *n.* foliage (*the ordinary term*), foliation, foliature (*R*), leafery (*R*), frondescence (*tech.* or (*R*); *spec.* vernation.

leafing, *n.* leaving (*a variant*), foliation, frondescence (*tech, or R*).

leaflike, *a.* foliaceous (*B or tech.*), foliar (*B or tech.*), foliated (*chiefly zoöl.*); *spec.* filiform (*R*), leafy.

leafy, *a.* **1.** *See* LEAFLIKE.
2. leaved, foliaceous (*tech. or B*), phylloid (*tech.*), leavy (*A or B*), foliose (*R*), folious (*R*), frondent (*R*); *spec.* bowery, foliate.
Antonyms: see BARE.

league, *v. t.* associate, ally, confederate (*chiefly spec.*).

leak, *v. i.* escape (*contex.*); *spec.* extravasate.

leakage, *n.* escape (*contex.*); *spec.* seepage, percolation.

leap year, bissextile (*tech.*).

learn, *v. t.* **1.** get (*contex.*); *spec.* con (*A or B*), master, prepare, have, acquire, memorize.
2. ascertain; *spec.* hear, see, read, infer; *see* DISCOVER.

learned, *a.* able (*contex.*), intelligent (*contex.*), lettered (*B or formal*), bookish, book-learned (*now usually disparaging*); *spec.* literate, erudite, bluestocking *or* blue (*cant or depreciatory*), scholarly, wise, profound (*emphasizing the depth of research or thought*), studied, accomplished, philosophical.
Antonyms: see IGNORANT, UNSCHOLARLY.

learning, *n.* **1.** knowledge, lore (*A or B; pertaining to a special subject, and often traditionary*); *spec.* erudition (*learning amassed from reading—esp. recondite*), scholarship (*exact learning*), pedantry (*learning made a matter of display, or of insistence on rules or details*), enlightenment, wisdom (*knowledge digested and available for right judgment*), opsimathy, clerkship (*A*), schoolcraft (*A*), mathesis (*A*), humanity, literature (*R*) science, art, religion, mathematics, languages, medicine, *etc.*
Antonyms: see IGNORANCE.
2. *See* DISCOVERY.

lease, *v. t.* **1.** grant (*contex.*), convey (*contex.*), let (*broader and less formal than* lease), farm (*R*), demise (*tech.*); *spec.* rent, conacre, sublease, sublet.
2. *In the sense of "to take a lease of":* take (*contex.*); *spec.* hire, rent, sublease.

leash, *n. Spec.* cord, thong, slip, couple, lune, lyam *or* lyme (*hist.*).

least, *a. Spec.* minimum, slightest, smallest, lowest, minimal.
Antonyms: see UTMOST.

least, *n.* minimum.

leather, *n. Spec.* kid, dogskin, calfskin, calf, cowhide, doeskin, pigskin, porpoiseskin, goose skin, morocco, cordovan, cordwain, Rutland, russia, buckskin, whitleather, cuir-bouilli (*French*), shagreen, saffian, skiver, buff.

leathern, *n.* coriaceous (*tech. or affected*), leathery.

leave, *n.* **1.** permission (*formally given*), sufferance (*tacitly given*); *spec.* furlough (*esp. of a soldier*).
2. *See* FAREWELL.

leave, *v. t.* **1.** *See* ABANDON, BEQUEATH, PERMIT, REFER, COMMIT, DEPOSIT, DESERT, STOP.
2. depart, quit, desert, abandon, flee, evacuate, forgo (*A*).

lecture, *n.* **1.** address, prelection (*R*).
2. reproof.

lecture, *v. t.* **1.** address; *spec.* sermon (*R*), sermonize, tutor, teach.
2. *See* REPROVE.

ledge, *n.* ridge (*contex.*), shelf (*contex.*); *spec.* berm, bench, ledging (*a collective*).

---

lazy fellow: *sluggard.*
league, *n.: agreement, association, confederacy.*
leak: *hole.*
lean, *v. i.: incline, rest, depend, hang.*
lean, *v. t.: rest.*
lean, *a.: thin, lanky, innutritious.*
leaning: *inclination.*
leap, *v. i.: jump, go, break.*
leap, *v. t. & n.: jump.*
least: *smallest.*
leave, *v. i.: depart, cease.*
leaven, *n.: ferment, admixture.*
leave-taking: *farewell.*
leavings: *residue.*
lecher: *dissipator.*
lecherous: *dissipated, lascivious.*

---

ledgy, *a.* shelfy, shelvy.

leech, *n.* doctor (*A*); *spec.* bloodsucker, parasite.

left, *a.* leftward (*R*), sinistral (*tech.*), sinister (*tech.*); *spec.* larboard (*naut.*), near (*C*), radical, red (*C*), leftist.
Antonyms: see RIGHT.

left-handed, *a. Spec.* sinistral (*tech.*), clumsy, ambiguous.

leftist, *a.* radical, red (*cant*), extremist.
Antonyms: see RIGHTIST.

leg, *n.* **1.** limb (*a term including both arms and legs*), stumps (*pl.; C*); *spec.* crus (*tech.*), jamb (*her.*), gamb *or* gambe (*her.*), shin, shank, leglet, drumstick, thigh, gigot (*R*), ham, podite (*tech.*), peg.
2. *See* BRANCH, BOW, BEAT, (*naut.*), SIDE.

leg, *a.* crural (*tech.*).

legacy, *n.* gift, bequest.

legal, *a.* **1.** law (*the noun used attributively*); *spec.* juridical, judicial.
2. *See* LAWFUL.

legalize, *v. t.* legitimate (*indicating that permission is given to do what has been unlawful;* legalize *refers esp. to making a thing conform to the law or to giving validity to forms or acts that hitherto were without legal validity*), legitimatize *or* legitimize (*chiefly spec.*); *spec.* formalize, authorize, regularize.

legate, *n.* diplomatic agent, ambassador.

legatee, *n.* grantee (*contex.*), donee (*contex.*), legatary (*R*); *spec.* collegatary (*R*), colegatee, institute (*Roman and Scots law*).

legend, *n.* **1.** story (*contex.*), saga (*a tale similar to the old heroic stories of Iceland*), myth (*dealing with gods or godlike men*); *spec.* folklore, haggadah.
2. inscription (*contex.*), lemma (*B*); *spec.* epigraph, motto.
3. *See* DEVICE.

legging, *n. Spec.* gramash (*Scot.*), gamash (*A or dial.*), gambado, gaiter, spats (*pl.*), puttee, gamashes (*pl.*), greaves (*pl.*), chaps (*pl.; western U. S.*).

legible, *a.* readable (*the Anglo-Saxon equivalent of "legible"*); *spec.* fair, decipherable.
Antonyms: see ILLEGIBLE.

legislator, *n.* lawgiver, lawmaker, legislatress (*fem.*), legislatrix (*fem.*); *spec.* thesmothete, filibuster, senator, representative, congressman, parliamentarian, magnate.

legislature, *n. Spec.* parliament, congress, senate, house of representatives *or* (*for short*) house, duma, diet, Commons, General Court.

legitimate, *a.* **1.** *See* LAWFUL.
2. *In reference to offspring:* lawful, kindly (*A or hist.*), mulier (*law*).
Antonyms: see ILLEGITIMATE.

leisure, *n.* **1.** freedom (*contex.*), ease, vacancy (*R or B*); *spec.* convenience.
2. time, by-time (*R*).

leisure, *a.* free (*contex.*), otiant (*R*), vacant (*R or B*), spare.

leisurely, *a. Spec.* leisured, deliberate, slow.
Antonyms: see BUSTLING.

lend, *v. t.* **1.** *See* LOAN; *spec.* bail (*law*), furnish.
Antonyms: see BORROW.
2. *See* GIVE, FURNISH.

length, *n.* **1.** distance, extent, longitude (*chiefly jocular or spec.*); prolixity (*R or humorous as physical length*); *spec.* measure, fly.
2. *Referring to time:* extent; *spec.* prolixity, quantity (*in prosody and phonetics*).
Antonyms: see BREVITY.
3. *Spec.* piece, roll, coil, ran, run.

lengthen, *v. t.* **1.** *See* EXTEND.
2. *In prosody and phonetics:* prolong.
Antonyms: see SHORTEN.

lengthwise, *adv.* lengthways (*less usual than "lengthwise"*), endlong (*A or dial.*); *spec.* fore and aft (*in reference to a vessel*), along, endwise, endways.
Antonyms: see CROSSWISE, SIDEWAYS.

lengthy, *a. Spec.* long, prolix, tall.
Antonyms: see SHORT, BRIEF.

lenient, *a.* **1.** soothing.
2. gentle; *spec.* indulgent, merciful.

lens, *n.* refractor; *spec.* eyepiece, bull's-eye, objective, eyeglass, crystalline, glass, magnifier, meniscus, pantoscope.

lens-shaped, *a. Spec.* lenticular, meniscal, meniscoid;—*all three B or tech.*

leopard, *n.* pard (*A or poetic*), panther (*chiefly* spec.), leopardess (*fem.*), pantheress (*fem.*), catamountain (*A or R*); *spec.* cheetah.

less, *a.* smaller (*with reference to size*); fewer (less *refers to quantity,* fewer *to number, as*— "fewer *people,*" "less *money*"); *see also* MINOR.

let, *v. t.* **1.** *See* ALLOW, CAUSE, PERMIT.
2. rent, hire (*neither in careful usage*), farm (*chiefly hist. or in matters of government finance*); *spec.* lend (*money;* let *is obs. in this sense*), lease, sublet.

letter, *n.* lessor, renter, hirer; *spec.* locator (*Civil and Scots law*), jobber *or* jobmaster (*Eng.*).

letter, *n.* **1.** symbol, character (*both contex.*); *spec.* initial, descender, italic, roman, nasal, labial, medial, guttural, cacuminal, dental, *etc.*, alpha, beta, *etc.*, digamma, cue.
2. communication, epistle (*formal, rhetorical, historical, or affected*), favor (*only in commercial usage*), missive; *spec.* note, billet, brief (*R or tech.*), line (*C*), billet-doux, poulet (*French*), bull (*papal*), notelet, drop letter (*U. S.*), valentine, pastoral, monitory.

---

leer, *v. i.: gaze.*
leer, *n.: look.*
legendary: *fabulous.*
lengthen: *extend* (referring to sounds); *prolong.*
lengthwise: *longitudinal.*
lengthy: *long, prolix.*
lenience: *indulgence, mercy.*
lenient: *indulgent, merciful.*
lessee: *grantee.*
lessen: *diminish, disparage, abate, shorten, moderate.*
lesser: *inferior, minor.*
lesson: *task, reading, reproof.*
lethal: *deadly.*
lethargy: *sleepiness, sleep, apathy, stupor, dullness.*

---

3. *In pl.:* see LITERATURE.
4. *See* TYPE.
letter, *v. t.* inscribe (*contex.*); *spec.* initial, sign.
letterbox, *n.* pillar box *or* pillar (*Eng.*).
letter carrier. *Spec.* postman, postboy, carrier.
letting, *n.* leasing, hiring, renting; *spec.* location (*Civil and Scots law*), conacre (*Irish land system*).
level, *n. Spec.* horizontal, elevation, equality, stage, drift, horizon.
level, *v. t.* **1.** *See* FLATTEN, DIRECT, AIM, ADJUST, LOWER, DEMOLISH.
2. repose (*contex.*), prostrate; *see* FELL, BOW, ABASE, OVERCOME, EXHAUST.
lever, *n.* prize (*chiefly dial. or A*), pry (*chiefly spec.*; *dial. U. S. and Eng. dial.*); *spec.* dog, crowbar, crow, sweep, swingle, brake, treadle, trigger, tumbler, tiller, tail, key, jack, pawl, pedal, garrot.
lever, *v. t.* prize (*now chiefly A or mech.*), pry (*U. S. or Eng. dial.*)
leverage, *n.* hold (*contex.*), purchase, prize (*chiefly Eng.*), pry (*U. S. or Eng. dial.*).
lewd, *a.* **1.** coarse (*contex.*), sensual (*contex.*), lecherous (*R*); *spec.* vile, filthy, impure, foul, ribald, Cyprian (*fig.*), lascivious, indecent, unchaste, licentious, dissolute, debauched.
Antonyms: see CHASTE, MODEST.
2. *See* LASCIVIOUS.
lexicographer, *n.* author (*contex.*), vocabulist (*R*); *spec.* glossarian, glossarist.
lexicographical, *a. spec.* glossarial.
lexicography, *n.* lexicology (*R*); *spec.* glossography *or* glossology.
liable, *a.* **1.** likely (*U. S., but best usage restricts* liable *to the sense of risk, or to implication of impending financial or other obligation;* likely, *to mere statement of possibility, as* "liable *to lose heavily,*" "likely *to rain.*"). *See* ACCOUNTABLE.
2. exposed, obnoxious (*B*), open, subject.
liar, *n.* prevaricator, story-teller (*C and euphemistic*), equivocator (*B or euphemistic*), falsifier (*R*), pseudologer (*R; chiefly humorous*); *spec.* cracker (*C*), fibber, fibster, bouncer, romancer.
liberal, *a.* **1.** *See* ABUNDANT, FRANK, GENEROUS, LAX, INCLUSIVE.
2. *Spec.* free, liberalistic, broad-minded (*commendatory*), open-minded, libertine (*R; usually derogatory*), broad (*of opinions, judgments, etc.*), broadish, catholic, latitudinarian (*often disparaging*), eclectic (*implying unfettered use of all that is available without conventional restraint*), tolerant, indifferent, democratic, *etc.*
Antonyms: see NARROW.
liberal, *n.* liberalist, libertine (*R, exc. spec.*); *spec.* free-thinker, Radical, Discomisado (*Spanish hist.*), Latitudinarian.
liberalize, *v. t.* broaden, catholicize, widen.
libertine, *n.* **1.** *See* LIBERAL, FREEDMAN.
2. *Spec.* debauchee, rake, lecher, Lothario (*chiefly with "gay"*), roué (*French*), rakehell (*A*), rip (*C*).
license or licence, *n.* **1.** authorization (*contex.*); *spec.* chop (*India and China*), purwanah (*India*), certificate, dispensation, imprimatur, warrant, passport, clearance, privilege, indult (*R. C. Ch.*), charter, patent.
2. freedom, liberty (*an inexact use*); *spec.* looseness, indulgence.
Antonyms: see RESTRAINT.
licentious, *a.* immoral (*contex.*), incontinent, dissipated (*contex.*); *spec.* broad (*in talk, manners, etc.*), free (*usually euphemistic*), libertine (*implying voluntary disregard of moral or conventional restraints*), loose, corrupt, lewd (*involving action sexually immoral and coarse*), lascivious, orgiastic, degenerate.
Antonyms: see CHASTE, MODEST.
lie, *n.* falsehood, equivocation (*spec. or euphemistic*), falsity (*R*), untruth (*often euphemistic*), story (*C and euphemistic*), mendacity (*R, exc. in an abstract sense*) *B, and lacking the offensiveness of "lie"*); *spec.* fib, romance, concoction, imagination, invention, sockdologer (*S, U. S.*), crack (*A*), prevarication.
Antonyms: see TRUTH.
lie, *v. i.* falsify, equivocate (*spec. or euphemistic*); *spec.* prevaricate, romance, fib, shuffle, quibble.
lie, *v. i.* **1.** recline (*the Latin and less emphatic equivalent of "lie"*); *spec.* couch (*A*), lair (*R, exc. of beasts*), bed, bunk (*C*), grovel, bundle.
Antonyms: see STAND.
2. *Referring more to the idea of support than to the idea of position:* rest; *spec.* repose, cuddle, nestle, seat, sit.
3. *See* EXTEND, BE, CONSIST, INHERE.
life, *n.* **1.** being, existence (*both contex.*), course (*fig.*); *spec.* vitality, breath, head (*fig.*), pilgrimage, journey (*fig.*).
Antonyms: see DEATH.
2. *See* ENERGY, LIVELINESS, ESSENCE, ESSENTIAL.
lifeless, *a.* **1.** inanimate (*often of that which never was alive*), inert, dead; *spec.* spiritless, breathless, bloodless, pulseless, defunct.
Antonyms: see LIVING.
2. *Referring to what seems lifeless: spec.* insensible, dull, motionless, insipid, sluggish, feckless (*Scot. or B*).
3. *Referring to coals that have been burning or "alive":* dead, extinct, extinguished, quenched.
lifetime, *n.* age, day.
lift, *v. t.* **1.** elevate, raise, heave (*spec., exc. A*); *spec.* boost (*C, U. S.*), heft, hoist, float, crank, crane.
Antonyms: see LOWER.
2. *See* DIGNIFY, ELEVATE, STEAL, PAY.
lift, *n.* **1.** elevation, heave (*spec., exc. A*); *spec.* boost (*C, U. S.*), hoist.
2. *See* LAYER, ELEVATOR.

levee: *dike, bank, quay.*
level, *a.: even, flat, horizontal, equal.*
levity: *lightness, frivolity.*
levy: *enlist, assess.*
libation, *sacrifice.*
libel: *defame.*
libelous: *defamatory.*
liberty: *freedom, license, right.*
libidinous: *lascivious.*
lick: *touch, wash, defeat.*
licking: *defeat.*
lid, *n.: cover.*
lien: *claim.*

3. *Referring to an act of assistance: spec.* cast (*Eng. or B*).
ligament, *n.* **1.** band, bondage.
2. *Anat.:* sinew (*chiefly spec.*), thew (*chiefly in pl.*); *spec.* tendon, whitleather.
light, *n.* **1.** ray *or* radiance (*chiefly poetic, exc. spec.*), levin (*B*), leam (*Scot. or dial.*); *spec.* glim (*S*), lamp (*fig.*), gleam, flare, phosphorescence, reflection, starlight, blink, iceblink, snowblink, daylight, candlelight, gaslight, glare.
Antonyms: see DARK.
2. luminary (*B, chiefly spec.*); *spec.* sun, planet, star, lamp, torch, mortar (*a kind of lamp or candle and candlestick*), will-o'-the-wisp, phosphorescence, comet.
3. *Referring to a window light:* pane; *spec.* bull's-eye, sash.
4. *See* ENLIGHTENMENT, VISION, ASPECT.
light, *v. t.* **1.** *See* IGNITE.
2. brighten, illuminate (*R*), lighten, emblaze (*R*), irradiate, ray (*R*), inflame, lamp (*R*), lantern (*R*), beacon; *spec.* relume.
Antonyms: see DARKEN.
light, *a. Spec.* ethereal, airy, foamy, yeasty, chaffy, feathery, weightless.
Antonyms: see HEAVY, BURDENSOME, DEEP.
See UNIMPORTANT, EASY, DIGESTIBLE, CHEERFUL, LOOSE, DISPARAGING, GENTLE, FRIVOLOUS, AMUSING, ACTIVE.
lighten, *v. t.* **1.** *Spec.* buoy (*with "up"*), levitate, uplift, disburden.
Antonyms: see BURDEN.
2. *See* ALLEVIATE, DIMINISH.
lighten, *v. t.* **1.** *See* BRIGHTEN, LIGHT.
2. fulmine (*R*), fulminate (*R*);—*both terms suggesting the accompanying thunderclap.*
lighter, *n. Spec.* candlelighter, spill, taper, fidibus, spillikin.
lighter, *n. Spec.* boat, scout, scow, gondola (*U. S.*).
lighthead, *n.* rattlebrain, rattlehead (*both S or C*); *spec.* butterfly (*fig.*).
lighthouse, *n.* pharos (*somewhat B or affected*), phare (*R*).
lightness, *n.* levity, flightiness, volatility; *spec.* airiness, *etc. Cf.* LIGHT. *See* FRIVOLITY.
lightning, *n.* levin (*B*), thunderlight (*A*), fire (*contex.*), fulgur (*R*), fulmination; *spec.* bolt, thunderbolt, wildfire.
lightning conductor. lightning rod.
like, *v. t.* approve, savor *or* savour (*A*), love (*C; properly implying a deeper feeling*), fancy; *spec.* relish, enjoy, conceit (*A or Eng. dial.*).
Antonyms: see ABHOR, ABOMINATE, DISLIKE.
likely, *a.* **1.** likable.
2. *See* CREDIBLE, GOOD-LOOKING.
liken, *v. t.* compare, assimilate.
likeness, *n.* **1.** *See* SAMENESS, SIMILARITY, HOMOGENEITY, APPEARANCE.
2. representation (*contex.*), presentment (*R*), counterpart (*contex.*), parallel; *spec.* eidolon (*B*), effigies (*R*), similitude (*rather rhetorical*), semblance, image, effigy, portrait, portraiture (*R*), mask.
likening, *n.* comparison, assimilation.
likewise, *adv. Spec.* similarly.
liking, *n.* approval, shine (*U. S.; S*); *spec.* affinity, fancy, palate (*of mental tastes*), relish, zest, stomach (*chiefly with a negative, as in "to have no stomach for"*), taste, gusto, swallow (*R*), inclination, affection, preference.
Antonyms: see DISLIKE, ABHORRENCE, AVERSION.
limb, *n.* **1.** extremity, member (*contex.*); *spec.* arm, leg, wing, paddle, flipper. *See* LEG.
2. *See* BRANCH.
limber, *v. t.* supple.
limestone, *n. Spec.* calp (*local Irish*), clunch, chalk, kunkur (*India*), tosca, travertin, scaglia, lias, lumachella, marble.
limit, *n.* **1.** boundary, bound, utmost, uttermost (*a less used, but emphatic, equivalent of "utmost"*); *spec.* circumscription (*R*), term, terminous (*R*), date, ne plus ultra (*Latin*), outside (*C*), end, stint, extreme, edge, side, list, qualification, bail, measure, condition. *See* BOUNDARY.
2. *See* PERIOD.
limit, *v. t.* bound; *spec.* circumscribe, condition, compass, stint, measure, qualify, define, tail, confine.
limitation, *n.* boundary; *spec.* circumscription boundedness, qualification, prescription, restriction, confinement, condition, measurement, finiteness.
limited, *a.* bounded, restricted; *spec.* circumscribed, confined, definite, qualified; *see* FINITE.
Antonyms: see INFINITE, BOUNDLESS, INEXHAUSTIBLE, UNQUALIFIED.
limp, *a. Spec.* limpsy (*C, U. S. or dial. Eng.*), flaccid (*wanting in elasticity*), flabby (*wanting in firmness*), loose, flaggy, flimsy (limp *because of unsubstantial construction*), slack, relaxed, lopping, dropping, flagging, hanging, pendulous, loppy.
Antonyms: see STIFF, BRITTLE.
limp, *v. i.* halt (*referring more to the outward effect as seen in the irregular or hesitating gait, while* limp *refers to the defective gait*), hitch (*implying a check or jerk in the gait*); *spec.* hobble (*implying great difficulty, and esp. suggestive of an up and down motion*), hirple (*Scot.*), hop.
line, *v. t.* cover (*contex.*); *spec.* ceil, dress, wad, wainscot, fur, fillet, bush, quilt, fettle, feather, double (*A, exc. her.*), lath, lead, fill.
line, *n.* **1.** band (*contex.*); *spec.* cord, thread, rope, hair, fishline, cable, buntline, string, knittle, towline.

---

light, *a.: bright, blond, pale.*
like, *n.: counterpart.*
like, *conj.: as.*
like, *v. i.: please.*
liked: *acceptable.*
liken: *compare.*
limitable: *terminable.*
limiting: *confining, qualificatory, determinative.*
limitless: *boundless, infinite.*
limn: *describe, depict.*
limpid: *clear.*

2. *Spec.* crease, boundary, transit, score, stroke, cordon, chain, scotch, stria (*tech.*), striation (*tech.*), chord, radius, dash, hyphen, taw, directrix (*math.*), outline, plan, hatch, team, string, queue, seam, creance, verse, equator, fortune, trench, lineage, degree, isobar, isocheim, isodynamic, isocrymal, isogeotherm, isogen, isogonic (*phys. geog.*), isothere, isotherm, isothermal, isotheral, loxodrome.
3. *See* AGREEMENT, COURSE, DIRECTION.
4. file, cue, row, queue, train, string (*C*).
lineal, *a.* linear; *spec.* direct, running.
linen, *n. Spec.* thread, cloth (*collective*), napery (*R, Scot. or U. S.*), line (*A*), écrue (*French*), cuttance (*Anglo-Indian*), lingerie (*collective; French*), lawn, holland, crash.
linen, *a. Spec.* flaxen, hempen (*R*), lawny.
linguist, *n. Spec.* philologist, glossologist (*R*), polyglot, pantoglot.
linguistic, *a. Spec.* philological, Glottic (*R*), glottological *or* glossological.
linguistics, *n.* philology, glottology *or* glossology (*chiefly spec.; R*), linguistry (*R*), logonomy (*nonce word*); *spec.* grammar, phonology, accidence.
lining, *n.* **1.** *Spec.* hatching, ruling, rosework, grating.
2. *Spec.* interlining, facing, inlayer, sheathing, doubling (*chiefly naut.*), doublure (*of a book; ornamental*), wainscot, wadding, brattice *or* brattish, bush, bushing.
link, *n.* bond (*contex.*), juncture (*R or spec.*); *spec.* couple, coupler, bar, ring.
links, *n. pl. or collective sing.* grounds (*pl.; contex.*), golflinks.
lion, *n.* **1.** cat (*contex.*); *spec.* lioness (*fem.*), cub, whelp, lioncel (*chiefly her.*), lionel (*her.*), leopard (*her.*).
2. *See* CELEBRITY.
lip, *n.* **1.** labium (*tech.*); *spec.* harelip, chiloma (*tech.*).
2. edge (*contex.*), labium (*tech.; often spec.*), labrum (*tech.; chiefly spec.*); *spec.* labellum (*tech.*).
lip-shaped, *a.* labiate (*tech.*), labelloid (*R*).
liquefied, *a.* liquid (*contex.*); *spec.* fusile (*R*), molten.
liquefy, *v. t. & i.* fluidify (*contex.; R*), liquidize (*R*); *spec.* fuse, melt, thaw, flux (*old chem.*), liquesce (*R; esp. in v. i.*), deliquesce, liquate, condense, run (*v. i.*).
Antonyms: see SOLIDIFY, COAGULATE, CONGEAL.
liquescent, *a.* liquefying.
liqueur, *n.* liquor (*contex.*), cordial; *spec.* benedictine, chartreuse, curaçao *or* (*less correct*) curaçoa, maraschino, kirschwasser, hippocras (*A or hist.*), ratafia, cherrybounce, persico, persecot, rasolio.
liquid, *a.* **1.** fluid (*applies both to liquid and to gaseous matter*), liquiform (*R*); *spec.* mobile.
Antonyms: see SOLID, VAPOROUS.
2. *See* CLEAR, SMOOTH, CONVERTIBLE.
liquidate, *v. t.* **1.** settle (*the amount due*), fix (*a loose usage*); *see* DETERMINE.
2. settle, acquit (*R*); *spec.* pay.
liquidity, *n.* liquidness, fusion.
liquor, *n.* drink (*contex.; C*), bottle (*fig.; esp. with "the"*), bouse *or* booze (*S*); *spec.* tipple, supernaculum (*B; humorous term*), ribbon (*S*), creature (*B or dial.*), grog, gin, Hollands, schnapps, hogwash (*contemptuous*), liqueur, samshoo, sake, moonshine, spirit, tizwin, tafia, raki, rotgut (*U. S.; S*), rum, nappy, ale, beer, wine, mescal, mead, broo (*Scot.*), bree (*Scot.*), whisky.
list, *n.* **1.** *See* EDGE, STRIP, LIMIT, INCLOSURE, ARENA.
2. *Spec.* inventory, roll (*of members*), muster (*of troops*), series, catalogue, schedule, scroll, scheme, file, brief (*A*), calends (*pl.; R*), panel, docket (*U. S.*), screed, register, ticket (*of candidates*), slate (*of candidates*), row, calendar (*of items to be attended to at a certain date*), nomenclature, cadre (*mil.; French*), bulletin, canon, tariff, schedule, collation, manifest, roster, rota (*Latin*), poll.
list, *v. t. Spec.* inventory, inventorize (*R*), catalogue, schedule, register, inscribe, enter, enroll, enlist, admit, invoice (*commerce*), post (*bookkeeping*), book, bill, slate, leet (*British and chiefly Scot.*), matriculate, manifest (*commerce*), empanel, bulletin, docket, calendar, poll.
listen, *v. i.* attend (*contex.*), list (*A*), hark (*A or B*), hearken *or* harken (*formal or B*), hear, eavesdrop.
listen, *v. t.* hear; *spec.* eavesdrop.
listening, *n.* listen (*chiefly used in "on the listen"*), hearkening; harkening; *spec.* eavesdropping, auscultation; *see* LISTEN.
literally, *adv.* literatim (*Latin*), verbatim et literatim (*Latin*), verbatim (*Latin*).
literary, *a.* educated, learned, literate (*relatively R*), literose (*R; disparaging*), paper (*depreciatory*), inky (*depreciatory*), bookish (*often derogatory*), bluestocking *or* (*for short*) blue (*depreciatory*).
Antonyms: see COLLOQUIAL.
literate, *n.* literatus (*R*), terato (*Italian*), literati (*pl.; scholars or educated men*), clerisy (*collective pl.; A*). "*Literate*" *as a noun is R.*
Antonyms: see IGNORAMUS.
literature, *n.* **1.** *In reference to writings characterized by artistic form or expression:* belles-lettres (*often called "polite literature"*) *or* (*for short*) letters.
2. prospectus, advertising (*commercial*).
litigant, *n.* suitor.
litigation, *n.* contention (*contex.*), lawing (*R or Scot.*); *spec.* law, vitilitigation.
litter, *n.* **1.** couch (*contex.*); *spec.* doolie *or*

lineage: *descent, family, ancestry.*
lineament: *feature, outline.*
linger, *v. i.: delay.*
lingo: *dialect, jargon.*
link, *v. t.: connect, couple, associate.*
listless: *languid, apathetic, dull, faint, sluggish.*
literal: *verbal.*
literate: *learned, literary.*
lithe: *flexible.*

dooly (*Anglo-Indian*), sedan, travail (*R*), dandy, palankeen *or* palanquin, norimono, stretcher, cacolet.

2. *See* BEDDING, ACCUMULATION, DISORDER, BIRTH, OFFSPRING.

little, *n. Spec.* modicum, trifle, whit, jot (*chiefly used in "jot nor tittle"*), tittle (*R, exc. as used with "jot"*), bit (*C*), drop, dab, dash, pittance, touch, pinch, handful, pennyworth (*Eng.*), halfpennyworth (*Eng.*). *"Little" is often used generically, without "a," like "much."*

Antonyms: see MUCH.

littoral, *a.* coastal.

live, *v. i.* **1.** exist (*contex.*), abide (*A; contex.*); *spec.* survive, move (*fig.*), breathe, quicken, number, subsist (*B*).

Antonyms: see DIE.

2. *Referring to the manner or conditions of living: spec.* fare, grow, move, flourish, go, walk, vegetate, crawl, drone, den.

3. *See* FEED, DWELL, FLOAT.

liveliness, *n.* activity, life, vivacity, *etc.*

lively, *a.* **1.** active, alive, spirited, animated (*referring only to mental or emotional activity*), vivacious (*referring to persons only; R, exc. spec.*); *spec.* dashing, effervescent, brisk, quick, buxom (*A*), breezy (*C*), spanking, sparkling, warm, racy, rousing, sharp, sprightly (*often suggesting animation of spirit or wit*), spry (*C, U. S.*), bright, frisky, frisk, volatile, crisp, dapper, pleased, cheerful, gay (*suggests overflowing light-heartedness*), strong.

Antonyms: see INACTIVE, MOTIONLESS, STILL.

2. *See* STIMULATING, BRIGHT, RESPONSIVE, SPIRITED.

liveryman, *n.* stableman (*contex.*), letter, jobber (*Eng.*), jobmaster (*Eng.*).

livid, *a.* leaden, blae (*Scot.*); *spec.* cyanotic.

living, *a.* **1.** alive (*always postpositive or predicative*), live, quick (*A*); *spec.* breathing, organic (*biol.*), organized (*biol.*).

Antonyms: see LIFELESS, DEAD.

2. *See* FLOWING, BURNING, PRESENT.

living, *n.* livelihood (*less concrete, but often more definite, than "living"*), subsistence *or* sustenance (*B*), support, sustentation (*R*), sustainment (*R*), maintenance, cohabitation, cohabitancy (*R*), benefice. *"Living" is R, exc. in "to get, earn, make," etc., "a living."*

lizard, *n.* saurian (*tech.*), lacertian (*tech.*); *spec.* newt, eft, asp, snake, skink, tarentola, marblet, dart, hardim, heloderm, iguana, geitje, gecko, gila monster, galliwasp, guana, dragon, stellion.

lizard, *a.* saurian (*tech.*), lacertine (*tech.*), lacertian (*tech.*).

lizardlike, *a.* sauroid, saurian, lacertiform, lacertian, lacertine;—*all tech., exc.* lizardlike.

load, *n.* **1.** burden; *spec.* cargo, freight, draft, pack, freightage, cargason (*A*), loading (*R*), jag (*U. S. or Eng. dial.*), lading, charge.

2. *See* BURDEN, CHARGE, PRESSURE, RESISTANCE.

load, *v. t.* **1.** burden, lade (*now esp. of a ship, exc. in p. p. "laden"*), weight; *spec.* pile, cumber, freight, hamper.

2. charge (*more formal than load*); *spec.* double-shot, slug, shot, lead, overcharge.

Antonyms: see DISCHARGE.

3. *See* ADULTERATE.

loaded, *a.* **1.** burdened, laden (*spec. "heavily laden"*), heavy, freighted.

2. *Referring to a firearm:* charged; *spec.* live, shotted.

loadstone, *n.* lodestone, lode (*A or R*), magnet (*min.*).

loaf, *n. Spec.* twist, cob, brick, loaflet, manchet (*A*), roll, block.

loafer, *n.* idler; *spec.* larrikin, wharf rat (*cant*), lazzarone (*Italian*), beggar, bum (*S, U. S.*).

loan, *v. t.* lend. *These words commonly used interchangeably in U. S.; but* loan *properly implies a financial transaction only whereas* lend *is unrestricted. The noun* loan *applies both to what is* loaned *and to what is* lent.

lobby, *n.* hall (*contex.*), foyer (*chiefly spec.; French*); *spec.* hallway (*U. S.*), anteroom, entrance.

lobe, *n.* division (*contex.*); *spec.* fluke, lappet, auricle, insula, wing.

lobed, *a.* divided (*contex.*), lobate, lobated, auriculate, invected (*chiefly her.*).

lobster, *n.* decapod (*contex.*); *spec.* homarine, shedder, crayfish (*chiefly Eng.*).

local, *a. Spec.* regional, regionary (*R*), sectional, provincial, topical *or* topic (*R or tech.*), territorial, epichorial (*R*).

Antonyms: see GENERAL, UNIVERSAL, WIDESPREAD, WORLDWIDE.

localize, *n. Spec.* territorialize, provincialize, concentrate, limit, place.

lock, *n. Spec.* tress, flake (*A*), ringlet, curl, cowlick, elflock, forelock, flock (*of a tuft or bunch that clings together*).

lock, *n.* fastening (*contex.*); *spec.* padlock, latch, bolt, key.

lock, *v. t.* **1.** fix (*contex.*), fasten (*contex.*); *spec.* latch, bolt, padlock.

2. fasten (*contex.*); *spec.* embrace, close, grapple, interlock, interlink.

lodge, *n.* **1.** *See* HOUSE, COTTAGE.

2. *Referring to any place where one lodges or rests: spec.* camp, canton, quarter, doss (*S or cant*), bench, burrow, tent, dwelling.

3. *See* BRANCH.

lodge, *v. t.* **1.** accommodate; *spec.* bed, house, inn (*R*), burrow, billet, quarter, kennel (*often fig.*), nestle, nest (*a more literal word than "nestle"*), embower, tent, guest.

2. *See* DEPOSIT, SHELTER, VEST.

lodge, *v. i.* **1.** dwell, roost (*C*), harbor (*A or*

live, *a.: living, energetic, burning, electrified, loaded.*
loaf, *v. i.: idle.*
loath: *unwilling.*
loathe: *dislike, abhor.*
loathing: *aversion, abhorrence, disgust.*
loathsome: *abominable, disgusting.*

R); *spec.* room (*U. S.*), bunk, bed, night (*R*), cabin, quarter, hut.
2. *Spec.* fall (*contex.*), settle, light, alight, lie (*A*), nestle, nest.
lodger, *n.* roomer (*U. S.*), dosser (*S or cant*).
lodging, *n.* **1.** lodgment; *spec.* depositing.
2. *In pl.* lodgment (*R*), accommodation; *spec.* dwelling, apartment, housing, barracks (*pl.*), cantonment, rooms (*pl.; C*).
loft, *n.* **1.** *Spec.* attic, traverse (*architecture*), gallery, fly, jube, haymow, hayloft, factory, warehouse (*N. Y.*).
2. *See* STOREROOM.
log, *n.* **1.** *Spec.* block, stump, stock (*A or B*).
2. *See* RECORD.
logic, *n.* **1.** *Spec.* dialectic *or* (*more commonly*) dialectics.
2. *See* REASONING.
logical, *a.* sound (*of correct reasoning*), legitimate (*of being permitted or proper because showing good reasoning*), valid; *spec.* raisonné (*French*), competent, correct, clear-headed, argumentative, dialectic.
Antonyms: see ABSURD, ILLOGICAL, INCONSEQUENT, INCONSISTENT.
logician, *n.* *Spec.* Ramist, logicaster (*R*), dialectician.
loin, *n.* reins (*pl.*), fillet (*esp. of an animal*); *spec.* griskin.
loincloth, *n.* pagne (*French*), dhoti *or* dhootie (*Anglo-Indian*), lungi (*East Indian*).
lonely, *a.* **1.** *See* ALONE.
2. unfrequented, lone (*B or A*), solitary (*suggests the feeling of isolation*), forlorn (*A*), lonesome (*unhappy for lack of companionship*), lorn (*B or A*), only (*R or dial.*); *spec.* desolate, retired.
3. depressing, lonesome (*less common than "lonely" in this sense*), dreary, drear (*R*), bleak, drearisome (*R*); *spec.* gloomy, fearful, dismal.
4. *See* DEPRESSED.
long, *a.* *Spec.* longish, lengthy (*too* long, *or rather* long), extended, elongate *or* elongated, great, long-drawn, far (*idiomatically used as in "a far way," "a far cry," etc.*), prolix (*R, exc. in reference to discourse*), mortal (*implying tedium; S*).
Antonyms: see SHORT, BRIEF.
long, *v. i.* yearn (*more rhetorical than "long"*), repine, hunger (*fig.*), thirst (*fig.*); *spec.* pine, hanker (*C*), crave, lust, pant, groan, yawn, sigh, weep, cry, moan, *etc.*
long-headed, *a.* **1.** *Spec.* dolichocephalic, macrocephalic, macrocephalous;—*all three tech.*
2. *See* DISCERNING.
longing, *n.* desire, yearning, hunger (*fig.*), thirst (*fig.*); *spec.* hankering (*C*), craving, panting, lust, dipsomania, appetite, *etc.*
Antonyms: see AVERSION.
longing, *a.* yearning, hungry (*fig.*), thirsty (*fig.; spec.*), panting, hankering (*C*), wistful, craving, lustful, *etc.*
longitudinal, *a.* lengthwise, endwise.
long-lived, *a.* longevous (*B*), longeval (*R*), longæval (*R*), macrobian (*R*), vivacious (*R*).
Antonyms: see EPHEMERAL.
look, *v. i.* **1.** *See* SEE.
2. behold (*A or B*), see (*obs., exc. imperative*); *spec.* peep, peer, gaze, squint, retrospect, introspect, outpeep (*poetic*).
3. *See* APPEAR, EXAMINE, EXPECT, FACE, ATTEND.
look, *n.* **1.** *See* SIGHT.
2. regard (*R*), eyebeam (*A and R*), eye (*fig.*), looking, eyeshot (*R, exc. spec.*); *spec.* blush, glance, cast (*by turning the eye, esp. momentarily*), ken (*R*), retrospect, introspect, languish, gaze, peep, peer, squint, ogle, lookout, leer.
3. *See* EXPRESSION, FRONT, APPEARANCE, ASPECT.
lookout, *n.* **1.** *See* LOOK.
2. *Referring to the place:* outlook, observatory; *spec.* gazebo, belvedere, tower, cupola, crow's-nest.
loom, *v. i.* *Spec.* appear, bulk.
loop, *n.* fold (*contex.*), bend (*contex.*), ring; *spec.* hank (*as of yarn*), bight (*in a rope*), link, bow, billet, pearl, coil, crupper, ear, buckle, staple, coque, eye, picot, noose, purl, sling, frog.
loop, *v. t.* **1.** fold (*contex.*), bind (*contex.*), ring; *spec.* noose, coil, kink.
2. *See* ENCIRCLE.
loophole, *n.* hole (*contex.*), aperture (*contex.*), vent (*R*); *spec.* meuse *or* muse (*R*), embrasure.
loose, *a.* **1.** free (*from attachment, restriction, etc.*); *spec.* open, light, disconnected, slack, incoherent, detached, incompact *or* uncompacted, graspless, crank *or* cranky, uncombined.
Antonyms: see TIGHT, FIRM.
2. *Referring to the bowels:* lax (*less emphatic than "loose"*), open, relaxed; *spec.* dysenterical, diarrheal, scoury (*C*).
Antonyms: see CONSTIPATED.
3. *See* INEXACT, EASY, IMMORAL, LAX, DISCURSIVE.
loose, *v. t.* **1.** free, unloose (*more emphatic than "loose"*), unloosen (*R*); *spec.* release, slacken, slack, unrein, disengage, undo, untie, unbolt, unlock, unbind, unpack, unfix, slip, unclasp, unbrace, unhasp, untether, unbuckle, unsling, unshackle, unscrew, unstring, unstick, unharness, unyoke, untruss, untrace, unchain, trip, unmoor, unpin, unlace, unlash, unanchor, uncord.
Antonyms: see BIND, FASTEN, CLUTCH, CONFINE.

lofty: *high, elevated, exalted, generous, bombastic, dignified.*
loiter: *delay.*
loll: *droop, idle.*
lone: *alone, unmarried, lonely.*
lonesome: *lonely.*
longevity: *long-livedness.*
long-suffering: *patient.*
long-winded: *prolix.*
loot: *plunder.*
lop, *v. t.: cut, chop.*
lope, *n.: gait.*
lope, *v. i.: go.*

2. *Spec.* free, release, disengage, relax, *etc.*
lord, *n.* lording (*esp. in address; A or an equiv. of "lordling"*); *spec.* master, proprietor, liege, seignor, thakur (*East India*), laird (*Scot.*), kami (*Japanese*), samurai (*Japanese*), suzerain, señor (*Spanish*), signor (*Italian*), husband, Jehovah, Christ.
Antonyms: see VASSAL, SUBJECT.
lordship, *n.* **1.** *See* RULE.
2. estate (*contex.*), domain, lairdship (*Scot.*); free, suzerainty, seigniory, seignory, signory, mesnalty, castellany.
3. *See* DOMAIN.
lorry, *n.* van (lorry *and* van *are chiefly Brit.*), truck, vehicle (*contex.*), rolley (*dial. Eng.*).
lose, *v. t.* **1.** *See* DEPRIVE, FORFEIT.
2. *Spec.* drop (*S*), sink, miss, sacrifice (*cant*), pretermit, waste, dice.
Antonyms: see CLEAR, RECOVER, WIN.
loss, *n.* **1.** *See* RUIN.
2. detriment; *spec.* sacrifice (*cant*), cost, hurt, forfeiture, average, deperdition (*R*), penalty, damage, leakage, death, casualties (*pl.; military*), disadvantage. *"Deprivation" as compared with "loss" considers the detriment from the point of view of the one deprived.*
Antonyms: see GAIN, ACQUISITION, COMPENSATION, PROFIT.
lost, *a. Spec.* forfeit, unredeemed, astray, absent; *see* ABANDONED, RUINED.
lot, *n.* **1.** counter, sors (*Latin; pl.* sortes).
2. *Spec.* division, share, destiny, quantity, plot, dole.
lottery, *n.* gamble; *spec.* tombola, little-go (*hist.*), raffle.
loud, *a.* **1.** big (*used esp. of the voice or of a noise*), strong (*as requiring or suggesting strength or violence*); *spec.* heavy, high, stentorian (*very loud*), clamant (*B*), crying, roaring, clamorous, sonorous, noisy, outspoken, strident; flashy, ostentatious (*of taste in clothing, etc.*).
Antonyms: see SILENT.
2. *Referring to what makes a loud noise: spec.* noisy, clamorous, sonorous.
Antonyms: see SILENT.
3. *See* VIVID, FLASHY.
loudly, *adv.* aloud, loud, big, bigly (*R*); *spec.* heavily, forte. (*Italian*).
loud-voiced, *a.* stentorian.
louse, *n.* parasite (*contex.*), creeper (*vulgar*); *spec.* cootie (*S*), nit, ked, crab (*S*).
lousiness, *n.* pediculosis, phthiriasis;—*both tech.*
lousy, *a.* pedicular (*R*), pediculous (*tech.*); *spec.* nitty (*R*), poor (*S*), inferior (*S*).
lovable, *a.* amiable (*slighter in appeal than* lovable, *which implies that which is worthy of love*), lovesome (*A*); *spec.* loveworthy.
lovableness, *n.* amiability, loveworth, lovesomeness (*A*); *spec.* loveworthiness, honey (*referring to one's manner*).
love, *n.* **1.** amour (*obs.*), feeling (*contex.*), attachment; *spec.* affection, adoration, idolism *or* idolatry, idolization, passion, fondness.
Antonyms: see HATRED, DISLIKE, ABHORRENCE, AVERSION, ILL-WILL.
2. *As personified: spec.* Eros (*Greek*), Amor (*Latin*), Cupid (*Latin*), Venus (*R*).
3. beloved (*A or formal*), inamorata (*fem.*), inamorato (*masc.*), *both Italian; spec.* idol, ladylove.
4. *See* AMOUR, LIKING.
5. *In tennis, etc.:* nothing.
love, *v. t.* **1.** belove (*chiefly in passive*), cherish; *spec.* adore, idolize, idolatrize.
Antonyms: see HATE, ABHOR, ABOMINATE.
2. *See* LIKE.
loved, *a.* dear, beloved, lief (*A*).
love letter, *n.* billet-doux (*French*).
love making, *n.* courtship (*usually referring to honorable love making*), gallantry (*esp. illicit*), service (*A*).
lover, *n.* admirer (*contex.*), sweetheart, steady (*S; vulgar*), servant (*A*), leman (*A or B*); *spec.* beau, gallant, squire (*A*), cavalier (*A*), follower (*C*), chamberer, spark (*C*), idolizer, Daphnis (*fig.*), inamorato (*masc.; Italian*), ladylove, truelove, cicisbeo (*Italian*), cavaliere servente (*Italian*), paramour.
lovesick, *a.* languishing (*contex.*), lovelorn.
low, *v. i.* cry (*contex.*), bellow, moo (*less usual than "low"*), boo (*R*).
low, *a.* **1.** short (*as opposed to tall*), little (*as opposed to big*), base (*A*); *spec.* depressed, down.
Antonyms: see HIGH.
2. *Referring to relative position: spec.* abject, depressed, profound, basal.
Antonyms: see HIGH.
3. *See* LOWLY, DEGRADED, COARSE, DEPRESSED, WEAK, BASE.
4. *Emphasizing the absence of, or incompatibility with, refinement or good ideals:* unrefined, vulgar; *spec.* plebeian, base, lousy (*fig.; contemptuous and vulgar or undignified*), dirty (*coarsely contemptuous*), contemptible, depraved.
Antonyms: see EXALTED.
5. *Referring to pitch of sound:* grave, deep, heavy; *spec.* flat, bass.
Antonyms: see HIGH, SHRILL.
6. *In reference to audibility of sound:* weak, gentle, still; *spec.* subdued.
lower, *a.* inferior, nether (*B*); *spec.* under, subjacent.
Antonyms: see HIGHER.
lower, *v. t.* **1.** *Spec.* depress, demit (*R*), dip, flatten, lay (*naut.*), shorten (*naut.*), couch, douse (*naut.*), sink, duck, drop, strike.
Antonyms: see RAISE, LIFT.

lord, *v. i.: domineer.*
lounge, *v. i.: idle, rest.*
lour: *frown, threaten.*
lout: *boor.*
love affair: *amour.*
lovely: *lovable, agreeable, beautiful.*
loving: *affectionate.*
low-born: *humble.*
low-bred: *boorish.*
lower, *v. i.: frown, threaten.*

2. *See* ABATE, DEGRADE, DEPRECIATE, DIMINISH, ABASE.
3. *Referring to sound:* deepen, grave (*R*); *spec.* flatten.
lower, *v. i. Referring to the countenance:* fall, cloud, threaten.
lowest, *a.* lowermost (*more formal than "lowest"*), nethermost (*B or R*), last (*chiefly spec.*).
Antonyms: see HIGHEST.
lowland, *a.* lallan (*Scot.*).
lowland, *n.* lallan (*Scot.*); *spec.* valley.
Antonyms: see UPLAND.
lowliness, *n.* humbleness, ignobleness (*R or spec.*), ignobility (*R*), lowlihead (*R or A*), humility, *etc.*
lowly, *a.* **1.** humble (*implying self-depreciation*), ignoble (*lacking in worthiness or honor*), base, low, mean, vulgar (*primarily spec.; A*); *spec.* small, obscure.
Antonyms: see NOBLE.
2. *See* INFERIOR, MODEST.
low-necked, *a. Spec.* décolleté (*French*).
low-priced, *a.* cheap.
lozenge, *n. Spec.* pastil, tabloid, tablet, tablette, drop, peppermint.
lozenge, *n.* rhombus *or* rhomb (*geom.*), diamond (*used esp. in reference to decorative features*).
lozenge-shaped, *a.* rhomboidal, rhomboid, rhombeous (*R*), rhombic;—*all B or tech.*
l-shaped, *a.* lambdoid *or* lambdoidal (*tech.*).
lubricant, *n.* lubricator, dope (*U. S.; S*); *spec.* oil, grease, graphite, slush, *etc.*
Antonyms: see ABRASIVE.
lubricate, *v. t.* lubrify (*R*), dope (*S; U. S.*); *spec.* oil, grease, slush.
luminescent, *a.* luminous (*contex.*); *spec.* phosphorescent, phosphoreous (*R*), phosphoric, fluorescent, noctilucent *or* noctilucous (*R*), triboluminescent.
Antonyms: see DARK.
luminosity, *n.* self-luminousness, luminousness; *spec.* brightness, brilliance, shine, shining, splendor, refulgence, effulgence, bright (*B*), lightfulness (*R*), fulgor, lightness, lightsomeness, lucency (*both R*), lucidity, lucidness, illumination, fire, flame, flare, glare, brilliance, blaze, dazzle, dazzlingness, incandescency, luminescence.
luminous, *a.* **1.** self-luminous (*full of its own light*), radiant (*shedding brightness; chiefly spec.*), radiative (*R*); *spec.* bright (*contex.*), brilliant, shining, lucid (*B or tech.*), splendid, splendorous *or* splendrous, fulgent, effulgent (*used esp. with a good connotation*), refulgent, lucible (*R*), lucent (*R*), luculent (*R*), incandescent *or* candescent, breme (*A or B*), lightful (*R*), glaring, flaring, glowing, illuminated (*made bright by light shed on it*), sparkling, coruscant, dazzling, flaming, sunny, burning.
Antonyms: see DARK.
2. *See* CLEAR, INTELLIGIBLE.
lump, *n.* **1.** mass; *spec.* collection (*contex.*), hunk, clot, clod, clout (*R or dial.*), clump, nugget, pat, knot, dab, chunk.
2. *See* PROTUBERANCE.
lumpy, *a. Spec.* cloddy, clumpy, flaky, clumpish (*R*), lumpish, clubbed, knotty, cloggy.
lunacy, *n. See* DERANGEMENT, ANGER, ECSTASY, FOOLISHNESS.
lunar, *a.* lunary (*R*), Cynthian (*B*); *spec.* crescent-shaped.
lunch, *n.* meal (*contex.*), luncheon, déjeuner (*French*); *spec.* snack, tiffin (*Anglo-Indian*).
lung, *n.* lights (*pl.; now chiefly or only spec.*).
lung, *a.* pulmonary, pulmonal (*R*), pulmonic (*R*);—*all* (*B*) *or tech.*
lurk, *v. i.* **1.** hide (*contex.*), snook *or* snoke (*chiefly northern Eng. or Scot.*), harbor (*A*); *spec.* skulk, couch.
2. *See* BE, SNEAK.
luster, *n.* **1.** *Referring to reflected light: spec.* shining, brightness, sheen (*suggesting strong and steady light*), brilliance (*intense light*), gloss (*of a smooth or polished surface, esp. as artificially produced or differing from the texture of the substance beneath*), glaze, reflet (*French*), lucency (*R*), refulgence, refulgency, splendor, resplendence, bright (*B*), burnish, dazzle (*baffling to the eyes*), dazzlingness, gleam, sparkle, fire, glitter (*hard and cold sparkle*), silver, gold, schiller.
2. *See* FAME, BEAUTY.
lustrous, *a.* **1.** *Referring to reflection of light: spec.* bright (*contex.*), brilliant, shining, clear (*implying purity and evenness of luster*), nitid (*R*), burnished, glossy, shiny, vivid (*very bright*), lusterful, sheeny, chatoyant (*of changeable light*), silken, silky, satiny, glittering, silvery, golden, coruscant, polished, pearly.
Antonyms: see DEAD.
2. *See* FAMOUS, BEAUTIFUL.
luxuriant, *a.* **1.** lusty (*A*), thrifty; *spec.* exuberant (*implying excess beyond bounds*), effuse, rank (*implying coarse, offensive or unhealthy growth*), gross, flourishing, lush (*implying succulence, esp. such as pleases*), jungly, wild, rampant.
Antonyms: see BARREN.
2. *See* PRODUCTIVE, ABUNDANT, FLORID.
luxurious, *a.* **1.** *Spec.* elegant (*refined*), rich, voluptuous, sumptuous (*implying great expense, often ostentation*), sybaritic *or* sybaritical,

---

low-spirited: *depressed.*
loyal: *constant.*
lubber: *clown, seaman.*
lucid: *luminous, clear, intelligible.*
luck: *chance, fortune.*
lucky: *fortunate.*
lucre: *profit, wealth.*
lucubrate: *work, discourse.*
ludicrous: *laughable, absurd.*
lug, *v. t.: draw.*
luggage: *baggage.*
lugubrious: *depressing, depressed, mournful, sorrowful.*
lull, *n.: intermission.*
lumber, *n.: refuse, timber.*
lump, *v. t.: gather, unite, dislike.*
lumpish: *lumpy, dull.*
lunatic, *n.: deranged person.*
lurid: *ghastly, cloudy, fiery.*
lurking: *hidden.*
luscious: *pleasant, sensuous.*
lush: *luxuriant.*
lust, *n.: desire.*
lust, *v. i.: long.*
lustful: *desirous, lascivious.*

Corinthian, Lydian, mollitious (*R*), high, epicurean, downy, silken, superb, splendid.
Antonyms: see SIMPLE.
2. *See* COMFORTABLE.
luxury, *n.* **1.** *Spec.* elegance, elegancy, richness, voluptuousness, sumptuousness, luxuriousness, sybaritism, delicacy, epicureanism.
Antonyms: see SIMPLICITY.
2. *See* COMFORT, ENJOYMENT.
lye, *n.* lixivium (*tech.*); *spec.* buck, bate, bittern.
lying, *a.* equivocatory (*R and spec. or euphemistic*), pseudology (*R*), false, truthless, mendacious (*B; given to false statement*); *spec.* fabulous, fabling.
Antonyms: see FRANK.
lying, *n.* equivocation (*spec. or euphemistic and less offensive than "lying"*), falsehood, mendacity (*learned and less offensive than "lying"*); *spec.* fabling, prevarication; *cf.* LIE.
lying-in, *n.* accouchement (*French*).
lyre, *n.* shell (*B*); *spec.* trigon.
lyre-shaped, *a.* lyriform (*B or tech.*), lyrate *or* lyrated (*tech.*).
lyric, *n.* poem (*contex.*); *spec.* epode, madrigal, canzone (*Italian*), melic.

M

machine, *n.* **1.** contrivance (*contex.*), apparatus, gin (*A, exc. spec.*); *spec.* automaton, lever, lathe, motor, loom, crab, vehicle, press, die, billy, *etc.*
2. *See* PERSON, ORGANIZATION.
machinery, *n.* **1.** *See* MEANS.
2. apparatus, enginery (*chiefly fig. or spec.*); *spec.* clockwork.
machinist, *n.* mechanist (*R*), mechanic, mechanician.
mad, *a.* **1.** *See* DERANGED, FRANTIC, INFATUATED, GAY, ANGRY.
2. *Referring to dogs:* rabies (*tech.*).
madam, *n.* ma'am (*C*), madonna (*Italian*), signora (*Italian*), senhora (*Portuguese*), señora (*Spanish*), madame (*French*).
madman, *n.* bedlamite (*A or B*); *spec.* raver.
madness, *n.* **1.** *See* DERANGEMENT, ANGER, ECSTASY, FOOLISHNESS.
2. *Referring to dogs:* rabies (*tech.*)
magic, *n.* thaumaturgy (*B; performance of miracles and wonders*); *spec.* necromancy (*chiefly prophecy through consulting spirits of the dead*), black art, black magic, enchantment (*emphasizing use of charms*), sorcery, diabolism, devilry, deviltry *or* diablerie, Magianism, witchcraft *or* witchery (*emphasizing the use of* spells), bewitchery, conjuration *or* conjury, incantation, glamour, glamoury *or* (*revived in B use by Scott*) gramarye (*chiefly used in "cast a glamour over"*), pishouge (*Irish*), wizardry, malefice (*A*), goety (*A*), cantation (*R*), fascination (*A or hist.*), myalism (*West Indies, etc.*), obeah *or* obi (*negro*), epode (*R*), voodoo, hoodoo (*U. S.*), exorcism, theurgy, spell.
See JUGGLERY, INFLUENCE.
magical, *a.* thaumaturgic *or* thaumaturgical (*B*), enchanting; *spec.* sorcerous, necromantic, Chaldean, diabolic, diabolical, occult (*as being hidden from the general*), mystical, druidic *or* druidical, talismanic, hermetic *or* hermetical (*because Hermes Trismegistus was reputed a magician*), incantatory, alchemical.
magician, *n.* *Spec.* conjurer, necromancer, sorcerer, sorceress, wizard, diabolist, incantator, witch, evocator *or* evocatrix, seer, tregetour (*A*), warlock, enchanter, enchantress, archimage, mage (*A*), pellar *or* peller (*dial.*), exorcist, fetishere *or* fetisher, medicine man, Magus, powwow, voodoo, Druid, Circe, diviner, divineress, Magian, Shaman.
magic lantern, stereopticon; *spec.* megascope.
magistrate, *n.* authority (*a fig. use*); *spec.* duumvir, triumvir, decemvir, eponym, burgomaster, bencher, prefect, president, mayor, consul, recorder, tribune, sovereign, warden, vizir, vizier, landdrost, demiurge, doge, ephete, ephor, proprætor, kotwal, judge, *etc.*
magnate, *n.* *Spec.* grandee (*orig. Spanish or Portuguese*), panjandrum (*derisive*), Mogul (*fig.*), bashaw (*fig.*), Magnifico (*ancient Venetian*), tycoon (*C; U. S.*), king (*C; U. S.*), baron (*C; U. S.*).
Antonyms: See NOBODY.
magnify, *v. t.* **1.** *See* PRAISE, EXAGGERATE.
2. enlarge; *spec.* microscope (*R*), gigantize.
maid, *n.* virgin, spinster. *See also* MAIDSERVANT.
maidservant, *n.* servant (*contex.*), maid, girl, help, wench (*contemptuous or humorous*); *spec.* handmaid *or* handmaiden (*A or fig.*), abigail (*fig.*), ancilla (*a Latinism*), biddy (*Irish; C*), bonne (*French*), slavey (*S, contemptuous, or Brit. C*), matranee (*India*), housemaid. *See also* MANSERVANT.
mail, *n.* *As a collective sing.:* letters (*pl.*), matter, post (*chiefly Eng.*); *spec.* tappal (*East India*).
mail, *v. t.* post; *spec.* drop.
maim, *v. t.* cripple, bemaim (*intensive*); *spec.* deface, mutilate (*both contex.*), truncate, pinion, hamstring.
maiming, *n.* crippling, mayhem (*law*), demembration (*chiefly Scots law*); *spec.* truncation.
mainland, *n.* land, main (*A*), continent (*chiefly spec.*).

M

macaronic: *confused, burlesque.*
made: *artificial.*
made-up: *artificial, false.*
madhouse: *asylum.*
magisterial: *arrogant, dogmatic, authoritative, commanding, dictatorial.*
magnanimous: *generous.*
magnet: *loadstone, attraction.*
magnetic: *hypnotic, attractive.*
magnetism: *energy, attraction, hypnotism.*
magnificent: *grand, imposing, elevated, exalted, fine.*
magniloquent: *bombastic.*
magnitude: *size, extent, quantity.*
maid: *girl, virgin, domestic.*
mail, *v. t.: post.*
maim: *mutilate.*
main, *a.: powerful, chief, utmost.*

Antonyms: see ISLAND.

maintain, *v. t.* (*keep in some particular state or condition*). *Spec.* sustain, continue, defend, support, preserve, vindicate, assert, fight, insist (*often with "that"*), keep, hold, retain.

Antonyms: see ALTER, ABJURE.

maintenance, *n. Spec.* continuation, defense, vindication, support, assertion, aid, living, keeping, holding.

maize, *n.* grain, Indian corn (*U. S.*), corn (*U. S.*), mealies (*pl.; South Africa*).

majority, *n.* **1.** adulthood.

2. mass (*esp. in "the masses and the classes"*), bulk, preponderance; *spec.* plurality.

Antonym: see MINORITY.

make, *v. t.* **1.** *Spec.* produce, cause, effect, form, manufacture, feel, constitute, confect (*affected, after French*), do, fashion, forge, establish, attempt, enact, consider, count, advance, clear, construct, contract, create, prepare, traverse, compose, turn (*as, to turn one sick, black, etc.*), strike (*a bargain, etc.*), take, brew (*often fig.*), levy, pick, cut, light, bore, coin, paint, draw, execute (*as a painting*), work, *etc.*

making, *n.* doing (*contex.*), facture (*B*), manufacture.

malcontent, *n. Spec.* agitator, irreconcilable, malignant (*R*).

male, *a.* **1.** he (*opposed to "she"; chiefly used attributively*), masculine.

Antonyms: see FEMALE.

2. *See* MANLY.

male, *n.* he; *spec.* tom- (*in combination*), jack- (*in combination*), man, boy, ox, bull, rooster, milter, dog, stag, buck.

Antonyms: see FEMALE.

malevolence, *n.* dislike (*contex.*), malignance, rancor, venom, ill-will; *spec.* hate, hatred, despite.

Antonyms: see COMPASSION.

malevolent, *a.* (*disposed to do evil or to injure*), black (*fig.*), black-hearted, malign, malignant, ill, rancorous, virulent, viperish, reptile; *spec.* evil, hateful, baleful, fiendish.

Antonyms: see BENEVOLENT, KINDLY, COMPASSIONATE.

malfeasance, *n.* evildoing, delinquence (*contex.*); *spec.* criminality, misdemeanance, malversation (*tech.*).

malfeasor, *n.* evildoer, malfeasant (*tech.*), delinquent (*contex.*); *spec.* criminal, convict, felon, bushranger, gallows, gallowsbird, *etc.*

mallet, *n.* hammer; *spec.* gavel (*U. S.*).

man, *n.* **1.** *See* PERSON, MANKIND, HUSBAND, VASSAL, SERVANT, EMPLOYEE, MANLINESS, PIECE.

2. gentleman (*only in address or by way of courtesy; used chiefly in pl.*), fellow (*familiar*), groom (*A*), boy (*in familiar address*), microcosm (*B, or philosophical*); *spec.* heart, buck (*S*), egg (*S*), Caliban, Betty, Molly, Peggy, cot, cotbetty (*U. S.*).

Antonyms: see WOMAN.

man, *v. t. Spec.* garrison, people.

manacle, *n.* band (*contex.*), handcuff (*the ordinary informal term*), snitcher (*S*), nippers (*pl.; S*), wristlet (*humorous*).

manage, *v. t.* **1.** control, conduct, order, boss (*S*), regulate; *spec.* direct, handle, guide, misgovern, operate (*chiefly U. S.*), negotiate (*chiefly C or S*), swing, administer, manipulate, wield (*often fig.*), engineer, navigate, maneuver, nurse, fight, hold, work.

2. *See* ACCOMPLISH, AFFORD, CONTRIVE.

manage, *v. i. Spec.* frame, do, shift (*by using makeshifts*), contrive.

manageable, *a. Spec.* governable, conformable, tractile, tractable, gentle (*of an animal*), flexible (*implying a ready yielding to others*), ductile, docile, buxom (*A*), pliable, pliant, handy (*naut.*), wieldy, toward *or* towardly (*A*), advisable (*R*), teachable, *etc.*

Antonyms: see UNMANAGEABLE, UNRULY, INTRACTABLE, OBSTINATE, PERVERSE, UNWIELDY.

management, *n.* **1.** control, regulation, carriage (*chiefly Eng.*); *spec.* conduct, guidance, administration, operation (*chiefly U. S.*), economy, operation, husbandry, ordinance (*R or A*), dispensation, diplomacy, *etc.*

2. *See* ACCOMPLISHMENT.

3. *Spec.* board, directory, directorate.

manager, *n.* controller; *spec.* conductor, operator, guide, dispenser (*A*), wielder, impresario (*Italian*), economist, manoeuvrer, engineer, curator, overseer, steward.

manger, *n. Spec.* cratch (*A*), crib, trough, box.

mangle, *v. t.* **1.** (*implying bruises or dismemberment as by repeated blows*), deface; *spec.* cut, slash, mince, hash, butcher, hasp.

2. *Referring to words, music, etc.: spec.* murder, mouth, gargle, bungle, mutilate.

manhater, *n.* misanthrope, misanthropist.

man-hating, *a.* misanthropic.

Antonyms: see AMATORY.

manhood, *n.* **1.** *As distinguished from "womanhood":* virility (*learned*).

2. *See* MANLINESS, COURAGE.

manifold, *v. t.* multiply; *spec.* graph (*C*), hectograph.

manifold, *n.* copy; *spec.* graph (*C*), cyclostyle, polygraph, hectograph, mimeograph.

manipulate, *v. t.* **1.** *See* HANDLE, FINGER, MASSAGE, WIELD.

2. manage; *spec.* jockey, shuffle, rig (*S or C; suggesting quick changes in price made by secret dealings*), milk (*cant or S*).

mankind, *n.* man (*less formal than "man-*

---

mainstay: *support.*
majestic: *dignified, grand.*
majesty: *dignity, grandeur.*
major: *greater, adult.*
make, *v. i.: constitute.*
makeshift, *a.: provisional.*
make-up: *composition, arrangement.*
malady: *disease.*
malice: *ill-will.*
malignity: *malevolence, ill-will.*
mandate: *bidding.*
manhandle: *move, handle.*
maniac, *n.: deranged person.*
manifestation: *appearance, disclosure, show.*
manifold: *diversified.*

kind"), men (*pl.*), humanity, humankind (*unusual*), flesh (*fig.*), earth (*with "the"*).
Antonyms: see WOMANKIND.
manliness, *n.* manhood (*A*), manlihood (*R*), masculinity, mannishness, manlikeness, virility.
Antonyms: see EFFEMINACY, FEMININITY.
manly, *a.* (*stressing the more admirable attributes*), male, masculine (*chiefly spec.*), manful (*often spec.*), virile (*stressing attributes of developed manhood*), manlike (*chiefly spec.; referring to weak or unworthy qualities, such as assertiveness, cocksureness, etc.*), mannish (*chiefly spec. and contemptuous, implying qualities of men out of place in, or affected by, a woman or child*).
Antonyms: see CHILDISH, FEMININE, WOMANLY, LADYLIKE.
manner, *n.* **1.** *See* KIND.
2. way, mode, sort (*A*), fashion (*R, exc. spec. with "after," "in," etc.*).
3. *In pl.:* etiquette; *spec.* breeding.
4. *See* CUSTOM, AIR, BEHAVIOR.
man-of-war, *n.* ship (*contex.*); *spec.* battleship, cruiser, dreadnought, superdreadnought, torpedo boat, aircraft carrier, destroyer, gunboat, submarine, submersible.
manservant, *n.* man (*contex; C*); *spec.* footman, flunky *or* flunkey, valet, gyp (*cant; Eng.*), boy (*chiefly South African or Anglo-Indian*), butler, waiter, cook, *etc.; see* LACKEY.
Antonyms: see MAIDSERVANT.
mantle, *n.* **1.** cloak; *spec.* chasuble (*eccl.*), toga, tallitto, pelisse, chuddar (*Anglo-Indian*).
2. *See* COVER, ENVELOPE, FOAM.
3. mantelpiece, chimneypiece.
manure, *n.* fertilizer (*contex.*), dung (*R*), muck, soil (*R or A*); *spec.* folding (*Eng.*), tankage, guano.
manure, *v. t.* fertilize (*contex.*), soil (*R or A*), dung (*R*), bedung (*intensive; R*).
manuscript, *n.* **1.** document (*contex.*); *spec.* palimpsest, codex, opisthograph (*tech.*).
Antonyms: see PRINT.
2. *See* WRITING.
many, *a.* numerous; *spec.* frequent, multiplied, manifold, multitudinous, multifold.
Antonyms: see FEW, ALL.
many-colored, *a.* polychromic, polychromatic, polychrome;—*all* (*B*) *or tech.*
Antonyms: see ONE-COLORED.
many-footed, *a.* multiped, multipede;—*both learned or tech.*
many-headed, *a.* polycephalic (*R*).
many-jointed, *a.* multiarticulate (*tech.*).
many-named, *a.* polyonymous (*R*), pœcilonymic (*R*).
many-seeded, *a.* polysperm (*R*), polyspermous (*R*), polyspermatous (*R*).
many-sided, *a.* polyhedral (*tech.; geom.*), polyhedric (*R*), polyhedrous (*R*), multilateral (*less usual than "polyhedral" in geom., but often fig.*), polygonal (*geom*).
Antonyms: see ONE-SIDED.
many-stringed, *a.* polychord (*R*).
many-voiced, *a.* polyphonic (*tech.*).
map, *n.* **1.** delineation (*contex.*); *spec.* chart, plat (*now chiefly U. S.*), plan, diagram, mappemonde (*hist.*), planisphere. *"Map" is especially used of geographical delineations.*
2. face (*S*).
map, *v. t.* delineate (*contex.*), chart, plot; *spec.* diagram.
mapper, *n.* delineator (*contex.*), chartographer *or* cartographer (*tech.*).
marauder, *n.* (*suggestive of roving in quest of plunder*), plunderer, desperado (*contex.*), reaver *or* reiver (*the Scottish spelling "reiver" is the more usual*); *spec.* pirate, boothaler (*A*), freebooter, brigand, refugee (*hist.*), cateran (*Scot.*).
marble, *n.* **1.** limestone; *spec.* rance, cipolin, giallo antico (*Italian*), verdantique, ophicalcite, brocatello (*Italian*).
2. *Spec.* sculpture, statue, frieze, *etc.*
3. *Spec.* bonce (*Eng.*), taw, alley.
marble, *a.* marmorean *or* marmoreal (*poetic and rhetorical*), marmoraceous (*R*).
march, *v. i. & t.* **1.** (*move with ordered steps*), go (*contex.*), walk (*contex.*); *spec.* troop, process (*C*), parade, file, defile, countermarch.
2. *See* ADVANCE.
march, *n.* **1.** walk (*contex.*); *spec.* file, defile, countermarch.
2. step (*contex.*); *spec.* quick, double-quick.
mare, *n.* gillie (*R or S*), lass (*playful or affectionate*).
marginal, *a.* *Spec.* border, coastal, littoral, shore, limbic (*anat.*).
marine, *a.* sea (*the noun used attributively*), thalassian (*R*), thalassic (*R*); *spec.* oceanic (*in reference to what characterizes or affects an ocean or oceans*), maritime (*referring to what relates to the sea, esp. lands bordering it or commerce upon it. The term* marine *denotes a closer relation than* maritime, *as,* marine *insurance, against the perils of the sea;* maritime *commerce, or c. carried on over the sea, in which the sea is a mere means of travel not an object of primary consideration. So, also,* marine *is generally used by biologists, etc., as* marine *life, etc.*), nautical.
Antonyms: see TERRESTRIAL.
marine, *n.* **1.** *See* FLEET, PICTURE.
2. gulpin (*S*), jolly (*British; S or C*), shipman (*R*), devil-dogs (*S of U. S. marines*).
marital, *a.* **1.** *See* MATRIMONIAL.
2. husbandly (*less formal*).
mark, *n.* **1.** *See* AIM, OBJECT.
2. *Referring to a thing shot at:* target (*primarily spec.*); *spec.* butt (*orig. archery*), bull's-eye, carton (*the disk or center in the bull's-eye*), white, crease (*cricket*), cock (*curling*), Jack-a-

manual, *n.: handbook, keyboard.*
manufacture, *n.: making, product.*
mar: *deface, impair.*
margin: *n.: edge, room, security.*

Lent (*Eng.*), Aunt Sally (*Eng.*), parrot, rover (*archery*), cockshy, quintain (*tilting*), jack (*bowls*), tee (*bowling*).
3. *Spec.* character, line, spot, stain, scratch, scar, brand, impression, impress, imprint, blur, label, print, dent, badge, device, note, hyphen, check (*for identification*), crisscross, diacritic (*printing*), chalk, charcoal, earmark (*esp. as a sign of ownership*), tally, score, tick, signature (*R*), cross, cachet (*French*), cognizance (*heraldry or formal*), demerit, difference (*R, exc. her. or logic*), chop, mintage.
4. *In punctuation:* character, stop; *spec.* comma, semicolon, colon, period, question mark, dash, parentheses, brackets, quotation marks.
5. *See* SIGN, BADGE, DISTINCTION.
mark, *v. t.* **1.** *Spec.* inscribe, line, dirty, stain, brand, countermark (*for additional authentication*), countersign (*for identification or reference*), scribe (*largely tech.*), postmark, star, bestar, letter, ink, enseam (*R*), buoy, cross, becross (*an intensive*), tick, tattoo, rubricate, label, inscribe (*as a monument*), enstamp (*R*), blaze (*a path or tree*), earmark, bespot (*an intensive*), scrawl, bescrawl (*an intensive*), rule, score, stigmatize (*esp. as a mark of disapproval*), sign, imprint, print, impress.
2. *See* DISTINGUISH, DENOTE, EMPHASIZE, CONSIDER.
market, *n.* **1.** marketplace, marketstead (*A*); *spec.* emporium (*often rhetorical or affected*), mart, vent (*A or tech.*), factory, exchange, rialto (*R*), cheap (*A*), bazaar, bezesteen (*Oriental*), forum (*Roman antiq.*), cross (*obs. or local Eng.*), curb, fair, staple, gunge *or* gunj.
2. *See* DEMAND.
market, *a.* nundinal (*R*).
market, *v. t.* mart (*R*); *spec.* offer, sell.
marking, *n.* *Spec.* delineation, gorgelet (*R*), feathering, gorget, interstriation (*R*), inscription (*anat.*), mirror.
marksman, *n.* *Spec.* toucher (*archery*), sharpshooter, franc-tireur (*French*).
marriage, *n.* **1.** *Referring to the state or relation:* matrimony (*chiefly formal or affected*), wedlock (*a word of finer connotation than "matrimony" or "marriage"*), conjugality, spousehood (*R*), connubialism (*R*), spousage (*A*), hymen (*R*).
2. *Referring to the ceremony:* union, matrimony (*formal or solemn*), nuptials (*pl.*), spousal (*chiefly in pl.*), wedding (*the Anglo-Saxon term*), match, bridal (*orig. spec.*), espousal (*chiefly in pl.; the fuller form for "spousal"*), hymen (*R*), hymeneals (*pl.; B*); *spec.* remarriage, intermarriage, coemption (*Roman law*), opsigamy (*R*), mesalliance *or* misalliance, confarreation (*Roman law*), bigamy, deuterogamy, hierogamy (*nonce word*), hetærism *or* hetairism, lobola, endogamy, exogamy, polyandry, polygamy, polygyny, morganatic marriage.
Antonyms: see DIVORCE.
marriage, *a.* hymeneal, hymenean (*R*).
marriageable, *a.* marriable; *spec.* nubile (*R*), viripotent (*R*).
marriage song, hymeneal (*B or formal*), epithalamium.
married, *a.* mated (*esp. with "ill-" or "well-", referring to the compatibility of the parties*), settled, conjugate (*R*); *spec.* farreate (*R; Latin antiq.*).
Antonyms: see UNMARRIED.
marrow, *n.* **1.** medulla (*anat.*); *spec.* pith.
2. *See* ESSENCE.
marry, *v. t.* **1.** wed, espouse (*chiefly used of the man*); *spec.* wife, husband (*both R*).
Antonyms: see DIVORCE.
2. *With two persons as the subject:* unite (*contex.; often in "unite in holy wedlock"*), join (*contex.*), wed (*formal*), pair (*R; being chiefly used of animals*), couple (*R; being, like "pair," chiefly used of animals*), espouse, tie (*C*), match, splice (*S*); *spec.* intermarry, remarry.
marry, *v. i.* unite (*contex.*), join (*contex.*), match (*C*), wed (*formal*), pair (*R*), couple (*R*), intermarry; *spec.* wife, husband (*both R*), remarry.
marsh, *n.* *Spec.* quagmire, quag, morass (*B*), slough (*a place of deep mire*), mire, bog, fen (*chiefly Eng.*), marish (*A*), swamp, maremma (*Italian*), marshland, moss (*chiefly Scot.*), pocosin *or* poquosin (*southern U. S.*), flow (*Scot.*), carr (*local Eng.*), corcass (*Ireland*), mash (*local U. S.*).
marshy, *a.* paludal (*B*), paludine (*R*), palustrine (*B*), squashy (*C*); *spec.* morassy, miry, plashy, fenny (*chiefly Eng.*), fennish (*chiefly Eng.*), swampy, boggy, marish (*A*), moory (*Eng.; chiefly local or dial.*).
martial, *a.* (*suggesting warlike pomp or display*). *Spec.* military, warlike (*referring to disposition of mind*).
mask, *n* **1.** *See* DISGUISE, MASKER, CLOAK, BALL.
2. *Referring to the cover or disguise for the face: spec.* visor, domino (*both a disguise for the face and a costume*), umberer (*R*).
masker, *n.* mask (*fig.*); *spec.* masquerader, mummer, domino, guisard (*chiefly Scot.*), guiser (*Scot. and Eng. dial.*).
mason, *n.* cowan (*Scot.; derogatory*); *spec.* stonemason, bricklayer.
masonry, *n.* *Spec.* stonework, ashlar, brickwork, rubblework, studwork, rubble.
mass, *n.* *Spec.* body, aggregate, quantity, number, bulk, size, lump, cake, clot, flake, majority, people, assemblage, crowd, cloud (*suggesting cloudlike consistence, a hovering, enveloping or the like*), block (*implying solidity and compactness*).
Mass, *n.* Eucharist; *spec.* canon, requiem.

---

marked: *distinguished, conspicuous, intense.*
marketable: *salable.*
marshal, *v. t.: arrange, escort.*
martyr: *sufferer.*
marvel: *wonder.*
masculine: *male, manly.*
mash, *v. t.: crush.*
mask, *v. t.: hide, disguise.*
masque: *ball, drama.*
mass, *v. t.: unite, gather.*

massacre, *n.* killing (*contex.*), scupper (*mil. S*); *spec.* magophony (*R*), pogrom, populicide (*R*).

massacre, *v. t.* butcher, slaughter (*both contex.*); *see* MURDER.

massage, *n.* shampoo (*R*); *spec.* percussion, stroking, rubbing, kneading, *etc.*

masseur, *n. Spec.* rubber.

massive, *a.* **1.** big, massy (*less formal and more B than "massive"*), substantial, bulky (*less suggestive of weight than of size*), beamy (*R or A*), Cyclopean (*fig.*), heavy, solid, ponderous (*more emphatic or intensive than "heavy"*).

Antonyms: see UNSUBSTANTIAL, GRANULAR.

2. *See* LOUD.

mast, *n.* stick (*humorous*), pole; *spec.* pine, mainmast, foremast, mizzen, mizzenmast, jurymast, jigger.

master, *n.* **1.** *Spec.* controller, owner, lord; *see* CONTROLLER, CONQUEROR, EMPLOYER, EXPERT, WORKMAN, CAPTAIN, TEACHER.

Antonyms: see SLAVE.

2. *As a courtesy title:* dan (*A*), don, sir (*used only in address*), sirrah.

master, *a.* **1.** *Spec.* chief, controlling, commanding.

Antonyms: see SUBORDINATE.

2. *Pertaining to a master:* herile (*R*).

masterpiece, *n.* masterwork (*less used than "masterpiece," and having less concrete suggestions*), chef-d'œuvre (*French*).

masterstroke, *n.* coup (*French*), coup d'état (*French*).

mastiff, *n.* bandog (*A*).

mat, *n.* fabric (*contex.*); *spec.* paunch (*naut.*), rug, felt, glib (*hist.*), bass.

match, *n.* **1.** fuze; *spec.* lunt.

2. *Spec., referring to the matches in ordinary use:* fusee *or* fuzee, Congreve, loco-foco (*U. S.*), lucifer, vesuvian.

match, *n.* **1.** equal, antagonist, Roland (*fig.*).

2. contest; *spec.* bonspiel (*Scot.*), main, twosome (*R*), threesome (*golf*), foursome (*golf*), shoot, roll, *etc.*

3. *See* COUNTERPART, MARRIAGE, EQUALITY, AGREEMENT.

match, *v. t.* **1.** *See* MARRY, EQUAL, COMPARE, OPPOSE, FIGHT, ADAPT.

2. *Spec.* pair, mate, duplicate.

matchmaker, *n. Spec.* marriage broker, shatchen.

mate, *n.* associate (*contex.*), fere (*A*); *spec.* fellow, match (*implying equality or adaptation*), schoolfellow, schoolmate, consort; husband, wife (*both R*). (*"Mate" is not properly used of persons, husband or wife, except as implying compatibility; but it is regularly of animals*).

mate, *v. t.* & *i.* pair, match; *see* MARRY.

material, *a.* **1.** *Spec.* corporeal (*emphasizing contrast of body and spirit*), carnal (*A, exc. spec.*), corporal (*B, R*), bodily, physical (*referring to the world perceived by the senses, in contrast to the "immaterial" or non-physical, and lacking the likenesses and contrasts implied by "corporeal," "bodily," "earthly," etc. "Physical" is therefore a word of somewhat hard, colorless character*), objective, earthy (*often suggestive of grossness*), earthly, hylic (*R*), tangible, sensible.

Antonyms: see IMMATERIAL, MENTAL.

2. *See* IMPORTANT, RELATIVE, CONSIDERABLE, SENSUOUS.

material, *n.* **1.** substance, stuff (*often somewhat contemptuous*), matter; *spec.* metal, mettle, body, timber, stock, component, fabric, feed, staple.

2. data; *spec.* notes, facts, information.

materiality, *n. Spec.* corporeality, bodiliness, corporeity.

materialize, *v. t.* materiate (*R*); *spec.* externalize, externate *or* externize (*R*), exteriorize, embody, precipitate.

Antonyms: see SPIRITUALIZE.

maternal, *a.* parental (*contex.*); *spec.* motherlike, motherly.

maternity, *n.* maternality (*R*); *spec.* motherliness, motherhood.

Antonyms: see BARREN, VIRGINITY.

mathematician, *n. Spec.* arithmetician, geometrician, trigonometrician, geodesist, actuary.

matrimonial, *a.* conjugal, connubial (*less common than "matrimonial"*), nuptial (*primarily spec.*), marital (*primarily spec.*), sponsal (*R or B*), spousal, conjugial (*used by Swedenborgians*), genial (*R*); *spec.* internuptial.

matrix, *n.* **1.** *See* WOMB.

2. form (*contex.*); *spec.* mold, bed, cast, coffin, ceroplast.

matron, *n.* **1.** dowager (*humorous*); *spec.* wife, widow, mother.

2. *See* HOUSEKEEPER.

matter, *n.* **1.** *Spec.* stuff, body, substance.

2. *See* MATERIAL, PUS, QUANTITY, COPY, IMPORTANCE, SUBJECT, AFFAIR, CIRCUMSTANCE, MAIL.

3. *Referring to what is stated in a book, speech, etc.:* substance, gear (*A*), stuff (*often somewhat contemptuous*), body.

matter, *v. i.* weigh, bulk, import, count, skill (*A*).

matter-of-fact, *a.* literal, sober, prosy, prosaic *or* (*less usual*) prose; *spec.* practical, unsentimental, unimaginative, simple.

Antonyms: see FANCIFUL, VISIONARY, EXTRAVAGANT.

maunder, *v. i.* **1.** *See* WANDER.

2. Flapdoodle (*C; contemptuous*), maudle (*R*).

master, *v. t.: control, defeat, overpower, learn.*
masterful: *authoritative, domineering.*
masterly: *able.*
mastership: *control, skill.*
mastery: *control, skill.*
match, *v. i.: marry, agree.*
matchless: *unequaled.*
matronly: *wifely, grave.*
mature, *a.: ripe, grown, due, deliberate.*
mature, *v. i. & t.: develop, ripen, complete, accrue.*

maverick, *a.* & *n.* **1.** unbranded (*Western U. S., used esp. of motherless calves*).
2. *fig.:* free-lance, independent, mugwump.
maximize, *v. t.* maximate, increase, improve, magnify.
Antonyms: see MINIMIZE; *cf.* BELITTLE, DIMINISH, DISPARAGE.
maximum, *n.* limit, greatest, highest.
maybe, *adv.* possibly.
meadow, *a.* pratal (*R*), meadowy.
meager, *a.* **1.** *See* THIN.
2. *Referring to what is scarcely sufficient:* poor; *spec.* scanty, slender, slight, slim, thin, spare, sparing, lean, deficient, bare.
Antonyms: see ABUNDANT.
meal, *n.* flour (*contex.*); *spec.* groats (*pl.*), hominy grits (*pl.*), pinole (*U. S.*).
meal, *n.* **1.** *Referring to food eaten at one time:* repast (*rather formal*); *spec.* refection (*B*), spread (*C*), collation (*formal*), snatch (*C*), snack (*C or dial.*), snap (*R*), ordinary (*Eng.*), table-d'hôte (*French*), coffee, breakfast, dinner, tea, supper, lunch, luncheon, tiffin (*Anglo-Indian*), feast, mess (*U. S. or Eng. dial.*), morsel, pot luck (*C*).
2. *Referring to the act:* feed (*C or vulgar*); *spec.* feast, gorge, refection, repast, collation, regale (*R*), breakfast, dinner, supper, tea, lunch, luncheon.
mean, *v. t.* **1.** *See* INTEND, SIGNIFY.
2. signify, intend, purport, import, bear (*A*); *spec.* denote, connote, argue, imply, symbolize, indicate.
mean, *a.* **1.** *See* UNDIGNIFIED, INFERIOR, SHABBY, LOWLY, BASE, CONTEMPTIBLE, WORTHLESS, ORDINARY, WRETCHED.
2. *As denoting an unworthy spirit: spec.* little-minded *or* (*more freely of things as well as persons*) little, small, petty, shabby, scurvy, sorry, sordid, wretched, beggarly, rascally, currish, dirty (*often a cheap or vulgar term of reproach*), unhandsome, caitiff (*B*), sneaking, spying, scoundrelly, malevolent, tattling, *etc.*
Antonyms: see GENEROUS, GRAND, NOBLE.
meaning, *n.* **1.** *See* INTENTION.
2. signification (meaning *arising from natural or conventionally established signs or symbols*), significance *or* significancy (*less usual equivalents of* signification *often suggesting an important* meaning, *esp. in relation to some specific thing or condition*), import (*emphasizing the idea of* meaning *as inferrible or deducible, often with reference to the effect upon, or relation to, something else*), power (*R*), purport (meaning *with relation to intention or pretension*); *spec.* substance, amount, upshot, spirit, interpretation, intent *or* intention, intendment, drift, content, sense, value, denotation (*the thing directly* meant), connotation (meaning *as attaching by inference or association to the direct meaning or denotation; thus the denotation of dog includes spaniel, collie, etc.; the* connotation, *those inferred qualities of faithfulness, etc.*), consignificance, by-sense, force, heart, effect, significate, comprehension, implication (*where the* meaning *is conveyed from speaker or writer to hearer or reader*), inference (*where the hearer or reader grasps or supplies a* meaning; *a passage* implies *what the reader is at liberty to* infer), burden. Meaning *is the general term, with no special implications, except that it often is used as suggesting a sense as intended.*
meaningless, *a.* empty, unmeaning, senseless, insignificant; *spec.* unimportant.
Antonyms: see EXPRESSIVE, SIGNIFICANT.
means, *n.* **1.** agency, mean (*A*), instrument (*chiefly spec.*); *spec.* agent, machinery, wherewithal (*C*), wherewith (*C*), foison (*chiefly Scot.*), medium, receipt (*fig.*), engine (*B*), organ (*A*).
2. *As a pl.:* resources, faculty (*obs. or hist.*); *spec.* income, wealth.
meanwhile, *adv.* meantime.
measurable, *a.* measurable (*more tech.*); *spec.* fathomable, gaugeable.
Antonyms: see INFINITE.
measure, *n.* **1.** *See* MEASUREMENT.
2. standard (*contex.*); *spec.* gauge, mile, rod, fathom, yard, foot, inch, hand, ell, cubit, line, acre, bushel, peck, degree, quart, pint, gill, hour, minute, cube, lea, pound, stone, ounce, pennyweight, grain, *etc.*
3. *See* DIMENSION, STANDARD, EXTENT, DEGREE, QUANTITY, ACTION, DANCE.
measure, *v. t.* **1.** mensurate (*tech. and R*); *spec.* span, gauge, mete (*now poetic, exc. in allusion to Matt. vii, 2*), quantity (*R or tech.*), calibrate, line, girt *or* girth, tape, divide, caliper, dial, pace, step, inch, space.
2. *See* LIMIT, ASSIGN, TRAVERSE, REACH, COMPARE.
measurement, *n.* **1.** measure (*R*), mensuration (*more tech.*); *spec.* mete (*R*), metage, horometry, autometry, quantification (*R*), photometry, æsthesiometry, calorimetry, micrometry, *etc.*
2. *See* SIZE, EXTENT, QUANTITY.
measurer, *n.* mensurator (*R*); *spec.* eriometer, gauger, micrometer, meter, burette, pipette, alcoholometer, gasometer, galactometer, æsthesiometer, *etc.*
measuring, *a.* mensurative (*R*).
meat, *n.* **1.** food (*contex.*); *spec.* lean, junk, bouilli (*French*), biltong, cabob, mincemeat, forcemeat, jerky, jerk, charqui, pemmican, cecils (*pl.*).
2. *See* FLESH.
meatmarket, *n.* shambles (*R or B*).
mechanic, *n.* workman (*contex.*); *spec.* machinist, mechanician, mechanist.
mechanical, *a.* machinelike; *spec.* automatic, unthinking, perfunctory.

---

maximum, *a.: greatest.*
maybe: *possibly.*
maze, *n.: labyrinth, tangle.*
meadow: *grassland.*
meaning, *a.: expressive.*
meantime, *adv.: meanwhile.*
meantime, *n.: interval.*
measured: *uniform, deliberate.*
measureless: *infinite, fathomless.*
meaty: *pithy.*

Antonyms: see MENTAL.
mechanics, *n. Spec.* statics, dynamics.
mechanism, *n.* machinery, apparatus, works; *spec.* movement, escapement, motion, gearing, clockwork.
medal, *n.* medallion (*large*); *spec.* medalet, jetton, badge, contorniate.
meddlesome, *a.* officious, meddling, pragmatic, busy, polypragmatic (*R*); *spec.* inquisitive.
mediatory, *a.* intermediary, mediatorial (*R*), mediative; *spec.* intercessory, intercessive (*R*).
medical, *a.* iatric (*R*), iatrical (*R*), physical (*R*), Galenic (*jocular*).
medication, *n.* dosage, medicamentation (*R*).
medicinal, *a.* curative (*contex.*), medicamentary (*R*), medicinable (*A*), medicatory (*R*); *spec.* druggy.
medicine, *n.* **1.** leechcraft (*A*), leechdom (*A*), therapy (*chiefly in combination*); *spec.* loimology, pharmaceutics, pharmacology, pharmacy.
2. drug (*properly spec.*), physic (*A or spec.*), medicament, dope (*chiefly spec.; S*); *spec.* simple (*A*), elixir, lincture *or* linctus, electuary, nostrum, druggery (*a collective*), abstract, extract, demulcent, triturate, drops, tisane.
medicine man. *Spec.* powwow (*North American Indian*), piache (*French; African*), peai.
meditative, *a.* considerative, contemplative, ruminative.
medium, *n.* **1.** mean (*usually spec.*), average, mediocrity (*R*).
2. *See* INTERMEDIARY, AGENT, AGENCY.
3. *In hypnosis, etc.:* subject; *spec.* psychic, hypnotic, oracle.
medley, *n.* (*suggesting heterogeneous elements*), mixture; *spec.* jumble, confusion, mess, disorder, hash, hodgepodge, hotchpot (*R*), farrago (*about equivalent to "hodgepodge"; B*), gallimaufrey (*about equivalent to "hodgepodge"; R*), muddle, mishmash (*R*), mélange (*French*), porridge, olio, olla podrida (*an olio; Spanish*), potpourri, macaroni (*R*), mob (*R*), pasticcio (*Italian*), pastiche (*French*), omniumgatherum (*C*), pell-mell (*R*), cento, charivari.
meet, *v. t. Spec.* encounter, rencounter (*R*), front, face, cross, cope (*A*), match, see, join, intersect, oppose, fight, experience, defray, satisfy, overcome.
Antonyms: see AVOID.
meet, *v. i.* **1.** *See* JOIN, COLLIDE, AGREE.
2. assemble, gather, collect, forgather (*chiefly Scot.; chiefly spec.*); *spec.* convene, rally, rendezvous, congress (*R*), congregate, caucus, muster, parade, troop, hill, gam, reassemble, reconvene.
Antonyms: see SEPARATE, SCATTER.
3. *In reference to time:* coincide, concur, strike.
meeting, *n.* **1.** *Spec.* encounter, rencounter (*R*), facing, fronting, joining, junction, intersection, opposition, fight.
2. *See* SATISFACTION, COLLISION, AGREEMENT, APPOINTMENT.
3. assembly, gathering, collection; *spec.* congress, convention, concourse, congregation (*R or eccl., except of the act alone*), conclave, cabal, conference, meet (*sports*), rendezvous, conventicle, congression, conversazione (*Italian*), turnout (*C*), sabbath, séance, rally, eisteddfod, caucus, duel, muster, parade.
Antonyms: see SEPARATE, SCATTER.
4. coincidence, concurrence.
meeting, *a.* **1.** *Spec.* concutient (*implying a concussion*).
Antonyms: see SCATTERING, SEPARATIVE.
2. coincident, concurrent, simultaneous.
melodious, *a.* (*pleasing as to sequence of pitch*), euphonious (*B, pleasing as to tone-quality*), harmonious, sweet-sounding, mellisonant (*A*), mellifluent *or* mellifluous, musical, sweet, mellow, sirenic (*fig.; R*), Orphic (*fig.*); *spec.* songful, rich, silvery, tunable.
Antonyms: see DISCORDANT, HARSH.
melody, *n. Spec.* air, diapason, descant, lay, plainsong, counterpoint, carillon, chant, chime, sweetness, run.
Antonyms: see DISCORD.
member, *n.* **1.** part (*contex.*), organ; *spec.* limb, branch, joint, colon, private parts.
2. socius (*Latin and tech.; chiefly spec.*); *spec.* fellow, conventioner, conventionist, incorporator, founder.
membrane, *n.* film; *spec.* skin, pia mater, decidua, caul, chorion, arachnoid, dura mater, meninges (*pl.*), hyaloid, mesogaster, epithelium, endocardium, endocarp, endoderm, meninx, web, tympan, conjunctiva, drumhead.
membrous, *a.* membraniform (*tech. or B*), membranoid (*tech.*); *spec.* epithelial, cuticular, webby, weblike, skinny, membranaceous, membraneous.
memorable, *a.* rememberable (*R*); *spec.* noteworthy.
memorandum, *n.* note, notandum (*R*); *spec.* minute (*chiefly in pl.*), jurat, abstract, tezkere, agenda (*pl.*).
memorial, *n.* remembrance (*R*); *spec.* memorandum, cahier (*French*), monument, factum (*a Gallicism*), hoarstone (*chiefly hist.*), ebenezer, trophy, souvenir.
memory, *n.* **1.** reminiscence, recollection.
2. *In reference to the act or to the time to which the memory runs:* remembrance (*state or fact of being remembered*), recalling.

---

meddle: *interpose.*
meddling: *meddlesome.*
medial: *intermediate, average.*
median: *intermediate.*
mediate, *v. i.: interpose.*
mediate, *v. t.: arrange.*
mediocre: *ordinary.*
meditate: *consider.*
medium, *a.: intermediate, fair, ordinary.*
meek: *submissive, humble.*
melancholy: *depressed, depressing, sad.*
mellow: *ripen, soften, intoxicate.*
melt: *liquefy, diminish, vanish, soften.*
memorize: *learn.*

---

menagerie, *n. Spec.* zoo (*C or humorous*).
mental, *a.* subjective; *spec.* intellectual (*as belonging to, requiring, or characterized by, the understanding or reasoning faculties, and so distinguished from "emotional"*), intellective (*suggesting relation or or the presence of reasoning, and a term of more technical use*), psychic *or* psychical (*as relating to the soul, and so distinguished from "physical," but including both "intellectual" and "emotional"*), immaterial, inner, inward, interior *or* internal, cognitive (*tech.*), epistemonic (*tech.*), intentional (*Scholastic philosophy*), purposive, reasoning, *etc.*
Antonyms: see MATERIAL, MECHANICAL.
mental healing, psychotherapy, psychopathy (*R*); *spec.* hypnotherapy, psychiatry, psychoanalysis.
mentally, *adv. Spec.* intellectually, psychically, emotionally, internally, interiorly, inly, inward, inwardly.
mention, *v. t.* enumerate (*one by one, "mention" usually specifically suggesting a brief or casual notice*), numerate (*R*), relate, recount, specify; *spec.* name, designate, individualize (*R*), particularize, rehearse (*implying mention one by one of a number, esp. to emphasize their character or numerousness*), retail (*giving petty details, mentioning tediously or repetitiously*), recite, note, overname (*R*), nominate, tell (*by way of giving information*), quote, remember, recommend, cite (*suggesting a naming with particularity, esp. by way of authority, proof, etc.*), itemize, notice, margin, narrate.
Antonyms: see DISREGARD, IGNORE, OMIT.
mention, *n.* enumeration, numeration (*R*), relation, recounting, recountment (*R*), specification; *spec.* rehearsal, recital, naming, designation, noting, note, particularization, retailing, recitation, nomination, telling, quoting, quotation, citation, tale, remembrance, dinumeration (*R*), itemization, notice, narration.
mercenary, *a.* venal (*implying usually corruption or immorality*), sordid; *spec.* hireling (*implying contempt*), salable, purchasable, hired. *"Mercenary" suggests a sordid regard for money interests alone.*
mercenary, *n.* hireling; *spec.* pensioner *or* pensionary, myrmidon, Hessian (*U. S.; a political or military hireling*), lansquenet, bashi-bazouk.
merciful, *a.* kind, clement (*not usually suggestive of sympathy*), lenient (*suggesting overindulgence*), gracious (*of a superior toward an inferior*), humane, gentle, mild.
Antonyms: see IMPLACABLE, CRUEL, UNFEELING, RELENTLESS.
mercury, *n.* quicksilver (*the popular name; meaning silver that is alive, or "quick"*), hydrargyrum (*tech.*).
mercy, *n.* clemency, lenity *or* lenience, graciousness, grace, goodness; *spec.* forbearance, quarter (*mil.*).
Antonyms: see CRUELTY, UNKINDNESS, RETRIBUTION.
mere, *a.* bare, bald, simple, naked, plain, sole, single; *spec.* dry.
merely, *adv.* barely, only, alone, simply, *etc.*
meridian, *n.* **1.** acme (*R*), mid-sky (*poetic*), mid-heaven (*astron. and astrol.*).
2. *See* HEIGHT, CIRCLE.
mermaid, *n.* seamaid(en) (*poetic*), merrow (*Anglo-Irish*); *spec.* merwoman (*R*).
merman, *n.* seaman (*R or poetic*); *spec.* marmennill.
merry-go-round, *n.* carrousel, roundabout (*Eng.*), whirligig, turnabout.
merrymaking, *n.* gayety, merrymake (*A*), merriment; *spec.* riot, conviviality, festivity, revel, Comus (*a personification*), gaudeamus, jollification (*C*), jubilee, high jinks (*C*), frolic, Maying.
Antonyms: see LAMENTATION.
message, *n.* communication (*contex.*); *spec.* dispatch, express, evangel (*R, exc. of the Gospel*), embassage *or* embassade (*A*), letter, telegram, telepheme, telelogue, telephone, cablegram, cable, heliogram, radiogram.
message-conveying, *a.* nunciative, Mercurial (*fig.*), messenger, ambassadorial (*chiefly spec.*); *spec.* internuncial, internunciary.
messenger, *n. Spec.* emissary, envoy, nunciate (*R*), nuncio (*R*), nuntius (*R*), Mercury (*fig.*), bode (*A*), internuncio (*R*), express, herald, post (*chiefly hist.*), poster, courier, intelligencer, chuprassy (*Anglo-Indian*), runner, peon (*India*), hircarra (*India*), chiaus (*Turkish*).
messmate, *n.* associate (*contex.*), comrade (*contex.*), buddy (*C*), commensal (*B or R*), pal (*S*), side-kick (*C*), mate.
metal, *n.* element (*contex.*), ore (*chiefly poetic; chiefly spec.*); *spec.* bullion, gate, pig, sow, regulus.
metallic, *a.* **1.** ory (*R*), metalline (*a general term, not indicating metal qualities so closely as "metallic"*); *spec.* brazen, silvery, gilt, golden, aureate, coppery, leaden, stannic, *etc.*
2. *See* HARSH.
metaphorical, *a.* (*implying comparison that imaginatively identifies one thing with another*), figurative, allegorical (*usually more spec.*), parabolic (*R*), transumptive (*R*).
metaphysics, *n. Spec.* ontology, epistemology.
meteor, *n.* **1.** phenomenon (*contex.*); *spec.* wind, cloud, rain, hail, snow, *etc.*
2. *Spec.* (*referring to the concrete object*) fire ball, bolide, falling star, shooting star, meteorite, exhalation (*A*), Andromedid, Lyraid, Leonid, Perseid, *etc.*

men: *mankind.*
mend, *v. t.: improve, cure, expiate, repair.*
mend, *n.: repair.*
menial, *a.: base.*
menial, *n.: servant, wretch.*
mentality: *intelligence, mind.*
merely: *hardly.*
merit: *worth due.*
merited: *deserved.*
merriment: *gayety, merrymaking.*
merry: *gay, cheerful.*
mesmerize: *hypnotize.*
mess, *n.: dish, meal, medley.*
mess, *v. t.: feed, confuse.*
mess, *v. i.: eat, dabble.*
messy: *confused.*
metaphysical: *immaterial, abstract.*

meteoric, *a. Spec.* atmospheric, transitory, flashing.
meteorite, *n.* meteor, meteorolite, cloud stone.
meteorological, *a. Spec.* atmospherical.
method, *n.* manner, mode; *spec.* procedure (*esp. with reference to successive actions of the agent*), process (*esp. with reference to a system or series of activities tending to some end, but taken apart from any agent or individual*), plan, order, system, scheme, rule.
Antonyms: see CONFUSION.
methodical, *a. Spec.* orderly, systematic, regular, businesslike.
Antonyms: see CONFUSED.
methodize, *v. t.* order, systemize; *spec.* regularize.
mew, *v. i.* cry (*contex.*), miaow, miaul, mewl, caterwaul.
microbe, *n.* microörganism, germ; *spec.* bacterium, microphyte, microzyme.
middle, *a.* central, centric *or* centrical (*R, B or tech.*), mid (*tech., B*), midway (*R, B*), middlemost (*superl.*), middest (*superl.; R*), midmost (*superl.*), mesial (*tech.*), mesian (*tech.*); *spec.* equatorial.
Antonyms: see BORDER, *n.*, CIRCUMFERENCE.
middle, *n.* center, mid (*R, B*), midmost (*the exact or nearest approachable middle*), middlemost (*R*); *spec.* midst, thick, midships, saint (*her.*), bull's-eye, cazimi (*astrol.*).
Antonyms: see BORDER, VERGE, CIRCUMFERENCE, RIM.
middle class, *n.* bourgeois (*esp. the shopkeeping middle class*). *As adjective, the word is often contemptuously synonymous with* common, vulgar, tasteless, ordinary, *etc.*) *but it more frequently connotes the conventional virtues of "the backbone of the nation."*
middleman, *n. Spec.* intermediary, broker, go-between, regrater, butty (*dial.*), bummaree (*Eng.*), salesman, saleswoman.
midshipman, *n.* middy (*C*), reefer (*S*); *spec.* guinea pig (*Eng. naut., S*), oldster, youngster.
midwife, *n.* obstetrician, accoucheuse (*French*), Lucina (*fig.*), obstetrix (*R*).
midwife, *v. t.* attend (*often euphemistic or affected*), accouche (*R*), deliver (*often with "of"*).
migrate, *v. i.* transmigrate (*R*), trek (*South African or C*), wander (*fig. or spec.*), nomadize (*R*); *spec.* run (*of fish*), emigrate, immigrate.
migrating, *a.* migrant, migratory, transmigrant (*R*); *spec.* emigrant, immigrant.
migration, *n.* transmigration (*R*), trek (*South African or C*); *spec.* rush, run, passage, emigration, immigration, intermigration.
mild, *a.* **1.** *See* GENTLE, MERCIFUL, MODERATE.
2. *In reference to weather, balmy climate, etc.:* temperate; *spec.* balmy, smooth (*R*), green (*as in "a green winter"*), clement, soft (*chiefly Scot. and dial.*), summery.
Antonyms: see SEVERE, ROUGH.
milden, *v. t.* **1.** ameliorate.
2. *See* SUBDUE, RELAX.
military, *n.* soldiery, sword (*fig.*); *spec.* militia, marines, infantry, troops, *etc.*
milk, *n. Spec.* buttermilk, skim, colostrum, beestings, foremilk, strippings.
milk, *v. t. Spec.* extract, exploit, nurse.
milky, *a.* lacteal (*tech.*), lacteous (*R*), lactary (*chiefly spec.*), galactic (*R*); *spec.* lactescent.
mill, *n. Spec.* crusher, stamper, brake, malaxator (*R*), quern, windmill.
millenarian, *n.* millenary, chiliast (*R*).
millennium, *n.* millenary, chiliad (*R*).
milliner, *n.* modiste (*French*).
millstone, *n. Spec.* buhrstone, quernstone, runner.
mince, *n.* mincemeat; *spec.* forcemeat *or* (*R*), force, hash.
mind, *n.* **1.** *See* REMEMBRANCE, CONSCIOUSNESS, SOUL, INTENTION, WILL, SPIRIT, COURAGE, THINKER.
2. *Referring to the mental faculty:* mentality; *spec.* head, heart, intellect, nous (*tech.*), brains (*pl.; C*).
Antonyms: see BODY.
mine, *n.* meum (*B*).
mine, *n.* **1.** *Referring to place where minerals, ores, precious stones, etc., are got: spec.* pit, shaft, placer, colliery.
2. *See* STORE.
3. *In mil. use: spec.* countermine, fougasse (*French*), caisson, case.
mineral, *n. Spec.* ore, rock.
Antonyms: see VEGETABLE, ANIMAL.
minister, *n.* **1.** agent; *spec.* councilor, diplomatic agent, dewan (*Anglo-Indian*), pander.
2. clergyman (*the general technical term*), parson (*C, familiar, or depreciatory, exc. as used spec. by the English*), pastor; *spec.* ecclesiastic, preacher, priest, rector, curate (*A, exc. as the name of a clergyman*), vicar, clerk (*now chiefly legal or hist.*), cleric, father (*a title, esp. of common reverential address among Roman Catholics*), patrico (*cant*), churchman, gownsman (*R*), divine, angel, reverend (*R; a term of respectful or deferential address or reference*), domine *or* dominie (*obs. in U. S., except in*

metropolitan: *capital.*
mettle: *energy, courage.*
mettlesome: *energetic, courageous.*
midget: *dwarf.*
midst: *middle.*
midway, *n.: middle.*
midwifery, *n.: obstetrics.*
might: *energy, power, force.*
mighty: *energetic, powerful, forceful, able, big, great.*
mildew: *stain, blight.*
militant: *fighting, combative.*
mill, *v. i.: grind, go.*
mimic, *a.: imitative, imitated.*
mimic, *n.: imitator, buffoon.*
mimic: *v. t.: imitate.*
mince, *v. t.: chop, mangle.*
mince, *v. i.: go, talk.*
mincing: *affected.*
mind, *v. t.: attend, notice, obey, consider.*
minded: *disposed.*
mindful: *attentive, careful.*
mine, *v. i.: burrow.*
mingle: *mix, associate.*
minimize: *diminish, belittle.*
minimum: *least.*
minion: *creature.*

Dutch Reformed Church), chaplain, liturgist (*R*), cassock (*C*), curé (*French*), prophet, padre (*Italian*), presbyter, predikant, deacon, helper, regular, canon *or* canonic, druid.

minister, *v. i.* **1.** *See* ATTEND, CONTRIBUTE, SERVE.

2. *Spec.* pander.

ministerial, *a.* **1.** *See* ATTENDANT.

2. *Spec.* clerical, clerkly, priestly, parsonic *or* parsonical *or* parsonish (*often C or depreciatory*), pastoral.

Antonyms: see LAY.

ministry, *n.* **1.** *See* AGENCY, COUNCIL.

2. *In relation to the duties, office, or character of a clergyman: spec.* administration, cure, itinerancy, rectorship, vicarage, curacy, priesthood.

3. *Meaning clergymen collectively:* clergy; *spec.* priesthood, parsondom (*C or depreciatory*), pulpit (*fig.*), frock (*fig.*), cloth (*fig.; with "the"*), council.

Antonyms: see LAITY.

minor, *a. Spec.* less, by *or* bye, lesser (*esp. in importance*).

minor, *n.* infant (*technical in this sense*); *spec.* ward, pupil.

minority, *n.* childhood (*contex.*), infancy (*technical in this sense*), minorage (*R*), nonage (*relatively unusual*); *spec.* pupilage, wardship.

Antonyms: see BULK, MAJORITY.

minstrel, *n.* entertainer (*contex.*); *spec.* bard (*Celtic*), gleeman (*A*), jongleur (*French*).

minus, *a. Spec.* less, wanting, lacking.

minute, *a.* small, tiny (*popular; often deprecatory, excusatory, or the like*); *spec.* atomic, wee (*C*), microscopic *or* microscopical, nice, minikin, smallest.

Antonyms: see IMMENSE, LARGE, GREAT.

minute, *a. Spec.* circumstantial (*as giving details*), trifling (*unimportant details*), particular (*all details*), elaborate (*minuteness in details arising from continual labor and pains*).

Antonyms: see GENERAL.

mire, *v. t.* **1.** bemire, lair (*Scot.*); *spec.* embag.

2. *See* DIRTY.

mirror, *n. Spec.* glass, looking-glass, speculum, pier-glass.

mis-. *This prefix implies positive error, perversion, or mistake;* mal- *and* caco- (*relatively R*) *imply faultiness or imperfection which may be of any degree, slight or great.*

misanthrope, *n.* misanthropist; *spec.* cynic, Timonist (*fig.; R*).

Antonyms: see PHILANTHROPIST.

misanthropy, *n.* misanthropism; *spec.* cynicism, cynism (*R*).

misbecome, *v. t.* mis-suit.

Antonyms: see BECOME.

misbehave, *v. t.* misconduct.

misbehavior, *n.* behavior (*contex.*), misconduct, disorder (*R*), misdemeanor (*chiefly spec.*); *spec.* malfeasance, malversation.

Antonyms: see DECORUM.

misbelief, *n.* error; *spec.* unbelief, delusion.

miscalculate, *v. t. Spec.* miscount, miscompute, misreckon.

miscarry, *v. i.* **1.** *See* FAIL.

2. abort (*tech.; referring only to animals*), slip (*C*), slink, warp, pick (*dial. Eng.*).

miscellaneous, *a.* mixed, farraginaceous (*B*), indiscriminate, promiscuous, heterogeneous; *spec.* hotchpotch, general.

Antonyms: see PARTICULAR.

miscellany, *n.* mixture; *spec.* medley, miscellanea (*pl.*), collectanea (*pl.*).

mischief, *n.* **1.** *See* HARM, INJURY, DETRIMENT.

2. *Referring to the action of mischief making: spec.* destruction, ruination, roguery (*playful*), devilry *or* devilment.

mischief-maker, *n.* mischief (*R*), fire-brand (*fig.*), hempy (*jocular*), rogue (*playful*); *spec.* breedbate (*A*).

Antonyms: see PEACEMAKER.

mischievous, *a.* **1.** *See* HARMFUL, INJURIOUS.

2. playful (*contex.*), roguish, wicked (*C*); *spec.* arch, impish, puckish, elfish *or* elvish, tricksy, prankish, urchin (*R*), waggish.

misdo, *v. t.* do (*contex.*); *spec.* misperform, misexecute.

misesteem, *v. t.* **1.** *See* DISRESPECT.

2. misjudge, misvalue, misrate, mismeasure, misappreciate.

misfire, *n.* miss, fizzle; *spec.* sputter;—*used of a firearm.*

misform, *v. t. Spec.* misshape, miscreate.

misfortune, *n.* mischance, mishap, accident, adversity (*misfortune which consists in or tends to produce a settled state opposed to well being or prosperity*); *spec.* disaster, calamity, scourge, catastrophe (*implying dramatic and irretrievable disaster*), affliction, misventure (*A*), reverse, casualty, misadventure, contretemps (*French*), ill, down (*C*); *used esp. in "ups and downs"*), illth (*R*), blow, fatality, sorrow, cross, infelicity, infliction, visitation, tragedy, fate, destruction.

Antonyms: see FORTUNE.

misinterpret, *v. t. Spec.* misexplain, misrender, misunderstand.

misjoin, *v. t. Spec.* misally, mismarry, mismate, misyoke.

misjudge, *v. t.* misdeem (*A*).

mismanage, *v. t. Spec.* misdirect, misguide, mishandle, misconduct, fumble, blunder, botch.

misname, *v. t.* miscall, misterm, mistitle, misstyle, misnomer (*R*), becall (*R*); *spec.* befool, beknave, beslave, nickname.

misplace, *v. t.* **1.** mislay, mis-set.

2. *See* DISPLACE.

mispronounce, *v. t.* mis-speak (*R*), missound; *spec.* mangle.

---

mint, *v. t.: coin.*
minus: *less, wanting.*
minute, *n.: moment, memorandum.*
mire, *n.: marsh, mud, dirt.*
mirth: *gayety.*
misconstrue: *pervert.*
miscreant: *unbeliever, rascal, wretch.*
misdemeanor: *transgression.*
miser: *niggard.*
miserable: *distressing, lamentable, calamitous, wretched.*
misgiving: *distrust, fear.*
misinform: *deceive.*
mislay: *misplace.*
mislead: *deceive.*

---

mispronunciation, *n.* mis-speech (*R*), cacoepy (*tech.*), cacology (*R; tech.*); *spec.* manglement.
misquote, *v. t.* misgive (*R*), miscite, misrepeat (*R*); *spec.* misrecite.
misrelate, *v. t. Spec.* misreport, mistell, misrecite.
misrepresent, *v. t.* belie (*literally "to give the lie to"*), color, miscolor (*less euphemistic than "color"*), disguise, falsify; *spec.* caricature, disparage.
miss, *n.* mademoiselle (*French*), signorina (*Italian*), senhorita (*Portuguese*), señorita (*Spanish*), Fräulein (*German*).
miss, *v. t. Spec.* lose, muff, mistake, cut, escape, slip, omit, want, overlook, overpass, pass.
Antonyms: see GET, PERCEIVE.
miss, *v. i. Spec.* fail, deviate, misaim, misfire, miscue, err (*R*).
miss, *n. Spec.* oversight.
missed, *a.* lost; *spec.* astray.
missile, *n.* projectile; *spec.* dejectile (*R*), arrow, bullet, ball, shell, shot, slug, bomb *or* bombshell, squib, boomerang, bolas (*Span. & Port.*), dart.
misstate, *v. t. Spec.* misrelate, misreport, misword, garble.
misstep, *v. i. & n. Spec.* slip, stumble, stub, trip.
mister, *n.* monsieur (*French*), signor (*Italian*), senhor (*Portuguese*), señor (*Spanish*), Herr (*German*).
mistress, *n.* **1.** *In a romantic, chivalric, or tender sense, of the one loved and wooed:* ladylove, sweetheart.
2. *In the sense of head, governing or directing figure: spec.* teacher, wife, head.
3. *In the sense of a woman living with or supported by a man:* paramour.
4. *In the sense of more casual relationships, see* HARLOT. *In this sense, however,* mistress *is not correct.* Mistress *implies a certain amount of reciprocal esteem and affection; the various senses of* harlot *none.*
misunderstand, *v. t.* mistake; *spec.* miscomprehend, misconstrue, misknow, misapprehend, misconceive, misperceive.
misusage, *n.* **1.** *Spec.* misuser (*law*); *see* ABUSE, PERVERSION.
2. *Referring to words:* barbarism; *spec.* catachresis (*rhet.*).
mitigate, *v. t.* **1.** soothe, subdue, temper, soften, allay, ease, alleviate, ameliorate, assuage, palliate (*a wrong*), quiet, quieten (*the fears; R*), relieve.
Antonyms: see AGGRAVATE.
2. *See* RELAX.
mitigating, *a.* mitigatory, soothing, softening, alleviating, ameliorating, palliative (*of wrong*), assuasive, balmy.
mitigation, *n.* subdual, allayment, alleviation, amelioration, assuagement, palliation (*of wrong*), relief.
mix, *v. t. & i.* **1.** *Spec.* blend (*implying interpenetration of the elements brought together*), combine, intermingle (*implying that the combined elements keep their identity*), intermix (*intensive for "mix"*), interfuse, mell (*A*), temper, interlard, (*fig.*), co-mingle *or* commingle (*intensive*), coalesce (*suggesting a fusion of elements*); contemper, braid (*dial.*), compose, confection, immingle (*R*), immix, commix (*A or poetic; intensive for "mix"*), caudle, hotchpotch (*R*), confound, confuse, interlace, intergrade, distemper, amalgamate, alloy, interplait, shuffle, intertangle, pie, beat, gauge, cross, mélange, poach, levigate, puddle, blunge.
Antonyms: see SEPARATE, CLASSIFY.
2. *See* ASSOCIATE.
mixed, *a. Spec.* blended, combined, immixed, medley, tempered, confused, diversified, heterogeneous.
mixture, *n. Spec.* mingling, mingle, minglement, minglemangle (*chiefly contemptuous*), blend, blendure (*R*), compound, combination, composition, compounding, commixture (*intensive for "mixture"*), commixtion (*R or tech.*), mix (*C*), immixture (*intensive for "mixture"*), admixture, alloy, hodgepodge, hotchpotch, amalgam, intermixture (*intensive for "mixture"*), cross, hash, jumble, eucrasy (*B*), concoction, mélange (*French*), chowchow, confusion, shuffle, interfusion, interfluence (*R*), medley, motley, theocrasy, interflow (*R*), batter, paste, mush, intertanglement, levigation, interlacement, intertexture, interlacery. *See* MIX.
mob, *n.* **1.** rabble, canaille (*French; contemptuous*), clamjamphrie (*Scot. and dial. Eng.*); *spec.* ruck, raff, riffraff, rag-tag, rag-tag and bobtail, dregs.
2. *See* CROWD, PEOPLE.
model, *n.* form; *spec.* pattern, design, example, dummy, manikin, last, cast, phantom (*anat.*), miniature, copy, type.
moderate, *a. Spec.* temperate, reasonable, indifferent (*as not affecting the mind with any special attitude of liking or disliking*), passable, mild, low (*as contrasted with "high" or "intense"*), sparing, slack (*of heat, energy, etc. as not being violent in effect*), easy, chaste (*implying freedom from what offends the taste*), modest, gentle, fair, ordinary, merciful, decent, light (*said of a sparing meal*).
Antonyms: see EXTREME, EXORBITANT, EX-

mistake, *v. i.: err.*
mistake, *n.: error.*
mistreat: *ill-treat.*
mistrust: *distrust, guess, forebode.*
misty: *foggy, hazy, dim, cloudy.*
misuse: *ill-treat.*
moan: *groan, mourn.*
mob, *v. i.: crowd.*
mob, *v. t.: attack.*
mobile: *movable, liquid, changeable.*
mobilize: *assemble.*
mock, *v. t.: ridicule, defy, deceive, imitate.*
mock, *v. i.: jeer.*
mock-heroic: *burlesque.*
model, *a.: exemplary.*

TORTIONATE, OUTRAGEOUS, EXTRAVAGANT, STEEP.

moderate, *v. t.* diminish, lessen, slack, slacken, slake (*of thirst, and fig., of ambition, etc.*), allay, abate (*esp. emphasizing idea of previous excessive action*); *spec.* alloy, alleviate, sober, temper, qualify.

Antonyms: see AGGRAVATE.

moderately, *adv.* temperately, indifferently, pretty, fairly, somewhat.

modern, *a. Spec.* present, present-day, late, recent, up-to-date (*C*), up-to-the-minute (*C*), neoteric (*B*), fin-de-siècle (*French*), twentieth-century, new-fashioned, newfangled, fresh.

Antonyms: see ANCIENT.

modernity, *n.* modernness, neoterism (*chiefly spec.; B or tech.*).

Antonyms: see ANTIQUITY.

modest, *a. Spec.* diffident (*not sure of one's self*), demure (*affectedly modest*), decorous, decent (*suggestive of good taste and judgment as to what is proper, while "decorous" suggests a mere observance of convention*), delicate, retiring, quiet, bashful, humble, unpresumptuous, unpretending, unobtrusive, unostentatious, inobtrusive (*R*), boastless, unassuming.

Antonyms: see SHOWY, LEWD, INDECENT, ASSUMING, BOASTFUL, BOLD, LICENTIOUS, CONCEITED, OPINIONATE, GAUDY.

modesty, *n. Spec.* diffidence, decorum, *etc.*

Antonyms: see BOLDNESS, BOASTFULNESS.

modulate, *v. t.* adjust (*contex.*); *spec.* inflect, tongue (*music; to modulate with the tongue*), accentuate, pitch.

modulation, *n.* adjustment (*contex.*); *spec.* accent, pitch, inflection, brogue, cadence, tonguing.

Mohammed, Muhammed, *n.* Mahomet (*now obsolescent*), Baphomet (*a medieval cabalistic corruption*), Mahound (*the usual name in the Middle Ages*), Prophet (*with "the," "our," etc.*).

Mohammedan, Muhammedan, *a.* Mussulman, Moslem *or* Muslim, Mahometan, Turkish, Islamic, Islamitic, Islamitical, *or* Islamistic, paynim (*an archaic Christian term of reproach or contempt*), Saracenic, Saracenical, Moorish (*C; India and Ceylon*).

Mohammedan, Muhammedan, *n.* Mussulman (*a derivative from the source of Moslem; pl. "Mussulmans"*), Moslem *or*, more *accurately,* Muslim (*from the source of Islam*), Mahometan (*R*), Moorman (*East India*), Islamist, Islamite, Saracen (*esp. in reference to the crusades*); *spec.* sufi, Motazilite, Karmathian *or* Carmathian, Kadarite, Shiite *or* Shiah, Sunnite, shereef *or* sherif, Moor, Ismaelian *or* Ismailian.

Mohammedanism, *n.* Islam (*the proper name of orthodox Mohammedanism*), Islamism, Mahometanism (*obsolescent*), Muanmetry (*A*).

moist, *a. Spec.* wet, damp (*suggesting unpleasantness to touch or feeling*), humid (*chiefly poetic or rhetorical exc. as applying to the atmosphere*), dank (*suggesting unhealthfulness*), dankish, muggy, wettish, uliginose *or* uliginous (*R*), roscid (*R*), dewy, oozy, vaporous.

Antonyms: see DRY.

moisten, *v. t. & i.* wet; *spec.* bemoist (*an intensive*), dampen *or* (*less usual*) damp, humidify (*R*), baste, dew, sponge.

Antonyms: see DRY.

moisture, *n.* moistness (*chiefly of the state*), wetness; *spec.* dampness, damp, humidity, mugginess, breath, dew.

Antonyms: see DRYNESS.

molasses, *n.* treacle (*more usual in Eng.*).

mold, *n.* fungus (*tech.*); *spec.* must, mustiness, mother.

mold, *v. i.* must (*R or Eng. dial.*), fust (*obs. or dial.*).

moldable, *a. Spec.* figuline *or* fictile.

molded, *a.* moulded (*a variant*), fictile.

molding, *n.* **1.** casting.

2. ornament; *spec.* bead *or* astragal, reed *or* reeding, chaplet, cyma, cavetto, congé (*French*), quarter-round *or* ovolo, ogee, cornice, scotia, thumb, torus, torsade, tringle, round, roundel, fillet, cable, bolection *or* bilection, casemate *or* casement, surbase, platband.

moldy, *a.* molded, mucid (*R*), mucidous (*R*), mucedinous (*bot.; R*); *spec.* mothery, stale, musty, foisty, frowzy.

mole, *n. Referring to the animal:* moldwarp *or* moldiwarp (*chiefly Eng. dial.*), wanty (*obs.*).

mole, *n.* nævus (*tech.*); *spec.* birthmark.

molecular, *a. Spec.* Brownian.

molecule, *n.* particle; *spec.* monad, dyad, triad, tetrad, pentad, hexad, heptad, octad.

molt, *v. t.* shed (*the usual term, except of birds*); *spec.* cast, slough, mew (*tech., or A*), exuviate (*a tech. equivalent of "slough"*), throw.

molting, *n.* molt; *spec.* ecdysis (*tech.*), cast, sloughing, slough.

moment, *n.* **1.** *Spec.* instant (*point of time too short to reckon by ordinary observation*), minute, flash (*esp. with reference to action*), trice (*now only in "in a trice"*), crack, gliff (*Scot. or C*), jiffy (*C*), shake (*C*), handclap, eyewink, blink, wink, twinkling.

Antonyms: see ETERNITY, AGE.

2. *See* IMPORTANCE, MOMENTUM.

momentum, *n.* energy, moment, impetus.

monarch, *n.* sovereign *or* (*B*) sovran, autocrat (*emphasizing idea of unrestricted power, while "monarch" refers esp. to one who rules alone, or without sharing his rule with others*), king, crown (*fig.*), monocrat (*R*); *spec.* kinglet, kingling (*less contemptuous than "kinglet"*), Cæsar (*hist. or fig.*), emperor, queen, monarchess (*R; fem.*), empress, sovereigness (*R; fem.*), roitelet (*A*), prince (*A*), princess (*A*), royalet (*R*), imperator (*Latin form of "emperor"; chiefly hist.*), Kaiser (*German; hist.*), czar (*Russian; hist.*), Mikado (*Japanese*), raja

modify, *v. t.: change.*
modish: *stylish, affected.*
mold, *v. t.: work, form.*
molest: *disturb, harm.*
momentary: *temporary.*

or rajah (*East Indian*), Pharaoh (*hist.*), shah, sultan, Bretwalda (*hist.*).
Antonyms: see SUBJECT.

monarchical, *a.* autocratic, kingly, monarchial (*R*), monarchic (*R*), monocratic (*R*); *spec.* imperial.
Antonyms: see DEMOCRATIC.

monarchism, *n.* autocratism, Cæsarism, absolutism; *spec.* imperialism.

monarchy, *n.* autocracy, kingdom, royalty (*R, exc. as a characterizing term*), realm (*chiefly rhetorical or tech.*), reign (*fig.*), princedom (*R*), principality (*R*), regality (*R*).
Antonyms: see DEMOCRACY.

monastery, *n.* convent; *spec.* charterhouse, borzery (*R*), lamasery, vihara, monkery, cell.

monastic, *a.* conventual, monachal, monkish (*often a term of reproach*), monkly (*R*).

monasticism, *n.* monachism (*B*), monkism (*R*), monkhood, monkery (*chiefly contemptuous*).

monetary, *a.* financial, pecuniary (*chiefly spec.*), fiscal (*chiefly spec.*).

money, *n. Spec.* currency (*money actually accepted in general use*), cash (*primarily specie or coin on hand*), funds (*pl.*; *money at disposal, suggesting a considerable amount*), specie, coin (*a collective*), coinage (*more formal for "coin"*), chink (*S*), rhino (*S*), tin (*S*), dust (*S*), brass (*S or dial.*), barrel (*political S*), copper (*C*), gingerbread (*S*), tender, wampumpeag, wampum, wakiki, larin, coat money (*hist.*), cowrie.

Mongolian, *a.* Mongolic, Mongol (*properly spec.*), Mogul (*chiefly hist.*); *spec.* Chinese, Japanese, Samoyed, Lappish, Lapponian, Lapp.

monism, *n.* theism, unitism (*R*), henism (*R*).

monk, *n.* ecclesiastic (*contex.*), conventual, monastic (*more technical than "monk"*), friar (*a loose use*), religieux (*French*); *spec.* cœnobite, anchoret, prior, caloyer, santon, santo, Benedictine, talapoin, Sarabaite, Cluniac, cloisterer, hospitaler *or* hospitaller, marabout, Mekhitarist, lama, palmer.

monkey, *n.* simian, jackanapes (*A*); *spec.* entellus, guariba, sagoin, marimonda, mangabey, marmoset, marikina, sapajou, teetee, vitoe, tota, langur, chacma, kahau, lar, macaque, macaco, grivet, howler, hoolock.

monkeylike, *a.* pithecoid (*tech.*); *spec.* cebocephalic.

monogram, *n.* cipher.

monologue, *n. Spec.* soliloquy.

monopolize, *v. t. Spec.* engross, corner (*cant*).

monopoly, *n.* staple (*hist.*), soleship (*R*); *spec.* monopolism.

monotone, *n. Spec.* drone, singsong.

monotone, *v. t. Spec.* intone, drone.

monotonous, *a.* dull, flat, samely (*R*); *spec.* singsong (*suggesting continued sameness in rise and fall of pitch, where "monotonous" suggests sameness of pitch*), wearisome, jogtrot (*C*), dreary *or* drearisome *or* (*R*) drear (*B*) (*with repellent implication*), routine.
Antonyms: see VARIED.

monotony, *n.* monotone (*chiefly spec.*), sameness, sameliness (*R*); *spec.* humdrum, dreariness, drearihead (*A*), dreariment, drearihood.
Antonyms: see VARIETY.

monster, *n.* **1.** *Referring to mythical or legendary beings: spec.* dragon, drake (*A*), dragonet, behemoth, leviathan, hydra, lamid, sphinx, chimæra, mermaid (*fem.*), merman (*masc.*), centaur, Frankenstein, Scylla *and* Charybdis, Cyclops, Erinnyes, harpy, siren, ogre (*masc.*), ogress (*fem.*), bucentaur, mariche, manticore, hircocervus, hippocampus, hippogriff, kylin (*of China and Japan*), chichevache (*French; obs.*), griffin, wyvern (*her.*).
2. *Referring to what is abnormal in shape:* monstrosity, freak, cacogenesis (*tech.*); *spec.* hodmandod, terata (*pl.; med.*), abortion, mooncalf (*A*), miscreation.
3. *Referring to a being of unnatural cruelty:* fiend, devil, shaitan (*Mohammedan*).

monstrosity, *n.* **1.** abnormality, freak; *spec.* atrocity, teratology.
2. *See* MONSTER.

monstrous, *a.* **1.** (*abnormal in size*), colossal, gigantic, prodigious (*suggesting an astonishing scale*), enormous, Cyclopean, Cyclopian, *or* Cyclopic. *See* GREAT.
2. unnatural, abnormal, freaky; *spec.* teratological (*med.*), teratical (*med.*), malformed, misshapen, miscreated.
Antonyms: see NATURAL, NORMAL.
3. See FLAGRANT, OUTRAGEOUS, IMMENSE.

month, *n.* moon (*fig.*); *spec.* lunation, ramadan (*Mohammedan*).

monthly, *a.* menstrual (*tech.*), mensual.

monument, *n.* **1.** memorial; *spec.* gravestone, sepulcher, cromlech (*archæol.*), lech (*archæol.*), dagoba (*Buddhist.*), cenotaph, lat (*East India*), antiquity, pyramid, menhir (*archæol.*), tombstone, tomb, trophy, megalith, monolith, trilith *or* trilithon, marble, document.
2. *See* BOUNDARY, DOCUMENT.

moon, *n.* **1.** Phœbe (*poetic; personified*), Cynthia (*poetic; personified*), Luna (*poetic or tech.; personified*); *spec.* plenilune (*chiefly poetic*), crescent, decrescent (*R*), sickle, increscent (*chiefly her.*).
2. *See* MONTH, MOONLIGHT.

moonlight, *n.* moonshine (*poetic or R*), shine (*contex.*), moon, moonbeam (*chiefly in pl.*); *spec.* earthlight.
Antonyms: see DARK.

moonlight, *a.* moonshiny (*R*), moony (*R*).
Antonyms: see DARK.

moor, *n.* moorland; *spec.* heath, bent, brier.

Moor, *n.* Moorman, Moresco (*chiefly spec.*); *spec.* Marrano (*hist.*), Maugrabee *or* Maugrabin.

---

mood: *disposition.* | **moody:** *changeable.* | **morale:** *spirit.*

---

moor, *v. t. Spec.* berth, anchor.
mooring, *n. Spec.* berthage, moor (*R*).
Moorish, *a.* Moresco, Moresque (*fine arts*).
moral, *a.* ethical *or* (*R*) ethic (*chiefly referring to morals as a subject of scientific discussion or consideration; "moral" being used esp. in reference to morals taken as an attribute of a person*).
morning, *n.* morn (*B*), forenoon, morningtide (*R or B*), morrow (*A*).
Antonyms: see EVENING.
morning star, daystar, Lucifer, Phosphor (*poetic*), Phosphorus (*R*).
Antonyms: see EVENING STAR.
morsel, *n.* **1.** *Spec.* bite, bit, titbit, sop.
2. *See* FRAGMENT, PARTICLE.
mortal, *a.* **1.** *Being subject to death:* earthborn, corporeal, ephemeral.
Antonyms: see IMMORTAL.
2. *See* DYING, DEADLY, GREAT, HUMAN, IMPLACABLE, LONG.
mortal, *n.* earthling, deathling (*R*).
mortgage, *n.* pledge (*contex.*), charge (*contex.*), encumbrance (*contex.*); *spec.* dip (*C*), bottomry, wadset (*Scot.*), bond, debenture.
mortgage, *v. t. Spec.* pledge, charge, encumber.
mortgagee, *n.* encumbrancer.
mortify, *v. t.* **1.** crucify (*fig.*); *spec.* humble.
2. *See* EMBARRASS.
mortify, *v. i.* gangrene.
mortise, *n.* hole (*contex.*); *spec.* gain, dovetail, cocket, cog.
mosaic, *n.* inlay; *spec.* tarsia (*tech.*).
mosaic, *a.* inlaid, tessellated *or* tessellate (*tech. or B*), musive (*R*).
mosquito, *n. Spec.* gallinipper (*chiefly U. S.*), Anopheles, Culex, wriggler.
mother, *n.* parent (*contex.*), mamma *or* mama (*chiefly in the vocative or preceded by a possessive pronoun*), genetrix *or* genitrix (*R*), dam (*as used of human beings only, contemptuous*), mammy (*a child's word*), mam (*C; a childish word*), matriarch (*jocular*), motherkin (*a dim., chiefly in affectionate use*), author (*contex.*), head (*contex.*), venter (*tech.; law*).
Antonyms: see CHILD.
motherhood, *n.* mother, motherhead (*R*), mothership, maternity.
motif, *n.* idea (*contex.*), motive (*the less used Eng. equivalent of the French "motif"*); *spec.* theme.
motion, *n.* **1.** movement (*suggesting a definite motion directed toward a particular purpose, as regulated by rule or law; "motion" is the act considered as a phenomenon with reference to its existence or qualities as such*), stir; *spec.* pass, move (*a change of position from stationary esp. as a step in the accomplishment of a purpose*), drift, drive (*suggesting a violent voluntary motion, esp. one intended to overcome opposition*), driftage, play, course, dash, rush (*headlong, often lacking purpose*), dart (*quick, sudden, light and momentary motion*), fling, flirt, onset, flight, flicker, career, dodge, excursion (*physics; motion of a body that will return*), travel, sweep, creep, set (*implying a steady, often irresistible motion*), hitch, flow, countermotion, flux, throw, gesture, translation, locomotion, walk, run, jump, hop, *etc.*
Antonyms: motionlessness (*cf.* MOTIONLESS).
2. *See* ACTION, PROPOSAL, OFFER, EVACUATION.
motionless, *a.* **1.** still, immovable; *see* STILL.
Antonyms: see LIVELY, RESTLESS, FLOWING.
2. stationary, immotile, stock-still, immobile (*chiefly spec.*); *spec.* quiescent, quiet, fixed.
Antonyms: see BOISTEROUS, LIVELY.
motionlessness, *n.* stillness, rest, immobility, quiescence, repose.
motion picture, *n.* moving picture, cinema, movie (*C*), flicks (*S; Brit.*), pictures (*C*); *spec.* talkies (*C*), news-reel, shorts (*cant*), Westerns, features, *etc.*
motive, *n.* **1.** cause (*contex.*), spring; *spec.* reason, purpose; *see* REASON.
2. *See* MOTIF.
mound, *n. Spec.* hill, heap, bank, tumulus, barrow, tell (*Arabic*), kurgun (*archæol.*), cache, esker (*geol.*), hornito, rampart (*fort.*), barbette (*fort.*), terp (*Friesland*), teocalli (*Mexican religion*), pyramid.
mount, *v. t.* **1.** *See* CLIMB, SET.
2. *Spec.* back (*a horse*), remount, horse (*a person*), bestride (*a horse*).
mountain, *n.* elevation (*contex.*), hill (*chiefly spec.*), heap, highland, mount (*B or A*); *spec.* sierra, jokul (*Icel.*), chain, range.
Antonyms: see PLAIN, VALLEY.
mourn, *v. t.* regret (*contex.*); *spec.* deplore, lament, bewail, wail (*R*), bemoan, moan (*less emphatic than "bemoan"*), greet (*Scot.*), condole (*R*), keen (*Irish*), dirge, behowl (*R*), besigh (*R*), sigh, overweep, elegize.
mourn, *v. i.* (*suggesting manifested sorrow*), regret (*contex.*); *spec.* lament (*implying expressed plaint or regret*), sigh, wail, greet (*Scot.*), keen (*Irish*), cry, weep, plain (*A*), sorrow, grieve (*suggesting deep mental pain*).
Antonyms: see EXULT, REJOICE.
mourner, *n. Spec.* lamenter, weeper, howler, mute, keener (*Irish*), *etc.*
mournful, *a.* **1.** regretful (*contex.*); *spec.* lugubrious, lamenting, lamentatory (*R*), plangorous (*a rhetorical term*), woeful, sad, moanful (*R*), plaintive, flebile (*R*), doleful, dismal,

morality: *virtue, ethics.*
morass: *marsh.*
moratorium: *deferment.*
morbid: *ailing, gloomy, deranged.*
mordant: *corrosive.*
more, *a.: additional, greater, else.*
more, *adv.: also.*
morgue: *dead house.*
morn: *daybreak.*
morose: *ill-tempered.*
mortify: *gangrene.*
mortuary: *dead house.*
most, *adv.: chiefly.*
most, *a.: greatest.*
mostly: *chiefly.*
mote: *particle.*
motherly: *maternal.*
motion, *v. i.: gesture.*
motion, *v. t.: guide, direct, summon.*
motley, *a.: party-colored, composite.*
mould: *mold.*
mount, *v. t.: rise, climb, increase.*
mount, *n.: hill, mountain, horse.*

sorrowful, elegiac, dirgeful, tearful, lachrymal, threnodic *or* threnodical, wailful (*R*), Lenten.
Antonyms: see FESTIVE.
2. *See* LAMENTABLE.
mourning, *n.* **1.** regretting (*contex.*), sorrow; *spec.* lamentation, deploration (*R*), wailing, moaning, *etc.*
Antonyms: see REVELRY, EXULTATION, REJOICING.
2. weeds (*esp. of a widow*); *spec.* crêpe (*French*), crape, armozeen.
mouselike, *a.* myoidal (*R*).
mouth, *n.* **1.** jaws (*pl.*), gob (*dial. or S*), reb (*chiefly Scot.*).
2. *See* GRIMACE.
3. opening (*contex.*), aperture (*contex.*); *spec.* estuary, debouchment (*R*), muzzle, crater, entrance, outlet, orifice.
mouth, *v. t.* **1.** *See* UTTER, DECLAIM, MANGLE
2. *To touch, rub, etc., with the mouth; spec.* mumble, lip, kiss.
mouthful, *n.* gob (*vulgar*).
mouthpiece, *n.* **1.** *Spec.* bit.
2. *See* SPOKESMAN.
movable, *a.* **1.** motionable (*R*), changeable; *spec.* mobile (*characterized by ready movement*), traveling.
Antonyms: see IMMOVABLE.
2. *See* IMPRESSIBLE, CHANGEABLE.
move, *v. t.* **1.** *Spec.* transport, transfer, translate (*B*), carry, convey, bear, take, remove, manhandle, hitch, flirt, dislodge, shake, sweep, stir, start, drift, edge, steal, play, pole, warp (*naut.*), daudle, walk, actuate (*tech.*), eloin *or* eloign (*obs., exc. as used with the reflexive or as a law term*), impel, drive, throw, cart, wheel, chariot (*R*), motor, charioteer (*R*), channel (*R*), operate, shift, flutter, tilt, jiggle, change, turn, displace, disturb, *etc. For sense-discriminations cf.* MOTION.
2. *See* AFFECT, ROUSE, COMPEL, IMPEL, ASK.
move, *v. i.* **1.** *Spec.* pass, drift, lob, locomote (*C*), career, drive, snail (*R*), stream, streak, lumber, travel, squib (*R*), budge, clip (*C*), run, rumble, hum (*C, implying lively action*), flitter, creep, crawl, draggle, drop, drawl (*R*), shift, steal, tilt, pole, jerk, advance, retreat, drumble (*R or dial.*), hitch, burst, bounce, edge, idle, startle, circulate, stir, start, vibrate, remove, trend, flow, go, turn, rush, dash, fling, falter, flirt, flicker, whisk, sail, float, fly, skip, hop, whip, swing, shiffle, flounce, lounge, castle (*chess*), bowl, operate, play, poke.
2. *See* DEPART, LIVE, ACT.
movement, *n.* **1.** motion, conduction (*now esp. of natural processes, sap, etc.*); *spec.* pass.
2. *Referring to the act of moving something: spec.* transfer, transferal, transport (*chiefly commercial*), carriage, conveyal (*R*), conveyance, boatage, cartage, disturbance, displacement.
3. *Referring to a definite motion, esp. as tending toward, or intended to produce, a certain result: spec.* maneuver, evolution, operation, figure, inversion.
4. *Referring to action of some kind by many or by people generally: spec.* crusade, war, propaganda, drive (*C*), revolt.
5. *See* ACTION, ACT, ACTIVITY, MECHANISM.
mover, *n. Spec.* transporter, carrier, conveyer, teamster, drayman, carman, expressman, *etc.*
moving, *a.* **1.** *Spec.* shifting, drifting, running, stirring, flitting, darting, astir, locomotive, live, changeful, *etc.*
2. *Spec.* motive, motory, material (*R*), motor, transfer (*of carriers or materials for carrying*).
3. *See* AFFECTING, COMPULSORY.
much, *n.* mickle (*A or Scot.*); *spec.* considerable (*chiefly U. S.*), heaps (*C; pl.*), lot (*C*).
Antonyms: see LITTLE, NOTHING.
much, *adv. Spec.* largely, enormously, highly, extremely, considerably, muchly (*jocular*), greatly.
mucous, *a.* pituitous (*tech.*), pituitary (*tech.*).
mucus, *n. Spec.* phlegm, pituita (*tech.*), snivel, mucilage.
mud, *n.* earth (*contex.*), dirt (*contex.*); *spec.* mire, muck, slush, sludge, clabber (*dial.*), slime, ooze, moya (*geol.*), lute, gumbo (*U. S.; C*).
muddy, *a.* **1.** earthy (*contex.*), dirty (*contex.*), muddish (*chiefly spec.*); *spec.* oozy, slushy, sludgy, slimy, uliginous *or* uliginose (*R*), limous (*R*), lutose (*R*), cloudy, gritty, roily, sandy, turbid.
Antonyms: see CLEAR.
2. *See* DARK, INTOXICATED, FOUL, DULL, CONFUSED.
muddy, *v. t.* **1.** dirty (*contex.*); *spec.* mire, bemire (*intensive for "mire"*), slime, slush, puddle, roil.
2. *See* DARKEN, CONFUSE.
mud-guard, *n.* fender, wing (*chiefly Brit. for the front* mud-guards *only*).
muff, *n.* **1.** *Spec.* cover, bungle, bungler, muffer, clown.
2. *In games:* miss; *spec.* fumble, bungle.
muff, *v. t. & i. In games:* miss; *spec.* fumble, bungle.
Antonyms: see CATCH.
muffer, *n. In games:* misser; *spec.* fumbler, bungler, butterfingers (*C*).
muffled, *a.* dull (*contex.*); *spec.* puffy.
muffler, *n.* wrap (*contex.*), muffle; *spec.* scarf, veil, tippet, disguise.
mug, *n.* cup (*contex.*); *spec.* Bellarmine, tankard, toby.
mulatto, *n.* hybrid, half-breed; *spec.* griff (*local, U. S.*).

---

movie, *n.: motion-picture.*
mow, *n.: heap.*
muck: *manure, dirt, earth.*
muddle, *v. t.: confuse, stupefy.*
muddle, *n.: confusion, disorder.*
muffle, *v. t.: cover, wrap, deaden.*
mulct, *v. t.: fine, deprive.*

---

mule, *n.* horse (*contex.*), hybrid (*contex.*), half-breed (*contex.*); *spec.* mute (*dial. or cant*).
mullion, *n.* munnion, monial (*both R*).
multiform, *a.* diversified, various (*diverse in kind as well as in form*), variform (*R*), diversiform; *spec.* protean *or* (*less usual*) proteiform, amœbiform, polymorphous *or* (*less usual*) polymorphic, metamorphotic, multiphase.
Antonyms: see UNIFORM.
multiplier, *n.* multiplicator (*R*), facient (*tech.*); *spec.* coefficient.
multiply, *v. t.* increase (*contex.*); *spec.* decuple (*tech.*), decuplate (*tech.*), cube, double, centuplicate, tenfold, quadruple, triplicate.
multitude, *n.* **1.** (*implying merely great numbers*). *Spec.* crowd (*implying many in a close, unordered formation*), throng (*suggesting an active concourse of people*), army, swarm, pack, flock, world, host, mob (*chiefly disparaging*), heap (*C*), pile (*obs. or inelegant*), hive, legion, herd (*derogatory*), power (*dial. or C*), plurality (*R*), sight (*C or S*), ruck (*derogatory*), assembly, troop, cloud.
2. numerousness, multitudinousness. *See* MANY, *a.*
mumble, *v. i.* **1.** mump, mutter.
2. *See* CHEW.
municipal, *a.* civil (*contex.*); *spec.* city, town, village, *etc.*
murder, *n.* assassination (*killing by treacherous violence*), homicide (*contex.*); *spec.* massacre, butchery, thuggee, thuggism, lynching.
murder, *v. t.* **1.** kill (*contex.*); *spec.* massacre, butcher, burke, bishop, morganize (*U. S.*), suppress, assassinate, thug, lynch.
2. *See* DESTROY, MANGLE.
murderer, *n.* killer (*contex.*), homicide (*contex.*); *spec.* cutthroat, gunman (*C*), butcher, assassin, thug, lyncher.
murmur, *n.* **1.** *Spec.* babble, prattle, frumescence (*R*), sough, souffle (*med.*), purl, hum, rustle, whisper.
2. *See* COMPLAINT, MUTTER.
murmur, *v. i.* **1.** *Spec.* babble, bicker, brawl, hum, sough, curr (*R*), prattle, purl, curmur (*imitative; R*), rumor (*R*), rustle, whisper.
2. *See* COMPLAINT, MUTTER.
murmuring, *a.* murmurous, murmurish; *spec.* babbling, brawling, babbly, purling, frumescent, rustling, whispering.
muscle, *n.* thew.
muscular, *a.* musculous (*R*), torous (*obs.* or *R*); *spec.* brawny, beefy (*C*).
museum, *n.* repository (*R*); *spec.* pinæcotheca.
mushroom, *n.* fungus; *spec.* truffle, champignon, chanterelle, flap, morel, whitecap, puffball, *etc.*
music, *n.* *Spec.* melody, harmony, descant (*part music*), chime, rondo.
musical, *a.* **1.** *Spec.* harmonic (*obs. or spec.*), Orphean (*fig.*), singing, canorous (*R*), philharmonic; *see* HARMONIOUS, MELODIOUS.
Antonyms: see UNMUSICAL.
2. *See* CLEAR.
musician, *n.* player, musicianer (*now chiefly illiterate*), harmonist (*B*); *spec.* luter (*hist.*), bard (*Lowland Scot.*), minstrel, wait, gleeman (*hist.*), lyrist, lutanist, violinist, oboist, drummer, bugler, *etc.*
musket, *n.* *Spec.* culverin, caliver, matchlock, musketoon.
mustache, *n.* mustachio (*B*), whiskers (*pl.; A*).
mute, *n.* dummy (*reproachful*); *spec.* deaf-mute.
mutilate, *v. t.* **1.** *In the sense of disabling or destroying a member or organ: spec.* maim, dismember, disarm, bemaim (*intensive term*), law, expeditate (*R*), truncate, pinion, hamstring.
2. *See* DEFACE, MANGLE, PERVERT.
mutilation, *n.* **1.** *Spec.* maiming, mayhem (*law*), concision, dismemberment, demembration (*chiefly Scots law*), lawing, expeditation, truncation.
2. *See* DEFACEMENT.
mutter, *v. i. & t.* *Spec.* grumble, mumble, murmur.
mutter, *n.* mumblement (*R*); *spec.* grumble, mumble, murmur, growl, snarl (*both implying primarily a warning of displeasure or a threat*).
mutual, *a.* common (mutual *implies reciprocal interest, action, or effect;* common, *joint or shared interest, etc., as "mutual esteem," "common friends"*), commutual (*chiefly poetic; emphatic for* mutual); *spec.* reciprocal, interactive, interurban, international, interstate, intertribal, *etc.*
Antonyms: see INDIVIDUAL.
muzzle, *n.* **1.** *Spec.* muffle, mouth.
2. mouth (*of a gun*).
my, *a.* mine (*A, exc. predicative*).
myriad, *a.* innumerable, ten thousand.
mysterious, *a.* hidden (*contex.*), enigmatic, enigmatical, sphinxlike.
mystic, *n.* *Spec.* cabalist, occultist, gnostic, quietist, sufi, therapeutæ (*pl.*).
mysticism, *n.* secrecy (*contex.*); *spec.* ontologism, Orphism, quietism, cabala.

N

nadir, *n.* bottom;—*no good synonyms.*
Antonyms: see ZENITH, APOGEE.
nail, *n.* **1.** ungula (*tech.*), unguis (*tech.*); *spec.* talon (*of beast or bird of prey*), claw (*the sharp, horny nail of some animals*).
2. *Spec.* tack, hobnail, spike, spud, stub, sparable, sprig, brad, clout nail, counterclout.
naked, *a.* **1.** bare, exposed, nude (*a term less suggestive of impropriety or disadvantage than*

mulish: *intractable.*
multiply: *v. i.: increase.*
mum, *a.: silent.*
murderous: *homicidal, fierce, deadly.*
muse: *consider, gaze.*
mushy: *soft, emotional.*
musing: *thoughtful, abstracted.*
muss, *n.: confusion, disturbance, disorder.*
muster, *v.: convene.*
muster, *n.: assembly, list.*
musty: *moldy.*
mutiny: *n.: disobedience, insurgence.*
mystery: *art, trade, association.*
mystic: *hidden.*
mystify: *perplex.*
mythical: *fictitious.*

N

naive: *artless.*

"naked"), stark-naked (*an intensive*), stark (*obs. or R for "stark-naked"*), in cuerpo (*used humorously in the predicate*), garmentless (*R*), unclad (*suggesting the previous removal of the clothes, or that they have not been put on*), unclothed *or* ungarmented (*chiefly euphemistic*), unarrayed *or* unappareled (*a dignified equiv. of "ungarmented"*); *spec.* bare-backed.

Antonyms: see CLOTHED.

2. *See* EVIDENT, MERE, HELPLESS.

name, *n.* **1.** title (*often spec.*), term (*precise or technical in sense, esp. in science*), denomination (*affected or obsolescent as used of individual names*), designation (*often spec.*), denotation (*now R or A; exc. spec.*); *spec.* alias, appellation (*a descriptive or characterizing name of a person or thing as belonging to a class; more suggestive than* appellative *of a name given in address*), appellative (*a name of any of a class, or one emphasizing more than* appellation *the idea of mere characterization*), epithet (*a name implying some particular significance*), firm, style (*implying particular reference to the formal or proper manner of designation, esp. of a titled person, business house, etc.*), compellative (*R*), compellation (*R*), nickname, nomenclature (*R*), cryptonym (*R*), pseudonym, byname, toname, caconym, sobriquet (*often suggesting a fanciful name*), prænomen, forename, nomen, cognomen, agnomen, surname, addition (*obs., exc. law*), binomial, patronymic, protonym, toponym; *see* NOUN.

2. *See* REPUTATION, CELEBRITY.

name, *v. t.* **1.** call (*of ordinary designation*), term (*of more precise or technical naming*), style, denominate, entitle, title (*R*), intitule (*A, equiv. of "entitle"*), nominate (*R*), nomenclate (*R*), nomenclature (*R*), clepe (*A*); *spec.* dub (*often humorous or contemptuous*), cognomen (*R*), cognominate (*R*), christen (*C*), count, epithet, epithetize (*R*), surname, design (*A and chiefly law*), nickname.

2. *See* MENTION, APPOINT.

named, *a.* called, hight (*A*), denominate, denominated, *etc.*

namely, *adv.* videlicet (*B*), even (*A or Biblical*), scilicet (*law*), to wit (*more formal than "namely"*).

namesake, *n.* homonym (*tech. or B*); *spec.* name child, name son, *etc.*

nap, *n.* pile (*chiefly spec.*); *spec.* shag, down, silk, wool, villi (*pl.*), villosity, fleece, cotton.

nape, *n.* poll (*R or A*), scruff *or* (*dial. Eng.*) scuff (*chiefly used in "scuff" or "scuff of the neck"*), nucha (*tech.*).

napkin, *n.* serviette (*affected*); *spec.* doily.

nappy, *a.* rough (*contex.*), napped, pily (*chiefly spec.*); *spec.* shaggy, downy, villous, fleecy, cottony, woolly.

narcotic, *a.* anæsthetic (*lessening feeling*), anodyne (*reducing pain*), soporific, stupefacient, dope (*S or C*); *spec.* bhang, hashish, hemp, ganja, opiate (nicotine, heroin, chloral, *etc.*).

Antonyms: see STIMULANT.

narrate, *v. t. Spec.* tell (*with idea of disclosure, or of giving information to the recipient*), retell, relate (*suggesting giving a connected account*), rehearse (*suggesting going over again, esp. in detail*), recite (*giving familiar details that may be tedious, or of little interest*), recount, state (*suggesting methodical relation, with or without details, for consideration by another, as by a court*), discourse (*A*), retail, report, record, delate (*R or B*), chronicle, circumstantiate, repeat. Narrate *suggests esp. the idea of a series of events or a story told in connected form often for its own interest, esp. in writing or print.*

narration, *n.* **1.** *Spec.* relation, rehearsal, recitation, repetition, statement, record, report, recital.

2. *See* NARRATIVE, ACCOUNT.

narrative, *n. Referring to the thing narrated: spec.* statement, account, narration, history, novel, story, yarn (*C*), fable, romance, tale, saga.

narrator, *n. Spec.* reciter, rehearser, recounter, chronicler, sayer (*A*), anecdotist, raconteur.

narrow, *a.* **1.** confined (*suggesting restraint within close limits*), strait (*now A or with Biblical reference*), incapacious, limited; *spec.* constricted, cramped, tight, close, crammy (*C*), pinched, scanty (*suggesting a deficiency, but not such as to prevent use or the like*), scant.

Antonyms: see VAST, WIDE, BOUNDLESS, SPACIOUS, ROOMY.

2. *In reference to an escape:* near, close, bare, hairbreadth.

3. illiberal, little (*suggesting inability to conceive large things*); *spec.* prejudiced, fanatical, bigoted, hidebound (*depreciatory*), uncomprehensive, insular, provincial, parochial, untraveled, clannish, cliquish, *etc.*

Antonyms: see WIDE, GENERAL, INCLUSIVE, LIBERAL, COMPREHENSIVE.

narrow, *n. Referring to a narrow waterway: spec.* strait, tidegait, gut. *The plural form "narrows" is common.*

narrow, *v. t.* **1.** straiten (*R exc. A or B*); *spec.* constrict, contract, lessen.

Antonyms: see WIDEN.

2. *See* DIMINISH.

nasality, *n.* twang.

natal, *a.* **1.** birth;—*the noun used attributively.*

2. *See* NATIVE.

nation, *n.* people, nationality (*fig.*), folk; *spec.* tribe.

nationality, *n.* nationalism. (Nationality *suggests esp. the character which makes a people a nation;* nationalism *suggests more the feeling of devotion to, or advocacy of, the national character and interests*).

nameless: *obscure, anonymous, abominable.*
nap: *sleep.*
narrowing: *constriction, contraction.*
narrow-minded: *intolerant, mean.*
nasality: *resonance.*
nasty: *dirty, filthy, foul, ill-tempered, dangerous.*

native, *a.* **1.** *See* INNATE.

2. *In reference to belonging by birth or origin:* original; *spec.* autochthonous (*B*), indigenous (*naturally belonging*), natural (*suggesting what is due to nature*), natal (*chiefly poetic*), aboriginal, live (*said of rocks* in situ), innate (*said of minerals, rocks, etc.*), endemic *or* (*less common*) endemical (*said of a place of natural or ordinary habitat or prevalence*), vernacular (*R, exc. spec.*), home-born, home-bred.

Antonyms: see FOREIGN, FALSE.

3. *See* DOMESTIC.

native, *n.* aborigine (*an etymologically indefensible sing. of "aborigines," pl.; but fairly common in use*), autochthon (*B*), indigene (*R*); *spec.* creole, countryman, countrywoman.

Antonyms: see FOREIGNER.

natural, *a.* **1.** normal, ordinary (*contex.*), regular.

Antonyms: see SUPERNATURAL.

2. *See* INNATE, ILLEGITIMATE, NATIVE, ACCUSTOMED, PHYSICAL, UNREGENERATE.

3. *In reference to what is in accordance with one's nature: spec.* constitutional (*implying inherence in or accordance with, one's constitution, or inmost and fixed nature; suggesting difficulty or impossibility of change*), inartificial, connatural (*B and emphatic*), customary, physic (*R*), easy, unlabored, artless, lifelike, unrestrained, unstudied, born (*as a born actor, etc.*)

Antonyms: see ARTIFICIAL, UNNATURAL, MONSTROUS, AFFECTED.

naturalize, *v. t.* **1.** *See* ENFRANCHISE, DOMESTICATE.

2. *In reference to adapting a person or plant to a country or environment: spec.* acclimate, acclimatize, creolize, domesticate, habituate.

nature, *n.* **1.** *In reference to that which is the source of life and being:* kind (*A as in "Dame kind," "the law of kind"*).

2. *See* UNIVERSE.

3. character, constitution, quality, inbeing (*R*), indoles (*R*); *spec.* grain, kind, type, form, mold, inside, interior, disposition, structure, idiom, heart.

4. naturalness.

nausea, *a.* **1.** disgust (*contex.*), sickness (*R in this restricted sense*); *spec.* qualm, seasickness, queasiness.

2. *See* DISGUST, ABHORRENCE, AVERSION.

nauseate, *v. i.* sicken, rise (*of the stomach*), turn (*of the stomach*), spleen (*R*).

nauseate, *v. t.* **1.** sicken, turn (*of the stomach*), revolt (*implying a revulsion of disgust*); *spec.* drug.

2. *See* DISGUST.

nauseous, *a.* **1.** offensive (*contex.*), qualmish *or* (*R*), qualmy, queasy (*R*), sickish, sickly (*less emphatic than "sickish"*), sickening; *spec.* mawkish (*suggesting esp. a faint but insipid taste or odor*), emetic, nasty.

2. *See* DISGUSTING.

nautical, *a.* (*referring esp. to the art of navigation*), naval (*chiefly as pertaining to a navy*), nautic (*poetic or rhetorical*), tarrish (*fig.*; *R*).

navigable, *a.* **1.** sailable (*R*).

Antonyms: see UNNAVIGABLE.

2. *In reference to balloons: see* DIRIGIBLE.

navigate, *v. t.* **1.** sail, pernavigate (*R; an intensive*); *spec.* cruise.

2. *See* STEER, MANAGE.

near, *adv.* **1.** by, about, forby (*A or Scot.*), around (*C, U. S.*), fast (*B, now only in "fast by"*), hard (*B, now only in "hard by"*), close (*only in "close by"*), nigh (*A or dial.*), nearhand (*Scot.*).

Antonyms: see FAR.

2. closely (*stronger than* near).

near, *prep. Spec.* by, beside, about, around (*C, U. S.*), on, at, along.

near, *a.* **1.** *Referring to space relations: spec.* close (*chiefly predicative*), nigh, proximate (*B or tech.*), warm (*C*), nearby, neighboring, vicinal (*a more learned equivalent of "neighboring"*), propinquent (*R*), adjacent (*implying immediate nearness, though not contact*), contiguous (*implying contact*), adjoining (*touching*). Near *and its improper synonyms apply to what is not in contact.*

Antonyms: see DISTANT.

2. *Referring to time relations: spec.* close (*chiefly predicative*), immediate, instant (*an emphatic equiv. of "immediate"*), impending, imminent.

3. *Fig.* close, tight (*S*); *see* STINGY.

Antonyms: see DISTANT.

nearest, *a.* next, proximal, proximate, hithermost (*R*).

Antonyms: see EXTREME.

nearly, *adv. Spec.* about, toward, nighly (*R*), almost.

nearness, *n. Spec.* adjacency, closeness, nighness (*A*), neighborhood, appropinquity (*R*), proximity (*in more common use than "proximateness"*), vicinity, propinquity (*B*).

Antonyms: see DISTANCE.

near-sighted, *a.* short-sighted, myopic (*tech.*)

Antonyms: see FAR-SIGHTED.

necessarily, *a.* needs (*used chiefly with "must"*).

necessary, *a.* **1.** indispensable, vital, needful, need (*R*), requisite, essential, inevitable, behoveful *or* behooveful (*A*).

Antonyms: see UNNECESSARY, ACCIDENTAL.

2. *See* CONSEQUENTIAL, AXIOMATIC, UNAVOIDABLE.

necessary, *n.* indispensable, requisite (*as demanded by circumstance*), requirement, essential (*as indispensable to the very nature of a thing*), necessity, needment (*chiefly in pl.; chiefly Eng. and spec.*); *spec.* estovers.

Antonyms: see SUPERFLUITY.

necessity, *n.* **1.** indispensableness, requisiteness, needfulness, need, inevitableness.

Antonyms: see CHANCE.

---

naturalize: *enfranchise, adopt, domesticate, accustom, acclimate.*
near, *v. i.: approach.*
neat: *pure, elegant, skillful, orderly, compact, shapely.*
necessitate: *compel, cause.*

---

2. *Referring to what compels or must be:* compulsion, must*: see* FATE, FATALITY.
Antonyms: see CHANCE.
3. *See* NECESSARY, *n.*
neck, *n.* **1.** cervix (*tech.*), jugulum (*tech.*), scrag (*S, exc. spec.*), hals (*Scot. and dial. Eng.*), gullet (*a loose, depreciatory term*); *spec.* rach (*dial.*), nape, clod, ewe neck (*fig.*). *The adjective for "neck" is* jugular.
2. *See* CONSTRICTION, CHANNEL, ISTHMUS.
neckcloth, *n.* (*obsolescent in modern use*), neckpiece, *spec.* neckerchief, kercher (*obs. or dial.*), cravat, scarf, waterfall, overlay (*R*), soubise, whisk, tie, gimp, stomacher, four-in-hand, choker, (*S*), *etc.*
necklace, *n.* gorget (*R*); *spec.* chaplet, sultana, carcanet (*A*).
necklace-shaped, *a.* moniliform (*B*).
neck-shaped, *a.* trachelate (*tech.*).
necrological, *a. Spec.* obituary.
necrology, *n. Spec.* obituary.
nectar, *n. In reference to plants:* honey, honeydew (*B and fig.*).
need, *n.* **1.** necessity (*implying something of compulsion*); *spec.* occasion, commodity (*A*), convenience, turn (*need as felt for some special act at occasion*), want (*suggesting more than* need *the element of feeling to be needed*), privation, use, exigency, distress, lack.
2. *See* POVERTY, NECESSITY.
need, *v. t.* require, claim, demand, take; *spec.* crave (*sometimes fig.*), lack, want (*esp. in Eng. in sense of lack*).
needle, *n. Spec.* bodkin, blunt, sharp, between, darner, straw.
needlework, *n.* stitchery (*usually contemptuous*); *spec.* embroidery, insertion, knotwork.
ne'er-do-well, *n.* good-for-nothing, losel (*A*).
negative, *n.* **1.** *See* DENIAL.
2. *Of words expressing negation: spec.* nay (*A, exc. as used in deliberative bodies*), no (*the usual word expressing denial, dissent, or refusal*), non placet (*used in voting "no" in some assemblies*).
neglectful, *a.* disregardful; *spec.* forgetful, derelict (*U. S.*), culpose; *see* CARELESS, INATTENTIVE.
Antonyms: see CAREFUL.
negligence, *n.* (*suggesting a habit of neglect*), disregard (*contex.*), remissness (*implying a lack of attention to duty*), slackness (*implying easy-going habit, leaving things "at loose ends"*); *spec.* laxity, looseness, laches, carelessness, omission, inattention.
Antonyms: see CARE.
negligent, *a.* remiss (*contex.*), neglective (*R*), slack; *spec.* lax, loose, supine.
Antonyms: see CAREFUL, THOROUGH, FASTIDIOUS.
negro, *n.* black, blacky (*C*), nigger (*C*), Sambo (*a nickname*), blackamoor (*now only as a nickname*), quashee (*primarily a negro proper name; R*), coon (*S, U. S.*), darky *or* darkey (*C*), smoke (*S, U. S.*), chocolate (*S, U. S.*), dinge (*S, U. S.*), midnight (*S, U. S.*); *spec.* negress, negrillo, melanian, creole.
neigh, *v. i. & n.* cry (*contex.*), whinny, hinny (*R; used only as a verb*), whinner (*dial.*), nicher (*Scot.*).
neighborhood, *n.* **1.** *See* NEARNESS.
2. region (*contex.*), vicinity (*usually including more than the immediate proximity suggested by "neighborhood"*), vicinage (*more definite or technical than "neighborhood" in meaning*); *spec.* precinct, environs (*pl.*), outskirts (*pl.*), venue, presence.
3. *See* COMMUNITY, DISTRICT.
nerve, *n.* **1.** chord *or* cord (*now chiefly in "spinal chord" or "cord"*); *spec.* ganglion, nervule, vagus.
2. *See* STRENGTH, BOLDNESS, COURAGE, VEIN.
nerve, *v. t.* **1.** *literally:* innervate.
2. *Fig.: see* EMBOLDEN, STRENGTHEN.
nest, *n.* **1.** *In reference to birds: spec.* hammock, aerie (*often fig.*).
2. *In reference to insects, small animals, etc.:* nidus (*tech.*); *spec.* bike (*Scot.*), vespiary.
3. *See* LAIR, GROUP, RESORT.
nest, *v. i.* **1.** nidify (*B or R*).
2. *See* LODGE.
nestling, *n.* bird (*contex.*), nestler (*R*); *spec.* garlin (*Scot.*).
net, *n.* **1.** toil (*now usually in pl.*); *spec.* drift, seine, flue, *or* flew, fyke (*U. S.*), pound, pod, scringe, trammel, tuck, tunnel.
2. fabric (*contex.*), mesh, meshwork, network; *spec.* bobbinet, lace.
3. *See* NETWORK.
netlike, *a.* retiform (*tech.*), reticular (*tech.*), reticulary (*R*), reticulose (*R*).
netting, *n.* **1.** net (*contex.*); *spec.* bobbinet, lace.
2. *See* NETWORK.
network, *n. Referring to interlacing lines or filaments of any kind:* net, netting, reticulation (*tech.*), reticulum (*chiefly spec.*), meshwork (*R*), mesh (*chiefly fig.*), system (*of nation-wide radio* networks); *spec.* cobweb, plexus *or* (*less common*) plexure, fret.
neural, *a.* nerve (*the noun used attributively*), nerval (*R*).
neuter, *n.* **1.** *See* NEUTRAL.
2. *Referring to bees, etc.:* worker, neutral (*R*).
neutral, *a.* neuter (*less usual than "neutral"*); *spec.* indifferent, colorless (*often fig.*), inert.
neutralize, *v. t. Spec.* negative, drown, cancel, offset; *see* DEFEAT, COUNTERACT, DESTROY, OVERPOWER.
never, *adv.* ne'er (*B*).
Antonyms: see ALWAYS, SOMETIME, SOON, SOMETIMES.
new, *a.* novel (*strikingly different from that*

---

needless: *unnecessary.*
neglect, *n.: disregard, negligence.*
negotiate, *v. t.: transfer, effect, accomplish, overcome, jump.*
negotiate, *v. i.: treat, bargain.*
nervous: *forcible, excitable, apprehensive.*
nervy: *strong, bold, courageous.*
nestle, *v. i.: lie, lodge, snuggle.*
nestle, *v. t.: lodge.*
net, *a.: clear.*
net, *v. t.: catch.*

previously familiar), unusual, recent (*near to the present*), fresh, late, original, newfangled, brand-new, unheard-of, up-to-date (*C*), modern.
Antonyms: see OLD, SHABBY, ANCIENT, OBSOLETE, IMITATED.

newcomer, *n.* comeling (*A*), newcome (*R*); *spec.* arrival, tenderfoot (*S or C*), jackaroo (*Australia*), new chum (*C, Australia*), recruit, parvenu (*in sense of coming to a hitherto unfamiliar status to which one is naturally unsuited*).

new-fashioned, *a.* new, newfangled (*depreciative*); *spec.* neologistis.
Antonyms: see OLD-FASHIONED.

newness, *n.* unusualness (*contex.*), novelty; *spec.* recency, originality, modernity.
Antonyms: see ANTIQUITY.

news, *n.* information, intelligence, tidings (*chiefly rhetorical or poetical*); *spec.* gospel, gossip, report.

newspaper, *n.* paper, gazette (*R, exc. as a proper name or spec.*), courant (*now usually a proper name*), courier (*only as a proper name*), journal; *spec.* sheet, tabloid, picture paper, rag, yellow journal, hearstpaper (*cant*).

nice, *a.* **1.** *See* FASTIDIOUS, PARTICULAR, FINE, DIFFICULT, DANGEROUS, SCRUPULOUS, ACCURATE, DISCRIMINATIVE, ELEGANT, EXACT, AGREEABLE, MINUTE, CAREFUL, SENSITIVE, REFINED, PALATABLE.
2. *Referring to that which demands or requires great skill, acumen, or the like, in doing, handling, understanding, etc.: spec.* delicate (*suggesting esp. need for care or tact*), subtle *or* (*R*), subtile (*implying difficulty in perceiving the right thing to do*), curious (*implying special care or attention, and suggesting the phase of interest or strangeness as being involved*), fine (*implying necessity for sharpness of mental distinction and suggesting that what is referred to is either commendable or excellent of its kind*), dainty (*implying the need or use of nice taste*), discriminating.
Antonyms: see CRUDE, GROSS.

niceness, *n.* **1.** *As a general equiv.:* nicety (*more suggestive than "niceness" of what is specific and concrete*).
2. *Spec.* fastidiousness, particularity, fineness, difficulty, scrupulousness, accuracy, discrimination, elegance, exactness, agreeableness, minuteness, carefulness, sensitiveness, refinement.
3. delicacy, subtlety *or* (*R*), subtilty, subtleness *or* (*R*), subtileness, curiousness, fineness, finesse, daintiness.
Antonyms: crudity (*cf.* CRUDE), *grossness* (*cf.* GROSS).

nicety, *n.* **1.** *See* NICENESS.
2. *In the sense of a thing that is nice: spec.* subtlety *or* (*R*), subtilty, refinement, distinction, elegance, delicacy, accuracy, discrimination, *etc.*
Antonyms: see CRUDITY.

niche, *n.* recess; *spec.* tabernacle, fenestella, kiblah.

nickname, *n.* name (*contex.*); *spec.* by-word, hypocorism (*R*).

niggard, *n.* curmudgeon (*esp. with "old"; contemptuous*), skinflint (*contemptuous*), churl, carl (*Scot.*), nipper (*R*), pincher (*C*), hunks (*C; contemptuous*), money-grubber (*S*), pinchpenny (*obs. or dial.*); *spec.* miser.
Antonyms: see SPENDTHRIFT, WASTER.

night, *n.* **1.** nighttime, nighttide (*B or A*).
Antonyms: see DAY.
2. *See* DARKNESS, SUNSET.

nightclothes, *n. pl.* night gear (*A*), nightdress (*chiefly spec.*); *spec.* nightgown, nighty (*a nursery or familiar term*), night robe (*dignified for "nightgown"*), nightshirt, bedgown (*R*), pajama *or* pyjama.

nightingale, *n.* Philomel *or* Philomela (*B*), nightbird (*contex.*); *spec.* bulbul.

nightly, *a.* **1.** nocturnal (*more B or tech. than "nightly"*), night (*the noun used attributively*).
2. *See* DARK.

nightmare, *n.* **1.** *See* HORROR.
2. dream, incubus (*more B than "nightmare"*), ephialtes (*R*), night hag (*R*).

night piece, night scene, nocturne (*tech. or B*).

nimble, *a.* **1.** active (*implying energetic, quick action that is kept up*), lively, agile (*implying smooth and easy dexterity of limb*), light; *spec.* brisk (*implying vigorous, animated movement*), lightsome, quick, ready, tripping, light-heeled, light-foot, light-footed, light-limbed, alert.
Antonyms: see SLUGGISH.
2. *Referring to the mind: see* READY.

nine, *a.* novenary (*R*); *spec.* ninefold, nonary.

nine, *n. As naming a group of nine:* novenary (*R*), nonary (*R*), ennead (*usually spec.*).

nine-faced, *a.* enneahedral (*tech.*).

nipper, *n.* **1.** claw.
2. *Chiefly in pl.: spec.* pliers (*pl.*), pincers (*pl.*), pinchers (*pl.*), forceps (*pl.*), tenaculum.

nipple, *n.* **1.** mamilla (*tech.*), teat (*now referring to the nipple of a quadruped exc. dialectally or contemptuously of a woman*), tit (*now chiefly dial. or vulgar*), dug (*now only in reference to animals; exc. contemptuously in reference to women*), pap (*chiefly B and A*), papilla (*R*).
2. *See* PROTUBERANCE.

nipple-shaped, *a.* mamilliform (*tech.*); *spec.* papilliform.

nobility, *n.* **1.** *See* DIGNITY, GENEROSITY, GRANDEUR.
2. aristocracy, gentility (*now chiefly depreciatory*), noblesse (*French*), classes (*pl.*), patriciate, peerdom, peerage; *spec.* baronage, dukedom, earldom.
Antonyms: plebeianism (*cf.* PLEBEIAN), *lowliness* (*cf.* LOWLY); *see* PEOPLE.
3. *Referring to the quality or state:* nobleness, noblesse (*French*), peerage, peerdom (*R*), gen-

next, *a.: nearest, immediate.*
next, *adv.: immediately.*
nib: *beak, point.*
niece: *relative, bastard.*
niggardly: *stingy.*
nip, *v. t.: squeeze, clip, bite, blight.*

tility (*now chiefly depreciatory*); *spec.* lordliness, kingliness, *etc.*
Antonyms: baseness (*cf.* BASE), *meanness* (*cf.* MEAN).
noble, *a.* **1.** *See* DIGNIFIED, ELEVATED, GENEROUS, GRAND.
2. aristocratic, gentle (*now including the well-born who are not of noble rank*), genteel, nobiliary (*R*), generous (*R*), gentilitial (*R*); *spec.* patrician, lordly, lordlike (*R*), kingly, princely, regal, royal, cidevant (*French; B*).
Antonyms: see VULGAR, BASE, PLEBEIAN, LOWLY, MEAN.
noble, *n.* well-born, aristocrat, nobleman, patrician (*orig. spec. only*), noblewoman (*fem.*), peer *or* (*fem.*) peeress (*spec. in Great Britain and Northern Ireland*), illustrissimo (*Italian*); *spec.* duke, marquis, earl, viscount, baron *or* (*fem.*) baroness, baronet, count *or* (*fem.*) countess, Junker, Herzog, thane, daimio, wildgrave, starost, douzepers (*pl.; A or hist.*), fidalgo, hidalgo, nawab, atheling.
Antonyms: see PLEBEIAN.
nobody, *n.* **1.** no man (*a more definite term*), nix (*S*), none (*often used as sing., also as a plural*).
Antonyms: see SOMEONE.
2. nonentity, cipher (*fig.*), lay figure, nought (*an equiv. of "cipher"*), nothing, insignificant (*R*), obscurity (*R*).
Antonyms: see PERSONAGE, MAGNATE.
nocturnal, *a.* nightly (*of that which happens or recurs by night*); *spec.* (*of birds, insects, etc.*), solifugous (*tech.*).
Antonyms: see DAILY.
noise, *n.* sound (*contex.*); *spec.* report, clamor, din, clash, clatter, rattle, crash, hubbub, garboil (*A equiv. of "hubbub"*), pandemonium, clutter (*chiefly A or dial.*), coil (*A or dial.*), racket, hullabaloo, hubbuboo (*R*), clam, bruit (*A*), gabblement, clack, caterwauling, chirm, brawling, grating, hum, jingle; *see* OUTCRY.
Antonyms: see CALM, SILENCE.
noisy, *a.* sounding (*contex.*), loud, noiseful (*R*); *spec.* dinsome (*Scot.*), fremescent (*R*), pandemoniacal, rackety; *see* CLAMOROUS, UPROARIOUS, BOISTEROUS.
Antonyms: see SILENT.
no-license, *a.* dry (*C*).
nominal, *a.* name *or* named, titular; *spec.* cognominal; moderate, minimum. Nominal *implies being in name only, and thus not actual; hence the derived senses of* trifling, negligible, *etc.*
nominate, *v. t.* **1.** *See* APPOINT.
2. propose, name (*a less formal term*), propound (*now U. S. and eccl.*); *spec.* present, postulate.
nominee, *n. Spec.* appointee, postulate, presentee.
none, *pron.* not any, not one.
Antonyms: see ALL.
nonentity, *n.* **1.** *See* NONEXISTENCE, NOBODY.
2. negation, nothing, nonexistence, nonexistent (*R*).
nonexistence, *n.* nonentity, non-being (*R*), no-being (*R*), inexistence (*R*), nothingness, not-being (*R*), nihility (*R*), nihilism (*chiefly spec.*), nullity (*chiefly spec.*), non esse (*a philosophical term*).
Antonyms: see BEING.
nonexistent, *a.* inexistent (*R*), null (*chiefly spec.*), minus (*C*); *spec.* (*predicatively, as used of fire, etc.*) out.
Antonyms: see EXISTENT, BEING.
nonexplosive, *a.* inexplosive (*R*), inert.
nonplus, *v. t.* stop (*contex.*), confound, get (*S*), gravel, pose, floor, beat (*C*), ground (*A or R*); *see* PERPLEX.
Antonyms: see ENLIGHTEN.
nonsense, *n.* (*often without the contemptuous implications of the synonyms that follow*). *Spec.* drivel, slaver (*a less refined term for "drivel"*), twaddle, balderdash, trumpery, rubbish, claptrap (*S or C*), froth, trash (*an equiv. of "rubbish," but a weaker term*), flimflam (*S*), fee-faw-fum, flummery, bosh (*contemptuous*), fudge (*a less emphatic equiv. of "bosh"*), stuff (*contemptuous*), fooling, absurdity, silliness, moonshine, amphigory, linsey woolsey (*fig.*), havers (*pl.; Scot.*), shenanigan (*S*), rigmarole, riddlemaree, gammon (*C or S*), rot (*vulgar S, or very contemptuous*), flapdoodle (*C; contemptuous*), stultiloquy (*R*), hokum (*S, U. S.*), baloney (*S, U. S.*), bull (*S, U. S.*).
nonsense! bosh! (*S or C*), tollyvally! (*A or R*), fudge! (*C*), tut!, tush!, fiddledeedee!, fiddlesticks!, rubbish!, *etc.*
nonsensical, *a.* meaningless; *see* ABSURD.
nonsensicalness, *n.* nonsense, no-meaning (*R*); *spec.* absurdity.
nonvocal, *a.* silent, mute, surd, voiceless.
nook, *n. Spec.* nooklet, byplace; *see* ANGLE, INLET.
noon, *n.* **1.** midday, noonday (*rather more definite and formal than "noon"*), noontide (*B*), midnoon (*B; strictly considered, pleonastic*).
Antonyms: see MIDNIGHT.
2. *See* HEIGHT.
noon, *a.* midday, noonday, meridional (*R*), meridian (*R*).
noose, *n. Spec.* bewet *or* bewit, hitch.
normal, *a.* **1.** ordinary, natural; *see* AVERAGE.
Antonyms: see ABNORMAL, MONSTROUS, PRETERNATURAL.
2. *See* PERPENDICULAR.
normality, *n.* **1.** normalcy (*an illiterate neologism foisted upon the language, but not in good usage*).
2. *See* ORDINARINESS, PERPENDICULARITY.

---

noiseless: *silent.*
noisome: *harmful, foul, ill-smelling.*
noncommittal: *careful.*
noncompliant: *disobedient.*
nonconformist: *dissenter, schismatic.*
nonessential: *accidental.*
noose, *v. t.: loop, catch.*
norm: *standard, pattern.*
normal, *n.: average.*

---

north, *n.* **1.** septentrion (*B*), northward *or* (*R*) norward.
Antonyms: see SOUTH.
2. northland *or* (*R*) norland.

northern, *a.* north (*less narrow in meaning than "northern"*), northerly (*less definite than "northern"*), septentrional (*B*), boreal *or* (*R*) borean (*now chiefly used in bot. and zool.*), high, northernly (*R*); *spec.* northward *or* (*R*) norward, northwardly (*less definite than "northward"*), hyperborean (*B*), arctic, polar.
Antonyms: see SOUTHERN.

northman, *n.* hyperborean (*B or tech.*).

northward, *adv.* norward (*R*), north *or* (*less definite*) northerly; *spec.* northwardly, poleward, polewards, up (*chiefly in "up north"*).

north wind, wind (*contex.*), norther, north (*chiefly poetic*), Boreas (*poetic*).

nose, *n.* **1.** snout (*as referring to man, contemptuous*), nese (*Scot.*), smeller (*S*), proboscis (*humorous or spec.; suggesting esp. a long nose*), beak (*fig.; humorous*), neb (*R or Scot.*).
2. *See* SMELL.

nostril, *n.* nosehole (*chiefly dial.*), tunnel (*R*), nare (*A, exc. as a hawk*), nares (*Latin, pl.; anat.*), breather (*S*); *spec.* blowhole, spiracle (*tech.*).

nosy, *a.* (*given to nosing*) snouty (*vulgar*).

notable, *a.* noticeable, distinguished, remarkable; *spec.* noteworthy, prominent, observable; *see* CONSPICUOUS.

notary, *n.* scrivener (*A*), greffler (*Eng.; chiefly spec.*); *spec.* prothonotary *or* protonotary.

notation, *n.* symbolology; *spec.* chorography (*R*), graphology.

notch, *n.* **1.** indentation (*contex.*); *spec.* nick, crena, gap, nock, dent, gain, score, cut.
Antonyms: see PROJECTION, TOOTH.
2. *See* PASS.

notch, *v. t. Spec.* crenate (*R*), mill, score, nock, nick.

notched, *a.* dentate; *spec.* nicked, crenulate, gapped, emarginate (*R or tech.*), crenate, scalloped.

note, *n.* **1.** *In music: spec.* semibreve, minim, crotchet, quaver, semiquaver, demisemiquaver, hemidemisemiquaver, pedal.
2. (*a tone of definite pitch*), sound (*contex.*); *spec.* strain, toot, pipe, peek, mote *or* moot (*A*); *see* CALL, TONE.

note, *n.* **1.** *Spec.* jotting; *see* MEMORANDUM, ANNOTATION, ABSTRACT.
2. *See* SIGN, LETTER, DISTINCTION, FAME.

note, *v. t.* **1.** *See* NOTICE, MENTION.
2. *Spec.* record, jot, dot (*less usual equiv. of "jot"*).

notebook, *n. Spec.* sketchbook.

nothing, *n.* **1.** *As implying the absence of anything whatever:* nought (*B*), naught (*A*), nil (*used predicatively*), nix (*S*), zero.
Antonyms: see THING, MUCH.
2. *See* NONENTITY, NOBODY, CIPHER.

nothingness, *n.* nullity.

notice, *v. t.* **1.** perceive (*implying merely that the mind recognizes the existence of the thing noticed*), animadvert (*R*), observe (*more formal than "notice"*), mark (*B or R as a mere synonym of "notice"*), remark, heed (*emphasizing the idea of voluntary attention, esp. such as weighs the value, import, or authority of what is noticed*), regard, reck (*a B equiv. of "heed"*), note (*more emphatic than "notice"*), hear (*fig. or spec.*), see (*fig. or spec.*), feel (*fig. or spec.*), mind.
Antonyms: see IGNORE, MISS.
2. *Referring to treatment of a person:* recognize, acknowledge, see; *spec.* patronize.
3. *See* MENTION, ADVERTIZE.

notice, *n.* **1.** perception, cognizance (*tech. or B*), observation, remark (*R*), mark (*R*), note, animadversion (*R*), advertence (*R*); *spec.* heed, regard, sight, hearing, feeling, touch.
2. *See* INFORMATION, MENTION, ATTENTION, CARE, ANNOUNCEMENT, ADVERTIZEMENT.
3. *Referring to the thing embodying an act of information or notification:* advertizement (*chiefly spec.*), notification (*chiefly spec.*); *spec.* sign, placard, program, playbill, poster, warning, advice, announcement.

noticeable, *a.* perceivable, perceptible, observable, striking, *etc.*; *see* NOTABLE, CONSPICUOUS.
Antonyms: see UNNOTICEABLE.

notoriety, *n.* **1.** notoriousness (*of that which is widely and unfavorably known*), proverbialness.
Antonyms: see OBSCURITY; *cf.* UNKNOWN.
2. *See* FLAGRANCY.

notwithstanding, *prep.* despite (*implying what is actively opposed, or strongly adverse*).

noun, *n.* term (*contex.*), name (*chiefly spec.*), substantive.

nourish, *v. t.* **1.** nurture (*more B than "nourish"*), nutrify (*R*); *spec.* conourish, feed.
Antonyms: see STARVE.
2. *See* FOSTER.

nourishing, *a.* nutritious, nutrient (*a more B or tech. equiv. for "nourishing" and "nutritious"*), nutritive; *spec.* eutrophic (*R*), foodful (*R and B*), substantial, sustentative (*R*), hearty, polytrophic (*very nourishing; R*).
Antonyms: see INNUTRITIOUS.

novice, *n.* **1.** *In the religious sense: spec.* probationer, neophyte, novitiate, initiate, chela (*Anglo-Indian*).
2. *In the general sense:* beginner, tyro (*suggesting one who has not yet learned a skill*), apprentice; *spec.* neophyte (*B*), initiate, débutant (*French; masc.*), débutante (*French; fem.*), entrant, greenhorn, greeny (*S or C*), greenhead (*A*), gosling (*C*), freshman, kid (*sporting or criminal cant*), puny (*Eng.*), youngling, colt (*C or S*), newcomer.
Antonyms: see EXPERT.

---

notable: *celebrity.*
noted: *distinguished, famous.*
noteworthy: *notable, considerable.*
notify: *inform, announce, warn.*
notion: *idea, caprice, opinion, fancy.*
notorious: *well-known, conspicuous, flagrant.*

---

now, *adv.* **1.** *In the present time: spec.* here, presently (*obs., Scot., or dial.*), yet, to-day.
Antonyms: see BEFORE, HEREAFTER, AFTERWARDS.
2. *See* IMMEDIATELY.
noway, *adv.* noways (*the usual form*), nowise (*more formal, or flavoring of archaism*), nohow (*dial.*).
nowhere, *adv.* nowhither (*nowhere in direction*).
Antonyms: see SOMEWHERE, EVERYWHERE.
nowhere, *n.* dreamland (*fig.*), Utopia, Erewhon, no man's land.
nullify, *v. t. Spec.* abolish, negative (*R*), negate, null (*R*), irritate (*Roman and Civil law*), cancel; *see* INVALIDATE, ANNIHILATE, DESTROY, COUNTERACT. *Neither "neutralize" nor "defeat" is a close synonym of "nullify."*
Antonyms: see CREATE.
numb, *a.* **1.** insensible (*contex.*), benumbed, deadened; *spec.* asleep, dull.
Antonyms: see SENSITIVE.
2. *See* DULL, *a.*
numb, *v. t.* **1.** benumb, deaden; *spec.* dull.
Antonyms: see STIMULATE, ROUSE.
2. *See* DULL.
number, *n.* **1.** *Spec.* total (*all there are*), aggregate (*made up of elements or parts combined into one mass or unit*), sum (*a number reached by combining two or more*), fraction, mass (*a number compacted together*), tally (*esp. a number taken as a unit in reckoning or computation*), tale (*a number considered as made up by taking all, esp. as representing what must be or has been accounted for*), quota, quotum (*R*), enumeration (*a number told over*), integer, indiction, radix, prime, folio, census, figurate. Number *is often used to suggest many, but not a multitude.*
2. *See* FIGURE, VERSE.
number, *v. t.* **1.** *See* COMPUTE, CLASS.
2. mark (*contex.*); *spec.* paginate, page, foliate.
numberless, *a.* innumerous (*A*); *spec.* innumerable, countless.
Antonyms: see FEW.
numbness, *n.* **1.** insensibility, sleep, deadness; *spec.* dullness.
2. *See* DULLNESS.
numeral, *a.* numerical; *spec.* numerary.
nun, *n.* ecclesiastic (*contex.*), sister, religieuse (*French*), sanctimonial (*R*); *spec.* conventual, cloisterer, discalceate, Clare, Gilbertine, *etc.*
nurse, *n.* attendant (*contex.*), nutrice (*R*), mammy (*a child's name of affection; often spec. in southern U. S.*); *spec.* fosterer (*R*), foster (*A*), fostress (*fem.*), rocker (*A*), dry nurse, wet nurse, Gamp (*fig.*), parabolanus (*R*), sister, nursemaid, bonne (*French*).
nursery, *n.* **1.** brattery (*contemptuous*); *spec.* crèche (*French*).
2. *See* GARDEN.
nut, *n. Spec.* nutlet, mast (*a collective sing.*), kernel; *see* FOOL.
nutrition, *n.* **1.** *Referring to the act:* nourishment (*less formal than "nutrition"*), nouriture (*R*), nurture (*R*); *spec.* alimentation, eutrophy (*tech. or R*), dystrophy (*tech.*).
Antonyms: see FAMISHMENT.
2. *See* FOOD.
nuzzle, *v. t. & i.* nose (*implying merely action with the nose, while "nuzzle" suggests a gentle, often repeated action*); *see* NESTLE.
nymph, *n.* nymphid (*R*); *spec.* nymphlet, dryad, oread, oceanid, naiad, mænad, hamadryad, hydriad (*R*), nepheliad, nais (*pl. naides*), ephydriad (*R*), houri, nixie.
nymphal, *a.* nymphish, nymphean, nymphic, nymphical *or* nymphine (*R*).

O

oar, *n. Spec.* scull, paddle, sweep.
oarsman, *n.* oar (*a term smacking a little of cant*), rower, bencher (*R*); *spec.* bowman, stroke.
oaten, *a.* avenaceous (*tech.*); *spec.* oaty.
oath, *n.* **1.** *See* INVOCATION, PROMISE.
2. expletive; *spec.* curse (*properly an utterance of a malediction with invocation or adjuration of the deity; hence, any blasphemous expletive; the term most suggestive of vulgar profanity*), imprecation, cuss (*U. S.; S or C*), rapper (*chiefly dial.*); *also* (*A*) 'swounds, zounds, zooks, 'sblood, *etc.*
obedience, *n.* biddableness (*R*), obediency (*R*), submission, submissiveness (*referring to the quality only*), compliance, compliancy (*R*); *spec.* complaisance, fulfillment (*R*), subservience, obsequiousness (*R*), dutifulness, duteousness, obeisance, piety (*A*), morigeration (*R*), buxomness (*A*).
Antonyms: see DISOBEDIENCE.
obedient, *a.* biddable (*A or B*), commandable (*chiefly spec.*), submissive (*implying absence of resistance*), compliant (*suggesting ready or voluntary obedience*); *spec.* complaisant (*implying a desire to please, often on the part of one who could refuse*), subservient (*obedience that leads one to put himself at the service of another; often suggesting servile or degrading conduct*), dutiful (*implying a careful regard to do or observe what is due to a superior*), duteous (*an equiv. of "dutiful," but less suggestive of the feeling, more of the outward act*), obeisant (*humble obedience*), obsequious (*rare as meaning "actually obedient"*), pious (*A equiv. of "duteous"*), morigerous (*R*), morigerate (*R*), buxom (*A*); *see* COMPLAISANT.

---

nucleus: *center.*
nuisance: *annoyance.*
null: *invalid, trifling, nonexistent.*
numerous: *many.*
nuptial: *marriage.*
nurse, *v. t.: suckle, foster, cherish, entertain, manage, embrace.*
nurture: *nutrition, food.*

O

oarlock: *rowlock.*
obdurate: *wicked, obstinate, unfeeling, unyielding.*
obeisance: *deference, obedience, bow.*

Antonyms: see DISOBEDIENT, OBSTINATE, DEFIANT, DICTATORIAL, UNDUTIFUL.

obelisk, *n.* column (*contex.*), guglio (*Italian*), needle (*C*).

obey, *v. t.* hear (*A or R*), mind, heed, obtemperate (*R*); *spec.* follow, fulfill.

Antonyms: see DISOBEY, DEFY.

obey, *v. i.* comply, conform, yield.

Antonyms: see DISOBEY, REFUSE.

obituary, *n.* **1.** obit (*R*).

2. *See* NECROLOGY.

object, *n.* **1.** *In reference to what is, or may be, perceived by the physical senses:* thing; *spec.* individuality (*R*), individual, percept, something, particular.

2. *The thing to the achievement of which efforts, intentions, or feelings are directed:* aim (*suggesting esp. definite intention and deliberate action directed toward its achievement*), intention, intent (*obs. exc. in "to all intents and purposes"*), purpose (*suggesting esp. the mental conception of what is intended or desired*), butt (*B*), end, mark (*an equiv. of "aim"*); *spec.* study (*an object, esp. in relation to conduct or mental life*), view, thought, effort, objective (*suggesting a more remote end than does "object"*), destination (*implying foreordination or predetermination*), goal, errand (*object or purpose on which one is sent or goes*), quarry (*the object of chase or pursuit*).

object, *v. i. Spec.* demur (*implying an objection made only by way of argument or delay till shown to be wrong or till overruled; in law, to admit facts but deny sufficiency*), except (*implying a denial of sufficiency, validity, etc.*), boggle (*used with* at, over, about, *etc.*; *implying fright, scruple, etc., as the cause of objection*), challenge, kick (*C*), spurn, repugn (*R*), reluct (*R*), protest, remonstrate.

Antonyms: see AGREE.

objection, *n.* **1.** *Referring to the act: spec.* demur, exception, boggle, challenge, kick (*C*), objectation (*R*), drawback, protest, protestation, remonstrance.

Antonyms: see AGREEMENT.

2. *Referring to the thing offered by way of objecting: spec.* exception, kick (*C*), boggle (*R*), demurrer, dislike, difficulty, fear, *etc.*

objectionable, *a.* objectable (*R*); *spec.* harmful, exceptionable, censurable, culpable, horrid (*C*).

objective, *a.* external, subjective (*the use of medieval philosophy*); *see* MATERIAL.

Antonyms: see SUBJECTIVE.

obligation, *n.* **1.** *Referring to the act of obligating: see* BINDING, COMPULSION.

2. *Referring to orally or mentally constraining force: spec.* bond, tie, sanction, obstriction (*R*), incumbency (*R*); *see* DUTY.

Antonyms: see PRIVILEGE.

3. *Referring to something to be done or forborne: spec.* burden, debt, liability; *see* DUTY.

4. *Referring to the state of being obligated: spec.* indebtedness, indebtedment (*R*).

5. *Referring to that by which obligation is created: spec.* agreement, bond, chirograph, contract, mortgage, hypothecation, pledge.

oblige, *v. t.* **1.** *See* BIND, COMPEL.

2. *Spec.* accommodate (*implying meeting one's requirements*), convenience (*implying saving trouble or avoiding difficulty*), favor, gratify, please.

obliging, *a. Spec.* kind, considerate, accommodating, serviceable (*R*); *see* COMPLAISANT.

Antonyms: see OBSTINATE.

obliquely, *adv.* sideways, sideway, sidelong, askance, askant, slantwise, slant; *see* INCLINED.

Antonyms: see VERTICALLY.

oblong, *a.* elongate.

obscuration, *n.* **1.** *See* DARKENING, HIDING.

2. *Spec.* camouflage, clouding, shrouding, disguising, obscurement (*R*), shading (*R*), obnubilation (*R*), obfuscation (*R*), glossing, *etc.*

obscure, *a.* **1.** *See* DARK, HIDDEN, QUESTIONABLE, PERPLEXING, INDISTINCT, INDEFINITE, DULL.

2. *Referring to persons having no fame nor notoriety: spec.* humble (*obscure as belonging to a low estate*), unknown, nameless, unsung (*B*), inglorious (*R*), recondite (*R*), inconspicuous (*lacking prominence*), undistinguished, uncelebrated, unnoticed, fameless, *etc. See* LOWLY.

Antonyms: see DISTINGUISHED, FAMOUS, CONSPICUOUS.

obscure, *v. t.* **1.** *See* DARKEN, HIDE.

2. *Referring to a making vague to the understanding or unintelligible: spec.* cloud (*implying lack of clear conception*), shroud (*implying esp. an intentional concealing*), disguise, shade (*R*), gloss (*implying fair but false explanations or interpretations*), becloud (*intensive for "cloud"*), befog (*intensive*), bemist (*intensive*), obfuscate (*R*), nubilate *or* obnubilate (*R; equiv. of "cloud"*).

Antonyms: see EXPLAIN, INDICATE.

obscurity, *n. Spec.* humbleness, namelessness. *Cf.* OBSCURE, *a.*

Antonyms: see FAME.

obsequious, *a.* servile; *spec.* abject (*emphasizing utter absence of spirit of independence and often of self-respect*), cringing (*idea of yielding through fear*), fawning (*involving self-abasing servility, flattery, etc., not necessarily suggesting any sense of fear, but rather one of recognized inferiority and submission*), compliant (*with idea of ready and unquestioning obedience;* compliance *may or may not arise from* obsequiousness), truckling (*implying a show of servility or favor-currying, esp. for reasons of personal advancement*), sycophantic (*implying insincere flattery, esp. by one who lives upon the bounty of another in return for praising his benefactor and abusing or betraying others*), sycophantish (*R*), pickthank (*A*), parasitic (*R; equiv. of* sycophantic), supple, subservient.

obligate: *bind.* | **oblique:** *inclined, indirect, unfair.* | **obloquy:** *abuse, discredit.*

Antonyms: see ARROGANT, IMPUDENT, SELF-IMPORTANT, SELF-SATISFIED, SELF-ASSERTIVE, DOMINEERING.

observance, *n.* **1.** *See* ATTENTION, CEREMONY, FORM.

2. observation (*R*), holding, keeping; *spec.* celebration, solemnization, sanctification.

Antonyms: see DISREGARD.

observe, *v. t.* **1.** *See* NOTICE, COMMENT.

2. hold, keep, respect (*contex.*); *spec.* follow, celebrate, solemnize, sanctify, hallow, solemn (*R*).

Antonyms: see DISREGARD, VIOLATE.

obsess, *v. t.* beset (*contex.*), besiege (*contex.*); *spec.* haunt.

obsolescence, *n.* disappearance (*contex.*), dying, waning.

obsolescent, *a.* disappearing (*contex.*), dying, waning.

obsolete, *a.* disused; *spec.* discarded, exploded, demoted (*R or affected*), passé (*French*), outworn, out-of-date, ancient, dead, extinct, past.

Antonyms: see CUSTOMARY, RECENT, NEW.

obstacle, *n.* obstruction, prevention (*chiefly fig.*); *spec.* barrage, impediment, snag, rub, block, difficulty, apex (*R*), stumbling-block, baffle.

obstetrics, *n.* midwifery (*chiefly Brit. usage for obstetrics*), tocology (*R*).

obstinacy, *n.* obstinateness (*esp. of the quality*), obstinance *or* obstinacy (*R*); *spec.* intractability, perversity, stubbornness, obduracy, obdurateness, obduration (*R*), unyieldingness, contumacy, contumaciousness, setness, willfulness, self-will, doggedness, cantankerousness, asininity, mulishness, headstrongness, headiness, bullishness, dourness (*Scot.*), sturdiness, protervity (*R*), induration (*R*), pervicacity (*R*), hard-heartedness, unfeelingness, cussedness (*C*), *etc.*

obstinate, *a. Spec.* intractable, refractory, stubborn (*suggesting esp. unreasoning or unthinking refusal*), obdurate (*implying unyielding, esp. hard-hearted, refusal to be influenced by persuasion, entreaty, the appeal of pity*), unyielding, contumacious (*implying contempt of rightful or* de facto *authority*), set (*implying a fixed attitude of mind incapable of being influenced*), willful, self-willed, dogged (*implying an unyielding, sullen or grim persistence in face of opposition, discomfort, or injury*), stiff-necked, cantankerous (*C; ill-natured or perverse obstinacy*), asinine, mulish, hardened, headstrong *or* (*C*) heady, bullish, pig-headed (*C*), dour (*Scot.*), sturdy (*A*), persistent, pervicacious (*R*), indurate (*R*), hard-hearted, camelish, unfeeling, cussed (*C*), *etc.*

Antonyms: see COMPLAISANT, OBEDIENT, OBLIGING, MANAGEABLE.

obstruct, *v. t. Spec.* block (*implying primarily a physical obstacle to be removed before progress is possible*), stop, choke (*implying a filling up of a confined passage by, usually, a number of small objects that prevent passage*), clog (*implying esp. hindrance of passage by what clings or adheres to the walls of the channel*), glut (*obstruction by what overcrowds*), jam (*obstruction by what is forcibly wedged in because too large for free passage*), shut, occlude (*chiefly tech. or B, and referring to pores, channels of communication, etc.*), hedge (*obstruction by what screens or protects*), dam, foul (*implying impediment that prevents free or proper action, as of a gun barrel with rust*), barricade (obstruct *by interposition of physical obstacles as a means of preventing passage or attack*), blockade (*implying a closure by hostile forces either to egress or ingress*), engorge, obturate, overgrow, silt, oppilate (*B*), gob (*cant*), scotch, encumber *or* cumber.

Antonyms: see OPEN.

2. *See* HINDER.

obstruction, *n.* **1.** *Referring to the act: spec.* blocking, choking, clogging, glutting, jamming, shutting, occlusion (*chiefly tech.*), blockade, engorgement, obturation, encumbrance, encumberment, embolism, *etc.*

2. *See* HINDRANCE, OBSTACLE.

obtainable, *a.* gettable (*inelegant*), procurable.

occasional, *a.* **1.** *Of what belongs only to the occasion: spec.* extemporary, extemporaneous, ephemeral, accidental, nonce.

Antonyms: see CUSTOMARY, HABITUAL.

2. *See* INFREQUENT.

occupant, *n.* occupier (*less formal than "occupant"*); *spec.* tenant, roomer, lodger, inmate, transient, interne, terretenant.

occupation, *n.* **1.** occupancy; *spec.* holding, tenancy, tenure, habitation, inhabitation.

2. employment, engagement, employ (*chiefly in the phrases "in employ" and "out of employ"*), conversation (*R, B*), work, engagement.

3. *See* BUSINESS.

occupied, *a.* employed, busy (*now spec.*).

Antonyms: see INDOLENT.

occupy, *v. t.* **1.** *Spec.* hold, keep, fill, beset, garrison, inhabit, tenant, take (*as a building, a city, etc.*).

2. *Spec.* busy, engage (*now chiefly in the passive*), exercise, employ, beset, interest, absorb.

Antonyms: see VACATE, EVACUATE.

occur, *v. i.* **1.** be; *spec.* fall (*chiefly with "in" or "upon"; A used alone or with "out"*), befall (*A as used alone or with "to," "unto," or "upon"; usually with an indirect object*), betide (*now only in 3d person*), arise *or* (*less usually*) rise; *spec.* come, pass, worth (*A*), intervene, transpire (*not in good usage for* occur. Transpire *implies leaking out or becoming public, as*

observant: *attentive.*
observation: *notice, comment.*
obstreperous: *clamorous.*
obstructionist: *filibuster.*
obtain: *gain, get.*
obtrude: *intrude.*
obvious: *evident, intelligible.*
occasion: *cause, induce.*

"*The marriage* occurred *last year, but did not* transpire *till last week.*"), supervene, eventuate; *see* HAPPEN.
2. *See* BE.
occurrence, *n.* **1.** *Referring to the action of taking place: spec.* happening, coming, falling, fall (*R*), chancing, arising, rise, passing, intervention, transpiration (*an erroneous use*), intercurrence (*R*), supervention, event (*now used chiefly in "in the event of"*).
2. *Referring to what takes place: spec.* happening, instance, chance, event (*anything taking place in time, esp. as considered to be the result of preceding events; often used of distinctive or important occurrences*), occasion (*a particular occurrence considered by itself, as marking a juncture, or as being the cause of something*), contingency (*arising by chance and not contemplated or necessarily expected*), circumstance (*an occurrence viewed as a matter of detail in a course of events, or often, vaguely, any fact or event of secondary importance*), incident (*secondary, or part of, but not necessary to, some action or course of events; also an occurrence or separate event which has befallen one*), fact (*an occurrence considered as a reality of experience*), phenomenon, prodigy, thing (*contex.*), eventuality (*what may come to pass, esp. as culmination of other events*), scene, episode (*an occurrence separable but naturally arising from some other event or course of events*), landmark (*an occurrence as marking a point or time of change, etc.*), memorabilia (*pl.*).
odd, *a.* **1.** *Spec.* unmatched, unmated, peerless.
2. *See* EXTRA.
3. unusual (*contex.*), peculiar, funny (*C*), strange (*suggesting what is not familiar*), bizarre, singular (*suggesting something that stirs puzzlement or curiosity*), eccentric, erratic (*both implying extreme divergence from the normal*); *spec.* cranky, outré (*French*), quaint, outlandish, oddish, queer; *see* FANTASTIC.
Antonyms: see USUAL, CUSTOMARY, COMMONPLACE.
oddity, *n.* **1.** peculiarity, oddness, singularity, singularness, eccentricity, erraticness; *spec.* crankiness, quaintness, queerness, outlandishness.
2. *Referring to what is odd:* quality, fantastic, crank, queerity (*R*), oddness (*R*).
Antonyms: see COMMONPLACE.
oddments, *n. pl.* odds and ends, manavilins (*S, R*); *spec.* remnants, scraps, litter (*sing.*).
odor, *n.* **1.** *See* SMELL.
2. repute, opinion, estimation.
odorous, *a.* odoriferous (*usually spec.; often humorous*), odorant (*R*), odorate (*R*); *spec.* redolent (*chiefly used with "of" or "with"*), opulent (*R*), enodic (*R*), rich, savory, smelly (*C*), stinking, stenchy (*R*), putrid, mephitic, olent (*R*), odoriferant, aromatic. *Cf.* SMELL.
Antonyms: see INODOROUS.
œstrus, *n.* **1.** *See* FRENZY.
2. *Referring to sexual appetite:* heat, rut, rage, passion.
offal, *n.* **1.** *Refuse parts in dressing an animal:* garbage, cagmag (*dial.*); *spec.* slumgullion (*U. S.*).
2. *See* REFUSE, DREGS.
offend, *v. t.* displease; *spec.* affront, spite, pique, hurt, huff (*chiefly in the passive; C*), grate, mislike (*B*), miff (*C*).
Antonyms: see PLEASE.
offense, offence, *n.* **1.** *See* TRANSGRESSION, ATTACK.
2. *Referring to the act of giving offense to a person:* offending, displeasing, affront, affronting, *etc.*
3. *Referring to the state or feeling of one offended:* displeasure; *spec.* pique, hurt, huff (*C*), miff (*C*), umbrage, snuff (*A*), displicence (*R*), displacency (*R*).
Antonyms: see PLEASURE.
offensive, *a.* **1.** *See* AGGRESSIVE.
2. unpleasant, displeasing, ungracious, disagreeable; *spec.* rank (*now chiefly spec.*), obnoxious (*B; suggesting what is strongly displeasing*), repugnant (*implying something repellent to one's nature*), objectionable, ill-favored, mephitic, horrid (*C, exc. in the R or B sense of "revolting" or "abominable"*), distasteful, unsavory; *see* ILL-SMELLING, HATEFUL, REPELLENT, NAUSEOUS.
Antonyms: see AGREEABLE, PLEASANT, UNOBJECTIONABLE, INOFFENSIVE.
offer, *v. t.* **1.** *See* SACRIFICE, PROPOSE.
2. *Spec.* tender, present, proffer (*chiefly a B equiv. of "offer" suggesting more heartiness*), prefer (*A*), bid, submit, advance, volunteer, market, cheap (*A*).
Antonyms: see REFUSE, DEMAND.
offer, *n.* **1.** *See* TENDER, SACRIFICE, PROPOSAL, ENDEAVOR.
2. *Spec.* presentation, presentment (*R*), proffer (*ch. B*), bid, submission, advance, overture, eirenicon (*R*), ultimatum, motion.
Antonyms: see DEMAND.
office, *n.* **1.** *See* SERVICE, POSITION, FORM, CEREMONY.
2. *Spec.* duty, business, function, part.
3. place (*contex.*); *spec.* headquarters, bureau, branch, countinghouse (*A*), department, room, suite.
officeholder, *n.* placeman (*chiefly derogatory*).
office-monger, *n.* barrator, simoniac (*eccl.*), simonist (*eccl.*).
officer, *n.* office bearer, officiary (*R*); *spec.* official, Dogberry (*fig.*), bureaucrat.
official, *a.* functional, functionary (*R*); *spec.* authoritative, public, curule; *see* FORMAL.
Antonyms: see PRIVATE, INFORMAL.
officialism, *n.* bureaucratism, officiality (*R*), red-tapeism, functionaryism (*R*); *spec.* beadledom, Bumbledom (*R*).

ocean: *sea.*
octave: *eighth, eight.*
odds: *difference, advantage.*
ode: *poem.*
odious: *disgusting, hateful.*
odium: *hatred.*
offhand, *extemporaneous, abrupt, careless.*

offspring, *n.* **1.** *Referring to one individual:* birth (*A*); *spec.* bairn (*Scot., dial. Eng., or R*), bantling (*now chiefly depreciatory*), branch (*A or humorous*), brattling *or* bratchet (*contemptuous*), descendant, imp (*A; esp. in "imp of the Devil"*), cadet, year-old *or* yearling, bed (*fig.*), olive branch *or* olive (*fig., and now humorous*), chit (*C*), brat (*more or less contemptuous*), sprig (*often slightly disparaging*), slip, scion (*B*); *see* CHILD, LAMB, KID, COLT, CALF, CUB, CHICK.

Antonyms: see PARENT.

2. *Referring to a single individual or collectively to two or more:* product (*contex.*), progeny (*more formal than "offspring"*), issue (*chiefly legal*), generation, increase (*chiefly collective as to animals; poetical as to a single human offspring*), race (*chiefly poetic*), seed (*chiefly Bib.*), get (*now only of animals*), produce (*R; esp. of animals*), hatch, pullulation (*R*), progeniture (*R*), spawn (*chiefly a collective; contemptuous*).

Antonyms: see ANCESTOR, PARENT.

3. *Referring to two or more (usually) animal young:* brood (*now somewhat contemptuous as used of human offspring*), litter (*sometimes contemptuously used of human twins, triplets, etc.*), fry (*of small offspring or contemptuously of young or insignificant creatures*); *see* CHILDREN.

Antonyms: see PARENT.

often, *adv.* frequently (*more formal and somewhat more emphatic than "often"*), oft (*A or B*), oftentimes (*chiefly B*), ofttimes (*A or B*), oftly (*R*). *"Repeatedly," "recurrently," etc., are synonyms of "often" if the repetitions or recurrences come near enough together.*

Antonyms: see INFREQUENTLY.

oily, *a.* **1.** fatty, lubricous (*B*), oleaginous (*chiefly tech.*), oleose (*R*), oleous (*R*); *spec.* greasy.

2. *Referring to a person's manners or speech: see* SMOOTH, UNCTUOUS.

ointment, *n.* unguent (*more tech. than "ointment"*), unction (*R*); *spec.* oleamen, cerumen, balm, nard, malabathrum (*hist.*), collyrium, salve, pomade, pomatum.

old, *a.* **1.** *Referring to what has existed for a long time:* aged (*more emphatic than "old"*), vetust (*R*); *spec.* ancient, antique (*A, exc. as meaning "old-fashioned"*), antiquated (*R when used of persons*), olden (*R or B*), eld (*A and B*), early, elder, senior, elderly, hoar *or* (*more commonly*) hoary, venerable, dateless, rusty (*depreciatory*), moss-grown (*fig.; chiefly depreciatory or contemptuous*), oldish, crusted (*humorous*), primeval, Ogygian (*fig.*), patriarchal, overold, overaged, gray, gray-headed, centuried, stale, oldest, experienced.

Antonyms: see YOUNG, YOUTHFUL.

2. *Referring to what formerly existed or to the time when it existed: spec.* ancient, olden (*B or A*), elder, aged, senile, eldern (*A*), primitive (*often depreciatory*), pristine (*the commendatory equiv. of "primitive"*), primeval.

Antonyms: see NEW.

oldest, *a. Superl. of old: spec.* eldest, firstborn.

old-fashioned, *a.* old, old-fangled (*R; depreciatory*), antique; *spec.* antiquated (*no longer appropriate*), archaic (*having the character or savor of an earlier era*), fusty, primitive (*suggesting the simplicity of an early period*), fogyish *or* fogeyish, obsolete.

Antonyms: see NEW-FASHIONED, STYLISH.

old man, graybeard (*often contemptuous*), grandsire (*fig. and A*), grayhead, hoarhead (*R or B*), cuff (*contemptuous; chiefly used with "old"*), grisard (*R*); *spec.* patriarch, Nestor (*fig.*), doyen.

Antonyms: see YOUTH.

old woman, beldame (*spec. or A*); *spec.* patriarchess (*R*), oldwife, luckie (*Scot.*), gammer (*rural Eng.*), grimalkin, grannam (*obs. or dial.*), granny (*familiar or endearing or often contemptuous*), grandam (*A*).

omission, *n.* **1.** *Spec.* preterition, pretermission, skip, exception, exclusion, elimination, apocope, ellipsis, apostrophe, elision, lipography, metemptosis; *see* EXCEPTION.

Antonyms: see INCLUSION (*cf.* INCLUDE).

2. *See* FAILURE.

omit, *v. t. Spec.* pretermit (*omit to mention, as in a narrative*), neglect, skip, slip, spare (*suggesting idea of avoiding something disagreeable as reason for omission*), hide, except (*omit as being different from the general run*), exclude (*omit as not belonging to, or desired in, what is included*), miss (*omit by oversight or neglect*), eliminate (*omit as undesirable*), drop (*of words or syllables, to omit by inadvertence; otherwise same sense as* eliminate), pass *or* (*R*) overpass; overlook, forget, overslaugh, elide, apocopate; *see* EXCEPT.

Antonyms: see INCLUDE, REMEMBER, MENTION.

omnibus, *n.* bus *or* (*R*) 'bus; *spec.* motor coach, char-à-bancs (*French; chiefly Brit. and Continental; often without the final "s"; usually restricted in sense to sightseeing vehicles*).

omnipotent, *a.* all-powerful (*more emphatic than "omnipotent"*), almighty (*chiefly spec.*), cunctipotent (*R*).

omnipresent, *a.* ubiquitous (*showing itself—esp. unexpectedly—in any and all places*), abroad (*contex.*).

omniscient, *a.* all-knowing (*simpler and more emphatic than "omniscient"*).

omnivorous, *a.* pantophagous (*R*), pamphagous (*R*).

on, *a. "Upon" and "on" are, in general, interchangeable; but "on" is commonly used except*

officious: *meddlesome.*
offish: *distant.*
offset, *v. t.: neutralize, counterpoise, branch.*
oil, *v. t.: anoint, smear.*
omen: *sign.*
ominous: *significant, threatening.*

where demand for greater emphasis, more formality, dignity or euphony leads to the use of "upon" instead.

one, *a. Spec.* singular.

one-celled, *a.* unicellular (*chiefly biol.*), unilocular (*chiefly bot.*).

one-chambered, *a.* unicamerate (*tech.*).

one-colored, *a.* unicolor *or* unicolorous (*R*), monochrome; *spec.* self-colored.
Antonyms: see PARTY-COLORED.

one-eyed, *a.* monoculous *or* (*less usual*) monocular (*both B or tech.*), single-eyed, monophthalmic (*R*).

one-footed, *a.* uniped, monopodous (*R*).

one-horned, *a.* unicorneous (*R*), monocerous (*R*).

one-layered, *a.* unilamellate, unilaminar, unilaminate;—*all three tech. or B.*

one-rowed, *a.* unifarious, uniserial;—*both tech. or B.*

one-sided, *a.* unilateral (*more formal or tech. than "one-sided"*).
Antonyms: see MANY-SIDED.

only, *a.* alone (*postpositive or predicative*).

onomatopœia, *n.* echoism (*R*), onomatopoësis (*R*).

onomatopœic, *a.* onomatopoëtic, echoic.

oozy, *a.* **1.** weepy (*C or dial.*), spewy.
2. *See* MOIST, MUDDY.

opaque, *a.* opacous (*R*), nontranslucent, beclouded, dim, obscure. *See* DULL, DARK.
Antonyms: see TRANSLUCENT, TRANSPARENT.

open, *a.* **1.** ope (*A or B*); *spec.* patulous (*chiefly tech.*), patulent (*R*), patent, yawning, gaping, wide, ajar, agape, unclosed, expanded, *etc.*
Antonyms: see CLOSED.
2. *See* UNCONCEALED, EXPOSED, UNINCLOSED, FRANK, EVIDENT, INTELLIGIBLE, LIABLE, LOOSE, FREE, ACCESSIBLE, GENEROUS.

open, *v. t.* **1.** ope (*A or B*); *spec.* unclose, reopen, divaricate, expand.
Antonyms: see CLOSE, SHUT.
2. *Referring to a process of unfastening, as in order to make free for passage, of separating or spreading apart what is joined, interlocked, rolled up, etc.:* undo (*emphasizing the process more than the result, which "open" suggests*), dup (*A*); *spec.* separate, unlock, unclench, unpick, unroll, unseal, pick, unclutch, unfold, unstop, deobstruct (*R*); *see* DISCLOSE.
Antonyms: see OBSTRUCT.
3. *Referring to vessels holding liquors, and hence in fig. uses having the idea of making a first beginning on: spec.* broach (*orig. to pierce*), tap, uncork.
Antonyms: see CLOSE, STOPPER.
4. *See* BEGIN.

open, *v. i.* **1.** *Spec.* yawn, gape, expand, split, crack, part, unclose, dehisce.
2. *See* EXPAND, SPREAD, BEGIN.

open-air, *a.* al-fresco (*chiefly predicative; learned*), hypœthral *or* hypethral (*R*); *spec.* plein-air.
Antonyms: see INDOOR.

opening, *n.* **1.** hole; *spec.* perforation, puncture, gape, gaping, orifice, aperture, foramen, gulf, open (*R*), rift, breach, tear, lumen, placket hole, intake, gate, fistula, micropyle, drop (*U. S.*), bole (*Scot.*), interspace, interstice, spiracle, blowhole, bay, pore, port, hatch, machicolation, loophole, dehiscence, bunghole, crater, hazard, embrasure, lunette, skylight, scuttle, scupper, cut; *see* GAP, MOUTH, CLEARING.
2. *See* OPPORTUNITY, BEGINNING, INITIAL, CLEARING, GLADE.

openly, *adv. Spec.* plainly, frankly, aboveboard.

opera glass, lorgnette, (*R*) lorgnon (*both Fr.*).

operate, *v. i.* **1.** *See* ACT, WORK.
2. *To take effect:* go, work; *spec.* run.

opinion, *n.* **1.** idea, thought; *spec.* preconception, prejudice (*opinion pre-formed, or obstinately maintained in the face of reason*), judgment (*emphasizing the idea of the weighing of reasons*), belief (*emphasizing the settledness of opinion to which the mind holds; generally speaking* belief *denotes a fuller faith and less reference to reason than does* opinion), view (*emphasizing idea of mental consideration, or of various aspects of a thing, of which one is that entertained*), notion (*more or less depreciatory or apologetic*), mind (*emphasizing the element of the will, the way of thinking, etc.*), dogma, verdict (*primarily legal*), think (*C*), tenet (*primarily referring to a religious, political, philosophical or other doctrine or belief held by a party, sect, etc.*), conceit (*obs., exc. in various phrases*), doxy (*C and usually humorous*), heterodoxy, orthodoxy, cacodoxy, cry (*implying an emphatic general utterance by the public*), doctrine, apprehension (*an opinion causing or caused by anxiety*), speculation (*a casual or chance opinion ventured perhaps for argument's sake*).
Antonyms: see CAPRICE.
2. *See* CONSIDERATION, ADVICE.

opinionated, *a.* opinionative (*suggesting more the tendency or general character in actions;* opinionated *emphasizing more the mere state or condition of the mind*), opiniative (*R*), opinionate, opinative (*R*), opinioned (*R*); *spec.* dogmatic, pragmatic *or* pragmatical, doxastic (*B and R*).
Antonyms: see MODEST.

opponent, *n.* antagonist, adversary (*more formal than "opponent" and implying more hostility or sharpness of contest*), oppugner (*R*), opposite (*R*); *spec.* withstander, opposition (*a collective*), oppositionist, counteractant *or* counteragent (*R*), enemy, con.
Antonyms: see ALLY, PARTNER.

---

once, *a.: formerly.*
onerous: *burdensome.*
onslaught: *attack, rush.*
onus: *burden.*
onward: *forward.*
open-hearted: *frank, generous.*
open-minded: *liberal.*
operate: *effect, manage, conduct, exercise, work.*
operative, *a.: active, effective.*
opiate: *narcotic.*
opine: *consider.*

opportunity, *n.* chance (*chiefly spec.*); *spec.* turn, occasion, room, space, place, opening, liberty, leisure, scope, show (*C, U. S.*), time.

oppose, *v. t.* **1.** *In the sense of "to place opposite, over against, or before physically," without implying resistance:* present; *spec.* contrast, confront, front.

2. *In the sense of "to set against (another) in opposition":* counterpose *or* contrapose (*R*); *spec.* match, countermatch, pit, pitch (*R*), measure, play.

3. counter; *spec.* resist (*suggests striving against aggression*), withstand, meet, attack (*suggests assuming the initiative in hostile action*), beard, breast, front, gainstand (*A*), head, fight (*literally and fig.*), antagonize, oppugn (*R*), repugnate (*R*), buck (*S, U. S.*), hinder (*suggests the putting of difficulty in the way*), check, stem, contradict, obstruct, defend, gainsay (*B*), cross, countervail, contravene, traverse, counteract, counterplot, countermine.

Antonyms: see ADVOCATE, AID.

opposed, *a. Spec.* averse, adverse, opponent (*R*), antagonistic, counter, opposite, hostile, inimical (*a stronger word than "hostile"*); *see* UNFRIENDLY, OPPOSING, UNWILLING.

Antonyms: see DISPOSED, FAVORABLE.

opposing, *a.* **1.** *Spec.* contrastive.

2. *Spec.* opposed, repugnant (*R*), resistant, resistive, oppugnant (*R*), adverse, counter, contrary, cross, crossing.

opposite, *a.* opponent (*R*); *spec.* antipodal, polar, converse, confronting, obverse (*R, exc. spec.*).

Antonyms: see ANALOGOUS.

opposite, *n. Spec.* inverse, converse, antipode, counterpoint, counterpole, vis-à-vis (*French*), counterpart, obverse, contrary, contrast.

Antonyms: see ANALOGUE.

opposition, *n.* **1.** *Spec.* presentation, contrariety, contrast.

Antonyms: see ANALOGY.

2. *Spec.* resistance, withstanding, breasting, meeting, fight, antagonism, oppugnance (*R*), confrontation, crossing, oppugnation (*R*), hindrance, obstruction, encounter, defiance, counteragency (*R*), counterinfluence, contravention, contradiction, load, friction.

Antonyms: see AID, YIELDING.

3. *Referring to the feeling or quality: spec.* aversion (*a turning away from, in the sense of loathing*), antagonism (*an active standing out against*), hostility, antinomy, renitency (*R*), inimicalness, opponency (*R*), oppugnancy (*R*).

Antonyms: see FRIENDLINESS.

oppress, *v. t.* **1.** *Spec.* burden, overburden, overweigh, crush, bow, depress (*suggesting that something makes the spirits or vigor sink, whereas* oppress *emphasizes more the sense of being passively crushed by a burden*).

2. press (*R*); *spec.* afflict, aggrieve, load, grind, overpress, overbear, screw, squeeze, gripe, pinch, compress (*A*), grieve, overtax, overburden, rack.

Antonyms: see ENCOURAGE.

3. *Spec.* SWELTER.

oppressive, *a.* **1.** burdensome, onerous (*more B than "burdensome"*), heavy, hard, grinding, sore; *spec.* inquisitorial, racking, tyrannical.

2. *See* CLOSE (*in reference to atmospheric conditions*).

option, *n.* contract, privilege; *spec.* straddle, spread, put, call.

optional, *a.* voluntary, elective, non-obligatory. *Spec.* facultative, discretionary.

Antonyms: see COMPULSORY.

oracular, *a.* **1.** oraculous (*R*); *spec. or fig.* Delphian, Orphic, *etc.*

2. *See* HIDDEN, INFALLIBLE, AMBIGUOUS.

oral, *a.* spoken, vocal, parol (*now law only*), word of mouth, nuncupative (*chiefly of wills*), nuncupatory (*R*), verbal (*an erroneous use*), unwritten (*a loose use*); *spec.* acroamatic.

Antonyms: see WRITTEN.

orally, *adv.* vocally, viva voce (*Latin*), by word of mouth, nuncupatively (*chiefly of wills*).

orator, *n.* speaker (*contex.*), rhetor (*R*).

oratory, *n.* **1.** *See* ELOQUENCE.

2. proseucha (*chiefly a word of antiquarians*); *spec.* chapel, cubiculum, crypt.

orchard, *n. Spec.* peachery (*R*), orangery (*R*), grove, pomery (*A*).

ordain, *v. t.* **1.** *See* APPOINT, DECREE, DESTINE.

2. frock, priest (*R*), japan (*S*).

Antonyms: see DEGRADE.

order, *n.* **1.** *See* ASSOCIATION, RANK, CLASS, DECREE, BIDDING, COURSE, GROUP, METHOD, ARRANGEMENT, DICTATION, DECISION, CONDITION, SYSTEM, FORM.

2. *In business usage: spec.* commission, draft, bill of exchange *or* (*briefly*) bill, check.

3. *Referring to the conduct of society or of a gathering:* orderliness; *spec.* quiet, obedience, regularity, form, discipline.

order, *v. t.* **1.** *See* ARRANGE, BID, APPOINT, CLASSIFY, DECREE, DESTINE, MANAGE, CONTROL.

2. *Referring to the ordering of goods, etc.: spec.* bespeak, engage.

orderly, *a.* **1.** *Spec.* neat, tidy, well-conducted, methodical, well-behaved, shipshape, ataunt *or* atraunto, regular, systematic, planned, harmonious, cosmic (*R*), settled.

Antonyms: see UNSYSTEMATIC, DISORDERLY, CONFUSED, UNTIDY.

2. *See* LAW-ABIDING.

ordinariness, *n.* mediocrity (*the more usual word*); *spec.* normality, customariness, *etc.*

ordinary, *a. Spec.* average, medium, mean (*R as an adjective, exc. math.*), medial (*equiv. of "medium"*), middling (*slightly depreciatory*), mediocre (*more formal than "middling," and more depreciatory or patronizing*), second-rate,

---

opportune: *timely.*
oration: *address.*
orb, *n.: ball, eye, circle.*
orchestra: *band.*
ordeal: *trial.*
ordinance: *arrangement, law, appointment, destiny, decree, ceremony.*

---

second-class, giftless, undistinguished; *see* COMMON, NORMAL, USUAL, CUSTOMARY, COMMONPLACE, EVERYDAY. *Cf.* FAIR.

Antonyms: see UNUSUAL, ABNORMAL, SPECIAL, WONDERFUL.

ore, *n.* mineral; *spec.* mine (*iron ore*), chat, float (*U. S.*), calmine, prill, slimes (*pl.*).

organ, *n.* **1.** *In music: spec.* organette, hydraulicon, reed organ, regal. *Also* (*referring to groups of stops*): *spec.* great organ, choir organ, swell organ, solo organ, pedal organ.

2. *Referring to bodily structures:* part; *spec.* vitals (*pl.*), instrument, medium, viscera (*pl.*), gland, eye, brain, hand, *etc.*

organic, *a.* organized.

Antonyms: see INORGANIC.

organism, *n.* organization, system; *spec.* animal, plant.

organization, *n.* **1.** arrangement, systematization, ordonnance (*referring esp. to the way parts are composed with reference to each other and to the whole*); *spec.* coördination, incorporation, regimentation, economy.

Antonyms: see DISORGANIZATION.

2. *See* ORGANISM.

3. *Spec.* machine (*chiefly U. S. politics*), system, association, band, army, regiment, brigade, clique.

organize, *v. t.* **1.** arrange, systematize, systemize; *spec.* coördinate, correlate, incorporate, embody, brigade, regiment, enregiment (*R*), district.

Antonyms: see DISORGANIZE.

2. *See* FORM.

organized, *a.* organic (*less usual*), systematic, systematized, *etc.*

orgiastic, *a. Spec.* corybantic.

origin, *n.* **1.** *Referring to the act: see* BEGINNING, DESCENT.

2. *In reference to that from which a thing springs or arises:* beginning (*R; here not in the sense of "the first part of a thing"*), source, fountainhead (*an equiv. of "source," but more formal*), fountain (*R*), parent (*fig.*); *see* CAUSE.

Antonyms: see RESULT.

original, *a. Spec.* first, initial (*suggesting esp. more to follow, often by way of development or completion*), earliest, primary (*first in a series or process; suggesting often the idea of independence, or of having other subsequent things in dependence*), primitive (*as being the first of its kind; often suggesting esp. a crude, rudimentary, or fundamental relation in respect of what follows*), pristine (*suggesting freshness, virginity*), primal, prime, fontal (*B*), primordial (*absolutely the first in history or development*), radical (*original in sense of being root, source, or foundation of what follows*), prototypal *or* prototypical, archetypal (*an equiv. of "prototypal"*), protoplastic *or* (*R*), protoplast, aboriginal, oldest; *see* INNATE, NEW.

Antonyms: see IMITATED, COMMONPLACE.

original, *n.* **1.** *In reference to a thing from which another is copied or on which it is patterned: spec.* copy, prototype (*the pattern of all that follows; often suggestive of a simple, primitive, or fundamental character*), archetype (*an equiv. of "prototype"*).

Antonyms: see COPY.

2. *See* CHARACTER.

originate, *v. t. Spec.* begin, start; *see* INVENT, CAUSE, CREATE.

Antonyms: see COPY, IMITATE.

originate, *v. i.* begin; *see* RESULT, ARISE, PROCEED.

originative, *a. Spec.* inceptive, inventive, imaginative; *see* CREATIVE, PRODUCTIVE.

ornament, *n.* **1.** ornation (*R*); *spec.* decoration, adornment, figure, embellishment, trim, garnish *or* garnishment, grace, bedizenment, fallal, offset *or* set-off, glory (*an ornament of great beauty or such as lends distinction*), flourish (*a showy or ostentatious embellishment*), knickknack, kick-shaw, gaud, drapery (*R*), illumination, fret, clasp, fringe, gem, jewel.

2. *See* HONOR.

ornament, *v. t. Spec.* beautify, adorn (*a term more elevated in idea than* ornament, *but chiefly applied to things that are extrinsic, appended, set upon, associated, or, fig., manifested in connection or intimate relation with, what is adorned;* adorn *is therefore more often used in fig. senses, referring to mental or spiritual graces;* ornament *often refers also to change or fixed addition, but is less suggestive of added beauty, and perhaps more suggestive of an inherent or intrinsic, æsthetically pleasing quality, thus we would say the tomb was* ornamented *with beautiful carvings and* adorned *with many statues*), decorate (*implying changes or accessories made or added for purposes of ornamentation; but not implying anything as to whether they are in good taste or not*), embellish (*implying adventitious or extraneous ornamentation, esp. elaborate or showy*), garnish (*now rhetorical or with allusion to Matt. xii:44*), grace, deck *or* (*intensive*) bedeck (*clothing or covering with decorative objects*), set (*contex.*), beautify, bedizen (*implying clumsiness or vulgarity*), daub *or* (*intensive*) bedaub, bedight (*A or B for "bedeck"*), prank, trick (*often used with "out"*), dress, trim, blazon *or* emblaze, figure, embroider (*rhetorical, exc. of needlework*), chase *or* enchase, set, engrail, guard, broider (*A*), paint, paper, panel, festoon, lace, illumine *or* illuminate, illustrate, gild *or* (*emphatic*) engild, carve, couch, hemstitch, incrust (*emphatic*), tool, tinsel, pipe, pink, scallop, flounce, fringe.

Antonyms: see DEFACE, STRIP.

ornamental, *a.* ornamentive; *spec.* adorning, decorative, fancy, dressy.

ornamentation, *n.* **1.** *Referring to the act: spec. see under* ORNAMENT, ADORNMENT, *etc.*

2. *Referring to ornaments collectively or to ornamental work: spec.* garnish, work (*much used in composition*), pride (*A*), bravery (*A*), finery,

---

organic: *living, constitutional, structural, organized.*

orgy: *rite, carouse, dissipation.*

orient, *n.: east.*

originator: *creator.*

garniture, trappings (*pl.*), turnery. *See also under* ORNAMENT.
orphan, *a.* parentless, twice-bereaved (*contex. and rhetorical*); *spec.* fatherless, motherless, unmothered.
orthodox, *a.* sound, standard; *spec.* canonical, conventional.
Antonyms: see HERETICAL.
orthodoxy, *n.* soundness; *spec.* canonicalness.
Antonyms: see HERESY.
other, *a. Spec.* else, another, additional; *see* DIFFERENT.
Antonyms: see SAME.
otherwise, *adv.* othergates (*dial.*), or, elsewise, *etc.*; *spec.* alias.
Antonyms: see LIKEWISE.
out, *adv.* **1.** forth (*stronger and more formal than "out"*).
Antonyms: see IN.
2. *See* ALOUD.
out, *n.* quondam (*A*), has-been (*S*).
outbreak, *n.* **1.** burst, eruption, outburst (*intensive for "burst"*); *spec.* round (*of applause*); *see* EXPLOSION.
2. *Referring to the outward exhibition of repressed activity, feeling, passion, etc.* (*the terms in sense* **2** *being used also fig.*); *spec.* storm, flare-up, blaze, roar, outleap, peal, explosion, volley, flash; *see* FIT.
3. *See* DISTURBANCE.
outcast, *n.* **1.** *See* EXILE.
2. *Referring to social status: spec.* pariah, Ishmael (*fig.*), derelict, dregs (*pl.*)
outcome, *n.* issue, end, termination, fruit (*fig.*), effect, hatch (*R*), event, sequel, upshot, final; *see* PROCEEDS, RESULT.
Antonyms: see BEGINNING, SOURCE.
outcrop, *n.* emergence (*contex.*), basset; *spec.* gossan.
outcry, *n.* noise (*contex.*), clamor, vociferation *or* (*R*), vociferance (*chiefly spec.*), rumor (*A*), bruit (*A*), exclaim (*R*); *spec.* exclamation, uproar, bellow, bawl (*chiefly derogatory*), dirdum (*Scot.*), shout, din, ecphonesis, brawling, scolding, *etc.*
Antonyms: see CALM.
outdate, *v. t. Spec.* antiquate.
outdo, *v. t.* exceed, overdo (*A*); *spec.* outgo, outwrangle, outwork, outweep, outshout, outhowl, outswear, outsee, outvoice, outthunder, outroar, outlie, outleap, outjump, outbrave, outbrazen, outbray, outdrink, outdare, outcharm, outswagger, outboast, outbluster, out-Hector, outjuggle, outblush, outgive, outeat, outdress, outshine, *etc.*
outdoor, *a.* extraforaneous (*pedantic*).
Antonyms: see INDOOR.
outdoors, *adv.* outdoor (*used only in combination, as in "outdoor-grown"*).
outface, *v. t.* face (*contex.*), outlook, outfront (*R*); *spec.* outstare, outfrown, defy.
outflow, *v. i.* outgo, outpour (*chiefly poetic*), flow (*contex.*); *spec.* outstream, outwell, ebb.
outflow, *n.* **1.** outgo (*contex.*), flow (*contex.*); *spec.* effluence, efflux, effluxion, outpour, outpouring, effusion, outgush, outrush, escape.
Antonyms: see INCOMING.
2. *Referring to what flows out: spec.* effluence, escape, efflux, effluxion, effluvium, issue (*R*), effluent, lasher (*chiefly local Eng.*).
Antonyms: see INFLOW.
outfly, *v. t.* outsoar, oversoar (*R*), overfly (*R*).
outgo, *n.* **1.** outgoing; *spec.* emanation, reflux, ebb, sally, sortie; *see* OUTFLOW.
Antonyms: see INCOME.
2. *See* EXPENDITURE.
outgrowth, *n.* excrescence *or* (*R*) excrescency (*of an abnormal outgrowth*), enation (*R*); *spec.* caruncle, condyloma, apophysis.
outhouse, *n.* skilling (*Eng.*); *spec.* office, outoffice; *see* TOILET.
outlaw, *n.* proscript (*formal*), wolf's head (*tech.*), Robin Hood (*fig.*).
outlaw, *v. t.* proscribe (*formal*).
outlet, *n.* opening (*contex.*), issue (*R*); *spec.* exit, egress, loophole, meuse *or* muse (*now dial.*), offlet (*R*), emissary (*obs. or Roman antiq.*), port, porthole, floodgate, sluice, penstock, escape.
Antonyms: see INLET.
outline, *n.* **1.** contour (*chiefly spec.*), line (*usually in pl., "lines"*); *spec.* lineament (*often in pl., "lineaments"*), lineation (*R*), relief, silhouette, profile; *see* BOUNDARY.
2. *Referring to a drawing of the general lines of something:* delineation (*less definite but more formal than "outline"*); *spec.* sketch, draft, skeleton.
3. *Referring to a crude or incomplete statement, which may be elaborated:* description (*Contex.*); *spec.* draft, scheme, conspectus, sketch, minute, skeleton.
outline, *v. t.* **1.** delineate (*contex.*); *spec.* contour, sketch, crayon, block, profile, skeleton, silhouette.
2. describe (*contex.*); *spec.* sketch, draft, minute, skeleton, skeletonize (*R*).
outmaneuver, *v. t.* outgeneral (*primarily mil.*); *spec.* outplan, outplot (*R*), outflank, outjockey.
outnumber, *v. t.* overcount (*R*); *spec.* outman, outvote.
out-of-the-way, *a.* devious; remote, isolated, *etc.*
outrage, *n.* **1.** *See* INJURY, INSULT, ABUSE.
2. *Spec.* atrocity, enormity.
outrageous, *a.* **1.** excessive, purple (*fig.; B*), great (*contex.*), rank, precious (*ironical*); *hence, with the underlying idea of an extreme that in*

orthodox: *conventional.*
oust: *deprive, expel, eject.*
outbreak: *v. t. & i.: burst.*
outcast, *a.: abandoned.*
outer: *exterior.*
outfit, *n.: equipment, group.*
outfit, *v. t.: equip.*
outlandish: *foreign, eccentric.*
outlast: *survive.*
outlay, *n.: expenditure.*
output: *product.*
outrage: *injure, ill-treat, abuse, insult.*
outrank: *precede.*

some way violates propriety: spec. monstrous, egregious, atrocious, black (*fig.*), heinous, enormous, horrible (*often C in a milder sense*), awful (*C or S*), arrant (*chiefly a term of abuse or reprobation*), ungodly (*S*), absurd; *see* FLAGRANT, UNREASONABLE.

Antonyms: see MODERATE, GENTLE.

2. *See* ABUSIVE.

outrigger, *n.* extension (*contex.*); *spec.* cop (*obs. or dial.*), float, rave, lade (*local Eng.*), whisker.

outshine, *v. t. In literal or figurative use:* overshine (*R*), eclipse; *spec.* outbeam (*R*), outluster, outflash, outflame (*R*), outray (*R*), outblaze, outbrave, outglitter, outdazzle, outsparkle, outglow, outglare.

outside, *adv. & prep.* without (*now becoming A or formal, esp. as a preposition*), beyond (*used only to indicate relation to one within*).

outsider, *n. Spec.* outlier, nonmember, extern, exoteric; *see* FOREIGNER.

outskirt, *n.* edge; *spec.* suburb, purlieu;—*all much used in pl. form.*

outstrip, *v. t.* pass (*contex.*), *spec.* distance, outdistance (*emphatic for "distance"*), devance (*R*), cote (*fig.*), outrun, overrun (*R*), lose, outgo (*A*), forespeed (*R*), outpace, forereach, forerun (*R or fig.*), outspeak, outsail, outrow, outwing, outswim, outstream, outtrot, outsoar, outride, outfly, outfoot, outgallop, outmarch, overfly, outwalk.

outweigh, *v. t.* outbalance *or* overbalance, overweigh, outpoise *or* overpoise (*chiefly fig.*), downweigh (*R*).

outwork, *n. Spec.* outfort, ravelin, redoubt, demilune, bawn, *etc.*

oven, *n. Spec.* kiln, dryer, baker (*U. S.*).

over, *adv. & prep. Spec.* above, by, beyond, upon, throughout, up, across, *etc.*

over, *adv. Spec.* across, throughout, again. *Also see* EXCESSIVELY.

overbear, *v. t.* **1.** *See* INTIMIDATE, BULLY.

2. overcome; *spec.* overwhelm, overrule, override, overtop, supersede.

overburden, *v. t.* burden (*contex.*), surcharge (*B*), overweigh.

overcoat, *n.* greatcoat, topcoat, wraprascal (*A, Eng.*); *spec.* spencer, Raglan, tabard, surtout (*formerly not spec.*), ulster, Inverness, peajacket, Chesterfield, mackinaw, *etc.*

overcome, *v. t.* conquer (*implying strenuous effort and counter-effort, as in war or in fighting tendencies or habits*), vanquish (*more emphatic than* conquer, *implying an overcoming which removes the possibility of resistance in the immediate or near future*); *spec.* crush (*implying utter breaking down of strength and power of action*), bow (*implying depression of feelings such as humbles or takes away pride, independence, etc.*), defeat (*implying frustration of a purpose, while* overcome *does not necessarily suggest any purpose present or implied in what is* overcome; *thus one* overcomes *bad habits, difficulties, etc. but* defeats *the enemy, a conspiracy, etc.*), rout, surmount (*suggests rather the use of resources, powers, or force to accomplish a purpose, than any direct action*), obviate (*implying a going around or avoiding difficulty*), overpower, overwhelm, prostrate, subdue (overcome *by reducing to at least outward calm or quiet*), subject (overcome *so as to impose one's will upon*), quell, subjugate, meet (*to satisfy the demands of, or* overcome *the objections to, a situation*), master *or* (*intensive*) overmaster, outmaster (*R*), overmatch, overthrow, overwhelm (overcome *by suddenness and quantity, amount or degree; often used where there is subsequent recovery and renewed opposition*), overbear (overcome *by pressure, intimidation, etc.*), exhaust, rush, weather (*lit. of ships that survive the storm; fig., of surviving opposition as a ship outrides a storm*), overrule, negotiate (*a use easily shading into C or S*), superate (*R*), overman (*R*); *see* CONFUTE, DEFEAT, OBVIATE, OVERBEAR.

overcome, *a.* conquered, vanquished; *spec.* crushed, defeated, heartbroken, brokenhearted.

overdo, *v. t.* **1.** *Spec.* overtire, overfatigue, overweary, overtax, overtask, overwork, overwalk, overdrive, exhaust, drive, override, overstrain.

2. *Spec.* overcarry (*a matter, proceedings, etc.*), overact.

3. *See* EXAGGERATE.

overflow, *v. t.* **1.** *Spec.* flood, overflood (*R; emphatic for "flood"*), inundate, deluge, overrun, overbrim, overboil, overwash (*R*), wash, overspill (*R*); *see* FILL.

2. *In the sense of "to cause to be overflowed": spec.* flood, float, flow.

overflow, *v. i.* **1.** *Spec.* inundate, exundate (*R*), debord (*R*), overstream, overspill (*R*), overwhelm.

2. *Referring to the vessel or other thing that is overflowed: spec.* swim.

3. *See* ABOUND.

overflow, *n.* **1.** *Referring to the act: spec.* flooding, inundation, deluge.

2. *Referring to that which overflows: spec.* wash; *see* FLOOD.

overhang, *v. i.* impend (*B or R*); *spec.* beetle, overlean (*R*), jut.

Antonyms: see RECEDE.

overhang, *n. Spec.* eaves, overbrow.

overhanging, *a.* hanging, pendent *or* pendant; threatening, portentous.

overlap, *v. t.* ride *or* override, interlap (*R*).

overlapping, *a. Spec.* equitant, imbricated.

overlay, *v. t.* cover (*contex.*); *spec.* ground, hide, coat, whip, seize, wrap, pave, sand, veneer; *see* COAT, PLATE, HIDE.

overlie, *v. t. Spec.* cap, crown, overlap, override.

overload, *v. t.* overburden, overcharge, over-

outright: *adv.: entirely.*
outright: *a.: thorough, unqualified, frank.*
outrun: *outstrip.*
outspoken, *blunt, frank, loud.*
outward: *exterior, formal.*
outwear: *exhaust.*
outworn: *exhausted.*
overawe: *intimidate, abash.*
overbearing: *arrogant.*
overcast, *a.: cloudy.*
overconfidence: *assurance.*
overdone: *excessive.*
overdue: *accrued, late.*
overflowing: *excessive.*

weight, overlade (*R*); *spec.* overfreight, overballast.

overloaded, *a.* overfraught (*R*).

overlook, *v. t.* **1.** command, oversee (*R*); *spec.* rake, give upon.

2. *See* EXAMINE, IGNORE, EXCUSE, MISS, OVERSEE.

overlying, *a.* superincumbent, superjacent (*R*).

overpower, *v. t.* **1.** overcome (*contex.*), force; *spec.* neutralize, master.

2. *See* DAZZLE.

overrate, *v. t.* overestimate, overprize, overvalue; *spec.* (*all with suggestion of* overrating *with intent to profit by the results*) puff, ballyhoo (*C*), push.

Antonyms: see UNDERRATE, UNDERVALUE.

overreach, *v. t.* deceive (*contex.*), outwit; *spec.* outtrick, jockey *or* (*more emphatic*) outjockey, best (*C*), circumvent, outknave (*R*).

overreach, *v. i.* interfere (*contex.*), forge.

overreaching, *n.* outwittal, overreach (*R*); *spec.* jockeying, circumvention, besting.

oversee, *v. t.* overlook (*less usual and definite*); *spec.* superintend, supervise, overseer (*R*).

overseeing, *a.* supervisory, supervisal (*R*); *spec.* superintendent.

overseeing, *n.* supervision, supervisal; *spec.* superintendence.

overseer, *n.* overlooker (*R*), boss (*S*), supervisor, surveyor (*R*); *spec.* superintendent, superintender, foreman, forewoman (*fem.*), driver, intendant, manager, maistry (*Indian*), censor, floorwalker, matron, gauger, provost, reeve, tackler, boatswain.

overshoe, *n. Spec.* galosh, rubber, gum (*chiefly local and C; usually in pl.*), patten, India-rubber (*obsolescent*), arctic (*U. S.*). Galosh *and* arctic *refer generally to a heavy canvas and rubber footgear for snow; but in New England this is called an* overshoe.

oversight, *n.* **1.** care (*contex.*), supervision, supervisal (*R*); *spec.* superintendence, intendance, management, superintendency, censorship.

2. *See* MISS.

overspread, *v. t.* cover (*contex.*), spread; *spec.* overcome (*R*), mantle *or* (*emphatic*) overmantle, immantle (*R*), overcast, lay, film, suffuse, perfuse (*R*), dip (*R*), bespread (*emphatic*), pall, whelm, smear.

overstay, *v. t.* outstay.

oversupply, *v. t.* overstock, glut.

overtake, *v. t.* catch, overhaul (*chiefly naut.*).

overtire, *v. t.* overdo, overfatigue, overweary; see TIRE, WEARY, OVERDO, EXHAUST.

overtire, *n.* overfatigue, overweariness; *spec.* exhaustion.

overturn, *v. t.* **1.** *In a physical sense:* overthrow, throw (*chiefly spec.*), capsize, upset, overset (*R*), overbalance; *spec.* coup (*Scot.*), culbut (*R*), upturn, topple, tumble, evert (*A*), cast, fling, overtopple, prostrate, down, overblow.

Antonyms: see BALANCE.

2. *In a nonphysical sense: see* CONFUTE.

overturn, *n.* overthrow, capsize, upset, overset (*R*); *spec.* overbalance, upturn, eversion (*A*), cast, fling, throw, prostration.

overwhelm, *v. t.* **1.** *See* COVER, OVERFLOW, OVERCOME.

2. *Referring to immaterial things that are heaped or forced upon (something) to excess: spec.* swamp, deluge, flood, drown, kill (*colloq.*), oppress.

overwork, *v. t.* overdo, overlabor, overtoil, overply (*R*); *spec.* overstudy.

own, *a.* **1.** peculiar (*now formal and always implying exclusiveness*), german (*used in "brother german," "sister german," etc.*), private.

2. *See* APPROPRIATE.

own, *v. t.* **1.** have, possess (*more formal*), hold (*often spec.*).

2. *See* ACKNOWLEDGE.

owner, *n.* holder, proprietor (*more formal and, in business, more usual*), proprietress (*fem. equiv. of "proprietor"*); *spec.* bearer, occupant, master, lord (*rhetorical, or a term of feudalism*), esquire.

ownership, *n.* possession, property, possessorship, proprietorship, proprietary (*R*); *spec.* hand, dominion, title.

owning, *a.* proprietary, possessory.

ox, *n.* beef, bullock (*now always an ox; formerly a young bull*); *spec.* stot, steer.

oxhead, *n. Spec.* bucrane *or* bucranium.

oxidation, *n.* oxygenation (*chiefly spec.*), oxidization; *spec.* eremacausis, combustion.

oxidize, *v. t.* oxidate, oxygenate (*chiefly spec.*), oxygenize (*R*); *see* RUST, BURN.

P

pace, *v. i.* **1.** *See* GO.

2. amble, rack, single *or* single-foot (*U. S.*). *See* GAIT.

pachyderm, *n. As applied to persons:* thickskin, ironclad, hog-in-armor.

pacifiable, *a.* pacificatory (*R*), appeasable, placatory (*R*), propitiable, propitiatory, placable.

pacific, *a.* **1.** pacificatory, peacemaking; *spec.* mollifying, soothing, appeasing, placatory, propitiatory, propitiative, conciliatory, conciliative, irenical *or* (*less usually*) irenic.

Antonyms: see VEXATIOUS, COMBATIVE.

2. *See* PEACEABLE.

pacify, *v. t.* **1.** *Spec.* mollify, soothe, placate (*implying that demands, etc., are satisfied without implying the production of an actively kindly or favorable spirit*), appease (*implying complete*

override: *overlie, overbear.*
overrule: *overbear, abrogate.*
overrun: *overflow, frequent.*
oversea: *foreign.*
overshadow: *darken, cloud.*
overstatement: *exaggeration.*
overstep: *cross, exceed.*
overthrow, *v. t.: overturn, overcome, abolish, confute.*
overtire, *overdo, exhaust.*
overweening, *a.: arrogant, conceited.*
owed: *due.*
owing: *due, accrued, attributable.*

P

pace, *n.: step, gait, speed.*

placation), propitiate (*implying a making well disposed or gracious, and suggesting the superiority in the one propitiated, and usually the fear of some great evil*), conciliate (*implying the gaining of favor*), pacificate (*R*), satisfy, content.

Antonyms: see ANNOY, AGITATE, DISTURB, IRRITATE, VEX.

2. *See* CALM.

pack, *n.* **1.** *See* BUNDLE, SET, MULTITUDE, FLOCK, HERD, KENNEL.

2. *Referring to playing cards:* deck, stack.

pack, *v. t.* **1.** *See* BUNDLE, FILL, CROWD, FAKE.

2. arrange (*contex.*), stow.

packing, *n.* **1.** package (*R*), impaction *or* impactment (*R or tech.*).

2. *Referring to what is used in packing: spec.* stuffing, gasket, dunnage.

packsaddle, *n.* saddle (*contex.*), bat; *spec.* aparejo (*local, U. S.*).

paddle, *n.* **1.** *See* OAR.

2. *A board at the circumference of a wheel:* float.

page, *n.* attendant (*contex.*); *spec.* buttons (*C*), ichoglan (*Turkish*), footboy, henchman (*hist.*), donzel (*A*).

pail, *n. Spec.* bowie (*shallow; Scot.*), piggin (*chiefly dial. Eng.*).

pain, *n.* **1.** *See* DISTRESS.

2. discomfort (*contex.*), distress (*contex.*), anguish (*A, exc. spec.*), suffering (*contex.*); *spec.* hurt, ache, agony, bale (*B*), torment, torture, pang, smart, lancination, sting, stitch, twinge, throe, gripe, dolor (*B or R*).

3. *In. pl.: see* WORK, CARE, CHILDBIRTH.

pain, *v. t.* **1.** *See* GRIEVE.

2. distress (*contex.*), anguish (*formerly not spec.; R*); *spec.* hurt, agonize, torment, torture, rack, twinge, pang (*R*), sting, smart, gripe, bite.

Antonyms: see PLEASE.

pain, *v. i. Spec.* twinge, shoot, rage, rankle, pang (*R*).

painful, *a.* **1.** *See* DEPRESSING, CAREFUL, DIFFICULT, ANNOYING, AFFLICTIVE.

2. distressing (*contex.*), fell (*chiefly poetic*), severe, sharp (*pain*); *spec.* hurtful, pungent, agonizing, poignant, tormenting, torturous, evil, dolorous *or* dolorific (*B, R*), sore, baleful (*B, R*), biting (*fig.*); *see* TROUBLESOME.

Antonyms: see PLEASANT.

paint, *v. t.* **1.** depict (*contex.*); *spec.* limn (*B or A*), bepaint, image (*contex.*), daub, grain, fresco, wash, raddle *or* reddle, pencil (*A*), flat, impaste, miniate, distemper.

2. *See* COLOR, DESCRIBE.

paint, *v. i. Spec.* blot, smear, wash, rouge.

painter, *n.* depicter (*contex.; formal or R*), brush (*cant*), brushman (*R*); *spec.* limner (*B or A*), paintress (*fem.*), dauber *or* daubster, plein-airist (*cant.*), primitive, landscapist.

painting, *n.* **1.** *Spec.* depiction (*contex.; formal or R*), limning (*B or A*), daubery, imagery (*contex.*), easeldom (*a nonce word*).

2. *See* DESCRIPTION.

palatable, *a.* tasteful (*R, a stronger word than "palatable"*), gustable (*A or R*), tasty (*C*); *spec.* savory, relishable, dainty, nice, delicate, Epicurean (*B*), toothful (*R*), toothsome, toothy (*C*), appetizing, delicious, ambrosial *or* ambrosian (*fig.*), racy, nectarean *or* nectareous *or* nectared *or* nectarine (*fig.*), savorous (*R*), sapid, sipid (*R for "sapid"*).

Antonyms: see UNPALATABLE, TASTELESS.

pale, *a.* **1.** light; *spec.* pallid (*chiefly referring to the bloodless appearance of the face*), wan (*nearly an equiv. of "pallid"*), wannish, paly (*chiefly poetic*), pasty, ghastly (*suggesting death or horror*), spectral, blanched, colorless, doughy (*C equiv. of "pasty"*), lunar (*fig.*), mealy, blank (*R*), bloodless, cadaverous, waxy, deathlike, sickly-looking, sickly, white-faced, whey-faced, white.

Antonyms: see BLUSHING, FLUSHED, RED, RED-FACED, DARK.

2. *See* DIM.

pale, *v. t. Spec.* whiten, white, sickly, blanch.

pale, *v. i.* whiten, blanch.

Antonyms: see BLUSH.

pallor, *n.* paleness; *spec.* bloodlessness, ghastliness, *etc. Cf.* PALE, *a.*

Antonyms: see FLUSH.

palm, *n.* **1.** *Referring to part of the hand:* flat (*C*), thenar (*tech.*).

2. *See* HANDLE, HANDBREADTH.

palmist, *n.* chiromant *or* chiromancer (*less usual*), palmister (*R*).

palmistry, *n.* chiromancy (*less usual*).

paltry, *a.* mean (*emphasizing the idea of pettiness, stinginess, or poverty of spirit*); *spec.* contemptible, trivial, scurvy, scald (*A, an equiv. of "scurvy"*), cheap, woeful, pitiful *or* (*less usually*) pitiable, worthless, rubbishy, trashy, scrubby, footy (*C, Eng.*), foolish (*A*).

Antonyms: see GENEROUS.

pan, *n.* **1.** *Spec.* skillet, Turk's-head, tache, heater, pattypan.

2. *Referring to part of a balance:* scale.

3. *See* HOLLOW, SUBSOIL.

panacea, *n.* remedy (*contex.*), cure-all *or* heal-all (*C or disparaging*), catholicon (*A or B*), panpharmacon *or* pampharmacon (*R*), panace *or* panax (*R*), polychrest (*A or R*), panchreston (*obs.*).

pancake, *n.* flapjack (*dial. or U. S.*); *spec.* froise *or* fraise (*Eng.*).

pane, *n.* **1.** *See* COMPARTMENT.

---

packed: *compact, full, crowded.*
pact: *agreement, contract.*
pad, *v. t.: cushion.*
pad, *n.: cushion, foot, tablet.*
paddle, *v. i.: dabble, row.*
pageant: *device, float.*
paint, *n.: pigment, cosmetic.*
pair, *v. t.: double, match, marry, mate.*
pair, *v. i.: match, marry, mate.*
pal: *mate, accomplice.*
palate: *taste, liking.*
pale, *n.: stake, fence, inclosure, bound.*
pale, *v. i.: fade.*
palm: *foist, handle.*
palmy: *prosperous.*
palpable: *evident, intelligible.*
pamper: *indulge.*
pander: *go-between, bawd, minister.*
pant, *v. i.: breathe, blow, gasp, long, pulsate.*

2. *Referring to a window glass: spec.* quarrel *or* (*R*) quarry, quirk.

panel, *n.* **1.** *See* LIST, JURY, INSERTION.

2. *Spec.* compartment, table, tablet, frontispiece, medallion.

pantomime, *n.* **1.** actor (*contex.*); *spec.* pantomimist, mute.

2. *See* DRAMA, GESTURE.

pantry, *n. Spec.* buttery (*an old-fashioned term for "pantry"*), butlery (*often used as a more pretentious name of any "pantry"*), cuddy (*naut.*).

pants, *n.* trousers, breeches (pants *is C, U. S.; in Brit. usage* pants *signifies underdrawers*).

papacy, *n.* pontificate, popeship, popedom *or* popehood (*less usual terms*).

papal, *a.* pontifical (*formal*), apostolic, papistic *or* papistical (*usually hostile or opprobrious*), papish (*usually hostile*).

paper, *n. See* DOCUMENT, NEWSPAPER, COMPOSITION, ARTICLE.

papery, *a.* paper (*the noun used attributively*), chartaceous *or* (*R*) cartaceous (*chiefly tech.*), papyraceous (*B*).

papilla, *n.* pimple, papule; *spec.* papillule.

pappus, *n. Spec.* plume, plumule, clock, egret.

parable, *n.* allegory, similitude (*less usual, and not technical*); *spec.* haggada.

paradise, *n.* **1.** Eden (*emphasizing the idea of innocent simplicity; while "paradise" emphasizes the idea of unalloyed happiness*).

2. *See* HEAVEN.

paragon, *n.* nonesuch (*a homelier Anglo-Saxon term*), nonpareil, phœnix (*fig.*), flower (*fig.*), pink (*fig.*), rose (*fig.*), queen (*fig.*).

paragraph, *n.* **1.** *Referring to the mark or character:* pilcrow (*A*).

2. *See* PART.

parallel, *v. t.* **1.** follow.

Antonyms: see CROSS.

2. *See* COMPARE.

parallel, *a.* **1.** equidistant; *spec.* concentric, collateral.

Antonyms: INTERSECTING, INCLINED, DIVERGENT.

2. *See* ABREAST, ANALOGOUS, EQUAL.

3. concurrent.

paralysis, *n.* paralyzation (*R*), palsy (*chiefly spec.*), palsification (*chiefly spec.*), sideration (*R*); *spec.* stroke, hemiplegia, diplegia, paresis, paraplegia.

paralyze, *v. t.* **1.** palsy (*now chiefly fig. or spec.*), palsify (*R*), impalsy (*R*); *spec.* benumb, freeze (*often fig.*), lethargize (*often fig.*).

Antonyms: see ANIMATE, STIMULATE.

2. *See* ENERVATE, DISABLE.

paralyzed, *a.* paralytic, palsied (*chiefly spec. or fig.*); *spec.* paretic.

paramour, *n.* lover (*contex.*); *spec.* ladylove, mistress, concubine, hetæra. *"Paramour" now is mostly used in reference to one who takes the place, without the rights, of a husband or wife. For discriminations see* BAWD, HARLOT, MISTRESS.

parapet, *n. Spec.* babette, battlement, bartizan, glacis, esplanade, breastwork.

paraphrase, *n.* repetition (*contex.*), rendering (*contex.*), rewording, rehash (*contemptuous*), restatement.

paraphrase, *v. t.* reword, repeat (*contex.*), restate.

parasite, *n.* **1.** *See* HANGER-ON.

2. *Spec.* entozoön, epizoön, epiphyte, commensal.

parasol, *n.* sunshade.

parboil, *v. t.* cook (*contex.*), boil (*contex.*), coddle (*chiefly spec.*).

parchment, *n.* **1.** skin (*contex.*), sheepskin; *spec.* forel, pell.

2. *See* DOCUMENT.

pare, *v. t.* cut (*contex.*); *spec.* slice, shave, skive, beat (*Eng.*), dole.

parent, *n. Spec.* father, mother.

Antonyms: see OFFSPRING, CHILD, SON, DAUGHTER.

paring, *n.* cut (*contex.*); *spec.* slice, shave, shaving, skive, skiving, chip.

park, *n.* paradise (*chiefly referring to Oriental parks*); *spec.* common, Prado.

parlor, *n.* **1.** *A room in which to hold conversation: spec.* locutory.

2. best room, drawing-room, living-room, foreroom (*A*).

parochial, *a.* parish (*the noun used adjectively; and not having the secondary connotations of parochial*).

paroxysmal, *a. In geology: spec.* catastrophic, cataclysmic.

parquet, *n.* **1.** *See* FLOOR.

2. auditorium, orchestra (*chiefly U. S.*).

parrot, *n.* **1.** popinjay (*A*), poll (*orig. an equivalent for "Mary"; conventionally used as the proper name of any parrot*), polly (*dim. of "poll"*).

2. *See* IMITATOR.

parsonage, *n. Spec.* benefice, rectory, parsonium (*southern U. S.*), manse.

part, *n.* **1.** parcel (*A or law*); *spec.* portion, proportion, member, division, subdivision, section, segment, fragment, piece, snatch, scrap, crumb (*fig.*), installment, callop, cantle (*chiefly Eng.*), moiety (*a loose use; properly, "one half"*), element; *see* SHARE, FRAGMENT, REMNANT, JOINT, ORGAN, DIVISION.

Antonyms: see ALL, WHOLE.

2. *Referring to the parts of printed matter: spec.* number, book, passage, chapter, section, paragraph, clause, comma (*Greek and Latin prosody*).

---

parade, *n.: show, disclosure, march.*
parade, *v. t.: show, disclose, march.*
parallel, *n.: analogue, counterpart.*
parallelism: *comparison, analogue, analogy, equality.*
parent: *father, mother, origin.*
parity: *equality, analogy.*
parley, *n.: conversation, conference, discussion.*
parole, *v. t.: free.*
paroxysm: *fit, ecstasy, spasm.*
parry, *v. t.: avert.*
parry, *v. i.: fence.*
part, *v. i.: separate, break, depart.*

---

3. *Referring to a character acted in a play or in real life:* rôle, cue, pageant (*A*), lines (*pl.*), cast.
4. *See* SOME, OFFICE, SIDE, DEPARTMENT, PLACE, FRAGMENT.

partake, *v. i.* **1.** *See* SHARE.
2. participate (*with "in"*). *"Partake" is followed by "of."*

partial, *a.* **1.** *Spec.* biased, one-sided, interested, unfair, prejudiced; *see* FOND.
Antonyms: see IMPARTIAL.
2. fractional, component, portional (*R*); *spec.* half, incomplete.
Antonyms: see ABSOLUTE, COMPLETE, THOROUGH.

partiality, *n. Spec.* bias, one-sidedness, interest, unfairness, prejudice, favor, favoritism, prepossession, nepotism; *see* FONDNESS.
Antonyms: see IMPARTIALITY.

partially, *a.* partly; (*though commonly used interchangeably,* partially *ought properly to imply bias or favoritism,* partly *to be used always in the simple sense of incompletely, not wholly*); *spec.* fractionally, incompletely, restrictedly.
Antonyms: see WHOLLY.

particle, *n.* **1.** *Spec.* bit (*often somewhat C*), atom (*very emphatic*), snip (*C*), atomy (*R*), iota (*a sense arising from, and often alluding to, Matt. v: 18, "iota" being etymologically equivalent to "jot"*), jot (*a sense arising from, and often alluding to, Matt. v: 18*), tittle, whit (*mostly with a negative expressed or implied*), trifle (*often in "jot or tittle"*), mite (*C*), morsel, scintilla (*usually fig. and used with a negative*), rap (*used with a negative; used esp. in "without a rap" or "not a rap"*), smitch (*C, U. S.*), grain, drop, moteling (*R*), molecule, corpuscle, corpuscule, granule, shred, dust (*R*), nip, glimmer, spark, speck, fleck, crumb, stiver, driblet, electron, ion, sup.
Antonyms: see BIG THING.
2. *In grammar: spec.* preposition, conjunction, interjection, inflex, prefix, suffix, enclitic, proclitic, *etc.*

particular, *a.* **1.** special, especial (*equiv. of "special," but A in this sense*), specific; *spec.* restricted; *see* DEFINITE.
Antonyms: see MISCELLANEOUS, GENERAL.
2. *Spec.* nice (*B implying emphasis on finespun accuracy of distinction*), dainty (*often with negative or disapproving implication of capriciousness or over-fussiness*), close, circumstantial, narrow, minute, detailed.
3. *See* SPECIAL, FASTIDIOUS, CAREFUL, INDIVIDUAL, INTIMATE, CONSCIENTIOUS, MINUTE.

particular, *n. Spec.* detail, circumstance, respect (*used with "in," as in "in this one respect"*), regard, point.

particularize, *v. t. Spec.* detail, itemize, specify.

partition, *n.* **1.** *Referring to the act: see* DIVISION, DISTRIBUTION.
2. *Referring to the dividing thing: spec.* fence, wall, septation (*R*), phragma, septum, septulum, dissepiment, diaphragm, brattice *or* brattish, interseptum, bulkhead, panel, mediastinum, perpend. *See* DIVISION.

partizan, *n.* adherent (*contex.*), partisan (*a variant*), sider, factioneer (*R*), sectionary (*R*), sectionist (*R*), fautor (*R*), partialist.

partizanship, *n. Spec.* party, dissension, fautorship (*R*); *spec.* ministerialism, politicalism, cliquism, cliquishness, partyism.

partner, *n.* associate; *spec.* copartner (*more formal*), halver (*fig.*), accomplice, cavalier, sharer.
Antonyms: see OPPONENT.

partnership, *n.* association; *spec.* copartnership, sharing.

parturient, *a.* travailing (*A*).

party, *n.* **1.** association (*contex.*), group (*contex.*); *spec.* division, interest, side, faction, clique (*a term of contempt or reproach*).
2. *See* COMBINATION, PARTIZANSHIP, GROUP, PERSON, DETAIL.
3. *Referring to a social affair:* assembly (*contex.*); *spec.* rout (*chiefly hist.*), reception, ball, dance, *etc.*

party-colored, *a.* parti-colored (*a variant*), variegated; *spec.* mottled, motley, piebald, pied, pinto (*southwestern U. S.*), skewbald.
Antonyms: see ONE-COLORED.

pass, *n.* passage; *spec.* defile, notch (*U. S.*), gap, neck, gut, cut, gate, ghaut *or* ghat (*Anglo-Indian*), kotal (*East India*); throw (*in football, basketball, etc.*); glance, allurement, gesture (*all three C, U. S., as in "She made a pass at him."*)

pass, *v. i.* **1.** *See* GO, MOVE, CHANGE, OCCUR, DIE, CIRCULATE, DECIDE, DESCEND, THRUST.
2. *In reference to time:* elapse (*chiefly formal or technical*), lapse (*R*), go; *spec.* flit (*usually with an adverb, as "by," "over," etc.*), glide (*usually with "by"*), slip (*usually with an adverb, as "by," "away," etc.*), expire, run, wear (*often with "on"*), flow (*with "by"*).
3. *Referring to the going by, away, or the like, of some state, emotion, etc.:* go, overpass (*R*), sink, slip, overblow.
4. *Referring to the transfer of rights from one to another:* go, devolve, fall, descend.

pass, *v. t.* **1.** *See* CROSS, DELIVER, EXTEND, OUTSTRIP, EXCEED, ENACT, MISS, IGNORE, APPROVE, PROMISE, THROW, *v. t.*
2. *In the sense of "to get by or go by": spec.* clear, skirt, leap, overpass, transmeate (*A or R*), stride.
3. *In the sense of "to let go, or cause to go":* allow, permit, let; *spec.* frank, graduate.
4. *Referring to time:* spend, overpass (*R*), wear (*often with "away"*), use, while *or* wile (*usually with "away"*); *spec.* beguile, moon, languish (*usually with "out" or "away"*), drowse.

---

particularity: *individuality.*
particularize: *mention, infer.*
parting, *n.: departure, death, division, farewell.*
partition: *divide, distribute.*
partly: *partially.*
parvenu: *upstart.*

---

pass, *n.* **1.** *See* STATE, THRUST, DEATH, MOTION, MOVEMENT.
2. authorization (*contex.*), permission (*contex.*); *spec.* order (*Eng.*), passport, purwanah (*East Indian*).

passable, *a.* **1.** pervious (*R*); *spec.* fordable.
Antonyms: see IMPASSABLE.
2. *See* MODERATE, FAIR.

passage, *n.* **1.** passing (*emphasizing the idea of the action*); *spec.* going, motion, movement, change, exchange, encounter, enactment, migration, evacuation.
2. *In reference to time:* lapse, elapse (*R*), tract (*R*), efflux (*B*), effluxion (*B*); *spec.* course, revolution, expiry, run.
3. way (*contex.*); *spec.* shoot, cut, communication, defile, corridor, gallery, hall, entry, door, gate, mouth, cloister, heading, drift, level, tunnel, winze, shaft, flue, chimney, caponier, cuniculus (*archæol.*), sap, iter, chute, vomitory (*chiefly hist.*), slype.
Antonyms: see IMPASSE.
4. *Referring to literature: spec.* commatin (*Gr. prosody*), pericope (*chiefly in writing on Biblical literature*), commonplace, collectanea (*pl.*). *Also see* PART.
5. *Referring to music: spec.* bar, measure, phrase, melody, coda, *etc.*

passenger, *n.* passager (*A*); *spec.* fare.

passer, *n.* passer-by (*emphatic*), by-passer (*equiv. of "passer-by"*), passenger (*R*).

passing, *a.* **1.** *In the physical sense: spec.* transmigratory, transient.
Antonyms: see ENDURING.
2. *Fig.: spec.* current, fleeting, revolving; *see* CURSORY, TRANSIENT, GREAT, HASTY.

passing, *n.* **1.** *See* PASSAGE.
2. *Fig.: spec.* transition (passing, *as in a discussion, a movement, or a historical sequence from one stage to another without reference to advance or decline*), graduation (passing, *as in* transition, *but with the implication of changed levels of time, achievement, etc.*), lapse (passing *by virtue of inaction or the automatic operation of forces in motion*), elapse; *see* DEATH, OCCURRENCE.

passive, *a.* **1.** nonresistant, patient (*R*).
2. *See* INACTIVE.

passiveness, *n.* **1.** passivity, nonresistance, irresistance (*R*), patience (*R*).
2. *See* INACTIVITY.

passover, *n.* pasch (*A or hist.*)

passport, *n.* pass (*contex.*), license (*contex.*); *spec.* credentials (*pl.*), dustuck *or* dustuk (*East Indian*).

password, *n.* countersign *or* (*for short*) sign, word (*short for "password"*), shibboleth (*spec. or fig.*); *spec.* watchword, parole.

past, *a.* bygone, gone (*R, exc. as used predicatively*), preterite (*R, exc. as a grammatical term*), bypast (*emphatic equiv. of "past"*), foregone (*A*), ancient (*A, exc. spec.*); *spec.* ago (*predicative*), agone (*A*), overpassed, elapsed, preterlapsed (*R*); *see* FORMER, OBSOLETE.
Antonyms: see PRESENT, FUTURE.

past, *n.* foretime (*R*), heretofore (*R*); *spec.* history, yesterday.
Antonyms: see PRESENT, FUTURE.

paste, *n.* **1.** *In cookery:* dough (*chiefly spec.*); *spec.* batter, brioche, macaroni, spaghetti, vermicelli.
2. *Referring to any of various things suggesting the paste of cookery: spec.* pastel, dope, electuary, magma, strass; *see* COSMETIC, CEMENT.

pasteboard, *n.* board (*short for "pasteboard"; chiefly cant*), carton (*R or spec.*); *spec.* cardboard, millboard, strawboard, binder's board.

pastoral, *n.* **1.** composition (*contex.*), eclogue; *spec.* idyl, bucolic (*chiefly in pl.*).
2. *See* CROSIER.

pastry, *n.* bakemeat (*obs.*), pâtisserie (*French*); *spec.* pie, cake, tart, puff, *etc.*

pasture, *n.* **1.** pasturage; *spec.* grass, grazing.
2. *Referring to the land:* grassland; *spec.* grazing, lea (*dial. or Eng.*), range (*U. S.*), cowgate (*Eng.*), yard (*U. S. and Canada*).

pasture, *a.* pascual (*R*), pascuous (*R*); *spec.* grazing.

pasty, *a.* **1.** doughy.
2. *See* SOFT, STICKY.

patchy, *a. Spec.* spotty (*painter's cant*).

paternity, *n.* fatherhood, fathership, sireship (*R*).

path, *n.* **1.** way (*contex.*); *spec.* track, footpath, trail, berm.
2. *See* WALK, COURSE.

pathless, *a.* unpathed (*R*); *spec.* untracked (*R*), trackless.

pathological, *a. Spec.* morbid, morbific.
Antonyms: see HEALTHFUL.

patience, *n.* patiency (*R*), patientness (*R*); *spec.* endurance, forbearance, long-suffering, sufferance, longanimity (*R*), forbearing.
Antonyms: see UNEASINESS; *also cf.* IRASCIBLE.

patient, *a.* self-restrained (*contex.*); *spec.* enduring *or* (*R*), endurant, long-suffering, longanimous (*B*), magnanimous (*R*).
Antonyms: see IRASCIBLE, INTOLERANT, UNEASY.

patient, *n.* **1.** *In medicine:* subject, case; *spec.* clinic.
2. *Referring to one acted upon in any way:* subject.

patriot, *n. Spec.* compatriot, jingo (*contemptuous*), Chauvinist, patriotess (*fem.*).
Antonyms: see TRAITOR.

---

passé: *obsolete, worn-out, faded.*
passion: *suffering, anger, frenzy.*
passionate: *intense, angry, frantic.*
past, *adv.: by, beyond.*
pastime: *diversion.*
pat, *a.: appropriate.*
pat, *n.: stroke, lump, caress.*
patch, *n.: repair, piece, spot, field.*
patch, *v. t.: repair.*
patent, *a.: open, evident.*
paternal: *fatherly, inherited, descended.*
paternity: *fatherhood, descent.*
pathetic: *affecting.*
pathos: *suffering, compassion, lamentableness.*
patrician, *a.: noble, aristocratic.*

---

patter, *v. i.* **1.** strike (*contex.*), pit-a-pat, pit-pat, pitter-patter;—*all but "strike" being imitative.*
2. *See* DABBLE.
patter, *n.* pit-a-pat, pattering, pit-pat, pitter-patter.
pattern, *n.* **1.** form (*contex.*), original (*contex.*); *spec.* model, block, norm *or* (*Latin*) norma, copy, type, archetype, exemplar (*R*), paradigm (*R*), mold *or* mould, template *or* templet, curb *or* kerb, plan, last.
2. *In a figurative or secondary sense: spec.* ensample (*A*), paragon, mirror (*R*), idea.
3. *See* EXAMPLE, DESIGN.
pave, *v. t.* cover (*contex.*), lay (*contex.*); *spec.* cobble, causey (*chiefly Scot.*), pitch, slab, concrete, flag, brick, flint, pavement (*chiefly in p. p. "pavemented"*), floor.
paved, *a.* paven (*chiefly B*), pavemented (*R*); *spec.* flagged.
pavement, *n.* pave (*chiefly U. S.*), paving; *spec.* flagging, cobbles (*pl.*), causey (*chiefly Scot.*).
paver, *n.* pavior (*more formal*), paviner (*R*); *spec.* flagger.
pawn, *v. t.* pledge (*contex.*); *spec.* (*in reference to putting with a pawnbroker to secure a loan*) spout (*C or S*), sweat (*S*), hock (*S*).
Antonyms: see FREE.
pawnbroker, *n.* broker (*contex.*), lumberer (*A or S*), uncle (*S*).
pawnshop, *n.* pawnbrokery (*R*), spout (*S*), popshop (*S*).
pay, *v. t.* **1.** *With the person as the object: spec.* compensate (*implying equality of the pay with the work done*), remunerate (*suggesting ample pay, such as is not obligatory*), satisfy, repay, prepay, reward, requite (*suggesting esp. paying what is due or merited; often used ironically*), reimburse, indemnify, stipend, recoup (*often used reflexively*), recompense, stand (*C*), fee, tip (*extra payment to a servant, guide, messenger, etc.*), salary.
2. *With the debt, obligation, or cause of indebtedness as the object:* discharge (*contex.*), satisfy, settle (*contex.*), liquidate, quit, acquit (*A*); *spec.* sink, lift, compound, foot, honor, defray, meet, discount.
Antonyms: see REPUDIATE, DISHONOR.
3. *With what is given in payment as the object:* give (*contex.*), render; *spec.* tribute.
pay, *v. i. Spec.* fine (*Eng.*), toll.
pay, *n.* profit (*contex.*); *spec.* compensation, reward, requital, recompense, remuneration, stipend, prebend, satisfaction, perquisite, percentage, brokerage, commission, freight; *see* HIRE, PAYMENT.
paying, *a. Spec.* compensatory, compensative, remuneratory, remunerative, profitable.
payment, *n.* **1.** *The act of paying a person: spec.* compensation, remuneration, satisfaction, repayment, reward, requital, reimbursement, recoupment, recompense, fee, stipend, tip, emolument, honorarium, pay, salary, wages, hire.
2. *The act of paying a debt:* discharge (*contex.*), settlement (*contex.*), satisfaction; *spec.* liquidation, quittance, acquittance, sinking, lifting, compounding, settlement, defrayal, discount.
3. *That which is given by way of payment:* render; *spec.* blood money, salvage, scot, royalty, earnest, gale (*R or U. S.*), garnish (*hist.*), relief (*hist.*), prestation, heriot; *see* FEE, INSTALLMENT.
peace, *n.* **1.** *Spec.* concord, accord (*R*), harmony, amity, frith (*obs. or hist.*), truce, friendliness.
Antonyms: see DISSENSION, WAR.
2. *Referring to a person's mental condition, actual or seeming: spec.* equanimity, composure, placidity *or* placidness (placidness *suggests more the mental quality or characteristic;* placidity *more the individual or concrete example or condition; so with* quiet, quietness, *etc.*), calmness *or* calm (calmness *implies absence of outward show of agitation, often with accompanying mental quiet;* calm, *a less usual equivalent of* calmness, *is more suggestive of the individual or concrete instance*), quiet *or* quietness, quietude (*a less usual, but rather stronger equivalent for* quietness), rest, requiem (*R*), tranquillity *or* tranquilness (*implying merely freedom from mental disturbance*), repose, peacefulness, imperturbation (*R*).
Antonyms: see ACTIVITY.
peaceable, *a.* **1.** peaceful (*R*); *spec.* pacific, quiet, gentle, bloodless.
Antonyms: see IRASCIBLE, COMBATIVE, PUGNACIOUS, QUARRELSOME.
2. *See* PEACEFUL.
peaceful, *a.* **1.** amicable, peaceable, concordant, harmonious.
2. *Spec.* equanimous (*R*), composed, placid, calm, quiet, restful, tranquil.
Antonyms: see AGITATED.
peacemaker, *n.* makepeace (*A*), pacificator (*R*), peacemonger (*opprobrious*); *spec.* dove (*fig.*).
Antonyms: see MISCHIEF-MAKER.
peace message, irenicon (*R*), olive branch (*fig.*).
peacocklike, *a.* pavonian, pavonine.
peak, *n.* **1.** *See* POINT, SUMMIT.
2. *Referring to a mountain summit ending in a point: spec.* pinnacle, horn (*R or consciously fig.*), pike (*now local Eng., or used in proper names*), butte (*U. S.*), cone, cusp (*R*), ben (*Scot.; chiefly used in proper names*), nunatak.
Antonyms: see BOTTOM, PLATEAU.
pearl, *n.* **1.** margarite (*A*); *see* DROP.
2. nacre (*B or tech.*).
pearly, *n.* **1.** perlaceous (*R*); *spec.* nacreous, nacrous (*R*).

patrol, *n.: guard, watchman.*
patron: *defender, benefactor, customer, saint, deity.*
patronage: *aid, custom.*
patronize: *protect, aid, notice.*
patter, *n.: babble, chatter, dialect.*
paunch: *abdomen.*
pavilion: *tent, bell, canopy, building.*
paw, *n.: hand, foot, handwriting.*
paw, *v. t.: handle.*
peal, *n.: ringing, set, outbreak.*

2. *See* LUSTROUS, GRAY.

pear-shaped, *a.* pyriform, obconic (*math.*).

peasant, *n.* countryman (*contex.*), boor (*obs., exc. of Dutch, German, or other foreign peasants*), bucolic (*humorous*), peasantess (*fem.*); *spec.* cotter, cottar, cottier (*Great Britain and Ireland*), muzhik *or* moujik, ryot, fellah.

pea-shaped, *a.* pisiform (*tech.*).

pebble, *n.* stone (*contex.*); *spec.* chuckie (*a quartz pebble; Scot.*), plum.

peck, *v. t.* strike (*contex.*), beak (*R*); *spec.* pecket (*R*), peckle.

peculiar, *a.* **1.** own, proper (*R, exc. spec.*), individual, idiosyncratic; *spec.* appropriate, idiomatic. *See* OWN.

2. *See* ODD, SPECIAL.

peculiarity, *n.* **1.** properness (*R*), idiosyncrasy, individuality; *spec.* idiom.

2. *See* ODDITY.

pedant, *n.* precisian (*contex.*); *spec.* bluestocking (*fem.; usually contemptuous*), morosoph, pedantess (*fem.*).

pedantic, *a.* pedantical (*R*), budge (*B*); *spec.* bluestocking *or* (*for short*) blue (*usually contemptuous*), bookish.

Antonyms: see COLLOQUIAL.

peddle, *v. t.* sell (*contex.*); *spec.* canvass (*usually less derogatory than "peddle"*), hawk, cadge (*dial. or S*).

peddler, *n.* seller (*contex.*), pedlar (*a variant*), peripatetic (*humorous and contex.*); *spec.* canvasser, hawker, cadger (*dial. or S*), costermonger *or* coster (*Eng.*), haggler (*Eng.*), huckster *or* (*R*) hucksterer (*chiefly a term of local use in specific senses*), hucksteress *or* huckstress (*fem.*), faker (*S*), cheap Jack (*S, contemptuous*), cheap John (*S, contemptuous*), packman, duffer (*S*).

pedestrian, *a.* peripatetic (*chiefly humorous, exc. spec.*), perigrinator (*R*); *spec.* tramp, itinerant, hiker, walker, runner.

pedigree, *n.* ancestry, genealogy, descent, lineage; *see* THOROUGHBRED.

pediment, *n.* frontal; *spec.* frontispiece, fronton (*R or A equiv. of "frontispiece"*).

peek, *v. i. & n.* look (*contex.*), peep, squint; *see* GLANCE.

peeker, *n.* peeper; *spec.* Paul Pry, Peeping Tom.

peekhole, *n.* eyehole, eyelethole (*R*), eyelet (*R*), loophole; *spec.* squint, hagioscope, Judas, oillet (*hist.*).

pellet, *n. Spec.* pebble, hailstone, bullet; *see* GLOBULE, GRAIN.

pelt, *v. t.* strike (*contex.*); *spec.* pepper, bepepper (*an intensive*), bepelt (*an intensive*), stone, egg, pellet, lapidate (*R*), bombard.

pen, *n.* style (*B or rhetorical*), stylus (*R equiv. of "style"*); *spec.* quill, goose quill.

pen, *n.* inclosure (*contex.*); *spec.* fold, penfold *or* pinfold (*chiefly Eng.*), coop, hutch, sty, cruive (*Scot.*), crib, stall, pit, cage, crawl, pound.

penalty, *n.* **1.** *Referring to what is inflicted in order to punish:* punishment; *spec.* chastisement, whipping, flogging, fine, forfeiture; *see* FINE.

Antonyms: see REWARD.

2. *See* DISADVANTAGE, HANDICAP.

pencil, *n.* **1.** *See* BRUSH.

2. marker (*contex.*); *spec.* crayon, chalk, charcoal, keelivine (*Scot.*).

pendant, *n.* drop; *spec.* flap, tag, pendicle (*R*), pendule (*R*), coachwhip (*naut.*), lobe, lob (*R*), flag, eardrop, tassel, jag, tippet, bulla; *see* CHANDELIER.

penetrate, *v. t.* **1.** *In a sense implying force: spec.* interpenetrate, impenetrate (*R*), compenetrate, cut, sink, invade, interdigitate (*R*), interosculate (*R*), bore, burrow, *etc.*; *see* PIERCE, PERFORATE.

2. *See* ENTER, PERVADE, INDENT, AFFECT, UNDERSTAND, PERCEIVE.

penetrative, *a.* **1.** penetrant, penetrating; *spec.* insinuating (*winding a way deviously into an object or idea*); *see* PERMEATIVE, PIERCING.

2. *See* SHARP, PIERCING, SUBTLE.

pennon, *n. Spec.* pennoncel (*hist.*), streamer; *see* FLAG.

penny, *n.* **1.** copper (*contex.*).

2. *See* CENT.

pensioner, *n.* pensionary (*often in a sinister sense*); *see* MERCENARY.

penthouse, *n.* lean-to; *spec.* pluteus (*Roman antiq.*).

people, *n.* **1.** *Referring to a body of persons constituting a nation, tribe, race, or the like:* folk (*chiefly spec.*); *spec.* landfolk (*R*), countryfolk, country, race, tribe, heritage, nation, state.

2. *Referring to persons standing in some special relation or having some characteristic by which they are classed together:* folk (*less formal than "people"*); *spec.* city, town, village, boys (*pl.*), girls (*pl.*), men (*pl.*), women (*pl.*), company, public.

3. *The ordinary people as distinguished from the nobility or from the wealthy or educated:* populace (*sometimes, more invidiously, equiv. to "mob"*), commons, commonalty (*a collective*), commonality (*R*), commonage (*R*), commune (*hist.*), proletariat, masses (*pl.*), mass (*used with "the"*), generality *or* (*with "the"*) general (*A*), vulgar (*R; used with "the"*), multitude (*used with "the"*), democracy, demos (*B or tech. or spec.*); *spec.* crowd, mob, gentry.

Antonyms: see NOBILITY.

peck, *v. i.: strike, eat.*
pecuniary: *monetary.*
pedestal: *support.*
peel, *n.: skin, bark, hull.*
peel, *v. t.: skin, decorticate, hull, strip.*
peep: *peck, glance, emerge, chirp.*
peer, *n.: equal, noble.*
peer, *v. i.: look, emerge.*
peerless: *unequaled.*
peevish: *complaining, irascible.*
pellucid: *clear, intelligible.*
pelt, *v. t.: throw, drive.*
pelt, *v. i.: strike.*
penalize: *punish, handicap.*
pendent: *drooping, hanging, undecided.*
pending, *prep.: during.*
pension, *n.: allowance.*
penury: *poverty, deficiency.*

4. folks *or* folk (*"folks" is now the commoner term, and is C; "folk" is A, exc. spec.*), they (*an indefinite use of the pronoun*), men (*properly, male people*).

people, *v. t.* **1.** populate, empeople (*intensive; B*); *spec.* settle.
Antonyms: see DEPOPULATE.
2. *See* INHABIT.

perceive, *v. t.* see; *spec.* seize, catch, apprehend (*implying esp. perception accompanied by a mental consciousness, often a grasp of the understanding*), appreciate, discern (*implying acuteness of perception or subtlety*), apperceive (*R, exc. tech.*), read, find, penetrate, pierce, descry, tell, observe, recognize, cognize (*R or tech.*), sense, detect, spot, smoke (*A*), trace, scan (*R*), hear, feel, snuff, sniff, smell; *see* UNDERSTAND, DISTINGUISH, NOTICE.
Antonyms: see MISS.

perceive, *v. i.* (*Implies deep intuitive understanding*), *spec.* know (*intellectually*), understand (*take into the mind with sympathy*), feel.

perceiver, *n.* percipient; *spec.* observer, discerner, *etc.*

percentage, *n. Spec.* pay (*contex.*), backwardation (*Eng. Stock Exchange*), contango (*Eng. Stock Exchange*), factorage.

perceptible, *a.* perceivable; *spec.* apprehensible, appreciable, discernible, detectable, tangible, sensible, observable; *see* VISIBLE.
Antonyms: see IMPERCEPTIBLE, UNPERCEIVABLE.

perception, *n.* **1.** *Referring to the act:* seeing; *spec.* seizure, apprehension, discernment, penetration, descrial (*R*), observation, recognition, percipience (*R*), apperception, knowledge, cognition (*act of knowing*), cognizance (*implying the conscious action of the understanding*), detection, illusion, sensation, vision (*suggesting esp. the range or capacity of mental or physical perception*), intuition, feeling, hearing, smell, sight.
2. *Referring to the faculty:* senses, sensation, perceiving, ken (*A or B*); *spec.* eye, telæsthesia, touch, feeling, hearing, smell, sight, consciousness; *see* INSIGHT.

perceptive, *a. Spec.* apprehensive, intuitive, intuitional, *etc.*

perch, *n.* rest (*contex.*), roost (*spec.*).

perch, *v. i.* rest (*chiefly spec.*); *spec.* alight, sit, roost.

perching, *a.* insessorial.

perennial, *a.* eternal, enduring, never-failing, persistent, annual (*being, strictly speaking, once a year, or for a year only, whereas* perennial *implies for more than a year, or continuing indefinitely*). *See* LASTING, ANNUAL.

perfect, *a.* consummate, ideal; *spec.* utter; *see* COMPLETE, FAULTLESS.

perfect, *v. t. Spec.* consummate; *see* COMPLETE, IDEALIZE.

perfection, *n.* **1.** *Referring to the act or action: spec.* completion, idealization, consummation.
2. *Referring to the state:* perfectness, perfectiveness (*R*), perfectivity (*R*); *spec.* finish, faultlessness, utterness; *see* EXCELLENCE, CORRECTNESS, HOLINESS.
Antonyms: see IMPERFECTION.
3. *Of one that is perfect:* perfect (*R*); *spec.* crown (*fig.*), bloom *or* flower (*fig.*).

perforate, *v. t.* penetrate (*contex.*), pierce (*contex.*), foraminate (*R*); *spec.* terebrate (*R*), riddle, tunnel, trepan *or* trepanize, transforate, prickle, pink, punch, prick.

perforated, *a. Spec.* fenestrate *or* fenestrated, foraminated.

perform, *v. t.* **1.** do, discharge, fulfill; *see* DO.
2. *See* FILL, ACT, OBSERVE, ACCOMPLISH.

performance, *n.* **1.** doing, discharge, fulfillment; *spec.* act, action, accomplishment, ceremony.
2. *Referring to a play, part, etc.: spec.* play, concert, sing (*R or C*), matinée, vaudeville; *see* SHOW.

performer, *n.* **1.** *See* DOER.
2. *Spec.* executant, soloist, duettist, singer, balancer, acrobat, equilibrist, contortionist, *etc.; see* PLAYER.

perhaps, *adv.* perchance (*formal; B*), possibly, peradventure (*A or B*), maybe (*less dignified than "perhaps"*); *spec.* probably, possibly, belike (*A*), haply (*A or B*), happily (*A; R*).

period, *n.* **1.** time (*contex.*); *spec.* epoch (*a period of considerable length, of history, life, development, marked by distinctive conditions, decidedly different from what preceded*), eon, era (*considered as marked by any particular condition, as of good will, crime, etc.*), age (*considered esp. in its relation to life or its conditions, as in the* age *of fishes, the golden* age, *etc.*), span, spell, stage, cycle (*a period in which a round of events or of phenomena recurrently take place*), eternity, season, term, limit, interval, epact, luster *or* lustrum, kalpa, manvantara, indiction, semester, hour (*of class, lecture or recitation* period).
2. *See* END.

periodic, *a. Spec.* epochal, seasonal, cyclic, serial, secular, termly, centennial; *see* INTERMITTENT.
Antonyms: see IRREGULAR.

periodical, *n.* publication (*contex.*); *spec.* serial, weekly, monthly, quarterly, magazine, bulletin, gazette.

perjure, *v. t. Used reflectively:* manswear (*A*), forswear.

perjured, *a.* forsworn, mansworn (*A*).

perk, *v. i.* **1.** *Spec.* strut.
2. *See* SPRUCE.

permanence, *n.* permanency; *spec.* immovableness, fixity, fixture (*A*), constancy, durableness, lastingness.

---

percussion: *stroke, shock.*
peremptory: *commanding, dogmatic, decisive, absolute.*
perform, *v. i.: act.*
perfume, *n.: smell, scent.*
perfume, *v. t.: scent.*
perfunctory: *formal, indifferent.*
peril, *n.: danger.*
peril, *v. t.: endanger.*
perilous: *dangerous.*

Antonyms: see TRANSIENCE.

permanent, *a. Spec.* fixed, standing, irremovable, immovable (*literally or fig.*), pucka *or* pakka (*Anglo-Indian*); *see* LASTING, CONSTANT, UNFADING, DURABLE.

Antonyms: see TRANSIENT, TEMPORARY, SHIFTING, PROVISIONAL.

permissible, *a.* allowable, free; *spec.* open, sufferable, unprohibited, admissible, dispensable (*eccl.*).

permission, *n.* allowance, permit (*R*), leave; *spec.* sufferance, toleration, favor, license, liberty, congé (*French*) *or* congee (*R*), grace (*Eng. univ.*), exeat, dispensation, *see* AUTHORIZATION.

Antonyms: see FORBIDDANCE.

permissive, *a. Spec.* facultative (*B*); *spec.* dispensative *or* dispensatory.

permit, *v. t.* allow; *spec.* let (*with an infinitive, usually used without "to"*), tolerate, leave (*with an objective and the infinitive*), suffer (*now A*), license, have (*only with a negative, as in "he will not have it mentioned"*), facultate (*R*); *see* AUTHORIZE.

Antonyms: see FORBID.

permit, *n. Spec.* chop (*in Chinese and East Indian trade*), firman (*Turkish*); *see* LICENSE, PASSPORT.

permitted, *a.* licit (*B*); *spec.* welcome (*contex.*).

perpendicular, *a.* **1.** *See* ERECT, PRECIPITOUS.

2. *In geometry:* normal (*more technical than "perpendicular"*), cathetal (*R*); *spec.* vertical.

perplex, *v. t.* **1.** puzzle, bepuzzle (*an intensive*), fog (*fig.*); *spec.* mystify, nonplus, set, corner, get (*C*), divide (*R*), embarrass, stagger, metagrabolize (*R*); *see* CONFUSE.

Antonyms: see ENLIGHTEN.

2. *See* COMPLICATE.

perplexed, *a.* doubtful (*contex.*), puzzled; *spec.* nonplussed, embarrassed, *etc.*

perplexing, *a. Spec.* puzzling, embarrassing, knotty, obscure, *etc.*; *see* CONFUSING.

perplexity, *n.* **1.** doubt (*contex.*), perplexedness, puzzle, puzzlement (*R*), puzzledom (*R*); *spec.* nonplus, quandary, embarrassment, fog (*C*); *see* CONFUSION.

2. *Referring to what perplexes:* difficulty (*contex.*), puzzle; *spec.* cobweb (*fig.*).

3. *See* COMPLEXITY.

persecute, *v. t.* **1.** oppress, pursue; *spec.* (*often fig.*) dragoon, dragoonade.

Antonyms: see INDULGE.

2. *See* AFFLICT, BESET, URGE.

persistent, *a.* **1.** *Spec.* sedulous, willful, assiduous; *see* OBSTINATE.

2. *See* CONSTANT, CONTINUING.

person, *n.* **1.** *In the sense of "a human being":* man (*now only in indefinite phrases, as "every man," etc., and understood as including women by implication*), individual (*chiefly a C vulgarism or disparaging*), party (*spec., exc. when vulgar or S as a simple equivalent of "person"*), fellow (*chiefly C, undignified, or even vulgar*), body (*familiar*), piece (*A or dial.*), wight (*A. exc. in "luckless wight," "hapless wight"*), chap (*familiar and undignified*), human (*now chiefly humorous or affected or used as a neuter in gender*); *spec.* (*as viewed in a certain way*) spirit, beast, presence, animal, personage, nature, soul, homo (*tech.; generic*), creature (*often depreciating, condescending, or pitying*), figure, form, guy (*C*), shape, hand, mind, mouth, machine, chit, card (*S*), bloke (*S*), egg (*S*), chal (*Gypsy*), billy, billie (*Scot.*), birkie (*familiar or jocular; Scot.*), buckie (*Scot.*), smarty (*C, U. S.*), hulk, worthy, worm *or* earthworm (*in contempt*), egoist *or* egotist, dry-as-dust, dragoon, dog (*in contempt or abuse*), disreputable, insect (*in contempt*), wagtail (*contemptuous; R*), deceiver, dupe, blockhead, *etc.*

2. *In theology, of the Deity:* hypostasis, personality; *spec.* Father, Son, Holy Ghost.

3. *In law:* university (*chiefly Roman or Civil law*), universitas (*Lat. equiv. of "university"*), corporation, body (*C*).

4. *See* PERSONALITY.

personage, *n.* **1.** person (*in this sense chiefly with a qualifying word or words*), somebody (*C*), figure, bigwig (*humorous or contemptuous*), character (*contex.*), buzzwig (*derisive; R*), big bug (*S*), tycoon (*C, U. S.*); *see* MAGNATE.

Antonyms: see NOBODY.

2. *See* CARRIAGE.

personal, *a.* **1.** individual; *spec.* intimate; *see* BODILY, PRIVATE.

2. *Of property:* movable.

3. *In theology:* essential, hypostatic.

personality, *n.* character, individuality, it (*S*).

personate, *v. t.* impersonate (*usually spec.*), personify (*R*); *see* ACT, COUNTERFEIT.

personate, *v. i. Spec.* masquerade.

personify, *v. t.* **1.** *In the sense of representing as a person, or symbolizing by a human form:* impersonate, personation, personalize (*R*), impersonify (*R*);—*"personify" being the most common.*

2. *See* EMBODY.

perspiration, *n.* excretion (*contex.*), water (*contex.*); *spec.* exhalation, sweat, sweating, diaphoresis (*tech.*).

perspire, *v. i. & t.* excrete (*contex.*); *spec.* exhale, sweat, swelter, glow (*obs. euphemism*).

pervade, *v. t.* penetrate, permeate, fill (*contex.*), commeate (*R*); *spec.* interfuse (*in a nonphysical sense*), imbue, impregnate, infiltrate. *See* ANIMATE.

---

permeate: *pervade.*
permutation: *interchange.*
pernicious: *destructive, harmful, ruinous.*
perorate: *declaim, end.*
perpetual: *constant, eternal, endless.*
perpetuate: *continue, eternalize.*
perpetuity: *constancy, eternity.*
persist: *continue.*
persistence: *continuance, constancy.*
persistent: *constant, continuing.*
personable: *good-looking.*
perspicacity: *discernment.*
persuade: *induce.*
pert: *impudent.*
pertain: *belong, relate.*
pertinent: *belonging, relative.*
perturb: *disturb.*

perverse, *a.* **1.** *See* WICKED, PERVERTED.
2. *Implying a going counter to what is reasonable or demanded:* froward (*B*), wayward, cross-grained, cantankerous, untoward *or* (*R*) untowardly, oblique *or* obliquitous (*both R*), contrarious (*B*), contrary (*C*), wrong-headed, cussed (*S, U. S.*); *primarily a euphemistic oath*), thwart (*R*); *see* INTRACTABLE, OBSTINATE.
Antonyms: see COMPLAISANT, MANAGEABLE.

perversion, *n.* **1.** *In the sense of a change or difference from the original form or purpose*: distortion; *spec.* wrench, twist, misuse, misusage, misrepresentation, misappropriation, misapplication, misconstruction, misdirection.
2. *Implying that the change is for the worse*: degeneration, depravation, degradation, corruption.

perversity, *n.* **1.** *See* WICKEDNESS.
2. perverseness, frowardness (*B*), waywardness, untowardness, obliquity (*R*), contrariousness (*B*), wrong-headedness, mulishness, cussedness (*S, U. S.*), thwartness (*R*); *see* INTRACTABILITY, OBSTINACY.
Antonyms: complaisance (*cf.* COMPLAISANT), *manageableness* (*cf.* MANAGEABLE).

pervert, *v. t.* **1.** distort; *spec.* wrest, wrench, twist, misuse, warp, writhe (*R*), torture, strain, wiredraw (*fig.*), wry (*A*), wring (*A*), misapply, misturn (*R*), mutilate, misdirect, corrupt, misconstrue, sophisticate, garble, misrepresent.
2. deprave, degrade, degenerate, corrupt.

perverted, *a.* distorted, perverse, wry (*B*), misdirected, *etc.*

pervious, *a.* penetrable; *spec.* permeable, diathermanous.
Antonyms: see IMPENETRABLE.

pessimist, *n. Spec.* cynic, malist, miserabilist.

pest, *n.* **1.** *See* DISEASE.
2. *Referring to something inflicting harm or distress:* bane, curse; *see* TROUBLE.
Antonyms: see GOOD.

pesthouse, *n.* hospital, lazaretto *or* (*less common*) lazaret (*chiefly spec. and referring to foreign, esp. Oriental, countries*).

pestle, *n.* pounder (*contex.*), muller, brayer.

pet, *n.* dear, fondling, darling, duck (*chiefly a term of endearment*), daut (*Scot.*), favorite; *spec.* dotage, cosset, cade.

pet, *a.* cherished, favorite, fond, cosset, cockney (*A or R; Eng.*), darling.

pet, *n.* fit, huff, tiff, peeve (*C or S*).

petrify, *v. t.* lapidify (*R*), lithify (*R*); *spec.* fossilize, calcify, gorgonize, enmarble *or* immarble, terrify (*fig.*), horrify (*fig.*), frighten (*fig.*).

petroleum, *n.* rock oil; *spec.* kerosene, petrol (*Eng.*), gasoline (*U. S. equiv. of Eng. "petrol"*), naphtha, maltha, *etc.*

petticoat, *n. Spec.* balmoral, crinoline, fustanella (*in Greece*).

pew, *n.* **1.** *Referring to the inclosed seat: spec.* box.
2. *Referring to the uninclosed seat:* bench; *spec.* slip (*U. S.*).

philanthropist, *n.* philanthrope (*R*); *spec.* humanitarian (*often contemptuous*), benefactor.
Antonyms: see MISANTHROPE.

Philistine, *n.* Philister (*a Germanism*), gigman (*so used by Carlyle*), Babbitt (*so used by Sinclair Lewis*).

philosopher, *n.* philosoph (*R*), philosophaster (*derogatory*); *spec.* philosopheress (*fem.; humorous; R*), metaphysician, peripatetic, cynic, Scholastic, Lockian, Hegelian, *etc.*

philosophy, *n.* metaphysics, philosophism (*derogatory*), *spec.* epistemology, empiricism, idealism, teleology, ontology, *etc.*

phonetic, *a.* **1.** phonic, phonal (*R*); *spec.* phonographic.
2. *See* SONANT.

phonograph, *n.* gramophone (*Brit.*), talking-machine, victrola, graphophone.

photograph, *n.* photo (*C*), print (*contex.*), snapshot, still (*movie tech.*); *spec.* minette, daguerreotype (*obs.*), portrait.

physic, *v. t.* **1.** *See* DRUG.
2. *Spec.* purge, drench.
Antonyms: see CONSTIPATE.

pianist, *n.* pianiste (*fem.; cant*), pianofortist (*formal*); *spec.* cembalist (*R*).

piano, *n.* pianoforte (*formal*); *spec.* pianette, pianino, grand, upright, vertical.

pick, *v. t.* **1.** *See* STRIKE, PIERCE, CHOOSE, MAKE, EAT, PLAY.
2. detach (*contex.*), pluck (*chiefly spec.*); *spec.* cull, gather, pull, cut.
3. *Referring to a fowl, bird, etc.:* clean (*contex.*), pluck; *spec.* plume (*R*).

pickle, *n. Spec.* brine, marinade, dip.

pickle, *v. t.* do (*contex.*), preserve (*contex.*); *spec.* brine, souse, marinade, corn, salt.

pickpocket, *n.* thief (*contex.*), gonoph (*cant*), robber (*contex.*), wire (*cant; Eng.*); *spec.* cutpurse, dip (*cant*), pickpurse (*A*), dipper (*cant*), swell-mobsman (*S*).

picture, *n.* **1.** *These words imply the actual physical* picture: piece (*contex.*); *spec.* scene,

---

pervert, *v. i.: apostasize.*
pervert, *n.: apostate.*
pesky: *unpleasant.*
pester: *annoy.*
pestiferous: *morbific, harmful, destructive, deadly, infectious.*
pestilence: *disease.*
pet, *v. t.: indulge, caress.*
petition, *n.: asking, address.*
petition, *v. i.: ask, appeal.*
pettifogging: *prevarication, trickery.*
petty: *unimportant, mean, inferior.*
petulant: *irascible.*
phantasm: *fancy, apparition, ghost.*
phase: *appearance, state.*
phenomenal: *apparent, extraordinary.*
phenomenon: *occurrence, appearance.*
philology: *linguistics.*
phlegmatic: *calm, dull, sluggish.*
phrase, *v. t.: describe.*
phraseology: *expression, diction, language.*
physical: *material, corporeal.*
physician: *doctor.*
physique: *build, constitution.*
pick, *v. i.: choose, eat.*
pick, *n.: stroke, choice, best.*
picket, *n. stake, detail, watcher, post.*
picket, *v. t.: fence, guard, station.*
picnic: *cf.* EXCURSION.
pictorial: *graphic.*
picture, *v. t.: depict, imagine, describe.*
pictures, *n. cf.* MOTION PICTURE.

---

daub, tableau, miniature, monochrome, monotint, perspective, drawing, etching, engraving, pastel, cartoon, caricature, sketch, illustration (*often of a* picture *in a book or magazine*), tableau (*often a stage* picture *or pantomime*), icon, painting, oil, watercolor, print, primitive, landscape, skyscape, marine, seascape (*a less proper equiv. of "marine"*), lithograph, photograph, portrait, portraiture, chromograph, zincograph, cyclorama, panorama, diorama, *etc.*

2. *These words cover the abstract or figurative senses of the idea,* picture: counterpart, likeness, portrayal, delineation, reproduction, study (*all suggesting the truth or accuracy of the* picture *under consideration*); scene, emblem (*a* picture *that represents an idea or conveys a message*), embodiment (*pictorialization of an abstraction*); description, account (*these two senses widely used in U. S. as "a* picture *of the situation"*); *in the phrase "out of the* picture,*" the word implies plan or calculation, the phrase implying the sense of "irrelevant" or "ignored." See also* IMAGE, COUNTERPART.

pie, *n.* pastry (*contex.*); *spec.* patty, pattycake, bury.

piece, *n.* **1.** *Spec.* hunk, hunch, junk, chunk, chuck, rag, lump, chump, mammock (*A*), shred, scrap, snatch, chip, cantle, cantlet, patch, flap, gobbet, end, bit, block, blad (*Scot.*), clip, cutting, bite, mouthful, print, pat, cut, slice, cutlet, chop, fragment, clout (*A or dial.*), cabbage (*a collective*). *See* PART.

2. *In games:* man; *spec.* blot, draught, pawn, king, knight, castle, queen, bishop.

3. *Referring to land:* plot, plat, lot (*chiefly U. S.*), area, patch, canton (*A or R*); *spec.* field, square, bed, gore, circle, block, corner.

4. *See* EXAMPLE, COIN, FIREARM, COMPOSITION, ARTICLE, STATUE, PICTURE, SCULPTURE.

piecemeal, *a. Spec.* limbmeal (*A*).

pier, *n.* **1.** support (*contex.*); *spec.* post, buttress, pillar, foundation.

2. *Referring to a pier in the water: spec.* mole, quay, jutty, jetty, dike (*local Eng.*), groin, dock (*C*); *see* WHARF.

pierce, *v. t.* **1.** penetrate (*contex.*), empierce (*B and intensive*); *spec.* impale, prick, pink, transpierce, transfix, puncture, pick, breach, hole (*R*), terebrate (*R*), lance (*B or spec.*), drill, bore, brog (*dial.*), gore, spear, dock (*cookery*), needle, gimlet, skewer, javelin; *see* PERFORATE (*which implies the making of a hole clear through*).

2. *See* AFFECT, ENTER, PERCEIVE.

piercing, *a.* **1.** penetrative, penetrating, perceant (*A, B*), perforative; *spec.* cutting.

2. *See* SHARP, AFFECTING, PAINFUL, HIGH (*in sound*), DISCERNING, SARCASTIC.

pig, *n.* swine, hog, porker; *spec.* roaster, whinnock, Tantony (*dial.*), sow.

pigeon, *n.* dove (*in ordinary usage a somewhat narrower term than "pigeon"*); *spec.* duffer, culver, cushat (*chiefly Scot. and dial. Eng.*), squab, piper, homer, fantail, pouter, tumbler.

pigeonlike, *a.* columbine (*B or tech.*), dovelike.

pigment, *n.* color (*contex.*); *spec.* dye, paint, wash, tincture (*R*).

pigsty, *n.* swinery, hogsty, sty, piggery.

pilgrim, *n.* **1.** *See* JOURNEYER.

2. devotee, palmer (*hist. or A*; *properly spec.*), peregrinator (*affected*).

pill, *n.* ball (*C or contex.*); *spec.* bolus, globule (*from its shape*), pellet (*a small pill*), pilule (*a small pill*), dose (*contex.*), punishment (*C, contex.*).

pillar, *n.* **1.** pier, column (*properly spec.*); *spec.* shaft, post, stanchion, stanchel, jamb, pilaster, atlas, caryatid, stele, needle, obelisk, herm, columella, standard, newel.

2. *See* SUPPORT.

pillory, *n.* **1.** *Referring to the instrument of punishment: spec.* jougs (*Scot.; hist.*), cangue (*used in China*).

2. *Referring to the form of punishment: spec.* cyphonism (*Greek antiq.*).

pimple, *n. Spec.* papula, papule, pustule, chalazion, wheal, ruby, carbuncle.

pimply, *a.* pimpled; *spec.* pustular, pustulate, pustulous.

pin, *n.* **1.** peg; *spec.* nog, bolt, cog, spill, bodkin, gnomon, forelock, norman (*chiefly naut.*), wrist, kevel, duledge, tongue, tang, fin, broach, needle, dowel, toggle, thole, treenail, skewer, spile, style.

2. *In games: spec.* skittle, tenpin, ninepin, duckpin, candlepin.

pincerlike, *a.* forcipate (*tech.*).

pincers, *n. pl.* pinchers, tweezers, claw (*sing.*), forceps; *spec.* pincette (*sing.*), crowbill *or* crow's-bill (*sing.*).

pioneer, *n.* **1.** *See* ENGINEER.

2. forerunner, dewbeater (*dial. or R*); *spec.* planter, settler, colonist.

pipe, *n.* **1.** *Referring to a kind of musical instrument: spec.* fife, chanter, straw (*C*), pipes (*pl.*), flute, flageolet, oboe, shawm, hornpipe.

2. *Referring to the smoker's pipe: spec.* meerschaum, callean *or* calean, hubblebubble, narghile, chibouk, hookah, dudeen, peacepipe, calumet (*Amer. Indian*).

3. *See* TUBE, CASK.

pirate, *n.* **1.** sea robber *or* (*for short and contex.*) robber, marauder (*contex.*), corsair (*chiefly spec.*), rover (*contex.*), picaroon (*R*), seadog (*chiefly spec.*), seathief (*R*), sea wolf (*a pseudo-*

piebald: *party-colored.*
piece, *v. t.: join repair.*
piety: *religiousness, obedience.*
piggish: *swinish, gluttonous, greedy.*
pile, *n.: hair, nap.*
pile, *n.: heap.*
pile, *v. t.: heap, load, furnish, accumulate.*
pillow: *cushion.*
pilot, *n.: steersman, guide, guard, aviator.*
pin, *v. t.: fasten, hold, bind.*
pinch, *v. t.: squeeze, oppress, straighten, force, famish, extort, arrest.*
pine, *v. i.: languish, long.*
pink, *v. t.: pierce, perforate, indent.*
pipe, *v. t.: tube, utter.*
pipe, *v. i.: whistle, speak, sing, play.*

archaism), marooner (*R*), buccaneer; *spec.* privateer, viking.

2. *Referring to the vessel: spec.* sallee-man, privateer.

pirate, *v. i.* maraud (*contex.*), rob (*contex.*), picaroon (*R*); *spec.* privateer.

pistol, *n.* firearm (*contex.*), flute (*S*), gun (*C*), shooting iron (*S*), *spec.* revolver, snaphance, bulldozer, petronel, dag, derringer.

piston, *n. Spec.* plunger, ram, bucket.

pit, *n.* **1.** *See* HOLE, TRAP, AUDITORIUM, HELL, ABYSS.

2. *Referring to a surface depression as on the body:* hollow (*contex.*); *spec.* alveolus, puncture.

pitch, *v. i.* **1.** *See* DESCEND, FALL, ENGAGE.

2. *Referring to a ship's head on a downward motion:* plunge.

Antonyms: see ROLL.

pitch, *n.* **1.** *See* THROW, SLOPE, DEGREE, INTENSITY, MODULATION.

2. *Of a ship:* plunge.

pitcher, *n.* ewer (*B or A*), jug (*Eng.*); *spec.* urceus (*tech.*), urceolus (*tech.*).

pitcher-shaped, *a.* urceolate (*tech.*).

pith, *n.* **1.** heart (*contex.*), core (*contex.*); *spec.* pulp, cord, medulla (*tech.*).

2. *See* ENERGY, ESSENCE, FORCE.

pith, *v. t.* decerebrize (*tech.*).

pithy, *a.* **1.** porous (*contex.*); *spec.* corky.

2. *Referring to literature, etc.:* substantial, meaty, matterful (*C*), pithful (*R*); *see* CONCISE, FORCIBLE.

Antonyms: see EMPTY.

pitted, *a.* variolate, punctate, puncturate, foveate, foveolate *or* foveolated, alveolate, lacunose (*R*), favose, cuppy; (*all but "pitted" and "cupped" B or tech.*).

pivot, *n.* **1.** axis, gudgeon (*chiefly spec.*); *spec.* jewel.

2. *Fig.: see* CENTER.

place, *n.* **1.** *Referring to the general conception of extension in space: see* SPACE.

2. *Referring to a definite portion of space, of greater or less extent and occupied or unoccupied:* space; *spec.* home, house, spot, part, locality, situation, location, side, region, quarter, scene (place *where something occurs*), tract, corner, locale *or* (*less commonly, but more properly*) local, provenience (place *from which derived, hence origin, source*), district (*implying a more or less accurate marking off, esp. a tract having some characteristic as a whole*), division (*referring to a region or part marked off for some purpose*), latitude, longitude, neighborhood; *see* BOUNDS.

3. *Referring to a particular locality as being a center of population and modified or more or less determined in character by local usages, customs, etc.: spec.* city, town, hamlet, village, dorp, borough, vill, *etc.*

4. *Referring to a place as occupied by a body:* position, locality, location, situation; *spec.* seat, site *or* (*R*) situs, station, locus (*tech.*), emplacement *or* (*R*) placement, post, pitch (*R*), whereabout *or* whereabouts.

5. *Referring to a portion of the earth's surface: see* TERRITORY.

6. *With "in":* in lieu, in stead.

7. *See* POSITION, ABODE, RESORT, RANK, OPPORTUNITY.

place, *v. t.* **1.** locate, situate; *spec.* set, lay (1. *implying esp. a putting for security, to get rid of, in proper position;* 2. *as the scene, etc.*), rest, fix (*immovably*), slip, emplace, dispose (*implying a placing in a proper or predetermined* place, *esp. of things with reference to each other*), bestow, pitch (*a tent, town, etc.*), station, stand, install, plant, collocate, perch, pose, impose (*A*), deposit, orientate *or* orient, rank, tee (*golf*); *see* PACK.

2. *Referring to the determination of the position of a thing:* locate, localize, allocate; *spec.* lodge.

3. *Referring to finding a position,* berth, billet, job.

4. *See* DATE, CLASS, ATTRIBUTE, PUT, APPOINT, BESTOW.

placing, *n.* **1.** placement, emplacement (*B or tech.*); *spec.* fixation, resting, stationing, depositing, installation, bestowal (*A*), preposition (*R*), postposition, bedding, orientation.

2. location, allocation (*tech. or B*), localization.

placket, *n.* opening (*contex.*), placket hole, slit, font (*chiefly dial. Eng.*).

plagiarist, *n.* plagiator (*R*), plagiary (*R*), transcribbler (*contemptuous*), cribber (*C or spec.*).

plagiarize, *v. t. & i.* abstract (*contex.*), crib (*C or spec.*), steal (*extremely opprobrious*).

plaid, *n.* pattern (*contex.*), checker *or* chequer; *spec.* tartan.

plain, *n.* flat, champaign (*B*) champian *or* champion (*dial., or A*), level, *spec.* prairie, steppe, tundra, llano, pampa (*chiefly in pl.*), sebka (*North Africa*).

Antonyms: see HILL, MOUNTAIN.

plainsong, *n.* melody, counterpoint, cantilena (*Italian; tech.*), canto (*music*).

plan, *n.* **1.** delineation (*contex.*); *spec.* diagram, chart, layout (*U. S.*), ichnography; *see* MAP.

2. idea, method, conception, design, scheme, system, program; *spec.* contrivance, device, arrangement, line, lay (*S or cant*), game, plot, rede (*A or B*), project, trick, forecast (*R*), intrigue, conspiracy.

plan, *v. t.* **1.** *See* DELINEATE, DIAGRAM.

2. contrive, arrange, study, design; *spec.* pro-

---

pit, *v. t.: fight, oppose.*
pit, *v. t.: hollow, indent.*
pitch, *n.: resin.*
pitch, *v. t.: erect, establish, throw, modulate, arrange.*
piteous: *compassionate, lamentable.*
pitiable: *lamentable, paltry, contemptible.*
pitiful: *compassionate, lamentable, paltry, contemptible.*
pity, *n.: compassion.*
pivotal: *axial, central.*
placard, *n.: notice, advertizement.*
placard, *v. t.: publish, advertize.*
placate: *pacify.*
plague, *n.: disease, annoyance.*
plague: *v. t.: trouble, annoy.*
plain, *n.: clear, evident, intelligible, simple, homely, mere, dull, artless, crude, uniform.*
plain-spoken: *blunt, frank.*
plaint: *lamentation, complaint.*
plaintiff: *accuser.*
plaintive: *mournful.*

---

vide, set, lay, concert (plan *jointly*), calculate (*A*), project, program (*R*), premeditate, devise, block (*chiefly with "out"*), shape, cast, plot, forecast (*R*), maneuver, conspire.

plan, *v. i.* devise, shape, contrive; *spec.* arrange, study, scheme.

plane, *n.* **1.** plain (*A*), flat; *spec.* horizon.
2. *See* DEGREE.
3. *See* AIRPLANE.

plane, *v. t.* smooth; *spec.* mill, traverse.

planet, *n.* star (*contex.*), light (*contex.*); *spec.* primary, secondary (*a less usual equiv. of "satellite"*), satellite, significator, lord, hyleg, Mercury, Venus, Earth, Mars, Jupiter, Saturn, Uranus, Neptune.

planking, *n.* plank (*a collective*); *spec. and collectively*) berthing, skin, compartition (*R*).

planning, *n.* contriving, arrangement, study, *etc. See* PLAN, *v. t.*

plant, *n.* **1.** organism (*contex.*), wort (*A or R, exc. in combination*); *spec.* herb, set, vegetable, plantlet, exotic, seedling, flower, flora (*a collective; tech.*), quick (*a collective; A or R*) herblet.
2. *See* APPARATUS, EQUIPMENT, ESTABLISHMENT.

plant, *v. t.* **1.** set (*chiefly with "out"*); *spec.* transplant, sow, prick, tub, ridge, replant.
Antonyms: see UPROOT, EXTIRPATE.
2. *See* FIX, HIDE, DEPOSIT, PUT, COLONIZE, SETTLE.

plantation, *n.* **1.** *A group of cultivated plants: spec.* basket, pinetum, pinery, nopalry, vineyard.
2. *See* ESTATE, FARM.

plant-eating, *a.* herbivorous, phytophagous (*tech.*), phytivorous (*a hybrid term*).

plaster, *n.* **1.** *In medicine: spec.* cataplasm (*obs.*), charge, sinapism, diachylon.
2. *Spec.* cement, parget, paste, stucco, staff, mortar, daub, mud.

plaster, *v. t.* beplaster (*an intensive*); *spec.* parget, daub, cement, tarras *or* trass, mortar, stucco, staff.

plasterwork, *n. Spec.* stucco, staff, pargeting, scagliola.

plastic, *a.* **1.** *See* CREATIVE.
2. moldable, fictile, formable, ductile.
Antonyms: see ELASTIC, RIGID.

plate, *n.* **1.** *Spec.* sheet, lamella (*tech.*), paten (*R*), web, plaque, escutcheon, fish plate *or* (*for short*) fish, slab, scute *or* scutum, vamplate, tile, planch, salamander; *see* LAMINA.
2. dish (*contex.*), paten (*A or hist., exc. spec.*); *spec.* platter, griddle *or* girdle (*Scot.*).
3. *See* ENGRAVING.

plate, *v. t.* **1.** overlay; *spec.* gild, silver, platinize, nickel, *etc.*
2. *In printing: spec.* electrotype, stereotype.

plateau, *n.* highland, platform, tableland; *spec.* mesa (*southern U. S.*), field, paramo (*chiefly So. Amer.*), puna.
Antonyms: see VALLEY, PEAK.

plate-shaped, *a.* placoid (*tech.*).

platform, *n.* **1.** floor (*contex.*), dais (*R, exc. spec.*), stage, pulpit (*A or spec.*); *spec.* scaffold, suggestum (*Roman antiq.*), emplacement, perron, catafalque, footboard, drop, roundtop, top, turntable, stand, bridge, predella; *see* DAIS, ROSTRUM.
2. *See* STATEMENT.

platter, *n.* plate, charger (*B or tech.*), trencher (*obs. or hist.*); *spec.* grail.

plausible, *a.* **1.** specious, fair-seeming, colorable, colored.
2. fair-spoken, smooth, suave, bland.

play, *v. i.* **1.** move (*contex.*); *spec.* lap, lick, dance, caper, jiggle, flutter, wave, ripple; *see* CAPER, WAVE.
2. idle, disport (*B*), sport (*chiefly spec.*); *spec.* toy, wanton, trifle, flirt; *see* FROLIC, TOY.
Antonyms: see WORK, STUDY.
3. perform (*formal*); *spec.* act, melodize (*chiefly humorous or jocular*), flourish, descant, pipe, drum, finger, pick, pluck, blow, chime, harp, flute, fiddle, doodle (*Scot.*), duet (*R*), thrum, smite (*the harp; B*).
4. *In playing cards: spec.* crossruff (*cant*), seesaw, nig (*S*), renege, revoke, discard.
Antonyms: see PASS.
5. *See* SHINE, GAMBLE.

play, *v. t.* **1.** move (*contex.*); *spec.* wield, ply, operate, dribble (*in football, basketball, etc.*); *see* FIRE, THROW, EXERCISE.
2. *Referring to the playing of a musical instrument:* touch (*chiefly with "strings," "keys," etc., as the object*); *spec.* sweep, pick, pluck, tune, breathe, bow, finger, twang, twangle, bang (*contemptuous*), pound (*contemptuous*), doodle (*chiefly Scot.*), drum, thrum.
3. *Referring to the playing of a card or piece in a game: spec.* throw, table, move, discard, sacrifice.
4. *See* ACT, EXECUTE, OPPOSE, DISCHARGE.

play, *n.* **1.** motion (*contex.*); *spec.* wielding, lap, lick, lambency, dance; *see* JIGGLE, CAPER, FLUTTER, WAVE, RIPPLE, EXERCISE.
2. *Spec.* disport, sport, fun, toy, toying, trifling, flirting; *see* FROLIC.
Antonyms: see WORK.
3. *See* DIVERSION, SPORT.
4. sport, fun; *see* JEST.
Antonyms: see EARNESTNESS.
5. *Referring to a game: spec.* throw, move, sacrifice, crossruff, seesaw, renege.
6. *A theatrical play:* piece, drama, comedy, tragedy, revue; *see* DRAMA.
7. *See* TURN, DISCHARGE, FREEDOM, DRAMA, ACTION, GAMBLING, PERFORMANCE.

player, *n.* **1.** performer; *see* MUSICIAN, ACTOR, ACROBAT.
2. *See* GAMBLER.

playful, *a.* sportive, playsome (*R*); gamesome

platitude: *commonplace.* | **playbill:** *notice, program.* | **playfellow:** *comrade.*

(*B*); *spec.* kittenish, wanton, half-serious, toyful, toysome; *see* FROLICSOME, MISCHIEVOUS.
Antonyms: see EARNEST, SERIOUS.

playground, *n.* playstead (*R*); *spec.* court.

plaything, *n.* sport, toy, whimwham (*A or R*); *spec.* hewgag (*U. S.*), doll, puzzle, whirligig, kite.

pleading, *n.* allegation, plea; *spec.* bill, answer, complaint, duply (*obs. or hist.*), duplication, demurrer, reply, rebutter, surrebutter, *etc.*

pleasant, *a.* **1.** pleasing (*suggesting a positive giving of pleasure, while* pleasant *is more vaguely used*), pleasurable, agreeable, acceptable; *spec.* comfortable (*of tranquil enjoyment, esp. the absence of emotional disturbance or physical discomfort*), likable *or* likeable, admirable, enjoyable, delightful, delightsome (*B*), delicious (*implying a stronger and less refined pleasure than* delightful, *more suggestive of sensuousness*), delectable (*affording great pleasure, esp. of the lighter kind; often ironical or humorous*), delectate (*R*), lovely, charming, fascinating, captivating, entrancing, prepossessing, pretty, nice, sweet, blessed, luscious, attractive, gracious, desirable, satisfactory, dulcet, joysome (*R*), joyful, gladsome, good, welcome, seemly, gratifying, flattering, pleasureful (*R*), lustly (*A*), glorious (*C*), jolly (*C*), goluptious (*S or humorous*); *see* ACCEPTABLE.
Antonyms: see TORTUROUS, UNPALATABLE, UNPLEASANT, OFFENSIVE, ABOMINABLE, SHOCKING, DISGUSTING, UNBEARABLE.
2. *Referring to a person's conduct toward others: see* AGREEABLE.

pleasantry, *n.* **1.** play, banter, raillery, badinage (*French*), dicacity (*A*), persiflage, chaff; *spec.* jesting, pleasance (*A*), drollery, facetiousness.
2. *Of the act exhibiting pleasantry:* banter, drollery, rally, raillery, roast (*C*), facetiæ (*pl.; Latin*); *see* JEST.

please, *v. t.* pleasure (*R*), take; *spec.* delight, oblige, charm, captivate, enchant, enamour (*chiefly used with "of"*), gratify, flatter, tickle, satisfy, ecstasize, enrapture, titillate, enravish (*B*), hit (*C, as in the phrase, "to hit it off"*), suit, regale (*R*); *see* ELATE, GLADDEN.
Antonyms: see PAIN, OFFEND, ANGER, DISGUST, GRIEVE, DISPLEASE.

please, *v. i.* like.

pleased, *a. Spec.* delighted, glad, gladsome, gladful, jubilant, gladly (*A*), fain, happy, joyful, joyous, joyant (*R*), gleeful, high, satisfied, eudemonic (*R*), blithe *or* blithesome (*chiefly B*), elate, exultant, blissful, blessed, blest, heavenly, paradisiacal, paradisial, proud.
Antonyms: see ANGRY, BLANK; *also cf.* OFFEND.

pleasure, *n.* **1.** *Referring to the mental state or emotion:* pleasedness (*R*), pleasance (*A and B*); *spec.* delight, delectation (*affected or humorous for "delight"*), happiness, gladness, gladsomeness, joy, joyfulness, joyance, joyancy, felicity, bliss, blissfulness, liking, gratification, satisfaction, enjoyment, elation, jubilance, jubilancy, jubilation, jubilee (*R*), beatitude, blessedness, blitheness, paradise, glory, elysium, heaven, heyday, jocundity (*R*), eudemony (*R*); *see* REJOICING, ADMIRATION.
Antonyms: see ANGER, OFFENSE, CALAMITY, DISGUST, PAIN, TORTURE, DISPLEASURE.
2. *Referring to the thing that pleases: spec.* delight, joy, gratification, satisfaction, enjoyment, treat, diversion, entertainment.
Antonyms: see TORTURE.
3. *See* WILL.

pleasure, *v. i.* **1.** *Spec.* delight, joy, jubilate; *see* REJOICE.
2. *See* WILL, DESIRE.

plebeian, *a.* **1.** baseborn *or* base, proletarian, popular (*R*), gregal *or* gregarian (*R*), ignoble (*B*), vulgar, common, middle-class, mean, infra dig. (*Latin*).
Antonyms: see ARISTOCRATIC, NOBLE, KINGLY.
2. *See* COMMONPLACE, LOW, COARSE.

plebeian, *n.* proletarian, proletary, pleb (*S*); *spec.* client (*Roman hist.*).
Antonyms: see NOBLE.

pledge, *n.* **1.** security, plight (*R*), gage, pawn; *spec.* hostage, deposit, collateral, wager (*A*), stake.
2. *See* EARNEST, TOAST, PROMISE.

pledge, *v. t. & i* **1.** deliver (*contex.*), plight (*chiefly B or rhetorical, now R*); *spec.* deposit, wage (*A*), pawn, impawn (*A or emphatic*), gage (*A*), hypothecate, mortgage, impledge (*R*), impignorate (*chiefly Scots law*), pignorate (*R*), dip (*C equiv. of "pawn"*), borrow (*obs.*), stake.
Antonyms: see FREE.
2. *See* BIND, PROMISE, TOAST.

pledget, *n.* stupe, dossil, tent, tampion, plug.

pleonasm, *n.* superfluity (*contex.*), redundancy, verbosity; *spec.* tautology, diffuseness.

pleonastic, *a.* superfluous (*contex.*), redundant.

plow, plough, *v. t.* **1.** ear (*A*), till, break, fallow (*spec.* or *R*); *spec.* subsoil, rib, ridge, rafter, hack.
2. *See* CLEAVE.

plower, plougher, *n.* plowman, tiller, plowjogger (*humorous or contemptuous*), clodhopper (*derogatory*).

plowing, ploughing, *n.* earing (*A*), tilling; *spec.* coaration (*R*).

pluck, *n.* **1.** *See* PULL, JERK.
2. viscera, haslet *or* harslet, gather (*obs.; chiefly spec.*).

---

playhouse: *theater.*
playmate: *comrade.*
plea: *allegation, defense, claim, excuse, appeal.*
plead, *v. i.: appeal, answer.*
plead, *v. t.: defend, state.*
plenary: *absolute.*
plenipotentiary, *a.: absolute.*
plenipotentiary, *n.: diplomatic agent.*
plenitude: *abundance, fullness.*
plenty, *n.: abundance.*
plethoric: *full-blooded, bombastic.*
pliable: *flexible, adaptable, manageable.*
pliant: *flexible, yielding, complaisant, adaptable, manageable.*
plod: *walk, drudge.*
plot, *n.: piece, diagram, plan, conspiracy, intrigue.*
plot, *v.: diagram, plan, devise, conspire, intrigue.*

3. courage, spirit (*C*), *see* DECISION.

plug, *n.* douk (*chiefly Scot.*); *spec.* dowel, dottle, plunger, wad, tampion; *see* STOPPER, PLEDGET.

plumage, *n.* feather (*chiefly in pl.*), feathering, plume (*chiefly in pl.*); *spec.* hackle *or* heckle, down, downiness, mantle, mirror, mail.

plume, *n.* **1.** feather, plumage (*R*); *spec.* plumet, egret, culgee (*Anglo-Indian*).

2. panache; *spec.* crest.

plummet, *n.* weight (*contex.*), lead, bob, plumb.

plump, *a.* **1.** fat, full, rotund, chubby, chuff (*obs. or dial. equiv. of "chubby"*), full-figured, buxom, sleek, pudgy, plumpy (*R*), opulent (*a Gallicism*).

Antonyms: see THIN.

2. *See* DIRECT, BLUNT.

plumpness, *n.* fatness, rotundity.

plunder, *v. t.* **1.** *With the person or thing from which plunder is taken as its object:* pillage; *or* (*A*) pill; *spec.* harry, devastate, rifle, ravage, loot, rob, desolate, sack, spoil, despoil, strip, maraud, raid, ransack, flay, ravish, spoliate, pluck, fleece, foray, gut, dacoit (*India*), pirate, picaroon (*R*), boothale (*A*), pilfer.

Antonyms: see PROTECT, ENRICH.

2. *With the thing as object which is taken away:* pillage; *or* (*A*) pill; *spec.* rifle, harry, loot, rob, strip, ransack (*R*), pirate, ravish, scoff (*S*), pilfer (*R*).

plunder, *v. i.* pillage, raven, reave *or* (*Scot.*) reive; *spec.* maraud, rob, depredate, boothale (*A*), loot, foray, forage, pirate, freeboot, prey, pilfer.

plunder, *n.* **1.** *Referring to the action:* pillage; *spec.* rapine, ravin, sack, sackage (*R*), harrying, prey (*A*), spoil, despoliation, spoliation, expilation (*R*), reave *or* (*Scot.*) reive, plunderage (*R*), freebooting, devastation, desolation; *see* ROBBERY.

2. *Referring to what is taken:* booty, pillage, plunderage (*R*), spoil, loot, ravin (*R or B*), rapine (*R or B*), creagh *or* creach (*Scot. and Ir.*).

plundering, *a.* predatory, depredatory, ravenous.

ply, *v. t.* **1.** *See* EXERCISE, PLAY, ATTACK, URGE.

2. belabor (*as with arguments or questions; R*) assail; *spec.* overwhelm.

pocket, *n.* **1.** *See* HOLLOW, CUL-DE-SAC, BIN.

2. *Referring to a pocket in a garment or attached to the person:* placket (*R*); *spec.* fob, burse.

pocket, *v. t.* pouch (*R or A*); *spec.* appropriate, steal.

pocketbook, *n.* wallet, purse; handbag (*spec.*); notebook (*Brit.*).

poem, *n.* poesy (*A*); *spec.* ballad, cycle, dit (*A*), ditty, duan (*Gaelic*), eclogue, epic, epigram, epilogue, epithalamium, epode, fabliau (*French*), georgic, idyll *or* idyl, limerick, lyric, madrigal, melody, monody, mythopoem, ode, odelet, partheniad (*R*), pastoral, quatorzain, rhapsody, rondeau, rondel, rune (*Finnish*), satire, sestina *or* sestine, sirvente (*Italian*), song, sonnet, triolet, virelay, *etc.*

poet, *n.* maker (*A*), epopœist (*R*), versifier *or* verseman (*contemptuous*), bard, poetaster (*depreciatory*); *spec.* rimer *or* rhymer, rimist *or* rhymist (*R*), rimester *or* rhymester (*depreciatory*), poeticule, poetling, bardling, poetess (*fem.*), druid, elegist, epicist, gnomic, lyricist, lyrist, minnesinger, scop (*hist.*), skald, sonneteer, sonnetist (*R*), troubadour, trouvère.

Antonyms: see PROSAIST

poetic, *a.* poietic (*R or B*), poetical, creative, imaginative; *spec.* elegiac, epic *or* epical, epodic, idyllic.

poetry, *n.* poesy (*A*), Muse, verse; *spec.* rime, song, epos, ghazal, macaronic, minstrelsy (*R*).

point, *n.* **1.** *Spec.* needle, style, pin, tang (*now dial. or spec.*), prong, spike, nib, neb, tine, pointrel (*R*), pike, gad, prickle, fin, beakiron, aciculus, spicule, spine, tag, calk, calkin, bodkin, fang.

2. *Referring to any more or less angular end: spec.* tip, apex, cusp (*chiefly tech.*), angle, peak, neb, nib, toe, spout.

Antonyms: see SIDE.

3. *See* DOT, PLACE, DEGREE, PARTICULAR, FEATURE, EFFECTIVENESS, MOMENT, LACE, TIP.

point, *v. t.* sharpen (*contex.*), acuminate (*R*).

pointed, *a.* **1.** sharp; *spec.* acute, cusped, cuspated *or* cuspidate, mucronate *or* mucronated, mucronulate, peaked, peaky, picked (*A*), piked, beaked, aciculate, spiry.

Antonyms: see BLUNT.

2. *See* DIRECT, EFFECTIVE, SHARP.

pointer, *n.* **1.** directer; *spec.* finger, gnomon, hand, arm, fescus, index, tongue.

2. *See* TIP.

poison, *n.* **1.** virulence, venom (*A or spec.*), toxicant (*tech.*), virus (*tech. or B*); spec. toxin, contagion, drug.

Antonyms: see ANTIDOTE.

2. *See* CORRUPTION.

poison, *a.* toxic, venomous; *see* POISONOUS.

poison, *v. t.* **1.** intoxicate (*R*), venom (*A or spec.*), envenom (*B and intensive; chiefly fig.*), venenate (*R*), empoison (*rhetorical or a B intensive; often fig.*); *spec.* drug, veratrize, vitriolize.

Antonyms: see DISINFECT.

2. *See* EMBITTER.

poisonous, *a.* venomous (*A or spec.*), virulent (*chiefly spec.*), poisoning, virous (*R*), venenous (*R*), venenose (*R*), toxicant (*tech.*), toxic (*tech.*); *spec.* mephitic. *The word* poisonous *is often used in the* (*S*) *sense of* disagreeable.

Antonyms: see INNOCUOUS, HEALTHFUL.

---

plume, *v. t.: feather, spruce, congratulate.*
plump, *v. t.: fatten, distend.*
plump, *v. i.: fall, blurt.*
plump, *adv.: directly, suddenly.*
plunge, *n.: thrust, dive, dip, descent, throw, gamble.*
plunge, *v.: sink, thrust, dive, dip, descend, throw, gamble.*
plunger: *gambler, piston.*
plurality: *multitude, majority, excess.*
ply, *v. t.: fold.*
ply, *n.: fold, layer.*
ply, *v. t.: exercise, play, attack, urge.*
pod: *hull.*
poignant: *painful, pungent, intense.*
poise, *n.: balance, carriage.*

---

poke, *v. t.* **1.** push (*contex.*), thrust, prod, jab (*C*), job (*C*), punch; *spec.* pole.
2. *See* PROTRUDE.

pole, *n.* **1.** stick, beam, mast (*chiefly spec.*); *spec.* shaft (*R*), spile, pile, stave, sprit, staff, stang (*Scot. and dial.*), caber (*Scot.*), upher (*Eng.*), quant (*Eng.*).
2. *Referring to the pole of a vehicle:* tongue, reach, shaft, staff, nib, neap (*U. S.*), disselboom (*South Africa*).

policeman, *n.* copper (*C*), bluebottle, bluecoat, cop (*C, U. S.*), bulk *or* bulky, bobby (*Brit.*), peeler (*Brit.*), runner, Robert (*R, Eng.*), trap (*all S or C*); *spec.* constable, gendarme, patrolman, roundsman (*U. S.*), sergeant, pointsman (*Eng.*), officer.

polish, *v. t.* **1.** smooth (*contex.*), shine, slick; *spec.* scour, burnish, furbish, glance (*tech.; U. S.*), glaze, planish, levigate, buff, pumice.
Antonyms: see ROUGHEN.
2. *See* REFINE.

polish, *n.* **1.** shine; *spec.* burnish, glaze, glazing.
2. *See* REFINEMENT, ACCOMPLISHMENT, ELEGANCE.

polished, *a.* **1.** burnished, glossy.
Antonyms: see ROUGH, DEAD.
2. *See* REFINED, ELEGANT.

polisher, *n. Spec.* burnisher, rubber, bob, skive, jigger, buff, runner, dolly, lapper.

polite, *a.* **1.** civil, courteous, genteel, gentle, mannerly; *spec.* soft, gracious, attentive, gentlemanly *or* (*less usual*) gentlemanlike, urbane, courtly, gallant, chivalrous, debonnair; *see* RESPECTFUL.
Antonyms: see IMPOLITE, CONTEMPTUOUS, IMPUDENT, UNGENTLEMANLY, UNMANNERLY, BOORISH, ROWDYISH.
2. *See* REFINED, ELEGANT.

politeness, *a.* civility, courtesy, courteousness, gentilesse (*A*), comity (*B or legal*); *spec.* devoir (*A or B*), gallantness, gallantry, breeding, graciousness, urbanity, mannerliness, attentiveness, respect.
Antonyms: see IMPOLITENESS, CONTEMPT, IMPUDENCE.

pond, *n.* lake (*contex.*), Atlantic Ocean (*contex. C*); *spec.* pondlet, cistern (*R*), tank (*dial. or local*), pool, carr (*local Eng.*), piscina *or* piscine (*R*), decoy; *see* POOL, VIVARIUM.

pony, *n.* hobby (*A or hist.*); *spec.* chelty (*Scot.*), goonhilly (*Eng.*), merlin, tat *or* tatt (*Anglo-Indian*), crib.

pool, *n.* pond (*contex.*); *spec.* fresh, plash, puddle, linn (*chiefly Scot.*), tank, Bethesda, natatorium, jheel (*East India*), decoy (*hunting*).

poor, *a.* **1.** *These senses all imply lack of means:* impecunious (*especially without money or ability to get it*), impecuniary (*R*), needy (*generally lacking in goods and services*), needful (*R*); *spec.* beggarly, destitute (*implying state of being forsaken or of having lost means once possessed*), penniless, indigent (*A in sense of lacking; now implies poverty with age and weakness*), moneyless, poverty-stricken, dollarless (*a nonce word*), fortuneless.
Antonyms: see RICH, PROSPEROUS.
2. *See* DEFICIENT, IMPERFECT, MEAGER, THIN, UNPRODUCTIVE, HUMBLE, INFERIOR, INSIGNIFICANT, UNSKILLFUL.

poorhouse, *n.* workhouse, almshouse.

poorly, *adv.* **1.** ill; *spec.* imperfectly, defectively, indifferently, inadequately, badly, wretchedly, sorrily, meanly, miserably, insufficiently, scantily, pitifully.
Antonyms: see WELL.
2. *Spec.* piteously, humbly, weakly, abjectly, contemptibly, despicably, *etc.*

pope, *n.* bishop (*contex.*), popeling (*diminutive and contemptuous*), papa (*obs.*), high priest (*R*).

popularize, *v. t.* vulgarize (*R*), generalize (*R*), democratize, familiarize (*R*).

porch, *n.* **1.** entrance (*contex.*), stoop (*a loose or erroneous use; U. S.*); *spec.* galilee, distyle.
2. *See* VERANDA.

pork, *n.* **1.** *The flesh of swine: spec.* pig, hog (*R*), swine (*R or contemptuous*), gammon, sparerib, souse, bacon, *etc.*
2. graft (*U. S., C, in political sense*).

porous, *a.* holey, open.
Antonyms: see COMPACT.

porridge, *n. Spec.* gruel, loblolly (*obs. or dial. equiv. of "gruel"*), pap, mush, flummery, stir about, hasty pudding, crowdie *or* crowdy (*Scot. & dial. Eng.*), burgoo, brochan (*Scot.*), drammock (*Scot.*), panada *or* panade, polenta, sagamite (*Amer. Indian*).

port, *n.* **1.** *See* GATE.
2. opening (*contex.*), porthole, embrasure (*R*).

port, *n. Nautical:* larboard (*obs.*).

portable, *a.* portative (*chiefly hist.*), carriageable (*R*).
Antonyms: see FIXED.

porter, *n.* redcap (*U. S.*), concierge (*Fr.*); *see* DOORKEEPER, GATEKEEPER.

portico, *n.* colonnade; *spec.* stoa, parvis, exedra, proaulion, xyst, veranda, prostyle, *etc.*

pose, *v. t.* place (*contex.*), posture, posturize (*R*), set.

pose, *v. i.* posture, attitudinize (*chiefly depreciatory*), posturize (*R*); *spec.* peacock (*R*).

position, *n.* **1.** place, situation, station, set, standpoint, bearing; *spec.* gauge.
2. posture (Posture *refers to* position *with reference to the relation of one part to another of the*

---

polemic, *n.: disputant, dispute.*
policy: *wisdom, art, expediency.*
politic: *wise, artful, expedient, time-serving.*
polity: *government, state.*
poll, *n.: head, list.*
poll, *v. t.: top, cut, list.*
pollute: *dirty, foul, contaminate, desecrate.*
pomp: *grandeur, show.*
pool, *n.: fund, association.*
pool, *v.: combine.*
pop, *v. t.: explode, present.*
popular: *public, plebeian, lay, common, acceptable, accepted, cheap.*
populate: *people.*
pore, *v. i.: gaze, consider.*
portal: *doorway, gate.*
portent: *sign, wonder.*
portentous: *significant, extraordinary, wonderful.*
portion, *n.: part, share, fate, dower.*
portion, *v. t.: apportion, endow, dower.*
portly: *dignified, fat.*
portrait: *picture, likeness, description.*
portraiture: *depiction, picture, description.*

object concerned, esp. as temporarily and intentionally assumed and subject to change at will; while position *includes the idea of the way in which a body is disposed in reference to other objects, or of a fixed position; thus, we would speak of a person or a post as being in a leaning* position, *or of a person being tied or constrained in an awkward* position; *but we would say that is an ungraceful* posture, *a* posture *of defiance, humility, etc.*).

3. place, situation, billet, post, berth; *spec.* office, bed, incumbency, dignity, intendancy, magistrature, magistracy, mastership, portfolio, countship, professorship, judgeship, *etc.*

4. *Referring to the place one holds in public estimation or customary consideration:* place, status (*tech. or B*), situation, standing, dignity, honor; *see* RANK.

5. *Referring to the mental view taken or professed: see* ATTITUDE.

possess, *v. t.* **1.** *See* HAVE, OWN, INFORM, CONTROL, KEEP, AFFECT, CONVINCE.

2. *Referring to possession by spirits:* diabolize, demonize, bespirit; *spec.* bedevil, obsess (*only in the passive*).

possession, *n.* **1.** having; *spec.* seizin, tenure.

2. *See* HOLD, OWNERSHIP, PROPERTY, CONVICTION.

3. theolepsy, enthusiasm (*R*); *spec.* bedevilment, obsession.

possessor, *n.* haver, holder; *spec.* bearer.

possibility, *n.* **1.** potentiality, potency; *spec.* practicability, feasibility, workability.

Antonyms: impossibility (*cf.* IMPOSSIBLE).

2. *See* CONTINGENCY.

3. *Referring to the thing:* potential, maybe (*C*).

possible, *a.* **1.** *Referring to capability of being brought into existence:* potential; *spec.* compossible (*R or B*), practicable, feasible, workable, doable (*C*); *see* PRACTICAL.

Antonyms: see IMPOSSIBLE.

2. *Referring to what is capable of being (that is of being, or not being, true; or of coming, or not coming, to pass) so far as the mind can see: see* CONTINGENT, THINKABLE.

possibly, *adv.* potentially, *etc.*, maybe; *see* PERHAPS.

post, *n.* **1.** *Spec.* stake, picket, baluster, stud, jamb, sidepost, cheek, newel, bollard, puncheon, bitts (*pl.*), loggerhead, dolphin, rymer, stump, heel, harre (*dial. Eng. equiv. of "heel" of a gate*); *see* PILLAR, PIER.

2. position, office.

3. headquarters, settlement (*chiefly mil.*).

post, *v. t.* **1.** mail (*U. S.*), drop.

2. *See* LIST, INFORM, PUBLISH.

3. enter, record.

postcard, *n.* postal.

postdate, *v. t.* mistime (*contex.*).

Antonyms: see ANTEDATE.

posterior, *n.* **1.** *See* BACK.

2. rear; *spec.* crissum; *see* RUMP, BUTTOCKS.

postern, *n.* doorway (*contex.*).

postscript, *n.* addition (*contex.*), envoy (*B*), subscript, subscription.

Antonyms: see PREFACE.

posture, *n.* **1.** position, attitude, pose, set (*C*); *spec.* decumbence *or* decumbency (*B or tech.*), decubitus, squat, guard.

2. *See* ATTITUDE, POSITION, STATE.

pot, *n. Spec.* crock, kettle, bicker, craggan (*archæol.*), posnet (*A*), jar, jardinière (*French*), jackshay *or* jackshea (*Australia*).

potter, *v. i.* putter, fiddle, trifle, fiddle-faddle, poke, niggle, dabble, dawdle; *see* TRIFLE.

pottering, *a.* trifling, poky, *or* poking (*C*).

pound, *n.* inclosure (*contex.*), greenyard (*Eng.*), penfold, pinfold.

pour, *v. t.* **1.** flow (*contex.*); *spec.* decant, souse, pump (*fig.*), effund (*R*), effuse (*R*), transfuse (*R*), flood, superfuse (*R, B*), cascade, cataract, libate.

2. *See* LAVISH.

pouring, *n.* pour (*R*); *spec.* decantation, effusion, transfusion (*R*), regurgitation, circumfusion, perfusion (*R*), libation.

poverty, *n.* **1.** *For senses implying lack of means, see* POOR.

Antonyms: see WEALTH.

2. *Spec.* deficiency, meagerness, humbleness.

powder, *n.* dust; *spec.* flour, meal, grit, pulvil (*R*), farina (*R*), bloom, diapasm (*A*), putty, rouge, pounce; *see* EFFLORESCENCE, DOSE, COSMETIC, DUST.

powder, *v. t.* **1.** sprinkle (*contex.*), bepowder (*intensive*), dust; *spec.* flour, meal (*R*), dredge, pounce, frost.

2. *See* PULVERIZE.

powdery, *a.* dusty, pulverulent, pulveraceous *or* pulverous (*R*); *spec.* floury, mealy, farinaceous (*obs., exc. med.*).

power, *n.* **1.** *Referring to a capacity for exerting physical force or achieving results:* strength, might (*B or rhetorical*), force (*R*), energy, virtue (*fig. B, as of a medicine's* virtue), puissance (*B*), potency *or* potence (*R*), reach; *spec.* leverage, arm (*fig.*).

Antonyms: see WEAKNESS.

2. *Referring to exerted physical power, or power in action: see* FORCE.

3. authority; *spec.* (*in the sense of "power of attorney"*) procuration (*R, exc. spec.*), carte blanche (*French*), warrant, proxy.

4. potentiate; *see* STATE, RULER.

5. *See* ABILITY, INFLUENCE, FACULTY, CONTROL, MEANING, INTENSITY, COGENCY, MULTITUDE, STATE, RULER.

powerful, *a.* **1.** strong, energetic, forceful, forcible, potent (*chiefly B or rhetorical*), mighty (*rhetorical*), mightful (*A*), main (*now*

post, *n.: place, fortification, garrison, branch, position, stage, station, settlement, goal.*
poster: *notice.*
postpone: *defer, subordinate.*
postulate, *n.: condition, proposition, assumption.*
postulate, *v. t.: ask, assume.*
potency: *power, intensity, influence.*
potent: *powerful, intense, influential.*
pounce, *v. i.: swoop, jump, dart, descend.*

obs. or R), puissant (*B*), potential (*R*); *spec.* prepotent (*intensive*), multipotent (*R*), Herculean, armipotent, bellipotent (*jocose or ironical*).

Antonyms: see WEAK, FAINT, POWERLESS.

2. *See* ABLE, FORCIBLE, INFLUENTIAL, COGENT.

powerless, *a.* weak, strengthless, impotent, forceless, mightless (*A*); *spec.* helpless, paralytic.

Antonyms: see POWERFUL, STRONG.

practicable, *a.* workable, usable, possible. *Often confused with* practical, *q. v.*

practical, *a.* **1.** *Refers to what is suited for use or action as opposed to the theoretical or ideal; whereas* practicable *is limited to the sense of actual capability in use; as "a* practical *man," "*practical *ethics," "a* practical *machine" and "a* practicable *plan."* positive, practic (*A*), operative, pragmatical *or* pragmatic (*obs., exc. in theol.*), hard-headed *or* (*R*) hard; *see* MATTER-OF-FACT.

Antonyms: see VISIONARY, IMAGINATIVE.

2. *See* USEFUL, VIRTUAL, WORKING.

practice, practise, *v. t.* **1.** *See* DO, EXERCISE, PURSUE.

2. *To do or perform habitually in order to acquire skill:* do (*contex.*), perform, rehearse, record; *spec.* repeat.

practice, practise, *n.* **1.** *See* EXERCISE, PURSUIT, CUSTOM, HABIT, ARTIFICE.

2. performance, rehearsal, recording; *spec.* repetition.

3. *Referring to the active or absolute sense of carrying on or conducting something, as opposed to "theory":* performance, orthopraxy (*R*), conduct; *see* CEREMONY, USAGE.

4. *Referring to the intransitive sense of a way of action or proceeding: see* PROCEDURE.

prairie, *a.* plain (*U. S. and colonial British; chiefly in pl.*); *spec.* steppe, savannah, prairillon (*R*).

Antonyms: see FOREST.

praise, *v. t.* approve (*contex.*), applaud (*chiefly spec.*); *spec.* bepraise, puff, laud, exalt, flatter, extol, bless, magnify, glorify, celebrate, commend, acclaim, eulogize, collaud (*R*), crack (*C*), preconize (*R*), doxologize, sing, carol, chant (*B*), hymn, compliment.

Antonyms: see SCOLD, REPROVE, CENSURE, CONDEMN, ABUSE, DEFAME, DISPARAGE, RIDICULE.

praise, *n.* approval (*contex.*), applause (*chiefly spec.*); *spec.* acclaim, acclamation, laud (*R*), laudation, puff, blurb (*cant for a publisher's praise of his book on the dust-jacket*), puffery (*extravagant or undeserved* praise), extolment, exaltation, magnification, glorification, celebration, commendation (*restrained* praise), collaudation (*R*), doxology, compliment *or* complimentation; *see* EULOGY.

Antonyms: see SCOLDING, REPROOF, DISPARAGEMENT, RIDICULE, CENSURE, CONDEMNATION, ABUSE.

praiser, *n.* approver, applauder, puffer, *etc.; spec.* eulogist, encomiast.

praiseworthy, *a.* good (*contex.*), commendable.

Antonyms: see CONTEMPTIBLE.

praising, *a.* approving, applausive, *etc. Cf.* PRAISE.

Antonyms: see CENSORIOUS, ABUSIVE, CONDEMNATORY.

prance, *v. i.* **1.** *Referring to horses:* spring, tittup, caper, brank (*Scot. or dial.*), curvet, cavort (*U. S.; C*).

2. *See* RIDE, CAPER, SWAGGER.

prayer, *n.* **1.** *See* APPEAL.

2. *Referring to an appeal to God:* bead (*obs.*), orison (*A, B*), oration (*hist.*), invocation; *spec.* paternoster *or* (*for short*) pater, litany, rosary, complin, suffrage, oremus (*R*), miserere, confiteor, memento, grace, collect, kyrie eleison, *etc.*

preach, *v. i. Spec.* exhort (*contex.*), sermonize, evangelize, homilize, preachify (*C; contemptuous*).

preacher, *n.* discourser (*contex.*), sky pilot (*C, S*); *spec.* sermonizer, homilist, homilete, Boanerges, Devil dodger (*humorous and contemptuous*), preacheress (*fem.; R*), predicator (*R*), pulpitarian (*R*), pulpiteer *or* pulpiter (*chiefly contemptuous*), sermoneer (*R*), predicant (*R*), evangelist, lecturer, rounder, circuit rider; *see* MINISTER.

preaching, *a.* predicatory (*R*), predicant (*R*).

preaching, *n.* discourse (*contex.*); *spec.* pulpitry, sermonizing, homiletics (*pl.*), preachment (*chiefly contemptuous*), predication (*A*), evangelization.

prearrange, *v. t.* arrange (*contex.*); *spec.* preorder (*R*), preconcert, precontract.

prearranged, *a.* cut-and-dried (*C; chiefly depreciatory*).

prearrangement, *n. Spec.* preconcert (*R*), precontract.

precede, *v. t.* **1.** antecede, forego (*B, A*); *spec.* forerun, prevene (*R*), usher (*B*); *see* LEAD, INTRODUCE.

Antonyms: see FOLLOW.

2. outrank, rank.

3. *See* ANTEDATE, PREFACE.

precedence, *n.* **1.** precedency, antecedence, predecession (*R*), precession (*R*); *spec.* lead, priority.

Antonyms: see FOLLOWING.

2. precedency, priority; *spec.* preference, preaudience; *see* ADVANTAGE.

precedent, *n.* ensample (*A*); *see* AUTHORITY.

preceding, *a. For sense discriminations see* PREVIOUS. precedent (*R*), foregoing, antecedent; *spec.* precursory, prodromal, prior, prodromic, last; *see* PAST, INTRODUCTORY, SUPERIOR.

Antonyms: see FOLLOWING, SUCCESSIVE.

---

practised, practiced: *experienced.*
prank, *n.: frolic, caper, jest.*
prate: babble, chatter.
prattle: *babble, chatter, murmur.*
preach, *v. t.: proclaim, teach, utter.*
preamble: *preface, introduction.*
prebend: *pay, benefice.*
precarious: *uncertain.*

precious, *a.* **1.** *See* VALUABLE, COSTLY, ESTIMABLE, OUTRAGEOUS.

2. precise (*contex.*), bluestocking (*of women*), priggish, prudish (*R*), precisian, purist.

precipitation, *n.* **1.** *See* HASTENING, HASTE.

2. deposit (*contex.*); *spec.* rainfall, rain, dewfall, dew, snowfall, snow, hail.

Antonyms: evaporation (*cf.* EVAPORATE).

precipitous, *a.* steep (*contex.*), perpendicular, sheer; *spec.* cliffy, craggy, scarry (*R*); hasty, ill-considered, headlong (*all three fig. and contex.*).

Antonyms: see GENTLE.

precisian, *n.* **1.** *Spec.* puritan, stickler.

2. *Referring only to language:* précieuse (*French; a sing. or a collective; properly fem. sing.*), prig, bluestocking (*fem.*); *spec.* formalist; *see* PEDANT.

precision, *n.* accuracy, exactness (*q. v. for discriminations*), preciseness (*implying over-fussiness or over-punctiliousness, as contrasted to the commendatory sense of* precision).

precocious, *a.* forward, advanced, premature.

Antonyms: see BACKWARD, DULL, STUPID.

predacious, *a.* predatory, raptorial, rapacious, ravening; *see* CARNIVOROUS.

predecessor, *n.* antecessor, foregoer (*A, R*); *spec.* forerunner, harbinger (*A, B*), herald, precursor; *see* ANCESTOR.

Antonyms: see FOLLOWER.

predicable, *a.* affirmable.

predicament, *n.* condition (*contex.*), dilemma, quandary, corner, hole (*C*), mess, scrape, fix, impasse (*French*), pickle (*C*), plunge (*obs. or dial.*).

predict, *v. t.* **1.** foretell, forecast, cast (*B or obsolescent*), fore-announce (*R*), forespeak (*R*); *spec.* prognosticate, prophesy, forebode, bode (*A*), presage, divine, augur, vaticinate (*R*), foresay (*R*), foredoom (*R*), portend (*R*), harbinger (*R*), fatidicate (*R*).

2. *See* GUESS.

predict, *v. i.* soothsay, forecast; *spec.* prophesy.

prediction, *n.* **1.** *Spec.* prognostication (*simple foretelling*), prognostic, presage (*R*), foreboding (*with sense of uneasiness as to future*), forebodement, boding (*obsolescent*), forecast (*implies a reasoned statement as to future likelihood on basis of past data*), cast (*obsolescent*), prophecy, augury (*these two with religious overtones*), prognosis (*med.*); *see* DIVINATION.

2. *See* GUESS.

predictive, *a.* soothsaying; *spec.* prophetic.

predictor, *n.* foreteller, forecaster, caster (*B*), seer; *spec.* prophet, *etc. See* PREDICT.

preface, *n.* introduction, foreword, preamble (*R, exc. spec.*), prologue (*B*), foretalk (*R*), proem (*B*), exordium (*R*), prolegomenon (*B*), induction (*R*), preambulation (*R*).

Antonyms: see POSTSCRIPT.

preface, *v. t.* precede (*contex.*), preamble (*R, exc. spec.*), prologue, premise (*R*).

Antonyms: see FOLLOW.

prefatory, *a.* introductory, prefacial (*R*), prefatorial (*R*), proemial (*R*), preambulatory (*R*), preambular (*R*), preambulary (*R*).

Antonyms: see FOLLOWING.

prefigure, *v. t.* **1.** indicate, show, shadow, foreshow, foretype (*R*), prefigurate (*R*), pretypify (*R*); *spec.* foreshadow, adumbrate.

2. *See* IMAGINE.

prefix, *n.* affix, addition (*contex.*), prefixture (*R*); *spec.* inflex (*R*).

Antonyms: see SUFFIX.

prefix, *v. t.* affix, add (*contex.*).

prefixing, *n.* prefixture, prefixtion (*R*); *spec.* prosthesis, prothesis.

pregnancy, *n.* gestation (*more tech. than "pregnancy"*), gravidity (*R*), gravidness (*R*), heaviness (*contex.*), ingravidation (*R*).

pregnant, *a.* **1.** gravid, heavy (*contex.*), great (*usually in "great with child"*), big (*usually in "big with young"*), big-bellied, teeming (*A*), gestant (*R*), impregnant (*R*).

2. *See* PRODUCTIVE.

prehensile, *a.* seizing (*contex.*), prehensive (*R*), prehensory (*R*).

prejudice, *v. t.* incline, bias, prepossess, partialize (*R*), turn (*chiefly with "against" or, less commonly, "for"*), malignify (*R*), earwig (*fig.*), preëngage (*R*).

prejudiced, *a.* inclined, biased, *etc.*; *see* PARTIAL, NARROW.

Antonyms: see IMPARTIAL.

prelude, *n.* **1.** *In music:* preamble (*B*), prolusion (*R*), descant (*hist.*); *spec.* overture, voluntary, ritornello (*Italian*) *or* ritornel.

2. *See* INTRODUCTION, FORERUNNER.

premium, *n. Spec.* reward, payment, gift, fee, agio.

preparation, *n.* **1.** *Referring to the act:* provision; *spec.* concoction, composition, confection, mixture, adaptation, dressing, equipment, strengthening, cooking, make-up, make-ready (*printing*) formation, *etc.*

2. *Referring to the state: see* PREPAREDNESS.

preparatory, *a.* preparative; *spec.* dispositive, introductory, concoctive, warning, strengthening, *etc.*

prepare, *v. t.* **1.** ready (*R*), dight (*A or B*), fit (*C, U. S.*), dispose (*A*), make, work, boun (*A or Scot.*), busk (*A or Scot.*); *spec.* gird; *see*

---

preceptor: *teacher.*
precinct: *inclosure, neighborhood, boundary, district.*
precipitate, *a.: falling, rushing, hasty.*
precipitate, *v. t.: throw, send, drive, hasten, deposit.*
precise: *definite, fastidious, diametric, exact, accurate.*
precisely: *exactly.*
preconception: *opinion, anticipation.*
predetermine: *appoint, destine, decide.*
predominant: *controlling, prevalent.*
preference: *advancement, choice, liking, precedence.*
prejudice, *n.: injury, detriment, partiality, opinion.*
prejudicial: *injurious.*
preliminary, *n.: introduction.*
prelude, *v. t.: introduce, forerun.*
premature: *untimely, precocious.*
premier, *a.: chief, first.*
preoccupation: *absorption.*

ADAPT, DRESS, LEARN, MAKE, COOK. *"Prepare" is used as a general synonym of very many words indicating a process or action that is intended to bring something into a state of readiness for some given purpose, as for "warm, heat, cool, dry, train, educate, load, prime," etc.*
2. *Spec.* (*referring to making a person ready with a retort, reply, speech, or the like, for a given occasion*): load, charge, prime.
3. provide, make-up, concoct; *spec.* mix, confection; *see* MAKE, FURNISH, FORM, COMPOSE, *etc. "Prepare" in this sense is used for many terms* (*as in sense* **1**), *as for "develop, complete, plan," etc.*
prepare, *v. i.* frame (*R*), fit (*R*), boun (*A or Scot.*), busk (*A or Scot.*).
prepared, *a.* ready, fit; *spec.* ripe.
preparedness, *n.* preparation (*R*), readiness.
preparing, *a. Spec.* afoot, making;—*the use of the present participle "preparing" in this sense being by many considered contrary to good usage.*
presence, *n.* **1.** *State or fact of being present in a place:* presentiality (*R*), presentness; *spec.* attendance, company, face.
Antonyms: see ABSENCE.
2. *See* NEIGHBORHOOD, CARRIAGE.
present, *a.* **1.** presential (*R*), here (*R*).
Antonyms: see ABSENT.
2. instant (*A, exc. spec.*), current, now (*R*), living (*as in "a living issue"*); *see* MODERN.
Antonyms: see PAST, FUTURE.
3. *See* AVAILABLE.
present, *n.* now;—*both words used with "the."*
Antonyms: see PAST, FUTURE.
present, *v. t.* **1.** *See* SHOW, INTRODUCE, OPPOSE, NOMINATE, OFFER, ADVANCE, EXPRESS, SUGGEST, GIVE.
2. *With the person as the object:* gift (*R*), gratify (*A*); *spec.* tip (*C*), compliment, fee.
Antonyms: see DEPRIVE.
3. express (*contex.*), lay, bring, put, prefer, submit, adduce, pop (*C*).
presentation, *n.* presentment (*R*); *see* SHOW, GIFT, OFFER.
preservation, *n.* **1.** *See* PROTECTION, SAVING, KEEPING.
2. conservation, conservancy (*chiefly British*), saving, cherishment (*R*), embalmment (*R*).
3. confection (*mostly spec.*), cure; *spec.* ensilage, mummification, smoking, canning (*U. S.*), *etc.*
preserve, *v. t.* **1.** *See* PROTECT, SAVE, MAINTAIN, KEEP.
2. *Referring to the keeping in existence or to the prevention of destruction, waste, or the like:* conserve, conservate (*R*), incorrupt (*R*); *spec.* save, cherish, enshrine (*often fig.*), embalm, balm (*A or R*), file, record.
Antonyms: see WASTE, DESTROY, ABATE, ANNIHILATE, EXTINGUISH.
3. keep (*contex.*), conserve, do (*contex.*); *spec.* confect, process, cure, season, ensilage, ensile, ensilate (*R*), barbecue, bloat, kipper, smoke, kyanize, tin (*chiefly British*), can (*U. S.*), pot, candy, embalm, mummify, jerk; *see* PICKLE, DRY.
preserve, *n.* **1.** conserve; *spec.* sweetmeat, confection, compote, marmalade, jam, jelly, sauce, goggles (*pl.; R*), dun (*chiefly in pl.*).
2. *Spec.* warren.
president, *n.* presider (*less formal*), head, preses *or* præses (*chiefly Scot.*); *spec.* chairman, dean, deacon, prefect, moderator, provost, speaker, toastmaster, rector, reeve (*Canada*), prexy (*univ. S, U. S.*).
press, *v. t.* **1.** crush, cram (*C*), crunch; *spec.* screw, crowd, cylinder, roll, roller, calender, tread, iron, goose, mangle; *see* PUSH, SQUEEZE, CRUSH, TREAD.
Antonyms: see STRETCH, EXPAND.
2. *See* CONSTRAIN, URGE, DISTRESS, ENLIST, CROWD.
pressure, *n.* **1.** press, oppression (*B*); *spec.* bearing, crowding, crowd, crushing, crush, crunching, crunch, screw, load, counterpressure, pression (*R*), impressure (*R*), impressment (*R*); *see* PUSH, SQUEEZE, CRUSH.
2. *See* DISTRESS, URGENCY, EXIGENCY.
pretend, *v. t.* **1.** feign, sham, simulate, affect, act, make-believe, counterfeit, gammon (*S or C*), dissemble (*R or obs.*); *spec.* profess.
2. *See* IMAGINE.
pretend, *v. i.* feign, feint, dissemble, make-believe, sham, play possum (*C, U. S.*), fake (*C*).
pretended, *a.* pretensive (*less common than "pretended"*), sham, feigned, feint (*R*), dissembled, counterfeit, affected, simulated, ostensible, spurious, colorable, dummy, bogus (*C*), false, imitated, acted, imitation, artificial, hypocritical; *spec.* shoddy; *see* FALSE.
pretender, *n.* feigner, simulator, make-believer, dissembler, actor, panjandrum, counterfeiter; *spec.* sciolist, antichrist; *see* DISSEMBLER, DECEIVER, QUACK, CLAIMANT, HYPOCRITE.
pretense, *n.* **1.** *Referring to the action, habit, or fact:* pretension, affectation, feigning, simulation, mummery, masquerade, imitation, mockery, falsity, show, sham, gloze (*R*), make-believe; *spec.* profession, puppetry, euphuism, bluff, shoddyism; *see* DECEPTION, DISSEMBLING.
2. *Referring to the thing embodying or used for pretense:* pretension, veil, show, sham, affectation, mask, guise, imitation, make-believe;

preponderant: *controlling, prevalent.*
prepossessing: *attractive.*
prepossession: *absorption, partiality.*
preposterous: *absurd.*
prerequisite: *condition.*
prerogative: *right.*
prescience: *foreknowledge, foresight.*
prescription: *dictation, appointment, limitation, formula, custom.*
prescriptive: *customary.*
presentable: *proper.*
presentiment: *foreboding, anticipation.*
press, *n.: pressure, constraint, distress, haste, crowd, cupboard.*
pressing: *urgent.*
prestige: *influence, reputation.*
presume, *v. t.: venture, assume, infer.*
presumption, *n.: assumption, inference, arrogance, impudence, assurance.*
presumptive: *probable, assumed.*
presumptuous: *venturesome, arrogant, assured, impudent.*

spec. mockery, shoddy (*C*), tinsel, profession.
3. *See* CLAIM, PRETEXT.

pretentious, *a.* affected, airy, Tartuffian (*fig.*), topping, high, big (*C*), brassy (*C*), important, fastuous (*R*); *spec.* high-sounding, high-hat (*C*), highbrow (*C*); *see* AMBITIOUS, SHOWY.
Antonyms: see UNAFFECTED, HUMBLE.

pretentiousness, *n.* airs (*pl.*), side (*S*), bigness.

preternatural, *a.* nonnatural; *see* UNNATURAL, SUPERNATURAL.
Antonyms: see NORMAL.

pretext, *n.* pretense, subterfuge, cover, color, cloak, veil, blind.

pretty, *a.* **1.** *Spec.* cute (*C*), cunning.
2. *See* GOOD-LOOKING, BEAUTIFUL, CONSIDERABLE.

prevail, *v. i.* **1.** predominate, preponderate, reign (*chiefly spec.*), rule, obtain, subsist; *spec.* rage.
2. *As used with "on" or "upon," or "with": see* OVERCOME, SUCCEED, CONTROL.

prevalence, *n.* predominance, currency, reign.

prevalent, *a.* predominant, preponderant, prevailing, general, current; *spec.* rife, regnant (*R*), ruling, running.

prevaricate, *v. i.* equivocate, palter, quibble, shuffle, whiffle (*R*), dodge, shift, tergiversate, sophisticate, quirk (*R*), pettifog (*R*), ergotize (*R*).

prevarication, *n.* **1.** *Referring to the action, practice, etc.:* equivocation, paltering, shuffling, quibbling, evasion, tergiversation, sophistry, casuistry, pettifogging.
2. *Referring to an instance of exhibiting prevarication:* equivocation, evasion, quirk, quip, quibble, dodge, shuffle, quillet (*R*). *A "prevarication" may or may not be a "lie"; a "lie" may or may not involve a "prevarication."*

prevaricator, *n.* sophist, sophister, shuffler, quibbler, *etc.*

prevent, *v. t.* preclude, deter, help, debar, stop, save (*with "from"*), forestall (*obsolescent*), forbid, prohibit, interdict, hinder, foreclose (*R*), inhibit, shield (*A*), forfend (*A*), help; *spec.* veto, restrain, bar; *see* ESTOP.
Antonyms: see AID, CAUSE, CONCLUDE, INCITE.

prevention, *n.* preclusion (*R*), inhibition, stoppage, prohibition, determent, forestalling, restraint, *etc.*; *see* OBSTACLE, ESTOPPEL.
Antonyms: see AID, PREVENTION, INCITEMENT.

preventive, *a.* preventative, preclusive, inhibitory, inhibitive, deterrent, prohibitive, prohibitory, hindering; *spec.* prophylactic.
Antonyms: see CONTRIBUTORY.

previous, *a.* antecedent (*referring to what has gone before in time, and sometimes also in the progression of a logical succession*), anterior (*before in space*), preceding (*immediately before in time*), precedent (*refers to the thing on whose going before some following matter depends*), prior (*whereas* previous *primarily implies earlier in time,* prior *implies first, not necessarily in time, but in importance or obligation*), foregone, fore (*obs.*), preallable (*R*), early (*a C sense of* previous, *implying too much before in time, hence anticipatory*); *see* FORMER.
Antonyms: see SUBSEQUENT.

previousness, *n.* antecedence, anteriorness, priority, *etc.*

previsional, *a.* previsionary, foresightful (*R*).

prey, *n.* **1.** quarry, ravin (*B*), kill; *spec.* pelt.
2. *See* VICTIM.

prey, *v. i.* **1.** *See* PLUNDER.
2. *Referring to the animal:* ravin; *spec.* kill (*R*).

price, *n.* charge, rate; *spec.* quotation, fiars (*pl.; Scot.*), ransom.

prick, *n.* **1.** *See* DOT, WOUND, STING.
2. point (*contex.*), pricker; *spec.* prod, goad, brog (*dial.*), prickle.

prickle, *n.* prick (*contex.*); *spec.* thorn, spine, acicule, spicule, needle, thistle.

prickly, *a.* pricky (*R or dial.*); *spec.* aculeate, aciculate, spiny, thorny, thistly, echinate, echinated, echinulate, burry.
Antonyms: see SMOOTH.

pride, *n.* **1.** self-esteem, proudness, disdainfulness, haughtiness. *"Vanity" is not a synonym of "pride."*
Antonyms: see HUMILITY.
2. *See* ARROGANCE, ELATION.

pride, *v. t.* plume; *see* CONGRATULATE.

priest, *n.* minister (*contex.*); *spec.* hierophant, priestlet *or* priestling (*chiefly contemptuous*), father, patrico (*cant*), confessor, pope (*Greek Church*), levite, lama, brahmin, brahman, bonze, Brehon, fetial, pontiff, pontifex, flamen, corybant, corybantian, fulgurator, druid, hierarch, sacrificer, seminarist, protopapas, protopope, powwow, poonghie, papa.
Antonyms: see LAYMAN.

priestess, *n. Spec.* nun, vestal, Pythia.

priesthood, *n.* ministry (*contex.*); *spec.* clergy, pontificate, pontificality (*R*).

priestly, *a.* ministerial (*contex.*); *spec.* hieratic, pontifical, pontific, levitical.
Antonyms: see LAY.

prim, *a. spec.* prudish, precise; *see* STIFF, FORMAL.

prime, *n.* **1.** *See* HOUR, BEGINNING, SPRING, ACCENT.
2. *Referring to the early period of life, when the flush of feeling is strong:* springtime, bloom (*fig.*), flower (*fig.*), heyday, May (*B and fig.*).
3. *Referring to the period of greatest activity*

pretty, *adv.: moderately.*
priceless: *invaluable.*
prick, *v. t.: pierce, perforate, sting, choose, appoint, erect.*
prick, *v. i.: thrust, ride, rise, sting.*
prig: *precisian.*
priggish: *fastidious, precious, conceited.*
primacy: *headship.*
primal: *original, first.*
primary, *a.: original, first, immediate, elementary, chief.*
prime, *a.: first, original, first-class, chief.*
prime, *v. t.: prepare, coat.*

and vigor, usually in the middle age of life: zenith (*fig.*), height, floruit (*R*).

prince, *n.* **1.** monarch, princelet (*dim.*), princeling (*dim.*), princekin (*dim.*); *spec.* pendragon, cardinal, duke, mirza, emir, elector.

2. *Referring to a male member of a royal family; esp. a son or grandson of the monarch:* infant; *spec.* infante, czarevitch *or* tsarevitch, dauphin.

3. *See* CHIEF.

princess, *n.* **1.** *See* MONARCH.

2. *Referring to a female member of a royal family, esp. a daughter or granddaughter of the monarch: spec.* infant, infanta, czarina *or* tsarina, dauphiness.

principal, *n.* **1.** *See* CHIEF.

2. *Referring to a person for whom another acts: spec.* client, consigner, constituent, constituency (*a collective*).

Antonyms: see AGENT, GO-BETWEEN.

3. *Referring to a sum of money as distinguished from increase or interest:* capital, corpus (*tech.*) body.

Antonyms: see INTEREST.

print, *v. t.* **1.** impress, imprint, engrave (*fig.*), stamp; *see* BRAND, INDENT.

2. *Referring to marking with or as with type, an engraved figure, etc.:* type (*R*); *spec.* reprint, lithograph, prove *or* (*less usual*) proof, pull, discharge.

print, *n.* **1.** form (*contex.*), figure (*contex.*), impression, imprint, impress, stamp; *see* BRAND, INDENTATION.

2. *Referring to matter printed with or as with type:* typography, letterpress.

Antonyms: see MANUSCRIPT.

3. *Referring to a particular thing printed:* impression, impress; *spec.* reprint, proof, pull, lithograph, xylograph, zincograph, zincotype, chromograph, cuneiform, negative, positive, vignette.

4. *See* DESIGN.

printer, *n. Spec.* typesetter, pressman, compositor.

prison, *n. Spec.* prisonhouse, dungeon, pit (*obs. or hist.*), jail, penitentiary, reformatory, lock-up, jug (*S*), roundhouse (*hist.*), calaboose *or* calaboza (*local, U. S.*), crib (*local, Eng.*), kitty (*S*), loga (*pl.; S, Australia*), can (*S, U. S.*), hell (*R*), gehenna (*R*), college (*S, Eng.*), hoosegow (*S, U. S.*), cooler (*S, U. S.*), choky (*Anglo-Indian*), bagnio, clink (*S, Eng.*), quod (*S*), cage (*C*), guardhouse, guardroom, bullpen (*S*), stockade (*S*), blackhole, counter (*obs. or hist.; Eng.*), vault, hulk, Newgate, bridewell, compter (*Eng.*).

prisoner, *n.* captive (*B, or fig.*), caitiff (*obs.*); *spec.* jailbird, collegian (*S, Eng.*), culprit, cageling.

privacy, *n. Referring to avoidance of, or freedom from, publicity:* privateness, intimacy (*R or spec.*), intimity (*R*).

Antonyms: see PUBLICITY.

private, *a.* **1.** privy (*A*), nonpublic (*R*), nonofficial (*R*), unofficial; *spec.* personal.

Antonyms: see OFFICIAL, PUBLIC.

2. *See* HIDDEN, SECRETIVE, OWN, SECLUDED, CONFIDENTIAL.

privilege, *n.* right, franchise (*legal*); *spec.* liberty, indulgence, charter, regality, regale, soke, license, monopoly, refusal, frank, prevention; *see* OPTION.

Antonyms: see OBLIGATION, DUTY.

prize, *n.* **1.** reward, trophy, premium, meed (*B or rhetorical*), booty (*C*), palm (*fig. or spec.*) plum (*C*); *spec.* blue ribbon, sweepstakes, plate, medal, cup.

2. *See* ADVANTAGE, STAKE.

probable, *a.* **1.** presumable, presumptive, likely, like (*R; C or dial.*), verisimilar (*B*), verisimilous (*R*), on the cards (*used predicatively; C, cant*).

Antonyms: see IMPROBABLE, IMPOSSIBLE.

2. *See* CREDIBLE.

probably, *adv.* belike (*A, R*), likely; *see* PERHAPS.

probationary, *a.* probative (*R*).

proboscis, *n. Spec.* trunk, snout, neb, tongue, haustellum, antlia, promuscis.

procedure, *n.* **1.** proceeding, course; *spec.* practice, way, conduct, policy, form; *see* CUSTOM.

2. *See* ACTION, METHOD.

proceed, *v. i.* **1.** *See* GO, ARISE, CONTINUE, ADVANCE, EMANATE, RESULT.

2. act. do, go (*usually with "on"*); *spec.* hugger-mugger; *see* PROGRESS.

proceeds, *n. pl.* outcome (*R*), avails (*pl.*), (*pl.*), profit, result, issue (*obs., exc. legal*), produce (*R*), income.

process, *n.* outgrowth, projection, protuberance, prominence, appendage; *spec.* apophysis, condyle, condyloma, caruncle, comb, barb, barbel, barbule, wattle.

procession, *n.* **1.** *See* GOING, MARCH.

2. *Referring to the body of people in procession:* parade, cavalcade (*chiefly spec.*), train; *spec.* triumph, ovation, funeral, skimmington.

proclaim, *v. t.* **1.** *Referring to official announcement by outcry:* announce (*contex.*), cry, call (*R*); *spec.* herald.

2. *Referring to loudly making known:* publish, cry, call, sing (*primarily spec.*), enounce; *spec.* preach, knell; *see* TRUMPET.

3. *See* SHOW, STATE.

proclamatory, *a.* annunciatory.

produce, *n.* **1.** *See* PRODUCT, YIELD.

2. *Referring to the yield from plants:* product,

primitive, *a.: original, old, old-fashioned, crude.*
principle: *assumption, basis, cause, constituent, element, force, rule, truth.*
prior, *a.: preceding, previous, former, superior.*
prize, *v. t.: esteem, value, lever.*
probation: *trial.*
probe, *v. t.: examine.*
probity: *uprightness.*
problem: *question, proposition.*
process, *v. t.: preserve, prosecute.*
proclivity: *inclination.*
procreate: *generate, create.*
procurable: *obtainable.*
procure: *get, induce.*
prodigal, *a.: extravagant, generous, wasteful, abundant.*
prodigal, *n.: spendthrift, waster.*
prodigy: *sign, wonder, occurrence.*
produce, *v. t.: generate, create, cause, show, form, furnish, make, grow, bear, compose, extend, develop.*

yield, crop (*chiefly spec.*); *spec.* truck, gardenage (*R*), emblements (*pl.*), grain, vegetable, harvest; *see* FRUIT.

producer, *n.* **1.** *See* INTRODUCER, GENERATOR, CREATOR, CAUSE, AUTHOR, *etc.*

2. *Referring to one who grows plants for their yield:* grower, raiser, culturist (*chiefly spec.*); *spec.* agriculturist, horticulturist.

product, *n.* production, result, produce (*R*), yield; *spec.* by-product, staple, outcome, origination, output, turnout, fruit, make, work, issue (*R*), birth (*fig.*), development, harvest, manufacture; *see* GROWTH, OFFSPRING.

productive, *a.* rich, fruitful, prolific, plenteous (*B*); *spec.* fructuous (*R*), proliferous, fertile, generative, fat, luxuriant, elaborative, originative, quick, pregnant; *see* CREATIVE, CAUSATIVE, ORIGINATIVE, FRUITFUL.

Antonyms: see BARREN.

profession, *n.* **1.** *See* ACKNOWLEDGMENT, AFFECTATION, PRETENSION, BELIEF, BUSINESS, DECLARATION.

2. *Referring to those in a profession:* calling (*R*), faculty (*A or spec.*); *spec.* law, ministry.

Antonyms: see LAIETY.

professional, *a.* *Spec.* trade, business;—*no good synonyms.*

Antonyms: see AMATEURISH, LAY.

profit, *n.* **1.** *See* BENEFIT.

2. gain, clearance (*R*), lucre, fruit; *spec.* perquisite, velvet (*S*), graft; *see* PAY.

Antonyms: see LOSS.

profitable, *a.* **1.** *See* ADVANTAGEOUS.

2. gainful, lucrative, remunerative, remuneratory, paying, emolumentary (*R*), fat (*C or S*), rewardful (*R*).

Antonyms: see UNPROFITABLE.

profitless, *a.* gainless, useless; *see* UNPROFITABLE.

program, *n.* **1.** playbill. *See* NOTICE.

2. plan, prospectus, syllabus, agenda. (*These senses suggest an orderly arrangement of procedure to be followed.*)

progress, *n.* **1.** *See* ADVANCE.

2. *Referring to a going on, taking place, happening, etc.:* advance, process, passage, movement, move, course, procession, progression; *spec.* passage, boom; *see* DEVELOPMENT, REFORM.

Antonyms: see RECESSION, DECLINE.

progress, *v. i.* **1.** *See* ADVANCE, REFORM.

2. advance, proceed, move, go, grow, wag (*C*), work, speed; *spec.* boom; *see* DEVELOP.

Antonyms: see RECEDE, DECLINE.

progressive, *a.* forward, advanced; *spec.* forward-looking.

Antonyms: see BACKWARD.

prohibition, *a.* dry (*C*).

prohibition, *n.* interdiction (*by order or edict*), proscription (*implies written* prohibition), prevention, stoppage, inhibition (*implying inner check or restraint, as contrasted with the outer check of* prohibition).

project, *v. t.* **1.** *See* PLAN, DEVISE.

2. propel (*contex.*); *spec.* deliver, cast, eject, hurl, hurtle, bolt, shoot, fire, serve, bowl; *see* THROW.

3. *Referring to a shadow, light, figure, etc.:* throw, cast.

project, *v. i.* extend; *spec.* jut, shoot, outshoot (*R*), poke, butt, jutty (*A*), peak (*R*), knob (*R*); *see* PROTRUDE, PROTUBERATE.

projecting, *a.* projective; *spec.* protrusive, protrudent (*R*), prominent, salient, exsurgent (*R*), extant (*A*), bold, outstanding (*R*), astrut (*A*), emersed, underhung, exserted, excurrent, protruding, protuberant.

Antonyms: see HOLLOW.

projection, *n.* **1.** *See* PLANNING.

2. propulsion; *spec.* throw, cast, hurl, throwing, ejection, shooting, firing, *etc.*, delivery, service; *see* THROW.

3. projectile, project (*R*); *see* MISSILE.

4. *Referring to the fact or condition of projecting: spec.* relief (*chiefly an art term*), relievo, jut (*R*), eminence, salience, protuberance, protrusion.

5. *Referring to a thing or part that projects:* extension; *spec.* protrusion, protuberance, prominence *or* (*R*) prominency, spur, elevation, eminence, salience, rising, outshoot, outshot (*R*), snag, jag, elbow, point, projecture (*R*), finger, shoulder, jut (*R*), jutty, outjet (*R*), outjut (*R*), rag, headland, outgrowth, process.

Antonyms: see HOLE, CAVITY, HOLLOW, RECESS.

6. *Referring to various projecting forms in carpentry, machinery, etc.:* tenon, cog, coak, tusk, tooth, shoulder, shouldering, bolster, fang, ear, speer, burr, pallet, kern, kick, cam, knuckle.

prolix, *a.* lengthy, long-winded (*often contemptuous*), verbose, wordy; *spec.* diffuse, exuberant.

Antonyms: see BRIEF, CONCISE.

prolixity, *n.* lengthiness, verbosity, wordiness; *spec.* diffuseness.

Antonyms: see BREVITY, CONCISENESS.

prolong, *v. t.* **1.** *See* EXTEND.

2. *Referring to sounds:* extend, lengthen, hold carry, continue, protract.

prolongation, *n.* **1.** *See* EXTENSION, ADDITION

2. *Referring to sounds:* lengthening, holding

profane, *a.: impious, unhallowed, vulgar.*
profane, *v. t.: desecrate, violate.*
profess: *state, avow, affect, pretend.*
proficient, *a.: skillful, accomplished.*
proficient, *n.: expert.*
profit, *v. t.: benefit.*
profligate, *a.: dissipated, extravagant, abundant.*
profound, *a.: deep, abstruse, learned, subtle, intense, dense, low.*
profound, *n.: deep.*
profusion: *extravagance, abundance expenditure.*
progenitor: *ancestor.*
progeny: *offspring.*
prognostication: *prediction, fore knowledge, sign.*
progression: *advance, progress.*
prohibit: *forbid, prevent.*
project, *n.: plan, enterprise, device.*
proletarian: *plebeian.*
proletariat: *people.*
prolific: *fruitful.*

prolongment (*R*), continuation, continuance; *spec.* hang, cipher.

prominent, *a.* **1.** *See* PROJECTING, NOTABLE, FAMOUS, CONSPICUOUS.

2. prognathous (*spec. of the jaw*).

promise, *n.* **1.** agreement, engagement, word; *spec.* pledge, undertaking, affiance, sacrament, preëngagement, vow, oath, parole, plight (*A*), pollicitation, subscription; *see* CONTRACT, BETROTHAL.

2. *See* EARNEST, AUSPICIOUSNESS.

promise, *v. t.* agree, engage, undertake; *spec.* plight (*B or rhetorical*), preëngage, vow, swear, pass, subscribe; *see* CONTRACT, BETROTH.

promising, *a.* **1.** *See* AUSPICIOUS.

2. *Referring to a person or thing that bids fair to turn out well:* likely; *spec.* flattering.

Antonyms: see UNPROMISING.

prompter, *n.* reminder.

pronounce, *v. t.* **1.** *See* UTTER, STATE.

2. *Referring to utterance of words:* utter, speak, say, articulate, frame, enunciate, enounce (*R*), form; *spec.* clip, garble, burr.

pronunciation, *n.* utterance, enunciation, saying, *etc.*; *spec.* orthoepy.

Antonyms: see MISPRONUNCIATION.

proof, *n.* **1.** *See* EVIDENCE, TRIAL, STANDARD.

2. probation (*R*), verification, averment (*R*), demonstration, apodeixis (*B or tech.*), substantiation, show.

Antonyms: see DISPROOF.

3. print (*contex.*); *spec.* pull, slip, revise.

prop, *v. t.* support; *spec.* block, shore, underpin, underset.

prop, *n.* support; *spec.* block, shore, underpin.

propel, *v. t.* force, drive, impel, impulse (*R*), put, send; *spec.* push, dash, thrust, shoot, screw, paddle, row, pole, sail, stream, cycle, wheel; *see* PROJECT, PUSH, THRUST.

proper, *a.* **1.** *See* OWN, INHERENT, INDIVIDUAL, ACCURATE, APPROPRIATE, FASTIDIOUS, GOOD-LOOKING. Proper *implies propriety or suitability as contrasted to the more restricted senses in the following group.*

2. *Referring to conformity to social convention:* accurate, correct, becoming, respectable, decent, decorous (*implying outward conformity*); *spec.* demure (*implying affected or constrained decorum or gravity*), chaste, prudish, presentable, elegant (*implying refinement and polish of manners*), delicate (*implying a nice sense or appreciation of what is becoming and modest*), right, rightful (*R*), correct (*C*), due; *see* TIMELY.

Antonyms: see IMPROPER, UNTIMELY.

property, *n.* **1.** *See* OWNERSHIP.

2. possession *or* (*generic pl.*) possessions, belonging *or* (*generic pl.*) belongings; *spec.* appurtenance, appurtenant (*R*), havings (*pl.*), estate, assets, holding (*chiefly in pl.*), stocks (*pl.*), personalty, chattels, goods, realty, land, shares.

prophet, *n.* **1.** *As being an inspired person:* oracle; *spec.* druid, Merlin, sibyl.

2. *See* PREDICTOR.

prophetess, *n.* **1.** *As being an inspired person:* Voluspa (*erroneous*), sibyl, Cassandra.

2. *See* PREDICTOR.

prophetic, *a.* **1.** oracular, oraculous (*R*), fatidical (*B*), fatidic (*R*), fatiloquent (*R*), vatic (*B*); *spec.* Dodonean, sibylline, druidic *or* druidical.

Antonyms: see BLIND.

2. *See* PREDICTIVE.

prophylactic, *a.* preventive, synteretic (*R*).

proportion, *n.* **1.** *See* PART, RATIO, DIMENSION, SHARE, EXTENT.

2. commensuration, commensurateness; *spec.* eurythmy, match.

Antonyms: see DISPROPORTION.

3. scale, rate, ratio, quota.

proportionate, *a.* proportional, proportionable, commensurate, according (*predicative*).

Antonyms: see DISPROPORTIONATE.

proposal, *n.* statement, proposition (*often with a commercial implication*), offer, advancement, submission, overture, motion; *spec.* nomination (*see* NOMINATE).

propose, *v. t.* **1.** state (*contex.*), propound, advance, present, move, offer, overture (*R*), submit, pose (*R*), propone (*obs. or Scot.*), put; *see* NOMINATE, MENTION.

2. *See* INTEND.

proposition, statement (*contex.*); *spec.* axiom, postulate, problem, thesis.

propriety, *n.* **1.** *Spec.* accuracy, suitability, fastidiousness.

2. becomingness, respectability, decency, decorousness, decorum; *spec.* demureness, chasteness, elegance, delicacy, seemliness, rightness, prudery, correctness; *see* TIMELINESS.

Antonyms: untimeliness (*cf.* UNTIMELY).

propulsion, *n.* pulsion (*R*), propelment (*R*); *spec.* drift, push, dash, impulse (*R*), putting, sending; *see* PROJECTION, PUSH.

prosaic, *a.* **1.** prosy.

Antonyms: see FLORID.

2. *See* COMMONPLACE, MATTER-OF-FACT, DULL, UNIMAGINATIVE.

prosaist, *n.* proseman (*R*), proser.

Antonyms: see POET, VERSIFIER.

prose, *v. t. & i.* prosify (*chiefly humorous*), beprose (*intensive*); *spec.* depoeticize (*R*), depoetize (*R*).

Antonyms: see POETICIZE, VERSIFY.

prosecute, *v. t.* **1.** *See* PURSUE, EXERCISE.

2. *In the sense of "to follow up or attempt to en-*

---

promenade: *walk, dance.*
promiscuous, *a.: mixed, confused.*
promotion: *advancement, aid.*
prompt, *a.: ready, immediate.*
prompt, *v. t.: incite, remind, suggest.*
prone: *prostrate, inclined, disposed.*
pronounced: *decided, great, broad.*
pronouncement: *utterance, statement.*
propaganda: *movement.*
propensity: *inclination.*
prophecy, *n.: inspiration, prediction.*
propinquity: *nearness, relation.*
proposition: *statement, proposal.*
proscribe: *outlaw, forbid.*
prose: *composition, commonplace, matter-of-fact.*
proselyte: *convert.*
prosiness: *dullness; for commonplaceness, cf.* COMMONPLACE.

force": push, drive, urge, pursue; *spec.* exchequer (*Eng.; cant*), law (*R*), libel, arraign.
3. sue, implead (*A or hist.*), process (*chiefly Scot.*).
prospect, *n.* **1.** *See* VIEW, EXPLORATION, FORESIGHT.
2. *Referring to what is to come or happen:* outlook, lookout (*R*), perspective; *spec.* expectations (*pl.*).
prosper, *v. i.* flourish, thrive, increase (*A*), cotton (*obs.*); *spec.* succeed, boom, flower (*fig.*), bloom (*fig.*).
prosperity, *n.* prosperation (*R*), prosperousness, thriving, flourishing, well-being, fortune, flourish (*R exc. with "in"*), felicity (*R*); *spec.* success, flower (*fig.*), bloom (*fig.*), boom.
Antonyms: see CALAMITY.
prosperous, *a.* **1.** flourishing, thrifty, thriving, golden, palmy, happy, swimming; *spec.* successful, booming; *see* FORTUNATE, RICH.
Antonyms: see UNSUCCESSFUL, UNFORTUNATE, POOR.
2. *See* AUSPICIOUS.
prostrate, *a.* **1.** flat, prone (*properly spec.*), flatling (*obs.*); *spec.* supine, groveling, cumbent, procumbent, decumbent, couchant, recumbent.
Antonyms: see VERTICAL.
2. *See* HELPLESS, DEPRESSED.
protect, *v. t. Spec.* defend, fend (*A or B for "defend"*), guard, preserve, champion, save, shield, buckler, shelter, screen, hedge, safeguard, secure, bulwark, bestride (*A*), patronize (*R*), fence (*A*), shadow, flank, bield (*Scot.*), sheathe, dike, cushion, shoe, arm, bush, *etc.: see* GUARD, HIDE, CHERISH, COVER.
Antonyms: see ATTACK, ASSAIL, EXPOSE, HARASS, PLUNDER, ILL-TREAT, RUIN, DESTROY.
protection, *n.* **1.** *Referring to the act; spec.* defense, saving, guard, fence (*A or B*), safeguard, championship, security, ward, care, patronage, coverture, manus; *see* CARE, GUARD.
Antonyms: see ATTACK, EXPOSURE, PLUNDER; *also cf.* ASSAIL, *etc.*
2. *The thing that protects: spec.* defense, guard, fence, screen, shelter, shield, sheath, shadow, safeguard, preservative, wall, hedge (*fig.*), bulwark, cover, covert, rock (*fig.*), cage, bracer, buckler, resist.
protective, *a.* protecting; *spec.* defensive, tutelar, guarding, shielding, *etc.*
protector, *n.* protecter, protection, preserver; *spec.* defense, warder, ward, guard, shelter, shielder, shield, buckler, guardant (*R*), keeper, pastor, safeguard, palladium, champion, promachos (*Greek antiq.*), ghazi (*Mohammedan*), bully, patron.
protest, *v. i.* object (*contex.*), remonstrate, demur, expostulate, reclaim (*R*), obtest (*R*), kick (*C*).
protrude, *v. t. & i.* extend (*contex.*), project, exsert (*R*), protend (*R*); *spec.* shoot, poke, peep, loll, pout, evaginate.
protrusile, *a.* extensible (*contex.*), protrusible, exsertile (*R*), emissile (*R*); *spec.* evaginable.
Antonyms: see RETRACTILE; *also see* FIXED.
protuberance, *n.* projection (*contex.*), protuberancy; *spec.* convexity, roundness, bulge, bulging, swell, swelling, whelk, weal, bilge, bunch, head, lump, hump, hunch, knot, node, gnarl, nodosity, hummock, boss, nipple, embossment, bosset, gibbosity (*B or tech.*), belly, bump, tuberosity, tubercle, bull's-eye, bud, buttress, capitulum, capitellum, torus, mamilla, papilla, inion, rose; *see* PROCESS.
Antonyms: see CAVITY, HOLLOW.
protuberant, *a.* **1.** *Referring to something projecting from what surrounds it:* projecting (*contex.*); *spec.* convex, bulging, swelling, extuberant (*R*), hummocky, lumpy, knotty, nodose, bossy, goggle, rounded.
Antonyms: see HOLLOW, HOLLOWED.
2. *Referring to what has protuberances upon it or a protuberating part: spec.* gibbous, torous, swelling, bulgy, bumpy, lumpy.
protuberate, *v. i.* project (*contex.*), rise; *spec.* bulge, swell, bunch, round, hump.
proud, *a.* **1.** *As implying an attitude of superiority to, and contempt for, another or others:* arrogant, haughty, haught (*A*), supercilious, vain, cavalier, uppish (*C*), high-minded (*A*) orgulous *or* orgillous (*A*), prideful (*chiefly Scot.*), exalted; *spec.* proudish; *see* HAUGHTY.
Antonyms: see HUMBLE.
2. *See* PLEASED, GRAND.
prove, *v. t.* **1.** show, demonstrate (*chiefly spec.*), establish (*make positive*), verify (prove *by comparative test or examination*), sustain (*support*), substantiate (*support by proof*); *spec.* speak, document (prove *by adducing written verification*), instruct (*Scots law*), aver (*obs., exc. spec.*), probate.
Antonyms: see CONFUTE, DISPROVE.
2. *See* TRY, EXPERIENCE.
provide, *v. i.* **1.** *See* PREPARE, PLAN, STIPULATE.
2. purvey, cater.
provision, *v. t.* furnish, (*contex.*), victual; *spec.* ration, fodder, provender, forage, revictual.
provisional, *a.* **1.** temporary, provisionary (*R*); tentative, makeshift.
Antonyms: see PERMANENT.
2. *See* CONDITIONAL.
prowl, *v. i.* wander, raven, mouse.
prudence, *n.* discretion, prudentiality, thoughtfulness, judiciousness, circumspection, care,

---

prostitute, *n.: harlot.*
prostitute, *v. t.: degrade.*
prostitution: *harlotry, degradation.*
prosy: *prosaic, matter-of-fact, commonplace, dull.*
protean: *multiform.*
protestation: *statement, protest.*
prototype: *original.*
protract: *extend.*
provenance: *source.*
provenience: *source.*
proverb: *saying, byword, talk, drama.*
provide, *v. t.: prepare, furnish.*
province: *division, domain, jurisdiction, sphere, department, function.*
provincial: *local, narrow.*
provision: *furnishing, preparation, condition, equipment, food, supply, action.*
proviso: *clause, condition.*
provocation: *incitement, excitation, incentive, irritation.*
provoke: *incite, excite, anger, irritate.*
provoking: *irritating.*

considerateness (*obs.*), counsel (*A*); *see* EXPEDIENCY.
Antonyms: carelessness (*cf.* CARELESS).

prudent, *a.* discreet, prudential, thoughtful, careful, circumspect, chary, judicious, considerate (*obs.*), worldly-wise; *see* TIME-SERVING.
Antonyms: see CARELESS.

public, *a.* **1.** popular (*R and chiefly or only in legal use*), general, common; *spec.* political, civil, national, state, provincial, nationwide, statewide.
Antonyms: see PRIVATE.
2. *Open to the public:* patent (*R*), exoteric (*R*).
3. *See* UNCONCEALED.

publication, *n.* **1.** announcement, advertizement (*chiefly spec.*), disclosure, divulgation (*B*), publishment (*R*); *spec.* celebration (*B*), report, proclamation, promulgation, ventilation, pervulgation (*R*), emblazonment.
2. *Referring to a book:* issue, issuance (*R*), evulgation (*R*).
3. *Referring to the thing that is published: spec.* review, bulletin, gazette, magazine; *see* PERIODICAL.

publicity, *n.* publicness (*R*); *spec.* daylight, limelight (*C*), spotlight (*C*).
Antonyms: see PRIVACY.

publish, *v. t.* **1.** announce, advertize (*chiefly spec.*), disclose, divulgate (*B*); *spec.* bruit, celebrate (*B*), report, proclaim, promulgate, promulge (*A*), ventilate, blow, emblazon, pervulgate (*R*) trumpet, preconize (*R*), bulletin, post, placard.
2. *Referring to a book:* issue, evulgate (*R*).

pucker, *v. t. & i.* wrinkle, contract, corrugate (*chiefly spec.*), gather, pinch, shrivel; *spec.* knit, purse, bulge, cockle, gauge, ruckle (*R*), crape, shirr.
Antonyms: see SMOOTH.

pucker, *n.* wrinkle, gathering, gather, corrugation (*chiefly spec.*); *spec.* cockle, shirr, crease.

puckered, *a.* wrinkled, puckery; *spec.* pursy, knit, cockly.

pugnacious, *a.* combative; *spec.* militant, quarrelsome, bellicose, contentious.
Antonyms: see PEACEABLE.

pug nose, *n.* snub, snub nose, flat nose.

pug-nosed, *a.* snub, snub-nosed, puggy, camois *or* camus (*obs.*).
Antonyms: see AQUILINE.

pull, *v. t.* **1.** *In this sense implying an actual separation or motion produced by means of applied force; that is, a result equivalent to that denoted by using words in def.* **2** *with an added adverb, such as "away," "off," "out," etc.:* separate (*contex.*), detach, pluck, wrest, rive; *spec.* epilate; *see* PICK.
2. *In this sense implying only an applied force merely tending to move something toward the source or place from which the force acts (as distinguished from "push") and not necessarily implying any resulting separation or motion, that idea being carried by added adverbs, as "away," "off," "out," etc.: spec.* drag, tug, tear, wrench, haul, pluck, tweak, twang, twitch, lug, strain, heave; *see* DRAW, JERK.
Antonyms: see PUSH.
3. *See* ATTRACT, DRINK, TRANSPORT.

pull, *n.* **1.** *Spec.* drag, draw, tug, tear, wrench, haul, pluck, twitch, tweak, twang, strain, lug (*C*), draft (*obs. or dial.*); *see* JERK.
Antonyms: see PUSH.
2. *See* DRINK, ROW (*pron.* rō), ATTRACTION, INFLUENCE.

pulp, *n.* **1.** *See* FLESH.
2. mash, mush (*C*), pap, paste; *spec.* mucilage, pomace.

pulp, *v. t.* **1.** mash, pulpify (*R*); *spec.* masticate.
2. dispulp (*R*).

pulpit, *n.* **1.** platform (*contex.*), rostrum (*B; contex.*), tub (*S, Eng.*).
2. *See* MINISTRY.

pulpy, *a.* pultaceous (*R*), pulpous, pasty, pappy (*R*), mushy.
Antonyms: see WOODY.

pulsate, *v. i.* **1.** beat, throb; *spec.* thump, pant, quiver, palpitate, pit-a-pat, pit-pat, shudder, tremble.
2. *See* VIBRATE.

pulsation, *n.* beating, beat, throb, stroke, shudder, tremble, palpitation, *etc.; spec.* pant, quiver, pit-a-pat, pit-pat, ictus, rhythm, accent.

pulverize, *v. t.* powder; *spec.* triturate, levigate, grind, pound, crumble, stamp, flour (*R*), meal.

pump, *n. Referring to the act of eliciting information from a person:* tap (*C*).

pun, *n.* paronomasia (*B*), conceit, equivoque (*B*), clinch (*R*), quibble, quillet.

punctuate, *v. t.* **1.** point; *spec.* interpunctuate *or* interpoint.
2. *See* DOT, EMPHASIZE.

pungency, *n.* **1.** *See* ACRIMONY.
2. irritatingness (*R*), keenness, penetrativeness (*R*), penetration, poignancy (*R*), sharpness; *spec.* heat, pepperiness, piquancy, stimulation; *see* ACRIDITY.

pungent, *a.* **1.** *See* PAINFUL, AFFECTING, ACRIMONIOUS.
2. irritating, keen, penetrative, penetrating, poignant (*R*), sharp; *spec.* hot, peppery, piquant, stimulating; *see* ACRID.
Antonyms: see BLAND.

punish, *v. t.* Punish *implies mere infliction of penalty for violation of law, or wrongdoing.* correct (*euphemistic*), lesson (*B*), reward (*B or ironical*), pay; *spec.* chastise (*especially to* punish *physically*), chasten (*spiritual punishment, especially moral suffering leading to reformation*), discipline, castigate, whip, dress

---

prudery: *propriety, preciousness.*
prudish: *prim.*
prune: *trim, abbreviate.*
pry, *v. i.: examine.*
prying, *a.: curious.*
psychic, psychical: *mental.*
public, *n.: people.*
puff, *n.: blow, breath, cloud, praise, gesture, wind.*
puffy: *gusty, swollen, inflated, fat, full, muffled, short-winded.*
punch, *v.: strike, poke.*
punctilious: *formal, scrupulous.*
puncture, *v. t.: pierce.*
puncture, *n.: opening.*

(*chiefly with "down"*), trim, smite, haze, decimate, centesimate (*R*), ferule, tar, impale, rusticate, masthead, hang, penance, pepper, draw, Tartarize, torture, proctorize, penalize, fine, mulct, imprison.

Antonyms: see ABSOLVE, REWARD, EXCUSE.

punishment, *n.* **1.** correction (*euphemistic*), reward (*B or ironical*), animadversion (*A*), punition (*R*), payment, pay; *spec.* lesson, toco (*S, Eng.*), chastening, chastisement, discipline, castigation, whipping, retribution, rod, penance, penitence (*R*), impalement, cyphonism, censure, dispensation, vengeance, fine, imprisonment.

Antonyms: see ABSOLUTION, REWARD, EXCUSE.

2. *Referring to what is inflicted in order to punish: see* PENALTY.

punitive, *a.* corrective (*euphemistic*), punitory, disciplinary, castigatory, castigative (*R*), retributive, vindictive (*R*), vindicatory (*R*).

puppet, *n.* **1.** lay figure, poppet (*obs.*), marionette (*operated by strings or wires, as contrasted to* puppet, *operated by hand; but the two terms are loosely used as close synonyms*), fantoccini (*pl.; Italian*), neuropast (*tech. or R*); *spec.* Polichinelle (*French*), Punchinello (*Italian*), Punch, Judy.

2. tool, yes-man (*C, U. S.*), jackstraw (*A or obs.*), Jack-a-Lent subordinate, vassal (*A*); *spec.* creature.

purblind, *a.* dim-sighted, starblind, mole-eyed (*R*), cecutient (*R*).

Antonyms: see CLEAR-SIGHTED.

pure, *a.* **1.** *In a physical sense:* simple, unmixed, unalloyed, unadulterated, clear, absolute, fine, neat (*spec.*), clean (*obs., exc. spec.*); *spec.* unstained, refined, unsullied, uncorrupted, uncontaminated, *etc.*

Antonyms: see SOILED.

2. *See* SMOOTH (*as in sound*), FULL-BLOODED (*in reference to lineage*), ABSOLUTE (*in an intensive sense*), CORRECT.

3. *In reference to freedom from moral defilement:* innocent, guiltless, guileless, sincere, clean, chaste, white, stainless, candid (*A*), seraphic, immaculate, honest, virgin, incorrupt *or* uncorrupt, incontaminate (*R*) *or* incontaminated, untainted, undefiled, unblemished; *see* CHASTE.

Antonyms: see CORRUPT, LASCIVIOUS.

purificatory, *a.* **1.** cleansing, depurant (*med.*), depurative, purgative (*R*), purgatory (*R*), cathartic.

2. *In reference to morals:* cleansing, purgatorial (*R*), purgatorian (*R*); *spec.* lustratory, lustral, lustrative.

Antonyms: see CORRUPTIVE.

purify, *v. t.* **1.** cleanse; *spec.* purge, rarefy, refine, fine, clear, depurate, defecate, edulcorate, wash, expurgate (*R*), epurate (*R*), sublime, retort, rectify; *see* CLEAN.

Antonyms: see ADULTERATE, DIRTY, ALLOY, SOIL.

2. *In reference to moral or spiritual cleanness:* cleanse, purge, chasten, sublime (*fig.*), sublimate (*fig.*), refine, fine (*fig.*); *spec.* clarify, catharize (*R*), reconcile.

Antonyms: see CONTAMINATE, CORRUPT, SULLY.

purity, *n.* **1.** *In a physical sense:* clearness, simpleness, absoluteness, fineness, neatness (*R or spec.*), cleanness.

Antonyms: see DIRT.

2. *See* CORRECTNESS.

3. pureness, innocence, guiltlessness, guilelessness, sincerity, cleanness, whiteness, immaculateness, immaculacy, honesty, virginity, incorruptness, incorruptibility, chastity *or* chasteness (*esp. in sexual matters or in style*); *see* CHASTITY.

Antonyms: see CORRUPTION; *also cf.* LEWD, LICENTIOUS.

purple, *a.* **1.** purplish, purply, purpurate (*A*), purpurean (*R*), porphyrous (*R*), Tyrian (*B or cant*); *spec.* violaceous, hyacinthine, murrey (*A*).

2. *See* BLOODY, BRILLIANT, OUTRAGEOUS.

purple, *n. Spec.* purpur, murrey (*hist. or A*), mauve, puce, violet, lilac, hyacinth, cudbear, damson, gridelin, heliotrope, magenta, solferino, *etc.*

purposeless, *a.* idle, intentionless (*R*), aimless, endless, driftless, chance.

purse, *n.* bag, pocket (*R*), burse (*A*), pouch (*A or B*), sparron (*Scot.*); *spec.* gipser (*A*).

pursue, *v. t.* **1.** follow (*contex.*), hunt, chase; *spec.* course, halloo, chevy *or* chivy (*Eng.*), stalk.

2. prosecute, push, practice, drive, follow, cultivate.

3. *See* CONTINUE.

pursuit, *n.* **1.** following, hunting, hunt, chase; *spec.* chevy *or* chivy (*Eng.*), course.

2. *A seeking to attain:* pursuance, quest; *see* SEARCH.

3. prosecution, practice, cultivation, conduct, business.

4. *See* BUSINESS, FAD.

purulent, *a. Spec.* puslike, suppurative, mattery, festering, pussy (*C*), sanious.

pus, *n.* humor, matter, purulence; *spec.* empyema.

push, *v. t.* press, propel, thrust, shove.

Antonyms: see DRAW, PULL.

push, *v. t. & i.* **1.** *Spec.* poke, detrude (*R*), boost (*C, U. S.*), shuffle, hustle, jostle, jog,

---

pupil: *scholar.*
purchase, *n.: buying, buy, advantage, tackle.*
purge, *v. t.: clean, purify, remove, evacuate, acquit, expiate.*
purge, *n.: cathartic, diarrhea, cleaning.*
purport, *n.: meaning.*
purpose, *n.: object, intention.*
pursy: *short-winded, fat, puckered, rich.*
purview: *body, scope, view.*
push, *v. i.: advance.*

---

crowd, elbow, butt, nudge, shoulder, bunt, punt, pole, spoon.
Antonyms: see PULL.
2. propel (*contex.*); *see* THRUST, DRIVE, CONDUCT, ADVANCE, PROSECUTE, PURSUE, URGE.
push, *n.* **1.** pressure, press, propulsion; *spec.* thrust, shove, poke, trusion, detrusion (*R*), shuffle, jostle, jog, impulse, impulsion, boost, trustion (*R*), nudge, bunt, butt, cant.
Antonyms: see PULL.
2. propulsion (*contex.*); *see* THRUST, EFFORT, ENTERPRISE, AMBITION, ADVANCE.
push button, *n. Spec.* pressel.
pusher, *n.* hustler, rustler (*C, U. S.*), hummer (*S or C*), go-getter (*C, U. S.*), booster (*C, U. S.*).
put, *v. t.* **1.** place; *spec.* lay, set, thrust, cast, hustle, stick, clap, rest, repose, impose, throw, fling, collocate; *see* DEPOSIT.
2. *In a sense not implying the translocation of anything:* place, lay, rest, repose, cast, fix, plant, set.
3. *See* TRANSLATE, BASE, ATTRIBUTE, APPLY, PROPOSE, ADD, INVEST.
puzzle, *n.* **1.** *See* PERPLEXITY, QUESTION.
2. *Referring to a thing that puzzles: spec.* puzzlement (*R*), tangram, trifle, ring, rebus.
pygmy, *n.* atomy; *see* DWARF.
Antonyms: see GIANT.

Q

quack, *v. i.* cry (*contex.*), quackle.
quack, *n.* pretender (*contex.*), charlatan, mountebank, quacksalver (*obs.*), medicaster (*R*); *spec.* empiric.
quack, *a.* charlatan, circumforaneous (*R*), quacky (*R*), charlatanish, quackish; *spec.* empirical *or* empiric, mountebank.
quackery, *n.* imposture (*contex.*), charlatany, charlatanism, mountebankery (*R*), quackism; *spec.* empiricism.
quadrangle, *n.* quadrilateral, quad (*C*), tetragon; *spec.* trapezium, parallelogram, *etc.*
qualification, *n.* **1.** change, modification, limitation.
2. *See* QUALITY, ADAPTATION.
3. condition (*contex.*), fitness, capacity, eligibility, competency.
Antonyms: see DISQUALIFICATION.
4. *In reference to the act of qualifying:* capacitation, habilitation.
qualified, *a.* **1.** able, fit, adapted, competent, eligible.
2. *See* LIMITED.
Antonyms: see UNQUALIFIED.
qualify, *v. t.* **1.** *See* DESCRIBE, MODERATE, ABATE, CHANGE, RESTRICT.
2. fit, adapt, capacitate (*for office*), habilitate (*R*); *spec.* rehabilitate, recapacitate, entitle.
Antonyms: see DISQUALIFY.
quality, *n.* **1.** attribute, property, characteristic, character, feature, singularity, trait, peculiarity, affection (*obs.*), proprium (*logic*), mark, tinge (*fig.*), color (*fig.*), flavor (*fig.*), savor (*fig.*), object (*R*); *spec.* accident, spirit, virtue, timbre, qualification; *see* ODDITY.
2. *See* NATURE.
3. stamp, caliber; *see* CLASS, BRAND, RANK.
quantity, *n.* **1.** amount (quantity *implies a measurable more or less;* amount *and* sum *are absolute concepts*), quantum (*B or tech.*), sum, volume, measure, magnitude, measurement, matter, mass, block, length, feck (*Scot.*), body, bulk, contiguity (*B*), lot (*not C, exc. spec. often somewhat depreciatory*); *spec.* deal (*used usually with "good," "great," "vast," etc.*), batch (*chiefly depreciatory; C*), cast (*tech. or dial.*), size, abundance, driblet, pittance, grist (*C, U. S.*), bunch (*S*), pot, wad (*C*), lick (*C*), bundle, complement (*R*), parcel, quota, quotum, quotiety (*R*), journey (*Eng.*), floor, malt, baking, washing, *etc.*
2. *See* SIZE, DURATION.
quarrel, *n.* disagreement (*contex.*), row (*C*), disturbance, difference (*euphemistic*); *spec.* fight, contention, contest, controversy, wrangle, squabble, brawl, misunderstanding, discord, embroilment, imbroglio, feud, bicker, miff (*C*), tiff, huff, spat (*C*), discord (*obsolescent*), breeze (*C*), brangle (*R*), branglement (*obs.*), brabble *or* brabblement (*A*), brigue (*obs.*), collieshangie (*Scot.*), cample (*Eng. dial.*), pique (*obsolescent*).
Antonyms: see AGREEMENT.
quarrel, *v. i.* disagree (*contex.*), differ (*contex.; often humorous*), row (*C*); *spec.* contend, wrangle, squabble, brawl, strive, fight, tiff, huff, bicker, spat (*C*), fratch (*chiefly dial.*), fray (*A*), cangle (*Scot.*), cample (*Eng. dial.*).
Antonyms: see AGREE.
quarrelsome, *a.* combative; *spec.* contentious, dissentious, discordant, pugnacious, wranglesome (*R*), cat-and-dog (*C*), quarreling, cantankerous (*C*), currish, ugly (*U. S.; C*), unpeaceable (*R*), litigious (*spec.*).
Antonyms: see PEACEABLE.
quarters, *n. pl.* billet, cantonment.
quartz, *n.* silicon (*tech.*); *spec.* flint, crystal, amethyst, citrine, false topaz, chert, chalcedony, onyx, jasper, *etc.*
quay, *n. Spec.* levee (*southern and western*

---

pushing: *enterprising, ambitious.*
putrid: *decomposed.*
puzzle, *v. t.: perplex.*
puzzle, *v. i.: grope.*
pygmy: *dwarf, small.*

Q

quadruple, *a.: fourfold.*
quadruple, *v. t.: multiply.*
quaff, *n.: drink.*
quagmire: *marsh.*
quail, *v. i.: shrink.*
quail, *v. t.: intimidate.*
quaint: *odd.*
quake, *v. i.: tremble.*
qualm: *fit, nausea.*
qualmish: *nauseous, sick.*
quandary: *perplexity, predicament.*
quarantine: *isolate.*
quarry, *n.: prey, object.*
quarry, *n.: excavation.*
quarry, *v. t.: dig.*
quarter, *n.: fourth, place, territory, lodge, abode, mercy, direction.*
quarter, *v. t.: divide, lodge.*
quarter, *v. i.: lodge.*
quartet: *four.*
quash: *invalidate, abolish, suppress.*
queasy: *sensitive, scrupulous.*

U. S.), bund *or* bunder (*the far East*); *see* PIER.

queen, *n.* **1.** monarch (*contex.*), princess (*A*), begum (*Anglo-Indian*); *spec.* Kaiserin, czarina.
2. *See* PARAGON.

queen, *a.* royal, regal, reginal (*R*); *see* KINGLY.

question, *n.* **1.** *Referring to the action or act:* inquiry *or* enquiry, quest (*obs. or R*), inquest (*chiefly tech.*), interrogation; *spec.* quiz (*U. S.*), docimasy, cross-question, interpellation; *see* EXAMINATION.
2. *Referring to what is asked:* inquiry, query, interrogation, interrogatory, quære (*Latin*); *spec.* demand, puzzle, conundrum, poser, problem, carriwitchet (*obs. or R*), puzzler, tickler (*C*), vote (*parliamentary*); *see* RIDDLE.
Antonyms: see ANSWER.
3. *Referring to a subject that gives rise to, or is the subject of, question: spec.* problem, puzzle, conundrum, enigma, knot, sphinx, mystery.
Antonyms: see ANSWER.
4. *See* DOUBT, AMBIGUITY.

question, *v. t.* **1.** ask, inquire *or* enquire, interrogate, query; *spec.* catechize, quiz (*U. S.*), heckle, cross-hackle (*chiefly Eng.*), cross-question, cross-examine, cross-interrogate, interpellate, pump (*S or C*), interview, wonder (*v. i.*); *see* EXAMINE.
Antonyms: see ANSWER.
2. dispute, challenge; *spec.* recuse.
3. *See* DOUBT.

question, *v. i.* ask (*usually with "after," "about," or "of"*), inquire *or* enquire, wonder.

questionable, *a.* doubtful, uncertain, disputable, debatable, arguable, controvertible, controversial, equivocal, problematical, fishy (*S or C*); *spec.* suspicious; *see* AMBIGUOUS, OBSCURE.
Antonyms: see UNQUESTIONABLE.

quick, *a.* **1.** *See* LIVELY, READY, IRASCIBLE, NIMBLE, RAPID.
2. speedy (*as in "a speedy result"*).

quicken, *v. i.* **1.** *See* LIVE.
2. *Also v. t.* accelerate, brisk (*often used with "up"*); *spec.* raise.
Antonyms: see SLOW, RETARD.

quid, *n.* chew, cud (*vulgar*).

quiet, *a.* **1.** still, tranquil, placid, unmoved, quiescent.
Antonyms: see AGITATED.
2. *See* PEACEFUL, PEACEABLE, CALM, INACTIVE, MOTIONLESS, SILENT.

quill, *n.* **1.** *See* SPOOL.
2. *Referring to part of a feather:* shaft, barrel, tube, beam, quillet, rib.

quitter, *n.* craven, turncoat, welcher (*cant or C*), crawfish (*S*), yellow-belly (*C*).

quiver, *n.* shake (*contex.*), tremble, quaver, flutter, flicker; *spec.* twitter, shiver, twitch, twitteration (*R*), palpitation; *see* VIBRATION, PULSATION, SHUDDER.

quiver, *v. i.* shake (*contex.*), tremble, quaver, flutter, flicker; *spec.* twitter, shiver, twitch, palpitate, tirl (*chiefly Scot.*); *see* VIBRATE, PULSATE, SHUDDER.

quotation, *n.* **1.** citation, selection, excerpt, extract, excerption (*R*); *spec.* cutting, clipping, analect, tag, text, epigraph; *see* COMMONPLACE.
2. *See* MENTION, PRICE.

quote, *v. t.* excerpt, extract, cite, take.

R

rabbit, *n.* cony (*rare, exc. in statutes, among gamekeepers, poachers, cooks, etc.*), bunny (*a pet name*), bun (*C for "bunny"*); *spec.* doe, drummer, cottontail, jack *or* jackrabbit.

race, *n.* **1.** breed, group, line, brood, stock, strain, folk, stem, tribe, nation (*i. e., as of common stock*), people, family, kind (*referring esp. to animals*), phylum (*tech.*); *spec.* clan, tribe; *see* FAMILY, BREED.
2. *See* KIND.

race, *n.* **1.** *See* CURRENT, CHANNEL.
2. competition, career, course (*A*); *spec.* handicap, derby, sweepstakes, broose *or* brooze (*Scot.*), regatta.

racecourse, *n.* course (*contex.*), track, cursus (*tech.*); *spec.* hippodrome.

racecourse, *a.* dromic *or* dromical (*B*).

racer, *n.* competitor (*contex.*), entrant (*contex.*); *spec.* runner, walker.

racial, *a.* phyletic (*biol.*), gentile.

rack, *n.* frame; *spec.* crib, heck (*Scot. & dial. Eng.*), cratch (*obs. or Eng. dial.*), stand, flake, brake (*hist.*), torture.

radiation, *n.* **1.** *See* EMISSION, RAY.
2. *In an intransitive sense:* radiature (*R*), emanation, irradiation, irradiance *or* (*R*) irradiancy; *see* SHINING.
Antonyms: see ABSORPTION.

---

queer: *odd.*
quell: *suppress, overcome.*
quench: *extinguish, appease.*
quenchless: *inextinguishable.*
querulous: *complaining.*
query: *question.*
quest, *n.: pursuit, search, expedition.*
quest, *v. i.: search.*
question, *v. i.: doubt.*
quibble, *v. i.: prevaricate.*
quibble, *n.: prevarication.*
quick, *adv.: rapidly.*
quicken, *v. t.: animate, excite, enliven, kindle.*
quickly, *adv.: readily, rapidly.*
quiescent: *motionless.*
quiet, *n.: peace, calm, silence.*
quiet, *v. t.: calm, still, silence.*
quietness: *peace, calm, stillness, silence.*
quietude: *peace, silence.*
quip: *sarcasm, witticism, conceit, caprice, prevarication, gewgaw, oddity.*
quirk: *witticism, prevarication, conceit, caprice, flourish.*
quit, *a.: free.*
quit, *v. t.: behave, abandon, stop, leave, pay.*
quit, *v. i.: desert.*
quite, *adv.: completely, truly, exactly, very.*
quits, *a.: equal.*
quixotic: *visionary.*
quiz, *n.: jester, hoax.*
quiz, *v. i.: jest.*
quiz, *v. t.: question, examine.*
quizzical: *laughable, jesting.*
quota: *quantity, share.*
quoth: *said.*

R

race, *v. i.: hasten.*
race, *v. t.: run.*
rack, *v. t.: pain, distress, strain, oppress.*
rack, *v. i.: go.*
racket, *n.: din, carouse, frolic.*
rackety: *noisy, lively.*
racking: *wearing.*
racy: *palatable, lively, stimulating.*
radiant: *luminous, pleased.*
radiate, *v. i.: shine, diverge.*

(*A*) *archaic.* (*B*) *bookish, poetic, literary or learned.* (*C*) *colloquial.* (*Contex.*) *contextual.* (*R*) *rare.* (*S*) *slang.*
See pp. viii–ix.

radical, *a.* basic, fundamental; *spec.* extreme, ultra, red (*C*), wild, Bolshevik, *etc.* (Radical *and its specific synonyms are often loosely used to mark the user's disagreement with the thing so stigmatized*).

radio, *n.* wireless telegraphy, wireless (*chiefly British*).

raft, *n.* vessel, float, floatboat (*R*); *spec.* crib, kelek, catamaran, jangada, jangar.

rafter, *n.* beam; *spec.* principal, couple, chevron, spar.

rag, *n.* clout (*A or dial.*), tatter, raggery (rags *collectively*); *spec.* stitch, ribbands (*pl.*).

ragamuffin, *n.* ragged robin (*fig.*), tatterdemalion, ragabash (*Scot. & dial. Eng.*).
Antonyms: see DANDY.

rage, *v. i.* **1.** storm, rave; *spec.* rampage, ramp, boil, smoke, mad (*R*), debacchate (*obs. or R*); *see* BLUSTER.
2. *See* STORM, DESIRE, PAIN, BURN.

raging, *a.* **1.** raving, rampant; *see* FRANTIC.
Antonyms: see CALM.
2. *See* VIOLENT, BURNING.

ragpicker, ragman; *spec.* bunter.

rail, *n.* **1.** *See* BAR.
2. *Spec.* tram, point, gully (*Eng.*), racer;—*referring to a rail in a track.*

railing, *n.* barrier; *spec.* balustrade, banister.

railroad, *n.* railway, rail (*chiefly in "by rail"*), road; *spec.* tram (*Great Britain*), tramway (*these two of street* railways), switchback, telpher. *See* STREET CAR.

rain, *n.* **1.** meteor (*contex.; tech.*), fall (*contex.*), wet (*contex.*); *spec.* shower, cloudburst, pour, downpour, plash, flood, sprinkle, mizzle, rainfall, drizzle, flurry, drencher, mist, raindown, flash, drisk (*U. S.*), skit, dash, brash (*chiefly dial.*), clash (*Scot.*), drops (*pl.*).
2. *See* FLIGHT

rain, *v. i.* **1.** *Spec.* pour, sprinkle, shower, drizzle, mist, mizzle, spit (*C*).
2. *See* FALL.

rain, *v. t. See* LAVISH.

rainbow, *n.* bow (*R or contex.*), iris (*R*); *spec.* watergall, weathergall.

rainy, *a.* wet (*contex.*), pluvious (*R*), pluvial (*R*), pluviose (*R*), juicy (*S*); *spec.* showery, drizzly, mizzly, drizzling, dripping, drippy, droppy (*now dial.*).
Antonyms: see CLEAR, SUNNY.

raise, *v. t.* **1.** *See* ERECT, ADVANCE, REVIVE, EXCITE, CAUSE, BUILD, INTENSIFY, BREED, GROW, CREATE, ENNOBLE, ELEVATE, INCREASE, BRIGHTEN, GET, EXPECTORATE, EMBOSS, STRENGTHEN, UTTER, BEGIN.
2. elevate, lift, rise (*R*), hoist, heave (*A, exc. spec.*), upheave, boost, uplift (*an intensive*), upraise, uphold (*R*), rear, uprear (*R*), upbear (*R*), weigh (*chiefly spec.*), upwhirl (*R*), higher (*R or illiterate*), height (*A*); *spec.* mount, exalt (*R*), sublime (*rhetorical or R*), float, crane, crank, windlass, jack, brail, rope, cathead, cat, trip, pulley, levitate, turn.
Antonyms: see LOWER, FELL, SINK.
3. *Referring to notes or tones:* elevate; *spec.* sharp.
4. *As in "to raise a question, a discussion, etc.":* stir (*used with "up"*).
5. *See* ADVANCE.

raising, *n.* **1.** *See* ERECTION, REVIVAL, *etc.*
2. elevation, lift, heave (*R, exc. spec.*); *spec.* boost (*S*), uplift (*an intensive*), hoist, exaltation (*A or rhetorical*), sublimation (*R*), floating, *etc.*, levitation, increase (*a popular and incorrect synonym for* raise, *i.e.*, rise, *in salary*).

rake, *v. t.* **1.** *See* GATHER, CULTIVATE, SEARCH, SCRAPE.
2. *In military usage:* enfilade.

ram, *v. t.* **1.** beat; *spec.* tamp, pun, block.
2. *See* DRIVE, CROWD.

rampart, *n.* circumvallation, rampire (*A*), wall, vallum (*chiefly spec.*).

range, *n.* **1.** *See* ROW, GRAZING, AREA, PERIOD, EXTENT, SCOPE, BOUND, COMPASS, VIEW, MOUNTAIN.
2. distance, reach, throw, fire, cast, shot, gunshot, sweep; *see* SIGHT, HEARING.

rank, *n.* **1.** *See* ROW, CLASS.
2. *Referring chiefly to social position:* position, place, parking space (*local in parts of Great Britain and U. S.*), order, sphere, gradation, grade, estate, station, standing, condition, class, quality (*obsolescent*), status (*tech. or B*), caste, degree; *spec.* distinction; *see* PLEBEIANISM, NOBILITY.

rank, *a.* **1.** *See* LUXURIANT, OFFENSIVE, OUTRAGEOUS.
2. ill-smelling (*contex.*), high, strong; *spec.* rancid; *see* FOUL, FETID.
Antonyms: see FRAGRANT.

rape, *n.* ill treatment (*contex.*), violation, ravishment, stupration (*R*), devirgination (*R*), violence (*contex.*).

rape, *v. t.* ill-treat (*contex.*), violate, ravish, force, devirginate (*R*), deflower.

rapid, *a.* **1.** fast, swift, quick, fleet (*B*), brisk, smart, lively, speedy, raking (*R*), apace (*pred-*

---

radiogram: *message.*
radius: *line, circle.*
raffle: *lottery.*
rage: *derangement, anger, frenzy, violence, fad.*
raid, *n.: invasion, attack.*
raid, *v. t.: attack, plunder.*
rail, *v. i.: scold, revile.*
raillery: *pleasantry.*
raiment: *clothing.*
rake, *n.: libertine.*
rakish: *dissipated.*
rally, *v. t.: gather, recover, concentrate, rouse, stimulate, banter.*
rally, *v. i.: meet, recover, rouse.*
ramble, *v. i.: wander.*
ramble, *n.: wander, excursion.*
rambling, *a.: wandering, discursive.*
rampant: *boisterous, raging, violent, luxurious.*
ramshackle: *rickety.*
ranch: *house, farm.*
rancid: *ill-smelling, rank.*
rancor, rancour: *ill-will.*
range, *v. t.: align, arrange, traverse, classify.*
range, *v. i.: go, wander, stray, extend, change, vary, cruise.*
rank, *v. t.: arrange, class, place, precede.*
rankle, *v. i.: fester, pain.*
ransom, *n.: freeing, expiation, price.*
ransom, *v. t.: free, expiate, buy.*
rant, *v.: declaim.*
rant, *n.: bombast.*
rapacity: *greed.*
rapine: *plunder.*

icative); *spec.* spanking, electric (*fig.*), running, round, arrowy.

Antonyms: see SLOW, SLUGGISH.

2. *See* HASTY, FREQUENT, QUICK, ACTIVE.

rapid, *n.* shoot, sharp (*R*), rifle (*U. S.*), sault (*local American*); *spec.* dalles (*U. S. & Canada*).

rapidity, *n.* celerity, speed.

rapidly, *adv.* fast, quick, quickly, express, post (*A*), briskly, roundly, apace; *spec.* electrically (*fig.*).

rare, *a.* **1.** sparse, thin, infrequent.

Antonyms: see ABOUNDING.

2. *See* UNUSUAL, INFREQUENT.

rascal, *n.* rogue, scoundrel, blackguard, villain, scamp, miscreant (*R or B*), scalawag (*C*), scapegrace, rapscallion *or* rascallion (*R*), vagabond, reprobate, knave (*often opposed to "fool"*), imp, limb (*C*), sinner (*in trivial use*), varlet (*A*), shyster (*vulgar or cant; U. S.*), spalpeen (*Irish*), scab (*S*), skellum (*A or South Africa*), comrogue (*A*), canter (*A*), rautener (*obs.*).

rascality, *n.* scoundrelism, roguery, blackguardism, villainy, vagabondage, varletry (*A*), reprobacy, knavery.

rascally, *a.* scoundrelly, villainous, scampish, roguish, knavish, reprobate.

rash, *a.* hare-brained, reckless, unadvised (*contex.*), temerous (*R*), temerarious (*B*); *spec.* adventurous, hot-headed, hot-brained, madbrain, madcap; *see* HASTY, VENTURESOME, CARELESS.

Antonyms: see CAREFUL.

rashness, *n.* recklessness, temerariousness, *etc.*

Antonyms: see CARE.

rather, *adv.* **1.** more;—*not idiomatically synonymous.*

2. more, sooner, preferably.

rational, *a.* **1.** sane, natural, reasoning, reasonable (*R*).

Antonyms: see IRRATIONAL, DERANGED, UNREASONING.

2. *See* REASONABLE.

rationalist, *n. In religious matters:* neologist, neologian.

rattening, *n.* sabotage (*French*).

rattle, *v. i.* **1.** clatter, ruckle, chatter, clack, brattle (*chiefly Scot.*), bicker.

2. *See* CHATTER, DRIVE.

rattle, *n.* **1.** rattler, clack; *spec.* fiddle, crotalum *or* crotal.

2. clatter, ruckle, clack, chatter, brattle (*chiefly Scot.*), bicker.

3. *See* DIN, CHATTER.

rave, *v. i.* wander.

ravine, *n.* cleft (*contex.*), gap (*contex.*); *spec.* gorge, gulch (*a deep and narrow* ravine, *esp. the bed of a torrent*), gully (*one made by water, esp. in a hillside*), defile, gulf (*a vast* ravine *or gorge*), gill (*dial. Eng.*), clough (*now chiefly dial. Eng.*), cleuch *or* cleugh (*Scot.*), waterfall, linn (*chiefly Scot.*), kloof (*South Africa*), khor (*Arabian*), nullah (*Anglo-Indian*), khud (*East India*).

raw, *a.* **1.** *See* UNCOOKED.

2. *See* CRUDE, INEXPERIENCED, BLEAK.

3. *Referring to sores, wounds, etc.:* bare, excoriated, fresh, green.

ray, *n.* **1.** beam, radiation (*rare or tech.*), shaft, emanation (*chiefly of light*), irradiation (*R or rhetorical*), rayon (*R*); *spec.* raylet, sunbeam, moonbeam, streamer.

2. *See* LIGHT, TRACE, GLANCE.

reach, *v. t.* **1.** *See* EXTEND, TOUCH, GRASP, AFFECT.

2. make, arrive (*A*), attain, fetch, gain, win; *spec.* soar (*R*), recover (*R*), regain.

3. touch, make;—*referring to an amount, etc.*

reach, *v. i.* **1.** *See* EXTEND, CARRY.

2. come, arrive, accede (*R*), attain; *see* ARRIVE.

react, *v. i.* return; *spec.* recoil.

reaction, *n. Spec.* retroaction, revulsion, backlash, response (*a C sense of* reaction).

reactionary, *a.* revulsive; *spec.* conservative.

read, *v. t.* **1.** peruse (*B*); *spec.* decipher, revolve (*R*), see, interpret, thumb, overlook (*A*), line, deacon, call.

2. *See* PERCEIVE, INTRODUCE, LEARN, UTTER.

read, *v. i.* **1.** *See* STUDY, SEEM.

2. go, run;—*as in "the passage reads like this."*

reader, *n.* peruser; *spec.* elocutionist, lector, gospeler, lectress *or* lectrice (*R*), droner, liner.

readily, *adv.* ready (*now only in the comparative or superlative, exc. colloq. or dial.*), quickly. immediately, summarily, promptly, forwardly.

reading, *n.* **1.** *Referring to the action:* perusal (*formal or B*), lecture (*A*), lection (*obs.*); *spec.* perlection (*R*), lining, deaconing.

2. *Referring to that which is read: spec.* lection, lesson, periscope.

ready, *a.* **1.** *See* PREPARED, WILLING, AVAILABLE, FLUENT, QUICK-WITTED, ACCESSIBLE.

2. prompt, quick, forward (*implying prompt or even eager willingness*), facile (*implying ease in execution of work*), free, swift, clever, speedy, handy, adroit, apt, offhand, easy, nimble, alacritous, alert, habile (*B*); *spec.* punctual.

Antonyms: see SLOW, HESITATING.

3. suitable, ripe.

realism, *n.* **1.** *In philosophy, "naturalism," "realism," "conceptualism," and "nominalism" are related, but not synonymous.*

Antonyms: see IDEALISM.

2. *In literature and art:* naturalism; *spec.* Zolaism.

Antonyms: see IDEALISM, ROMANTICISM.

3. *See* ACTUALITY.

realistic, *a.* naturalistic, descendental (*chiefly*

rapt: *ecstatic, absorbed, abducted.*
rapture, *n.: ecstasy, frenzy, rhapsody.*
rapture, *v. t.: transport, frenzy.*
rate, *n.: value, price, charge, proportion, class, speed.*
rate, *v. t.: consider, value, class, tax.*
rate, *v. t.: scold.*
ration, *n.: allowance, food.*
ration, *v. t.: provision.*
raving, *a.: delirious, deranged, raging.*
ravish: *abduct, transport, rape, plunder, frenzy.*
ravishment: *ecstasy, rape.*
raw: *uncooked.*
raze: *demolish.*
real: *actual, genuine.*

spec.); *spec.* unideal, picturesque, positive, graphic *or* (*R*) graphical; *see* DESCENDENTAL.

realize, *v. t.* **1.** *See* ACTUALIZE, UNDERSTAND, EXPERIENCE, BRING.

2. *To conceive in the mind as being objectively actual:* externalize, objectify, objectize (*R*), entify (*R*).

3. *Of accomplishment of a goal, profit, etc.:* get, make, clear, net.

ream, *v. t.* enlarge, drift, broach.

rear, *v. t.* **1.** *See* BUILD, ERECT, RAISE, GROW, ESTABLISH.

2. *Referring to bringing up by care and nurture:* raise, breed, foster, educate, nurture; *spec.* cradle. *The usual term now is "to bring up."*

reason, *n.* **1.** ground, motive, wherefore (*C*), score, matter (*grounds for fear, hope, etc.*), occasion, foundation, cause, basis, root, argument, rationale (*tech.*); *spec.* gist, pretense, consideration; *see* EXCUSE.

2. *Referring to the faculty:* intelligence, rationality, sense, sanity; *see* INTELLIGENCE.

3. *See* GROUND, BASIS.

reason, *v. i.* think, ratiocinate (*R or tech.*), rationate (*R*), intelligize (*R*), intellectualize (*R*), logicize (*R*), paralogize (*R*); *spec.* syllogize, philosophize, argue.

reasonable, *a.* **1.** *In the sense of "agreeable to reason":* rational, logical, sensible, sane, just; *spec.* well-founded; *see* FAIR.

Antonyms: see IRRATIONAL, ABSURD, GROUNDLESS.

2. *See* MODERATE, RATIONAL.

reasoning, *n.* ratiocination, syllogization, discursion *or* discourse (*A*), logic (*tech.*); *spec.* fallacy, sophistry.

reassuring, *a. Spec.* comforting, assuring, encouraging, cheerful.

rebirth, *n.* renascence.

rebuild, *v. t.* build (*contex.*), reform (*contex.*), reconstruct, reërect, reëdify.

recall, *v. t.* **1.** revoke (*obs. or R*); *spec.* encore.

2. retract, swallow (*C*), withdraw, unsay, recant, renounce, abnegate, deny; *spec.* repudiate, reject (*R*), abjure.

3. *In the sense of "to bring back" (to some state or condition):* restore, revive, revoke (*R*), reclaim (*R*).

Antonyms: see DISMISS.

4. *In the sense of "to bring back to the mind or as an object of memory"):* retrace (*R*), commemorate (*R or spec.*), revive.

Antonyms: see FORGET.

5. *See* REVOKE, UNDO, REMEMBER, REVIVE, COMPOSE.

recall, *n.* **1.** revocation (*obs. or R*), recallment (*R*); *spec.* encore, lure (*of the thing that recalls; falconry*).

2. retraction, unsaying, recantation, withdrawal, withdrawment (*R*); *spec.* abjuration.

3. restoration, revocation (*R*), reclamation (*R*).

4. retracement (*R*), commemoration (*R*), revival.

5. *See* REVOCATION, REMEMBRANCE, REVIVAL.

recast, *v. t.* **1.** *Referring to metal:* cast (*contex.*), refound.

2. *See* REFASHION.

recede, *v. i.* **1.** *In the sense of "to go back":* retrocede (*R*), retrograde, regress, retrogress, retire, retreat, return; *spec.* ebb.

Antonyms: see ADVANCE, OVERHANG, PROGRESS.

2. *See* SLOPE, DEPART, WITHDRAW, DECLINE.

receive, *v. t.* **1.** accept, get, take, catch, have, acquire; *spec.* reset (*A*), embrace, greet.

Antonyms: see DECLINE, REJECT.

2. *See* ADMIT, BELIEVE, EXPERIENCE, ENDURE, UNDERSTAND, SHELTER, HOLD, HEAR, CONSIDER.

3. *In the sense of "to allow to come into one's presence or to give audience to":* see.

receiver, *n.* recipient, receptor (*R*); *spec.* donee (*tech.*), donatary (*esp. Scots law*), grantee, donatee (*R*), hopper, fence, resetter (*A*), treasurer, collector, teller, *etc.*

recency, *n.* recentness, lateness, newness, youth, lowness, neoterism (*tech. or B*); *see* MODERNITY, NEWNESS, FRESHNESS.

Antonyms: see ANTIQUITY.

recent, *a.* late, new, young, low (*of a date*), neoteric (*tech. or B*); *see* NEW, MODERN, FRESH.

Antonyms: see ANCIENT, OBSOLETE.

recently, *adv.* lately, latterly, newly, new (*chiefly used in combination*), late (*R or B*).

receptacle, *n.* **1.** receiver, repository, vessel, reservoir, container (*chiefly commercial*), continent (*A*); *spec.* encasement, custodial, bin, locker, drip, well, cist, saveall, sink, cibarium, trough, boot, tabernacle, safe; *see* BASIN, BOX, CASE, BAG, CASK, *etc.*

2. support (*contex.*), base; *spec.* torus, thalamus.

reception, *n.* **1.** acceptance, recipience *or* recipiency (*R*), receipt, getting, taking, *etc.*

2. *See* ADMISSION, BELIEF, SHELTER, HOLDING.

3. *Spec.* matinée (*French in form, but Anglicized in usage*), levee, soirée (*French*), at-home, drawing-room, durbar (*East-Indian*), ruelle.

reception room. *Spec.* parlatory.

receptive, *a.* recipient, suscipient (*R*); *spec.* hospitable, open-eyed; *see* SUSCEPTIBLE.

Antonyms: see UNRECEPTIVE.

receptivity, *n.* recipiency (*R*), receptiveness; *spec.* hospitableness, hospitality.

recess, *n.* **1.** *See* INTERVAL, RETREAT, RECESSION, INTERIOR, INLET.

---

realm: *domain, sphere.*
reap: *cut, harvest, gain.*
rear, *n.: back, posterior, tail.*
rear, *a.: hind.*
reared: *bred, trained.*
reassure: *encourage.*
rebate, *n.: deduction, diminution.*
rebel, *a.: insurgent, disobedient.*
rebel, *n.: insurgent.*
rebellious: *insurgent, disobedient.*
rebound, *v. i.: bound.*
rebuff, *n.: repulse, check.*
rebuke, *v. t.: reprove.*
recalcitrant: *disobedient.*
recension: *editing.*

---

2. hollow, cover, nook, alcove, niche, retreat; *spec.* pigeonhole, cubbyhole, oriel; *see* CLOSET.
Antonyms: see PROJECTION.
recess, *v. t.* **1.** *See* HOLLOW.
2. niche;—*to put in a recess.*
recession, *n.* withdrawal, retirement, retiral, regression, regress, retrocession, retreat, retrogression, depression, recess (*chiefly of motion, esp. of a body of water or of a heavenly body*), return; *spec.* retrogradation; *see* RETREAT.
Antonyms: see ADVANCE, PROGRESS.
recessive, *a.* regressive, retrogressive; *see* BACKWARD.
reciprocal, *a.* correspondent, corresponding, cross, correlative, complementary; *spec.* equivalent; *see* MUTUAL.
reciprocal, *n.* correlate; *spec.* return, equivalent, counterpart, *etc.*
reciprocate, *v. i.* **1.** correspond, correlate.
2. *Referring to motion:* alternate, gig (*chiefly U.S.*), shuttle, seesaw.
reciprocate, *v. t.* **1.** *See* INTERCHANGE, REQUITE, RETURN.
2. shuttle, seesaw (*R*).
reciprocation, *n.* **1.** *Referring to the relation:* correspondence, reciprocality, correlation, reciprocity; *spec.* mutuality.
2. *Referring to motion:* alternation, to-and-fro, seesaw, shuttle (*R*).
3. *See* EXCHANGE, RETURN.
reciprocity, *n.* correspondence.
recitation, *n.* **1.** repetition, rehearsal, recital, saying; *spec.* declamation, intonation, intonement, pattering, cantillation (*R*).
2. *See* ACCOUNT, MENTION.
recite, *v. t.* **1.** repeat, rehearse, say; *spec.* declaim (*chiefly U. S.*), intone, patter, cantillate (*R*), chant, monotone, rhapsodize.
2. *See* NARRATE, MENTION.
reckless, *a.* **1.** *See* CARELESS, RASH.
2. *Implying heedless rashness:* careless (*contex.*), rash, harum-scarum, wild, wanton, madcap, hare-brained, hare-brain, hot-headed, bold, devil-may-care (*C*), dare-devil, temerous (*R*), temerarious (*B*); *spec.* desperate; *see* VENTURESOME.
Antonyms: see CAREFUL, AFRAID.
recklessly, *adv.* disregardfully, carelessly, rashly, *etc.*; slap-bang (*C*), slap-dash (*C*).
recklessness, *n.* carelessness (*contex.*), rashness, *etc.; spec.* desperation. *Cf.* RECKLESS.
reclaim, *v. t.* **1.** *See* REFORM, TAME, CIVILIZE.
2. *Referring to land:* recover, redeem.
recognition, *n.* **1.** *See* ACKNOWLEDGMENT, NOTICE, ACCEPTANCE, KNOWLEDGE.
2. perception (*contex.*), identification; *spec.* diagnosis, diagnostication (*R*), exequatur.
recognize, *v. t.* **1.** *See* ACKNOWLEDGE, NOTICE, ACCEPT.
2. perceive (*contex.*), know, identify; *spec.* diagnose, diagnosticate (*R*).
recoil, *v. i.* **1.** return (*contex.*), rebound, resile (*R*), kick (*chiefly spec.*), reverberate (*R*); *spec.* double, tail.
2. *See* RETREAT, SHRINK.
recoil, *n.* **1.** return (*contex.*), rebound, resile (*R*), spring, kick (*chiefly spec.*), resilience, reverberation (*R*); *spec.* repercussion, backstroke, bricole.
2. *See* RETREAT, SHRINK.
recommendation, *n.* **1.** *See* ADVICE.
2. *Referring to a letter or document that recommends:* testimonial, reference.
reconciled, *a.* resigned.
reconsider, *v. t.* consider, rethink (*R*), revise, review.
record, *n.* **1.** account; *spec.* minutes, diary, journal, proceedings, memorandum, score, memorial, file, cartulary, docket, iter, logbook *or* log, itinerary, dufter (*Anglo-Indian*), protocol; *see* HISTORY, REPORT.
2. *Referring to the record made by self-recording instruments:* register; *spec.* trace, tracing, phonogram, thermograph, sphygmograph, *etc.*
record, *v. t.* memorandum (*R*), minute, score, enter, enregister (*R*), mark, note, monumentalize, chronicle, inscroll (*R*), memorize (*R*), notch, nick, journal, journalize, diarize, catalogue, log; *see* HISTORICIZE.
recorder, *n.* **1.** *Spec.* registrator (*R*), register (*R*), registrer (*R*), chronicler, registrar, registrary (*R*), clerk, notary, prothonotary, secretary, griffier (*Eng.*), historiographer.
2. *Referring to a device or instrument: spec.* marker, scorer, tracer, electrograph, sphygmograph, phonograph, multigraph, dictaphone.
recover, *v. t.* **1.** get (*contex.*), regain, reacquire, retrieve, reobtain, repossess, reoccupy, reget (*R*), rewin; *spec.* revindicate (*R*), replevin (*now U. S.*), replevy, reconquer, recapture, reseize.
Antonyms: see LOSE.
2. *Referring to the regaining or resuming of a state, condition, quality, etc.:* regain, resume, reestablish, recuperate (*R*).
3. *In the sense of "to bring back from a state, condition, etc.":* reclaim, recall, rally, rescue, retrieve, right (*a reflexive*); *see* RECLAIM.
4. *In the sense of "to get better from" (a sickness, etc.):* recuperate (*obs. or R*), retrieve (*R*).
5. *See* CURE, REVIVE, RETRIEVE, COMPOSE.
recover, *v. i.* **1.** recuperate, retrieve (*recover what was lost*), recruit (*replenish weakened*

---

recipe: *formula.*
reciprocate: *interchange, return.*
recital: *recitation, account, mention, concert.*
reckon: *compute, consider, class, anticipate.*
reckoning: *computation, consideration, anticipation, account.*
recollection: *remembrance, memory.*
recompense, *n.: pay, payment, compensation, reward.*
reconcile: *conciliate, reunite, harmonize.*
recondite: *abstruse.*
recount: *compute.*
recount: *narrate, mention.*
recounting: *account, mention.*
recoup: *deduct, pay, compensate, retrieve.*

---

forces), rally (recover *after decline, with sense of gathering force*); *spec.* convalesce.
2. *In the sense of "to regain one's footing," position, previous state, etc.:* rally, rise, brace (*used with "up"*); *see* REVIVE.
Antonyms: see DECLINE.

recovery, *n.* **1.** getting, regainment (*R*), retrieval, repossession, reoccupation; *spec.* revindication (*R*), recapture, replevin.
2. *Referring to the act of the person or organism in getting better after sickness or other evil:* cure (*complete* recovery), recuperation, recruital (*R*), recruitment (*R*), rally; *spec.* convalescence (*the continuing process of* recovery); *see* REVIVAL.
Antonyms: see DECLINE.
3. *Referring to the action of something exterior bringing a person into a better state after sickness or evil:* restoration, revival.
4. *See* REVIVAL, RETRIEVAL, CORRECTION, RECLAMATION.

re-create (*pron.* rē-krē-āt'), *v. t.* create (*contex.*), new-form, new-create, new-make, renew.

rectangular, *a.* orthogonal (*tech.*), rectangulate (*R*), normal (*R*); *spec.* square.

recur, *v. i.* **1.** return, reappear; *spec.* repullulate (*R*); *see* REPEAT.
2. *See* REVERT.

recurrence, *n.* **1.** return, reappearance, crebrity (*R*); *spec.* frequence, repullulation (*R*), atavism; *see* REPETITION.
2. *See* REVERSION.

recurrent, *a.* discontinuous, returning, reappearing; *spec.* frequent (*implying numerousness*), cyclic, haunting (*of memories*), rolling, atavistic, repetitory, intermittent, periodical.

red, *a.* **1.** *Spec.* reddish, reddy (*R*), rubric (*A*), incarmined (*R*), rufous, ferruginous, rufescent, glowing, burning, bloody, sanguineous (*B equiv. of "bloody"*), gory, pink, pinkish, pinky, cardinal, miniate (*R*), miniatous, miniaceous (*R*), copperish, coppery, incarnadine (*B*), laky, foxy, coral, coralline, vinaceous, carroty, roseate, rosal (*R*), rosy, ruby, rubied, rubious (*R*), sandy, puniceous (*R*), bricky, auroral, lateritious (*R*); *see* CRIMSON.
2. *Referring to complexion: spec.* florid, blowsy *or* blousy, blowzed, ruddy, rubicund (*R; theatrical or rhetorical*), frowsy, hectic, blushing, blushful (*R*); *see* RED-FACED, FLUSHED.
Antonyms: see PALE.
3. *Referring to animals: spec.* tawny, chestnut, bay, sorrel.
4. *See* BLOODY, BLOODSHOT, ANARCHISTIC, FIERY, VIOLENT, RADICAL.

red, *n. Spec.* scarlet, cherry, cerise, kermes, garnet, stammel (*obs.*), sanguine, hectic, terracotta, carmine, crimson, cramoisy (*A*), vermilion, vermeil (*R*), damask, cochineal, sericon, orchil, magenta, gules (*tech. or B*), pompadour, gridelin, reddle, *etc.*

redden, *v. t.* **1.** rubify (*R*); *spec.* fire, ruddy, ruby, empurple, inflame, vermilion, rubricate or (*R*) rubric, rouge, rose, crimson, encrimson (*R*), coral (*R*), incarnadine (*B*), rosy (*R*), flush (*R*).
2. *Referring to the complexion:* flush.

redden, *v. i.* **1.** *The words under "redden," v. t.,* **1.** *are largely used as v. i.*
2. *Referring to the complexion:* flush; *see* BLUSH.

reddening, *a.* rubescent, erubescent (*R*), flushing.

red-faced, *a.* red (*contex.*), florid, ruddy, rubicund (*theatrical or rhetorical*), ruddy-faced, frowsy; *see* FLUSHED.
Antonyms: see PALE.

redness, *n.* **1.** ruddiness, rubor (*tech.*), rubescence, rufescence (*R*), rud (*A*); *spec.* rosiness, *etc.*
2. *Of the complexion:* flush; *spec.* rash, heat.

redress, *n.* rectification, redressment (*R*), amendment, righting, correction, satisfaction, remedy, repair, relief, reparation.

redress, *v. t. Referring to the setting right of what is wrong:* right, amend, remedy, rectify, correct, repair, relieve.
Antonyms: see AGGRAVATE

reduce, *v. t. Spec.* diminish, shorten, abbreviate, contract, comminute, grind, convert, bring, commit, decompose, dilute, smelt, subdue, capture, compel, cut, curtail, subject, subjugate.

reed, *n.* **1.** *The plant: spec.* rush, flag, bent.
2. *As part of a musical instrument: spec.* tongue.

reedlike, *a.* reedy, reeden (*R*), arundinaceous (*tech.*), calamiform (*R*); *spec.* flaggy, rushy.

reedy, *a.* **1.** calamiferous (*R*); *spec.* flaggy, rushy.
2. *See* REEDLIKE, COARSE.

reef, *n.* ledge, key *or* (*Eng.*) cay (*chiefly spec.*), scar (*Brit.*); *see* HEADLAND.

reef, *v. t.* shorten (*sail*).

reëstablish, *v. t.* establish, resettle, replace, restore; *spec.* replant, refound, rehabilitate, redintegrate (*R*), reinstate, revest, reinstall, reinthrone, renew, regenerate, revive, revivify, remonetize; *see* RECOVER.

refashion, *v. t. Spec.* reshape, recast, reform, new-cast, new-mold, new-form, remold, remodel, reframe, recompose, rearrange, reconstruct, reforge (*fig.*), regenerate, revolutionize.

refashionment, *n. Spec.* reshaping, recast, reconstruction, new-modeling, *etc.*

refer, *v. t.* **1.** *See* ATTRIBUTE.

---

recreant, *a.: cowardly, treacherous, apostate.*
recreate, *v. t.: refresh, divert.*
recreation: *refreshment, diversion.*
recreative: *refreshing, diverting.*
recruit, *v. t.: strengthen, renew, refresh, enlist.*
recruit, *v. i.: recover.*
rectify: *correct, reform, redress, purify.*
rectitude: *uprightness, correctness.*
rector: *minister.*
rectory: *parsonage.*
redeem: *buy, free, reclaim, compensate, expiate.*
redemption: *buying, freeing, compensation, expiation.*
redound: *contribute, accrue.*
redundance: *excess, pleonasm.*
redundant: *excessive, pleonastic.*
reek, *n.: smoke, vapor, exhalation.*
reel, *n.: spool.*
reel, *v. i. & n.: whirl, stagger, sway, totter.*
reel, *v. t.: wind, unwind.*
reënforce: *strengthen.*

---

2. *In the sense of "to place among others of its kind":* assign (*with "to"*).
3. commit, leave, submit, relegate; *spec.* send, recommit, remit, relate.
4. send (*contex.*), direct.

refer, *v. i.* 1. *See* RELATE, APPEAL.
2. allude, advert, glance, touch, point.

reference, *n.* 1. *See* ATTRIBUTE, RELATION.
2. commitment, committal, relegation, recommission, submission, remission; *spec.* remit (*R*), relation.
3. allusion, advertence, glance.
4. mark; *spec.* asterism, asterisk, parallel, dagger, obelisk.

referential, *a.* 1. allusive; *spec.* fiducial (*tech.*).
2. *See* RELATIVE.

refine, *v. t.* 1. *See* PURIFY, CLEAR.
2. cultivate, polish, subtilize (*R or spec.*), bolt (*fig.*), decrassify (*R*); *spec.* spiritualize, humanize; *see* CIVILIZE, IDEALIZE, PURIFY, ELEVATE.
Antonyms: see BRUTALIZE.

refine, *v. i.* hair-split, wiredraw, subtilize (*R or spec.*).

refined, *a.* 1. *See* FINE.
2. cultured (*possessing the fruits of culture*), cultivated (*implies training or the product of training*), polished, polite (*in certain collocations only*), fine, Attic (*B*), nice, delicate, elegant; *spec.* ethereal, courtly, unrude (*R*), over-refined, elevated, ladylike, gentlemanly, high-minded, well-bred, spiritual, accomplished.
Antonyms: see VULGAR, UNPOLISHED, UNREFINED, COARSE, BOORISH, CRUDE, GROSS, ROWDYISH, VILE.

refinement, *n.* 1. *See* NICETY, ACCOMPLISHMENT, SUBTLETY.
2. culture, cultivation, polish, polishedness (*R*), refinedness (*R*), politeness (*R*), delicacy, nicety, niceness, elegance; *spec.* courtliness, ethereality, overrefinement, elevation, spirituality.
3. hair-splitting, subtilization (*B*), micrology (*R*).
Antonyms: see COARSE, BOORISH, *etc.*

reflect, *v. t.* 1. *See* TURN, BRING, CURVE.
2. return, reverberate, flash; *spec.* mirror, glass, image; *see* ECHO.
Antonyms: see ABSORB.

reflected, *a.* reflex, reflexed, reflective (*R*), borrowed; *spec.* introverted, introrse.

reflection, *n.* 1. *Referring to the action:* return, reverberation, reflex.
Antonyms: see ABSORPTION.
2. *Referring to the image formed by reflection:* reflex, shadow, idol (*B*), image, glade (*chiefly in "moonglade"*), specter (*R*); *see* ECHO.
3. *See* CONSIDERATION, BLAME, DISPARAGEMENT, THINKING.

reflector, *n.* reverberator; *spec.* mirror, speculum.

reflow, *v. t.* flow (*contex.*), ebb (*spec. or fig.*).

reflux, *n.* flow (*contex.*), reflow, refluence, ebb (*spec. or fig.*); *spec.* backwater; *see* OUTGO.

reform, *n.* progress (*contex.*); *spec.* amendment, reconstruction.

re-form, *v. t.* 1. remake, renew, reproduce, reconstitute, reconstruct, regenerate; *see* REBUILD.
2. *See* REFASHION.

re-form, *v. i. Spec.* regrow, regenerate.

reform, *v. t.* 1. *See* AMEND, CORRECT, ABOLISH.
2. *Referring to the correction of bad habits:* amend, mend (*A*), reclaim, rectify, regenerate.
Antonyms: see CORRUPT.

reform, *v. i.* progress; *spec.* amend, regenerate.

reformable, *a.* amendable, corrigible.

reformation, *n.* 1. *Spec.* amendment, correction, abolition.
2. amendment, reclamation, recovery, regeneration.

re-formation, *n.* remaking, renewal, reproduction, reconstitution, reconstruction, regeneration.

reformative, *a.* reformatory, reformational; *spec.* progressive.
Antonyms: see CORRUPTIVE.

reformed, *a.* regenerate (*with sense of being born again or made anew, as contrasted with simpler sense of "altered" for* reformed).

reformer, *n.* reformist, reformado (*R*); *spec.* come-outer (*S, U. S.*), progressive, progressist (*R*).

refractory, *a.* 1. *See* INTRACTABLE, OBSTINATE.
2. *Of objects:* obstinate, intractable, incoercible; *spec.* unworkable, infusible (*R*), unmeltable.
Antonyms: see DUCTIBLE, FUSIBLE.

refrain, *n.* repetend (*R*), burden, bob, overword (*Scot.*); *spec.* tag, chorus, falderal *or* folderol (*R*), lullaby, faburden (*hist.*), lillibullero, ritornello *or* ritornel.

refresh, *v. t.* 1. *see* FRESHEN.
2. freshen, invigorate, reinvigorate, recreate, renew, renovate, recruit, revive, revivify, refreshen (*R*), refocillate (*R*), regale; *spec.* rejoice (*R*), recomfort (*R*), refect (*with food and drink; chiefly reflexive*), breathe, slake; *see* DIVERT.
Antonyms: see TIRE, EXHAUST.

refreshing, *a.* recreative, invigorating; *spec.* restful, refective (*R*).
Antonyms: see WEARISOME.

refreshment, *n.* 1. reinvigoration, revival, recreation, renewal, renovation, recreance (*R*), refection (*spec. or fig.*), regalement, regale (*R*), refocillation (*R*); *spec.* relaxation, diversion.
2. *Chiefly in pl.:* provisions (*pl.*), bait; *spec.* charity, bever (*Eng.*).

refuge, *n.* 1. *Referring to the fact or state: see* SHELTER.
2. *Of the place:* retreat, shelter, haven, harbor; *spec.* asylum, sanctuary, grith (*hist.*), hiding (*R*), bield (*Scot.*), stronghold, resort (*contex.*), den, earth.

---

referee: *arbitrator.*
reflect, *v. i.: consider.*
refrain: *abstain.*
refund: *repay.*

---

refurnish, *v. t.* furnish, refit, reëquip.

refusal, *n.* **1.** *See* REJECTION.

2. declination, nonacceptance, declension; *spec.* regret (*chiefly in pl.*).

Antonyms: see ACCEPTANCE.

3. denial, debarment, disallowance, nay, no, nay-say (*R or Scot.*).

refuse, *v. i.* **1.** decline.

Antonyms: see OBEY.

2. balk.

3. renege, nig (*S*), revoke, renounce (*R*).

refuse, *v. t.* **1.** *See* REJECT.

2. *With the infinitival "to":* decline.

3. *With the thing refused as object or the double objective of thing refused and the person:* deny, debar, disallow.

Antonyms: see OFFER, ATTRIBUTE.

refuse, *a.* rubbishy, recrementitious, quisquilious (*R*); *spec.* trashy, discarded, useless, worthless, waste, dreggy, drossy.

refuse, *n.* rubbish, recrement (*R*), rejectamenta (*pl.; B, R*), trash, lumber, garbage, offal (*tech.; chiefly spec.*), offscouring, outcast (*R*); *spec.* brash, dross, dregs, crumble, chaff, breeze, sweepings (*pl.*), pomace, rough (*chiefly in pl.*), dunder, discard, tare, rummage, gurry (*chiefly U. S.*), culls (*pl.; cant*), rape, burr.

regenerate, *v. t.* **1.** *See* CONVERT, RE-FORM, REESTABLISH.

2. *In the spiritual sense:* renovate, renew, resurrect, resuscitate (*R*); *see* REFORM, REËSTABLISH.

regenerate, *a.* regenerated, new-born (*fig.*), reborn.

regeneration, *n.* **1.** *See* CONVERSION, REFORMATION.

2. *In the spiritual sense:* renovation, renewal, palingenesy *or* palingenesis *or* palingensia (*B*), resuscitation (*R*); *see* REFORMATION.

Antonyms: see DEGENERATION.

regret, *v. t.* **1.** *With the implication of mental distress over something lost or some evil: see* MOURN.

2. *With the implication of mental distress over one's own acts that one would now have undone:* repent, rue.

regret, *v. i.* **1.** *See* MOURN.

2. repent, rue.

regret, *n.* **1.** *Referring to the feeling of one who mourns: see* SORROW.

2. *Referring to the feeling of one who repents his own acts:* repentance, penitency (*R*), remorse, contrition, compunction (*originally a strong* remorse; *now only formal* regret), ruth (*A*), rue (*A*), resipiscence (*R*), worm (*fig.*).

regretful, *a.* **1.** *See* MOURNFUL.

2. repentant (*showing pain or sorrow for sin*), penitent (*feeling pain or sorrow for sin*), remorseful (*whereas* regretful *may convey only a formal or slight sense of* compunction, remorseful *implies overwhelming self-contrition*), compunctious, compunct (*obs.*), contrite (*completely penitent*), conscience-stricken, penitential (*R*), sorry, rueful (*often spec.*).

Antonyms: see IMPENITENT.

regular, *a. Spec.* systematical, systematic, symmetrical, even, methodical, constant, habitual, normal, correct, ordinary, qualified, orderly.

Antonyms: see IRREGULAR.

regularize, *v. t.* normalize, standardize; *spec.* grammaticize.

regulate, *v. t.* shape, settle; *spec.* time, police, throttle; *see* CONTROL, ADJUST, MANAGE.

regulation, *n.* **1.** shaping, settlement; *spec.* police; *see* CONTROL, MANAGEMENT.

2. *See* RULE.

rein, *n.* **1.** band, lines (*pl.*), strings (*pl.; S*), ribbons (*pl.; C or S*).

2. *See* CONTROL, RESTRAINT.

reject, *v. t.* **1.** discard, disallow, deny, repugn (*R*); *spec.* cashier (*fig.*), disapprove, recuse, explode (*now chiefly used in the p. p.*), cast, scout, negative (*chiefly U. S.*), repudiate, pluck (*Univ. S, Eng.*), veto, respue (*R*), plow (*Univ. S, Eng.*), flunk (*Univ. S, U. S.*); *see* ABJURE, DISBELIEVE, DISMISS, FAIL.

Antonyms: see ENTERTAIN.

2. *Implying the refusal to accept something offered:* refuse, decline, spurn, repel; *spec.* jilt, check.

Antonyms: see ACCEPT, BEG, CHOOSE, RECEIVE.

rejected, *a.* discarded, cast-off.

rejection, *n.* **1.** *Spec.* disallowance, denial, discard, dismissal, cashierment, repudiation, veto, reprobation, disbelief, disapproval.

Antonyms: see ACCEPTANCE.

2. refusal, declination, declension, spurning, repulse.

Antonyms: see CHOICE, ACCEPTANCE.

rejoice, *v. i.* exult, triumph, vaunt, insult (*A*), gloat, crow (*C*), joy, jubilate.

Antonyms: see SORROW, MOURN, COMPLAIN, CRY, WAIL.

rejoicing, *n.* rejoicement (*R*), exultation, exultance, exultancy, elation, joy, triumphing, vaunting, jubilance, jubilation, jubilee, gratulation (*R*).

Antonyms: see LAMENTATION, MOURNING, SORROW.

rejoicing, *a.* gratulant (*R*), exultant.

Antonyms: see SORROWFUL.

rekindle, *v. t.* kindle (*contex.*), relight, reinflame, reignite, reillume (*R*), relume (*B*), relumine (*R*).

rekindle, *v. i.* kindle (*contex.*), reflame.

relapse, *v. i.* regress, backslide, slide (*R*), fall, revert, weaken, recidivate (*chiefly spec.*); *see* APOSTATIZE.

relapse, *n.* regress, regression, fall, reversion, throwback, recidivation (*chiefly spec.*); backsliding; *see* APOSTASY.

---

refutation: *disproof.*
regale: *feast, entertain, refresh.*
regard, *n.: particular, attention, care, notice, consideration, deference, esteem, affection* (in pl.), *respect.*
regard, *v. t.: notice, consider, esteem.*
register, *n.: list, record, compass.*
rehabilitate: *restore, reëstablish.*
rehearsal: *recitation, account, mention, practice.*
reign, *n.: control, rule, prevalence.*
rein, *v. t.: check, guide, control.*
reinstate: *reëstablish, replace.*
rejoice, *v. t.: gladden.*
rejoin, *v. t. reunite.*
rejoinder: *answer.*

relate, *v. t.* **1.** *See* NARRATE, MENTION.
2. connect, correlate, interrelate; *spec.* apply.
relate, *v. i.* refer, pertain, appertain (*chiefly tech.*), belong (*A*), bear (*used with "on"*).
related, *a.* **1.** *Referring to things:* connected, correlative, correlated, collateral, cognate, connate (*R*), allied, congeneros (*B*), congenial (*R*), connatural (*B*); *spec.* conjugate (*of words, directly from some stem or root, and usually of kindred meaning*), akin, affinitive, paronymous.
Antonyms: see UNRELATED, UNCONNECTED.
2. *Referring to persons:* akin, allied (*R or spec.*), sib (*A and chiefly Scot.*), consanguineous *or* (*chiefly tech.*) consanguine, consanguinean (*R*), cognate (*implying relation through the mother*), agnate (*implying relation through the father*); *spec.* affinal, german (*predicative*).
Antonyms: see UNRELATED.
relation, *n.* **1.** *See* NARRATION, ACCOUNT, MENTION.
2. apposition, connection (*implying esp. natural or necessary relation*), relationship, bearing, respect (*in "in this respect," "in one respect," etc.*); *spec.* relevancy *or* (*R*) relevance, pertinency *or* (*R*) pertinence, alliance, reference, rapport, interrelation, interconnection, bearing, correlation, affinity, concern *or* (*R*) concernment (*the particular respect in which a thing has to do with something else*), business, respect, propinquity, privity, contingency (*R or Scot.*), proportion.
3. relationship, kinship, kinsmanship (*R*), kin, blood, connection (*esp. by family ties or distant consanguinity*), consanguinity, cognation (*esp. through females*), agnation (*esp. through males*), cousinship (*spec., exc. as loosely used*), sib (*R*), alliance, sibness (*obs. or Scot.*), interrelationship; *spec.* affinity (*relation by marriage*), nearness (*close kinship*).
4. *See* RELATIVE.
relative, *a.* referential, pertinent, appertaining (*chiefly tech.*), apposite (*used with "to"*), relevant, germane (*B or formal*), connective, material, proportional, correspondent; *see* COMPARATIVE.
Antonyms: see IRRELEVANT.
relative, *n.* relation, kinsman, kinswoman (*chiefly B*), connection (*chiefly spec.*), cognate (*chiefly spec.*), agnate (*chiefly spec.*), belonging (*contex.*), friend (*only in pl.; R or obs.*), cousin (*A or familiar; spec. exc. as loosely used*); *spec.* collateral, affine, father, blood (*a collective*), mother, brother, sister, niece, *etc.*; *see* KIN.
relax, *v. t.* **1.** *In a physical sense:* loosen, unbrace (*B or spec.*), unstrain (*R*), unstring (*fig. or spec.*); *spec.* unbend, unthread (*R*).
Antonyms: see TIGHTEN.
2. *Of immaterial things, as effort, attention, severity, etc.:* loosen, milden, slacken, slack, diminish; *spec.* mitigate, dispense (*R*); *see* ABATE, SOFTEN.
Antonyms: see INCREASE, INTENSIFY.
relax, *v. i.* **1.** loosen, slacken.
2. loosen, unbend, slack, slacken, milden; *spec.* soften; *see* ABATE,
Antonyms: see INCREASE, INTENSIFY.
relaxation, *n.* **1.** loosening, unbracing, *etc.*; *spec.* resolution (*R*), laxation (*R*), diastole.
2. loosening, slackening, *etc.*, diminution, unbending; *see* SOFTENING.
3. *See* DIVERSION.
relaxed, *a.* loosened, slackened, lax; *see* LIMP.
relay, *n.* shift, squad, relief; *spec.* dawk (*Anglo-Indian*), translator (*R*).
relent, *v. i.* yield, soften, bend.
relentless, *a.* unyielding, obdurate, stern, unrelenting, remorseless, unappeasable; *see* UNCOMPASSIONATE, UNFEELING.
Antonyms: see MERCIFUL, COMPASSIONATE.
reliable, *a.* dependable, trustworthy, sure, certain, authentic (*R*), secure, safe, unfailing; *see* CONSTANT, SOLVENT.
Antonyms: see UNRELIABLE, UNTRUSTWORTHY.
reliance, *n.* **1.** dependence, recumbency; *see* TRUST.
Antonyms: see DISTRUST.
2. *See* SUPPORT.
reliant, *a.* defendant, recumbent; *see* TRUSTFUL.
Antonyms: see DISTRUSTFUL.
relic, *n.* remain; *spec.* halidom (*A*), survival, antiquity; *see* REMINDER, REMAINS.
relief, *n.* **1.** projection, relievo, alto-relievo, mezzo-relievo, half-relief, bas-relief.
2. composition; *spec.* embossment, bas-relief, high relief, *etc.*
3. *See* DISTINCTNESS, VIVIDNESS.
relief, *a.* raised; *spec.* repoussée, embossed.
relief, *n.* **1.** *See* AID, FREEING, MITIGATION, REDRESS.
2. *Referring to the mind, feelings, etc.:* easement (*the act*), ease, lightening, relaxation; *see* DIVERSION, COMFORT, REST.
Antonyms: see DISTRESS.
3. *Referring to one on duty:* rest, respite, release; *spec.* spell.
relieve, *v. t.* **1.** *See* AID, FREE, MITIGATE, DEPRIVE, REDRESS.
2. *Referring to the mind, spirits, or feelings:* ease, respite, lighten, relax; *see* COMFORT, REST.
Antonyms: see DISTRESS.
3. *Referring to one on duty, as on guard, at work, etc.:* rest, release, free, respite, spell (*now U. S.*), relay.
religion, *n.* piety (*B*).
religious, *a.* **1.** devout, pious, godly, solemn, religionary (*R*), righteous, good (*chiefly contex.; often more or less sarcastic*); *spec.* pietistic (*emotionally or affectedly* religious), devotional, God-fearing, holy, heavenly-minded, otherworldly, prayerful, divine.
2. *See* CONSCIENTIOUS.
Antonyms: see IRRELIGIOUS.

release, *v. t.: free, loose, relinquish.*
release, *n. freeing, loosing, relinquishment.*
relegate: *expel, refer.*
relevancy: *relation.*
relevant: *relative.*
reliability: *constancy.*

religious, *n.* religieuse (*French; fem. or masc.*), religieux (*French; masc.*); *spec.* cenobite, anchoret, hospitaler, Culdee (*Scotch-Irish*).

relinquish, *v. t.* abandon, surrender, yield, concede, cede, resign, renounce, deliver, waive, release; *spec.* demit, disgorge, regorge; *see* ABDICATE.
Antonyms: see KEEP.

relinquishment, *n.* abandonment, surrender, yielding, concession, cession, resignation, renunciation, delivery, waiving, waiver (*tech.*), release; *spec.* dimission, regorgement (*R*), abdication.

rely, *v. i.* depend, rest, count, reckon, build, bank, found, trust (*used with "to"*), calculate; *spec.* lean.

remainder, *n.* surplus, residue, rest (*sing. or a collective pl.*), residuum, residual (*R*), others (*pl.; contex.*), leavings (*pl.*), remain (*R*), relict (*R*), remanet (*R*), remanence (*R*), balance (*commercial*); *spec.* remnant, surplusage, rump, dreg, caput mortuum (*B and fig.*), tally, difference, shadow, fossil.

remaining, *a.* surplus, residual, residuary, behind, residuous (*R*), remanent (*R*), odd.

remains, *n. pl.* relics, relicts, remain (*sing.; R*), reliquiæ (*B or tech.*); *spec.* disjecta membra (*Latin*), bones, fossil, ashes; *see* BODY.

remedy, *n.* **1.** cure (*an entirely successful* remedy), help, boot (*A*); *spec.* specific, elixir, nostrum (*a* remedy *of doubtful efficacy because recommended wholesale by its proposer*), treacle (*R or fig.*), vulnerary; *see* PANACEA, ANTIDOTE.
Antonyms: see DISEASE.
2. *See* REDRESS.

remember, *v. t.* **1.** recollect, recall, mind (*A or dial.*), bethink (*obs., exc. with a clause or reflexive*), think, retain, treasure, keep, have.
Antonyms: see FORGET, OMIT.
2. *See* MENTION.

remembrance, *n.* **1.** recollection, recall, memory, retention, mind, rememoration (*R*), reminiscence.
2. *See* MEMORY, MENTION, REMINDER.

remind, *v. t.* prompt, mind (*R*), remember (*A*), jog.

reminder, *n.* **1.** *Referring to persons:* monitor, prompter, remembrancer (*chiefly spec.*), flapper (*so used in ridicule, after Swift*).
2. *Referring to things:* memento, remembrance, remembrancer; *spec.* memorial, souvenir, keepsake, relic, relict (*R*), trophy.
3. *Referring to the action of one who reminds:* prompt (*chiefly theatrical cant*), jog.

removal, *n.* **1.** remotion (*R*), transfer, shift, change, estrangement (*A or R*), sequestration, deportation (*R, exc. spec.*), remove (*R, exc. spec.*), removement (*R*); *spec.* dislodgment, extraction, eloignment, abstraction, sublation (*R*); *see* WITHDRAWAL, EJECTION, DISPLACEMENT.
Antonyms: see INSERTION.
2. *Spec.* elimination, clearance, detergency (*R*), purging, discharge, retrenchment, draft, dispelling, dislodgment, expulsion, dispossession, excision, effacement, *etc.*
3. *Spec.* devestment, retrenchment, abolition; *see* DEDUCTION.
4. *See* DISPOSITION, DISCHARGE, DEPARTURE.

remove, *v. t.* **1.** *Referring to the direct physical moving of an object from one place to another:* move, transfer, shift, take (*chiefly used with "from," "away," etc., and often esp. contrasted with "bring"*), change (*contex.*); *spec.* draw, abstract, estrange (*somewhat A*), sequester, deport, dislodge, extract, eloign (*legal, reflexive, or obs.*), quit (*R*), sublate (*R*), unship, wipe (*chiefly used with "away," "off," etc.*), bear, wash (*chiefly used with "away," "off," etc.*); *see* MOVE, EXTRACT, ABSTRACT, WITHDRAW, EJECT, UPROOT, DISPLACE.
2. *In physical senses in which the sense of actual direct bodily transferal is not distinctly or immediately present: spec.* eliminate, clear (*chiefly used with "away," "off," etc.*), deterge, purge, leach (*used with "out," "away," etc.*), dislodge, rid (*R*), discharge, scour (*chiefly used with "away," "off," etc.*), dress, draft, raze; *see* DISPEL, EXPEL, DISPOSSESS, EXCISE, EFFACE, ASSASSINATE.
3. doff (*B*), cast, douse (*C*); *spec.* slip (*with "off"*).
Antonyms: see DON.
4. *In a nonphysical sense: spec.* divest *or* devest (*R*), retrench, fordo (*A*); *see* ABOLISH, EXTINGUISH, DEDUCT.
5. *See* RETIRE, DEPOSE, DISCHARGE.

rend, *v. t.* **1.** *As used with "away," "off," "up," etc.: see* TEAR.
2. *As implying a tearing to pieces:* tear, lacerate, dilacerate (*B; an intensive*), disrupt, dismember, dispiece (*R*), discorp (*R*), divellicate (*R*); *spec.* divide, break, burst, shatter, split, chew (*used with "up," "to pieces," etc.*).
3. *See* DESTROY.

rendezvous, *n.* **1.** tryst (*B; chiefly spec.*); *see* RESORT.
2. *See* MEETING.

rending, *n.* **1.** *See* DIVISION, BREAKING, BURSTING.
2. divulsion (*B*), dilaceration (*B*), disruption, dismemberment, discerption (*R*), divellication (*R*).

renegade, *a.* tergiversant (*R*), apostate, changeling (*A*).

renew, *v. t.* **1.** renovate (*chiefly implies freshening of material things, whereas* renew *is unlimited in the sense of doing over or starting*

---

relish, *n.: taste, liking, flavoring, enjoyment.*
relish, *v. t.: enjoy, like.*
relish, *v. i.: taste, savor.*
reluctant: *unwilling.*
remand: *consign.*
remark, *v. t.: notice, comment.*
remark, *v. i.: comment.*
remark, *n.: notice, comment.*
remarkable: *notable, extraordinary.*
remedy, *v. t.: cure, redress, correct.*
remembrance: *reminder.*
remit: *excuse, forgo, abate, consign.*
remonstrate: *object.*
remorse: *regret.*
remote: *distant, unrelated, secluded, small.*
remuneration: *payment, pay.*
rend, *v. t.: divide, break, burst, split, tear, disunite.*

afresh), restore, refresh, repair, reintegrate, revive, resuscitate (*R*), furbish (*fig.*), refurbish (*fig.*); *spec.* rejuvenate, recruit, replenish, recuperate, resurrect; *see* REËSTABLISH, RENOVATE, REGENERATE, REFRESH, RE-CREATE, REFORM, REPAIR.
Antonyms: see CONSUME.
2. recommence, resume, reopen, continue.
3. *See* REPEAT, FRESHEN.
renew, *v. i.* **1.** recrudesce, return, regrow, reappear; *spec.* re-form, regenerate.
Antonyms: see DECAY.
2. *See* BEGIN.
renewal, *n.* **1.** restoration, refreshment, reparation, revival, repair, repairment (*R*), renovation, redintegration, continuation, resuscitation (*R*); *spec.* rejuvenation; *see* RENOVATION, REGENERATION, REFRESHMENT, RE-FORMATION, REPAIR.
Antonyms: see DECAY.
2. recommencement, resumption, continuation, continuance.
3. recrudescence, return, regrowth, reappearance, renascence; *see* RE-FORMATION.
Antonyms: see DECAY.
4. *See* REPETITION, BEGINNING.
renovate, *v. t.* **1.** renew (*q. v. for discrimination*), furbish (*orig. spec.*), refurbish (*orig. spec.*), revamp, recoct (*R*), retouch; *see* REPAIR.
2. *See* REFRESH, REGENERATE.
renovation, *n.* **1.** renewal, furbishment (*R*), refurbishment, recoction (*R*), revamping; *see* REPAIR.
2. *See* REFRESHMENT, REGENERATION.
rent, *n.* return, render, payment, rental, rentage (*R*); *spec.* quitrent, fee-farm, mail (*obs. or Scot.*), canon, gale (*Eng.*), gavel (*hist.*), rack-rent, stallage; *see* HIRE.
repair, *v. t.* **1.** restore, renew, renovate, mend, botch (*now spec.*); *spec.* tinker, patch, piece (*C*), cobble *or* (*dial. Eng.*) clobber, vamp, clout, bushel, darn, finedraw, seat, toe, heel, half-sole, tap.
2. *See* RENEW, CORRECT, REDRESS.
repair, *n.* **1.** *Referring to the act:* renewal, restoration, renovation, mend (*R*), mending, reparation (*R*).
2. *Referring to the place mended:* mend; *spec.* patch, tinker (*R*), darn, bushel, vamp.
3. *See* RENEWAL, CORRECTION, REDRESS, RESTORATION.
reparative, *a.* amendatory, satisfactive, corrective, reformatory, remedial.
repay, *v. t.* **1.** return (*contex.*), refund, reimburse, restore, retaliate (*R*), retribute (*R*).
2. *See* PAY, COMPENSATE, REWARD, RETRIBUTE.
repeat, *v. t.* **1.** reiterate, recapitulate, iterate (*R, exc. spec.*); *spec.* rote, din, echo, reëcho, cuckoo, ingeminate (*R*), battologize (*R*), reword, retell, remurmur; *see* RECITE, PARAPHRASE.
2. reduplicate, redouble, renew, duplicate; *see* DOUBLE, PRACTICE.
3. *See* NARRATE.
repeat, *v. i.* **1.** tautologize (*B*).
2. recur; *spec.* circulate (*referring to fractions, etc.*).
repel, *v. t.* **1.** repulse, rebuff, ward, rebut, fence, fend, defend, repercuss.
2. *See* REJECT.
3. *In the sense of to cause aversion in:* repugn (*R*); *spec.* disgust; *see* FRIGHTEN.
Antonyms: see ATTRACT, FASCINATE, CAPTIVATE, ENTICE.
repellent, *a.* **1.** repellant (*R*), repulsing (*in the act of* repelling), repercussive.
Antonyms: see ATTRACTIVE.
2. uninviting, repugnant, horrid, repulsive (*of the nature to* repel), repellant (*R*); *spec.* grim *or* (*A*) grimly, forbidding, harsh, chilling, gaunt, stern, unsightly, ugly, cold, frigid, stiff, freezing, abhorrent; *see* DISGUSTING.
Antonyms: see CAPTIVATING, ENTICING, INGRATIATING, ATTRACTIVE.
repetition, *n.* **1.** repeat (*R*), reiterance (*R*), iterance (*R*), iteration (*literally,* repetition *a second time*); *spec.* recapitulation, reëcho, echo, ingemination (*R*), encore, dilogy (*R*), tautology (*a literary fault, of* repetition *of meaning in numerous similar words*), battology, alliteration (repetition *of initial sound*), place, palilogy; *see* PRACTICE.
2. *Referring to repeated words or expressions: spec.* tautology, dilogy (*R*), dittogram, dittograph, jingle.
3. renewal, iteration (*B*), iterance (*R*), recurrence, duplication, conduplication (*B*), reduplication; *see* FREQUENCY, PRACTICE.
4. *See* NARRATION.
repetitive, *a.* repetitious, repetitionary, repetitional, reduplicative, reduplicatory (*R*), reiterant (*chiefly spec.*), recurrent; *spec.* (*in rhetoric*) tautological, tautologous.
replace, *v. t.* **1.** restore (*contex.*), reimplace (*R*), return, reduce (*obs., exc. spec.*), replant, reimplant (*R*), reset; *spec.* reinstate, reseat, reinstall, relay, remount; *see* REËSTABLISH.
Antonyms: see DISPLACE.
2. displace, supersede, supplant; *spec.* novate.
replacement, *n.* **1.** restoration, reimplantation (*R*), return, reinstatement, reinstallment, reposition (*chiefly spec.*); *spec.* reduction (*obs., exc. spec.*).
Antonyms: see DISPLACEMENT.

---

renown: *fame.*
renowned: *famous.*
rent, *v. t.: let.*
rent, *n.: tear, cleft, breach.*
rent, *a.: torn, broken.*
renunciation: *relinquishment, disclaimer, self-denial;* also *cf.* ABANDON (for *abandonment*).
reparation: *renewal, correction, redress.*
repast: *meal.*
repeal, *v. t.: revoke.*
repeal, *n.: revocation.*
repent: *regret.*
replica: *duplicate.*
reply: *answer, echo.*

(*A*) *archaic.* (*B*) *bookish, poetic, literary or learned.* (*C*) *colloquial.* (*Contex.*) *contextual.* (*R*) *rare.* (*S*) *slang.*
See pp. viii–ix.

2. displacement, supersedure, supersession (*R*), replacing, supplantation; *spec.* novation.
report, *n.* **1.** *In the generic sense, as in "if we may trust report," and without any pl.:* rumor, talk, hearsay, bruit (*R*); *see* GOSSIP.
2. *In a concrete sense, with the article "a" or "an" and having a pl., as in "a false report of you came to us":* rumor, bruit (*B*), news (*construed both as a pl. and as sing.*), talk (*R*); *spec.* canard, misreport, cry (*A or R*), hearsay (*R*).
3. statement (*contex.*); *spec.* delation, return (*tech.*), bulletin, record.
4. *See* ACCOUNT, NOISE, EXPLOSION.
report, *v. t.* **1.** *See* NARRATE.
2. rumor, noise, bruit (*B*), fame, cry (*R*); *spec.* circulate.
3. state, tell; *spec.* delate, repeat, take (*cant*), return.
report, *v. i.* return (*chiefly law*).
repository, *n.* repositary (*R*), repertory, treasury, thesaurus, salvatory (*R*); *spec.* sacristy, museum, shed; *see* RECEPTACLE, STOREHOUSE, WAREHOUSE.
reprehensible, *a.* reprehendable (*R*), censurable, blamable, blameworthy, culpable, reprovable, condemnable, illaudable, uncommendable (*R*).
Antonyms: see BLAMELESS.
representative, *n.* **1.** agent (*contex.*); *spec.* delegate, deputy, depute (*Scot.*), deputation, commissioner, commissionaire, representant (*R*), lieutenant, vicar, substitute, locum-tenens, vice (*R*), secondary (*R*), vicegerent, viceroy, undersheriff, tipstaff, burgess, commoner, congressman, congresswoman, senator, proctor, legate.
2. *See* EXAMPLE.
repress, *v. t.* **1.** *See* RESTRAIN, SUPPRESS.
2. suppress, silence, choke (*chiefly used with "down"*), check, crucify, mortify, deaden, smother, dull, stifle, retund (*R*); *see* HIDE, CHOKE.
Antonyms: see ADVANCE.
repression, *n.* suppression, crucifixion, mortification, deadening, check, smothering, *etc.*
reprieve, *v. t. & n.* respite.
reproach, *v. t.* **1.** *See* REPROVE.
2. upbraid, taunt, twit.
reproof, *n.* **1.** criticism, reprehension, reprimand, censure, rebuke, reproach, chiding, objurgation (*B*), castigation, upbraiding, exprobation (*R*), admonition, monition, lecture, blame, blaming (*the action only*), lesson (*B*), correction, rating, dressing (*chiefly used with "down"; C*), increpation (*R*), reproval (*R*), monishment (*A*), trimming (*S*), dirdum (*Scot.*), slap (*C*); *spec.* snub, rate, bawling-out (*S*).
Antonyms: see PRAISE, COMPLIMENT.
2. *See* CENSURE.
reprove, *v. t.* **1.** *In the sense referring to censure addressed to the person criticized:* criticize, reprehend, reprimand, rebuke, censure, reproach, chide (*B*), castigate (*chiefly spec.*), objurgate, upbraid, blame, admonish, monish (*A*), lecture, lesson (*B*), correct, rate, dress (*chiefly used with "down"; C*), trim (*S*); *spec.* slash, bawl out (*S*).
Antonyms: see PRAISE, APPROVE, COMPLIMENT.
2. *In the sense in which adverse criticism is made on or about something:* censure, dispraise (*R*), mispraise (*R*), inculpate (*R*).
Antonyms: see PRAISE, APPROVE, COMPLIMENT.
reproving, *a.* admonitory, reproachful.
reptile, *a.* **1.** *See* CREEPING, ABJECT, MALEVOLENT, TREACHEROUS.
2. *Spec.* lacertian (*referring to ordinary lizards, geckos, chamaleons, etc.*).
reptile, *n.* reptilian; *spec.* dragon, hydra; *see* SNAKE, CROCODILIAN.
reputable, *a.* creditable; *see* HONORABLE.
reputation, *n.* name, fame (*usually in a good sense*), credit (*esp. in a good sense*), repute, prestige, character, report (*now only with "good," after the Biblical usage*); *spec.* memory; *see* FAME.
resemblance, *n.* **1.** simulation, favoring, nearness; *spec.* assonance, alliteration, imitation, mimicry.
Antonyms: see DIFFERENCE.
2. *See* SIMILARITY.
resemble, *v. t.* simulate; *spec.* favor (*C*), facsimile (*R*), copy, imitate, counterfeit, mimic, feature (*a R or dial. equiv. of "favor"*), reproduce, follow, echo, duplicate.
resembling, *a.* **1.** simulative, imitative, simular (*R*), simulant (*R*), mimicking.
2. *See* SIMILAR.
resentment, *n.* displeasure, anger, choler, umbrage (*heavy, portentous* displeasure), dudgeon (*implies, with* pique, *upset temper*), pique, heartburn, heartburning, indignation, animosity (*a hostile spirit*), malice (*active ill will with evil intent*), spite (*a petty* malice), grudge (*sullen hostility*), rancor (*deep-seated* malice *or* spite).
Antonyms: see THANKFULNESS.
reservation, *n.* **1.** *Spec.* exception, appropriation.

---

repose, *v. t.: prostrate, rest, put.*
repose, *v. i.: lie, rest.*
repose, *n.: rest, peace, calm, inactivity, ease.*
represent: *act, depict, describe, example, express, show, typify, symbolize.*
reprisal: *retaliation.*
reproach, *n.: reproof, discredit.*
reprobate, *a.: abandoned, rascally.*
reprobate, *n.: sinner, rascal.*
reprobate, *v. t.: condemn, censure.*
reproductive: *generative.*
repudiate: *reject, disclaim, divorce.*
repugnance: *inconsistency, dislike aversion.*
request, *n.: asking, demand*
request, *v.t.: ask.*
requisite: *necessary.*
requisition, *n.: demand.*
requisition, *v. t.: demand, impress.*
requite, *v. t.: return, pay, compensate, reward, retaliate.*
rescind: *revoke.*
rescue: *deliver, free, recover.*
research, *v. t.: investigate.*
resent: *dislike.*
reserve: *v. t.: keep, defer, appropriate.*

---

2. *Referring to a district or tract of land:* reserve.

reserve, *n.* **1.** *See* STORE, FUND, CONSTRAINT, SELF-CONTROL, DISTANCE, RETICENCE.

2. *Referring to land:* reservation.

reservoir, *n.* receiver, receptacle; *spec.* basin, tank, standpipe, waterback, lodge, fountain, font, magazine, forebay.

residence, *n.* **1.** *Referring to the fact or action:* abode (*B or A*), dwelling, habitation (*B*), habitancy (*R*), inhabitation (*R, exc. with "of"*), inhabitancy.

2. sojourn (*chiefly spec.*), sojournment (*R*), abidancy (*R*); *spec.* commorancy (*R*), commoration (*R*), stay, stop, tarrying (*R*), tarriance (*R*), rest (*R or spec.*).

3. *See* DWELLING (*the house which is the place of residence*), ABODE (*time or period of residence*).

resignation, *n.* **1.** *Spec.* abandonment, relinquishment, abdication, consignment.

2. acquiescence, resignment, resignedness, submission; *spec.* compliance.

resigned, *a.* acquiescent, reconciled, philosophical, submissive; *see* COMPLIANT.

Antonyms: see DEFIANT.

resin, *n.* rosin (*chiefly spec.*); *spec.* pitch, fat.

resinous, *a.* resined, resinous, rosiny, resinaceous (*R*); *spec.* pitchy, fat.

resist, *v. t.* **1.** *In a physical sense:* withstand.

2. *See* OPPOSE.

resist, *v. i. In an immaterial sense:* recalcitrate (*R*), reluctate (*R*).

resistance, *n.* **1.** *In a physical sense:* withstanding, renitency (*R*); *spec.* reluctance, reaction, load.

2. *See* OPPOSITION.

resistance, *a.* **1.** *In a physical sense:* withstanding, renitent (*R*), resistive.

2. *See* OPPOSING.

resonance, *n. Spec.* roar, boom, clang, roll, thunder, din, rumble, *etc.; spec.* nasality, twang.

resonant, *a.* sonorous, resounding, plangent, vibrant, roaring, rumorous (*A*), canorous (*B*); *spec.* rotund, clangorous, rebellant (*R*), thundering, booming, thunderous, remugient (*R*), reverberant; *see* RINGING, NASAL.

resort, *n.* **1.** *See* EXPEDIENT, APPLICATION.

2. *Referring to the act of going:* going, repair, recourse (*obs. or R*).

3. place (*contex.*), retreat, haunt, rendezvous; *spec.* dive, harbor, nest (*as of traitors, etc.*), joint (*S*), hangout (*S*), walk, soil (*a miry place of* resort *by deer*), lie (resort *of an animal*), lounge, wallow; *see* REFUGE.

resort, *v. i.* **1.** *See* GO, APPLY.

2. *In the sense of "go habitually or often":* repair, recourse (*obs. or R*).

3. *In the sense of "carry one's action":* go, turn, proceed.

resound, *v. i.* vibrate, peal (*chiefly spec.*), thunder, boom, roar; *spec.* bump, roll; *see* RING, ECHO.

resourceful, *a.* shifty, competent, able.

respect, *v. t.* **1.** *In the sense of "to have reference or relation to":* regard, contemplate.

2. *Spec.* venerate; *see* ESTEEM.

3. *See* CONSIDER, OBSERVE.

respect, *n.* **1.** *See* RELATION, PARTICULAR, ATTENTION, CONSIDERATION, POLITENESS.

2. *Spec.* veneration; *see* ESTEEM.

3. *In pl.: as a term denoting a complimentary message of regard or esteem:* regards, commendations, greetings, devoirs, compliments, service (*obs. or R*).

respectable, *a. Spec.* honorable, presentable; *see* ESTIMABLE, PROPER, CONSIDERABLE, FAIR.

respected, *a. Spec.* venerable, esteemed.

respectful, *a.* reverent, reverential, deferential; *see* POLITE.

Antonyms: see DISRESPECTFUL, CONTEMPTUOUS, IMPUDENT.

responsive, *a.* **1.** respondent, lively, responsorial (*R*); *spec.* appealable; *see* EXCITABLE, SYMPATHETIC, SENSITIVE.

Antonyms: see UNRESPONSIVE.

2. interlocutive (*R*), responsorial (*R*).

rest, *n.* **1.** repose, respite, relief, requiem, quiet, resting, breath, breathing, comfort; *spec.* siesta, meridian, sabbatism; *see* SLEEP, PEACE, CALM.

Antonyms: see ACTION, WORK.

2. *See* MOTIONLESSNESS, SUPPORT, BEARING.

rest, *v. t.* **1.** repose, refresh, relieve, breathe; *spec.* wind.

Antonyms: see WEARY, TIRE, WORK, EXHAUST.

2. lay, set, repose, settle, couch; *spec.* bed, recline, level, lean, pillow; *see* CUSHION.

3. *See* PLACE, PUT, BASE.

rest, *v. i.* **1.** repose, breathe; *spec.* sabbatize; *see* SLEEP.

Antonyms: see WORK.

2. lie, set, repose, stand; *spec.* bed, pillow, ride, lean, perch, lounge.

3. *See* RELY, DEPEND, STAY, WAIT, CONTINUE.

restate, *v. t.* state, reword, recapitulate; *see* PARAPHRASE.

restful, *a.* reposeful, easy, comfortable.

Antonyms: see TIRESOME.

rest house, hospital (*obs. or R*), hospitium (*R*), resting (*R*); *spec.* hospice, choultry (*India*), khan (*Arabian*), caravansary, caravanserai, dak bungalow (*India*).

---

reserved: *self-controlled, reticent, distant.*
reside: *dwell, inhere.*
residuary: *remaining.*
resign: *relinquish, consign, abdicate.*
resolute: *determined, courageous.*
resolution: *decomposition, conversion, determination, courage, decision, analysis* (mental).
resolve, *v. t.: decompose, convert, explain, analyze* (mentally), *decide, dispel, assure.*
resolve, *v. i.: decompose, decide.*
resolved: *determined, deliberate.*
resounding: *resonant.*
respect, *n.: relation, particular, attention, consideration, esteem, politeness.*
respectable: *estimable, proper, presentable, considerable, fair.*
respite, *v. t.: relieve, reprieve, defer.*
respond: *answer.*
restful: *comfortable.*
restive: *balky, intractable.*

---

restless, *a.* **1.** *In a physical sense:* active, unsteady, unquiet (*esp. spec.*), unresting; *spec.* astatic.

Antonyms: see MOTIONLESS, STILL.

2. *Referring to mental conditions: see* UNEASY.

restlessness, *n.* **1.** activity, unsteadiness, unquiet, unquietness, inquietude, unrestingness (*R*).

2. *See* UNEASINESS.

restoration, *n.* **1.** return, restitution, reduction (*R*), reddition (*obs. or R*), restoral (*R*); *spec.* redelivery, remitter, repayment.

Antonyms: see DEPRIVATION.

2. recovery (*R, in the active sense*), repristination (*R*), restitution (*R*), repair, instauration (*R*), renewal, renovation, retrieval (*R*); *see* CURE, REVIVAL.

3. *See* RENEWAL, RECOVERY, REPAIR, REPLACEMENT, RECALL.

restorative, *a.* recuperative, recuperatory (*R*); *see* CURATIVE.

restore, *v. t.* **1.** return, regive, reduce (*R*), restitute (*R*), redeliver; *see* REPAY.

2. *In the sense of "to bring a person or part of the body back to some previous, usually better, condition":* recover (*R*), repair (*R*), retrieve, recuperate, repristinate (*R*), renew, rehabilitate; *see* CURE, REVIVE.

Antonyms: see TIRE, EXHAUST.

3. *See* RETURN, RENEW, REPAIR, REPLACE, RECALL, REËSTABLISH.

restrain, *v. t.* **1.** *In the sense of "to bring to a complete cessation of activity" or "to withhold from activity":* check, arrest, stop, stay, withhold, deter, rebuff, refrain (*R*), keep, hold, repress, inhibit (*B or tech.*), bind, cramp, cohibit (*R*), cork (*fig. and chiefly C or S*), bottle (*fig.; C or S*); *see* PREVENT, HINDER.

Antonyms: see IMPEL, INCITE.

2. *In the sense of "to hold back from putting forth full activity":* check, contain, govern, rule, constrain (*B*), control, bridle, curb, bit (*consciously fig.*), rein, temper, shackle (*fig.*), yoke (*consciously fig.*), hold, discourage (*C*), coarct (*R*), compesce (*R*), trash (*obs. or R; orig. spec.*); *see* CONTROL, CONFINE.

Antonyms: see IMPEL, INCITE, DRIVE, URGE.

3. *In the sense of "to hold back (desire, enthusiasm, feeling, or other form of activity)":* check, repress, deaden, damp, dampen, chill, chasten (*B*), lessen, control, govern, constrain (*B*), bridle, curb, hold, bit (*consciously fig.*), confine.

4. *See* RESTRICT.

restraint, *n.* **1.** check, arrest, stopping, staying, withholding, deterrence, determent, keeping, repression, inhibition; *see* PREVENTION, FORBIDDING.

2. *Referring to the action:* check, government, control, containment (*R*), rein, discouragement (*chiefly C*); *see* CONTROL, CONFINEMENT, CONSTRAINT.

Antonyms: see URGING, INCITEMENT.

3. *Referring to the thing that restrains:* check, control, bridle, curb, bit (*consciously fig.*), rein, shackle, discouragement (*C*), deterrent.

Antonyms: see INCITEMENT.

4. check, repression, control, government, confinement, bridling, curbing, cramp, binding, *etc.*

Antonyms: see LICENSE.

5. *See* RESTRICTION.

restrict, *v. t.* **1.** *In reference to confinement of a body within a certain space: see* CONFINE.

2. *Referring to the limitation of the scope or extent of the operation of activities, causes, etc.:* confine, restrain, limit, constrain, straiten, astrict (*R*), restringe (*R*); *spec.* tie, qualify, circumscribe.

restricted, *a.* limited, strait (*A*), strict; *see* PARTICULAR, CONFINED.

Antonyms: see ABSOLUTE.

restriction, *n.* **1.** *See* CONFINEMENT.

2. confinement, restraint, limitation, constraint; *spec.* qualification, embargo.

restrictive, *a.* limiting, limitative; *spec.* circumscriptive, qualificatory; *see* CONFINING.

result, *n.* **1.** effect (*viewed as immediately following from a cause*), consequence (*viewed esp. as a thing or circumstance, or in its relations to those affected by it, or as being worth consideration*), sequel, sequela (*B; chiefly tech. and chiefly spec.*), outcome, fruit, product, resultant, creature (*disparaging or contemptuous*), sequent (*R*), resultance (*R*), end (*contex.*); *spec.* corollary, superconsequence, dregs (*pl., the sequence of disease*); *see* PRODUCT.

Antonyms: see CAUSE.

2. *In pl.: see* PROCEEDS.

3. *In mathematics: see* COMPUTATION.

result, *v. i.* **1.** *Referring to the cause: see* EVENTUATE.

2. *Referring to what arises from the cause:* follow, come, arise, originate, redound, proceed.

resulting, *a.* resultant, consequent, sequent (*R*), consequential, emergent (*implying an arising from something else*), arising, appendant.

resume, *v. t.* **1.** retake, reassume, recall, revoke; *spec.* reoccupy; *see* RECOVER.

2. *See* RENEW, SUMMARIZE.

resumption, *n.* **1.** retaking, reassumption, recall; *spec.* reoccupation, recaption; *see* RECOVERY.

2. *See* RENEWAL, SUMMARIZATION.

retaliate, *v. t.* return, requite, repay, retribute, retort. "*Retaliate*" *is used only with reference to the return of evil.*

retaliation, *n. For discriminations see* RETRIBUTION. return, reprisal, requital, retribution, payment, retortion, talio *or* talion (*tech.*), pay (*R*).

Antonyms: see ABSOLUTION.

retard, *v. t.* **1.** restrain, delay, slow, forslow (*A*), slacken, slack (*R*).

Antonyms: see HASTEN, QUICKEN.

retail: *sell, mention, narrate.*
retain: *keep, engage, remember, hold, detain.*
retainer: *adherent.*
retainer: *fee.*

2. *See* HINDER.
retardation, *n.* **1.** restraint, delay, retard (*R; used in "in retard"*), retardment (*R*), slowing, slacking; *spec.* lag.
2. *See* HINDRANCE.
retch, *v. i.* reach (*now dial.*), heave, wamble (*dial.*), keck (*R*), gag.
retentive, *a.* **1.** *Spec.* keeping, continent (*R*).
2. *In reference to the mind's power to remember:* tenacious.
Antonyms: see FORGETFUL.
reticence, *n.* reserve, silence, dumbness, secrecy, mumness, reservedness, taciturnity, reticency, secretiveness, closeness, seclusion. *Cf.* COMMUNICATIVE, TALKATIVE.
reticent, *a.* reserved, uncommunicative, silent, dumb, secretive, close, taciturn, mum, secret, dark (*implying concealment, suggestive of evil*), private.
Antonyms: see COMMUNICATIVE, TALKATIVE.
retinue, *n.* following, attendance, tail, train, trail, suite, suit (*A*), rout, people (*contex.*); *spec.* court, cortège (*French*), bodyguard.
retire, *v. i.* **1.** withdraw, retreat.
Antonyms: see ADVANCE.
2. bed (*R*), lair (*of an animal*), go to bed.
3. *See* RECEDE.
retire, *v. t.* **1.** withdraw; *spec.* seclude.
Antonyms: see ADVANCE.
2. remove, shelve (*fig.*); *spec.* pension (*often used with "off"*), superannuate; *see* DISCHARGE.
retirement, *n.* **1.** *Referring to the act:* withdrawal, retire (*R*), retiral (*R*), seclusion, reclusion.
2. *Referring to the state:* withdrawal, retreat; *spec.* seclusion, reclusion.
retreat, *n.* **1.** recession, withdrawal, recoil (*R, exc. spec.*), retrograde (*R*), retrogradation, katabasis (*B; used in reference or allusion to Xenophon*); *spec.* rout; *see* RETIREMENT.
Antonyms: see ADVANCE, INVASION.
2. recess, place (*contex.*), cove, retirement (*R*), retire (*R*); *spec.* hold, niche, shadow, reclusion, hibernaculum *or* hibernacle (*R*), grotto; *see* REFUGE.
3. *See* RECESS.
retreat, *v. i.* **1.** recede, withdraw, retrograde, recoil (*R, exc. spec.*), go (*contex.*); *see* RETIRE.
Antonyms: see ADVANCE.
2. *In an immaterial sense: see* WITHDRAW.
retreating, *a.* recessive, retrograde; *spec.* retiring.
retribute, *v. t.* **1.** *See* RETALIATE.
2. compensate, repay, avenge, revenge, wreak (*A*). *The verb "retribute" is less usual than its synonyms.*
retribution, *n.* **1.** *With sense of a return by way of punishment:* avengement, reprisal (*especially used in war or conflict*), revenge, retaliation, revengement, vengeance, Nemesis (*the goddess of vengeance*), nemesis (*vengeance in general*).
2. *With simple sense of a just return for losses suffered or caused:* recompense, compensation, requital, reparation.
Antonyms: see FORGIVENESS, MERCY.
retributive, *a.* retributory, avenging, requiting.
retrieval, *n.* **1.** *See* RECOVERY.
2. *In the sense of "a making up for":* recovery.
retrieve, *v. t.* **1.** *See* RECOVER.
2. *In the sense of "to make good"; "to make up for":* recover, recoup.
retroactive, *a.* retrospective, regressive; *spec.* expost facto (*Latin*).
return, *v. t.* **1.** *Referring to a sending, conducting, or putting back to, toward, or in a previous position or place:* restore; *spec.* reconduct, volley, boast, redart; *see* REPLACE, REFLECT, ECHO, RECOMMIT.
2. give (*contex.*), reciprocate, requite, repay, respond (*R*); *see* RETALIATE.
3. *See* REPAY, REPORT, ANSWER, ELECT, YIELD.
return, *v. i.* **1.** *In the sense of "to come back to or toward an original position":* recover, regress (*R*); *spec.* retrograde, revolve, remigrate; *see* RECEDE.
2. *See* ANSWER, RECUR, REPORT, RENEW, RECOIL, REACT, REVERT.
return, *n.* recovery, regress (*R*), regression; *spec.* reëntry, retrogression, retrogradation, countermarch; *see* RECESSION.
return, *n.* **1.** *Spec.* volley; *see* REPLACEMENT, REFLECTION, ECHO.
2. reciprocation, restoration, requital, repayment; *see* RETALIATION.
3. *See* RECURRENCE, RENEWAL, REPORT, REPAYMENT, RENT, YIELD, REVERSION.
reunite, *v. t. & v. i.* **1.** unite (*contex.*), rejoin, recompound, recompose, recombine, recompact (*v. t. only*).
2. reconcile.
revel, *v. i.* **1.** disport; *spec.* riot, roister.
2. *See* DELIGHT, ABOUND.
revelation, *n.* **1.** *Referring to divine communications:* disclosure, oracle; *spec.* apocalypse, gospel (*R*).
2. *See* DISCLOSURE.
revelatory, *a.* disclosing, apocalyptic (*chiefly spec. and Bib.*).
reveler, *n.* merrymaker; *spec.* mænad, bacchant, roisterer *or* (*A*) roister, Bacchanal, Bacchanalian.
reveling, *a.* merrymaking; *spec.* Bacchic, Bacchanalian, roystering, roisterous (*R*), Bacchanal.
revelry, *n.* merrymaking, revel-rout (*A*), revel-

retention: *keeping, remembrance, memory, holding, detention.*
retired: *secluded, lonely.*
retrace: *delineate, draw, follow, recall.*
retract, *v. t.: withdraw, recall, revoke.*
retrench: *v. t.: diminish, remove, delete.*
retrench, *v. i.: diminish, economize.*
retrenchment: *diminution, removal, economy.*
retrogression: *recession, decline, degeneration.*
retrospect, *n.: look, view, consideration.*
reveal, *v. t.: disclose, show, confess.*
revenge, *v. t.: vindicate, retribute.*
revenue: *income.*

ment; *spec.* carnival, deray (*A*), Bacchanal, Bacchanalia (*pl.*), orgy.
Antonyms: see MOURNING, LAMENTATION.
reversal, *n.* **1.** abrogation, annulment; *cf.* INVALIDATE.
2. inversion, reversement (*R*).
reverse, *a.* **1.** *See* BACK, BACKWARD.
2. turned, inverted, inverse; *spec.* retrorse, retrograde.
reverse, *n.* **1.** contrary.
2. *Referring to the side of medal, coin, etc., that does not bear the main device:* back, counterpart, verso, tail, pile (*A*).
3. misfortune, adversity, backcast, down (*C; chiefly used in "ups and downs"*), backset, check, comedown (*C*), set-back, pull-back (*C*); *see* DEFEAT.
4. inverse.
reverse, *v. t.* **1.** turn, revert (*R*), invert; *spec.* retrograde, transpose, intussuscept, invaginate.
2. *See* INVALIDATE.
reversion, *n.* **1.** *In law:* return; *spec.* escheat.
2. *In thought, discourse, etc.:* recurrence, retrospect, retrospection.
3. *See* RELAPSE.
4. throwback, atavism.
revert, *v. i.* **1.** *In law:* return; *spec.* escheat.
2. *To go back in thought, discourse, etc.:* return, recur, retrospect, remount (*R*).
3. *See* RELAPSE, BACKSLIDE.
revile, *v. i.* vituperate, rail, slang (*C*).
revival, *n.* **1.** restoration, reanimation, raising, revivement (*R*), recovery, resurrection, resuscitation, revivification, recall (*contex.*); *spec.* animation.
2. *In an intransitive sense:* resurrection, resuscitation, rising, revivescence (*R*).
3. *In the sense of "bringing again to knowledge, notice," etc.:* recall, renewal, restoration, rekindling, resurrection, revivement (*R*), revivification (*R*); *spec.* reëstablishment. *See* REËSTABLISH.
4. *In the sense of "coming again into notice, currency," etc.:* resurrection (*R*), renascence, renaissance, revivement (*R*), revival.
5. *In a religious sense:* reawakening.
6. *See* RECALL, STRENGTHENING, RENEWAL, REFRESHMENT.
revive, *v. t.* **1.** restore, recover, reanimate, wake (*religious or poetic*), requicken (*R*), resuscitate, raise, resurrect, revivify, recall (*contex.*); *see* ANIMATE.
Antonyms: see KILL.
2. *In the sense of "to bring again into existence, notice, or currency":* renew, recall, restore, revivify (*R*), rekindle, resurrect; *see* REESTABLISH.
3. *See* RESTORE, RENEW, RECALL.
revive, *v. i.* **1.** recover, resurrect, resuscitate, rise.
Antonyms: see DIE, FAINT.
2. *See* FRESHEN.
reviving, *a.* **1.** *In an active or transitive sense:* resuscitative, resurrective, revivifying.
2. *In an intransitive sense:* revivescent (*R*).
revocation, *n.* recall, rescission, repeal.
revocatory, *a.* revocative, rescissory, abrogative.
revoke, *v. t.* annul, retract, renege (*cards*), abrogate, repeal (*chiefly spec.*), cancel, rescind, raise (*an embargo, etc.*), recall, countermand, counterorder (*R*); *spec.* unpray (*R*), unpromise (*R*), disenact, abolish.
Antonyms: see ENACT.
revoke, *v. i.* *In cards:* renege.
revolution, *n.* **1.** gyre (*B*), turn, wheel, circuit, circulation, round, circumvolution, whirl.
2. overthrow, overturn, upset.
3. *See* INSURGENCY, PASSAGE.
revolutionary, *a.* **1.** revolutional (*R*), red (*fig.*), sansculottic (*fig.*), unusual (*a weakened, journalistic sense*); *see* INSURGENT.
2. *See* REVOLVING.
revolve, *v. i.* **1.** *Referring to an orbit or, fig., to what returns to its starting-place in a circuit:* circle, roll, circuit, orb (*R*), turn, round, wheel, swing, gyrate, circumgyrate, circumvolve (*R*), circulate.
2. *See* ROTATE.
revolve, *v. t.* **1.** roll, wheel.
2. *See* CONSIDER, ROTATE.
revolving, *a.* revolutionary, gyral, voluble (*R*), gyratory.
reward, *v. t.* **1.** recompense, requite, reguerdon (*R*), premiate (*R*); *spec.* remunerate, gratify (*A*), repay, remember, flesh, *see* PAY.
Antonyms: see PUNISH.
2. *See* PUNISH.
reward, *n.* **1.** *Referring to the act:* recompense, requital, remuneration, gratification (*A*), repayment, remembrance; *see* PAYMENT.
Antonyms: see PUNISHMENT.
2. *Referring to the thing that rewards:* recompense, return, remuneration, remembrance, premium, crown (*fig.*), bounty, meed (*B or rhetorical*), guerdon (*B*), gratification (*A*), reguerdon (*R*); *spec.* honorarium, pay, hire, prize.
3. *See* PUNISHMENT.
Antonyms: see PENALTY.
rewrite, *v. t.* rescribe (*R*); *see* COPY.
rhapsody, *n.* effusion, rapture.
rhetoric, *n.* **1.** *As the name of the art:* eloquence (*R*).
2. *As the name of a form of language: see* DICTION.
rhythm, *n.* number, cadence, cadency, rhythmus (*tech.*), pulsation (*R*); *spec.* chime, run, lilt (*chiefly B*), swing, meter, measure.
rhythmic, *a.* metrical, metric, numerous (*B; R*), cadent.

---

reverberate: *reflect, echo.*
revere: *esteem.*
review, *v. t.: examine, consider, discuss, reconsider, criticize.*
revile, *v. t.: abuse.*
revise: *edit, reconsider.*
revolt, *n.: insurgence, movement.*
revolt, *v. i.: insurrect, shrink.*

rib, *n.* **1.** *In anatomy:* costa.
2. ridge, ribbet (*R*), cord; *spec.* groin, ogive, lierne; *see* FEATHER, BRACE.
3. *See* VEIN, QUILL, RIDGE.
ribbed, *a.* costate.
ribbon, *n.* **1.** ribband (*A*), band (*contex.*); *spec.* cordon, galloon.
2. *See* STRIP, BADGE.
rich, *a.* **1.** prosperous (*contex.*), wealthy, opulent, affluent, well-to-do, moneyed, solid, flush, pursy (*C*), pecunious (*R*), dollared (*a nonce word*), snug (*chiefly Irish dial.*), warm (*C, Eng.*).
Antonyms: see POOR.
2. *See* VALUABLE, LUXURIOUS, MELODIOUS, DEEP, ABOUNDING, ABUNDANT, PRODUCTIVE, ODOROUS.
rich person, moneybags (*pl.; humorous or contemptuous*), Dives (*cf. Luke xvi: 19-31*), richling (*R*), Crœsus (*fig.*), Midas (*fig.*); *spec.* millionaire, multimillionaire, billionaire.
Antonyms: see BEGGAR.
rickety, *a.* **1.** *See* WEAK.
2. shaky, ramshackle, ramshackled (*R*), tumbledown, ramshackly (*R*), cranky, crank, crazy.
Antonyms: see FIRM.
riddle, *n.* **1.** question (*contex.*), conundrum (*properly spec.*), enigma, griph (*obs. or R*); *spec.* logogriph, logogram *or* logograph (*an erroneous usage*), rebus, charade.
2. *See* SECRET.
ride, *v. i.* **1.** *Spec.* lark, prick (*A*), bucket, pump, tool (*S or cant*), walk, trot, gallop, canter, prance, spank, grind (*Eng. univ. S*), hack, jumble (*R*), jolt, cavalcade, spur, tantivy (*obs. and R*), jackass (*R*).
2. *To ride in or on a vehicle:* vehiculate (*R*), cycle, wheel; *spec.* caroche, chariot; *see* DRIVE.
3. *See* REST, FLOAT.
ride, *v. t.* **1.** *Spec.* bucket, pump, walk, amble, trot, canter, lark, prance, hunt.
2. *See* SIT, TRAVERSE, EXPEL.
3. bestride (*as spectacles do the nose*).
rider, *n.* **1.** horseman (*masc.*), horsewoman (*fem.*), equestrian, equestrienne (*fem.; R*), pricker (*A*), rideress (*fem.; R*); *spec.* jockey, galloper, ambler, postillion *or* postilion, courier.
2. *A clause appended to a document after its drafting: spec.* tack (*Eng.*).
ridge, *n.* **1.** *Spec.* ridgelet, keel, carina, rib, carination, fret, fillet, spine, crest, ripple, seam, burr, inion, back, zastruga; *see* RIB, WRINKLE, WEAL.
Antonyms: see CHANNEL.
2. *Referring to a ridge of land: spec.* chine, spine, crest, bridge, kame *or* kaim (*Scot. & North of Eng.*), hogback, sowback (*R*), horseback (*U. S.*), thank-you-ma'am (*C, R, U. S.*), saddle, ledge; *see* BANK, BAR, HILL.
Antonyms: see CHANNEL.
ridged, *a.* ridgy; *spec.* keeled, carinate, cristate, crested, corded, twilled, wrinkled.
ridicule, *n.* derision, mockery, irony (*ridicule by juxtaposition of inequalities or absurdities, but though biting, not intentionally cruel*), sarcasm (*with implication of intentional cruelty*), mock (*R*), mocking, game (*used only in "to make game of"*), irrison (*R*), roasting (*C; the action*), roast (*C; a specific act*); *spec.* imitation; *see* SATIRE.
Antonyms: see PRAISE.
ridicule, *v. t.* contemn (*simple condemnation, which, like* ridicule *does not necessarily imply malice*), deride (*implies mockery*), mock, bemock, guy (*orig. theatrical S*), roast (*C*), scout; *spec.* monkey (*R*), sneer (*R*), skit, burlesque, hoot, satirize, taunt, chaff, quiz (*the latter two C, implying good-natured banter*).
Antonyms: see PRAISE.
ridiculing, *a.* sardonic (*said of a smile or grin*).
right, *n.* **1.** *See* JUSTICE, UPRIGHTNESS, TRUTH.
2. interest, part, claim, title, droit (*law; chiefly in "droits of admiralty"*); *spec.* equity, patent; *see* DUE.
3. liberty, privilege, prerogative.
right, *a.* **1.** *See* JUST, CORRECT, APPROPRIATE, TRUE, CONVENTIONAL, PROPER, ADVANTAGEOUS, SANE, ACTUAL, GENUINE, STRAIGHT.
2. dextral, dexter.
Antonyms: see LEFT.
3. droitural; *spec.* contractual.
righteous, *a.* just (*now chiefly Bib.*), godly, god-fearing, good, right (*R*); *spec.* goody (*C*); *see* SINLESS, UPRIGHT, RELIGIOUS.
Antonyms: see IMMORAL.
right-handed, *a.* dexterous *or* dextrous (*R.*)
rightist, *a.* conservative, white (*cant*).
Antonyms: see LEFTIST.
rightless, *a. In law:* dead (*fig.*), unlawed.
rigid, *a.* **1.** stiff, indeformable (*R*), implastic, marbly (*fig.*), inflexible, firm, unyielding; *see* HARD.
Antonyms: see DUCTILE, FLEXIBLE, SOFT, PLASTIC.
2. *See* UNYIELDING, STRICT, FORMAL, AUSTERE.
rigidity, *n.* **1.** stiffness, rigidness, implasticity, inflexibility, firmness, unyieldingness; *see* HARDNESS.
2. *Spec.* unyieldingness, strictness, formality, austerity.
rim, *n.* edge; *spec.* felloe *or* felly, chime *or* chimb, ring, flange, girdle, curb.
Antonyms: see BODY, CENTER, MIDDLE.
rime, rhyme, *n.* **1.** crambo (*contemptuous*); *spec.* assonance.
2. *See* VERSE, POETRY.

ribald: *abusive, irreligious, coarse, lewd.*
rid, *v. t.: clear, free.*
ridiculous: *laughable, absurd.*
rife: *prevalent, current, abundant.*
rifle: *plunder.*
rift, *n.: cleft, opening.*
rig, *n.: equipment, costume, team.*
rig, *v. t.: equip, adjust, clothe.*
rightful: *lawful, deserved, due.*
rigor: *severity, austerity.*
rigorous: *severe, austere, strict.*
rim, *v. t.: edge.*

rime, rhyme, *v. t.* berime *or* berhyme (*an intensive*); *see* VERSIFY.

rime, rhyme, *v. i.* **1.** *Of words:* chink (*R or contemptuous*).
2. *Of a person: see* VERSIFY.

rimose, *a.* cleft, rimous, rifty, chinky, clefty (*R*).

ring, *v. i. & v. t.* **1.** resound; *spec.* tinkle, jingle, jangle, dingle (*R*), twang, clink, clank, clang, peal (*v. i. only*), sing (*v. i. only*), tintinnabulate (*B*), chinkle (*R*), toll, knell, knoll (*A or dial.*), jow (*Scot.*); *see* CHIME, PLAY, DIN.
2. *As a v. i.; referring to the ears:* sing, hum, buzz, tingle.

ring, *n.* **1.** resonance; *spec.* tinkle, jingle, jangle, dingle (*R*), twang, chink, clank, clang, clangor, ringing, tintinnabulation (*B*), chinkle (*R*), tinnitus, ding-dong (*imitative*), peal, knell, knoll (*A or dial.*), toll, curfew.
2. *See* SET.

ring, *n.* **1.** circle, annulus (*B or tech.*), cirque (*B*), round, roundel (*R*), hoop; *spec.* gimmal *or* gemel, eyelet, circlet, ringlet, keeper, grummet *or* grommet, whorl, cringle, traveler, torque, thimble, discus, vervel *or* varvel, washer, burr, terret, manilla, lasket, collar, collet; *see* LOOP, FERRULE, COIL, CROWN, WREATH, GIRDLE, RIM.
2. *See* SET, COMBINATION, ARENA.

ring, *v. t.* **1.** *See* SURROUND, GIRDLE.
2. *In the sense of "to put a ring on or around":* enring (*R*); *spec.* girdle.

ringing, *a.* resonant; *spec.* tintinnabulant (*R*), tinkling, clanging, *etc.*

ringing, *n.* **1.** resonance; *spec.* tintinnabulation (*B*), tinkling, *etc.*, curfew, peal.
2. buzz (*of the ears*).

riparian, *a.* riverside, riverine, ripal (*R*), riparial (*R*), riparious (*R*); *spec.* estuarine.

ripe, *a.* **1.** *Of fruit:* mature (*obs. or R*); *spec.* mellow, soft, overripe.
Antonyms: see UNRIPE.
2. *Of persons, judgment, scholarship, etc.:* mature, developed.
3. *See* GROWN, ADVANCED, PREPARED, COMPLETED.

ripen, *v. i.* **1.** *Of fruit:* ripe (*R*), mature (*also fig.*); *spec.* mellow (*also fig.*).
2. *Of a boil:* gather, head.
3. *See* DEVELOP.

ripen, *v. t.* **1.** enripen (*R*), mature, mellow.
2. *See* DEVELOP, CURE.

ripple, *n.* **1.** agitation (*contex.*), play (*contex.*), wave (*contex.*), wavelet, dimple, ruffle, curl, crinkle, lipper (*cant*); *spec.* ring, ripplet, ripple.
2. *See* WAVE.

ripple, *v. i.* **1.** play (*contex.*), wave, lap, dimple, ruffle, curl, crinkle, lipper (*cant*).
2. *See* FLOW, WAVE, FRET.

ripple, *v. t.* **1.** agitate, wave, dimple, ruffle, curl, crinkle.
2. *See* WAVE.

ripply, *a.* **1.** agitated, wavy, dimply, ruffly (*R*), crinkly, ruffled.
2. *See* WAVY.

rise, *n.* **1.** ascent, ascension, ascendance, uprising (*R*), levitation (*often spec.*), heave, tower (*R*), mount (*R*); *spec.* flow, soaring, break; *see* EMERGENCE, ASCENT.
Antonyms: see DESCENT, FALL.
2. *See* HILL, INCREASE, ADVANCE, OCCURRENCE.

rise, *v. i.* **1.** ascend, uprise, mount, levitate (*chiefly spec.*), lift (*chiefly spec.*), arise (*B*); *spec.* soar, climb, clamber, upclimb (*R*), upleap, scale, rear, tower, ramp, spring, spire, aspire (*R*), heave, upheave (*R*), remount, resurge (*R*), heighten (*R*), rouse (*R*), break, upflow (*R*), exsurge (*R*), upsoar (*R*), emerge.
Antonyms: see DESCEND, ALIGHT, FALL.
2. *In the sense of "to get up or take a more erect position":* arise; *spec.* bristle, prick, stand.
Antonyms: see STOOP.
3. *Referring to the flowing up of water:* flow, head (*chiefly U. S.*), swell.
4. Insurrect (*R*), insurrectionize (*R*), rebel, mutiny, revolt.
5. *Referring to the spirits, passions, etc.:* kindle, wax, mount, tower.
6. *See* ADVANCE, ARISE, APPEAR, OCCUR, PROTUBERATE, INCREASE, RECOVER, REVIVE, ADJOURN, DECAMP.

rising, *a.* **1.** ascendant, ascending, mounting, resurgent (*R*); *spec.* orient.
Antonyms: see DESCENDING, FALLING.
2. *See* HILLY, ADVANCING.

risky, *a.* **1.** *See* DANGEROUS.
2. scabrous (*B, R*), risqué (*French*), off-color.

rite, *n.* form, ceremony, ritual (*chiefly in pl.*); *spec.* hierurgy, liturgy, service, cult, sacrament, sacramental, use, baptism, proper, mass, form, orgies (*pl.*).

rival, *n.* corrival *or* corival (*R*); *see* COMPETITOR.

river, *n.* stream (*contex.*); *spec.* rivulet, riveret, riverling (*R*), tributary, affluent, anabranch (*Australia*); *see* RIVULET.

river, *a.* fluvial, fluviatile, riverain, riverine, potamic (*R*).

rivulet, *n.* river (*contex.*), stream (*contex.*), streamlet (*contex.*), run (*chiefly U. S.*), runnel, creek (*British colonies & U. S.*), runlet, riverlet (*R*); *see* BROOK.

road, *n.* **1.** way, passage, roadway, highway, street, avenue, turnpike, pike; *spec.* boulevard, ride, track, drive, causeway, ridgeway, corduroy, trail; *see* TRACK.
2. *See* ANCHORAGE, RAILROAD, COURSE, DIRECTION.

roar, *n.* **1.** cry (*contex.*), rout; *see* BELLOW, SHOUT, OUTCRY.
2. resonance, thunder, fremitus (*R*), buller

---

ringleader: *chief.*
rinse, *v. t.: wash, gargle.*
riot, *n: dissipation, merrymaking, disturbance.*
riotous: *merry, boisterous, lawless.*
rising: *rise, insurgence, hill, projection.*
risk, *n.: danger, chance, venture.*
risk, *v. t.: endanger, venture, wager.*
roam, *v. i.: wander.*

(*Scot.*), rote (*U. S.*), swough (*obs. or A*); *spec.* rut (*U. S.*), echo.
3. *See* OUTBREAK.
roar, *v. i.* **1.** cry (*contex.*), rout; *see* BELLOW, SHOUT.
2. *See* RESOUND.
roar, *v. t.* cry, rout (*R*); *see* BELLOW.
roaring, *a.* **1.** crying (*contex.*), routing; *see* BELLOWING.
2. *See* LOUD, BOISTEROUS.
roast, *n.* **1.** cook (*contex.*);—*said of the operation or its result.*
2. *Of meat: spec.* barbecue, cabob (*primarily Anglo-Indian*), sirloin, rump, sparerib, *etc.*
3. torrefaction (*R*); *spec.* calcination, decrepitation, parch; *see* BAKE.
4. *See* RIDICULE, GLOW.
roast, *v. t.* **1.** cook (*contex.; R*); *spec.* barbecue, bake.
2. heat (*contex.*), torrefy; *spec.* calcine, burn, decrepitate, frit, parch; *see* BAKE.
3. *See* RIDICULE.
robber, *n.* desperado, plunderer, thief; *spec.* highwayman, footpad, bandit, dacoit (*India*); *see* PICKPOCKET, BURGLAR, PIRATE.
robbery, *n.* thievery, plunder, hold-up, stick-up (*S*); *spec.* dacoity (*India*), piracy.
robe, *n.* **1.** garment (*contex.*), gown; *spec.* cassock, chrisom, dalmatic, colobium, dolman, surcoat, peplum *or* peplos *or* peplus, prætexta, toga, trabea, manga, cymar, chimer, kimono; *see* CLOAK.
2. *See* COVER, (*in pl.*) CLOTHING.
rock, *n.* **1.** *Referring to a large mass of stone:* stone (*contex.*); *spec.* crag, bowlder *or* boulder, sarsen, dolman, monolith, *etc.*
2. *Referring to the hard, massive substance in general:* stone; *spec.* burr, trap, tufa, clint, slate, asbestos, dolomite, lava, flint, pumice.
rock, *v. t.* **1.** cradle.
2. *See* SWAY.
rocky, *a.* **1.** stony; *spec.* craggy, bowldery.
2. *See* UNFEELING.
rod, *n. Spec.* tie, bull, pontil, spindle, slat, shaft, cue, verge, ferule, ferula, pole.
rodlike, *a.* virgate, veretilleous (*R*), veretilliform (*R*), rhabdoid;—*all tech.*
roe, *n.* eggs (*pl.*); *spec.* botargo, caviare.
roll, *v. t.* **1.** *In the sense of "to turn over or rotate an object with the result of forward motion or with reference to its motion relative to what supports it" (contrasting with "rotate," which refers simply to the turning round of the object about a central line):* wheel, trundle, truckle (*R*); *spec.* bowl, devolve (*A*); *see* REVOLVE.
2. *In the sense of "to fold continuously on itself," esp. with "up" or with an adverb of direction or manner:* infold, enroll; *spec.* furl.
Antonyms: see UNROLL.
3. *See* FLOW, TURN, SWAY, ACCUMULATE, CURL, WIND, WRAP, UTTER, SPREAD, SMOOTH.
roll, *v. i.* **1.** wheel, trundle, trindle (*A*), truckle (*A*); *spec.* grind, wallow, welter, run; *see* BOWL, REVOLVE.
2. *See* GO, WANDER, RIDE, PASS (*of time*), CURL, FLOW, WAVE, RESOUND, SOUND, TURN, DELIGHT, SWAY, SWAGGER.
roll, *n.* **1.** *Of a paper, parchment, or the like, bearing a record:* scroll, volume (*A or hist.*); *spec.* pipe (*Eng.*).
2. *Referring to anything rolled up in cylindrical form: spec.* collar, furl, bolt, fillet, rove *or* row.
3. *Referring to the action:* trundle, trindle (*A*); *spec.* bowl, devolution *or* devolvement (*A*), run.
4. *See* LIST, CYLINDER, ROLLER, COIL, LOAF, WINDLASS, TURN, GAIT, RESONANCE.
roller, *n.* cylinder, roll, rundle (*chiefly spec.*), trendle (*R; chiefly spec.*), truck, trundle (*chiefly spec.*); *spec.* bowl, runner, barrel, mill, drum, jigger, beam, doctor, jack, trolley; *see* WHEEL.
romance, *n.* **1.** narrative, romant (*tech.*), cycle *or* cyclus (*R*).
2. *See* NARRATIVE.
romantic, *a. Spec.* imaginative, idealistic, fantastic, wild, picturesque.
romanticism, *n. Spec.* imaginativeness, idealism, wildness, *etc.*
rondeau, *n.* poem (*contex.*), roundel (*often spec.*), rondel (*often spec.*).
roof, *n.* **1.** cover (*contex.*); *spec.* thatch, tortoise, tiler, cupola, tile, laquear, canopy, hip roof, mansard, dome, awning, saddleback, chopper (*Anglo-Indian*), deck (*U. S.*).
2. *See* CEILING, PALATE.
roof, *v. t.* cover (*contex.*); *spec.* shingle, slate, tile, thatch.
roofing, *n.* roofage; *spec.* tiling, tile, shingling, slate, thatch.
room, *n.* **1.** apartment, chamber (*rhetorical or spec.*); *spec.* den, salon (*French*), saloon, stew, rotunda, conclave, cuddy, cubbyhole, cenacle, gloriette, consistory, divan, crypt, cabinet (*A*), wardrobe, library, study, closet, cabin, boudoir, bower (*A*), berth, cellar, stanza, buffet, ward, surgery, cell, zeta (*A*); sala (*R*), lodge; *see* CHAMBER, CELL, ROOM, HALL, BEDROOM.
2. space, roomage (*R*), scope (*chiefly fig.*), pace (*A*), capacity, accommodation; *spec.* margin, headway, seaway, leeway, elbowroom.
3. *See* OPPORTUNITY, LODGING.
roommate, *n.* comrade (*contex.*); *spec.* chum, tentmate.
roomy, *a.* spacious, large, wide, broad, capacious, roomthy (*now dial.*), commodious, roomful (*R*); *spec.* comfortable.

---

rob, *v. t.: plunder, steal, deprive.*
rob, *v. i.: steal, plunder, pirate*
robber: *thief, pirate.*
robust: *hardy, vigorous, energetic.*
robustious: *hardy, vigorous, strong, self-assertive.*
rogue: *rascal, mischief-maker.*
roguish: *rascally, mischievous.*
rôle: *part.*
romance, *v. t.: exaggerate.*
roomer: *lodger.*

Antonyms: see NARROW.
root, *n.* **1.** *Spec.* rootlet, radical, radicle, radication (*R*), tap, taproot, hand, race.
2. *Referring to hairs, the tongue, nails, teeth, etc.:* base, origin.
3. *In philology:* radical, etymon (*tech.*).
4. *See* SOURCE, ANCESTOR, BOTTOM, REASON.
root, *v. i.* strike;—*said of plants.*
root, *v. i.* dig (*contex.*), nuzzle, grout, rootle (*R*), grub.
rope, *n.* line (*contex.*); *spec.* fast, earing, guy, halliard *or* halyard, stay, halter, hawser, cable, cablet, painter, swifter, sheet, gad, gasket, ratlin, guesswarp, guest-rope, foreganger, foretack, foresheet, lanyard, boltrope, brail, span, runner, downhaul, forerunner, messenger, lunge, roband *or* robbin (*R*), buntline, tackle, bowline, cord, tack, lariat, lasso, timenoguy, spring; *see* HALTER.
ropelike, *a.* funiform (*tech. or B*).
rope-walker, *n.* acrobat (*contex.*), funambulator (*R*), funambulist (*rhetorical*).
rose, *n.* **1.** *Referring to the plant:* rosier (*B*); *spec.* roselet.
2. red (*contex.*); *spec.* crimson, solferino.
roseate, *a.* **1.** rose-colored, rose, rosy.
2. *See* HOPEFUL.
rose garden, *n.* rosary, rosarium.
roselike, *a.* rosaceous.
rostrum, *n.* platform (*contex.*), stage, stand, tribune; *see* PULPIT.
rotary, *a.* **1.** *See* CIRCULAR.
2. rotative, rotatory, revolutionary (*R*); revolving (*R*), peristrephic (*R*); *spec.* whirling.
rotate, *v. i. & t.* **1.** turn, revolve, run (*contex.*) roll, wheel, whirl, twist, spin, round (*v. i.*), twirl, pirl (*A or dial.*), purl (*R or dial.*), birl (*Scot.*), circumrotate (*R and tautological*).
2. *See* ALTERNATE.
rotation, *n.* **1.** turn, revolution, round, roll (*R, exc. of a single instance*), wheel, whirl, twist, twirl, spin, circumrotation (*R*), circumvolution, whirligig (*R*), volubility (*R*).
2. *See* ROUND, SUCCESSION, ALTERNATION.
rough, *a.* **1.** uneven, coarse (*chiefly spec.*), harsh, unsmooth (*R*), ragged, roughish, broken, rugged, horrid (*B*); *spec.* salebrous (*R*), scabrous, bushy, burry, scraggy; *see* STUBBY, BURRY, CRAGGY, SCRATCHY.
Antonyms: see SMOOTH, DELICATE, POLISHED.
2. *Referring to weather, the winds, etc.:* bumpy (*of air travel*), foul, severe, violent, turbulent, harsh, rigorous (*B*), boisterous, tumultuous, rugged, wild; *see* STORMY.
Antonyms: see MILD.
3. *Referring to the water, as of the sea:* agitated (*contex.*), wavy, turbulent, tumultuous, broken; *spec.* fretful, chopping, stormy, wild, uproarious, rampageous (*R*), roaring, boisterous.
Antonyms: see CALM.
4. *Of, or referring to, the hair, fur, etc.:* shaggy, ragged, bushy, hirsute (*B*); *spec.* unkempt; *see* UNSHORN, NAPPY.
Antonyms: see SMOOTH, SMOOTH-HAIRED.
5. *Referring to one's treatment of others or to the course of life as it affects one:* ungentle, harsh, acid, acrimonious, hard, dure (*R*), ungenial (*R*), untender (*R*), blunt, brutal, rude, round, astringent (*R*), seamy (*fig.; after Shakespeare*); *spec.* brutish, churlish, sharp, savage (*C*), crude, coarse, brute, surly, sour, foul, gruff, brusque, boisterous; *see* IMPOLITE, SEVERE.
Antonyms: see SMOOTH, GENTLE, SOFTSPOKEN.
6. *Referring to style or quality in diction, art, etc.:* imperfect, rude, coarse, unfinished, unpolished, crude, rugged, gross, hirsute (*fig. use*), borrel *or* borel (*A*).
7. *See* HAIRY, COARSE, CRUDE, CLUMSY, UNREFINED, ACRID, ASTRINGENT, DISORDERLY, ASPIRATED, APPROXIMATE, DISCORDANT.
roughen, *v. t.* rough, coarsen (*R*), ruffle (*chiefly spec.*), enrough (*R*), engrail (*B*); *spec.* depolish (*R*); *see* FRET, GRAIN.
Antonyms: see SMOOTH, POLISH.
roughness, *n. Spec.* unevenness, horror (*B or rhetorical; R*), harshness, asperity, crudeness, rudeness, gruffness, brutality, bruteness, grossness, acidity, *etc. See* ROUGH, *a.*
round, *n.* **1.** *See* CIRCLE, BALL, RING, OUTBURST, CURVE, COIL, REVOLUTION, ROTATION, RUNG, GROUP, CIRCUMFERENCE, DISCHARGE, CIRCUIT, ROUTINE, WATCH.
2. *Referring to a single complete turn of some kind as at play, horse-racing, etc.:* turn, spell, bout (*now chiefly spec.*), cycle, rotation; *spec.* rally, run, lap, game, hand, wrestle, pass, heat.
3. *In music:* catch, troll (*R*).
round-up, *n.* rodeo (*Amer. Spanish*).
rouse, *v. t.* **1.** *See* START, WAKE, EXCITE, STARTLE, STIMULATE.
2. *Referring to rousing from inactivity or inattention to a state of activity or attention:* stimulate, arouse, move, bestir, stir, inspire, wake, awake, waken, awaken, raise, shake, inactuate (*R*).
Antonyms: see NUMB, SILENCE, STILL, STUPEFY.
3. *Referring to bringing into action the energies, spirits, etc.:* raise, arouse, call (*used esp. with "up," "together," etc.*), summon, rally, brace, draw (*used esp. with "out," "forth," etc.*).
Antonyms: see STUPEFY, CALM, SILENCE, STILL.
rouse, *v. i.* **1.** *See* AWAKE.
2. move, stir, uprouse (*R*); *spec.* rally.
roused, *a.* up (*used predicatively*).
rousing, *a.* lively.
rout, *v. t.* **1.** flight *or* fley (*obs. or A*), stampede (*orig. spec.*); *see* CHASE, SCATTER, DISPERSE.
2. *See* OVERCOME.

---

root, *v. t.: fix, establish, uproot, destroy.*
rooted: *fixed, chronic.*
rosy: *roseate, hopeful, auspicious.*
rotten: *decomposed, crumbly, corrupt, immoral.*
rotund: *circular, spherical, plump, full, resonant.*
rough, *n.: rowdy.*
round, *a.: blunt, circular, complete, spherical.*
round, *v. t.: curve, circuit, surround, traverse, finish, collect.*
round: *v. i.: curve, revolve, rotate, circuit, go.*

---

routine, *n.* course, round, path, rut, rota (*R*), groove (*often depreciatory*).
row, *n.* line, series, string, chain, queue, file, rank, range (*R*), tier (*chiefly spec.*); *spec.* degree, cordon, bank, team, swath, windrow; *see* LIST.
row, *v. i.* remigate (*R*), oar (*R*), paddle (*chiefly spec.*), pull; *spec.* scull, bucket, skiff, tub.
row, *v. t.* **1.** propel (*contex.*), oar (*R*), pull; *spec.* scull.
2. *See* TRANSPORT.
row, *n.* pull, paddle; *spec.* scull.
rowdy, *n.* desperado (*contex.*), tough (*C*), rough, ruffian, blackguard, hoodlum (*U. S.; S or C*), Hooligan (*S*), larrikin (*Australia*); *spec.* highbinder.
rowdyish, *a.* disorderly (*contex.*), ruffianly, ruffianish, hoodlumish (*U. S.; S or C*).
Antonyms: see LAW-ABIDING, POLITE, REFINED.
rowdyism, *n.* disorderliness (*contex.*), ruffianism, blackguardism, hoodlumism (*U. S.; S or C*), larrikinism (*chiefly Australia*), ruffianry (*R*).
rower, *n.* oarsman, oarman (*R*), oar, oarswoman (*fem.*), benchman (*R*); *spec.* bowman, bow-oar, stroke, sculler, galleyman.
rowing, *n.* oarage, remigation (*R*).
rowlock, *n.* oarlock, thole.
royal, *a.* **1.** sovereign; *spec.* kingly, queenly, imperial; *see* NOBLE, KINGLY.
2. *See* GENEROUS, IMPOSING.
royalty, *n.* **1.** sovereignty; *see* MONARCHY.
2. *See* GENEROSITY.
3. payment; *spec.* percentage, gale (*local Eng.*).
rub, *v. t. Spec.* chafe, fret, gall, grate, grind, grit, pumice, frictionize (*R*), fridge (*chiefly dial.*), friz, stroke; *see* GRAZE, FRAY, SCRUB, WIPE.
rub, *v. i. Spec.* chafe, fret, grate, grind; *see* GRAZE.
rub, *n.* **1.** chafe, fret, grate, grind, friction (*R exc. of the action*); *see* ABRASION, GRAZE.
2. *See* OBSTACLE.
rubber, *n.* **1.** *See* MASSEUR.
2. caoutchouc; *spec.* ebonite, vulcanite.
rubber, *n. A decisive game:* odd; *spec.* bumper.
rubbing, *n.* friction.
rubbish, *n.* **1.** stuff, débris, brash, truck *or* litter; *spec.* trumpery, rubble; *see* REFUSE.
2. *See* NONSENSE.
ruin, *n.* **1.** overthrow, fall, downfall, wreck, shipwreck, subversion, wrack, rack (*chiefly in "to go to rack and ruin"*), crash, loss, ruination (*chiefly referring to the action*), undoing (*the action*), perdition (*R*), decay, mischief, damnation (*moral or spiritual ruin*); *spec.* destruction, devastation, demolition, dilapidation, desolation, violation.
Antonyms: see SAVING.
2. *Referring to what is left of a ruined thing; chiefly in pl., except as used to designate a ruined structure as a unit:* remains (*pl.; R*); *spec.* carcass, wreck, débris.
3. bane;—*referring to what ruins.*
4. *See* HARM.
ruin, *v. t.* overthrow, overturn, subvert, ruinate (*R*), sap, wreck, shipwreck, damn (ruin *spiritually*), sink, undo, break, blast, shatter, mine, lose (*chiefly in p. p. "lost"*), do (*C*), confound (*A*), cook (*S*), diddle (*S*), dish (*S*); *spec.* demolish (*fig.*), dash; *see* DESTROY, DEMOLISH, IMPAIR, DESOLATE.
Antonyms: see SAVE, PROTECT.
ruined, *a.* ruinate (*formal or R*), gone (*C*), lost, flat, ruinous.
ruinous, *a.* **1.** *See* RUINED.
2. pernicious, damnatory (*spiritually* ruinous), wreckful (*A*); *spec.* subversionary, subversive, Cadmean, Pyrrhic; *see* DILAPIDATIVE, DISASTROUS, DESTRUCTIVE.
Antonyms: see BENEFICIAL, HELPFUL.
rule, *n.* **1.** canon (*a system of* principles), principle (*the general basis of* rules), maxim, axiom, precept (*these three are neatly expressed* rules, *moral or ethical*), regulation (*a specific minor* rule), law, formula (*orig. spec.*), convention (*usually an unwritten, generally agreed upon* rule, *but sometimes a formal body of* rules *in international law*); *spec.* philosopheme (*R*), gnomology (*R*), capitular *or* capitulary; *see* LAW, DECREE, CODE.
2. control, dominion, government, governance (*B or A*), regnancy (*R*), regency (*R*), reign (*R*), jurisdiction; *spec.* lordship, interregnum, interreign (*R*), condominium, raj (*Anglo-Indian*); *see* MONARCHY, AUTOCRACY.
3. *See* CONTROL, HABIT, RULER.
rule, *v. t.* **1.** control, govern, judge (*Bib.*), rein (*R; fig.*); *spec.* lord (*R*), king (*R*), overlord (*R*), misgovern, misrule.
2. *See* CONTROL, RESTRAIN, DECREE, DECIDE.
rule, *v. i.* **1.** control, domineer, reign; *spec.* monarchize, lord (*used esp. with "it"*), royalize, king (*used esp. with "it"*), queen (*used esp. with "it"*).
2. *See* PREVAIL.
ruler, *n.* **1.** controller (*contex.*), lord (*chiefly spec.*), sovereign, potentate, regent (*R*), sire (*R*), gubernator (*R*), governor; *spec.* power, dynast (*B*), dey, interrex, diabolarch, decarch, coregent, coloniarch (*R*), cosmocrat (*R*), cryptarch (*R*), decemir, duumvir, triumvir, hierarchy (*a collective*), ecclesiarch, hierarch, sultan, caliph *or* calif, tinea, gerent (*R*), pendragon, heptarch, harmost, meridarch, ethnarch, exarch, elector, thalassocrat, tetrarch, khedive, emir, sultan, genearch (*R*), khan, hakim, decan, hyleg, Kaiser, czar, king; *see* CHIEF, GOVERNOR.
Antonyms: see SUBJECT.
2. strip, rule; *spec.* clicker, straightedge.

---

row, *n.: quarrel, disturbance.*
rude: *rough, crude, imperfect, impolite, unrefined, undeveloped, artless, discordant.*
rudiment: *element, beginning.*
rudimentary: *elementary, initial, imperfect, undeveloped.*
rugged: *rough, hardy, unrefined, austere.*

(*A*) *archaic.* (*B*) *bookish, poetic, literary or learned.* (*C*) *colloquial.* (*Contex.*) *contextual.* (*R*) *rare.* (*S*) *slang.* *See pp. viii–ix.*

ruling, *a.* controlling, governing, regnant, regent; *spec.* ignipotent, omnipotent.
Antonyms: see SUBORDINATE.

rumble, *n.* grumble, growl, rumbling; *spec.* borborygmus; *see* RESONANCE, DIN.

rump, *n.* **1.** hip, rumple (*Scot. & dial. Eng.*), posterior (*contex.*); *spec.* croup *or* crupper, podex.
2. *See* REMAINDER.

run, *n.* **1.** race (*obs. or Scot.*), cursitation (*R*); *spec.* burst, scamper, scud, scour, scorch, scurry, sprint, scuttle, lope, flutter (*cant*), helter-skelter.
Antonyms: see STANDSTILL.
2. *See* GAIT, AVERAGE, GRAZING, CONTINUANCE, SCHOOL, ROLL, TRACK, MELODY, DIRECTION, JOURNEY, TREND, FLOW, STREAM, SCORE, MIGRATION, DEMAND, COURSE.

run, *v. i.* **1.** go (*contex.*), cursitate (*R*); *spec.* sprint, scour, scorch, scurry, scuttle, scud, lope, scamper, bolt, course, career, scutter (*C*), scram (*S*), skir (*Eng.*); *see* FLEE.
Antonyms: see WALK.
2. *See* MOVE, FLOW, PASS, GLANCE, WAG (*of the tongue*), ROLL, FLEE, EXTEND, CLIMB, DISCHARGE, CREEP, COAGULATE, CONTINUE, CIRCULATE, LIQUEFY, GO, MIGRATE, APPLY, READ, AVERAGE, TREND, SPREAD, SAIL, CHASE.

rung, *n.* stick, round, roundle *or* rundle (*obs. or R*); *spec.* spoke, stave (*now chiefly dial.*), degree (*obs., exc. heraldry*).

running, *a.* **1.** *See* FLOWING, HASTY, RAPID, CREEPING, SUPPURATIVE, CONSTANT, LINEAR.
2. *Referring to one that runs:* current (*now R*).
3. *Of handwriting:* current, cursive.
4. *Of the feet or legs of animals:* cursorial.

rural, *a.* **1.** rustic (*now R*), country, agrarian, bucolic (*often humorous*), landward (*Scot.*), back (*usually disparaging*), Arcadian (*B*); *spec.* pastoral, woodland, silvan, sylvan; *see* AGRICULTURAL.
Antonyms: see URBAN.
2. *See* SIMPLE, ARTLESS.

rush, *n.* **1.** motion (*contex.*), movement (*contex.*); *spec.* onrush, precipitancy *or* precipitance (*R as referring to action*), precipitation (*B or affected*), hurry (*R*), brastle (*Scot.*), debacle, stampede, route, tear, spirt, fly, rampage, scutter (*C*), scurry, onset, swoop, surge, lunge, plunge, estampede (*R*), whirlwind (*fig.*), hurry, whish (*R*), whir (*R*), whiz (*R*), dash, start.
2. *See* FLOW, MIGRATION, HASTE, BODY.

rush, *v. i.* move (*contex.*), speed; *spec.* precipitate, career (*B*), rouse (*R*), charge, sweep, lunge, plunge, dive, dash, drive, storm, hurtle, smoke, launch, lash (*often used with "at"*), rage, gush, swoop, dart, bolt, shoot, fling, flounce, spring, hurl, boom, surge, smash (*C*), skelter, scurry, hurry-scurry, helter-skelter, tumble, rampage, clap (*R*), hurricane (*fig.; R*), whisk, whiz, whistle; *see* FLOW.
Antonyms: see LAG.

rushing, *a.* precipitate, precipitant; *spec.* dashing, tearing, hurtling, helter-skelter, *etc.*

rushlike, *a.* rushy, junciform (*tech.*).

rust, *v. t.* corrode (*contex.*), oxidize (*contex.*).

rust-colored, *a.* rusty, rubiginous (*tech. or B*), ferruginous (*tech. or B*).

rustic, *a.* **1.** *See* RURAL.
2. *As suggesting a lack of elegance, refinement, education, or, usually, of conventionally good breeding:* country, countrified, geoponic (*humorous*), farmerish, boorish, loutish, clodhopping (*depreciatory*), cloddish (*depreciatory*), churlish, hobnailed (*fig.*), clownish, carlish (*B*), borrel (*A*), swainish (*R*), inurban (*R*), uplandish (*R*), backwoods, woolen (*R*), rurigenous (*R*), yokelish (*R*); *spec.* Doric.
Antonyms: see URBAN, ACCOMPLISHED.
3. *See* UNREFINED, VULGAR, COARSE, SIMPLE.

rustic, *n.* countryman (*masc.*); peasant, churl, clodhopper, landman (*B*), homespun, chawboor, carl (*A or Scot*), rural (*R*), ruralist (*R*), lout, clout, hind (*B or historical*), hobnail, clodhopper, landman (*B*), homespun, chawbacon (*vulgar*), bumpkin, loblolly (*dial. or vulgar*), lob (*dial. or vulgar*), yokel, hayseed (*U. S.; humorous*), swad (*R*), kern (*R*). *Also personifications, as* Hodge, Hob (*A*), Joan (*fem.*), Jack (*Scot.*), Corydon (*from pastoral poetry after classic literature*); *spec.* carter, farmer.
Antonyms: see TOWNSMAN.

rusticate, *v. i.* retire, ruralize.

rusticate, *v. t.* **1.** rusticize (*R*); *see* PUNISH, SUSPEND.
2. *See* COUNTRIFY.

rusticity, *n.* **1.** clownishness, boorishness, churlishness, rurality (*R*), rusticness (*R*).
2. *See* AWKWARDNESS, IGNORANCE.

rustle, *n. Spec.* swish, swish-swash, whisper, susurration *or* susurrus (*B*), bustle, lisp; *see* MURMUR.

rustle, *v. i.* **1.** *Spec.* swish, whisper, bustle, lisp; *see* MURMUR.
2. *See* HASTEN, BUSTLE.

rustling, *a.* rustly (*R*); *spec.* swishing, susurrant *or* susurrous (*R*); *see* MURMURING.

rusty, *a.* **1.** rusted, rubiginous (*R*), ferruginous (*tech. or B*).
2. *See* RUST-COLORED, GRATING, SHABBY.

S

Sabbath, *n.* **1.** Lord's day;—*referring to the seventh day of the week, or Saturday.*
2. *See* SUNDAY.

sac, *n.* bag, cyst (*often spec.*), utricle, vesica (*tech.*), pouch, pocket; *spec.* saccule *or* sacculus, cysticle, follicle, bursa, bladder, theca.

saccular, *a.* saclike, saccate, utricular, utriculate, vesiculate.

sacerdotalism, *n.* priestism (*in hostile use*); *see* CLERICALISM.

---

rumpus: *disturbance.*
runaway: *fugitive, deserter, eloper.*
runner, *racer, messenger, courier, smuggler, creeper, solicitor.*
rupture, *v. t.: break, burst.*

S

sack, *n.: bag.*
sack, *v. t.: plunder.*

---

sacrament, *n.* **1.** rite; *spec.* (*with most Protestants*) baptism, Eucharist; (*with others, as before the Reformation and still in the Eastern Church*) baptism, confirmation, Eucharist, penance, extreme unction, orders (*pl.*), matrimony.

2. *See* RITE.

sacrifice, *n.* **1.** *Referring to the act:* oblation, offer; *spec.* immolation, libation, lustration.

2. victim, offering; *spec.* libation, heave offering, host, hostie (*A*), holocaust, corban, hecatomb, taurobolium, lustrum, lectisternium, krioboly, idolothyte (*R*), chiliomb.

3. *See* SELF-DENIAL, LOSS.

sacrifice, *v. t.* offer, oblate (*R*); *spec.* immolate, libate, holocaust, molochize (*R*).

sad, *a.* **1.** depressed, pensive, melancholy, melancholic, grievous, disconsolate, trist (*A*), subtrist (*R; A or obs.*), uncheerful, joyless, cheerless, mirthless, unjoyful (*R*), unsportful (*R*), dreary (*A*); *see* UNHAPPY, SORROWFUL.

Antonyms: see AMUSING, GAY, VIVACIOUS, GLAD.

2. *See* DISTRESSING, LAMENTABLE, MOURNFUL, BAD, DULL (*colors*).

sadden, *v. t.* distress, depress, contrist (*obs. or A*); *see* GRIEVE.

Antonyms: see GLADDEN, CHEER.

saddle, *n.* seat (*contex.*), sell (*A*); *spec.* pad, bat, panel, demipique, pillion, somerset.

safe, *a.* **1.** *See* UNHARMED, RELIABLE, CAREFUL, HARMLESS.

2. secure, unexposed, dangerless, sure (*R*).

Antonyms: see DANGEROUS, UNSAFE.

safe-conduct, *n.* **1.** safeguard, cowlo (*Anglo-Indian*).

2. *See* PROTECTION.

safety, *n.* security (*implies being freed from anxiety or concern, a state obtainable through such means as locking up, taking care, making advance provision;* safety *implies escape, release, or freedom from danger*), safeness.

Antonyms: see DANGER.

said, *pret.* quoth (*A*)

sail, *n.* **1.** rag (*derogatory, contex.*), wing (*of a ship*), canvas (*a collective*); *spec.* flyer (*of a windmill*), course (*lower sail on a ship*).

2. excursion, cruise; *see* VOYAGE.

sail, *v. i.* **1.** navigate, ride (*contex.*); *spec.* boat, run, make (*to a certain place on a course or in a certain direction*), fetch, spank, coast, quarter, scud, yacht.

2. *See* FLY, GLIDE.

sail, *v. t.* **1.** *Referring to a place or region:* traverse, navigate, range; *spec.* circumnavigate, coast.

2. *Referring to a vessel:* drive; *spec.* run, pinch.

sailing, *n.* navigation; *spec.* voyaging, seafaring.

sailor, *n.* sailer (*obs.*), seaman, mariner, navigator (*chiefly spec.*); *spec.* hand (*contex.*), sea dog (*chiefly with "old"; C*), Jack Tar (*humorous or affected*), water dog (*C*), true blue (*Eng.; a landsman's term*), tarpaulin (*A or R; C*), shellback (*S*), lubber, bluejacket, runner (*cant*), lascar (*East Indian*), privateer, lithsman, galiongee, guinea-pig (*S*), midshipman, middy (*C*), mate, captain, *etc.*

Antonyms: see LANDSMAN.

saint, *n. Spec.* saintling (*cant*), patron, patroness, pir, sainterrant (*ironical; obs. or a nonce use*).

sake, *n. In "for the sake of":* account (*of either persons or things, where* sake *is said of persons*), purpose, end, reason.

salable, *a.* vendable, saleable (*a variant*); *spec.* marketable, merchantable, commerciable (*R*), staple.

Antonyms: see UNSALABLE.

sale, *n.* **1.** disposal (*contex.*), trade (*contex.*), vendition (*R*); *spec.* retail, wholesale, auction, wash (*cant*).

Antonyms: see BUYING.

2. *See* DEMAND.

salesman, *n.* seller (*R*); *spec.* salesperson, clerk (*U.S.*), counterjumper (*S*), shopman, drummer.

saliva, *n.* water (*contex.*); *spec.* froth; *see* SLOBBER, SPIT.

salivate, *v. t.* **1.** *Referring to a person:* ptyalize (*tech.*).

2. *In the sense of "to put saliva upon":* insalivate, wet (*contex.*).

salivating, *a.* salivant, sialagogic (*tech. or R*).

sallow, *a.* **1.** *See* YELLOW.

2. *Of the complexion:* thick, muddy.

Antonyms: see CLEAR.

saloon, *n.* **1.** *See* DRAWING-ROOM, HALL.

2. bar, dramshop, shebeen (*Irish & Scot.*), grogshop (*S or contemptuous; U. S.*), groggery (*S or contemptuous; U. S.*), drunkery (*R; contemptuous*), drinkery (*R*); exchange (*local U. S.*), sample room (*obs.*); *spec.* tavern, jerry-shop *or* jerry (*Eng.*), pub (*Eng.*). *The term* saloon, *an Americanism which carries usually a suggestion of offensiveness, is disappearing as the result of the new conditions set up since the repeal of prohibition.* Bar *or* cocktail bar *thus becomes a new word, for the new form the popular drinking place has assumed. See* BARROOM.

salt, *a.* saline, salty; *spec.* saltish, brackish, briny.

salt, *v. t. Spec.* souse; *see* PICKLE.

salutation, *n.* **1.** *Spec.* salaam, hail, ave, Ave *or* (*in full*) Ave Maria, salute, bow, farewell, adieu.

2. *See* GREETING.

salute, *v. t.* **1.** *Spec.* knee, salaam.

2. *See* GREET.

salver-shaped, *a.* hypocrateriform, salverform, hypocraterimorphous;—*all three tech.*

same, *a.* identical, one, ditto (*a commercial term; C or cant*), selfsame, like.

sacred: *holy, inviolable.*
saddening: *depressing.*
saintly: *holy.*
salary: *hire.*
sally, *n.: issue, flight, burst, excursion, outbreak, witticism.*
sally, *v. i.: issue, burst, start.*
salute, *n.: greeting, discharge.*

Antonyms: see DISTINCT, OTHER, DIFFERENT.

sameness, *n.* **1.** identity, identicalness, oneness, likeness, selfsameness, unity; *spec.* connature, connaturalness, connaturality, homogeneity.

Antonyms: see DIFFERENCE.

2. *See* MONOTONY.

sample, *n.* example (*contex.*); *spec.* trypiece, swatch (*cant*), relish, prospect; *see* EXAMPLE.

sanction, *n.* **1.** *See* AUTHORIZATION, APPROVAL, CONFIRMATION.

2. enforcement, punishment, agreement (*all senses of international action taken to implement or apply international law, or of the law itself*).

sanctuary, *n.* **1.** sanctum, sanctorium (*R*); *spec.* Bethel (*fig.*), harem, sacrarium, sanctum sanctorium, Holy of Holies, Holy Place, oracle; *see* CHANCEL, ALTAR, SHRINE.

2. *Referring to the inner, or sacred, part of a church or temple: spec.* cella, adytum, naos, penetralia (*pl.*), penetral (*R*).

sandy, *a.* earthy (*contex.*), gritty, sabulous (*tech.*), sabulose (*R*); *spec.* tophaceous.

sane, *a.* **1.** sound, right; *see* RATIONAL.

Antonyms: see DERANGED.

2. *See* REASONABLE.

sanitary, *a.* sanatory (*with the force of "curative," "healing," where* sanitary *means simply "pertaining to health"*), sanitarian, hygiastic (*R*), hygienic, hygeic (*R*).

Antonyms: see UNHEALTHFUL.

sanity, *n.* **1.** *See* HEALTH.

2. soundness, saneness, rightness (*R*), balance; *see* REASON.

Antonyms: see DERANGEMENT.

sap, *n.* juice (*contex.*), blood (*B; fig*); *spec.* latex, milk

sarcasm, *n.* **1.** quip, cut, nip, hit, stroke, braid (*obs.*); *see* JEER, RIDICULE (*for distinction from* irony).

2. *See* ABUSE, ACRIMONY.

sarcastic, *a.* sarcastical (*R*), piercing, abusive (*contex.*), acrimonious, slashing, biting, cutting, mordant, sharp; *spec.* ironical; *see* SATIRIC.

sash, *n. The frame for a window:* frame (*contex.*), casement.

satire, *n.* **1.** *See* RIDICULE.

2. *Referring to a particular ridiculing composition: spec.* lampoon, pasquil, pasquinade, skit, squib.

satiric, *a.* satirical, sarcastic (*contex.*), Juvenalian (*R*); *spec.* cynic, ironical, Pantagruelian; *see* RIDICULING.

satirical, *a.* **1.** *See* SATIRIC.

2. *Of persons: spec.* cynic.

satirist, *n.* iambist (*hist.*), sillograph (*R; chiefly spec.*); *spec.* lampoonist, pasquinader, Pantagruelist.

satirize, *v. t.* lash (*contex.; fig.*); *spec.* lampoon, pasquinade; *see* ABUSE, RIDICULE.

satisfaction, *n.* **1.** *See* PAYMENT, PAY, EXPIATION, REDRESS, CONVICTION.

2. *Referring to satisfying a person or the mind: spec.* contentment, contentation (*R*), satiation.

3. *Referring to the fact or state of being satisfied: spec.* contentment (*a less abstract or generic word than "content"*), satiety; *see* PLEASURE.

Antonyms: see DISCONTENT.

4. *Referring to satisfying of wishes, desires, etc.: spec.* meeting, sating, satiation, appeasement, fulfillment, answering; *see* GRANT.

5. *Referring to the satisfying of conditions, requirements, etc.: spec.* meeting, answering, fulfillment, discharge.

satisfactory, *a.* **1.** *See* ADEQUATE, CONVINCING.

2. good, well (*used predicatively*); *see* PLEASANT, COMFORTABLE.

satisfiable, *a. Spec.* appeasable, satiable, placable.

satisfied, *a.* **1.** content; *see* CONTENTED, PLEASED.

Antonyms: see DISCONTENTED.

2. sated, satiate (*R*), satiated (*R*), full (*chiefly A or vulgar*).

satisfy, *v. t.* **1.** *See* PAY, CONVINCE.

2. *Referring to a person or the mind:* sate (*implying repletion*), glut (*suggests the result of greed*), satiate; *spec.* content; *see* PLEASE, PACIFY, APPEASE.

3. *Referring to satisfaction of wishes, desires, etc.:* appease; *spec.* meet, sate, satiate, glut, fulfill, answer; *see* GRANT.

4. *Referring to the satisfaction of conditions, requirements, etc., to be met: spec.* meet, answer, fulfill, discharge.

saturate, *v. t.* fill, imbue (*R*), supersaturate; *see* IMPREGNATE.

sauce, *n.* **1.** dressing; *spec.* vinaigrette, dip (*local Eng. and U. S.*), gravy.

2. *See* IMPUDENCE.

sausage-shaped, *a.* botuliform (*tech.*).

sauté, *v. t.* fry (*contex.*), toss, jump (*R*).

savage, *n. Spec.* barbarian, Goth (*fig.*), Hun (*fig.*), vandal (*fig.*), Tartar (*fig.*).

save, *v. t.* **1.** keep (*contex.*), preserve (*implying exerted power*); *spec.* rescue, recover, snatch, redeem, deliver, salve, salvage (*R*); *see* DELIVER.

Antonyms: see RUIN, WRECK.

2. *See* PROTECT, PRESERVE, KEEP, PREVENT, STINT.

3. keep, hoard, store.

4. *Referring to the protecting or keeping from fatigue, wear, etc.:* favor (*C*), spare.

saver, *n.* preserver, salvor, Savior *or* Saviour (*chiefly cap. and used of Christ*).

saving, *n.* **1.** keeping (*contex.*), preservation;

---

sanctify: *consecrate, observe.*
sanction, *v. t.: confirm, authorize, approve, enforce.*
sanguine: *red, hopeful.*
sap, *v. t.: undermine, destroy, ruin.*
sapid: *palatable.*
sardonic: *ridiculing.*
sash: *scarf, girdle.*
satanic: *devilish.*
sated: *full, satisfied.*
satisfy, *v. i.: suffice.*
saucy: *impudent, smart.*
saunter, *v. i.: stroll.*
sausage, *n.: frankfurter*
savage, *a.: wild, uncivilized, fierce, cruel, rough.*
save, *v. i.: economize.*

spec. rescue, salvation, recovery, redemption, salvage.

Antonyms: see RUIN.

2. *See* PROTECTION, PRESERVATION, EXCEPTION.

3. thrift; *see* ECONOMY.

4. *In pl.:* store, hoard, thrift (*A*).

Antonyms: see WASTE.

savor, *v. i. In the sense of "to show the influence of or presence of":* relish, smack;—*used with "of."*

say, *n.* **1.** *See* DICTUM.

2. voice, floor (*cant*); *spec.* vote;—*used with "to have," or "to have no."*

saying, *n.* **1.** *See* PRONUNCIATION, RECITATION.

2. expression (*contex.*), statement (*contex.*); *spec.* apothegm, epigram, logion; *see* DICTUM, WITTICISM.

3. proverb, adage, saw, mot (*A, B, or considered as French*), byword, commonplace, gnome (*R*), text (*R*), dict (*obs. or A*); *spec.* maxim, aphorism, epigram, precept, apothegm.

scab, *n.* **1.** slough, crust, eschar (*tech.*).

2. *As used by trade-unionists:* strike-breaker, rat, knobstick (*Eng.*), blackleg, snob (*dial. Eng.*).

scab, *v. i.* slough, crust, incrust (*contex.; B*).

scabby, *a.* scald (*A*), sloughy.

scale, *n.* **1.** *Referring to a balance:* pan, dish, basin.

2. *In pl.:* balance, beam (*fig.*); *spec.* trebuchet.

scale, *n.* **1.** squama (*tech.*), lamella (*tech.*), plate, flake; *spec.* urostege, cinder; *see* LAMINA.

2. *See* FILM.

3. *In botany: spec.* hull, ramentum, lodicule, palea, pale, bract.

scale, *n.* **1.** *In music:* genus (*ancient Greek music*); *spec.* gamut, mode, diapason, tetrachord, pentachord, hexachord, diatonic, chromatic, *etc.*

2. *See* SERIES, STANDARD, PROPORTION.

scale, *v. t.* **1.** unscale (*R*).

2. flake.

scale, *v. i.* desquamate (*tech.*), shed, exfoliate, flake, pill (*of skin, bark, etc.*).

scalelike, *a.* squamous, squamoid, squamiform; —*all three tech.*

scaling, *n.* flaking, peeling, desquamation (*tech.*).

scalp, *n.* epicranium (*tech*).

scaly, *a.* squamous, ramentaceous (*bot.*), scutate (*chiefly zoöl.*), imbricate (*having overlapping scales*); *see* SCURFY.

scanty, *a.* **1.** meager, scant (*of quantity*), sparse (*of numbers scattered thinly*), poor (*contex.*), scrimpy, scrimp, pinched, spare, sparing, skimp, exiguous (*R*), exile (*A*), frugal; *spec.* niggard, stingy, niggardly.

Antonyms: see ABUNDANT, UNSTINTED.

2. *See* DEFICIENT, NARROW.

scar, *n.* cicatrix (*tech.*), cicatrice (*R*); *spec.* cicatricle, hilum.

scar, *v. t.* cicatrize, disfigure (*contex.*), *spec.* pit.

scarecrow, *n.* **1.** deedman (*dial.*).

2. *See* BOGY.

scarf, *n.* **1.** sash; *spec.* cornet; *see* GIRDLE.

2. *Referring to a broad strip worn variously for ornament or comfort: spec.* fichu, muffler, cloud, throw, veil, tippet, tallith, lambrequin.

scarlet, *a.* red (*contex.*), bow-dyed (*Eng.; R*), cochineal, Babylonian *or* Babylonic (*cf. Rev. xvii:* 4; *B*); *spec.* pink (*cant*).

scatter, *v. t.* separate (*contex.*), disperse, dispel, diffuse, dissipate, disseminate (*fig. or spec.*); *spec.* strew (*spread loosely*), shake, spread, spill, shed, sprinkle, broadcast (*throw so as to* scatter *widely*), sow, ted (*often fig.*), rout, melt (*as clouds, a crowd, etc.; implying an almost imperceptibly slow process*), strow, radiate, spatter, sparse (*R*), litter (*to* scatter *in disorder*), resolve, disband (*from a state of union or association*), dot; *see* INTERPOSE, SPRINKLE, SPRAY, DISTRIBUTE.

Antonyms: see GATHER, COLLECT, ACCUMULATE, CONCENTRATE, CONVENE, CONVERGE.

scatter, *v. i.* disperse, dissipate; *spec.* melt, dissolve, spread, radiate, lift (*as fog, clouds, mist, etc.*); *see* STREW, STROW, SPATTER, SPILL, DISBAND.

Antonyms: see MEET, GATHER, CONGREGATE, CONVENE, CONVERGE, CROWD.

scattered, *a.* diffuse, strewn, strown, dissipated, disseminated; *spec.* dispersed, broadcast, *etc.; see* INFREQUENT.

Antonyms: see COLLECTIVE, BUNCHY.

scattering, *a.* dispersive, dispellent (*R*), diffusive, dissipative; *spec.* discutient, resolvent.

scattering, *n.* separation (*contex.*), dispersion, dispelling, diffusion, *etc. Cf.* SCATTER.

Antonyms: see COLLECTION, MEETING, CONVENTION.

scene, *n.* **1.** *Referring to a piece of theatrical property used in making up the pretended view:* scenery (*collective*); *spec.* profile, hanging, slide, curtain, flat, *etc.*

2. *Spec.* panorama, tableau, phantasmagoria *or* (*R*) phantasmagory, pageant; *see* PICTURE, SITUATION, VIEW.

3. *See* DISTURBANCE, OCCURRENCE.

scenery, *n.* **1.** *See* SCENE.

2. view; *spec.* landscape, seascape.

scent, *v. t.* **1.** smell; *spec.* wind;—*chiefly referring to animals, as dogs.*

2. *See* FOLLOW, TRACK.

scent, *v. t.* perfume, fume (*R*), odorize (*R*); *spec.* incense, cense (*R*), fumigate (*B*), embalm; *see* FUMIGATE.

---

savor, *n.: taste, trace.*
savory: *palatable, odorous.*
scaffold: *platform.*
scald, *v. t.: burn, boil.*
scale, *v. t.: climb.*
scale, *v. i.: rise.*
scamp, *n.: rascal.*
scamper, *v. i.: run.*
scan: *analyze, examine, consider.*
scandal: *discredit.*
scandalize: *disparage, shock, defame.*
scandalous: *discreditable, defamatory, abusive.*
scant, *a.: deficient, scanty, narrow.*
scant, *v. t.: stint.*
scarce: *deficient, infrequent.*
scathe: *harm.*

---

scepter, *n.* **1.** rod (*contex.*); *spec.* bauble, mace. **2.** *See* SUPREMACY.

scheming, *a. Spec.* designing, planning, diplomatic; *see* CALCULATING.

schismatic, *a.* nonjuring, nonconformist.

schismatic, *n.* separatist, nonjuror, nonconformist, sectary (*chiefly hist.*), sectarian (*chiefly hist.*).

scholar, *n.* **1.** student (*U. S.*), learner, pupil, disciple (*A, rhetorical, or jocular, exc. in ref. to personal follower*); *spec.* classman, sophomore, freshman, junior, senior, schoolboy, schoolgirl, undergraduate, graduate (*U. S.*), postgraduate (*orig. U. S.; a more common term than "graduate"*), grade (*a collective*), master, monitor, bluecoat (*Eng.*), demy (*Oxford University; Eng.*); *see* STUDENT.

2. savant (*masc.; chiefly spec.*), savante (*fem.; chiefly used of Frenchwomen; French*), clerk (*A*), bookman (*R*), doctor (*A*), polyhistor (*R*), polymath (*R*); *spec.* Greek, Græcist, Hebraist, moolvee (*East Indian*), pundit (*Hindu*), philologist, ethnologist, *etc.*

Antonyms: see IGNORAMUS, BLOCKHEAD.

scholarly, *a.* academic (*stressing the institutional conventions of schools, where* scholarly *stresses the standards of disciplined learning*), learned (*stresses amassed knowledge*).

scholarship, *n.* **1.** studentship (*R*), pupilage, pupilship (*R*), discipleship (*R or spec.*), discipulate (*R*).

2. *Referring to what is given to a scholar for his maintenance: spec.* fellowship, bursary, grant.

3. *See* LEARNING.

school, *n.* **1.** phrontistery (*fig. and usually contemptuous or humorous*); *spec.* kindergarten, primary school, common school, grade school, high school, junior high school, junior college, academy, institute, lyceum, lycée (*French*), seminary, college (*U. S., C*), university (*U. S., C*), conservatory, gymnasium (*Continental Europe*).

2. *See* EXERCISE, MANAGE, SECT, GROUP.

school, *n.* **1.** *Referring esp. to fish or cetaceans:* shoal, run (*chiefly spec.*); *spec.* gam, pod (*of seals or whales*), herd.

2. *See* FLOCK.

schoolman, *n. Hist.:* scholastic.

schooner, *n. Spec.* jack, tern, quart, quint, sext.

science, *n.* **1.** *See* KNOWLEDGE.

2. *Referring to a branch or knowledge:* discipline (*A*); *spec.* trivium (*a collective*), quadrivium (*a collective*).

scissors, *n. pl.* forfex (*humorously pedantic*); *spec.* shears (*more common than* scissors *in dignified metaphor*).

scissorslike, *a.* forficate *or* forficated (*tech.*).

scold, *v. i.* chide, row (*S*), rail, storm; *see* COMPLAIN.

scold, *v. t.* reprove (*contex.*), chide, rate, berate, dress (*C; chiefly with "down"*), trim (*S or C*), wig (*C*), huff (*R*), bounce (*C, R*), tongue (*A or C*), score (*U. S., C*), strafe (*C*), row (*S*).

Antonyms: see PRAISE.

scolding, *n.* reproof (*contex.*), rating, dressing (*C; chiefly with "down"*), wigging (*C*), trimming (*C or S*).

Antonyms: see PRAISE.

scope, *n.* **1.** reach, range, field, purview, sphere, stretch, limit, bound, tether (*fig.*), amplitude, span, extension, diapason (*fig.*); *spec.* incidence.

2. *See* EXTENT, AREA, ROOM, OPPORTUNITY.

score, *n.* **1.** *See* NOTCH, MARK, LINE, ACCOUNT, CHARGE, RECORD, MATTER, REASON, TWENTY.

2. *A gaining of a point, or a particular amount scored: spec.* duck's egg *or* duck egg (*S*), goose egg (*S*), run, notch (*R*), bye, hole, bogy, love, string, *etc.*

scorn, *n.* **1.** *See* CONTEMPT.

2. *Referring to what is despised*: scoff.

Scotsman, *n.* Scotchman, Scot, Sawney (*C and derisive*).

Scottish, *a.* Scotch, Scots, Caledonian (*B or rhetorical*).

scour, *v. t.* **1.** rub (*contex.*); *spec.* holystone, scrape, fettle; *see* POLISH.

2. *See* REMOVE, CLEAR, WASH, EVACUATE, CLEAN, SWEEP.

scramble, *n.* **1.** *See* CONTENTION.

2. scrabble, sprawl, clamber.

scramble, *v. i.* **1.** *See* CONTEND.

2. scrabble, scrawl (*obs. or dial.*), sprawl; *see* CLAMBER.

scrape, *v. t.* **1.** abrade (*formal or tech.*); *spec.* rake, rasp, grind, grate, scrabble (*implying repeated slight* scraping), scuff (*as with the feet*), file, bark, sclaff, squilgee, paw, curry (*of horses, and implying pleasurableness*); *see* GRAZE, SCRATCH, SCOUR.

Antonyms: see SMOOTH.

2. *See* ACCUMULATE.

scrape, *n.* **1.** scraping (*referring to the action; "scrape" refers esp. to a single act*), abrasion; *spec.* attrition, scratch, grind, grate, scrabble, rasp, rake, scuff, file, sclaff; *see* GRAZE, SCRATCH, SCOUR.

2. *Referring to the effect of the act:* break (*contex.*), abrasion, rub (*contex.*); *spec.* gall, raw, fleck, fox.

3. *See* BOW, PREDICAMENT.

scratch, *v. t.* **1.** scrape (*contex.*); *spec.* bescratch, scrabble, furrow, scarify, rake, rasp, score, claw, bite (*often fig.*), race, card; *see* GRAZE.

---

scheme, *n.: outline, plan, list, method, table, system.*
scholastic, *a.: academic, pedantic.*
school, *v. t.: teach, exercise, train.*
scientific: *expert.*
scoff: *jeer.*
scoop, *n.: ladle, bucket, hollow, beat.*
score, *v. t.: cut, gash, scratch, groove, mark, arrange, record, count.*
scorn, *v. t.: contemn.*
scornful: *contemptuous.*
scoundrel: *rascal.*
scourge, *n.: lash, calamity.*
scout, *n.: survey, watcher.*
scout, *v. t.: ridicule, reject.*
scowl: *frown.*
scrabble, *n.: scrawl, scribble.*
scraggy: *rough, thin.*
scrappy: *unconnected.*

Antonyms: see SMOOTH.
2. *See* SCRAWL, SCRIBBLE.
scratch, *n.* **1.** scrape (*contex.*); *spec.* rake, rasp, scarification, claw; *see* GRAZE.
2. *Referring to the effect of the act:* mark (*contex.*), line (*contex.*), scrape (*contex.*); *spec.* furrow (*contex.*), striation.
3. *See* GRATE, FIGHT, SCRIBBLE, SCRAWL.
scratchy, *a.* rough (*contex.*), scrapy, rasping, abradent (*B or tech.*).
Antonyms: see SMOOTH.
scrawl, *v. t.* **1.** *See* SCRIBBLE.
2. *Referring to drawing, painting, etc.:* scratch, scrabble.
scrawl, *n.* **1.** *See* SCRIBBLE.
2. *Referring to a delineation or picture:* scratch, scrabble.
scream, *v. i. & t.* cry (*contex.*), shout (*contex.*), screech (*harshly, as with fright*), screak (*R*), ululate (*R; chiefly spec.*); *spec.* scritch (*A*), squall, squawk, squeal, shriek.
scream, *n.* cry (*contex.*), shout (*contex.*), screech, screak (*R*), ululation (*R; chiefly spec.*); *spec.* squall, squeal (*as a pig, shrilly*), squawk, scritch (*A*), shriek.
screamy, *a.* screechy (*C*), ululant (*chiefly spec.*), screaky (*R*).
screen, *n.* **1.** *Spec.* curtain, medium, sconce, blind, blindage, blinding, shade, tat *or* tatty (*East Indian*), shield; *see* PROTECTION.
2. partition (*contex.*); *spec.* parclose, iconostasis, reredos, mask, lattice.
scribble, *v. i. & t.* **1.** write (*contex.*), scrawl, scrabble, scratch.
scribble, *n.* scrawl, scrabble, scratch, scribblement (*R*); *spec.* pothook.
2. *See* COMPOSITION.
scribbly, *a.* scrawly.
scrimmage, *n.* **1.** *See* CONTEST, FIGHT, DISTURBANCE.
2. *In football:* mêlée (*French*); *spec.* bully (*Eton football*), rush (*U. S.*), rouge (*Eton school; Eng.*).
scripture, *n.* **1.** Word (*with "the"*), Bible, Holy Writ, Book (*with "the"*). *Often used in pl., "Scriptures," and with "the" prefixed.*
2. *Referring to any sacred writings:* oracles (*pl.*), canon.
scroll, *n.* **1.** *See* ROLL, LIST.
2. *Referring to a convoluted or spiral ornament:* cartouche; *spec.* volute.
3. *Referring to a ribbonlike strip, often bearing a motto: spec.* escroll.
scrub, *v. t.* rub (*contex.*); *spec.* pumice, holystone.
scrupulous, *a.* **1.** strict, queasy, nice, meticulous (*suggests a finicking care for details*), punctilious (*stresses precise observance of requirements*), religious.
Antonyms: see UNPRINCIPLED.
2. *See* CONSCIENTIOUS, FASTIDIOUS, HESITATING, EXACT.
scullion, *n.* menial, drudge, servant (*contex.*).
sculptor, *n.* artist (*contex.*), sculptress (*fem.*), insculptor (*R*); *spec.* statuary.
sculpture, *n.* **1.** sculpturing, sculpturation (*R*); *spec.* toreutics; *see* CARVING, MOLDING.
2. piece (*contex.*), figure (*contex.*); *spec.* relief, bas-relief, statuary, figurine, bust, torso, grotesque, marble, glyph; *see* STATUE.
sculpture, *v. t.* carve (*contex.*), insculp (*R*), insculpture (*R*), sculpt (*R or jocular*), sculp (*C or jocular*); *spec.* statue (*R*); *see* MOLD.
sculptured, *a.* carved, glyphic (*R*).
scum, *v. i.* despumate (*R or tech.*).
scurf, *n.* scales (*pl.*); *spec.* dandruff *or* dandriff, furfur.
scurfy, *a.* scaly, impetiginous (*tech.*), scruffy, farreous (*R*), furfuraceous (*chiefly med.*).
scurvy, *n.* scorbutus (*tech.*).
sea, *n.* **1.** ocean, main (*B*), deep (*B or rhetorical; used with "the"*), brine (*chiefly B; used with "the"*), blue (*B; used with "the"*), wave (*B; used with "the"*), pond (*humorous; used with "the"*), herring pond (*humorous; used with "the"*); *spec.* archipelago, hyaline (*B; used with "the"*), offing, mediterranean (*R*).
Antonyms: see LAND.
2. *See* LAKE, WAVE.
seacoast, *n.* seashore, seaboard, seaside (*chiefly spec.*), ripe (*R*).
seal, *n.* **1.** sigil (*R*); *spec.* bull *or* bulla, signet, cocket (*Eng.*), chop (*India, China, etc.*), wafer, impression.
2. *See* STAMP, CONFIRMATION, EVIDENCE.
seal, *v. t.* **1.** sigillate (*R*), obsignate (*R*); *spec.* enseal (*A*).
Antonyms: see UNSEAL.
2. *See* CONFIRM, AUTHENTICATE, FASTEN, FIX.
seam, *n.* **1.** juncture (*contex.*), junction (*contex.*), line (*contex.*); *spec.* suture, commissure, raphe, cicatrix, furrow, harmonia.
2. *See* INTERSPACE, RIDGE.
seam, *v. t.* line (*contex.*); *see* FURROW.
seamanship, *n.* navigation, seacraft (*R*).
search, *v. t.* **1.** examine (*contex.*), ensearch (*A*), rake (*spec. or fig.*), explore (*B*); *spec.* ransack, rummage, hunt, ferret, seek, sweep, drive, draw, drag, frisk (*C*).
2. *See* INVESTIGATE, SEEK.
search, *v. i.* explore (*contex.*); *spec.* hunt (*eagerly or strenuously*), ransack, rummage, seek, grub (*in a mean or abject way*), grope, rake, nose, pry, quest, mouse, forage (*as in*

---

scrawny: *thin.*
screech: *scream, creak.*
screen, *v. t.: protect, hide, shade, shelter.*
screw, *n.: twist, spiral, distortion, niggard, pressure.*
screw, *v. t.: attach, fasten, stretch, strain, propel, oppress, extort, press, twist, distort.*
scribe, *n.: clerk, amanuensis, author.*
scrimp, *v. i.: economize.*
script: *handwriting.*
scrubby: *dwarf, shabby, bushy.*
scruple, *n.: hesitation.*
scrutinize: *examine, investigate.*
scuffle: *contest, fight.*
scum, *n.: film, foam, dregs, dross.*
scurrilous: *coarse, abusive.*
scurry, *v. i.: run, rush, hasten.*
sear: *dry, burn, blight.*

---

search *of supplies*), delve, drag, draw, fossick (*Australia*); see GROPE, INVESTIGATE.

search, *n.* **1.** examination (*contex.*), exploration; *spec.* hunt, quest, research, rummage, perquisition (*R*), scrutation (*R*), beat-up, jerque, pursuit (*used with "of"*). *"Search" is used with "for."*

2. *See* INVESTIGATION.

searching, *a.* **1.** sharp (*contex.*), scrutinous, scrutinizing.

2. *See* ATTENTIVE, DISCERNING, SHARP.

seasickness, *n.* nausea (*contex.*), mal-de-mer (*French*).

season, *n.* **1.** period (*contex.*); *spec.* spring, summer, autumn *or* fall, winter, harvest.

2. *See* TIME.

seat, *n.* **1.** sitting (*R or spec.*); *spec.* chair (*implying comfort, ease, dignity or authority*), cathedral, divan, bench, bleacher (*U. S.*), ottoman, howdah, bottom, box (*a driver's* seat), gradin *or* gradine, thwart, bank (*A, exc. of a* seat *for rowers*), dicky box *or* (*for short*) dicky (*S*), tribunal, thronelet, settee, stall (*in a church or theater*), stool, form, throne, sofa, saddle, pew.

2. *See* BUTTOCKS, CAPITAL, PLACE, COUNTRY HOUSE.

seat, *v. t.* **1.** accommodate (*contex.*), set; *spec.* bench, throne, cushion.

2. *To cause to be seated:* set.

3. *In the passive: see* LIE.

seaward, *adv.* seawards (*less common than seaward*), offshore, off, oceanward, oceanwards, offward *or* offwards (*R*).

Antonyms: see LANDWARD.

seaweed, *n.* fucus (*tech.*), ooze (*R*); *spec.* wrack, fucoid, dulse, kelp, tang, tangle, whipcord, ware.

seclude, *v. t.* withdraw (*contex.*), sequester (*R, exc. spec.*); *spec.* embower (*B*).

Antonyms: see EXPOSE.

secluded, *a.* remote, retired, secret, covert, sequestered, private (*A*), secluse (*R*), recluse (*R*), solitary, hidden; *spec.* screened, outlying, back.

secondary, *a.* **1.** subordinate, collateral, by *or* bye, second-rate, subsidiary (*suggesting esp. the idea of aid or help*); *see* INDIRECT.

Antonyms: see CHIEF.

2. *See* AUXILIARY.

secrecy, *n.* **1.** *See* HIDDENNESS, RETICENCE, RETIREMENT, CONFIDENTIALNESS.

2. concealment, clandestineness (*R*), mystery, furtiveness, surreptitiousness, stealthiness, covertness, hugger-mugger (*A*), cabbalism (*S*).

secret, *a.* **1.** *See* HIDDEN, RETICENT, SECLUDED, CONFIDENTIAL.

2. *Referring to actions, conduct, agreements, etc., done with the intention of concealment, the motive being more emphasized than the result, which may not be achieved:* furtive, concealed, clandestine (*implies intent to elude observation*), surreptitious (*implies craft or deceiving*), underhand, sly, dark, covert (*of what is not avowed*); *see* STEALTHY.

Antonyms: see FRANK.

secret, *n.* **1.** secrecy (*A*), concealment (*obs.*); *spec.* riddle, mystery, deep.

2. *See* ESSENTIAL, EXPLANATION, CONFIDENCE.

secretary, *n.* **1.** clerk, scribe (*ancient history*), scrivener (*B or tech.*); *spec.* protonotary.

2. bureau (*contex.*), desk, writing desk.

secrete, *v. t.* **1.** *See* HIDE, APPROPRIATE.

2. secern, produce (*R*), separate (*contex.*).

secretion, *n.* **1.** *See* APPROPRIATION, HIDING.

2. *Referring to the physiological action:* separation, production (*R*), secernment (*R*).

3. *Referring to what is secreted:* product (*contex.*), secrement (*obs. and R*); *spec.* lymph, saliva, juice, bile, gall, chyle, chyme, sweat, urine; *see* EXCRETION.

secretive, *a.* private; *see* RETICENT.

secretly, *adv.* **1.** *Cf.* HIDDEN.

2. *Referring rather to the mind's intent:* inly, privily (*B or A*), clandestinely, *etc.*

sect, *n.* division (*contex.*), school, schism, faction, heresy (*obs. or R*); *see* DENOMINATION.

sectarian, *a.* sectarial, schismatic; *see* DENOMINATIONAL.

secularize, *v. t.* laicise; *spec.* deconsecrate (*R*).

secure, *v. t. In commercial use:* margin.

security, *n.* **1.** *See* CARELESSNESS, SAFETY, HARMLESSNESS, FIRMNESS, PLEDGE, GAGE, GUARANTY.

2. surety; *spec.* pledge, collateral, share, bond, consol, debenture, mortgage, scrip, floater, margin.

sedative, *a.* assuaging, assuasive, soothing, calmative (*chiefly med.*), calmant (*med.*).

Antonyms: see STIMULATING, EXCITING.

seduce, *v. t.* **1.** betray, debauch, ruin (*a woman*); *see* VIOLATE.

2. *Referring to what seduces: see* ATTRACT.

seduction, *n.* betrayal, debauchment, ruin, ruination; *see* VIOLATION.

see, *v. t.* **1.** perceive (*contex., with sense of understanding*), sight, vision (*R*), ken (*A*), behold (*formal or A*); *spec.* survey, discern (*implying an express effort, and emphasizing the idea of distinguishing from other things*), distinguish (*to* see *distinctly or as separate from other things*), view, descry (*implying observation, attentive gazing, and a catching sight of from a distance*), espy (*implying a conscious effort and a sudden* seeing *by chance*), witness, spot (*S*), glimpse (see *momentarily, faintly, imperfectly*), drink (*chiefly with "in"; fig.*), notice, contemplate; *see* MAKE.

2. *See* PERCEIVE, NOTICE, LEARN, ESCORT, MEET, READ, EXPERIENCE, EXAMINE, INSURE, CONSIDER.

seed, *n.* **1.** seedling, grain; *spec.* stone, pip, pippin (*obs. or dial.*), gin, nucule, grapestone; *see* GRAIN.

---

season, *v. t.: flavor, acclimatize, cure, preserve, enliven.*
secede: *withdraw, apostatize.*
section, *n.: cutting, division, part, territory, diagram, slice.*
secure, *a.: careless, safe, confident, firm.*
sedulous: *active, constant, persistent, diligent, industrious.*

2. *See* GERM, OFFSPRING.

seek, *v. t.* **1.** search (*R and B, exc. with "out"*); *spec.* hunt, court (*fig.*), woo (*fig.*).

2. *In the sense of "to try to obtain":* pursue, court (*fig.*), woo (*fig.*).

3. *See* ENDEAVOR.

seem, *v. i.* appear, show (*C*), look (*orig. spec.*), beseem (*R or A*); *spec.* read, feel.

seer, *n.* **1.** *See* SPECTATOR.

2. *Spec.* speculator (*obs. or A*), rishi (*Sanskrit*); *see* CLAIRVOYANT, CRYSTAL-GAZER, PROPHET.

seesaw, *n.* teeter (*U. S. and dial. Eng.*).

seesaw, *v. i.* **1.** teeter (*U. S. and dial. Eng.*), teetertotter (*U. S. and dial. Eng.*).

2. *In cards, referring to alternate taking of tricks by partners:* crossruff (*tech.*), saw.

seize, *v. t.* **1.** *In law: see* INVEST.

2. *Referring to taking possession of by legal process: spec.* sequester, sequestrate, extend, impound, distrain, distress, arrest; *see* IMPRESS, CONFISCATE.

3. take (*contex.*), hent (*A*), possess (*A*), apprehend (*A*); *spec.* snatch, catch, clutch (*implying eagerness, force and quickness, avidity, convulsive action, or the like*), grab (*implying sudden and sharp, firm action*), grip (*to seize firmly with a prehensile organ, or to take firm hold of*), clasp, gripe (*chiefly B*), clench (*implying firmness or violence*), clinch (*U. S.*), grapple, snap, rape (*B*), pounce (*often fig.*), swoop (*often fig.*), hook, grabble (*R*), braid (*obs.*), nab (*S or C*), nip (*chiefly dial. or S*), nobble (*S*), cleek (*Eng. dial.*), cleck (*chiefly dial.*), cly (*thieves' cant*), tail, finger (*A*), bag, intercept, chop, tong, foot.

4. *See* GRIP, FASTEN, CATCH, CAPTURE, AFFECT, PERCEIVE, UNDERSTAND, USE, USURP.

seizure, *n.* **1.** *Spec.* sequestration, caption (*esp. Scots law*), extent, distress, confiscation; *see* IMPRESSMENT, ARREST.

2. taking, apprehension (*A*); *spec.* snatch, grab, grip, clutch, snap, ereption (*R*), prehension; *see* INTERCEPTION.

3. *See* GRIP, CATCH, CAPTURE, PERCEPTION, UNDERSTANDING, USE, USURPATION.

self-approval, *n.* self-commendation, self-approbation; *spec.* self-applause, self-conceit, self-admiration, elation (*R*); *see* SELF-SATISFACTION.

self-assertive, *a.* assured, positive, bumptious (*C*), robustious (*B*), dogmatic *or* dogmatical *spec.* forward, perky *or* perk.

Antonyms: see OBSEQUIOUS, ABJECT.

self-begotten, *a.* self-produced, autogeneal (*R*), autogenous (*chiefly tech.*), self-begot (*R*), self-born, parthenogenetic (*tech.*).

self-control, *n.* reserve, restraint, self-restraint, possession (*R*), self-government (*R*), control, self-possession, self-command; *spec.* constraint, collection, patience, continence, self-repression, coolness, retention (*R*); *see* CALM.

Antonyms: see EXCITEMENT, CONFUSION.

self-controlled, *a.* reserved, self-restrained, restrained; *spec.* undemonstrative, self-possessed, cool, collected, recollected (*R*), continent (*esp. as to bodily, sensual, appetites*), patient; *see* CALM.

Antonyms: see EXCITED, CONFUSED.

self-deception, *n.* self-delusion, self-abuse (*R*).

self-denial, *n.* sacrifice, self-sacrifice, self-giving, renunciation, self-renunciation; *spec.* kenosis.

Antonyms: see SELFISHNESS.

self-existence, *n.* absoluteness, aseity (*tech.*), autotheism, innascibility (*R*), perseity (*R*).

self-existent, *a.* absolute, ingenerate, innascible (*R*), unoriginal (*R*), unoriginated (*R*), uncreated, unbegotten.

self-governing, *a.* autonomous.

self-gratifying, *a.* self-indulgent.

Antonyms: see ABSTEMIOUS, ASCETIC, AUSTERE.

selfhood, *n.* selfdom, proprium (*B*), seity (*R*), ipseity (*R*).

self-importance, *n.* importance (*contex.*); *spec.* arrogance (*implying an attitude offensive to others*), vaingloriousness, consequentialness, consequence, pomposity (*implying an ostentatious bearing*), stiltedness, self-consequence, consequentiality (*R*).

self-important, *a* consequential; *spec.* pompous, arrogant, vainglorious, cocky (*C*).

Antonyms: see OBSEQUIOUS.

selfish, *a.* self-centered, self-interested, sordid (*B*), mercenary (*fig.*), egoistic (*B*), self-regarding (*B*); *spec.* factious (*implying regard for party interests*), piggish (*contemptuous; C*), hoggish (*very contemptuous; C*); *see* EGOISTIC.

Antonyms: see UNSELFISH, GENEROUS.

selfishness, *n.* self-interest, self-partiality (*R*), self-regard, self-love, egoism (*ethics*), selfcentration (*R*), selfism (*R*), selfness (*R*), suicism (*R*), selffulness (*R*); *spec.* piggishness *or* (*R*) piggery (*contemptuous; C*), hoggishness (*very contemptuous; C*); *see* EGOISM.

Antonyms: see SELF-DENIAL, GENEROSITY.

self-made, *a. Spec.* self-educated, self-taught, autodidact, parvenu, nouveau riche (*both French*).

self-moving, *n.* locomotor (*R*), motile; *see* AUTOMATIC, AUTOMOBILE.

self-moving, *a.* motile, locomotory (*R*), locomotive; *spec.* self-acting, self-active; *see* AUTOMATIC, AUTOMOBILE.

self-regard, *n.* egoism (*ethics*); *spec.* self-pity; *see* SELFISHNESS.

self-righteous, *a.* Pharisæan (*R*), Pharisaic, Pharisaical.

self-satisfaction, *n.* self-approval (*contex.*), complacency *or* complacence, self-content; *see* CONCEIT.

---

seeming: *apparent.*
seeming: *appearance.*
seemly: *good-looking, becoming.*
seldom: *infrequently.*
select, *a.: chosen, choice.*

---

self-satisfied, *a.* self-approving, smug, complacent; *see* CONCEIT.
Antonyms: see OBSEQUIOUS.

sell, *v. t.* **1.** market (*suggests a course of commercial activity*), vend (*suggests dealing in small articles*), place (*contex.*), furnish (*contex.*); *spec.* prostitute (*fig.*), retail, wholesale, unload, dump, peddle, hawk, auction.
Antonyms: see BUY.
2. *See* HOAX, BETRAY.

seller, *n.* vender (*chiefly tech. or B*); *spec.* auctioneer, retailer, wholesaler, saleswoman; *see* SALESMAN, PEDDLER.

selvage, selvedge, *n.* edge (*contex.*), list, listing, forel (*R*).

send, *v. t.* **1.** *Spec.* dispatch (*implying haste, expedition or promptitude to meet some purpose or for some urgent or strongly impelling reason*), speed, hurl (send *impetuously*), bundle (*to* send *off people hastily and together, or bag and baggage*), fling (*as troops, suddenly*), drive (*implying force or compulsion*), forward, rush, flash (*as by a telegraphic message, hence with quickness*), emigrate, mission.
Antonyms: see BRING.
2. *See* REFER, PROPEL, FRANK, COMMUNICATE.
3. *In the sense of "to cause to be carried forward": spec.* ship, mail, express (*U. S.*), transmit.

sending, *n.* **1.** *Spec.* dispatch, speeding, hurling, *etc.*, mission.
2. *See* REFERENCE, PROPULSION, COMMUNICATION.
3. forwarding, transmission, transmittal; *spec.* shipment, expressage (*U. S.*).

senior, *n.* **1.** *See* SCHOLAR.
2. dean, elder (*implying greater actual age, where* senior *may refer simply to longer tenure*); *spec.* doyen (*French*).
Antonyms: see JUNIOR.

sensation, *n.* **1.** feeling, sense (*of something less material and objective than* sensation *implies—usually with "of" and in reference to some specific object*)), impression; *spec.* creep, crawl, aura.
2. *See* FEEL, EMOTION, PERCEPTION, CONSCIOUSNESS.
3. *Referring to excited feeling:* excitement, impression, thrill, yellowness (*S*).

sensational, *a.* **1.** sense (*the noun used attributively*), sensory, sensible, sensitive, sensatory, sensative (*R*), sensatorial (*R*).
2. impressive, thrilling, thrillful (*R*), lurid (*chiefly disparaging*), yellow (*S*); *spec.* sensationish (*R*), spicy.

senseless, *a.* **1.** *See* INSENSIBLE, UNWISE, FOOLISH.
2. *Referring to the absence of the faculty of sensation:* insensate, unfeeling; *see* INANIMATE.
Antonyms: see SENSITIVE.

sensitive, *a.* **1.** *See* SENSORY, SENSUOUS, SENTIENT.
2. sensible (*implying a delicacy of feeling*), impressionable (*often used with "by"*), alive (*used with "to"*), susceptible (*because so constituted as to be unresistant—used with "to"*), sore, responsive (*used with "to"*), appreciative (*used with "of"*), susceptive (*R*); *spec.* delicate (*implying an exquisitely fine perception*), queasy, thin, thin-skinned, tender, hyperæsthetic, supersensitive, passible; *see* SYMPATHETIC, APPRECIATIVE, IRRITABLE.
Antonyms: see SENSELESS, NUMB, DULL, INSENSIBLE.
3. *Referring to the touch, scientific instruments, etc.:* acute, nice, delicate, fine; *spec.* exquisite, sore.

sensory, *a.* sensitive, sensible, sensual (*R*), sensorial, sensuous (*R*).

sensual, *a.* **1.** voluptuous (*implying indulgence in sensual enjoyment*), voluptuary, gross, earthy, animal, brutish, brute, brutal (*R*), boarish (*R*), fleshly, carnal, sensuous (*not implying the derogatory force of* sensuous); *spec.* sexual, bestial, Epicurean, Epicurish (*R*); *see* GLUTTONOUS, LASCIVIOUS.
Antonyms: see SPIRITUAL.
2. *See* SENSORY.

sensualist, *n.* voluptuary (*implying a deliberate concern to make the most of sensual pleasures*), animal, brute; *spec.* Epicurean; *see* GLUTTON.

sensualize, *v. t.* coarsen, carnalize, encarnalize (*R an intensive*), brutify.
Antonyms: see SPIRITUALIZE.

sensuous, *a.* **1.** *See* SENSORY.
2. sensitive, material, luscious, delicious; *spec.* Epicurean; *see* SENSUAL.
Antonyms: see ASCETIC, SPIRITUAL.

sentence, *n.* **1.** *See* OPINION, DECISION, CONDEMNATION.
2. *In grammar, rhetoric, etc.:* period, ensample (*A*), proposition.

sentient, *a.* **1.** *See* CONSCIOUS.
2. feeling, sensible, sensate, sensitive, sensive (*R*).
Antonyms: see INSENSIBLE.

sentiment, *n.* **1.** *See* FEELING, IDEA.
2. *Spec.* toast.

separate, *a.* distinct (*implying absolute and evident separateness such as gives individuality*), discrete (*implying individual distinctness; that is, distinct or absolute, but not necessarily wide separation*), dividual (*implying the fact or capacity of being separated from other things, B*), sejugate (*R*), segregate (*R*); *spec.* particular, individual, definite, disembodied, alone, infrequent, different, disconnected, unconnected, distant, divided, apart.

---

sense, *n.: faculty, meaning, perception, understanding, intelligence, reason, sensation, consciousness, opinion, essence, direction, common sense.*
sense, *v. t.: perceive, discover, value, understand.*
sensible: *sensational, aware, perceptible, tangible, visible, reasonable, judicial, intelligent, conscious, sensitive, appreciative, sentient.*
sentence, *v. t.: condemn.*
sententious: *concise.*
sentience: *consciousness, feeling.*
sentimental: *emotional.*

Antonyms: see JOINED, ADJACENT, COLLECTIVE, JOINT.

separate, *v. t.* **1.** *Referring to the causing of two or more things to come apart or to be more apart from one another, or to the withdrawing of one thing from another: spec.* divide, sever (*implying sharp and abrupt separation of things naturally joined*), disunite, dissever (*B and emphatic equiv. of "sever"*), sunder, dissunder (*an emphatic equiv. of "sunder"; B or R*), cut (*used with "off," "away," etc.*), part, dispart (*B*), isolate, eliminate, sequester, sequestrate, segregate, seclude, detach (*implying the breaking of not very firm or intimate connection*), bite (*off*), dissociate *or* (*less usual*) disassociate, single (*R*), winnow (*fig.*), divorce (*fig.*), disintegrate, demarcate, unfellow (*R*), discombine (*R*), inquartate (*R*), seclude (*R*), prescind (*R*), discorporate (*R*), disintricate (*R*), distance (*R*), space, tease, eliquate, disaggregate, untwine, trunk, severalize (*R*); *see* DISCONNECT, SCATTER, STRAIN, SIFT, DISENGAGE, ALIENATE, LOOSEN, OPEN, WITHDRAW, PULL, SPACE, UNFOLD, WINNOW, SECRETE, DIVORCE.

Antonyms: see MIX, ATTACH, BLEND, COLLECT, CONCENTRATE, CONVENE, GATHER, MEET.

2. *See* DIVIDE, DISTINGUISH.

separate, *v. i.* divide, sever, disunite, dissever (*B*), sunder, dissunder (*R*), part; *see* SEPARATE, *v. t.*

Antonyms: see CONGREGATE, CONVENE.

separative, *a. Spec.* divulsive, divellent, segregative, separatory, diazeuctic, bursting, dissilient (*R*).

Antonyms: see JOINING, MEETING.

sequel, *n.* **1.** sequence, train; *spec.* sequelæ (*pl. med.*).

2. *See* RESULT, OUTCOME, CONTINUATION.

sequence, *n.* **1.** *See* SEQUEL.

2. *In cards:* run.

series, *n.* succession (*in order of time, place, or number*), *spec.* list, gradation, scale, train, stream, thread, range, concatenation (*B or tech.*), chain, course (*implying a connected run of items in a line*), progression, sequence (*suggesting some principle of logical or regular succession*), set, rotation, order (*A*), beadroll (*fig.*), combination, coil.

serious, *a.* **1.** earnest, grave (*chiefly spec.*), sober, solemn, severe (*R*), owlish (*fig.*).

Antonyms: see AMUSING, PLAYFUL, VIVACIOUS.

2. *See* SOBER, DANGEROUS, IMPORTANT, DEEP, MATTER-OF-FACT.

sermon, *n.* discourse (*contex.*), address (*contex.*), preachment (*chiefly contemptuous*); *spec.* homily, sermuncle (*R*), sermonette *or* sermonet (*R*), khutbah.

serum, *n.* humor, water (*contex.*); *spec.* whey, chyle, lymph.

servant, *n.* **1.** *See* AGENT.

2. help (*cant or C; generic or a collective*), servitor (*A*), servitress (*R*), servitude (*a collective; R*), servature (*a collective; R*), loafeater (*hist.*), sergeant (*hist.*), hind (*obs.*), feeder (*obs. and R*); *spec.* man, boy, boots (*Eng.*) menial (*implying degrading work*), factotum, do-all (*C*), buttons (*C*), domestic, biddy (*C*), butler, sewer, ferash (*Anglo-Indian*), maty *or* mate (*Anglo-Indian*), striker (*cant*), waiter, cook, *etc.*; *see* MANSERVANT, MAIDSERVANT, SCULLION.

Antonyms: see EMPLOYER.

serve, *v. i.* **1.** minister (*often used with "to"*), help, assist, attend, subserve (*R*); *spec.* lackey, slave; *see* WORK.

2. *Referring to waiting upon those at table:* attend, wait; *spec.* skink (*A*).

3. answer (*used with "to" and the infinitive, or with "for"*), do (*used with "for"*), avail (*used only with the infinitive denoting the use or purpose*).

4. *See* ACT, SUIT, SUFFICE, CONTRIBUTE.

serve, *v. t.* **1.** *See* AID, HELP, BENEFIT, SUFFICE, SUPPLY, TREAT, DELIVER, WORK.

2. *Referring to waiting upon those at table:* attend, help.

3. *Referring to serving food or drink:* help; *spec.* dish, skink (*A*), pour, ladle, *etc.*

4. *In games:* deliver; *spec.* bowl, pitch, throw.

service, *n.* **1.** *Referring to the state or condition:* employ, employment (*R*); *spec.* waiterage.

2. *Referring to the action or fact of serving:* work (*contex.*), serving, ministration (*formal*), ministry (*eccl., except as colored by eccl. use*); *spec.* duty, function, office (*used chiefly in pl., and with "good," "kind," etc.*), exercise, eyeservice.

3. *Spec.* attendance, tendance (*R*), attention; *spec.* waiting.

4. *Referring to the portion served:* help, helping, go (*S or C*).

5. *See* AID, BENEFIT, WORSHIP, RITE.

serviceable, *a.* **1.** *Referring to persons: see* USEFUL.

2. *Referring to things:* helpful; *spec.* convenient, handy, commodious (*A equiv. of "convenient"*), beneficial, improvable (*R*); *see* DURABLE.

Antonyms: see USELESS.

servile, *a.* **1.** *Referring to what belongs or is appropriate to a slave or slaves:* slavish, thrall-like, thralled (*R*).

Antonyms: see DOMINEERING, HAUGHTY.

2. *As designating the condition of a slave:* subject (*contex.*), slave, slavish, bond, unfree (*formal*), thrall, enslaved, villain *or* (*hist.*) villein (*R or A*), vernile (*R*).

3. *See* BASE, OBSEQUIOUS, IMITATIVE.

session, *n.* meeting, sitting; *spec.* diet, court, assize, school.

set, *n.* **1.** *See* GROUP, COMPANY, FORCE.

2. clique (*stresses an attitude of exclusiveness*), circle, coterie (*implies congeniality*), ring, crowd (*C or S*), gang (*C esp. of spontaneously formed youth-groups, often with antisocial pro-*

---

serial, *n.: periodical.* | **set,** *a.: appointed, deliberate, formal,* | *fixed, obstinate.*

---

pensities), push (*cant, S or Australian*), pack (*contemptuous*), tribe (*contemptuous*), platoon (*fig.; R*); *spec.* clan, covey (*R*), junto, junta, cabal, class, *etc.*; *see* COMBINATION.
3. number, collection, lot, kit (*C*); *spec.* pack, packet, stand, nest, service, shook, train, gang, book; *see* SERIES, SUITE, BOOK.
4. *Referring to bells tuned to one another for ringing:* suite, peal, ring; *spec.* chime, carillon.

set, *v. t.* **1.** *See* SEAT, PUT, PLACE, FIX, PLANT, PLAN, FRAME, ADJUST, POSE, STAND, REST, APPOINT, MODULATE, CLENCH, DIRECT, ESTABLISH, ORNAMENT, COMPOSE, HARDEN, COAGULATE, CONGEAL.
2. start (*used chiefly with "at"*), put (*used chiefly with "to"*). *"Set" is chiefly used with "to" or "at."*
3. reduce (*a fractured bone*).
4. *Of a trap, noose, etc.:* adjust, lay.
5. *In jewelry*: fix, mount, enchase (*B or fig.*); *spec.* collet.
6. *Of a guard, watch, etc.:* put, place, establish; *spec.* clap, impose.
7. spread (*the table*), lay, serve (*R*).

set, *v. i.* **1.** fix; *see* HARDEN, SOLIDIFY.
2. *See* DESCEND, GERMINATE.

set, *n.* **1.** *See* MOTION, POSTURE, ATTITUDE, TENDENCY, INCLINATION, BUILD, POSITION, ATTACK.
2. hang, fit.

setting, *n.* **1.** *Spec.* congelation, coagulation, planting, *etc.*
2. monture (*R*), mounting; *spec.* collet, ouch, chape.

settle, *v. t.* **1.** *See* REST, COLONIZE, CLEAR, CALM, ESTABLISH, APPOINT, CONSOLIDATE, REGULATE, PAY, LIQUIDATE, FIX, DECIDE, ARRANGE, UNDO, ADMINISTER.
2. root, plant, domiciliate (*R or B*), domicile (*R or B*), locate (*chiefly U. S.*); *spec.* resettle; *see* COLONIZE.
3. *In law: spec.* entail, jointure.

settle, *v. i.* **1.** *See* DESCEND, ALIGHT, LODGE, SUBSIDE.
2. domicile (*R or B*), domiciliate (*R*), plant (*R*), locate (*chiefly U. S.*).
3. pay, account, answer.

settlement, *n. Spec.* colony, post, factory.

settler, *n.* **1.** *See* DWELLER, COLONIST, IMMIGRANT, SQUATTER.
2. *Of that which* settles *or concludes:* finisher, clinker, clincher, corker, trimmer, sockdologer (*S, U. S.*), staggerer, poser, squelcher; (*all C or S*).

seven, *a.* septenary (*R or B*), septimal (*R*).

seven, *n.* septenary (*R*), heptad (*R or spec.*).

sevenfold, *a.* septuple (*R*).

seventy, *a.* septuagesimal (*B or spec.*), septuagenary (*chiefly spec.*).

severally, *adv.* **1.** apiece.
2. respectively.

severe, *a.* **1.** *Referring to the act of imposing, or to the tendency to impose, extreme penalties, reproof, criticism, etc.:* rigorous, stern, iron (*fig.*), iron-handed (*fig.*), hard, dure (*B or A*), unsparing, dour (*Scot.*); *spec.* Draconic *or* Draconian (*R; fig.*); *see* UNSPARING.
Antonyms: see EASY, GENTLE.
2. *See* STRICT, CRUEL, VIOLENT, EXTREME, STRENUOUS, AUSTERE, DISTRESSING, PAINFUL, DEEP.
3. *Referring to climate, weather, etc.:* distressing, hard, inclement, rigorous, bad (*C*), intemperate; *spec.* bitter, extreme, cold, hot, dry, wet; *see* ROUGH
Antonyms: see MILD.

severity, *n.* **1.** rigor, rigorism, sternness, iron (*fig.*), iron-handedness (*fig.*), hardness; *spec.* Draconism (*fig.*).
Antonyms: see GENTLENESS, INDULGENCE.
2. *See* STRICTNESS, CRUELTY, VIOLENCE, EXTREMITY, STRENUOUSNESS, AUSTERITY, DEPTH, HARDNESS.
3. distressingness, inclemency, rigor, badness (*R*), intemperateness (*R*), distemperature (*R*), hardship; *spec.* bitterness, extremity (*R*), roughness, heat, drought.
Antonyms: mildness (*cf.* MILD.)

sew, *v. t. & i.* stitch, needle (*R*); *spec.* baste, backhand, whip, overhand, tack, finedraw, run, seam, buttonhole, fell, embroider, quilt.
Antonyms: see RIP.

sewage, *n.* (*designating the waste matter carried off*), refuse (*contex.*), soil, drainage, sewerage (*now R, as designating the system of sewers*); *spec.* seepage.

sewed, *a.* stitched, sutile (*R*).

sewer, *n.* stitcher, sewster (*fem.; obs., exc. Scot.*); *spec.* seamstress *or* sempstress, needlewoman, hemmer, feller, *etc.*

sewing, *n.* stitching, suture (*B or tech.*).

sex, *n.* sexuality (*R*), persuasion (*jocular*), gender (*jocular, exc. as referring to word-forms in grammar*).

sexless, *a.* asexual (*tech.*), agamic (*biol.*), nonsexual.

shabby, *a.* **1.** inferior (*contex.*), mean (*contex.*); *spec.* seedy, dowdy, mangy, scrubby, scaly (*S*), rusty; *see* WORN, FADED.
Antonyms: see NEW, DANDY.
2. *See* MEAN.

shackle, *n.* **1.** bonds (*pl.; contex.*), hamper, fetter (*orig. and usually spec.*); *spec.* irons (*pl.*), gyve, clog, hopple *or* hobble, trammel (*obs. or R*), bilbo, chains (*pl.*), bolt; *see* MANACLE.
2. *See* RESTRAINT, COUPLING.

shackle, *v. t.* **1.** restrain (*contex.*), hamper; *spec.* manacle, fetter, iron, gyve, clog, hamshackle, trammel (*obs. or R*), hobble, clog, incatenate (*R*), enchain (*R*); *see* MANACLE.
Antonyms: see FREE.
2. *See* RESTRAIN, COUPLE.

shade, *n.* **1.** darkness (*contex.*), shadow (shade *defined by outline of body intercepting the*

---

setback: *reverse.*
settled: *constant, habitual, fixed, married, orderly.*
sever, *v. t.: divide, separate, amputate, distinguish.*
sever, *v. i.: separate.*
several: *individual, distinct.*

light), umbra (*tech.*), umbrage (*B*), twilight (*fig.*).
Antonyms: see SUNLIGHT.
2. *Referring to a thing that shades:* protection, umbrage (*B*), screen; *spec.* blind (*U. S.*), canopy, curtain, globe, shutter.
3. *See* DEGREE, TINT, KIND, TRACE, SHADOW, GHOST.

shade, *v. t.* **1.** protect, screen, shadow (*obs. or B*), obtenebrate (*R*), umbrage (*R*); *spec.* overshadow *or* (*less usual*) overshade, curtain, canopy, beshadow *or* (*less usual*) beshade (*intensive*).
2. change (*contex.*), gradate.
3. *In painting and drawing: spec.* cross-hatch, hachure, stipple.
4. *See* DARKEN.

shade, *v. i.* pass, change, gradate (*chiefly spec.*).

shadow, *n.* **1.** *See* SHADE.
2. *Referring to the figure cast:* shade (*R or B*), umbra (*B or tech.*); *spec.* penumbra, silhouette; *see* IMAGE.
3. *See* REFLECTION, GUEST, ATTENDANT, SYMBOL, REMAINDER, APPEARANCE, GHOST, APPARITION, SPY.

shady, *a.* dark (*contex.*), shaded, shadowy, umbrageous (*B*); *spec.* shadowish (*R*), bowery, bushy.
Antonyms: see SUNNY.

shaft, *n.* **1.** rod (*contex.*); *spec.* truncheon (*R*), loom, diaphysis; *see* QUILL, POLE.
2. *Referring to a column:* body (*contex.*), scape (*tech.*), trunk.
3. *See* ARROW, AXLE, STEM, PILLAR.
4. *Referring to wagon shafts:* thill.

shaft, *n. Referring to a form of excavation or passage:* well; *spec.* pit.

shake, *v. t.* **1.** move (*contex.*), agitate (*with a violent, irregular perturbation*), rock (*with slower, less violent and more regular motion*), sway (*with a heavy, swinging motion*); *spec.* concuss (*R*), hustle, quiver, tremble, convulse, wabble, coggle (*C*), conquassate (*obs. or R*), diddle (*C or dial.*), succuss (*R*), flap, jar, jolt, jerk, stagger; *see* VIBRATE, WAVE, WORRY, FLOURISH.
2. *See* DISTURB, WEAKEN, TRILL, ROUSE, SCATTER.

shake, *v. i.* move (*contex.*), wabble; *spec.* quiver, flap, jar, jolt, jerk, stagger; *see* TREMBLE, TOTTER, VIBRATE, WAVE. *"Shake," as distinct from "oscillate," "vibrate," "undulate," "wave," usually implies irregular motion.*

shake, *n.* motion (*contex.*), agitation (*formal or B*); *spec.* concussion, wabble, conquassation (*R*), quiver, flap, jar, jolt, jerk, wave; *see* TREMBLE, VIBRATION, FLOURISH.

shaky, *a.* **1.** *Spec.* quaky, shackly (*C*), jiggly, jerky, jolty, rickety.
Antonyms: see FIRM.
2. *See* UNCERTAIN, TREMBLING.

shall, *v.* will (*implying volition when used in the first person;* shall *in the second or third person suggests authority or compulsion on the speaker's part*).

shallow, *a.* **1.** shoal, depthless, fleet (*chiefly dial. and agric.*); *spec.* skin-deep.
Antonyms: see DEEP, FATHOMLESS.
2. *See* SUPERFICIAL.

shallow, *n.* shoal; *spec.* flat; *see* FORD.
Antonyms: see DEEP.

shallowness, *n.* shoalness, depthlessness.
Antonyms: see DEPTH.

sham, *v. i.* pretend; *spec.* malinger.

shameless, *a.* immodest, blushless, barefaced, brazen, unblushing, cynopic (*nonce word*); *see* ABANDONED, IMPUDENT, INDECENT.
Antonyms: see BASHFUL, MODEST.

shape, *n.* **1.** *See* FORM, FIGURE, IMAGE, APPARITION, APPEARANCE, ARRANGEMENT, STATE.
2. *Referring to an object made in a certain shape, in manufacturing, building, etc.: spec.* bend, facet, turn, bar, column, girder, angle iron, block, ball, band, *etc.*

shape, *v. t.* **1.** form; *spec.* rough, build, roughcast (*often fig.*), roughhew (*often fig.*), bend, block, last, machine, dome, carve, cut, turn, scapple, mold, blow, forge.
2. *See* PLAN, ADAPT, ADJUST, REGULATE, DEVISE, DESTINE.

shapely, *a.* well-shaped, clean, neat, well-made, trim; *spec.* concinnous (*R*), decent (*A*); *see* GOOD-LOOKING.
Antonyms: see DEFORMED.

share, *n.* part, portion, division; *spec.* proportion, cup (*fig.*), allotment, deal, quantum, quota, contingent, lot, dividend, divvy (*S or C*), dole (*A, B*), partage (*R*), purparty (*A*), legitim; *see* DOWER, DOWRY, ALLOWANCE.

share, *v. t.* **1.** divide (*contex.*), part (*R*), divvy (*S or C; esp. with "up"*), whack (*S; esp. with "up"*); *see* DISTRIBUTE.
2. participate, partake (*R*), divide; *see* EXPERIENCE.

share, *v. i.* participate, engage, partake, enter.

sharing, *n.* division (*contex.*), participation, partaking, community; *spec.* intercommunity (*R*), cahoot (*used in "in cahoot," "go cahoots"; S*); *see* PARTNERSHIP.

sharp, *a.* **1.** cutting (*contex.*), keen (*of a cutting edge, where* sharp *refers either to an edge or a point*), edged, edgy (*R*), keen-edged, trenchant (*A and B*), cultrate (*nat. hist.*); *spec.* fine.
Antonyms: see BLUNT.
2. *Referring to a person or to the mind:* sharp-witted, acute, keen, clever (*C*), smart (*chiefly spec.; U. S.*), bright, canny (*somewhat contemptuous or sneering*), quick-witted; *spec.* shrewd.
Antonyms: see DULL, STUPID.

---

shadow, *v. t.: shade, protect, cloud, hide, foreshadow, symbolize.*
shadowy, *a.: shady, unreal, imaginary, ghostly.*
shaggy: *rough, unkempt, unshorn, nappy, bushy, bristling.*
shaken: *agitated, broken* (in health).
sham, *n.: deceit, counterfeit.*
sham, *a.: pretended, counterfeit.*
shame, *v. t.: abash.*
shameful: *discreditable, flagrant.*

---

3. *Referring to language:* severe, cutting (*with intent to hurt feelings*), penetrative, caustic (*fig.*), piercing, pointed, trenchant (*with energy and clear-cut definiteness*), stinging, biting, pungent, piquant (*R*), crisp, mordant (*R*), acid, acidulous, lancinating (*as criticism*), stimulating, dry, brisk; *see* BITTER, CRUEL, SARCASTIC.

Antonyms: see SMOOTH, GENTLE, KIND, KINDLY, AFFECTIONATE.

4. *Referring to the look:* keen, piercing, penetrating; *spec.* searching.

5. *Referring to pain:* keen, excruciating, piercing; *spec.* lancinating, shooting, darting.

6. *See* ANGULAR, ABRUPT, PUNGENT, HARSH, PAINFUL, VIGOROUS, HIGH, LIVELY, VIOLENT, INTENSE, COLD, DISCERNING, INTELLIGENT, VIGILANT.

sharpen, *v. t.* **1.** edge (*chiefly fig.*), sharp (*R*); *spec.* strop *or* strap, reset, resharpen, grind; *see* POINT.

Antonyms: see BLUNT.

2. *See* INTENSIFY.

sharpener, *n.* sharper (*R*); *spec.* stone, bone, whetstone, rifle.

sharp-featured, *a.* thin (*contex.*), hatchety (*C*).

sharpness, *n.* **1.** cut (*R*), keenness, trenchancy (*R*), edge; *spec.* fineness.

2. acuteness, cleverness (*C*), smartness (*chiefly spec.*), brightness, dexterity.

3. severity, incisiveness (*R*), edge, causticness (*fig.*), causticity (*fig.*), trenchancy, sting, crispness, stimulatingness (*R*), piquancy, pungency, piquantness (*R*), dryness, acidity; *spec.* bitterness, cruelty, acrimony.

Antonyms: see GENTLENESS, KINDNESS.

4. *Spec.* angularity, abruptness, pungency, distinctness, discernment, intelligence, intensity, *etc.*

sharpshooter, *n.* rifleman, sniper (*both contex.*).

sharp-sighted, *a.* eagle-eyed; *spec.* all-seeing.

shatter, *v. t.* **1.** destroy (*contex.*), break (*contex.*), smash (*under heavy impact*), crash (*with noise of breakage*), rend, shiver (*into splinters or small pieces*), dash; *spec.* dynamite.

2. *See* RUIN, IMPAIR, DERANGE.

shave, *v. t.* **1.** *See* PARE, GRAZE, CHEAT.

2. cut (*contex.*), scrape (*jocular*), mow (*jocular*), razor (*R*).

shaving, *n. Spec.* whittling, excelsior (*a collective*); *see* PARING.

shawl, *n.* mantle (*contex.*); *spec.* whittle (*A or dial.*).

sheaf, *n.* **1.** bundle, reap (*agric. or dial.*); *spec.* grab (*obs. or hist.*).

2. *See* BUNDLE.

sheaf, *v. t.* bind (*contex.*), sheave.

shears, *n. pl.* clip (*sing.*), clippers (*pl.*); *see* SCISSORS. *In dignified figurative use "shears" is more common than "scissors."*

sheath, *n.* covering (*contex.*), case; *spec.* vagina, stall, thumbstall, fingerstall, lorica, boot, theca, ocrea, fascia, hose, coleorhiza, elytron, aponeurosis, cot, scabbard.

sheathe, *v. t.* cover (*contex.*), incase, ensheathe (*R*); *spec.* scabbard, vaginate (*R*), muzzle, clapboard.

shed, *n.* **1.** shelter (*contex.*), cover, hovel (*dial. Eng.*), skilling (*Eng.; chiefly spec.*); *spec.* box, cot, hangar, lean-to, penthouse, cote, byre, roundhouse, skillion.

2. *See* HOUSE.

shed, *v. t.* **1.** *See* SCATTER, EMIT, DIFFUSE, SPILL, SCALE.

2. *Referring to tears:* emit, rain (*fig.*), weep, drop.

3. *Referring to shedding an old skin, shell, etc.:* slough, throw, cast, exuviate (*tech.*); *spec.* mew (*tech. or A*), exfoliate.

4. *Referring to plants:* exfoliate (*tech.*), drop, cast; *spec.* deoperculate.

sheep, *n.* mutton (*jocular*), fleece (*fig.*), bleater (*C*), fold (*a collective sing.*), jumbuck (*Australia; C*); *spec.* down, hog, hogget, hogling, yearling, herdwick, burrel (*East Indian*), ram; *see* EWE, LAMB.

sheepcote, *n.* sheepshed, sheepy (*dial.*).

sheepskin, *n.* pelt (*contex.*); *spec.* basan *or* bazan, basil *or* bazil, roan, parchment, diploma.

sheet, *n.* **1.** *Spec.* folio *or* folium, card, lap, blanket, web, folder (*U. S.*), flake, floe, foil; *see* LAMINA, PLATE.

2. *See* EXPANSE.

shelf, *n.* **1.** *Spec.* bracket, gradin, gradine, desk, retable, degree.

2. *See* LEDGE.

shell, *n.* **1.** test (*R or tech.*); *spec.* frustule, pen univalve, bivalve.

2. *Referring to the hard outer covering of various animals:* case; *spec.* elytron, carapace, shard.

3. *Referring to missiles:* case; *spec.* shrapnel, grenade, bomb, carcass, grenado (*A*), dud (*S*); *see* MISSILE.

4. *See* CASE, CRUST, HULL.

shell, *v. t.* **1.** *See* HULL.

2. attack, bombard.

shell-bearing, *a.* conchiferous (*tech.*).

shellfish, *n.* mollusk (*tech.; most "shellfish" are "mollusks"*).

shell-shaped, *a.* conchiform, conchate, conchylaceous (*R*);—*all three tech. or B.*

shelly, *a.* chitinous, conchylious, testaceous;—*all three tech. or B.*

shelter, *n.* **1.** protection (*contex.*), cover (*contex.*), screen (*for concealment*), shield, bulwark (*B or rhetorical*); *spec.* covert, shadow, shroud, crow's-nest, houseroom, canopy, bower, box, lee, cab, guardhouse, dugout; *see* REFUGE.

2. *Referring to the fact or state of being sheltered:* refuge (*as in "to seek refuge"*).

---

shear, *v. t.: cut, clip, cleave, deprive.*
shed, *v. i.: fall.*
shed, *n.: divide.*
sheen, *n.: luster, shine.*
sheepish: *bashful, abashed.*

Antonyms: see EXPOSURE.
3. *Referring to giving shelter:* harboring, reception; *spec.* housing.
4. *See* PROTECTOR.
shelter, *v. t.* **1.** protect, cover, screen, bescreen (*an intensive*), shield; *spec.* ensconce, shroud, shadow, overshadow.
2. *Spec.* (*referring to giving asylum or safety to one seeking refuge*) receive, refuge (*R*), harbor, haven (*R*), lodge, hive, ensconce, embosom (*B; fig.*), embower, reset (*A*), sanctuarize (*R*); *see* ENTERTAIN, HOUSE.
Antonyms: see ASSAIL, ATTACK, EXPOSE.
sheltered, *a.* protected, screened, covert, cozy; *spec.* cloistered, sequestered, lee, leeward.
Antonyms: see EXPOSED, SHELTERLESS.
sheltering, *a.* protecting, screening, shielding, cozy.
shelterless, *a.* unprotected (*contex.*), shieldless, screenless; *spec.* exposed, houseless.
Antonyms: see SHELTERED.
shepherd, *n.* herder (*contex.*), shepherdess (*fem.*), pastor (*R or classical*); *spec.* Endymion (*fig.*), Daphnis (*fig.*), shepherdling (*R*).
shield, *n.* **1.** protection; *spec.* targe (*A and B*), buckler, pelta, roundel, target, hielaman (*Australia*).
2. *Referring to a protective covering of various animals: spec.* buckler, cuirass, scute, scutellum.
3. *See* SHELTER, PROTECTOR, ESCUTCHEON.
shield-shaped, *a.* scutiform, scutate; *spec.* clypeate, peltate;—*all four tech.*
shifting, *a.* fugitive, flitting, ambulatory (*B or tech.*), deambulatory (*R*); *spec.* floating, unsettled.
Antonyms: see PERMANENT.
shilling, *n.* bob (*S*), thirteener (*R*), twelvepence.
shine, *v. t. Spec.* polish, glaze, burnish, brighten.
shine, *v. i.* radiate, beam, sheen (*A*); *spec.* play, irradiate (*B*), lighten, gleam (*implying esp. the subduing effect of distance or an intervening medium, or implying momentariness or repeated interruption*), blaze, flame, flare (*to* shine *with a spreading, unsteady flame*), glimmer (gleam, *on a smaller scale*), glimpse (*R*), glare, burn, glow (*as if intensely heated*), beacon (*R*), glisten, glister, glitter (*with bright unsteady reflection from a hard surface*), brighten (*R*), blink, effulge (*B*), flash (*with a sudden burst of light*), brandish (*R*), resplend (*R*), luster *or* lustre (*R*), gloze (*R*), ray (*R*), outbeam (*R*), lamp (*R*), moon.
shine, *n. Spec.* polish, brightness, sheen, luster, glare, glaze.
shining, *a.* **1.** radiant, bright (*contex.*), beaming; *spec.* irradiant (*B*), refulgent, fulgent (*R or B*), resplendent, glittering, gleaming, lambent (*with a clear, soft, and not very hot light*), orient (*like the dawn*), burning, flaming, nitent (*R*), relucent (*R*), splendent (*R*), flaring, interlucent, luminous (*as not involving any conscious reference to the action*), flashing.
Antonyms: see DARK.
2. *See* LUSTROUS, DISTINGUISHED.
shining, *n.* **1.** radiance, radiation; *spec.* refulgence, flash, lambency *or* (*R*) lambence, glitterance (*R*), irradiance *or* irradiancy (*B*), irradiation (*B*); *see* LUMINOSITY.
2. *See* LUSTER.
ship, *n.* vessel, hulk (*A, exc. spec.*); *spec.* castle (*B or rhetorical*), argosy (*historical or B*), runner, leviathan (*rhetorical*), liner, roller, screw, razee, carvel, brig, brigantine, barkentine *or* barquentine, frigate, galleon, junk, schooner, sloop, yawl, yacht, ketch, lugger, dromond, consort, prow, clipper, buss.
ship, *v. t.* **1.** embark.
2. *Spec.* export; *see* SEND, TRANSPORT.
shipping, *n.* ships (*collective pl.*), marine, tonnage.
shirk, *v. t.* avoid, evade, balk, blink, blench.
shirk, *v. i.* soldier, soger (*C*), skulk; *spec.* malinger.
shirker, *n.* quitter (*U. S.*), skulk, slacker (*C*), soger (*C*); *spec.* eyeservant, rogue.
shirt, *n.* sark (*Scot.*), shift (*obs. or R, exc. spec.*); *spec.* chemise, smock, vest, camise, guernsey.
shirt front, dicky (*S or C*), sham, plastron (*R*).
shoal, *v. i.* shallow (*R*).
shock, *v. t.* **1.** strike (*contex.*), concuss (*R*); *spec.* jar, jolt, jounce.
2. *Spec.* scandalize, horrify, jar (*S*), stun, stagger, jolt (*chiefly S or C*), disedify (*R*).
shock, *n.* **1.** *See* ENCOUNTER.
2. impulse, concussion (*only of material bodies, where* shock *may be either material or mental*), brunt; *spec.* crash, slam, dash, percussion, water hammer; *see* EARTHQUAKE.
3. *See* START, THRILL.
shock, *n.* **1.** *See* GROUP.
2. shag, mat, mop, shog (*Scot. and dial.*).
shocking, *a. Spec.* horrible, horrific, ghastly, ghast (*A or B*), ghastful (*A*); *see* HORRIBLE, ABOMINABLE, DISGUSTING.
Antonyms: see PLEASANT.
shoe, *n.* **1.** *Spec.* boot, bootee (*a trade name*), half-boot, bottine, bootikin, buskin, cothurnus, sock, solleret, startup, clodhopper, clog, chaussure (*A or French*), balmoral, sandal, pump, brogan, brodekin (*obs.*), chopine *or* chopin, galosh *or* golosh (*R in U. S.*), patten, oxford, crakow, brogue, moccasin, stogy (*C*), leathers (*a collective pl.*).
2. *See* FERRULE.
shoe, *v. t.* **1.** *Spec.* boot, sandal.
2. *See* FERRULE.
shoeblack, *n.* boots (*cant or C*).

---

shelve: *retire, defer.*
shield, *v. t.: protect, shelter.*
shift, *n.: expedient, evasion, device, turn, trick, removal, displacement, relay, change, substitution.*
shift, *v. i.: dodge, contrive, displace, change, prevaricate, gybe.*
shine, *n.: luminosity, luster, polish, sunlight, moonlight.*
shiver, *v. t.: shatter, splinter, crash.*
shiver, *v. i.: quiver, shudder.*

---

shoemaker, *n.* cordwainer (*obs., exc. cant*), crispin (*fig.; sometimes cant*), souter (*obs. or Scot.*), snob (*dial. Eng.*).

shoemaking, *n.* cordwainery (*B*).

shoe-shaped, *a. Spec.* sandaliform (*B*).

shoot, *n.* **1.** *See* GROWTH, DART, RAPID, CHUTE.

2. branch, sprout, graff (*A; primarily spec.*), chit (*obs. or dial.*); *spec.* bine, tendril, tiller, braird (*Scot.*), browse (*a collective*), dag (*obs.*), layer, turion; *see* GRAFT.

shoot, *v. t.* **1.** *See* PROJECT, PROPEL, DISCHARGE, EMIT, EXTEND, PROTRUDE, EXPEL, VARIEGATE, UTTER, WOUND.

2. *Referring to the shooting of missiles:* discharge; *spec.* catapult.

3. strike (*contex.*), hit, plug (*S*); *spec.* rifle (*R*), pot, hull, flight, pistol, snipe, pelt.

shooter, *n.* **1.** shot, marksman (*contex.*), markswoman (*contex.*), gun (*cant*); *spec.* gunman (*cant or S*), rifleman, sharpshooter; *see* GUNNER.

2. *See* GUN.

shop, *n. In Brit. use, the generic term; in U. S. tends to be confined to smaller or smarter establishments.* **1.** repository (*R, exc. spec.*), store (*the generic term in U. S.; but in Britain reserved for large establishments*), emporium (*a loose and grandiloquent use*), market (*chiefly spec.*); *spec.* confectionary, cutlery, sutlery, canteen, grocery, creamery, *etc.*

2. *See* FACTORY, BUSINESS.

shop, *v. i. Spec.* market.

shopkeeper, *n.* tradesman, shopman; *spec.* bourgeois (*French*).

shore, *n.* strand (*B or poetical*), coast (*only along the sea*), foreshore (*between high and low water*), waterside *or* side (*contex.*), water (*contex.*), ripe (*R*), rivage (*B*), brim (*A*); *spec.* seashore, bank (*implies steeply sloping margin to running water*), beach (*implies sandy or pebbly surface*), sands (*chiefly Brit.*).

short, *a.* **1.** brief, curtate, curtal (*A*), curtailed, cutty (*Scot.*); *spec.* curt, close.

Antonyms: see LONG, ENDLESS, LENGTHY.

2. *See* LOW, BRIEF (*in time*), CRUMBLY, CONCISE, CURT (*in language*), DEFICIENT.

shorten, *v. t.* **1.** diminish, abridge, reduce, abbreviate (*R, exc. as to time*), lessen; *spec.* curtail, dock, cut, breviate (*obs.*); *see* TRIM.

Antonyms: see EXTEND, LENGTHEN.

2. *See* DIMINISH, ABBREVIATE, CONTRACT, BEGUILE, LOWER (*prices*), DEPRIVE.

shortened, *a. Spec.* curtate (*tech.*), abridged.

short-headed, *a.* brachycephalic (*tech.*).

short-lived, *a.* transitory, transient (*R*), ephemeral (*properly spec.*).

shortness, *n.* brevity.

short-winded, *a.* dyspnœic (*tech.*); *spec.* puffy, pursy, pursive (*A*), breathless, asthmatic.

shot, *n.* **1.** *Referring to an act of shooting:* shoot (*R*); *spec.* inner, carton, bull's-eye, bowshot.

2. *In games:* shoot; *spec.* throw, inwick (*Scot.*); *see* CAROM.

3. *Referring to a kind of missiles: spec.* buckshot, swanshot, canister, grapeshot.

4. *See* SHOOTER, MISSILE, EXPLOSION, AIM.

shoulder blade, scapula (*tech.*), bladebone (*now chiefly a butcher's term*), omoplate (*R*).

shoulder piece. *Spec.* epaulet *or* epaulette, pouldron *or* pauldron.

shout, *v. i.* cry (*contex.*), exclaim (*formal; chiefly spec.*), yell (*somewhat depreciatory*), scream, screech, bellow, vociferate (*B*); *spec.*, thunder, bawl, mouth, roar, clamor, whoop; *see* HOLLO, EXCLAIM, CHEER.

Antonyms: see WHISPER.

shout, *v. t.* cry (*contex.*), exclaim (*formal, chiefly spec.*), scream (*chiefly spec.*), vociferate (*B*), yell (*depreciatory*); *spec.* roar, acclaim (*R*), thunder, bawl, bellow, mouth (*R*), clamor; *see* EXCLAIM.

Antonyms: see WHISPER.

shout, *n.* cry (*contex.*), yell (*depreciatory*), scream (*chiefly spec.*), vociferation (*B*); *spec.* thunder, bawl, bellow, roar, clamor, whoop acclaim (*R*); *see* OUTCRY, HOLLO, EXCLAMATION, CHEER.

Antonyms: see WHISPER.

shouter, *n.* stentor.

shovel, *n. Spec.* peel, battledore, plow, scoop, skeet, slice.

show, *n.* **1.** *See* DISCLOSURE, SIGHT, PROOF, PRETENSE, OPPORTUNITY, APPARITION, AIR.

2. *Referring to the act of showing to others:* display, exhibition, presentation; *spec.* demonstration (*implying a public or lively display in reference to its effect on others*), manifestation, theophany, epiphany.

Antonyms: see HIDING.

3. *Referring to a public show, as in a theater: spec.* performance, exhibition, exposition, waxworks (*pl.*), movies, cosmorama, cyclorama, gaff (*Eng. S and colonial*); *see* FAIR.

4. spectacle, pageant, display, set-out (*C or informal*); *spec.* masque, procession, games (*pl.*).

5. *In a concrete sense, referring to the objects shown:* display, exhibit, layout, spread, set-out.

6. *Referring to ostentatious display:* display, showiness, ostentation, ostentatiousness, pretension, pageantry, pomp, parade, bravery (*A or B*); *spec.* bravura (*implying brilliancy or daring in execution*), bubble, dash (*a less formal equiv. of "bravura"*), vanity, vainglory, glazonment *or* blazonry, gallantry, moonshine (*fig.; depreciatory*), éclat (*French*), gayety, dazzle, garishness (*excessive display*), tinsel (*fig.*), clinquant (*B or artistic*), flash, flourish, frippery, splurge (*C*), figure (*A*), flare, glare, gaudiness, gaudery (*R*), gaud (*R*), ostent (*R*).

show, *v. t.* **1.** *In a sense implying an intentional bringing into sight:* exhibit (*as something markworthy*), present, produce, display (*for public inspection*); *spec.* spring (show *suddenly*), reveal, manifest, proclaim, flaunt (show *with pride, arrogance, or defiance*), flare, flash (*S*), parade, air, demonstrate, outshow (*B*), discover (*A*), blazon, wear, stage, represent, unfold, meld.

2. *In a sense not implying any intention:* exhibit, evince, present, display, manifest; *see* DISCLOSE.

3. *Referring to showing by inference from outward acts, signs, etc.:* evidence, exhibit, display, disclose, bear, evince, manifest, give (*as in "to give signs of life"*); *spec.* demonstrate, betray.

4. *Referring to obedience, thanks, etc.:* render (*used with "obedience"*), do (*used chiefly with "obedience"*), pay, give.

5. *See* EXERCISE, EVIDENCE, PROVE, GUIDE, DISCLOSE, TEACH, INDICATE, PRE-FIGURE, EXPRESS, REPRESENT.

shower, *n.* **1.** scud, brash (*chiefly dial.*); *spec.* fall, flurry; *see* RAIN.

2. *See* FLIGHT, FALL.

showing, *n.* **1.** disclosure, display, exhibition; *spec.* manifestation, *etc.*

2. *See* STATEMENT.

showy, *a.* ostentatious, brave (*A or B*), pretentious; *spec.* ambitious, dashing (*C*), vain, spectacular, theatrical, clashy (*C*), gay (*R*), peacocky (*C*), loud, braw (*Scot.*), showish (*R*), branky (*Scot.*), garish (*offensively dazzling*), tawdry (*as something cheap and flimsy*), splendid (*C*), gaudy (*suggesting overconspicuous and tasteless gay colors*), flashy (*suggesting cheap, meretricious display*), sparkish (*R*), bright, flaunty (*R*), gallant, gorgeous (*C or S*), splendiferous (*C or S*), flash (*cant*), smart (*C*), gewgawish (*R*), gingerbready (*C*), flary (*R*), glaring, magnificent (*C*), sumptuous (*C*), ambitious; *see* GAUDY.

Antonyms: see MODEST, SIMPLE.

shrew, *n.* termagant (*of brawling or boisterous habit*), virago, vixen (*implying confirmed ill-temper*), cotquean (*A*), frump (*of a dowdy and old-fashioned cross woman*), brimstone (*fig.*), hellcat (*implying witchlike evil or spite*), hag, harridan, fish-wife, rantipole (*R*); *spec.* scold.

shrewd, *a.* **1.** clever (*general sense*), discerning, intelligent (*contex.*), sagacious (*implying more dignity than the mere implication of native cleverness in* shrewd), perspicacious, sage (sagacious *and* perspicacious *suggest discernment;* sage *suggests wisdom or age*), sapient (*the implication of wisdom is often ironical*), knowing (*real ability or the impression of* it).

Antonyms: see DULL, STUPID.

2. subtle, artful, astute (*diplomacy, artfulness, craft*), wily, cunning, sly, acute, cute (*C*), canny (*a sense based on qualities attributed by the English to the Scotch*), long-headed, hard-headed, tricky (*C*).

3. close, hard, evil (*A*); harsh, biting, keen (*the latter three often fig. of wind or weather*); *see* SHARP.

4. *See* ILL-TEMPERED.

2. intelligent (*contex.*), discerning, knowing, astute (*with implied sagacity or craft*), astucious (*R*), canny (*a sense based on qualities attributed by the English to the Scotch*), keen, cute (*C*), long-headed, hard-headed; *see* SHARP.

Antonyms: see DULL, STUPID.

shrewish, *a.* harridan, vixenish, boisterous, tumultuous, scolding, quarrelsome.

shrill, *a.* high, thin, sharp, acute, keen, small, penetrative, penetrating, clarisonous (*R*); *spec.* stridulous, treble, pipy (*R*).

Antonyms: see DULL, LOW, SWEET.

shrill, *v. i.* sound, pipe; *spec.* stridulate; *see* CRY, EXCLAIM.

shrine, *n.* *Of a receptacle for relics:* sanctuary (*contex.*), reliquary, relicary (*R*); *spec.* feretory *or* feretrum (*R*), tabernacle (*obs.*), tester (*R*), martyry, lararium, durgah (*East Indian*), pir (*Mohammedan*), phylactery (*Hebrew*), nymphæum.

shrink, *v. i.* **1.** *See* CONTRACT, DIMINISH, HESITATE.

2. contract (*contex.*), scringe (*C or dial.*), cringe, huddle (*usually with "together"*).

Antonyms: see EXPAND, BLOAT, SWELL.

3. recoil (*contex.*), wince, cringe, scringe (*C or dial.*), quail, cow, flinch, blench *or* (*A*) blanch, funk (*S*); *spec.* boggle, revolt, start; *see* SHY.

shrink, *n.* **1.** *See* CONTRACTION, HESITATION, DIMINUTION.

2. contraction, scringe (*C or dial.*), cringe, bundle.

3. recoil (*contex.*), revolt, resilience (*R*), revulsion, wince, cringe, scringe (*C or dial.*), funk (*S*), flinch; *spec.* gabble, start; *see* SHY.

shroud, *n.* **1.** *See* GARMENT, DISGUISE, SHELTER.

2. cerecloth, cerement (*R*), winding sheet, sheet (*short for "winding sheet"*), sindon (*hist. or A*).

shrub, *n.* bush, frutex (*R; tech.*).

shrubby, *a.* **1.** bushy, frutescent (*tech.*), fruticose (*tech.*), fruticous (*R*); *spec.* fruticulose (*R*), suffruticose.

2. *See* BUSHY.

shudder, *v. i.* shake (*contex.*), quiver, horror (*chiefly med.*), shiver.

shudder, *n.* shake (*contex.*), quiver, horror (*chiefly med.*), shiver.

shuddering, *n.* shaking, quivering, horrent (*R or B*), horrescent (*R*).

shuffle, *n.* **1.** *See* EXCHANGE, TRICK, PREVARICATION, EVASION, PUSH.

2. *Referring to the gait:* scuff, scrape; *see* DANCE.

shuffle, *v. i.* **1.** scrape, scuff.

2. *See* PREVARICATE, DODGE.

shut, *v. t.* **1.** *Referring to a door, gate, etc.:* close; *spec.* snap, slam, clap;—*these last specific synonyms being contextual senses.*

Antonyms: see OPEN, UNFOLD.

2. *See* CLOSE, OBSTRUCT.

shy, *v. i.* shrink, skit, skew, boggle.

shy, *n.* shrink, boggle;—*referring to horses.*

sick, *a.* **1.** *See* AILING, DISEASED, DEPRESSED, SPOILED.

shrivel: *contract, wrinkle.*
shroud, *v. t.: disguise, hide.*
shuffle, *v. t.: push, mix, manipulate.*
shy, *a.: distrustful, timid, bashful, elusive.*
shy, *n. & v. t.: throw.*

2. qualmish, nauseated, ill (*though* sick *and* ill *are used interchangeably, nice usage confines* sick *to implication of nausea, leaving* ill *as the generic term*); *spec.* seasick.

3. tired (*used with "of"*), weary (*used with "of"*), disgusted (*used with "with"*).

sicken, *v. i.* **1.** fail, invalid; *see* LANGUISH.

2. *Referring to a becoming weary of a thing:* tire (*used with "of"*), weary (*used with "of"*).

sicken, *v. t.* **1.** indispose, craze (*A*); *see* NAUSEATE.

2. tire, weary; *see* DISGUST.

sickle-shaped, *a.* falciform (*tech.*), falculate (*R*).

sickly-looking, *a.* peaky (*C*), peaked (*chiefly C*), peakish (*C; R*).

sickness, *n.* **1.** illness (*of a particular person at some time and place*), indisposition (*a slighter illness that incapacitates one for the time*), ill health, morbidity, invalidship (*R*), invalidism, indisposedness (*R*); *see* NAUSEA.

2. *See* AILMENT, DISEASE.

side, *n.* **1.** pleuron (*anat.*), paries (*anat.*); *spec.* flitch, flank.

2. surface (*contex.*), face (*contex.*); *spec.* aspect, lee, leeboard, broadside, front, bottom, top, interior, exterior, slope, shore.

Antonyms: see POINT.

3. hand;—*as in "on either side" or "hand."*

4. cause, part, party (*R*), behalf.

5. *See* LIMIT, EDGE, PARTY, ALTERNATIVE, DIRECTION, PLACE.

sideboard, *n. Spec.* cellaret, buffet, dresser.

sideway, *a.* lateral, sidelong, sideling, sideways (*C*), sidewise, sideward; *see* BROADSIDE.

sideways, *adv.* sidelong, sidewise, laterally, sideward, sidewards, sideway, collaterally; *see* BROADSIDE, CROSSWISE, OBLIQUELY.

Antonyms: see LENGTHWISE.

siding, *n.* track (*contex.*), sidetrack (*orig. U. S.*); *spec.* pass-by.

sidle, *v. i.* side (*R*), edge, skew; *spec.* crabsidle.

siege, *n.* investment, beleaguerment, leaguer (*B*), besiegement (*R*), blockade (*chiefly spec.*).

siesta, *n.* rest (*contex.*), nap; *spec.* meridian (*R*).

sieve, *n.* tense (*obs. or dial.; chiefly spec.*), search (*obsolescent*), cribble (*obsolescent*); *spec.* screen, bolter, colander, drum, grate, grating, riddle, griddle, grizzly, harp (*Scot.*); *see* STRAINER.

sievelike, *a.* cribriform (*tech.*), cribrate (*tech.*), cribrose (*tech.*), coliform (*R*); *spec.* ethmoid.

sift, *v. t.* **1.** separate (*contex.*), sieve, searce (*obs.*), cribble (*obs.*); *spec.* bolt, screen, riddle, garble; *see* STRAIN.

2. *See* DISCOVER, EXAMINE, DISCUSS.

sigh, *n.* breath, suspiration (*R*); *spec.* heigh-ho, sob, aspiration (*R*).

Antonyms: see LAUGH.

sigh, *v. i.* **1.** breathe (*contex.*), suspire (*R*), sough (*B or dial.*); *spec.* heigh-ho, sob.

2. *See* LONG, SORROW, MOURN.

sight, *n.* **1.** *Referring to that which is seen:* vision (*suggesting a significant appearance, as to one in dream or exalted contemplation*), view (*suggesting a prospect or something spread before the eye*), show (*implying intended display*), beholding (*A*), spectacle; *spec.* gawk, fright, eyesore, guy; *see* SPECTACLE, VIEW.

2. *Referring to the act of seeing something:* perception (*contex.*), vision, view, spectacle, look, glimpse; *spec.* notice, contemplation.

3. *Referring to the faculty or power of seeing:* vision, eyesight, seeing, view (*R*), light (*B or rhetorical*).

Antonyms: see BLINDNESS.

4. *Referring to the area open to sight:* range, eyeshot, view, eye (*now only fig., as in "out of one's eye"*).

5. *Spec.* target, vane, dispart, pinnule, notch, leaf.

sightsee, *v. i. & t. Spec.* lionize, slum, tour, travel, rubberneck (*C*).

sign, *n.* **1.** *See* GESTURE, VESTIGE.

2. indication, signification (*B*), mark, significative (*R or B*), token, note, signal (*arbitrarily contrived to convey notice of something*), denotation (*R*), ensign (*A*), signature (*R or tech.*), significant (*R*); *spec.* direct, diæresis, collar (*implying servitude*), charact (*A*); *see* BADGE, NOTICE, COUNTERSIGN, PASSWORD, SYMBOL.

3. *Referring to a business sign: spec.* device, signboard, shingle (*C*), post, bush (*chiefly hist.*), winebush (*chiefly hist.*), pole.

4. *Referring to what indicates coming events:* omen, portent, auspice (*chiefly spec.*), augury, prognostication, presage, token, foretoken, presignification (*R*), prognostic, boding, bodement (*R*), prodigy (*R*), ostent (*R*); *see* SYMPTOM.

sign, *v. t.* **1.** *See* SIGNAL.

2. confirm (*contex.*), subscribe; *spec.* countersign, letter, cross, initial, indorse.

signal, *n.* **1.** *See* SIGN.

2. sign, token (*R*); *spec.* beacon, whistle, cry, cue (*theater*), catchword (*chiefly theater*), enunciator, flare-up, light, target (*U. S.*), telegraph, semaphore, wave, wigwag, balk, assembly, reveille, taps, tattoo, beat, flam, troop, watchword; *see* GESTURE, ALARM.

signal, *v. t.* **1.** inform (*contex.*), notify (*contex.*), sign (*R*), signalize (*R*), signify; *spec.* fugle, flame, whistle, flag.

2. *See* ANNOUNCE, DISTINGUISH.

signaler, *n.* signalman; *spec.* flagman, trumpeter, operator, sentinel, *etc.*

signaling, *n. Spec.* beckoning, waft (*R*), wafture (*R*), *etc.; spec.* heliography, telegraphy.

signatory, *a.* signing, signatary.

signature, *n.* **1.** *Referring to the mark:* subscription, subscript (*R*), autograph, sign manual, hand (*chiefly tech.*); *spec.* mark, cross, frank, countersignature; *see* INDORSEMENT.

2. *Referring to the act or action:* subscription, signing, signation (*R*), indorsement.

---

sickening, *a.: nauseous, disgusting.* | **sickly:** *ailing, faint, diseased, unhealthy, nauseous.* | **sign,** *v. i.: gesture.*

---

significant, *a.* **1.** *See* EXPRESSIVE, IMPORTANT, EMPHATIC.
2. expressive (*charged with meaningfulness*), indicative, suggestive, significative; *spec.* presageful, ominous, prognostic, boding, bodeful, oracular, portentous, sinister, consignificant; *see* THREATENING.
Antonyms: see EMPTY, MEANINGLESS.

signify, *v. t.* **1.** *See* EXPRESS, INDICATE, MEAN, ANNOUNCE, SIGNAL.
2. indicate, denote, mean, betoken, augur, omen, portend (*esp. evil*), presignify (*R*), preindicate, promise, foretoken, foreshow, foresignify (*R*); *spec.* bode, symbolize, forebode, nod, announce, harbinger, prognosticate; *see* FORESHADOW.

silence, *n.* **1.** speechlessness, silentness, mumness, hush (*imposed or enforced silence*); *see* RETICENCE.
Antonyms: see SPEECH, TALK.
2. noiselessness, silentness, quiet, quietness, quietude, stillness, still, hush; *spec.* dead (*of night*).
Antonyms: see NOISE, DIN, SOUND, SOUNDING, UPROAR.

silence, *v. t.* **1.** *Referring to speech:* hush, quiet, dumb, mum (*C or R*), muzzle (*spec. or fig.*), throttle (*spec. or fig.*).
2. *Referring to the prevention of noise or of the perceptibleness of noise:* still, hush, quiet, quieten (*R*), deafen *or* (*A*) deaf, drown.
Antonyms: see ROUSE.
3. *See* DISABLE, SUPPRESS, CONFUTE.

silence, *v. i.* quiet, hush.

silencer, *n. Spec.* mute, sordine, silentiary (*R*), choker (*S*), muffler.

silent, *a.* **1.** speechless, mute (*not speaking; spec.*), voiceless, dumb (*deprived of speech*), quiet, mum (*refraining from speech*), husht (*A*), whist (*A or R*), tacit (*R*), conticent (*R*), wistful (*R*); *spec.* tongueless; *see* RETICENT.
Antonyms: see UPROARIOUS, CLAMOROUS, BOISTEROUS, NOISY.
2. noiseless, quiet, still, dumb, inaudible, stilly (*B*), hush (*A*), dumb (*emphatic and suggesting normal presence of noise*); *spec.* hushful, echoless (*B or rhetorical*), tuneless.
Antonyms: see LOUD, BOISTEROUS, NOISY, SILENT.
3. *See* NONVOCAL.

silently, *adv.* speechlessly, dumbly, mutely, noiselessly, *etc.*
Antonyms: see ALOUD, NOISILY.

silky, *a.* **1.** silken, sericeous (*tech.*), flossy; *spec.* satiny.
2. *See* INGRATIATING, SMOOTH, SOFT, DOWNY.

sill, *n. Spec.* threshold.

silly, *n.* featherhead, goosey;—*all three C; see* SIMPLETON.

silver, *n.* argent (*A, B or her.*), white metal (*journalistic cant*).

silver, *a.* argental (*B or tech.*), argentine (*R*), silvern (*A or B*), white (*obs. or A*).

silver-haired, *a.* white-haired, silvered.

silvery, *a.* **1.** silver (*chiefly B*), argent (*B or tech.*), argenteous (*R*), argentine (*R*).
2. *See* CLEAR, MELODIOUS.

simian, *a.* apelike, apish; *spec.* baboonish, catarrhine.

simian, *n.* ape (*chiefly spec.*), monkey, jackanapes (*A*); *spec.* baboon, gorilla, catarrhine.

similar, *a.* resembling, resemblant (*R*); *spec.* like (*very* similar), alike (similar *in almost or entirely all respects*), such, consimilar, conspecific, conformable; *see* ANALOGOUS.

similarity, *n.* resemblance, similitude (*R*); *spec.* likeness, alikeness (*R; a predicative*), consimilarity (*R*), parity (similarity *in nature, tendency, etc.*); *see* ANALOGY.

similarly, *a.* likewise (*as in "to do likewise," etc.; A*).

simple, *a.* **1.** *See* ARTLESS, INSIGNIFICANT, MERE, UNAFFECTED.
2. simple-minded, innocent, unsophisticated, onefold (*R*), guileless, inartificial, silly (*A*); *see* UNSUSPECTING.
Antonyms: see AFFECTED, ARTFUL.
3. plain; *spec.* homely, homelike, russet, rustic, rural, frugal, natural, native, homespun (*fig.*), Attic.
Antonyms: see AMBITIOUS, SHOWY, LUXURIOUS, ELABORATE, FANTASTIC, GAUDY, ORNAMENTAL.
4. uncompounded, unmixed, incomposite (*B or R*), single, elemental *or* elementary, incomplex (*R*); *see* PURE, UNADULTERATED.
Antonyms: see COMPLEX, COMPOSITE.
5. easy, plain, uninvolved, straightforward.
Antonyms: see UNSOLVABLE.

simpleton, *n.* lighthead, simple, stupid, wantwit (*A or B*), jay (*S or C*), nincompoop (*contemptuous; C or S*), geck (*obs. or dial.*), gaby (*C or dial.*); *spec.* gawky *or* (*undignified*) gawk, greenhorn (*C*), gander, gulpin, gull, noddy, gump (*U. S.; vulgar*), tony (*R or A*), ninny, ninnyhammer, idiot (*C*), soft *or* softy (*S*), ass, simpkin (*R*), clown, Gothamist *or* Gothamite (*R; fig.*), booby (*C or S*), juggins (*S*), jobbernowl (*C*), innocent (*euphemistic*), goose (*C*), noodle, goof (*S*), boob (*C*), simp (*S*), sap (*S*), halfwit (*C*); *see* BLOCKHEAD (*referring esp. to the lack of understanding*), FOOL (*extremely deficient in the faculty of understanding*).

simplicity, *n.* **1.** *Spec.* artlessness, humbleness, lowliness, unaffectedness.
2. simple-mindedness, simpleness, innocence, unsophisticatedness, unsophistication, naiveté, simplesse (*A*), silliness (*A*); *spec.* unsuspiciousness, ignorance.
Antonyms: cf. the adjectives mentioned under SIMPLE, **2.**

---

significance: *meaning, importance.* | **signification:** *expression, meaning, sign.* | **silly:** *foolish, imbecile, unwise, absurd.*

---

3. plainness, simpleness, homeliness, simplesse (*A*), rusticity, frugality, naturalness.
Antonyms: see LUXURY.
4. uncompoundness (*R*), incompositeness (*R*); *see* PURITY.
5. easiness, plainness, straightforwardness.

simplify, *v. t.* disintricate (*R*); *spec.* abbreviate (*math.*).
Antonyms: see COMPLICATE.

sin, *n.* transgression (*implying violation of command or law, where* sin *stresses the lost moral standing of the wrongdoer*), offense (*contex.*), wrong, wickedness, crime (*referring to offenses publicly prescribed and punishable*), piacle (*R*), iniquity (*implying gross or heinous wrongdoing*), debt (*Biblical*), trespass (*R or Biblical*), error (*contex.*), peccancy (*R*); *spec.* peccadillo.

sin, *v. i.* transgress (*formal or B*), offend, trespass (*Biblical*), err (*esp. in "to err is human, to forgive divine"*).

since, *adv.* **1.** *See* AGO.
2. subsequently, later, afterwards.

sincere, *a.* **1.** *See* PURE.
2. *In the sense of "not containing any element of insincerity":* real, true, genuine, unfeigned, single (*B*), unaffected, simple, honest, deceitless (*R*).
Antonyms: see INSINCERE, SPECIOUS, TRIFLING.
3. *In the sense of "characterized by sincerity," and referring to persons, their actions, etc.:* honest, honorable, hearty, cordial, simple (*R or B*), single (*B*), direct, straight (*C*), straightforward, candid, unfeigned, frank, undeceitful, fraudless (*R*), plain-dealing, single-hearted, whole-hearted, single-minded, heart-whole (*R*), single-eyed (*R*), heartful (*R*), unaffected; *spec.* devout.
Antonyms: see AFFECTED, INSINCERE.

sincerity, *n.* **1.** *See* PURITY.
2. reality, truth, trueness, genuineness, singleness (*B*), simplicity, honesty, sterlingness.
Antonyms: see INSINCERITY.
3. honesty, honorableness, heartiness, cordiality, cordialness, singleness (*B*), single-heartedness, single-mindedness, whole-heartedness, devotion, simplicity (*R or B*), integrity, directness, plain-dealing, straightforwardness.
Antonyms: see INSINCERITY.

sinewy, *a.* **1.** wiry, stringy (*C*), whipcordy (*R*), nervous (*R*), nervy (*R*).
2. *See* STRONG, FORCIBLE.

sinful, *a.* transgressive (*R*), wicked, wrong, wrongful, piacular (*R*), peccant (*B*), sinning, peccable (*B*); *spec.* blamable, corrupt.
Antonyms: see SINFUL, BLAMELESS, HOLY, INNOCENT.

sing, *v. i.* **1.** *Spec.* lilt, melodize (*R*), descant, warble, chant (*A or B*), carol (*chiefly B*), melody (*R*), choir (*B*), trollol (*R*), yodel, hum, troll, singsong (*R*), hymn, psalmodize.
2. *Referring to birds:* flute, whistle, pipe; *spec.* warble, lilt, carol, crow.
3. *See* CRY, HUM, RING.

sing, *v. t.* **1.** utter (*contex.*), raise (*contex.*), *spec.* lilt, chant (*A or B*), carol (*chiefly B*), warble, bear (*in "to bear a part"; A*), modulate (*R*), choir (*B*), yodel, troll, intone, cantillate (*R*), monotone, succent (*R*), hum, timbrel, quaver.
2. *See* INTONE, CELEBRATE, PROCLAIM.

singer, *n.* **1.** *Referring to males or females:* vocalist (*R*), voice, songster; *spec.* descanter (*R*), chanter (*chiefly B*), melodist (*R*), warbler, caroler, chorister, precentor, orpheonist.
2. *Referring to males:* songman (*R*), cantator (*R*); *spec.* bass, barytone, tenor, falsetto, warbler, yodler, minstrel, bard, minnesinger, troubadour, gleeman, hymner, hymnist, Iliadist (*fig.*), rhapsodist, psalmodist, cantor, succentor, precentor.
3. *Referring to females:* songstress; *spec.* chantress (*B or A*), soprano *or* (*R*), sopranist, alto, contralto, nightingale (*fig.*), siren, prima donna.
4. *Referring to birds:* song bird, songster, songstress (*fem.*); *spec.* warbler, whistler.

singing, *a.* cantatory (*R*).

singing, *n.* **1.** *Spec.* modulation (*R*), charm, cantillation (*R*), intonement, humming, minstrelsy, hymnody.
2. *See* INTONATION.

single, *a.* **1.** *See* ALONE (*as being apart from others*), INDIVIDUAL (*as being considered separately*), ONE (*as being the only one*), SIMPLE (*as being made up of one part only*), SINCERE, MERE.
2. sole; *spec.* celibate.

sink, *n.* **1.** *Spec.* cesspool, hollow, drain, basin.
2. *Referring to a place where things sink in and are lost: spec.* slough, mire, quicksand, hole.
3. *Referring to a place of moral degradation:* cloaca (*fig.*), sewer (*fig.*), den (*contex.*).

sink, *v. i.* **1.** submerge (*R*), subside (*R*); *spec.* founder, poach (*in walking*).
Antonyms: see EMERGE, FLOAT.
2. *Referring to a giving way, as under emotion, etc.:* fail, collapse, subside (*chiefly spec.*); *spec.* drop, lapse; *see* FALL.
3. *See* SUBSIDE (*referring to the lowering, as of a body of water, etc.*), PENETRATE, DESCEND, FALL, DEGENERATE, LANGUISH, DISAPPEAR, CHANGE.

sink, *v. t.* **1.** submerge, submerse (*R*); *spec.* plunge, founder, swamp; *see* DROWN.
Antonyms: see RAISE, FLOAT.
2. *See* LOWER, INSERT, IGNORE, DEPRESS, LOSE, DEGRADE, ABASE, PAY, RUIN.

sinklike, *a.* colluvial (*R*).

sinless, *a.* innocent, righteous, impeccable, blameless, unspotted; *see* HOLY.
Antonyms: see WICKED, SINFUL, BLAMABLE, CORRUPT.

sinner, *n.* transgressor (*which see*), trespasser, offender, wrongdoer, malfeasant; *spec.* reprobate.
Antonyms: see INNOCENT.

---

single, *v. t.: separate, distinguish.*
singleness: *sincerity, celibacy.*
singular: *one, individual, odd, extraordinary, unique.*
sinister: *dishonest, harmful, wicked, significant, threatening, unfavorable, ill-omened, left.*

---

sinuosity, *n.* curve (*contex.*), crook (*contex.*), sinuation (*R*), bend (*contex.*); *spec.* undulation, wave, wind, winding, flexuosity, crinkle.

sinuous, *a.* crooked, curved, curving, sinuate, sinuated (*R*), sinuose (*R*), winding, undulating, wavy, zigzag (*contex.*); *spec.* flexuous (*chiefly tech.*), flexuose, vermicular, vermiculate, tortuous, circuitous, serpentine, anfractuous (*R*).
Antonyms: see STRAIGHT.

sip, *v. i. & n.* sup.

sister, *n.* **1.** *Spec.* cadette.
2. associate (*contex.*); *spec.* nun.

sisterhood, *n.* **1.** sistership.
2. association (*contex.*), sisternity (*R; a barbarism*); *spec.* nunnery.

sit, *v. i.* **1.** *Spec.* set (*referring to a hen—a rustic usage*), incubate (*tech.*), squat; *see* PERCH.
Antonyms: see STAND, KNEEL, LIE, BUSTLE.
2. *Referring to a body convening for business:* meet.
Antonyms: see RISE.
3. *See* STAY, LIE, POSE.

sit, *v. t. Spec.* ride.

sitting, *a.* sedent (*R*), sedentary (*spec.*).

sitting, *n.* **1.** *Referring to the act:* session (*R*).
Antonyms: see STANDING.
2. *See* SESSION, SEAT.

situation, *n.* **1.** *See* PLACE, POSITION, STATE.
2. juncture, scene.

six, *n.* **1.** *Spec.* sise *or* size (*A or R*).
2. sextuplet (*chiefly spec.*), hexad.

six-angled, *a.* hexagonal *or* (*R*) hexangular (*B*).

six-columned, *a.* hexastyle (*architecture*).

sixfold, *a.* sextuple (*B*).

sixfold, *v. t.* sextuple (*R*), sextuply (*obs. or R*).

sixpence, *n.* kick (*S*), tizzy (*S*), size (*S; obs. or R*).

six-sided, *a.* hexahedral (*B or tech.*).

sixty, *n.* threescore; *spec.* sexagenary.

size, *n.* **1.** magnitude (*suggesting definite and measurable greatness*), bulk (*suggesting unwieldy or unsymmetrical bigness*), volume, bigness, greatness, grossness, quantity (*obs. exc. math.*), amplitude (*formal or B*); *spec.* measure, measurement, content, folio; *see* WIDTH.
2. *See* EXTENT, AREA.

size, *v. t.* **1.** *Spec.* adjust, gauge.
2. *See* CLASSIFY, ARRANGE.

skein, *n. Spec.* bottom, hank, hasp.

skeleton, *n.* **1.** anatomy (*A, exc. spec.*), atomy (*A*).
2. *Referring to a very thin person or animal:* scrag, gangrel (*A*), anatomy (*A*), atomy (*obs. or jocular*).
3. *See* STRUCTURE, OUTLINE.

skeptic, *n.* doubter, freethinker, minimifidian (*R*); *spec.* PYRRHONIST.
Antonyms: see BELIEVER (*cf.* BELIEVE).

skeptical, *a.* doubtful, skeptic; *spec.* PYRRHONIAN *or* PYRRHONIC.
Antonyms: see BELIEVING.

skepticism, *n.* doubt; *spec.* PYRRHONISM, nihilism.
Antonyms: see BELIEF.

skill, *n.* **1.** ability, expertness, dexterity, proficiency, cleverness, address, expertness, mastery, mastership (*R*), masterhood (*R*), technique (*tech.*), featness (*A*), cunning (*A*), sleight (*A*); *spec.* perfection, science, art, craft (*A*), handicraft (*R*), adroitness, handiness, deftness, adeptness, virtuosity.
2. *See* TACT.

skillet, *n.* saucepan, stewpan.

skillful, *a.* able (*contex.*), skilled, expert (*exceptionally proficient by virtue of specialized experience*), habile (*B*), canny (*Scot.; A*), clever (*implying a native aptitude*), proficient (*implying advanced training*), slick (*S*), facile (*B*), dexterous (*implying light and sure manipulation*), good (*contex.*); *spec.* adept, masterly, clean, neat, perfect, deft, adroit, handy, ingenious, feat (*A*), cunning (*A*), artful (*A*), crafty (*A*), knacky (*C*), wise, workmanly, workmanlike, scient (*R*), sleighty (*A*), tight (*chiefly dial.*), dædal (*B*), Dædalian; *see* TACTFUL, TRAINED.
Antonyms: see UNSKILLFUL, AWKWARD, CLUMSY, CRUDE.

skim, *v. t.* **1.** scum (*R*), despumate (*R*); *spec.* cream.
2. *See* COVER, SLIGHT.

skimmed, *a. Referring to milk:* fleet (*chiefly dial.*).

skin, *n.* **1.** *Referring to the integument of a vertebrate:* covering (*contex.*), integument (*tech. or B*); *spec.* membrane, coat, hide (*esp. of large quadrupeds*), pelt (*referring to furry, wooly, or hairy surface*), fell, rind, leather (*S*), case (*R*), jacket (*C*), buff, felt (*dial.*), peltry (*a collective*), derma *or* (*less usual*) dermis, epidermis, cutis, cuticle, corium, scarf skin, sheath, parchment, mort, crop, kip, shagreen, butt, woolfell, parfleche, lambskin, deacon; *see* FUR.
2. *Referring to the skin of various animals other than the vertebrates:* covering (*contex.*), coat, integument; *spec.* tunic.
3. *Referring to the covering of fruits: spec.* integument, peel, rind, epicarp (*tech.*), jacket (*C or S*), parings (*pl.*); *see* HULL, BARK.
Antonyms: see FLESH.
4. *See* FILM, FACING, ENVELOPE, MEMBRANE, EXUVIUM.

skin, *a.* dermal (*tech.; often spec.*), cuticular (*often spec.*), integumental, cutaneous (*often spec.*); *spec.* epidermal (*tech.*), epidermic (*tech.*), epidermatous (*R, tech.*).

skin, *v. t.* **1.** strip (*chiefly contex.*), flay, bark (*S*); *spec.* hide (*R*), excoriate (*esp. of bark,*

skinflint: *niggard.*
skip, *n.: jump, caper, glance, intermission, interval, interspace, omission.*
skip, *v. i.: jump, caper, glance, depart.*
skip, *v. t.: omit, ignore, jump.*

peel, or rind), decorticate (*fig.*), pelt (*obs.*), case (*cant or obs.*), scalp, cheat (*contex.*).
2. *Spec.* peel, pare, pill (*A*), rind (*R*), bark; *see* DECORTICATE.
3. *See* COVER.
skinlike, *a.* dermatoid, dermoid, dermoidal;—*all three tech.*
skinned, *a.* bare (*contex.*), excoriated (*B or tech*), raw.
skinny, *a.* **1.** cutaneous, membranous.
2. *See* THIN.
skirmish, *v. i.* fight, pickeer (*A*).
skirmisher, *n.* fighter; *spec.* sharpshooter.
skirt, *n.* **1.** *Spec.* overskirt, petticoat, crinoline, hoopskirt, basque, lappet, kilt, draggle-tails *or* (*obs. or dial.*) daggle-tails (*pl.*), fustanella.
2. *See* BORDER, EDGE, SUBURB.
skittish, *a.* **1.** *See* FROLICSOME.
2. *Of a horse:* shy (*R*), bogglish (*R*).
skull, *n.* head (*contex.*), headpiece (*A or C*); *spec.* cranium (*tech.*), brainpan (*A or tech.*), braincase, skullcap, death's-head.
slag, *n.* **1.** cinder, clinker, clink.
2. *See* LAVA.
slant, *n.* slope, inclination; *spec.* bias, steep; *see* SLOPE, INCLINATION.
slap, *n.* **1.** stroke (*contex.*), blow (*contex.*); *spec.* smack, cuff, clap, dab, box, sidehit, spank (*chiefly spec.*).
2. *See* CLAP, REPROOF.
slap, *v. t.* **1.** *Of a blow with the open hand:* strike (*contex.*), hit (*contex.*); *spec.* smack, cuff, clout, (*cuff heavily*), clap, box, spank.
2. *Spec.* reprove, clap.
slap, *v. i.* *Spec.* slipslop, slipslap; *see* FLAP.
slattern, *n.* sloven, slut, drab, trollop, dowdy, dab (*R; C*), trapes (*C, or dial.*), draggle-tail (*C*), dolly (*C*), slammakin (*chiefly dial.*).
slatternly, *a.* slovenly (*which see*), sluttish, drabbish, dabbish (*R*).
slaughter, *n.* **1.** *Referring to the killing of animals for food:* butchering, butchery (*now chiefly or only as an attrib., as in "butchery business"*).
2. killing (*contex.*), butchery, carnage, slaughter; *spec.* bloodshed, massacre, holocaust, hecatomb.
slaughter, *v. t.* **1.** *See* BUTCHER.
2. kill (*contex.*), massacre.
slaughterer, *n.* butcher, butcherer, flesher (*chiefly Scot.*); *spec.* knacker.
slaughterhouse, *n.* butchery, abattoir (*French; chiefly spec.*), shambles (*pl.; obs. or fig.*).
slave, *n.* **1.** bondman, bondsman, neif (*hist.*), serf (*chiefly spec.*), bondmaid (*fem.*), bondwoman (*fem.*), bondslave, thrall (*B or hist.*), theow (*A or hist.*); *spec.* contraband (*U. S.*), black bird (*C*), galley slave, native (*hist.*), gallerian (*R*), odalisque, hierodule (*Greek hist.*), mameluke (*hist.*), villein (*hist.*), carl (*obs. or hist.*), vassal (*hist.*), helot (*Greek hist.*), peon (*Spanish American*), captive (*hist.*).
Antonyms: see MASTER.
2. *See* SUBJECT.
slavery, *a.* **1.** bondage, servitude, serviture (*R*), thralldom (*B*), enthrallment (*R*), enthralldom (*R; chiefly fig.*), thrall (*A*), yoke (*fig.*), slavedom (*R*), serfdom *or* serfage *or* serfhood (*chiefly spec.*); *spec.* villeinage (*hist.*), vassalage (*hist.*), helotism (*Greek hist.*), peonage (*Spanish American*), captivation.
Antonyms: see FREEDOM.
2. *See* DRUDGERY.
sled, *n.* **1.** sledge, drag, boat (*chiefly in "stoneboat"*).
2. sledge (*chiefly British*), sleigh (*chiefly spec.*); *spec.* bobsled, bobsleigh, carriole (*Canada*), cutter (*U. S.*), pung (*U. S.*), train (*Canada*), toboggan, jumper (*U. S. and Canada*).
sleep, *n.* **1.** rest (*contex.*), repose (*contex.*), slumber (*chiefly spec. or used in pl.*), balmy (*S*), dormancy (*R or B*), sopition (*R*), hypnosis; *also* (*giving forms of profound sleep, in order of increased intensity*) sopor, coma, stupor, lethargy, carus.
2. [*cap.*] *Referring to the personification of sleep:* Morpheus, Somnus, Hypnos (*Greek myth.*), Dustman (*C used with "the"*), Sandman (*C with "the"*).
3. *Referring to a time or occasion of sleeping:* rest (*contex.*), doss (*S or cant*); *spec.* slumber, drowse, doze, nap, snooze (*C*), nod, wink (*C*), dog sleep, catnap, siesta.
4. *See* DEATH, NUMBNESS.
sleep, *v. i.* **1.** rest (*contex.*), repose (*formal or affected; contex.*); *spec.* slumber, doze, drowse, nap, nod, snooze (*C*), bundle, lie.
2. numb (*R*).
sleepiness, *n.* sluggishness (*contex.*), drowsiness, heaviness, lethargy (*B or spec.*), dullness (*contex.*), somnolence *or* somnolency (*R*), oscitancy (*R*), oscitation (*R*); *spec.* doziness, hypnæsthesis (*med.*), kef *or* keif *or* kief (*B or Oriental*).
sleeping, *a.* asleep; *spec.* slumbering, dozing, dead, unwakeful (*R*), dormant (*B*).
sleeping, *n.* slumbering, dozing, *etc.*, dormition (*R*); *spec.* incubation (*Greek religion*).
sleepless, *a.* slumberless, wakeful, insomnious, insomnolent (*R*).
sleeplessness, *n.* wakefulness, insomnia.
sleepwalker, *n.* somnambulist, somnambule (*R*), somnambulator (*R*).
sleepwalking, *a.* somnambulant.

---

skirt, *v. t.: border, edge, pass.*
skit, *n.: satire, rain.*
slab: *plate, flag, board, table.*
slack, *v. t.: moderate, loose, relax, slow, appease, abate.*
slack, *v. i.: moderate, relax, slow, abate.*
slacken, *v. t.: retard, moderate, relax, loose, abate.*
slacken, *v. i.: moderate, loose, relax, abate.*
slake, *v. i.: moderate.*
slake, *v. t.: moderate, appease, extinguish.*
slam, *n.: blow, impact.*
slam, *v. t.: dash, shut, strike.*
slander, *n.: disparagement, defamation.*
slang, *n.: jargon, language.*
slant, *v. i.: glance, fall, diverge.*
slant, *v. t.: incline, slope.*
slash, *n.: blow, gash, slit, switch.*
slash, *v. t.: gash, reprove, switch.*
slash, *v. i.: strike.*
slave, *v. i.: enslave, drudge.*
slay: *kill.*

sleepy, *a.* slumbery, slumberous (*often implying faculties or latent forces in repose*), drowsy (*of one who is heavy with sleep*), heavy, heavy-headed, lethargic *or* (*R*), lethargical (*B suggesting a state of torpid indifference*), Morphean (*fig.*), oscitant (*R*); *spec.* dozy, nodding, dozing, *etc.*, comatose (*R*), somnolent (*suggesting sluggishness*) *or* somnolescent (*B*), dull.
Antonyms: see WAKEFUL.

sleeve, *n.* **1.** arm; *spec.* gigot, union (*tech.*), manche (*obs., antiquarian, or her.*), mancheron (*her.*).
2. *In machinery:* tube; *spec.* gland, thimble, bush.

slender, *a.* **1.** *Referring to spare or poor animals: see* THIN.
2. *Referring to an object:* attenuated (*B*), small, thin, slim; *spec.* slimmish, slight, gracile, lithe, fine, exile (*A*), delicate, tenuous, exiguous (*R*), elongate, linear, waspy, spindling, threadlike.
Antonyms: see BIG, COARSE.
3. *See* MEAGER, SCANTY.

slenderness, *n.* **1.** *See* THINNESS.
2. attenuation (*B*), thinness; *spec.* tenuity, tenousness, slimness, slightness, gracility (*R*), fineness, exility (*A*), delicacy, exiguity (*R*).
3. *Spec.* meagerness, scantiness.

sleuth, *n.* detective, bloodhound, G-man (*C, U. S.*), dick (*S*). Sleuth *often carries humorous implication.*

slice, *n.* **1.** piece (*contex.*), section (*contex.*), cut (*contex.*); *spec.* shaving, cantle, collop, bard, steak, rasher, flitch, chop, divot (*Scot.*), plit; *see* PARING.
2. *See* KNIFE, BAR, SHOVEL.

slice, *v. t.* section (*contex.*), cut (*contex.*), sectionize (*R*); *spec.* leach (*A*), *see* PARE.

slide, *n.* slip, glide; *spec.* coast (*U. S.*), skid, glissade.

slide, *v. i.* **1.** move (*contex.*), pass (*contex.*), glide, slip; *spec.* coast (*U. S.*), skid, toboggan, avalanche, glissade.
Antonyms: see ENGAGE.
2. *See* STEAL.

slide, *v. t.* move (*contex.*), pass (*contex.*), slip; *spec.* skid.

slight, *a.* **1.** *See* SLENDER, GENTLE, SMALL, MEAGER, UNIMPORTANT.
2. weak, frail, flimsy, delicate, unsubstantial.

slight, *v. t.* **1.** *See* DISREGARD.
2. *Referring to failure in doing something:* neglect, scamp, skim, slur.
3. *Referring to treatment of others:* neglect, snub, cold-shoulder (*C*); *spec.* cut, ignore.

slime, *n.* **1.** mud, ooze.
2. *Referring to animal or vegetable substances:* glair, gleet (*R, exc. spec.*); *spec.* mucus, semen.

slimy, *a.* viscous (*B or tech.*), slippery (*contex.*), lubricous (*B*), limous (*R*); *spec.* slobbery, mucous, muculent (*R*), oozy.

sling, *n.* **1.** slingshot; *spec.* catapult (*British*), shanghai (*Australia*), staffsling.
2. *See* THROW.

sling, *n.* loop; *spec.* parbuckle.

slipper, *n.* pantofle (*chiefly hist.*); *spec.* mule, papoosh *or* papouche *or* pabouch, pump.

slipper-shaped, *a.* soleiform, calceiform, calceolate;—*all three tech. or* (*B*).

slippery, *a.* **1.** smooth, lubricous (*B*), slippy (*C*), gliddery (*dial.*), slithery (*dial.*), slither (*dial.*), sliddery (*C*), lubric (*R*), lubricate (*R*); *see* SLIMY.
2. *See* UNCERTAIN, ELUSIVE, DISHONEST, EVASIVE.

slit, *n.* **1.** cut (*contex.*); *spec.* (*in a dress*) slash, pane, pink, jag (*hist.*).
2. *See* CLEFT.

slit, *a.* cut (*contex.*), slashed, jagged (*hist.*), pinked.

slobber, *v. i.* slaver, drivel, slabber, dribble, drool (*dial. or C; U. S.*).

slobber, *v. t.* **1.** dirty (*contex.*), slaver, slabber, beslobber (*an intensive*), beslaver (*an intensive; chiefly dial.*), drivel (*R*), bedrivel (*an intensive; R*).
2. *See* UTTER.

slobber, *n. Spec.* saliva (*B or tech.*), slaver, drivel, dribblings (*pl.*), slabber, dribble, drool (*dial. or C; U. S.*).

slope, *n.* **1.** slant (*contex.*), ramp (*chiefly tech.*); incline, inclination (*R as applied to the surface*), cant (*chiefly tech.*); *spec.* pitch, declivity (*considered as sloping downward*), acclivity (*considered as sloping upward*), grade (*U. S.*), gradient (*Eng.*), bevel, batter, bezel, talus, esplanade, counterslope, glacis, calade, hillside; *see* DESCENT, ASCENT.
2. *Referring to the fact or condition: see* INCLINATION.

slope, *v. i.* incline, slant, cant (*chiefly tech.*); *spec.* recede, tilt; *see* DESCEND, ASCEND.

sloping, *a.* inclined, slant, sloped, aslant, aslope (*R; only predicative*), declivitous (*chiefly spec.*); *spec.* shelving, shelvy, bevel, descending, ascending.

sloven, *n.* slouch (*C or S*), slob (*C and inelegant*), Grabian (*B, R*); *see* SLATTERN.
Antonyms: see DANDY.

slovenliness, *n.* untidiness, frowziness, sluttishness (*contemptuous*), sluttery (*obs.*), slatternliness, *etc.*

slovenly, *a.* **1.** untidy, unkempt, frowzy, blowzy, blowzed, sloppy (*C*), slobbery (*C*), slouchy (*C*), grubby (*C*), slipshod (*primarily spec.*), sluttish (*very contemptuous*), tacky (*C*); *see* SLATTERNLY.
2. *See* CARELESS.

---

sling, *v. t.: throw.*
sling, *n.: loop, hoist.*
slip, *n.: leash, gown, inattention, error, slide, glide, misstep, avalanche, blunder.*
slip, *v. i.: glide, slide, steal, pass, escape, err, misstep, blunder.*
slip, *v. t.: slide, place, remove, withdraw, free, loose, displace, miss, omit, avoid.*
slouch, *n.: clown, sloven, gait, droop, stoop.*
slouch, *v. i.: droop, walk.*
slouch, *v. t.: incline.*

Antonyms: see DANDY.

slow, *a.* **1.** *See* DULL, SLUGGISH, LATE, DELIBERATE.

2. unready, unhasty (*R*), behindhand, behind.

Antonyms: see READY.

3. sluggish, slack, tardy (*of one who is behindhand*), dilatory (*of one habitually behindhand or procrastinating*), lazy, unspeedy (*R*), testudinous (*R; fig.*); *spec.* gradual.

Antonyms: see SUDDEN, RAPID.

slow, *v. t.* slacken, slack; *see* RETARD.

Antonyms: see QUICKEN.

slow, *v. i.* slacken, slack. *"Slow" is chiefly used with "up."*

Antonyms: see QUICKEN.

sluggard, *n.* slug (*R or A*), dolittle (*C*), drone (*fig.*), slugabed (*A*), lurdan (*A*).

sluggish, *a.* **1.** inactive, dull, inert, slow, listless, sluggard, heavy, sleepy (*fig. or spec.*), drowsy, dopey (*S*), torpid, torpent (*R*), logy (*U. S.; C*), sullen (*B*), languid (*fig. and B*), languishing (*fig. and B*), lentitudinous (*R*), lymphatic (*R; fig.*), phlegmatic (*R, fig.*).

Antonyms: see ACTIVE, ALERT, NIMBLE, RAPID.

2. *See* DULL, INSENSIBLE, SLOW.

sluggishness, *n.* inactivity, dullness, torpor, inertness, *etc.*

sluice, *n.* **1.** gate; *spec.* hatch, waste, floodgate.

2. *See* CHANNEL.

slush, *n.* sludge, slosh; *see* MUD.

slushy, *a.* sludgy, sloshy (*R*), plashy, sloppy, slipsloppy (*R*); *see* MUDDY.

small, *a.* **1.** *See* SLENDER.

2. *Referring to physical size:* diminutive (*more emphatic than* small), little, lilliputian (*fig. or allusive*); *spec.* smallest, petite, dapper, pygmy *or* pigmy, fine, puny, elfin (*fig.*), minikin, miniature, lesser, toyish (*R*), comminuted; *see* MINUTE, DWARF.

Antonyms: see LARGE, IMMENSE, BIG, COARSE, ENORMOUS, GRAND.

3. *Referring to quantity or to some mental aspect or consideration:* little, slight, narrow, limited, trifling, inextensive (*R*), slender, light; *spec.* least, faint *or* (*less emphatic*) faintish, inconsiderable, dribbling, smallest, infinitesimal, petty, remote, less, nice, evanescent, skin-deep.

Antonyms: see LARGE, GREAT, CONSIDERABLE, GRAND, ENORMOUS.

4. *See* FEW, LOWLY, FAINT, SHRILL, INSIGNIFICANT, WEAK, MEAN.

small-headed, *a.* microcephalic, microcephalous;—*both tech.*

smallpox, *n.* pox (*obs.*), variola (*tech.*).

smart, *a.* **1.** *See* BRISK, VIGOROUS, RAPID, INTELLIGENT, CLEVER, SHARP, STYLISH.

2. spruce, trim, fine, dapper, showy, natty (*C*), chic (*French*), gallant (*A*); *spec.* smartish, stylish, saucy, rakish, perk (*C*), elegant (*C*), nobby (*S*).

smatter, *n.* knowledge (*contex. or euphemistic*), smattering, smatch.

smatter, *v. i.* dabble.

smear, *v. t.* **1.** *See* ANOINT.

2. *Spec.* smirch (*so as to leave dirty or stained*), smudge (*as by the grime of smoke*), smutch, smut, stick, splotch, daub (*as bad artists*), bedaub (*intensive*), plaster, beplaster (*intensive*), besmear (*intensive*), besmutch (*R*), besmudge (*intensive*), blur, gum, moil (*A*), coat, gaum (*dial. or C*), clam (*obs. or dial.*), inunct (*R*), oil, grease, begrease, rosin, butter, ruddle, pay, pitch, lime.

Antonyms: see CLEAN.

smear, *n.* smudge, smirch, smutch, splodge (*R of thick and heavy smear*); *spec.* daub, plaster, blur, coat, glair.

smearing, *n.* smudging, smirching, smutty, *etc.; spec.* illinition (*obs. or R*), unction (*B*).

smeary, *a.* smudgy, smirchy (*R*); *spec.* dauby, splotchy, blottesque, *etc.*

Antonyms: see CLEAN.

smell, *n.* **1.** *Referring to the sense or faculty:* nose, scent, flair (*French*).

2. *Referring to the act:* sniff, snuff, scent, olfaction (*R*).

3. odor, scent (*not so strong as* odor); *spec.* stink, stench, reek (*these three violently unpleasant* smells), fume, mephitis (*tech.*), malodor, tang, perfume (*of matter that is sweet-smelling*), aroma (*implies a delicately spicy and characterizing scent*), incense, flavor, redolence, fragrance *or* (*less usual*) fragrancy (*suggesting freshness, as from flowers*), nosegay, savor, essence (*A*), bouquet, incense, attar, effluvium, hogo (*obs. or dial.*), drag, nidor (*obs. or R*), empyreuma.

4. *See* TRACE.

smell, *v. t.* **1.** scent, nose (*R*), savor (*R*); *spec.* snuff, sniff.

2. *See* DISCOVER, SUSPECT.

smell, *v. i.* **1.** nose (*R*); *spec.* sniff, snuff, scent.

2. savor (*A*), scent (*R*); *spec.* reek, stink, draw.

smelt, *v. t.* fuse, melt, reduce, run.

smile, *v. i.* grin (*spec. or depreciatory*); *spec.* smirk, simper, fleer, sneer.

Antonyms: see CRY, FROWN.

smiling, *a.* grinning (*spec. or depreciatory*); *spec.* smirking, *etc.*

smith, *n.* worker (*contex.*), forger, Cyclops (*fig.; classical myth.*), hammerman (*R*), hammersmith (*R*); *spec.* striker, tilter, blacksmith, whitesmith, goldsmith, silversmith, locksmith.

smoke, *n.* **1.** fume (*A*), smudge (*now U. S.*), reek (*B or Scot. & dial.*); *spec.* smolder, smother, suffumigation (*R*), pother (*R*), funk (*S*); *see* INCENSE.

---

slut: *slattern, bitch.*
sly: *artful, stealthy, hidden.*
smack, *v. t.: sound, slap, kiss.*
smack, *n.: taste, trace.*
smack, *v. i.: taste, savor.*
smack, *v. t.: taste.*
smash, *v. t.: shatter, crush, strike, destroy, overwhelm.*
smash, *v. i.: dash, crash, strike, shatter, fail.*
smash, *n.: blow, collision, crash, failure.*
smirch, *v. t.: soil, stain, smear, discredit.*
smirch, *n.: smear, stain, discredit.*
smite, *v. t.: strike, kill, affect, afflict, enamor.*
smite, *v. i.: strike.*

2. *See* HAZE, EXHALATION, DUST.
smoke, *v. i.* **1.** fume, reek (*B or Scot. & dial.*); *spec.* smolder, smudge (*R*), smother (*contex.*), funk (*S*), lunt (*Eng.*).
2. *See* RUSH, RAGE.
smoke, *v. t.* **1.** fumigate, fume, reek (*B or Scot. & dial*); *spec.* besmoke, smudge, suffumigate (*R*), tobacconize.
2. *Referring to tobacco or opium:* puff.
smoker, *n.* puffer, tobacconalian (*nonce word*); *spec.* piper (*R*), pipeman (*nonce word*).
smoky, *a.* **1.** fumy, fuliginous (*B*), fumose (*R*); *spec.* reeky, smudgy.
2. *See* HAZY, SPRAYLIKE.
smooth, *a.* **1.** *See* EVEN.
2. *Referring to absence of physical roughness to the feeling: spec.* sleek (*of that which is both smooth and soft*), sleekish, slick, silky, satin, satiny, soft, velvet, velvety, glossy (*of that which is both smooth and shining*), unruffled, ivory (*fig.*), glabrous, glare (*U. S.*), polished, levigate (*tech.*), spineless, fine-grained, glair; *see* SLIPPERY, GREASY.
Antonyms: see WRINKLED, ROUGH, BRISTLY, PRICKLY, SCRATCHY.
3. agreeable (*which see*), easy, bland, suave, fair-spoken, soft-spoken, smooth-spoken, smooth-tongued, silken (*fig.*), silky (*fig.*), unctuous, unctious (*R*), oily, sleek, slick, glib; *see* PLAUSIBLE, INGRATIATING, AGREEABLE.
Antonyms: see ROUGH, SHARP, BLUNT, CRABBED.
4. *In reference to the voice or a musical sound:* euphonious (*B*), pure, clear, soft, liquid, running, flowing, velvet, silky (*fig.*); *spec.* harmonious.
Antonyms: see HARSH.
5. *See* CALM, UNEVENTFUL, BLAND.
smooth, *v. t.* **1.** *See* EVEN.
2. smoothen (*R*); *spec.* slick, sleek, sleeken, iron, pumice, roll, file, pounce, float, unknit, velure, unwrinkle, dub, plane, hammer, planish; *see* POLISH.
Antonyms: see SCRATCH, ROUGHEN, SCRAPE, CORRUGATE, DISHEVEL, PUCKER.
3. *See* GLOZE, HANDLE, CALM, FLATTER, EASE.
smooth-haired, *a.* leiotrichous, lissotrichous; —*both tech. or B.*
Antonyms: see ROUGH.
smuggled, *a.* uncustomed (*R*), run (*cant*).
smuggler, *n.* freetrader (*contex. or hist.*), runner (*cant*), contrabandist (*R or B*), bootlegger.
smuggling, *n.* free trade (*contex. or hist.*), contraband (*B*), bootlegging.
smut, *n.* **1.** mark, black (*esp. in pl.*), smudge, crock; *see* SMEAR.
2. *See* SOOT.
snaffle, *n.* bridle; *spec.* bridoon.
snail, *n.* gastropod, hodmandod *or* dodman (*now chiefly dial.*).
snail-like, *a.* limaceous (*tech.*).
snail-shaped, *a.* cochleate (*tech.*).
snake, *n.* reptile (*contex.*), serpent (*now chiefly used of the larger or more venomous species, or rhetorical*), ophidian (*tech.*), worm (*A*); *spec.* viper, dipsas, Hydra (*Greek myth.*), Python (*Greek myth.*), constrictor.
snake, *a.* serpent, serpentine, ophidian (*tech.*), ophic (*R*), colubrine.
snake-charming, *a.* psyllic (*R*).
snakelike, *a.* snaky, serpentiform (*R*), serpentine, colubrine (*tech.; chiefly spec.*); *spec.* viperine, crotaline.
snap, *v. t.* **1.** *See* BITE, SEIZE, SNATCH, SHUT, FIRE, BREAK.
2. sound, crack; *spec.* crackle; *see* CLICK.
3. jerk (*contex.*), flip, fillip; *spec.* flick, whip.
snap, *v. i.* **1.** *See* BITE, GRASP, UTTER, SPEAK.
2. sound, crack; *spec.* click.
3. jerk (*contex.*), flip, fillip; *spec.* flick, whip.
snap, *n.* **1.** *See* BITE, GRASP, BREAK, FROST, FORCE.
2. sound (*contex.*), crack, report; *spec.* crackle; *see* CLICK.
3. jerk (*contex.*), fillip, flip; *spec.* flick, whip.
snare, *n.* **1.** trap (*contex.*), noose, springe, snarl (*obs. or dial.*); *spec.* springe.
2. *Fig.: see* TRAP.
snare, *v. t.* **1.** trap (*contex.*), ensnare, catch, noose (*R*), snarl (*obs. or dial.*); *spec.* wire.
2. *See* TRAP.
snarl, *v. i.* growl, gnar (*R or dial.*), girn (*obs. or dial.*).
sneak, *v. i.* **1.** skulk, slink, lurk, crawl, slip (*R*), miche (*obs. or dial.*).
Antonyms: see STALK.
2. *See* CRINGE.
sneak, *n.* sneaker, skulker, slinker, sneaksby (*R or obs.*).
sneaking, *a.* **1.** furtive (*B*), sly, sneaky, slinking, skulking.
Antonyms: see FRANK.
2. *See* ABJECT, MEAN.
snell, *n.* snood. "*Snell*" *is an Americanism.*
sniff, *v. i.* **1.** spurn (*B*), snuff (*obsolescent*).
2. *See* INHALE.
snivel, *v. i.* sniffle; *spec. see* WHINE, CANT.
snob, *n.* flunkey, lackey, toady.
Antonyms: see GENTLEMAN, LADY.
snobbery, *n. Spec.* flunkeydom, flunkeyism.
snort, *v. i.* snore (*dial.*), snortle (*dial.*).
Antonyms: see SNUFF.
snow, *n.* meteor (*tech.; contex.*), fleece (*fig.*); *spec.* flurry, slush, sleet.
snowfall, *n.* snow; *spec.* snowstorm, flurry (*contex.*), blizzard, buran.
snowy, *a.* snowish, niveous (*R*).

smother, *v. t.: suffocate, hide, repress, suppress, deaden, extinguish.*
smother, *v. i.: suffocate, smoke, burn.*
smother, *n.: smoke, fire, dust, haze.*
smutty, *a.: blackened, smeary, indecent.*
snack: *lunch, meal.*
snag: *stump, projection, obstacle, tooth.*
snaky: *snakelike, deceitful, treacherous, winding.*
snatch, *v. t.: seize, save.*
snatch, *n.: seizure, piece, meal, song, strain.*
sneer: *smile, laugh, jeer.*
sniff, *v. t.: inhale, examine, perceive, smell, suspect, utter.*

Antonyms: see CLEAR.
snub, *a. Referring to the nose:* snubby, troussé (*French*), rhinocerical (*obs.*).
Antonyms: see AQUILINE.
snuff, *v. t.* **1.** *Referring to a candle:* crop, snift (*R*).
2. *See* EFFACE.
snuff, *v. i.* **1.** inhale (*contex.*), sniff, snift (*now chiefly dial.*); *spec.* snuffle.
Antonyms: see SNORT.
2. *See* SMELL.
snuggle, *v. i.* snug, nestle, nuzzle, cuddle, hug, crowd, snozzle (*R*).
soak, *v. i.* **1.** seethe, steep; *spec.* souse.
Antonyms: see DRY.
2. *See* DRINK.
soak, *v. t.* **1.** drench (*by pouring upon*), saturate (*to complete absorption*); *spec.* infuse (*R or tech.*), steep (*subject to a penetrative soaking process*), seethe, sodden, souse, sop, sob (*Eng. dial. and U. S.*), macerate.
Antonyms: see DRY.
2. *See* DRENCH, ABSORB.
3. *Referring to plying with drink:* liquor (*S*), liquefy (*S or jocular*).
soaked, *a. Spec.* sodden, soggy, pappy, poachy, soppy.
Antonyms: see DRY.
soapiness, *n.* saponacity (*jocular; R*).
soapy, *a.* saponaceous (*tech. or B*); *spec.* lathery.
soar, *v. i.* **1.** fly (*contex.*), plane (*R, exc. of an aëroplane*).
2. *See* FLY, RISE.
sob, *n.* cry (*contex.*), singult (*A*), singultus (*R*).
Antonyms: see LAUGH.
sobbing, *a.* singultient (*R*).
sober, *a.* **1.** *See* MODERATE, SERIOUS, ABSTEMIOUS, CALM, DULL, ACTUAL, MATTER-OF-FACT.
2. sedate, serious, staid, grave (*implying a weight of serious matter on the mind*), solemn (*implying an occasion of deep seriousness*), demure; *spec.* matronly, matronal, heavy.
Antonyms: see AMUSING.
3. unintoxicated (*formal or R*).
Antonyms: see DRUNKEN, INTOXICATED.
sober, *v. t.* **1.** solemnize, soberize (*R*), steady.
Antonyms: see INTOXICATE.
2. *See* MODERATE, DULL.
sobriety, *n.* sedateness, seriousness, solemnity.
sociable, *a.* companionable, social, conversable, intersocial (*R*), intercommunicative (*R*); *see* AFFABLE, CONVIVIAL.
Antonyms: see UNSOCIABLE.
social, *a.* sociable, gregarious; *spec.* republican.
socialism, *n.* collectivism (*standing for the control of industry by government*), communism (*extreme Marxian socialism*), communalism, bolshevism.
society, *n.* **1.** *See* COMPANIONSHIP, ASSOCIATION.
2. *Referring to the state:* community (*R*); *spec.* democracy, aristocracy.
3. company (*now less usual than "society"*), fashion, monde (*French*).
sock, *n.* **1.** *See* SHOE.
2. half-hose.
socket, *n.* hole, pan (*R*), nozzle (*R*), pit; *spec.* bucket, alveolus, budget (*hist.*), tabernacle, step, pad, orbit, gudgeon, pyxis, acetabulum, cotyle, crapaudine.
sod, *n.* **1.** *Referring to a piece:* clod, turf, divot (*Scot.*).
2. *Referring to the surface of the ground:* grass, turf, sward, grassland, greensward.
sofa, *n.* couch, settee (*chiefly spec.*); *spec.* squab.
soft, *a.* **1.** *See* GENTLE, MILD, FAINT, EASY, POLITE, SMOOTH, EUPHEMISTIC, EFFEMINATE, FOOLISH, AFFECTIONATE, KIND, IMPRESSIBLE, COMPLAISANT.
2. yielding (*contex.*); *spec.* mellow, mushy, pasty, squashy, waxen, silky, silken, velvet, velvety, crummy, doughy, downy, creamy, fleecy, flabby, flaccid, pulpy, plastic; *see* CRUMBLY.
Antonyms: see HARD, RIGID.
soften, *v. t.* **1.** *See* MITIGATE.
2. mollify (*esp. of the allaying of temper*), milden, sweeten, attemper (*B, implies moderating, often by admixture*), mellow (*implying the sweetness and gentleness of maturity*), tender (*R*), humanify, humanize, melt, touch, dulcify (*B*), unstarch (*R; fig.*), relax, gentle (*R*); *see* ENERVATE, EFFEMINATE.
Antonyms: see EMBITTER, HARDEN.
3. *Referring to physical softness:* mollify (*R*), tender (*tech. or spec.*), malaxate (*R*), intenerate (*R*); *spec.* relax, mellow, macerate.
4. *Referring to the removal of harsh qualities:* modify (*contex.*), edulcorate (*chiefly tech.; R*), sweeten, tame; *spec.* scumble, dull.
Antonyms: see CONGEAL, HARDEN, SOLIDIFY.
soften, *v. i.* **1.** *See* MITIGATE.
2. mollify, milden, sweeten, mellow, melt, dissolve, relax; *see* RELENT.
softening, *n.* **1.** *See* MITIGATION.
2. mollification, sweetening, attemperation (*R*), mellowing, dulcification (*R*), relaxation.
3. mollification (*R*), tendering (*chiefly tech.*), malaxation (*R*), inteneration (*R*), relaxation; *spec.* emollition (*R*), emollescence, malacia, maceration.
soft-spoken, *a.* mincing, mealy *or* mealy-mouthed; *see* GENTLE, PLAUSIBLE, SMOOTH.
Antonyms: see ROUGH, SURLY, BLUFF.
soil, *n.* **1.** earth (*contex.*), dirt (*contex.; C*); *spec.* mold *or* mould (*B or spec.*), loam, humus, fay, malm, marl, green.
2. *See* COUNTRY.
soil, *v. t.* **1.** dirty, sully (*chiefly B or elevated*); *spec.* foul, befoul, defile, besoil (*an intensive*), besully (*an intensive*), deface, begrime, pollute, muck (*now vulgar*), tar, grease, bespit, thumb, fingermark, finger, track, grease,

snub, *v. t.: reprove, slight, check.*
snug, *a.: comfortable, compact, hidden.*
soaring: *ambitious, high, elevated.*
soil, *n.: discoloration, stain, contamination, sewage, excrement.*

smear, smirch, stain, muddy, slobber, draggle, daggle, blacken, slop.
Antonyms: see CLEAN, PURIFY.
2. *See* CONTAMINATE.
soiled, *a.* dirty, sullied, soily; *spec.* greasy, thumbed, fingermarked; *see* SMEARY, MUDDY, DRAGGLED, BLACKENED.
Antonyms: see DIRTY, CLEAN, PURE, SPOTLESS.
soiling, *n.* dirtying, soilure (*R*); *spec.* defilement, befoulment (*R*), defacement, pollution.
solar, *a.* heliac *or* heliacal (*R*).
solder, *v. t.* cement (*R; contex.*), conferruminate (*R*); *spec.* soft-solder, braze.
Antonyms: see BREAK.
soldier, *n.* warrior (*B or elevated*), man-of-war (*A or jocular*), man-at-arms (*A or jocular*), sojer (*dial. or C*), swad *or* swaddy (*S; British*), salamander (*S; British*), guffy (*sailors' S*), martialist (*R*); *spec.* private, recruit, conscript, volunteer, martinet, brigander (*hist.*), buffcoat, carabineer, carbineer, carmagnole (*French Revolution*), carpet knight, cataphract (*Greek hist.*), darter, duck (*Anglo-Indian S*), effective, fencible, franctireur (*French*), bersagliere (*Italian*), fugleman, fusilier (*British*), galloglass (*obs. or hist.*), gendarme (*French*), grayback (*U. S.*), confederate (*U. S.*), grenadier, guardsman, harquebusier *or* aquebusier, hayduck, hoplite (*Greek hist.*), imperial, jayhawker (*U. S.*), janizary *or* janissary (*Turkish hist.*), javelineer, jemadar (*East Indian*), kern, lance, lancer, lansquenet, lascar (*East Indian*), linesman, lobster (*S; British*), mameluke (*hist.*), marine, militarist, miner, mousquetaire (*French*), musketeer, musketoon, myrmidon, partizan, peltast (*Greek hist.*), peninsular, provincial, petardeer *or* petardier, pioneer, pistoleer, pontonnier, prætorian (*Roman hist.*), ranger, rapparee, redcoat, regular, rifleman, rutter (*A*), saber, sapper, sebundy (*Anglo-Indian*), sentinel, sepoy, silladar (*Anglo-Indian*), servitor (*obs. or A*), sowar, spahi, spearman, striker (*cant*), targeteer, territorial, timariot (*Turkish hist.*), Turco, uhlan, velite (*Roman hist.*), voltigeur (*French*), jager, yeoman (*British*), Zouave, Hessian (*hist.*), amazon, Tommy Atkins *or* (*for short*) Tommy (*British*), doughboy (*U. S.*), boche (*S; a German soldier*), poilu (*a French soldier*); *see* INFANTRYMAN, CAVALRYMAN.
soldierly, *a.* warlike, military, martial.
soldiery, *n.* military, legion (*primarily Roman hist. and spec.*), troops (*pl.*), forces (*pl.*); *spec.* rank, ranks (*pl.*), line, militia, trainband, immortals (*pl.*), Ironsides (*pl.*), rifle, horse, gendarmery (*French*), lootie (*Anglo-Indian*), lashkar (*East Indian*), musketry, chariotry, landsturm (*Ger., Swedish, etc.*), landwehr (*Ger., Swedish, etc.*), opalchenie (*Russia*), reserves (*pl.*), redif (*France*).
sole, *n.* tread; *spec.* insole, outsole, clump;—*referring to a shoe.*
sole, *v. t.* tap; *spec.* half-sole, cork.
sole, *a.* plantar (*tech.*).
solicit, *v. i. Spec.* canvass, drum, tout (*cant*).
solicitation, *n.* importunity (*implying continued asking, pressed to the point of annoyance*).
solicitor, *n.* **1.** *See* LAWYER, ASKER.
2. *Spec.* canvasser, drummer, runner, tout (*cant*), touter (*cant*).
solid, *a.* **1.** cubic (*math.*); *spec.* hard, congealed, frozen; *see* CONCRETE.
Antonyms: see FLUID, LIQUID, VAPOROUS.
2. *Spec.* massive (*which see*), compact (*which see*).
Antonyms: see HOLLOW.
3. *See* FIRM, STRONG, UNINTERRUPTED, UNMIXED, ACCOUNTABLE.
solidification, *n.* hardening, concretion, consolidation, *etc.*
solidify, *v. t.* **1.** harden, concrete (*chiefly spec.*), set, consolidate, fix; *spec.* plot; *see* CONGEAL, COAGULATE, CONDENSE, PETRIFY, CRYSTALLIZE.
Antonyms: see SOFTEN, EVAPORATE.
2. *See* UNITE.
solitude, *n. Spec.* loneliness, seclusion, desert.
solstice, *n.* sunstead (*A*), standing (*A*).
soluble, *a.* dissolvable.
Antonyms: see INSOLUBLE.
solution, *n.* **1.** resolution (*formal or tech.*); *spec.* unriddling, unraveling; *see* EXPLANATION, ANSWER.
2. *See* END, TERMINATION, DISSOLUTION, DISSOLVING.
3. *Spec.* decoction, apozem (*R*), cremor (*R*), sirup, lixivium, alloy.
solve, *v. t.* **1.** resolve (*implies* solving *by getting at the elements or first principles*), do (*contex.*), unravel, unriddle, work (*C*); *see* ANSWER, EXPLAIN.
2. *See* TERMINATE, DISSOLVE, DISCHARGE.
solvent, *a.* **1.** *In finance:* sound, solid, good, reliable, responsible.
2. *Referring to the dissolving of something:* resolvent, dissolvent, resolutive, diluent;—*all tech. or less usual than "solvent."*
solvent, *n.* resolvent, menstruum, dissolvent, diluent;—*all tech. or less usual than "solvent."*
somehow, *adv.* someway *or* someways (*now chiefly dial.*).
someone, *n.* somebody, quidam (*R*); *spec.* so-and-so.
Antonyms: see NOBODY.
sometime, *adv.* somewhen (*R*).
Antonyms: see NEVER.
sometimes, *adv.* sometime (*R*), somewhile *or* somewhiles (*A, R*).

---

sole, *a.: single, alone, unique, exclusive, mere.*
solecism: *barbarism, impropriety, error, blunder.*
solemn: *religious, formal, serious, sober, impressive.*
solicit, *v. t.: ask, court, attract, canvass, try, ply.*
solicitous: *anxious, careful.*
solitary, *a.:* alone, secluded, lonely.
somber: *dark, depressed, depressing, dull.*

Antonyms: see NEVER.
somewhat, *adv.* something, rather, slightly, some (*C, U. S. or dial.*).
somewhere, *adv. Referring to motion:* somewhither (*R, A*).
Antonyms: see NOWHERE.
son, *n.* **1.** child (*contex.*); *spec.* cadet, dauphin; *see* INFANT.
Antonyms: see PARENT, FATHER, MOTHER.
2. *See* DESCENDANT.
sonant, *a.* sounding; *spec.* phonetic; *see* VOCAL.
song, *n.* **1.** *Spec.* carol, descant (*B*), chant, ditty, note (*B*), lay, strain, pæan, snatch, canticle, rune, aubade, canzonet, carmagnole, catch, choral, chorus, dithyramb, dithyrambic, epinicion (*B*), glee, hunt's-up, jorram lay, lilt (*chiefly Scot.*), lullaby, madrigal, Marseillaise, matin, noël, Orphic, prothalamium, round, roundelay, scolion, serenade, chanty, warble, hymn, dirge; *see* BALLAD.
2. *See* POETRY, POEM.
sonorous, *a.* sounding; *spec. see* RESONANT.
soon, *adv.* **1.** presently, quickly, shortly, anon (*A*), forthwith (*emphatic*), betimes (*R, exc. B, implying some particular time of reference*).
Antonyms: see NEVER.
2. *See* EARLY.
soot, *n.* carbon, smut, crock (*R*), coom (*Scot. or local Eng.*), fuliginosity (*R*).
sooty, *a.* **1.** corky, smutty, fuliginous (*B*).
2. *See* DARK.
sop, *n.* morsel (*contex.*), sippet.
sophomore, *a.* junior sophister (*Eng.*), student (*contex.*), soph (*C*). *"Sophomore" and "soph" are U. S. only.*
soporific, *a.* somniferous (*R*), somnific (*R*), somnifacient, slumberous (*R*), dormitive (*R*), soporiferous, hypnotic (*R*), papaverous (*fig.*), soporous (*R*); *see* NARCOTIC.
Antonyms: see STIMULATING.
soprano, *n.* descant (*hist.*), canto (*cant*).
sore, *n. Spec.* raw, ulcer, abscess, fistula, pimple, canker, gangrene, impostume (*R*), fester, felon, boil, carbuncle, exulceration (*R*), blain, crepance, *etc.*
sore, *a.* **1.** *See* PAINFUL, SENSITIVE, OPPRESSIVE, INTENSE, ANGRY.
2. *Spec.* raw, ulcerated, ulcerous, cankered, gangrened.
sorority, *n.* society (*contex.*), club (*contex.*), sorosis; *spec.* Dorcas society, sisterhood.
sorrow, *n.* **1.** *Referring to the mental state, or experience:* distress, pain, grief, mourning, lamentation, woe, woefulness, regret, dole (*A, B*), dolor (*B*), heartache, heartbreak, bale (*B, R*), disconsolation, disconsolateness, ruth (*A*), rue (*A*), grame (*A*), teen (*A*), discomfort (*R*).
Antonyms: see REJOICING.
2. *Referring to what causes sorrow:* distress, grief, pain, heart-sore (*R*), heartbreak, discomfort (*R*).
3. *Referring to the outward manifestation: see* MOURNING.
sorrow, *v. i.* **1.** *Referring to the mental state:* grieve, lament, mourn; *spec.* sigh.
Antonyms: see REJOICE.
2. *Referring to outward acts: see* MOURN.
sorrowful, *a.* **1.** sad, grievous, grieved (*implying poignant sadness with a definite cause*), afflicted (*esp. by loss or misfortune*), mournful (*implying manifested grief*), sorry (*R, B*), grieful (*R*), lugubrious (*often implying forced or theatrical woefulness*), heartsore, broken-hearted, woeful, woebegone, trist (*A*), doleful, dolorous (*B*), lamentable (*R*), funereal.
Antonyms: see GLAD.
2. *See* LAMENTABLE.
sortilege, *n.* sortition (*R*); *see* DIVINATION.
soul, *n.* **1.** spirit, breath (*obs. or hist.*), pneuma (*hist.*), shade (*obs. or hist.*), shadow (*A or hist.*), nephesh (*Heb.; hist.*), entelechy (*R*), psyche (*B or myth.*), mind, interior, ghost (*A*).
Antonyms: see BODY.
2. heart.
3. *See* FEELING, ESSENCE, PERSON, SPIRIT.
soulless, *a.* **1.** *Spec.* inanimate, brute.
2. *See* UNFEELING, BASE, EXPRESSIONLESS.
sound, *a.* **1.** *See* HEALTHY, SANE, VALID, LOGICAL, ORTHODOX, INTACT, HONEST, SOLVENT, DEEP, SWEET.
2. uninjured, unimpaired, incorrupt (*R, A*).
sound, *v. t.* **1.** *Referring to water:* examine, plumb, fathom.
2. *See* EXAMINE.
sound, *n.* **1.** noise (*esp. without agreeable resonance*); *spec.* bang, beat, blare, blast, boom, bourdon, buzz, cacophony, chime, chink, chirm, chir, clang, clank, clap, clash, clatter, click, clink, cloop, clunk, crack, crackle, crepitation, creak, crick, crunch, decrepitation, din, ding-dong, discord, drone, drum, dub, flump (*C*), gluck, glug, guggle, gurgle, harmony, hem, hurtle, jangle, jar, jingle, jingle-jangle, jow (*Scot. or Eng. dial.*), klop, knell, lisp, melody, moan, murmur, muffle, pat, phone (*tech.*), plash, plunk (*C*), purl, roll, shrill, smack, voice (*often fig.*), splash, souse, stroke, swish, tang, tap, thud, tick, ticktack, toll, tone (*implying musical resonance*), toot, trumpet, twang, volley, wash, whistle, word, zip; *see* NOISE, WHISPER, MURMUR, RUSTLE, HUM, CLICK, NOTE, MELODY, JINGLE, HISS, RING, *etc. The foregoing list is partial.*
Antonyms: see SILENCE.
2. *See* HEARING.
sound, *v. i.* go (*contex.*), consonate (*R*), speak (*fig. or transferred sense*); *spec.* bang, beat, blare, blow, boom, buzz, chime, chink, chirm,

soothe: *pacify, calm, mitigate.*
soothing: *calming, sedative, mitigating.*
sophism: *argument, fallacy.*
sordid: *foul, filthy, mean, selfish, stingy, mercenary, base.*
sorry: *sorrowful, regretful, mean, contemptible.*
sort, *v. t.: classify, pick.*
sort, *v. i.: associate.*
sort, *n.: kind, class, manner.*

chir, clang, clank, clop, clap, clash, clatter, click, clink, crack, crackle, crepitate, creak, crick, crick-crack, crump, crunch, decrepitate, din, ding-dong, drone, gluck, guggle, gurgle, hum, jangle, jar, jingle, jow (*Scot. or Eng. dial.*), knell, lisp, moan, murmur, outring (*B*), pat, plash, plunk (*C*), purl, roll, roop, shrill, smack, speak, splash, strike, swish, tang, tap, thud, tick, toll, toot, trumpet, twang, volley, whistle, hiss, ring, *etc.*

sound, *v. t.* **1.** *Spec.* bang, beat, strike, blare, blow, boom, bugle, buzz, chime, chink, chirm, clang, clank, clap, clapper, click, clink, crack, creak, crunch, decrepitate, drone, gurgle, hum, jangle, jar, jingle, jow (*Scot. or Eng. dial.*), lisp, pat, play, pluck, plunk (*C*) roll, shrill, smack, speak, tap, tick, toll, toot, twang, whistle, wind, ring, hiss, *etc.*

2. *See* ANNOUNCE, CELEBRATE.

sounder, *n.* **1.** leadsman (*tech.*).

2. *See* LEAD.

sounding, *a.* **1.** sonorific (*B, R*); *spec.* crepitant, crepitating, horrisonant, drony, ringing, melodious, jingling, *etc.; see* NOISY.

Antonyms: see SILENT.

2. *See* BOMBASTIC, PRETENTIOUS.

sounding, *n.* sonation, sonifaction;—*both R and tech.*

Antonyms: see SILENCE.

soup, *n.* potage (*French*), pottage, broth; *spec.* purée, consommé, bouillon;—*all French.*

sour, *a.* **1.** acid (*suggests biting or caustic*), acrid (*of irritating sharpness*), tart (*suggests pungent quality*), sharp; *spec.* vinegarish, vinegary, vinaigrous (*R*), foxy, dry; *see* ACID.

Antonyms: see SWEET, SUGARY.

2. *See* ILL-TEMPERED, ROUGH, DISAGREEABLE, ACRIMONIOUS.

sour, *v. t.* **1.** turn; *spec.* prick, vinegar (*R*), verjuice, fox (*cant*), acidulate (*tech. or B*).

2. *See* EMBITTER.

Antonyms: see SWEETEN.

source, *n.* **1.** *Referring to the place from which water flows:* origin, spring, headspring, springhead, fountainhead, fountain (*R*), head (*contex.*), wellspring (*rhetorical or R*), wellhead (*R*), issue (*R*).

2. *Referring to that which affords or gives rise to something:* origin, original (*R*), beginning (*R*); *spec.* parent (*fig.*), birthplace, cradle (*fig.*), cunabulum (*B*), nidus (*fig.; B*), root, radix (*R*), fountain (*R*), fountainhead (*rhetorical; fig.*), wellspring (*B, fig.*), provenance *or* provenience (*B or tech.*), seminary (*R or tech.*), derivation, hand (*fig.*), primordium (*R*).

Antonyms: see OUTCOME.

southern, *a.* south, southerly, austral (*B*), southron (*chiefly Scot.*), meridian (*R*), meridional, high (*contex.*); *spec.* southward.

Antonyms: see NORTHERN.

southerner, *n.* southron (*chiefly Scot.*).

south wind, *n.* south (*B*), Notus (*R*).

sovereign, *n.* **1.** *See* RULER, MONARCH.

2. *Referring to the British coin:* shiner (*S*), chip (*S*), James (*S*), goldfinch (*S*), quid (*S*).

sovereignty, *n.* **1.** *See* SUPREMACY.

2. *Spec. referring to the position, power, etc., of a monarch:* sporanty (*B*), crown (*fig.*), royalty, scepter (*fig.*), regality (*R*), throne (*fig.*), reign, principality (*R*), kingship, despotism.

Antonyms: see DEPENDENCY.

sow, *v. t.* **1.** *Referring to the depositing of seed:* scatter, seminate (*A*); *spec.* cast, drill, dibble, broadcast.

Antonyms: see HARVEST.

2. *Referring to the land:* seed (*often used with "down"*).

3. *See* SCATTER.

spa, *n.* watering-place, hydro (*Brit.*), resort; soda-fountain (*loc., U. S., esp. New England*).

space, *n.* **1.** *See* TIME.

2. *Referring to the generic idea:* place (*now A or rhetorical, and chiefly in contrast to "time"*), expansion (*A*), extension (*B or tech.*).

3. *Often admitting of being used with the article "a" or "an":* place, region; *spec.* plenum, infinity, heavens, ether.

4. *See* DISTANCE, GAP, PLACE, ROOM, AREA.

spacious, *a.* **1.** wide, broad; *spec.* vast, vasty (*R*), extensive; *see* ROOMY.

Antonyms: see NARROW.

2. *See* ABOUNDING.

spade, *n.* shovel; *spec.* slice, spud, didle (*local*), loy (*Anglo-Irish*).

spadelike, *a.* palaceous (*tech.*).

span, *v. t.* **1.** *See* MEASURE, ENCIRCLE.

2. extend (*contex.*), overspan (*R*), overreach (*R*); *see* ARCH.

spangle, *n.* paillette (*tech. or R*); *spec.* star.

spar, *n.* pole; *spec.* (*naut.*): mast, boom, gaff, bowsprit, yard, sprit.

spare, *a.* **1.** additional (*contex.*), extra (*C*), subsecive (*R*); *see* EXCESSIVE, UNNECESSARY.

Antonyms: see DEFICIENT.

2. *See* LEISURE, SCANTY, THIN, MEAGER.

spare, *v. t.* **1.** *Referring to refraining from injuring or destroying a thing:* forbear (*A R*), respect (*contex.*).

2. *Referring to avoidance of inflicting or visiting upon:* save (*as in "save him all you can"*).

3. *See* SAVE, ECONOMIZE, WITHHOLD.

sparrowlike, *a.* passeriform (*tech.*).

spasm, *n.* **1.** *Referring to muscular contraction:* paroxysm, convulsion, throe, cramp, crick, seizure, grip, gripe; *spec.* eclampsia, hiccup, entasia, flurry (*a collective*), laryngismus, tetanus, holotony.

---

span, *n.: period, width, arch, range.*
sparing, *a.: frugal, economical, meager, moderate, scanty, forbearing.*
spark, *n.: fire, trace, particle, flash.*
spark, *n.: blade, lover.*
spark, *v. t.: court.*
sparkle, *n.: flash, trace, witticism, brightness, twinkle.*
sparkle, *v. i.: flash, bubble, twinkle.*
sparkling: *lively, witty.*
sparse: *infrequent, few.*

---

2. *Referring to sudden convulsive action:* see FIT.

spasmodic, *a.* **1.** paroxysmal, convulsive, paroxysmic (*R*), spastic (*tech.*), catchy (*R*).
2. *See* INTERMITTENT.

spatter, *v. t.* **1.** *See* SCATTER, SPRINKLE.
2. spot (*contex.*); *spec.* bespatter (*intensive*), sprinkle, besprinkle (*intensive*), oversprinkle (*R*), splash, splutter (*R*).

spawn, *n.* **1.** eggs (*collective pl.*), spat, roe; *spec.* brood, redd (*Scot. or dial.*).
2. *See* OFFSPRING.
3. Mycelium (*tech.*).

speak, *v. i.* **1.** talk (*implies speaking in connected discourse*), word (*R*); *spec.* outspeak (*R*), snap, pipe, dulcify (*humorous*), sputter, splutter, drawl, sniff, sniffle, snuffle, perorate, lisp, wharl (*R*), whisper, murmur, shout, intone, sing.
2. discourse (*implying elaboration of a theme*), (*C, R*), patter (*S or cant*), orate (*usually humorous or sarcastic*), oratorize (*R equiv. of "orate"*), stump, speechify (*contemptuous*), speechmake (*R*), spout (*C*); *spec.* lecture; *see* CONVERSE, DECLAIM.
3. *See* SOUND, BARK.

speak, *v. t.* **1.** utter (*contex.*), say, pronounce (*formal or spec.*); *spec.* mutter, mumble, discourse, enunciate, sputter, sniff, snuff, snuffle, splutter, dictate.
2. *Referring to the use of a tongue as a spoken language:* talk, use.
3. *See* STATE, EXPRESS, PRONOUNCE, DISCLOSE, ADDRESS, PROVE.

speaker, *n.* **1.** talker; *spec.* drawler, lisper, *etc.*
2. discourser, speechifier (*contemptuous*), voice (*fig.*), orator, rhetorician, oratress (*fem.*), oratrix (*fem.; R*), concionator (*R*); *spec.* elocutionist, droner, lecturer, lecturess (*fem.*), demagogue, spouter (*C*), patterer (*cant or C*), Boanerges (*fig.*), valedictorian, thunderer; *see* DECLAIMER, SPOKESMAN.
3. *See* CHAIRMAN.

speaking, *n.* utterance (*contex.*), talk, discourse; *spec.* patter (*S or cant*), longiloquence, mumble, prolocution (*R*), dictation, declamation, pronunciation.

speaking, *a.* loquent (*R*); *spec.* dulciloquent (*R; chiefly humorous*).
Antonyms: see SILENT.

spear, *n.* lance; *spec.* bourdon, gaff, pike, leister, trident, harpoon, dart.

spear-shaped, *a.* hastate (*technical or B*), hastiform (*R*); *spec.* lanceolate (*chiefly tech.*), lanceolar (*chiefly tech.*).

special, *a.* **1.** exceptional, peculiar, individual (*stressing what is characteristic*), particular (*stressing special concern with the given one as against others of the sort*), express (*suggesting selection for a particular purpose*), especial (*not now used predicatively*), marked; *spec.* intimate.
Antonyms: see ORDINARY, USUAL.
2. *See* PARTICULAR, INTIMATE.

specialize, *v. t.* **1.** *See* MENTION.
2. *Referring to a rendering specific or investing with a specific character:* separate, individualize, differentiate (*chiefly biol.*), distinguish (*R*), specificize (*R*), specify (*R*).

specially, *adv.* express, expressly.

specious, *a.* colorable, flimsy, colored (*R*); *see* PLAUSIBLE.
Antonyms: see SINCERE.

spectacle, *n.* **1.** *See* SHOW.
2. sight, object, gazingstock (*chiefly depreciatory*); *spec.* guy.
3. *Spec.* preserves, goggles.

spectator, *n.* beholder, onlooker, observer, seer (*R*), viewer, gazer, watcher, witness; *spec.* bystander, groundling, gallery god, kibitzer (*C*).

speculation, *n.* **1.** *See* CONSIDERATION, OPINION.
2. venture; *spec.* flyer (*U. S.*).

speculative, *a.* speculatory, notional (*tech.*); *see* INFERENTIAL, ACADEMIC.

speculator, *n.* **1.** *See* REASONER.
2. *Spec.* bear, bull, lamb, lame duck, long, short.

speech, *n.* **1.** *Referring to the act:* utterance (*contex.*), talk, loquency (*R*); *spec.* declamation, sputter, splutter, parlance (*A*), parle (*A*), whisper, shout, roar, sing, *etc.*
Antonyms: see SILENCE.
2. *Referring to what is said:* utterance (*contex.*); *spec.* word, talk, discourse, locution (*R*), parle (*A*), palaver (*chiefly spec. or contemptuous*), whisper; *see* CONVERSATION.
3. *Referring to the faculty or power:* tongue, language (*R*).
4. *Referring to a more or less formal discourse to others:* address, oration (*suggests rhetorical elaboration and an important occasion*), rhesis (*R*); *spec.* declamation, dithyramb, exhortation, speechlet (*dim.; C*), defense, eulogy, dirge; *see* HARANGUE.
5. *See* LANGUAGE.

speed, *n.* **1.** *See* RAPIDITY.
2. *Referring to the rate of motion or action:* rate, velocity (*chiefly tech.; mech.*), pace (*spec. or fig.*); *spec.* music, tempo, time, haste.
Antonyms: see DELAY.

speed, *v. i.* go (*contex.*); *spec.* race, ramp, scud, skirr (*Eng.*), scurry, pelt (*C*), peg (*C or dial.*), lick (*dial. or C; U. S. and Australia*); *see* RUSH.
Antonyms: see DELAY.

spelling, *n.* orthography (*properly spec.*); *spec.* transliteration, homography, phonography (*R*), cacography, misspelling.

spendthrift, *n.* **1.** spender (*contex.*), prodigal, spend-all (*R*), scapethrift (*A*), scattergood (*A, R*), unthrift (*R*).
Antonyms: see NIGGARD.
2. *See* WASTER.

speed, *v. t.: send, hasten, advance.*
speedy: *rapid, ready, quick.*
spell, *n.: magic, influence, bewitchery.*
spell, *n.: round, period, turn.*
spell, *n.: fit.*
spell, *v. t.: relieve.*
spell, *v. t.: bewitch.*
spend: *expend, exhaust, pass, bestow.*

spent, *a. Referring to a fish:* shotten, spawned.
sphere, *n.* **1.** *See* BALL, RANK, SCOPE.
2. *Referring to the place or domain in which something acts or prevails:* realm (*of influence or function*), domain (*over which dominion is in force*), province, kingdom, circuit, round (*R*), arena, element, field, scope, range, walk, department, bound;—*mostly spec. or fig.*
spherical, *a.* sphere-shaped, orbicular (*rhetorical or technical*), round *or* rounded (*contex.*), globose (*tech.*), spheral (*R*), spheric (*R*), rotund (*R*), orbed (*B or spec.*), globy (*R*), globous (*R*); *spec.* globoid (*R*), globulous (*R*), orbiculate (*R*), orbic (*R*), spherular, spheroid, spheroidal *or* (*R*) spheroidical, bulbous, circular.
spider, *n.* arachnid, spinner (*now dial. or rhetorical*).
spike, *n.* gad (*obs. or hist.*); *spec.* nail, spikelet, dag, gadling, boss.
spike-shaped, *a.* spiciform.
spill, *v. t.* **1.** *Referring to blood:* shed, let, broach.
2. slop, drip, drop, bespill (*intensive*), overflow.
3. *See* SCATTER.
spill, *n.* **1.** slop.
2. *See* FALL.
spinal, *a. Spec.* vertebral.
spindle-shaped, *a.* fusiform;—*tech. or B.*
spine, *n.* **1.** point (*contex.*), thorn; *spec.* spinula, thornlet, quill, ray, neurapophysis; *see* PRICKLE.
2. *See* BACKBONE, RIDGE.
spinner, *n.* spinster (*usually fem.*), spinstress (*fem.*).
spiny, *a.* **1.** spinous, spinose (*tech.*), thorny, spinescent; *see* PRICKLY.
2. spine-shaped, thorny, spinose; *spec.* spinulate.
3. spinigerous (*tech.*), spiniferous (*tech.*), spinose (*tech.*), thorny
spiral, *n.* **1.** *Referring to a curve in a single plane:* curl, coil (*tech.*), helix (*R*), winding.
2. *Referring to a screwlike coil:* helix, twist, screw, coil.
spiral, *a.* **1.** curled, winding, coiled, helical (*R*).
2. helical, twisted, screw-shaped, coiled.
spire, *n.* **1.** *See* GROWTH.
2. *Referring to a conical or tapering end or body: spec.* steeple, branch, broach, flêche (*French*), aiguille.
spirit, *n.* **1.** *See* SOUL, GHOST, DEITY, DEMON, ANGEL, GENIUS, FORCE, ENERGY, MEANING, DISPOSITION, ESSENCE, PERSON, BRAVERY, QUALITY.
2. liveliness, soul, decision, vigor; *spec.* spice, morale *or* (*the proper French form*) moral, mind, dash, pith, mettle, courage, pluck, esprit (*French*), sprightliness, enterprise, go (*C*), ginger (*S*), spunk (*C*), devil (*C*), heart, bravura.
3. *Referring to strong distilled alcoholic liquid: spec.* proof; *also in pl. form* (*spirits*) whisky, gin, brandy, faints (*pl.*), schnapps (*pl.*), *etc.*
spirited, *a.* high-spirited, animated, high-strung (*implies tense nerves and high sensitivity*), mettlesome *or* mettled (*implies energy and ardent readiness for activity*), eager (*implies keen specific desire*), keen, sharp, crank, cocky (*S*), lusty, strenuous, proud (*chiefly B*), beany (*C*), galliard (*A*), spunky (*C*), fiery, enterprising; *see* LIVELY.
Antonyms: see APATHETIC.
spiritual, *a.* immaterial, supersensible (*contex.*), psychical, ethereal, ghostly (*B, A*), inner, interior, internal, inward, high-minded, pneumatical (*R*), pneumatic (*R*), unworldly; *spec.* Platonic; *see* DIVINE, REFINED.
Antonyms: see ANIMAL, WORLDLY, COARSE, EARTHLY, BODILY, SENSUAL, SENSUOUS.
spiritualist, *n.* spiritist (*R*), rappist (*R*).
spiritualize, *v. t.* enspiritualize (*R*), etherealize, uncarnate (*R*); *see* IDEALIZE.
Antonyms: see MATERIALIZE, BRUTALIZE, EMBODY, SENSUALIZE.
spit, *v. i.* **1.** spawl (*obs.*); *spec.* splutter, drivel, drool, slobber, salivate (*tech.*), expectorate.
2. *See* EJECT.
spit, *n.* spawl (*obs.*); *spec.* spittle, saliva (*tech.*), water (*contex.*), froth, slobber, drivel.
spit, *n. Referring to the depth of earth that is turned up by a spade or plow:* cut (*contex.*), graft.
spit, *n.* broach.
spittoon, *n.* cuspidor (*U. S.*); *spec.* spit-box.
splash, *v. i.* plash (*less usual than "splash"*), splurge (*U. S.*), splodge, splatter (*chiefly U. S. or dial. Eng.*), slush, spatter (*R*); *spec.* dabble, swash, swish, wash, dash, squatter, swish-swash, plap, plop; *see* SPATTER.
splash, *v. t.* **1.** wet (*contex.*), plash (*less usual than "splash"*), dash (*contex.*), splatter (*chiefly U. S. or Eng. dial.*), slush; *spec.* squash, swash, wash; *see* SPATTER.
2. *Referring to the liquid acted upon:* plash (*less usual than "splash"*), splatter (*chiefly U. S. or dial. Eng.*); *spec.* dash (*contex.*), bedash (*R*), squatter, slush, swash, swish, wash, swish-swash; *see* SPATTER.
splash, *n.* plash (*less usual than "splash"*), splatter (*chiefly U. S. or dial. Eng.*), splurge (*U. S.*); *spec.* dash (*contex.*), slush, swash, swish, wash, swish-swash.
spleen, *n.* **1.** entrail (*contex.*), milt (*R*).
2. *See* ILL TEMPER, ILL WILL, DEPRESSION.
splenic, *a.* splenetic, lienal (*R*).
splice, *v. t.* join, marry; *spec.* plank.
splinter, *n.* fragment (*contex.*), sliver (*often spec.*), shiver, spill, splint (*now R or dial.*), chip, flinder (*chiefly in pl.*); *spec.* spall, spillikin.

spin, *v. t.: rotate, devise, fabricate, attenuate, continue.*
spirt, *n.: rush, effort.*
spirt, *n. & v. i.: spout, jet.*
spirt, *v. t.: spout, emit.*
spite, *n.: ill will, grudge.*
spite, *v. t.: ill-treat, irritate, offend.*
splendid: *grand, fine, showy, luxurious, impressive, luminous, bright.*
splendor, splendour, *n.: grandeur, luster, brightness.*

splinter, *v. t. & i.* split, sliver, shiver, chip; *spec.* spall.
split, *v. i.* divide (*contex.*), cleave; *spec.* fissure, rend, rive; *see* CRACK, SPLINTER.
split, *v. t.* divide (*contex.*), cleave; *spec.* rend, rive, rift, fissure, wedge; *see* CRACK, SPLINTER.
split, *n.* division (*contex.*), cleft; *spec.* rent, fissure, rift; *see* CRACK, BREACH (*in a fig. sense*).
splitting, *n.* division (*contex.*), cleavage, rending, fission (*tech.*).
spoil, *v. t.* **1.** *See* PLUNDER, DEPRIVE, DESTROY, IMPAIR, DEFORM, DEFEAT, INDULGE.
2. *Referring to destruction or impairment of the good qualities of a thing:* mar, ruin, vitiate (*formal*), butcher (*C*), murder (*C*), mangle (*C*); *spec.* demolish.
Antonyms: see AMEND, IMPROVE.
spoiled, *a.* damaged, impaired, injured, sick (*spec. or fig.*).
spokesman, *n.* speaker, mouthpiece, mouth (*fig.*), prolocutor (*R or spec.*), spokeswoman (*fem.*).
sponger, *n.* sponge, bloodsucker (*C or contemptuous*), sucker (*C*), dead beat (*S, U. S.*), deadhead (*orig. U. S.*), beat (*S*), piker (*S*), *spec.* smell-feast, trencher friend, sorner.
Antonyms: see ENTERTAINER, BENEFACTOR.
spontaneous, *a.* natural, free; *see* INTENTIONAL, AUTOMATIC, EXTEMPORANEOUS.
Antonyms: see LABORED.
spool, *n.* reel (*chiefly spec. or tech.*); *spec.* bobbin, quill, pirn, cop, bottom, wharve *or* wherve.
spoon, *n.* **1.** *Spec.* cochleare, labis.
2. *See* SIMPLETON.
spoon-shaped, *a.* cochlear, cochleariform, spatulate, spatuliform;—*all four tech. or B.*
sport, *n.* **1.** *See* DIVERSION, PLAY, PLAYTHING, FREAK, BUTT, FROLIC, SPORTSMAN, JEST.
2. *In a generic sense:* play, game, fun; *spec.* joke, jest.
3. *Referring to a flashy or dashing young fellow:* blood (*S*), flash man (*cant*), swell (*S*); *see* GAMBLER.
sporting, *a.* flash (*cant*).
sportsman, *n.* hunter, sport (*R*), sportswoman (*fem.*); *spec.* pothunter.
spot, *n.* **1.** mark (*contex.*); *spec.* brand, dot, dab, speck, speckle, macula, maculation, dash, cast (*R*), daub, drop, blotch, spatter, splotch, moil (*B or A*), pock, blur, blot, fleck, mottle, clouding, dapple, spangle, patch, facula, blaze, mole, fleece, mottle, smear, discoloration, stain, eye, freckle, pip.
2. *Referring to a natural marking on an animal, esp. on the face: spec.* snip, cloud, blaze, star.
3. *See* SULLY, PLACE.
spot, *v. t.* **1.** *See* SULLY.
2. mark (*contex.*); *spec.* stud, speck, speckle, spatter, bespatter (*intensive*), dab, maculate, dash, daub, dot, drop (*A*), splotch, pock, blur, blot, blotch, fleck, mottle, dapple, sprinkle, besprinkle (*intensive*), bespot, pepper, measle (*R*), smear, stain, discolor, freckle.
3. *See* SULLY, DISCOVER, PERCEIVE.
spotless, *a.* **1.** immaculate (*B or rhetorical*); *spec.* stainless, smearless (*R*); *see* CLEAN.
Antonyms: see DIRTY, SPOTTED, STAINED, SOILED.
2. *See* UNSULLIED.
spotted, *a.* spotty; *spec.* splotchy, specky, specked, mottled, speckled, dotted, dappled, blotchy, flecky, maculose, maculated, macular, measly, guttate *or* guttated, fleecy, flecked, fleckered, flea-bitten, mealy, ocellated, ocellate, oculated, bimaculate; *see* PARTY-COLORED.
Antonyms: see SPOTLESS.
spouse, *n.* associate (*contex.*), consort (*chiefly spec. or rhetorical*), companion (*contex.*), partner (*chiefly dial. or uneducated*), mate, espousal (*obs. or R*), fere (*A*); *see* HUSBAND. "*Spouse*" *is chiefly formal or official.*
spout, *n.* **1.** outlet (*contex.*); *spec.* pipe, nozzle, snout, beak, waterspout, monitor, jet, gargoyle; *see* COCK.
2. issue, spirt, spurt, spire (*R*), gush, squirt, jet; *spec.* waterspout, sandspout.
spout, *v. t. & i.* **1.** eject, emit (*contex.*), issue (*R as a v. t.*), spirt, spurt, spire (*R*), squirt, gush, jet; *spec.* blow.
2. *See* DECLAIM.
sprain, *n. & v. t.* strain, overstrain (*emphatic*); *spec.* wrench, rick.
spray, *n.* mist (*contex.*); *spec.* (*referring to water blown or thrown up from the waves, etc.*) scud, foam, spume, spindrift, drizzle.
spray, *v. t.* scatter (*contex.*), nebulize (*chiefly spec.;*) *spec.* atomize.
spraylike, *a.* sprayey, misty, smoky, hazy; —*the last three contex. uses.*
spread, *v. t.* **1.** *In a physical sense: spec.* open, stretch, roll, unroll, run, drive, couch, ted; *see* EXPAND, DISTRIBUTE, DIFFUSE, SCATTER, FLARE.
2. *See* OVERSPREAD.
3. *Referring to a report, rumor, etc.:* tell, circulate; disseminate, propagate (*both implying desired growth of that which is spread*); *spec.* rumor.
4. *Referring to the extending of the parts, esp. of a person or animal, so as to reach out widely, esp. in confusion, aimlessly, or awkwardly:* sprawl, splay, display (*chiefly spec.*); *spec.* explanate (*R*).
spread, *v. i.* **1.** *In a physical sense: spec.* open, run, stretch, strike, trail, creep, crawl, gape, flange, flare, flanch, mantle, fan (*R*); *see* EXPAND, DIFFUSE, SCATTER.
2. *To extend or reach out loosely, etc.:* sprawl; *spec.* straddle.
3. *Referring to rumors, reports, etc.:* circulate, run, go (*contex.*); *spec.* canard, fly.
spread, *n.* **1.** *See* EXPANSE, DIFFUSION, SHOW, MEAL, BEDCOVER.

spoil: *plunder, graft, acquisition.* | **sport,** *v. i.: frolic, play.*

2. sprawl, splay; *spec.* straddle (*C*).
spreading, *a.* diffusive (*formal*), patent (*R*); *spec.* patulous (*B*), effuse.
spring, *n.* **1.** *Spec.* source prime.
2. *Referring to a flow of water from the earth, primarily a natural one:* fountain (*A*, *B or fig.*), font (*B*), fount (*chiefly B*), wellspring (*A*), wellhead (*R or A*); *spec.* fresh, deerlick, seep (*R*), spa, gipsies (*pl.; local Eng.*), geyser, Castalia *or* Castalic (*fig.*), Hippocrene (*fig.*).
3. prime (*R*), springtime, springtide (*A or B*); *spec.* seedtime.
4. *See* JUMP, RECOIL, START, DART, MOTIVE.
springy, *a.* **1.** fountainous (*R*), fountful (*R*, *B*).
2. *See* ELASTIC.
sprinkle, *v. t.* **1.** *Referring to the thing dispersed:* strew, scatter, sparge (*chiefly Scot.*); *spec.* spatter, powder, dust, dredge, sand.
2. *Referring to that upon which something is sprinkled:* strew, scatter, asperse (*B or spec.*); *spec.* besprinkle, bedew, spatter, flour, powder.
3. *See* DOT.
sprinkled, *a.* besprent (*A*, *B*); *spec.* dotted.
sprinkler, *n.* *Spec.* dredger, aspergillum.
sprinkling, *n.* aspersion (*B or tech.*).
spruce, *v. t. & i.* dress, smarten, titivate (*C*), perk, plume, prink, prune, preen, trim (*chiefly* spec.), lick (*S*). *"Spruce" is chiefly used with "up."*
spur, *n.* **1.** *The spur of a rider:* point, pricker, prick, ripon (*local or hist.*).
2. *The spur of a fowl or bird:* heel, calcar (*tech.*), claw (*R*); *spec.* gaff.
3. *See* INCENTIVE, STIMULANT, PROJECTION, BRANCH.
spur, *v. t.* **1.** prick (*A*), rowel.
2. *See* INCITE, HASTEN, URGE.
spurlike, *a.* calcariform, calcarine;—*both tech.*
spurred, *a.* spicate, calcarate, spiciferous (*R*); —*all three tech. or* (*B*).
spy, *n.* watcher (*contex.*); *spec.* intelligencer, scout, shadow, lurcher (*B*), tout (*S or cant*), smeller (*S*), beagle (*Eng. cant*), plant (*S*), nose (*S*), emissary, hircarra (*East India*).
spy, *v. i.* **1.** watch (*contex.*), espy (*R*); *spec.* scout, pry, nose (*S*), smell (*S or consciously fig.*), tout (*R*).
2. *See* OBSERVE, DISCOVER.
square, *n.* **1.** rectangle, quadrate (*tech.*); *spec.* pane.
2. *Referring to buildings: see* BLOCK.
3. *Referring to an open area:* plaza, piazza, parade (*Eng.*).
square, *a.* **1.** rectangular (*formal*), four-square, quadrate (*tech.*), quadratic (*R*); *spec.* squarish.
2. *See* RECTANGULAR, JUST, HONEST.
square, *v. t.* **1.** quadrate (*R*).
2. *See* ADJUST, ADAPT, BALANCE.
squat, *a.* thickset, stocky, pudgy, podgy, squidgy (*R*), punchy, stumpy, dumpy, squatty, spuddy (*R*), tubby (*C*), tubbish (*C*), squab *or* squabby.
Antonyms: see LANKY.
squeamish, *a.* *Spec.* sick, fastidious, distant, priggish.
squeeze, *v. t. & i.* **1.** press, compass, pinch (*chiefly spec.*), wring, coarct (*R*); *spec.* nip. clutch, crush; *see* CONSTRICT.
Antonyms: see STRETCH.
2. *See* FORCE, EXPRESS, OPPRESS, EXTORT.
squeeze, *n.* **1.** pressure, compression, coarctation (*R*); *spec.* nip, pinch, vise (*R*); *see* CRUSH, CONSTRICTION.
2. *Spec.* forcing, expression, oppression, extortion.
squelch, *v. t.* **1.** *See* CRUSH, FLATTEN, SUPPRESS.
2. quelch, quash, squatter, squish, squash.
squelch, *n.* quelch, quash, squatter, squidge (*R*), squish, squash.
squelchy, *a.* squashy, quashy, squishy.
squint, *v. i.* **1.** look (*contex.*); squinny, goggle, skew, slant (*all R*).
2. *See* PEEK, REFER, TEND.
squint, *n.* **1.** look (*contex.*), cast (*R or A*), squinny (*R*), goggle (*R*); *spec.* strabismus, cross-eye.
2. *Spec.* peek, reference, inclination, tendency.
squint-eyed, *a.* strabismic (*tech.*), squint (*R*), goggle-eyed (*R*), squinting; *spec.* cross-eyed.
squire, *n.* **1.** *Referring to the knight's attendant:* esquire (*A*), armiger (*tech.*), henchman (*hist.*); *spec.* page.
2. *Referring to a landed proprietor:* esquire (*A; Eng*); *spec.* squireen, squirelet, squireling.
squirrel, *n.* rodent, sciurine (*tech.*), bunny, bun (*R*), con (*Eng. dial.*).
s-shaped, a. doubly-curved, sigmoid (*tech.*).
stab, *v. t.* **1.** pierce (*contex.*), stick, job, jab (*C*), dig (*C*), pink, broach (*B or fig.*); *spec.* poke, prick, prong (*R*), bayonet, dirk, knife, spear, stiletto, creese *or* crease *or* kris, poniard, dagger, paunch, gore.
2. *See* AFFECT.
stab, *n.* job, jab (*C*); *spec.* prick, dig (*C*), poke.
stable, *n.* stall (*R as referrihg to horses*); *spec.* mew (*a collective*), mews (*pl.*).
staff, *n.* **1.** *See* POLE.
2. rod (*contex.*), wand, baton (*chiefly tech.*); *spec.* truncheon, caduceus, crook, crosier, cross, crutch, mace, lituus, warder, thyrsus (*R*), thyrse, tipstaff, cowlstaff.
stag, *n.* deer (*contex.*); *spec.* royal, brocket.
stage, *n.* **1.** *See* STORY, DEGREE, PLATFORM, ROSTRUM, DRAMA, LEVEL, PERIOD.

---

spring, *v. i.: dart, rush, prance, issue, flow, rise, arise, descend, grow, deform, appear.*
spring, *v. t.: start, displace, deform, bend.*
sprite: *ghost, demon, fairy, goblin.*
spur, *v. t.: goad, incite, hasten, urge.*
spurn, *n.: kick, rejection.*
spurn, *v. t.: tread, reject.*
spurn, *v. i.: object.*
squash, *v. t.: crush, flatten, splash, squelch.*
squash, *n.: squelch.*
stable, *a.: firm, lasting, constant.*
stack, *n.: heap, group, chimney.*
stack, *v. t.: heap, gather.*

---

2. *Referring to a division in a journey:* post, reach; *spec.* manzil.
3. stagecoach, coach; *spec.* diligence, omnibus.
4. scene (*classical antiq.*), footlights (*cant*); *spec.* proscenium (*antiq.*), postscenium (*antiq.*), parascene (*antiq.*).
stagnant, *a.* **1.** still, motionless, dead, standing.
Antonyms: see AGITATED, FLOWING.
2. *See* INACTIVE.
stain, *n.* **1.** discoloration (*contex.*), soil (*R*), soilure (*R*); *spec.* tarnish, splotch, blur, blot, blotch, cloud, smirch, smutch, crock.
2. *See* SULLY, CONTAMINATION.
stain, *v. t.* **1.** discolor (*implying change to a color less natural or pleasing*), distain (*A*), soil (*suggesting impurity*); *spec.* tarnish (*implying loss of luster*), bestain (*intensive*), splotch, blot, blotch, smirch, smutch, besmutch (*intensive*), smut, dye, engrain (*R*), imbrue (*B*), blacken, mildew, ink.
2. *See* SULLY, CONTAMINATE, DYE.
stained, *a.* discolored (*contex.*), soiled, imbrued (*B, R*); *spec.* smudgy, smirchy, spotted.
Antonyms: see SPOTLESS.
stair, *n.* flight, grece (*obs. or dial.*), staircase, stairway; *spec.* winder, companionway, escalator. *In England and America the pl. form "stairs" is now generally used, but in Scotland the sing. form "stair" is still the ordinary form.*
stake, *n.* stick (*contex.*); *spec.* bar, rod, stock, post, pale, pile, palisade, picket, palisado (*R*), snub.
stake, *n.* **1.** hazard, prize (*chiefly spec.*), risk (*R*); *spec.* bank; *see* PLEDGE, WAGER.
2. *See* VENTURE.
stake, *v. t.* hazard, risk; *see* PLEDGE, WAGER.
stale, *v. t.* hackney, hack (*R*).
stalk, *v. i.* go (*contex.*), sweep; *spec.* strut.
Antonyms: see SNEAK.
stalk, *v. t.* hunt (*contex.*), still-hunt.
stalk, *n.* **1.** stem, caulis (*tech.*), caudex (*tech.*); *spec.* spear, spire, shaft, caulicle, culm (*esp. of grass*), helm (*Eng. or dial. of grain*), haulm (*Eng.*), bun (*dial.*), boon, bent, bennet, straw, stipe, stipes, stipule, cane, pedicel, footstalk, beam, castock (*Scot.*), pedicle, peduncle, petiole, gynophore, funiculus, funicle, scape, tigella *or* tigelle, stipel.
2. *See* STEM.
stalked, *a. Spec.* pediculated, petiolate, pedicellate, tigellate, pedunculate, pedunculated, stiped, *etc.;—all tech.*
stall, *n.* **1.** *See* STABLE.
2. *Referring to the division or compartment for accommodating one animal:* travis (*Scot.*); *spec.* crub (*obs. or R*), box stall *or* box, cote.
3. stand, booth, crame (*Scot.*); *spec.* bulkhead (*Eng.*), bulk (*Eng.*), pandal (*Anglo-Indian*).
stalwart, *a.* **1.** strong, stout, sturdy.
2. *See* DETERMINED.

stand, *v. i.* **1.** *There are no direct synonyms:* remain (*contex.*), stay (*contex.*).
Antonyms: see FALL, LIE, SIT.
2. *See* REST, CONTINUE, BE, HESITATE, STOP, BRISTLE.
standard, *n.* **1.** flag (*contex.*), ensign (*mil. or naval; chiefly spec.*), oriflamme (*spec. or fig.*), vexillum (*Roman antiq.*), gonfalon, labarum.
2. measure, norm *or* norma (*tech. or B*); *spec.* canon, scale, gauge, diapason, vernier, metewand (*B*), proof, assize, criterion, test.
3. *See* EXAMPLE, CANDLESTICK, UPRIGHT.
standard-bearer, *n.* ensign, signifer (*R*), vexillator (*R*); *spec.* cornet, gonfalonier.
standing, *n.* **1.** *Referring to the action or condition:* station (*now tech.*).
2. *See* POSITION, CONTINUANCE, ENDURANCE, RANK.
standstill, *n. Referring to the fact or state:* stand, station (*R*), deadlock (*only fig.*), stay (*A*).
Antonyms: see RUN.
stanza, *n.* stave, staff, strophe (*R*); *spec.* sixain, terzina, tercet, pennill, quatrain, englyn, envoy, tristich, tetrastich, *etc.*
star, *n.* **1.** light (*contex.*), luminary (*B or rhetorical*), twinkler, starlet (*dim.*), planet (*astrol. or spec.*); *spec.* sun, nova, vesper, shooter (*R*), primary, comet.
2. *Referring to the figure or image: spec.* pentacle, pentagram, pentangle, pentalpha, mullet (*her.*), asterisk.
3. *See* DESTINY, SPANGLE.
starchy, *a.* **1.** farinaceous.
2. *See* STIFF.
staring, *a.* **1.** *Referring to the look:* gazing, glaring, fixed.
2. *See* CONSPICUOUS.
starling, *n.* cutwater.
starred, *a.* **1.** stellular.
2. *See* CRACKED.
starry, *a.* **1.** *Full of stars:* constellate (*B*).
2. astral (*tech. or formal*), stullular, stellar (*formal or tech.*), sidereal, starlike.
3. star-shaped, stellate, stelliform, stellular;—*the last three tech. or* (*B*).
start, *n.* **1.** spring, shock, startle (*R*), jump, braid (*obs.*); *see* SHRINK.
2. beginning, go-off (*C*), outset, offset, setoff; *spec.* break, breakaway (*cant*), get-away (*cant or S*); *see* RUSH.
3. impulse (*contex.*), send-off (*C*).
4. lead;—*referring to an advantage of position, as in racing.*
5. *See* DISPLACEMENT, BRANCH.
start, *v. i.* **1.** spring, jump, startle (*R*), braid (*obs. or A*); *see* SHRINK.
2. break, put (*U. S.; C*), sally (*B, rhetorical, or humorous*), boun (*A*); *spec.* burst, flash, sail.
3. *See* BEGIN, ENTER.

---

stagger, *v. t.: perplex, shake, shock, zigzag, weaken.*
stale, *a.: tasteless, moldy, commonplace.*
stanch, *a.: strong, firm, constant, courageous.*
stand, *v. t.: station, place, endure.*
standard, *a.: authoritative, average.*
standing, *a.: upright, stagnant, permanent.*
standpoint: *position, viewpoint.*
stark: *absolute, naked, unmitigated, stiff.*

start, *v. t.* **1.** *Referring to game:* rouse, spring; *see* FLUSH.
2. *See* BEGIN, SET, DISPLACE.

startle, *v. t.* surprise, rouse, electrify (*fig.*), jump (*R*); *see* FRIGHTEN.

state, *n.* **1.** *Referring to the circumstances or condition of affairs in which a thing exists:* condition, status (*B*), situation, estate (*A, B*), posture (*R*), pass, case, plight (*R, exc. spec.*), disposition, circumstance *or* (*usually*) circumstances (*pl.*).
2. *Referring to the condition in which a person or thing is:* condition, estate (*A, B*), form, shape, fettle, trim (*chiefly cant or C*), keeping, kelter *or* kilter (*C or dial.*), case (*R*), tone, order, affection (*R or A*).
3. *Referring to a mode of existence:* phase, stage, mode (*tech.*), modus (*tech.*).
4. government, commonwealth (*chiefly spec.*) country, polity (*tech. or B*); *spec.* power, potentate (*rhetorical for "power"*), democracy, aristocracy, republic, monarchy, toparchy, dictatorship, federation, confederation, confederacy; *see* REPUBLIC, MONARCHY. *Most of the synonyms of "government" are also used for a state having such a government.*

state, *v. t.* **1.** *See* EXPRESS, NARRATE, REPORT, PROPOSE, RESTATE.
2. affirm, have, assert; *spec.* (*or in a transferred sense*) declare, insist, asseverate, protest, predicate, aver, allege, expound, avow, avouch, vouch (*R*), warrant, profess, say, speak, pronounce, enounce, proclaim, testify (*Biblical*), premise (*logic*), preface (*R*), plead, bulletin, swear.
Antonyms: see ABJURE.

statecraft, *n.* diplomacy, statesmanship, policy; *spec.* courtcraft.

stated, *a.* **1.** fixed, settled, given.
2. fixed, set.

statement, *n.* **1.** *See* EXPRESSION, ACCOUNT, PROPOSITION.
2. affirmance, affirmation, assertion; *spec.* (*or in a transferred sense*) declaration, insistence, asseveration, protestation, proposition, predication, protest (*R*), averment, allegation, avowal, exposition, vouch (*R*), vouchment (*R*), predicament (*tech. or R*), pretension (*R*).
Antonyms: see DENIAL.
3. *Referring to what is stated: spec.* allegation predicate, protest, thesis (*tech. or spec.*), pronouncement, saying, testification (*Biblical*), pronunciamento, platform, affidavit, pleading, scheme, schedule, memorial, case (*law*), ipse dixit, dictum, theorem (*a proposition viewed as something to be proved, where* problem *implies something to be done*), bulletin; *see* SAYING, REPORT, PROPOSAL, FORMULATION, NARRATIVE.
4. *Referring to a document setting forth a status of financial facts: spec.* bill, budget, showing (*chiefly U. S.*).

statesman, *n.* politician, politicaster (*contemptuous*), statist (*A*), politico (*R*).

station, *n.* **1.** *See* PLACE, POSITION, DIGNITY, RANK.
2. *Spec.* post, depot (*mil.*), camp, encampment, garrison, factory.
3. stopping place, stop; *spec.* stand, depot (*U. S.*), terminal (*U. S.*), stationette (*a nonce word*).

station, *v. t.* place, post, stand, plant; *spec.* garrison, quarter, lodge, picket.

statue, *n.* image, piece (*contex.*); *spec.* statuette, sculpture, bronze, colossus, term, terminus, figurine.

stay, *v. i.* **1.** remain, rest, stop (*not in good usage in this sense*), continue, abide (*B or R*), bide (*A*), lie, sit, keep, dwell (*A*); *spec.* hang, sojourn, nestle, sist (*Scots law*); *see* DELAY.
Antonyms: see DEPART, FLEE.
2. *See* CONTINUE, DESIST.

stay, *n.* **1.** remain (*R*), continuance, rest, stop (*not in good usage in this sense*), abode (*B or R*); *spec.* sojourn; *see* DELAY.
2. *Spec.* continuance, desistance.

steal, *v. t.* **1.** appropriate (*contex.*); *often euphemistic*), thieve (*R*), lift, purloin, crib (*C*), take (*contex.*), convert (*contex.*), snatch (*contex. or S*), rifle, plunder, filch, cabbage (*S or tailors' cant*), cly (*thieves' cant*), convey (*a euphemism*), nobble (*S*), nim (*A*), pinch (*S*), abstract (*S*), bob (*S or cant*), prig (*S or cant*), hook (*S or cant*), rob (*R or spec.*), bone (*S*); *spec.* misappropriate, pilfer, peculate (*R*), finger.
2. *See* MOVE.

steal, *v. i.* **1.** thieve, lift, purloin, rob (*R or spec.*), crib (*C*), filch (*referring to objects that can be carried off*), pilfer (*esp. of petty theft*), peculate, shoplift; *spec.* embezzle.
2. move, slip, slide, slink, sneak, creep, lurk (*R*).

steamer, *n.* puffer (*C or contex.*), steamboat (*chiefly spec.*); *spec.* steamship, tug, propeller, sidewheeler, greyhound. *"Steamer" is chiefly spec.*

steep, *a.* hilly (*contex.*), declivitous, high-pitched, brant (*obs. or dial.*), steepy (*R*), arduous (*fig.*), heavy, abrupt, bold, proclivous (*R*); *spec.* hanging (*as in "hanging gardens"*); *see* PRECIPITOUS.
Antonyms: see MODERATE.

steeplechase, *n.* grind (*Eng. university S*).

steer, *v. t.* **1.** guide (*contex.*), direct, navigate, con *or* cond *or* cund (*tech.*), helm (*chiefly spec.*), pilot (*often spec.*).
2. *See* GUIDE.

steer, *v. i.* stand, course (*R*), point.

steerage, *n.* **1.** steering, guidance, direction,

---

stately: *dignified, imposing, grand.*
stay, *n.: support, brace.*
stay, *n.: stoppage, stop.*
stay, *v. t.: stop, fix, restrain, detain, defer.*
steady, *a.: firm, constant, uniform, sober.*
stealthy, *a.: secret, thievish.*

---

pilotage (*often spec.*), pilotism (*R*), pilotry (*R*).
2. *See* GUIDANCE.
steersman, *n.* steerer, helmsman, pilot (*often spec.*); *spec.* coxswain, hoveler *or* hoveller (*Eng.*), manjee (*Anglo-Indian*), nobbler (*Eng.*), patroon (*R*), patron (*R*), wheelman, sluer.
stem, *n.* **1.** stock, caudex (*tech.*), axis (*tech.*); *spec.* cane, kex (*obs. or dial.*), creeper, runner, brier *or* briar, pedestal, caulome (*tech.*); *see* STALK, TRUNK.
2. bow, cutwater.
3. *In philology:* base, theme (*tech.*), thema (*R*).
4. shank, shaft, stalk, pillar.
5. *See* RACE.
step, *v. i.* **1.** tread; *spec.* tramp, clamp, clump (*heavy and stolid*), stride, trip, pace.
2. *See* GO, WALK.
step, *n.* **1.** tread, footstep; *spec.* tramp, stride, pace, clamp (*chiefly dial.*), footstep, trip.
2. *Referring to dancing: spec.* chassé, whirl, coupee (*dancing*), drag, *etc.*
3. *Referring to a rest for the foot, as in stairs:* tread, pace (*R*), degree (*obs., exc. heraldry*); *spec.* flyer, gradin *or* gradine, half-pace, winder, rung, stile.
4. *See* GAIT, MARCH, FOOTPRINT, ACTION, DEGREE, INTERVAL.
stepfather, *n.* good-father (*Scot.*).
stepmother, *n.* good-mother (*Scot.*). *The adjective for "stepmother" is "novercal."*
sterilize, *v. t.* asepticize, aseptify (*R*); *spec.* disinfect.
stern, *a.* **1.** unyielding, grim, grimmish (*R*), grimly (*A*), gaunt (*B or A*), dour (*Scot.*), hard; *see* RELENTLESS, REPELLENT.
Antonyms: see AFFECTIONATE, GENTLE, KINDLY.
2. *See* AUSTERE, SEVERE, SHARP, FIERCE, RELENTLESS, MERCILESS.
stern, *n. Referring to a vessel:* buttocks (*R*); *spec.* counter, poop.
stevedore, *n. Spec.* roustabout (*U. S.*), hobbler (*Eng.*), longshoreman.
stew, *v. t.* cook (*contex.*), boil, coddle, seethe, simmer; *spec.* curry.
stew, *n.* **1.** *Referring to the action:* boil, seethe, simmer.
2. *Referring to the dish: spec.* hodgepodge, olio, ollapodrida, curry, colcannon, lobscouse, pepperpot.
3. *See* FRET.
steward, *n.* **1.** agent (*contex.*), stewardess (*fem.*); *spec.* bailiff, husband, hind (*local Eng.*), dewan (*Anglo-Indian*), chamberlain, seneschal major-domo, khansamah *or* khansaman, sirkar (*Anglo-Indian*), maître d'hôtel (*French*).
2. purser.
stick, *n.* **1.** *Referring to a piece of wood, usually one long in relation to its breadth or diameter: spec.* spar, billet, cue, rod, walking-stick, cane; *see* BRANCH, TWIG, STAKE, POLE, SWITCH, MAST, RUNG, CLUB.
2. *Spec.* hesitation, stickiness, stab.
stick, *v. t.* **1.** *See* STAB, THRUST, PUT, TRANSFIX, SMEAR, FASTEN.
2. agglutinate (*R or B*); *spec.* wafer, cement, freeze.
stick, *v. i.* **1.** adhere, cling, take (*chiefly cant*); *spec.* cleave, hold, mire, freeze, jam.
2. *Referring to mental action:* adhere, hold, cleave, cling, abide, hang, persist.
3. *See* BIND, HESITATE.
sticky, *a.* adhesive, tenacious, clingy (*R*), clinging, cohesive, viscous (*B or tech.*), viscid (*B or tech.*), glutinous (*B or tech.*) agglutinative (*B*); *spec.* clammy, clam (*dial.*), gluey, pasty, stringy, ropy, cledgy (*Eng. dial.*), gummy, dauby, cementitious (*R*), fat, strong, tacky (*chiefly cant*), smeary (*R*), clarty (*dial.*), cloggy, plastery, mucilaginous.
stiff, *a.* **1.** firm, rigid, unlimber (*R*), unpliant (*R*), crisp; *spec.* stark (*suggesting the rigidity of death*), heavy (*chiefly dial.*); *see* UNYIELDING, TENSE.
Antonyms: see FLEXIBLE, LIMP, WILLOWY.
2. *Referring to what is hard to overcome:* hard, obstinate, pertinacious; *see* UNYIELDING, DIFFICULT.
3. *Referring to manners, style, etc.:* constrained, cramped, budge (*obs. or A*), buckram (*fig.*), prim, starch, starched; *see* FORMAL.
Antonyms: see UNCONVENTIONAL, HOMELIKE.
4. *See* HIGH, STRONG, REPELLENT, CONVENTIONAL.
stiffen, *v. t.* **1.** *In a physical sense:* rigidify (*R*); *spec.* buckram, bone, size, starch, glue, *etc.*; *see* HARDEN, BRACE.
2. *Referring to prices:* harden.
3. *Referring to the mind, feelings, etc.: see* HARDEN.
stiffening, *a.* rigescent (*R*).
stiffness, *n. Spec.* firmness, rigidity, hardness, constraint, *etc. Cf.* STIFF.
still, *a.* **1.** motionless.
Antonyms: see AGITATED, LIVELY, RESTLESS, FLOWING.
2. *See* SILENT, CALM, STAGNANT, LOW.
3. *Referring to wines, beer, etc.:* dead.
still, *v. t.* **1.** quiet, bestill (*R*), immobilize (*R*).
Antonyms: see ROUSE, AGITATE.
2. *See* CALM, SILENCE.
still, *n.* stillatory (*R*); *spec.* retort, worm, serpentary, serpentine.
stimulant, *n.* **1.** *In a general sense:* stimulus (*more dignified than "stimulant"*), tonic (*fig.*), stirring; *spec.* fillip, sting, whetstone (*fig.*) incentive, encouragement, spur.
2. *In medicine:* cordial, tonic, cardiac; *spec.* restorative.
Antonyms: see NARCOTIC.
3. intoxicant; *spec.* liqueur, bracer, pick-me-up, eye-opener.
stimulate, *v. t.* **1.** excite, stir, goad, prick, actuate (*R*), brace, liven, rally; *spec.* elec-

stifle, *v. t.: suffocate, extinguish, repress, suppress.*
stifle, *v. i.: suffocate.*
stigma: *brand, extravasation, blotch, sully.*
stillness: *motionlessness, silence, calm.*

trify (*fig.*), sting, pique, fan, rouse, nettle; *see* ENCOURAGE.

Antonyms: see NUMB, DULL, PARALYZE.

2. *See* ROUSE.

stimulating, *a.* **1.** stimulant, stimulative, exciting; *spec.* inspiring, biting, lively, racy, spicy (*C*), electric (*fig.*), stinging, bracing, poignant, piquant, inflammatory (*fig.*), pungent (*fig.*); *see* SHARP.

Antonyms: see SEDATIVE, SOPORIFIC.

2. cardiac, cordial, tonic; *spec.* restorative.

sting, *v. t.* **1.** prick, urticate (*R*); *spec.* nettle.

2. *Referring to what causes a sharp tingling, as liquors or cold:* bite, nip.

3. *See* PAIN.

sting, *v. i.* **1.** prick, prickle, tingle; *spec.* nettle.

2. *Referring to the sensation:* tingle.

sting, *n.* **1.** *Referring to a stinging organ: spec.* ovipositor, dart, nettle.

2. *See* STIMULANT, PAIN.

3. *Referring to liquor, as wines, etc.:* bite, tang, edge, sharpness, zest, nip (*Scot. or C*).

4. *Referring to the feeling of being stimulated, often pleasantly:* tingle.

stinging, *a.* *Referring to speech, wit, etc.:* poignant, pungent, salt (*R*).

stingy, *a.* **1.** illiberal, close, miserly, niggardly *or* (*less usual, but more emphatic*) niggard, mean, parsimonious, penurious, sordid, close-fisted (*C*), pinching, cheese-paring (*C or contemptuous*), near (*R or A*), economical (*a euphemism*), miser (*A*), churlish (*A or B*), sparing, grudging, close-handed (*A*), hard-fisted (*C, R*), tight (*C*), hard, uncommunicative (*R*).

Antonyms: see GENEROUS, EXTRAVAGANT, WASTEFUL.

2. *See* SCANTY.

stint, *v. t.* **1.** *See* LIMIT.

2. economize, save (*euphemistic or contex.*), scant, scrimp, skimp, pinch.

Antonyms: see LAVISH, WASTE.

stipulate, *v. t.* arrange, provide, bespeak (*R or B*), condition.

stir, *v. t.* **1.** *See* MOVE, ROUSE, STIMULATE, EXCITE, RAISE.

2. *Spec.* stoke, poke, pole, spoon, beat, poker.

stirrer, *n.* *Spec.* poker, pole, strike, rabble, paddle, swizzle-stick (*C*).

stirrup-shaped, *a.* stapedial (*tech., or B*).

stitch, *n.* **1.** *See* PAIN.

2. *Spec.* backstitch, cross-stitch, blindstitch, hemstitch, feather stitch, tent stitch, petit point, tack, diamond, prickseam, overhand.

stock, *n.* **1.** *See* STAKE, TRUNK, STEM, ANCESTOR, RACE, FAMILY, BREED, FUND, MATERIAL, CAPITAL.

2. butt, thick; *spec.* handle.

3. supply, store (*suggests a quantity laid up against need, where* stock *suggests what is laid up as a basis of operations*), accumulation, budget; *spec.* repertoire (*French*), repertory.

stocky, *a.* thick-set, stumpy, stubby, stout, portly (*R*), close; *spec.* bunting; *see* FAT, SQUAT.

Antonyms: see LANKY.

stomach, *n.* belly (*not now in refined usage*), maw (*now only of animals, exc. ludicrous or contemptuous*), abdomen (*S or incorrect*), craw (*chiefly humorous or derisive, exc. spec.*); *spec.* ingluvies, proventriculus, gizzard, gorge, rumen *or* paunch, reticulum *or* bonnet, omasum, psalterium, manyplies, abomasum.

stomachic, *a.* gastric (*tech.*), gasteral (*R*).

stone, *n.* **1.** *In a collective or generic sense: spec.* metal, rubble; *see* ROCK, GRAVEL.

2. *Referring to a stone of any size:* rock (*Australia and C, U. S.*); *spec.* meteorite, megalith, hog, whetstone, grindstone; *see* GRAVESTONE.

3. *Referring to a small piece of rock:* pebble, cobble, cobblestone, coggle (*obs. or dial.*).

4. *Referring to the stone of a fruit:* pyrene (*tech.*), pit (*U. S.*).

5. *See* CALCULUS, GEM.

stone, *v. t.* **1.** *Spec.* pebble (*R*), cobble, pave, gravel.

2. lapidate (*R*).

stone, *a.* lithic (*tech.*), lithoid (*tech.*).

stony, *a.* **1.** rocky, petrous (*R exc. fig.*), lapideous (*R*), saceous (*R*), lapidose (*R or tech.*); *spec.* bowldery, pebbly, gravelly, shingly, gritty.

2. *See* UNYIELDING, UNFEELING, UNCOMPASSIONATE, COLD.

stool, *n.* **1.** *Spec.* tabouret, cricket, commode, nightchair, close, stool, cuckingstool, cutty-stool (*Scot.*), standrest, footstool.

2. *See* EXCREMENT.

stoop, *v. i.* **1.** lean, bend, incline, bow; *spec.* cower, slouch; *see* CROUCH.

Antonyms: see RISE.

2. *See* YIELD, CRINGE, SWOOP, CONDESCEND.

stoop, *n.* **1.** bend, inclination, stooping; *spec.* slouch, crouch, cower.

2. descent, condescension, vouchsafement, condescendence.

3. *See* SWOOP.

stooping, *a.* crouching, cowering, slouchy.

Antonyms: see ERECT.

stop, *v. t.* **1.** *See* CLOSE, OBSTRUCT.

2. *Referring to action not put forth by the person or thing that causes the stop:* check, arrest (*formal or B*), hold, stay (*B*); *spec.* resist (*contex.*), halt, intercept, bar, block, embar (*obs. or A*), stall (*obs. or R exc. spec., as when the engine of a car is stopped through being forced to too much load*), cease (*R*), belay (*sailors' S*), discontinue, pawl, field (*baseball*); *see* PREVENT, INTERRUPT, RESTRAIN, SUPPRESS, NONPLUS.

Antonyms: see IMPEL.

---

stir, *v. i.: move, rouse, bustle, act.*
stir, *n.: motion, activity, disturbance, commotion, bustle, fuss.*
stirring, *a.: exciting, stimulant, about.*

(*A*) *archaic.* (*B*) *bookish, poetic, literary or learned.* (*C*) *colloquial.* (*Contex.*) *contextual.* (*R*) *rare.* (*S*) *slang.* *See pp. viii–ix.*

3. *Referring to stopping one's own action:* cease, discontinue, quit (*U. S.*), belay (*sailors' S*), drop (*S; chiefly in "drop it"*), leave (*A*); *spec.* arrest, abandon.
Antonyms: see CONTINUE.
stop, *v. i.* **1.** desist (*chiefly B*), cease, surcease (*B, R*), stay (*B or formal and chiefly in the imperative*), discontinue (*formal*); *spec.* die (*usually with "out"*), pause, halt, leave, hesitate, breathe (*fig.*), stall, intermit; *see* END.
Antonyms: see CONTINUE.
2. *Referring to a cessation of a physical journey or progress:* stand, halt, prop (*Australia*), touch; *spec.* bait, noon, lodge, tarry.
3. *See* DELAY.
stop, *n.* **1.** stoppage, check, cessation, stay (*now B or tech.*), cease (*obs. exc. in "without cease"*), discontinuance, surcease (*B*); *spec.* block, desistance, pause, hesitation, halt, hitch (*C*), cæsura, intermission.
Antonyms: see CONTINUANCE.
2. stand, prop (*Australia*), jib (*R*); *spec.* check.
3. *In music:* register; *spec.* diapason, cromorna *or* cremona, tuba, celeste, flageolet, flute, *etc.*
4. *See* STATION, MARK, STOPPER, DELAY.
stop, *interj.* soft, hold, avast (*naut.*), quit (*C U. S.*); *spec.* silence, whoa, cut it out (*C*), pipe down (*C*).
stoppage, *n.* **1.** stop (*R*), stopping, stay (*chiefly legal*), arrest (*formal*), arrestment (*R*), discontinuance; *spec.* check, checking, resistance, interception; *see* END, PREVENTION, INTERRUPTION, SUPRESSION, CLOSURE, RESISTANCE.
Antonyms: see IMPULSE, CONTINUANCE, CONTINUATION.
2. *See* STOP.
stopper, *n.* stop, stopple; *spec.* cork, bung, plug, spigot, shive.
stopper, *v. t.* close, stop, stopple; *spec.* cork, spike, plug.
Antonyms: see OPEN.
storage, *n.* storing, stowage; *spec.* warehousing, tankage.
store, *n.* **1.** *See* STOREHOUSE, STOREROOM, SHOP.
2. supply, stock, accumulation, treasure (*B*); *spec.* mine, reserve, garner, hoard, magazine, cache, clamp (*cant*); *see* SAVING, FUND.
store, *v. t.* **1.** *See* FURNISH, ACCUMULATE, HOARD.
2. deposit, reposit (*R*), hive (*fig. only*), garner, treasure (*B, R*), entreasure (*R*); *spec.* magazine (*R*), hide, bury, cache, reserve, tank (*R*), reservoir, bottle, sack, warehouse.
storehouse, *n.* depository, repository, store (*U. S. and British colonies*), repertory (*B or R*), repertorium (*R*), treasury (*B*); *spec.* magazine (*mil.*), hive (*fig.*), golah (*Anglo-Indian*); *see* GRANARY, WAREHOUSE.
storeroom, *n.* depository, store; *spec.* loft (*U. S.*), cellar, larder.
stork, *n.* crane (*local*).
stork, *a.* pelargic (*R*).
storm, *n.* **1.** tempest (*B or rhetorical*), bluster (*fig.*), rack (*obs. or R*); *spec.* hurricane, cyclone, anticyclone, blizzard, blow (*S or C*), gale, brickfielder (*Australia*), tornado, whirlwind, squall, typhoon, snowfall, rainfall, *etc.*
Antonyms: see CALM.
2. *See* OUTBREAK, FLIGHT.
storm, *v. i.* **1.** *Referring to the elements:* rage, rave (*R*); *spec.* snow, rain, blow, hail, *etc.*
2. *See* RAGE, SCOLD, RUSH.
storm, *v. t. Spec. see* ASSAIL, ATTACK.
stormy, *a.* **1.** foul, rough, severe, tempestuous (*formal*), wild, dirty (*used esp. of wet weather at sea*); *spec.* oragious (*R*), breme (*obs. or B*), uproarious, rampant, rampageous (*C*), roaring, rainy, snowy, sleety, *etc.*; *see* WINDY, ROUGH.
Antonyms: see CALM.
2. *See* VIOLENT.
story, *n.* floor, stage, contignation (*R*); *spec.* basement, clerestory, loft, flat, mezzanine.
stove, *n.* **1.** *Spec.* heater, range, cockle, furnace, kiln.
2. *See* GLASSHOUSE.
straddle, *v. t. & i.* bestraddle (*v. t. only; an intensive*), stride (*R*), bestride (*v. t. only*), cross (*v. t. only; C*).
straggle, *v. i.* **1.** *See* WANDER.
2. draggle, tail, string, stretch.
Antonyms: see CROWD.
straight, *a.* **1.** right, direct; *spec.* straightlined, rectilinear, (*of hair*) lank, lanky.
Antonyms: see ANGULAR, BENT, CURVED, CROOKED, DEVIOUS, SINUOUS, ZIGZAG.
2. *See* ERECT, UPRIGHT, INFERABLE.
straight, *adv.* **1.** directly, dead, right, forthright (*A*), outright (*A*).
2. *See* IMMEDIATELY.
straightedge, *n.* staff; *spec.* strickle, strick.
straighten, *v. t.* straight (*R*).
Antonyms: see CURVE.
strain, *n.* **1.** *See* RACE, FAMILY, TRACE, NOTE, SONG.
2. *In music:* diapason (*tech.*), fit *or* fytte (*R*), stave, snatch, point (*A*).
3. *Referring to conduct, way of talking, etc.:* passage, flight, movement, vein, tone.
strain, *v. t.* **1.** stress; *see* STRETCH, BEND, DEFORM, PERVERT.
2. bend, tax, task.
3. overstrain (*intensive*), try, outstrain (*R*), overtax; *spec.* overexert, screw, rack, wrench, outstretch (*R*), overstretch (*R*); *see* SPRAIN.
4. separate (*contex.*), percolate, transcolate (*R*); *spec.* colander, elutriate; *see* FILTRATE.
strain, *n.* **1.** stress, tension, tensity; *see* FORCE, EFFORT.
2. tax, burden, task.
3. overstrain, overtax; *spec.* wrench; *see* SPRAIN.
strainer, *n.* sieve, colature (*R*), colatory (*R*); *spec.* bolter, physeter, colander, filter.

---

stop-gap: *expedient.*
story: *account, history, narrative, legend, fable.*
stout: *firm, big, fat, brave, courageous, hardy, stalwart, strong.*
stow: *pack, hide, furl, hold.*

strand, *n.* **1.** string, twist; *spec.* sliver.
2. *See* FIBER.
stranger, *n.* unknown.
Antonyms: see ACQUAINTANCE.
strap, *n.* band (*contex.*), strip, strop (*chiefly spec.*); *spec.* enarme (*armor*), crupper, jess (*falconry*), martingale.
strategy, *n.* **1.** *Spec.* generalship, tactics.
2. *See* ARTIFICE.
stratified, *a.* stratiform (*tech. or B*), layered; *see* LAMINATE.
stratum, *n.* layer; *spec.* (*in geol.*) post, measure, magma.
straw-colored, *a.* yellow, stramineous (*B*), festucine (*R*).
stray, *v. i.* **1.** deviate, exorbitate (*A*), estray (*A*), extravagate (*R*), range, err (*chiefly fig.; now A*); *see* WANDER.
Antonyms: see GATHER, CONVENE.
2. *See* ERR.
stray, *a.* **1.** deviating, strayed, astray, errant (*B*); *see* WANDERING
2. *See* ACCIDENTAL
streak, *n.* **1.** stripe, vein, fleck, flake, stria (*tech.*), striation (*tech.*); *spec.* thread, band, line, interstriation, slick, vitta (*tech.*), penciling, seam, ridge, furrow.
2. *See* TRACE.
streak, *v. t.* stripe, vein, fleck, flake, striate (*tech.*); *spec.* pencil, tabby, line, bestreak (*intensive; R*), band.
streaked, *a.* striped, veined, striate (*tech.*), flecked; *spec.* lined, rowy, penciled *or* (*tech.*) pencilate, brinded, brindled, tabby.
stream, *n.* **1.** flow, run, current, rindle (*R or dial.*), fleet (*local Eng.*), flood (*obs. or B*), fresh, kill (*local U. S.; chiefly in proper names*); *spec.* coulee, confluent, affluent; *see* RIVER, RIVULET, BROOK, TRIBUTARY, STREAMLET.
2. *See* FLOW, SERIES.
stream, *v. i.* **1.** flow, run, rindle (*R or dial.*), rill (*R*); *spec.* drill (*R or dial.*), trickle, discharge, spout.
2. *See* MOVE, HANG, EXTEND.
streamlet, *n.* stream, rill, trickle, drill (*R or dial.*); *see* RIVULET, BROOK.
street car, *n.* trolley car, tram (*chiefly Brit.*).
street-cleaner, *n.* scavenger (*formal*), orderly (*Eng.*), white-wing (*S; local U. S.*).
strength, *n.* **1.** *Referring merely to capacity to exert force: see* POWER.
2. *Referring to the capacity of man or beast to exert force:* sinew *or* (*pl.*) sinews, nerve, muscle, brawn, stamina, thew *or* (*pl.*) thews (*A*), sturdiness (*R*), stoutness, foison (*chiefly Scot.*), main (*obs. exc. in "with might and main"*), doughtiness (*B; A or humorous*); *spec.* arm (*fig.*); *see* STALWARTNESS. *See also the general terms under* POWER.
Antonyms: see WEAKNESS.
3. *Referring to the mere capacity to resist force:* solidity, toughness, stoutness, stanchness, robustiousness (*R or humorous*); *see* FIRMNESS.
Antonyms: see WEAKNESS.
4. *Referring to the wind:* freshness, briskness.
5. *Referring to alcoholic liquors:* body, potency (*formal*), potence (*R*), authority (*humorous*), kick (*S*); *spec.* proof.
6. *Spec.* adhesiveness, stickiness, effectiveness, hardiness, vigor, determination, activity, decidedness, violence, intensity, acuteness, brilliance, ability, influence, loudness, depth, energy, cogency, emphasis, stress, durability.
strengthen, *v. t.* **1.** *Referring to a physical structural strengthening:* fortify (*R exc. spec.*), reinforce *or* reënforce, support, buttress (*fig. or spec.*); *see* BRACE.
Antonyms: see WEAKEN.
2. *Referring to an increase in power, or capacity to exert force:* invigorate, invigor (*R*), potentiate (*R*), reënforce *or* reinforce, fortify; *spec.* recruit, enforce, reman, flank, fortify, gird, freshen.
Antonyms: see WEAKEN, EXHAUST, BLIGHT, ENERVATE.
3. *Referring only to the strength of man or animal:* indurate, sinew, nerve, vitalize, harden, brace. *See also def.* **2**, *above.*
Antonyms: see WEAKEN, ENERVATE, EXHAUST.
4. *Referring to a making more secure, unchangeable, or probable in respect of ideas, habits, opinions, etc.:* confirm, fortify, roborate (*R*), encourage, clench, clinch, corroborate (*R*); heighten.
Antonyms: see WEAKEN.
5. *Referring to the voice:* raise, rear (*R, A*).
6. *See* AID, INTENSIFY, SUPPORT, CHEER, ENCOURAGE, CONCENTRATE.
stretch, *v. t.* **1.** *See* EXTEND, EXAGGERATE, EXCEED.
2. strain (*contex.*), draw (*contex.*), pull (*contex., exc. as with "out"*), tense (*R*), tenter; *spec.* screw, brace, beam, rack, finedraw, wiredraw (*often fig.*), crane; *see* EXPAND, DISTEND, BEND.
Antonyms: see CONTRACT, SQUEEZE, PRESS.
stretched, *a.* tense, taut, strict.
stretcher, *n.* **1.** *Spec.* tent, tenter, temple.
2. *See* LITTER.
stretching, *a.* tensive.
strict, *a.* **1.** *See* TIGHT, STRETCHED, ACCURATE, RESTRICTED.
2. unyielding, inflexible, unswerving, uncompromising, stringent, severe, exact, rigorous, rigid, strait (*A*), precise, nice, punctual (*A*), scrupulous, extreme.

strange: *foreign, unfamiliar, surprising, odd, inexperienced, distant, bashful, distrustful.*
stranger: *foreigner, visitor, intruder.*
strenuous: *energetic, spirited, vigorous.*
stress, *v. t.: strain, accent, emphasize.*
stress, *n.: force, constraint, strain, height, effort, importance, accent, emphasis.*
stretch, *n.: scope, effort, expanse, flight.*
stricken: *blighted.*
stricture: *censure.*
stride, *v. i.: step, walk.*
strife: *emulation, contention, dissension, dispute.*

Antonyms: see LAX.
3. *Referring only to morals, religious practices, etc.:* strait-laced, puritanical, blue; *see* SCRUPULOUS, CONSCIENTIOUS, AUSTERE.
Antonyms: see LAX.

strike, *v. t.* **1.** *In the general sense of to cause to be impinged upon:* impinge (*R or tech.*), hit, smite (*A or rhetorical*), verberate (*R*), take (*contex.*).
2. *With special implications:* bang, baste (*C*), thwack, bethwack (*intensive*), belabor, box, buffet, clour (*Scot. or dial.*), cob (*C*), crack (*chiefly S*), dash, flail, hurtle (*R*), job, smash, pash (*A or R*), pick, plug (*S*), punch, rap, slam, slash, slug (*C*), smack, swipe (*C*), whang (*dial. or C*), whop (*C*), fisticuff, clout, saber, sabre, cut, bunt, bowl, dolly, stamp, butt, cane, cannon, foul, nob (*boxing S*), knee, brake, beat, cudgel, fist, flap, flip, harpoon, knock, lash, peck, pelt, pound, punch, shock, shoot, slap, percuss, switch, drum, tap, thrash, whip.
3. *In the sense of to cause (a thing) to impinge:* impinge (*R*), hit, smite (*A or rhetorical*), collide (*R*); *spec.* bang, bound, crack (*S*), drive, dash, hurtle, rap, slam, slash, smack, stamp, beat, clash, flap, knock, lash, pelt, pound, slap, switch, drum, tap, thrash, whip.
4. *See* DEAL, IGNITE, HOOK, LOWER, AFFLICT, BLIGHT, DISCOVER, ASSUME, SOUND, MAKE, MEET, AFFECT, FLATTEN.

strike, *v. i.* **1.** impinge (*R*), hit, smite (*A or rhetorical*); *spec.* buffet, cannon, clash, clatter, crash, smash, dash, drive, jar, knock, pat, patter, peck, pelt, spat (*C*), tattoo, thud; *see* GLANCE.
2. *To make a stroke (at): spec.* smite (*A or rhetorical*), slash, smash.
3. *See* COLLIDE, GO, HAPPEN, ROOT, SOUND.

strike, *n.* **1.** *See* STROKE, DISCOVERY.
2. turnout, walkout (*cant*), tie-up (*C, U. S.*).

striking, *a.* **1.** percussive, percutient (*R*).
2. *See* NOTICEABLE.

striking, *n.* strike (*R*), percussion, verberation (*R*), illision (*R*).

string, *n.* **1.** band (*contex.*), line, cord, snare (*chiefly spec.*), thread (*chiefly spec.*), chord (*now B*); *spec.* twine, cordon, cordonnet, cordeliere, braid, bride, gut, lace, leash, lead, lanyard, mese (*Greek music*), tape, wire (*music*).
2. *Referring to a series of things:* chain, estoon, rope; *spec.* chaplet, rosary.
3. *Spec.* gang, coffle, stud, file. *"String" is* (*C*).
4. *See* ROW, HOAX.

string, *v. t.* **1.** cord, rope; *spec.* shard, wire.
2. *See* FILE, EXTEND, HOAX.

string, *v. i.* **1.** rope, fibrillate.
2. *See* STRAGGLE.

stringcourse, *n.* table, tablet *or* tablette (*R*), tablement (*R*); *spec.* ledgment *or* ledgement.

stringy, *a.* **1.** cordy (*R*), ropy; *see* FILAMENTOUS.
2. *See* STICKY.

strip, *n.* **1.** slip, ribbon *or* ribband (*chiefly spec. or tech.*); *spec.* ligula (*tech.*), ligule (*R*), counterlath, rand (*obs. or dial.*), skelp, list, rod, lath, label, welt, tape; *see* STRAP, THONG.
2. stripe; *spec.* screed, headland, listel, fillet; *see* BAND.

strip, *v. t.* **1.** *See* DEPRIVE, PLUNDER, HULL, SKIN.
2. bare, disfurnish (*R*), deplenish (*R*), displenish (*Scot.*), disinvest (*R*), divest, skin (*C or spec.*); *spec.* dismantle, peel, disgarnish (*B*), disarm, defoliate, deforest, disflower, deflorate, dismast, plume (*R*), displume (*R*), glean; *see* DISMANTLE.
Antonyms: see COVER.
3. bare, undress, disrobe, disvest (*B or tech.*), divest (*B*), disinvest (*R*), denude, disarray (*B*), peel (*C or S*); *spec.* uncloak.
Antonyms: see CLOTHE.

strive, *v. i.* **1.** endeavor, strain, labor.
2. *See* CONTEND, QUARREL.

stroke, *n.* **1.** strike (*R*), smite (*A or rhetorical*), impact, hit, percussion (*chiefly spec.*); *spec.* BLOW, KNOCK, GLANCE, DRUMBEAT, TAP, SLAP, SWITCH, LASH, FLAP.
2. *With more special implications: spec.* chuck, pick, peck, pat, flick, bob, lick, bunt, touch, rap.
3. *In games:* shot, hit; *spec.* follow, return, fluke, hazard, jenny, masse, screw, string, snick, take-off, roquet, boast, foul, cut, foozle, loft, putt *or* put, lob.
4. action, hit.
5. *See* ATTACK, PARALYSIS, PULSATION, MOVEMENT, CARESS, LINE, SOUND, FLOURISH, SARCASM.

stroke, *v. t. Spec.* palm, lick, pat, flick, peck; *see* RUB, CARESS.

stroll, *v. i.* saunter, loiter, lounge, troll (*R*), spatiate (*R*), dander (*Scot.*); *spec.* ramble.

stroll, *n.* saunter, loiter, lounge, spatiation (*R*); *spec.* ramble.

stroller, *n.* saunterer, loiterer, *etc.*

strolling, *n.* sauntering, *etc.*

strong, *a.* **1.** *Referring merely to the capacity to exert force: see* POWERFUL.
2. *Referring to the strength of man or beast:* sinewy, nervy, sinewous (*R*), nervous (*spec., exc. fig.*), muscular (*spec., exc. fig.*), brawny, sturdy, stout, husky (*C, U. S.*), doughty (*B, A or humorous*), robustious (*chiefly A; often humorous*), Herculean (*fig.*), Atlantean (*fig.*), buckra (*S, southern U. S.*); *spec.* tough; *see* STALWART. *See also the general words under* POWERFUL.
Antonyms: see WEAK, EXHAUSTED, POWERLESS, WEAKLY.
3. *Referring to the mere capacity to resist force:* solid, tough, stout, stanch, robustious (*R or humorous*); *see* FIRM.
Antonyms: see WEAK, BRITTLE, CRUMBLY, FLIMSY.
4. *Referring to the wind:* powerful, lively, smart, virent (*R*); *spec.* brisk, fresh, freshish.
Antonyms: see WEAK.

---

stripe, *n.: band, streak, strip, kind.*

5. *Referring to alcoholic liquors:* full, solid (*R*) nappy, bodied, stiff, heavy, hard, powerful.
6. *Referring to an odor or smell: spec.* gamy, high, hot; *see* RANK.
7. *Referring to the feelings:* powerful, forcible, masterful; *see* INTENSE.
8. *See* STICKY, HARDY, VIGOROUS, DETERMINED, ACTIVE, DECIDED, VIOLENT, ABLE, BRIGHT, INFLUENTIAL, LOUD, DEEP, ENERGETIC, EMPHATIC, COGENT.
"Strong" can be used as a synonym of very many words that denote more than usual activity, intensity, or the like.
stronghold, *n.* hold, fastness; *see* FORTIFICATION, REFUGE.
struck, *p. a.* smitten (*A or rhetorical*).
structural, *a.* constructional, constitutive (*R, exc. spec.*), conformational (*R*), textural, organic; *spec.* geotectonic, tectonic, architectural.
structure, *n.* **1.** *These senses relate to the conceptual idea of the material, organization or plan by which something is made. They are analytical in approach*: make, build, frame, constitution (*as determining its character*), composition, construction, organization, make-up, texture (*the finer sense of the arrangement of parts of the* structure), conformation (*relation of parts*), nature (*contex.*), tissue (*chiefly spec.*), schematism (*R*), physique (*chiefly spec.*), organism (*R*), framing; *spec.* malconformation; *see* ARCHITECTURE.
2. *These senses relate to actual material parts of the material concept,* structure: frame, framework, fabric, texture (*the actual arrangement of the minute parts of material in* structure), work, shell, case, skeleton, carcass, corpus, machine (*R*), erection, compages (*B*); *spec.* contignation (*R*), superstructure, network, cradle, trestle, truss, crib, chassis, creel, grillage, cage, gridiron, grid, cortex; *see* BUILDING.
structureless, *a.* unformed, unorganized.
struggle, *v. i.* **1.** reluctate (*R*), sprawl (*obs. or R*), reluct (*R*), agonize (*R*); *spec.* wrestle, tussle, scramble, scuffle, wriggle, kick; *see* CONTEND.
Antonyms: see YIELD.
2. *See* ENDEAVOR.
struggle, *n.* **1.** reluctation (*R*), reluctance (*R*); *spec.* wrestle, scramble, wriggle, scuffle; *see* CONTEST.
2. *See* ENDEAVOR, EFFORT.
struggling, *a.* reluctant (*R*).
strut, *v. i.* cock (*fig.*), prance, swell, major, peacock (*fig.*), flaunt, bestrut (*an intensive*), brank (*A or Scot.*), perk; *see* SWAGGER.
strut, *n.* cock, prance; *see* SWAGGER.
stub, *n.* **1.** *See* STUMP, END.
2. *Remainder of a check, etc.:* counterfoil.
stub, *v. t.* **1.** *See* CLEAR.
2. *Referring to the toe:* strike, stump (*C*).
stubble, *n.* eddish (*tech.; Eng.*).
stubby, *a.* **1.** rough, stubbly.
2. *See* STOCKY.
stud, *v. t.* **1.** *See* SUPPORT, SPOT.
2. boss, emboss, bestud (*an intensive*), set, beset (*an intensive*), knot (*R*).
studded, *a.* bossy, bossed, embossed, set, beset; *spec.* naily.
student, *n.* **1.** pupil, scholar (*in U. S.* scholar *is used chiefly of mature persons of wide intellectual powers and achievement; but in Brit. usage* scholar *implies also commonly a person enrolled in school or college; in the latter sense* student, *while general in the U. S., is R in Brit.*), undergraduate, studier (*R*), bookman (*R*), lucubrator (*R*).
2. *Of earnest or good* students: bookworm, grind, shark (*C*), dig (*S*), sap (*S*), opsimath (*R*); *see* SCHOLAR.
Antonyms: see TEACHER.
studio, *n.* workroom, atelier (*French*).
studious, *a.* **1.** booky, bookish.
2. *See* ATTENTIVE, DILIGENT.
study, *n.* **1.** lucubration (*B*); *spec.* cram, pilpul.
2. *See* CONSIDERATION, EXERCISE, OBJECT, SKETCH.
study, *v. i.* **1.** lucubrate (*R*), read (*contex.*), con (*A or dial.*); *spec.* pore (*chiefly with "over"*), grind, sap (*school S*), dig (*C*), cram (*S*).
Antonyms: see PLAY.
2. *See* CONSIDER.
study, *v. t.* **1.** read (*contex.*); *spec.* grind (*C*), dig (*C or S*), con (*A or dial.*), cram (*S*).
2. *See* CONSIDER, PLAN.
stuff, *v. t.* fill (*contex.*), ram, cram; *spec.* pad, pack, wad, flock, lard.
Antonyms: see EMPTY.
stuffing, *n. Spec.* padding, wadding, excelsior, dressing.
stultify, *v. t.* besot, duncify (*R*), idiotize (*B or fig.*).
stumblingblock, *n.* offense (*A*), scandal (*a religious term*).
stump, *n.* **1.** stub, snag (*chiefly spec.*), scrag (*chiefly dial.*), stool (*R*); *see* LOG.
2. remnant, stub; *spec.* dock.
3. *See* CHALLENGE.
stunt, *v. t. Referring to growth:* check, cramp, nip; *see* DWARF.
stunted, *a.* undergrown, checked, nipped, runtish, scrubby; *spec.* dwarfish.
stupefaction, *n.* **1.** confusion, bewilderment, petrifaction (*R*), paralysis (*chiefly spec.*), dazing, obfuscation (*R*), stunning, *etc.*
2. *See* STUPOR, INTOXICATION.
stupefactive, *a.* stupefacient, confusing, *etc.*, torporific (*R*), carotic (*R*), narcotic, dazing; *spec.* intoxicating, dazzling.
stupefied, *a.* confused, dazed, benumbed, dazy (*R*), stupent (*R*); *spec.* comatose, intoxicated.
Antonyms: see ALERT.

studied: *deliberate, elaborate.*
stumble, *v. i.: misstep, falter, blunder, err, happen.*
stumble, *n.: misstep, falter, blunder, error.*
stun: *stupefy, shock, deafen, surprise.*

stupefy, *v. t.* confuse, confound (*A*), obfuscate (*R*), obstupefy (*R*), dull; *spec.* bewilder, stun, daze, muddle, besot (*chiefly spec.*), benumb maze (*A*), bemuse (*A*), dare (*obs. or dial. Eng.*), daver (*Eng. dial.*), deaden, petrify, paralyze, dullify (*C*), entrance, narcotize, opiate (*R*), drug, intoxicate, dazzle.

Antonyms: see ROUSE.

stupid, *a.* unintelligent, witless, thoughtless (*R*), stolid, heavy, brainless, vacant, empty, dull, inept (*B*), senseless, dull-witted, dense, inane, fatuous (*B*), slow, obtuse, insulse (*R*), crass, asinine, doltish, fat (*C*), fat-headed (*C*), flat, incapacious, wooden, wooden-headed, headless (*R*), dotish *or* doatish (*R*), doting *or* doating (*R*), dumpish, anserine (*R*), purblind, cloddish, blockish, oafish (*R*), addle (*R*), addle-headed, fiddle-headed (*R*), pig-headed (*C*), buffle-headed, sottish (*chiefly spec.*), donkeyish (*R*), heavy-headed, dotardly (*R*), daft (*obs. or dial.*), Bœotian (*fig.*), stockish (*R*), hebete (*R*), hebetudinous (*R*); *spec.* foolish, idiotic, imbecile, driveling (*extremely contemptuous*).

Antonyms: see INTELLIGENT, CLEVER, SHARP, SHREWD, PRECOCIOUS, WITTY.

stupid, *n. See* SIMPLETON.

stupidity, *n.* witlessness (*R*), ineptitude (*B*), crassitude (*B*), density, opacity (*B, R*), inanity, fatuousness *or* fatuity (*B*), noodleism (*contemptuous*), noodledom (*contemptuous*), jackassery (*R, contemptuous*), jobbernowlism (*C*), hebetude (*R*), senselessness, dullness, *etc.*

Antonyms: see INTELLIGENCE, DISCERNMENT; *also cf.* CLEVER, SHARP, *etc.*

stupor, *n.* stupefaction, daze, confusion (*contex.*), lethargy, mazement (*R*), dazedness (*R*), dazement (*R*), deadness (*R*), lull (*R*); *spec.* narcotism, coma; *see* SLEEP.

style, *n.* **1.** *See* POINT, PEN, NAME.

2. mode, fashion, genre (*French*), manner, character, form, taste; *spec.* histrionism, gusto.

3. *Relating to expression:* diction, wording, phraseology; *spec.* cacology, euphuism, preciosity, Gongorism, Guevarism, journalese (*C*).

4. *Relating to a conventional standard, esp. in social relations, dress, etc.: spec.* fashion, pattern, model, vogue, chic (*French or S*), fashionableness, format, get-up, make, wear (*R or cant*), block, cut.

styliform, *a.* stylate, styloid, pen-shaped.

stylish, *a.* fashionable, modish, elegant, chic (*French or S*), genteel (*chiefly sarcastic*), high-toned (*a cheap or contemptuous term*), tony (*S or C; U. S. and colonial Eng.*), alamode; *spec.* dressy (*C*), smart.

Antonyms: see OLD-FASHIONED.

subdivide, *v. t.* divide (*contex.*), redivide.

subdual, *n.* subjection, subjugation, reduction, subduement (*R*); *spec.* downing (*C*), taming, *etc.; see* OVERCOMING, INTIMIDATION, MITIGATION.

subdue, *v. t.* subject, subjugate, allay; *spec.* down, milden, tame, curb, reduce, bend, bow, break; *see* OVERCOME, INTIMIDATE, MITIGATE, SUPPRESS.

subdued, *a.* subjected, reduced, redact (*obs. or R*); *spec.* chastened, dispirited.

Antonyms: see UNSUBDUED.

subject, *n.* **1.** *In a political sense:* liege, people (*a collective; contex.*). *A "citizen" is not a "subject."*

Antonyms: see LORD, RULER, MONARCH.

2. *Referring to one subjected to some action, power, or habit:* slave, patient.

Antonyms: see ACTOR.

3. *In hypnotism, spiritualism, etc.:* patient, medium, sensitive, sympathetic; *spec.* psychic, hypnotic.

4. matter, theme, topic, question, head, subject matter, object matter, text (*chiefly spec.*), locus (*a Latinism; R*); *spec.* lemma, food, leitmotiv (*German*), testo, dux.

5. *In logic:* premise.

6. *In metaphysics:* ego.

7. *In medicine: see* PATIENT.

subject, *v. t.* **1.** master, subjugate, break, enslave; *see* SUBDUE, OVERCOME.

2. expose, submit, surrender, abandon, put; *see* SUBORDINATE.

subjective, *a.* **1.** inner, interior, objective (*the use of the older medieval philosophy*).

Antonyms: see OBJECTIVE.

2. *See* INTROSPECTIVE, DECEPTIVE.

sublet, *v. t.* let (*contex.*), sublease, underlease, underlet, underset (*Eng.*).

submerge, *v. t.* **1.** *See* SINK.

2. whelm, drown, bury, submerse (*R*); *see* OVERFLOW.

submissive, *a.* yielding, passive, meek, tame, slavish, humble; *see* DEFERENTIAL, COMPLAISANT, RESIGNED, OBEDIENT.

Antonyms: see UNSUBMISSIVE, DEFIANT, ARROGANT, AUTHORITATIVE.

subordinate, *n.* inferior, sub (*C*), understrapper (*contemptuous*), underling (*depreciatory*); *spec.* subaltern (*chiefly mil.*), dependent.

subordinate, *a.* subsidiary, ancillary (*chiefly tech. or fig.*), servient (*chiefly tech.*); *spec.* dependent, understrapping (*R*); *see* SECONDARY, COLLATERAL.

Antonyms: see CHIEF, MASTER, RULING.

subordinate, *v. t.* subject, submit, postpone, postposit (*R*).

subordination, *n.* subjection, submission, subservience, servitude (*R*), subordinacy (*R*); *spec.* postponement.

subscribe, *v. t.* **1.** underwrite, undersign, postscribe; *see* SIGN.

2. *See* INSCRIBE, PROMISE.

---

sturdy: *determined, strong, hardy, stalwart.*
subject, *a.: servile, conditional.*
subjugate: *subdue, subject, overcome.*
sublimate, *v. t.: purify, idealize.*
submission: *yielding, offer.*
submit, *v. t.: subject, propose, present, offer, refer.*
submit, *v. i.: yield.*
suborn: *induce, bribe.*
subscription: *postscript, signature, accession, contribution.*

subsequent, *a.* **1.** *Referring to order or time:* following, sequent, after (*chiefly referring to time*), posterior, sequacious (*R*), sequential (*R*), latter, succeeding, successive, attendant (*contex.*).
Antonyms: see FORMER, PREVIOUS.
2. *Referring to time only:* later, future (*a loose usage*), postliminary (*R*), postliminious (*an erroneous use*).
Antonyms: see FORMER.
subside, *v. i.* **1.** *See* SINK.
2. lower, sink, settle, fall, drop, lapse.
subsidy, *n.* gift, grant, aid, allowance, contribution, subvention, bounty;—*all contex.*
Antonyms: see TAX.
subsoil, *n.* earth (*contex.*), substratum, undersoil; *spec.* pan.
substance, *n.* **1.** *See* ESSENCE, MATTER, MATERIAL, MEANING, WEALTH, ACTUALITY.
2. matter, substratum, essence (*tech.*), hyle (*obs. or tech.*), hypostasis (*tech.*), stuff.
3. body, sum, gist, heart, core, fullness, volume, gravamen (*tech.*), pith, content.
substitute, *n. Spec.* makeshift, apology, duplicate, succedaneum (*R*), surrogate (*R or spec.*), vicar, understudy, double (*these two chiefly in theater parlance*), representative, change, ghost (*C, for one who writes or prepares what another publishes or speaks*).
substitute, *v. t.* exchange (*contex.*), supposite (*R*), suffect (*R*), substiture, subrogate (*R or spec.*), surrogate (*R*).
substituted, *a.* vicarial (*R*), vicarious (*chiefly spec.; B*), suffected (*R*), subrogated (*R or spec.*).
substitution, *n.* exchange *or* change (*contex.*), shift, subrogation (*R or spec.*), surrogation (*R*); *spec.* enallage, novation.
subtle, *a.* **1.** *See* ATTENUATED, PENETRATIVE, ELUSIVE, NICE, DELICATE, INTELLIGENT, INGENIOUS, DISCERNING, ARTFUL.
2. profound, fine, refined, fine-spun, wire-drawn (*fig.*), superfine, nice, delicate, deep, subtile (*R if not extinct in current use*), astute, sharp, witty (*chiefly spec.*), serpentine (*B, fig.*), keen, exile (*A*).
Antonyms: see CRUDE.
subtlety, *n.* **1.** *See* ATTENUATION, NICENESS, NICETY, DELICACY, INTELLIGENCE, ART.
2. profundity, fineness, refinement, profoundness, delicacy, subtleness, subtileness (*R*), subtility (*R*), nicety, depth, astuteness, sharpness, wittiness (*chiefly spec.*), keenness, exility (*R*).
Antonyms: see CRUDENESS; *cf.* CRUDE.
3. *Referring to an argument, distinction, etc.:* profundity, quiddity (*R*), refinement, nicety.

suburb, *n.* outskirt, skirt (*often in pl.*).
subway, *n.* tube, underground (*chiefly Brit.*).
succeed, *v. t.* follow; *spec.* inherit, replace.
succeed, *v. i.* **1.** *See* FOLLOW.
2. *Referring to a person:* prosper, speed (*A*), prevail, cotton (*obs.*), win.
Antonyms: see FAIL.
3. *Referring to a thing:* go, do, take (*R or med.*), prevail.
Antonyms: see FAIL.
success, *n.* **1.** *See* FORTUNE.
2. prosperity, speed (*A*), hit (*C; often spec.*), go (*chiefly U. S.; C*).
Antonyms: see DEFEAT, FAILURE.
3. *Referring to what succeeds:* go (*chiefly U. S.; C*), hit (*C; often spec.*).
succession, *n.* **1.** following, sequence, consecution, consequence, rotation, seriality (*R*), procession, train (*usually with "of thought"*).
2. *See* DESCENT, SERIES.
3. inheritance; *spec.* reversion, entail (*R*).
successive, *a.* sequent, sequential, consecutive, serial, progressive, successional, contiguous; *spec.* ordinal; *see* FOLLOWING.
Antonyms: see PRECEDING.
successively, *a.* consecutively, serially, *etc.*, seriatim.
suck, *v. t.* **1.** draw (*contex.*), pull; *spec.* drink, inhale.
2. *See* ABSORB.
suck, *n.* draw, pull, suction (*formal or tech.*); *spec.* exsuction.
sucker, *n. Spec.* suckling, proboscis, haustellum, acetabulum, bothrium, haustorium, surculus.
sucking, *a.* **1.** sugent (*R*).
2. suctorial (*formal*), sugescent (*R; tech.*), suctional (*R*); *spec.* haustellate.
suckle, *v. t.* feed (*contex.*), nurse.
suckle, *v. i.* draw, suck, nurse, pull (*C*).
suckling, *n.* lactation.
sudden, *a.* **1.** abrupt, precipitant (*R*), subitaneous (*R*).
Antonyms: see GRADUAL, SLOW.
2. *See* ABRUPT.
suddenly, *adv.* slap (*C*), plump, presto, smack (*C*), pronto.
sudorific, *a.* sudoriferous, sudoriparous, hidrotic;—*all tech.*
sudorific, *n.* diaphoretic (*tech.*), sudatory (*tech.*), sweater.
suds, *n. pl.* lixivium (*tech.*).
suffer, *v. t.* **1.** experience (*contex.*), bear, endure, sustain, undergo; *spec.* receive, pay, get, take.
2. *See* ENDURE, PERMIT.

subservient: *subordinate, obsequious, obedient, serviceable, contributory, complaisant.*
subsidiary: *auxiliary, subordinate, accidental.*
subsidize: *bribe, aid.*
subsist, *v. i.: be, continue, consist, inhere, live, prevail, apply.*
substantial: *essential, important, considerable, massive, actual, influential, virtual, nourishing, pithy.*
substantialize: *actualize.*
substantiate: *actualize, embody, prove, confirm.*
subterfuge: *artifice, pretext, expedient.*
subtract: *deduct, abstract.*
subvention: *subsidy.*
successful: *fortunate, prosperous.*
succinct: *concise.*
sue, *v. t.: prosecute, court.*
sue, *v. i.: ask, court, appeal.*

suffer, *v. i.* groan, smart, agonize, sweat (*S*), smoke (*spec. or fig.*); *spec.* pay.
sufferance, *n.* permission.
sufferer, *n.* patient (*R*); *spec.* martyr, protomartyr.
suffering, *n.* **1.** sufferance (*A*), experience (*contex.*), endurance, bearing, sustainment, undergoing; *spec.* receiving, *etc.*, passion (*obs., exc. of Christ on the cross and of his agony in the Garden of Gethsemane*), pathos (*B*), teen (*A*), martyrdom; *see* PAIN.
2. *Spec.* endurance, permission.
suffice, *v. i.* serve, do, satisfy.
suffix, *n.* affix (*contex.*), ending, termination, postfix, addition (*contex.*), terminant (*R*).
Antonyms: see PREFIX.
suffix, *v. t.* affix (*contex.*), postfix.
suffocate, *v. t.* **1.** choke, smother, strangle (*chiefly spec.*), stifle, asphyxiate (*tech.*), spiflicate (*S*), scomfish (*Scot.*); *spec.* drown, overlie (*v. t. only*), charcoal; *see* CHOKE.
2. *See* EXTINGUISH.
suffocate, *v. i.* **1.** choke, smother, strangle (*chiefly spec.*), stifle, asphyxiate (*tech.*); *spec.* gulp.
2. *See* DIE.
suffocation, *n.* choking, smothering, asphyxiation, *etc.*
suffocative, *a.* choky, choking, stifling, smothery, strangly (*C*), pothery (*R*).
suffrage, *n.* **1.** *See* ACCESSION.
2. vote.
sugary, *a.* sweet, saccharine (*tech.*), saccharous (*R*); *spec.* honeyed.
Antonyms: see SOUR.
suggest, *v. t.* present, prompt, inspire; *see* INTIMATE, ADVANCE.
suggestion, *n.* **1.** presentation, prompting, inspiration, prompture (*R*); *see* INTIMATION, ADVANCE.
2. *Referring to what is suggested:* inspiration, cue (*chiefly spec.*), prompt (*R*); *see* INTIMATION.
suicide, *n.* **1.** homicide (*contex.*), self-destruction, self-murder, self-homicide (*R*), felo-de-se (*a loose use; Latin*), self-slaughter (*R*); *spec.* hara-kiri (*not "hari-kari"*), seppuku (*R*).
2. self-murderer, felo-de-se (*tech.; Latin*), self-destroyer.
suit, *v. i.* agree, fit, serve (*chiefly spec.*), sort (*A*).
suite, *n.* **1.** *See* RETINUE.
2. *Referring to rooms, furniture, etc.:* set, suit; *spec.* apartment, flat, conclave.
suitor, *n.* **1.** lover (*contex.*), beau, attendant (*contex.*), wooer, protestant (*R*), steady (*S or dial.*). *"Suitor" is formal.*
2. *See* LITIGANT.
sulk, *v. i.* pout, pet, mope, mump (*R*), grump (*R, C*), boody (*R*).
sulk, *n.* fit, pout, pet.
sullen, *a.* ill-tempered (*contex.*), sulky, glum, grum, glumpy (*R*), morose, moody, mumpish, dogged, doggish (*R*), cloudy.
Antonyms: see GOOD-NATURED, GAY, CHEERFUL, VIVACIOUS.
sullenness, *n.* ill temper, sulkiness, sulks (*pl.; C*), sullens (*pl.; C*), glumness, *etc.*
sully, *v. t.* **1.** *In a physical sense: see* SOIL, FOUL.
2. *In an immaterial sense:* stain, soil, blemish, tarnish, stigmatize (*R or B*), blot, blur, spot, cloud, blacken, darken, defile, foul, smirch, defame, asperse (*R*), denigrate (*R*), disluster *or* dislustre (*R*), dusk (*R*), attaint.
Antonyms: see PURIFY.
3. *See* CONTAMINATE.
sully, *n.* stain, stigma, blemish, tarnish, blot, blur, spot, cloud, smirch.
sullying, *n.* staining, soiling, defilement, *etc.*
sulphurous, *a.* sulphury, brimstony (*R*), hepatic (*tech.*).
sum, *n.* **1.** *See* AGGREGATE, QUANTITY, HEIGHT, SUBSTANCE.
2. amount, purse.
summarization, *n.* abridgment, summarizing, recapitulation, summing (*chiefly with "up"*), resumption.
summarize, *v. t.* abridge (*contex.*), sum (*chiefly with "up"*); *spec.* resume, abstract, recapitulate.
summary, *n.* abridgment, brief; *spec.* résumé (*French*), précis (*French*), abstract, capitulation, breve, breviate (*R*), breviary (*obs. or R*), continent (*A*), conclusum (*a term of diplomacy*).
summer, *n.* summertime, summertide (*B*); *spec.* midsummer.
Antonyms: see WINTER.
summer, *v. i.* æstivate (*tech. or B; chiefly spec.*).
Antonyms: see WINTER.
summer, *a.* æstival (*tech. or B*).
summerhouse, *n. Spec.* mahal (*East Indian*), kiosk.
summon, *v. t.* **1.** call, bid (*A*), cite, invoke (*R, exc. spec.*), summons (*C*), demand (*R*), ask; *spec.* drum, preconize (*R*), motion, bugle, muster, knell, lure, ring, subpœna, avoke, pipe; *see* CONVOKE, INVOKE.
2. *See* ROUSE, CALL (*in law*).
summoning, *a.* citatory, invocatory;—*both tech. or B.*
summons, *n.* call, bid (*A or S*), invocation, citation, calling; *spec.* alarum, larum (*A*), roll-call, subpœna; *see* CONVOCATION, INVOCATION.
sumptuary, *a.* expense.
sun, *n.* **1.** sol (*mythol. or B*), Phœbus (*fig. or Greek myth.*), daystar (*B*), Titan (*fig. or Greek myth.*); *spec.* mock sun, parhelion.
2. *See* SUNLIGHT, SUNRISE.
sun, *v. t.* solarize (*R*), insolate (*tech.*).
Sunday, *n.* Lord's Day, Sabbath, First Day.
sunlight, *n.* sunshine, sun (*fig.*), daylight, day (*contex.*), shine (*contex.*), light (*contex.*).
Antonyms: see SHADE.

---

sufficiency: *adequacy, ability, fortune, conceit.*
suit, *v. t.: adapt, answer, become.*
suitable: *agreeable, appropriate, becoming, applicable, worthy, ready.*
sulky: *ill-tempered, sullen.*
summary, *a.: concise.*
summit: *top, height.*

---

sunny, *a.* **1.** sunshiny; *see* CLEAR.
Antonyms: see SHADY, RAINY.
2. *See* CHEERFUL.
sunrise, *n.* sun (*contex.*), sun-up (*C, U. S.*).
sunset, *n.* sundown, nightfall, night, evensong (*A*), set (*B*).
sunwise, *a.* clockwise.
superficial, *a.* **1.** *See* SURFACE.
2. *Referring to mental qualities:* shallow, meretricious; *see* CURSORY.
Antonyms: see DEEP.
superfluity, *n.* **1.** *See* EXCESS.
2. *A superfluous thing:* neednot (*R*), fifth wheel (*fig.*).
Antonyms: see NECESSARY.
superhuman, *a.* preterhuman (*R*), transhuman (*R*); *spec.* seraphic (*B*), angelic, divine.
Antonyms: see HUMAN.
superior, *a.* **1.** *See* HIGHER, FINE, BETTER, ADVANTAGEOUS.
2. *Referring to superiority in general:* supreme, preëminent, paramount, palmary (*R*), topping, supereminent.
Antonyms: see INFERIOR.
3. *Referring to superiority in rank or office:* higher, upper, over, above; *see* DISTINGUISHED.
4. *Referring to precedence of rights:* precedent, senior, elder, preferent, prior.
superior, *n.* chief, head, boss, top-sawyer (*C*), higher-up (*S*); *spec.* mahaut (*East Indian*), suzerain, lord, liege *or* liege lord, domina, major, prior, prioress guardian.
Antonyms: see INFERIOR.
supernatural, *a.* preternatural (*formal or B*), supranatural (*R*), transnormal (*R*), marvelous, unearthly, hyperphysical, miraculous, metaphysical (*R*); *spec.* superhuman, superorganic.
Antonyms: see NATURAL.
supernumerary, *n.* supe *or* super (*C*); *spec.* figurant (*masc.*), figurante (*fem.*).
superpose, *v. t.* impose, superimpose.
supersensible, *a.* metaphysical; *spec.* spiritual, supernatural.
supersensual, *a.* supersensuous, supersensory.
superstition, *n.* believingness (*contex.*), belief (*contex.*); *spec.* (*and contextually*) tradition, idea, fear.
superstitious, *a.* believing (*contex.*); *spec.* (*and contextually*) fearful, credulous.
supplementary, *a.* additional, supplemental, suppletive, suppletory, parergal (*R*); *spec.* accessory.
supply, *n.* **1.** *See* STORE, STOCK, FURNISHING, FUND, SUBSTITUTE.
2. *Chiefly in pl.:* stores, crop, provision, stock; *see* AMMUNITION.
support, *v. t.* **1.** *The material senses:* bear, sustain, carry, uphold (*chiefly B*), hold; *spec.* corbel (*used with "out" or "off"*), cradle, pillow, truss; *see* PROP, BRACE, FLOAT.
2. *Referring to giving aid or favor to a person, cause, etc.:* strengthen, uphold, sustain, succor, maintain, second, back (*C*), champion (*primarily spec.*), patronize, reënforce *or* reinforce (*R*), float (*fig.*), tide (*with "over"*), sustentate (*R*); *spec.* grubstake, prop, bolster, patron (*R*), favor; *see* APPROVE, AID, DEFEND, ADVOCATE, JUSTIFY.
3. *Referring to provision of the upkeep of a person or thing:* maintain, subsist, keep; *spec.* winter, feed.
4. *Referring to making more probable by evidence, etc.:* strengthen, uphold, sustain; *see* EVIDENCE, CONFIRM, PROVE.
5. *See* ENDURE, STRENGTHEN, ACT, CONTINUE.
support, *n.* **1.** *Referring to the action of physically supporting:* sustentation, upholding, upbearing, sustenance (*R*), sustainment (*formal or R*), bearing.
2. *Referring to what supports physically:* rest, base; *spec.* bearing, bottom, seat, underpinning, bolster, prop, brandreth (*dial.*), stay, guy, potent (*A*), buttress, undersetter (*R*), pier, pillar, pedestal, bed, bedding, back, stud, tread, trestle, leg, stilt, block, dog, triangle, yoke, easel, buoy, float, saddle, hanger, trammel, truss, straddle, shore, stirrup, step, bush, skid, ran (*chiefly Scot.*), cushion, pillow, cant, caryatid, atlantis, cantilever, horse, gantry *or* gauntry, footman (*dial. Eng.*), chaplet; *see* FOUNDATION, BEARING.
3. *Referring to the act of supporting a person, cause, etc.:* strengthening, backing, maintenance, behalf, championship (*primarily spec.*), sustentation (*formal*); *spec.* reënforcement *or* reinforcement (*R*), prop (*R*), patronage; *see* APPROVAL, AID, DEFENSE, ADVOCACY.
4. *Referring to the person or thing from which one receives support:* strength, pillar, prop, stay, mainstay, dependence, trust, reliance; *spec.* understudy (*cant*).
5. *Referring to the act of upkeep:* maintenance, upkeep, keep.
6. *Referring to that which is supplied for upkeep:* upkeep, keep; *see* LIVING.
7. *See* EVIDENCE, CONFIRMATION, ENDURANCE.
supporter, *n.* maintainer, upholder, seconder, stand-by (*C*), patron (*chiefly spec.*), patroness (*fem.; chiefly spec.*); *spec.* espouser, champion, partizan, defender, approver, countenancer; *see* ADHERENT.
Antonyms: see HANGER-ON.
supposed, *a.* **1.** *See* ASSUMED.
2. suppositive (*R*), supposititious (*formal or B*), suppositional (*R*), suppositionary (*R*),

---

sunshine: *sunlight, cheerfulness.*
superannuate: *disqualify, retire.*
superb: *fine, grand, imposing, luxurious.*
supercilious: *proud, haughty, contemptuous.*
superfluous: *unnecessary, excessive.*
supernal: *higher, heavenly.*
supersede: *replace.*
superstitious: *fearful, believing, timid.*
supervise: *oversee.*
supple, *a.:* *flexible, complaisant, obsequious.*
supplement: *addition, counterpart.*
supplicant, *n.:* *asker.*
supply, *v. t.:* *furnish.*
suppose: *assume, imagine, believe, imply.*

---

believed (*R*), putative (*chiefly tech.*), reputed, reputative' (*R*); *spec.* conjectural, hypothetical, tentative.
Antonyms: see ACTUAL.

suppress, *v. t.* **1.** subdue, destroy (*contex.*), stop, check, quell, quench, squelch, quelch (*R*), quash (*R*), stifle, strangle, repress, allay, extinguish, smother, cushion (*R*), retund (*R*), kill, burke (*R*), hush, eliminate, silence; *see* SWALLOW, HIDE;—*mostly fig. uses.*
Antonyms: see ADVANCE.
2. *See* ABOLISH, REPRESS, MURDER.

suppurate, *v. i.* maturate (*tech. or B*), mature (*R*), ripen (*R or dial.*), fester, putrefy (*R*), gather.

suppuration, *n.* maturation, fester, pyosis (*R*), diapyesis (*R*), impostumation (*R or obs.*), purulence *or* purulency.

suppurative, *a.* **1.** festery, running, purulent.
2. *See* PURULENT.

supremacy, *n.* **1.** supremity (*R*), supremeness, sovereignty, sovranty (*B*), principality (*R*), principate (*R*), paramountcy, primacy; *see* HEADSHIP.
2. authority, sovereignty, paramountcy, primacy, scepter.

supreme, *a.* **1.** highest, sovereign, sovran (*B*), paramount, hegemonic (*R*); *spec.* imperial.
2. *See* EXTREME.

surety, *n.* **1.** *See* CONFIDENCE, SECURITY.
2. sponsor (*formal*), guarantee, guarantor, security; *spec.* gage, warrantor, insurer (*R*), voucher, fidejussor (*R or spec.*), pledge (*hist.*), mainpernor (*hist.*), bond, bail.

surf, *n.* breach (*R*), breakers (*pl.*).

surface, *n.* **1.** exterior, face, superficies (*tech. or B*), periphery (*tech.*), rind (*R or spec.*); *spec.* top, outside, inside, brim (*A*), bosom, flesh, flat, concavity, convexity; *see* SIDE, FINISH.
Antonyms: see INTERIOR.
2. *See* APPEARANCE.

surface, *a.* exterior, superficial (*formal*), superficiary (*R*), peripheral (*tech.*); *spec.* peripheric (*R*), epigene, epipolic.
Antonyms: see INTERIOR, DEEP.

surfeit, *n.* **1.** feeding, satiety, glut, gorge, cloy, engorgement (*R*), crapulation (*R*), gorging, cramming, *etc.*
2. fullness, satiety, cloy, crapulence; *see* NAUSEA.
Antonyms: see APPETITE, HUNGER.

surfeit, *v. t.* feed, overfeed, sate (*B*), satiate (*formal*), cram (*C or spec.*), stuff, overcram (*intensive*), cloy (*B; often used fig.*), overcloy (*intensive*), gorge, engorge (*R*), overgorge (*intensive*), glut, englut (*A*), crapulate (*R*).

surfeit, *v. i.* overeat, cram, gorge.
Antonyms: see HUNGER, THIRST.

surfeited, *a.* satiated, crapulent (*B*), stuffed.
Antonyms: see HUNGRY, UNSATISFIED.

surge, *v. i.* **1.** *See* BILLOW.
2. sway, sweep, swing, rush.

surgeon, *n.* doctor (*contex.*), chirurgeon (*A*), sawbones (*S*); *spec.* orthopedist, laparotomist.

surgery, *n.* *Spec.* orthopedy *or* orthopædy, orthopraxy, autoplasty, laparotomy, *etc.*

surly, *a.* ill-tempered (*contex.*), ungracious, churlish (*B*), cynical *or* cynic (*R*), grumpy (*C*), grum (*R*), doggish (*R*), dogged (*R*), snarling, rusty (*R*).
Antonyms: see SMOOTH-SPOKEN, AFFABLE, AGREEABLE, GRACIOUS.

surmount, *v. t.* **1.** overmount (*R*), rise (*chiefly U. S.*), overpass (*R*), overget (*R*), overclimb (*primarily spec.*).
2. *See* TOP, OVERCOME.

surpass, *v. t.* exceed (*merely to be larger than*), excel (*implies superior worth or attainment*), beat (*sense of defeating rival*), cap (*fig.*), top, ding (*A or dial.*), transcend, overtop, outmatch, distance, better, outvie, outrival, outclass (*sporting*), pass (*A*), lick (*S*), outpeer (*R*), overpeer (*R*), best (*C*), overpass (*R*), outpass (*R*), outbid (*R*), outbrave (*R*), overcome (*A*), pretergress (*R*), outdo, outnumber.

surprise, *v. t.* **1.** *See* ATTACK, STARTLE.
2. astonish, astound, stound (*obs. or A*), astony (*A*), steen.

surprise, *n.* **1.** *See* ATTACK.
2. surprisal, surprisement (*R*), astonishment, astoundment (*R*), amazement, mazement (*R*), wonder, marvel (*A*).

surprised, *a.* **1.** startled.
2. astonished, thunderstruck, thunderstricken (*R*), wonderstricken (*R*).

surprising, *a.* astonishing, astounding, mazing (*R*), marvelous, strange (*contex.*), miraculous, tremendous, mirific (*R and jocular*); *spec.* startling.

surrender, *v. t.* **1.** yield, render, deliver, betray, sacrifice.
2. *See* RELINQUISH, ABANDON, SUBJECT, DEDICATE.

surrender, *v. i.* yield, capitulate (*chiefly mil.*), flinch (*now obsolescent*), fall (*chiefly mil.*), succumb.

surrender, *n.* **1.** yielding, rendition, delivery, capitulation (*chiefly mil.*), fall (*chiefly mil.*), dedition (*R*).
2. *Spec.* relinquishment, subjection, abandonment, dedication.

surround, *v. t.* encircle (*completely surrounding, taken passively, as woods about a pond; or taken actively, implying the act of completely surrounding*), circle, inclose, enclose, encompass, compass, girdle, beset, invest, hem (*chiefly used with "in" or "round"*); *spec.* sphere, ensphere, skirt, hedge, clip (*R or spec.*), cincture (*R*), encincture (*R*), enwreathe *or* inwreathe (*often fig.*), embay, enring (*R*), girth (*R*), gird, begird (*intensive*), begirt (*intensive*), beleaguer, round (*R*), invest, circumvent (*R or B*), brace (*R*), collar, twine, ring,

sure: *confident, reliable, unquestionable, unquestioning, unerring, certain.*
surmise, *n.: guess, suspicion.*
surplus, *n.: excess, remainder.*
surreptitious: *hidden, stealthy, secret.*

rim, orb (*elevated*), loop, enwind *or* inwind, cordon, circumsept (*R*); *see* INCLOSE, INVEST.

surrounded, *a.* inclosed; *spec.* cinct (*R*), girt, circumcinct (*R*), bestead (*B*).

surrounding, *a.* inclosing, encompassing; *spec.* ambient, circumjacent, circumambient.

surrounding, *n.* **1.** surroundal (*R*), inclosure, enclosure, encompassment, *etc.*

2. *In pl.:* environs, environment (*a collective*), externality (*R*), milieu (*French*), neighborhood.

survey, *v. t.* **1.** examine, view; *spec.* sweep, reconnoiter, scout, pickeer (*A*), perambulate.

2. *See* SEE, EXAMINE.

survey, *n.* examination, view; *spec.* sweep, reconnoissance, reconnaissance, reconnoiter, scout, panorama (*R*), conspectus, perambulation.

survive, *v. t.* **1.** outlive, overlive (*R*).

2. outlast, outlive (*fig.*), outwear, outgrow; *spec.* outride.

susceptible, *a.* receptive, susceptive (*R*), capable, open, passionate (*B*).

Antonyms: see INSENSIBLE, APATHETIC.

suspect, *v. t.* **1.** surmise, imagine, think, mistrust, smell (*fig.*), suspicion (*dial.*), doubt (*A*), misdoubt (*A*), jalouse (*Scot.*), sniff; *see* GUESS.

2. *See* DISTRUST.

suspend, *v. t.* **1.** *See* HANG, INTERMIT, ADJOURN, DEFER.

2. dismiss; *spec.* rusticate.

suspenders, *n. pl.* braces (*chiefly Brit.*), gallows, gallowses (*Scot., dial., or U. S.*);—*all pl.*

suspicion, *n.* **1.** surmise, imagination (*R*), mistrust, smell (*fig.; C*), inkling, jealousness *or* jealousy (*now dial., exc. spec.*), misdoubt (*A*); *see* GUESS.

2. *See* DISTRUST, TRACE.

suspicious, *a.* **1.** doubtful, distrustful; *spec.* thunderstruck.

Antonyms: see UNSUSPICIOUS.

2. *See* QUESTIONABLE.

sutlery, *n.* canteen.

swagger, *v. i.* **1.** strut, roll, swash, swell, renown (*R*), flourish, brandish, ruffle (*A*); *spec.* prance.

Antonyms: see CRINGE.

2. *See* BLUSTER.

swagger, *n.* **1.** strut, roll, flourish, brandish, ruffle (*A*), swashing, swash.

Antonyms: see CRINGE.

2. *See* BLUSTER.

swallow, *n.* progne (*B*).

swallow, *v. t.* **1.** gulp, ingurgitate (*B*), englut (*A*), take (*contex.*), consume (*contex.*), slabber (*chiefly dial.*), deglute (*R*), bolt (*C*), paunch (*R*), gobble (*C or humorous as used of human beings*), swill (*contemptuous*) regorge (*R*); *spec.* pouch.

Antonyms: see VOMIT.

2. engulf *or* ingulf, involve, devour, gulf (*R*).

Antonyms: see EMIT, ERUPT.

3. *See* ENDURE.

swallow, *n.* **1.** deglutition (*tech.*), ingurgitation (*R*), gulp, bolt (*C*), gobble (*C or humorous of human beings*), glutition (*R*).

2. *Referring to what is swallowed:* gulp.

3. engulfment *or* ingulfment, involution, devourment.

swallowing, *a.* deglutitious, deglutitory, deglutitive (*R*);—*all tech.*

swan, *n.* cygnet (*R, exc. B*); *spec.* pen (*female*), cob (*male*).

swanlike, *a.* swanny, cygneous (*R*), cycnean *or* cygnean (*R*).

swarm, *n.* **1.** crowd, brood; *spec.* (*referring to bees*) colony, hive, cast.

2. *See* CROWD.

swarm, *v. i.* **1.** *See* CROWD, FLOCK.

2. abound, teem, swim, formicate.

swarming, *a.* abounding, teeming, swimming (*fig.*); *spec.* crawling, full, alive.

swastika, *b.* gammadion, fylfot, triskele, cross cramponee.

swathe, *v. t.* bind, enswathe, swaddle, bandage (*chiefly spec.*), cocoon (*fig.*); *spec.* clothe.

sway, *v. t.* **1.** swing; *spec.* roll, rock, wag, waggle; *see* SWING, WAVE.

2. *See* TURN, INFLUENCE, CONTROL.

sway, *v. i.* swing; *spec.* roll, rock, reel, wag, waggle, wabble, wobble, waddle; *see* SWING, SURGE, WAVE.

swear, *v. i.* **1.** affirm, depone (*tech.*).

2. curse, oath (*R*), cuss (*vulgar or euphemistic; U. S.*), objure (*R*).

swear, *v. t.* **1.** affirm, depone (*tech.*), depose; *spec.* vow.

2. bind (*contex.*), objure (*R*).

3. *See* PROMISE.

sweaty, *a.* sudorous (*R*).

sweep, *v. t.* **1.** besom (*R, B*), brush.

2. *See* TOUCH, MOVE, FLOURISH.

3. *Referring to guns or gunfire, etc.:* scour, rake, enfilade (*tech.*).

4. *See* SEARCH, PLAY, CLEAR, SURVEY.

sweep, *n.* **1.** brush (*C*); *spec.* whisk, brush-up.

2. *See* MOVEMENT, FLOURISH, SURGE, DRIVE, RANGE, COMPASS, AMPLITUDE, LEVER, CURVE, OAR.

sweet, *a.* **1.** mellifluous (*R*), dulcet (*A*), honey (*R, exc. spec.*), honeyed *or* honied (*R, exc. spec.*); *spec.* candied; *see* SUGARY.

Antonyms: see SOUR.

2. *Of the voice, etc.:* pleasant, soft, mellifluous (*B*), honeyed *or* honied (*fig.*), sugared (*fig.*),

---

suspicious: *distrustful.*
sustain: *support, act, approve, aid, defend, maintain, prove, suffer, continue, confirm, endure.*
sustained: *continued, constant.*
sustenance: *support, aid, continuation, endurance, suffering.*
swarm, *v. t.: crowd, climb.*
sweat, *n.: exudation, perspiration.*
sweat, *v. i.: perspire.*
sweat, *v. t.: exude, perspire, fleece, work.*
sweep, *v. i.: rush, stalk, surge.*

Hyblæan (*fig.; B*) Hyblan (*R*); *see* PLEASANT, KINDLY, MELODIOUS.

3. *Referring to food, fruits, etc.:* sound, wholesome; *see* FRESH.

Antonyms: see DECOMPOSED, TAINTED.

4. *See* FRAGRANT, FAIR, FRESH.

Antonyms: see HARSH, SHRILL.

sweetbread, *n.* burr (*R*); *spec.* pancreas, thymus.

sweeten, *v. t.* **1.** dulcify (*B or R*), sugar, saccharize (*tech.*), honey (*R or spec.*), disembitter (*R*), disacidify (*R*); *spec.* candy, sirup.

Antonyms: see BITTER, SOUR.

2. *See* SOFTEN.

sweetheart, *n.* lover (*always masc. exc. in pl.*), love (*chiefly feminine*), flame (*now jocular*), boyfriend, girlfriend (*vulgar*), sweetie (*vulgar*); *spec.* valentine; *see* LOVER, LADYLOVE.

sweetmeat, *n.* tidbit, dainty, confection, confectionery (*a collective*), confectionary (*R*), goody (*chiefly in pl.*), sucket (*obs. or dial.*), comfit, confect, candy, tuck (*S*), sweeties (*pl.*), bonbon; *spec.* conserve, sugar plum, ice, compote, caramel, preserve.

sweetness, *n.* **1.** dulcitude (*R*); *spec.* honeyedness, sugariness, honey.

2. *See* MELODY.

swell, *v. i.* **1.** *See* ENLARGE, INCREASE, RISE, PROTUBERATE, BILLOW, BLUSTER, SWAGGER.

2. expand, bulk, volume (*R*), distend, turgesce (*R*), puff (*spec. or fig.*), plim (*R or dial.*), tumefy (*R*); *spec.* bloat, intumesce, heave.

Antonyms: see WITHER, SHRINK.

3. *Referring to swelling with pride:* peacock (*R*).

Antonyms: see CONTRACT.

swell, *v. t. Spec. see* INCREASE, DISTEND, INFLATE.

swell, *n.* **1.** *See* INCREASE, PROTUBERANCE, HILL, BILLOW.

2. Corinthian (*R or humorous*). "*Swell*" *is colloq.*

swelling, *a.* **1.** *See* PROTUBERANT.

2. tumescent, intumescent (*R*), turgent (*R*), turgescent (*R*), bulging; *spec.* swollen, puffy, bloated, baggy, tumefacient (*R*), bunting (*dial.*), surging, surgent (*R*).

swelling, *n.* **1.** *See* INCREASE, INFLATION, PROTUBERANCE.

2. tumefaction (*R or tech.*), intumescence (*R or tech.*), turgescence (*R or tech.*), ebullience (*R*).

3. *In medicine: spec.* gathering, bump, clour (*Scot. and north Eng. dial.*), wen, tumor, goiter, boil, carbuncle, capelet.

swim, *v. i.* **1.** *Spec.* paddle, overhand.

2. dizzy (*R*).

swine, *n.* grunter (*R or humorous*), porcine (*R*), baconer (*R*), grice (*A or Scot.*); *spec.* hog, pig, piggy (*dim. or humorous*), gruntling, brawn (*dial.*), pigling, hogling, hoggery (*a collective*), sow, boar, farrow (*now dial.*), galt *or* gilt (*now dial.*), shoot *or* shot *or* shote (*Eng. dial. and U. S.*), hogget, razorback.

swineherdship, *n.* sybotism (*R*).

swing, *v. i.* **1.** *Referring to a movement of a body, as a pendulum, a horse's tail, a play swing, etc., about or as if about a center at one end of it or beyond it:* sway, switch, swish, pendulate (*R*), sweep; *spec.* dangle, dingle-dangle, flap, flop, gybe.

2. *See* REVOLVE, ROTATE, MOVE.

3. *Referring to a regular back-and-forth, or reciprocating, motion, between regular or fixed limits:* fluctuate (*a flowing, easier movement*), vibrate (*a nervous, intense, quick motion*), oscillate (*swing regularly back and forth*), wave, pendulate (*R*), undulate.

swing, *v. t.* **1.** sway, switch, swish, sweep; *spec.* dangle; *see* FLOURISH.

2. *See* MANAGE, HANG.

3. wave, vibrate, oscillate, fluctuate, undulate (*R*).

swing, *n.* **1.** sway, sweep, swish, switch, *see* FLOURISH.

2. *See* MOVEMENT, GAIT, RHYTHM, FREEDOM.

3. fluctuation, vibration, oscillation, wave, undulation, pendulation (*R*).

4. *Spec.* trapeze.

swinish, *n.* **1.** hoggish, piggish, porcine (*R*), suilline (*R*); *spec.* boarish.

2. *See* COARSE, CRUEL.

switch, *n.* **1.** rod, twig, stick, wattle, withe, wand; *spec.* birch, hickory, rattan *or* ratan; *see* WHIP.

2. stroke, slash, scutch (*dial.*), cut.

3. shunt (*chiefly British*); *spec.* by-pass (*elec.*).

4. *See* SWING.

switch, *v. t.* **1.** strike, whip, cut, scutch (*chiefly dial.*), slash; *spec.* birch.

2. shunt (*chiefly British*), turn (*contex.*); *spec.* sidetrack.

3. *See* SWING.

swollen, *a.* **1.** big (*contex.*), swoln (*chiefly predicative,*) tumid (*B or tech.*), turgid (*B or tech.*); *spec.* puffy, bloat, bloated, gouty (*fig.*), blown (*fig. or spec.*), gummy, baggy, plethoric, varicose, proud, blowzy, blobber.

Antonyms: see WITHERED.

2. *See* PROTUBERANT, SWELLING, INFLATED, ELATED, BOMBASTIC.

swoop, *v. i.* **1.** descend (*contex.*), stoop (*R*), pounce, souse; *spec.* fly (*contex.*).

2. *See* RUSH.

swoop, *n.* **1.** descent, stoop, pounce, souse.

2. *See* RUSH.

sword, *n.* brand (*A or B*), glaive (*A or B*), falchion (*B, exc. spec.*), slasher (*C*); *spec.* rapier, cutlass, scimitar *or* scimiter, saber, sabre, foil, hanger, broadsword, backsword, point, verdun, damascus, wafter, bilbo, diego (*obs. or hist.*).

sword-shaped, *a.* ensate, gladiate, ensiform;—*all three tech. or B.*

swordsman, *n.* spadassin (*R*); *spec.* fencer.

syllabify, *v. t.* syllabicate, syllabize (*R*), syllable (*R*).

swelter: *perspire, glow.*
swift: *rapid, ready, brief.*
swill, *v. t.: drink, swallow.*
sycophant: *fawner.*
syllabus: *abstract.*

syllogism, *n. Spec.* elench *or* elenchus, sorites, enthymeme, epicheirema, trilemma, prosyllogism.
symbol, *n.* representation, sign, significative (*R*), emblem, figure, type, token, shadow (*fig.*), ensign (*B*), presentation (*R*), sacrament (*R*); *spec.* palm, pictograph, totem, badge, character, letter, exponent, word, image, picture.
symbolic, *a.* representative, significative, typical, emblematic, emblematical; *spec.* sacramental (*R*), figurative, mystical *or* mystic (*a term of religion*), ideographic *or* ideographical, hieroglyphic *or* hieroglyphical.
symbolize, *v. t.* represent, present (*R*), signify, mean, typify, figure, emblemize, emblem (*R*), emblematize (*R*), shadow (*fig.*), symbolify (*R*), similize (*R*); *see* SIGNIFY, EXPRESS.
symmetrical, *a.* **1.** symmetral (*R*), regular, even; *spec.* radiate.
2. *See* PROPORTIONATE.
symmetry, *n.* regularity, evenness; *spec.* radiation, radiism (*R*), peloria.
sympathize, *v. i.* **1.** condole.
2. *See* HARMONIZE.
sympathizer, *n.* compassionator (*R*), condoler, sympathist (*R*).
sympathy, *n.* communion, compassion (*these three imply spiritual comprehension and agreement*), understanding (*implying both intellectual and intuitive* sympathy).
symptom, *n.* indication, sign, prognostic (*R*).
synonym, *n.* equivalent (*contex.*), duplicate (*R*), polyonym (*R*), pœcilonym (*R*).
An antonym *of any word is a word of opposite meaning; a* homonym *of any word is a word having the same sound but a different meaning; a* heteronym *of any word is a word having the same spelling but a different sound and a different meaning. Thus,* intelligent *is an antonym of* stupid; *it is also an antonym of* dull *as said of a boy, but not of* dull *as said of a knife;* pair, pear, *and* pare *are homonyms; and the noun* sow, *a female pig, is a heteronym of the verb,* sow, *to scatter seed.*
system, *n.* **1.** *See* ORGANISM, ORGANIZATION, UNIVERSE.
2. regimen, régime, scheme; *spec.* dispensation, economy (*used chiefly in theology*); *see* PLAN, METHOD, ORDER.
Antonyms: see CONFUSION.
systematize, *v. t.* **1.** *See* ORGANIZE, ARRANGE.
2. systemize, regularize, regiment (*R or tech.*).

T

table, *n.* **1.** slab, tablet (*dim.*); *spec.* board; *see* TABLET.
2. board (*contex.*), tabling (*a collective*); *spec.* stand, teapoy (*Anglo-Indian*), tabaret, mahogany, credence, desk, mensa (*eccl.*), Pembroke, dresser (*now R*), tripod, toilet, sideboard.
3. statement (*contex.*), tabulation, chart, scheme, schema (*R*); *spec.* ephemeris, tariff, schedule.
4. *See* PANEL, FARE, FACET.
tablecloth, *n.* cover, cloth (*C*), tapis (*only in "on the tapis"*).
tablet, *n.* **1.** *See* TABLE.
2. table (*contex.*), tablature (*R*), tabula (*antiq.*), slab (*R, exc. spec.*); *spec.* slate, palette *or* pallet, board (*contex.*), brass, cartel, cartouche, plaque, plaquette, medallion, diptych, pax, diglyph, parapegm, tessera, pad.
3. tabula *or* tabella (*chiefly med.*); *spec.* cake, lozenge, wafer.
tabular, *a.* tabulary, tabulate, tabuliform;—*all tech. or formal.*
tabulate, *v. t.* schematize, chart.
tack, *v. t.* **1.** *See* ATTACH, ADD.
2. beat, ply, stay, claw, board (*R*), busk (*obs. or A*), lave (*obs., exc. B*); *spec.* boxhaul, clubhaul, gybe.
tack, *n.* **1.** *See* NAIL, COURSE.
2. trip (*contex.*), beat, board, leg, reach; *spec.* gybe.
tackle, *n.* **1.** purchase; *spec.* fish, cat, garnet, whip, jigger, jeer, fall, burton, halliard *or* halyard.
2. *See* CORDAGE, EQUIPMENT.
tact, *n.* skill, address, diplomacy, savoir faire (*French*).
tactful, *a.* skillful, diplomatic; *spec.* adept.
Antonyms: see AWKWARD.
tactual, *a.* tactile, tactic (*R*).
tag, *n.* **1.** tab, tail, taglet (*dim.*); *see* LABEL, PENDANT.
2. *See* ADDITION, REFRAIN.
tail, *n.* **1.** rear, back.
Antonyms: see HEAD.
2. appendage (*humorous*), tailpiece (*humorous*), narrative (*humorous*); *spec.* flag, fud, flap *or* flapper, trundletail, brush, fantail, dock, scut, bunt (*Eng.*), single, pole, wreath.
3. end (*contex.*); *spec.* train, liripipe (*hist.*); *see* TAG, END, CUE, RETINUE.
4. *See* REVERSE.
tailor, *n.* sartor (*humorously pedantic*), needleman (*R*), snipper (*contemptuous*), whipcat (*C*), pricklouse (*derisive; dial.*).
tailor, *a.* sartorial, sartorian (*R*);—*both* (*B*).
tail-shaped, *a.* caudiform, caudate;—*both tech. or* (*B*).
taint, *v. t.* **1.** *See* CONTAMINATE.
2. *In a physical sense, and implying some deleterious change;* affect (*contex.*), infect, touch, corrupt (*R*), spoil; *spec.* mildew, cork, flyblow.

---

syllogize, *v. i.: reason.*
sympathetic: *compassionate, harmonious.*
synchronous: *contemporaneous.*
syndicate, *n.: combination.*
syndicate, *v. t.: combine.*
synod: *council, assembly.*
synopsis: *abstract.*
synthesis: *composition.*
systemize: *organize, arrange, methodize, systematize.*

T

table, *v. t.: play, defer.*

(*A*) *archaic.* (*B*) *bookish, poetic, literary or learned.* (*C*) *colloquial.* (*Contex.*) *contextual.* (*R*) *rare.* (*S*) *slang.* *See pp. viii–ix.*

taint, *n.* **1.** *See* CONTAMINATION, IMPERFECTION.
2. touch, infection; *spec.*

tainted, *a.* touched, infected, strong, spoiled *or* spoilt; *spec.* corked, flyblown, decayed.
Antonyms: see SWEET.

take, *v. t.* **1.** grasp, seize; *spec.* pocket, reave (*A*), whip (*"out," as a knife*), sack (*S*); *see* SEIZE, RECEIVE, STEAL.
Antonyms: see BESTOW.
2. *See* APPROPRIATE, WITHDRAW, ACCEPT, NEED, ADOPT, GET, ASSUME, QUOTE, REMOVE, CHOOSE, ATTRACT, AFFECT, ACT, PLEASE, STRIKE, MAKE, JUMP, MOVE, CATCH, CAPTURE, BUY, EXACT, DERIVE, CONSUME, COPY, CONSIDER, CONTRACT, INHERIT, BREATHE, OCCUPY, USE.

take, *v. i.* **1.** *See* GO, STICK, WORK.
2. cotton (*Eng. or C*).

taking, *n.* **1.** take (*R*), grasp, seizure, caption (*R*); *see* SEIZURE, RECEPTION.
2. *See* ACCEPTANCE, DERIVATION, ASSUMPTION, CAPTURE, APPROPRIATION.

talent, *n. Implies large capacity for a certain thing. Should not be confused with* genius *which is creative, rare and spontaneous as contrasted to* talent: ability (*capability of a good sort*), aptitude (ability *directed along a particular channel*), gift (*native* ability), endowment (*native* ability *more formally considered than in* gift), faculty (*native ease in accomplishment*).

talk, *n.* **1.** *Referring to the act simply or to what is said: see* SPEECH.
2. *In the generic sense:* discourse (*formal*), palaver, parley (*B, R*), gas (*S*), vapor (*S*), buzz (*C or S*), haver (*Scot.*), jaw (*S or C; contemptuous and usually inelegant*), gab (*inelegant and contemptuous*), chin (*S and contemptuous*), bull (*S, U. S.*), baloney (*S, U. S.; both in sense of intemperate, aimless, or exaggerated* talk), tongue (*contemptuous*); *spec.* loquacity, slackjaw (*vulgar S*), chatter, gossip; CONVERSATION, ADDRESS, BABBLE.
Antonyms: see SILENCE.
3. *See* REPORT, CONFERENCE.
4. proverb, byword, fable (*R*), fame (*R*).

talk, *v. i.* **1.** *See* SPEAK.
2. palaver, jaw (*S and often contemptuous*), parleyvoo (*humorous or S*), gab (*inelegant and contemptuous*), chin (*S and contemptuous*), noise (*contex.*); gammon (*S or C*), chirp, patter (*S*); *spec.* splutter, smatter, honey (*A or U. S.*), snarl, mince, babble, chatter; *see* CONVERSE, GOSSIP.
3. *See* CONSULT, COMMUNICATE.

talkative, *a.* loquacious (*B*), garrulous, voluble, babbly, tonguey (*C or vulgar*), lubrical (*R*), windy (*C*), mouthy (*S and coarse*), gaggling (*contemptuous*), gabby (*vulgar or Scot.*), irreticent (*R*), multiloquent (*R*), narrative (*R*), conversable (*a dignified term*); *spec.* glib (*C*), conversational, leaky.
Antonyms: see RETICENT.

talkativeness, *n.* loquacity, garrulity, volubility, polylogy (*R*), *etc.*
Antonyms: see RETICENCE.

talker, *n.* **1.** *See* SPEAKER.
2. palaverer, palaverist (*R*), mag (*C*), gabber (*undignified and contemptuous*), blatherskite *or* bletherskite (*dial. or C; U. S.*), blatterer (*C*), chatterbox, windbag (*C or S*); *spec.* babbler, chatterer; *see* CONVERSATIONALIST.

tall, *a.* high, lofty; comely, excellent, fine (*all three A*); brave, bold (*obs.*); grandiloquent, exaggerated (*C, of stories*); unusual, fine, big (*all three C*).

tambourine, *n.* drum (*contex.*); *spec.* timbrel, tympanum.

tame, *a.* **1.** domesticated *or* domestic, broken, mansuete (*A*), familiar (*R*).
Antonyms: see WILD.
2. *See* SUBMISSIVE, COMMONPLACE, DULL.

tame, *v. t.* **1.** domesticate, domesticize (*R*), break, bust (*horse-training cant; western U. S.*), reclaim (*R or B*), man, gentle, meeken (*R*), entame (*R*).
2. *See* SUBDUE.

tangible, *a.* **1.** sensible, material, palpable, touchable, tactile.
Antonyms: see INTANGIBLE.
2. *See* ACTUAL, PERCEPTIBLE.

tangle, *n.* **1.** *See* ENTANGLEMENT, CONFUSION.
2. tanglement, snarl, snare; *spec.* knot, maze, ravel, twist.

tank, *n.* **1.** *See* POND.
2. *Spec.* cistern, boiler.

tap, *n.* stroke (*contex.*), touch (*contex.*), spat (*C*), pat, tip; *spec.* peck, sick, dab, patter, chuck; *see* CLICK.

tap, *v. t. & i.* strike (*contex.*), touch (*contex.*), pat, tip; *spec.* tick, peck, dab, spat (*C*), bob, dib, chuck, bepat, virginal (*v. i. only; nonce use*), percuss; *spec.* elect (*local, Yale Univ.*); *see* CLICK.

tape, *n. Spec.* inkle, ferret.

tapering, *a.* taper, spiry, fastigiate (*tech.*), conical; *spec.* pyramidal.

tapestry, *n.* drapery (*contex.*), arras; *spec.* verdure.

tapster, *n.* skink (*R*), skinker (*A*); *spec.* bartender, barmaid.

tarry, *v. i.* **1.** abide, bide (*ch. A*), sojourn, stop (*C*), harbor (*A*), rest, stay, lodge; *spec.* camp; *see* DWELL, STOP.
Antonyms: see DEPART.
2. *See* DELAY.

task, *n.* **1.** labor, work, stint, business, chore (*chiefly spec.*), job, lay (*S*); *spec.* duty, lesson, exercise, assignment, pensum (*R; a school term*), imposition.
2. *See* STRAIN.

taskmaster, *n.* tasker (*R*), exactor (*R*), taskmistress (*fem.*); *spec.* overseer.

tastable, *a.* gustable.

taste, *n.* **1.** *Referring to the act:* gustation, gust (*R*), degustation (*R*).
2. *Referring to the sense or faculty:* palate, tooth (*fig.*), gusto, gust (*A*).

---

tangle, *v. t.: entangle, involve, trap.*
tantalize: *deceive, tease.*
tardy: *slow, late.*
target: *shield, mark, butt, aim.*
tariff: *charge, table.*
tart: *sour, acrimonious, curt.*

3. *Referring to the quality of what is tasted:* sapor (*chiefly tech.*), savor, smack, smatch (*R*), gust (*R*); *spec.* tang, relish, flavor, piquancy, subflavor.
4. *Referring to a little that is eaten:* smack, smitch, taster; *spec.* sip.
5. *See* FONDNESS, EXPERIENCE, TRACE, JUDGMENT, STYLE.
taste, *a.* gustative, gustatory, degustatory (*R*); —*all B.*
taste, *v. t.* **1.** savor, smack, degust *or* degustate (*R*), palate (*R*); *spec.* sip.
2. *See* FEEL, EXPERIENCE.
taste, *v. i.* savor, relish, smack, smatch (*A*).
tasteless, *a.* **1.** insipid, flat, savorless, vapid, mawkish, unsavory, dead, stale; *spec.* silent, watery, waterish.
Antonyms: see PALATABLE.
2. *See* CRUDE.
tasty, *a.* appetizing, palatable, delicious, *etc.; also* (*C*) *for* tasteful.
tattle, *v. i.* **1.** *See* GOSSIP.
2. inform, tell, blab (*coarse or contemptuous*), babble, snitch (*S*), peach (*S*), round, buzz (*R*).
tattle, *v. t.* tell, divulge (*contex.*), blab (*coarse or contemptuous*), blat (*coarse or contemptuous*), babble, buzz (*R*), betray.
tattle, *n.* **1.** *See* GOSSIP.
2. babble, tittle-tattle.
tattler, *n.* **1.** *See* GOSSIP.
2. informer, telltale, talebearer, blab (*inelegant or coarse*), clatterer (*R*), blabber, cackler (*contemptuous*), whisperer, pickthank (*A*), tittle-tattle (*R*), snitcher (*S*).
taunt, *v. t.* reproach, twit, upbraid, mock, flout, jeer.
taunt, *n.* reproach, twit, scorn (*A*), cut.
tax, *n.* **1.** charge, assessment, due, taxation (*R*), rate, toll, levy, mail (*obs. or Scot.*), gild (*hist.*), duty, impost (*obs., exc. as equiv. to "duty"*), gabelle (*obs., exc. spec.*), cess (*A or local, exc. as equiv. to "rate" in Eng.*); *spec.* capitation, carnatch (*Arabian*), carucage (*feudal*), chancer, choky (*Anglo-Indian*), contribution, danegeld, decimation (*R or hist.*), fifteenth, fumage, geld, groundage, hidage (*hist.*), lastage, lockage, poll, poundage, quarterage, quint, quinzième (*hist.*), rate (*chiefly in pl.*), saladine, sayer (*India*), scavage, scot, seignorage, surtax, supertax, tallage, tithe, tribute, tonnage, tunnage; *see* DUTY.
Antonyms: see SUBSIDY.
2. *See* STRAIN.
tax, *v. t.* **1.** assess, rate (*chiefly spec.*), cess (*obs. or local, exc. spec.*); *spec.* tariff, excise, surtax, tonnage, tithe.
2. *See* ACCUSE, BURDEN, STRAIN.
taxable, *a.* assessable, ratable (*chiefly spec.*); *spec.* customable, dutiable, tithable.
taxation, *n.* assessment, imposition; *spec.* decimation (*R, exc. hist.*), capitation, pollage (*R*), tollage.

teach, *v. t.* **1.** *See* INFORM.
2. instruct, educate, inform (*R*), lesson (*R*), learn (*obs. or vulgar*); *spec.* school, show, indoctrinate *or* (*A*), doctrinate, catechize, ground, regent (*R*), tutor, dry-nurse (*C or cant*), lecture, cram (*C*), coach, college.
3. *Referring to an inculcation of knowledge in:* inculcate, preach, indoctrinate (*R*); *spec.* profess.
teachable, *a.* **1.** instructible (*R*), docile, docible (*R*), educable (*R*), disciplinable, tractable.
Antonyms: see UNTEACHABLE.
2. *See* COMMUNICABLE.
teacher, *n.* **1.** *See* INFORMER.
2. instructor (*masc. or fem.*), instructress (*fem.*); *spec.* schoolmaster, schoolmistress, school teacher, schoolmarm, preceptor, preceptress, pedagogue (*often depreciatory*), educator (*somewhat pompous and affected*), dominie (*largely local*), doctor (*A*), master, mistress (*these two more common in U. S. for* teachers *in private schools*), governess, inculcator, professor, dame (*obs.*), tutor, coacher, crammer (*C*), mystagogue, usher, drillmaster, guru (*India*), principal, pædotribe, khoja, lecturer, catechist, sophist, sophister, Sopherim (*pl.*), rhetor, docent, oracle, assistant, teaching fellow, apprentice. *In the U. S. the* teachers, *collectively, of a given institution constitute the* faculty; *but this sense of* faculty *is not in Brit. usage.*
Antonyms: see STUDENT.
teaching, *n.* **1.** *See* INFORMATION.
2. instruction; *spec.* tutelage, tuition, inculcation, grounding, discipline, education, edification, catechesis, catechizing, tutory (*R*), indoctrination, lesson, lecture, *etc.*
3. *The art or science:* pedagogy (*tech.*), pedagogics (*tech.*), education, didactics *or* didascalics (*R and tech.*), didacticism (*R*), protreptic (*R*); *spec.* mystagogy.
4. *That which is taught:* doctrine, lore.
team, *n.* **1.** rig; *spec.* span, line, tandem, swing.
2. *Spec.* nine, eleven, fifteen, four, *etc.*
tear (*pron.* tēr), *n.* **1.** *See* DROP.
2. drop, pearl (*B*), brine (*a collective*), dew (*B; a collective*).
tear (*pron.* tair), *v. t.* **1.** rend.
2. pull, draw, rip, rend; *spec.* wrench, claw, shred.
3. *See* DISTRESS.
tear (*pron.* tair), *n.* **1.** tearing, rending, pull, rip; *spec.* wrench, laceration, dilaceration (*R*).
2. rent, rip.
3. *See* RUSH.
tear bottle, lachrymatory.
tearful, *a.* watery (*contex.*), teary (*C*), mournful (*contex.*), lachrymose *or* lachrymous (*both B or tech.*), liquid, maudlin (*A*), wet (*contex.*), moist (*B; contex.*), larmoyant (*R*); *spec.* swimming.
Antonyms: see TEARLESS.

tasteful: *palatable, æsthetic.* | **tawdry:** *gaudy.* | **tawny:** *fulvous, red, dark.*

tearless, *a.* dry (*contex.*).
Antonyms: see TEARFUL.
tear-shaped, *a.* lachrymiform (*tech.*).
tease, *v. t.* **1.** *See* DISENTANGLE.
2. annoy, trouble, harass, bother, pester, torment, plague, vex; *spec.* lark, badger, bullyrag, haze (*U. S.*), tantalize.
technique, *n.* **1.** *See* EXECUTION, SKILL.
2. technique, technics (*pl. or collective sing.*), technology.
teeth, *n. pl. Referring to artificial teeth:* set (*contex.*), denture (*cant*).
telegram, *n.* message (*contex.*), telegraph (*obs. or R*); *spec.* cablegram, marconigram, radiogram, heliogram, wire (*C*), cable (*C*).
telegraph, *n. Spec.* wire (*C*), cable (*C*), heliograph, marconigraph, wireless (*C*), radiograph, radiotelegraphy.
telegraph, *v. i.* communicate (*contex.*); *spec.* wire (*C*), cable (*C*), radiograph, heliograph.
telescope, *n.* tube (*C*); *spec.* reflector, refractor, glass (*C*), finder, photohelioscope, equatorial.
tell, *v. i.* **1.** babble, inform; *see* TATTLE.
2. count, make, act.
temper, *n.* **1.** *See* CALMNESS, DISPOSITION.
2. *Referring to actual frame of mind at a given time:* mood, tone, vein, humor, frame, cheer, spirits; *see* ILL TEMPER.
temper, *v. t.* **1.** *See* MIX, ALLOY, MITIGATE, MODERATE, RESTRAIN.
2. *Referring to metals, glass, etc.:* anneal.
3. *Referring to clay, etc.:* work, pug, puddle.
temple, *n.* **1.** house (*contex.*), sanctuary, tabernacle, fane (*A, B*), naos (*tech.*), templet (*dim.*), delubrum (*Latin*), church (*a loose usage*); *spec.* pantheon, pagoda *or* (*R*) pagod, sacellum, hecatompedon, dipteros.
2. *See* CHURCH.
temporal, *a.* **1.** *Of or relating to time:* chronal (*R*), temporaneous (*R*); *see* CHRONOLOGICAL, WORLDLY.
2. *See* TEMPORARY.
temporary, *a.* temporal (*R*), momentary, short-lived, momently (*R*), flashing; *spec.* interimistic; *see* PROVISIONAL.
Antonyms: see ETERNAL, LASTING, PERMANENT.
temporize, *v. i.* **1.** *Referring to indulgence in opportunism:* diplomatize; *spec.* trim.
2. *See* HEDGE.
ten, *n.* **1.** *Referring to the number:* decad.
2. *Referring to a set, group, etc.:* decad, dicker (*cant*), decad (*R*).
tenacious, *a.* **1.** firm, strong, holding, holdfast (*R*), fast, unyielding.
2. *See.* STICKY, CONSTANT, PERSISTENT, RETENTIVE.
tenant, *n.* holder, tenantry (*collective pl.*), tenementer (*R*); *spec.* leaseholder, renter, vassal (*feudalism*), termor; *see* OCCUPANT.
tend, *v. t.* **1.** *See* ATTEND.
2. *Referring to cattle, etc.:* herd, guard, tail (*Australia*); *spec.* shepherd, graze.
tend, *v. t.* **1.** *See* INCLINE, CONTRIBUTE.
2. lean, incline, head, lead, point, gravitate, look, conduce; *spec.* squint.
tendency, *n.* **1.** *See* INCLINATION.
2. leaning, inclination, gravitation, gravity, set, tendency (*R*); *spec.* bias.
tender, *v. t.* **1.** *In law:* offer, delate (*obs. or Roman law*).
Antonyms: see DEMAND.
2. *See* OFFER.
tender, *n. In law:* offer.
Antonyms: see DEMAND.
tenfold, *a.* decuple (*chiefly math.*).
tenon, *n.* projection (*contex.*); *spec.* dovetail, cog, dowel.
tense, *a.* **1.** *See* STRETCHED, TIGHT, INTENSE, EXCITED.
2. high-strung, strung-up (*chiefly predicative*), strained.
ten-sided, *a.* decagonal (*literally "ten-angled"*), decahedral;—*both tech.*
tent, *n.* pavilion (*chiefly spec.*), tilt; *spec.* marquee, marquise, prætorium (*Roman antiq.*), canvas, booth, kibitka, tepee, wigwam, lean-to.
tenth, *n.* tithe, decima (*R*), denary (*R*), tithing (*obs. or R*).
tenure, *n.* tenement (*R*), holding, tenancy, tenantship, tenantry (*R*); *see* OCCUPATION.
term, *n.* **1.** *See* LIMIT, DURATION, PERIOD, NAME, EXPRESSION.
2. *In logic: spec.* subject, predicate, major, minor, conclusion.
3. *In math.: spec.* mean, extreme.
4. *In academic use: spec.* semester.
terminable, *a.* limitable, lapsable *or* labile, determinable; *see* FINITE.
Antonyms: see ENDLESS.
terminology, *n.* nomenclature (*tech.*), glossology (*R*), orismology (*R*), technology; *spec.* toponomy.
terrestrial, *a.* **1.** earthly (*R, exc. in contrast with "heavenly"*), earthy (*obs., exc. spec.*), tellurian (*B*), terrene (*B*), worldly (*chiefly in contrast to "heavenly"*), mundane, sublunar *or* sublunary, subastral, terranean (*R*), telluric (*R*), tellural (*R*).
Antonyms: see HEAVENLY.
2. *See* WORLDLY.

---

tedious: *dull, tiresome.*
tedium: *ennui.*
tell, *v. t.: compute, disclose, communicate, mention, narrate, express, report, tattle, assure, inform, announce, evidence, perceive, distinguish, bid, confess.*
temerity: *cf.* RASH.
temperament: *constitution, disposition.*
temperance: *moderation, abstinence.*
temperate: *moderate, abstemious, mild.*
tempt: *provoke, attract, entice.*
tend, *v. i.: attend.*
tender, *a.: delicate, weak, weakly, unstable.*
tenement: *tenure, holding, abode, dwelling.*
tension, *n.: tightness, force, strain, excitement, intensity.*
tensity, *n.: tightness, strain, intensity.*
termination: *ending, end, outcome, suffix.*
terrible: *fearful, alarming.*
terrific: *alarming.*
terrified: *afraid.*
terrify: *frighten.*

For explanation of terms used, see pp. viii–ix; for abbreviations, see p. x.

territory, *n.* **1.** extent (*contex.*), region, place, land, tract, quarter, district, locality; *spec.* division, side, countryside, part, section, terrain, terrane, corner, latitude, confine, ambit, domain, bound (*chiefly in pl.*), coast (*obs.*), climate, clime (*B*), fatherland, Cockaigne, El Dorado, realm.
2. *politically:* domain, dominion, demesne, empire, diocese (*obs. or hist., exc. spec.*); *spec.* enclave, exclave; *see* DIVISION.
testator, *n.* legator (*R*), bequeather (*chiefly spec.*), deviser (*chiefly spec.*).
Antonyms: see LEGATEE.
testify, *v. t.* **1.** state (*contex.*), swear, attest, depose, depone (*a less usual equiv. of "depose"*); *spec.* witness.
2. *See* EVIDENCE, AVOW.
testimonial, *n.* **1.** credential.
2. *See* GIFT.
tether, *v. t.* fasten (*contex.*), tie (*contex.*); *spec.* bush, picket, stake.
text, *n.* **1.** composition, wording, scripture (*R*); *spec.* context, mantra (*East Indian*), hexapla, libretto.
2. *See* SUBJECT.
texture, *n.* **1.** *See* FABRIC, STRUCTURE, COMPOSITION.
2. constitution, fabric, fiber, grain, contexture (*R*); *spec.* grit.
thank, *v. t.* bless (*usually ludicrous or hyperbolic*).
thankful, *a.* grateful.
Antonyms: see UNGRATEFUL, THANKLESS.
thankfulness, *n.* gratitude, gratefulness.
Antonyms: see RESENTMENT.
thanks, *n. pl.* blessings (*usually ludicrous or hyperbolic*); *see* GRACE.
thanks, *interj.* gramercy (*A*).
thanksgiving, *a.* eucharistic (*B*).
that, *pron. & a.* thilk (*A*); *spec.* yonder, yon (*B*).
thatch, *a. Spec.* haulm (*Eng.*), cadjan (*Anglo-Indian*), reed, grass.
theater, *n.* **1.** playhouse, house (*contex.*).
2. *See* DRAMA.
theatrical, *a.* **1.** *Referring to the stage or stage playing:* histrionic (*tech. or B*), dramatic (*relating to the inherent qualities of drama, as opposed to the more artificial implications of* theatrical, histrionic *and* stagy), stagy (*derogatory*), dramaturgic *or* (*R*) dramaturgical (*both B, with reference to the art of play construction*), scenic *or* scenical.
2. *See* DRAMATIC, SHOWY, ARTIFICIAL.
theft, *n.* **1.** steal (*R*), stealing, conversion (*contex.*), larceny (*often spec.*), depredation (*contex., often euphemistic*), thievery, thiefdom (*R*); *spec.* pilfer (*obs. or R*), pilferage (*R*), pilfery (*obs. or R*), pickery *or* picking (*obs. or Scots law*), cribbage (*C*), robbery, burglary. *"Theft" is not properly a synonym of "embezzlement."*
2. *The thing stolen:* steal (*R*), filch (*R*); *spec.* pilfer, pilferage (*R*), pilfery (*obs. or R*), crib, mainour (*hist.*).
theist, *n. Spec.* deist, monotheist, polytheist, pantheist.
theologian, *n.* theologer (*R*), theologaster (*derogatory*), theologue (*R*), theologist, theolog (*S or C*); *spec.* divine.
theology, *n.* divinity; *spec.* isagogics, dogmatics, homiletics.
theoretical, *a.* theoretic, speculative, notional (*logic or philos.*), doctrinaire, paper (*fig.*); *spec.* ideal; *see* CONJECTURAL, ACADEMIC.
theorist, *n.* speculator (*R*), doctrinaire (*often used in reproach*), doctrinarian, notionalist (*logic or philos.*).
theorize, *v. i.* speculate, doctrinize; *see* GUESS.
theory, *n.* **1.** *Implying what is opposed to fact or practise. See* IDEA.
2. hypothesis (*in science a preliminary supposition, as contrasted to* theory, *which is a verified* hypothesis), speculation (*implying unverified guessing more or less intelligently performed*), doctrine, system, ism (*chiefly disparaging; C*), principle, philosophy; *spec.* theosopheme; *see* GUESS.
there, *adv.* **1.** thereat (*a formal term*).
2. thither (*B*).
thereabout, *adv.* **1.** thereabouts, therebesides (*A or B*), thereby (*A or dial.*). *There is no decided choice between the two forms, "thereabout" and "thereabouts."*
2. thereupon (*A or formal*), thereon (*formal*), thereanent (*R*).
therefore, *adv. & conj.* thus, consequently, hence, so, ergo (*tech. or Latin*), wherefore; *spec.* henceforward, then.
thereon, *adv.* thereupon (*more formal or emphatic or employed for euphony*).
thermometer, *n.* calorific (*a loose use*); *spec.* mercury, glass, Fahrenheit, Centigrade, Reaumur.
thick, *a.* **1.** *Referring to extension from one surface to the opposite:* heavy, crass (*obs.*); *see* DEEP.
Antonyms: see THIN.
2. *Referring to that which consists of visible separate parts or objects, as hair, a forest, etc.:* dense, thickset, crowded; *spec. see* BUSHY.
Antonyms: see THIN.
3. *Referring to fluids:* stiff, inspissated, viscid, viscous, grumous *or* (*R*) grumose (*chiefly tech.*), crass (*R*); *spec.* clotted.
Antonyms: see THIN.
4. *See* COARSE, CLOUDY, FOGGY, HAZY, FREQUENT, ABUNDANT, HOARSE, GUTTURAL.
thicken, *v. t.* thick (*R*), stiffen, inspissate

---

terse: *concise.*
test, *n.: examination, trial, standard, assay.*
testament: *will.*
theme: *subject, composition, stem.*
then: *afterwards, therefore.*
theorem: *statement, rule.*
thesaurus: *dictionary.*
thesis: *statement, composition, proposition.*

(*tech. or B*), inviscate (*R*), incrassate (*R*); *spec.* embody (*paints*); *see* CONDENSE, COAGULATE.

Antonyms: see THIN, DILUTE.

thickening, *n.* **1.** stiffening, inspissation, incrassation (*R*), inviscation (*R*); *see* CONDENSATION.

2. *Referring to what makes thick:* stiffening, binding; *spec.* liaison (*cookery*).

thickening, *a.* stiffening, inspissant (*R*), incrassative (*R*).

thicket, *n.* brush, underbrush, thickset (*R*), bosk (*B*), boscage (*B*), covert, brake; *spec.* chaparral (*southwestern U. S.*), fernshaw (*R*), canebrake, jungle.

thickness, *n.* **1.** thick (*R*), crassness *or* crassitude (*R*), heaviness; *spec.* grist, diameter.

2. density, crowdedness.

3. stiffness, consistence *or* (*less usual*) consistency, spissitude (*B or tech.*), viscosity, crassness *or* crassitude (*R*).

thick-skinned, *a.* **1.** pachydermatous, pachyderm;—*both tech.*

2. *See* INSENSIBLE.

thief, *n.* stealer, purloiner (*chiefly spec.*), larcener (*R*), pilferer (*chiefly spec.*), filcher (*chiefly spec.*), lurch (*R; A*), robber (*chiefly spec.*), lifter, depredator (*contex.*), micher (*obs. or dial.*), prig *or* prigger (*S or cant*), nimmer (*A*), snatcher (*obs. or R*), snapper (*obs. or R*), hooker (*S, obs., or spec.*); *spec.* picklock, pickpocket, shoplifter, kleptomaniac, pickpurse (*R or hist.*), cutpurse (*hist.*), light horseman, burglar.

thievish, *a.* larcenous, furacious (*pedantic or humorous*), stealthy (*R*), furtive (*R*), mercurial (*fig.; B*), light-fingered, pilfering (*chiefly spec.*), pitchy (*fig.; said esp. of the claws, finger, etc.*), sticky (*fig., like "pitchy"*), theftierous (*R*).

thievishness, *n.* thievery, furaciousness *or* furacity (*R*); *spec.* kleptomania.

thigh, *n.* ham (*chiefly in pl., exc. spec.*), hock *or* hough (*spec. and chiefly Scot. as applied to man*).

thighbone, *n.* femur (*tech.*); *spec.* crossbones (*pl.*).

thighpiece, *n. In armor:* cuisse *or* cuish.

thimble, *n. Spec.* thumbstall.

thin, *a.* **1.** *See* SLENDER, SENSITIVE, SHRILL, UNSUBSTANTIAL, FAINT.

Antonyms: see THICK.

2. rare, rarefied, crude (*R*), exile (*A*), subtle *or* (*R*) subtile, tenuous (*B or formal*), tenuious (*R*), unsubstantial (*contex.*).

3. *Spec.* thinnish, dilute; *see* WATERY.

Antonyms: see THICK, VISCID, CROWDED.

4. lean, leanish (*R*), slim, poor, spare, meager (*B*), pinched, slender; *spec.* thinnish, peaked (*C*), spindling, emaciated, spindly (*C*), gaunt, lank, lanky, scraggy, scrawny (*U. S.*), hollow, shrunken, macilent (*R*), haggard, bony, fleshless, lathy (*C*), skinny (*very emphatic or loose and C; often contemptuous*), skeletal, scrannel (*R or obs.*), raw-boned, squinny (*R*).

Antonyms: see FAT, PLUMP.

thin, *v. t.* **1.** rarefy, attenuate, extenuate (*R*), subtilize (*R*).

Antonyms: see THICKEN.

2. *Spec.* water, dilute, adulterate.

3. *See* EMACIATE.

thing, *n.* **1.** *See* DEED, CONCERN, MATERIAL, ARTICLE, ITEM, OBJECT, SUBJECT, CREATURE, PERSON, CHATTELS, GOODS.

2. article, affair, arrangement, production, contrivance, concern, commodity, business (*C*), shebang (*S, U. S.*), dodge (*C or S*).

3. entity (*B or tech.*), individuum (*tech.*), *spec.* non-ego, monad, something.

think, *v. i.* **1.** cogitate (*tech. or B*), ween (*A*); *spec.* misthink; *see* REASON.

2. *To form a conception (of):* dream (*used with "of"*).

3. *As in "to think well of," "to think a good deal of":* reckon (*R*).

think, *v. t.* conceive, ideate; *spec.* imagine, understand, realize.

thinkable, *a.* cogitable (*B*), conceivable, possible; *spec.* imaginable.

thinker, *n.* mind, intellect, intelligence *or* intelligency (*R*); pundit, philosopher.

thinking, *a.* cogitating (*B or tech.*), reasoning, cogitative (*B or tech.*), cogitant (*B*); *see* REASONABLE.

Antonyms: see UNTHINKING.

thinking, *n.* **1.** cogitation (*tech. or B*), thought, brainwork; *spec.* conception, reflection; *see* CONSIDERATION, REASONING, IMAGINATION.

2. *See* BELIEF.

third, *a.* tertiary, ternary, ternal (*R*);—*all B or tech.*

third, *n.* tierce (*obs. or spec.*); *spec.* ditone, terza.

thirst, *n.* **1.** appetite (*contex.*), longing (*contex.*), drought *or* drouth (*A*); *spec.* dipsomania, polydipsia.

2. *See* GREED.

thirsty, *a.* **1.** *Having thirst:* athirst (*A or B*), thirstful (*R*), droughty *or* drouthy (*A*), dry (*C or vulgar*).

2. *Causing thirst:* dry (*C or vulgar*), dipsetic (*tech.*).

3. *See* DESIROUS.

thong, *n.* strip, band, range (*R*); *spec.* riem *or* rheim (*So. Africa*), lasso.

thoracic, *a.* pectoral.

thorn, *n.* **1.** spine; *spec.* brier *or* briar; *see* PRICKLE.

2. *See* ANNOYANCE.

thorough, *a.* complete, absolute, unqualified, straight-out, regular, ingrained, out-and-out, downright, right-down (*C*), outright (*R*), unmitigated (*C*), good (*contex.*); *spec.* radical; *see* EXHAUSTIVE, DEEP.

Antonyms: see NEGLIGENT, INCOMPLETE, PARTIAL.

thoroughly, *adv.* completely, well, up, good (*C*), downright; *spec.* radically.

thoughtful, *a.* **1.** considerative (*tending to thought or contemplation*), reflective, pensive (*R*), cogitabund (*R*), deliberate, musing, contemplative.

Antonyms: see BLANK, THOUGHTLESS, UNTHINKING.

2. *See* CAREFUL, PRUDENT, ATTENTIVE, KINDLY.

thoughtless, *a.* **1.** unthinking, unreflecting, irreflective (*R*), unweighing (*R*), vacant, blank, vacuous (*B*), unideaed (*R*), unideal (*R*), lightheaded (*R*), inconsiderate (*R*), scatter-brained.

2. *Referring to what is done thoughtlessly:* unthinking, unweighed, casual.

Antonyms: see THOUGHTFUL, DELIBERATE.

3. *See* BLANK, CARELESS, STUPID.

thoughtlessness, *n.* unthinkingness, unreflectingness, vacuousness, blankness, *etc.*

Antonyms: see CONSIDERATION.

thousand, *a.* millenary (*B*); *spec.* MILLENNIAL.

thousand, *n.* chiliad (*B*), millennium (*B or spec.*), millenary (*R*), milliad (*R*).

thrash, *v. t.* **1.** strike, beat, thresh (*obs. or R*), curry (*fig.*), comb (*S*), dust (*obs. or C*), wallop (*S*), whale (*C*), trim (*S*), drub, trounce (*C*); *spec.* belt, strap.

2. *See* DEFEAT.

thread, *n.* **1.** string (*contex.*), filament (*contex.*); *spec.* yarn, cotton, linen, purl, lisle, twine, twist, tram, shute, lingel *or* lingle (*dial.*).

2. *The thread of a screw:* fillet.

3. *See* FILAMENT, STREAK, SERIES, CHANNEL, COURSE.

thread, *v. t.* **1.** *Naut.:* reeve.

2. *Referring to a screw: spec.* tap.

3. trace; *spec.* (*of dancing*) braid.

4. *See* FILE.

threadlike, *a.* linear (*chiefly tech.*); *see* HAIRLIKE.

thready, *a.* setuliform (*tech.*); *see* FILAMENTOUS.

threat, *n.* **1.** menace, thunder (*fig.*), thunderbolt (*fig.*), commination (*B*); *spec.* denunciation (*B*).

2. *Referring to the aspect of the sky:* lower *or* lour.

threaten, *v. t.* **1.** menace, threat (*A*), comminate (*R*); *spec.* denounce (*R*), warn.

2. *With the thing held out by way of a threat, as object:* menace; *spec.* vow.

3. *See* FOREBODE.

threaten, *v. i.* overhang, lower *or* lour.

threatening, *a.* **1.** significant (*contex.*), minatory (*B*), menacing, sinister, dark (*contex.*), black (*contex.*), ominous, comminatory *or* (*R*) comminative (*B*), ill-boding, direful, dire, threatful (*R*); *spec.* thundery (*fig.*), denunciatory (*B*).

2. *Referring to the sky, clouds, etc.:* lowering *or* louring, lowery *or* loury.

3. *See* FOREBODING.

three, *n.* trio, ternion (*B*), triad (*chiefly tech.*), trinity (*B or spec.*), trine (*R*); *spec.* triumvirate (*chiefly fig.*), triplet.

three-cornered, *a.* triangular, triangle (*R*), triangled;—*all three tech. or formal.*

threefold, *a.* triple, triplicate, treble, ternary, ternal (*R*), triplasic (*tech.*), triplasian (*obs. or R*), trine (*R*), triadic, trinary; *spec.* trimerous.

threefold, *adv.* triply, trebly.

three-footed, *a.* tripod, tripodal, tripodic (*R*); —*all B or formal.*

three-headed, *a.* tricephalous (*tech.*).

three-hundredth, *a.* tercentennial, tercentenary;—*both B.*

three-legged, *a.* tripod.

three-parted, *a.* tripartite, triparted; *spec.* trichotomous;—*all tech. or B.*

three-sided, *a.* trilateral (*tech. or B*), triquetrous (*chiefly spec.; tech. or B*).

thresh, *v. t. Referring to the threshing of grain:* thrash (*R*); *spec.* flail.

threshold, *n.* **1.** sill, groundsel, doorsill.

2. *See* BORDER, BEGINNING.

3. *In psychology:* limen (*tech.*).

thrill, *n.* sensation (*contex.*), shock, flush, tingle, tickle, electrification (*fig.*), dirl (*Scot. & Eng. dial.*).

thrill, *v. t.* affect (*contex.*), rouse, tingle, tickle, electrify (*fig.*), dirl (*Scot. & Eng. dial.*).

thrilling, *a.* sensational, electric (*fig.*), tinglish (*R*).

thrive, *v. i.* **1.** *See* PROSPER.

2. flourish, batten, boom.

3. grow, flourish; *spec.* bloom, vernate.

throat, *n.* gullet (*a loose, depreciatory use*), throttle (*chiefly dial.*), thropple (*Scot. & dial.*), gorge (*A of the exterior front of the throat; rhetorical of the internal throat*), maw (*chiefly spec.*), lane (*S*), hals (*Scot.*), fauces (*tech.*).

throat, *a.* faucal (*tech.*), guttural (*chiefly tech.*), gular (*zoöl.*), faucial (*R*).

throaty, *a.* hoarse (*contex.*), guttural.

through, *prep.* **1.** thorough (*A*), throughout.

2. *See* BY, DURING.

throw, *v. t.* **1.** *See* PROJECT.

2. *Referring to projection by the motion of the arm or hand:* project, cast (*chiefly B or used in games*), pitch (*chiefly spec.*), sling, fling; *spec.* deliver, hurl, hurtle, launch, skim, lance (*R or B*), elance (*A and R*), toss, chuck (*often C or S*), dash, shy, jaculate (*R*), lob, heave (*naut. or C*), cob, pelt, pitchfork (*fig. or spec.*), sky (*S*), reject (*R*), retroject (*R*), jettison, jerk, quoit, fork, flirt, flip, play, pass.

Antonyms: see CATCH.

3. *Meaning to throw off or down:* cast, tumble,

---

thought: *thinking, intelligence, idea, fancy, opinion, intention, expectation, consideration, attention, care.*
throb, *v. i.: pulsate.*
throne: *seat, chair, cathedra, sovereignty.*
throng, *n.: crowd, multitude, crowding.*
throng, *v. i.: crowd, congregate.*
throng, *v. t.: crowd.*
throw, *v. i.: gamble, flounce.*

---

cant, flap (*C*), flop (*C*), fling; *spec.* wrestle (*cowboy's cant; western U. S.*), hipe; *see* FELL, UNHORSE.
4. precipitate, fling, plunge.
5. *See* OVERTURN, DISCHARGE, PUT, BRING, DEFEAT, EMIT, PLAY, SHED.
throw, *n.* **1.** *See* PROJECTION.
2. *Referring to projection by the motion of the arm:* projection, throwing, cast (*chiefly B or used in games*); *spec.* delivery, pitch, sling, fling, hurl, toss, chuck; dash, shy, jaculation (*R*), put (*Scot. or cant*), lob, rejection, downcast, flip.
3. *See* PLAY; *spec.* crab, nick, cast, main.
4. precipitation, throwing, plunge, pitch.
5. *Meaning a casting off or down:* cast, cant, tumble, fall (*chiefly spec.*), fling; *spec.* buttock, backcast, nelson, hipe.
throwing, *a.* jaculatory (*R*).
thrum, *v. i.* **1.** strum; *see* DRUM.
2. *See* HUM.
thrum, *v. t.* strum; *spec.* thumb; *see* PLAY.
thrum, *n.* **1.** strum.
2. *See* HUM.
thrushlike, *a.* turdiform (*tech.*).
thrust, *n.* **1.** *See* PUSH.
2. push, pass (*chiefly fencing and pugilism*), dub (*C*); *spec.* dab, jab (*C*), job, plunge, lunge.
thrust, *v. t.* **1.** *See* PUSH.
2. push, propel, stick, poke, run; *spec.* plunge, lunge (*R*), ram, jam, jab (*C*), perk, strike (*contex.*).
Antonyms: see DRAW.
3. punch, dig; *see* POKE.
4. *See* PROPEL, PUT.
thrust, *v. i.* **1.** push, pass; *spec.* lunge, poke, job, jab (*C*), prick, dab, foil (*A*), foin (*R or obs.*).
2. push, poke; *spec.* lunge, pass (*chiefly fencing and pugilism*), plunge, ram, job, jab (*C*).
3. punch, dig (*C*), dub; *spec.* stab, poke.
thumb, *n.* digit (*formal or B*), pollex (*tech.*).
thunder, *v. i.* **1.** detonate (*R*), fulmine *or* fulminate (*R*).
2. *See* RESOUND, SHOUT.
thunderbolt, *n.* thunder (*B or A*), thunderstone (*A*), thunderstroke.
thunderclap, *n.* thunder (*B or rhetorical*), thunderblast.
thunderous, *a.* **1.** thundering, fulminatory (*R*), thundery.
2. *See* RESONANT.
ticket, *n.* **1.** *Spec.* coupon, ballot; *see* LABEL, LIST.
2. *Referring to a ticket of admission:* pasteboard (*S*), billet (*A or obs.*); *spec.* ivory (*S or cant*).
ticking, *n.* *The sound:* tick-tock (*C*).
tickle, *v. t.* **1.** *See* PLEASE, DIVERT.
2. titillate, curry (*fig.*); *spec.* ginnel.
tickling, *n.* titillation.
ticklish, *a.* **1.** tickly, kittly (*Scot. and local U. S.*).
2. *See* DANGEROUS.
tidied, *a.* redd (*Scot.; chiefly with "up"*).
tidy, *n.* antimacassar (*R or obs.*).
tidy, *v. t.* arrange, groom, redd (*Scot. or dial.; chiefly with "up"*).
Antonyms: see DISARRANGE.
tie, *n.* **1.** *See* BAND, BOND, FASTENING, OBLIGATION, EQUALITY.
2. *In music, typography, and writing:* ligature, slur (*music*).
tiger, *n.* cat (*in zoölogical classification*), pussy (*humorous*), Johnny (*sportsman's cant*); *spec.* whelp.
tight, *a.* **1.** *See* COMPACT, FIRM, NARROW, IMPASSABLE, CLOSE, STINGY.
2. tense, taut *or* taught (*chiefly naut.*), strict (*R or tech.*), strait (*R or B*), hard (*contex.*); *spec.* snug.
Antonyms: see LOOSE.
tighten, *v. t.* **1.** draw (*contex.*), tauten; *spec.* lace.
Antonyms: see LOOSE, RELAX.
2. *Spec.* flag.
tightness, *n.* tension, tensity, *etc.*
tile, *n.* plate; *spec.* quarl, head, pantile.
timber, *n.* **1.** wood (*contex.*); *spec.* lumber (*chiefly U. S.*), raff, pilework, piling, stumpage (*cant, U. S.*).
2. *See* BEAM, MATERIAL.
timbre, *n.* *In music:* clang tint *or* (*for short*) clang.
time, *n.* **1.** tide (*A*), space (*R, exc. contex.*), day (*fig.*), days (*pl.; less fig. than "day"*); *spec.* long, eve, usance, breathing, bit; *see* DATE, PERIOD, LEISURE, OPPORTUNITY, EXPERIENCE.
2. *Referring to a particular instant in time, without reference to duration:* point, instant, moment; *spec.* bell; *see* HOUR.
timely, *a.* **1.** appropriate, seasonable, opportune, tempestive (*A*), convenient (*A*), timeous (*obs. or tech.*); *spec.* fortunate, acceptable.
Antonyms: see UNTIMELY, IMPROPER.
2. *See* EARLY.
timely, *adv.* **1.** acceptably, seasonably, opportunely, apropos.
2. *See* EARLY.
timepiece, *n.* timekeeper, horologe (*tech.*), horologium (*R*), chronometer (*chiefly spec.*), clock (*chiefly spec.*); *spec.* watch, water glass, journeyman, clepsydra, hydroscope, regulator, repeater.
timeserver, *n.* opportunist, temporizer, trimmer.
timeservice, *n.* opportunism (*chiefly politics*).
timeserving, *a.* opportunist, temporizing, politic, diplomatic.
time-table, *n.* schedule (*chiefly U. S.*).
timid, *a.* fearful, timorous (*B or formal*), meticulous (*obs.*), scary (*C*), pavid (*R*), tremulous (*R or spec.*), unhardy (*R*); *spec.* shrink-

thumb, *v. t.: handle, read.*
tide, *n.: flow.*
tide, *v. i.: float, flow.*
tide, *v. t.: transport.*
tie, *v. t.: bind, fasten, knot, equal, confine, attach, restrict.*
tiff, *n.: pet, quarrel.*
tilt, *n.: inclination, fight, contest.*

ing, shy, diffident, faint-hearted, faint, half-hearted, cow-hearted (*R*), creepmouse (*fig.; chiefly in nursery talk*), cowardly, superstitious, heartless (*R*), spiritless (*R*), spineless (*fig.*), inadventurous (*R*), ghastful (*A*), funky (*S*); *see* BASHFUL.

Antonyms: see ASSURED, BOLD, CONFIDENT, VENTURESOME.

timidity, *n.* timidness, fearfulness, timorousness (*B or formal*), meticulousness (*obs.*); *spec.* shyness, cowardice, cowardliness, diffidence, faint-heartedness, *etc.; see* BASHFULNESS.

Antonyms: see ASSURANCE, BOLDNESS, *etc.*

tinkle, *n.* ring, tinkling, ting-a-ling (*C*), tintinnabulation (*B*), ting (*R*), tingle (*R*), tink (*R*); *see* RING.

tinkle, *v. i.* ring, tink (*R*), ting (*R*).

tinner, *n.* tinsmith, tinman, whitesmith (*R or obsolescent*).

tint, *n.* color (*contex.*), shade, tinge, tincture (*R*), tinct (*A or B*), tone, cast.

tint, *v. t.* color (*contex.*), shade, tinge, tinct (*A or B*), tincture (*R*).

tip, *v. t. & i.* **1.** *See* TAP, INCLINE, INFORM.

2. fee, remember (*euphemistic*), pouch (*S or C*), dash *or* dashee (*African coast*), baksheesh (*Oriental*).

tip, *n.* **1.** *See* TAP, INCLINATION.

2. point, pointer (*C, U. S.*), hint.

3. gift, fee, dash *or* dashee (*African coast*), baksheesh (*Oriental*), bonus, pourboire (*French*), gratuity.

tipple, *v. i.* drink, nip.

tippler, *n.* drinker, nipper, bencher, sipper.

tirade, *n.* discourse (*contex.*), harangue, declamation, screed, rant.

tirade, *v. i.* discourse (*contex.*), harangue, declaim, rant, screed (*R*).

tire, *n.* **1.** *See* DRESS.

2. tyre (*the usual British spelling*); *spec.* pneumatic.

tire, *v. t.* **1.** weary, fatigue, tucker (*C; New Eng. usually in p. p. with "out"*), forweary (*A*); *spec.* jade, fag, bore, exhaust.

Antonyms: see DIVERT, REFRESH, REST, RESTORE.

2. *See* SICKEN.

tire, *v. i.* **1.** weary, flag; *spec.* jade, fag.

2. *See* SICKEN.

tired, *a.* wearied, weary, fatigued, pooped (*S*), bushed (*S*), fagged (*A*), washed out (*C*); *spec.* tiry (*C and R*).

Antonyms: see FRESH.

tiresome, *a.* **1.** wearisome, fatiguing, tedious; *spec.* fagging.

Antonyms: see RESTFUL.

2. *See* DULL.

tissue, *n.* **1.** *See* FABRIC, STRUCTURE.

2. *In biology: spec.* web, membrane, parenchyma, prosenchyma, cartilage, cinenchyma, muscle, *etc.*

to, *prep.* **1.** toward.

2. *See* AT, BY, UNTIL, AFTER.

toad, *n.* batrachian, paddock (*A*), toadlet *or* toadling (*dim.*).

toast, *v. t.* **1.** *Spec. see* BROWN, WARM.

2. drink, bumper (*R*), pledge.

toast, *n.* **1.** pledge, pledging, wassail (*obs. or A*), skoal (*A*); *spec.* sentiment, health.

2. *See* GLOW.

tobacco, *n.* weed (*C*), nicotian (*R*), Nicotiana (*a personification*).

toddle, *v. i.* walk, waddle, paddle.

toe, *n.* digit (*tech.; humorous or affected in ordinary language*), dactyl *or* dactylus (*tech.*); *spec.* heel, hallux.

together, *adv. Spec.* mutually, reciprocally, unitedly, conjointly, contemporaneously.

Antonyms: see APART.

toilet, *n.* **1.** attire, dress, dressing.

2. *Spec.* table.

3. *Spec.* room, wardrobe (*A*), powder-room (*euphemism*), cabinet (*French*), water-closet (*A*), W. C. (*C, B*), Ajax (*A, B*), Vespasien (*A, French*), jakes (*A, B*), privy, outhouse, backhouse (*C*), comfort-station (*U. S. euphemism*), restroom, bathroom, lavatory, latrine (*military*), washroom, No. OO (*Continental*), can (*C, U. S.*), jo (*C, U. S.*), john (*C*).

tolerant, *a.* **1.** *See* ENDURANT.

2. forbearing, indulgent; *see* LIBERAL.

Antonyms: see INTOLERANT.

tolerate, *v. t.* **1.** *See* ENDURE, PERMIT.

2. indulge.

toleration, *n.* **1.** *See* ENDURANCE, PERMISSION.

2. tolerance, forbearance, indulgence; *spec.* liberality.

tomb, *n.* **1.** *See* GRAVE.

2. sepulcher *or* sepulchre (*hist. or rhetorical*), sepulture (*A*), bier (*R*), cist (*archæol.*); *spec.* mausoleum, charnel, charnel house, feretory, mastaba *or* mastabah, vault.

to-morrow, *n.* morrow (*B*), to-morn (*obs. or dial.*).

tone, *n.* **1.** *See* SOUND.

2. *Referring to a sound of a definite musical pitch:* note; *spec.* second, third, fifth, *etc.*, touch, hypate (*ancient Greek music*), toot, monotone.

3. *Referring to vocal pitch or modulation:* strain, key, accent, intonation; *spec.* singsong.

4. *Referring to the sentiment of discourse:* strain, key, spirit, accent (*often in pl., as in "in accents mild"*).

5. *See* TEMPER, STRAIN, HEALTH, STATE, HUE.

---

tinge, *n.: tint, quality, trace, admixture.*
tinge, *v. t.: tint, dye, impregnate.*
titillate: *please, tickle.*
title, *n.: heading, name, right, ownership.*
toady, *n.: fawner.*
toil, *n.: net.*
toil, *n. & v.: work.*
token: *sign, symbol, badge, evidence.*
tolerable: *endurable, fair, inferior, considerable.*
tolerance: *endurance, toleration.*
tolerate: *endure, permit, indulge.*
toll: *ring.*
toll: *tax.*
tomboy: *hoyden.*

---

tongue, *n.* **1.** lingua (*tech.*), clapper (*S*), clack (*S*).
2. *Referring to a tonguelike part: spec.* lingua, lingula, languet (*chiefly mach.*), examen (*R*), doab *or* daub, clapper.
3. *See* LANGUAGE, POLE, POINTER, HEADLAND.
tongue-shaped, *a.* lingulate, linguiform;—*both tech. or B*).
tooth, *n.* **1.** ivory (*S*), dental (*humorous*); *spec.* game (*pl.; Scot.*), fang, snag, tang, gang tooth, pearl (*fig.*), incisor, molar; *see* TUSK.
2. projection (*contex.*), dent (*tech.*), jag; *spec.* denticle, denticulation, dentil *or* dentel (*A*), cog, spur, sprocket.
3. *See* TASTE.
toothless, *a.* edentate (*tech.; chiefly spec.*), edentulate, edentulous (*R*), anodont (*R*); *spec.* fangless.
tooth-shaped, *a.* dentiform (*tech.*), odontoid (*R*);—*both tech. or B.*
top, *n.* **1.** *See* HEAD, CROWN.
2. summit, head, cop (*obs. or dial.*), crown, apex, upside (*R*); *spec.* tiptop.
Antonyms: see BOTTOM.
3. *Referring to a top sloping to a point or edge:* apex, peak, vertex, fastigium (*chiefly architecture; R*), pitch; *spec.* crest, edge.
Antonyms: see BOTTOM.
4. *Referring to the piece or covering forming the top:* head, headpiece (*chiefly in spec.*), heading, cap, capping, crown, cumulus (*R*), topping, capital (*chiefly architecture*); *spec.* drumhead, lid, capstone, cornice, corona, larmier, coping.
top, *v. t.* **1.** cover, cap, tip, crown, head, surmount, crest, ride.
2. ascend, surmount, rise (*chiefly U. S.*), crest (*R*).
3. head; *spec.* crop, pollard, pall.
4. *See* CROWN, SURPASS.
top, *a.* **1.** highest, topmost, apical (*B or tech.*), culminal (*R*), culminant (*R*), uppermost, overmost.
2. *See* CHIEF.
top-shaped, *a.* turbinate (*tech.*).
torch, *n.* link (*B, R*), brand (*B*), flambeau, mussal (*Anglo-Indian*); *spec.* lampion, light.
torchbearer, *n.* linkman *or* linkboy (*R or B*), lampadephore (*Greek antiq.; R*), mussalchee (*Anglo-Indian*).
torn, *a.* rent, riven (*B*), lacerate *or* lacerated (*tech. or B*), mangled, broken.
Antonyms: see INTACT.
tort, *n.* delict (*civil and Scots law*); *spec.* trespass.
torture, *v. t.* **1.** pain (*a contex. sense*), agonize, torment, excruciate, anguish (*R*); *spec.* impale, martyr *or* (*R*) martyrize, strappado, rack, roast, burn, card, pincer, boot.
2. *See* GRIEVE, PERVERT.
torture, *n.* pain, torment, excruciation; *spec.* impalement, martyrdom, strappado, estrapade, fire, boot, screws, rack, sling, *etc.*
Antonyms: see PLEASURE.
torturer, *n.* tormenter, excruciator.
torturous, *a.* painful, excruciating (*often humorous*), agonizing.
Antonyms: see PLEASANT.
totter, *v. i.* **1.** *See* FALTER.
2. *Referring to what seems about to fall from weakness or instability:* shake, reel, stagger, rock, titubate (*R*), waver, tremble.
totter, *n.* **1.** *See* FALTER.
2. shake, reel, stagger, rock, titubation (*R*), waver, tremble.
tottering, *a.* shaky, labefact (*R*), titubant (*R*), staggering, *etc.*
Antonyms: see FIRM.
touch, *v. t.* **1.** *Spec.* reach, impinge (*tech.*), kiss, lick, sweep, brush, glance, graze, feel, handle, palm, toe, finger, join, adjoin.
2. *See* AFFECT, INJURE, IMPAIR, CARESS, ANNOY, SOFTEN, PLAY, TAINT, REACH, IRRITATE.
touch, *v. i.* **1.** contact (*R and tech.*); *spec.* impinge, kiss, glance, graze, brush, lap, border, adjoin, join, osculate.
2. *See* STOP.
touch, *n.* **1.** contact, impact (*tech.*), trait (*A; now chiefly fig.*), tangence (*R*), attaint (*A*); *spec.* feel, kiss, graze, glance, brush, osculation, tickle, button; *see* IMPACT.
2. sensation, feel, feeling.
3. *Referring to a quality of a player or artist:* hand, stroke; *spec.* finger.
4. *See* CARESS, ACTION, EXECUTION, STROKE, LITTLE, DASH, TRACE, FIT, IMPERFECTION.
touching, *n.* contingence (*R or tech.*), joinder (*R*), tangence *or* tangency (*tech.; chiefly spec.*); *spec.* adjacence, adjacency.
touching, *a.* **1.** tangent (*tech.; chiefly spec.*); *spec.* adjacent.
Antonyms: see APART.
2. *See* AFFECTING.
toughen, *v. t.* strengthen (*contex.*); *spec.* indurate, inure; *see* ANNEAL, HARDEN.
tournament, *n.* **1.** fight, tourney; *spec.* hastilude (*hist.*), carrousel, justs *or* jousts.
2. *See* CONTEST.
tousle, *v. t.* **1.** ill-treat (*contex.*), tumble, touse (*R*), maul, mishandle, manhandle (*S*), mouse *or* mousle (*A*).
2. *See* WORRY, DISHEVEL.
tow, *v. t.* **1.** draw (*contex.*), drag, cordelle (*U. S. & Canada*); *spec.* tug, track.
Antonyms: see PUSH.
2. *See* DRAW.
tow, *n.* **1.** draw, drag;—*referring to the act of towing a vessel.*
2. towline, cordelle (*U. S. & Canada*).

tool, *n.: instrument, puppet.*
tool, *v. i.: drive, bowl.*
torment, *v. t.: pain, torture, distress, tease, annoy, trouble.*
tortuous: *sinuous, indirect.*
toss, *v. t.: throw, agitate, annoy, bandy.*
total, *a.: whole, absolute.*
total, *n.: whole, sum.*
total, *v. i.: amount.*
total, *v. t.: add, constitute.*
tough, *a.: strong, intractable, hardy, difficult, troublesome, violent.*
tough, *n.: rowdy.*
tour, *v. i. & t.: sightsee.*

toward, *prep.* towards (*less usual than "toward"*), to.
Antonyms: see FROM.
towel, *n.* cloth (*contex.*), wiper (*R*), diaper (*R or obs.*), napkin (*R*); *spec.* lavabo (*eccl.*), rubber.
tower, *n. Spec.* towerlet, sikhra, vimana, pyramid, pagoda, pylon, bastile, lantern, peel, donjon, dungeon, barbican, bartizan, beacon, tracker, turret, helepole (*hist.*), belfry, castle, keep, spire.
town, *n.* burg (*C or S; U. S.*), wick (*obs., exc. in place names*); *spec.* borough, city, burgh (*now Scot.*), pueblo, hamlet.
townsman, *n.* citizen (*contex.*), towny (*S*), urbanite (*humorous*), urban (*R*), oppidan (*R*), burgher (*A*), snob (*university cant; Eng.*), Philistine (*a term of dislike or contempt*), cit (*short for "citizen"*); *spec.* cad (*Eng.*).
Antonyms: see RUSTIC.
toy, *v. i.* **1.** *See* PLAY.
2. play, dally, dalliance (*R*), trifle, fondle, wanton, daff (*chiefly Scot.*); *spec.* finger, fiddle, twiddle, twaddle (*R*).
trace, *n. Part of a harness:* tug.
trace, *n.* **1.** *See* TRACK, FOOTPRINT, EVIDENCE, DRAWING, DELINEATION.
2. mark, impression, vestige, vestigium (*tech.*).
3. trifle, taste, savor, smack, smatch, shadow, shade, smell, tang, touch, suspicion (*C*), flavor, suggestion, hint, tinge, cast; *spec.* ray, trick, strain, streak, spark, sparkle, tincture; *see* DASH.
trace, *v. t.* **1.** follow; *spec.* retrace.
2. *See* TRACK, DELINEATE, DESCRIBE, COPY, PERCEIVE.
3. derive, track, fetch (*obs. or R*), deduce.
track, *n.* **1.** trace, trail, wake, vestige (*R*), slot (*A or spec.*), run (*R*), rack (*R*); *spec.* tail (*tech.*), file, spoor, furrow, footing (*R*), scent; *see* FOOTPRINT, PATH.
2. way (*contex.*), road (*contex.*), run, runaway, rails (*collective pl.*); *spec.* tramway (*Eng.*), tram (*Eng.*), plate; *see* SIDING.
3. *See* ROAD, COURSE.
track, *v. t.* **1.** trace, trail, spoor, slot (*R, exc. spec.*); *spec.* pad, foot (*R*), prick, pug (*Anglo-Indian*), scent, road, draw (*hunting*).
2. *See* TRACE.
trade, *n.* **1.** *See* BUSINESS, ASSOCIATION, BARTER, TRAFFIC, SALE.
2. craft, handicraft, mystery (*A*).
tradesman, *n.* dealer; *spec.* shopkeeper.
tradition, *n.* **1.** *See* DELIVERY.
2. *Spec.* folklore, sunna.
traditional, *a.* traditive (*B*), traditionary (*R*), unwritten.
traffic, *n.* **1.** *See* DEALING.
2. business (*contex.*), trade, trading, operations (*pl.*), mongering (*chiefly A or depreciatory*), dealing, commerce (*implies, along with the broader sense of* trade, *a large scale or general view; whereas other senses of* traffic *are restricted to smaller or more specific* business dealings), merchantry (*R*), truck, merchandry (*A*), nundination (*R*), chapmanry (*obs. or A*), chaffer (*obs.*); *spec.* simony, huckstery, arbitrage, contraband, barter.
traffic, *v. i.* **1.** trade, deal, operate, merchandise, merchant (*R*), chaffer (*obs. or A*); *spec.* huckster, bucket, truck, barter, commerce.
2. *See* DEAL.
tragedian, *n.* actor (*contex.*), Thespian (*B or humorous*).
tragedy, *n.* drama (*contex.*), buskin (*fig.*).
Antonyms: see BURLESQUE.
tragic, *a.* dramatic, cothurnal (*fig.*), Thespian (*B*), buskined (*fig.*).
Antonyms: see COMIC.
trail, *n.* **1.** train (*chiefly spec.*), drag, tail.
2. *See* TRACK, PATH.
train, *n.* **1.** *See* TAIL, PROCESSION, SERIES, SET, RETINUE, SEQUEL.
2. *Referring to persons or things following or attending:* entourage, cortège (*French*); *spec.* coffle (*Oriental*).
3. *Spec.* local, express, accommodation, freight.
train, *v. t.* **1.** teach, discipline, drill, educate, school (*chiefly spec.*), form (*R*); *spec.* make (*cant*), rehearse, pace, gait; *see* ACCUSTOM, EXERCISE.
2. *In horticulture: spec.* espalier.
3. *See* AIM.
trained, *a.* skilled, disciplined, educated (*contex.*); *spec.* thorough-paced, reared.
Antonyms: see UNTRAINED.
trainer, *n.* educator (*contex.*), drill *or* driller (*chiefly mil.*), coach (*chiefly spec.*); *spec.* roughrider, walker, lanista (*Roman antiq.*).
training, *n.* discipline, drill, drilling, school (*chiefly military; cant*), manage (*equestrianism, A*), making (*tech.; hunting*), education; *see* EXERCISE.
training, *a.* educative (*contex.*).
traitor, *n.* betrayer, proditor (*obs. or R*), snake (*fig.*), serpent (*fig.*), traitress (*fem.*), Iscariot (*fig.*), Judas (*fig.*), renegade, turncoat; *spec.* parricide (*fig.*), deserter.
Antonyms: see PATRIOT.
tramp, *v. i.* go (*contex.*); *spec.* walk, hike, plod, trudge.
trample, *v. t.* tread (*contex.*), betrample (*intensive*), tramp, overtread (*R*), over-trample (*R*); *spec.* hobnail, poach.
trampled, *a.* trod *or* trodden (*chiefly used in composition*).
trance, *n.* ecstasy (*hist.*), rapture (*obs.*), catalepsy, hypnosis, coma.
transaction, *n.* **1.** *See* DOING.
2. act, action, affair, job, deal (*U. S.*).

---

traceable: *attributable.*
tractable: *adaptable, manageable.*
trail, *v. t.: draw, draggle, track, hunt.*
trail, *v. i.: draw, hang, float, flow, creep.*
trait: *touch, characteristic, quality.*
traitorous: *treacherous, treasonable.*
tramp, *n.: step, tread, walk, pedestrian, vagrant.*
transcendent: *excessive, fine, unequaled.*

---

transcribe, *v. t.* **1.** write (*contex.*), copy; *spec.* exemplify, engross, estreat.
2. *See* TRANSLITERATE.
transcriber, *n.* writer, copyist, scrivener, scribe (*B or specific*); *spec.* literalist.
transcript, *n.* writing (*contex.*), copy, transcription; *spec.* exemplification, engrossment, estreat.
transcription, *n.* **1.** *Referring to the action:* writing, copying, transcribing; *spec.* exemplification, engrossment.
2. *Referring to the copy: see* TRANSCRIPT.
transfer, *v. t.* **1.** *See* REMOVE, COPY.
2. convey, cede (*formal or tech.*), alienate (*tech.*), grant (*R or tech.*), divest (*B*), pass (*contex.*), transmigrate (*R*); *spec.* devise, bequeath, consign, assign, lease, charter, will, demise, give, negotiate, mancipate.
3. *Referring to intangible things:* pass, remove, devolve, devolute (*R*), translate (*chiefly spec.*), transfuse (*fig.*), transmit, shift, transplant (*chiefly fig. or spec.*), post, carry; *see* DELEGATE.
transfer, *n.* **1.** *See* REMOVAL, MOVEMENT, COPY.
2. transference, transferal, conveyance, cession (*R or tech.; often spec.*), assignment (*often spec.*), assignation (*R*), alienation (*tech.*), disposal, disposure (*R*), grant (*chiefly tech.*), passing (*contex.*); *spec.* deed, devise, devisal, bequest, bequeathment (*R*), bequeathal (*R*), lease, demise, mancipation (*R*), commendation, negotiation, gift.
3. *Referring to intangible things:* transferal, transference, removal, devolvement, devolution, translation (*chiefly spec.*), transfusion (*fig.*), transplantation (*chiefly fig. or spec.*), transmission, transmittal, shift; *spec.* convection, metonymy, metaphor.
transferable, *a.* conveyable, assignable, disponible (*Scot.*), *etc.; spec.* bequeathable, devisable, negotiable.
transferee, *n.* assignee (*often spec.*), grantee; *spec.* consignee, indorsee, legatee, devisee, donee.
transfix, *v. t.* pierce, impale, transpierce (*R*); *spec.* spit, broach, stake (*R*), spear, skewer, pin.
transform, *v. t.* (*Implies a fundamental change in nature or appearance*) change (*contex.*), transfigure (*implies exaltation, with religious overtones*), transfigurate (*R*), convert (*changing from one state to another, either material or spiritual*), metamorphose (*utterly change, often by enchantment*), translate (*chiefly spec.*), transverse (*R*), transmute (*a change in essential nature or substance, especially from lower to higher*), transpeciate (*R*), transnature (*R*), transmogrify (*humorous or contemptuous*), transshape (*R*); *spec.* transubstantiate, bedevil, revolutionize, resolve.
transformation, *n.* change (*contex.*), transfiguration, transfigurement, conversion, metamorphosis (*chiefly spec.*), translation (*chiefly spec.*), transmutation (*chiefly spec.*), version (*R*), transmorphism (*R*), transnaturation (*R*), transpeciation (*R*), transmogrification (*humorous or contemptuous*), metastasis (*R*); *spec.* resolution, diagenesis.
transgress, *v. i.* offend, trespass (*A or B*), slip, fault (*A*), misdo (*R*); *see* SIN.
transgression, *n.* **1.** *See* VIOLATION, DISOBEDIENCE.
2. offense, trespass (*A or B*), slip, misdeed, fault, delinquency (*chiefly B or tech.*), crime, delict (*tech.; chiefly a term of Roman or Civil law or of French law*); *spec.* enormity, misdemeanor; *see* SIN.
transgressor, *n.* offender, offendant (*R*), trespasser (*B or A*), misdoer, delinquent, culprit, misfeasor; *spec.* malefactor, criminal, misdemeanant; *see* SINNER.
Antonyms: see INNOCENT.
transience, *n.* **1.** transientness (*R*), transiency, temporariness, evanescence (*chiefly fig.*), fugacity *or* fugaciousness (*B*), caducity (*R*), impermanence *or* impermanency, ephemerality, ephemeralness, passingness (*R*), fleetingness (*R*), preterience (*R*), volatility (*R*); *see* BREVITY.
Antonyms: see PERMANENCE.
2. cursoriness (*cf.* CURSORY).
transient, *a.* **1.** transitory (*emphasizing the brief duration of a passing, as contrasted to* transient *which implies the fact of quick passing*), temporary, momentary, fleeting, passing, impermanent, ephemeral (*short-lived*), ephemerous (*R*), evanescent (*quickly vanishing*), caducous (*R*), evanid (*A*), fugitive, volatile (*B*), fleet (*B*), meteoric (*fig.*), cometary (*fig.*), fugacious (*B*), preterient (*R*); *spec.* transeunt, transitive, monohemerous (*med.*), deciduous; *see* BRIEF, SHORT-LIVED.
Antonyms: see IMPERISHABLE, PERMANENT, CONSTANT.
2. *See* PASSING, CURSORY.
transient, *n.* ephemeron (*B*), rolling stone (*fig. and spec.*).
transition, *n.* change (*contex.*), transit (*R*), passing, passage; *spec.* leap, jump, break, graduation, saltation (*B*), saltus (*R*), play, rise, fall, metastasis, metabasis.
transitional, *a.* passing; *spec.* gradual, metabatic.
translate, *v. t.* **1.** *See* MOVE, TRANSFER, TRANSFORM.
2. *Referring to being carried to heaven without death:* transport, ravish (*R*), enheaven (*R*).
3. render, turn, do (*contex.*), put (*contex.*), throw (*contex.*), construe (*a loose use*); *spec.* retranslate, retrovert (*R*), transdialect (*R*), interpret, English, paraphrase, metaphrase (*R*), decipher, decode (*cant*).
translation, *n.* **1.** *See* MOTION, TRANSFER, TRANSFORMATION.
2. *Referring to the action:* rendition (*U. S.*), version, construction (*a loose use*), turning.
3. *Referring to the result:* version, construe (*a*

transfigure: *transform, dignify, idealize.*
transfuse: *pour, transfer, inject.*
transgress, *v. t.: violate, disobey.*
transitory: *trancient, shortlived.*

loose use); *spec.* metaphrase, paraphrase, interpretation; *see* CRIB.
translator, *n.* renderer, doer (*contex.*), versionist (*R*); *spec.* interpreter.
transliterate, *v. t.* transcribe; *spec.* decode.
translucent, *a.* **1.** *See* TRANSPARENT.
2. semitransparent, semiopaque, semidiaphanous (*R*), translucid (*R*).
Antonyms: see OPAQUE.
transmigrate, *v. i.* **1.** *See* MIGRATE.
2. metempsychosize (*R*), transcorporate (*R*).
transmission, *n.* **1.** *See* COMMUNICATION.
2. *In physics:* transmittal, transmitment (*R*), propagation, conveyance, conduction (*chiefly spec.*); *spec.* convection, radiation, circulation, communication.
transmit, *v. t.* **1.** *See* SEND, TRANSFER, COMMUNICATE.
2. *In physics:* convey, propagate, conduct; *spec.* radiate, communicate.
transparency, *n.* **1.** clearness, transparence, diaphaneity *or* diaphanousness (*B or tech.*), lucidity *or* lucidness (*B*), limpidity (*B*), lucency (*R*), pellucidness *or* pellucidity (*B*); *spec.* thinness, cloudlessness.
2. *Referring to a transparent object:* transparence, diaphane (*B*); *spec.* diapositive.
transparent, *a.* **1.** *Referring to what can be seen through:* diaphanous (*B or tech.*), clear, translucent (*allowing light only to pass through*), lucid (*B*), pellucid (*B*), limpid (*implying clearness as of water; B*), transpicuous (*R*), crystal (*fig.*); *spec.* thin, cloudless, white.
Antonyms: see OPAQUE.
2. *Referring to what can be seen through mentally:* flimsy, thin.
transpire, *v. i.* **1.** *See* EXHALE, OCCUR.
2. escape (*contex.*), leak out.
transplant, *v. t.* **1.** plant, replant; *spec.* repot.
2. *In surgery:* graft.
transport, *v. t.* **1.** move (*contex.*), carry, take (*contex.*), convey, transfer, bear (*primarily spec.*), translate (*B*); *spec.* conduct, lug (*C*), smuggle, row, pull, boat, tide, ship, raft, trail, float, wagon, cart, truck, coach, chair, horse, telpher, vehicle, buck (*C, U. S.*), waft, wheel, transship, tram, pack, portage, sled (*chiefly U. S.*), sledge, roll, bowl, run, drive, wing, whirl, drog (*R, Eng.*), whisk, freight, ferry; *see* TRANSLATE, EXPEL, ABDUCT.
2. overpower, ravish, enravish (*R*), enrapture, entrance, trance (*R*), imparadise *or* emparadise (*fig.; B*), rapture (*R*), rape (*R*), rap (*R*), rapturize (*R*); *spec. see* FRENZY.
transport, *n.* **1.** *See* MOVEMENT, TRANSPORTATION, VESSEL.
2. ravishment, transportation (*R*), rape (*R or A*), rapture (*R*).
3. *See* FRENZY.
transportation, *n.* movement (*contex.*), carriage, transportal (*R*), conveyance, bearing (*primarily spec.*), transporting, transport, transit (*R*), transference, translation (*B*); *spec.* fare (*obs.*), lug (*C*), traduction (*R*), transvection (*R*), convection (*R*), shipment, transshipment, ferriage, telpherage, portage, truckage, porterage, freight, gestation (*R; tech.*); *see* EXPULSION.
transported, *a.* entranced, ravished, spellbound (*rather C or spec.*); *see* FRANTIC, ECSTATIC.
transporter, *n.* carrier, bearer, conveyer; *spec.* porter, shipper.
transporting, *a.* entrancing, ravishing, Orphic (*fig.*).
transpose, *v. t.* interchange, transverse (*R*); *spec. see* REVERSE.
trap, *n.* **1.** gin (*A*); *spec.* snare, net, pit, springe, trapfall, deadfall (*chiefly U. S.*), creel, pot, cruive (*British*), mousetrap.
2. *In a figurative sense:* snare, gin (*B*), net, trepan *or* trapan (*A*), ambush.
trap, *v. t.* **1.** catch, entrap (*R or B*), gin (*A*); *spec.* snare, springe; *see* SNARE, NET.
Antonyms: see FREE.
2. *In a figurative sense:* catch, snare, insnare *or* ensnare, tangle, trepan *or* trapan (*A*), gin (*B*), enmesh.
trap, *v. t.* adorn, caparison.
trapping, *n.* **1.** *For a horse:* caparison, bard.
2. *In pl.: see* DRESS, ORNAMENTATION.
travel, *v. i.* **1.** go (*contex.*), itinerate (*R or spec.*), journey; *spec.* rail, railroad (*U. S.*), tram (*Eng.*), tramp, rogue (*now R*), drive, wheel (*C*), stage, camel, cab, caroche (*obs.*), roll, gig, sledge, sled (*U. S.*), train, post, motor, boat, canoe, sail, steam, trek (*South Africa or C*), pad; *see* JOURNEY.
2. *See* MOVE, JOURNEY.
traveler, *n.* **1.** goer (*contex.*), ganger (*A*), viator (*R*), wayfarer, passenger, itinerant (*R or spec.*); *spec.* polytopian (*to many places; R*), sleigher, rider, excursionist, roadster, trekker.
2. *See* JOURNEYER.
traveling, *a.* **1.** going (*contex.*), travel, journeying, itinerant (*R, exc. spec.*), errant (*A, exc. spec.*).
2. *See* MOVABLE.
traveling, *n.* **1.** going (*contex.*), journeying, travel, itineration (*R*), itinerancy (*B*), itineracy (*R*).
2. *See* GOING.
traveling salesman, *n.* drummer, traveler (*Brit.*).
traverse, *v. t.* **1.** *See* CROSS, TURN, OPPOSE, CONTRADICT.
2. travel, make (*contex.*), cover (*chiefly contex.*), transit (*R*), overgo (*R*), overpass (*R*), peregrinate (*R*), pervade (*R*), itinerate (*R*), peragrate (*R*); *spec.* run, round, range, quarter, march, ride, walk, retravel, retraverse, patrol, promenade, perambulate, wander, scour, track, measure, overmeasure (*R*), wing, procession (*R*), sail, boat, cruise, shoot, over-

transmute: *change, transform.* | **transpire,** *v. t.: exhale, occur.* | **trash:** *refuse, nonsense.*

sail (*R*), override (*R*), overwalk (*R*), overwander (*R*), navigate, swim, trot, thread, tramp, trace (*R or obs.*), ply, percur (*R*).

tray, *n. Spec.* box, plateau, galley, coaster, trencher, voider, salver, server.

treacherous, *a.* **1.** faithless, traitorous, traitor, false, perfidious, untrue, recreant (*B*), reptile (*fig.*), snaky (*fig.*), Iscariotic *or* Iscariotical (*fig.; R*), trappy (*C*), serpentine (*fig.*), proditorious (*R*), trustless (*R*), treasonable (*chiefly spec.*), Punic (*fig.*), treasonous (*R*); *see* TREASONABLE.

Antonyms: see CONSTANT.

2. *See* DECEITFUL, UNRELIABLE, UNSAFE.

treachery, *n.* faithlessness, traitorousness, treason (*chiefly spec.*), infidelity (*formal; often spec.*), perfidy, falsity, falseness, recreancy (*B*), prodition (*R*), *etc.*

tread, *v. t.* walk, pace, foot (*R or C*), press (*contex.*), pad (*R*), stamp, spurn (*B*); *spec.* full (*tech.*), tramp; *see* TRAMPLE.

tread, *v. i.* step, go (*contex.*), pace (*often spec.*); tramp, trample, dance, trip, walk, run.

treason, *n.* treachery (*contex.*), parricide (*fig.*), prodition (*R*), lese-majesty (*Civil law*).

treasonable, *a.* treacherous (*contex.*), traitorous, proditorious *or* proditious (*R*).

Antonyms: see CONSTANT.

treasurer, *n.* receiver, bursar (*tech.*), cofferer (*hist.*); *spec.* dewan (*Anglo-Indian*).

treasury, *n.* fisc (*chiefly spec.*), bursary (*tech.*), exchequer (*Eng. or B*), coffer.

treat, *v. i.* **1.** deal, negotiate, capitulate (*R*); *spec.* parley, temporize; *see* BARGAIN, DISCOURSE.

2. entertain (*contex.*); *spec.* shout (*S*).

treat, *v. t.* **1.** handle, serve (*now chiefly C*), use; *spec.* work; *see* DISCUSS, DOCTOR.

2. entertain (*which see*); *spec.* shout (*S; U. S. & Australia*).

treat, *n.* **1.** *See* PLEASURE.

2. entertainment (*which see*); *spec.* shout (*S; U. S. & Australia*), set-up (*S, U. S.*).

treatise, *n.* composition (*contex.*), discourse (*contex.*); *spec.* commentary, tract, tractate, tractlet (*dim.*), monograph, handbook.

treatment, *n.* **1.** dealing; *spec.* negotiation, bargaining.

2. handling, dealing, use, usage; *spec.* service, detail; *see* DISCUSSION.

3. therapy (*mostly in comp.*); *spec.* hydrotherapy, serotherapy, aerotherapy, *etc.*

treaty, *n.* agreement (*contex.*); *spec.* accord, concord.

treble, *n.* soprano.

treble, *v. t.* triple, triplicate (*R or formal*).

tree, *n.* **1.** dryad (*fig.*); *spec.* pollard, stand, sapling, rampike (*U. S. or dial*), cordon (*hort.*), scrub, snag, espalier, Yggdrasil (*myth.*).

2. *In genealogy:* stemma (*tech.*); *spec.* Jesse.

treelike, *a.* arboreal (*B*), dendriform (*tech.*), arborescent, dendritic *or* dendritical (*tech.*), dendroid (*tech.*).

tremble, *v. i.* shake, shiver (*chiefly spec.*), quake, quiver, quaver (*R*), tremulate (*R*), dither (*chiefly dial.*), didder (*now dial.*), dirl (*Scot. & dial. Eng.*); *see* TOTTER, QUIVER, SHUDDER, PULSATE.

tremble, *n.* shake, tremor, quiver, quaver (*R*), quake, tremulation (*R*), trepidation (*R*), tremblement (*R*); *spec.* twitter, twitteration, tremolo (*music*); *see* QUIVER, TOTTER, SHUDDER, PULSATION.

trembling, *a.* shaking, shaky, tremulous (*B or formal*), quivering, quavering (*R*), quaking, trembly (*C*), palsied, tremulant, aspen (*fig.*); *spec.* trepid (*R*), vibratory.

tremulous, *a.* **1.** *See* TREMBLING, VIBRATORY.

2. shaky, quivery, quavery (*R*), trembly (*R*); *spec.* tottery.

trench, *n.* ditch, fosse (*tech., often spec.*), furrow (*chiefly spec.*), line (*contex.*), cutting (*contex.*); *spec.* parallel, zigzag, boyau (*mil.*), sap, cunette (*mil.*).

Antonyms: see DIKE.

trend, *v. i.* tend (*R of persons*), gravitate (*formal or B*), set, drift, strike (*R or spec.*); *spec.* lean, run, go (*contex.*).

trend, *n.* course, direction (*contex.*), bent, set, determination (*B*); *spec.* run, tide.

trespass, *v. i.* **1.** *See* SIN, ENCROACH.

2. *Referring to intrusion on land:* intrude (*R*), enter (*contex.*), encroach; *spec.* poach.

trespass, *n.* **1.** *See* SIN, ENCROACHMENT.

2. *Referring to land:* intrusion (*R*), entrance (*contex.*), encroachment.

trial, *n.* **1.** hearing, doom (*A*), judgment (*R, exc. in reference to God, as in "the Last Judgment"*); *spec.* ordeal, mistrial.

2. test, probation (*R, B or pedantic*), try (*R*), proof; *spec.* prospect, van.

3. experiment, experimentation, tentation (*tech., R*), try (*R*).

4. distress, ordeal, cross, denial; *see* AFFLICTION.

5. *See* ENDEAVOR.

trial, *a.* experimental, probative, probationary, probatory (*R*), empirical, peirastic (*R*), tentative.

triangle, *n.* trigon (*R*), delta (*chiefly spec.*); *spec.* gore, gusset.

triangular, *a.* trigonal (*R*), triquetrous (*R; B or tech.*), deltoid.

tribal, *a.* tribual (*R*), tribular (*R*), gentile (*R or tech.*).

tribunal, *n.* **1.** bench (*contex.*), chair (*contex.*); *spec.* dais.

2. *See* COURT.

tributary, *n.* stream, affluent, feeder, influent (*R*); *spec.* leader.

trick, *n.* **1.** artifice, ruse, shift, stratagem, wile, subterfuge, bilk (*R*), device, game (*C*), dodge (*C*), fob (*S*), rig (*S or C*), trap, fake (*S*), cantel (*A*), jape, shave (*fig.; esp. in "a clean shave"*), sleight (*now R, exc. spec.*), braid (*obs.*); *spec.* cog, bunco *or* bunko, double, shuffler, flim-

tremendous: *immense, fearful, surprising.* | **tremor:** *tremble, vibration.* | **trenchant:** *sharp, energetic.*

flam; *see* HOAX, CAPER, FROLIC, ARTIFICE, EXPEDIENT, PLAN, HABIT.

2. *In wrestling:* trip, chip, click; *spec.* mare, nelson, half-nelson, hip, *etc.*

trick, *v. t.* **1.** deceive, cheat, fob, jockey; *spec.* trap, intrigue (*R*), *see* HOAX.

2. *See* ORNAMENT.

trickery, *n.* deception, artifice; *spec.* claptrap (*contemptuous*), sleight (*now R, exc. of* trickery *in legerdemain*), hocus-pocus, pettifogging (trickery *in legal practice*), hocus (*A or R*), trap (*C or S*), buncombe *or* bunkum, practice (*R*); *see* CHICANERY.

Antonyms: see ARTLESSNESS, SINCERITY.

trickiness, *n.* deceit, deceitfulness, evasiveness, art, artfulness, shiftiness, crookedness.

trickster, *n.* deceiver, cheat, hocus-pocus, shifter (*R*), juggler.

tricky, *a.* deceitful, evasive, artful, pawky (*chiefly humorous; Scot. or dial.*), tricksy (*R*), shifty, shifting, crooked, quirky (*R*).

Antonyms: see ARTLESS.

tried, *a.* proved, proven, tested, proof.

Antonyms: see UNTRIED.

trifle, *n.* **1.** nothing, bagatelle, folderol *or* falderal, fillip, fig, fico (*A*), straw, bean, fiddle-faddle (*chiefly in pl.*), fidfad, bubble, fiddlestick, flimflam, feather (*R*), toy, triviality, vanity (*R*), breath, doit (*fig.; B or A*), minim (*R, B*), frivolity, nihility (*R*), nothingism (*R*), bawbee (*fig.; Scot.*); *see* GEWGAW.

2. *See* PARTICLE, TRACE.

trifle, *v. i.* **1.** fool, shilly-shally, frivol (*C*), niggle (*chiefly Eng.*), moon (*C*), dawdle, dally, toy, dillydally, fiddle-faddle, fribble (*contemptuous*), palter, peddle (*R*), piddle (*R or C*), trick (*R*), tomfool (*C*), flimflam (*C*); *see* IDLE, POTTER.

2. *See* PLAY.

trifle, *v. t.* fool, frivol (*C*), dawdle, fribble (*contemptuous*), palter, fritter, toy, flimflam (*C*).

trifler, *n.* dawdler, fribble (*contemptuous*), frivoler (*C*), shilly-shallier, tomfool (*R*); *spec.* idler, potterer, butterfly (*fig.*).

trifling, *a.* idle, foolish, silly (*R, exc. spec.*), trivial, finicking; *spec.* null; *see* FRIVOLOUS.

Antonyms: see EARNEST, SINCERE.

trifling, *n.* **1.** fooling, dalliance (*B*), play, fidfad (*R*), fiddle-faddle, frivolity, flummery, *etc.; spec.* flimflam, boy's play, girl's play.

2. *See* PLAY.

trill, *n.* quaver, vibration; *spec.* roll, burr, rhotacism, shake, tremolo, vibrato, tremblement, warble.

trill, *v. i.* quaver, vibrate; *spec.* roll, shake, warble, tremble.

trim, *v. t.* **1.** *See* ORNAMENT, ADJUST, ARRANGE, DEFEAT.

2. *In nautical use:* adjust, fill.

3. cut, clip, lop (*R or spec.*); *spec.* crop, poll, shear, prune, shrub, pare, dub, skirt, barber, list.

trim, *n.* **1.** *See* STATE, ADJUSTMENT, ARRANGEMENT, DRESS.

2. cut, clip; *spec.* crop.

trimming, *n.* **1.** cutting, clipping; *spec.* pruning, inlucation, cropping, *etc.*

2. *See* REPROOF.

trinity, *n.* **1.** *Of the state or quality:* triunity, triplicity (*R*).

2. *Of what constitutes three in one:* triunity, triplicity (*R*), trine (*R*), triad. "*Trinity*" *is especially applied to Deity.*

trinket, *n.* bauble; *spec.* jewel, jingle-jangle; *see* GEWGAW.

trip, *v. t.* **1.** stumble (*R*).

2. *See* CATCH.

tripod, *n.* tripos (*R*), trivet (*chiefly spec.*); cat, teapoy (*Anglo-Indian*).

trivial, *a.* **1.** *Pertaining to a crossroads where three ways meet:* compital;—*both R.*

2. insignificant, unimportant, trifling, light, little, petty, small, slight, slim, niggling (*chiefly Eng.*), picayune (*C*), picayunish (*C, U. S.*), flimsy (*chiefly spec.*), sixpenny (*Eng.*), futile (*formal or B*), empty, frothy (*fig.*), nugatory (*B*), quotidian (*R*), nugacious (*R*), minute (*R*), immemorable, worthless, gimcrack (*chiefly spec.*), trumpery (*chiefly spec.*), sapless (*fig.*); *spec.* paltry, doggerel; *see* NOMINAL.

Antonyms: see IMPORTANT.

triviality, *n.* insignificance, unimportance, nugatoriness (*B*), flimsiness (*chiefly spec.*), futility (*formal or B*), emptiness, fiddle-faddle (*in a generic sense*).

tropical, *a.* tropic (*R*), intertropical *or* intratropical.

trouble, *n.* **1.** distress, disquiet, worry, worriment (*C*), pain, vexation, torment, affliction, care, cross, cark (*A*), teen (*A*), sore (*obs.*), cumber (*A*), fash *or* fashery (*Scot. and dial. Eng.*), molestation (*R*), perplexity (*R or obs.*); *spec.* sorrow, misfortune, anxiety, fear.

2. *In a loose sense referring to any degree, however slight of discomfort or inconvenience:* bother, botherment, ado, pother, fuss, annoyance, vexation (*a loose use*), discomfort; *see* EMBARRASSMENT, INCONVENIENCE.

3. *Referring to what causes trouble:* distress, vexation, torment, cross, curse, thorn, bale, pest, plague, bane, bother, chagrins (*pl.*); *spec.* care, burden, misfortune, sorrow.

Antonyms: see COMFORT.

4. *See* EFFORT, AILMENT, DISTURBANCE.

trouble, *v. t.* **1.** distress, disquiet, ail, worry, pain, vex, torment, plague, afflict, harass, agitate, excruciate *or* (*A*) cruciate (*R*), crucify (*fig.*), cut (*fig.*), infest (*R*), cumber (*A or*

tricky: *shrewd.*
trim, *v. i.: hedge, temporize.*
trim, *a.: elegant, smart, shapely.*
trip, *n.: step, excursion, journey, errand, circuit, error.*
trip, *v. i.: step, misstep.*
triumph, *n.: celebration, victory, exultation, accomplishment, hymn.*
triumph, *v. i.: celebrate, rejoice, exult.*
troop, *n.: body, company, multitude, flock, herd.*
troop, *v. i.: meet, march.*

obs.), cark (*A*), perplex (*R or obs.*), molest (*A*); *spec.* frighten, oppress; *see* GRIEVE.

2. *In a loose sense:* bother, pother, ail, fuss (*R or S*), curse, annoy, pester, dun; *see* EMBARRASS, TEASE.

troubled, *a.* **1.** distressful, disturbed, *etc.*, troublous, careful (*A*).

2. *See* UNSETTLED.

troublesome, *a.* **1.** distressful, disturbing, distressing, troublous (*R*), afflictive, grievous, painful, worrisome, cruel (*often in C use as a mild intensive*), troubling, spiny (*fig.*), thorny (*fig.*), tough (*C*), vexatious, bad, cumbersome (*A or dial.*), molestful (*R*), fashious (*Scot.*); *spec.* burdensome; *see* CALAMITOUS.

2. *In a loose sense:* distressful, discomfortable (*R*), bothersome, pestiferous (*C or humorous*), pestilent *or* pestilential (*C or humorous*); *spec.* inconvenient, difficult, unwieldy.

troubling, *n.* distressing, agitation, worriment (*R*), vexation, affliction, harassment, excruciation *or* (*A*) cruciation, molestation (*A*).

trough, *n.* **1.** *Spec.* manger, hutch, launder.

2. *See* CHANNEL, TUBE.

trousers, *n. pl.* pantaloons (*orig. spec.*), breeches (*C*), pants (*vulgar or cant*), kickseys (*S*), inexpressibles, innominables (*last two humorous, Victorian*), sacks (*S*), unmentionables (*humorous*), ineffables (*humorous*), kicks (*S*), continuations (*S*), slacks, bags; *spec.* slops, bloomers.

truce, *n.* **1.** armistice.

Antonyms: see WAR.

2. *See* DELAY.

true, *a.* **1.** *See* CONSTANT, ACCURATE, CORRECT, GENUINE, SINCERE, JUST, FULL-BLOODED, ACTUAL, TRUTHFUL.

2. *Referring to agreement with reality:* right, accurate, correct, substantial, sooth (*A*).

Antonyms: see UNTRUE, ABSURD, ERRONEOUS, FALSE.

trueness, *n.* **1.** *See* CONSTANCY, ACCURACY, CORRECTNESS, SINCERITY, ACTUALITY, TRUTHFULNESS.

2. rightness, substantiality, soothness (*A*).

truly, *adv.* **1.** *Spec.* constantly (*"truly" in this sense is A*), accurately, correctly, purely, actually, sincerely, justly.

2. *By way of emphasis, or, sometimes, as a mere expletive:* assuredly, indeed, quite, sooth (*A*), soothly (*A*), forsooth (*now only ironical and used parenthetically*), verily, yea (*A*), iwis (*A*), perfay (*A*).

trumpet, *n.* trump (*A*), horn (*often spec.*); *spec.* lituus (*Roman antiq.*), lure (*Scot.*), conch.

trumpet, *v. i.* blow, toot (*chiefly spec.; often contemptuous*); *spec.* tootle.

trumpet, *v. t.* proclaim, blow, blare; *see* CELEBRATE, ADVERTIZE.

trumpeter, *n.* blower (*contex.*), tooter (*chiefly contemptuous or humorous*), blazer (*A*); *spec.* tootler.

trunk, *n.* **1.** stem, body, bole, stock, bouk (*Scot.*), truncheon (*R*), butt, caudex (*tech.*), axis (*tech.*).

Antonyms: see BRANCH.

2. *See* SHAFT, BODY.

3. box (*contex.*), chest (*contex.*), peter (*thieves' cant*); *spec.* imperial.

4. proboscis (*tech.*), snout (*C*).

5. *Referring to the body or main part: spec.* beam, synangium (*anat.*).

truss, *v. t.* **1.** *See* BIND.

2. *Referring to fastening the wings or legs (as of a fowl) for baking: spec.* skewer.

trust, *n.* **1.** confidence, faith, reliance, affiance (*B*); *see* BELIEF.

Antonyms: see DISTRUST, DOUBT.

2. *See* HOPE, CREDIT, DUTY, ASSOCIATION.

trust, *v. i.* **1.** confide, lippen (*chiefly Scot.*); *see* RELY, BELIEVE.

Antonyms: see DOUBT.

2. *See* HOPE.

3. tick (*C*).

trusted, *a.* confidential, bosom, undoubted, unsuspected.

trustee, *n.* depositary, fiduciary (*R*); *spec.* garnishee.

Antonyms: see GRANTOR.

trustful, *a.* confiding, confident (*R*), unsuspicious, reliant, trusting, credent (*R*), undoubting, questionless (*R*), unquestioning, fiducial (*theol.*); *see* BELIEVING.

Antonyms: see DOUBTFUL.

trustworthy, *a.* faithful, trusty, faithworthy (*R*), responsible; *see* RELIABLE, CREDIBLE, CONSTANT.

truth, *n.* **1.** *See* CONSTANCY, ACCURACY, CORRECTNESS, AUTHENTICITY, SINCERITY, JUSTICE, ACTUALITY, TRUTHFULNESS.

2. *Referring to conformity with what is actual:* fact, reality, verity (*B*), accuracy, correctness, trueness, right, troth (*A*), sooth (*A*).

Antonyms: see ERROR.

3. *Meaning a thing that is true or in conformity with reality:* fact, reality, oracle, principle; *spec.* præcognita (*R*), generalia (*pl.*).

Antonyms: see UNTRUTH, ERROR, FALLACY, LIE.

truthful, *a.* true, veracious (*B*), veridical (*B*), veridicous (*R*), soothfast (*A*).

Antonyms: see UNTRUTHFUL.

truthfulness, *n.* truth, trueness, veracity (*B*), veridicality *or* veridicalness (*R*), fidelity.

try, *v. t.* **1.** *See* ATTEMPT, STRAIN, AFFLICT, JUDGE.

2. examine, test, prove (*A or tech.*), essay *or* assay (*B or A*); *spec.* sample, taste, ring (*a coin*), sift (*a person*), smell; *see* EXPERIENCE.

3. tempt, solicit.

4. hear (*as a case in court*).

---

truck, *n.: rubbish, intercourse, produce.*
truck, *n.: wheel, roller, lorry.*
truckle, *v. i.: fawn, cringe.*
truckling: *obsequious.*
truculent: *fierce, cruel.*
trumpery, *a.: worthless, frivolous, trivial.*
truncate: *dock, maim.*
trust, *v. t.: hope, credit, expect, commit.*
trust, *a.: fiduciary.*

try, *v. i.* **1.** *See* ENDEAVOR.
2. seek, fish.
tub, *n.* keeve *or* kive (*Eng. or tech., and chiefly spec.*); *spec.* cowl (*A or dial.*), bowie (*Scot.*), kit, corf (*mining*), beck (*brewing*).
tube, *n.* **1.** pipe, duct (*chiefly spec., anat., or bot.*), tuba (*tech.*), trough (*R or dial. Eng.*), tubulus (*tech.*), tubule (*dim.*); *spec.* bore, catheter (*med.*), hose, chimney, lead, trap, tuyère *or* twyer, worm, fistula, quill *or* quillet, lull (*whaling*), pipette, bronchus, bronchiole, tubulure.
2. subway, tunnel, underground (*chiefly Brit.*).
3. valve (*chiefly Brit. for a radio* tube).
tube, *v. t.* pipe.
tuber, *n. Spec.* tubercle *or* tubercule (*dim.*) *"Bulb," "corm," and "tuber" are not, in exact usage, synonymous.*
tubercular, *a.* **1.** tuberculous (*R*); *spec.* verrucose, verrucous.
2. *See* TUBERCULOUS.
tuberculous, tubercular (*R*); *spec.* consumptive, hectic, phthisical (*R*), phthisicky (*R*), scrofular.
tubular, *a.* tube-shaped, tubate (*R or tech.*), tubiform (*R*), pipy (*R*); *spec.* tubuliform, tubulous, tubulose, vasiform (*tech.*), fistulous, fistulose, fistuliform, fistular, capillary, canalicular, canaliculate.
tuck, *n.* fold, pleat, plait, wimple (*obs. or A*), take-up (*cant; C*).
tuck, *v. t.* **1.** fold, pleat, plait, wimple (*obs. or A*).
2. *See* CROWD.
tuft, *n.* **1.** bunch, brush, feather; *spec.* tussock, pompon, spear, fetlock, scopa, penicil, floccus, topknot, coma, cirrus, verricule, villus; *see* FLOCK, CREST, CLUMP.
2. hassock, tussock, hag (*Scot. and dial. Eng.*), bog (*Scot. and dial. Eng.*).
tufted, *a.* **1.** tufty; *spec.* penicillate, plumed, floccose.
2. tussocky, hassocky.
tumble, *v. i.* **1.** roll, wallow, welter; *see* FLOUNCE.
2. *See* RUSH, DEPRECIATE.
tumble, *n.* **1.** *See* FALL, FLOUNCE.
2. roll, wallow, welter.
tumor, *n.* tumefaction (*R or B*); *spec.* neoplasm, boil, carbuncle.
tune, *v. t.* **1.** adjust, modulate; *spec.* temper, disattune (*R*).
2. *See* PLAY.
tunnel, *n. Spec.* tube (*C*), drift (*mining*).
turban, *n.* headdress, mandil (*Arabian*); puggree *or* puggaree (*Anglo-Indian*).
turbid, *a.* **1.** thick, muddy, cloudy, roily (*U. S. & dial. Eng.*), riley (*U. S.*), drumly (*chiefly Scot.*), lutulent (*R*), unsettled; *see* DREGGY.
2. *See* CONFUSED.
Antonyms: see CLEAR.
turfy, *a.* grassy, soddy (*R*), cespititious (*R*), cespitose *or* cespitous (*R*), turfen (*R*), turbinaceous (*R and erroneous*).
turkey, *n.* gobbler (*masc.*).
turn, *n.* **1.** *See* ROTATION, REVOLUTION.
2. *Referring to a change in position only:* turning; *spec.* twirl, roll, swing, twist, troll (*chiefly spec.; R*), anteversion, antroversion, retroversion, retortion (*R*), cock-up, volution (*R*), cast, return, counterturn; *see* TWIST.
3. *Referring to a change of direction or course:* deflection (*B or tech.*), diversion (*B*), flexure (*R or tech.*); *spec.* slue, slew, bend, swing, wheel, double, doubling, demivolte, volte, refraction, blanch, canceleer, contraversion (*R*), caracole; *see* DEVIATION, WIND.
4. *Referring to the motion of the eyes:* roll, cast, cock, goggle.
5. *Referring to speech:* twist, crank, crankle, crankum (*B*).
6. spell, shift, tour, trick, try (*C*), go (*C or S*), inning (*orig. spec. in sports*); *spec.* hand (*games*), watch; *see* ROUND, OPPORTUNITY.
7. *See* BEND, TWIST, CURVE, CIRCUIT, ROUND, CHANGE, COIL, NEED, CRISIS, COURSE, FIT, INCLINATION, FOLD.
turn, *v. t.* **1.** *See* ROTATE, REVOLVE.
2. *Referring to change in position only:* sway, bend, swivel, cast, twist, twirl, wheel; *spec.* traverse, crank, grind, trip (*naut.*), sphere; *see* BEND, TWIST, FOLD, REVERSE, CURVE.
3. *Referring to change in the direction of motion:* sway, roll, swerve, deflect, divert, flex (*R or tech.*); *spec.* reflect, retract, refringe, slue, slew, antrovert, introvert (*chiefly fig.*), topsyturn (*R; also fig.*), brace, round (*R*), avert, haul; *see* REVERSE, DRIVE, WIND, SWITCH.
4. *Referring to the eyes:* roll, cock, cast; *spec.* goggle, troll.
5. *Referring to remarks, arguments, etc.:* direct, retort.
6. *See* ADAPT, DISSUADE, CONVERT, MAKE, DIRECT, CONSIDER, AVERT, PREJUDICE, NAUSEATE, SOUR.
turn, *v. i.* **1.** *See* ROTATE, REVOLVE.
2. *Referring to a change in position:* move, bend, roll, shift, twist, twirl, wry (*A*); *spec.* grind; *see* TWIST.
3. *Referring to a change in direction of motion:* bend, sway, swing, roll, deflect (*formal or B*); *spec.* veer, slue, slew, cast, double, deviate, swerve, maneuver, jib, broach, tack, haul, warp, elbow (*R*), wear (*naut.*), return, wind, shy, goggle.
4. *Referring to mental action:* advert.
5. *See* BECOME, RESORT, NAUSEATE, DEPEND, APPLY, APPEAL.
turnable, *a.* versable (*R*), versatile (*tech.*); *see* DIRECTABLE.

---

try, *n.: attempt, endeavor, effort.*
tryst: *appointment, rendezvous.*
tumble, *v. t.: throw, overturn, tousle, disarrange, dishevel.*
tumid: *swollen, bombastic.*
tune, *n.: melody, harmony.*
turbulent: *disorderly, boisterous, rough, violent.*
turgid: *swollen, inflated, bombastic.*
turmoil: *disturbance, commotion, agitation, activity.*

---

turned, *a. See* REVERSE.
turnip-shaped, *a.* napiform (*tech.*).
turret, *n.* tower, pinnacle, tourelle (*R*); *spec.* gazebo, lantern, belvedere, cupola, serac, louver.
tusk, *n.* tooth, tush (*chiefly A or dial.*), ivory (*spec. or S; C or tech.*); *spec.* scrivello.
twang, *n.* **1.** ring (*contex.*), twangle, twank (*dial.*).
2. *See* NASALITY.
twang, *v. i. & t.* **1.** ring (*contex.*), twangle, twank (*dial.*).
2. *See* PULL.
twelve, *a.* duodecimal (*tech. and chiefly spec.*), duodenary (*arith.*).
twelve, *n.* dozen.
twentieth, *a.* vigesimal (*tech. or B*), vicenary (*R*).
twenty, *n.* score.
twice, *adv.* bis (*tech.*); *see* DOUBLY.
twiddle, *v. i.* **1.** *See* FIDGET.
2. twirl, wiggle, fiddle, play.
twiddle, *v. t.* twirl, fiddle, wiggle, play.
twig, *n.* stem (*contex.*), shoot, stick, switch, rod, sarment (*R*); *spec.* slip, withe.
twiggy, *a.* **1.** virgal (*R*), viminal *or* vimineous (*both tech.*).
2. *See* BRANCHY.
twilight, *n.* **1.** dusk, candlelight (*fig.*), crepuscle *or* crepuscule *or* crepusculum (*all three tech. or B*), gloaming (*B*), gloam (*R*), glooming (*R*), dimmit (*dial. Eng.*), nightfall. *The time from daybreak to sunrise is seldom called "twilight."*
2. *See* SHADE.
twilight, *a.* crepuscular (*chiefly tech.*), crepusculine (*R*), crepusculous (*R*).
twin, *n.* gemini (*pl.; Latin*); *fig.* Dromio (*in Shak.*), Antipholus (*in Shak.*), Castor (*classical*), Pollux (*classical*).
twinkle, *v. i.* **1.** flash, sparkle, spangle, scintillate, twink (*R*).
2. *See* FLIT.
twinkle, *n.* twinkling, flash, sparkle, scintillation, twink (*R*).
twist, *n.* **1.** *See* CORD, THREAD, ROTATION, SPIRAL, WIND, COIL, PERVERSION, DISTORTION, INCLINATION, ATTITUDE, TURN, CONVOLUTION, TANGLE.
2. *Referring to the making of thread, yarn, cord, etc.:* spin, spinning, throwing (*tech.*), purling (*A*); *spec.* lay.
3. torsion, torque (*tech.*), screw, twine (*R*), twirl (*R, exc. spec.*), wreath (*R, exc. spec., as in "a wreath of smoke"*); *spec.* curl, turn (*contex.*), crinkle, intorsion (*R*), kink, buckle, kinkle.
twist, *v. t.* **1.** *Referring to thread, yarn, cord, etc.:* spin, throw (*tech.*), purl, pirl (*A*), twine (*R or A*), wreathe (*R*); *spec.* slub, lay.
2. *Referring merely to torsion:* screw, twine (*R, exc. spec.*), twirl (*R*), wring, turn (*contex.*), entwist (*emphatic; B*); *spec.* kink, crinkle (*dim.*), curl, coil (*R*), wreathe (*R, exc. fig.*), wry (*R*), intort (*R*).
Antonyms: see UNTWIST.
3. *See* ROTATE, WIND, COIL, INTERLACE, TURN, CONTOUR, DISTORT, PERVERT.
twist, *v. i.* **1.** *Referring to motion of torsion:* turn, spin (*chiefly spec.*), kink (*chiefly spec.*), twirl.
2. *See* ROTATE, WIND, TURN, COIL.
twisted, *a.* **1.** crooked (*contex.*), screwed, twisty, torqued (*tech.*), tortulous (*tech.*), tortile (*R*), tortive (*R*), wreathen (*B and chiefly fig.*), wreathy (*R; B and chiefly fig.*); *spec.* convolute, kinky.
2. *See* SPIRAL.
two, *a.* twain (*A, B*).
two, *n.* **1.** twain (*B, R*); *spec.* both.
2. *Referring to two things taken as a unit:* dyad (*chiefly tech.*), duad (*B*), pair; *spec.* couple, couplet, doublet (*tech., cant, or C*), brace, match, span, yoke, cast.
3. *Referring to cards, dominoes, etc.:* deuce.
two-colored, *a.* dichroic, dichromic, dichromatic, dichroöus;—*all four tech.*
two-edged, *a.* ancipital (*R*), ancipitous, ancipitate (*R*);—*all three* (*B*).
two-faced, *a.* **1.** bifacial (*tech.*), bifront (*R*);—*both* (*B*).
2. *See* DECEITFUL.
two-handed, *a.* bimanous (*tech.*).
two-headed, *a.* double-headed, dicephalous (*R*), bicephalous (*R*), bicipitous (*R; chiefly spec.*), bicipital (*chiefly spec.*).
two-horned, *a.* bicorn, bicorned, bicornous, bicornute, dicerous;—*all five* (*R*) *or spec.*
two-legged, *a.* bicrural (*R*).
two-paired, *a.* bigeminal (*esp. in anat.*), bigeminate (*esp. in bot.*), bijugate (*esp. in bot.*),
two-rowed, *a.* biserial *or* biseriate (*tech.*). distichous *or* (*R*) distich (*tech. or B*); *spec.* bifarious (*R*).
two-sided, *a.* bilateral (*tech. or B*).
type, *n.* **1.** *See* SYMBOL, PATTERN, KIND, NATURE.
2. example, representative, ideal, model, pattern, beau ideal.
3. *Referring to any block used in printing: spec.* letter, figure, member, character, *etc.*
4. *Collectively: spec.* letters (*pl.*), letter (*tech.*), form, script, roman, italic, text, clarendon, brevier, *etc.*
typical, *a.* **1.** *See* SYMBOLIC.
2. exemplary, representative, true, ideal, model.
typify, *v. t.* **1.** *See* SYMBOLIZE.
2. exemplify, represent, type (*R*), idealize, image; *spec.* impersonate, embody; *see* PREFIGURE.
tyrannical, *a.* pendragonish (*R*), tyrannous, arbitrary; *see* DOMINEERING, OPPRESSIVE.
tyrannize, *v. i.* despotize (*R*), tyrant (*R*); *see* DOMINEER.

turpitude: *baseness, wickedness.*
tutor, *n.: guardian, teacher, coach.*
tutor, *v. t.: teach, coach, discipline.*
twine, *v. t.: twist, wind, interlace, encircle.*
twine, *v. i.: wind, coil.*
twine, *n.: string, coil, wind.*
twirl, *v. i.: twist, rotate, turn, twiddle.*
twitch, *n.: jerk, pull, pluck, quiver.*
tyrannous: *autocratic, tyrannical.*

tyranny, *n.* **1.** *See* AUTOCRACY.
2. arbitrariness, despotism, harshness; *see* DOMINEERING, OPPRESSION.
tyrant, *n.* **1.** *See* AUTOCRAT.
2. oppressor (*contex.*), despot, liberticide (*R*).

U

udder, *n.* bag (*only of cows, goats, etc.*).
ugly, *a.* **1.** unsightly, hideous; *spec.* hard-favored (*A*), evil-looking.
Antonyms: see BEAUTIFUL.
2. *See* REPELLENT, ILL-TEMPERED, ILL-SHAPED.
ulcerate, *v. i.* fester (*chiefly spec.*).
ulcerous, *a. Spec.* cankerous.
umbrella, *n. Spec.* gingham, gamp, chatta (*Anglo-Indian*), parasol.
umpire, *n.* arbitrator, referee; *spec.* linesman.
umpire, *v. t.* referee (*sports*).
unaccented, *a.* atonic (*tech.*), unstressed, toneless, weak.
unacceptable, *a.* unwelcome, disagreeable; *spec.* unpopular.
Antonyms: see ACCEPTABLE.
unaccommodating, *a.* disobliging, noncompliant, incompliant.
Antonyms: see COMPLAISANT.
unaccountable, *a.* irresponsible, unanswerable.
Antonyms: see ACCOUNTABLE.
unaccustomed, *a.* unusual, unused, strange, foreign (*R*).
Antonyms: see CUSTOMARY.
unadorned, *a.* plain, simple, bare, unornamented, ungarnished; *spec.* unvarnished (*fig.*), naked, blank.
unadulterated, *a.* pure, clear, simple, sincere (*R or B*), honest; *spec.* undiluted, neat.
unadvisable, *a.* inadvisable, inexpedient, impolitic.
Antonyms: see ADVANTAGEOUS, WISE.
unaffected, *a.* **1.** untouched, unmoved, unchanged; *spec. see* INTACT.
Antonyms: see AFFECTED.
2. simple, plain, natural, native, inartificial.
Antonyms: see AFFECTED, PRETENTIOUS.
unaided, *a.* unsupported, unseconded; *spec.* singly (*predicative*), single-handed, helpless.
unallowable, *a.* inadmissible, impermissible.
unambitious, *a.* humble, unaspiring (*R*).
Antonyms: see AMBITIOUS.
unanimous, *a.* agreeing, consentaneous, consentient, solid (*chiefly S; in political usage; U. S.*).
unappealable, *a.* final.
unappeasable, *a.* inappeasable, implacable, deadly, mortal; *spec.* inexpiable; *see* RELENTLESS.
Antonyms: see COMPASSIONATE.
unappreciative, *a.* inappreciative, unapplausive (*R*).
Antonyms: see APPRECIATIVE.
unarmed, *a.* weaponless, inerm (*R or bot.*).
Antonyms: see ARMED.
unascertainable, *a.* indeterminable.
unassailable, *a.* invulnerable (*often fig.*), inoppugnable (*R*).
unatonable, *a.* inexpiable.
unauthorized, *a.* illegitimate, bastard.
unavoidable, *a.* inevitable, certain, necessary, ineluctable (*B*), escapeless (*R*); *spec.* inavertible (*R*), indispensable, unpreventable.
unaware, *a.* unknowing, ignorant.
Antonyms: see KNOWING.
unawareness, *n.* ignorance.
unbaked, *a.* raw, crude; *spec.* green, unfired, unburnt.
unbearable, *a.* intolerable, insupportable, insufferable, unendurable.
Antonyms: see ENDURABLE, PLEASANT.
unbecoming, *a.* unbeseeming (*B or A*), unseemly, unworthy, misbecoming (*R or B*), uncomely (*R*), unmeet, unsuitable, unfitting, indecent (*R*); *spec.* incorrect; *see* IMPROPER.
Antonyms: see BECOMING.
unbelief, *n.* heresy (*tending to create schism*), miscreance (*A*), disbelief, miscredit (*R*), discredence (*R*), infidelity (*chiefly eccl.*), incredulity, incredulousness.
Antonyms: see BELIEF.
unbelievable, *a.* incredible, disbelievable (*R*); *spec.* inconceivable.
Antonyms: see BELIEVABLE.
unbeliever, *n.* disbeliever, infidel (*chiefly eccl.*), heretic (*chiefly eccl.*), miscreant (*A*), misbeliever; *spec.* minimifidian (*R*), nullifidian (*R*), free-thinker, zendik (*Oriental*), nothingarian (*eccl.; R*).
Antonyms: see BELIEVER.
unbelieving, *a.* incredulous; *spec.* infidel, disbelieving.
Antonyms: see BELIEVING.
unbosom, *v. t.* unburden, unbreast (*R*), open.
unbreakable, *a.* infrangible (*B*), irruptible (*R*).
Antonyms: see BRITTLE.
unbreathable, *a.* irrespirable.
unbroken, *a.* **1.** even; *spec.* blind, dead (*level*).
2. *See* CONSTANT, UNINTERRUPTED.
uncalled, *a.* uninvited.
uncanny, *a.* unnatural, weird.
unceremonious, *a.* abrupt, bluff, blunt, offhand, brusque, curt, gruff, informal; *spec.* familiar.
Antonyms: see FORMAL.
uncertain, *a.* doubtful, indeterminate; *spec.* precarious, problematical, shaky, slippery, equivocal, insecure, mistakable.
Antonyms: see CERTAIN.
uncertainty, *n.* doubt; *spec.* precariousness, insecurity.

U
ubiquitous: *omnipresent.*
ulterior: *distant, additional.*

(*A*) *archaic.* (*B*) *bookish, poetic, literary or learned.* (*C*) *colloquial.* (*Contex.*) *contextual.* (*R*) *rare.* (*S*) *slang.*
See pp. viii–ix.

Antonyms: see CERTAINTY.

unchangeable, *a.* unalterable, immutable.

unchaste, *a.* wanton; *see* LASCIVIOUS.

uncivilized, *a.* savage, barbarous, barbarian, barbaric, low (*contex.*), uncivil (*R*), raw (*R*).

Antonyms: see CIVILIZED.

uncle, *n.* nuncle (*obs. or dial.*), nunk (*obs. or dial.*).

uncomfortable, *a.* distressing, uneasy (*obs. or R*).

Antonyms: see COMFORTABLE.

uncompassionate, *a.* unkind, unfeeling, pitiless, stony, relentless, ruthless, fierce, cruel, impiteous (*R*).

Antonyms: see COMPASSIONATE.

unconcealed, *a.* open, public, overt.

Antonyms: see HIDDEN.

uncongenial, *a.* incongenial (*R*), incompatible.

unconnected, *a.* **1.** separate, disparate, distinct, disjunct; *spec.* individual.

2. *Referring to knowledge, facts, etc.:* unrelated, incoherent, scrappy, disjointed, loose.

Antonyms: see RELATED.

unconquerable, *a.* **1.** invincible, indomitable, unsubduable, irreducible (*R*), inexpugnable.

Antonyms: see CONQUERABLE.

2. *See* IMPREGNABLE.

unconscious, *a.* insensible, unaware (*only in pred., with "of"*), inconscious (*R*), inconscient (*R*), nonconscious, incognizant (*R*), brute (*B*).

Antonyms: see CONSCIOUS, AWARE, AWAKE.

uncontrol, *n.* freedom (*contex.*).

uncontrollable, *a.* ungovernable, incontrollable, unrestrainable, wild; *spec.* rampant, rampageous; *see* UNMANAGEABLE.

Antonyms: see MANAGEABLE.

uncontrolled, *a.* unbridled, unbitted, reinless, wild, intemperate.

unconventional, *a. Spec.* unofficial, unaccustomed; *see* INFORMAL.

Antonyms: see CONVENTIONAL, CUSTOMARY, STIFF.

unconvincing, *a.* weak.

Antonyms: see CONVINCING, COGENT, IMPRESSIVE.

uncooked, *a.* raw.

uncorrupted, *a.* honest, innocent, untarnished, uncorrupt (*R*).

Antonyms: see CORRUPT.

uncover, *v. t.* open, discover, disclose; *spec.* undrape, unveil, uncurtain, unsheathe, discase (*A*).

Antonyms: see COVER.

uncovered, *a.* open, bare, naked, undisguised.

unction, *n.* **1.** anointing, aneling (*esp. as a religious rite*).

2. *See* EMOTIONALISM.

unctuous, *a.* **1.** bland, smooth; *spec. see* EMOTIONAL.

2. smooth (*contex.*), oily (*fig.*), greasy (*fig.; contemptuous*).

Antonyms: see HARSH.

uncultivated, *a.* **1.** wild, untilled, unreclaimed, unhusbanded (*R*); *spec.* fallow.

2. homely, home-bred, rough, unrefined; *spec.* uncultured, uncouth, crude.

uncultured, *a.* artless, rural, Philistine; *see* BOORISH.

undeceive, *v. t.* disillusion, disabuse, disillude (*R*), unbefool (*R*).

Antonyms: see DECEIVE.

undecidable, *a.* indeterminable.

undecided, *a.* **1.** uncertain, undetermined, irresolute, unresolved, unsettled; *spec.* open, pendent, drawn (*battle, etc.*).

2. *See* DOUBTFUL, HESITATING.

undefended, *a.* unguarded, unprotected, guardless, naked (*fig.*), exposed.

undefiled, *a.* **1.** *See* CLEAN.

2. inviolate, unpolluted, unfiled (*R*).

undeniable, *a.* unquestionable, incontestable, indisputable, incontrovertible, irrefutable, irrefragable.

under, *prep.* below, beneath, underneath.

Antonyms: see UPON.

underbrush, *n.* undergrowth, underwood; *see* THICKET.

underclothes, *n.* underwear, undergear (*C*); *spec.* flannels, underlinen.

undercurrent, *n.* underset, underflow (*R*); *spec.* undertow.

underground, *a.* subterraneous, subterranean, subterrane (*R*), subterrestrial (*R*), catachthonian (*R*).

underhung, *a. Spec.* undershot.

underlying, *a.* subjacent (*to*).

Antonyms: see INCUMBENT.

undermine, *v. t.* **1.** mine, sap, underwork (*R*); *spec.* honeycomb.

2. *See* WEAKEN.

underrate, *v. t.* depreciate, underestimate, disparage (*R*), extenuate (*R, A*); *see* UNDERVALUE.

Antonyms: see OVERRATE.

undersong, *n.* refrain, bourdon, burdoun, burden (*hist. or R*), faburden (*hist.*).

understand, *v. t.* know, comprehend (*to know clearly*), perceive, catch, grasp (*to become completely cognizant of*), penetrate (*implying a thorough* understanding, *or one reached only after overcoming obstacles*), seize, realize, sense (*C*), apprehend, conceive, twig (*S*), receive, have, sympathize with (understanding *that implies agreement*), intelligize (*R*), ken (*Scot. or obs.*), wool (*S*), tumble to (*S*), take (*R*); *spec.* decipher, interpret, construe, follow (*keep up with and* understand), fathom (*implying thoroughness*), bottom.

understandable, *a.* knowable, comprehensible, apprehensible, penetrable, intelligible, fathomable; *spec.* interpretable.

understanding, *n.* knowledge, sense, comprehension, conception, perception, head, intellec-

uncouth: *awkward.*
undergo: *suffer, experience, endure.*
underhanded: *hidden, deceitful, stealthy.*
underling: *subordinate, wretch.*
understanding, *a.: intelligent.*
understanding, *n.: intelligence, agreement, sympathy.*

tion (*R or B*); *spec.* grip, appreciation, sympathy.
understudy, *n.* substitute, devil (*C or cant*).
undertake, *v. t.* accept, attack, tackle (*C*), assume, enterprise (*A*); *see* ATTEMPT, PROMISE, GUARANTEE, CONTRACT.
Antonyms: see AVOID.
undertaker, *n. Spec.* projector, entrepreneur (*French*); *see* CONTRACTOR.
undertaking, *n.* enterprise (*a bold, arduous or momentous* undertaking), emprise (*A*), affair, assumption, venture, contract (*spec. or S*); *see* ATTEMPT, GUARANTY.
undervalue, *v. t.* underrate, deconsider (*R*), underprize, depreciate, disappreciate (*R*), misprize, underestimate.
Antonyms: see OVERRATE.
underwater, *a.* subaqueous (*B or tech.*); *spec.* submarine.
underworld, *n.* **1.** antipodes (*pl.; B*).
2. *See* HELL.
undeserving, *a.* deserveless (*R*), unworthy, desertless, indign (*A*).
undeveloped, *a. Spec.* rudimentary, embryonal, rude, embryonary, embryonic, primordial, perennial, immature, unbaked.
undevelopment, *n.* immaturity.
undignified, *a.* belittling, mean; *spec.* degrading.
Antonyms: see DIGNIFIED.
undiscriminating, *a.* indiscriminate, indiscriminative, promiscuous.
undisputed, *a.* unquestioned, uncontroverted, uncontested.
undissolvable, *a.* irresoluble, insoluble, insolvable (*R*).
undisturbed, *a.* **1.** sound, unmolested.
2. *See* CALM.
undo, *v. t.* **1.** *Spec.* unknit, unrip, untie, unplait, unpick, unhook, unlace, unbutton, unspin, unwork (*R*), unweave, untuck, unwreathe (*R*), unmake.
2. *See* OPEN, INVALIDATE, RUIN.
undress, *v. i.* unrobe, unclothe, disrobe (*B, formal, or affected*), devest (*obs. or R*), discase (*A*), unapparel (*R*), disarray (*B*); *spec.* disgown; *see* STRIP.
Antonyms: see DRESS.
undress, *v. t.* disrobe, strip (*C*), peel (*S*), unattire (*R*).
Antonyms: see DRESS.
undress, *n.* disarray (*B or formal*); *spec.* negligée, dishabille *or* deshabille (*state of negligent dress or partial* undress), mufti (*plain clothes worn by one who might wear a uniform*).
undressed, *a.* **1.** *See* CRUDE.
2. *Of stone:* unhewn, self-faced (*tech.*).
undulate, *v. i.* **1.** *Spec.* fluctuate (*R*), wave, ripple, roll (*of prairie land*), pulsate, pulse, wimple, crisp, crimp, crimple.
2. *See* SWING, BILLOW.
undulate, *v. t.* agitate; *spec.* wave, crinkle, ripple, roll.
undulating, *a.* undulous, fluctuant; *spec.* rolling, rippling, wavy; *see* BILLOWY, SINUOUS.
undulation, *n.* **1.** agitation, wave, billow (*chiefly spec.*), rolling; *spec.* crispation, pulsation, pulse.
2. *See* SINUOSITY, SWING.
undulatory, *a.* wavy, rolling, rippling, ripply, crinkly.
undutiful, *a.* dutiless (*R*), remiss; *spec.* disobedient.
Antonyms: see OBEDIENT.
uneasiness, *a.* restlessness, unrest, unquiet, unquietness, unrestingness (*R*), intranquillity (*R*), inquietude, disquiet, unrestfulness (*R*), dispeace (*chiefly Scot.*); *spec.* impatience, impatiency (*R*), fidgetiness, fidgets (*C*), perturbation, agitation, discomposure; *see* DISCOMFORT.
uneasy, *a.* **1.** restless, unreposing (*R*), unresting, disturbed, inquiet (*R*); perturbed, disquieted discomposed; *spec.* queasy, sleepless, twitchy, impatient, excited, fidgety, feverish.
Antonyms: see CALM, COMPOSED, PATIENT.
2. *See* DISTRESSING, DIFFICULT, AGITATED.
uneatable, *a.* inedible, inesculent (*B or formal*).
Antonyms: see EATABLE.
uneducated, *a.* ignorant, untaught, illiterate, letterless (*R*); *spec.* untutored, untrained.
Antonyms: see EDUCATED.
unemotional, *a.* cold, cool, apathetic, icy, dry (*chiefly spec.*), impassive, unimpassioned.
Antonyms: see DEMONSTRATIVE, EFFUSIVE.
unemployed, *a.* idle; *spec.* loafing.
Antonyms: see INDUSTRIOUS.
unemployment, *n.* idleness, nonemployment; *spec.* loafing.
unengaged, *a.* **1.** unemployed; *spec.* briefless (*law*).
2. free, heart-whole.
unequal, *a.* inequal (*R*), disparate, inadequative, inequitable (*with an implication of injustice not necessarily suggested by* unequal).
Antonyms: see UNIFORM.
unequaled, *a.* fellowless (*R*), matchless, inimitable, unparalleled, unpeered (*R*), unexampled, unpatterned (*R*), nonpareil, peerless, incomparable, transcendent, unmatched (*R*), unique, unrivaled, unapproached; *spec.* unmatchable (*R*).
unerring, *a.* **1.** *See* INFALLIBLE.
2. accurate, sure, inerrant (*R*); *spec.* dead (*shot, etc.*).
unescapable, *a.* ineludible (*B*), inevitable, inevasible (*R*), inescapable (*R*), unavoidable; *spec.* unexcludible (*R*), inexcusable (*R*).
unessential, *a.* **1.** meaningless, pithless.
2. dispensable; *see* UNNECESSARY.
uneven, *a.* **1.** rough (*contex.*), tumbly, variable.

undertow: *current.*
underwrite: *subscribe.*
undue: *improper, excessive.*
unearth: *disinter, disclose, expose.*
unequivocal: *definite.*

lumpy, stony, cuppy, pitted, hilly, holey, broken.
Antonyms: see EVEN, UNIFORM, PLAIN.
2. *Of numbers:* odd.

uneventful, *a.* smooth, eventless.
Antonyms: see EVENTFUL.

unexaggerated, *a.* true, real.

unexcitable, *a.* imperturbable, calm.
Antonyms: see EXCITABLE.

unexhausted, *a.* inexhausted (*R*); *see* FRESH.

unexpected, *a.* sudden, unlooked-for, unforeseen.

unexperienced, *a.* **1.** *See* INEXPERIENCED.
2. untasted, unfelt.

unexplainable, *a.* insoluble, inexplicable, unaccountable, inexplainable (*R*); *spec.* sphinxlike (*fig.*).

unexploded, *a.* live.

unexposed, *a.* protected, unobnoxious (*R*); *spec. see* SAFE.
Antonyms: see EXPOSED, UNPROTECTED.

unexpressed, *a.* unworded (*R*); *spec.* unwritten, unsaid.

unfading, *a.* fast, fadeless, immarcescible (*R*), amaranthine (*B*), permanent.

unfailing, *a.* **1.** infallible.
2. *See* RELIABLE.

unfair, *a.* inequitable, unjust, oblique (*B*, *R*), unequal; *spec.* foul; *see* PARTIAL.
Antonyms: see IMPARTIAL.

unfaithful, *a.* faithless, recreant, dishonest, derelict (*R*), unleal, illoyal (*R*), false, untrue, disloyal (*implying faithlessness to allegiance, now occasionally used of ties of friendship and honor*), untrusty (*R*), perfidious.
Antonyms: see CONSTANT.

unfamiliar, *a.* strange, novel, new, unacquainted, inconversant; *spec.* outlandish, bizarre.
Antonyms: see FAMILIAR, COMMON.

unfasten, *v. t.* loose, unloose, loosen, unloosen (*R*); *spec.* unscrew, unbind, unhitch, unhasp, unpin, disglue, untack, unlace, unspar (*R*), unclasp, unfix, unlink.
Antonyms: see FASTEN.

unfathomable, *a.* **1.** bottomless, soundless, unplumbed (*R*).
2. *See* UNINTELLIGIBLE.

unfavorable, *a.* unfriendly, sinister, adverse, disadvantageous; *spec.* ill, inauspicious, unlucky, indisposed, foul, contrary; *see* INAUSPICIOUS.
Antonyms: see FAVORABLE.

unfeeling, *a.* merciless, pitiless, unpitiful (*R*), unmerciful, hard, hard-hearted, hard-boiled (*C*), cold, cold-blooded, cold-hearted, obdurate (*B*), careless, heartless, soulless, inhuman, inhumane (*R*), dispiteous (*B*), granitic (*fig.*; *R*), unimpressionable, callous, incompassionate (*R*), rocky (*fig.*), stony, marbly (*fig.*), marble (*fig.*) flinty (*fig.*), bloodless, dispassionate, iron (*fig.*), bowelless; *spec.* hollow, emotionless, relentless, adamantine, empty; *see* SENSELESS, INSENSIBLE; CRUEL, DULL.
Antonyms: see KINDLY, MERCIFUL, COMPASSIONATE.

unfinished, *a.* crude, incomplete, incondite (*R*); *spec.* raw, sketchy, inelegant; *see* ROUGH.
Antonyms: see FINISHED.

unfitness, *n.* unsuitability, disqualification; *spec.* ineligibility, disability.

unfold, *v. t.* open, undo, display (*R or spec.*), unroll, evolve (*chiefly B*), expand; *spec.* undouble (*R*), spread, unfurl, disinvolve (*R*), separate; *see* DEVELOP.
Antonyms: see FOLD, CLOSE, SHUT, WRAP.

unfolding, *n. Spec.* evolution (*said, literally, of what is wrapped up; implying a certain orderliness or gradual succession of events*), disclosure, display; *see* DEVELOPMENT.

unforeseeable, *a.* incalculable, unforeknowable.

unforgiving, *a.* implacable, unrelenting, inexorable, unappeasable; *spec.* rancorous, merciless, pitiless; *see* RELENTLESS.
Antonyms: see FORGIVING.

unfortunate, *a.* ill, unlucky, disastrous, destructive, ruinous, fatal (*hyperbolical*), hapless (*A*, *B*), ill-starred; *spec.* fortuneless, misfortunate (*now chiefly Scot. & dial. U. S.*), luckless, evil, unsuccessful.
Antonyms: see FORTUNATE, PROSPEROUS.

unfounded, *a.* proofless, unevidenced; *see* GROUNDLESS.
Antonyms: see WELL-FOUNDED.

unfrequented, *a.* solitary (*implies both absence of people and remoteness*), desolate (*suggests barrenness or ruggedness unfit for habitation*), desert, deserted, forsaken (*implies breaking off of dear or familiar associations*), abandoned (*suggests a giving up as useless or unserviceable*), lonely, lone (*A or B*), lonesome; *spec.* uninhabited; *see* UNINHABITED, LONELY.

unfriendliness, *n.* hostility.

unfriendly, *a.* hostile, inimical, ill-affected (*R*), enemy (*R, exc. spec.*), opposed (*contex.*), indisposed.
Antonyms: see FRIENDLY.

unfurnished, *a.* bare, naked, unequipped, ungarnished.

ungallant, *a.* unchivalrous, unchivalric; *spec.* caitiff.
Antonyms: see BRAVE, POLITE.

ungentlemanly, *a.* uncivil, impolite, coarse; *see* BOORISH.
Antonyms: see POLITE.

ungirt, *a.* zoneless, unzoned (*R*), uncinctured, discinct (*R*).

ungovernable, *a.* unruly, uncontrollable, unmanageable.

ungoverned, *a.* **1.** unbridled, uncontrolled.
2. *See* ANARCHICAL.

ungrateful, *a.* ingrate (*B*), unthankful, thankless.

---

unfit, *a.: improper.*
unfit, *v. t.: disable, disqualify.*
unfruitful: *barren, unproductive.*
ungainly: *awkward.*
ungracious, *a.: impolite, offensive.*

Antonyms: see THANKFUL.
unguarded, *a.* unwatched, uncared-for; *spec.* blind (*side*).
unhallowed, *a.* profane, unsanctified, unbaptized (*spec. or fig.*).
Antonyms: see HALLOWED.
unhappy, *a.* **1.** miserable, wretched, sad, infelicitous (*B or formal*), disconsolate, unblessed (*R*), unblissful (*R*), unjoyful, joyless; *spec.* heartsick (*intensely grieved*), inconsolable, dismal.
Antonyms: see HAPPY.
2. *See* CALAMITOUS.
unharmed, *a.* uninjured, unhurt, safe, scatheless, immune, scotfree, harmless (*R*).
unharness, *v. t.* **1.** unrope (*local U. S.*), untackle (*R*), unhitch; *spec.* outspan (*So. African*), unsaddle.
Antonyms: see HARNESS.
2. *See* LOOSE.
unhealth, *n.* infirmity, morbidity (*R*), sickness, cacochymy (*med.; used by the old humorists*), feeblesse (*A*), valetudinarianism; *spec.* disease.
Antonyms: see HEALTH.
unhealthful, *a.* unwholesome, insalubrious, healthless, insanitary.
Antonyms: see HEALTHFUL, SANITARY.
unhealthy, *a.* ailing, morbid, sickly, insalubrious (*chiefly of places or climate*), healthless (*R*), morbose (*R*), valetudinarian.
Antonyms: see HEALTHY.
unheeded, *a.* unobserved, unregarded; *spec.* ignored.
unholy, *a.* **1.** unsanctified, profane; *see* UNHALLOWED.
2. ungodly, godless, impious; *see* IRRELIGIOUS.
Antonyms: see HALLOWED.
unhorse, *v. t. Spec.* throw, unsaddle, buck; *see* DISMOUNT.
uniform, *a.* equal (*R as to physical things, and then equivalent to "equable"*), steady, constant, even (*of surfaces and lines*), smooth (*of color, quality, etc.*), equable (*A of temper, mind, etc.*), unvarying, regular, same, dead (*implying absence of relieving change*), plain, level; *spec.* flat, unbroken (*color*), measured, solid, undiversified, jog-trot (*of action*), pure (*of color*), self (*of color*), undeviating, homogeneous, correspondent; *see* EVEN.
Antonyms: see VARIED, UNEQUAL, UNEVEN, DIVERSIFIED, MULTIFORM, VARIEGATED.
uniform, *n.* livery, regimentals (*pl.; spec. or fig.*); *see* COSTUME.
uniformed, *a. Spec.* liveried.
uniformity, *n.* constancy (*which see*), evenness, regularity, sameness; *spec.* steadiness, monotony, homogeneity, homogeneousness, unity.
Antonyms: see VARIETY, DIVERSITY.
unimaginable, *a.* inconceivable, unthinkable, impossible.
Antonyms: see THINKABLE.
unimaginative, *a.* prosaic, unromantic, fanciless (*R*); *see* MATTER-OF-FACT.
Antonyms: see IMAGINATIVE, FANCIFUL.
unimpassioned, *a.* cold, passionless, dispassionate, bloodless (*S or C*), cold-blooded; *see* UNEMOTIONAL, CALM.
Antonyms: see EXCITED, ANGRY.
unimportant, *a.* immaterial, inconsequent (*R*), inconsiderable, insignificant, light, inconsequential, slight; *spec.* inessential, petty, small, inferior, inappreciable, meaningless, minor, indifferent, immomentous (*R*), nonessential.
Antonyms: see IMPORTANT, FLAGRANT, GREAT.
uninclosed, *a.* open; *spec.* fenceless.
Antonyms: see CONFINED.
uninfluenced, *a.* unswayed; *spec. see* IMPARTIAL.
uninformed, *a.* **1.** unapprised, ignorant.
2. *See* IGNORANT.
uninhabitable, *a.* untenantable, unlivable.
Antonyms: see HABITABLE.
uninhabited, *a.* unfrequented, lifeless, desolate, desert (*R*), unsettled, peopleless (*R*); *spec.* waste, abandoned.
uninjured, *a.* whole, unprejudiced; *see* SOUND, INTACT.
unintelligent, *a.* unapprehensive (*R*), mindless (*R*); *spec.* impenetrable; *see* STUPID.
Antonyms: see INTELLIGENT, CLEVER.
unintelligible, *a.* inexplicable, inscrutable, unfathomable, fathomless, blind, inconceivable, incomprehensible, hidden.
Antonyms: see INTELLIGIBLE, CLEAR.
unintentional, *a.* unmeant (*R*), indeliberate (*R*), undesigned, inadvertent, spontaneous, unpremeditated.
Antonyms: see INTENTIONAL.
uninteresting, *a.* dry (*implying absence of details or ornament that give extrinsic interest*), dreary, drearisome, arid, barren, flat, jejune; *spec.* featureless, dry-as-dust, tasteless; *see* DULL, INSIPID.
Antonyms: see INTERESTING.
uninterrupted, *a.* continuous, unbroken, solid.
uninvited, *a.* unasked, unbidden, uncalled.
union, *n.* **1.** *Referring to the act or action:* uniting, joining, interunion (*R*), unition (*R*); *spec.* conjunction, conjuncture, connection, fusion, combination, incorporation, consolidation, coalescence, inosculation; *see* ATTACHMENT.
Antonyms: see DIVISION.
2. *See* COUPLING.
3. *Referring to a vital process, as of growth: spec.* conjugation, fusion, symphysis, inosculation, synartesis (*R*), synosteosis, ankylosis, coössification, synizesis, synechia (*mostly tech.*).
4. association (*contex.*), federacy, alliance, confederacy (*usually a looser or more temporary*

unhinge: *derange, unseat.*

(*A*) *archaic.* (*B*) *bookish, poetic, literary or learned.* (*C*) *colloquial.* (*Contex.*) *contextual.* (*R*) *rare.* (*S*) *slang.* *See pp. viii–ix.*

union than a "confederation"), coalition (*especially in politics*); *spec.* guild, craft, trade union *or* union; *see* ASSOCIATION, MARRIAGE.

unique, *a.* singular, only, sole, single (*R*). *In good usage* unusual, rare, *etc.*, *are not synonyms of* unique *which implies only one of the kind.*

unison, *n.* unisonance, homophony (*music, tech.*); *see* HARMONY.

unisonous, *a.* unisonant, unisonal (*R*), unison (*R*), homophonic *or* homophonous (*tech.*).

unit, *n.* one, unity, monad (*chiefly tech. and spec.*), monas (*R*); *spec.* item (*as included in a list*), integer (unit *of measure*), module, standard, point.

unitary, *a.* monadic, monadical;—*both tech. or* (*B*).

unite, *v. i.* **1.** combine, join, conjoin; *spec.* connect, incorporate, couple (*to join two or more*), marry (*fig.*), inosculate, interosculate, fuse, cement, consubstantiate, consolidate (*implying union in a single fund, system, etc., having one law or viewed as one*), blend, interlace (*chiefly fig.*), anastomose, coalesce, conjugate, syncretize (*R*), solidify, regelate, agglutinate; *see* JOIN.

Antonyms: see DISUNITE.

2. combine, join, coalize (*R or tech.*), solidify (*fig.*), league, confederate, federate, consolidate, inone (*R*); *spec.* ally, interleague (*R*), pair, couple, mate, fraternize, harmonize, mass, center, club, wed (*fig.*), amalgamate; *see* ASSOCIATE, MARRY.

Antonyms: see BREAK, DIVIDE.

unite, *v. t.* **1.** combine, join, conjoin (*R, formal, or intensive*); *spec.* connect, couple incorporate, concentrate, conflate (*B*), marry (*fig.*), fuse, aggregate, cement, consolidate, center, unify, solidify, lump, dovetail, agglutinate; *see* ADD, ATTACH.

Antonyms: see DISUNITE, COMMINUTE, DIVIDE.

2. combine, join, conjoin (*R or emphatic*); *spec.* ally, solidify, league, confederate, federate, harmonize, mass, amalgamate; *see* ASSOCIATE, MARRY.

Antonyms: see DISUNITE.

united, *a.* **1.** combined, joined, consolidate *or* consolidated, conjunct (*R or emphatic*), conjoint (*R or emphatic*); *spec.* connected, conjunctive, attached, indiscrete (*B*), conjugate, connate.

Antonyms: see DIVIDED.

2. combined, joined, conjoint (*R or emphatic*); *spec.* federal, confederate, allied, leagued, amalgamated (*fig.*), corporate.

uniting, *a.* **1.** combinatory, conjunctive; *spec.* concrescive, connective (*R*), additive, coalescent.

2. federative, confederative, incorporative, coalescent (*R*).

unity, *n.* **1.** oneness, singleness, undividedness, indivision (*R*); *spec.* compages (*often fig.; B or tech.*); *see* SAMENESS.

2. oneness, singleness, harmony, concord, solidarity.

universal, *a.* **1.** cosmic *or* cosmical; *see* GENERAL, COSMIC.

Antonyms: see LOCAL.

2. catholic, ecumenical *or* œcumenical.

3. *Spec.* pandemic, encyclopedic.

universe, *n.* world, creation, cosmos (*B or tech.*), system, nature; *spec.* macrocosm, megacosm.

unjointed, *a.* inarticulate, inarticulated; *spec.* unhinged.

unjust, *a.* unwarranted, unrighteous, unright (*A*), unequal, unrightful (*R*), ill, inequitable, iniquitous (*chiefly intensive*).

Antonyms: see JUST.

unjustifiable, *a.* unwarrantable, inexcusable.

unkempt, *a.* disordered, disarranged, disheveled, shaggy; *see* DISHEVELED, SLOVENLY.

unkind, *a.* unfeeling, hard-hearted; *spec.* pitiless, merciless, harsh, cruel, atrocious, brutal, ferocious, savage, inhuman, barbarous; *see* ILL-NATURED.

Antonyms: see KIND.

unkindness, *n.* unfeelingness, *etc.*; *spec.* cruelty, atrociousness, atrocity, brutality, ferocity, inhumanity, barbarity, *etc.*

Antonyms: see KINDNESS, MERCY.

unknown, *a.* unascertained, hidden, mysterious, unbeknown (*R*), undiscovered, dark; *spec.* untold, incognita (*fem.*), incognito (*masc.*); *see* ANONYMOUS, OBSCURE.

unknown, *n.* incognita (*fem.*), incognito (*masc.*); *spec.* mystery; *see* STRANGER.

unladen, *a.* disburdened, light.

unlamented, *a.* unmoaned, unmourned; *spec.* unwept.

unlawful, *a.* illegal, illegitimate, illicit; *spec.* unconstitutional.

Antonyms: see LAWFUL.

unless, *prep.* except.

unlimited, *a.* boundless, limitless, illimitable, unbounded, illimited (*R*), indefinite, absolute; *spec.* unconfined, confineless; *see* INFINITE, ENDLESS.

Antonyms: see CONFINED.

unload, *v. t. & i.* discharge (*more formal than "unload"*), disburden *or* (*A*), disburthen, disemburden *or* disemburthen (*both R*), disload (*R*), unlade (*R*), disencumber, discumber (*R*), off-load (*South Africa*); *spec.* unship, empty, dump.

Antonyms: see ENCUMBER.

unlucky, *a.* **1.** unhappy, unfortunate, mischanceful (*B, R*), mischancy (*chiefly Scot.*), misadventurous.

Antonyms: see FORTUNATE.

2. *See* INAUSPICIOUS.

unmake, *v. t.* **1.** uncreate, unform; *see* ANNIHILATE.

Antonyms: see CREATE.

2. *See* INVALIDATE.

---

unlikely: *improbable.* | **unlovely,** *a.: homely, unpleasant, ill-tempered.*

unman, *v. t.* **1.** *Spec.* disgarrison.
2. *See* EMASCULATE.
unmanageable, *a.* difficult, wieldless (*R*), unworkable (*R*), unwieldy; *see* UNGOVERNABLE.
Antonyms: see MANAGEABLE.
unmannerly, *a.* ill-mannered, mannerless, ill-bred; *spec.* caddish, rude, rustic; *see* BOORISH.
Antonyms: see POLITE.
unmarked, *a.* blank.
unmarried, *a.* single, celibate (*chiefly tech. or B*), lone, unwed (*B*); *spec.* wifeless, husbandless, discovert (*law*).
Antonyms: see MARRIED.
unmentionable, *a.* indescribable; *spec.* ineffable; *see* UNSPEAKABLE.
unmentioned, *a.* unnamed, nameless, untouched.
unmitigated, *a.* unredeemed, unrelieved, stark, perfect, utter, absolute, sheer, mere.
unmixed, *a.* pure, unmingled, sheer, solid, clear, unalloyed, simple, straight, neat (*both S, of drinks*).
unmoral, *a.* nonmoral.
unmusical, *a.* rude, musicless (*R*).
Antonyms: see MUSICAL.
unmutilated, *a.* immutilate (*R*), unmaimed.
unnamed, *a.* **1.** innominate (*R or tech.*).
2. *See* UNMENTIONED, ANONYMOUS.
unnatural, *a.* nonnatural, foreign, abnormal, prodigious (*R*); *spec.* preternatural, contranatural, subternatural, subnatural, cataphysical (*R*), infranatural; *see* MONSTROUS, ARTIFICIAL, AFFECTED.
Antonyms: see NATURAL.
unnecessary, *a.* needless, inessential, superfluous, dispensable, supererogatory, spare, unneedful (*R*), supervacaneous (*R*).
Antonyms: see NECESSARY.
unnerved, *a.* upset (*C*); *spec.* flighty.
unnoticeable, *a.* inconspicuous, unobservable, unobtrusive, inobservable.
Antonyms: see CONSPICUOUS.
unnoticed, *a.* unobserved, unnoted, unperceived, unremarked, noteless (*R*).
unobjectionable, *a.* inoffensive, unexceptionable.
Antonyms: see OFFENSIVE.
unobservant, *a.* careless, disregardful, unobserving; *see* INOBSERVANT, CARELESS, INATTENTIVE.
Antonyms: see ATTENTIVE, CAREFUL.
unobstructed, *a.* open, fair, clear, free.
unoccupied, *a.* **1.** vacant, unpossessed; *spec.* tenantless.
2. *See* IDLE.
unpaid, *a.* *Spec.* unsatisfied, unsalaried, unfeed, feeless, unsettled.
unpalatable, *a.* distasteful, untoothsome (*R*); *spec.* bitter, sour, *etc.*
Antonyms: see PALATABLE.
unpardonable, *a.* unforgivable, irremissible (*R*), inexcusable.
Antonyms: see EXCUSABLE.
unperceivable, *a.* incognizable; *spec.* unseeable, intangible, indiscernible.
Antonyms: see PERCEPTIBLE.
unpleasant, *a.* displeasing, bad, unpleasing, distasteful (*implying disagreeable effect on feelings or sense, causing aversion, not pain or suffering*), offensive, unlovely, disagreeable, pesky (*C or dial.; U. S.*), displacent (*R*), unagreeable (*R*); *spec.* indelectable (*R*), nasty, brackish (*fig.*), ungracious, disgustful, sickening, jarring (*spec. or fig.*), noisome; *see* OFFENSIVE.
Antonyms: see PLEASANT.
unpleasantness, *n.* **1.** displeasure, disagreeableness; *spec.* noisomeness, jarringness (*spec. or fig.; R*), insuavity (*R*), surliness.
2. time (*as in "to make a time about a thing"*), stink (*S; vulgar*).
unpolished, *a.* **1.** *See* ROUGH.
2. rude, ill-bred, crude; *spec.* cubbish; *see* COARSE.
Antonyms: see REFINED.
unprecedented, *a.* unexampled.
unpretentious, *a.* modest, simple, unassuming; *spec.* unambitious, homelike, homely.
Antonyms: see ASSUMING.
unprincipled, *a.* *Spec.* dishonest, crooked (*C*), fraudulent, thievish, rascally, scampish, roguish, lawless; *see* ABANDONED.
Antonyms: see UPRIGHT, CONSCIENTIOUS, SCRUPULOUS.
unproductive, *a.* **1.** fruitless, unfruitful, sapless, dead, poor, waste; *see* BARREN.
Antonyms: see FRUITFUL.
2. futile, barren, nugatory, otiose (*R*); *spec. see* INEFFECTUAL.
Antonyms: see EFFECTIVE.
unprofitable, *a.* profitless, bootless, unbeneficial (*R*), ungainful (*R*).
Antonyms: see PROFITABLE.
unprogressive, *a.* improgressive, backward; *spec.* vegetative (*fig.*), stagnant; *spec. see* CONSERVATIVE.
unpromising, *a.* unlikely.
Antonyms: see PROMISING.
unprotected, *a.* defenseless, naked, fenceless (*R*), unfenced (*obs. or spec.*); *spec.* unguarded.
Antonyms: see UNEXPOSED.
unprovable, *a.* undemonstrable, indemonstrable.
unproved, *a.* unauthenticated.
unpunished, *a.* scatheless (*B*), immune.
unqualified, *a.* **1.** straight, outright, out-and-out, thoroughgoing; *see* THOROUGH, ABSOLUTE.
Antonyms: see LIMITED.
2. disqualified (*less general than "unqualified"*), unsuited, unfit, ineligible (*legally disqualified*).
Antonyms: see QUALIFIED.

---

unmindful: *careless, forgetful, inattentive.*
unmoved: *constant, insensible.*
unofficial: *informal.*
unorganized: *structureless, inorganic.*
unpropitious: *inauspicious.*

unquestionable, *a.* indubitable, sure, indisputable, questionless, unimpugnable (*R*), certain, dead (*as in "dead certainty"*); *see* UNDENIABLE.
Antonyms: see AMBIGUOUS, CONJECTURAL, DISPUTABLE, QUESTIONABLE.

unquestioned, *a.* undoubted, undisputed.

unquestioning, *a.* implicit, sure.

unquiet, *a.* unpeaceful, disquiet (*R*), inquiet (*R*), peaceless; *spec.* unquiescent; *see* RESTLESS.
Antonyms: see AGITATED.

unravel, *v. t.* **1.** ravel, unweave; *spec.* feaze; *see* DISENTANGLE.
Antonyms: see ENTANGLE.
2. *See* DEVELOP, EXPLAIN.

unreal, *a.* illusionary, illusory, imaginary, fictitious, shadowy, aërial (*fig.*); *spec.* fanciful, spectral, dreamlike; *see* UNSUBSTANTIAL.
Antonyms: see ACTUAL.

unreasoning, *a.* irrational, unthinking, brutal, brute, brutish, animal, unreasonable (*R*).
Antonyms: see RATIONAL.

unrefined, *a.* **1.** rude, gross, rough, coarse, inelegant, unpolished, vulgar, rustic, rural, uncultivated, uncultured, incult (*R*), Gothic (*fig.*), common, vulgate (*R*); *spec.* rugged, Doric; *see* LOW.
Antonyms: see REFINED.
2. *See* CRUDE.

unregenerate, *a.* natural, irregenerate (*R*).

unrelated, *a.* irrelative, irrelate (*R*), disrelated, foreign, alien, remote, apart (*predicative; used with "from"*).
Antonyms: see KINDRED, RELATED.

unreliable, *a.* unsure, uncertain, ticklish, fallible (*liable to error*); *spec.* treacherous, inconstant, inauthentic; *see* UNTRUSTWORTHY, UNSTABLE.
Antonyms: see CONSTANT, RELIABLE, TRUSTWORTHY.

unremovable, *a.* ineradicable, inextirpable, inerasable.

unrequited, *a.* unreturned, unanswered.

unresisting, *a.* nonresistive, nonresistant, yielding, resistless; *spec.* frictionless.

unrest, *n.* disquiet, disquietude.
Antonyms: see MOTIONLESSNESS; *cf.* MOTIONLESS.

unrestrainable, *a.* irrestrainable (*R*), irrepressible.

unrestrained, *a.* **1.** untrammeled, unbounded, unbridled, unchecked, uncurbed; *spec.* unconfined, fetterless, unfettered; *see* FREE.
Antonyms: see CAREFUL.
2. incontinent, broad, wanton, inordinate (*of persons, as to passions, etc.*), licentious (*R*), lawless, lax, loose (*as a* loose *tongue*), effuse (*A*), wild, rampant, reinless; *spec.* ruleless.

unripe, *a.* immature, crude.
Antonyms: see RIPE.

unroll, *v. t.* open, outroll (*R*).
Antonyms: see ROLL.

unruly, *a.* **1.** obstreperous, unmanageable, wanton, insubordinate, fractious, refractory, rowdy (*R*), breachy (*of cattle*).
Antonyms: see MANAGEABLE.
2. *See* LAWLESS, DISOBEDIENT.

unsafe, *a.* insecure, precarious, uncertain; *spec.* treacherous.
Antonyms: see SAFE.

unsalable, *a.* dead (*implying inactivity in effecting its proper purpose*), unmarketable, unmerchantable.
Antonyms: see SALABLE.

unsatisfiable, *a.* insatiable, insatiate.

unsatisfied, *a.* **1.** insatiate, unstanched (*R*).
Antonyms: see SURFEITED.
2. *Spec.* unperformed, undischarged, unrendered, unpaid.

unsatisfying, *a.* empty, hungry (*of fare, food, etc.; R*).

unscalable, *a.* insurmountable.

unscholarly, *a.* ignorant, illiterate, illiberal, bookless (*B*).
Antonyms: see LEARNED.

unseat, *v. t. Spec.* unship, unhinge, unhook.

unselfish, *a.* self-sacrificing, self-forgetful, disinterested, altruistic, selfless, self-renounced, generous.
Antonyms: see SELFISH, EGOISTIC.

unsettle, *v. t.* **1.** disarrange, disturb, dissettle (*R*), upset; *spec.* unstring, unhinge.
Antonyms: see FIX.
2. *See* DERANGE.

unsettled, *a.* **1.** indeterminate, unfixed; *spec.* troubled, unnerved, afloat; *see* SHIFTING.
2. *Spec.* pendent, pendant, pending, outstanding, unpaid.

unshaped, *a.* unfashioned, unformed.

unsheathe, *v. t.* bare.

unsheathed, *a.* bare, naked.

unshorn, *a.* uncut, rough, shaggy.

unskilled, *a.* inexpert, rough, rude (*A*), unversed.

unskillful, unskilful, *a.* skilless, bungling, clumsy, poor, ill, inapt; *spec.* unpracticed.
Antonyms: see CLEVER, SKILLFUL.

unsociability, *n.* reserve, aloofness, unsocialism (*R*), unsociality (*R*).

unsociable, *a. Spec.* reserved, distant, retiring, shy, dissociable, insociable, insocial, segregative (*R*), morose, sour.
Antonyms: see SOCIABLE.

unsolvable, *a.* insoluble, insolvable, irresoluble (*R*).
Antonyms: see SIMPLE.

unspeakable, *a.* ineffable (*not to be described in words, with the implication, always favorable, that the subject defies description through some gossamer or fleeting quality*), indescribable (*usually implying merely inability to describe, without implication as to the quality of the object*), unutterable, inexpressible (*like* indescribable, *these two take their color, whether*

unreasonable: *illogical, excessive, unreasoning.*
unshod: *barefoot.*
unsolicited: *groundless.*
unsophisticated: *simple.*
unsound: *diseased, deranged, decayed, incorrect, imperfect.*

favorable or unfavorable, from the object modified; unutterable *is rarely used predicatively;* inexpressible, *used alone, often implies, like* ineffable, *great delicacy or fineness, unless specific context controls otherwise; thus "the view was* inexpressible" *carries favorable connotation*), unmentionable (*always carries unfavorable implication, and so is a synonym of a spec. use of* unspeakable, *which, used attributively, takes its color from the word described, but used absolutely, carries unfavorable implication; as* "unspeakable *kindness,*" "unspeakable *horror*"; *but "his behavior was* unspeakable" *means that it was exceedingly bad*).

unspoken, *a.* tacit.

unstable, *a.* changeable, inconstant, infirm, instable (*R*), variable, fluctuant (*fig.*), wavering (*fig. or spec.*); *spec.* fluid, labile, crank, tender, topheavy.
Antonyms: see CONSTANT.

unsteady, *a.* **1.** *In a physical sense:* vacillating, tottery, shaky, tottlish (*C*), ticklish, tipply (*C*), wavery, wabbly, drunken (*fig.*), rocky (*S*), coggly (*C*); *spec.* unballasted, wayward, faltering, jumpy.
Antonyms: see FIRM.
2. wavering, fluctuating, trembling, shifting, desultory.
Antonyms: see CONSTANT, FIRM.
3. *See* RESTLESS.

unstinted, *a.* abundant (*contex.*), prodigal, profuse, profusive (*R*), lavish; *see* ABOUNDING.
Antonyms: see SCANTY.

unsubdued, *a.* unbowed, untamed, unbroken.
Antonyms: see SUBDUED.

unsubmissive, *a.* insubmissive, unruly, ungovernable; *see* DISOBEDIENT.
Antonyms: see SUBMISSIVE.

unsubstantial, *a.* **1.** bodiless, slight, insubstantial, unsolid (*R*), nonsubstantial; *spec.* gaseous, imponderable, thin, pasteboard; *see* SLIGHT, FLIMSY.
Antonyms: see MASSIVE.
2. tenuous, vague, flimsy, vaporous, windy, airy, frothy, vain, shallow, yeasty, fungous (*fig.*), mushroom (*fig.*), moonshiny (*C*), dreamlike (*fig.*); *spec.* unreal; *see* EMPTY.

unsuccess, *n.* insuccess (*R*); *see* FAILURE.

unsuccessful, *a.* **1.** unprosperous, thriveless (*B*); *see* UNFORTUNATE.
Antonyms: see PROSPEROUS, FORTUNATE.
2. *See* INEFFECTUAL.

unsuitable, *a.* **1.** ill-adapted, improper, unbeseeming, inapplicable, dissuitable (*R*), unchancy (*chiefly Scot.*), inappropriate, malappropriate (*R*), malapropos, infelicitous, misappropriate, unbecoming, inapt, unapt, bad, inapposite, impertinent, inept (*R or A*), incongruent, incongruous.
Antonyms: see AGREEABLE, APPROPRIATE, BECOMING.
2. *See* UNTIMELY.

unsullied, *a.* **1.** *See* INTACT.
2. spotless, immaculate.
Antonyms: see SULLIED: *cf.* SULLY.

unsupported, *a.* *Spec.* unbacked, naked.

unsuspected, *a.* unguessed, undoubted.
Antonyms: see KNOWN.

unsuspicious, *a.* unsuspecting, simple, undoubtful (*R*); *see* TRUSTFUL.
Antonyms: see SUSPICIOUS, DISTRUSTFUL.

unsystematic, *a.* disorderly, planless (*R*); *spec.* haphazard.
Antonyms: see ORDERLY.

unteachable, *a.* ineducable (*R, B*).
Antonyms: see TEACHABLE.

unthinkable, *a.* inconceivable, insupposable, incogitable (*R, B*).
Antonyms: see THINKABLE.

unthinking, *a.* incogitative (*tech.*), incogitant (*B*); *spec.* mechanical, automatic; *see* UNREASONING, THOUGHTLESS, CARELESS.
Antonyms: see THINKING, THOUGHTFUL.

untidy, *a.* *Spec.* dowdy, frumpy, slatternly, mussy (*U. S.*), mussed (*U. S.*), littery, disorderly, helter-skelter; *spec., see* SLOVENLY.
Antonyms: see ORDERLY.

untie, *v. t.* *Spec.* unknit (*R*), unknot; *see* LOOSE.

until, *prep. & conj.* till (*less formal than "until"*); *spec.* to.

untimely, *a.* unsuitable (*contex.*), inopportune, ill-timed, ill-placed, unseasonable, timeless (*R*), intempestive (*R*); *spec.* immature, premature, late, inconvenient.
Antonyms: see TIMELY, APPROPRIATE, PROPER.

untiring, *a.* indefatigable, unfatigueable, unweariable, fatigueless, unwearied, tireless, unwearying; *spec.* unremitting, unrelaxing.

untrained, *a.* raw, green; *spec.* unbroken, unbacked (*of colts*).
Antonyms: see TRAINED.

untried, *a.* virgin (*fig.*), maiden (*fig.*), untested, unassayed (*R*), unattempted; *see* INEXPERIENCED.
Antonyms: see TRIED.

untrodden, *a.* untrod, unbeaten.

untrue, *a.* inaccurate, wrong, false; *see* ERRONEOUS, INCORRECT.
Antonyms: see TRUE, CORRECT.

untrustworthy, *a.* unreliable, slippery; *see* dishonest, unreliable.
Antonyms: see TRUSTWORTHY, RELIABLE.

untruth, *n.* **1.** *See* INCORRECTNESS, ERROR.
2. fabrication, fudge (*C*), deceit, fable, falsehood, tale, story (*C and euphemistic*), cog (*obs.*), rapper (*chiefly dial.*), taradiddle *or* tarradiddle (*S or C*), lie; *spec.* mistake (*often euphemistic*), imposture, fib (*often euphemistic*), flam; *see* LIE.
Antonyms: see TRUTH.

untruthful, *a.* false, unveracious, lying, faithless, inveracious.
Antonyms: see TRUTHFUL.

untoward: *perverse.* | **untroubled:** *careless, calm.* |

untruthfulness, *n.* **1.** falsehood, hollowness.
2. falsehood, fibbery, lying, leasing (*A*), unveracity, inveracity.
untwist, *v. t.* disentwine, untwine; *spec.* unlay (*a rope*), unwreathe.
Antonyms: see TWIST.
unused, *a. Spec.* virgin (*fig.*), maiden (*fig.*), idle, waste, disused.
Antonyms: see USED.
unusual, *a.* abnormal, exceptional, extraordinary, uncommon, out-of-the-way, unordinary (*R*), inusitate (*R*), unwonted, unaccustomed, especial (*only attributively*), exceptionable (*a misuse*), rare, supernormal (*R*), singular, extra; *spec.* curious, peculiar.
Antonyms: see USUAL, ORDINARY, COMMON, COMMONPLACE.
unutterable, *a.* unspeakable, incommunicable; *spec. see* INEXPRESSIBLE, ABOMINABLE, UNSPEAKABLE.
unuttered, *a.* unvoiced, unvented (*R*); *spec.* unsyllabled, unpronounced.
unwieldy, *a.* heavy, ponderous, cumbersome (*troublesome from weight or bulk*), cumbrous, elephantine (*fig.*), hulking (*C*), hunky (*C*), unwieldsome (*R*), megatherial (*fig.*), hippopotamic; *see* CLUMSY.
Antonyms: see WIELDY, MANAGEABLE.
unwilling, *a.* disinclined, indisposed, reluctant, averse, loath, backward.
Antonyms: see WILLING, DISPOSED.
unwillingness, *n.* disinclination, reluctance.
unwind, *v. t.* uncoil; *spec.* reel, unreel, untwine, ravel.
Antonyms: see COIL.
unwisdom, *n.* insipience (*R*); *spec.* foolishness, silliness, imbecility, indiscretion, injudiciousness, folly, senselessness.
Antonyms: see WISDOM.
unwise, *a.* injudicious, unwary, imprudent, ill-judged, ill-advised, unadvised; *spec.* silly, goosish (*R*), senseless, brainless, stupid, witless, reasonless, crazy, mad, insane, insensate, empty, foolish, impolitic, inexpedient, indiscreet, inconsiderate, absurd, insipient (*R*), imbecile, fatuous, idiotic, weak.
Antonyms: see WISE, ADVANTAGEOUS, JUDICIAL.
unyielding, *a.* **1.** *Spec.* immovable, unbending, adamantine (*fig.*), inductile; *spec. see* RIGID.
Antonyms: see YIELDING, DUCTIBLE.
2. indomitable, immovable, grim, inflexible, obdurate (*B*), inexorable, relentless, uncompromising, hard, stiff (*fig.*), rigid, rocky (*fig.*), stony, iron (*fig.*), steel (*fig.*), steely (*fig.*); *spec.* unconquerable, incoercible, stubborn; *see* STERN, TENACIOUS, STRICT, OBSTINATE.
Antonyms: see YIELDING, ADAPTABLE, COMPELLABLE, COMPLAISANT.
up, *adv.* upward, upwards, upways (*C*), heavenward, skyward; *spec.* aloft, uphill, upstream.
Antonyms: see DOWN.
upheaval, *n.* **1.** agitation, upthrow, upthrust, uplift, upcast; *spec.* cataclysm; *see* CATASTROPHE.
2. *In a nonphysical sense: spec.* cataclysm, debacle, paroxysm.
upland, *n.* **1.** ridge, down (*usually in pl.*); *spec.* fell.
Antonyms: see LOWLAND.
2. *See* INLAND.
upon, *prep.* on, over. *"Upon" does not essentially differ from "on," except in being more formal or emphatic and in some places more euphonious.*
upright, *a.* **1.** *See* VERTICAL.
2. conscientious, honorable, righteous, straight (*C*), incorrupt, honest, upstanding, stand-up (*C*), rightful (*R*), perpendicular (*B; R*); *see* JUST.
Antonyms: see UNPRINCIPLED, IMMORAL.
upright, *n.* standard, vertical, perpendicular; *spec.* post, stile.
upright, *adv.* endlong, endwise.
uprightness, *n.* **1.** erectness, perpendicularity, verticalness, verticality.
2. righteousness, rightness, goodness, morality, honesty, honor, right, rectitude, probity, integrity.
uproar, *n.* discord, tumult, hubbub, pother (*C*), hullabaloo (*C*), pandemonium; *spec.* larum, Bedlam (*a scene of mad confusion*), ferment, din, clamor, embroilment, bruit, hurly-burly; *see* OUTCRY, DISTURBANCE.
Antonyms: see SILENCE.
uproar, *v. i.* hurricane (*R*), hurly-burly (*R*).
uproarious, *a.* noisy, tumultous; *see* BOISTEROUS, CLAMOROUS, FESTIVE.
Antonyms: see SILENT.
uproot, *v. t.* **1.** root, grub (*used chiefly with "up"*), disroot (*R*), displant (*R*); *spec.* muzzle, stub.
Antonyms: see PLANT.
2. *See* EXTIRPATE.
uprush, *v. i.* rise (*contex.*), upsurge (*R*).
upset, *v. t.* **1.** overtumble (*R*), overthrow, overset (*R*); *see* OVERTURN.
Antonyms: see BALANCE.
2. overthrow, subvert, overset (*R*).
3. *See* DISCONCERT, DERANGE.
4. *In metallurgy:* jump.
upset, *a.* **1.** topsyturvy, confused.
2. disconcerted.
upstart, *n.* parvenu, mushroom, start-up (*R*).
upturned, *a.* raised, elevated.
Antonyms: see DOWNCAST.
urban, *a.* town (*the noun used attributively*), townish, oppidan (*R*).
Antonyms: see RURAL, RUSTIC.
urge, *v. t.* press, push, drive; *spec.* hound, spur, egg, solicit, exhort, crowd, importune, incite, ply, persecute, bucket, yoick (*a term in hunting*), goad; *see* ENCOURAGE, DRIVE, EXHORT, HASTEN, PROSECUTE.
Antonyms: see RESTRAIN.
urge, *v. i.* press, push, drive; *spec.* insist.
urgency, *n.* push, pressure, drive, press, instancy (*B*), instance (*R*); *spec.* goad (*fig.*),

clamorousness, importunity, drive, cogency (*R*), haste.

urgent, *a.* pressing, importunate, instant (*B*); *spec.* cogent (*R*), imperative, crying, clamant (*chiefly Scot.*), exigent; *see* EXIGENT.

urging, *n.* pressure, exhortation, cohortation (*R*), prosecution; *spec.* encouragement.
Antonyms: see RESTRAINT.

urinate, *v. i.* stale (*obs. or dial.*), micturate (*an erroneous use*).

urine, *n.* water (*contex. and usually euphemistic*), lant (*obsolescent*), stale (*now only of horses and cattle*).

usable, *a.* utile (*R*); *spec.* applicable, practicable, consumable, available.
Antonyms: see USELESS.

usage, *n.* practice, fashion (*prevailing* usage, *esp. of a people, place or time*), custom (*established by long continuance, esp. in a locality, trade, society, etc., implying intention; i.e., voluntary practice*), consuetude (*chiefly Scot. or law*), mode, ordinance (*chiefly eccl.*); *see* CUSTOM, HABIT.

use, *n.* **1.** usage (*R*), employment, employ (*R*), occupation, entertainment (*R*); *spec.* nonce (*as in "for the nonce"*), *see* FREQUENTATION.
Antonyms: see DISUSE.
2. avail, service, advantage.
3. *See* CUSTOM, HABIT, NEED, FORM.

use, *v. t.* **1.** employ (*more literary and rhetorical than* use *and often more suggestive of some special purpose*), utilize (*tech., B*); *spec.* improve (*to take advantage of*), take (*resort to as a means, etc.*), seize, condemn, christen (*fig.*), handsel (*for the first time*), borrow, brook (*obs. or A*), handle, spare, do (*contex.*), treat, waste; *see* EXERCISE, EXPEND, PASS, APPLY.
Antonyms: see DISUSE.
2. *See* ACCUSTOM, FREQUENT.

use, *v. i.* wont.

used, *a. Spec.* second-hand, worn.
Antonyms: see UNUSED.

useful, *a.* serviceable, practical, advantageous, valuable.
Antonyms: see USELESS.

useless, *a.* unserviceable, worthless, bootless; *spec.* waste, unprofitable, impracticable, helpless, inutile (*R*), fruitless, otiose (*R*), inapplicable, dead; *see* IDLE, PROFITLESS, INEFFECTUAL.
Antonyms: see USABLE, SERVICEABLE, USEFUL.

uselessness, *n.* inutility.
Antonyms: see UTILITY.

usher, *v. t.* announce, introduce; *spec.* ring, induct.

usual, *a.* customary, habituary, wonted, ordinary, general, usitate (*R*), regular, normal, unexceptional (*R*); *see* CUSTOMARY, HABITUAL.
Antonyms: see UNUSUAL, ODD, SPECIAL.

usurp, *v. t.* seize, accroach (*R*).

usury, *n.* interest (*contex.*), gombeen (*Anglo-Irish*).

utility, *n.* value, usefulness, serviceableness, use.
Antonyms: see USELESSNESS.

utilize, *v. t.* **1.** *See* USE.
2. exploit, use (*C*).

utmost, *a.* **1.** *See* EXTREME, HIGHEST.
2. main, supreme, superlative, greatest, highest, last, full.
Antonyms: see LEAST.

utter, *a.* stark, downright, sheer, blank, absolute; *see* DIAMETRIC, PERFECT.

utter, *v. t.* **1.** voice, emit, give, fetch (*a sigh, a laugh, etc.*), tell (*dial. or C*), tongue (*R*), breathe, raise, mouth (*A*); *spec.* deliver, articulate, bespout, blat, blate, bleat (*fig.*), blunder (*usually with "out"*), blurt (*usually with "out"*), hurl, bolt, brawl, bray, call, cast (*obs.*), chime, consummate, coo, cough, crack, cry (*often with "out"*), dictate, discourse, draw, drivel, drone, drop, ejaculate, enounce, enunciate, fulminate, grind (*usually with "out"*), gabble, giggle, gasp, groan, gurgle, harp, heave, hiss, hollo, hollow, holla, howl, hum, hymn, jabber, jangle, jerk, keckle, launch, lip, lisp, low, mumble, oracle, outspeak (*R*), pass, peal, phonate (*tech.*), pipe, prate, pronounce, prattle, preach, pule, rattle, rave, read, resound (*R*), rip (*used with "out"*), roar, roll, rumble, say, shoot, shriek, sigh, slobber, snap, snarl, sniff, sniffle, snuff, splutter, spout, syllable, tang, twang, whimper, whine, whisper, yawn, yowl, express, fling, grate, hoot, scream, shout, sing, speak.
2. *See* ISSUE.

utterance, *n.* **1.** emission (*R*), deliverance, delivery, breathing, elocution (*R, exc. spec.*), vent (*as in "to give vent to"*), voice, parol (*now only law*); *spec.* articulation, blurt, chorus, drawl, effusion, ejaculation, fulmination, gibber, heave, hiss, scream, hum, humph, phonation (*tech.*); *see* PRONUNCIATION, SPEECH.
2. *Referring to what is uttered: spec.* breath, whisper, speech, dictamen (*R or B*), dictum, pronouncement, dixit (*B*), effusion, observation, remark, wind.

V

vacancy, *n.* **1.** vacuity, emptiness (*R*), voidance (*R*), vacuousness.
Antonyms: see FULLNESS.
2. opening (*for a position*).
3. *See* ABSENT-MINDEDNESS, GAP, EMPTINESS, LEISURE.

vacate, *v. t.* **1.** *See* INVALIDATE.
2. disoccupy (*R*), quit, void (*R*), abandon.
Antonyms: see OCCUPY.

vacillate, *v. i.* **1.** oscillate.
2. fluctuate (*of persons, opinions, etc.*), waver, wabble (*C*), sway, stagger.

utterly, *adv.: absolutely.*

V

vacation: *invalidation, holiday.*

(*A*) *archaic.* (*B*) *bookish, poetic, literary or learned.* (*C*) *colloquial.* (*Contex.*) *contextual.* (*R*) *rare.* (*S*) *slang.* *See pp. viii–ix.*

Antonyms: see CONTINUE.
vacillating, *a.* willy-nilly, shilly-shally.
Antonyms: see CONSTANT.
vacillation, *n.* **1.** oscillation.
2. wavering, faltering, wabbling (*C*), wabble (*C*).
Antonyms: see CONSTANCY.
vacuum, *n.* void, vacancy (*R*), vacuity (*R*), voidness (*R*); *see* EMPTINESS.
vagabond, *n.* wanderer, stroller, tramper, tramp, lurdan (*A*), loafer (*A*), palliard (*A*), shack (*dial.*), canter (*A*), landloper *or* landlouper (*B*), gangrel (*A*); *see* RASCAL, BEGGAR.
Antonyms: see WORKER.
vagabond, *a.* wandering, landloping *or* landlouping (*B*), truant (*now usually spec.*).
vagrancy, *n.* wandering, vagabondage, vagabondism.
vagrant, *a.* wandering, vagabond, roving, gangrel (*A*), circumforaneous (*R*), vagrom (*an allusive Shakespearianism*), arrant (*A*).
vagrant, *n.* wanderer, vagabond, tramp (*now chiefly spec.*), floater (*R or spec.*); *spec.* caird (*Scot.*), hedgebird (*Eng.*), gaberlunzie (*Scot.*).
valet, *n.* attendant, body-servant, tireman (*obs. or A*), lackey (*chiefly spec.*); *spec.* footman.
valid, *a.* **1.** well-grounded, solid, sound, good; *see* LOGICAL.
2. legal, sound, just, good, effectual (*tech. or B*).
Antonyms: see INVALID.
valley, *n.* hollow, basin, vale (*B*), bottom (*now obsolescent or local*); *spec.* cañada (*Span.*), cañon *or* canyon, clough (*Eng.*), col, coomb (*Eng. or Scot.*), corrie (*Scot.*), coulee, dale (*chiefly B or dial.*), dean *or* dene (*local Eng.*), dell, dumble (*dial. Eng.*), donga (*South Africa*), dingle, glen, gully, gorge, gap, park (*U. S.*), pocket, ravine, rille, slade (*Eng.*), swale, swire; *see* GLEN.
Antonyms: see HILL, MOUNTAIN, PEAK.
valuable, *a.* **1.** rich, precious, prizable *or* prisable (*R*); *see* COSTLY.
Antonyms: see WORTHLESS.
2. *See* ESTIMABLE.
valuation, *n.* appraisal, appraisement, estimate; *spec.* assessment, appreciation, extent.
value, *n.* **1.** worth, importance, rate, valuation.
Antonyms: see WORTHLESSNESS; *cf.* WORTHLESS.
2. *See* MEANING.
value, *v. t.* estimate, sense, appraise, apprise, treasure, mete (*A*), rate, price (*A or spec.*), ponderate (*R*); *spec.* prize, assess, extend (*Eng.*); *see* APPRECIATE.
valve, *n.* **1.** *Spec.* flap, poppet, butterfly, cock, ventil, piston, pallet, valvula, portal.
2. *See* LEAF.
valvular, *a.* valvate, valviform.
van, *n.* **1.** *See* FRONT.
2. wagon (*contex.*), caravan (*chiefly spec.*); *spec.* pantechnicon (*Eng.*).
vandalic, *a.* barbarous.
vandyke, *n.* beard (*contex.*), pick-de-vant (*obs.*).
vane, *n.* **1.** beard (*of a feather*).
2. *Of an arrow:* feather.
3. *See* WEATHERVANE.
vanish, *v. i.* disappear (*contex.*); *spec.* melt, evaporate, fleet, fly, sink, die (*usually with "away" or "out"*), vamoose (*S*).
Antonyms: see APPEAR.
vanishing, *a.* disappearing, dewy (*fig.; B*).
vanity, *n.* **1.** windiness, inanity (*of human desires, etc.*); *see* EMPTINESS, SHOW, FOOLISHNESS, CONCEIT, INEFFECTIVENESS.
2. trifle (*a vain thing*).
vapor, *n.* **1.** exhalation, reek, steam, fume, brume (*B*), halitus (*R*); *spec.* cloud, mist.
2. *See* FANCY, BOAST, BLUSTER.
vapor, *v. i.* **1.** exhale, reek, steam, fume.
Antonyms: see CONDENSE.
2. *See* BLUSTER.
vaporous, *a.* reeky (*R*), steamy, smoky, fuming, reeking, fumose (*R*), fumy, vapory, halituous (*R*); *spec.* moist.
Antonyms: see LIQUID, SOLID.
varied, *a.* diversified; *spec.* dædal (*B*), checkered (*often fig.*).
Antonyms: see UNIFORM, MONOTONOUS.
variegate, *v. t.* diversify, counterchange (*R*), variate, vary, varify (*R*); *spec.* freak (*usually in p. p. or p. a.; R*), shoot (*usually in p. p. "shot"*), lace, interlace, fret, diaper, water, camlet, intershoot (*R*), mottle, streak, spot.
variegated, *a.* diversified, varied (*tech. or R*); *spec.* motley, multicolored, harlequin (*fig.*), dappled, dædal (*B*), discolor *or* discolorate *or* discolorous (*biol.*), varicolored, varicolorous, laced, intershot (*R*), mottled, streaked, spotted, party-colored, checked.
Antonyms: see UNIFORM.
variety, *n.* **1.** diversity, assortment, variation.
Antonyms: see UNIFORMITY, MONOTONY.
2. subspecies, race;—*both tech*
3. *See* GROUP.
variolous, *a.* pocky (*now obsolescent or C*).
various, *a.* different, manifold, sundry, divers (*now chiefly in scriptural or legal use*); *spec.* omnifarious; *see* DIVERSIFIED, MULTIFORM, DIFFERENT.
varnish, *v. t.* **1.** *Spec.* megilp, lacquer shellac, japan, enamel.
2. *See* GLOZE.
vary, *v. i.* change (*contex.*), fluctuate, veer, range; *spec.* depart; *see* DIFFER, DEVIATE.
vase, *n.* **1.** *Spec.* tazza, lachrymatory, murrhine, epergne, urn, beaupot, boughpot. *In*

---

vacuous: *empty, blank, thoughtless.*
vagary: *caprice.*
vague: *indefinite, discursive.*
vain: *empty, conceited, showy, proud, ineffectual.*
vainglory: *show, boasting.*
valediction: *farewell.*
valetudinarian: *ailing.*
valiant: *brave, courageous.*
validate: *confirm.*
vandalism: *barbarism, destruction.*
vanquish: *overcome.*
vapid: *tasteless, dull.*
variable: *changeable, changing, floating, capricious.*
variance: *difference, disagreement.*
variant: *changeable, different.*
variation: *difference, alternation, change, deviation, diversity.*
vary, *v. t.: change, alternate, diversify, variegate.*

Greek antiq.: amphora, crater, cylix, lecythus.
2. *In architecture:* basket, bell, drum.
vaseline, *n.* petrolatum (*British*).
vassal, *n.* feodary, liege, man (*contex.*), subject (*contex.*), feudary, bondman; *spec.* vavasor, subvassal; *see* FEUDATORY.
Antonyms: see LORD.
vast, *a.* wide; *spec.* monumental (*loose or contemptuous*); cosmic; *see* ENORMOUS, SPACIOUS, IMMENSE.
Antonyms: see NARROW.
vat, *n. Spec.* tun, hopper, buddle, union.
vault, *n.* arch; *spec.* dome, cupola, crypt, cope, dungeon, round; *see* CELL.
vault, *v. t.* arch; *spec.* dome.
vaulted, *a.* arched; *spec.* domed, domical (*R*), domic (*R*), dome-shaped, cupolar, cathedraled.
vegetable, *n.* plant, produce (*a collective*), truck (*a collective*); *spec.* greens (*pl.*), salading, sauce (*pl.; chiefly U. S.*), fruit (*a collective*), legume, fruitage (*R; a collective*), fruitery (*a collective; R*).
vegetable, *a.* vegetal, vegetative, halophytic (*tech.*), *spec.* olitory (*R*).
Antonyms: see ANIMAL, MINERAL.
vehemence, *n.* force (*contex.*), hardness; *spec.* passion; *see* ARDOR, IMPETUOSITY.
Antonyms: cf. IMPASSIVE.
vehicle, *n.* **1.** carriage (*now chiefly spec.*), conveyance (*esp. for persons, as passengers*); *spec.* caravan, caroche (*A or hist.*), cart, catafalque, chair (*A*), chariot, chaise, coach, equipage, float, hackney, hack (*now U. S.*), hearse, rattletrap, sled, sledge, sleigh, taxi, trap (*C*), tumbrel, van, wagon, wagonette, car, *etc.*
2. *See* AGENCY.
vehicular, *a.* vehiculatory (*R*), curricular (*R*).
veil, *n.* **1.** film (*contex.*); *spec.* yashmak (*Turkish*), muffler, fall, mask.
2. *See* PRETENSE, GLOSS, CURTAIN, COVER, DISGUISE.
veil, *v. t.* **1.** enveil (*R*), shroud, overveil (*R*).
2. *See* COVER, DISGUISE, GLOZE.
vein, *n.* **1.** vena (*tech.*); *spec.* veinlet.
2. nerve, nervure; *spec.* veinlet, venule, venula, veinule, rib, midrib.
3. *In mining: spec.* leader. ledge, lode.
4. *See* DISPOSITION, TEMPER, STRAIN, STREAK.
veined, *a.* netted, reticulate.
vendor, *n.* institor (*chiefly Roman & Scots law*); *spec.* hawker, peddler, cramer (*Scot.*), consigner.
venous, *a.* venosal (*R*), venose.
vent, *n.* **1.** opening (*contex.*), orifice (*contex.; B*); *spec.* bung, bunghole, fumarole, femerell, touchhole, bouche, bush, hydrant, plug.
2. *See* EXPRESSION, MARKET.
vent, *v. t.* **1.** emit (*contex.*), exhale, breathe.
2. *See* EXPRESS.
ventilate, *v. t.* air, aërate (*R or spec.*), perflate (*R*).
ventilator, *n.* aërator (*R*); *spec.* louver, transom, funnel.
ventral, *a.* stomachal (*tech.*), sternal (*tech.*); *see* ABDOMINAL.
venture, *n.* **1.** chance, risk, stake, slap (*C or S*); *spec.* flyer.
2. *See* DANGER, SPECULATION.
venture, *v. t.* chance, risk, hazard, presume, dare, adventure, undertake; *see* ATTEMPT, ADVANCE.
venturesome, *a.* rash (*contex.*), bold, adventurous, venturous; *spec.* reckless, foolhardy, presumptuous.
Antonyms: see CAUTIOUS, TIMID.
veranda, *n.* stoop (*incorrect, U. S.*), porch (*local, U. S.*).
verbal, *a.* word (*the noun used attributively*); *spec.* literal, wordy.
verbalist, *n.* wordsman (*R*); *see* CRITIC.
verbose, *a.* wordy, wordish, expletive (*R*); *spec.* talkative; *see* PROLIX.
Antonyms: see CONCISE.
verdant, *a.* green (*contex.*), verdurous; *spec.* viridescent; *see* GREENISH.
verdict, *n.* decision, deliverance.
verdure, *n.* foliage, green (*chiefly in pl. and spec.*), greenness (*R*), greenery (*R*), vegetation, greenth (*R*); *spec.* vert.
verge, *n.* edge (*contex.*), rim (*of the horizon, the sea, etc.; chiefly B*), brink (*of an action*); *see* BOUNDARY, BORDER.
Antonyms: see CENTER, MIDDLE.
verge, *v. i.* border (*upon*), approach.
verify, *v. t.* confirm (*contex.*), support, substantiate, aver (*R*); *spec.* actualize, number; *see* PROVE.
Antonyms: see DISPROVE.
verily, *adv.* so, actually, truly.
vernacular, *a.* living (*said of languages*), vulgar (*R, B*), trivial (*tech.*); *see* NATIVE.
vernal, *a.* spring.
versatile, *a.* mobile (*R*), mercurial (*B*), many-sided, two-handed (*fig.*), ambidextrous (*fig.*), polytropic (*R*); *see* ADAPTABLE.
verse, *n.* **1.** line, stave (*tech. or B*), bob (*prosody*), stitch *or* stichos (*tech.*), number; *spec.* heroic, versicle, verselet, echo; *see* DIVISION.
Antonyms: see PROSE.
2. numbers (*pl.*); *spec.* rime *or* rhyme, doggerel; *see* POETRY.
versed, *a.* conversant, versant (*R*); *spec.* accomplished.
versification, *n.* orthometry (*tech.*), prosody (*tech.*).

---

vast, *a.: spacious, immense.*
vasty: *immense.*
vault: *arch, curvet.*
vaunt: *boast, rejoice, exult.*
vegetate: *germinate, grow.*
vegetation: *growth, herbage.*
venal: *mercenary.*
veneer, *n.: facing, gloss, disguise.*
veneer, *v. t.: face, gloze, disguise.*
venerable: *respected, old.*
venerate: *respect, esteem.*
venial: *excusable.*
venom, *n.: poison, ill will, malevolence.*
venue: *neighborhood.*
verdict: *opinion, decision.*
verification: *proof, confirmation.*

---

versifier, *n.* poet, versificator (*R*); *spec.* rimer, rimester, jingler, rhymester, rhymist, lyrist.
Antonyms: see PROSAIST.

versify, *v. i.* meter (*R or obs.*), metrify (*R*); *spec.* rime *or* rhyme.
Antonyms: see PROSE.

vertical, *a.* upright, perpendicular, plumb, downright; *see* ERECT.
Antonyms: see HORIZONTAL, PROSTRATE, INCLINED.

verticality, *n.* uprightness, perpendicularity.

verticalize, *v. t.* plumb.

vertically, *adv.* perpendicularly, plumb, downright (*A*).
Antonyms: see OBLIQUELY.

very, *adv.* right (*A or dial.; or C, U. S.*), quite, hugely, vastly, exceedingly (*stronger than "very"*), excessively (*stronger than "exceedingly"*), full, jolly (*C*), uncommon (*illit. or vulgar*), parlous (*C*), enormously (*spec. or C*), wondrous (*spec. or C*), wondrously (*spec. or C*), horribly (*C*), terribly (*C*), frightfully (*C*), woundy (*A and C*), woundily (*A and C*); *spec. see* EXTREMELY.

vesicle, *n.* bladder, bleb, pompholyx (*tech.*); *spec.* bulla, blain, blister, follicle, vacuole, blotch; *see* BLISTER.

vesicular, *a.* vesiculate, vesiculose, vesiculous, cystic (*tech.*), vesical, blebby, bullate (*tech.*), bullous; *spec.* vacuolar, vacuolate, follicular, folliculose, folliculous.

vespers, *n.* evensong (*tech.*).

vessel, *n.* **1.** boat, craft (*a collective*); *spec.* hulk, coffin (*an unseaworthy vessel, C or S*), tub, bark, blackbirder, catamaran, cockle, cockleshell, coaster, collier, convoy, hooker, lapstreak, razee, slaver, tender, transport, tramp, whaleback, whaler; *see* SHIP, RAFT.
2. receptacle; *spec.* horn, dish, canteen, crock, glass, pot de chambre (*French*).
3. *In anatomy: spec.* vein, artery, capillary.

vest, *n.* waistcoat (vest *is C, U. S.; in Brit. usage it signifies an undershirt*); *spec.* caftan (*Oriental*).

vest, *v. t.* **1.** lodge (*as a power*); *spec.* revest.
2. *See* CLOTHE, ADMIT.

vest, *v. i.* inhere, rest; *spec.* see ACCRUE.

vestibule, *n.* entrance, propylæum (*R*), porch (*R*); *spec.* hall, lobby, prothyrum, pronaos, narthex, tambour, anteroom.
Antonyms: see BODY.

vestige, *n.* evidence, sign; *see* FOOTPRINT, TRACE.

vestment, *n.* garment; *spec.* stole, dalmatic, pallium, maniple, succinctorium (*eccl.*), cope, chasuble, pall, tunicle.

veterinarian, *n.* farrier, vet (*C*); *spec.* hippiatric, horseshoer.

veto, *n.* **1.** intercession (*Roman hist.*).
2. *See* FORBIDDANCE.

veto, *v. t.* **1.** intercede (*Roman hist.*).
2. *See* FORBID.

vex, *v. t.* disquiet (*contex.*), disturb (*contex.*), gall, harass, irritate, pester, plague, spite, irk (*A*), chagrin, nip (*R*); *see* TEASE, TROUBLE, ANNOY.
Antonyms: see PACIFY.

vexation, *n.* **1.** disquiet, spite; *see* ANNOYANCE, TROUBLE, TROUBLING, ANGER, EMBARRASSMENT, DISTURBANCE.
2. disquiet, chagrin (*implying disappointment, irritation or failure*), mortification; *see* ANGER.

vexatious, *a.* annoying, disturbing, pesterous (*R*), pestilent (*humorous*); *see* ANNOYING, TROUBLESOME.
Antonyms: see PACIFIC.

viaduct, *n. Spec.* trestlework *or* (*for short*) trestle.

vibrant, *a.* oscillating, oscillant, undulous, librating, *etc.*

vibrate, *v. i. & t.* oscillate, librate, waver (*R*), sway, shake, undulate (*R*), quiver, pulsate (*R*); *spec.* nutate, dirl (*Scot. & dial. Eng.*), jar, tirl (*chiefly Scot.*), thrill, trill (*of sound*), tremble (*fast and short*); *see* SWING.

vibration, *n.* oscillation, libration, undulation (*R*), shaking (*contex.*), shake (*contex.*), quiver, wavering (*R*), wag (*spec. or C*), pulsation (*R*), pulse (*R*); *spec.* jar, fremitus, thrill (*R*), tremor, tremble, trepidation (*R*), vibratiuncle (*R*); *see* SWING.

vibrational, *a.* undulatory, oscillatory, libratory, shaking (*contex.*), vibrative (*R*), vibratile (*R*), motatorious *or* motatory (*R*), pulsatile (*tech. or R*), pulsatory (*tech. or R*), pulsative (*tech. or R*), seismic.

vibrator, *n. Spec.* trembler, oscillator, diaphragm.

viceroy, *n.* prorex (*obs.*); *spec.* exarch, regent.

vice versa, contrariwise, conversely, turn about.

victim, *n.* prey; *spec.* dupe, hoaxee (*R; jocular*); *see* SACRIFICE.

victor, *n.* conqueror, triumpher, victress (*fem.*), victrix (*fem.*), master; *spec.* winner, pancratiast, champion, conquistador (*Spanish hist.*).

victorious, *a.* conquering, triumphant, triumphal, prevalent (*R*).

victory, *n.* conquest, triumph, palm (*fig.*), mastery; *spec.* walkover (*C*), pushover (*C*), epinician (*Greek literature*), gammon.
Antonyms: see DEFEAT.

vie, *v. i.* contend, strive.

view, *n.* **1.** *Referring to what is seen by the eye:* prospect, survey, sight, outlook, vista, purview, range, scene, spectacle (*chiefly spec.*); *spec.* picture, eyeshot, command, lookout, perspective, cloudscape (*R*), seascape, landscape, offscape (*R*), offskip (*R*), scape; *see* SCENERY.
2. *Referring to mental view, the view of the mind's eye:* look, outlook, conspectus (*formal*), light (*as in "to come to light"*); *spec.* retrospect, retrospection, review, purview, foreglance (*R*),

---

verve: *energy, ardor.*
very, *a.: actual.*
vicarious: *substituted.*
vice: *immorality, corruption, fault.*
vicinity: *neighborhood, nearness.*
vicious: *immoral, corrupt.*
viciousness: *immorality, corruption.*
vicissitude: *change.*

---

glimpse (*faint and momentary*), panorama; *see* SURVEY, OPINION.
3. *See* SIGHT, VISION, OBJECT, CONSIDERATION, ASPECT.

view, *v. t.* **1.** *Referring to beholding with the eye:* see, behold (*look at voluntarily, A*); *spec.* eye (*often with a word or phrase implying some special emotion or attitude*), gaze (*fixedly, R*), contemplate, envisage (*look directly at, R*), consider (*implying care or attentiveness, A*), meditate (*implying interest or intentness, R*); *see* SURVEY.
2. *Referring to mental vision: see* CONSIDER.

viewer, *n.* seer, beholder, observer, surveyor, onlooker, *etc.*

viewpoint, *n.* point of view, ground, standpoint.

viewy, *a.* **1.** sightly, showy.
2. *See* VISIONARY.

vigil, *n.* watch; *spec. in pl.* devotions, pernoctation (*R*).

vigilant, *a.* watchful, jealous, sharp, unslumbering; *see* CAUTIOUS.

vigor, *n.* **1.** activity, vehemence, strenuousness, strength, vim (*C*), freshness, forcibleness, intensity, intenseness, intension (*R*), strenuosity (*R*), severity; *spec.* cordiality, heartiness, boldness, eagerness; *see* ACTIVITY, ENERGY, SPIRIT.
Antonyms: see WEAKNESS.
2. virility, smartness, stamina (*originally a pl.; now mostly construed as a sing.*), lustihead (*A*), lustihood (*A*), lustiness, dewiness (*R*), pith (*fig.*), strength, flower (*fig.*), nerve, energy, vitality, health; *spec.* hardiness.
Antonyms: see WEAKNESS.

vigorous, *a.* **1.** active, strong, lustful, lusty, robust, robustious, fresh (*as showing unabated vigor*), hale, stout, flourishing, smart, entire (*A*), vegete (*R*); *spec.* buxom (*plump and comely*); *see* ROBUST.
Antonyms: see AILING, WEAK, WEAKLY.
2. active, energetic, strong, strenuous, smart, sharp (*of a conflict, skirmish*), quick, crank (*dial.*), hot (*of a fight, battle*), severe, sturdy, stout; *spec.* bold (*of conception, etc.*), cordial, nervous (*as in "nervous English"*), hearty, masculine, virile.
Antonyms: see WEAK.

vile, *a.* **1.** *See* DIRTY.
2. base, filthy, contemptible, discreditable, ugly, lousy (*in contempt; usually vulgar, but also common in the mild C sense of "not very good"*), dirty, obscene, (*R or spec.*); *spec.* slavish, degraded, piggish, hoggish, brutish; *see* BEASTLY, ABOMINABLE, LEWD.
Antonyms: see ELEVATED.

village, *n.* wick (*obs., exc. in place names*), thorp (*A or hist.*), settlement; *spec.* vill (*chiefly hist.*), hamlet, dorp, clachan (*Scot. & Irish*), rancho, kampong (*Malay*), kraal (*South Africa*), bustee (*Anglo-Indian*), compound.

villain, *n.* blackguard, miscreant, sliphalter (*A*), nithing (*A*); *spec.* ruffian; *see* RASCAL.

villainous, *a.* miscreant; *spec.* ruffianly; *see* CRIMINAL, RASCALLY.

villainy, *n.* miscreancy (*R*), doggery (*fig.*); *spec. see* WRONG, RASCALITY.

vindicate, *v. t.* defend (*contex.*), right, avenge, maintain; *spec.* assert, revenge.

vindictive, *n.* retaliative, revengeful, grudgeful (*R*), vengeful.

vine, *n. Spec.* liana, grape.

vinery, *n.* grapery.

violate, *v. t.* **1.** desecrate (*implying a taking away the sacred character of, or treating as if not sacred*), defile (*emphasizing the polluting effect on the thing desecrated*), profane (*referring esp. to* violation *by heathen religious rites, or impious or irreverent action*), dishonor; *spec.* deflower (*implying, fig., the taking away of the chief freshness, bloom, or beauty*), abuse, force.
Antonyms: see HONOR.
2. infringe, invade, contravene (*tech. or B*), break, infract, transgress.
Antonyms: see OBSERVE.
3. *See* ILL-TREAT, RAPE.

violated, *a.* broken; *spec.* breached, desecrated.

violation, *n.* **1.** desecration, defilement, deflowering (*fig.*).
2. infraction (*formal or B*), transgression, breach, infringement, contravention (*tech. or B*), breaking.
3. *See* RAPE.

violence, *n.* force (*contex.*), fury, furiousness, furiosity (*R*), heaviness (*contex.*), rage, headiness (*fig. or R*), strength (*contex.*), severity (*contex.*), rampage, rudeness (*R*), brunt, turbulence, ferocity, ferociousness; *spec.* strain, flagrancy, desecration, excess, intensity, desperateness.
Antonyms: see GENTLENESS.

violent, *a.* furious, forcible (*contex.*), forceful, strong, fierce, raging (*of disease, storm, etc.*), extreme (*of pain, suffering, etc.*), severe, rabid (*B*); *spec.* sharp (*as rain, storm, wind*), grievous (*A*), rampant, high, wild, tough (*C*), smart, hot, heavy, hard, heady (*dust, current, etc.*), rank, impetuous, rude (*B or R*), rough, roaring (*R*), sore, impetuous, stormy, boisterous (*rough, but good-natured*), drastic (*once implying* violent *effect upon the intestines; now used figuratively*), desperate, outrageous (*R*), virulent, vicious (*C*), tearing, towering, stiff, red (*fig.*), turbulent, passionate; *see* ROUGH, FLAGRANT, BURNING, INTENSE.
Antonyms: see GENTLE.

violin, *n.* fiddle (*now C, familiar, or depreciatory*), viol (*R, B*), catgut (*fig.*); *spec.* crowd, rebeck, kit (*R*).

violin, *v. i.* fiddle (*familiar, often cant*).

violinist, *n.* fiddler (*except as denoting the*

vim: *force.* | **vindication:** *defense.* | **vintage:** *harvest.*

violinist in action, C or derogatory) scraper (*derogatory*); *spec.* crowder.

virgin, *a.* **1.** maiden, maidenly, virginal, vestal, parthenian (*R*), parthenic (*R*); *spec.* vestal.
2. *See* PURE.

virgin, *n.* maiden, maid (*A*), may (*B and A*); *spec.* vestal.

virtual, *a.* potential, practical, substantial; *spec.* moral.

virtue, *n.* **1.** rectitude, uprightness, morality, worth, honor, goodness; *spec.* cardinal virtues (justice, prudence, temperance, fortitude, *as distinguished from the theological virtues of* faith, hope, *and* charity; *the last also with modern writers being called "cardinal virtues"*); *see* CHASTITY, HONESTY.
Antonyms: see WICKEDNESS, DISHONESTY.
2. *Referring to a virtue:* grace.
3. *See* POWER, EFFECTIVENESS.

virtuoso, *n.* connoisseur, master (*contex.*), adept; *see* EXPERT.

virtuous, *a.* honorable, good (*being what it ought to be*), moral, honest (*chiefly B; often spec.*), upright; *spec.* goody (*virtuous in a weak or sentimental way*), goody-goody, exemplary; *see* CHASTE.
Antonyms: see WICKED, DISHONEST.

virulent, *a.* acrid, bitter; *see* ACRIMONIOUS, ACRID, MALIGNANT, POISONOUS.

viscera, *n. pl.* entrails (*now chiefly spec.*), insides (*C or dial.*), inwards, internals (*R*), numbles (*A*), guts; *spec.* inmeats, haslet *or* harslet.

visceral, *a.* splanchnic; *see* ABDOMINAL.

viscid, *a.* viscous, adhesive, sticky, mucilaginous, thick, stiff, tough, tenacious, slab (*B*); *spec.* glairy, glaireous (*R*), slimy, sizy, clammy, glutinous, thready, ropy, plastery; *see* SLIMY.
Antonyms: see THIN.

visible, *a.* visual, perceptible (*contex.*), open, seeable, unhidden, apparent; *spec.* megascopic, macroscopic, conspicuous (*clearly or noticeably* visible; *obvious to the eye*).
Antonyms: see INVISIBLE.

vision, *n.* **1.** *Referring to the faculty:* sight, eyesight, light (*fig.*); *spec.* diplopia; *see* SIGHT.
2. *Referring to the range of vision:* eyeshot, eyesight, eye, ken.
3. *Mental vision or comprehension:* foresight, prospect, view; *spec.* dream.
4. *See* SIGHT.

visionary, *a.* unreal, impractical, chimerical, absurd, Laputan (*fig.*), fantastic (*R*), viewy (*C*); *spec.* quixotic, Cervantic; *see* IMAGINARY.
Antonyms: see ACTUAL, PRACTICAL, MATTER-OF-FACT.

visionary, *n.* visionist (*R*), dreamer, fantast (*R*); *spec.* utopian; *see* IMAGINER.

visit, *n. Spec.* call.

visit, *v. t.* **1.** seek (*A*), do (*contex.*), *spec.* intervisit, haunt, lionize; *see* FREQUENT.
2. affect, afflict.

visitor, *n.* visitant, company (*a collective*); *spec.* caller, sojourner, incomer, stranger; *see* GUEST, IMMIGRANT.

visor, *n. Spec.* beaver.

visual, *a.* optical, ocular, optic (*R, exc. spec.*).

visualize, *v. t.* externalize, envisage, actualize.

vital, *a.* **1.** life (*the noun used attributively*); *spec.* biotic.
2. *See* ESSENTIAL, NECESSARY.

vitiation, *n.* **1.** *See* DEGRADATION, CORRUPTION.
2. contamination, corruption; *spec.* adulteration, spoiling.

vitrify, *v. t.* vitrificate (*R*); *spec.* glaze.

vivacious, *a.* **1.** *See* LONG-LIVED.
2. active, smart, lively, bright, breezy (*fig.*); *see* LIVELY, GAY.
Antonyms: see SAD, SULLEN, SERIOUS.

vivacity, *n.* vivaciousness, activity; *see* GAYETY.
Antonyms: see ENNUI.

vivarium, *n.* vivary (*R*), pond, stew (*obs. or dial. Eng.*), preserve, preservatory (*R*); *spec.* park (*for oysters*), pound (*for fish*), aquarium, mulletry, penguinery, pelicanry, insectarium (*R*), aviary.

vivid, *a.* fresh, lively, living, quick, clear, loud, brilliant, strong; *see* DESCRIPTIVE, DEFINITE, INTENSE.
Antonyms: see DULL.

vocabulary, *n.* **1.** language, terms (*pl.*).
2. *See* DICTIONARY.

vocal, *a.* **1.** sonant, voiceful (*R*), phthongal (*R*); *spec.* sonorescent (*R*).
2. *See* ORAL.

vociferate, *v. t.* bellow, bawl, yell, howl, clamor; *see* SHOUT.
Antonyms: see WHISPER.

vociferation, *n.* bellow, howl, bawl; *spec. see* OUTCRY.

vociferous, *a.* open-mouthed; *see* CLAMOROUS.

voice, *n.* **1.** tongue, tone, vox (*Latin*); *spec.* whisper, bass, baritone, tenor, alto, soprano, contralto, falsetto, pipe, breast (*A*), cry.
2. *See* SAY, SPEAKER, SINGER.

void, *a.* **1.** *See* EMPTY, DEVOID, INEFFECTUAL.
2. blank, null, invalid, inept (*law; R*).

void, *n.* **1.** blank; *spec.* chasm; *see* HOLE, ABYSS.
2. *See* EMPTINESS.

void, *v. t.* **1.** empty, clear; *see* EVACUATE, EJECT.
2. evacuate (*B*).

volatile, *a.* **1.** flyaway, flighty, mercurial (*B*), giddy, light-headed, inconstant, transient; *see* FRIVOLOUS, LIVELY.
2. incoercible (*gases*), evaporative.

volley, *n.* **1.** flight; *spec.* round, platoon, return, harquebusade; *see* DISCHARGE.
2. *See* OUTBREAK.

volplaning, *n.* flight, planing (*C*).

volume, *n.* **1.** content, bulk, bouk (*Scot.*), quantity, substance, size.
2. *See* QUANTITY.
3. book, tome (*B*); *see* ROLL.

---

virago: *shrew.*
virile: *forceful, manly.*
virulence: *poison.*
visitation, *n.: affliction, frequentation.*
vitality: *life.*
vituperate: *abuse, revile, denounce.*

voluminous, *a.* big (*contex.*), full; *spec.* discursive, flowing, ample, polygraphic (*B*).
voluntary, *a.* intentional, willing, deliberate, free, unconstrained.
Antonyms: see INVOLUNTARY.
voluptuary, *n.* pleasurist (*R*), softling (*obs. or R*), sensualist; *spec.* beast, brute.
voluptuous, *a.* voluptuary; *spec.* effeminate (*implying the surrender to luxury, ease and self-indulgence characteristic of women of fashion*), sybaritic; *see* SENSUAL, LUXURIOUS.
vomit, *v. t. & i.* **1.** eject (*contex.*), spew, disgorge (*contex.*), regorge (*R*), puke (*vulgar*), cast, egurgitate (*R*), eructate (*B or tech.*), throw up, chuck up (*C*), calf (*C*), shoot one's lunch (*S*).
Antonyms: see SWALLOW.
2. *See* EJECT.
voracious, *a.* ravenous, devouring, ravening (*B*), vulturous (*R*), rapacious, cormorant (*fig.*), bulimic (*chiefly med.*), bulimious (*R*), polyphagous (*R*), voraginous (*R*).
voracity, *n.* ravenousness, raven *or* ravin; *see* HUNGER.
vortex, *n.* whirl, tourbillion *or* turbillion (*R*), gyre (*B*).
votary, *n.* adherent (*contex.*), votarist (*C*), votaress (*fem.*); *spec.* Cytherean; *see* DEVOTEE.
vote, *n.* **1.** voice (*spec. or fig.*), say (*spec. or fig.*); *spec.* plebiscite, plebiscitum, plumper (*Eng.*), ballot.
2. franchise, suffrage, poll (*R*); *spec.* ballot.
voter, *n. Spec.* suffragist (*R*), floater, potwalloper (*Eng.*), potwaller (*Eng.*), plumper (*Eng.*), repeater (*U. S.*), elector; *see* CONSTITUENT.
votive, *a.* votary; *spec. see* DEDICATORY.
vouch, *v. t.* evidence; *see* GUARANTEE.
voyage, *n.* journey, trip; *spec.* cruise, navigation (*R*), sail, passage; *see* EXCURSION.
voyage, *v. i.* journey; *spec.* travel, sail, steam, row, passage.
vulgar, *a.* **1.** plebeian, popular, common, profane (*B*); *see* LOWLY.
Antonyms: see NOBLE.
2. base, cheap, rustic, suburban, raffish, carlish (*B*), gross, Bowery (*fig., U. S.*); *spec.* boorish, coarse, rabble; *see* LOW.
Antonyms: see REFINED.
vulgarize, *v. t.* plebeianize, plebify (*R*); *see* POPULARIZE.
vulnerable, *a.* assailable, woundable.
Antonyms: see INVULNERABLE.

W

wade, *v. t. Spec.* ford.
wading, *a. Spec.* grallatorial (*tech.*).
wafer, *n. Spec.* cachet, konseal, obley; *see* HOST.
wag, *v. t. & i.* **1.** *See* SWAY.
2. *Referring to the tongue:* run.
wager, *v. i.* gamble; *spec.* plunge (*S*), punt; *see* BET.
wager, *v. t.* gamble, stake, risk, set (*A*), go, adventure; *spec.* play (wager *in a game*); *see* GAMBLE.
wager, *n.* stake, gamble, risk; *spec.* bet, ante, raise, straddle, pot, jackpot; *see* GAMBLE.
wages, *n. sing. & pl.* pay, payment, stipend; *see* HIRE, EARNINGS.
wagon, *n. Spec.* truck; *see* VEHICLE.
wail, *v. t.* **1.** bewail (*an intensive*), behowl (*R*), beweep (*R*); *see* MOURN.
Antonyms: see REJOICE, LAUGH.
2. *See* ACCLAIM.
waist, *n.* **1.** *See* BODY.
2. *Referring to a garment:* body; *spec.* bodice, vest, basque, corsage, bolero, blouse, cuirass, corset (*now R*).
wait, *v. i.* **1.** rest, defer; *spec.* watch.
2. *See* ATTEND.
3. *To wait at table:* minister (*A or B*).
waiter, *n. Spec.* garçon (*French*), pannier (*Eng.*), skinker (*R*).
wake, *n.* wash (*of a vessel*); *see* TRACK.
wake, *v. t.* **1.** *See* ROUSE.
2. waken, awake, awaken, arouse, rouse, excite.
wakeful, *a.* waking, roused.
Antonyms: see SLEEPY.
walk, *n.* **1.** *Act of walking:* deambulation (*R, B*); *spec.* excursion, tramp, trudge, hike, pace, waddle, daddle, march, promenade, perambulation, plod, saunter, stroll, stalk, cakewalk; *see* GAIT.
2. *A distance walked: spec.* constitutional (*R*), hike, tramp, saunter, stroll, promenade, dander (*Scot. & dial. Eng.*), turn.
3. *Place where one walks: spec.* path, cloister, promenade, pergola, frescade (*R*), mall, deambulatory (*R*), boulevard, marina (*Spanish and Italian*), esplanade; *see* COURSE.
4. *See* SPHERE.
walk, *v. i.* **1.** deambulate (*R*), tread, pedestrianize (*R*), pedestrianate (*R*); *spec.* trample, tramp (*with heavy step*), trudge (*implying weariness or laboriousness*), stamp, hike, stump, stride, step, plod (*heavily*), poach, grind (*Eng. university S*), dade (*obs. or dial. Eng.*), leg (*esp. with "it"*), pad, falter (*unsteady, tottering, stumbling*), stalk, foot (*used with "it"*), mince, perambulate, saunter, stroll, lounge (*leisurely*), ramble (*with no definite destination, route or purpose*), tiptoe, shin (*C*), thump, trundle, roll, trapes *or* traipse (*C or dial.*), promenade, parade, shamble (*unsteadily or awkwardly*), pound; *see* MARCH, TODDLE.
Antonyms: see RUN.
2. *See* LIVE.
walk, *v. t.* **1.** traverse, tramp; *spec.* pace; *see* TREAD.
2. *See* MOVE.
walker, *n.* footman (*R*), footer (*R*), peripatetic (*chiefly humorous*); *spec.* pedestrian (*suggesting merely the fact of going on foot, often with reference to the manner*), dustyfoot

(*obs. or hist.; Scot.*), perambulator (*R*), trudger, tramper, hiker, *etc.*
walking, *a.* gradient (*tech.*), ambulant (*tech.*), gressorial (*tech.*), ambulatory (*tech.*); *spec.* pedestrian, trippant.
walking, *n.* pedestrianism, peripateticism (*humorous*), perambulation.
walking-stick, *n. Spec.* staff, cane, bourdon (*obs.*), palster (*A*), crutch.
wall, *n. Spec.* partition, bulkhead, bail *or* bailey, canaut (*Anglo-Indian*), counterscarp, parapet, escarp, revetment, countermure; *see* INCLOSURE.
wall, *v. t. Spec.* mure, inwall, countermure; *see* FORTIFY.
wallow, *v. i.* welter, muddle (*A*); *spec. see* TUMBLE.
wand, *n.* stick (*contex.*), rod; *spec.* rodlet, baton, caduceus, scepter; *see* STAFF, SWITCH.
wander, *v. i.* **1.** ramble, roam, rove, stray, straggle, range, meander, maunder, stroll, prowl, roll, trapes (*obs. or dial.*), spatiate (*R*), divagate (*B*); *spec.* gad (*used with "about"*), obambulate (*R*), expatiate (*R or fig.; B*), vagabondize (*R*), vagabond (*R*), scamander (*R*), estray (*R*), shack (*dial. or C*), truant, forage.
2. *Referring to mental wandering:* moon, ramble, gander (*dial. Eng.*); *see* RAVE.
3. *See* MIGRATE, DEVIATE.
wander, *n.* ramble, rambling, roam, rove, divagation (*B*); *spec.* prowl, gad (*dial. Eng. or C*), trapes (*C or dial.*), stroll (*B*).
wanderer, *n.* rambler, roamer, rover, strayer, *etc.*, runagate (*A*), vagabond (*R, B*), vagrant (*chiefly spec.*), scatterling (*A*), waif, gadabout (*C*), runabout (*C*); *spec.* nomad.
wandering, *a.* **1.** rambling, roaming, roving, *etc.*, stray, vagarish (*R*), vagarious (*R*), abroad (*predicative*); *spec.* nomadic, discursive (*going hither and thither irregularly, B*), floating, nomad, vagabond, migratory, multivagant (*R*), perambulatory, itinerant, devious (*suggesting a going out of the usual way, or out of one's natural or proper course*), vagrant, truant, cometic, aberrant (*from the right, or from the right way*), circumforaneous (*R*), erratic (*of pains, diseases, etc.; also of rocks, stars, etc.*), excursive, planetary (*fig.*), obambulatory (*R*).
2. *Referring to thought or discourse:* rambling, discursive.
Antonyms: see DIRECT.
3. *See* DEVIOUS, DELIRIOUS.
wandering, *n.* **1.** rambling, roaming, straying, *etc.*, error (*B*), divagation (*B*); *spec.* gadabout (*aimless or gossipy going about*), obambulation (*R*), discursion (*R*), extravagation (*R*), evagation (*R*).
2. *See* DEVIATION, DELIRIUM, ABERRATION.
waning, *a.* decrescent (*B or tech.*).
wanting, *a.* minus; *spec.* absent, gone, lost, destroyed, *etc.*

wanton, *n. Referring to a woman:* gill, flirt (*A*), baggage (*often playful*), bitch (*not now in decent use*), light-o'-love (*B*), light-skirts (*R*), Cyprian (*B*), skit (*chiefly Scot.*), bona roba (*B*); *see* FLIRT.
war, *n.* fight (*contex.*), hostilities (*pl.*); *spec.* warfare, guerrilla (*R*), jihad, jehad, crusade, gigantomachy (*R*).
Antonyms: see PEACE, TRUCE.
war, *v. i.* fight (*contex.*); *spec.* crusade, campaign.
war cry, slogan, battle cry, on-cry (*R*).
ward, *n.* **1.** alumnus (*masc.*), alumna (*fem.*);—*both tech. or B.*
2. *See* GUARD, PROTECTION, PROTECTOR, DIVISION, DISTRICT.
ward, *v. t.* fend (*R, A*), guard, drive (*used with "off"; A*); *spec.* stave (*used with "off"*), parry; *see* REPEL.
warden, *n. Spec.* herenach (*Anglo-Irish*), dizdar, disdar (*Oriental*); *see* GUARD, CUSTODIAN.
warder, *n. Spec.* gatekeeper, gateward (*A*); *see* GUARD, PROTECTOR.
wardrobe, *n.* **1.** clothing, vestiary (*R*); *spec.* vestry.
2. *See* CLOSET.
ware, *n.* **1.** *Spec.* crockery, earthenware, enamel, silver, plate, glass, *etc.*
2. commodity, truck (*a collective*), goods (*pl.*); *spec.* merchandise (*a collective*), import, export.
warehouse, *n.* repository, bankshall (*Oriental*), emporium (*a loose usage*); *spec.* hong (*Chinese*), godown (*in the Far East*), pantechnicon (*Eng.*), packhouse, storehouse.
warlike, *a.* belligerent, bellicose, belluent (*R*); *spec.* truculent, militant; *see* PUGNACIOUS.
warm, *a.* **1.** *Spec.* calid, tepid, lukewarm; *see* HEATED.
Antonyms: see COLD.
2. *See* LIVELY, GLOWING, FRESH, AFFECTIONATE, ARDENT.
warm, *v. t.* heat (*contex.*), calefy; *spec.* tepefy, roast, toast (*C*).
Antonyms: see COOL.
warm-blooded, *a.* hæmathermal, hæmathermous;—*both tech. or R.*
warmth, *n.* **1.** heat (*contex.*); *spec.* tepidity, tepidness; *see* GLOW.
Antonyms: see COLD.
2. *See* ARDOR.
warn, *v. t.* caution, admonish (*formal*), premonish (*R*), notify, inform, precaution (*R*), forewarn (*emphatic*), monition (*eccl.; R*), prewarn (*R*), advise (*chiefly spec.*), readvise (*R*).
warning, *a.* monitory (*formal*), cautionary, admonitory (*formal*), premonitory (*emphatic*); *spec.* sematic.
warning, *n.* caution, monition (*B*), premonition (*R or spec.*), monitor (*fig.*), forewarning (*emphatic*), preadmonition (*R*), notice, notification, information, admonition (*formal*), precaution (*R*), commonition (*R*), advice (*chiefly*

W

wane, *n.: decline.*
wane, *v. i.: abate.*
want, *n.: desire, deficiency, poverty, need, absence.*
want, *v. i.: lack.*
wanting: *deficient, absent.*

spec.), caveat (*now only fig.*); *spec.* example, exemplar, memento (*R*), ensample (*A*).

warp, *n.* stamen (*tech. or hist.*), web (*dial.*), chain, bend.

warp, *v. i. Spec.* hog, kedge, cast.

warring, *a.* belligerent (*tech.*), militant (*B*).

warrior, *n.* belligerent (*contex.; B*), brave (*now chiefly spec.*); *spec.* Hector, Amazon (*fem.*), berserker, crusader.

warship, *n. Spec.* battleship, cruiser, battle cruiser, destroyer, dreadnought, monitor, frigate.

warty, *a.* verrucous *or* verrucose (*both tech.*), warted (*R*).

wash, *n.* **1.** *Spec.* rinse (*C*), scrub, scour, swab; *see* BATH, CLEANING, SPLASH, GARGLE.

2. *Referring to the waves: see* BREAK.

3. *Referring to liquid with which to coat or wash: spec.* bath liquor, coat, calcimine, whitewash, pigment, paint, embrocation, liniment, lotion, eyewater, collyrium.

4. *In geology: spec.* alluvium, till, silt.

5. *Referring to an amount of clothes to be washed:* washing, batch, buck.

wash, *v. t.* **1.** clean (*contex.*), lave (*B*), bathe; *spec.* rinse, sluice, irrigate, launder, lick, lip.

2. coat (*contex.*); *spec.* calcimine, whitewash, paint.

3. *See* ABSOLVE.

wash, *v. i.* **1.** lave (*B*); *spec.* lip, rinse, scour (*usually jocular as used of the face*), scrub, flush, sluice; *see* BATHE, SPLASH.

2. *Referring to covering with a liquid: spec.* coat, elutriate (*R*), flush, edulcorate, gull (*dial. or tech.*), pan; *see* SPLASH, LAUNDER, GARGLE, PURIFY.

washer, *n.* burr (*of a rivet*).

washing, *n.* **1.** *The action:* ablution (*R*), lavage (*chiefly med.*), lavation (*B, pedantic, or tech.*); *spec.* elution (*R*), edulcoration, lavabo; *see* CLEANING.

2. *See* WASH.

washing, *a. Spec.* lavatory (*chiefly eccl.*); *see* TOILET.

washroom, *n.* lavatory (*formal or B*).

washstand, *n.* lavabo (*grandiose or cant*), wash-hand-stand (*Brit.*); *spec.* commode.

wasplike, *a.* vespine (*tech.*).

waste, *v. t.* **1.** lose, dissipate, squander, scatter (*A*), misspend, consume (*contex.*); *spec.* lavish, dilapidate (*R*), wanton, riot, lounge, fritter (*chiefly with "away"*).

Antonyms: see ECONOMIZE, STINT, PRESERVE.

2. *See* DEVASTATE, DESOLATE, EMACIATE.

3. emaciate, tabefy (*tech.*), forpine (*A*).

waste, *v. i.* tabefy (*tech.*), pine, dwine (*A or Scot.*); *spec.* molder.

Antonyms: see FATTEN.

waste, *n.* **1.** squander, ineconomy (*R*); *spec.* estrepement; *see* DECAY.

Antonyms: see ECONOMY.

2. *Referring to what is wasted:* wastage, offal (*tech.*), refuse, wastrel (*B or A*); *spec.* clum, debris, detritus, spilth, sands (*pl.*), slops, trash, wash, wilderness, dross, leakage, junk, alluvium, egesta.

Antonyms: see SAVING, *n.* **3.**

3. *See* DESERT, DEVASTATION.

wasted, *a.* **1.** lost (*contex.*); *spec.* squandered, misspent.

2. *See* EMACIATE.

wasteful, *a.* prodigal, unthrifty; *see* EXTRAVAGANT.

Antonyms: see ECONOMICAL, STINGY.

wastefulness, *n.* prodigality, unthrift.

waster, *n.* prodigal, wastrel, lavisher; *see* SPENDTHRIFT.

Antonyms: see NIGGARD.

wasting, *a.* **1.** tabescent (*tech.*).

2. *Causing wasting:* emaciative, tabific (*tech.*).

wasting, *n.* emaciation, tabefaction (*tech.*), contabescence (*R*); *spec.* maceration, marasmus, syntexis, colliquation, consumption, tabes.

watch, *n.* **1.** *Referring to the act:* observation (*contex.*), ward, guard, vigil (*formal or B*), outlook, espial (*R*), wake (*chiefly spec.*); *spec.* oversight (*R*), surveillance, dog watch, round; *see* GUARD.

2. *One who watches:* observer, ward; *spec.* sentinel, sentry (*the more technical military term*), picket; *see* GUARD.

3. *A timepiece:* tompion (*obs.*), ticker (*S*), tattler (*S*); *spec.* bull's-eye (*R*), hack.

watch, *v. i.* invigilate (*R or spec.*); *spec.* waken (*R*), mark, picket, preside, scout, float; *see* GUARD, SUPERVISE.

watch, *v. t.* **1.** observe (*contex.*), overwatch (*emphatic*), oversee (*R*), ward (*A*), attend (*R*), notice (*R*), espy (*A*), twig (*S*), stag (*S*), mark (*R or B*); *spec.* dragonize (*R*), follow, eye; *see* GUARD, SUPERVISE.

2. *See* AWAIT.

watchdog, *n.* bandog (*A*), porter (*fig.*); *spec.* Cerberus (*fig.*).

watcher, *n.* observer (*contex.*), guard (*R*); *spec.* lookout, crow (*thieves' cant*), spy, picket, scout, dragon *or* (*fem.*) dragoness, invigilator.

watchful, *a.* observing (*contex.*), vigilant, alert; *spec.* erect.

Antonyms: see CARELESS.

watching, *n.* vigilance; *spec.* surveillance, spying, espionage, invigilation.

watchman, *n.* watch, ward (*A*); *spec.* lookout,

watchman, *n.* watch, ward (*A*); *spec.* look-out, scout, runner, patrol, night watchman, Charley (*obs.*), dozener (*obs.*); *see* GUARD.

watchtower, *n.* beacon.

watchword, *n.* word, catchword, slogan, cry, shibboleth (*fig.*); *see* PASSWORD, COUNTERSIGN.

water, *n.* **1.** *Spec.* lymph (*rhetorical or B*), crystal (*B*), flood (*B or rhetorical*), steam.

warp, *v. t.: move, bend, distort, pervert.* | **warrant,** *v. t.: guarantee, state, assure, justify.* | **waste,** *a.: wild, desolate.*

2. *A body of water: spec.* dam, drink (*humorous; U. S.*), sluice, river, lake, pond, sea, ocean, pool, *etc.; see* FLOOD.

water, *a.* aquatic (*formal or tech.*), hydraulic (*tech.*).

water, *v. t.* **1.** wet; *spec.* damp, irrigate, flood, soak, sprinkle, moisten.

Antonyms: see DRY.

2. calender, moire, tabby, cloud.

water cooler, olla (*U. S. & formerly in Spain, etc.*), guggler, goglet, gugglet, gorgolette (*R*).

watercourse, *n.* run (*chiefly U. S. & North Eng. dial.*); *spec.* arroyo (*local, U. S.*), nullah (*Anglo-Indian*), inlet, lead, donga (*South Africa*).

water cure, hydrotherapy, hydrotherapeutics.

waterfall, *n.* fall; *spec.* cataract, cascade, force (*local, Eng.*), sault (*local, America*), Niagara (*fig.*), linn (*chiefly Scot.*).

watery, *a.* waterish, aqueous (*B or tech.*), liquid (*rhetorical*); *spec.* wheyish, thin (*contex.*), washy, serous.

wattle, *n.* gill, jowl, jollop (*R*); *spec.* dewlap, jewing.

wave, *n.* **1.** undulation (*B or tech.*); *spec.* bore, billow, comber, curl, decuman (*R*), eager *or* eagre, groundswell, heave, ripple, head, roller, ranger (*R*), ripplet, sea, seiche, surge, swell, wavelet, whitecap; *see* BILLOW, RIPPLE.

2. *A body of moving water: spec.* flood, flush.

3. *See* UNDULATION, SINUOSITY, SWING, SEA, GESTURE, FLOURISH.

4. *A wave of emotion, success, etc.:* flush, tide.

wave, *v. i.* **1.** undulate; *spec.* heave, wallow (*A*), ripple, fluctuate (*R*), roll, curl, crisp, crinkle; *see* RIPPLE.

2. swing (*contex.*), flaunt, tremble (*fig.*), shake, sway; *spec.* play, flow, ripple; *see* FLUTTER, UNDULATE.

3. *See* GESTURE, CURVE.

wave, *v. t.* swing (*contex.*), sway, shake; *spec.* flourish (wave *ostentatiously, as a weapon*), brandish (*originally of* waving *a weapon in threat or display*), flaunt (wave *gaily or proudly*), ripple, flash, flare (*R*), stream, flutter (*float loosely, as a flag*), *see* WAVER, RIPPLE, FLOURISH.

waver, *n.* **1.** wave (*contex.*), oscillation, fluctuation.

2. *See* FLICKER, FALTER, TOTTER.

waver, *v. i.* **1.** (*contex.*); *spec.* fluctuate (*implying change of position or view, but not necessarily hesitation or weakness*), oscillate (*like a pendulum*), pendulate (*R*); *see* FLICKER, TOTTER.

2. vacillate, balance, fluctuate; *see* HESITATE.

3. *See* FALTER.

waving, *n.* undulating (*B or tech.*); *spec.* flying, flourish.

wavy, *a.* **1.** undulant (*tech. or B*), undulatory (*tech. or B*); *spec.* surgy; *see* BILLOWY, RIPPLY, ROUGH, CHOPPING, FLICKERING.

2. *Marked with wavy lines:* undate (*tech.*), undulate (*chiefly tech.*), undose (*tech.*), undulated (*tech.*), repand (*tech.*); *spec.* flexuous, flamboyant, undé (*her.*), curly, crisp, crisped, crispy, gyrose; *see* RIPPLY, SINUOUS.

waxing, *a.* crescent (*tech. or B*).

waxy, *a.* **1.** waxen, cereous (*B*), ceraceous (*tech.*); *spec.* ceruminous.

2. *See* IMPRESSIBLE.

way, *n.* **1.** via (*Latin*); *spec.* passage, avenue, path (*as formed by the tread of man or beast; hence, esp., of uninclosed* way *incidentally formed by passage, as distinguished from one planned and constructed for traffic*), footway, walk, route, cut, lane, byway, midway, boulevard, driftway, canal, footpath, ferry, wireway, wheelway, waterway, fairway, thoroughfare, wynd (*Scot. & Eng.*), alley, defile (*narrow, deep pass or gorge, so that troops must go in file or narrow column*), causeway, gate, transit, descent; *see* TRACK, ROAD, PATH.

2. *See* DISTANCE, DIRECTION, CUSTOM, MANNER, PROCEDURE, COURSE.

wayside, *n.* roadside.

weak, *a.* **1.** *Having little power:* feeble (*implying great* weakness, *and suggesting pity or contempt*), weakly, feckless (*Scot. or B*), foisonless (*chiefly Scot.*), infirm, asthenic (*tech.*); *spec.* debilitated, impotent, decrepit (*implying esp. the effects of old age, or sometimes of sickness or other decay, wear, or use; primarily referring to living beings only*), inenergetic, shaky (*C*), strengthless, doddered, groggy (*S or farriery*), debile (*obs. or A*), crazed (*A*), crazy (*A*), imbecile (*R*), impuissant (*R*), brittle, weakling (*R*), poorly, languid, faintly, sickly, faint (*of things that act, as fire, breezes, etc., or of wishes, purposes, etc.*), feeblish, effeminate, enervated, dotty (*C, S*), low, atonic (*tech.*), remiss (*as the pulse, pain, etc.*), puny, forceless, nerveless, small (*voice*), spineless; *see* POWERLESS, EFFEMINATE, UNCONVINCING.

Antonyms: see STRONG, ABLE, COGENT, POWERFUL, FIRM, FORCIBLE, INTENSE, VIGOROUS.

2. *Having little power to resist:* unsubstantial, frail, slimsy (*C, U. S.*), delicate, soft, molluscous (*fig.*), slender, reedy (*fig.*), tender, infirm, spineless (*fig.*); *spec.* fragile, paper (*fig.*), brittle, rickety, boneless (*fig.*), sinewless, invertebrate (*fig.*), little; *see* SLIGHT, FRAGILE, BRITTLE, COMPLAISANT.

Antonyms: see STRONG, VIGOROUS.

3. *Referring to liquors:* thin, small, single (*A*), light, wash, washy.

weaken, *v. t.* **1.** enfeeble, feeble (*R or A*); *spec.* unstring, undermine, depotentiate (*R*), shake, reduce, imbecilitate (*R*), impair, debilitate (*implying esp. general impairment of the natural or healthy powers or vitalities*), retund (*R*), faint (*R*), disinvigorate (*R*), unsinew (*fig.; R*), devitalize (*implying impairment of vital qualities that give life in quick and effective action, of water, doctrine, etc.*), unman,

wax, *v. i.: rise, increase, become, grow.* | **wayward:** *disobedient, capricious,* | *perverse.*

emasculate, attenuate, enervate (*impair nervous tone or character, and hence mentally or morally*), indispose, disintensify, slacken, sap, stagger, blunt, bate, effeminate, effeminize, unnerve.
Antonyms: see STRENGTHEN, CONFIRM, ENERGIZE, FIRM, INTENSIFY.
2. *Reduce the resisting force of:* shake, impair; *spec.* fatigue, strain.
Antonyms: see STRENGTHEN.
3. *See* DILUTE, ADULTERATE.

weaken, *v. i.* **1.** decline, languish, flag, fail.
2. *See* BACKSLIDE.

weakened, *a.* enfeebled, broken, reduced, impaired, broken-down; *spec.* decrepit, emasculated, atonic (*tech.*), enervate (*fig. or B*), unmanly, effeminate.
Antonyms: see STRENGTHENED; *cf.* STRENGTHEN.

weakening, *a.* debilitating, debilitant (*R*), debilitative, asthenic (*tech.*); *spec.* exhausting.
Antonyms: see STRENGTHEN; *cf.* STRENGTHENING.

weakening, *n.* enfeeblement, impairment, impair (*A*), labefaction (*R*); *spec.* attenuation, effemination, debilitation.

weakling, *n.* jellyfish (*fig.*), squab (*fig.*).
Antonyms: see ATHLETE.

weakly, *a.* frail, tender, unhardy (*R*); *spec.* rickety; *see* DELICATE.
Antonyms: see STRONG, VIGOROUS, HARDY.

weak-minded, *a.* feeble-minded; *spec.* doting, dotish.

weakness, *n.* **1.** feebleness, impotence, impotency, impuissance, infirmity (*implying a specific bodily* weakness), infirmness, caducity (*B*); *spec.* decrepitude, superannuation, senility, atony (*tech.*), debility (*implying esp. general impairment of the vital functions, or in mental or moral qualities, and usually more or less permanent*), neurasthenia (*tech.*), faintness, languidness, languor, imbecility, puniness, attenuation.
Antonyms: see STRENGTH, ENERGY, INTENSITY, POWER.
2. frailty, frailness *spec.* invertebracy (*R*), delicacy; *see* EFFEMINACY.
Antonyms: see VIGOR.
3. foible, failing; *spec.* liking, besetment.
4. *See* AILMENT.

weal, *n. Spec.* welt, wale, ridge, fleabite, streak.

wealth, *n.* **1.** riches, fortune, substance, lucre (*chiefly depreciatory*), pelf (*depreciatory*), mammon (*Biblical*), gold (*rhetorical for large sums*), treasure, moneybags (*fig.*); *spec.* capital.
2. opulence, affluence, richness, wealthiness.
Antonyms: see POVERTY.
3. *See* ABUNDANCE.

weapon, *n.* arm (*chiefly in pl.*); *spec.* dagger gun, sword, *etc.*

wear, *v. t.* **1.** consume (*contex.*), eat, impair; *see* DETERIORATE, FRAY, EXHAUST.
2. carry (*as a watch, crutches, etc.*), bear (*as in defense or display*), sport (*C*), display (*C*).
3. *See* PASS.

wear, *n.* consumption (*contex.*), impairment; *spec.* detrition (*tech. or B*).

wearied, *a.* tired, fatigued, worn; *spec.* bored.
Antonyms: see FRESH.

weariness, *n.* fatigue, tire (*C*), tiredness (*R*); *spec.* ennui (*French, implying* weariness *caused by lack of mental occupation*), tedium, boredom, languor, lassitude, languishment, sickness, monotony.
Antonyms: see FRESHNESS, ENERGY.

wearing, *a. Referring to pain:* racking, grinding.

wearisome, *a.* weary, weariful (*R*), fatiguesome (*R*); *spec.* borish, tedious, boring, irksome; *see* TIRESOME.
Antonyms: see RESTFUL, REFRESHING.

weary, *v. t.* **1.** fatigue, tire, wear (*as with "out"*).
Antonyms: see REST.
2. *Referring to mental attitude:* bore, tire, irk (*A*); *spec.* glut, surfeit.
Antonyms: see DIVERT.

weary, *v. i.* tire; *see* SICKEN.

weary, *a.* **1.** *See* TIRED.
2. impatient, aweary (*B*); *spec.* careworn; *see* SICK, DISCONTENTED.

weathervane, *n.* weathercock, vane, cock.

weave, *v. t.* **1.** inweave (*R*), compose (*contex.*), loom (*R*); *spec.* twill, knit, tissue, damask.
2. *See* INTERLACE, DESIGN.

weaving, *n.* loom (*fig.*), weave (*cant*).

web, *n.* **1.** *Web of spiders, etc.:* cobweb, net; *spec.* tent, gossamer.
2. *See* FEATHER, MEMBRANE, PLATE, TISSUE.

webbed, *a.* vexillate (*tech.*).

web-footed, *a.* bicolligate (*R*), palmiped (*tech.*), totipalmate (*tech.*).

wedge, *n.* quoin *or* coin (*tech. or B*); *spec.* shim, cleat, slice, cotter, chock, block, forelock, froe, frow, glut, gore, bias.

wedge-shaped, *a.* spheroid (*chiefly tech.*), cuneiform (*tech. or B*), cuneal (*R*), cuneate (*chiefly tech.*), wedgy (*R*).

weeds, *n. pl.* sackcloth (*a collective*), sables (*pl.*), mourning.

week, *n.* sevennight (*B, R*), sennight (*A*), heptad (*R*), hebdomad (*chiefly spec.; R*).

weekly, *a.* hebdomadal *or* hebdomadary (*B; chiefly spec.*).

weep, *v. i.* **1.** cry (*originally implying inarticulate exclamation, esp. of grief, lament, or suffering; now not so strong a word as* weep), greet (*Scot.*); *spec.* blubber (*generally contemptuous and in ridicule*), blirt (*dial.*), boohoo (*contemptuous; often jocular*), wail; *see* CRY.
Antonyms: see LAUGH.
2. *See* DRIP, DROOP.

weeping, *n.* cry (*C, a fit of* weeping), greet (*Scot.*), lachrymation (*R*), tears (*pl.*), ploration (*R*), lachrymals (*pl.; R*), sobbing; *cf.* LAMENTATION.
Antonyms: see LAUGHTER.

---

wear, *v. i.: pass, endure.* | **weather,** *v. t.: overcome, disintegrate.* | **weather,** *v. i.: disintegrate.*

---

weeping, *a.* **1.** lachrymatory (*B or tech.*), ploratory (*R*).
Antonyms: see LAUGHING.
2. *See* DROOPING.
weigh, *v. t.* **1.** trutinate (*R*); *spec.* scale.
2. consider (*contex.*), prepend (*R*), ponderate (*R*), poise (*R*); *spec.* heft (*C*).
3. *See* RAISE.
weigh, *v. i.* **1.** scale (*R*); *spec.* counterweigh.
2. *To weigh on the mind:* press, sit.
3. count, talk (*S*); *see* MATTER.
weight, *n.* **1.** ponderousness (*R*), ponderance (*R*), ponderosity (*B; chiefly rhetorical*), heaviness, heft (*U. S. & dial. Eng.*); *spec.* tonnage, gravity.
2. *Spec.* plumb, sinker, counterbalance, pea, bob, plummet, counterpoise, halteres (*pl.*), bias; *see* PLUMMET, CLOG.
3. *See* BURDEN, EMPHASIS.
weight, *v. t.* ingravidate (*R and chiefly fig.*); *spec.* plumb, load, lead; *see* LEAD, LOAD, BURDEN.
weightless, *a.* imponderable.
weir, *n.* stop (*contex.*); *spec.* goryd (*local, Eng.*), lasher (*chiefly local, Eng.*), hedge, waste; *see* DAM.
weird, *a.* eerie *or* eery (*B*), unearthly, uncanny, witching, eldritch (*chiefly Scot.*); *spec.* elvish, elfish.
welcome, *v. t.* embrace (*spec. or fig.*), gratulate (*A*); *spec.* greet.
welcome, *n. See* GREETING.
welfare, *n.* weal, well-being; *spec.* commonwealth (*obs.*), commonweal (*obs.*).
well, *n.* **1.** eye (*A*); *spec.* cesspool, gusher.
2. *See* SHAFT.
well, *adv.* **1.** *Spec.* exemplarily (well *enough to be a model or pattern*), capitally, first rate (*C*), finely, gallantly, fairly (*implying a degree, extent or the like that gives a sense of only reasonable completeness of satisfaction*), clean, famously (*C*), splendidly (*C*), nobly, rarely, timely, properly, justly; *see* THOROUGHLY.
Antonyms: see POORLY.
2. *Spec.* conveniently, fortunately, agreeably, favorably (*cf.* CONVENIENT, FORTUNATE, *etc.*).
well, *a.* whole, sound, right (*R*), wholesome (*obs. or A*), bobbish (*dial. or S*); *see* HEALTHY.
Antonyms: see AILING.
well-balanced, *a.* level (*C, U. S.*).
well-being, *n.* good, welfare, health (*A*); *spec.* comfort; *see* PROSPERITY.
Antonyms: see DISCOMFORT.
well-born, *a.* thoroughbred (*C or fig.*); *see* NOBLE, GENTLE.
well-bred, *a.* genteel (*vulgar or depreciatory*); *spec.* gentlemanly, ladylike.
well-founded, *a.* reasonable, just.
Antonyms: see UNFOUNDED.
well-informed, *a.* intelligent, posted (*C*); *spec.* well-read, learned.
Antonyms: see IGNORANT.
well-known, *a.* familiar, notorious; *spec.* famous, renowned, celebrious (*A*), proverbial.
well-shaped, *a.* eumorphous (*R*); *see* SHAPELY.
Antonyms: see DEFORMED.
welsh, *v. i.* back out, jib, weaken, funk (*S*), crawfish (*fig.; C*).
welsher, *n.* funker, jibber (*R*), weakener, recreant.
wench, *n.* **1.** girl (*which see*); *spec.* (*in depreciation*) blowze, dowdy *or* dowdie, trull, slut (*not in polite use*).
2. *See* MAIDSERVANT.
werewolf, *n.* lycanthrope.
west, *n.* occident (*R, exc. spec. and with cap., "Occident"*), sunset.
Antonyms: see EAST.
western, *a.* west, westerly, westward, Hesperian (*poetic*), ponent (*obs. or R*), occidental (*R, exc. spec. and cap., "Occidental"*).
Antonyms: see EASTERN.
wet, *a.* madid (*R*); *spec.* drippy, dewy, rainy, sprinkly, drunken (*soaked or saturated with moisture, now R or B*), dripping, irriguous (*R*), nasty (*contex.*), soppy, sloppy, slushy, slobbery (*chiefly dial.*), wishywashy (*C*), spewy, squelchy, clammy, sour, dabby; *see* MOIST, FOUL.
Antonyms: see DRY.
wet, *v. t.* water (*chiefly in spec. senses*), moil (*A*), humidify (*R*), humect (*R*), humectate (*R*), humify (*R*); *spec.* dip, daggle, dew, bedew, drench, dabble, sluice, slaver, slobber, shower, bedraggle, bedrabble, bedabble, draggle, soak, saturate, moisten, irrigate, embathe (*B*), drown, bucket, buck (*R*), blubber, beweep (*R*), besplash, beslubber, bedrench, baste (*cookery*), hose; *see* MOISTEN.
Antonyms: see DRY.
wet, *n.* moisture; *spec.* humidity, wash, damp.
wetting, *n.* humectation (*R*); *spec.* drench, irrigation (*R, exc. spec.*), flushing.
wetting, *a. Spec.* irriguous (*R*), irrigational *or* irrigative (*R exc. spec.*).
whale, *n.* cetacean (*contex.*), cete (*B*); *spec.* cub, finner.
wharf, *n. Spec.* quay, pier (*a pier used as a wharf*), dock (*C & U. S.*), key (*obs.*).
whatever, *n.* whatsoever (*formal or A*), whatsomever (*dial. & illiterate*).
wheat, *n.* cereal (*contex.*), grain (*contex.*); *spec.* frumenty, spelt.
wheel, *n.* **1.** *Spec.* roller, balance, caster, bowl pulley, fusee, rowel, roulette, trundle, truck, trolley, lap, drum, sheave, disc (*B*), orb (*B*), scaife (*local*), skive, truckle; *see* CYCLE, CASTER, TURN.
2. *See* ROTATION, REVOLUTION, TURN.
wheel, *v. i.* **1.** *See* DRIVE, RIDE, PROPEL.
2. *See* FLY.
wheeler, *n. Referring to a horse:* poler, thiller.
wheel-shaped, *a.* rotate (*tech. or B*), rotiform.
wheezy, *a.* phthisicky (*humorous*).
whelp, *n.* cub, puppy, pup.
whence, *adv.* where, wherefrom (*formal*) whenceforth (*R*); *spec.* whencesoever.
where, *adv.* **1.** *Spec.* wherever.
2. whereto (*formal*), whither.
whereness, *n.* ubiety (*R*), ubication (*R*).

whetstone, *n. Spec.* rubstone, burr, hone, oilstone.

which, *pron.* whether (*A*).

whichever, *pron.* whether (*A*).

while, *conj.* whilst (*A*), whiles (*A*).

whine, *n.* cant, snivel.

whine, *v. i.* whimper, mewl, cant, pule; *spec.* snivel, nasillate (*R*).

whip, *n.* **1.** flagellum (*humorously pedantic*), scourge (*rhetorical or spec.*); *spec.* cat, cat-o'-nine-tails, kourbash *or* koorbash, knout, crop cowhide swinge, switch, dick (*S*), quirt (*U. S.*), bullwhack (*U. S.*), taws (*pl.*), sjambok, chabouk; *see* LASH.

2. *See* SNAP.

whip, *v. t.* **1.** beat (*contex.*), scourge (*rhetorical or spec.*), swinge, flagellate (*tech. or B*); *spec.* switch, rawhide, twig (*R*), cowhide, flog, knout, koorbash, lace, willow, thong, horse, birch, flick, breech, double-thong (*C*), horsewhip, tar, quirt, discipline (*R exc. spec.*), slash, lash.

2. *See* GATHER, DEFEAT, HURRY, SNAP, TAKE.

whipped, *a.* flagellate (*R*).

whipper, *n.* flagellator (*B*); *spec.* flagellant.

whipping, *a.* flagellatory (*B*), flagellative (*R*).

whipping, *n.* **1.** flagellation (*B or spec.*); *spec.* flogging, dusting (*C*), jacketing (*C*), quilting (*R*), bastinado, breeching.

2. *See* DEFEAT.

whippletree, *n.* crossbar, singletree, swingletree.

whip-shaped, *a.* flagellate (*B or tech.*).

whir, *n. Spec.* birr *or* burr, chirr *or* chir, whiz, whish (*R*).

whirl, *n.* **1.** rotation (*which see*); *spec.* vortex (*tech.*), reel, spin, pirouette, twirl, swirl.

2. *Referring to bodily motion in a circuit:* revolution, swirl, vortex (*tech.*); *spec.* eddy.

3. *Referring to a state of excitement, either pleasurable or bewildering:* dither (*S*), attention (*fig. C, as "he gave her a whirl,"* e. g. *"showed marked attention."*).

whirl, *v. i. & t.* **1.** rotate (*which see*); *spec.* reel, swirl, spin, pirouette, trundle, twirl, whip.

2. *Referring to bodily motion in a circuit:* revolve (*which see*), swirl; *spec.* eddy.

whirling, *a.* **1.** rotatory, vertiginous (*B*); *spec.* giddy, dizzy.

2. revolving, vortical (*B*), vorticose (*R*), vortiginous (*R*), swirling, swirly (*R*), eddying.

whirlpool, *n.* vortex (*B*), gurge (*R*), well (*R*), gulf (*now chiefly fig.*); *spec.* eddy, curl, gurglet, maelstrom, Charybdis (*fig.*).

whisker, *n.* **1.** hair; *spec.* vibrissa (*tech.*); *see* FEELER.

2. *In pl.: see* BEARD.

whisky, *n.* usquebaugh (*Irish or Scot. or humorous*), tanglefoot (*S, U. S.*); *spec.* poteen *or* potheen (*Irish*).

whisper, *n.* **1.** murmur, buzz.

Antonyms: see SHOUT.

2. *See* RUSTLE.

whisper, *v. i.* **1.** speak (*contex.*), round (*A*).

Antonyms: see SHOUT.

2. *See* RUSTLE.

whisper, *v. t.* speak (*contex.*), breathe, round (*A*).

Antonyms: see SHOUT, VOCIFERATE.

whispering, *a.* susurrous (*B*), susurrant (*R*); *spec.* rustling.

whistle, *n.* **1.** note (*contex.*); *spec.* call, catcall, siren, pipe, whew.

2. *The thing: spec.* hooter, pipe.

whistle, *v. i.* **1.** *Spec.* siffle (*R, B*), pipe, pule, flute, toot.

2. *See* SING.

white, *a.* **1.** candid (*A*); *spec.* whitish, silver, milky, whity (*R*), snowy, snowish, ivory, frosty, hoary, canescent, frosted, marmoreal (*fig.; B or rhetorical*), marmorean (*fig.; R*), chalky.

Antonyms: see BLACK.

2. *See* PURE.

white, *n.* **1.** glair (*of an egg*).

2. cracker (*a poor white; U. S.*).

white man. *Spec.* buckra (*a Negro term*), pakeha (*New Zealand*), paleface.

whiten, *v. t.* white, dealbate (*obs., exc. spec.*), blench (*R*), bleach (*spec. or fig.*), blanch (*spec. or fig.*); *spec.* pale, etiolate, besnow, grizzle, silver, ermine (*fig.; R*), hearthstone, frost.

Antonyms: see BLACKEN.

whiteness, *n.* **1.** *Spec.* canescence, hoariness, milkiness, frostiness, blink, grizzliness.

2. *See* PURITY.

whitening, *a.* canescent (*B*), incanescent (*R*), albescent (*tech. or B*).

whitening, *n.* dealbation (*R, exc. spec.*); *spec.* blanching, bleaching, bleach.

whitewash, *n. Spec.* parget (*R*), roughcast, calcimine.

whitewash, *v. t.* **1.** white; *spec.* calcimine.

2. *To make speciously fine by use of fair words:* gild, varnish (*S*).

whitewashed, *a.* white-limed.

whitish, *a.* white, albescent, whity (*R*).

whole, *a.* **1.** total, entire, complete, all (*with "the" or predicative*), integral (*R*), integrate (*B, R*), gross, indiscrete; *see* INTACT.

Antonyms: see BROKEN.

2. *See* WELL.

whole, *n.* totality, entirety, entire (*R*), all, ensemble, general (*A*), be-all (*R or spec.*), integer; *spec.* integral (*math.*), complex.

Antonyms: see ABSTRACT, PART.

wholeness, *n.* entirety (*which see*), completeness, totality, totalness, integralness, integrity, integrality (*R*), allness (*R*), omneity (*R*), omnitude (*R*); *spec.* universality, undividedness, intactness.

wholly, *adv.* entirely, clean, fully, altogether, quite, utterly, outright.

Antonyms: see PARTIALLY.

whore, *n. See* HARLOT.

whorl, *n.* volution (*tech.*), gyre (*R*); *spec.* involucre *or* involucrum.

why, *adv.* wherefore (*formal or A*).

wicked, *a.* evil, iniquitous, wrong, wrongful, bad, nefarious (*B*), nefandous (*B*), sinister, perverse, felon, dark (*implying absence of moral or spiritual light*), black, ill (*R*, *B*), nefast (*R*), unholy, unrighteous; *spec.* unregenerate, obdurate, ungodly, heinous, abominable, atrocious, black-hearted, infamous, facinorous (*A*), graceless, godless, devilish, flagitious (*extremely* wicked *and immoral*), horrible, corrupt, unprincipled, ungracious (*obs.*), vicious, villainous, criminal; *see* SINFUL, FLAGRANT.

Antonyms: see SINLESS, VIRTUOUS, INNOCENT.

wickedness, *n.* evilness, evil, turpitude, iniquity, perversity, depravity, darkness (*fig.*), ill (*R*), iniquitousness, unrighteousness, improbity (*B*), perverseness, pravity (*R*); *spec.* darkness, unregeneracy, corruption, villainy, criminality, crime, obduracy, corruption, putridity, gracelessness, godlessness, atrocity, devilry, deviltry, diabolism, malignity (*R*), enormity (*monstrous* wickedness); *see* SIN, IMPIETY, FLAGRANCY, IMMORALITY, HORRIBLENESS.

Antonyms: see VIRTUE, HOLINESS; *also cf.* SINLESS.

wide, *a.* **1.** broad, broadish, expanded; *spec.* heavenwide, statewide, nationwide.

Antonyms: see NARROW.

2. *See* SPACIOUS, ROOMY, COMPREHENSIVE, ASTRAY, INCLUSIVE, EXPANSIVE.

widely, *adv.* far.

widen, *v. t.* **1.** broaden, breadthen (*R*).

Antonyms: see NARROW.

2. *See* ENLARGE, EXPAND, EXTEND.

wideness, *n.* broadness; *see* EXPANSION, ENLARGEMENT, EXTENSION, WIDTH.

widening, *a.* broadening; *see* EXPANSIVE.

widespread, *a.* diffuse, rife; *spec.* world-wide, nationwide, statewide; *see* EXTENSIVE, GENERAL.

Antonyms: see LOCAL.

wide-spreading, *a.* effuse (*A*).

widow, *n.* relict (*legal*), matron (*contex.*); *spec.* jointress *or* jointuress, dowager, suttee.

widowed, *a.* viduous (*R*), husbandless (*contex.*), bereaved (*contex.*), unhusbanded (*R*).

widowhood, *n.* viduity, viduation, viduage;—*all* (*R*).

width, *n.* size (*contex.*), breadth, broadness, amplitude (*formal or B*), latitude (*obs. or humorous*), wideness; *spec.* tread, measure, diameter, beam, span, roominess, spaciousness.

wield, *v. t.* ply, manipulate, handle; *see* PLAY, EXERCISE, MANAGE.

wieldy, *a.* handy (*colloq.*).

Antonyms: see UNWIELDY.

wife, *n.* spouse (*contex.*), woman (*contex.; low, contemptuous, or dialect*), helpmate (*chiefly rhetorical or B; a corruption of the Biblical "helpmeet"*), rib (*humorous or in allusion to Gen. ii:21*), queen (*fig., exc. spec.*), matron (*contex.*), lady (*contex.; complimentary or deferential*), feme (*legal*); *spec.* concubine, Grizel, grass widow, bride, empress.

Antonyms: see HUSBAND, CELIBATE.

wifelike, *a.* wifely.

wifely, *a.* matronly (*contex.*).

wig, *n.* periwig (*obs. or historical*), jasey (*chiefly spec.; C and humorous*); *spec.* toupee, peruke, pigtail, tail, Ramillie, frizz; *see* GRIZZLE.

wig, *v. t.* periwig (*R*), bewig (*emphatic*); *spec.* peruke (*R*).

wiggle, *v. i. & t.* tweedle; *see* TWIDDLE.

wild, *a.* **1.** untamed, savage, untame, feral (*B*). ferine (*R*), undomesticated; *spec.* tameless.

Antonyms: see TAME.

2. uncultivated, wilding (*B*), incult (*R*); *spec.* desert, waste, rough, luxuriant, desolate, rude.

Antonyms: see CULTIVATED; *cf.* CULTIVATE.

3. *Of persons or conduct:* harum-scarum, harum (*R*); *see* EXCITED, FROLICSOME, GAY.

4. *See* STORMY, ROUGH, RECKLESS, BOISTEROUS, UNCULTIVATED, EXTRAVAGANT, DISSIPATED, ILL-CONSIDERED, UNCONTROLLED.

wild-looking, *a.* frenzied, haggard.

wildness, *n.* **1.** savageness, savagery, ferity (*R*).

2. uncultivation, naturalness, incultivation (*R*); *spec.* desolation.

willful, *a.* heady, headstrong, capitose (*R*), willyard (*Scot.*); *spec.* high-handed; *see* OBSTINATE, ARBITRARY.

will, *n.* **1.** volition, pleasure, mind, desire; *spec.* discretion; *see* INTENTION.

2. testament.

willing, *a.* **1.** *See* INTENTIONAL.

2. volitive (*R*), ready, forward, free (*chiefly spec.*).

Antonyms: see UNWILLING.

willingly, *adv.* readily, freely, lief (*B*).

will-o'-the-wisp, *n.* ignis-fatuus (*Latin*), jack-o'-lantern *or* jack-a-lantern, wisp, Fata Morgana (*Latin*).

willowy, *a.* supple (*contex.*), willowish (*R*); *see* FLEXIBLE.

Antonyms: see STIFF.

willy-nilly, *adv.* nolens volens (*Latin*).

wimple, *n.* gorget (*historical*).

win, *v. t.* **1.** gain, get (*R*), conquer (*get by overcoming opposition, obstruction or difficulty*), carry (*a victory, one's point, etc.*), gather, obtain (*A*), score (*fig. exc. spec.*); *spec.* steal, recover (*a favorable judgment*), take (*a prize, etc.*), make (*a trick, a point, etc.*).

Antonyms: see LOSE.

2. gain (*as friends, the court, the summit, etc.*), engage; *spec.* reclaim, recover, curry (*favor*), conciliate (*implying acts of concession, favor, attention or the like, that soothe, pacify, or induce friendliness*); *see* INDUCE.

Antonyms: see ESTRANGE.

3. *Spec.* reach, accomplish.

win, *v. i. Spec.* recover (*as a favorable judgment*), overcome; *see* SUCCEED.

wind, *n.* meteor (*tech.; contex.*), air (*chiefly spec.*); *spec.* aura, blow, blast, blare (*A*), blizzard, bluster, blusterer, Boreas, breath, flurry, breeze, buster, Cæcias, cat's-paw, coil, cyclone, east, Eurus, fanning (*R*), flaught (*chiefly Scot.*), flaw, fresh, fuff (*R or Scot.*), squall, gale (*naut., a storm; B and rhetorically, a gentle breeze*), gust, hurricane, monsoon, scud, puff, simoon, sirocco, siroc (*R*), slant, slap, sough, slat, snorter (*S or C*), storm, tornado, typhoon, waft, whiff, whiffle, whirlwind, whisk, windate, williwaw, windfall, zephyr, Zephyrus.

wind, *v. i.* twist, turn, wry (*A*); *spec.* twine, meander, serpentize (*R*), snake (*R*), coil, spool (*R*), circuit, bottom, curl, zigzag.

wind, *v. t.* **1.** turn (*contex.*), entwine (*emphatic or formal*); *spec.* twine, twist, involve, wreathe, coil, crank, roll, reel, quill.

2. *To wrap something around:* encircle (*contex.*); *spec.* serve, woold, gange, worm.

wind, *n.* curve (*contex.*), turn, twist; *spec.* twine, meander, coil, circuit, curl, curling, roll, crankle (*R or Scot.*), zigzag; *see* SINUOSITY, COIL.

winder, *n. Spec.* flyer, blow (*chiefly in "sidewinder"*).

windfall, *Spec.* obvention (*occasional or incidental, R; chiefly tech.*), legacy.

winding, *a.* crooked (*contex.*), twisting, turning, sinuous (*formal or B*), devious (*contex.*), voluble (*R*); *spec.* meandering, meandrous, serpentine, snaky, tortuose (*R*), tortuous, cranky, circuitous; *see* SINUOUS.

winding, *n.* **1.** twisting, turning, circuit; *spec.* twining, sinuation (*formal or B*), reeling, filature.

2. *That which winds:* twist, bend (*contex.*); *spec.* meander (*chiefly in pl.*), serpentry (*R*), circumvolution (*R*), crinkle-crankle, intervolution, crankle, insinuation (*R*); *see* SINUOSITY.

wind instrument, wind (*cant or C*); *spec.* brass wind, wood wind.

windlass, *n.* roll (*contex.*), roller (*contex.*); *spec.* capstan, hurdy-gurdy, winch, jack.

window, *n.* light, casement (*spec. or poetic*), fenestration (*a collective; B or tech.*), bole (*Scot.*); *spec.* fenestella (*R*), windowlet, dormer, lattice, oriel, bay, bow, bow-window, glass, transom, rosace, lychnoscope (*tech.*), bull's-eye.

windpipe, *n.* weasand (*A*), trachea (*tech.*), guggle (*S*).

windshield, *n.* windscreen (*chiefly Brit.*).

windy, *a.* **1.** airy, breezy, blowy; *spec.* blasty, gusty, blustery, blusterous, drafty, fretful, fitful, squally, stormy.

2. *See* FLATULENT, EXPOSED.

wine, *n.* **1.** *Spec.* cup, sherry, vidonia, sack, *etc.; see* ELEMENT.

2. *See* FEAST.

wine, *a.* vinic, vinous;—*both tech. or* (*B*).

wine cellar, *Spec.* catacomb.

wine-colored, *a.* vinous;—*tech. or B.*

wineshop, *n.* bodega (*Spanish*).

wing, *n.* **1.** sail (*B or tech.*), van (*R*); *spec.* pinion, poiser, alula, winglet, elytrum.

2. *Wing of an army:* horn (*R*).

3. *See* EXTENSION, LOBE, SAIL, FLIGHT.

winged, *a.* **1.** *See* ALAR.

2. pennate.

3. lofty, wingy, soaring, aspiring.

wingless, *a.* apterous (*tech.*), impennate (*chiefly spec.*), flightless.

wink, *n.* **1.** twinkle, blink.

2. *See* MOMENT.

wink, *v. i.* twinkle, blink; *spec.* nictate, nictitate.

winking, *a.* nictitant (*tech. or R*), blinking, intermittent (*of lights*).

winnow, *v. t.* **1.** separate, ventilate, wind (*R*); *see* FAN.

2. *See* FLAP.

winter, *n.*

Antonyms: see SUMMER.

winter, *a.* hiemal (*B*), hibernal (*R*).

winter, *v. i.* hibernate (*spec. or B*), shack (*local, U. S.*), overwinter (*R*), hiemate (*R*).

Antonyms: see SUMMER.

wintering, *a.* hibernating (*spec. or R*), latitant (*R*).

wintering, *n.* hibernation (*spec. or B*), hiemation (*R*), latitancy (*R*).

wintry, *a.* winterly, brumal (*B*), brumous (*B*).

wipe, *v. t.* rub, mop; *spec.* feak.

wiper, *n. Spec.* squeegee, wipe.

wisdom, *n.* **1.** sapience (*B and chiefly humorous*), advisability, policy, wiseness.

Antonyms: see UNWISDOM, FOOLISHNESS.

2. *See* LEARNING.

3. advisability, expediency, policy; *see* PRUDENCE.

wise, *a.* **1.** sapient (*B and chiefly humorous or ironical*), sage, Solomonic (*fig.*); *spec.* worldly-wise; *see* LEARNED, EXPERIENCE, SKILLFUL.

2. advisable, expedient, politic; *see* PRUDENT, JUDICIOUS.

Antonyms: see UNWISE, FOOLISH, UNADVISABLE.

wiseacre, *n.* **1.** sophist (*R*), sapient (*B and chiefly jocular*). *"Wiseacre" is now chiefly depreciatory.*

Antonyms: see BLOCKHEAD.

2. *See* SCHOLAR.

wishbone, *n.* furcula (*tech.*), furculum (*an incorrect form*), merrythought (*B*).

wit, *n.* **1.** *See* INTELLIGENCE, FUN.

2. *Referring to a witty person: spec.* droll.

witch, *n.* **1.** pythoness (*spec. or fig.*), sibyl (*spec. or fig.*), cummer (*Scot.*); *spec.* water witch; *see* MAGICIAN.

2. *See* HAG, CHARMER.

with, *prep.* **1.** *See* BY.

2. plus, besides.

withdraw, *v. i.* **1.** *See* RETIRE.

2. retreat (*contex.; spec.*), recede (*from a position, proposal, etc.*), retract, shrink, resile (*tech. as from a contract, or course of action*), inshell

wish: *desire.* | **wishful:** *desirous.*

(*R*), dissociate (*R*), secede; *see* RETIRE, RETREAT, DEPART.
Antonyms: see INTRUDE, EXTEND.
3. welsh, crawfish (*fig.; C, U. S.*); *spec.* resile (*tech.*).
withdraw, *v. t.* **1.** remove, separate, subduce, take; *spec.* sequester, retract, retire (*as troops, or as money, from circulation*), slip (*with "off" or "out"*), minish (*R*), abduce, subtract, extract, deduct, detract; *see* ABSTRACT, RETIRE.
Antonyms: see COMMIT, INSERT, INTRODUCE, INTRUDE.
2. *See* RECALL.
withdrawal, *n.* **1.** *See* RETIREMENT.
2. separation, removal, retraction; *spec.* drain (*implying constant, gradual* withdrawal, *and suggesting excessive or inconvenient amount*), subduction (*R*), subtraction, deduction.
Antonyms: see INSERTION, INTRODUCTION.
3. *See* RETIREMENT, DEPARTURE, RETREAT, RECESSION, ABSTRACTION, RECALL.
withdrawer, *n. Spec.* seceder, burgher (*Scot.*), secessionist (*U. S. hist.*), secesh (*U. S. hist.; C*).
withe, *n.* withy, wicker, osier, wattle; *see* SWITCH.
wither, *v. i.* **1.** wilt, shrivel, dry, fade, wizen, sear (*R*).
2. *See* DECLINE.
wither, *v. t.* wilt, shrivel, wizen, sear, blight (*contex.*), fade.
Antonyms: see SWELL.
withered, *a.* wilted, sear *or* sere, wizen, blighted (*contex.*); *spec.* sapless.
Antonyms: see SWOLLEN, FRESH.
withering, *a. Spec.* marcescent (*tech.*).
withhold, *v. t.* **1.** *Spec.* forbear (*uttering, using, etc.*), check, spare (*as not to spare words, expense, etc.*), detain (*chiefly legal*).
2. *See* RESTRAIN, KEEP.
within, *prep.* **1.** in, inside; *spec.* inboard.
Antonyms: see OUTSIDE.
2. *See* DURING.
within, *adv.* in, internally, interiorly, inside, withinside (*R*), ben (*Scot.*); *spec.* indoors.
without, *prep.* **1.** sans (*A*); *spec.* beyond.
2. *See* OUTSIDE.
without, *adv.* outwardly, externally; *see* OUTSIDE.
witling, *n.* witticaster (*B*), smart Alec (*S*).
witness, *n.* **1.** observer, overlooker, beholder, bystander.
2. testifier; *spec.* compurgator.
3. *See* EVIDENCE.
wits, *n. See* FACULTY.
witticism, *n.* saying, bon mot (*French*), quip, sally, flight, mot (*French*), jeu d'esprit (*French*), quirk, sparkle.
witty, *a.* clever (*contex.*), bright (*contex.*), funny (*C*), sharp (*contex.*), smart, sparkling.
Antonyms: see DULL, STUPID.
wolf, *n. Spec.* whelp, cub, wolfkin, wolfling, Isegrim *or* Isgrin (*B and A; a personification*), lobo, coyote, hyena (*often fig., as of a cruel, treacherous, rapacious person*).
wolfish, *a.* **1.** lupine (*B or tech.*), lupous (*R*).
2. *See* FIERCE, CRUEL.
woman, *n.* female (*contex.*), tabby (*contemptuous*), dona (*S*), maness (*R*), carline (*chiefly spec.; Scot.*), feminine (*R*), petticoat (*fig.*), femme (*French*), fair (*A or B*), burd (*obs.*), Amazon (*fig.*); *spec.* beebee (*Anglo-Indian*), beldam (*B*), Bellona (*fig.*), cailleach (*Gael.*), crone, cummer, *or* kimmer (*Scot.*), dame (*hist. or B*), damsel (*A, B, or playful*), damosel *or* damozel (*B or a word of the romances*), matronage (*a collective*), dowager (*implying dignity of carriage, suggestive of self-importance*), dowd, hag, dragon *or* dragoness (*fig.*), duenna, gib (*reproachful*), Gorgon (*fig.*), matron (*a married* woman), mother, nymph (*a beautiful* woman), squaw, sylph (*a slender and graceful* woman), Titaness (*fig.*), vixen, skirt (*S, U. S.*).
Antonyms: see MAN.
woman-hating, *a.* misogynous.
Antonyms: see AMATORY.
womanish, *a.* petticoat, feminine, effeminate; *spec.* haggish; *see* EFFEMINATE.
Antonyms: see MANLY.
womankind, *n.* woman, femininity, feminity (*R*), feminine (*A*), womanhood, distaff (*fig.; used with "the"*).
Antonyms: see MANKIND.
womanly, *a.* womanlike; *spec.* ladylike, matronal, matronly.
Antonyms: see CHILDISH, MANLY.
womb, *n.* uterus (*tech.*), matrix (*R*), venter (*tech.*), ventricle (*R*).
wonder, *n.* **1.** wonderment, astonishment, awe; *spec. see* SURPRISE.
2. prodigy, marvel, miracle, portent, phenomenon (*contex.*), wonderwork.
wonder, *v. i.* **1.** marvel.
2. *See* QUESTION.
wonderful, *a.* marvelous, miraculous, wondrous (*elevated*), prodigious, portentous, astonishing, stupendous.
Antonyms: see ORDINARY.
wondering, *a.* marveling, agape (*predicative*).
wonder-working, *a.* miraculous, thaumaturgic (*B*), mirific (*R and jocular*).
wood, *n.* **1.** hurst (*chiefly dial. or in combination*); *spec.* grove (*a small, shady* wood), shaw (*R or A*), thicket, bosk, bosket, hanger (*Eng.*), holt (*B*), covert (*a* wood *considered as sheltering animals*), carr (*Eng.*), coppice (*a small* wood *of undergrowth and small trees, grown for periodical cutting*), copse, spinney, spinny, greenwood (*a* wood *in leaf*).
2. *Spec.* brash, lumber, timber, loppings (*pl.*), lop (*Eng.*), driftwood.
wooded, *a.* overgrown (*contex.*); *spec.* busky, tufty (*R*).
wooden, *a.* **1.** ligneous (*chiefly jocular*).

withhold, *v. i.: abstain.*
withstand: *resist, endure, oppose.*
woeful: *sorrowful, depressing, depressed.*
wold: *down.*

3. *See* AWKWARD, STUPID, EXPRESSIONLESS.
woodland, *n. Spec.* bush; *see* FOREST.
woodland, *a.* silvan *or* sylvan; *spec.* forestal, forestial (*R*).
woodworker, *n. Spec.* carpenter, joiner, cabinetmaker, cartwright, wheelwright, bender, ebonist.
woody, *a.* **1.** ligneous (*tech.*), lignescent, lignose (*R*), xyloid.
Antonyms: see PULPY.
2. *Spec.* sylvan, bosky, silvestral (*R*), silvestrian (*R*), braky, nemorous (*R*), woodsy (*U. S.*).
woof, *n.* weft.
wool, *n.* **1.** fleece; *spec.* marling, brokes, matchings, slub.
2. *See* DOWN.
wool-bearing, *a.* laniferous, lanific, lanigerous;—*all tech. or B.*
woolly, *a.* **1.** fleecy, lanose (*tech.*).
2. *Bearing wool:* lanate (*tech.*); *spec.* ulotrichous.
3. *See* FLUFFY, FLOCCULENT.
word, *n.* **1.** *A unit of speech, having in modern writing a formal independence:* term; *spec.* name, vocable, monosyllable, folio (*a collective*), accents (*pl.*), antonym, metonym, synonym, heteronym, homonym.
2. *See* SPEECH, PROMISE, INFORMATION, CONVERSATION.
word, *a. Spec.* lexical; *see* VERBAL.
word, *v. t. To express in words: spec.* phrase.
wordy, *a.* verbose (*formal or B*); *spec.* diffuse, garrulous; *see* PROLIX.
Antonyms: see CONCISE.
work, *n.* **1.** toil, labor, moil (*A or B*), business (*chiefly spec.*), cark (*A*); *spec.* handiwork, handwork, hand, headwork, brainwork, journeywork, elbow grease (*humorous*), counterwork (*R*), slavery, grind, fag (*C*), drudgery, turn, Sisyphism (*fig.; B*), pain.
Antonyms: see INDOLENCE, REST, PLAY, DIVERSION.
2. *Concretely with "a":* labor, opus; *spec.* opuscule *or* opusculum (*B, often humorous*), bronze, statue, *etc.*
3. *See* TASK, OCCUPATION, SERVICE, STRUCTURE, EMBROIDERY, ORNAMENTATION, ACCOMPLISHMENT, EXERCISE.
4. *In military usage:* battery.
work, *v. i.* **1.** labor (*chiefly spec., as to* work *hard physically or against difficulties*); *spec.* peg (*C*), ply (*R*), toil, cark (*A*), root (*C, S; U. S.*), hustle (*C; U. S.*), moil (*A or B*), drudge (*implying slavish or hard and distasteful* work), poke, grind (*to* work *hard steadily and monotonously*), slave, scrub, fag (*to* work *wearisomely*), job, char (*Eng.*), chore (*U. S.*), devil (*cant or S*), grub (*to* work *laboriously or meanly*), lucubrate (*R or B*), push (*to* work *hard*), sweat, practice *or* practise (*to* work *usually at the profession of law or medicine*), doctor, serve, hammer (*to* work *hard*).
Antonyms: see IDLE, PLAY, REST.
2. operate; *spec.* act, go (*as a machine*), run, seethe, take (*as a vaccine*); *see* FERMENT.
3. *See* ACT, PROGRESS.
work, *v. t.* **1.** *To cause to work: spec.* employ, belabor, drive, busy, drudge (*R*), horse (*cant*), sweat.
2. *To put into operation:* operate (*chiefly U. S.*), play, run; *spec.* treadle, crank.
Antonyms: see REST, DIVERT.
3. *To shape, make, or alter by work: spec.* hammer, forge, tool, puddle, pug, knead, beat, rough, torture, mold.
4. *To give effect or expression to:* vent (*rage, fury, etc.*).
5. *See* ACCOMPLISH, MANAGE, CULTIVATE, EXPLOIT, EMBROIDER, EFFECT, BURROW, ACT, PREPARE.
workbag, *n. Spec.* reticule, hussy.
worked, *a.* wrought; *spec.* embroidered, chased, carved, inlaid, *etc.*
worker, *n.* **1.** *One who works:* laborer, toiler; *spec.* performer, moiler (*B*); drudge, slave, hack, artist, grubber, sweater, grinder, fagger, handicraftsman, jobber, handworker, practitioner, practician (*R*).
Antonyms: see IDLER.
2. *A worker at some occupation of the so-called working class:* laborer, labor (*a collective*), hand; *spec.* journeyman, operative, hind (*Scot. and local Eng.*), peon (*Spanish American*), coolie, cooly, docker, lumper, ditcher, diker, shoveler, heaver, doffer, brazier, kanaka paddy (*cant or S*), navvy, longshoreman, stevedore, proletarian.
Antonyms: see VAGABOND.
3. *See* AGENT, ARTIFICER, SMITH, NEUTER.
workhouse, *n.* bridewell (*Eng.*), union (*Eng.*).
working, *n.* **1.** operation.
2. *See* ACTION, EXERCISE, FERMENTATION.
working, *a.* practical.
working girl. grisette (*French*).
workman, *n.* wright (*obs., exc. in combination*); *spec.* master, workmaster (*R*), machinist, machiner, mechanic, journeyman, operator, hobo (*cant or S*), artisan, artificer, craftsman, mason, maistry (*East Indian*), brazier.
workmanlike, *a.* workmanly, masterly; *see* SKILLFUL.
workmanship, *n.* facture (*R*); *spec.* craftsmanship.
work place, works; *spec.* shop, room, factory, workroom, workshop.
workroom, *n.* work place; *spec.* shop, laboratory; *see* STUDIO.
workshop, *n.* officina (*R*), works (*sing.*); *spec.* plumbery, chapel (*a printer's* workshop), pottery, atelier (*French*), workroom; *see* FACTORY.

workmanly: *skillful.*

world, *n.* **1.** *See* EARTH.
2. *The inhabitants of the earth:* mankind, monde (*French*), earth; *spec.* microcosm.
3. *See* MULTITUDE, LIFE.
worldliness, *n.* secularism, temporalism, secularity, carnalness, mundanity (*R*), mundaneness (*R*);—*all six formal or R.*
worldly, *a.* temporal, terrestrial, secular, worldly-minded, terrene (*B*); *spec.* mundane, unspiritual, carnal (*A*), earthborn, fleshly (*R*), unregenerate, unsanctified.
Antonyms: see HEAVENLY, SPIRITUAL.
worldwide, *a.* cosmopolitan (*formal or B, implying freedom from national limitations or attachments*); *spec.* universal.
Antonyms: see LOCAL.
worm, *n.* helminth (*tech.*; *chiefly spec.*), vermin (*a collective*); *spec.* wormling (*chiefly fig.*), grub, larva.
worm-eaten, *a.* wormy, vermiculate (*tech. or B*).
wormlike, *a.* vermiform (*tech.*).
wormy, *a.* vermiculate (*tech. or B*), vermian (*R*), helminthoid (*R*), vermiceous (*R*), vermicular, vermiform (*tech.*), vermiculose (*R or tech.*), verminous (*R*); *spec.* grubby, maggoty.
worn-out, *a.* gone, passé (*French*).
Antonyms: see NEW.
worried, *a.* fretted, distressed, harassed.
worry, *v. t.* **1.** distress (*contex.*), touse (*R*), tousle, disquiet, beset, bait (*fig. or spec.*), harass, shake, harry, faze, bedevil; *see* TROUBLE, DISTURB, DRIVE.
Antonyms: see COMFORT.
2. tease, bait (*fig.*), badger; *see* TROUBLE.
worry, *v. i.* fidget, fuss, fume; *see* FRET.
worry, *n.* distress (*contex.*), cark (*A*), fret, fume, fuss; *see* DISTURBANCE.
worship, *n.* **1.** office (*chiefly tech.*), service, adoration (*formal or spec.*), laud, devotion, cult *or* cultus (*tech.*); *spec.* synaxis (*R*), incense, latria, prayer, order, chapel (*Eng.*), compline *or* complin, matin, Lychnic, hours, cosmolatry, ecclesiolatry, geolatry, gyneolatry, hagiolatry, hygeiolatry, iconolatry, idolatry, idolatrization, idolism, logolatry, lordolatry (*jocose*), Mariolatry, Marianolatry (*R*), martyrolatry, necrolatry, topolatry, zoölatry, zoömorphism, zoötheism.
2. *See* ESTEEM, HONOR.
worship, *v. t.* **1.** adore (*formal or B*), bless (*A*); spec. hymn, idolatrize, idolize, cense, incense; *see* DEIFY.
2. *See* ESTEEM, HONOR.
worshiper, *n.* adorer (*formal or spec.*); *spec.* idolater, idolatress (*fem.*), idolist, fetishist, iconolator, ignicolist (*R*), kneeler, hagiolator, Marian.
worshipful, *a.* **1.** adorable (*formal or R*), worshipable.
2. *See* HONORABLE.
worth, *n.* worthiness, value, merit, account, excellence, dignity (*a Latinism*); *spec.* nobleness, condignity; *see* DIGNITY.
Antonyms: see FAULT.
worthless, *a.* meritless, naught (*predicative*), unworthy, unvaluable (*R*), good-for-nothing (*chiefly spec.*), precious (*ironical*); *spec.* losel (*A*), chaffy, light, empty, ne'er-do-well, riffraff, refuse, rubbish, trumpery, mean, draffish, draffy, queer (*thieves' cant*), trashy, yeasty; *see* PALTRY, TRIVIAL.
Antonyms: see VALUABLE, INVALUABLE.
worthy, *a.* worthful (*R*); *spec.* noble, suitable, estimable; *see* HONORABLE, DESERVING.
wound, *n.* traumatism *or* trauma (*tech.*), breach (*R, exc. spec.*), gride (*A*); *spec.* hack, cut, scratch, stab, crepance, bite, prick, laceration.
wound, *v. t.* *Spec.* cut, shoot, bite, scratch, harrow (*R*), lance, wing, calk, tear, vuln (*chiefly heraldry*), lacerate.
wounded, *a.* vulnerose (*B*).
woven, *a.* textile.
wrap, *n.* envelope; *spec.* muffler, mantle, shawl, nubia, sontag, overwrap (*R*); *see* FOLD.
wrap, *v. t.* envelop *or* envelope (*formal or B*), fold, enwrap *or* inwrap (*B*); *spec.* involve, cere, bewrap (*intensive*), enswathe (*R*), impall, wind, whip, serve, seize, shawl, lap, roll, muffle, mob, furl (*R*), swathe, tuck, mantle, scarf; *see* FOLD.
Antonyms: see UNFOLD.
wrapper, *n.* **1.** envelope (*B, formal, or spec.*), wrapping, wrappage (*R*); *spec.* puddening *or* pudding (*naut.*).
2. *See* CONTAINER.
wrapt, *a.* absorbed, breathless.
wreath, *n.* ring (*contex.*); *spec.* bays (*pl.*), laurel, garland, crown, twist, torse (*heraldry; R*), festoon, coronet.
wreathe, *v. t.* twist (*contex.*), overtwine (*R*); *spec.* festoon, garland.
wreck, *v. t.* shipwreck (*originally spec.*); *spec.* dynamite.
Antonyms: see SAVE.
wreckage, *n.* flotsam, jetsam, ligan.
wrecker, *n.* *Spec.* salvager.
wrench, *n.* **1.** *Spec.* wrest; *see* STRAIN, PERVERSION, TEAR.
2. *Spec.* spanner, key, monkey-wrench, s-wrench.
3. *See* FORCE, PERVERSION.
wrench, *v. t.* **1.** wrest; *see* DEFACE, STRAIN, TEAR.
2. *See* DISTORT, PERVERT.
wrestle, *v. i.* struggle, tug;—*both contex.*
wretch, *n.* **1.** *A wretched person:* elf (*B*), devil (*used with "poor"*), soul (*used with "poor"*), caitiff (*A*); *spec.* menial, underling.
2. *As a term of reprobation:* miscreant, slubberdegullion (*obs. or dial.*), scab (*S; opprobrious or a term of abuse*), bugger (*low*), cullion (*B and A*), caitiff (*contemptuous*); *spec.* beggar (*fig.*), hound (*fig.*), skunk (*vulgar*), scrub, hilding (*A*), cur (*C; contemptuous*).

worm, *v.:* *crawl, insinuate.* | **wounding:** *cutting.* |

wretched, *a.* miserable, mean, forlorn; *see* DEPRESSED, MEAN.
wriggle, *v. i.* writhe, squirm (*chiefly U. S. & dial. Eng.*), worm; *spec.* busk.
wrinkle, *n.* **1.** *Spec.* crumple, rumple, ridge (*contex.*), ruga (*tech.*), crimple (*dial.*), furrow (*contex.*), ruck, crease, touse (*R*), rugosity, pucker, crimp, crinkle, crow's-foot; *see* FOLD, RUFFLE.
2. wrinkledness; *spec.* crumpledness, ruffledness.
3. *See* EXPEDIENT.
wrinkle, *v. t. & i. Spec.* rumple, crumple (*to* wrinkle *by force of compression, shrivelling, etc., implying often distortion or defacement*), corrugate (*implying parallel folds or ridges, not sharp as a rule, B or tech.*), crinkle (*to make minute* wrinkles), pucker, knit, furrow (*contex.*), crease, ruck, frumple (*obs. or dial.*), ridge (*contex.*), ruckle, crimp (*to make minute folds or flutings*), crape, shrivel; *see* RUFFLE.
wrinkled, *a.* rugose (*tech.*), corrugated (*B or tech.*), puckered, wrinkly, rugate (*tech.*); *spec.* crinkly, crimpy, crumpled, rugous (*tech.*), rugulose (*tech.*), oursed (*R*), puckered, rugged (*features*), knit, bent, shriveled.
Antonyms: see SMOOTH.
wrist, *n.* carpus (*tech.*).
wristlet, *n.* band, wrister (*local, U. S.*).
writ, *n.* brieve (*law; Scot.*), precept; *spec.* extent.
write, *v. t.* **1.** inscribe (*formal or B*), indite (*B*), set (*now always with "down"*), scriven (*R*); *spec.* engross (write *in large letters, or in a certain hand; hence, in legal form*), pencil, draw (*a check*), scrawl, hieroglyph, bescribble, record.
2. *See* COMPOSE.
write, *v. i.* **1.** inscribe; *spec.* cipher; *see* SCRIBBLE, DISCOURSE.
2. *In sense of "write up:" spec.* paper, paragraph, scribble.
writer, *n.* **1.** scribe, scriptor (*R*); *spec.* calligraphist, penman, penner, pen (*fig.*).
2. *See* AMANUENSIS, AUTHOR, CORRESPONDENT.
writhe, *v. i.* worm, twist, wring, contort, wry (*R*); *spec.* distort.
writhing, *a.* twisting, worming, serpentine.
writing, *a.* scriptory (*B*).
writing, *n.* **1.** inscription, engrossment.
2. manuscript, lucubration (*now usually derisive or playful*), writ (*chiefly used of Scriptures*, script (*obs.*); *spec.* legend, autograph, scroll, scribble, document.
3. *A style, manner, etc., of writing:* handwriting, hand; *spec.* cipher, lexigraphy, cuneiform, haplography, dittography, macrography.
writing desk, table (*contex.*); *spec.* davenport, escritoire.
writing room, scriptorium (*B or tech.*), scriptory (*R*).
written, *a.* scriptory (*R*), literal (*R*).
Antonyms: see ORAL.
wrong, *a.* **1.** amiss (*predicative*), erroneous, abroad; *see* INCORRECT.
Antonyms: see RIGHT.
2. *See* WICKED, IMPROPER, IMMORAL, CRIMINAL, SINFUL.
wrong, *n.* **1.** *See* ERROR.
2. *A wrong act or deed:* injury, injustice, tort (*law*), crime, grievance, gravamen (*R*); *spec.* unfairness, villainy; *see* INJURY, SIN.
Antonyms: see JUSTICE.

X

x-shaped, *n.* decussate, chiasmal;—*both tech. or B.*

Y

yard, *a.* inclosure (*contex.*); *spec.* court, curtilage, garth, bailey, farmyard, barton (*Eng.*), barnyard, bawn. *The word* yard *is used in U. S. for the grounds, no matter how modest, about a dwelling; the Brit. equivalent is usually* garden.
yarn, *n.* **1.** *Spec.* worsted, inkle, fingering (*Eng.*), crewel.
2. *See* NARRATIVE.
year, *n.* **1.** twelvemonth (*formal or emphatic*), sun (*fig.*); *spec.* indiction, jubilee.
2. *In pl.: see* AGE.
yeast, *n.* leaven; *spec.* barm, emptyings (*U. S.*), emptins (*dial. U. S.*).
yeasty, *a.* barmy (*A*).
yellow, *a.* xanthous (*tech.*); *spec.* buff, buffy, citrine *or* citrinous, cream, drab, fallow, flavescent, foxy, fulvous, icterine (*tech.*), isabelline, jaundiced, khaki, luteous (*tech.*), luteolous (*tech.; R*), lutescent (*tech.*), nankeen, ocherous, ochery, ochrous, ochry, orange, saffrony (*R*), sallow, sandy, sorrel, subflavous (*R*), vitelline, xanthochroic (*tech.*), xanthochroöus (*tech.*), yellowish, yellowy, flaxen; *see* STRAW-COLORED, GOLDEN, COWARDLY.
yellow, *n. Spec.* fustic, jonquil, massicot, orellin, saffron; *see* GOLD.
yeoman, *n.* goodman (*hist. or B*), laird (*Scot.*); *spec.* beefeater, duniwassal (*Scot.*), cocklaird (*Scot.; humorous*).
yes, *exclamation.* yea (*A*), aye (*A, Scot. or spec.*); *spec.* placet.
yesterday, *a.* pridian (*R*), hesternal (*R*).
yesterday, *n. Spec.* yestermorn, yestereve, yestereven, yesternight;—*all four A.*
yield, *n.* **1.** return, income, produce; *see* HARVEST.
2. bend, give (*C*).
yield, *v. i.* **1.** *In a physical sense:* give, budge, go (*as a bridge or barrier*); *spec.* fall, come, bend, sink, cave in, duck, start, ply (*R*).
2. succumb, meeken (*R*), weaken; *spec.* defer

Y

yawning, *a.: gaping, open.*

(*A*) *archaic.* (*B*) *bookish, poetic, literary or learned.* (*C*) *colloquial.* (*Contex.*) *contextual.* (*R*) *rare.* (*S*) *slang.* *See pp. viii–ix.*

(*to submit to acknowledged superior claims*), submit, cringe (*to show base or servile deference or submissiveness*), crouch, budge, stoop, melt; *see* SURRENDER, ACCEDE, ADMIT, RELENT.

Antonyms: see STRUGGLE.

yield, *v. t.* **1.** furnish (*contex.*), return, afford, bear, pan (*esp. with "out"; spec. or fig.*); *spec.* net; *see* PRODUCE.

2. *See* RELINQUISH, SURRENDER.

yielding, *a.* **1.** nonresistant, pliant, weak; *see* SOFT.

Antonyms: see UNYIELDING.

2. weak, pliable, acquiescent, passive, flexible, toward (*B, A*); *see* COMPLAISANT, SUBMISSIVE, RELENTING.

Antonyms: see UNYIELDING, AUTOCRATIC.

yielding, *n.* submission, submittal (*R*); *spec.* homage, acquiescence, fall (*succumbing to temptation or force*), lapse, deference, abandonment, relinquishment, submissiveness.

Antonyms: see OPPOSITION.

yodel, *v. t. & i.* warble (*U. S.*), carol, troll, trollol.

yonder, *adv.* beyond, yon (*B*).

yonder, *a.* yon (*B*).

young, *a.* **1.** youthful, youthy (*R*), youthsome (*R*), green (*fig.*); *spec.* juvenile, infant, immature, squab (*esp. of doves or pigeons*).

Antonyms: see OLD.

2. *See* RECENT.

younger, *a.* junior, puisne (*obs., exc. law*), less (*a Latinism used of those having the same name*); *spec.* minor (*in same use as* less; *Eng. schools*).

youth, *n.* **1.** childhood (*contex.*), children (*pl.; chiefly spec.*), juvenescence (*R*), youthhead (*A*), youthhood (*A*), youngness (*R*); *spec.* adolescence, boyhood, boyage (*R*), girlhood, immaturity, nonage.

Antonyms: see AGE.

2. *A boy or girl:* youngster (*chiefly familiar or contemptuous*), younker (*obsolescent*), youngling (*R*), sprig (*often somewhat contemptuous*), slip (*chiefly spec.*), kid.

3. *Referring to a boy:* stripling, lad (*usually familiar or spec.*), laddie (*a term of endearment; chiefly Scot.*), cockerel (*fig.*), springal (*chiefly Scot.*), grummet (*historical*), callant (*Scot.*), whelp (*contemptuous*), gossoon (*chiefly Anglo-Irish*); *spec.* cub, damoiseau (*obs. or A*), hobbledehoy (*C*), buckeen (*Anglo-Irish*), boykin (*dim.*), knave (*A*).

Antonyms: see OLD MAN.

4. *See* RECENCY.

youthful, *a.* childish (*contex.*), young (*contex.*), early (*contex.*), juvenile, youngly (*R*), green (*fig.; chiefly depreciatory*); *spec.* beardless, maiden, boylike, boyish, puerile.

Antonyms: see OLD.

youthfulness, *n.* childishness, juvenility, green (*as in "in the green"; often depreciatory*); *spec.* boyishness, boyism.

y-shaped, *a.* ypsiliform;—*tech. or B.*

Z

zeal, *n.* devotion, passion, jealousness (*A*), jealousy (*A*), zealotry, zelotypia; *see* ARDOR.

zealot, *n. Spec.* enthusiast (*often depreciatory*), religionist; *see* DEVOTEE, FANATIC.

zealous, *a.* ardent (*which see*), alacritous, jealous (*A*).

zenith, *n.* **1.** prime, apogee.

Antonyms: see HORIZONTAL, NADIR.

2. *See* HEIGHT.

zenithal, *a.* culminant (*literal or fig.*).

zero, *n.* **1.** *See* CIPHER.

2. nothing (*contex.*); *spec.* goose egg (*U. S.*), duck (*S*).

zest, *n.* **1.** flavor, salt (*fig.*).

2. *See* EDGE, FLAVORING, ENJOYMENT, STING, LIKING.

zigzag, *n. Spec.* dancette, boyau.

zigzag, *a.* crooked (*contex.*), sinuous (*contex.*), cranky (*R*); *spec.* zigzaggy, dog-legged (*said of a kind of staircase*), chevrony.

Antonyms: see STRAIGHT.

zigzag, *v. t.* stagger.

zonal, *a.* zonary, arthromeric (*tech.*), metameric (*tech.*).

zone, *n.* band (*contex.*); *spec.* zonula, zonule, zonulet; *see* GIRDLE.